Roger Ebert's
Movie Yearbook
2000

Other books by Roger Ebert

An Illini Century

A Kiss Is Still a Kiss

Two Weeks in the Midday Sun: A Cannes Notebook

Behind the Phantom's Mask

Roger Ebert's Little Movie Glossary

Roger Ebert's Movie Home Companion
annually 1986–1993

Roger Ebert's Video Companion
annually 1994–1998

Questions for the Movie Answer Man

Roger Ebert's Book of Film: An Anthology

Ebert's Bigger Little Movie Glossary

With Daniel Curley
The Perfect London Walk

With John Kratz
The Computer Insectiary

With Gene Siskel
The Future of the Movies: Interviews with Martin Scorsese, Steven Spielberg, and George Lucas

Roger Ebert's Movie Yearbook 2000

Andrews McMeel Publishing

Kansas City

This book is dedicated
to Robert Zonka, 1928–1985.
God love ya.

Printed in the United States of America.

For information write
Andrews McMeel Publishing,
an Andrews McMeel Universal company,
4520 Main Street,
Kansas City, Missouri 64111.

ISBN 0-7407-0027-8

All the reviews in this book originally appeared
in the *Chicago Sun-Times*.

Contents

Introduction

This *Movie Yearbook* for the year 2000 includes every review written in the thirty months starting on January 1, 1997, as well as most of the interviews, essays, festival reports, and Movie Answer Man entries published since the previous edition.

This new format, introduced last year, replaces the long-running series of *Companions* in which, year after year, I tried to decide what reviews to cut in order to make room for the new ones. The old book had reached its physical limit. I was writing 250 reviews a year, but there was room for only perhaps 150 of them in each new edition of the book, and that meant pruning 150 older titles. Inevitably, lower-profile movies got left behind, and yet a book like this should suggest titles you might not otherwise hear about.

The new format includes every review I write. Each edition, we drop the oldest twelve months to add the newest. That means 40 percent of the reviews and all of the other material is new: about 60 percent of the book. With the *Companion*, only about 25 percent was new every year.

I like running every review. The more obscure titles are often the most interesting, because they are very good, or offbeat, or very bad. You may already know everything you ever want to know about *Phantom Menace* or *Eyes Wide Shut*. But consider in this edition such titles as *The Brandon Teena Story, Children of Heaven, La Cucaracha, Drifting Clouds, Fireworks, God Said, "Ha!", SLC Punk!* or *King of Masks*. Titles like that never play in many cities. They find their audiences mostly on video. That's you.

Lovers of good movies look at current film exhibition patterns, and despair. The big releases open on 3,000 screens on the same day, propelled by $20 million media buys. There's a natural human tendency to believe that you have to see the most-hyped movie, or be missing something. Alternative films open in fewer theaters or only one, with smaller ads and no promo slots on the talk shows. They have to make their own way. Many become "one-weekend wonders," seven-day bookings that disappear just about the time you hear about them.

Yet somehow movie lovers persist in seeking out the more obscure new work. Takeshi Kitano is the best and most popular new director/star in Japan. Aki Kaurismaeki is the skewed comic genius from Finland. In the 1970s, they would have been as big worldwide as Godard (yes, Godard was big, once). Today's hype-driven American movie market doesn't even have a blip for them on its radar screen, but all over the country people are renting *Fireworks* or *Drifting Clouds*, and they find each other on the Internet. This process is necessary to the survival of the cinema as an art form and not simply as a distraction.

* * *

There is an audience for good movies, if it can only find them. In April 1999, I hosted the first annual Roger Ebert's Overlooked Film Festival at the University of Illinois in

Urbana-Champaign (my alma mater). We took over the landmark Virginia Theater, a downtown vaudeville palace, and showed films I believed had been (or would be) overlooked. Audiences were large and, much more important, enthusiastic. Marketing students did a survey and found that at least half of the ticket-buyers were not cinema buffs from the campus, but local and regional people. When we screened a title like Eric Rohmer's *Autumn Tale*, which conventional wisdom segregates into big-city art houses, the reception from this popular audience was warm and joyous.

You should have been there, too, when we showed Rolf de Heer's *Dance Me to My Song*, the wonderful Australian film about a woman imprisoned in a wheelchair by cerebral palsy. Unable to speak without the aid of a voice synthesizer, she wants to free herself from a cruel paid companion—and find a guy. The film was a major success on the 1998 festival circuit (it got a standing ovation at Cannes), and yet as I write it still hasn't been picked up for U.S. distribution. Why not? Maybe because distributors are afraid it won't attract the Friday night teenage boy audience that rules the American box office.

Heather Rose, who cowrote the movie and stars in it, herself suffers from cerebral palsy. Her performance transcends ordinary drama and moves into the realms of documentary truth, and yet the story also has the power of popular melodrama. As I experienced the audience's strong response, I knew this film had the power to reach out to almost anyone—if it ever got the chance to.

Other Overlooked titles included unreleased films such as David Williams's *Thirteen*, a docudrama about a young black girl's eventful entry into adolescence; Kevin Di Novis's *Surrender, Dorothy*, a strange underground film about forced gender change; and Jan Troell's *Hamsun*, about the Nobel Prize–winning poet who flirted with the Nazis. Also films that were released but should have found wider audiences, such as Dale Rosenbloom's *Shiloh*, a wonderful children's film; Hirokazu Kore-eda's *Maborosi*, a masterpiece of love, loss, and acceptance; and Nancy Savoca's spiritual odyssey, *Household Saints*. We also honored two overlooked genres: silent films (*Potemkin* played with a live score by Concrete, a western Michigan band), and 70mm *(Tron)*.

The second Overlooked festival will be held April 26–30, 2000. Information is at www.ebertfest.com.

* * *

Maybe this doesn't belong in a yearbook aimed at video viewers, but I believe the whole universe of film is at a dangerous crossroads.

It is taken as an accepted fact in some circles that film projection will be replaced in theaters by digital video projection, sometime in the next five years. Texas Instruments has the best projection system, and has won good reviews for its test screenings of *Phantom Menace*. Most viewers agree it is somewhere between 85 percent as good as film, and "about as good" as film.

Splendid, right? Especially since satellite delivery of movies would save the studios the cost of making and distributing prints?

Well, maybe not so good. Because satellite delivery would involve compression, so the picture quality might not be as high as in those *Phantom Menace* demos, when the projection booth was stuffed with Texas Instruments acolytes, fine-tuning their custom installation.

And maybe not so good for theaters, because satellite distribution might create the odd situation of low-paid projectionists being replaced in the booth by expensive computer systems engineers, who could expect salaries larger than the theater managers—or, in some cases, the owners.

And maybe not so good because this would further the tyranny of mass bookings. And because movies would start *exactly* on time, even if the lights were still on and the audience filing in.

And *especially* not so good because the movie industry has devoted zero research to the crucial question of whether film and video *are the same thing.* Some experts in the psychology of perception believe that film and video affect the mind in fundamentally different ways. Film creates an alpha, or reverie, state. Video creates a beta, or hypnotic, state. It may be that a video picture, no matter how "good," would not affect the subconscious in the same way—that a video movie in a theater would somehow subtly not reach us emotionally in the same way that film does. In that case, theatrical video projection could destroy the intangible relationship between the viewer and the screen.

Meanwhile, why settle for video "about as good" as film, when a new film projection system promises a picture more than twice as good? MaxiVision 48 uses forty-eight frames a second, not twenty-four, and has a picture area 32 percent larger (it recaptures the unneeded space used by the analog sound track). It incorporates existing technology, so is much cheaper than video projection. I've seen MaxiVision and video projection and, believe me, there's no comparison.

For more info: www.mv48.com.

* * *

The *Yearbook 2000* also includes:

• All the new Answer Man entries that are still relevant, arranged by movie title or topic. A little pointing finger at the end of a review means there are Answer Man questions on the film. I also included a few dozen AM entries that got squeezed out of the biweekly column.

• Selections from my daily film festival coverage from Telluride, Toronto, Sundance, and Cannes.

• A selection of new Glossary entries. *Ebert's Bigger Little Movie Glossary*, now in bookstores, was published in May 1999 with twice as many entries. But new contributions keep flowing in.

• Those interviews and "think pieces" I've done during the past twelve months. I don't attend as many junkets as I used to, because they're not a useful way of getting real information: They've been turned into assembly lines for sound bites, and cater to the "benevolent blurbsters" who can be counted on for burbles of ecstasy about every film they see. Sometimes I attend a premiere simply because the film is so widely anticipated (*Eyes Wide Shut*, for example). Other times, I get interviews during film festivals.

* * *

My reviews and articles can be found on-line on CompuServe (the go-word is "Ebert") and the Web (www.suntimes.com/ebert). I hang out in a section of the CompuServe Showbiz Forum (go-word "Showbiz"). From the TV program, audio (and soon video) of *Roger Ebert & the Movies* is on-line at www.ebert-movies.com.

* * *

Where should you start in compiling a movie library? *For Keeps*, by Pauline Kael, brings together a generous selection from her many previous books of reviews, providing an overview of the career of the most influential of film critics. The greatly revised and expanded edition of David Thomson's *Biographical Dictionary of Film* is an opinionated, informed, concise summary of hundreds of key careers. The late Ephraim Katz's *Film Encyclopedia* is an invaluable one-volume survey of the world of film. And *Distinguishing Features*, by Stanley Kauffmann, is the latest collection of reviews by the critic whose superb writing and scholarship have distinguished the *New Republic* for decades. Jonathan Rosenbaum's recent book *Movies as Politics* showcases the work of one of the best contemporary critics. David Bordwell's *On the History of Film Style* tells you more about how to look at a movie than any other book I have ever found.

For laser disc fans, there is no better guide than the *Laser Video Disc Companion*, by Douglas Pratt. For the critics who shaped today's film criticism, I recommend the collected works of Kael, Kauffmann, Manny Farber, Andrew Sarris, Dwight Macdonald, James Agee, and Graham Greene.

On the Web, the best critics include James Berardinelli, Peter Brunette, Tom Keogh, Scott Renshaw, Damien Cannon, Harvey S. Karten, Edwin Jahiel, and the excellent writers at Mr. Showbiz, Film.com, and Ain't It Cool. For parents in search of *detailed*, factual information about the contents of movies, supplied without a political or religious agenda, there is no better site than www.screenit.com. David Poland's Hot Button column at the TNT Rough Cut site is the best-informed daily report on the movie biz. Harry Knowles's Ain't It Cool site is the clearinghouse for insider information, rumors, gossip, and speculation, and has many good critics, especially "Moriarity." The two most valuable resources for finding material on the Web are the Internet Movie Database (http://us.imdb.com/search) and the Movie Review Query Engine (http://www.cinema.pgh.pa.us/movie/reviews).

* * *

When I speak to students of journalism and writing, I always give the same advice: "The Muse visits *during* the act of composition, not before." Those who stare at a blank sheet or screen waiting for inspiration are likely to stare forever. The Muse listens for the sound of actual work before whispering her psychic encouragements.

My own Muse is my wife, Chaz, who works in ways of her own. She offers an atmosphere of love and encouragement, enriching my life and work. She is a movie lover like myself, attending most of the screenings and festivals, helping me plow through the mob scenes at Cannes and survive the sneak previews (why do studios persist in believing that critics will like a movie better if it is screened in the evening in a theater filled with a disk jockey's noisy fans?). Chaz has a gift I can only wonder at: She remembers the names of all the characters. Not just Marsellus Wallace, but Doc Wallace. To her, my love and gratitude.

* * *

In February 1999, I lost my colleague, Gene Siskel. I have tried to express my feelings of loss in an essay elsewhere in this volume. He was irreplaceable. What any memorial essay is likely to miss is a feeling for his sense of humor. He cut to the bottom line with his favorite critical question: "Is this film more interesting than a documentary of the same actors having lunch?" I treasure an earlier edition of this book, which Gene autographed: "I disagree with every word in this beautifully-written volume."

ROGER EBERT

Acknowledgments

My editor is Dorothy O'Brien, tireless, cheerful, all-noticing. She is assisted by the equally invaluable Julie Roberts. My friend and longtime editor, Donna Martin, suggested this new approach to the annual volume. The design is by Cameron Poulter, the typographical genius of Hyde Park. My thanks to production editor Polly Blair, who renders Cameron's design into reality. I have been blessed with the expert and discriminating editorial direction of John Barron, Laura Emerick, Avis Weathersbee, and Mi-Ai Ahern, and the copyediting of Jeff Johnson, Jeff Wisser, Darel Jevens, and Miriam DiNunzio at the *Chicago Sun-Times*; Sue Roush at Universal Press Syndicate; and Michelle Daniel at Andrews McMeel Publishing. Many thanks are also due to the production staff at *Siskel & Ebert*, and to Marsha Jordan at WLS-TV. My gratitude goes to Carol Iwata, my expert office assistant, and to Marlene Gelfond, at the *Sun-Times*. And special thanks and love to my wife, Chaz, for whom I can only say: If more film critics had a spouse just like her, the level of cheer in the field would rise dramatically.

ROGER EBERT

Key to Symbols

★★★★	A great film
★★★	A good film
★★	Fair
★	Poor
	G, PG, PG-13, R, NC-17: Ratings of the Motion Picture Association of America
G	Indicates that the movie is suitable for general audiences
PG	Suitable for general audiences but parental guidance is suggested
PG-13	Recommended for viewers 13 years or above; may contain material inappropriate for younger children
R	Recommended for viewers 17 or older
NC-17	Intended for adults only
141 m.	Running time
1999	Year of theatrical release
☞	Refers to "Questions for the Movie Answer Man."

Reviews

A

Absolute Power ★ ★ ★ ½

R, 122 m., 1997

Clint Eastwood (Luther Whitney), Gene Hackman (President Richmond), Ed Harris (Seth Frank), Laura Linney (Kate Whitney), Scott Glenn (Bill Burton), Dennis Haysbert (Tim Collin), Judy Davis (Gloria Russell), E. G. Marshall (Walter Sullivan). Directed by Clint Eastwood and produced by Eastwood and Karen Spiegel. Screenplay by William Goldman, based on the novel by David Baldacci.

Clint Eastwood's *Absolute Power* is a tight, taut thriller with a twist. It's also about a father and daughter, estranged for years, who are finally able to become friends. Not many thrillers slow down to notice relationships, but this one does.

Eastwood stars as Luther Whitney, a burglar who breaks into a mansion in the dead of night and penetrates a hidden room filled with diamonds and cash. He's interrupted in the middle of his work by visitors. Hiding behind a two-way mirror, he sees a man and woman having sex. The play turns rough, the man beats her, the woman stabs him, and two men burst in and shoot her dead.

Eastwood watches, all but his eyes in shadow. He is about to intervene—risking discovery—when the gunshots ring out. He escapes from the mansion down a rope from a third-floor window, carrying with him the deadly knowledge that the woman was the younger wife of an eighty-year-old millionaire, and the man was the president of the United States.

What we have here is a setup that could be developed in a lot of ways. The recent and dreadful *Shadow Conspiracy* detailed a White House plot that was cheerfully absurd. *Absolute Power*, based loosely on a novel by David Baldacci, could have been as silly, but it's not, because Eastwood uses fine actors and a smart script by William Goldman to make it into something more.

A lot of the best qualities come from the thief's relationship with his daughter, Kate (Laura Linney), "the only kid in show-and-tell that got to talk about visiting day." Her dad was in prison most of her childhood, and now, as a prosecutor, she never sees him. But sometimes she senses he's watching her; one of the movie's best scenes has her discovering that he attended her graduation ceremonies. Why did he remain invisible? Having an ex-con for a father would not help her much.

The story behind the murder is developed briskly. Old Walter Sullivan (E. G. Marshall) is a prime backer of the president (Gene Hackman). He was happily married for forty-eight years, but after his wife's death he took a younger wife. The men who burst into the mansion bedroom and shot her were Secret Service agents (Dennis Haysbert and Scott Glenn). The cover-up is being orchestrated by a White House chief of staff (Judy Davis).

Seth Frank (Ed Harris), the cop on the case, immediately notices all sorts of suspicious loose ends: Two shots were fired but only one bullet was recovered, for example, and the gunshot trajectories don't match. He suspects this was more than a simple murder.

Most thrillers depend on chase scenes and shoot-outs. Some of the best scenes in *Absolute Power* involve dialogue. The cop immediately fingers Luther Whitney as a possible suspect (he's one of "only six guys alive" who could have gotten into the mansion), and interviews him at a museum dining room. Eastwood, wearing half-glasses and a cloth cap that accentuate his age, smiles laconically and says, "Go down a rope in the middle of the night? If I could do that, I'd be the star of my AARP meetings."

There is another good scene between Ed Harris and old E. G. Marshall, who tells the policeman the two-way mirror was installed in the bedroom at his wife's suggestion: "She thought I might have liked sitting there. I didn't." His is a poignant character, a self-made man who has spent his life giving money to charity, who has elected a president, and who now fears "I'll go out as the joke of the world."

Eastwood delivers a few nice set pieces as the suspense builds, including a rendezvous with his daughter in a public plaza, while two sets of gunmen train their sights on him. And we get hard-boiled dialogue in the Oval Office, as the president and his merciless chief of staff run the cover-up by ordering the Secret Servicemen to do things not covered in their job description (one is willing, one has qualms). Much depends on a hypocritical speech the president makes, which Luther sees at an airport bar just as he's about to flee the country. In a classic Eastwood moment, the thief's jaw hardens and he decides to stay and fight, rather than give a pass to a heartless liar.

Eastwood as a director is usually eclipsed by Eastwood the actor; he has directed almost twenty films, good enough and successful enough to make him one of Hollywood's top filmmakers, and yet his stardom overshadows that role. Here he creates scenes of pure moviemaking; scenes without dialogue or violence, that work only because we know the characters and because the direction, camera work (by Jack N. Green), and editing (Joel Cox) put them together into suspenseful montages. The opening sequence is especially effective.

But at the end what I remembered most was the relationship between father and daughter. By using this personal story as an arc to draw together the other elements in the film, Eastwood does a difficult thing: He makes a thriller that is not upstaged by its thrills. Luther Whitney is a genuinely interesting, complicated character—not just an action figure. What happens to him matters to us, and that's worth more than all the special effects in the world.

Addicted to Love ★★

R, 101 m., 1997

Meg Ryan (Maggie), Matthew Broderick (Sam), Kelly Preston (Linda), Tcheky Karyo (Anton), Maureen Stapleton (Nana), Nesbitt Blaisdell (Ed Green). Directed by Griffin Dunne and produced by Jeffrey Silver and Bobby Newmyer. Screenplay by Robert Gordon.

I have to train myself to stop expecting plausibility in films. After all, I'm the guy who argues that nothing is implausible in a film if it works, since it's all part of getting the job done. And yet, in the opening scene of *Addicted to Love* I was struggling. Astronomers have a telescope trained on a supernova. Then suddenly it's noon and the chief astronomer (Matthew Broderick) lowers the telescope until he can focus on the woman he loves (Kelly Preston) frolicking in a meadow with the students she teaches.

Huh? I'm thinking. They can see the stars through that telescope at high noon? I should have taken the clue right there. Then I wouldn't have been distracted a little later when Preston announces she wants to leave their small town and spend some time in New York City, and as her commuter plane taxis on takeoff, Broderick races beside it down the runway in his pickup truck, waving good-bye. I think that's against FAA regulations.

So look, I'm not being fair to the movie. It's obviously a romantic fantasy, and only a curmudgeon would nitpick. What bothered me more was that the characters are supposed to be intelligent, and yet they have the maturity of gnats. It is always a problem in a love story when the rival seems more interesting than the hero, and that's what happens here.

But let's back up. Broderick plays Sam, the astronomer, who follows his lifelong love, Linda (Preston), to the big city, where she has gone because she finds small-town life stagnating. Sam soon finds her by canvassing lots of residential hotels until he finds the right one (don't try this yourself unless you have lots of time). Then he discovers Linda is dating a French chef named Anton (Tcheky Karyo). In fact, she's moving in with him.

Sam sneaks into an empty building across the way and, using his astronomer's knowledge of lenses, builds a refracting gadget that projects an image of their apartment onto a wall in his (the technical term for his device is "camera obscura"). Later he bugs their place, so he can relax on his sofa and watch a moving picture of their private life, with sound. Using his scientist's training, he graphs their progress (there is even a chart showing her daily smile quotient) to predict when they will break up.

During this process, a mystery figure on a motorcycle turns up. It is an old rule in movie comedies that whenever a motorcyclist's head and face are completely obscured by a helmet, that motorcyclist is inevitably revealed to be a woman. True again this time: It's Maggie (Meg Ryan), who is the jilted lover of the French chef. Since Maggie and Sam have their losses in common, they team up to try to sabotage the two happy lovers across the way.

Among their tricks: They pull a pickpocket scheme to get lipstick on his collar. They bribe kids to use squirt guns to douse him with perfume. These clues are supposed to make Linda jealous. By this point in the film, I was squirming: What intelligence level is the story pitched at?

Sam eventually inveigles himself into the kitchen of Anton's restaurant as a dishwasher, so that he can masochistically observe his rival at close quarters. This leads to a conversation between the two men in which Anton seems so manifestly wiser and more grown up that I was reminded of a generalization I once heard: "European films are about grown-ups, and American films are about adolescents." Not true in all cases, of course, but it's dramatically true here that Anton has an adult's understanding of the world, and the Sam character thinks he's living in a sitcom.

How much more interesting this situation might have been if they'd forgotten about the reflecting lenses and the practical jokes, and tried to devise a comedy based on personalities and dialogue! That might have even led to an unexpected outcome. Instead, we get a plot so predictable that there cannot be a single person in the audience who doesn't know Broderick and Ryan are destined to fall in love with each other. Not simply destined, but absolutely required to by the bylaws of the Hollywood Code of Clichés.

The actors are very engaging. The production design (including the reflecting lenses) is artful and ingenious. The direction, by Griffin Dunne, is smooth and confident for a first-timer. There are nice supporting roles for Maureen Stapleton, as a wise grandmother, and Nesbitt Blaisdell as Linda's father, Mr. Green, who assigns himself to read her Dear John letters. There is, in fact, a lot of good stuff here, but it's all at the service of an imbecilic approach. It's like bright people got together to make the film and didn't trust the audience to keep up with them.

Affliction ★★★★

R, 114 m., 1999

Nick Nolte (Wade Whitehouse), Sissy Spacek (Margie Fogg), James Coburn (Glen Whitehouse), Willem Dafoe (Rolfe Whitehouse), Mary Beth Hurt (Lillian), Jim True (Jack Hewitt), Marian Seldes (Alma Pittman), Holmes Osborne (Gordon LaRiviere). Directed by Paul Schrader and produced by Linda Reisman. Screenplay by Schrader, based on the novel by Russell Banks.

Nick Nolte is a big, shambling, confident male presence in the movies, and it is startling to see his cocksure presence change into fear in Paul Schrader's *Affliction.* Nolte plays Wade Whitehouse, the sheriff of a small New Hampshire town, whose uniform, gun, and stature do not make up for a deep feeling of worthlessness. He drinks, he smokes pot on the job, he walks with a sad weariness, he is hated by his ex-wife, and his young daughter looks at him as if he's crazy.

When we meet Glen, his father, we understand the source of his defeat. The older man (James Coburn) is a cauldron of alcoholic venom, a man whose consolation in life has been to dominate and terrorize his family. There are scenes where both men are on the screen together, and you can sense the sheriff shrinking, as if afraid of a sudden blow. The women in their lives have been an audience for cruelty; of the older man's wife, it is said, "Women like this, it's like they lived their lives with the sound turned off. And then they're gone."

Affliction is based on a novel by Russell Banks, whose work also inspired *The Sweet Hereafter.* Both films are set in bleak winter landscapes, and both involve a deep resentment of parental abuse—this one more obviously, since Sheriff Whitehouse's entire unhappy life has been, and still is, controlled by fear of his father. We're reminded of other films Schrader wrote *(Taxi Driver, Raging Bull, The Mosquito Coast)* or directed *(Mishima, Hardcore),* in which men's violence is churned up by feelings of inadequacy. (He also wrote *The Last Temptation of Christ,* in which at least one line applies: "Father, why hast thou forsaken me?")

Wade Whitehouse is a bad husband, a bad father, and a bad sheriff. He retains enough qualities to inspire the loyalty, or maybe the sympathy, of a girlfriend named Margie (Sissy Spacek), but his ex-wife (Mary Beth Hurt) looks at him in deep contempt, and his brother Rolfe (Willem Dafoe), the film's narrator, has been wise to clear out of the town and its poisons.

Early in the film, Wade decides to show a little enterprise on the job. A friend of his has gone out as a hunting guide for a rich man and returned with the man's expensive gun, some bloodstains, and a story of an accident. Wade doesn't believe it was an accident, and like a sleepwalker talking himself back to wakefulness, he begins an investigation that stirs up the stagnant town—and even rouses him into a state where he can be reached, for the first time in years, by fresh thoughts about how his life has gone wrong.

Because there are elements of a crime mystery in *Affliction*, it would be unwise to reveal too much about this side of the plot. It is interrupted, in any event, by another death: Wade and Margie go to the old man's house to find that Wade's mother, Glen's wife, lies dead upstairs and Glen is unable to acknowledge the situation. It is even possible that the sick woman crawled upstairs and was forgotten by a man whose inner eye has long been focused only on his own self-diagnosis: not drunk enough, drunk just right, or too drunk?

Rolfe returns to town for the funeral and to supply missing elements from the story of their childhood, and the film ends in an explosion that seems prepared even in the first frame. Its meaning is very clear: Cruelty to a child is not over in a moment or a day, but is like those medical capsules embedded in the flesh, which release their contents for years.

Nolte and Coburn are magnificent in this film, which is like an expiation for abusive men. It is revealing to watch them in their scenes together—to see how they're able to use physical presence to sketch the history of a relationship. Schrader says he cast Coburn because he needed an actor who was big enough, and had a "great iconic weight," to convincingly dominate Nolte. He found one. Coburn has spent a career largely in shallow entertainments, and here he rises to the occasion with a performance of power.

There is a story about that. "I met with Coburn before the picture began," Schrader told me, "and told him how carefully Nolte prepares for a role. I told Coburn that if he walked through the movie, Nolte might let him get away with it for a day, but on the second day all hell would break loose. Coburn said, 'Oh, you mean you want me to really act? I can do that. I haven't often been asked to, but I can.'" He can.

Afterglow ★ ★ ★

R, 113 m., 1998

Nick Nolte (Lucky Mann), Julie Christie (Phyllis Mann), Lara Flynn Boyle (Marianne Byron), Jonny Lee Miller (Jeffrey Byron), Jay Underwood (Donald Duncan), Domini Blythe (Helene Pelletier), Yves Corbeil (Bernard Ornay), Alan Fawcett (Count Falco/Jack Dana). Directed by Alan Rudolph and produced by Robert Altman. Screenplay by Rudolph.

Julie Christie has the kind of face you find on the covers of romance novels, and surely one of the reasons she was cast in *Dr. Zhivago* was that she would look so good on the poster. She projects the wounded perfection of a great beauty who has had the wrong sort of luck. In *Afterglow*, only her third role in the 1990s, Alan Rudolph has given her the sort of character she knows inside out: bemused, sad, needful, mysterious.

She plays Phyllis Mann, a former B-movie actress specializing in horror roles, who now lives in Montreal with her husband, Lucky (Nick Nolte), a handyman equally at home with wrenches and wenches. Some great sadness from the past overshadows their marriage, and although Phyllis and Lucky are held together by love and understanding, he philanders, with her tacit permission, among the lonely housewives who phone for his services ("Plumbing and a woman's nature are both unpredictable, and filled with hidden mysteries," he philosophizes).

Nolte plays Lucky not as a sex machine, however, but as a tender, observant man who feels a certain sympathy with the women he has sex with. The deal with his wife is, he can fool around, as long as he doesn't get serious. One day seriousness threatens, when he meets Marianne Byron (Lara Flynn Boyle), a yuppie wife who yearns for the baby her husband will not, or cannot, give her. So deep is her need that she has hired Lucky Mann to convert an extra bedroom into a nursery, even as her cold, arrogant husband, Jeffrey (Jonny Lee Miller, Sick Boy in *Trainspotting*), vows he wants nothing to do with children.

The plot to this point could be the stuff of

soap opera, but there's always something askew in an Alan Rudolph film, unexpected notes and touches that maintain a certain ironic distance while permitting painful flashes of human nature to burst through. Imagine a soap in which the characters subtly mock their roles while the actors occasionally break down in grief about their offscreen lives.

Afterglow has a script that permits coincidence and contrivance; like many of Rudolph's films *(Choose Me, Trouble in Mind)*, it has characters who seem fated to share common destinies. As Lucky Mann falls into the pit created by Marianne's great need, Phyllis meets Jeffrey and allows herself to be drawn toward him in a mixture of curiosity and revenge.

Afterglow doesn't depend on a visible style as much as some of Rudolph's films; he seems so interested in the story, which he wrote himself, that he doesn't need to impose directorial distance. That may be because the characters are so poignant. Julie Christie, lounging on a sofa looking at her old horror films, has speeches in which she looks back on Hollywood with the fascination of an accident victim. Nolte's character is not a one-dimensional louse but a man whose sex life may reflect a deep sympathy for women—the same sympathy he feels for his wife, so steeped in sadness.

As for Christie, what's the story with her? She is so familiar a face from her early films *(Darling, McCabe and Mrs. Miller, Far from the Madding Crowd, Shampoo)*, but then her career drifted into unessential and forgettable films. Infrequent newspaper interviews reported on her happiness in solitude. Like the character Phyllis, she has a distance on her early career; unlike her, she uses it here to create something fresh and vulnerable. How mysterious and intriguing some performances can be.

Air Bud ★ ★ ★

PG, 97 m., 1997

Kevin Zegers (Josh Framm), Wendy Makkena (Jackie Framm), Bill Cobbs (Arthur Chaney), Michael Jeter (Norm Snively), Eric Christmas (Judge Cranfield). Directed by Charles Martin Smith and produced by William Vince and Robert Vince. Screenplay by Paul Tamasy and Aaron Mendelsohn.

"Are there ever movies you just hate the idea of going to see?" Yes, I say, there are—but sometimes I'm surprised. It happened again the other night. I dragged myself down to a multiplex to attend a sneak preview of a movie named *Air Bud*. I had seen the trailer, and knew it was about a dog who could play basketball. I was not impatient to see this movie.

I began to have stirrings of hope in the opening scenes, which involved an obnoxious and possibly drunken clown making a fool of himself at a children's party. His act was called "Clown and a Hound," and the dog seemed smarter and nicer than its master, and probably smelled better.

On the highway, the dog's cage bounces out of the clown's pickup, and through a series of adventures the dog makes friends with the young hero of the movie, Josh (Kevin Zegers). Josh has just moved to a small town with his mother (Wendy Makkena) and kid sister. (His father, a test pilot, has been killed in a crash, following the ancient Disney tradition that one dead parent is nice, and an orphan for a hero is best of all.)

Josh is lonely and depressed in the new town, and is an outcast at the junior high school, although eventually he gets to be manager of the basketball team. Could he be a player? He lacks the confidence to try out, although he practices for long hours in an abandoned court he's discovered behind an old church. (The church's notice board carries the ominous legend, EEK AN YE SHAL FIN.)

Josh names the dog Buddy. This is some dog. It has the ability to enter Josh's second-floor bedroom by jumping on a car, climbing a rose trellis, walking across the roof, and jumping in the window. And on the basketball court it turns out to be a star; pass Buddy the ball, and it can bounce it with its nose and make a basket (it doesn't miss once in the entire movie).

The school's aging janitor (Bill Cobbs) turns out to be a New York Knicks star from the 1950s, and when the regular coach is fired, he takes over the team and hands out advice like: "You take that dog. It doesn't give a rat's behind about his point average—he just likes to play the game!" Because by then, of course, Buddy has found the gymnasium, bounded on court during a game, and scored a basket.

There are predictable crises: Will Snively

the clown (Michael Jeter) come looking for his dog? Will Josh be promoted from water boy to player? Will the team's mean star and his overzealous dad spoil the fun? The movie touches those bases, but with freshness and energy. And the climactic scenes are not only absurd and goofy but also enormously entertaining. By the end of the film I was quietly amazed: Not only could Buddy play basketball, but I actually cared how the game turned out.

The movie was directed by Charles Martin Smith, himself the star of a much different kind of animal movie, the classic *Never Cry Wolf* (1983). He has the structure of a traditional story here, but makes it seem new with good performances, crisp editing, a lovable dog, and a new twist on the old movie tradition of the "big game." And then the movie just keeps getting better, with a very funny courtroom scene involving a judge (Eric Christmas) who never catches on that the dog is trained to bark when it hears a gavel pounding.

Now, then. Can this dog really shoot baskets? I doubt it. I especially doubt that the dog has a better average from the field than Michael Jordan. But I don't want to know what kind of trickery was used to create the dog's game scenes; whatever it was, it worked. The dog, by the way, wears its own little basketball shoes. Don't let your dog see the movie, or it'll want some.

Air Bud 2: Golden Receiver ★ ½

G, 91 m., 1998

Kevin Zegers (Josh Framm), Cynthia Stevenson (Jackie Framm), Gregory Harrison (Patrick Sullivan), Nora Dunn (Natalia), Perry Anzilotti (Popov), Shayn Solberg (Tom Stewart), Robert Costanzo (Coach Fanelli), Simon Isherwood (Ram's Coach). Directed by Richard Martin and produced by Robert Vince. Screenplay by Aaron Mendelsohn and Paul Tamasy.

Air Bud 2: Golden Receiver is a pale shadow of the entertaining 1997 family movie. It's a sequel that lacks the spirit and sweetness of the original. I went to the first *Air Bud* with a heavy heart, since movies about dogs that play basketball do not rank high on my wish list. But I was won over by the movie's charm, and its story about a new kid in town who is an outcast who practices basketball by himself until he realizes that his dog, Buddy, can play too.

There was some sadness in the setup; the boy, named Josh (Kevin Zegers), had just lost his dad, a test pilot killed in a crash. He and his mom and little sister had moved to a leafy Seattle coastal suburb. Josh was the manager of the school basketball team, and Buddy—well, Buddy hardly ever missed a shot, and eventually helped the school team win the big game.

Is it against the rules for dogs to play on school teams? The movie nimbly sidesteps that question, and this time Buddy turns his talents to football, trading in his little paw-sized basketball shoes for a jersey with padded shoulders, which makes him look weirdly deformed. Buddy, catching the ball in his mouth, flawlessly executes plays. He's never offside, always runs the patterns, inspires fumbles, and can outrun anyone on the field.

The human story is not quite as simple. Josh's mom, Jackie (Cynthia Stevenson), has started to date again and falls in love with the local veterinarian, Patrick Sullivan (Gregory Harrison). Josh and his buddy don't like this and do what they can to prevent the romance. Meanwhile, in a total miscalculation, the movie unwisely adds a lamebrained subplot about a couple of Russian petnappers who apparently plan to steal a lot of animals and use them to set up a zoo.

The chief pet thief, played by Nora Dunn, runs through people's yards after Buddy, wearing a slinky black dress and waving a big butterfly net that would certainly not attract the attention of a town alerted to dognapping. She and her sidekick tool around town in an ice-cream truck with an annoying little jingling bell, which would also certainly not attract attention. She finds out about Buddy through TV coverage of the dog's brilliant play in the basketball finals, which in this town are apparently held the day before football season opens.

There are way too many heartfelt scenes between Mrs. Framm and her fiancé. And not enough stunts by the dog (perhaps because the original and great Buddy, who could allegedly actually shoot baskets, died of cancer soon after the first film was completed). I did like Robert

Costanzo's performance as the football coach, a quaint creature who actually believes that schoolchildren should play sports for fun.

And there was another aspect of the film that amused me. Whenever Buddy scores a touchdown, he doesn't spike the ball (lacking the equipment to do so). Instead, he celebrates his score by rolling onto his back and luxuriously digging his shoulders into the turf.

Watching him do that, I was reminded of the classic dog novels of Albert Payson Terhune, which I read as a boy. He wrote about "Lad," as I recall, and revealed that when dogs don't like you, they engage in that shoulder behavior as a way of suggesting they're rolling in the putrefying flesh of their dead enemies.

Too bad the play-by-play announcer doesn't pick up on that, but then the announcers are not real sharp in this town. The first time Buddy runs onto the field, the announcer shouts, "It's a dog!" Don't you kinda think a play-by-play announcer in a small suburban town would recognize the golden retriever that had just won the basketball championship? A dog like that, it attracts attention.

Air Force One ★ ★ ½

R, 118 m., 1997

Harrison Ford (President James Marshall), Gary Oldman (Ivan Korshunov), Glenn Close (Vice President Kathryn Bennett), Wendy Crewson (Grace Marshall), Liesel Matthews (Alice Marshall), Paul Guilfoyle (Chief of Staff Lloyd Shepherd), Xander Berkeley (Agent Gibbs), William H. Macy (Major Caldwell), Philip Baker Hall (Attorney General). Directed by Wolfgang Petersen and produced by Petersen, Armyan Bernstein, Gail Katz, and Jon Shestack. Screenplay by Andrew W. Marlowe.

Harrison Ford is one of the most likable and convincing of movie stars, and he almost pulls off the impossible in *Air Force One.* I don't mean he saves the day; I mean he almost saves the movie. Here is a good example of how star power can breathe new life into old clichés—and *Air Force One* is rich with clichés.

You are familiar with the movie's premise because of all the commercials and coming attractions trailers and magazine covers and talk show appearances. You know that Gary Oldman plays the leader of a gang of terrorists who gain control of *Air Force One* as it's flying back home from Moscow. You know it's up to Ford, as President James Marshall, Vietnam combat hero, to battle the terrorists. You know his wife and children are among the hostages—and that he has just vowed that America will never negotiate with terrorists.

So. Since the movie has no macro surprises, does it have any micro ones? Has director Wolfgang Petersen *(Das Boot, In the Line of Fire)* found lots of neat little touches to make the movie work on a minute-by-minute basis, while on the larger scale it slogs to its preordained conclusion?

Sorta, sometimes. There's some neat stuff about *Air Force One,* although I don't know how much of it to believe. (Is it really bulletproof from the inside? Does it really have an escape pod onboard? Is there really a way to parachute out the back hatch? Can you really call Washington from Russia on a cell phone?) Many of the action scenes take place in the bowels of the plane, down in the galley and luggage areas.

There is also a counterplot set in Washington, where the vice president (Glenn Close) learns from the attorney general (Philip Baker Hall) that the president may be technically "incapacitated," and that she should consider taking over. And there are some good action sequences, in which people enter and leave airplanes at an altitude at which the practice is not recommended.

But mostly the movie is stapled together out of ingredients from many, many other films about presidents, terrorists, hijackings, hostages, airplanes, politics, and cat-and-mouse chases. It is inevitable, for example, that the terrorists will separate and go poking around on their own, so that they can be picked off one at a time. It is inevitable that there will be Washington press conferences, so that bones of information can be thrown to the seething press. It is inevitable that there will be personality flare-ups among the lesser politicians, and dire comments by their advisers ("The element of surprise is a formidable weapon").

The movie also resurrects that ancient and dependable standby, the Choosing of the Wires. In countless other movies, the bomb squad hesitates between "Red . . . or black? Red . . . or black?" This is a big-budget movie and presents us with five wires. It's an emergency, and the president needs to decide which two he should connect. See if you can guess the right two colors. The choices are green, yellow, red, white, and blue.

The movie is well served by the quality of the performances. Close is convincing as the vice president, and Gary Oldman has a couple of effective scenes as the terrorist ("Murder? You took 100,000 lives to save a nickel on the price of a gallon of gas"). And Harrison Ford is steady and convincing as the president, even while we're asking ourselves if a middle-aged chief executive would really be better at hand-to-hand combat than his Secret Service agents.

Some of the special effects scenes are effective, but others are distracting. In a key scene next to an open doorway on the plane, none of the actors convinced me they thought they were standing next to a 30,000-foot drop. (For one thing, they never looked down, which I think is more or less the first thing I would do.) A climactic explosion is less than convincing, visually. And scenes involving a Russian political prisoner are confusing.

Air Force One is a fairly competent recycling of familiar ingredients, given an additional interest because of Harrison Ford's personal appeal. At this point, however, I've had enough explosions, showdowns, stunts, and special effects. I saw a movie the other day about a woman in Paris who lost her cat, and know what? It was more exciting than this. At least when the cat got up on the roof, it knew enough to look down.

An Alan Smithee Film Burn Hollywood Burn no stars

R, 86 m., 1998

Ryan O'Neal (James Edmunds), Coolio (Dion Brothers), Chuck D (Leon Brothers), Eric Idle (Alan Smithee), Richard Jeni (Jerry Glover), Leslie Stefanson (Michelle Rafferty), Sandra Bernhard (Ann Glover), Cherie Lunghi (Myrna Smithee). Directed by Alan Smithee and produced by Ben Myron. Screenplay by Joe Eszterhas.

An Alan Smithee Film Burn Hollywood Burn is a spectacularly bad film—incompetent, unfunny, ill-conceived, badly executed, lamely written, and acted by people who look trapped in the headlights.

The title provides clues to the film's misfortune. It was originally titled *An Alan Smithee Film.* Then *Burn, Hollywood, Burn!* Now its official title is *An Alan Smithee Film Burn Hollywood Burn*—just like that, with no punctuation. There's a rich irony connected with the title. "Alan Smithee," of course, is the pseudonym that Hollywood slaps on a film if the original director insists on having his name removed. The plot of *AASFBHB* involves a film so bad that the director wants his name removed, but since his *real* name is Alan Smithee, what can he do? Ho, ho.

Wait, it gets better. The movie was directed by Arthur Hiller, who hated the way the film was edited so much that, yes, he insisted his name be removed from the credits. So now it really *is* an Alan Smithee film. That leaves one mystery: Why didn't Joe Eszterhas, the film's writer, take off his name too?

I fear it is because this version of the film does indeed reflect his vision. Eszterhas is sometimes a good writer, but this time he has had a complete lapse of judgment. Even when he kids himself, he's wrong. "It's completely terrible!" a character says of the film within the film. "It's worse than *Showgirls*!" Of course, Eszterhas wrote *Showgirls,* which got some bad reviews, but it wasn't completely terrible. I was looking forward to explaining that to him this week, but he canceled his visit to Chicago, reportedly because his voice gave out. Judging by this film, it was the last thing to go.

Have you ever been to one of those office parties where the PR department has put together a tribute to a retiring boss? That's how this film plays. It has no proper story line. No dramatic scenes. It's all done in documentary form, with people looking at the camera and relating the history of a doomed movie named *Trio,* which cost more than $200 million and stars Sylvester Stallone, Whoopi Goldberg, and Jackie Chan, who play themselves as if they are celebrity impersonators.

The film stars Eric Idle as Smithee, who eventually burns the print and checks into the Keith Moon Psychiatric Institute in England (ho, ho). Ryan O'Neal plays the film's producer. I love the way he's introduced. We see the back of a guy's head, and hear him saying, "Anything!" Then the chair swivels around and he says "anything!" again, and we see, *gasp!*—why, it's *Ryan O'Neal!* I was reminded of the moment in Mike Todd's *Around the World in 80 Days* when the piano player swivels around and, gasp!—it's *Frank Sinatra!*

These actors and others recount the history of the doomed film in unconvincing sound bites, which are edited together without wit or rhythm. One is accustomed to seeing bad movies, but not incompetent ones. Sophomores in a film class could make a better film than this. Hell, I have a movie here by Les Brown, a kid who looks about twelve and who filmed a thriller in his mother's basement, faking a fight scene by wrestling with a dummy. If I locked you in a room with both movies, you'd end up looking at the kid's.

In taking his name off the film, Arthur Hiller has wisely distanced himself from the disaster, but on the basis of what's on the screen I cannot, frankly, imagine any version of this film that I would want to see. The only way to save this film would be to trim eighty-six minutes.

Here's an interesting thing. The film is filled with celebrities playing themselves, and most of them manifestly have no idea who they are. The only celebrity who emerges relatively intact is Harvey Weinstein, head of Miramax, who plays a private eye—but never mind the role, just listen to him. He could find success in voice-over work.

Now consider Stallone. He reappears in the outtakes over the closing credits. Such cookies are a treat for audiences after the film is over. Here they're as bad as the film, but notice a moment when Stallone thinks he's off camera, and asks someone about a Planet Hollywood shirt. *Then* he sounds like himself. A second later, playing himself, he sounds all wrong. Jackie Chan copes by acting like he's in a Jackie Chan movie, but Whoopi Goldberg mangles her scenes in a cigar bar, awkwardly trying to smoke a stogie. It's God's way of paying her back for telling Ted Danson it would be funny to wear blackface at the Friars' Club.

Albino Alligator ★★

R, 97 m., 1997

Matt Dillon (Dova), Faye Dunaway (Janet), Gary Sinise (Milo), William Fichtner (Law), Viggo Mortensen (Guy), John Spencer (Jack), Skeet Ulrich (Danny), M. Emmet Walsh (Dino), Joe Mantegna (G. D. Browning). Directed by Kevin Spacey and produced by Brad Krevoy, Steven Stabler, and Brad Jenkel. Screenplay by Christian Forte. Photographed by Mark Plummer.

It's a basic movie situation. Desperate criminals are trapped and surrounded. They have hostages. The hard-boiled cop in charge issues an ultimatum. During a long and exhausting night, the tension builds while the men consider their options. And the hostages try to reason them out of a dangerous decision. In the old days it was always Pat O'Brien as the good Irish cop, a bullhorn to his mouth, shouting out a final ultimatum.

Why did the actor Kevin Spacey choose this formula for *Albino Alligator,* his first film as a director? Maybe because it's fun for the actors, who are required to move through plateaus of emotions. Maybe because by limiting the action mostly to one room, it eliminates distractions and allows for a closer focus. Maybe because he liked the screenplay by Christian Forte—even though it violates that old writer's rule, "Never quote your title in the dialogue."

Spacey does what can be done with the material, but it never achieves takeoff velocity. The heart of the problem, I think, is our suspicion that in real life these situations don't turn into long discussions. The crooks are likely to be too scared, too inarticulate or too confused for the kind of verbal jockeying that occupies most of *Albino Alligator.* The enterprise seems contrived—more like an actor's workshop than a drama.

The story takes place in New Orleans, where we see a group of law enforcers in a stakeout. Three robbers—not the ones the cops are looking for—botch a job at a warehouse and try to make a quick getaway. They have the bad luck to run directly into the police roadblock and a cop is killed (there's a nice shot here of a book of matches; he needed a light at just the wrong time).

In the car are Law (William Fichtner), who

is a cold psychopath; Milo (Gary Sinise), who seems more like your high school civics teacher than a criminal; and Dova (Matt Dillon), who is the leader of the gang but not necessarily in control. Two agents are killed when the chase goes wrong, and Milo is injured; the three stumble into an all-night dive poetically named Dino's Last Chance.

Dino is the owner, a phlegmatic old-timer played by M. Emmet Walsh. His bartender is Janet (Faye Dunaway). There are three customers in the bar: a kid playing pool (Skeet Ulrich), a guy in a suit who looks out of place (Viggo Mortensen), and a barfly (John Spencer). They all seem too sober to be drinking at 4 A.M., but if they were like most all-night drinkers, it would take Eugene O'Neill or Charles Bukowski to tell their story.

Dino's is quickly surrounded by cops, led by Browning (Joe Mantegna), who barks the usual orders and issues the usual ultimatums. There's no possible escape; the bar, which is below street level, has no back door and no windows. The criminals are doomed to be caught or killed, unless they come up with a bright idea. They do, sort of.

I will not be giving away plot secrets if I describe at this point the albino alligator connection. According to an anecdote told in the movie, alligators force an albino to go out first in order to flush out the opposition, after which they pounce from ambush. It's ingenious the way Forte's screenplay employs this principle, and interesting the way he develops the characters. Walsh and Dunaway try to reason with the desperadoes; the customers (who are not all exactly who they seem) have a turn; and there's a dynamic within the gang involving Sinise, who begins to think of his Catholic upbringing, Fichtner, who wants to blast everyone away, and Dillon, who tries to keep a level head.

It is all done about as well as it can be done, I suppose. Hostage movies follow such ancient patterns that it's rare to be surprised by one, and this one does have some surprises, none very rewarding. Occasionally the genre will be transformed by brilliant filmmaking, as it was in *Dog Day Afternoon*. Not this time.

Alien Resurrection ★ ½

R, 109 m., 1997

Sigourney Weaver (Ripley), Winona Ryder (Call), Dominique Pinon (Vriess), Ron Perlman (Johner), Gary Dourdan (Christie), Michael Wincott (Elgyn), Kim Flowers (Hillard), Dan Hedaya (General Perez), Brad Dourif (Gediman). Directed by Jean-Pierre Jeunet and produced by Bill Badalato, Gordon Carroll, David Giler, and Walter Hill. Screenplay by Joss Whedon.

Between *Alien* and *Aliens*, fifty-seven years passed, with Ellen Ripley in suspended animation. Between *Aliens* and *Alien3*, she drifted through space in a lifeboat, before landing on a prison planet. In all three films she did battle with vile alien creatures constructed out of teeth, green sinew, and goo. In *Alien3* she told this life form: "I've known you so long I can't remember a time when you weren't in my life."

I'm telling the aliens the same thing. This is a series whose inspiration has come, gone, and been forgotten. I'm aliened out. The fourth movie depends on a frayed shoestring of a plot, barely enough to give them something to talk about between the action scenes. A "Boo Movie," Pauline Kael called the second one, because it all came down to aliens popping up and going "boo!" and being destroyed.

I found that second film dark and depressing, but skillfully directed by James Cameron *(Terminator II)*. I lost interest with the third, when I realized that the aliens could at all times outrun and outleap the humans, so all the chase scenes were contrivances.

Now here is *Alien Resurrection*. Ripley (Sigourney Weaver) is still the heroine, even though 200 years have passed since *Alien3*. She has been cloned out of a drop of her own blood, and is being used as a brood mare: The movie opens with surgeons removing a baby alien from her womb. How the baby got in there is not fully explained, for which we should perhaps be grateful.

The birth takes place on a vast spaceship. The interstellar human government hopes to breed more aliens and use them for—oh, developing vaccines, medicines, a gene pool, stuff like that. The aliens have a remarkable body chemistry. Ripley's genes are all right, too:

They allow her reconstituted form to retain all of her old memories, as if cookie dough could remember what a gingerbread man looked like.

Ripley is first on a giant government science ship, then on a tramp freighter run by a vagabond crew. The monsters are at first held inside glass cells, but of course they escape (their blood is a powerful solvent that can eat through the decks of the ship). The movie's a little vague about Ripley: Is she all human, or does she have a little alien mixed in? For a while we wonder which side she's on. She laughs at mankind's hopes of exploiting the creatures: "She's a queen," she says of the new monster. "She'll breed. You'll die."

When the tramp freighter comes into play, we get a fresh crew, including Call (Winona Ryder), who has been flown all the way from Earth to provide appeal for the younger members of the audience. Ryder is a wonderful actress, one of the most gifted of her generation, but wrong for this movie. She lacks the heft and presence to stand alongside Ripley and the grizzled old space dogs played by Ron Perlman, Dominique Pinon, Dan Hedaya, and Brad Dourif. She seems uncertain of her purpose in the movie, her speeches lack conviction, and when her secret is revealed, it raises more questions than it answers. Ryder pales in comparison with Jenette Goldstein, the muscular Marine who was the female sidekick in *Aliens.*

Weaver, on the other hand, is splendid: strong, weary, resourceful, grim. I would gladly see a fifth *Alien* movie if they created something for her to do, and dialogue beyond the terse sound bites that play well in commercials. Ripley has some good scenes. She plays basketball with a crewman (Perlman) and slams him around. When she bleeds, her blood fizzes interestingly on the floor—as if it's not quite human. She can smell an alien presence. And be smelled: An alien recognizes Ripley as its grandmother and sticks out a tongue to lick her.

These aliens have a lot of stuff in their mouths; not only the tongue and their famous teeth, but another little head on a stalk, with smaller teeth. Still to be determined is whether the littler head has a still tinier head inside of it, and so on. Like the bugs in *Starship Troopers,* these aliens are an example of specialization. They have evolved over the eons into creatures adapted for one purpose only: to star in horror movies.

Mankind wants them for their genes? I can think of a more valuable attribute: They're apparently able to generate biomass out of thin air. The baby born at the beginning of the film weighs maybe five pounds. In a few weeks the ship's cargo includes generous tons of aliens. What do they feed on? How do they fuel their growth and reproduction? It's no good saying they eat the ship's stores, because they thrive even on the second ship—and in previous movies have grown like crazy on desolate prison planets and in abandoned space stations. They're like perpetual motion machines; they don't need input.

The *Alien* movies always have expert production design. *Alien Resurrection* was directed by the French visionary Jean-Pierre Jeunet *(City of Lost Children),* who with his designers has placed it in what looks like a large, empty hangar filled with prefabricated steel warehouse parts. There is not a single shot in the movie to fill one with wonder—nothing like the abandoned planetary station in *Aliens.* Even the standard shots of vast spaceships, moving against a backdrop of stars, are murky here, and perfunctory.

I got a telephone message that *Inside Edition* wanted to ask me about *Alien Resurrection,* and what impact the movie would have on the careers of Weaver and Ryder. Financially, it will help: Weaver remains the only woman who can open an action picture. Artistically, the film will have no impact at all. It's a nine-day wonder, a geek show designed to win a weekend or two at the box office and then fade from memory. Try this test: How often do you think about *Jurassic Park: The Lost World*?

American History X ★ ★ ★

R, 118 m., 1998

Edward Norton (Derek Vinyard), Edward Furlong (Danny Vinyard), Beverly D'Angelo (Doris Vinyard), Stacy Keach (Cameron Alexander), Jennifer Lien (Davina), Ethan Suplee (Seth), Fairuza Balk (Stacey), Avery Brooks (Bob Sweeney), Elliott Gould (Murray), Guy Torry

(Lamont). Directed by Tony Kaye and produced by John Morrissey. Screenplay by David McKenna.

American History X shows how two Los Angeles brothers are drawn into a neo-Nazi skinhead gang, and why one decides to free himself. In telling their stories, the film employs the language of racism—the gutter variety, and more sophisticated variations. The film is always interesting and sometimes compelling, and it contains more actual provocative thought than any American film on race since *Do the Right Thing*. But in trying to resolve the events of four years in one day, it leaves its shortcuts showing.

The film stars Edward Norton as Derek, a bright kid who has become the leader of a skinhead pack in Venice Beach; he's the lieutenant of a shadowy adult neo-Nazi (Stacy Keach). One night two black kids attempt to steal Derek's car as the result of a playground feud, and he shoots them dead. He's convicted of murder and sent to Chico for three years.

His kid brother, Danny (Edward Furlong), idolizes him, and to some degree steps into his shoes—although he lacks Derek's intelligence and gift for rabble-rousing rhetoric. Then Derek gets out of prison and tries to find a new direction for himself and Danny. Their backdrop is a family that consists of a chronically sick mother (Beverly D'Angelo) and two sisters. Their father, a fireman, was shot and killed by blacks while fighting a fire in a crack house in a black neighborhood.

On a TV news show, the grief-stricken Derek blamed his father's death on a laundry list of far-right targets. Later we learn it wasn't just his father's death that shaped him, but his father's dinner table conversation; his father tutors him in racism, but the scene feels like tacked-on motivation, and the movie never convincingly charts Derek's path to race hatred.

The scariest and most convincing scenes are the ones in which we see the skinheads bonding. They're led by Derek's brilliant speechmaking and fueled by drugs, beer, tattoos, heavy metal, and the need all insecure people feel to belong to a movement greater than themselves. It is assumed in their world (the beaches and playgrounds of the Venice area of L.A.) that all races stick together and are at undeclared war with all others. Indeed, the race hatred of the skinheads is mirrored (with different words and haircuts) by the other local ethnic groups. Hostile tribalism is an epidemic here.

The film, written by David McKenna and directed by Tony Kaye, uses black-and-white to show the recent past, and color to show the twenty-four-hour period after Derek is released from prison. In prison, we learn, Derek underwent a slow transition from a white zealot to a loner; a brutal rape helped speed the process. Meanwhile, young Danny and his friends (including a massive guy named Seth, played by Ethan Suplee) wreck a grocery run by immigrants. At school, Danny is a good student, as Derek was before him; both are taught by a black history teacher named Sweeney (Avery Brooks), who supplies the moral center of the film.

In the immediacy of its moments, in the photography (by Kaye) that makes Venice look like a training ground for the apocalypse, and in the strength of the performances, *American History X* is a well-made film. I kept hoping it would be more—that it would lift off and fly, as it might have with a director like Oliver Stone, Martin Scorsese, or Spike Lee. But it never quite does. Its underlying structure is too apparent, and there are scenes where we sense the movie hurrying to touch its bases.

One crucially underdeveloped area is Derek's prison experience. With a swastika tattooed on his chest, he fits in at first with the white power faction, but is disillusioned to find that all the major groups in prison (black, Hispanic, white) have a working agreement; that's too much cooperation for him. Fine, but is it that or a crucial basketball game that gets him into trouble? Not clear.

He's assigned to the laundry, where his black coworker (Guy Torry, in a wonderful performance) gradually—well, begins to seem human to him. But there's a strange imbalance in the conversion process. The movie's right-wing ideas are clearly articulated by Derek in forceful rhetoric, but are never answered except in weak liberal mumbles (by a Jewish teacher played by Elliott Gould, among others). And then the black laundry worker's big speech is not about ideas and feelings but about sex and how much he misses it. There is no effective spokesman for what we might still hopefully describe as American ideals. Well, maybe Derek wouldn't find one in his circles.

What we get, finally, is a series of well-drawn sketches and powerful scenes in search of an organizing principle. The movie needs sweep where it has only plot. And Norton, effective as he is, comes across more as a bright kid with bad ideas than as a racist burning with hate. (I am reminded of Tim Roth's truly satanic skinhead in *Made in Britain,* a 1982 film by Alan Clarke.)

Tony Kaye wanted to have his name removed as the film's director, arguing that it needs more work and that Norton re-edited some sequences. We will probably never know the truth behind the controversy. My guess is that the postproduction repairs were inspired by a screenplay that attempted to cover too much ground in too little time and yet still hasten to a conventional conclusion. Still, I must be clear: This is a good and powerful film. If I am dissatisfied, it is because it contains the promise of being more than it is.

An American Werewolf in Paris ★

R, 98 m., 1997

Tom Everett Scott (Andy), Julie Delpy (Serafine), Vince Vieluf (Brad), Phil Buckman (Chris), Julie Bowen (Amy), Pierre Cosso (Claude), Thierry Lhermitte (Dr. Pigot), Tom Novembre (Inspector LeDuc). Directed by Anthony Waller and produced by Richard Claus. Screenplay by Tim Burns, Tom Stern, and Waller, based on characters created by John Landis.

Now that *Scream* and *Scream 2* have given us horror film characters who know all the horror clichés, the time has come for a werewolf movie about characters who know they're in a werewolf movie. Not that such an insight would benefit the heroes of *An American Werewolf in Paris,* who are singularly dim. Here are people we don't care about, doing things they don't understand, in a movie without any rules. Triple play.

I was not one of the big fans of John Landis's original 1981 film, *An American Werewolf in London,* but, glancing over my old review, I find such phrases as "spectacular set pieces," "genuinely funny moments," and "sequences that are spellbinding." My review of the Paris werewolves will not require any of those phrases.

The new movie involves three callow Americans on a "daredevil tour" of Europe. Played by Tom Everett Scott (of *That Thing You Do*), Vince Vieluf, and Phil Buckman, they climb the Eiffel Tower by moonlight, only to find a young woman (Julie Delpy) about to leap to her death. They talk, she leaps, and Scott leaps after her, luckily while tethered to a bungee cord. (Hint: Always be sure the other end of a bungee line is tied to something else before tying this end to yourself.)

The girl survives, the lads track her to her home, she has blood on her hands, her friend invites them to a rave club, she's not there, Chris finds her locked in a cell in her basement, the ravers are werewolves, so is she, etc., etc. Please don't accuse me of revealing plot points: In a movie with this title, are you expecting that the girl who leaps from the tower is not a werewolf, her friends are exchange students, and the club is frequented by friendly tourists?

One of the pleasures of a film like this is the ritual explanation of the rules, in which we determine how werewolves are made, how they are killed, and how they spread their wolfiness. Here it doesn't much matter, because the plot has a way of adding new twists (like a serum that makes moonlight unnecessary for a werewolf transformation). By the end of the film, any plot discipline (necessary so that we care about some characters and not the others) has been lost in an orgy of special effects and general mayhem.

But let me single out one line of dialogue. After the three American college students are trying to figure out what happened at the tower, one says, "The kind of girl who jumps off the Eiffel Tower has issues, man." Starting with that line, a complete rewrite could be attempted, in which the characters are self-aware, know the werewolf rules, and know not to make the same mistakes as the characters in *An American Werewolf in London* (not to mention *The Howling, The Howling II: Your Sister Is a Werewolf, Howling III, Howling IV: The Original Nightmare, Howling V: The Rebirth,* and *Howling VI: The Freaks*). I even have a great title for them: *Howler.*

Amistad ★ ★ ★

R, 232 m., 1997

Morgan Freeman (Theodore Joadson), Anthony Hopkins (John Quincy Adams), Matthew McConaughey (Roger Baldwin), Nigel Hawthorne (Martin Van Buren), Djimon Hounsou (Cinque), David Paymer (Secretary Forsyth), Pete Postlethwaite (Saunders), Stellan Skarsgard (Tappan), Anna Paquin (Queen Isabella), Tomas Milian (Calderon), Austin Pendleton (Professor Gibbs). Directed by Steven Spielberg and produced by Spielberg, Debbie Allen, and Colin Wilson. Screenplay by David Franzoni.

Slavery could, I suppose, be seen largely as a matter of laws and property—at least to those benefiting from it. One of the astonishing facts contained in Steven Spielberg's *Amistad* is that seven of the nine U.S. Supreme Court justices in 1839 were slave-owning southerners. His new film centers on the legal status of Africans who rise up against their captors on the high seas and are brought into a Massachusetts court. Slavery itself is not the issue. Instead, the court must decide whether the defendants were born of slaves (in which case they are guilty of murder) or were illegally brought from Africa (and therefore had a right to defend themselves against kidnapping).

This legal distinction is not made as clear as it could be; the international slave trade had been outlawed by treaties by 1839, but those who were already slaves remained the property of their masters—as did their children. The moral hairsplitting underlying that distinction is truly depraved, but on it depends the defense of Cinque, the leader of the Africans, and his fellow mutineers.

The film opens on the ship *Amistad*, where Cinque (Djimon Hounsou) is able to free himself from shackles and release his fellow prisoners. They rise up against the Spanish crew of the ship, which is taking them from a Havana slave market to another destination in Cuba. The two men who bought them are spared, and promise to guide the ship back to Africa. But they guide it instead into U.S. waters, and the Africans find themselves in an American court.

Luckily, it is a northern court, or they would have little chance at all. They are not at first lucky in their defense team, which is led by Roger Baldwin (Matthew McConaughey), a real estate lawyer who bases his case on property law and only slowly comes to see his clients as human beings. The cause is supported by two Boston abolitionists, a former slave named Joadson (Morgan Freeman) and an immigrant named Tappan (Stellan Skarsgard). And eventually, on appeal, former U.S. president John Quincy Adams (Anthony Hopkins) argues eloquently for the freedom of the men.

Amistad, like Spielberg's *Schindler's List*, is not simply an argument against immorality. We do not need movies to convince us of the evil of slavery and the Holocaust. Both films are about the ways good men try to work realistically within an evil system in order to spare a few of its victims. *Schindler's* strategies are ingenious and suspenseful, and lead to a more gripping and powerful film than the legal tactics in *Amistad*, where lawyers in powdered wigs try to determine the origin of men whose language they do not speak.

Entirely apart from the moral issues involved, *Schindler's List* works better as narrative because it is about a risky deception, while *Amistad* is about the search for a truth which, if found, will be small consolation to the millions of existing slaves. As a result, the movie doesn't have the emotional charge of Spielberg's earlier film—or of *The Color Purple*, which moved me to tears.

The moments of greatest emotion in *Amistad* stand outside the main story. They include a horrifying scene where, when food runs low on the ship, the weaker slaves are chained together and thrown over the side to drown so that more food will be left for the rest. And another sequence in which the mechanics of the slave trade are examined, as Africans capture members of enemy tribes and sell them to the slave traders. And a scene where Cinque sees African violets in John Quincy Adams's greenhouse, and is seized with homesickness. And Cinque's memory of his wife left in Africa.

What is most valuable about *Amistad* is the way it provides faces and names for its African characters, who are so often in movies made into faceless victims. The slave called Cinque (his real name is Sengbe Pieh) emerges as a powerful individual, a once-free farmer who has lost his wife and family. We see his wife, and his village, and something of his life; we understand how cruelly he was ripped from his life and ambitions (since it was the policy of slavery to destroy African families, this is especially poignant).

He speaks no English, but learns a little while in prison, and a translator is found who helps him express his dismay at a legal system that may free him but will not affirm the true nature of the crime against him. He learns enough of Western civilization to see its contradictions, as in a scene where he uses an illustrated Bible to explain to a fellow slave how he can identify with Jesus. And there is a touching scene between lawyer and client in which Joadson at last talks to Cinque as a man, and not as a piece in a puzzle. "Give us free!" Cinque cries in a powerful moment in the courtroom, indicating how irrelevant a "not guilty" verdict would be to the real facts of his case.

Djimon Hounsou's performance depends largely on his screen presence, which is formidable. Some of the other performances are disappointing. I was surprised how little importance or screen time was given to the Morgan Freeman character, who in his few scenes indicates the volumes that remain concealed. Matthew McConaughey's character is necessarily unfocused as the defense attorney; he proceeds from moral blindness to a light that surprises no one, and while we are happy for him we are not, under the circumstances, much moved. Nigel Hawthorne plays Martin Van Buren, then the president of the United States, who is revealed as a spineless compromiser who wants only to keep the South off his back; the character is played in the same note as his pathetic old George III, when more shrewd calculation might have been effective.

The heart of the film, really, is in Anthony Hopkins's powerful performance as old John Quincy Adams, who speaks for eleven minutes in defense of the defendants, and holds the courtroom (and the audience) spellbound. It is one of the great movie courtroom speeches. But in praising it, I touch on the film's great weakness: It is too much about the law, and not enough about the victims.

Ever since Spielberg began *Amistad,* the story has been hyped and hailed as a great untold chapter in American history, an event to put beside Nat Turner's uprising. The story of Cinque certainly deserves more attention in textbooks, but it is not an ideal story to make into a film; Nat Turner would have been a better choice for Spielberg. That John Quincy Adams wins his big case is a great achievement for him and a great relief for Cinque and his fellows, but in the sad annals of American slavery it is a rather hollow triumph.

Among Giants ★ ★ ★

R, 94 m., 1999

Pete Postlethwaite (Ray), Rachel Griffiths (Gerry), James Thornton (Steve), Lennie James (Shovel), Andy Serkis (Bob), Rob Jarvis (Weasel), Alan Williams (Frank), Emma Cunniffe (Barmaid). Directed by Sam Miller and produced by Stephen Garrett. Screenplay by Simon Beaufoy.

Sometimes movies are simply about actors. There is a story, but only to give them something to talk about while being themselves. With the right actors, a film can essentially be about the way they talk, the look in their eye, their personal style and grace. *Among Giants* is a movie like that. It stars Pete Postlethwaite and Rachel Griffiths as an unlikely couple who fall in love, but mostly it just stars them being interesting.

Postlethwaite you may recall from *In the Name of the Father,* the 1994 Irish film where he won an Oscar nomination for playing the father of a man unjustly accused of being an IRA bomber. Griffiths was an Oscar nominee, playing the sister of a doomed musician in *Hilary and Jackie* (1998). I've seen them both several times; when you look at them you always know how their characters are feeling.

Among Giants was written by Simon Beaufoy, who also wrote *The Full Monty,* and once again combines working-class camaraderie and sex, this time in the same couple. Postlethwaite is Ray, the foreman of a freelance work gang that signs on to paint a long row of electrical power pylons that march across the British landscape. He's in his forties, wiry, ruddy, balding. Griffiths plays Gerry, a backpacker from Australia, making her way around the world and climbing peaks that interest her.

"How long you been out on the road?" he asks her when they meet.

"How long is a piece of string?"

"You get lonely?"

"Yeah, I do."

Something intangible passes between them, and soon she's back, asking for a job. Ray's gang is leery of a woman, but Gerry points out that she's a climber, not afraid of heights—or work. Ray hires her. It's the beginning of a long summer in which the men build campfires to brew their tea, and sleep in vans or tents, and spend their days high in the air with paint buckets (singing "Stand By Me" at one point).

Ray lives in a nearby town, and we learn that he has an estranged wife and kids. He considers himself divorced, but the formalities haven't taken place. Gerry lives in her tent. She is a strange, winsome loner: "All I've got is a whole bunch of people I'm never gonna see again, and a whole lot of places I'm never gonna go back to." One night Ray kisses her. They fall in love.

The complications of their romance provide the main line of the story. The counterpoint comes from details about the other characters in the work gang, especially a young man who relates to Ray as a surrogate father. The film is thick with atmosphere, and knows its way around blue-collar pubs where everybody wears jeans and cowboy shirts on Friday nights, the band plays C&W, and (in a scene that will seem realistic to British viewers and unlikely to Americans) the customers are skillful line dancers.

We are aware at some level that the whole story is a contrivance. The logistics are murky: Who is the man who hires the work gang, and why does he treat them like illegals, and why exactly is the power off now but scheduled to be turned on at the end of the summer? (No prizes for guessing that the uncertainty about power is the setup for his dramatic scene.) Those are questions that can be asked, but the answer is that the whole reality of the film is simply a backdrop to the relationship of these two characters.

They make an odd match. They're probably twenty years apart in age. They're prideful loners. Yet they have a certainty about their physical styles that makes them a good match. They both like to climb, they both work hard, and there is a scene where they frolic, not under a waterfall, but under a falling sheet of water inside the cooling tower of a power plant. Haven't seen that before.

One of the gifts of the movies is to allow us to guess what it might be like to be somebody else. As actors, Postlethwaite and Griffiths have the ability to evoke people it might be interesting to be, or know. The director, Sam Miller, uses this gift in unexpected ways. There is a scene where Gerry uses her climbing skills to traverse entirely around the four walls of a pub without ever touching the floor. Haven't seen that before, either.

Anaconda ★ ★ ★ ½

PG-13, 90 m., 1997

Jennifer Lopez (Terri Flores), Ice Cube (Danny Rich), Jon Voight (Paul Sarone), Eric Stoltz (Dr. Steven Cale), Jonathan Hyde (Warren Westridge), Owen Wilson (Gary Dixon), Kari Wuhrer (Denise Kalberg), Vincent Castellanos (Mateo). Directed by Luis Llosa and produced by Verna Harrah, Leonard Rabinowitz, and Carol Little. Screenplay by Hans Bauer, Jim Cash, and Jack Epps Jr.

"Alone among snakes, anacondas are unique. After eating their prey, they regurgitate in order to eat again."

This information is included in the opening titles of *Anaconda*, and as the words rolled across the screen I heard a chuckle in the theater. It came from me. I sensed with a deep certainty that before the movie was over, I would see an anaconda regurgitate its prey. Human prey, preferably.

Anaconda did not disappoint me. It's a slick, scary, funny Creature Feature, beautifully photographed and splendidly acted in a high adventure style. Its snakes are thoroughly satisfying. The most dreaded predator of the Amazon, we learn, the anaconda can grow to forty feet in length, and crushes its prey before engorging it whole (so whole that it eats an entire jaguar, leaving behind only a single poignant eyeball).

These insights into anaconda lore come mostly from a character named Sarone, played by Jon Voight as a slimy river rat with a dangerous gleam in his eye. "This river can kill you in a thousand ways," he intones, and we get the feeling that he can too. The propeller of his boat is broken, and he's rescued by a small expedition that hopes to make a documentary about the People of the Mist—a legendary lost Amazon tribe. "I know them," Sarone says. "They saved my life." And are probably still regretting it.

The leader of the expedition is Terri Flores (Jennifer Lopez, from *Selena*), who will direct the documentary. Ice Cube plays Danny, her cinematographer. Eric Stoltz is Dr. Steven Cale, a scientist. The other members include Jonathan Hyde as their fastidious British narrator, Owen Wilson as the sound man ("ever notice how the jungle makes you horny?"), Vincent Castellanos as the sinister boat pilot, and Kari Wuhrer as a production assistant. If the cast seems large, reflect that some, perhaps many, of these characters are required so that they can be eaten by snakes.

A movie like *Anaconda* can easily be dumb and goofy (see *Piranha*). Much depends on the skill of the filmmakers. Here one of the key players is the cinematographer, Bill Butler, who creates a seductive yet somehow sinister jungle atmosphere. The movie looks great, and the visuals and the convincing sound track and ominous music make the Amazon into a place with presence and personality: It's not a backdrop; it's an enveloping presence.

The acting is also crucial. Director Luis Llosa, whose *Sniper* (1993) was another good thriller set in the jungle, finds the right notes. He gives the members of the expedition plausible backgrounds (Lopez and Ice Cube say they met in the USC film school), and he allows Jon Voight to take some chances with his performance. Voight's river rat is always on the delectable edge of overacting. He sneers, he frowns, he grimaces, he utters ominous pronouncements ("So young—and yet so lethal," he says, as a baby snake sinks its teeth into a fingertip). This is a daring performance: Voight, a serious actor, isn't afraid to pull out the stops as a melodramatic villain, and his final scene, which he plays with a wink, will be remembered wherever great movie exits are treasured.

Now, as for the snakes. Several kinds of snakes are used in the movie: animated, animatronic and, for all I know, real. They are mostly convincing. There are a few moments when we know, if we bother to think about it, that special effects are being used (especially in a scene where a flaming snake attacks). But there are other moments that earn a gasp from the audience, including one where a giant snake captures its falling prey in midair. There are utterly convincing close-ups of an anaconda's head, its bright eyes glistening, its mouth gaping open to reveal fangs, its skin glistening with a terrible beauty. (Those shots are matched by a point-of-view shot from inside the snake, and by another in which we see the snake's belly skin stretched tautly over the body and face of one of its victims.)

The screenplay has nice authentic touches. The Eric Stoltz character lectures on the dangers of going into the water. He's less afraid of the snakes than of "the little catfish that swims up through your urethra, finds a nice warm spot, and spreads its thorny little spines." A scuba diver finds a poisonous wasp in his mouthpiece. An emergency tracheotomy is performed with a pocket knife. There's a mysterious wall built across the river, which they blow up with dynamite which Voight happens to have with him ("always good to be prepared"). And a protest that blowing up the wall will "upset the ecological balance of the river." Yeah, like the wall grew there.

Anaconda is an example of one of the hardest kinds of films to make well: a superior mass-audience entertainment. It has the effects and the thrills, but it also has big laughs, quirky dialogue, and a gruesome imagination. You've got to like a film where a lustful couple sneaks out into the dangerous jungle at night and suddenly the guy whispers, "Wait—did you hear that? Silence!"

Analyze This ★ ★ ★

R, 106 m., 1999

Robert De Niro (Paul Vitti), Billy Crystal (Ben Sobol), Lisa Kudrow (Laura MacNamara), Chazz Palminteri (Primo Sindone), Joe Viterelli (Jelly), Richard Castellano (Jimmy), Molly Shannon (Caroline), Max Casella (Nicky Shivers). Directed by Harold Ramis and produced by Paula Weinstein and Jane Rosenthal. Screenplay by Peter Tolan, Ramis, and Kenneth Lonergan.

"Do you know who I am?" the mobster asks the shrink.

"Yes, I do."

"No, you don't."

"No, I don't."

The psychiatrist is only too happy to please Paul Vitti, the boss of the New York mob. But Vitti is in a vulnerable position: He's lost his nerve, he has panic attacks, he breaks out crying during sentimental TV commercials. If his rivals find out, he's dead.

A comic situation like this depends on casting to elevate it from the environs of sitcom, and *Analyze This* has Robert De Niro and Billy Crystal to bring richness to the characters. Also a large, phlegmatic man named Joe Viterelli, as a bodyguard named Jelly who tries dimly to understand why the most feared criminal in America needs help from this little head doctor.

Analyze This is funny partly because De Niro and Crystal do what we expect them to do, and partly because they don't. De Niro kids his screen image from all those mob movies by Scorsese and others, making the psychiatrist compliments he cannot refuse.

"You're good."

"Well, I . . ."

"No! You're good!"

"I'm good."

Crystal's character, named Ben Sobol, is the kind of guy who figures if he can just keep talking, sooner or later he'll say the right thing. What we don't expect is that the characters take on a certain human dimension, and we care for them a little. This isn't a deeply involving human drama, you understand, but attention is paid to personalities, and the movie isn't all gag lines.

Of course there has to be a Meet Cute to explain how Ben Sobol meets the mob, and it's handled in a funny setup scene where the shrink's car rams the back of a car with an extra passenger in the trunk. The gangsters are only too happy to forget the incident, even though Crystal wants to call the cops; eventually Jelly accepts the psychiatrist's card, and still has it in his pocket when Vitti needs help.

Vitti's archenemy is a mobster named Primo Sindone (Chazz Palminteri), who would strike if he had any suspicion of his rival's weaknesses. That's why utter secrecy is important, and why Sobol is horrified when he discovers his son eavesdropping on their sessions. "You cannot tell a single person!" he shouts at the kid. "You mean," says the kid, "take it off the Internet?" Sobol is a divorced man about to remarry (to Lisa Kudrow), but Jelly comes for him even in the middle of a wedding, and it begins to look to his fiancée's parents as if he's a mobster himself.

Crystal can go over the top when he needs to, but here he wisely restrains his manic side, and gets into a nice rhythm with De Niro's fearful gangster. The movie surrounds them with fairly lively violence (the shrink himself ends up in a shark tank at one point), but a lot of the mob scenes are satires of *The Godfather* and its clones. There's even a dream sequence where the psychiatrist imagines himself being shot in the street in exactly the same way Don Vito Corleone was in the movie, with Vitti too slow to save him. He describes the dream to Vitti. "I was Fredo?" Vitti says. "I don't think so."

The director and cowriter is Harold Ramis, whose work ranges from broad comedy like *Caddyshack* to the fine-tuned observation of *Groundhog Day.* Here he's presented with all sorts of temptations, I suppose, to overplay the De Niro character and turn the movie into an *Airplane!*-type satire of gangster movies. I think he finds the right path—allowing satire, referring to De Niro's screen past, and yet keeping the focus on the strange friendship between two men who speak entirely different languages. (When Sobol explains Freud's theory that some men subconsciously want to kill their fathers and marry their mothers, Vitti's response is to the point: "You ever seen my mother?")

A movie like this will be thought of almost entirely in terms of De Niro and Crystal, with a nod to Palminteri and Kudrow, and yet I think what holds the parts together is the unexpectedly likable character of Jelly. Joe Viterelli makes the bodyguard not just a mobster, not just a tough guy, but an older man who is weary after many years in service, but loyal and patient with his weirdo boss. As Jelly patiently pads about trying to deal with the disturbing news that his boss is cracking up and seeing a shrink, he lends a subtle dimension to the movie; he gives Vitti a context, and someone who understands him. The comedy here isn't all on the surface, and Viterelli is one reason why.

Anastasia ★★★½

G, 94 m., 1997

With the speaking voices of: Meg Ryan (Anastasia), John Cusack (Dimitri), Kelsey Grammer (Vladimir), Christopher Lloyd (Rasputin), Hank Azaria (Bartok), Bernadette Peters (Sophie), Kirsten Dunst (Young Anastasia), Angela Lansbury (Dowager Empress Marie), and the singing voices of: Liz Callaway (Anastasia), Lacey Chabert (Young Anastasia), Jim Cummings (Rasputin), Jonathan Dokuchitz (Dimitri). An animated film directed and produced by Don Bluth and Gary Goldman. Screenplay by Susan Gauthier, Bruce Graham, Bob Tzudiker, and Noni White. Songs by Lynn Ahrens and Stephen Flaherty; score by David Newman.

The legend of Anastasia would seem like unlikely inspiration for an animated musical, but *Anastasia* picks and chooses cleverly, skipping blithely past the entire Russian Revolution but lingering on mad monks, green goblins, storms at sea, train wrecks, and youthful romance. The result is entertaining and sometimes exciting—a promising launch for Fox's new animation studio, which has declared war on Disney.

The movie's based loosely on the same speculative story as the 1956 feature film starring Ingrid Bergman; it assumes that when Russia's ruling Romanoff family was murdered in the upheaval of revolution, one child escaped the carnage and survived to make a valid claim for the throne. This was Anastasia (voice by Meg Ryan), beloved granddaughter of the Dowager Empress Marie (Angela Lansbury), who herself escaped to Paris and now wearily rejects one impostor after another.

Young Anastasia is seen wrapped in the warm bosom of her family; then disaster strikes, and she spends years in a cruel orphanage, losing all memory of her earlier days. Then, as a lithe and spirited teenager, she falls into the clutches of two con men named Dimitri (John Cusack) and Vladimir (Kelsey Grammer). They both worked in the royal court and have insider knowledge; their scheme is to tutor an impostor until she can fool the Dowager Empress. The irony, which the movie makes much of, is that this impostor is, in fact, the real thing.

Anastasia tells this story within what has become the almost rigid formula of the modern animated feature: The heroine and the hero both have sidekicks, the villain commands nasty little minions, and romance blooms but doesn't get too soppy. Much depends on how colorful the villain is, and the mad monk Rasputin (Christopher Lloyd) is one of the best cartoon villains in a long time. The real Rasputin became infamous for taking so long to die—he was almost unkillable—and this movie version likewise lingers between life and death. His spirit burns on, but his body parts have a disconcerting habit of falling off. His little sidekick Bartok, an albino bat voiced by Hank Azaria, tirelessly screws missing limbs back into place.

Anastasia has a friend, too: her little dog Pooka, who faithfully tags along. Indeed, every important character is assigned a sidekick; Dimitri has Vladimir, and the Dowager Empress has her faithful lady-in-waiting, Sophie (Bernadette Peters). By the movie's end Dimitri wins Anastasia, Vladimir wins Sophie, and I guess we can be relieved that the filmmakers spared us the Bartok-Pooka nuptials.

The film was produced and directed by former Disney artists Don Bluth and Gary Goldman, whose credits include *The Land Before Time* and *An American Tail*. Here they consciously include the three key ingredients in the big Disney hits: action, romance, and music. Only the songs disappoint (why didn't they do the obvious and license the title song from the 1956 film?).

There are three big action sequences: a storm at sea, as Anastasia sleepwalks perilously close to the briny deep; a runaway locomotive and a wreck, as Rasputin's little green goblins sabotage the train carrying Anastasia to Paris; and a final showdown between Rasputin and the forces of good. The action here is alive and energetic, and the train sequence is genuinely thrilling.

What won me over most of all, however, was the quality of the story: It's clearly set up, so that even younger viewers can understand Anastasia's fate and her hopes. ("I'm not exactly grand duchess material here," she says: "A skinny little nobody with no past and no future.") It gets a couple of neat twists out of the idea of making Anastasia a fraud who isn't a fraud. And the Dowager Empress, as played by Lansbury, creates real pathos with her weariness: How many more frauds must she endure?

Animation is the road less traveled for the movies. Although it offers total freedom over the inconveniences of space, time, and gravity, it's so tricky and difficult that animated features have always been rare—and Disney has always known how to make them best. With *Anastasia,* there's another team on the field.

Angel Baby ★ ★ ★

NO MPAA RATING, 105 m., 1997

John Lynch (Harry), Jacqueline McKenzie (Kate), Colin Friels (Morris), Deborra-Lee Furness (Louise), Daniel Daperis (Sam), Dave Argue (Dave), Geoff Brooks (Rowan), Humphry Bower (Frank). Directed by Michael Rymer and produced by Jonathan Shteinman and Timothy White. Screenplay by Rymer.

Watching *Shine,* I found myself wondering about the dynamics of the marriage between David and Gillian Helfgott. Could it have been so simple as a loving woman healing a troubled man?

At the same 1996 Sundance Film Festival that introduced *Shine* to North America, there was another Australian film, one that arrived with seven Australian Academy Awards, including best picture, actor, actress, and director. It also dealt with romance and mental illness. Yet somehow it didn't cause the same stir, perhaps because it was the very opposite of a feel-good movie.

Michael Rymer's *Angel Baby* tells the story of Harry and Kate, who meet at an outpatient clinic for mental patients, who fall in love, who seem for a time to be blessed with one another, and who then make the mistake of growing overconfident and discontinuing their medication.

The results are inevitable, but this is not the film of unredeemed dreariness that the story line would suggest; I have noticed in any number of Australian films a pull toward human comedy, an appreciation for the quirks and eccentric fillips of characters who may be doomed but rage cheerfully against the dying of the light. Even in their final downward spiral, Kate (Jacqueline McKenzie) and Harry (John Lynch) see hopeful omens.

But then Kate's whole life is controlled by omens, which she receives from her guardian angel, named Astral. His method of communication is the Australian version of *Wheel of Fortune.* As the letters are turned over and the underlying phrases are revealed, Kate takes careful notes; she learns she's pregnant, for example, when the Australian version of Vanna White turns over letters spelling out "Great Expectations." And she believes it is Astral who is resident in her womb.

The movie avoids many of the clichés often found in pictures about mental illness. The professionals in the film, for example, are sensitive and competent. And in the film's early scenes, it looks as if Harry and Kate might indeed be successful in their quest for love.

Harry is a nice man, who helps his young nephew banish monsters from the bedroom (he draws a magic chalk circle around the kid's bed), and when he's around Kate his face almost always reflects tender concern. She is more out of control; after a careless in-line skater in a mall store cuts her, she grows hysterical at her loss of blood and even licks some of it up off the floor. When they decide to move in together, the choice seems promising, but then they take the fateful decision to stop their medication.

John Lynch is an actor who is ready for wider recognition (you may remember him as a teenager in *Cal,* or as the hunger striker Bobby Sands in *Some Mother's Son*). In *Angel Baby* he has in some ways the more difficult role; Jacqueline McKenzie's Kate is on her own wavelength, but he has to gauge her condition, react to it, and somehow monitor his own health as well. And there is an intensity that goes along with loving anyone who is disturbed—an uncertainty during the happy moments that makes them seem poignant and precious. That's what the movie captures, and that's the tone that prevails even during the harrowing scenes of suffering.

Those who shed tears during *Shine* are likely to be dry-eyed during *Angel Baby.* The movie's only release is a touching fantasy in the last shot. No marriage is simple, and no love story is uncomplicated. Watching this film, I realized that while I admired *Shine* and was moved by it, *Angel Baby* comes closer to dealing honestly with a fraught relationship. As Tolstoy might have written if he had lived longer and seen more movies: All happy endings are the same, but every unhappy ending is unhappy in its own way.

Anna Karenina ★ ½

PG-13, 108 m., 1997

Sophie Marceau (Anna Karenina), Sean Bean (Count Vronshy), Alfred Molina (Constantin Levin), Mia Kirshner ("Kitty" Scherbatshy), James Fox (Alexi Karenin), Danny Huston (Stiva), Saskia Wickham (Dolly), Fiona Shaw (Lydia Ivanova). Directed by Bernard Rose and produced by Bruce Davey. Screenplay by Rose, based on the novel by Leo Tolstoy.

It's not the story but the style and the ideas that make Tolstoy's *Anna Karenina* a great novel and not a soap opera. There's no shortage of stories about bored rich women who leave their older husbands and take up with playboys. This new screen version of the novel makes that clear by focusing on the story, which without Tolstoy's wisdom is a grim and melodramatic affair. Here is a woman of intoxicating beauty and deep passion, and she becomes so morose and tiresome that by the end we'd just as soon she throw herself under a train, and are not much cheered when she obliges.

The film has been shot on location in Russia; we see St. Petersburg exteriors, country estates, and opulent czarist palaces whose corridors recede to infinity. It all looks wonderful, but the characters, with one exception, are clunks who seem awed to be in the screen adaptation of a Russian classic. The exception is Alexi Karenin, Anna's husband, who is played by James Fox with such a weary bitterness that I found myself caring for him even when he was being cruel to poor Anna.

The story: Anna (Sophie Marceau) and her husband live on a country estate, where their marriage is a dry affair. She goes to the city to counsel her rakish brother, Stiva (Danny Huston), who is treating his wife badly. She meets a slickster named Count Vronsky (Sean Bean), who has a mistress named Kitty (Mia Kirshner), but drops her the moment he sees Anna. He dances with her, she is intoxicated by his boldness, she leaves by train, and he stops the train in the middle of the night to say he must have her, etc. It is not a good sign that while he declares his love we are more concerned about how his horses could have possibly overtaken the train.

Back in the country, Vronsky pursues his ideal and Anna succumbs, after a tiny little struggle. Karenin observes what is happening, especially during a steeplechase when Vronsky's horse falls and Anna shrieks with concern that is unseemly in another man's wife. Soon Anna is pregnant by Vronsky, and Karenin, after a lapse (he tries to force himself on her), offers her a deal: If she stays with him and behaves herself, she can keep the child. Otherwise, she gets Vronsky but not the child.

As in all Victorian novels, this crisis leads to a sickbed scene, declarations of redemption and forgiveness, etc., while in the city a parallel romance is developing between the jilted Kitty and the kind but uncharismatic Levin (Alfred Molina). In the novel, Levin stands for Tolstoy, and also for the decency the other characters lack.

The challenge of any adapter of *Anna Karenina* is to make Anna sympathetic despite her misbehavior. Sometimes that is done with casting (how could we deny Garbo anything?), sometimes with writing. In this film, it is not done. I never felt sympathy for her, perhaps because Sophie Marceau (from *Braveheart*) makes her such a narcissistic sponge, while Fox makes her husband tortured but understandable. Toward the end, as Anna and Vronsky are shunned by society and live in isolation, she even gets on his nerves, especially after she becomes addicted to laudanum.

There is much more to Tolstoy's story. But not in this bloodless and shallow adaptation. Bernard Rose is a director of talent (his *Paper House* is a visionary film, and his *Immortal Beloved* was a biopic that brought great passion to the story of Beethoven). Here, shooting on fabulous locations, he seems to have lost track of his characters. The movie is like a storyboard for *Anna Karenina*, with the life and subtlety still to be added.

Another Day in Paradise ★ ★ ★

R, 101 m., 1999

James Woods (Mel), Melanie Griffith (Sid), Vincent Kartheiser (Bobbie), Natasha Gregson Wagner (Rosie), James Otis (Reverend), Branden Williams (Danny), Brent Briscoe (Clem), Peter Sarsgaard (Ty), Lou Diamond Phillips (Gangster). Directed by Larry Clark and produced by Stephen Chin, Clark, and James Woods. Screenplay by Christopher Landon and Chin, based on the book by Eddie Little.

Another Day in Paradise is a lowlife, sleazeball, drugs-and-blood road movie, which means its basic materials will be familiar to audiences of the post–*Easy Rider* decades. There's not much new here, but then there's so rarely something new at the movies that we're sometimes grateful to see the familiar done well.

What brings the movie its special quality is the work of James Woods and Melanie Griffith and their mirror images, played by Vincent Kartheiser and Natasha Gregson Wagner. Woods and Griffith play types they've played before, but with a zest and style that brings the movie alive—especially in the earlier scenes, before everything gets clouded by doom. Woods plays Uncle Mel, who describes himself: "I'm just a junkie and a real good thief. Kind of go together." Griffith is his woman, Sid. They met because he was her drug dealer.

The movie opens with the younger couple, Bobbie and Rosie (Kartheiser and Wagner). He breaks into a junior college to burgle a vending machine, gets in a struggle with a security guard, is badly wounded, and stabs the guard to death. Soon he's being treated by Uncle Mel. "Are you a doctor?" he asks. "Yeah, sure. I'm a doctor shooting you up with heroin," says Mel sarcastically.

As Bobbie recovers, Mel spins visions of the four of them as a family, setting out on a glorious adventure on the road. He's a spieler, a fast-talking spinner of visions, and Sid backs him up with warmth and encouragement. As a sample of the paradise ahead, she takes them on a shopping spree and then to a nightclub (where the kids get drunk and have to be hauled home by the grown-ups).

We know the good times can't last. Mel needs money too badly because he needs drugs—and because he needs drugs, he's willing to get money in dangerous ways. Soon Bobbie has learned about concealing himself in crawl spaces, and Mel is masterminding a particularly inept crime. The arc of the story is preordained: Early glorious scenes of freedom on the road, followed by lowering clouds, gathering omens, and the closing net of fate.

They do a lot of drugs in the movie. There are five scenes of shooting up and one of snorting, according to the invaluable "Screen It" Website (which helpfully adds that the f-word is used "at least" 291 times). The writer-director is Larry Clark, whose *Kids* (1995) told the harrowing story of young street teenagers in Manhattan, playing with sex and drugs as if they were harmless toys. Clark is drawn to decadence and marginal lifestyles, and he finds special interest in the tension generated by kids in danger.

In Kartheiser and Wagner, he finds performers in the tradition of Juliette Lewis and Brad Pitt in *Kalifornia* (1993) or, indeed, Martin Sheen and Sissy Spacek all those years ago in *Badlands* (1973). The underlying story structure is from *Bonnie and Clyde*, which itself was inspired by earlier road movies. The road and crime and doom seem to fit together easily in the movies.

If there are no new insights in *Another Day in Paradise*, at least there are old arias powerfully sung. James Woods and Melanie Griffith enjoy the possibilities of their characters—they enjoy the supercharged scenes of speed, fear, fantasy, and crime. Woods has played variations on this character many times (how many times have we seen him driving a car, smoking, and talking like a demented con man?). Griffith is like the last rose of summer: still fragrant, but you can see her energy running out, until finally it is more important for her to escape Uncle Mel than to have access to his drugs.

A movie like this reminds me of what movie stars are for. We see them many times in many movies over a period of years, and grow used to their cadences and their range. We invest in them. Those that we like, we follow. James Woods is almost always interesting and often much more than that. Melanie Griffith has qualities that are right for the role she plays here. The kids, Kartheiser and Wagner, are talented but new. It's a sign that you're a movie lover and not just a fan when you start preferring the fine older vintages to the flavors of the month.

Antz ★ ★ ★ ½

PG, 83 m., 1998

With the voices of: Woody Allen (Z), Dan Aykroyd (Chip), Anne Bancroft (Queen), Jane Curtin (Muffy), Danny Glover (Barbatus), Gene Hackman (Mandible), Jennifer Lopez (Azteca), Sharon Stone (Bala), Christopher Walken (Cutter), Sylvester Stallone (Weaver). Directed by Eric Darnell and Tim Johnson and produced by Brad Lewis, Aron Warner, and Patty Wooton. Screenplay by Todd Alcott, Chris Weitz, and Paul Weitz.

Antz rejoices in the fact that a cartoon can show us anything. It's so free, it turns visual cartwheels. It enters into a microscopic world—an ant colony beneath Central Park—and makes it into a world so vast and threatening that comparisons with *Star Wars* are not unjustified.

And it's sharp and funny—not a children's movie, but one of those hybrids that works on different levels for different ages. The kids will enjoy it when the hero and his girl get stuck in some gum on the bottom of a running shoe. Older viewers will understand the hero's complaint that it's not easy "when you're the middle child in a family of 5 million."

The movie is the first animated feature from the DreamWorks Studio and benefits from the input of studio partners Jeffrey Katzenberg, who earlier oversaw the renaissance in Disney animation, and Steven Spielberg, whose *E.T.* seems to have inspired the look of the hero's eyes and a crucial scene where a kiss brings him back to life. The movie is entirely computer-generated, incorporating a clever software program that makes the mouths of the insects look a little, but not too much, like morphs of the actors who voice their dialogue: Woody Allen, Sharon Stone, Sylvester Stallone, Jennifer Lopez, Gene Hackman, Christopher Walken, and others.

The story mixes adventure with political parable. As it begins, every ant in the colony goes dutifully about its age-old assignment, never thinking to question why some are workers, some are warriors, and only one can be the queen. Then the little ant named Z (voice by Allen) develops that attribute which an ant colony has no room for, a mind of his own. "I'm supposed to do everything for the colony?" he asks on a psychiatrist's couch. "And what about *my* needs?"

This is no time for individualism. The colony is engaged in an emergency project to dig a giant tunnel (in ant-scale, it looks as daunting as the Chunnel). Militarists led by General Mandible (Hackman) and Colonel Cutter (Walken) want to divert all resources to war. They even invent false reports of an approaching termite invasion, and convince the queen (Anne Bancroft) that they must strike first. Meanwhile, in a bar, Z meets the beautiful Princess Bala (Sharon Stone). All the other ants "dance" with a rigid precision that looks, well, insectlike. But Z breaks loose, and Bala, intoxicated with the sudden freedom of movement, regrets her engagement to Mandible. Like all ants, her fiancé is . . . predictable.

Z meets a warrior ant (Stallone) and arranges to switch jobs, just so he can impress Bala. Bad timing. Z finds himself hurled into battle against the vastly superior termites, in a microscopic version of the beach massacre in DreamWorks' previous release, *Saving Private Ryan.* Surviving, he returns to the colony and is the seed for a virus of individualism. Eventually Z and Bala find themselves alone on the surface, in search of the legendary Insectopia (a picnic), and threatened by vast creatures of man and nature, which loom overhead like Darth Vader's Death Star.

I have an abiding love of animation, all kinds of animation. (As a child, I naively thought it was "more real" than live action because the edges were sharper and the characters did things I could understand.) Modern animation embodies a certain irony: Although cartoons can literally show any imaginable physical action in any conceivable artistic style, most of the successful ones are contained within the Disney studio style, as it has evolved over the years.

That isn't a bad thing for Disney movies, and I treasure most of them, especially the early ones and the modern renaissance. But there are other ways a cartoon can look. The Japanese master Hayao Miyazaki *(My Neighbor Totoro, Kiki's Delivery Service)* has developed a look with the fanciful style of great children's book illustration. *Toy Story,* by Disney and Pixar, used computer animation to create a new world with a fresh, exciting look. Japanese anime titles like *Akira* and *The Ghost in the Shell* move closer to hard-edged science fiction.

And now look at the panoramic overhead shots of the ant colony in *Antz.* We could be looking at an alien life form, or the headquarters of one of James Bond's megalomaniac enemies. The scale and detail are astonishing. And consider the imagination involved in a sequence where most of the ants in the colony gather themselves into a giant ball, helped by a string of other ants, so that millions of individuals can become one collective tool.

Facts about the lives of real ants provide inspiration for many sequences. There is a scene where an ant is decapitated, and Z has a conversation with his head. Scenes of nursemaids in perpetual procession, as the queen delivers a newborn every five seconds. A funny scene where ants drink nectar from the hindquarters of aphids, and Z complains, "I may be crazy, but I have a thing about drinking from the anus of another creature." And a visually exciting sequence in which an ant is trapped inside a body of water, and struggles with the power of its surface tension.

The visuals are joined to a screenplay with wickedly amusing dialogue and lots of cross-references to current culture. ("All we are saying," chants an ant chorus, "is, give Z a chance!" And later the hero is told, "You de ant!") Eric Darnell and Tim Johnson, who codirected the film, and Todd Alcott, Chris Weitz, and Paul Weitz, who wrote it, lead a team of gifted animators in telling a fable with the resonance of *Animal Farm.* And we sense Woody Allen's satirical spirit sneaking through in some lines; instead of attacking the termites, he suggests, why not try subverting them with campaign contributions? ☞

The Apostle ★ ★ ★ ★

PG-13, 133 m., 1998

Robert Duvall (The Apostle E.F.), Farrah Fawcett (Jessie Dewey), Miranda Richardson (Toosie), Todd Allen (Horace), John Beasley (Brother Blackwell), June Carter Cash (Mrs. Dewey Sr.), Walter Goggins (Sam), Billy Joe Shaver (Joe), Billy Bob Thornton (Troublemaker). Directed by Robert Duvall and produced by Rob Carliner. Screenplay by Duvall.

There's a scene early in *The Apostle* where Robert Duvall, as a Pentecostal preacher from Texas, is having a talk with God, who has to do all of the listening. In an upstairs room at his mother's house, he rants and raves at the almighty, asking for a way to see reason in calamity: His cheating wife is stealing his church from him.

So far, the scene could be in a more conventional film. But then the phone rings, and it's a neighbor, complaining to his mother that someone is "carrying on like a wild man." The call establishes that the preacher lives in a real world, with real neighbors, and not on a sound stage where his life is lived in a self-contained drama. His mother tells the neighbor that her son has talked to God ever since he was a boy and she's not going to stop him now.

The Apostle sees its characters in an unusually perceptive light; they have the complexity and spontaneity of people in a documentary. Duvall, who not only plays the preacher but also wrote and directed the film, has seen this preacher—named Eulis "Sonny" Dewey—with great attention and sympathy.

Sonny is different from most movie preachers. He's not a fraud, for one thing; Hollywood tilts toward the Elmer Gantry stereotype. Sonny has a one-on-one relationship with God, takes his work seriously, and in the opening scene of the movie pauses at an auto accident to ask one of the victims to accept Jesus Christ, "who you're going to soon meet." He is flawed, with a quick temper, but he's a good man, and the film is about his struggle back to redemption after his anger explodes.

As the film opens, Sonny is spending a lot of time on the road at revivals (we see him at one of them, made convincing because Duvall cast all the extras from real congregations). His wife (Farrah Fawcett) has taken up with the youth minister, and one night, sitting in a motel room, Sonny figures that out, drives home through the darkness, finds her absent from her bed, and throws a baseball through the minister's bedroom window.

His wife wants out of the marriage. And through legal but shady maneuverings, she also deprives him of his church and his job. Sonny gets drunk, wades into a Little League game being coached by the youth minister, and bangs him on the head with a baseball bat. Then he flees town (there is an overhead shot of his car circling aimlessly around a rural intersection; he has no idea where to go). Eventually he ends up in a hamlet in the Louisiana bayou, where he spends his first night in a pup tent supplied by a man who wants to help him but isn't sure he trusts him.

Sonny changes his name to "The Apostle E.F.," and sets about rebuilding a small rural church given him by a retired black minister. His mostly black congregation is small at first, but grows as the result of broadcasts on the local forty-watt station. We see in countless little ways that Sonny is serious: He wants this church to work, he wants to save souls, he wants redemption. Like the documentary *Say Amen, Somebody,* the film spends enough time at the church services, listening to the music and the preaching, that we get into the spirit; we understand his feelings.

The Apostle became something of a legend in independent film circles, because Duvall was so long in getting it made. The major studios turned him down (of course; it's about something, which scares them). So did old associates who had always promised help, but didn't return his calls on this project. As he waited, Duvall must have rewritten the script many times, because it is astonishingly subtle. There isn't a canned and prefab story arc, with predictable stops along the way. Instead, the movie feels as alive as if it's a documentary of things happening right now.

Consider a sequence where the Apostle E.F., who is a man after all, asks the receptionist at the local radio station out on a date. How will he approach her? How does she see him? He wants to find a way to make his desires clear, without offending her. She knows this. As played by Duvall and Miranda Richardson, the sequence is a brilliant observation of social and sexual strategies.

Many of his scenes develop naturally, instead of along the lines of obligatory clichés. A confrontation with his wife, for example, doesn't end as we think it might. And a face-down with a redneck racist (Billy Bob Thornton) develops along completely unexpected lines. The Apostle E.F. is not easy to read; Duvall's screenplay does what great screenwriting is supposed to do and surprises us with additional observations and revelations in every scene.

Perhaps it's not unexpected that Duvall had to write, direct, and star in this film, and round up the financing himself. There aren't that many people in the film industry gifted enough to make such a film, and fewer still with the courage to deal honestly with a subject both spiritual and complex. (Simpleminded spirituality is no problem; consider the market for angels right now.) *The Apostle* is like a lesson in how movies can escape from convention and penetrate into the hearts of rare characters.

Apt Pupil ★ ★

R, 112 m., 1998

Ian McKellen (Kurt Dussander) Brad Renfro (Todd Bowden), Bruce Davison (Todd's father), Elias Koteas (Archie), Joe Morton (Dan Richler), David Schwimmer (Edward French). Directed by Bryan Singer and produced by Jane Hamsher, Don Murphy, and Singer. Screenplay by Brandon Boyce, based on the story by Stephen King.

Apt Pupil uses the horrors of the Holocaust as an atmospheric backdrop to the more conventional horror devices of a Stephen King story. It's not a pretty sight. By the end of the film, as a death camp survivor is quoting John Donne's poem about how no man is an island, we're wondering what island the filmmakers were inhabiting as they assembled this uneasy hybrid of the sacred and the profane.

The movie is well made by Bryan Singer *(The Usual Suspects)* and well acted, especially by Ian McKellen as Kurt Dussander, a Nazi war criminal who has been hiding in America for years. The theme is intriguing: A teenager discovers the old man's real identity and blackmails him into telling stories about his wartime experiences. But when bodies are buried in cellars and cats are thrown into lighted ovens, the film reveals itself as unworthy of its subject matter.

Brad Renfro is the costar, as Todd Bowden, a bright high school kid who after a week's study of the Holocaust notices a resemblance between a Nazi criminal and the old man down the street. Using Internet databases and dusting the old guy's mailbox for fingerprints, Todd determines that this is indeed a wanted man, and confronts him with a strange demand: "I want to hear all about it. The stories. Everything they were afraid to tell us in school. No one can tell it better than you."

The old man is outraged, but trapped. He shares his memories. And the film, to its shame, allows him to linger on details: "Although the gas came from the nozzles at the top, still they tried to climb. And climbing, they died in a mountain of themselves."

Soon the boy undergoes a transformation into a bit of a Nazi himself. He brings the old man a Nazi uniform, makes him put it on, and orders him to march around the kitchen: "Attention! March! Face right!" When the old man protests, young Todd barks: "What you've suffered with me is nothing compared to what the Israelis would do to you. Now move!"

The movie at least doesn't present the old man as repentant. Indeed, under the urging of the boy, he seems to regress to his earlier state, and there is the particularly nasty scene where he attempts to gas a neighbor's cat in his oven. (Does he succeed? The movie's shifty editing seems to permit two conclusions.) This scene is paired with another in which an injured bird is killed by a bouncing basketball.

Is there some kind of social message here? Some overarching purpose? If there were, then the material itself would not automatically be offensive. But the later scenes in the movie seem more, not less, exploitative. After the old Nazi tries to kill a spying bum and push him down the basement stairs, he calls on the kid to finish the job: "Now we see what you are made of!" We even get the tired cliché where a body seems to be dead and then rears up, alive. And of course victims being hit over the head with shovels.

All of this plays against a subplot where the kid tells lies at school, and even blackmails the old Nazi into posing as his grandfather at a counseling session. And at the end, after it is far too late for the film to change its nature, there is an attempt at moral balancing, including the poetry-quoting patient in the next hospital bed. That John Donne poem, about how no man is an island, about how we are all part of the larger humanity, ends with words that might profitably be considered by the filmmakers: "Never send to know for whom the bell tolls; it tolls for thee."

Armageddon ★

PG-13, 150 m., 1998

Bruce Willis (Harry S. Stamper), Billy Bob Thornton (Dan Truman), Ben Affleck (A. J. Frost), Liv Tyler (Grace Stamper), Keith David (General Kimsey), Chris Ellis (Walter Clark), Jason Isaacs (Ronald Quincy), Will Patton ("Chick" Chapple). Directed by Michael Bay and produced by Jerry Bruckheimer, Gale Anne Hurd, and Bay. Screenplay by Jonathan Hensleigh and J. J. Abrams.

Here it is at last, the first 150-minute trailer. *Armageddon* is cut together like its own highlights. Take almost any thirty seconds at random and you'd have a TV ad. The movie is an assault on the eyes, the ears, the brain, common sense, and the human desire to be entertained. No matter what they're charging to get in, it's worth more to get out.

The plot covers many of the same bases as the recent *Deep Impact*, which, compared to *Armageddon*, belongs on the AFI list. The movie tells a similar story at fast-forward speed, with Bruce Willis as an oil driller who is recruited to lead two teams on an emergency shuttle mission to an asteroid "the size of Texas," which is about to crash into Earth and obliterate all life—"even viruses!" Their job: Drill an 800-foot hole and stuff a bomb into it to blow up the asteroid before it kills us.

Okay, say you do succeed in blowing up an asteroid the size of Texas. What if a piece the size of Dallas is left? Wouldn't that be big enough to destroy life on Earth? What about a piece the size of Austin? Let's face it: Even an object the size of that big Wal-Mart outside Abilene would pretty much clean us out, if you count the parking lot.

Texas is a big state, but as a celestial object it wouldn't be able to generate much gravity. Yet when the astronauts get to the asteroid, they walk around on it as if the gravity is the same as on Earth. Sure, they're helped by back-mounted compressed-air nozzles, but how does that lunar buggy fly across a jagged canyon, Evel Knievel–style?

The movie begins with Charlton Heston telling us about the asteroid that wiped out the dinosaurs. Then we get the masterful title card, "65 Million Years Later." The next scenes show an amateur astronomer spotting the object. We see top-level meetings at the Pentagon and in the White House. We meet Billy Bob Thornton, head of Mission Control in Houston, which apparently functions like a sports bar with a big screen for the fans, but no booze. Then we see ordinary people whose lives will be Changed Forever by the events to come. This stuff is all off the shelf—there's hardly an original idea in the movie.

Armageddon reportedly used the services of nine writers. Why did it need any? The dialogue is either shouted one-liners or romantic drivel. "It's gonna blow!" is used so many times, I wonder if every single writer used it once, and then sat back from his word processor with a contented smile on his face, another day's work done.

Disaster movies always have little vignettes of everyday life. The dumbest in *Armageddon* involves two Japanese tourists in a New York taxi. After meteors turn an entire street into a flaming wasteland, the woman complains, "I want to go shopping!" I hope in Japan that line is redubbed as "Nothing can save us but Gamera!"

Meanwhile, we wade through a romantic subplot involving Liv Tyler and Ben Affleck. Liv is Bruce Willis's daughter. Ben is Willis's best driller (now, now). Bruce finds Liv in Ben's bunk on an oil platform and chases Ben all over the rig, trying to shoot him. (You would think the crew would be preoccupied by the semidestruction of Manhattan, but it's never mentioned after it happens.) Helicopters arrive to take Willis to the mainland, so he can head up the mission to save mankind, etc., and he insists on using only crews from his own rig—especially Affleck, who is "like a son."

That means Liv and Ben have a heartrending parting scene. What is it about cinematographers and Liv Tyler? She is a beautiful young woman, but she's always being photographed while flat on her back, with her brassiere riding up around her chin and lots of wrinkles in her neck from trying to see what some guy is doing. (In this case, Affleck is tickling her navel with animal crackers.) Tyler is obviously a beneficiary of Take Our Daughters to Work Day. She's not only on the oil rig, but she attends training sessions with her dad and her boyfriend, hangs out in Mission Control, and walks onto landing strips right next to guys wearing foil suits.

Characters in this movie actually say: "I wanted to say—that I'm sorry," "We're not leaving them behind!" "Guys—the clock is ticking!" and "This has turned into a surrealistic nightmare!" Steve Buscemi, a crew member who is diagnosed with "space dementia," looks at the asteroid's surface and adds, "This place is like Dr. Seuss's worst nightmare." Quick—which Seuss book is he thinking of?

There are several Red Digital Readout scenes, in which bombs tick down to zero. Do bomb designers do that for the convenience of interested onlookers who happen to be standing next to a bomb? There's even a retread of the classic scene where they're trying to disconnect the timer, and they have to decide whether to cut the red wire or the blue wire. The movie has forgotten that *this is not a terrorist bomb,* but a standard-issue U.S. military bomb, being defused by a military guy who is on board specifically because he knows about this bomb. A guy like that, the *first* thing he should know is, red, or blue?

Armageddon is loud, ugly, and fragmented. Action sequences are cut together at bewildering speed out of hundreds of short edits, so that we can't see for sure what's happening, or how, or why. Important special effects shots (like the asteroid) have a murkiness of detail, and the movie cuts away before we get a good look. The few "dramatic" scenes consist of the sonorous recitation of ancient clichés ("You're already heroes!"). Only near the end, when every second counts, does the movie slow down: Life on Earth is about to end, but the hero delays saving the planet in order to recite cornball farewell platitudes.

Staggering into the silence of the theater lobby after the ordeal was over, I found a big poster that was fresh off the presses with the quotes of junket blurbsters. "It will obliterate your senses!" reports David Gillin, who obviously writes autobiographically. "It will suck the air right out of your lungs!" vows Diane Kaminsky. If it does, consider it a mercy killing. ☞

Artemisia ★★★

R, 96 m., 1998

Valentina Cervi (Artemisia), Michel Serrault (Orazio), Miki Manojlovic (Agostino), Luca Zingaretti (Cosimo), Emmanuelle Devos (Costanza), Frederic Pierrot (Roberto), Maurice Garrel (The Judge), Brigitte Catillon (Tuzia). Directed by Agnes Merlet and produced by Patrice Haddad. Screenplay by Merlet.

Most painters draw life studies while looking at nude models. In the secretive opening scenes of *Artemisia,* a young woman uses herself as a model, sketching by candlelight, looking at her own body in a mirror. This is Artemisia Gentileschi, who wants to be a painter but lives at a time when the profession is forbidden to women. She sketches anyway, and when her nude drawings are discovered by the nuns and shown to her father, he responds with pride: "You are the child of a painter."

He is Orazio (Michel Serrault), a professional painter of considerable skills, although his craft is a little behind the new work being done in Florence. It is 1670, the Italian Baroque is flourishing, and he allows his beloved daughter to study in his studio—although he draws the line at letting her view nude males. She is direct and determined, and bribes the fisherman Fulvio with a kiss for letting her draw him.

Artemisia is played by Valentina Cervi, who you may remember as the dark-haired, bright-eyed love child of John Malkovich and Barbara Hershey in *Portrait of a Lady.* She looks older here but is still a coltish teenager, with an eager stride and impulsive courage. You like her right away, because you sense there's no deceit in her: Like all true artists faced with the nude form, she sees not the naughty bits but the technical challenge.

The famous artist Agostino Tassi (Miki Manojlovic) joins her father in carrying out a papal commission. He is more advanced in his work with light and shadow, and she wants to study under him. Tassi wants nothing to do with her until he sees her work. Then he accepts her. "Someday you'll take lessons from me," she tells him. It is foreordained that they will fall in love—and rather touching, since he is a man of the world (she spies on him through a brothel window). He's attracted to her not just for sexual reasons, but because he has literally never met anyone like her before: a woman who thinks for herself, is as talented and ambitious as a man, and says what she believes.

The film follows through on the inevitable consequences of their romance. There is an ecclesiastical trial in which the cardinal in charge, bored with the conflicting testimony, simply has her fingers wound tight with a leather thong until either they are cut off or someone tells the truth. In a sense, she shares the same fate as her sister to the north in *Dangerous Beauty,* another 1998 movie set a century earlier, about a Venetian woman who can be independent only by becoming a courtesan. She can't be a modern woman without her world getting medieval on her.

The difference—and this is the most important difference in the world—is that Artemisia gains her freedom not by selling herself, but by selling her work. She seems to have been the first professional woman artist in the Western world, the first to be commissioned, the first to be admitted to the Academy in Florence, the first to travel to England for employment. Her paintings hang in the museums of Europe, and the critic Harvey Karten says of her painting *Judith Beheading Holofernes* in a Florence gallery: "You don't have to look closely at it to guess that it's the work of a woman painter. Two women are standing over the bearded, defeated general Holofernes, one holding a sword at his neck, the other helping to hold him down to a bed." Not a favorite baroque male fantasy.

Artemisia is as much about art as about sex, and it contains a lot of information about techniques, including the revolutionary idea of moving the easel outside and painting from nature. It lacks, however, detailed scenes showing drawings in the act of being created (for that you need *La Belle Noiseuse,* Jacques Rivette's 1991 movie that peers intimately over the shoulder of an artist in love). And it doesn't show a lot of Artemisia's work. What it does show is the gift of Valentina Cervi, who is another of those modern European actresses, like Juliette Binoche, Irene Jacob, Emmanuelle Béart, and Julie Delpy, whose intelligence, despite everything else, is the most attractive thing about her.

As Good As It Gets ★★★

PG-13, 138 m., 1997

Jack Nicholson (Melvin Udall), Helen Hunt (Carol Connelly), Greg Kinnear (Simon Bishop), Cuba Gooding Jr. (Frank Sachs), Skeet Ulrich (Vincent), Shirley Knight (Beverly), Yeardley Smith (Jackie). Directed by James L. Brooks and produced by Bridget Johnson and Kristi Zea. Screenplay by Mark Andrus and Brooks.

There's something about Jack Nicholson that makes you want to grin. Maybe the anticipation that you'll see him get away with something. He's the guy who knows the angles. His screen persona was established for all time the moment he told the waitress to hold the chicken salad between her knees. *As Good As It Gets* takes that attitude as far as it will go in the direction it was already headed: He plays an obsessive-compulsive curmudgeon whose communication with the world is mostly limited to insults—not funny ones, but intended to wound.

It is some kind of twisted tribute to Nicholson that he's able to use this dialogue in what is, after all, a comedy. He hurls racist, sexist, homophobic, and physical insults at everyone he meets, and because it's Nicholson we let him; we know there has to be a payback somehow. If you see the movie, ask yourself how Nicholson's tirades would sound coming from any other actor. They'd bring the film to an appalled halt.

Nicholson plays Melvin Udall, a man who crouches in the apartment where he has ground out sixty-two romance novels for women. Asked how he writes the women characters so convincingly, he replies, "I think of a man. And I take away reason and accountability." He hates everyone in the building, and the movie opens with him hurling his neighbor's little dog down the garbage chute. Then he marches out to take his habitual meal in a nearby restaurant, where he lays out his own plastic cutlery.

"Sometimes you must try other people's clean silverware, as part of the fun of eating out," advises Carol the waitress (Helen Hunt). She waits on him but she doesn't like him, and when he makes a disparaging remark about her asthmatic son, she makes him withdraw it or she will never, ever serve him again. Since she's the only waitress who will serve him, and since this is the only restaurant he will eat in, he backs down. (Later, when he's thrown out of the restaurant, there's applause from the regulars.)

We meet Melvin's neighbor, the dog owner. He's a gay artist named Simon (Greg Kinnear), who is beaten up one day by the friends of one of his models. During his recovery, his agent and dealer (Cuba Gooding Jr.) insists that Melvin take care of the little dog, which has been rescued from the garbage. Melvin doesn't want to, but he does, and to his amazement (but not ours) he develops a grudging affection for the mutt.

As Good As It Gets was directed by James L. Brooks, whose films *(Terms of Endearment, Broadcast News)* show original characters in unexpected lights. This film, cowritten with Mark Andrus, creates memorable people but is not quite willing to follow them down unconventional paths. It's almost painful, watching the screenplay stretch and contort these characters to fit them somehow into a conventional formula—they're dragged toward the happy ending, screaming and kicking all the way.

If the movie had been either more or less ambitious, it might have been more successful. Less ambitious, and it would have been a sitcom crowd-pleaser, in which a grumpy Scrooge allows his heart to melt. More ambitious, and it would have touched on the underlying irony of this lonely man's bitter life. But *As Good As It Gets* is a compromise, a film that forces a smile onto material that doesn't wear one easily. Melvin is not a man ever destined to find lasting happiness, and the movie's happy ending feels like a blackout, seconds before more unhappiness begins.

Yet there's so much good here, in the dialogue, the performances, and the observation, that the movie succeeds at many moments even while pursuing its doomed grand design. Consider Melvin's decision to arrange for the medical treatment of Carol's son. The little boy suffers agonizing asthma attacks, but through Melvin, Carol is able to find a smarter doctor (Harold Ramis) who can do some good. The material here is right out of a silent weeper: Repentant Scrooge helps poor child to breathe again. But by casting the wonderfully droll Ramis as the doctor and skewing the dialogue just slightly, Brooks makes it new and screwy.

The main story line gets a similar treatment. It becomes clear that Melvin has been destined by the filmmakers to become a better man: First he accepts dogs, then children, then women, and finally even his gay neighbor. But Brooks and Andrus, having blocked out this conventional progression, then write against it, using rich irony so that individual scenes seem fresh even while the overall progress follows ancient custom. When Melvin goes back for a belated visit to his one-time therapist, for example, they give him a perfect line: "How can you diagnose someone as having obsessive-compulsive disorder and yet criticize him for not keeping an appointment?"

There were times, watching *As Good As It Gets,* when I hoped the movie might go over the top into greatness. It had the potential. The pieces were in place. It was sad to see the filmmakers draw back into story formulas. Maybe the studio, mindful of the $50 million price tag, required Brooks to channel his obstreperous material in a safe direction. One can imagine an independent filmmaker, with a smaller budget, taking dialogue and characters like these and following them into the wild blue yonder. One can imagine Brooks, Nicholson, and Hunt doing it too. That's why the film left me with such a sense of lost opportunities.

The Assignment ★ ★ ★ ½

R, 115 m., 1997

Aidan Quinn (Annibal Ramirez/Carlos), Donald Sutherland (Jack Shaw [Henry Fields]), Ben Kingsley (Amos), Claudia Ferri (Maura Ramirez), Celine Bonnier (Carla), Vlasta Vrana (KGB Head Officer), Liliana Komorowska (Agnieska), Von Flores (Koj). Directed by Christian Duguay and produced by Tom Berry and Franco Battista. Screenplay by Dan Gordon and Sabi H. Shabtai.

The Assignment is a canny, tricky thriller that could serve as an illustration of what a similar release, *The Peacemaker,* is not. Both films involve an international hunt for a dangerous terrorist, but *The Peacemaker* is a cartoon and *The Assignment* is intelligent and gripping—and *it has a third act!* Instead of an action orgy, it has more than enough story to see it through to the end and keep us absorbed the whole way. Yes, it ends with a deadly struggle, but as the setting for another stage of the movie's web of deceit.

The film is centered on a CIA plot to discredit and kill Carlos, the feared terrorist who operated for years despite the best efforts of the free world's security agencies to capture him. Donald Sutherland plays Fields, the CIA agent for whom Carlos has become an obsession, and when he finds a U.S. Navy officer named Ramirez (Aidan Quinn) who's a dead ringer for the terrorist, he devises a risky scheme: He'll train Ramirez to impersonate Carlos, then use the double to convince the KGB that their attack dog is disloyal. As a result, Carlos will either be dead or, almost as good, discredited in the eyes of his sponsors.

Fields works with an Israeli named Amos (Ben Kingsley) in training Ramirez, after first using psychological tactics to convince the reluctant navy man to leave his wife and family and become a counterterrorist. (The scene where Fields shows Ramirez a dying child in a hospital is a direct echo of *The Third Man.*) Then the false Carlos is sent into the field to work the deception, which I will not describe.

The Assignment is fascinating because its characters can be believed, because there is at least a tiny nugget of truth in the story, and because from the deceptive opening credits, this is a film that creates the right world for these characters to inhabit. Sutherland's CIA man is especially well drawn: "I don't have any family," he says, "and I don't have any friends. The only people I've ever cared about were the ones I've killed."

Quinn plays a dual role, as Ramirez and Carlos, and has some tricky scenes, especially one in which a former lover of Carlos's helps train him sexually so that he will be a convincing bedmate for another of the terrorist's lovers.

The screenplay, by Dan Gordon and Sabi H. Shabtai, has action scenes that grow from the story and are not simply set pieces for their own sake. It's impressive the way so many different story threads come together all at once near the end.

The director, Christian Duguay, is new to me. What he has is a tactile love of film, of images. He and the cinematographer, David Franco, don't use locations so much as occupy them; we visit Jerusalem, Paris, Vienna, Washington, Tripoli, and Moscow (or sets and effects that look like them), and yet the movie's not a travelogue but a story hurtling ahead.

I have seen so many lazy thrillers. They share the same characteristics: Most of the scenes involve the overpriced star, the villain is underwritten, and the plot is merely a setup for the special effects, the chases, and the final action climax. *The Assignment* gives us ensemble work by fine actors, it has a villain of great complexity (developed through the process of imitating him), and at the end there is a tantalizing situation for us to unravel as we leave the theater.

At First Sight ★★

PG-13, 124 m., 1999

Val Kilmer (Virgil Adamson), Mira Sorvino (Amy Benic), Kelly McGillis (Jennie Adamson), Steven Weber (Duncan Allanbrook), Bruce Davison (Dr. Charles Aaron), Nathan Lane (Phil Webster), Ken Howard (Virgil's Father), Laura Kirk (Betsy Ernst). Directed by Irwin Winkler and produced by Winkler and Rob Cowan. Screenplay by Steve Levitt, based on the story "To See and Not See" by Oliver Sacks, M.D.

The Oliver Sacks case study that inspired *At First Sight* tells the story of a man who has grown accustomed to blindness, and then is offered an operation that will restore sight. The moment when the bandages are removed all but cries out to be filmed. But to have sight suddenly thrust upon you can be a dismaying experience. Babies take months or years to develop mind-eye-hand coordination; here is an adult blind person expected to unlearn everything he knows and learn it again, differently.

The most striking moment in *At First Sight* is when the hero is able to see for the first time since he was three. "This isn't right," he says, frightened by the rush of images. "There's something wrong. This can't be seeing!" And then, desperately, "Give me something in my hands," so that he can associate a familiar touch with an unfamiliar sight.

If the movie had trusted the fascination of this scene, it might have really gone somewhere. Unfortunately, its moments of fascination and its good performances are mired in the morass of romance and melodrama that surrounds it. A blind man can see, and *still* he's trapped in a formulaic studio plot.

The buried inspiration for this film, I suspect, is not so much the article by Oliver Sacks as *Awakenings* (1990), another, much better movie based on another report by Sacks. Both films have similar arcs: A handicapped person is freed of the condition that traps him, is able to live a more normal life for a time, and then faces the possibility that the bars will slam shut again. *Charly* (1968), about a retarded man who gains and then loses normal intelligence, is the classic prototype.

In *Awakenings,* Robert De Niro played a man locked inside a rare form of Parkinson's disease. Under treatment by a brilliant doctor (Robin Williams), the disease goes into remission, and the man, who had not been able to speak or move for years, regains normal abilities. He even falls a little in love. Then the regression begins. In *At First Sight,* Val Kilmer plays a blind man who meets and falls in love with a woman (Mira Sorvino). She steers him to a doctor (Bruce Davison) whose surgical techniques may be able to restore his sight.

The woman, Amy, is a New York architect. She's left an unhappy relationship: "For the last five years I have lived with a man with the emotional content of a soap dish." She goes to a small resort town on vacation and sees a man skating all by himself on a forest pond. Later, she hires a massage therapist, who turns out to be the same person, a blind man named Virgil (Kilmer). The moment he touches her, she knows he is not a soap dish. She begins to cry as the tension drains from her.

Virgil knows his way everywhere in town, knows how many steps to take, is friendly with everybody. He is protected by a possessive older sister named Jennie (Kelly McGillis), who sees Amy as a threat: "We're very happy here, Amy. Virgil has everything he needs." But Amy and Virgil take walks, and talk, and make love, and soon Virgil wants to move to New York City, where Amy knows a doctor who may be able to reverse his condition.

The movie is best when it pays close attention to the details of blindness and the realities of the relationship. When the two of them take shelter from the rain in an old building, for example, he is able to sense the space around him by the sound of the rain outside. Some of his dialogue is sweetly ironic; when they meet for a second time, he says, "I was describing you to my dog, and how well you smelled."

All of this is just right, and Kilmer and Sorvino establish a convincing, intimate rapport—a private world in which they communicate easily. But the conventions of studio movies require false melodrama to be injected at every possible juncture, and so the movie manufactures a phony and unconvincing breakup, and throws in Virgil's long-lost father, whose presence is profoundly unnecessary for any reason other than to motivate scenes of soap-opera psychology.

The closing credits tell us the movie is based on the true story of "Shirl and Barbara Jennings, now living in Atlanta." My guess is that their story inspired the scenes that feel authentic, and that countless other movies inspired the rest. Certainly the material would speak for itself, if the screenplay would let it: Every single plot point is carefully recited and explained in the dialogue, lest we miss the significance. Seeing a movie like this, you wonder why the director, Irwin Winkler, didn't have more faith in the intelligence of his audience. The material deserves more than a disease-of-the-week docudrama simplicity.

Footnote: For a contrast to the simplified melodrama of At First Sight, *see* Hilary and Jackie, *which examines relationships and handicaps in a more challenging and adult way.*

Austin Powers: International Man of Mystery ★★★

PG-13, 88 m., 1997

Mike Myers (Austin Powers), Elizabeth Hurley (Vanessa Kensington), Mike Myers (Dr. Evil), Michael York (Basil Exposition), Mimi Rogers (Mrs. Kensington), Robert Wagner (Number Two), Seth Green (Scott Evil), Fabiana Udenio (Alotta Fagina), Charles Napier (Commander Gilmour). Directed by Jay Roach and produced by Suzanne Todd, Demi Moore, Jennifer Todd, and Mike Myers. Screenplay by Myers.

In the opening scenes of *Austin Powers: International Man of Mystery,* the British superagent has nearly won his war against the scheming Dr. Evil. But Evil escapes by boarding a rocket shaped like Bob's Big Boy and going into orbit around Earth—where he will wait, cryogenically frozen, until the time is right to resume his scheme for world domination. To counter this move, Austin Powers has himself frozen, and when Evil returns in 1997, Powers is defrosted too.

That's the simple but productive premise of *Austin Powers,* a funny movie that only gets funnier the more familiar you are with the James Bond movies, all the Bond clones, and countless other 1960s films. The joke is that both Powers and Dr. Evil are creatures of the 1960s, and time has passed them by.

Both roles are played by Mike Myers, who has the same spirit of getting away with something that was so infectious in *Wayne's World.* As Powers, he's a sex-mad male chauvinist pig who tries to seduce a 1990s woman like agent Elizabeth Hurley with words like "groovy," "trendy," and "with-it." He's doing his own thing. In an opening tribute to the immortal *Beyond the Valley of the Dolls,* he throws a party and cries out, "This is my happening and it freaks me out!"

Dr. Evil is similarly time-challenged. With a bald head and a sneer that make him look like a prototypical Bond villain, he pushes buttons to send underlings falling into an incinerator. But he's hopelessly out of touch. During his frozen decades, his operation has moved into legitimate businesses under the direction of Number Two (Robert Wagner), and no longer finds international blackmail profitable. (At one point, when Dr. Evil suggests a scheme involving a million-dollar ransom demand, his board members chuckle as they explain how little a million will buy these days.)

Modern times are not accommodating for these relics from the past. Dr. Evil discovers he has a son named Scott Evil (Seth Green), who resents him for spending all that time in orbit when he should have been performing his parenting duties. They end up at a twelve-step meeting for dysfunctional families.

The movie is based on variations of its theme:

James Bond meets Political Correctness. A lot of the laughs come from Elizabeth Hurley, as Vanessa Kensington, liberated feminist British secret agent, who reacts to Austin's seduction techniques as if he were a bug and she should squish him. One of the movie's funniest scenes takes place when Austin frolics nude in their hotel suite: Through elaborate choreography, his private parts are somehow always covered from the camera's point of view, saving the movie's PG-13 rating by a hair, while we find out that the British don't call their breakfast sausages "bangers" for nothing.

The movie, written by Myers and directed by Jay Roach, is smart enough to know the 1960s are funny without being exaggerated. In one sequence, a fashion photographer shoots sixties fashions, and the clothes, which look like outlandish science-fiction fantasies, are in fact identical to costumes worn during posing sessions in Antonioni's *Blow Up* (1967). Movie buffs will have fun cataloging all the references to other movies; I clocked *A Hard Day's Night* and *Sgt. Pepper's Lonely Hearts Club Band* in addition to *BVD* and all the Bond, Matt Helm, and *Our Man Flint* references. And, of course, those who remember Bond's adventures with Pussy Galore will be amused by his female antagonist this time, the sinister Alotta Fagina (Fabiana Udenio).

The cast is well chosen. Michael York is serious business as Basil Exposition, the British spymaster assigned to bring Powers up-to-date. Hurley again shows a nice comic flair (she regards her own sexuality with amusement). Charles Napier, from *BVD*, is the hard-edged Commander Gilmour, all teeth and grim concern. And Seth Green finds the right modern note in totally dismissing everything that his father has worked so long to destroy.

What is best is the puppy-dog earnestness and enthusiasm that Myers brings to his role. He can only imagine how exciting 1997 will be. Just think: When he was frozen, the world was embracing widespread promiscuity, one-night stands, recreational drugs, and mind expansion. He can only imagine what wonderful improvements have come along in the last thirty years.

Austin Powers: The Spy Who Shagged Me ★ ★ ½

PG-13, 95 m., 1999

Mike Myers (Austin Powers/Dr. Evil), Heather Graham (Felicity Shagwell), Elizabeth Hurley (Vanessa Kensington), Rob Lowe (Young Number Two), Michael York (Basil Exposition), Robert Wagner (Number Two 1999), Seth Green (Scott Evil), Gia Carides (Robin Swallows), Verne Troyer (Mini-Me). Directed by Jay Roach and produced by Suzanne Todd, Jennifer Todd, Demi Moore, and Eric McLeod. Screenplay by Mike Myers and Michael McCullers.

There are some big laughs in *Austin Powers: The Spy Who Shagged Me*, but they're separated by uncertain passages of noodling. You can sense it when comedians know they have dead aim and are zeroing in for the kill. You can also sense it when they don't trust their material. The first *Austin Powers* movie burst with confidence: Mike Myers knew he was onto something. This time, too many scenes end on a flat note, like those *Saturday Night Live* sketches that run out of steam before they end. *SNL* cuts to music or commercials; *Austin Powers* cuts to song-and-dance interludes.

The key to a lot of the humor in the first film was that Austin Powers had been transported lock, stock, and barrel from the sixties to the nineties, where he was a sexist anachronism. The other satirical target was the James Bond series. This second film doesn't want to be a satire so much as just zany, raunchy slapstick.

The Spy Who Shagged Me seems to forget that Austin is a man out of his time; there are few laughs based on the fact that he's thirty years past his sell-by date, and there's so much time travel in this movie that half of the time he's back in the sixties again. Even when he's in the nineties, however, the women seem to take him on his own terms. Myers and his collaborators, flush with the victory of the first film, have forgotten that Austin is a misfit and not a hero.

The plot again involves Austin and his arch-enemy, Dr. Evil (both played by Myers). Thirsting for revenge after being exiled into Earth orbit, Evil wants to travel through time to when Powers was cryogenically frozen, and steal his mojo. (In case you were wondering, a beaker of mojo looks like Kool-Aid with licorice ropes floating in it.)

I didn't use a stopwatch, but my guess is that Evil has more screen time than Austin this time. There are several revelations. Early in the movie, in a funny sequence set on *The Jerry Springer Show,* Dr. Evil's son, Scott (Seth Green), appears, complaining that he hates his dad. Later a secret of parentage is revealed, *Star Wars*–style. And Evil acquires a midget double named Mini-Me, played by Verne Troyer and inspired, Myers has said, by the miniature Marlon Brando in *The Island of Dr. Moreau.*

In a film with a lot of babes, Heather Graham plays the lead babe, Felicity Shagwell, a spy dedicated to her craft. In one scene that had the audience cringing when they should have been laughing, she goes to bed with a villain from Scotland named Fat Bastard, who wears a kilt, "weighs a metric ton," and is covered with greasy chicken bits. (Study the end credits for a surprise about the actor playing the F.B.)

There were some laughs (but more groans) during a scene where Austin mistakes a fecal brew for coffee; the movie is going for the kind of gross-out humor that distinguished *There's Something About Mary,* but what this sequence proves is that the grosser a scene is, the funnier it has to be to get away with it. I saw the movie with an audience recruited from the radio audience of Mancow Muller, Chicago's most cheerful vulgarian, and if *they* had a mixed reaction, middle America is likely to flee from the theater.

The movie succeeds, however, in topping one of the best elements in the first film, which was when Austin's private parts were obscured by a series of perfectly timed foreground objects. After Dr. Evil blasts off in a phallic spaceship, characters look up in the sky, see what the ship looks like, and begin sentences that are completed by quick cuts to other dialogue. (If I told you the names of some of the people you'd get the idea, but that wouldn't be fair to the movie.)

There is an underlying likability to Austin Powers that sort of carries us through the movie. He's such a feckless, joyful swinger that we enjoy his delight. Myers brings a kind of bliss to the Bond lifestyle. I also liked Seth Green as Evil's son, not least because he has obviously studied *Ebert's Bigger Little Movie Glossary* and knows all about the Fallacy of the Talking Killer (when Evil gets Powers in his grasp, Evil's son complains, "You never kill him when you have the chance to"). And the movie has fun by addressing the audience directly, as when Austin introduces Burt Bacharach and Elvis Costello, or later observes, during a scene set in the British countryside but shot in the Los Angeles hills, "Funny how England looks in no way like Southern California." Oh, and the tradition of homage to *Beyond the Valley of the Dolls* continues with a bit part for the Russ Meyer superstar Charles Napier.

Note: This film obtained a PG-13 rating—depressing evidence of how comfortable with vulgarity American teenagers are presumed to be. Apparently you can drink shit, just as long as you don't say it. ☞

B

Babe: Pig in the City ★★★★

G, 96 m., 1998

Magda Szubanski (Mrs. Hoggett), James Cromwell (Farmer Hoggett), Mary Stein (The Landlady), Mickey Rooney (Fugly Floom), Roscoe Lee Browne (Narrator). And the voices of: E. G. Daily (Babe), Danny Mann (Ferdinand), Glenne Headly (Zootie), James Cosmo (Thelonious), Stanley Ralph Ross (Bull Terrior). Directed by George Miller and produced by George Miller, Doug Mitchell, and Bill Miller. Screenplay by George Miller, Judy Morris, and Mark Lamprell.

"The first hazard for the returning hero is fame."

So we are assured by the narrator in the opening line of *Babe: Pig in the City*. And what is true of heroes is even more true of sequels. The original *Babe* was an astonishment, an unheralded family movie from Australia that was embraced and loved and nominated for an Oscar as Best Picture. Can the sequel possibly live up to it?

It can and does, and in many ways is more magical than the original. *Babe* was a film in which everything led up to the big sheepherding contest, in which a pig that worked like a dog turned out to be the best sheep-pig of them all. *Babe: Pig in the City* is not so plotbound, although it has the required assortment of villains, chases, and close calls. It is more of a wonderment, lolling in its enchanting images—original, delightful, and funny.

It doesn't make any of the mistakes it could have. It doesn't focus more on the human characters—it focuses less, and there are more animals on the screen. It doesn't recycle the first story. It introduces many new characters. It outdoes itself with the sets and special effects that make up "the city." And it is still literate, humane, and wicked. George Miller, who produced, directed, and cowrote the film, has improved and extended the ideas in *Babe* (1995), instead of being content to copy them.

The movie begins with Babe returning in triumph to the farm with his sheepdog trophy. Alas, he soon falls into the well, setting in motion a calamitous chain of events that ends with Farmer Hoggett (James Cromwell) laid up in bed, and Mrs. Hoggett (Magda Szubanski) forced to exhibit Babe at a state fair in order to save the farm from foreclosure. Alas again, Babe and Mrs. Hoggett miss their connecting flight (she is busted on suspicion of drug possession, that merry, apple-cheeked dumpling of a lady). And they are homeless in the cruel city, where hotels sniff at pigs.

What a city this is! I love imaginary cities in the movies, from *Metropolis* to *Dark City*, and here is one to set beside the great ones. Using elaborate sets that surround the buildings with a canal system, Miller uses f/x to create a skyline that impudently incorporates such landmarks as the Statue of Liberty, the Sydney Opera House, and the Hollywood sign. This is all cities. And in it, Babe finds himself at a boardinghouse whose landlady (Mary Stein) believes animals deserve rooms just like people do.

There is a large cast of animal characters, whose dialogue is lip-synched, and who are colorful and individual—not at all like silly talking animals. One of my favorite scenes involves Ferdinand the duck (voice by Danny Mann), attempting to keep up with the jet plane taking Babe to the city; the rear view of him flapping at breakneck speed is one of the funniest moments in the movie. (He's eventually given a lift by a pelican, who intones, "Go well, noble duck!")

In the boardinghouse, we meet chimpanzees, orangutans, cats, fish, and a dog paralyzed from the waist down, who propels himself on a little cart. Babe is tricked by some of his new housemates into distracting fierce dogs during a desperate raid for food; apparently facing doom, he turns, looks his enemy in the eye, and asks, "Why?" He has a close call with a bull terrier (voice by Stanley Ralph Ross, sounding like a Chicago gangster) who tries to kill him and ends up dangling headfirst in the canal. Babe saves him from drowning, and the dog becomes his fierce protector: "What the pig says, goes!"

The movie is filled with wonders large and small. Little gags at the side of the frame and big laughs in the center. It is in no way just a "children's movie," but one that extends the imagination of everyone who sees it, and there is a wise, grown-up sensibility to its narration, its characters, and a lot of the action. (Other action is cheerfully goofy, as when Mrs. Hoggett gets involved in a weird bungeelike session of chandelier swinging.)

Here is a movie that is all made up. The world and its characters materialize out of the abyss of the imagination, and in their impossibility they seem more real than the characters in many realistic movies. Their hearts are in the right places. And apart from what they do and say, there is the wonderment of the world they live in ("A place just a little to the left of the twentieth century"). I liked *Babe* for all the usual reasons, but I like *Babe: Pig in the City* more, and not for any of the usual reasons, because here is a movie utterly bereft of usual reasons. ☞

Baby Geniuses ½★

PG, 94 m., 1999

Kathleen Turner (Elena) Christopher Lloyd (Heap), Miko Hughes (voice) (Sly), Kim Cattrall (Robin), Peter MacNicol (Dan), Dom DeLuise (Lenny), Ruby Dee (Margo). Directed by Bob Clark and produced by Steven Paul. Screenplay by Clark and Greg Michael, based on a story by Paul, Francisca Matos, and Robert Grasmere.

Bad films are easy to make, but a film as unpleasant as *Baby Geniuses* achieves a kind of grandeur. And it proves something I've long suspected: Babies are cute only when they're being babies. When they're presented as miniature adults (on greeting cards, in TV commercials, or especially in this movie), there is something so fundamentally *wrong* that our human instincts cry out in protest.

Oh, you can have fun with a baby as a movie character. *Look Who's Talking* (1989) was an entertaining movie in which we heard what the baby was thinking. *Baby's Day Out* (1994), with its fearless baby setting Joe Mantegna's pants on fire, had its defenders. But those at least were allegedly real babies. *Baby Geniuses* is about toddlers who speak, plot, scheme, disco dance, and beat up adults with karate kicks. This is not right.

The plot: Kathleen Turner plays a woman with a theory that babies can talk to each other. She funds a secret underground lab run by Christopher Lloyd to crack the code. Her theory is based on the Tibetan belief that children have Universal Knowledge until they begin to speak—when their memories fade away.

This is an old idea, beautifully expressed by Wordsworth, who said that "heaven lies about us in our infancy." If I could quote the whole poem instead of completing this review, believe me, we'd all be happier. But I press on. The movie involves a genius baby named Sly, who escapes from the lab and tries to organize fellow babies in revolt. The nauseous sight of little Sly on a disco floor, dressed in the white suit from *Saturday Night Fever* and dancing to "Stayin' Alive" had me pawing under my seat for the bag my Subway Gardenburger came in, in case I felt the sudden need to recycle it.

Every time the babies talk to one another, something weird happens to make it look like their lips are in synch (think of talking frogs in TV commercials). And when the babies do things that babies don't do (hurl adults into the air, for example), we lose all track of the story while trying to spot the visual trick.

There's only one way the movie might have worked: If the babies had been really, really smart. After all, according to the theory, they come into this world "trailing clouds of glory" (Wordsworth again: the man can write). They possess Universal Knowledge. Wouldn't you expect them to sound a little like Jesus or Aristotle? Or at least Wayne Dyer? But no. They arrive to this mortal coil (Shakespeare) from that level "higher than the sphery chime" (Milton), and we expect their speech to flow in "heavenly eloquence" (Dryden). But when they open their little mouths, what do they say? "Diaper gravy"—a term used four times in the movie, according to a friend who counted (Cleland).

Yes, they talk like little wise guys, using insipid potty-mouth dialogue based on insult humor. This is still more evidence for my theory that the greatest single influence on modern American culture has been Don Rickles.

Bad Manners ★ ★ ★

R, 88 m., 1998

David Strathairn (Wes Westlund), Bonnie Bedelia (Nancy Westlund), Saul Rubinek (Matt Carroll), Caroleen Feeney (Kim Matthews), Julie

Harris (Professor Harper). Directed by Jonathan Kaufer. Screenplay by David Gilman, based on his play *Ghost in the Machine.*

Is this a dream or a nightmare? A man programs a computer to compose music at random. The computer gives him what he has asked for. But in the middle of all the binary coin-tossing, he discovers several perfect bars of Martin Luther's "A Mighty Fortress is Our God." How could this be? Did the computer have a serendipitous accident? Or did God himself reach down a bemused finger and stir the zeroes and ones?

There is another possibility that does not occur to the musicologist, who is a self-important middle-aged man named Matt (Saul Rubinek). His latest girlfriend is a brainy temptress named Kim (Caroleen Feeney), who is a computer expert. Could she have meddled with his program, just as she has reprogrammed his life? Do not hasten to choose the third possibility. It seems likely only because Kim is such a game-player anyway, a woman who draws out the worst in everyone around her for her private delight.

As the wickedly funny *Bad Manners* opens, Kim and Matt arrive as the house guests of a longtime married couple named Wes and Nancy Westlund (David Strathairn and Bonnie Bedelia). She is a successful academic. He is not. He has, in fact, just been denied tenure at a second-tier school, which hurts for a lot of reasons, among them: (1) Nancy has tenure at Harvard, and (2) the overbearing, condescendingly successful Matt is Nancy's former lover.

Matt is full of himself. He believes his computer program will make him as famous as if he had intercepted messages from distant galaxies. Wes also takes himself very seriously. He is pompous and easily wounded, and the dark-haired, chain-smoking young Kim immediately singles him out as a target. She observes that Wes and Nancy have no children, and asks him, "Firing blanks?" She uses his antique bowl as an ashtray. She wanders about the house wearing less than she should, and she seduces Wes once in a fantasy sequence and probably again for real, although the truth is obscured by much game-playing.

Bad Manners is based on the play *Ghost in the Machine,* by David Gilman, first performed at Chicago's Steppenwolf theater in 1993. Like work by that other Chicagoan, David Mamet, it toys with the integrity of its characters by subjecting them to devious games. In *Bad Manners,* the key game is one only two of the characters are playing—and perhaps they are playing it only with themselves. Wes is powerfully attracted to Kim but denies it, and when he discovers that a $50 bill is missing, he tells Nancy that Kim is the thief. At his urging, Nancy searches Kim's luggage and does indeed find a $50 bill, which appears to be concealed. But is it the same bill? The bill is removed, replaced, and doubled, in a fiduciary version of "Who's on First?" Sounds silly, but there's a way in which smart people can get obsessed with tiny, goofy matters of principle and blow them all out of proportion—and Wes goes weird over that bill.

Meanwhile, in the movie's best single scene, the proud Matt goes to visit the editor of a respected academic journal (Julie Harris). He has submitted a paper describing his computer miracle to her, and she tells him what she thinks of it. The Harris character is like a visitor from another world; the four main characters are trapped inside their rigid little dance, and she is not. She handles the interview with brutal directness.

Bad Manners, directed by Jonathan Kaufer, will remind some of *Who's Afraid of Virginia Woolf,* and others of Tom Noonan's oddly involving, overlooked *The Wife.* Like them, it is about intellectuals who would rather verbalize about their problems than solve them. But it doesn't choose to cut to the bone; the visitors will eventually leave, and perhaps routine will reestablish itself; the movie is more about games than about psychological reality, and all the more fun because of that.

There is a masochistic sense in which all of the characters are enjoying themselves with their mind games, especially Wes. And at least Kim, before she leaves, is able to provide Nancy with a useful suggestion.

Bang ★ ★ ★ ½

NO MPAA RATING, 98 m., 1997

Darling Narita (Woman), Peter Greene (Homeless Man), Michael Newland (Cop), David Allen Graff (Producer), Luis Guizar (Jesus). Directed by Ash and produced by Daniel M. Berger and Ladd Vance. Screenplay by Ash.

Bang is a powerful sleeper, convincing, provocative, and exciting—an adventure in "guerrilla filmmaking" that uses an unexpected story device to hold up a mirror to a big American city.

Bang tells the story of a desperate young woman who spends a day wearing the uniform of a Los Angeles policeman, and experiences some of the privileges and sorrows that go with being perceived as a cop. Because it's shot in a flat and realistic style, it's curiously convincing: The story doesn't hype manufactured scenes, but considers what might happen in such a situation. I found myself forgetting the structure and artistry, and simply being carried along with the flow.

The movie stars Darling Narita ("her real name," the press notes say) as an unnamed Japanese-American actress, about twenty-five, who has been evicted from her apartment for nonpayment of rent. Homeless and broke, she goes to an audition with a "producer" who drops the names of Julia and Dustin, tells her she looks "like an Asian Meryl Streep with brown hair," and then asks her to join him in a phony love scene. Is he a fake? Probably, but in Hollywood not necessarily.

She flees from the house, and runs into a homeless guy who lives in the bushes (Peter Greene, who played Zed in *Pulp Fiction* and was brilliant in the painful *Clean, Shaven*). He won a bronze medal in the '84 Olympics, he says, although he never takes it out of his brown paper bag.

Angered that she was mistreated, he destroys the producer's mailbox. The cops are called, and an officer leads her into the woods and demands sex. She grabs his gun, forces him to strip, and handcuffs him to a tree. Then she puts on his uniform, drives off on his motorcycle, and the real movie begins.

What would it be like to be a cop? To be hated or treasured by the people on the street, depending on their condition or need? To be seen as a law enforcer, medic, counselor, good guy, bad guy? She finds out.

The story of the making of *Bang* helps explain its curiously convincing quality. The film, written and directed by a British director named Ash ("his real name," the notes say), was shot for only $20,000 on the streets of Los Angeles, without permits or permissions; real L.A. police occasionally got involved in the filming because they thought the film's star was one of their own, and LAPD helicopters circle ominously overhead during some scenes.

What the actors and crew did was to turn up, film a scene quickly, and disappear. Some scenes were improvised on the spot, including one where the "cop" hands out money to homeless men and nearly starts a riot. Others show thought and depth. Despite its budget, *Bang* doesn't look cheap or rushed; that this film cost less than a single costume for *Batman and Robin* is some kind of a parable.

Darling Narita is an actress with a flat, uninflected style (she acts in a movie much like she does in the "audition"). She plays a woman who is depressed and fairly undemonstrative, who gets through scenes by saying as little as possible. The approach creates unexpected tension in a scene like the one where, wearing the uniform, she's eating breakfast in a diner when two real cops join her at her table. Will she be exposed as an impersonator? What can she possibly say? In a more facile movie she'd ad-lib her way out of danger; here, she's nearly speechless, and it plays a lot better.

Two sequences are especially strong. In one, she chases a drug dealer up to a roof, where he threatens to jump. "I'm not a cop!" she shouts, and the scene develops two unexpected but likely surprises. In another lengthy sequence, which is the heart of the movie, her cycle runs out of gas and she gets a lift to the gas station with two Latinos. For once she is able to unwind a little (with a beer and a joint, to their amazement), and then that scene also pays off surprisingly, with great unexpected drama.

The film is filled with other incidents: A run-in with a Japanese-American hooker, who thinks she is being arrested. An encounter with two people she finds making love in the Hollywood Hills. And eventually a return to the real cop, who has spent the day handcuffed to the tree and trying to deal with the homeless man.

Bang avoids obvious buildups and payoffs. It takes a simple premise—cop for a day—and treats it not as an excuse for a thriller, but as a window into the everyday life of the city. Its choice as heroine is a good one, because the woman is perceived by others through three lenses: female, Asian, cop. ("Where are you from?" the so-called producer asks. "Here," she says. "No, where are you really from?")

Knowing little about *Bang* before I saw it, except for its reputation as a low-budget film shot guerrilla-style on the streets, I confess I expected flashy sub-Tarantino GenX narcissism. What I didn't expect was a film so well made, so penetrating, so observant. And, like all films that really hold your attention, so entertaining.

B.A.P.S. no stars

PG-13, 90 m., 1997

Halle Berry (Nisi), Martin Landau (Mr. Blakemore), Ian Richardson (Manley), Natalie Desselle (Mickey), Troy Beyer (Tracy), Luigi Amodeo (Antonio), Jonathan Fried (Isaac), Pierre (Ali). Directed by Robert Townsend and produced by Mark Burg and Loretha Jones. Screenplay by Troy Beyer.

B.A.P.S. is jaw-droppingly bad, a movie so misconceived I wonder why anyone involved wanted to make it. As a vehicle for the talents of director Robert Townsend and actors Halle Berry and Martin Landau, it represents a grave miscalculation; I hope they quickly put it behind them.

The title stands for "Black American Princesses." Its two heroines are more like tacky Cinderellas. Berry and Natalie Desselle play vulgar and garish homegirls from Decatur, Georgia, whose artificial nails are eight inches long, whose gold teeth sparkle, and whose hairpieces are piled so high on their heads that the concept passes beyond satire and into cruelty.

There is a thin line between satire and offensiveness, and this crosses it. Its portraits of these two working-class black women have been painted with snobbery and scorn. The actresses don't inhabit the caricatures with conviction. The result is a hurtful stereotype, because the comedy doesn't work to redeem it. We should sense some affection for them from the filmmakers, but we don't—not until they receive a magic Hollywood makeover in the later scenes of the movie, and miraculously lose their gold teeth. The movie invites us to laugh at them, not with them, but that's a moot point since the audience I joined did not laugh at all, except incredulously.

The plot: Berry plays Nisi, a waitress, who hears on MTV about a contest to choose a dancer for a music video and national tour by a rap star named Heavy D. She shares this news with her friend Mickey (Desselle), a hairdresser, and it fits right into their plans for marrying rich guys and living on easy street. So they say good-bye to their shiftless boyfriends and fly to L.A. wearing hairstyles so extreme no one behind them on the airplane can see the movie. Funny? No. It could have been funny, but not when the reaction shots are of annoyed white businessmen asking to change their seats.

In L.A. they're spotted at the audition by a mysterious figure who makes them an attractive offer: room and board in a Bel Air mansion and $10,000. What's the deal? He represents Mr. Blakemore (Landau), a dying millionaire, who has experienced true love only once in his life, many years ago—with Lily, his family's black maid. Nisi will pose as Lily's granddaughter and cheer the old guy in his final days on Earth.

There's more to it than that, of course; it's all a scam. But Mr. Blakemore inexplicably takes to the women from the moment he sees them. (Nisi, dressed in pink latex and high heels, looks like a hooker, and Mickey looks like her coach.) The plot later reveals details that make it highly unlikely Mr. Blakemore would even for a second have been deceived by the story, but never mind; the movie's attention span isn't long enough for it to remember its own setup.

Even though the movie fails as a comedy, someone should have told Landau it was intended to be one. He plays Mr. Blakemore with gracious charm and great dignity, which is all wrong; his deathbed scene is done with such clunky sincerity that one fears Landau actually expected audiences to be moved by it. Not in this movie. The cause of his ill health is left a little obscure, and no wonder, because shortly before his dreadful deathbed scene he's well enough to join the women in a wild night of disco dancing. You have not lived until you've seen Martin Landau discoing. Well, perhaps you have.

Another key character is Manley (Ian Richardson), Blakemore's butler, who turns up his nose at the first sight of the women, but inevitably comes to like them. The message of the movie, I guess, is that two homegirls can find wealth and happiness if only they wear blond wigs, get rid of those gold teeth and country vocabularies, and are nice to rich old white men. It gets even better: At one point, the boyfriends from Georgia are flown out to L.A. to share the good luck, and they vow to get their acts together and Plan For Their Futures, in a scene that comes way too late in the film for us to believe or care.

The movie was written by the actress Troy Beyer, who has a small role as a lawyer. What was she thinking of? I don't have a clue. The movie doesn't work, but was there any way this material could ever have worked? My guess is that African-Americans will be offended by the movie, and whites will be embarrassed. The movie will bring us all together, I imagine, in paralyzing boredom.

Barney's Great Adventure ★ ★ ★

(Star rating for kids six and under; adults: bring your Walkman)
G, 75 m., 1998

Trevor Morgan (Cody Newton), Diana Rice (Abby Newton), Kyla Pratt (Marcella), George Hearn (Grandpa Greenfield), Shirley Douglas (Grandma Greenfield). Directed by Steve Gomer and produced by Sheryl Leach and Dennis DeShazer. Screenplay by Stephen White.

Since *Barney's Great Adventure* is intended for children six and below, I am writing this review to be read aloud:

Barney has his own movie. Not one of those videos you've watched a hundred times, but a real movie, more than an hour long. If you like him on TV, you'll like him here, too, because it's more of the same stuff, only outdoors and with animals and shooting stars and the kinds of balloons people can go up in.

The main character in the story, after Barney, is a boy named Cody, who is in about the first or second grade. He's just at that age when kids start to have their doubts about dinosaurs who look like large purple stuffed toys. Along with his sister Abby and her best friend, Marcella, he goes to visit Grandpa and Grandma on their farm. Cody doesn't think he'll like the farm, because his grandparents don't have cable TV, so how can he watch Nickelodeon? Plus Grandpa's pigpen is directly below Cody's bedroom window.

But then Barney turns up. He starts as a little toy, and then he becomes about eight feet tall, but looking just the same. He sings a song named "Imagine" and tells Cody that it was Cody's own imagination that made the toy dinosaur become the real Barney.

Cody plays a trick. He stops believing in Barney. Barney disappears. Then Barney plays a trick. He appears again, because *he* believes in Cody! That sort of makes sense.

Barney shows Cody a special wishing star. The star deposits an egg in Grandpa's barn. This is a wishing egg. It has different colored stripes on it. When all the stripes glow, the egg is about to hatch. The kids take the egg to Miss Birdfinch to find out about it.

But the egg gets in a lot of trouble. It falls into the back of a birdseed truck and is hauled off to town. Cody, Abby, and Marcella chase it, and get to be in a parade and see the balloons go up. To get to town they ride a pony.

Barney must not know any new songs, because mostly he sings old ones, like "Twinkle, Twinkle Little Star" and "Old McDonald" and "Clap Your Hands." It's sweet when Grandpa sings "Let Me Call You Sweetheart" to Grandma. Even though this is probably the first time you've heard that song, it's not new, either.

By the end of the movie, Cody believes in Barney, because it's pretty hard not to believe in something that's purple and eight feet tall and standing right there in front of you. The egg hatches and helps everyone have their wishes. Baby Bop and B.J., Barney's friends on television, have small roles. Baby Bop is always looking for her yellow blanket, which she calls a "blan-kee." Don't you think it's time for Baby Bop to get serious about learning to say "blanket"?

BASEketball ★ ½

R, 98 m., 1998

Trey Parker (Coop), Matt Stone (Remer), Yasmine Bleeth (Jenna), Jenny McCarthy (Yvette), Robert Vaughn (Cain), Ernest Borgnine (Denslow), Dian Bachar (Squeak), Bob

Costas (Himself), Al Michaels (Himself). Directed by David Zucker and produced by Zucker, Robert LoCash, and Gil Netter. Screenplay by Zucker, LoCash, Lewis Friedman, and Jeff Wright.

BASEketball is a major missed opportunity from the creators of the TV grosstoon *South Park.* It starts promisingly as an attack on modern commercialized sports, and then turns into just one more wheezy assembly-line story about slacker dudes versus rich old guys.

It does give you a taste, every now and then, of what a genuinely subversive, satiric comedy on pro sports would feel like. I laughed at an opening montage of sponsored sports domes ("Preparation H Arena"), and when the narrator talked about runaway sports teams and stars who care only about money, my ears perked up. But there's little follow-through, and the movie sinks quickly into sight gags about bodily functions.

Bodily functions can be funny. I recall with great affection the gas attack in Eddie Murphy's *The Nutty Professor* and the famous opening sequence in *There's Something About Mary.* But *BASEketball* thinks the functions *themselves* are funny. There's an enormous gulf between a joke built on peeing (opening scene of *Mary*) and the belief that peeing is a joke (an early scene in this film).

Thinking it's funny simply to show something—that it's hilarious just to be getting away with it—is junior high school humor. Once you outgrow that age, you kinda like the material to be taken to another level. Too much of this film is pitched at the level of guys in the back row of home room, sticking their hands under their armpits and making farting noises.

The movie stars Trey Parker and Matt Stone, creators of Comedy Central's *South Park,* as a couple of high school buddies who get desperate during a basketball grudge game, and invent baseketball, which combines basketball, baseball, and volleyball (it's a real game that David Zucker, the film's director, invented in the 1980s). Soon they're playing it in their driveway; then they start to draw a crowd, and an aging sports zillionaire (Ernest Borgnine) takes them pro.

The ideals of the first baseketball league are high. Teams will not jump from town to town in search of the highest bidder, and the players will all be paid the same. The sport catches on, and soon Bob Costas and Al Michaels (playing themselves) are announcing the games. The playing field consists of a big mockup of the heroes' original garage and driveway. The sport rewards the art of trash-talking your opponents, and players try to distract shooters by grossing them out.

The performances of Parker and Stone, who are onscreen in almost every scene, are surprisingly good, especially considering these guys don't have a lot of acting experience. They're goofy in a *Wayne's World* kind of way, and use the word "dude" so much that one conversation is conducted entirely in "dudes." Their long wet kiss toward the end of the film is not as funny as the tongue work between the neighbor and her dog in *There's Something About Mary* but at least they tried.

I liked the personal sports museum of another team owner (Robert Vaughn), who pays sports legends like Kareem Abdul Jabbar to sit in a glass case as an exhibit. And I guess it's sort of funny when the guys both fall for the sexy head of the Dreams Come True Foundation (Yasmine Bleeth) and treat her sick kids to a day with their baseketball heroes (the high point: sitting in a bar watching Jerry Springer on TV). The preview audience laughed at a scene where the guys visit poor little Joey after his liver transplant, inadvertently sit on his air tube, and then fry him with defibrillators; the movie's jaundiced attitude toward the deaths of kids is lifted straight from *South Park,* where little Kenny, of course, dies weekly and has been consumed by scavengers right there on the screen.

Famous faces float through the film. Jenny McCarthy plays Borgnine's mistress ("I gave him the best three months of my life!"), Robert Stack kids his work on *Unsolved Mysteries,* and Reggie Jackson turns up at the end. All of the guest stars are required to use four-letter words, but that takes us back to the original problem: It's not funny just *because* they say them; it has to be funny for another reason too.

Some commentators will no doubt seize upon *BASEketball* as further evidence of the deterioration of standards in our society. They will attack it as vulgar, offensive, disgusting, etc. That's not what bothers me. I think the movie is evidence of deteriorating *comic* standards in our society. It's not very funny, and tries to buy laughs with puerile shocks. My theory: Those who find it funny haven't advanced a whole lot from the sneaky-fart-noise evolutionary stage.

Batman & Robin ★★

PG-13, 126 m., 1997

George Clooney (Batman/Bruce), Chris O'Donnell (Robin/Dick), Arnold Schwarzenegger (Mr. Freeze), Uma Thurman (Poison Ivy), Alicia Silverstone (Batgirl), Michael Gough (Alfred Pennyworth), Pat Hingle (Commissioner Gordon), John Glover (Dr. Jason Woodrue), Elle Macpherson (Julie Madison), Vivica A. Fox (Ms. B. Haven), Jeep Swenson (Bane). Directed by Joel Schumacher and produced by Peter Macgregor-Scott. Screenplay by Akiva Goldsman, based on Batman characters created by Bob Kane and published by DC Comics.

Because of my love for the world of Batman, I went to Joel Schumacher's *Batman & Robin* with real anticipation. I got thrilled all over again by the Gothic towers of Gotham City. I was reminded of how cool the Batmobile is (Batman has a new one), and I smiled at the fetishistic delight with which Batman and Robin put on their costumes, sheathing themselves in shiny black second skins and clamping on lots of belts, buckles, shields, hooks, pulleys, etc. (How much does that stuff weigh? How do they run while they're wearing it?)

But my delight began to fade at about the thirty-minute mark, when it became clear that this new movie, like its predecessors, was not *really* going to explore the bizarre world of its heroes, but would settle down safely into a special-effects extravaganza. *Batman & Robin,* like the first three films in the series, is wonderful to look at, and has nothing authentic at its core.

There is a scene that illustrates what I mean. It comes during the dreary central section of the film. Bruce Wayne (George Clooney) dines at home with his fiancée for the past year, Julie Madison (Elle Macpherson). Julie says she would like to spend the rest of her life with Wayne. Bruce hems and haws and talks about his bachelorhood and the complications of his life. Julie looks like she has heard all of this before. The scene is interrupted by an emergency.

Watching it, I realized why it makes absolutely no difference who plays Batman: There's nobody at home. The character is the ultimate Suit.

Garb him in leather or rubber, and he's an action hero—Buzz Lightyear with a heartbeat. Put him in civilian clothes, and he's a nowhere man. I've always suspected they cast movie Batmans by their chins, which is all you see when the Bat costume is being worn, and Clooney has the best chin yet. But like Michael Keaton and Val Kilmer, he brings nothing much to the role because there's nothing much there. Most of the time he seems stuck for conversation. I think the way to get him started would be to ask about his technological gimmicks. This is a guy who would rather read the Sharper Image catalog than *Playboy.*

The series has been driven by its villains. They make some good memories: Jack Nicholson as the Joker, Danny DeVito as the Penguin, Michelle Pfeiffer as Catwoman, Tommy Lee Jones as Two-Face, Jim Carrey as the Riddler. In *Batman & Robin* we get Arnold Schwarzenegger as Mr. Freeze, a man who can survive only by keeping his body at zero degrees (Celsius? Fahrenheit? absolute?), and Uma Thurman as Poison Ivy, a botanist who turns into a plant and wages war against animals. They earn their places in the pantheon of Batman's enemies, but the screenplay doesn't do them justice: It meanders, and some of the big action sequences are so elaborate they're hard to follow (examples: the one where Freeze's men play hockey with a diamond, and a completely pointless motorcycle chase).

Listening to Schwarzenegger's one-liners ("The iceman cometh!") I realized that a funny thing is happening to the series: It's creeping irresistibly toward the tone of the 1960s TV show. The earlier Batman movies, especially the dark *Batman Returns* (1992), made a break with the camp TV classic and went for moodier tones. But now the puns and punch lines come so fast the action has to stop and wait for them, and although we don't get the POW! and WHAM! cartoon graphics, this fourth movie seems inspired more by the TV series than the Bob Kane comic character.

The plot: Mr. Freeze wants to freeze everybody ("First Gotham—then the World!") while bringing back to life the cryogenically frozen body of his beloved wife. Poison Ivy wants to destroy all animals and free the globe for her new kinds of genetically engineered plants. Ivy attracts Batman and Robin (and every other man in view) with her seductive perfume, and tricks Mr. Freeze into helping her, until he catches on. Thurman plays her with a languid drawl that suggests plants *can* have multiple orgasms.

Among the supporting characters is the faithful old butler, Alfred (Michael Gough), who seems to be dying, and asks poignant questions such as, "For what is Batman but an attempt to control the chaos that sweeps our world?" Midway in the action, Alfred's niece (Alicia Silverstone) turns up and finds herself a job as Batgirl, although the movie can never decide if Robin (Chris O'Donnell) is more attracted to her or to Poison Ivy. Another interesting character is a bionic muscleman named Bane (Jeep Swenson), who is Poison Ivy's pet monster. Chemicals pump his muscles to six times life size, and there are opportunities here for satire on Schwarzenegger's movie roles, but all of them are studiously avoided.

What I'll remember from the film are some of the images, such as the Gotham Observatory, which is inside a giant globe held aloft far above the city streets by a towering statue in the Grecian style. And I will remember Mr. Freeze sadly looking at a little music-box figure of his wife. And Alfred poignantly searching his family tree on his computer. And Ivy's leafy eyebrows.

My prescription for the series remains unchanged: Scale down. We don't need to see $2 million on the screen every single minute. Give the foreground to the characters, not the special effects. And ask the hard questions about Bruce Wayne. There is a moment in the film where we learn that the new telescope in the Gotham Observatory can look at any place on Earth. "Just don't point it at my bedroom," Bruce Wayne chuckles. What is he chuckling about?

Bean ★ ★ ½

PG-13, 90 m., 1997

Rowan Atkinson (Mr. Bean), Peter MacNicol (David Langley), Pamela Reed (Alison Langley), Sir John Mills (Chairman), Burt Reynolds (General Newton), Harris Yulin (George Grierson). Directed by Mel Smith and produced by Peter Bennet Jones, Tim Bevan, and Eric Fellner. Screenplay by Rowan Atkinson, Richard Curtis, and Robin Driscoll.

Bean is like a malevolent Ace Ventura in slow motion. Remember the Al Capp character who went everywhere with the dark rain cloud hovering over his head? For everyone he meets, Bean is that cloud. Since so many slapstick heroes are relentlessly cheerful or harmless, his troublesome streak is sort of welcome.

Bean, played by Rowan Atkinson, first came to life as the star of a British sitcom that quickly became the most popular comedy show in English-speaking markets all over the world. Only in America, where Bean hides out on PBS, is he relatively unknown. Now comes *Bean* the movie, which arrives in the United States having already grossed more than $100 million in the United Kingdom, Australia, Canada, etc.

Although the United States is the last market to play *Bean*, the film seems to have been tailored with an eye to Yank viewers; most of the action takes place in Los Angeles. The setup is in London, where Bean is employed as a guard at an art gallery and is "easily our worst employee," as the curator says at a board meeting where the first order of business is to fire him. When the ancient chairman (John Mills) vetoes that idea, the board gleefully ships Bean off to America as its representative at the unveiling of *Whistler's Mother.*

The famous painting has been purchased from a French museum by a rich retired general (Burt Reynolds), who is no art lover but hates the idea that the "Frenchies" own America's most famous painting. Bean's task will be to oversee the installation of the painting in L.A. and speak at the unveiling—tasks for which he is spectacularly unequipped.

The Bean character has his roots in the clowns of silent comedy, although few were this nasty. On TV he scarcely speaks at all, preferring wordlike sounds and swallowed consonants, but here he blurts out the odd expression, and in one of the funniest scenes gives a speech before assembled art experts. His adventures are a mixture of deliberate malice and accidental malice. (For example, when he inflates the barf bag on an airplane and pops it above the head of a sleeping passenger, that's malice. But the fact that it was filled with vomit—that was an accident.)

Bean's host in the United States is a young curator (Peter MacNicol), whose wife (Pamela Reed) and children move out of the house after about twenty minutes of Bean. MacNicol hangs in there, as he must: His boss (Harris Yulin) has warned him his job depends on it. Bean goes on a tour of L.A., succeeding in speeding up a virtual-reality ride so that it hurls patrons at the screen, and that's benign compared to what he eventually does to *Whistler's Mother.*

The movie gets in some sly digs as the California museum prepares to market the painting with tie-in products such as T-shirts, beach towels, and beer mugs. But most of the film consists of Bean wandering about, wrinkling his brows, screwing up his face, making sublingual guttural sounds, and wreaking havoc.

Who is Bean, anyway? Like the Little Tramp, he exists in a world of his own, perhaps as a species of his own. He combines guile and cluelessness (he knows enough to use an electric razor on his face, but not enough to refrain from also shaving his tongue). He knows how to perform tasks, but not when to stop (can stuff a turkey, but gets it stuck on his head). And he is not, in any sense, lovable (the movie gets a smile with MacNicol's attempt to tack on one of those smarmy moments where it's observed that Bean means well; he doesn't mean well).

There are many moments here that are very funny, but the film as a whole is a bit too long. Perhaps the half-hour TV form is the perfect length for Bean. When the art gallery episode has closed and the action shifts to a hospital operating room, I had the distinct feeling that director Mel Smith was padding. Maybe there's a rule that all feature films must be at least ninety minutes long. At an hour, *Bean* would have been nonstop laughs. Then they added thirty minutes of stops.

The Beautician and the Beast ★ ★

PG, 103 m., 1997

Fran Drescher (Joy Miller), Timothy Dalton (Boris Pochenko), Ian McNeice (Grushinsky), Patrick Malahide (Kleist), Lisa Jakub (Katrina), Michael Lerner (Jerry Miller), Phyllis Newman (Judy Miller), Adam LaVorgna (Karl). Directed by Ken Kwapis and produced by Howard W. "Hawk" Koch Jr. and Todd Graff. Screenplay by Graff.

Fran Drescher is a taste I have not acquired, but I concede that one could acquire it. It would help if she made a silent film. Her speaking voice is like having earwax removed with a small dental drill. And yet, doggone it, there's something lovable about her. I picture her making the coffee at Stuart Smalley's AA meetings, or doing the ringside announcements for pro wrestling.

You have seen her on *The Nanny* and on countless talk shows. Most talk show guests say something and then laugh, so you know it's supposed to be funny. She laughs, and then says something, so you know it was supposed to be a laugh and not a respiratory emergency. Not every role would be suitable for her. I cannot visualize her, for example, in *The English Patient,* saying, "Promise you'll come back for me." Or as Sheriff Marge Gunderson in *Fargo,* asking, "So, I guess that was your accomplice in the wood chipper?"

The Beautician and the Beast contains a role that seems to have been whipped up out of two parts of Drescher's public persona and one part of nothing else. She plays Joy Miller, who teaches beauty secrets in a Queens night school. After a smoking mishap leads to a wig fire and the school burns down, she is hailed on the front pages as a heroine (for saving the lab rats) and approached by a representative of the obscure central European nation of Slovetzia.

That nation has recently emerged from communism into a dictatorship controlled by Boris Pochenko (Timothy Dalton), a despot who wants to soften his image and thinks maybe importing an American tutor for his children might help. (Pochenko is also the name of the European exile who is killed at the beginning of *Shadow Conspiracy,* but I cannot think of anything to say about this coincidence, other than that they are both named after a popular Japanese pinball game.) Dalton plays the role as if he had somehow found himself the villain in a James Bond film instead of the hero.

Slovetzia is not an advanced nation. There are sheep on the runway of the national airport. Pochenko lives in a castle possibly mortgaged from Young Frankenstein. Joy makes a bad first impression when she is late for her official welcoming ceremony because she hasn't finished her hair and nails.

The dictator (known to his subjects as the "Beast for Life") has three children, who have grown restive under his iron fist while nevertheless managing to speak in American accents after their first few scenes. A daughter is unhappy about her approaching arranged marriage. The son bites his nails. "Don't do that!" Joy tells him. "Do you want to grow a hand in your stomach?"

Joy's wardrobe runs toward day-glo stretch pants and pullover blouses. She is sublimely indifferent to the veiled threats of Pochenko, so he tries unveiled ones, which she tut-tuts away. Meanwhile, she has the castle running like a catering kitchen, and is able to save precious currency reserves by planning a diplomatic reception around frozen Chung King egg rolls.

The trajectory of this story is clear from its title. The beautician will get the beast, and in the subplot Juliet will get her Romeo. The direction is by Ken Kwapis, whose *He Said, She Said* (1991) is invaluable for getting you from John Tesh to the Addams Family in the Kevin Bacon game. Kwapis tries to build suspense where none can possibly exist, which is always an annoyance; is it a crime for a movie to know as much about its story as the audience does?

But there are some genuine laughs here and there, and a certain charm emanates from Fran Drescher, who I suspect is easier to stand in real life than she lets on in her acting. And we are not disappointed in our wait for the Obligatory Transformational Entrance Scene, which all movies like this lead up to. After being an ugly duckling for three-quarters of the movie, the heroine turns up at the top of a staircase looking regal and beautiful, and descends while trying to keep one of those "are they looking at poor little me?" looks on her face.

The Beautician and the Beast made me laugh, but each laugh was an island, entire unto itself. They didn't tie together into anything very interesting. Drescher never really seems to be interacting with the other characters. Like Mae West or Groucho Marx, she eyeballs the stiffs while they're talking, and then delivers her zingers. We don't care about her character because we never feel she's really uncertain, insecure, or vulnerable. Here's a woman who will never grow hands in her stomach.

Beloved ★ ★ ★ ½

R, 175 m., 1998

Oprah Winfrey (Sethe), Danny Glover (Paul D), Thandie Newton (Beloved), Kimberly Elise (Denver), Beah Richards (Baby Suggs), Lisa Gay Hamilton (Younger Sethe), Albert Hall (Stamp Paid), Irma P. Hall (Ella). Directed by Jonathan Demme and produced by Edward Saxon, Demme, Gary Goetzman, Oprah Winfrey, and Kate Forte. Screenplay by Akosua Busia, Richard LaGravenese, and Adam Brooks, based on the novel by Toni Morrison.

The moment the man walks into the house, he senses that something is wrong: "Good God, girl, what kind of evil you got in there?" And she replies: "It ain't evil. Just sad." That explains the difference between *Beloved* and other stories of ghosts. The movie is not about the ghost, but about the feelings that bring it into existence.

The film tells the story of Sethe (Oprah Winfrey), who was a slave on a Kentucky plantation in the days before the Civil War. Now Sethe is free, and lives in a frame house on a few acres on the outskirts of Cincinnati—"124 Bluestone Road," the film informs us, as if it would be an ordinary house if it were not for the poltergeist that haunts it. When Paul D (Danny Glover), who knew Sethe years ago in Kentucky, enters the house, the air glows red and the walls and floor shake violently; the spirit resents this visitor.

But Paul D remains, and seems to quiet the poltergeist. Then the spirit appears again, waiting for them one day when they return to the house. It now manifests as a young woman in a black dress and (Paul makes note) shoes that don't look as if they've been walked in. Asked her name, she spells it out one painful letter at a time, in a gravelly voice that doesn't sound as if it's ever been used: B-E-L-O-V-E-D.

Thandie Newton, who plays Beloved, does an interesting thing with her performance. She inhabits her body as if she doesn't have the operating instructions. She walks unsteadily. She picks up things as if she doesn't quite command her grasp. She talks like a child. And indeed inside this young woman there is a child, the ghost of the young daughter that Sethe killed rather than have her returned to the plantation as a slave.

Like the Toni Morrison novel it is based on, *Beloved* does not tell this story in a straightforward manner. It coils through past and present, through memory and hallucination, giving us shards of events we are required to piece back together. It is not an easy film to follow. Director Jonathan Demme and his screenwriters have respected Morrison's labyrinthine structure—which does, I think, have a purpose. The complexity is not simply a stylistic device; it is built out of Sethe's memories, and the ones at the core are so painful that her mind circles them warily, afraid to touch. Sethe's life has not been a linear story, but a buildup to an event of unimaginable horror, and a long, sad unwinding afterward.

The film had a curious effect on me. I was sometimes confused about events as they happened, but all the pieces are there and the film creates an emotional whole. It's more effective when it's complete than during the unfolding experience. Seeing it more than once would be rewarding, I think, because knowing the general outline—having the road map—would deepen the effect of the story *and* increase our appreciation of the fractured structure.

The film, based on a true story, is about a woman who is raised as a slave and then tastes twenty-eight days of freedom before "on the 29th day, it was over." She has been beaten and raped by her employer, School Teacher, and boys under his care; there is a flashback in which the boys steal the milk from her breasts, and her chained husband looks on and goes mad. Faced with the prospect that her children will be returned to the degradation of slavery, she chooses to kill them—and is stopped only after she does kill the daughter now returned as Beloved.

Postwar life in Ohio contains its peaceful moments, of bringing in the laundry or shelling peas, but the house at 124 Bluestone Road is forever saddened by what Sethe did. Was it wrong? Yes, said the law: She was guilty of destroying property. The law did not see her or her child as human beings and thus did not consider the death to be murder. In a society with those values, to kill can be seen as life-affirming.

These are all feelings that churn up after the film. *Beloved,* film and novel, is not a genre ghost story but a work that uses the supernatural to touch on deep feelings. Like *The Turn of the Screw,* it has no final explanation. Spirit manifestations come from madness, and need not follow logical agendas. It is a remarkable and brave achievement for Demme and his producer and star, Winfrey, to face this difficult material head-on and not try to dumb it down into a more accessible, less evocative, form.

Winfrey plays Sethe as a woman who can sometimes brighten and relax, but whose spirit always returns to the sadness of what she did, and the hatred of those who forced her to it. It is a brave, deep performance. Supernatural events whirl around her, but she is accustomed to that: She's more afraid of her own memories. Thandie Newton, as Beloved, is like an alien (I was reminded of Jeff Bridges in *Starman*). She brings a difficult character to life by always remembering that the tortured spirit inside was still a baby when it died. Danny Glover, big and substantial, is the pool of caring that Sethe needs if she is ever to heal. And Kimberly Elise, as Sethe's grown daughter, plays the character as a battered child—battered not by her mother but by the emotional maelstrom of 124 Bluestone Road. And the legendary Beah Richards has an electric screen presence as Baby Suggs, Sethe's mother-in-law, who presides over haunting spiritualist ceremonies.

Demme's direction tells the story through mood and accumulation of incident, rather than through a traditional story line. His editor, Carol Littleton, takes on the difficult task of helping us find our way through the maze. Some audience members, I imagine, will not like it—will find it confusing or too convoluted. And it does not provide the kind of easy lift at the end that they might expect. Sethe's tragic story is the kind where the only happy ending is that it is over. ☞

Bent ★★

NC-17, 104 m., 1997

Clive Owen (Max), Lothaire Bluteau (Horst), Brian Webber (Rudy), Ian McKellen (Uncle Freddie), Mick Jagger (Greta). Directed by Sean Mathias and produced by Michael Solinger and Dixie Linder. Screenplay by Martin Sherman, based on his play.

Bent tells a heartrending love story, set against the backdrop of the Holocaust. I could describe the film in solemn pieties, but that would be too easy. The more deeply it descends into horror, the more alarming its agenda becomes, until finally I'd had enough: The material is not worthy of its setting.

The story involves a Berlin homosexual named Max (Clive Owen), who is swept up in the Nazi madness, forced to kill his lover, sent to a prison camp, and there finds true love with another man. Max has lied to qualify for a yellow star (signifying he is Jewish) instead of a pink one (homosexual). By the end he is proud to wear the pink star, but his decision is staged as a crowd-pleaser.

Bent is a movie very much about entertaining its audience (I have not seen the stage play by Martin Sherman). It opens with a gay orgy, hosted by the transvestite Greta (Mick Jagger), where bodies are strewn about in sexual congress. Some of the celebrants are either Nazis, or wear Nazi uniforms as a form of erotic enhancement (whether their own or the audience's is a tricky question).

Max goes home with a handsome young Nazi, and has sex with him to the dismay of Max's lover, Rudy (Brian Webber). It is the time of the purge of gay Nazis; storm troopers burst in to slit the Nazi's throat. Max and Rudy escape, hide in the woods, and are captured after a thrilling action scene. The scene exists for its own sake; the drama is suspended so the audience can thrill to the formula of pursuit.

On a train to prison camp, Max is forced to commit unspeakable acts and betray his friend. The underlying message is, it's every man for himself; the film will refute that. In the camp, Max is assigned to shift rocks from one pile to another. He's joined by Horst (Lothaire Bluteau), whom he met on the train. "Friendship lasts about twelve hours in this place," Horst tells him.

But soon, in the midst of dread and a bitter winter, they find erotic desire stirring, and there is a scene where they stand side by side, with no eye contact, and by describing their feelings verbally are able to arrive at simultaneous orgasm. This scene works like the chase scene: It drops out of the drama to stand alone as entertainment—as eroticism. A better film would have found a way to absorb the sexuality into the underlying theme; both scenes are crowd-pleasers, and so is a closing sequence, which seems staged more as a noble tableaux than as drama at all.

Max's personal victory we of course applaud, but does the film, with its methods, deserve the sentiment it requests? Sherman's stage version of *Bent* is, I am told, a moving experience. During the film there was scarcely a moment when I wasn't aware of the gears cleverly turning.

Besieged ★

R, 92 m., 1999

Thandie Newton (Shandurai), David Thewlis (Mr. Kinsky), Claudio Santamaria (Agostino). Directed by Bernardo Bertolucci and produced by Massimo Cortesi. Screenplay by Bertolucci and Clare Peploe, based on a story by James Lasdun.

Note: I've found it impossible to discuss this film without mentioning important plot points. Otherwise, as you will see, the review would be maddeningly vague.

Bernardo Bertolucci's *Besieged* is a movie about whether two people with nothing in common, who have no meaningful conversations, will have sex—even if that means dismissing everything we have learned about the woman. It is also about whether we will see her breasts. How can a director of such sophistication, in a film of such stylistic grace, tell such a shallow and evasive story?

But wait. The film also involves race, politics, and culture, and reduces them all to convenient plot points. The social values in this movie would not have been surprising in a film made forty years ago, but to see them seriously proposed today is astonishing. In a hasty moment I described the film as "racist," but it is not that so much as thoughtless and lacking in all empathy for its African characters, whose real feelings are at the mercy of the plot's sexual desires.

The film opens in Africa, with an old singer chanting a dirge under a tree. We see crippled children. A teacher in a schoolroom tries to lead his students, but troops burst in and drag him away. The young African woman Shandurai (Thandie Newton) sees this. The teacher is her husband. She wets herself. So much for the setup. The husband will never be given any weight or dimension.

Cut to Rome, where Shandurai is a medical student, employed as a maid in the house of Mr. Kinsky (David Thewlis). He will always remain "Mr. Kinsky" to her, even in a love note. He is a sardonic genius who plays beautifully upon the piano and occupies a vast apartment given him by his aunt and hung with rich tapestries and works of art. Given the size and location of the apartment, she was a very rich aunt indeed. The maid's quarters are spacious enough for a boutique, and Mr. Kinsky's rooms are reached by a spiral staircase to three or four levels.

Thandie Newton is a beautiful woman. She is photographed by Bertolucci in ways that make her beauty the subject of the shots. There's a soft-core undertone here: She does housework, the upper curves of her breasts swelling above her blouse. Little wisps of sweaty hair fall down in front of those wonderful eyes. There is a montage where she vacuums and Mr. Kinsky plays—a duet for piano and Hoover.

It is a big house for two people, very silent, and they move around it like stalkers. One day she drops a cleaning rag down the spiral staircase and it lands on Mr. Kinsky's head. He looks up. She looks down. Mr. Kinsky decides he loves her. There is a struggle. "Marry me! I'll do anything to make you love me!" She throws him a curve: "You get my husband out of jail!"

He didn't know she was married. Other things divide them, including their different tastes in music. He performs the classics, but one day plays rhythmic African rhythms for her. She smiles gratefully, in a reaction shot of such startling falseness that the editor should never have permitted it. Later Shandurai has a speech where she says how brave, how courageous, her husband is. Eventually we gather that Mr. Kinsky is selling his possessions to finance the legal defense of the husband. Even the piano goes.

All of this time the film has been performing a subtle striptease involving Shandurai, who has been seen in various stages of partial or suggested nudity. Now, at the end, we see her breasts as she lies alone in bed. I mention this because it is so transparently a payoff; Godard said the history of cinema is the history of boys photographing girls, and Bertolucci's recent films (like *Stealing Beauty*) underline that insight.

I am human. I am pleased to see Thandie Newton nude. In a film of no pretension, nudity would not even require any justification; beauty is beauty, as Keats did not quite say. But in *Besieged* we have troublesome buried issues. This woman is married to a brave freedom fighter. She says she loves and admires him. Now, because Mr. Kinsky has sold his piano to free her husband, she gets drunk and writes several drafts of a note before settling on one ("Mr. Kinsky, I love you"). She caresses herself and then steals upstairs and slips into his bed. Do they have sex? We don't know. In the morning, her freed husband stands outside the door of Mr. Kinsky's flat, ringing the bell again and again—ignored.

If a moral scale is at work here, who has done the better thing: A man who went to prison to protest an evil government, or a man who freed him by selling his piano? How can a woman betray the husband she loves and admires, and choose a man with whom she has had no meaningful communication?

To be fair, some feel the ending is open. I felt the husband's ring has gone unanswered. Some believe the ending leaves him in uncertain limbo. If this story had been by a writer with greater irony or insight, I can imagine a more shattering ending, in which Mr. Kinsky makes all of his sacrifices, and Shandurai leaves exactly the same note on his pillow—but is not there in the morning.

The film's need to have Shandurai choose Mr. Kinsky over her husband, which is what I think she does, is rotten at its heart. It turns the African man into a plot pawn, it robs him of his weight in the mind of his wife, and then leaves him standing in the street. *Besieged* is about an attractive young black woman choosing a white oddball over the brave husband she says she loves. What can her motive possibly be? I suggest the character is motivated primarily by the fact that the filmmakers are white.

The Beyond ½★

NO MPAA RATING, 88 m., 1998

Catriona MacColl (Liza Merrill), David Warbeck (Dr. John McCabe), Sarah Keller (Emily), Antoine Saint John (Schweik), Veronica Lazar (Martha), Al Cliver (Dr. Harris), Anthony Flees (Larry [painter]), Giovanni de Nava (Joe the Plumber). Directed by Lucio Fulci and produced by Fabrizio De Angelis. Screenplay by Dardano Sacchetti.

The Beyond not only used to have another title, but its director used to have another name. First released in 1981 as *Seven Doors of Death*, directed by Louis Fuller, it now returns in an "uncut original version" as *The Beyond*, directed by Lucio Fulci.

Fulci, who died in 1996, was sort of an Italian Hershell Gordon Lewis. Neither name may mean much to you, but both are pronounced reverently wherever fans of zero-budget schlock horror films gather. Lewis was the Chicago-based director of such titles as *Two Thousand Maniacs, She-Devils on Wheels*, and *The Gore-Gore Girls*. Fulci made *Zombie* and *Don't Torture the Duckling*. Maybe that was a temporary title too.

The Beyond opens in "Louisiana 1927," and has certain shots obviously filmed in New Orleans, but other locations are possibly Italian, as was (probably) the sign painter who created the big DO NOT ENTRY sign for a hospital scene. It's the kind of movie that alternates stupefyingly lame dialogue with special-effects scenes in which quicklime dissolves corpses and tarantulas eat lips and eyeballs.

The plot involves . . . excuse me for a moment while I laugh uncontrollably at having written the words "the plot involves." I'm back. The plot involves a mysterious painter in an upstairs room of a gloomy, Gothic Louisiana hotel. One night carloads and boatloads of torch-bearing vigilantes converge on the hotel and kill the painter while shouting, "You ungodly warlock!" Then they pour lots of quicklime on him, and we see a badly made model of his body dissolving.

Time passes. A woman named Liza (played by Catriona MacColl, who was named "Catherine" when the director was named "Louis") inherits the hotel, which needs a lot of work. Little does she suspect it is built over one of the Seven Doors of Evil that lead to hell. She hires a painter, who falls from a high scaffold and shouts, "The eyes! The eyes!" Liza's friend screams, "This man needs to get to a hospital!" Then there are ominous questions, like "How can you fall from a four-foot-wide scaffold?" Of course, one might reply, one can fall from anywhere, but why did he *have* a four-foot-wide scaffold?

Next Liza calls up Joe the Plumber (Giovanni de Nava), who plunges into the flooded basement, wades into the gloom, pounds away at a wall, and is grabbed by a horrible thing in the wall, which I believe is the quicklimed painter, although after fifty years it is hard to make a firm ID.

Let's see. Then there is a blind woman in the middle of a highway with a seeing-eye dog, which later attacks her (I believe this is the same woman who was in the hotel in 1927), and a scene in a morgue, where the wife of one of the victims (the house painter, I think, or maybe Joe) sobbingly dresses the corpse (in evening dress) before being attacked by acid from a self-spilling jar on a shelf.

But my favorite scene involves the quicklimed, decomposed corpse, which is now seen in a hospital next to an oscilloscope that flatlines, indicating death. Yes, the rotting cadaver is indeed dead—but why attach it, at this late date, to an oscilloscope? Could it be because we'll get a shot in which the scope screen suddenly indicates signs of life? I cannot lie to you. I live for moments like that.

Fulci was known for his gory special effects (the Boston critic Gerald Peary, who has seen several of his films, cites one in which a woman vomits up her intestines), and *The Beyond* does not disappoint. I have already mentioned the scene where the tarantulas eat eyeballs and lips. As the tarantulas tear away each morsel, we can clearly see the strands of latex and glue holding it to the model of a corpse's head. Strictly speaking, it is a scene of tarantulas eating makeup.

In a film filled with bad dialogue, it is hard to choose the most quotable line, but I think it may occur in Liza's conversations with Martin, the architect hired to renovate the hotel. "You have carte blanche," she tells him, "but not a blank check!"

Beyond Silence ★★★½

PG-13, 100 m., 1998

Sylvie Testud (Lara), Tatjana Trieb (Lara as a child), Howie Seago (Martin), Emmanuelle Laborit (Kai), Sibylle Canonica (Clarissa), Matthias Habich (Gregor), Alexandra Bolz (Marie), Hansa Czypionka (Tom). Directed by Caroline Link and produced by Thomas Wobke, Jacob Claussen, and Luggi Waldleitner. Screenplay by Link and Beth Serlin.

Beyond Silence is one of those films that helps us escape our box of time and space and understand what it might be like to live in someone else's. It tells the story of Lara, the child of deaf parents, who loves them and has been well raised by them, but must, as all children must sooner or later, leave her nest and fly on her own.

The movie isn't centered on a few manufactured plot points, but gives us a sense of the whole span of the family's life. It's not a sentimental docudrama but a hard and yet loving look at the way these people deal with their issues and incriminations. No one is the hero and no one is the villain; they are all doing the best they can, given the way life has made them.

Lara, played as a child by Tatjana Trieb and as a young woman by Sylvie Testud, moves effortlessly between the worlds of sound and sign. She sits beside the TV set, signing for her parents, and translates for them during a heated meeting with a banker. (At the end of the conference, when the banker says, "Thanks, Lara," she pointedly tells him, "My parents are your customers, not me.") She is not above mischief. At a parent-teacher conference, she shamelessly represses the teacher's critical observations about her schoolwork.

The crucial event in the film is a simple one: Lara's aunt, her father's sister, gives her a clarinet. This is a gift fraught with meaning. In a flashback, we see the father as a young deaf boy, watching as relatives crowd around to applaud his sister's first clarinet recital. Frustrated, he gives voice to a loud, painful noise, and is banished to a bedroom. It is the kind of exclusionary wound that shapes a lifetime, and although the father and sister as children communicated effortlessly, as adults they are cool and distant.

There is a ten-year gap (the actresses are so well matched we hardly notice it), and Lara, now nearly twenty, is encouraged by her aunt to attend music school. Her father is opposed, and there is a bitter argument. Lara, who is a gifted player, sits in with her aunt's group, takes classes, and one day sees a man signing to a boy in a park. She follows them, and is surprised to find that he is not deaf, but the child of a deaf father, and a teacher in a school for the deaf. They fall in love.

All of these events are seen with a particular clarity, as stages in Lara's discovery of herself. The opening shot of the movie places the camera underwater in a frozen pond, as skaters circle on the surface and muffled voices come from far away. The whole movie is a process of breaking through the ice into the air of communication.

Beyond Silence was one of the 1998 Academy Award nominees for Best Foreign Film, but I have not mentioned until now that this is a German film, because I know some readers have an irrational prejudice against subtitles. But, really, what language is this film in? The subtitles handle not only the spoken dialogue but also describe the music and the sound effects, like thunder; they are designed to be useful for deaf viewers. If the movie were in English, it would still be subtitled. So little does the movie depend on which language is spoken that Howie Seago, the actor playing the father, is an American (both he and Emmanuelle Laborit, as his wife, are hearing impaired).

The movie is alert to nuances of the politics of deafness. Characters talk about the historical prejudice against sign language in Germany, and Lara's grandmother frets that she was advised not to sign, in order to "force" her son to learn to talk: "If I hadn't listened to that pighead, my hands might be able to fly too."

But *Beyond Silence* is wise and complex about the limitless subject of deafness. It is about how hurts are formed in families and remain for decades. About how parents favor a hearing child over a deaf one. About how Lara and her parents have formed a symbiosis that must be interrupted if she is to have a life of her own. So much hinges on simple things, as when Lara wants her mother to ride a bicycle "like other mothers."

One night on TV, Tom Brokaw asked Harrison Ford if movies have grown mediocre because of their dependence on mindless action and special effects, and I raised up my hands in frustration. If such a question really mattered to Brokaw, he would do a segment about a film like *Beyond Silence*, instead of publicizing the latest mindless 'plex product. Of course, you have to be the kind of person to whom *Beyond Silence* just plain *sounds* more interesting than, say, *Godzilla*. Such people are rare, and to be valued.

Big Daddy ★ ½

PG-13, 95 m., 1999

Adam Sandler (Sonny Koufax), Joey Lauren Adams (Layla), Jon Stewart (Kevin Gerrity), Rob Schneider (Delivery Guy), Cole and Dylan Sprouse (Julian), Leslie Mann (Corinne), Allen Covert (Phil), Kristy Swanson (Vanessa), Josh Mostel (Arthur), Steve Buscemi (Homeless Guy). Directed by Dennis Dugan and produced by Sid Ganis and Jack Giarraputo. Screenplay by Steve Franks, Tim Herlihy, and Adam Sandler, based on a story by Franks.

Big Daddy is a film about a seriously disturbed slacker who adopts a five-year-old and tutors him in cynicism, cruel practical jokes, and antisocial behavior. It's not every film where an adult role model throws himself in front of a moving car just to cheer the kid up. "Man, this Yoo Hoo is good!" the adult tells the tyke. "You know what else is good? Smoking dope!"

On the way down in the elevator after the *Big Daddy* screening, a fellow critic speculated that the line about weed was intended not as a suggestion, but as a feeler: The hero was subtly trying to find out if the kid and his friends were into drugs. I submit that so few five-year-olds are into drugs that it's not a problem, and that some older kids in the audience will not interpret the line as a subtle feeler.

Big Daddy stars Adam Sandler as Sonny Koufax, a layabout who won $200,000 in a lawsuit after a cab ran over his foot, and now hangs around the Manhattan loft that he shares with his roommate, a lawyer played by Jon Stewart—who must be doing well, since the space they occupy would sell or rent for serious money. Sonny's girlfriend, Vanessa (Kristy Swanson), tells him to get a real job, but he says he has one: He's a toll-booth attendant, I guess, although the movie gives him nothing but days off.

Just after the roommate heads out of town, little Julian (played by twins Cole and Dylan Sprouse) is dropped at the door. He is allegedly the roommate's love child. Sonny tries to turn the kid over to Social Services, but they're closed for Columbus Day, and so he ends up taking Julian to Central Park for his favorite pastime, which is throwing tree branches in the paths of speeding in-line skaters. One middle-aged blader hits a branch, takes a nasty fall, and ends up in the lagoon. What fun.

The predictable story arc has Sonny and Julian bonding. This is not as easy as it sounds, since any Adam Sandler character is self-obsessed to such a degree that his conversations sound like interior monologues. It is supposed to be funny that Sonny has a pathological hostility against society; when McDonald's won't serve them breakfast, he throws another customer's fries on the floor, and when a restaurant won't let the kid use the rest room, he and the kid pee on the restaurant's side door.

The movie is filled to the limit with all the raunchy words allowed by the PG-13 rating, and you may be surprised how many and varied they are. There's a crisis when a social worker (Josh Mostel) turns up, and Sonny impersonates his roommate and claims to be the kid's dad. We're supposed to think it would be nice if Sonny could win custody of little Julian. I think it would be a tragedy. If the kid turns out like Sonny, he's probably looking at prison time or heavy-duty community service. Sonny is the first couch potato I've seen with road rage.

The film is chock-full of supporting characters. The most entertaining is Layla (Joey Lauren Adams), whose sister is engaged to Sonny's roommate. (The sister is an ex-Hooters girl, leading to more talk about hooters than a non-drug-using five-year-old is likely to require.) Adams, who was so good in *Chasing Amy*, is good here, too, bringing a certain sanity to the plot, although I don't know what a smart girl like Layla would see in this closed-off, angry creep. Even when Sonny tries to be nice, you can see the passive aggression peeking around his smile.

The final courtroom scene is one of those movie fantasies where the judge bangs her gavel while everyone in the movie grandstands—yes, even the homeless person (Steve Buscemi) who has tagged along for the ride, an old drunk from Sonny's local bar, and the gay lawyers Sonny knows from law school. (Like many gay characters in comedies, they kiss and hug at every opportunity; why don't they just wear signboards?)

There have been many, many movies using the story that *Big Daddy* recycles. Chaplin's *The Kid* used Jackie Coogan as the urchin; *Little Miss Marker* (versions by Shirley Temple and Walter Matthau) was about an innocent tyke and a bookie; James Belushi's *Curly Sue* has some of the same elements. What they had in common were adults who might have made good parents. *Big Daddy* should be reported to the child welfare office.

The Big Hit ★

R, 93 m., 1998

Mark Wahlberg (Melvin Smiley), Lou Diamond Phillips (Cisco), Christina Applegate (Pam Shulman), Avery Brooks (Paris), Bokeem Woodbine (Crunch), Antonio Sabato Jr. (Vince), China Chow (Keiko), Lela Rochon (Mistress), Lainie Kazan (Jeanne Shulman), Elliott Gould (Morton Shulman). Directed by Che-Kirk Wong and produced by Warren Zide and Wesley Snipes. Screenplay by Ben Ramsey.

Hollywood used to import movie stars from overseas. Then directors. Then they remade foreign films. Now the studios import entire genres. It's cheaper buying wholesale. *The Big Hit* is a Hong Kong action comedy, directed by Che-Kirk Wong *(Crime Story)*, starring an American cast, and written by Ben Ramsey, an American who has apparently done as much time in the video stores as Quentin Tarantino.

The movie has the Hong Kong spirit right down to the deadpan dialogue. Sample:

Hit Man: "If you stay with me you have to understand I'm a contract killer. I murder people for a living. Mostly bad people, but . . ."

Girl He Has Kidnapped: "I'm cool with that."

The characters in these movies exist in a twilight zone where thousands of rounds of ammunition are fired, but no one ever gets shot unless the plot requires him to. The bullets have read the screenplay.

As the film opens, we meet four buddies working out in a health club. They're played by Mark Wahlberg (of *Boogie Nights*), Lou Diamond Phillips, Bokeem Woodbine, and Antonio Sabato Jr. The guys are hunks with big muscles, which we can study during a locker-room scene where they stand around bare-bottomed while discussing Woodbine's recent discovery of masturbation, which he recommends as superior to intercourse, perhaps because it requires only one consenting adult.

Then they dress for work. They're all garbed as utilities workers, with hard hats, tool boxes, and wide leather belts holding wrenches and flashlights. As they saunter down the street to Graeme Revell's pumping sound track, they look like a downsized road company version of the Village People.

The plot: They attack the heavily defended high-rise stronghold of a rich pimp who has just purchased three new girls for $50,000 a head. They break in with guns blazing, and there's an extended action sequence ending with one of the heroes diving out of an upper floor on a bungee cord, just ahead of a shattering explosion. And so on.

They kidnap Keiko (China Chow), the daughter of a rich Japanese executive. Complications ensue, and she ends up in the hands, and later the car trunk, of the leader of the hit men, named Melvin Smiley (Wahlberg). This is most likely the first movie in which the hero hit man is named Melvin Smiley. But he does smile a lot, because his weakness is, "I can't stand the idea of people who don't like me." You would think a hit man would have a lot of people walking around not liking him, but not if he is a good enough shot.

Keiko falls in love with Melvin with astonishing rapidity. Sure, she tries to escape, but by the end she realizes her future lies with him. Will this complicate Melvin's life? Not any more than it already is.

He has a black mistress (Lela Rochon), who looks at a dismembered body in their bathtub and says, "He's kinda cute." And he has a Jewish fiancée (Christina Applegate), who is Jewish for the sole purpose of having two Jewish parents (Lainie Kazan and Elliott Gould) so they can appear in the middle of the movie like refugees from a Woody Allen picture and provide crudely stereotyped caricatures. Gould makes crass remarks about his wife's plastic surgery, gets drunk, and throws up on Lou Diamond Phillips, in a scene where both actors appear to be using the powers of visualization to imagine themselves in another movie.

Many more action scenes. Cars explode. Cars are shot at. Cars land in trees. They fall out of trees. Remember those old serials where someone got killed at the end of an installment, but at the beginning of the next installment you see him leap quickly to safety? That trick is played three times in this movie. Whenever anyone gets blowed up real good, you wait serenely for the instant replay.

I guess you could laugh at this. You would have to be seriously alienated from normal human values and be nursing a deep-seated anger against movies that make you think even a little, but you could laugh.

The Big Lebowski ★ ★ ★

R, 117 m., 1998

Jeff Bridges (The Dude), John Goodman (Walter Sobchak), Julianne Moore (Maude Lebowski), Steve Buscemi (Donny), David Huddleston (The Big Lebowski), Philip Seymour Hoffman (Brandt), Tara Reid (Bunny Lebowski), Ben Gazzara (Jackie Treehorn), John Turturro (Jesus), Sam Elliott (Narrator). Directed by Joel Coen and produced by Ethan Coen. Screenplay by Joel Coen and Ethan Coen.

The Coen brothers' *The Big Lebowski* is a genial, shambling comedy about a human train wreck, and should come with a warning like the one Mark Twain attached to *Huckleberry Finn:* "Persons attempting to find a plot in it will be shot." It's about a man named Jeff Lebowski, who calls himself The Dude, and is described by the narrator as "the laziest man in Los Angeles County." He lives only to go bowling, but is mistaken for a millionaire named The Big Lebowski, with dire consequences.

This is the first movie by Joel and Ethan Coen since *Fargo.* Few movies could equal that one, and this one doesn't—but it's weirdly engaging, like its hero. The Dude is played by Jeff Bridges with a goatee, a pot belly, a ponytail, and a pair of Bermuda shorts so large they may have been borrowed from his best friend and bowling teammate, Walter Sobchak (John Goodman). Their other teammate is Donny (Steve Buscemi), who may not be very bright, but it's hard to tell for sure since he is never allowed to complete a sentence.

Everybody knows somebody like The Dude—and so, rumor has it, do the Coen brothers. They based the character on a movie producer and distributor named Jeff Dowd, a familiar figure at film festivals, who is tall, large, shaggy, and aboil with enthusiasm. Dowd is much more successful than Lebowski (he has played an important role in the Coens' careers as indie filmmakers), but no less a creature of the moment. Both dudes depend on improvisation and inspiration much more than organization.

In spirit, *The Big Lebowski* resembles the Coens' *Raising Arizona,* with its large cast of peculiar characters and its strangely wonderful dialogue. Here, in a film set at the time of the Gulf War, are characters whose speech was shaped by earlier times: Vietnam (Walter), the flower power era (The Dude), and *Twilight Zone* (Donny). Their very notion of reality may be shaped by the limited ways they have to describe it. One of the pleasures of *Fargo* was the way the Coens listened carefully to the way their characters spoke. Here, too, note that when the In & Out Burger shop is suggested for a rendezvous, The Dude supplies its address: That's the sort of precise information he would possess.

As the film opens, The Dude is visited by

two enforcers for a porn king (Ben Gazzara) who is owed a lot of money by the Big Lebowski's wife. The goons, of course, have the wrong Lebowski, but before they figure that out one has already urinated on his rug, causing deep enmity: "That rug really tied the room together," The Dude mourns. Walter, the Vietnam vet, leads the charge for revenge. Borrowing lines directly from President Bush on TV, he vows that "this aggression will not stand," and urges The Dude to "draw a line in the sand."

The Dude visits the other Lebowski (David Huddleston), leaves with one of *his* rugs, and soon finds himself enlisted in the millionaire's schemes. The rich Lebowski, in a wheelchair and gazing into a fireplace like Major Amberson in *The Magnificent Ambersons,* tells The Dude that his wife, Bunny (Tara Reid), has been kidnapped. He wants The Dude to deliver the ransom money. This plan is opposed by Maude (Julianne Moore), the Big Lebowski's daughter from an earlier marriage. Moore, who played a porno actress in *Boogie Nights,* here plays an altogether different kind of erotic artist; she covers her body with paint and hurls herself through the air in a leather harness.

Los Angeles in this film is a zoo of peculiar characters. One of the funniest is a Latino bowler named Jesus (John Turturro), who is seen going door to door in his neighborhood on the sort of mission you read about, but never picture anyone actually performing. The Dude tends to have colorful hallucinations when he's socked in the jaw or pounded on the head, which is a lot, and one of them involves a musical comedy sequence inspired by Busby Berkeley. (It includes the first point-of-view shot in history from inside a bowling ball.)

Some may complain that *The Big Lebowski* rushes in all directions and never ends up anywhere. That isn't the film's flaw, but its style. The Dude, who smokes a lot of pot and guzzles White Russians made with half-and-half, starts every day filled with resolve, but his plans gradually dissolve into a haze of missed opportunities and missed intentions. Most people lead lives with a third act. The Dude lives days without evenings. The spirit is established right at the outset, when the narrator (Sam Elliott) starts out well enough, but eventually confesses he's lost his train of thought.

The Big One ★ ★ ★

PG-13, 96 m., 1998

A documentary directed by Michael Moore and produced by Kathleen Glynn. Screenplay by Moore.

Americans are happy with the economy. Unemployment is at an all-time low. Clinton gets high approval ratings despite scandals because times are good and we don't want to rock the boat.

Swimming upstream against this conventional wisdom, here comes Michael Moore, the proletarian in the baseball cap. In his new documentary, *The Big One,* he crisscrosses the country on a book tour and finds factories closing, corporations shipping jobs overseas, and couples working extra jobs to make ends meet. "It's like being divorced," a mother with three jobs tells him in Centralia, Illinois. "I only see the kids on weekends." Many locals have lost their jobs with the closure of, ironically, the Payday candy bar factory.

Moore became famous overnight in 1989 with his hilarious documentary *Roger and Me,* in which he stalked Roger Smith, president of General Motors, in an attempt to find out why GM was closing its plants in Flint, Michigan, and moving production to Mexico. The movie was filled with cheap shots and media manipulation, and proud of it: Part of the fun was watching Moore turn the imagery of corporate America against itself.

In 1989, though, we were in a slump. Now times are good. Is Moore's message outdated? Not necessarily. If unemployment is low, that doesn't mean the mother in Centralia is prosperous. And what about the workers at Johnson Products in Milwaukee, which celebrated $500 million in profits by closing its factory and moving to Mexico? Moore visits their factory and tries to present them with a "Downsizer of the Year Award" along with his check for eighty cents: "The first hour's wage for a Mexican worker."

He likes to write checks. He creates fictitious committees to make donations to 1996 presidential candidates: Pat Buchanan's campaign cashes a $100 check from "Abortionists for Buchanan," and Moore also writes checks from "Satan Worshippers for Dole," "Pedophiles for

Free Trade" (for Perot), and "Hemp Growers for Clinton." Watching Steven Forbes on TV, he notes that the candidate never blinks, and gets an NYU doctor to say, "That's not human."

The occasion for this documentary is Moore's forty-five-city tour to promote *Downsize This!* his best-seller about hard times in the midst of prosperity. We see him lecturing campus crowds, confronting security guards, sympathizing with the striking workers at a Borders bookstore. He's an unapologetic liberal, prounion, anti–fat cat; during an interview with Studs Terkel, he beams beatifically as Studs notes the sixtieth anniversary of the CIO's sit-down strikes against the carmakers.

The movie is smart, funny, and edited cleverly; that helps conceal the fact that it's mostly recycled information. There is little here that *Roger and Me* didn't say first and more memorably. But we get two docs for the price of one: The second one is about book tours, with Moore on a grueling schedule of one city a day, no sleep, endless talk shows and book signings, plus his guerrilla raids on downsizers.

He still wears the gimme caps and the blue jeans with the saggy seats, but the Moore of *Roger and Me* was an outsider, and the Moore of *The Big One* is a celebrity (flight attendants recognize him from his TV show, kids want his autograph). He's rueful about the "media escorts" hired by his publisher to accompany him in every city; at one point, he describes one of his escorts to security guards as a "stalker." She's forcibly led outside the building before the "joke" is revealed; I didn't find it as funny as Moore did.

She is, after all, a working person, too—and so are the security guards Moore banters with as they eject him from factories. Most of them don't even work for the companies they guard, but for temp agencies, and one of the movie's startling statistics is that the largest employer in America is not AT&T, not GM—but Manpower, the hourly temp agency.

Moore's goal in the film is to get at least one corporate big shot to talk to him on camera. He finally lands Phil Knight, CEO of Nike, whose shoes are famously manufactured in Indonesia by workers paid a few dollars a day. Knight is in a no-win situation, but at least he's willing to talk. He doesn't hide behind corporate security.

His case: Shoe factories are good for the Indonesian economy, which in another generation could bootstrap itself into more prosperity. And, "I am convinced Americans do not want to make shoes." But what about Indonesia's genocidal practices against minority groups? Moore asks. "How many people died in the Cultural Revolution?" asks Knight. That's not an answer, but it is a response.

Do Americans want to make shoes? Moore returns to his hometown of Flint and asks citizens to rally if they want a shoe job. It's a cold day, which may have kept the turnout down, but Moore is forced to use low-angle shots to conceal the fact that the crowd of eager shoe workers is not very large. Maybe the issue isn't whether poor Americans want to make shoes, but why poor Americans are charged $150 for a pair of shoes that Indonesians are paid pennies to manufacture.

Moore's overall conclusion: Large American corporations care more for their stockholders than for their workers, and no profit level is high enough to satisfy them. If he'd been able to get more top executives on camera, I have a feeling their response would have been: "Yes. And?"

Billy's Hollywood Screen Kiss ★★

R, 92 m., 1998

Sean P. Hayes (Billy), Brad Rowe (Gabriel), Paul Bartel (Rex Webster), Carmine D. Giovinazzo (Gundy), Meredith Scott Lynn (Georgiana), Bonnie Biehl (Connie Rogers). Directed by Tommy O'Haver and produced by David Mosley. Screenplay by O'Haver.

We wouldn't be fascinated by a routine Hollywood love story simply because the leading characters were heterosexual; we'd want them to be something else besides, like interesting or funny. The same standard isn't always applied to gay-themed movies, which sometimes seem to believe that gayness itself is enough to make a character interesting. It isn't, and the best recent movies with gay characters *(High Art* and *The Opposite of Sex)* have demonstrated that.

Billy's Hollywood Screen Kiss seems besotted by its sexuality, and wouldn't be able to pass this test: Would the film be interesting if it was about heteros? The story involves Billy (Sean P. Hayes), who announces at the outset, "My name is Billy, and I am a homosexual" (the movie misses its first gag when nobody replies, "Hi, Billy!"). Billy tells us he grew up in Indiana (montage of old snapshots of tousle-headed lad squinting into camera), and now lives in Los Angeles, where he rooms platonically with a gal-pal named George, for Georgiana (Meredith Scott Lynn).

Billy is a nice kid, well-played by Hayes, who never pushes the character further than the material will take him. Billy's got a cool, laid-back personality, is quietly bemused, goes everywhere with a Polaroid, and eventually works on a photo series re-creating famous Hollywood love scenes with drag queens.

One day a thunderbolt strikes. Billy meets the angelic Gabriel (Brad Rowe), an improbably handsome waiter, and falls in love with him. But Gabriel, alas, is straight—or says he is. Billy runs into him again at a party, and convinces him to pose in one of his re-creations of Hollywood's golden age. And after the plot does handstands and back flips to make it happen, the two men wind up spending the night in Billy's apartment. First Gabriel sleeps on the couch. Then it looks like it might be more comfortable in the bed. You know the drill.

Do they have sex? I would not dream of saying. Whatever they have, Gabriel is still not sure he is gay, and there's a heartfelt discussion of the Kinsey scale, which rates people from 1 to 6, 1 being completely hetero and 6 being completely gay. Billy is a perfect 6. If I were a judge, I'd hold up a card scoring Gabriel at 3.5.

The movie surrounds this plot with a lot of amusing window dressing, including celebrity walk-ons (director Paul Bartel is at a party accompanied by what seems to be his pet chortler, and Warhol superstar Holly Woodlawn plays herself—and Deborah Kerr). From time to time a chorus line of three drag queens appears to provide musical commentary, and one of them has a hilarious line, explaining that her earrings are miniatures of Milli Vanilli and John Tesh.

The will-he-or-won't-he plot spins out as long as the movie is able to sustain it, which is long after we have given up hoping that Billy and Gabriel will find the happiness they so earnestly deserve. And then the ending is a giant, soggy, wet blanket. I can't discuss it without revealing it, but let me say this: Does it make the whole movie a lie, or is it simply a case of a character with an attention span of six seconds?

Blade ★ ★ ★

R, 120 m., 1998

Welsey Snipes (Blade), Kris Kristofferson (Whistler), Stephen Dorff (Deacon Frost), N'Bushe Wright (Dr. Karen Jensen), Donal Logue (Quinn), Udo Kier (Dragonetti), Traci Lords (Racquel), Kevin Patrick Walls (Krieger). Directed by Stephen Norrington and produced by Peter Frankfort, Wesley Snipes, and Robert Engelman. Screenplay by David S. Goyer.

At a time when too many movies are built from flat, TV-style visuals of people standing around talking, movies based on comic books represent one of the last best hopes for visionary filmmaking. It's ironic that the comics, which borrowed their early visual style from movies, should now be returning the favor.

Blade, starring Wesley Snipes as a killer of vampires who is engaged in an armageddon for possession of Earth, is a movie that relishes high visual style. It uses the extreme camera angles, the bizarre costumes and sets, the exaggerated shadows, the confident cutting between long shots and extreme close-ups. It slams ahead in pure, visceral imagery.

Of course, anyone patiently attending the film in the hopes of a reasoned story line is going to be disappointed. Better to see it in comic book terms, as an episode in a master-myth in which even the most cataclysmic confrontation is not quite the end of things because there has to be another issue next month. The story, like so many comic myths, involves ordinary people who are connected through a superhero to an occult universe that lurks beneath reality—or, as Blade tells a young human doctor, "The world you live in is just a sugarcoated topping. There is another world beneath it—the real world!"

Blade, based on a Marvel Comics hero, is played by Snipes as a man on the border between human and vampire. Blade's origination story: His mother was bitten by a vampire in childbirth, infecting her child, who lived in the streets until being adopted by a man named Whistler (Kris Kristofferson), who masterminds a lonely war against vampires. Now Blade, raised to manhood, is the spearhead of that battle, as vampires spread their influence through the major cities. One of their chief gathering grounds: secret after-hours dance clubs where victims are lured by the promise of forbidden thrills, only to be bitten and converted.

The movie is based around a series of major action scenes; the first one features an update of an old friend from 1970s Hong Kong movies, the flying guillotine. This is a knife-edged boomerang that spins, slices, and returns to its owner. Very neat.

Blade encounters Dr. Karen Jensen (N'Bushe Wright), a blood specialist who has been bitten by a badly burned vampire brought in for emergency treatment. Can she be saved? He returns her to Whistler's secret lab for an injection of liquid garlic, which will give her a fighting chance. Blade himself lives under a daily reprieve; Whistler's serum keeps him on the human side, although he may be building up a resistance to it.

Arrayed against Blade are the forces of vampirism, represented by his archenemy Deacon Frost (Stephen Dorff), also half-human, half-vampire, who dreams of a final vampire uprising against humans, and world conquest. His rival within the vampire world is Dragonetti (Udo Kier), a pure vampire who prefers the current arrangement under which vampires secretly control key organizations to safeguard their interests.

There is a lot of mythology underlying Frost's plans, including the evocation of an ancient vampire god who may return to lead the creatures in their final conquest. The setting for the climactic scene is a phantasmagoric vampire temple where Blade, of course, must risk everything in a titanic showdown.

The movie, directed by Stephen Norrington, is another in a recent group of New Line movies that combine comic book imagery, *noir* universes, and the visual heritage of German Expressionism; I'd rank it third after *Dark City* and *Spawn.* This material is obviously moving in the direction of pure animation, which is the look it often tries to evoke, and there are some shots here that use f/x to evoke animation's freedom from gravity and other physical laws: Notice, for example, an unbroken shot where Blade takes Dr. Jensen in his arms and makes an improbable leap from a high window to a far rooftop. Can't be done—especially not with them seemingly floating down in midair to a safe landing—but the dreamlike feel of escape is effective.

Wesley Snipes understands the material from the inside out and makes an effective Blade because he knows that the key ingredient in any interesting superhero is not omnipotence, but vulnerability. There is always a kind of sadness underlying the personalities of the great superheroes, who have been given great knowledge and gifts but few consolations in their battle against evil. The fun all seems to be on the villain's side. By embodying those feelings, Snipes as Blade gives the movie that edge of emotion without which it would simply be special effects. Of course, you have to bring something to it yourself, preferably a sympathy for the whole comic superhero ethos. This is the kind of movie that gets better the more you know about the genre.

The Blair Witch Project ★ ★ ★

R, 88 m., 1999

Heather Donahue (Heather), Joshua Leonard (Josh), Michael Williams (Mike). Directed and edited by Eduardo Sanchez and Daniel Myrick. Screenplay by Sanchez and Myrick. Produced by Gregg Hale and Robin Cowie.

We're instinctively afraid of natural things (snakes, barking dogs, the dark), but have to be taught to fear walking into traffic or touching an electrical wire. Horror films that tap into our hard-wired instinctive fears probe a deeper place than movies with more sophisticated threats. A villain is only an actor, but a shark is more than a shark.

The Blair Witch Project, an extraordinarily effective horror film, knows this and uses it. It has no fancy special effects or digital monsters, but its characters get lost in the woods, hear noises in the night, and find disturbing stick figures hanging from trees. One of them discovers slime on his backpack. Because their imaginations have been inflamed by talk of witches, hermits, and child-murderers in the forest, because their food is running out and their smokes are gone, they (and we) are a lot more scared than if they were merely being chased by some guy in a ski mask.

The movie is like a celebration of rock-bottom production values—of how it doesn't take bells and whistles to scare us. It's presented in the form of a documentary. We learn from the opening titles that in 1994 three young filmmakers went into a wooded area in search of a legendary witch: "A year later, their footage was found." The film's style and even its production strategy enhance the illusion that it's a real documentary. The characters have the same names as the actors. All of the footage in the film was shot by two cameras—a color video camcorder operated by the director, Heather (Heather Donahue), and a 16mm black-and-white camera operated by the cameraman, Josh (Joshua Leonard). Mike (Michael Williams) does the sound. All three carry backpacks and are prepared for two or three nights of sleeping in tents in the woods. It doesn't work out that way.

The buried structure of the film, which was written and directed by Eduardo Sanchez and Daniel Myrick, is insidious in the way it introduces information without seeming to. Heather and her crew arrive in the small town of Burkittsville ("formerly Blair") and interview locals. Many have vaguely heard of the Blair witch and other ominous legends; one says, "I think I saw a documentary on the Discovery Channel or something."

We hear that children have been killed in the woods, that bodies have disappeared, that strange things happened at Coffin Rock. But the movie wisely doesn't present this information as if it can be trusted; it's gossip, legend and lore, passed along half-jokingly by local people, and Heather, Josh, and Mike view it as good footage, not a warning.

Once they get into the woods, the situation gradually turns ominous. They walk in circles. Something happens to their map. Nature itself begins to seem oppressive and dead. They find ominous signs. Bundles of twigs. Unsettling stick figures. These crude objects are scarier than more elaborate effects; they look like they were created by a being who haunts the woods, not by someone playing a practical joke. Much has been said about the realistic cinematography—how every shot looks like it was taken by a hand-held camera in the woods (as it was). But the visuals are not just a technique. By shooting in a chill season, by dampening the color palette, the movie makes the woods look unfriendly and desolate; nature is seen as a hiding place for dread secrets.

As fear and desperation grow, the personalities of the characters emerge. "We agreed to a scouted-out project!" one guy complains, and the other says, "Heather, this is *so* not cool!" Heather keeps up an optimistic front; the woods are not large enough to get lost in, she argues, because "this is America. We've destroyed most of our natural resources." Eventually her brave attitude disintegrates into a remarkable shot in which she films her own apology (I was reminded of Scott's notebook entries as he froze to death in Antarctica).

At a time when digital techniques can show us almost anything, *The Blair Witch Project* is a reminder that what really scares us is the stuff we can't see. The noise in the dark is almost always scarier than what makes the noise in the dark. Any kid can tell you that. Not that he believes it at the time. ☞

Blast From the Past ★ ★ ★

PG-13, 106 m., 1999

Brendan Fraser (Adam), Alicia Silverstone (Eve), Christopher Walken (Calvin), Sissy Spacek (Helen), Dave Foley (Troy), Joey Slotnick (Soda Jerk), Dale Raoul (Mom). Directed by Hugh Wilson and produced by Renny Harlin and Wilson. Screenplay by Bill Kelly and Wilson.

Blast From the Past opens with a cocktail party in 1962 at the home of Calvin and Helen Webber, where some of the guests whisper about how brilliant, but weird, Calvin is. Their host meanwhile mixes cocktails, tells bad jokes, and hints darkly that "I could take a simple yacht battery and rig it to last a year, easily."

Suddenly President Kennedy appears on TV to announce that Russian missiles in Cuba are aimed at targets in America. Calvin (Christopher Walken) hustles the guests out the door and hurries his pregnant wife (Sissy Spacek) into an elevator to take them down to his amazingly well-stocked bomb shelter, where fish grow in breeding tanks, and the decor of their surface home has been exactly reproduced—right down to the lawn furniture on the patio.

Calvin is a brain from Cal Tech who has been waiting for years for the big one to drop. His prudence is admirable but his luck is bad: There's no nuclear war, but a plane crashes on his house and sends a fireball down the elevator shaft, convincing him there is one. So he closes the heavy steel doors and informs Helen that the time locks won't open for thirty-five years—"to keep us from trying to leave."

That's the setup for Hugh Wilson's quirky comedy that turns the tables on *Pleasantville.* That was a movie about modern characters visiting the 1950s; this is about people emerging into the present from a thirty-five-year time warp. In the sealed atmosphere far below Los Angeles, nothing changes. Calvin and Helen watch kinescopes of old Jackie Gleason programs ("People will never get tired of watching these," Calvin smiles, while Helen's eyes roll up into her head). Tuna casserole is still on the menu. And unto them a son is born, named, of course, Adam, and played as an adult by Brendan Fraser.

Adam is trained by Calvin to speak several languages, and he masters science, math, and history, while his mother teaches him good manners and gives him a dance lesson every day. His dad even tries to explain the principles of baseball to him. Try it sometime. Calvin is pleased as punch with how well his shelter is functioning, but Helen grows quietly stir-crazy and starts to hit the cooking sherry. Her wish for her son: "I want you to marry a nice girl from Pasadena." His birthday wish for himself: "A girl. One who doesn't glow in the dark."

Eventually the locks open, and Adam is sent to the surface, where his family's pleasant neighborhood has been replaced by a ruined strip mall made of boarded-up storefronts and porno shops, and populated by drunks and transvestite hookers. "Subspecies mutants," he decides. Then he meets a real girl who doesn't glow in the dark, the inevitably named Eve (Alicia Silverstone). She can't believe his perfect manners, his strange clothes, his lapses of current knowledge, or his taste in music. But eventually, as is the custom in such movies, they fall in love.

Brendan Fraser has a way of suggesting he's only passing through our zone of time and space. He was the "Encino Man" and "George of the Jungle," and even in *Gods and Monsters* his haircut made him look a little like Frankenstein's creature. Here he fits easily into the role of a nice man who has a good education but is, to borrow the title of Silverstone's best movie, clueless.

Blast From the Past is the first screen credit for writer Bill Kelly, who coscripted with the director, Wilson *(The First Wives Club* and the overlooked *Guarding Tess).* It's a sophisticated and observant film that wears its social commentary lightly but never forgets it, as Adam wanders through a strange new world of burgeoning technology and decaying manners. His innocence has an infectious charm, although the worldly-wise Eve can hardly believe he doesn't know the value of his dad's baseball card collection (wait until she hears about his dad's stock portfolio).

The movie is funny and entertaining in all the usual ways, yes, but I was grateful that it tried for more: that it was actually about something, that it had an original premise, that it used satire and irony and had sly undercurrents. Even the set decoration is funny. I congratulate whoever had the idea of putting Reader's Digest Condensed Books on the shelves of the bomb shelter—the last place on Earth where you'd want to hurry through a book.

Bliss ★ ★ ★ ½

R, 98 m., 1997

Craig Sheffer (Joseph), Sheryl Lee (Maria), Terence Stamp (Baltazar Vincenza), Spalding Gray (Alfred), Casey Siemaszko (Tanner), Leigh Taylor Young (Redhead). Directed by Lance Young and produced by Allyn Stewart. Screenplay by Young.

Bliss is a daring movie not because of the sexuality it contains, but because it is so intent about it. You can snicker about anything sexual in our society, but sex, when it's taken seriously, makes people squirmy, and here's a movie that's grown-up, thoughtful, and surprisingly erotic.

The movie tells the story of two people who are in love with each other, but bring to their marriage many problems that prevent them from having a fulfilling sex life. Joseph (Craig Sheffer) and Maria (Sheryl Lee) are both apprehensive on their wedding day; he knows she's compulsive and neurotic, and while he's ostensibly better adjusted, that may be because he's better at hiding things. Within six months they're telling their problems to a therapist (Spalding Gray), who uses a traditional psychoanalytic approach, and before much longer Maria is sneaking to secret sessions with a sex therapist named Baltazar (Terence Stamp), who "operates on the edge of the law."

The movie is awkward at getting to this point, but once the Stamp character appears on screen, the film finds its rhythm and its confidence, and becomes the story of a search, not for the perfect orgasm, but for the healthiest route in that direction. Because the material is fraught with pitfalls, there's always the danger we might laugh to cover our embarrassment; what's remarkable is how well the actors handle scenes which, in the wrong hands, would have been unplayable.

Lance Young, who wrote and directed the film, moves confidently among enough sex-related topics to fill six months of *Cosmo* covers. Maria fakes her orgasms, Joseph claims he never masturbates, they love each other, but when they try getting closer it's so frightening to Maria that she insists Joseph move out. Eventually a repressed memory surfaces: She was abused by her father, whom she loved, and so she fears love because she fears betrayal. Meanwhile, Joseph has confronted Baltazar in anger but stayed to listen, and is being led through a course of sexual training that includes tantric theories, the art of "injaculation," and yoga breathing exercises while hanging by the heels.

This material could, with just a slight tilt, easily become a Woody Allen movie. Amazing, how good acting can find the truth in well-written material. Although Craig Sheffer and Sheryl Lee are courageous and convincing in very challenging scenes, the key to the film's success is Terence Stamp's performance. His character is written not only at the edge of the law but also at the edge of parody. He lives in an apartment out of *Architectural Digest*, plays violin in the symphony, and believes that the object of sex is bliss (which is nine on his personal scale) and not orgasm (which is down around four). He nevertheless makes the character believable because he plays it with a great and solemn conviction, and very sparingly—there are no unnecessary notes.

I'm sure professional sex counselors will find much to object to in the details of his therapeutic approach. But the details aren't the point. What makes *Bliss* remarkable is that it approaches sex openly and thoughtfully, doesn't fall into soap opera clichés, and avoids all the temptations to turn into a docudrama. It works as the story of these people. It stays focused. When Maria flashes back to episodes of abuse from her childhood, for example, we expect one of those tiresome, obligatory scenes where she confronts her father. Instead, the film accepts this new information, deals with it, and learns from it: The point is to move on, not to extract revenge. (I'm not saying she shouldn't confront her father; I'm saying that scene would be an unnecessary distraction in the progress of this movie.)

The film also avoids the temptation to pit the two therapists against one another. One approach obviously works better than the other for this couple, but when the two therapists meet in a hospital waiting room and learn important information, all the movie does, subtly, is have each man deal with this information in his own jargon. Truth is the objective, not proving who's right or wrong.

Sex is a currency in our society, sold on the basis of glib assumptions and glossy packaging. It's about bodies and functions, not about people. The lessons in *Bliss* are idealistic and romantic, but at the same time unblushingly grounded on specific physical processes and fairly clinical language.

This is Lance Young's first film. I learn from *Box Office* magazine that he went to USC on a golfing scholarship, was a financial analyst, and got into movies as a "production executive." This debut as a writer and director is very impressive. Some moments a more experienced director would have avoided (there are countless better ways to introduce Baltazar than with the silly gimmick involving a telescope at a construction site), and the character of Maria takes too long to be defined. But what's important is that *Bliss* is not an "adult film" but a film for and about adults: It's provocative, and it has a heart.

Blood and Wine ★ ★ ★ ½

R, 100 m., 1997

Jack Nicholson (Alex Gates), Stephen Dorff (Jason), Jennifer Lopez (Gabrielle), Judy Davis (Suzanne Gates), Michael Caine (Victor Spansky). Directed by Bob Rafelson and produced by Jeremy Thomas. Screenplay by Nick Villiers and Alison Cross, based on a story by Villiers and Rafelson.

Blood and Wine is a richly textured crime picture based on the personalities of men who make their living desperately. Jack Nicholson and Michael Caine are the stars, as partners in a jewel theft that goes wrong in a number of ways, each way illustrating deep flaws in the ways they choose to live. It's a morality play, really, but dripping with humid sex and violence.

Nicholson is a Florida wine dealer whose business is going broke, whose wife (Judy Davis) wants to leave him, and whose stepson (Stephen Dorff) hates him. He hooks up with a tubercular British exile (Michael Caine) to steal a million-dollar diamond necklace from the house of some rich people. But it is all so much more complicated than that, and includes Nicholson's sexual liaison with the rich family's nanny (Jennifer Lopez). That's just the setup. The plot gets *really* complicated.

Blood and Wine was directed and cowritten by Bob Rafelson, who directed Nicholson's first great picture (*Five Easy Pieces*, 1970) and also worked with him in *The King of Marvin Gardens* (1972), *The Postman Always Rings Twice* (1981), and the unsuccessful *Man Trouble* (1992). This is a return to the tone of their best work; all the major characters are villains or victims. The director Paul Schrader was telling me not long ago that movies have passed out of an existential period and into an ironic period. In that case, *Blood and Wine* is a throwback, because there is nothing ironic about these characters except what finally happens to them. The plot is lurid and blood-soaked beyond description, but is handled seriously as a string of events illustrating the maxim that bad things happen to bad people.

Much of the film's delight depends on what happens to the diamond necklace after Nicholson and Caine do finally steal it. The theft itself is not so hard. "Rich people are so cheap," the Caine character says. "They'll spend millions on a necklace and lock it in a tin box from Sears." I will not spoil the fun of discovery by describing the travels of the necklace once it is stolen. Instead, I'd like to observe some wonderful actors hard at work.

This is one of Nicholson's best performances, because he stays willingly inside the gritty, tired, hard-nosed personality of Alex Gates, who is failing at love, business, and crime. He nevertheless remains a romantic at heart, and his romance with young Gabrielle (Lopez) is genuine: They love one another, even though she is unwise to believe his stories about how they'll soon be unwinding in Paris. What makes the performance believable is in the details, in the way he tells his stepson to put on a shirt before leaving the house, or in the way he and his wife have a practiced shorthand, condensing all their old arguments into short, bitter trigger-words.

Michael Caine, who can sleepwalk through bad movies, can bring good ones a special texture. Here he is convincing and sardonically amusing as a wreck of a man who chain-smokes, coughs, spits up blood, and still goes through the rituals of a jewel thief because that is what he is. He is capable of sudden violence (pounding Nicholson with a golf club, he observes, "That was an acupuncture point"). But he almost inspires sympathy, as a crook who has labored a long time at a hard profession and has nothing to show for it.

The other roles are given almost equal weight; the supporting characters aren't atmosphere, but crucial to the story, and one sign of the good writing is in the way other relationships (the mother and her son, the son and Gabrielle) affect the outcome of the plot. In a bad crime movie, people do what they do to fit the plot. In a good crime movie, people are who they are, and that determines the plot. Judy Davis, for example, projects a fierce, wounded anger that adds a whole dimension to her marriage; she has given this man her money and trust and seen both thrown away.

Then there is the way Rafelson handles the movie's love triangle, if that is what it can be called. Gabrielle has no way of knowing the relationship between the man she loves and the man she is beginning to love, and Rafelson walks a fine line; when she's forced to choose, we honestly have no way of knowing which way she'll turn.

One early review of this film said it had a "seventies feel." Perhaps that means it takes its plot seriously and doesn't try to deflect possible criticism by hedging its bets, by pretending there is an ironic subtext. I like movies like this: I like the way the actors are forced to commit to them, to work without a net. When Rafelson and Nicholson find the right material, it must be a relief for them to fall back into what they know so well how to do, to handle hard scenes like easy pieces.

Blood Guts Bullets and Octane ★ ★ ½

NO MPAA RATING, 87 m., 1999

Joe Carnahan (Sid French), Dan Leis (Bob Melba), Ken Rudulph (FBI Agent Jared), Dan Harlan (Danny Woo), Kurt Johnson (Hillbilly Sniper), Mark S. Allen (FBI Agent Franks), Kellee Benedict (FBI Agent Little). Directed by Joe Carnahan and produced by Dan Leis, Leon Corcos, and Patrick M. Lynn. Screenplay by Carnahan.

I've had a busy day on the Tarantino beat. First I reviewed a movie named *Go* that seemed inspired by *Pulp Fiction,* then I had a cup of coffee, and here I am back at the keyboard reviewing *Blood Guts Bullets and Octane,* which is so indebted to QT's kinetic style that it doesn't even pause to put commas in its title. One thing you have to say about the long shadow of *Pulp Fiction:* In a season dominated by movies that end at the senior prom, at least the QT retreads are generally more energetic and inventive, and involve characters over seventeen.

The story behind *BGB&O* is an inspiring fable for would-be filmmakers. Its writer-director-editor-star, Joe Carnahan of Sacramento, shot it in three weeks for less than $8,000, and cheerfully let it be known at Sundance that his cast and crew were paid "partly in Doritos." Like Robert Rodriguez's *El Mariachi,* the bargain price was enough to make a video version for showing to distributors; Lions Gate ponied up a reported $100,000 in post-production sound and transfer work to get the movie into theaters in 35mm.

What Carnahan made for his money is a fabulous calling card: This movie shows that he can direct, can generate momentum even in the face of a problematic story, and knows how to find and cast natural actors, including himself. There is real talent here. The most engaging aspect of the film is its spoken dialogue, which largely involves used car salesmen and seems inspired by David Mamet's real estate agents in *Glengarry Glen Ross.* (Consider this line: "The best in this business are, by virtue, fabulous salesmen." Using "by virtue" without explaining by virtue of *what* is prime Mamet.)

The movie opens in a torrent of words, as two desperate used car salesmen named Sid and Bob (Carnahan and Dan Leis) try to close a sale while screaming into the phone to a supplier who hasn't delivered the cars he promised. They're going under fast, swamped by the TV ads of their powerful competitor, Mr. Woo (Dan Harlan). Then they're offered $250,000 to simply hang onto a vintage Pontiac Le Mans for two days—to just park it on their lot.

This is a car with a lot of history. An FBI agent has traced it from South America to California, and reckons thirty-four dead bodies are associated with it. There's something in its trunk, but the trunk, Sid and Bob discover, is wired to a bomb and can't be opened. The locked trunk functions for much of the movie like the trunk in *Repo Man* and the briefcases in *Pulp Fiction* and *Ronin;* it contains the MacGuffin.

Carnahan is nothing if not stylistically open-minded. He uses color, black-and-white, flash frames, tilt shots, weird points of view, whatever. True to the QT tradition, he also fractures his time line and moves back and forth between elements of his story. He ends up with a lot of icing and very little cake, and his ending is an exercise in narrative desperation, but for most of the way he holds our attention, if not our interest: If he can do this with smoke and mirrors, think what he might be able to accomplish with a real budget.

Blues Brothers 2000 ★ ★

PG-13, 121 m., 1998

Dan Aykroyd (Elwood Blues), John Goodman (Mighty Mack McTeer), Joe Morton (Cabel Chamberlain), J. Even Bonifant (Buster), Frank

Oz (Warden), Kathleen Freeman (Mother Mary Stigmata), B. B. King (Malvern Gasperon), Aretha Franklin (Mrs. Murphy). Directed by John Landis and produced by Landis, Dan Aykroyd, and Leslie Belzberg. Screenplay by Aykroyd and Landis.

Blues Brothers 2000 has a lot of good music in it. It would have had more if they'd left out the story, which would have been an excellent idea. The film is lame comedy surrounded by high-energy blues (and some pop, rock, and country and western). And don't stop watching: *after* the end credits James Brown does "Please, Please, Please."

It's as if director John Landis had such good James Brown footage he had to use it, even though there was no room in the main plot line, which mostly involves updates on characters in the original 1980 film. "I always thought there was another story to be told," Landis says in the film's notes. Fine; then tell one.

The first movie opened with Jake Blues (the late John Belushi) getting out of Joliet Prison and going with his brother Elwood (Dan Aykroyd) to the orphanage where they were raised, still presided over by the fearsome Sister Mary Stigmata. The new movie begins with Elwood getting out of prison and seeking out the aging nun, who still whacks Elwood when his manners stray.

Elwood wants to get the old band back together again. Sister Mary has another idea: He should do a little "mentoring" for Buster (J. Even Bonifant), a ten-year-old orphan. Buster gets his own Blues Brothers uniform, plays some harmonica, and gets Elwood charged with kidnapping—but what's he *doing* in this story? Apparently Landis originally conceived the role for Macaulay Culkin. Culkin outgrew it, and Landis should have too.

Seeking out old friends, Elwood goes to a strip joint where he encounters Mighty Mack (John Goodman), a bartender who has a good voice and is enlisted as Jake's replacement. Other band members are added along the way, during an interstate chase orchestrated by a state policeman (Joe Morton) who is more or less Elwood's stepbrother (the dialogue spends a lot of time explaining that "more or less").

The original (much better) film made great use of locations in the Blues Brothers' sweet home Chicago, but this one was shot mostly near Toronto and New Orleans, with a few shots of the Chicago skyline thrown in for effect. (Hint: Bars in Louisiana do not usually advertise that they are "licenced.")

The 1980 movie had neo-Nazi bad guys. This one has a right-wing militia group, with a leader whose pep talks are unnecessarily offensive. I've noticed a disturbing trend recently for lightweight comedies to toss in racist language under the guise of "establishing" the villains. Vile language doesn't require additional currency.

But I stray from the heart of the film, which is good blues music. Just as the 1980 film included show-stopping numbers by Aretha Franklin and Cab Calloway, this one has great musical segments by Aretha ("R.E.S.P.E.C.T."), Eddie Floyd ("634-5789"), John Popper and Blues Traveler ("Maybe I'm Wrong"), Lonnie Brooks and Junior Wells ("Checkin' Up On My Baby"), and the Paul Butterfield Blues Band version of "Born in Chicago."

What is amazing is that the numbers by the guest artists are outnumbered by the Blues Brothers (including little Bonifant), who are backed up by a terrific band. There is food for thought in the sight of the late, great Junior Wells playing backup to a couple of comedians. It's not so much that I didn't enjoy their numbers as that, let's face it, with backup like these guys get, Buddy Hacket and I could be the Blues Brothers.

Jonathan Eig wrote an article in *New Republic* that explains "How the Blues Brothers destroyed the Windy City's musical heritage." It opens in a smoky dive on the South Side where the true blues still live, and then sniffs at the upscale North Side clubs where suburbanites pay $8 entry fees to hear tarted-up and smoothed-down blues.

But surely it has always been thus? The true blues come from, and flourish in, a milieu of hard times—hard emotionally, economically, racially, and not infrequently in lifestyle and substance abuse choices. Move the music to an affluent, paying audience, contract the musicians to two shows a night, mix in some soul and r-&-b to lighten the blues' heavy load, and that's entertainment. The notion that a professional blues musician can be "authentic" on demand (i.e., depressed, angry, bereft, and forlorn) is amusing. It's like they say in the theater: The most important thing is sincerity, and if you can fake that, you've got it made.

What the Blues Brothers do is worse than Eig's complaint about the posh blues clubs. They take a musical tradition and dine out on it, throwing scraps to the real pros. If Junior Wells, Aretha Franklin, Wilson Pickett, John Popper, and James Brown want to sing in a Hollywood musical, they've got to be supporting characters for the brothers.

I don't suggest that Aykroyd and Belushi, in the 1970s, were not providing entertaining musical performances. I do suggest that the Blues Brothers schtick has outlived its usefulness. Watching *Blues Brothers 2000*, I found I had lost all interest in the orphanage, orphans, police cars, nuns, and mentoring. I wanted more music.

It's said that the climactic sequence of *BB2000*, a talent contest assembling many legendary musicians (even an ill-at-ease Eric Clapton), was a legendary jam session. No doubt. I'd love to see it as a concert film. With no chase scenes and no little kids. And really shot in Chicago. Or New Orleans would be okay. Not Toronto. I've heard Toronto called a lot of things, but not the home of the blues.

Boogie Nights ★ ★ ★ ★

R, 152 m., 1997

Mark Wahlberg (Eddie/Dirk), Burt Reynolds (Jack Horner), Julianne Moore (Amber Waves), John C. Reilly (Reed Rothchild), Heather Graham (Rollergirl), Don Cheadle (Buck Swope), Luis Guzman (Maurice T. Rodriguez), Philip Baker Hall (Floyd Gondolli), Philip Seymour Hoffman (Scotty J), Ricky Jay (Kurt Longjohn), William H. Macy (Little Bill), Nina Hartley (Bill's Wife), Robert Ridgely (The Colonel). Directed by Paul Thomas Anderson and produced by Lloyd Levin, John Lyons, Anderson, and Joanne Sellar. Screenplay by Anderson.

Paul Thomas Anderson's *Boogie Nights* is an epic of the low road, a classic Hollywood story set in the shadows instead of the spotlights, but containing the same ingredients: fame, envy, greed, talent, sex, money. The movie follows a large, colorful, and curiously touching cast of characters, as they live through a crucial turning point in the adult film industry.

In 1977, when the story opens, porn movies are shot on film and play in theaters, and a director can dream of making one so good that the audience members would want to stay in the theater even after they had achieved what they came for. By 1983, when the story closes, porn has shifted to video and most of the movies are basically just gynecological loops. There is hope, at the outset, that a porno movie could be "artistic," and less hope at the end.

Boogie Nights tells this story through the life of a kid named Eddie Adams (Mark Wahlberg) from Torrance, who is a dishwasher in a San Fernando Valley nightclub when he's discovered by a Tiparillo-smoking pornographer named Jack Horner (Burt Reynolds). "I got a feeling," Jack says, "that behind those jeans is something wonderful just waiting to get out." He is correct, and within a few months Eddie has been renamed "Dirk Diggler" and is a rising star of porn films.

If this summary makes the film itself sound a little like porn, it is not. Few films have been more matter-of-fact, even disenchanted, about sexuality. Adult films are a business here, not a dalliance or a pastime, and one of the charms of *Boogie Nights* is the way it shows the everyday backstage humdrum life of porno filmmaking. "You got your camera," Jack explains to young Eddie. "You got your film, you got your lights, you got your synching, you got your editing, you got your lab. Before you turn around, you've spent maybe $25,000 or $30,000."

Jack Horner is the father figure for a strange extended family of sex workers; he's a low-rent Hugh Hefner, and Burt Reynolds gives one of his best performances, as a man who seems to stand outside sex and view it with the detached eye of a judge at a livestock show. Horner is never shown as having sex himself, although he lives with Amber Waves (Julianne Moore), a former housewife and mother, now a porn star who makes tearful midnight calls to her ex-husband, asking to speak to her child. When Jack recruits Eddie to make a movie, Amber becomes his surrogate parent, tenderly solicitous of him as they prepare for his first sex scene.

During a break in that scene, Eddie whispers to Jack, "Please call me Dirk Diggler from now on." He falls immediately into star mode, and before long is leading a conducted tour of his new house, where his wardrobe is "arranged according to color and designer." His stardom is based on one remarkable attribute; "everyone is blessed with one special thing," he tells himself, after his mother has screamed that he'll always be a bum and a loser.

Anderson wisely limits the nudity in the film, and until the final shot we don't see what Jack Horner calls "Mr. Torpedo Area." It's more fun to approach it the way Anderson does. At a pool party at Jack's house, Dirk meets the Colonel (Robert Ridgely), who finances the films. "May I see it?" the silver-haired, business-suited Colonel asks. Dirk obliges, and the camera stays on the Colonel's face as he looks, and a funny, stiff little smile appears on his face; Anderson holds the shot for several seconds, and we get the message.

The large cast of *Boogie Nights* is nicely balanced between human and comic qualities. We meet Rollergirl (Heather Graham), who never takes off her skates, and in an audition scene with Dirk adds a new dimension to the lyrics "I've got a brand-new pair of roller skates, you've got a brand-new key." Little Bill (William H. Macy) is Jack's assistant director, moping about at parties while his wife (porn star Nina Hartley) gets it on with every man she can. (When he discovers his wife having sex in the driveway, surrounded by an appreciative crowd, she tells him, "Shut up, Bill; you're embarrassing me.") Ricky Jay, the magician, plays Jack's cameraman. "I think every picture should have its own look," he states solemnly, although the films are shot in a day or two. When he complains, "I got a couple of tough shadows to deal with," Jack snaps, "There are shadows in life, baby."

Dirk's new best friend is Reed (John C. Reilly). He gets a crush on Dirk and engages him in gym talk ("How much do you press? Let's both say at the same time. One, two . . ."). Buck Swope (Don Cheadle) is a second-tier actor and would-be hi-fi salesman. Rodriguez (Luis Guzman) is a club manager who dreams of being in one of Jack's movies. And the gray eminence behind the industry, the man who is the Colonel's boss, is Floyd Gondolli (Philip Baker Hall), who on New Year's Eve 1980 breaks the news that videotape holds the future of the porno industry.

The sweep and variety of the characters has brought the movie comparisons to Altman's *Nashville* and *The Player.* There is also some of the same appeal as *Pulp Fiction,* in scenes that balance precariously between comedy and violence (a brilliant scene near the end has Dirk and friends selling cocaine to a deranged playboy while the customer's friend throws firecrackers around the room). Through all the characters and all the action, Anderson's screenplay centers on the human qualities of the players. They may live in a disreputable world, but they have the same ambitions and, in a weird way, similar values as mainstream Hollywood.

Boogie Nights has the quality of many great films, in that it always seems alive. A movie can be very good and yet not draw us in, not involve us in the moment-to-moment sensation of seeing lives as they are lived. As a writer and director, Paul Thomas Anderson is a skilled reporter, who fills his screen with understated, authentic details. (In the filming of the first sex scene, for example, the action takes place in an office set that has been built in Jack's garage. Behind the office door we see old license plates nailed to the wall, and behind one wall of the set, bicycle wheels peek out.) Anderson is in love with his camera, and a bit of a showoff in sequences inspired by the famous nightclub entrance in *GoodFellas,* De Niro's rehearsal in the mirror in *Raging Bull,* and a shot in *I Am Cuba* where the camera follows a woman into a pool.

In examining the business of catering to lust, *Boogie Nights* demystifies its sex (that's probably one reason it avoided the NC-17 rating). Mainstream movies use sex like porno films do, to turn us on. *Boogie Nights* abandons the illusion that the characters are enjoying sex; in a sense, it's about manufacturing a consumer product. By the time the final shot arrives and we see what made the Colonel stare, there is no longer any shred of illusion that it is anything more than a commodity. And in Dirk Diggler's most anguished scene, as he shouts at Jack Horner, "I'm ready to shoot my scene *right now!*" we learn that those who live by the sword can also die by it.

Booty Call ★ ★ ★

R, 77 m., 1997

Tommy Davidson (Rushon), Vivica Fox (Lysterine), Jamie Foxx (Bunz), Tamala Jones (Nikki). Directed by Jeff Pollack and produced by John Morrissey. Screenplay by Takashi Bufford and Bootsie Parker.

In a world where vulgarity is the new international standard, where everyday speech consists entirely of things you wouldn't want your grandmother to hear, *Booty Call* nevertheless represents some kind of breakthrough. This is the raunchiest sex comedy I can remember—sort of an *Animal House Grosses Out.*

Did I laugh? Sure. Did I recount some of the more incredible episodes to friends? You bet. Is the movie any good? Does goodness have anything to do with it? I walk out of movies like this wishing my parents had sent me to more concerts instead of letting me read *Mad* magazine. I'm astonished at some of the things I laugh at. But laugh I do.

The action follows two couples on a double date. Rushon and Nikki (Tommy Davidson and Tamala Jones) have been dating for a while. Rushon gets Nikki to fix up his friend Bunz (Jamie Foxx) with her across-the-hall neighbor, Lysterine (Vivica Fox). Lysterine ("That's spelled with a 'y,' not an 'i'") is at first not enchanted by the dreadlocked Bunz ("That tarantula-head fool looks like Predator"). But her girlfriend talks her into coming along for the evening.

It is a long and very busy evening (the usually understated MPAA notes "nonstop sexuality, including sex-related dialogue and crude humor, and strong language"). During its course both couples reveal great enthusiasm for sex, but the sex scenes aren't detailed. Well, they're detailed, all right, but not about sex—the details are in the difficulties, the refinements, and what goes wrong or sometimes even right.

Consider, for example, Lysterine's peculiar turn-on. She likes to have sex while her partner does a Jesse Jackson imitation, and Bunz is happy to oblige with highlights from several speeches. (For afterplay, he cools down with Bill Cosby.) Lysterine is also into various kinky implements, props, and costumes. There are times when she enters the bedroom and Bunz reacts like a man about to have an orthoscopic examination.

"Safe sex" is the watchword of both women, and this leads to a scene where Rushon fights with Nikki's pet dog for possession of a condom. Rushon wins. That's funny in itself, but even funnier (and possibly unscripted) is the way the dog continues for the rest of the scene to leap desperately into the air, barking and snapping at the prize held just out of its reach.

This is some dog. It also figures in the funniest single scene in the movie, where it licks Lysterine's toes under the table, and Lysterine thinks it's Bunz. Later, Bunz makes a similar mistake, also involving the dog, which I will not recount here.

One of the movie's positive qualities is its hearty equality of the sexes. This is not about lustful male predators and female victims. All four characters are equally matched, and equally enthusiastic. And all four have a healthy cheerfulness about sexuality. Although the movie is a wall-to-wall exercise in bad taste, it somehow retains a certain innocence; it challenges and sometimes shocks, but for me at least it didn't offend, because its motives were so obviously good-hearted. I was reminded of Mel Brooks's defense of *The Producers:* "This movie rises below vulgarity."

Example: Toward the end of the movie, Rushon finds himself in a hospital about to be operated on. Through a sneaky mix-up in charts, his minor surgery is upgraded to removal of the testicles. Anesthetized and unable to speak, he looks in horror at the surgeon's preparations. His friends can't dissuade the grim doctor from the performance of his mission. Finally they hit upon the magic words that will stop any operation in mid-slice: "He doesn't have any insurance!" (The pre-op preparations lead, a little later, to a truly inspired recycling of the famous line, "Not only am I the president—I'm a client!")

To evaluate this movie, I find myself falling back on my time-tested generic approach. First, I determine what the movie is trying to do and what it promises its audiences they will see. Then, I evaluate how successful it is, and whether audiences will indeed see the movie they've been promised and enjoy it. *Booty Call* is being advertised as a raucous exercise in vulgarity. It is. I laughed. So I must, to be honest and consistent, award it three stars. In an era when so many movies have no taste at all, a movie in bad taste is at least sailing under its true colors.

The Borrowers ★ ★ ★

PG, 83 m., 1998

John Goodman (Ocious Potter), Jim Broadbent (Pod Clock), Celia Imrie (Homily Clock), Flora Newbigin (Arrietty Clock), Tom Felton (Peagreen Clock), Aden Gillett (Joe Lender), Mark Williams (Exterminator Jeff), Bradley Pierce (Pete Lender), Hugh Laurie (Officer Steady), Raymond Pickard (Spiller), Ruby Wax (Town Hall Clerk), Doon Mackichan (Victoria Lender). Directed by Peter Hewitt and produced by Tim Bevan, Eric Fellner, and Rachel Talalay. Screenplay by Gavin Scott and John Kamps, based on the novels by Mary Norton.

The Borrowers is a charming, whimsical family adventure about little people who live in the walls and under the floors of big people's houses, and support themselves by stealing—excuse me, "borrowing"—the necessities of life. Their needs are small: One pea is enough to make a cup of pea soup. They're the ones to blame for all those items that go missing: buttons, cuff links, salt shakers. Ever notice how ice cream disappears from the freezer?

Borrowing and Borrowers are the inventions of the British author Mary Norton, whose books have been adapted twice into TV movies, and now inspire this big-screen, big-budget version with special effects so amusing it's like *Toy Story* has come to life.

As the movie opens, two children of the tiny Clock family (average height: four inches) are on an expedition to the kitchen of the Lenders, the "beings" whose house they inhabit. The kids want ice cream, but things go wrong and one is trapped inside the freezing compartment. It's up to their dad, Pod Clock (Jim Broadbent), to rescue the kid with an emergency trip up the ice-cube chute—and when cubes come crashing down, they look like boulders.

The Lender family is in trouble. An aged aunt left them their house, but after her death the will is missing, and an evil lawyer (John Goodman) plans to destroy the house and build condos. But the Borrower kids get their hands on the will, and the lawyer comes after them with an exterminator.

The plot, and there's a lot more of it, is simply a way to lead us from one wonderfully imagined set after another. Like *The Incredible Shrinking Man* (and Lily Tomlin's shrinking woman), the Clocks live in a world where everyday items look gargantuan: A birthday candle is as big as a torch. Some of the effects will also remind you of *Honey, I Shrunk the Kids*, but the charm comes in the way *The Borrowers* makes its world look like a timeless storybook. The Lenders' new neighborhood looks like a British factory town, for example, but the skyline is an (obvious) matte painting of a metropolis of the future.

The humor is physical. Goodman, as the lawyer, gets a face full of insecticide, is nearly electrocuted, and has all kinds of things bounce off his head. Little Peagreen Clock (Tom Felton) has a harrowing time in a milk bottling plant (he's trapped in a bottle that's filled with milk and capped shut—a challenge for Houdini). Exterminator Jeff (Mark Williams) has a bloodhound that feeds on cheese and stinks up the place. And all of the Clocks face terrifying dangers, as when the kids fall out the bottom of a moving truck, and are almost sucked into a vacuum cleaner.

The film is wisely modest in its scope: It sets up the situation, involves us, has fun with the special effects and the cliffhanging adventures, and is over in eighty-three minutes. If the action and the physical humor are designed to appeal to kids, the look of the film will impress adults who know what to look for. The director, Peter Hewitt, made *Bill & Ted's Bogus Adventure* (1991) and exhibits the same wild visual imagination this time.

Consider the possibilities, for example, when little Peagreen is desperately clinging to a lightbulb, and the evil lawyer turns on the light. How long can he hang on before the bulb heats up? Can his sister rescue him with that spring-loaded retractable tape measure? There's something you don't see every day.

The Boxer ★ ★ ★

R, 105 m., 1998

Daniel Day-Lewis (Danny Flynn), Emily Watson (Maggie), Brian Cox (Joe Hamill), Ken Stott (Ike Weir), Gerard McSorley (Harry), Eleanor Methven (Patsy), Ciaran Fitzgerald (Liam), Kenneth Cranham (Matt McGuire). Directed by Jim Sheridan and produced by Sheridan and Arthur Lappin. Screenplay by Sheridan and Terry George.

The Boxer is the latest of Jim Sheridan's six rich stories about Ireland, and in some ways the most unusual. Although it seems to borrow the pattern of the traditional boxing movie, the boxer here is not the usual self-destructive character, but the center of maturity and balance in a community in turmoil. And although the film's lovers are star-crossed, they are not blind; they're too old and scarred to throw all caution to the wind.

The film takes place in a Belfast hungering for peace. It stars Daniel Day-Lewis (also the star of Sheridan's *My Left Foot* and *In the Name of the Father*) as Danny Flynn, an IRA member who was a promising boxer until he was imprisoned at eighteen for terrorist associations. Refusing to name his fellow IRA men, he was held captive for fourteen years, and is now back on the streets in a city where Joe Hamill (Brian Cox), the ranking IRA man, is trying to negotiate a truce with the British.

Danny was in love as a young man with Maggie (Emily Watson), Hamill's daughter. After his imprisonment, she married another IRA man, who is now in prison. IRA rules threaten death for any man caught having an affair with a prisoner's wife; Danny and Maggie, who are still drawn to one another, are in danger—especially from the militant IRA faction led by Harry (Gerard McSorley), a hothead who hates Hamill, fears Danny, and sees the forbidden relationship as a way to destroy them both.

Danny Flynn is no longer interested in sectarian hatred. He joins his old boxing manager, an alcoholic named Ike (Ken Stott), in reopening a local gymnasium for young boxers of all faiths. And he goes into training for a series of bouts himself, becoming a figurehead for those in the community who want to heal old wounds and move ahead. The story, which is constructed in a solid, craftsmanlike way by Sheridan and his cowriter, Terry George, balances these three elements—the IRA, boxing, and romance—in such a way that if elements of one goes wrong the other two may fail as well.

Sheridan is a leading figure in the renaissance of Irish films. His directing credits include *My Left Foot* (1989), with Day-Lewis in an extraordinary performance as Christy Brown, the poet who was trapped inside a paralyzed body; *The Field* (1990), which won Richard Harris an Oscar nomination as a man who reclaims land from a rocky coast; and *In the Name of the Father* (1993), nominated for seven Oscars and starring Day-Lewis as a Belfast man wrongly accused of bombings. He also cowrote Mike Newell's comedy *Into the West* (1993) and Terry George's *Some Mother's Son* (1996), about the mothers of hunger strikers in the Maze prison. George is his frequent collaborator.

His films are never exercises in easy morality, and *The Boxer* is more complex than most. Apart from Danny and Maggie, the film's key figure is Joe Hamill, played with a quiet, sad, strong center by Brian Cox as a man who has, in his time, killed and ordered killings—but has the character to lead his organization toward peace. Harry, the bitter militant, lost a child to the British and accepts no compromise; if Danny and Maggie act on their love for one another, they may destroy the whole delicate balance.

Against the political material, the boxing acts as a setting more than a world. We see how hot passions are passed along to a younger generation, how boxing can be a substitute for warfare, and (in an almost surrealistic scene in a black-tie private club in London) how the rich pay the poor to bloody themselves.

What's fascinating is the delicacy of the relationship between Maggie and Danny. Played by two actors who have obviously given a lot of thought to the characters, they know that love is not always the most important thing in the world, that grand gestures can be futile ones, that more important things are at stake than their own gratification, that perhaps in the times they live in romance is not possible. And yet they hunger. Day-Lewis and Watson (from *Breaking the Waves*) are smart actors playing smart people; when they make reckless gestures, it is from despair or nihilism, not stupidity.

The film's weakness is in its ambition: It covers too much ground. Perhaps—I hate to say it—the boxing material is unnecessary, and if the film had focused only on the newly released prisoner, his dangerous love, and the crisis in IRA politics, it might have been cleaner and stronger. There are three fights in the film, and the outcome of all three is really just a distraction from the much more important struggles going on outside the ring.

Box of Moonlight ★ ★ ★

R, 111 m., 1997

John Turturro (Al Fountain), Sam Rockwell (The Kid), Catherine Keener (Floatie Dupre), Lisa Blount (Purlene Dupre), Annie Corely (Deb Fountain), Alexander Goodwin (Bobby Fountain), Dermot Mulroney (Wick), Mike Stanley (Doob). Directed by Tom DiCillo and produced by Marcus Viscidi and Thomas A. Bliss. Screenplay by DiCillo.

Box of Moonlight tells the story of a man who lost the key to living, somewhere along the way. His name is Al Fountain, he's an engineer on an out-of-town factory job, and the foreman describes him as "one of those guys who goes through life like a robot." His wife calls him "Mr. Clockwork" because he always does exactly what he says he will do, precisely when he says he will do it.

John Turturro plays Al as a sad and lonely everyman in white shirts and black slacks. When the factory job is canceled and they're paid their bonuses and sent home, he doesn't go home. He rents a car and stays in the area, and asks the motel clerk if he's ever heard of Splatchee Lake—a place he remembers being taken to when he was a kid. God knows if Al has ever been happy since.

This is a man going through some kind of a crisis. He just got his first gray hair. He is beginning to see things backward: Water runs up into the tap; children pedal their bikes in reverse. He has commitments but no contacts; when he calls home, he doesn't even want to speak to his son, maybe because he has nothing to say to him or anyone else.

Splatchee Lake is a disappointment. An elderly couple tell him it's filled up with formaldehyde: "You step in it and it'll burn your feet off." It's not only nature that fails him. Sex and religion don't help either; he makes a baffling call to a phone sex service, and meets a man who has seen a vision of Jesus in the flames on a billboard barbecue grill.

Then Al meets The Kid (Sam Rockwell), who wears a coonskin cap and lives in a clearing in the woods, which he has decorated to resemble—oh, I dunno, a junkyard run by Daniel Boone. The Kid is a free spirit who encourages Al to shoot at things and go to a bar and break the rules of society. Among The Kid's possessions is a box of moonlight, although whether it has moonlight in it is a question to post alongside the details on the briefcase in *Pulp Fiction*. Eventually a couple of young women (Catherine Keener and Lisa Blount) join the little camp in the clearing, and Al makes sweet love with one of them. That seems kind of unfair to his long-suffering wife (Annie Corely), but maybe it falls under the heading of therapy.

Box of Moonlight was written and directed by Tom DiCillo, a filmmaker with a streak of magic realism in him. His *Johnny Suede* starred Brad Pitt as sort of a leftover 1950s icon. His next film, *Living in Oblivion*, made fun of more or less the exact kind of whimsical little indee film *Box of Moonlight* is, but so what? The fact that he knows what he's doing, and how close it is to parody, adds a sort of smile to the material.

There isn't a whole lot of story in *Box of Moonlight*. The film works by setting up Al Fountain as a mope, and then hurling gobs of life at him. Some stick. Turturro is good for the role because he can play both speeds: defeated salaryman, and reawakened dreamer. People keep asking him, "Are you all right?" Too bad about Splatchee Lake.

The Brandon Teena Story ★ ★ ★

NO MPAA RATING, 90 m., 1999

A documentary directed and produced by Susan Muska and Greta Olafsdottir.

Brandon Teena was a "good kisser" and "knew how to treat a woman," we are told, and even after Brandon's secret was revealed—"he" was a biological female born Teena Brandon—there is a certain wistfulness in the memories of her girlfriends. None of the women who dated Brandon seem particularly angry about the deception, and after we've spent some time in the world where they all lived, we begin to understand why: Most of the biological men in *The Brandon Teena Story* are crippled by a vast, stultifying ignorance. No wonder a girl liked a date who sent her flowers and little love notes.

Consider, for example, the sheriff in the rural area where Brandon Teena and two bystanders were shot dead. We hear his words on tape as he interviews Brandon, who was raped by those who would commit the murders a few days later. To hear the interrogation is to hear words shaped by prejudice, hatred, deep sexual incomprehension, and ignorance. I cannot quote most of what the sheriff says—his words are too cruel and graphic—but consider that he is interviewing, not a rapist, but a victim, and you will get some notion of the atmosphere in some corners of the remote Nebraska district where the murders occurred.

The sheriff did not like it one bit that a woman was pretending to be a man. There is the hint that a woman who behaves like this deserves whatever she gets; that it is natural for a red-blooded man to resent any poaching on his phallic preserve. The tapes also preserve the voice of Brandon, who was twenty or twenty-one at the time and sounds very young, insecure, and confused. "I have a sexual identity crisis," we hear at one point.

The documentary includes photos of Brandon, or Teena, at various ages, and although the clothing gradually becomes masculine and the haircut gets shorter, I must say that I never really felt I was looking at a man. Perhaps the deception would have worked only in a rural and small-town world far removed from the idea of gender transitions. The two men who were convicted of the murders were apparently deceived; they considered Brandon a friend, before growing suspicious and brutally stripping their victim of her clothes and, apparently, virginity.

But what about the women Brandon dated? Their testimony remains vague and affectionate. They were not lesbians (and neither was Brandon—who firmly identified with a male identity), but they were responsive to tenderness and caring and "good kissing." One woman in the film dated both one of the murderers and Brandon; given a choice between the narrow-minded dimness of the man and the imagination of someone prepared to cross gender lines, the more attractive choice was obviously Brandon.

The film itself is not slick and accomplished. It plays at times like home video footage, edited together on someone's computer. There are awkward passages of inappropriate music, and repeated shots of the barren winter landscape. Oddly enough, this is an effective style for this material; it captures the banality of the world in which individuality is seen as a threat. The testimony in the film is often flat and colorless (the killers are maddeningly passive and detached). Even the hero, Brandon Teena, was only slowly coming to an understanding of identity and sexuality.

Watching the film, I realized something. It is fashionable to deride TV shows like *Jerry Springer* for their sensational guests ("My boyfriend is really a girl!"). But as I watched *The Brandon Teena Story,* I realized that Brandon lived in a world of extremely limited sexual information, among people who assumed that men are men and women are women, and any violation of that rule calls for the death penalty. To the degree that they have absorbed anything at all from church or society, it is that homosexuals are to be hated. If tabloid TV contains the message that everyone has to make his or her own accommodation with life, sex, and self-image, then it's performing a service. It helps people get used to the idea that some people are different. With a little luck, Jerry Springer might have saved Brandon Teena's life.

Brassed Off ★ ★ ★

R, 107 m., 1997

Pete Postlethwaite (Danny), Tara Fitzgerald (Gloria), Ewan McGregor (Andy), Stephen Tompkinson (Phil), Jim Carter (Harry), Philip Jackson (Jim), Peter Martin (Ernie), Sue Johnston (Vera). Directed by Mark Herman and produced by Steve Abbott. Screenplay by Herman.

The central image in *Brassed Off* is that of a face: shiny, homely, dead serious. It is the face of a man who earnestly believes he is doing the most important thing in the world. The man's name is Danny, and he is the leader of a brass band made up of coal miners who work at a pit in Grimley, a Yorkshire mining town. The band was founded in 1881, and its rehearsal room is lined with the photographs of past bandmasters, looking down sternly on the current generation of musicians.

It is 1992, and the colliery is about to be closed. The Conservative government made a decision some years earlier to replace coal with nuclear power as a source of fuel, and as a result some 140 pits, representing more than 200,000 miners' jobs, were declared redundant. The closure of a pit means the death of a town, because a village like Grimley depends entirely on the wages of the miners, whose families for generations have gone down in the mines—and played for the band.

Brassed Off is a film that views the survival of the town through the survival of the band, and the survival of the band through the eyes of Danny (Pete Postlethwaite), who in some corner of his mind probably believes the mines exist only to supply him with musicians. The movie makes liberal use of storytelling formulas (there is a love story involving young people, and a crisis involving a married couple, and a health crisis involving Danny, a strategic use of "Danny Boy," and a national band contest at the Royal Albert Hall). But Postlethwaite's performance elevates and even ennobles this material.

He loves music. He is stern and exacting about it. His band members may labor in the pits all day, but when they come to rehearsal he expects seriousness and concentration. There is a fourteen-town competition coming up, and then the national finals, and this year he thinks the Grimley Brass Band has a real chance. If the pit closes, it will be a last chance.

Into the rehearsal hall one day comes a pretty young woman named Gloria (Tara Fitzgerald), who asks if she can sit in with her flugelhorn. She can. Her late father had been the band's best flugelhorn player, and her performance of "Rodrigo's Concerto" brings tears to the eyes of some of the band members—and a sparkle to the eye of young Andy (Ewan McGregor, from *Trainspotting*), who had a crush on her in school. Now she has gone away to London, and returned to Grimley (we learn) to make a study about the pit closure.

She pretends to have forgotten Andy, but later admits, "I did know your name—I just didn't want you to think it was etched forever on my brain." The love they felt when they were fourteen blossoms again, until it is revealed that she is working for the other side—for the government agency that would close the mine. She protests that she is on the miners' side and that her study might save the pit, but is told scornfully, "It's just a bloody P.R. exercise. They've already made their decision while you were at bloody college."

Another important figure in the story is Phil (Stephen Tompkinson), Danny's son, who struggles to make ends meet for his wife and large family. He wants to quit the band in order to save paying the dues, but lacks the nerve to tell his father. Phil moonlights as Chuckles the Clown, and brings a quick end to a children's birthday party with an uncontrolled outburst against Margaret Thatcher.

Brassed Off is a sweet film with a lot of anger at its core. The writer and director, Mark Herman, obviously believes the Tory energy decisions were inspired by the fact that coal miners voted Labour while nuclear power barons were Conservative. His plot tugs at every possible heartstring as it leads up to a dramatic moment in the Royal Albert Hall, which I will not reveal; it includes a speech against Thatcherism that some British critics found inappropriate, although it's certainly in character for old Danny.

One of the movie's great pleasures is the music itself. Brass bands are maintained by many different British institutions—schools, police forces, military units, coal miners, assembly-line workers—and their crisp music always seems gloriously self-confident. Some of the film's best shots show Pete Postlethwaite's face as he leads the band: his anger when members get drunk and miss notes, and his pride when everything is exactly right.

Acting is not accomplished only with words and emotion. Sometimes it is projected from within, into a stance or an expression. There is not a moment in *Brassed Off* when I did not believe Postlethwaite was a brass band leader—and a bloody good one.

Breakdown ★★★

R, 96 m., 1997

Kurt Russell (Jeff Taylor), J. T. Walsh (Red Barr), Kathleen Quinlan (Amy Taylor), M. C. Gainey (Earl), Jack Noseworthy (Billy), Rex Linn (Sheriff Boyd), Ritch Brinkley (Al), Moira Harris (Arleen). Directed by Jonathan Mostow and produced by Martha De Laurentiis and Dino De Laurentiis. Screenplay by Mostow and Sam Montgomery.

Breakdown is taut, skillful, and surgically effective, the story of a man who finds himself trapped in a surrealistic nightmare. The story's setup is more entertaining than the payoff; as Hitchcock observed, suspense plays better than action. But the film delivers—right up until a final moment I'll get to later.

Kurt Russell and Kathleen Quinlan star as a Massachusetts couple driving to California through the deserts of the Southwest. They've made two mistakes, as a character later helpfully explains: driving a brand-new red Jeep, and having out-of-state plates. In the middle of nowhere, the car breaks down, or so they think, and they are left at the mercy of the locals.

The locals do not come well advertised. Early in the film, the Jeep nearly sideswipes a dusty black pickup driven by a stringy-haired goon (M. C. Gainey) who looks like he belongs back home in the swamps of *Deliverance.* He later accosts them at a gas station, and Russell floors the Jeep in an attempt to put highway space between them. That may be a mistake during the new car's break-in period; it has an engine meltdown in the desert, and they seem to be at the mercy of the goon until a helpful semi driver (J. T. Walsh) happens along.

Now I will move carefully to conserve plot details. Walsh offers them a ride to a nearby diner, Russell chooses to stay with his car, and Quinlan accepts the offer so she can phone a road service. But when Russell later arrives at the diner, no one there has seen his wife. And when he stops the truck driver for a highway showdown with a deputy sheriff on hand, Walsh convincingly argues he has never seen the woman. Russell narrowly avoids being arrested, and is left standing by the side of his car in the middle of nowhere, baffled and angered by the disappearance of his wife.

The situation at this point resembles the opening dilemma of *The Vanishing* (1988), a brilliant Dutch-French thriller (accept no substitutes; the 1993 U.S. remake is a pale shadow). In that one, a couple paused at a highway rest stop, the woman walked inside, and was never seen again. There is a moment here when Russell stares at a wall of Missing Persons posters in the local sheriff's office, and realizes how common it is for people to disappear into thin air. (The sheriff cheerfully quotes discouraging statistics.)

What happened to his wife? I will tell no more than necessary, but stop reading now if you want total suspense. If *Breakdown* had the courage of *The Vanishing,* which was a chillingly nihilistic film, we would never find out—or, we would discover things we would rather not have known. But this is an American thriller, and so it is preordained that Russell will find himself on a desperate solo struggle to find his wife and save her. (The previews provided a large hint with a shot of him hanging onto a speeding truck's undercarriage.)

In the course of his quest, there are two scenes that don't work as well as they should. One is a scene in a small-town bank, which shows Russell behaving so awkwardly that opportunities for suspense are lost; the director, Jonathan Mostow, seems to have realized that, and cuts away from the bank abruptly without concluding the sequence. Another is a scene where Russell is being pursued by villains and unwisely drives his nice new Jeep down an embankment and into a river. In the TV ads it would power across to the other shore, but in the movie it floats downstream, allowing him to discover, in the vastness of the landscape, a single tiny doughnut wrapper that provides a (unnecessary) clue.

Those scenes raise questions. The others do not. For most of its length *Breakdown* functions so efficiently that we put logic on hold and go with the action. Russell makes a convincing, dogged, weary everyman, and the J. T. Walsh character is given some shades that are interesting (including his relationship with his wife and son).

I'm recommending *Breakdown,* but I have a

problem with the closing scene I mentioned above. It involves a situation in which a villain is disabled and powerless—yet a coup de grace is administered. There is (or was) a tradition in Hollywood thrillers that the heroes in movies like this kill only in self-defense. By ending as it does, *Breakdown* disdains such moral boundaries. I noticed, interestingly, that no one in the audience cheered when that final death took place. I felt a kind of collective wince. Maybe that indicates we still have an underlying decency that rejects the eye-for-an-eye values of this film. *Breakdown* is a fine thriller, and its ending is unworthy of it.

Broken English ★★★

NO MPAA RATING, 90 m., 1997

Rade Serbedzija (Ivan), Aleksandra Vujcic (Nina), Julian Arahanga (Eddie), Marton Csokas (Darko), Madeline McNamara (Mira), Elizabeth Mavric (Vanya), Jing Zhao (Clara), Yang Li (Wu), Temuera Morrison (Manu). Directed by Gregor Nicholas and produced by Robin Scholes. Screenplay by Nicholas, Johanna Pigott, and Jim Salter.

Broken English opens with news footage of the devastation in Croatia, and then it is three years later and we are in the green, quiet land of New Zealand. A family of Croatians, allowed to immigrate because the mother was born in New Zealand, have moved there. And far from home, the father enforces his unyielding standards on his family; he uses a baseball bat to chase off a man who is necking with one of his daughters.

Fathers who have a jealous obsession with the sex lives of their grown daughters are not new to the movies. But *Broken English* is about more than that. It is about ethnic identity transferred to a place where it cannot find nurture. The father, named Ivan (Rade Serbedzija), still nurses old wounds, and lingers over videotapes from home. He does not want his daughters to associate with the local men—but who else, really, is there for them to date?

The story focuses on Nina (Aleksandra Vujcic), who likes to dress in sexy clothes. She works in a Chinese restaurant, where she's attracted to the Maori cook named Eddie (Julian Arahanga). They fall into a passionate relationship. Meanwhile Ivan broods about the wrongs done to his people and is angered even when the pope visits the war zone to ask for peace and forgiveness. "We've left that madness behind," his wife cries. Ivan has not.

He brings his old mother over from Croatia and holds a feast to welcome her. Nina asks if she can bring "a friend," and Ivan, who has briefly met Eddie, says she can. But resentment against this man of another race is obviously brewing, and when Nina also turns up at the party with two Chinese friends, Ivan says the party has been invaded by "a bloody UN peacekeeping force."

As the Croatian music plays in Ivan's backyard, another festival with music is going on next door in the yard of a large Maori family. The Maoris, of course, have been in New Zealand longer than anybody else, which does not prevent Ivan from resenting the racket they're making. And then Ivan gets a surprise: Although Nina is dating Eddie, she has agreed to marry the Chinese man, who will pay her $16,000 because marriage will give him citizenship. When the would-be groom unwisely drinks too much and announces this fact to Ivan, there is a brief, brutal moment of violence that sets up the final passages of the film.

Like the powerful *Once Were Warriors*, this film is about how old wounds cause new ones, and is about male sexual jealousy mixed with alcoholism. The situation is not original, but the setting makes it seem so, and the director and cowriter, Gregor Nicholas, is alert to nuances of the characters.

Consider, for example, Nina's style. She likes to wear tight leather pants, she likes to appear sexy, and at the feast Eddie notices the way she flirts with her father and all the other men in the family. "Do you always sit on those guys like that?" he asks. She does. And we can intuit that she was taught to act like that at an early age; undeclared, unconsummated incest is a family style.

The acting is sometimes ragged but always effective. Rade Serbedzija, who plays Ivan, played a much different character in *Before the Rain*, a film in which he was the sad-eyed outsider observing ethnic hatreds. Aleksandra Vujcic, a newcomer, is effective as the flashing-eyed woman who wants to break loose from her family while remaining unaware of how closely she is still bound. Julian Arahanga's Maori character is able to find a certain thoughtful detachment from the situation, which leads to a better perspective. And I was touched by Zing Zhao, as the Chinese woman, who wants only to "have a little kiwi." (Temuera Morrison, unforgettable as the brutish husband in *Once Were Warriors,* has a smaller role as Arahanga's friend.)

We assume the movie will end in violence, but Nicholas finds a more thoughtful and probably more realistic conclusion. The underlying subject of the film is what might be called tribalism: The belief that a group depends for its existence on the exclusion and hatred of outsiders. Transplanted far from the ethnic conflicts that have ravaged their homeland, these characters still play the same tired tapes. If there are no Serbs to hate, then they will hate Maoris and Chinese. Of course, such feelings are not limited to Croatians. Serbians in the same situations might act the same. Or Maoris. Or Chinese. And all the rest of us. Tribalism is a universal human trait that has long outlived its usefulness.

A Brother's Kiss ★ ★ ★

R, 92 m., 1997

Nick Chinlund (Lex), Michael Raynor (Mick), Cathy Moriarty (Doreen), Rosie Perez (Debbie), Justin Pierce (Young Lex), Joshua Danowsky (Young Mick), Marisa Tomei (Missy), John Leguizamo (Drug Dealer). Directed by Seth Zvi Rosenfeld and produced by Bob Potter and E. Bennett Walsh. Screenplay by Rosenfeld.

A Brother's Kiss tells the harrowing story of two brothers—one a cop, one a crackhead—on a collision course. We've seen that before. What we haven't seen is how they got where they are; the movie's early scenes are heartbreaking in the way they show the brothers as kids.

They live with their mother, Doreen (Cathy Moriarty), who is at that delicate stage between being a tramp and becoming a hooker—the stage when a woman accepts presents from men, but doesn't exactly charge them. There's a parade of strange men through the East Harlem apartment, and Doreen even has the kids prepare some breakfast eggs for one of them.

She's not an unloving mother. She cares fiercely for them, and would do a better job of parenting if she had money, if she were not an alcoholic, and if she were not slowly dying of diabetes. The kids help her take her insulin shots, and they stir her martinis before they all sit down to a Scrabble game.

One day young Lex (Justin Pierce) and Mick (Joshua Danowsky) are coming home through the park when Mick, the smaller and weaker, is sexually assaulted by an off-duty cop. Lex, already strong as a man, stabs the cop, and this is the act that sets the course for his life: He is sent to reform school, and begins a long slide down into unemployment, drug addiction, and even stealing from his own brother's apartment.

As adults, Mick (Michael Raynor) becomes, curiously, a policeman. He remains a virgin; his sexuality is so confused after that night in the park (which they never mention to one another) that he has hidden his manhood behind a shield. Lex (Nick Chinlund) is a ladies' man, gets a girl (Rosie Perez) pregnant, has a kid, tries working as a bus driver, and eventually finds himself tied to the local dealer (John Leguizamo). Lex's problem is that he does more drugs than he sells, so that the dealer becomes a threat to his life—and to his supply.

A Brother's Kiss began life as a one-act play, also starring Chinlund and Raynor. I learn that the writer-director, Seth Zvi Rosenfeld, grew up with Raynor in the area shown in the movie, and Raynor met Chinlund when they were both eleven. So there is history and emotion embedded in the dialogue and performances.

Since what happens to the characters as adults is more or less preordained, what makes the movie work is the conviction of the performances. It's fascinating how Chinlund's character is simultaneously a screw-up and the dominant older brother, while Raynor's is simultaneously the responsible cop and the terrified kid. The roles that life has assigned them do not match their natures, and sooner or later the policeman will find himself in a situation where he has to decide what frightens him more—his brother, or his department superiors.

The supporting cast is good across the board. Marisa Tomei plays a disintegrating cocaine addict, Rosie Perez is touching as a woman who tries to protect her child, and Cathy Moriarty (immortal as Vicky LaMotta in *Raging Bull*) here takes a clichéd role and makes it fresh and heartbreaking. Watching the story of these two brothers, I was reminded of *Angels With Dirty Faces* (1938), with James Cagney and Pat O'Brien as two boys who get in trouble. One is caught, and becomes a killer. The other gets away, and becomes a priest. After the killer is executed, the priest says, "Let's say a prayer for a boy who couldn't run as fast as I could."

Buddy ★★

PG, 84 m., 1997

Rene Russo (Trudy Lintz), Robbie Coltrane (Dr. Lintz), Alan Cumming (Dick), Irma P. Hall (Emma), Peter Elliott (Buddy), Paul Reubens (Professor Spatz), John Aylward (Mr. Bowman), Mimi Kennedy (Mrs. Bowman). Directed by Caroline Thompson and produced by Steve Nicolaides and Fred Fuchs. Screenplay by Thompson, based on the book *Animals Are My Hobby* by Gertrude Davies Lintz.

Buddy is about a woman who is stark raving mad, and the filmmakers don't seem to know it. She lives in a rambling suburban mansion with six geese, five dogs, countless cats, tanks full of fish, a parrot, horses, and two chimpanzees, who she likes to dress up and take to the movies. One day she brings home a baby gorilla named "Buddy."

How does her husband react? Well, he's a doctor, and so he takes out his stethoscope, examines the infant simian, and gravely announces, "double pneumonia." But little Buddy recovers, and soon he is a full-sized gorilla, although the woman insists on treating him as a child (she tells a gorilla expert that a little chicken soup never hurts).

I watched this movie with steadily mounting incredulity. I was trying to find the category for it, and there isn't one. The posters make it look like a madcap family film about a zany couple and their lovable pets. But in a family film you don't expect subtle but unmistakable sexual undertones. Nor is it a serious wildlife film like *Gorillas in the Mist.* Not with Buddy wearing a suit and tie, and the chimps juggling meat cleavers in the kitchen. It could be a study of undiagnosed mental illness, if it weren't shot on perky 1930s sets, scored with upbeat music, and played by the actors like a *Thin Man* movie with Nick and Nora on Prozac.

The film, "based on a true story," stars Rene Russo as Trudy Lintz, who fills her home with animals. Robbie Coltrane plays her chubby, long-suffering and, I must say, remarkably patient husband. His job is to wear three-piece suits and pleasantly say, "Trudy, sweetheart? I wonder if I might have a word with you . . ." (It's inspired casting to put a fat man in this role: He knows a 900-pound gorilla can sit down wherever he wants to, but he always thought *he* was the gorilla.)

The household also includes a cook (Irma P. Hall) whose standard lines ("Don't you do that in my kitchen!") sound strange when addressed to apes, and a butler (Alan Cumming) whose tasks include extricating his mistress from Buddy's death grip by distracting the beast with bowls of milk. He also presumably cleans up around the house, if you get my drift, although that aspect of the situation is not explored.

More than once during the film, I was reminded of John Cassavetes's *Love Streams,* where the deeply disturbed Gena Rowlands character pulls up in a taxi with a duck, a goat, some chickens, a dog, and a parrot, having done a little compulsive shopping at a pet store. The difference is, *Love Streams* knows its heroine is nuts, and *Buddy* doesn't. One of the peculiarities of the film is the vast distance between the movie they've made and the movie they think they've made.

Consider, for example, a sequence where Trudy takes Buddy and the chimps to the Chicago World's Fair. "Sweetheart, I beg you not to take Buddy to the fair," says her sweet husband. "There will be hundreds of people there. He's not used to it." But she persists.

One of the chimps lets Buddy out of his cage and he wanders onto the midway, where there is an unintentionally hilarious sequence showing hundreds of people fleeing and screaming like extras in a *Godzilla* movie, while Buddy ambles about in confusion. (Later that night,

Trudy and a cop drive through the empty fairgrounds while she calls "Buddy! Buddy!"—as if a gorilla could remain undetected for hours at a world's fair.)

The story's underlying tragedy, of course, is that Buddy grows up. "He doesn't know his own strength," Trudy says. In one scene he hugs her so tightly we're afraid she'll be crushed. And what about the very peculiar scene where Trudy is asleep in a filmy negligee in her 1930s movie bedroom, and Buddy wanders in? The cutting, the pacing, and the music all suggest, very subtly, that some of the neglected themes in *King Kong* are about to get belated recognition.

Rene Russo plays Trudy as a sweet, resourceful, intelligent woman who is obviously on the edge of screaming hysteria. She smiles, she's the voice of reason, and we're thinking she ought to be shot with tranquilizer darts. Consider the scene where she walks out into the backyard and talks to her animals with a series of shrieks, growls, roars, whistles, and wild, bestial cries. The scene would be odd enough as I've described it. But now imagine it lasting about twice as long as you'd expect.

Robbie Coltrane's husband is a case study in an actor at sea. Why *would* a husband benevolently allow his wife to fill their home with dozens of messy, annoying, and somctimes dangerous animals? If the character were based on Jim Fowler, that would be one thing. But the husband is a doctor who, it appears, doesn't much care about animals one way or another. Coltrane handles this enigma by ignoring it. He addresses his wife always with calm and sweet reason. One day he will probably drop her into a bathtub filled with acid. If he shows the jury this movie, they might let him off with the minimum.

Buena Vista Social Club ★★

NO MPAA RATING, 101 m., 1999

A documentary featuring Ibrahim Ferrer, Compay Segundo, Ruben Gonzalez, Omara Portuondo, Luis Barzaga, Joachim Cooder, Ry Cooder, Pio Leyva, Manuel "Puntillita" Licea, Eliades Ochoa, and others. Directed by Wim Wenders and produced by Ulrich Felsberg and Deepak Nayar.

There's an overwhelming temptation to praise *Buena Vista Social Club* simply because it is about legendary performers and wonderful music. But that praise should really go to the Grammy-winning 1997 album of the same name, produced by Ry Cooder, who rediscovered an almost vanished generation of Cuban musicians in Havana and assembled them for a last hurrah. It is a touching story, and the musicians (some more than ninety years old) still have fire and grace onstage, but, man, does the style of this documentary get in the way.

Wim Wenders, who directed it, seems to have given his cameramen a few basic instructions that they follow over and over again for the entire movie. One shot of a camera circling a musician on a chair in a big room would have been splendid—especially since the interiors in the movie are of beautiful, decaying Havana locations. But the camera circles obsessively. In big empty rooms, in bars, on verandahs, in rehearsal halls, in a recording studio, it circles and circles annoyingly.

When it isn't circling, there's another problem. The credits say the film was made on two digital cameras; one seems to have been handheld by a cameraman with the shakes. One camera is level, smooth, and confident. The other has the jitters so badly that you can sense the editor cutting away from it as much as he can. The unstable handheld look can be an interesting choice in certain situations. As a style, it becomes a problem.

Then there is the question of how to show Ry Cooder in the film. Yes, he is the godfather of this project, and there would be no film and no Buena Vista Social Club without him. But the filmmakers seem too much in awe of him. When the musicians give concerts in Amsterdam and at Carnegie Hall, the onstage footage keeps returning to a single repetitive camera move: focus on musician, then pan up to Ry Cooder smiling benevolently. He is positioned in the top row of the onstage musicians, on the strong visual axis just to the right of center, and the camera keeps glancing up at him as if for approval from the teacher.

Then there's the problem of presenting the music. I didn't expect a concert film, but I did expect that I might be allowed to hear one song all the way through, with the cutting dictated by the music. No luck. The songs are intercut with biographical testaments from the veteran musicians. These in themselves are splendid: The stories of how these performers grew up, learned their music, flourished, were forgotten, and then rediscovered are sometimes amazing, always moving (as when we reflect that the singer Ibrahim Ferrer, "the Cuban Nat King Cole," dominating the orchestra and the audience at Carnegie Hall, was shining shoes when Cooder found him). But the movie's strategy is to show them in performance, then cut away to their story, leaving the songs stranded.

When the Social Club gets to New York, the Carnegie Hall concert should have been the climax. (Consider the emotional payoff of the not dissimilar *The Weavers: Wasn't That a Time!* Consider, too, Terry Zwigoff's magical documentary *Louie Bluie*, about Martin, Bogan, and the Armstrongs—also elderly musicians who were belatedly rediscovered.) Instead of pausing sometimes to simply listen to the music, Wenders intercuts Carnegie Hall with shots of the musicians visiting the Empire State Building and Times Square, looking in souvenir shop windows, talking about how wonderful it all is, as if they were on a school trip. This is condescending. The movie reminded me of a concert where somebody behind me is talking and moving around all the time. Let them play.

When they do, it is magical. We meet not only Ferrer, who has all of the ease and charisma of a born star, but a pianist named Ruben Gonzalez, who is eighty years old and complains of arthritis but has a strong and unmistakable piano style; Compay Segundo, a guitarist and singer, over ninety; and Omara Portuondo, "the Cuban Edith Piaf," luxuriating in the joy of the music. And many more; the faces become familiar, the music becomes seductive.

Wenders's visual texture for the film is interesting. He overexposes slightly with moderately high contrasts and then washes the picture out a little; it's like the watercolor technique where you finish the painting, let it dry, and then let it soak briefly in a pan of water so that the strong colors remain and others become more faded. It's a nice surface for the film, and appropriate.

But there's that constant humming undercurrent of adulation for Ry Cooder—who I am sure is a good man and a gifted musician and does not need to be shown so constantly that his presence becomes like product placement. I was reminded uncannily of those old *Amateur Hour* programs on TV, where the emcee beamed benevolently on one act after another. The musicians of the Buena Vista Social Club needed to be rediscovered, but that's all they needed: They came ready to play. I bought the album. You should, too. If this movie comes out on DVD, I hope the other side contains bonus concert footage.

Buffalo '66 ★ ★ ★

NO MPAA RATING, 110 m., 1998

Vincent Gallo (Billy Brown), Christina Ricci (Layla), Anjelica Huston (Janet Brown), Ben Gazzara (Jimmy Brown), Kevin Corrigan (Goon), Mickey Rourke (Bookie), Roseanna Arquette (Wendy), Jan-Michael Vincent (Sonny). Directed by Vincent Gallo and produced by Chris Hanley. Screenplay by Gallo.

Vincent Gallo's *Buffalo '66* plays like a collision between a lot of half-baked visual ideas, and a deep and urgent need. That makes it interesting. Most movies don't bake their visual ideas at all, nor do we sense that their makers have had to choose between filming them or imploding. Oh, and the film contains an astonishing performance by Christina Ricci, who seems to have been assigned a portion of the screen where she can do whatever she wants.

Gallo plays Billy Brown, who is being released from prison when we first see him. He waits outside a long time, and then knocks on the gates, asking a guard if he can come back in to use the john. Turned away, urgently needing to pee, he takes a bus into town, is turned away at the bus station and the restaurant, and then barges into a tap-dancing class. While he's there, he grabs one of the students, drags her out, tells her she's being kidnapped, and says she has to pretend to be his wife when he goes to visit his parents.

This is Layla (Christina Ricci), who is dressed like Barbie as a hooker, and takes the kidnapping in stride: "Are your parents vegetarians? I hope so, because I don't eat meat—ever!" At Billy's house, we meet the parents. Dad (Ben Gazzara) glowers but doesn't speak. Mom

(Anjelica Huston) has her eyes glued to the TV, where a tape of an old Buffalo Bills game is playing. She named her son for the team. The display of family photos includes Jack Kemp and O. J. Simpson. Eventually Dad warms up to Layla, grabbing her clumsily and cooing, "I love my little daughter. Daddy loves his daughter." Later, he mimes to a record by a Sinatra soundalike (actually, we learn from the end titles, Gallo's father).

Gallo shot these scenes in his childhood home in Buffalo, and has said the parents are based on his own. His memories are like an open wound. Consider, for example, a flashback where his mother *knows* he's allergic to chocolate doughnuts and feeds him some anyway, and his face swells up like the Pillsbury doughboy. The movie plays like revenge time.

But that's not all. Gallo, an angular and unshaven man with a haunted look, has acted for such offbeat and experimental directors as Abel Ferrara *(The Funeral)*, Bille August *(The House of the Spirits)*, Mika Kaurismaki *(L.A. Without a Map)*, Emir Kusturica *(Arizona Dream)*, Claire Denis *(Nenette and Boni)*, Mira Nair *(The Perez Family)*, and Kiefer Sutherland *(Truth or Consequences, N.M.)*. His career is proof that it is possible to work steadily and well in challenging and original films by gifted directors and remain almost completely unknown. Now, directing his own film at last, he seems filled with ideas that he wants to realize—sequences that spring to life even though they may have precarious attachments to the rest of the film.

Consider his visit to the local bowling alley, still with Ricci as his hostage (he has named her "Wendy Balsam" and explained that they met "while overseas on assignment for the CIA"). Although he was in prison for six or seven years, his old locker is still waiting for him (when they don't change your lock after you're sent to the Big House, that's a bowling alley with a heart). He bowls, brilliantly. She, dressed like a finalist for Little Miss Sunbeam, does a tap-dance routine right there on the hardwood, while a spotlight follows her. What's this scene doing in *Buffalo '66*? Maybe Gallo didn't have any other movie he could put it in.

We gradually learn a little of Billy's story, although nothing of Layla's. Carried away by the family obsession with the Buffalo Bills, he bet $10,000 he didn't have and lost it on a crucial missed field goal. His bookie (Mickey Rourke) forgave the debt on the condition he do the prison time for another guy. Now he wants revenge. Not on the bookie—on the placekicker.

There's probably a dark and violent ending looming for the film, although there's a good chance, we think, that it may avoid it: The movie has stepped nimbly around all sorts of other obligatory scenes. *Buffalo '66* isn't really about endings, anyway. Endings are about conclusions and statements, and Gallo is obviously too much in a turmoil about this material to organize it into a payoff.

What we get is more like improvisational jazz, in which themes are introduced from other movies, and this one does riffs on them. Christina Ricci is like a soloist who occasionally stands up and takes the spotlight while the other players recede into the shadows, nodding and smoking. Why does her character go along with the kidnapping? Why does she throw herself into the role of "wife" with such zeal—and invention? Well, it's more interesting than if she was merely frightened and trying to escape. That would be the conventional approach. There's not a thing conventional about this movie.

A Bug's Life ★ ★ ★ ½

G, 94 m., 1998

With the voices of: Dave Foley (Flik), Kevin Spacey (Hopper), Julia Louis-Dreyfus (Princess Atta), Hayden Panettiere (Dot), Phyllis Diller (Queen), Richard Kind (Molt), David Hyde Pierce (Slim), Joe Ranft (Heimlich), Denis Leary (Francis), Jonathan Harris (Manny), Bonnie Hunt (Rosie). Directed by John Lasseter and produced by Darla K. Anderson and Kevin Reher. Screenplay by Andrew Stanton, Donald McEnery, and Bob Shaw, based on the original story by Lasseter, Stanton, and Joe Ranft.

As ants struggle to gather morsels of food, a leaf falls and interrupts their procession. "I'm lost!" screams a worker in panic. "Where's the line?" Rescue workers quickly arrive: "We are going around to the *left!*" The harvest continues. "This is nothing compared to the twig of '93," an ant observes.

Enjoying this, I enjoyed too the use of animation to visualize a world that could not be seen in live action and could not be created with special effects. Animation contains enormous promise for a new kind of storytelling, freed from reality and gravity, but although the Japanese have exploited that freedom, too many American feature cartoons follow the Disney formula of plucky young heroes and heroines and comic sidekicks.

It's a formula that has produced wonderful movies. But the Pixar computer animation studio, a Disney coproducer, broke new ground with *Toy Story* in 1995, and again in *A Bug's Life* it runs free. The story, about an ant colony that frees itself from slavery to grasshoppers, is similar in some ways to the autumn's other big animated release, *Antz*, but aimed at a broader audience and without the in-jokes.

The film's hero is Flik (voice by Dave Foley), the smartest ant in the colony (the competition is not fierce). As the other ants labor to pile up "the Offering," a mountain of food for tyrannical grasshoppers, Flik perfects an invention to harvest grain more quickly; he's the Cyrus McCormick of the hymenopterous Formicidae. But he's still basically just an ant; the film is more about the fate of the colony and not so much about individuals like the Woody Allen hero of *Antz*.

There is a crisis. Flik spills the Offering, and Hopper (Kevin Spacey), the leader of the grasshoppers, is not pleased. Hopper has the kind of personality that makes him talk with his hands, and since he has four, Flik gets the message: Rebuild the Offering or face unspeakable consequences. What to do? Flik feels terrible because his clumsiness caused the trouble; he apologizes to the queen (Phyllis Diller), is encouraged by Princess Atta (Julia Louis-Dreyfus) and resolves to fight back.

Flik uses a dandelion pod as a sort of aircraft, and flies off on a hopeful quest to find mercenaries he can hire to defend the colony. He finds nine, including a walking stick named Slim (David Hyde Pierce), a praying mantis (Jonathan Harris), a caterpillar that looks military and sounds like a Nazi (Joe Ranft), a black widow (Bonnie Hunt), and others. How is he to know they aren't really warrior insects, but simply discontented performers from P. T. Flea's Circus?

The animators, led by director John Lasseter, provide rich images. A rainstorm feels like the colony is being water-bombed. A circus trick involves matches and flypaper. There are sneaky throwaway lines (when Flik visits a city, he encounters a beggar who explains, "A kid pulled my wings off").

Will *A Bug's Life* suffer by coming out so soon after *Antz*? Not any more than one thriller hurts the chances for the next one. *Antz* may even help business for *A Bug's Life* by demonstrating how many dramatic and comedic possibilities can be found in an anthill. And the Pixar animators, using later generations of the software that created such a fresh look in *Toy Story*, have made a movie that is always a pleasure to look at: There are glistening rounded surfaces, the sense of three dimensions, an eye for detail. And big laughs at the end, when the credits are interrupted by animated "outtakes" that satirize the blown lines and missed cues in live-action credit cookies.

Antz has a more sophisticated sensibility, and could play for adults attending by themselves. *A Bug's Life* is more clearly intended as a family film. Smaller children will respond to the threat from the Hoppers and the zaniness of the weird assortment of mercenaries hired by Flik.

Note: After seeing A Bug's Life, *you might want to rent that French documentary* Microcosmos, *which uses enormously magnified images to show us the insect kingdom. There's a whole other world down there. Be careful where you step.* ☞

Bulworth ★ ★ ★ ½

R, 108 m., 1998

Warren Beatty (Jay Bulworth), Halle Berry (Nina), Don Cheadle (L.D.), Paul Sorvino (Graham Crockett), Jack Warden (Eddie Davers), Sean Astin (Gary), Nora Dunn (Missy Berliner), Laurie Metcalf (Mimi), Oliver Platt (Dennis). Directed by Warren Beatty and produced by Beatty and Pieter Jan Brugge. Screenplay by Beatty.

What it comes down to is a politician who can no longer bring himself to recite the words, "America is standing on the doorstep of a new millennium." Over and over and over again he has repeated the same mindless platitudes, the same meaningless baloney, the same hot air. Now he sits in his office, playing one of his stupid TV commercials on an endless loop. He has not eaten or slept in three days. He is sick to the soul of the American political process.

These do not seem to be the makings of a comedy, but Warren Beatty's *Bulworth* made me laugh, and wince. You realize that if all politicians were as outspoken as Bulworth, the fragile structure of our system would collapse, and we would have to start all over again. The movie suggests that virtually everything said in public by a politician is spin. "Spin control" is merely the name for spin they don't get away with.

Bulworth is a onetime Kennedy liberal (like Beatty himself), an incumbent senator from California who is accused by an opponent of being "old liberal wine trying to pour himself into a new conservative bottle." The joke to Bulworth is that liberal and conservative, Democrat and Republican, are no longer labels that mean much: When it comes to national health care, for example, the insurance companies have both parties in their pockets (and both parties have their hands in the companies' pockets).

Bulworth is in trouble. He hates his job and his life, and has just lost millions in the market. So he puts out a contract on his own life and flies back to California thinking he has three days to live. His impending death fills him with a sense of freedom: At last he is free to say exactly what he thinks, and that's what he does. In a black church, he observes, "We all come down here, get our pictures taken—forget about it." Blacks will never have power within the establishment, he says, until they've spent the money to buy it like the whites do.

Bulworth's campaign manager (Oliver Platt) goes ballistic and hits a fire alarm to end the church service. But an hour later in Beverly Hills Beatty is insulting a mostly Jewish audience of movie moguls: "How much money do you guys really need?" he asks, observing that they produce "mostly crap." And so it goes. "That was good. Really good," he says. He's enjoying political speechmaking for the first time in his life.

Following Bulworth through his conversion is a posse of foxy young black women who pile into his limousine and direct him to an after-hours club, where he samples hip-hop and drugs. Lingering always nearby in the background is an attractive woman named Nina (Halle Berry), who eventually takes him home to her neighborhood, where he sees grade-school kids selling crack, and is treated to the truth of families where everybody has lost someone to gunfire.

Bulworth doesn't consist simply of the candidate making insults like a radical Don Rickles. There's substance in a lot of the dialogue, written by Beatty with a debt to the critiques of American society by such as Noam Chomsky. Beatty zeroes in on the myth that government is wasteful and industry is efficient by claiming that government runs Medicare for a fourth of the overhead raked off by insurance companies for equivalent health care. But why don't we have national health care like every other First World country? Because of insurance payoffs, Bulworth is only too happy to explain.

The movie fires shots in all directions. Some of them hit, some of them miss. When Bulworth asks Nina where all the black leaders have gone, her answer is as intelligent and plausible as a year's worth of op-ed columns. But when the movie presents black culture as automatically more authentic and truthful than white, that's a leftover knee-jerk; the use of blacks as repositories of truth and virtue is a worn-out convention in white liberal breast-beating. (There is even a mysterious old black man who follows Bulworth around reciting incantations that are meant, I guess, to be encoded universal truths.) It's better when Bulworth simply abandons political correctness and says what he thinks, however reckless, as when he theorizes that the solution to racial difficulties is for everybody to bleep everybody else until we're all the same color.

Bulworth seems to reflect a rising tide of discontent with current American political discourse. Like *Wag the Dog* and *Primary Colors*, it's disenchanted with the state of the system. No wonder. I can remember listening, as a child, to radio debates between those two old warhorses of Illinois politics, Paul Douglas and Everett Dirksen. They simply had at each other, like two opinionated guys talking off the tops of their heads. Now debates, like campaigns, are carefully hedged with rules and regulations designed to ensure that everyone stays timidly within the tradition of "doorsteps of the new millennium," etc.

Bulworth is not a perfect movie, nor could it be. It's too messy and takes too many risks. I didn't buy the romance between Bulworth and Nina; it's a recycling of the tired movie convention that a man in a fight for his life can always find time, in three days, to fall in love with a woman half his age. And I didn't much like the movie's ending—not the false ending, and not the real one that follows, either.

But those are minor complaints. *Bulworth* plays like a cry of frustrated comic rage. It's about an archetypal character who increasingly seems to stand for our national mood: the guy who's fed up and isn't going to take it anymore. Funny how in the twenty-two years since we heard those words in *Network*, we've kept right on taking it.

The Butcher Boy ★ ★ ½

R, 105 m., 1998

Stephen Rea (Da Brady), Fiona Shaw (Mrs. Nugent), Eamonn Owens (Francie Brady), Alan Boyle (Joe Purcell), Aisling O'Sullivan (Annie Brady), Sinead O'Connor (Virgin Mary). Directed by Neil Jordan and produced by Redmond Morris and Stephen Woolley. Screenplay by Jordan and Patrick McCabe, based on the novel by McCabe.

Neil Jordan's *The Butcher Boy* tells the story of a young Irish boy who turns violent and insane under the pressure of a tragic childhood and a sense of betrayal. By the end of the film, when he acts out his murderous fantasies, I was thinking, of course, about the shooting spree by the two young boys in Jonesboro.

This film is, in a sense, optimistic. It suggests that children must undergo years of horrible experiences before they turn into killers. The Jonesboro shooters were apparently more fortunate: more or less normal kids raised with guns, and unable to understand the consequences of their actions. We want to believe violent kids have undergone emotional torments like Francie Brady, the young hero of *The Butcher Boy*. If they haven't, then the abyss is closer than we think.

The film takes place in the early 1960s, in a small town in the west of Ireland. It is narrated by Francie, who is played by the newcomer Eamonn Owens in one of the cockiest and most confident performances I've seen by a young actor. Francie's home life is not happy. His father (Stephen Rea) is a drunk who turns violent, who kicks in the TV, who weeps for the lost innocence of his days before whiskey. His mother (Aisling O'Sullivan) is suicidal; one day Francie comes home from school to find a chair on the kitchen table, and his ma preparing to hang herself.

She has a "breakdown," and is sent to a mental institution, which Francie calls a "garage," because that's where you usually go with a breakdown. He meanwhile clings to the islands of reassurance in his fragile universe, especially his best friend, Joe (Alan Boyle). They hide out in a playhouse near the river, they live in the fantasies of comic books, and Francie feels a fierce, possessive pride in his friend.

Francie's archenemy is the hated Mrs. Nugent (Fiona Shaw), who speaks with an English accent and is a snob and a scold, and seems to delight in persecuting Francie. It's she who turns in Francie and Joe for stealing apples. Francie in his fantasies imagines dire consequences, and is occasionally comforted by the appearance of the Virgin Mary (Sinead O'Connor), who sometimes turns up on TV and is not above using the f-word (although always, to be sure, in a lilting Irish context).

Things fall apart. He's sent to a youth home, where the priest dresses him in girl's clothes before being caught and whisked away to another garage. Francie returns to a job as a butcher boy, cutting up pig carcasses. He has fantasies of nuclear disaster, of humans turned into beasts, of charred corpses. His dad dies, and Francie leaves him in his favorite chair for a long time, until the authorities break in. Joe betrays him and becomes the friend of Mrs. Nugent's hated son.

The closing passages of the film, which is based on a novel by Patrick McCabe, are the logical outcome of what has come before. Jordan doesn't exploit; his tone is one of sad regarding, in which Francie's defiant voice sounds brave and forlorn. This is a kid who keeps up a front while his heart is breaking.

Neil Jordan *(The Crying Game, Michael*

Collins) is a strong, passionate director, and *The Butcher Boy* is original work, an attempt to combine magic realism with everyday reality and tie it together with Francie's own brash, defiant personal style (he is not a dumb kid). Yet in some way the movie held me outside; I didn't connect in the way I wanted to, and by the end I was out of sympathy with the material.

Why was this? I can see, objectively, that this is a film of weight, daring, and visual invention. I was in a little awe of young Eamonn Owens's performance. I can understand any praise this film receives, but I cannot feel it. *The Butcher Boy* has been compared to Kubrick's *A Clockwork Orange*, an acknowledged masterpiece that I have also found myself standing outside of. Rationalize as I will, revisit the film as I have, I cannot feel the emotional shift that would involve me in the material: It remains for me an exercise, not an experience (odd that his detached, cerebral *2001* sweeps me so easily into its spell).

Am I simply out of sympathy with Francie? Would I have been more moved by a more realistic approach (like the treatment of the reform school boy in *The Loneliness of the Long-Distance Runner*), rather than this film with miracles and horrific mirages? I can't say. I know there is something substantial here. I can't recommend the film, and yet if it sounds intriguing to you, I certainly think you should see it.

C

Can't Hardly Wait ★ ½

PG-13, 98 m., 1998

Ethan Embry (Preston Meyers), Jennifer Love Hewitt (Amanda Beckett), Lauren Ambrose (Denise Fleming), Peter Facinelli (Mike Dexter), Seth Green (Kenny Fisher), Charlie Korsmo (William Lichter), Jenna Elfman (The Angel), Jerry O'Connell (Trip McNeely). Directed by Deborah Kaplan and Harry Elfont and produced by Jenno Topping and Betty Thomas. Screenplay by Kaplan and Elfont.

There's one character in *Can't Hardly Wait* who is interesting and funny. Maybe it was a mistake to write her in; she makes the other characters look like gnat-brained bozos. Her name is Denise, she is played by Lauren Ambrose, and she has a merry face, a biting tongue, and a sardonic angle on high school. Her classmates look like candidates for *Starship Troopers* or the *Sports Illustrated* swimsuit pictorial.

The early days of June seem to bring a movie like this every year, celebrating the graduation of the senior class and its ejection onto the conveyor belt of life. *Can't Hardly Wait* is a lesser example of the genre, which includes (in descending order of accomplishment) *Say Anything, American Graffiti, Dazed and Confused, Fast Times at Ridgemont High,* and *Porky's.*

The movie lumbers gracelessly from romantic showdowns to deep conversations to bathroom humor. The hero is Preston (Ethan Embry), a would-be writer who has lusted for four years after the class sexpot, Amanda (Jennifer Love Hewitt). He knew their destinies were entertwined when they both ate strawberry Pop Tarts during their first freshman class. But the class jock, Mike (Peter Facinelli), won her instead.

Now it is the night of graduation day, and Mike has dumped Amanda because he plans to move up from high school *girls* to college *women.* At a long (some would say endless) keg party, Preston tries to give Amanda a letter he has written, spilling out his innermost thoughts. This must be some letter. We never get to see what it says, no doubt because a letter good enough to win Amanda would have to be better than anything the screenwriters are capable of writing.

Meanwhile, Mike learns from last year's high school make-out champ, Trip McNeely (Jerry O'Connell), that college women are always talking about serious stuff and dating older guys. Bummer. So he tries to win Amanda back in a scene played before a hushed crowd, but is rejected. That's even though Amanda has earlier wailed, "If I'm not Mike's girlfriend, who am I? Nobody knows me as anything else. I don't even know me as anyone else."

Real poignancy there. My own rule of thumb, in high school and ever after, is that if a woman has little of interest to say, she is likely, over a span of time, to have less and less to say, until finally she will drive you mad. That is true even though she may, as Amanda does, have awesome boobs.

Now take Denise, on the other hand. She gets accidentally locked into the bathroom with Kenny (Seth Green), who talks like a black rap artist even though he's white, and wears goggles and thinks he's cool and will someday no doubt be a radio talk jock. Denise is cute and plucky, and has intelligent lips (don't pretend you don't know what I mean), and kids Kenny's affectations, and remembers that they were best pals until the sixth grade, when he dropped her because, she says, "I was in all the smart classes, and my parents didn't make a lot of money, and you desperately needed to sit at the popular table in the lunchroom."

Denise is the only person in this senior class that anyone of any taste would want to be friends with. Why don't the filmmakers know that? Why do they go through the tired old motions of making Denise the comic relief, and assigning the romantic leads to a couple of clueless rubber stamps?

You tell me. *Can't Hardly Wait* is the kind of movie that somehow succeeds in moving very, very slowly even while proceeding at a breakneck pace. It cuts quickly back and forth between nothing and nothing. It underlines every single scene with a pop song that tells us what the scene is about. It doesn't have the zing of life and subversion that the best high school movies always have. Or, if they don't have them, like *Porky's* didn't, at least they have mercy on us and throw in a shower scene.

Career Girls ★ ★ ★

R, 87 m., 1997

Katrin Cartlidge (Hannah), Lynda Steadman (Annie), Kate Byers (Claire), Mark Benton (Ricky), Andy Serkis (Mr. Evans), Joe Tucker (Adrian), Margo Stanley (Ricky's Nan), Michael Healy (Lecturer). Directed by Mike Leigh and produced by Simon Channing-Williams. Screenplay by Leigh.

The world of Mike Leigh is one of small victories, painfully earned. His characters don't have lives that are easily transformed; they can't remake themselves overnight as self-help success stories. They're stuck with who they are and what they started out with, and somehow they find the courage to carry out essential upkeeps and improvements.

Career Girls, Leigh's first film since the heralded *Secrets and Lies,* is about two thirtyish women who were roommates six years ago, when they were both students at a London college. Now they meet again. Have their lives improved? Yes. Are they where they want to be? No. Are they confident they can get there? Not very.

Annie (Lynda Steadman) takes the train to London to meet Hannah (Katrin Cartlidge), who still lives there. Annie is as taut as a guitar string; she doesn't talk, she jerks the words free from her inhibitions. She's better now, though, than she was on the first day when she came to see Hannah in response to a roommate-wanted ad. In those days Annie had a nasty skin condition that covered half her face, and it wouldn't take a specialist to guess the rash was connected to nerves.

Leigh likes to let scenes develop in their own time. They don't rush to a payoff, because how the characters talk is often more important than their conclusions. Both actresses are highly mannered (or Leigh directs them to be), and as we watch, we're reminded of how smooth and articulate most characters are in the movies—why, you'd almost imagine someone had written out all the words for them to memorize! Not Annie, who seems blazingly self-conscious, and not Hannah, who is so wound up that words come tumbling out like an assault. I was reminded of a good performance in a much different movie—Benicio del Toro's work in *Excess Baggage,* where he also finds a new tone for his dialogue, lazy and coiling. Distinctive speech styles can be an affectation, or they can be a gift from the actor: *Career Girls* is like a workshop on conversational self-defense.

The two women sit and chat, and decide to go out (Hannah is apartment-hunting). They run into some old friends from their school days, including a rental agent named Adrian (Joe Tucker), who uncannily reminded me of the scenes in *Trainspotting* when Renton, the Ewan McGregor character, puts on a suit and tie and works as a real estate agent. Adrian dated one of the roommates and then the other, but doesn't remember either one.

In a hilarious flashback, we see another page from their social life: A drink at a pub with Ricky (Mark Benton), who closes his eyes when he talks, the better perhaps to read the words off the insides of his eyelids. One of Leigh's favorite actors is Timothy Spall, who played the photographer in *Secrets and Lies;* it's not a stretch to see Ricky as a younger version of the same character.

As *Career Girls* advances, we gradually realize that there is not going to be much of a plot to resolve. Annie and Hannah are in midstream. They know where they came from, but it's pretty murky in the direction they're going. They are neither successes nor failures, neither happy nor particularly sad, and they have jobs which, for the moment, focus their lives. They are, in short, like most of the young jobholders in big cities, and to an important degree their self-images are defined by the apartments they live in. (Looking out the window of a high-rise shown by an estate agent, one observes, "You can see the class struggle from up here!")

What is the use of a film like this? It inspires reflection. Strongly plotted films provide a goal and reach it, and we can go home under the impression that something has been accomplished. Mike Leigh's films realize that for most people, most days, life consists of the routine of earning a living, broken by fleeting thoughts of where our efforts will someday take us—financially, romantically, spiritually, or even geographically. We never arrive in most of those places, but the mental images are what keep us trying.

Annie and Hannah have a game they play in the film. Holding a copy of Emily Brontë's *Wuthering Heights,* they chant "Miss Brontë, Miss Brontë . . ." and then ask her a question, as if she were a Ouija board. Then they stab at a page at random, and read what she says in response.

I recognized the edition they were using: the Penguin English Library paperback, first published in 1965. I have the identical edition on my shelf, so I took it down. "Miss Brontë, Miss Brontë," I chanted, "what is the bottom line on the characters in this movie?" I opened it to page 163, stabbed, and read: "Oh, I'm burning! I wish I were out of doors—I wish I were a girl again, half savage and hardy, and free . . . and laughing at injuries, not maddening under them!"

The Castle ★ ★ ★

R, 85 m., 1999

Michael Caton (Darryl Kerrigan), Anne Tenney (Sal Kerrigan), Stephen Curry (Dale Kerrigan), Anthony Simcoe (Steve Kerrigan), Sophie Lee (Tracey Kerrigan), Wayne Hope (Wayne Kerrigan), Tiriel Mora (Dennis Denuto), Eric Bana (Con Petropoulous), Charles "Bud" Tingwell (Lawrence Hammill). Directed by Rob Sitch and produced by Debra Choate. Screenplay by Santo Cilauro, Tom Gleisner, Jane Kennedy, and Sitch.

Early in *The Castle,* the happy Kerrigan family is served a chicken dinner by Sal, wife of proud Darryl and mother of daughter Tracey and three sons Dale, Steve, and Wayne; Wayne, currently in prison, is the only one missing from the table. Dad (Michael Caton) observes something on the chicken and asks his wife (Anne Tenney) what it is. "Seasoning," she says proudly. Dad beams: "Seasoning! Looks like everybody's kicked a goal."

And so life spins along at 3 Highview Crescent in Melbourne, where the Kerrigan home sits surrounded by its built-on rooms, screened-in porch, greyhound kennel, big-dish satellite, and carport. For Darryl, it is not so much a house as a shrine to one of the best darn families in the universe, and he proudly points out the plastic Victorian gingerbread trim and the fake chimney to an inspector—who is there, as it turns out, to condemn the property under the laws of public domain.

The Kerrigans don't want to move. They've been told that the three most important words in real estate are "location, location, location"—and how could they improve on their home's convenient location, so close to the airport? So close, indeed, that jumbo jets pass within inches of the property line and the house trembles when they take off.

The Castle, directed by Rob Sitch, is one of those comic treasures like *The Full Monty* and *Waking Ned Devine* that shows its characters in the full bloom of glorious eccentricity. The Kerrigans may be the proudest and happiest family you've ever met, what with Dad's prosperous tow-truck business, and the inventions of Steve (Anthony Simcoe), the "idea man," who specializes in fitting tools together so they can do two jobs equally badly. Tracey (Sophie Lee) is the only college graduate (from beauty school), and Dale (Stephen Curry) is the narrator, frequently quoting his dad, who observes, as he gazes up at pylons towering over the home, that "power lines are a reminder of man's ability to generate electricity."

Dad is a bit of an idea man himself, taking advantage of a narrow room by building an even narrower pool table for it. Meanwhile, Steve searches the *Trader* ad paper for bargains, making sudden discoveries: "Jousting sticks! Make us an offer!" So tightly knit is the family that Dale proudly reports that during mealtimes, "the television is definitely turned down." So it is with a real sense of loss that the Kerrigans discover they may be evicted from their castle, a fate they share with their neighbors Jack and Farouk.

The movie's comic foundation is the cozy if spectacularly insular family life of the Kerrigans. They think almost as one: When Darryl rises to offer the toast at his daughter's wedding, he begins expansively with, "Speaking as the bride's parents . . ." Australia seems to abound with peculiar households, and the Kerrigans are wholesome, positive-thinking versions of such strange samples of Aussie family life as the dysfunctional weirdos in *Muriel's Wedding* and the sisters in *Love Sere-*

nade, who date a disk jockey who is a fish. I can picture them in the audience to view the finals in *Strictly Ballroom.*

The film develops suspense with a big (or, actually, a very small) courtroom finale. The Kerrigans determine to mount a legal battle against eviction and hire an attorney named Dennis Denuto (Tiriel Mora) to represent them, against his own advice (he specializes in repossessions). When he approaches the bench, it is to ask the judge, "How am I doing?" or to whisper urgently, "Can you give me an angle?" He gives the case his best shot (Dale informs us he "even learned Roman numerals" for the appeal), but it isn't until a kindly old expert in constitutional law (Charles "Bud" Tingwell) comes on board that they have a prayer.

This is the sort of movie the British used to make in black-and-white, starring Peter Sellers, Alec Guinness, Terry-Thomas, and Ian Carmichael. It's about characters who have a rock-solid view of the universe and their place in it, and gaze out upon the world from the high vantage point of the home that is their castle. The movie is not shocking or daring or vulgar, but sublimely content—as content as the Kerrigans when Mom not only serves pound cake for dessert but is so creative she actually tops it with icing sugar. At a time like that, she doesn't need to be told she's kicked a goal.

Cats Don't Dance ★ ★ ★

G, 69 m., 1997

With the voices of: Scott Bakula (Danny), Jasmine Guy (Sawyer), Natalie Cole (Sawyer's Songs), Ashley Peldon (Darla Dimple), John Rhys-Davies (Woolie), Kathy Najimy (Tillie), Matthew Harried (Pudge), George Kennedy (Mr. Mammoth). Directed by Mark Dindal and produced by David Kirschner and Paul Gertz. Screenplay by Roberts Gannaway, Cliff Ruby, Elana Lesser, and Theresa Pettengill.

The words "Disney" and "animation" fit together so firmly in the public mind that a feature-length cartoon from any other studio has tough going. If it's not Disney, somehow parents don't feel automatically compelled to load up the family van and head for the multiplex.

Warner Bros. has been trying to change that perception, and its *Space Jam,* starring Michael Jordan and Bugs Bunny, was a box-office hit, even though it didn't break through the magic $100 million domestic box-office ceiling. Now the studio is back again, with *Cats Don't Dance,* a cute animated musical about Danny the Song and Dance Cat from Kokomo, Indiana, who hops on a bus to Hollywood in search of stardom, circa 1939.

The movie lacks the strong plotting and vividly defined characters that are typical of Disney movies, and it doesn't start with the death of one or more parents, which seems more or less obligatory in the genre. It plays, indeed, more like an animated version of an old Hollywood musical (there are elements of *Singin' in the Rain,* and the late Gene Kelly is credited with the animated choreography).

The opening is right out of countless showbiz tales. Danny arrives in Hollywood with a seven-day plan that starts with getting an agent and ends with getting the girl. He quickly discovers the hard facts of life: Animal actors aren't much in demand, and humans get all the best jobs.

He's lucky to land a one-liner ("Meow") in a new musical by Darla Dimple (voice by Ashley Peldon), legendary heroine of Mammoth Studios, where the formula for a box-office hit is "Simple! It's Dimple!" He works the meow up into an entire routine, and is in the process of stealing the show when an ominous presence looms high above him: Max, Darla's butler (lifted here, accent and all, from Erich von Stroheim in *Sunset Boulevard*).

Danny (voice by Scott Bakula) makes some new friends, including Woolie (voice by John Rhys-Davies), the elephant who serves as Mammoth's mascot and spends his off-hours playing piano in the gypsy caravan that doubles as his home. (There's nice animation in a scene where Woolie's slightest movement causes his home to tremble alarmingly.) And Danny falls in love with Sawyer (voice by Jasmine Guy, songs by Natalie Cole), a veteran feline actress. But after Max gets him all but blacklisted in Hollywood, he grows disheartened and starts to go back home—only to change his mind, return, and star in a triumphant impromptu production number at the premiere of Darla's new movie. Even the dreaded mogul L. B. Mammoth (voice by George Kennedy) is won over.

This scene, which mirrors *Singin' in the Rain* by making a new star at the cost of an older one, is well handled with a lot of energy. And Mark Dindal, the film's director, creates a fresh look for the animation: not Disney and not Loony Tunes, but a touch of Betty Boop and Max Fleischer. *Cats Don't Dance* is not compelling and it's not a breakthrough, but on its own terms it works well. Whether this will appeal to kids is debatable; the story involves a time and a subject they're not much interested in. But the Randy Newman songs are catchy, the look is bright, the spirits are high, and fans of Hollywood's golden age might find it engaging.

Note: The movie's curtain-raiser is "Pullet Surprise" (say it out loud), a six-minute color cartoon produced by the legendary animator Chuck Jones, and starring Foghorn Leghorn.

Caught Up ★ ★

R, 95 m., 1998

Bokeem Woodbine (Daryl), Cynda Williams (Vanessa), Joseph Lindsey (Billy Grimm), Clifton Powell (Herbert/Frank Lowden), Basil Wallace (Ahmad), Snoop Doggy Dogg (Kool Kitty Kat), LL Cool J (Roger), Tony Todd (Jake). Directed by Darin Scott and produced by Peter Heller. Screenplay by Scott.

Caught Up is the first movie directed by Darin Scott, who has written three earlier movies and has produced eight. I suspect he spent those years impatiently stashing away ideas and images for his own first film; *Caught Up* plays like Fibber McGee's closet—it opens and everything but the kitchen sink comes tumbling out. Scott is ambitious and not without talent, but he ought to ration his material a little; there's so much plot it's dizzying.

Caught Up stars Bokeem Woodbine as Daryl, a man who dreams of opening his own club to support his girlfriend and their son. He needs $10,000, and a friend offers to get it at the bank. Daryl realizes too late that the withdrawal is a robbery. In prison, Daryl reads Greek philosophy. "You wanna know what those five years were like?" he asks. And when he answers, "Hell!" Scott has flames shoot up from the bottom of the screen. It's that kind of film.

On the outside again, Daryl meets a woman named Vanessa (Cynda Williams, from *One False Move*), who looks uncannily like his former girlfriend (who he is "staying away from" until he has his act together). She tells his fortune (tarot cards are superimposed on the screen) and gets him a job as a limo driver, ferrying dubious people to unsavory destinations.

And then—well, at some point I have to bail out of the plot description because it begins to appear that Daryl is caught in an elaborate web of betrayal and deception, and nobody is quite who or what they seem. We get the rug pulled out from beneath us so many times we stop caring: What's the use of trying to figure things out when the story is toying with us?

Yet the film has qualities. I liked the stylized way the story was told, with narration and flashbacks, visual overlays and special effects. Even those phony flames from hell were entertaining just because the movie was trying something. You could sense the enthusiasm of the director.

What I didn't much like was the device of a mysterious man in black, his face concealed, who follows Daryl and tries to kill him. I didn't like him as a gimmick, and I liked him even less when I heard the ludicrous explanation of who he was and why he was mad. And my patience was running a little thin by the time a body was hurled through a glass window perfectly on cue—timed to be the punch line for dialogue that, of course, no one on the other side of the window could hear. I sort of liked the sulfuric acid scene, though.

Caught Up is a film by a man who wanted to make a movie more than he wanted to tell a story. The story is the excuse for visual gizmos and directorial virtuosity. It makes me curious to see Scott's next film, but next time he should remember that if the audience can't care about the characters it has a hard time caring about the style.

The Celebration ★ ★ ★

R, 105 m., 1998

Ulrich Thomsen (Christian), Henning Moritzen (Helge), Thomas Bo Larsen (Michael), Paprika Steen (Helene), Birthe Neumann (Elsa), Trine Dyrholm (Pia), Helle Dolleris (Mette), Therese Glahn (Michelle). Directed by Thomas

Vinterberg and produced by Birgitte Hald. Screenplay by Vinterberg and Mogens Rukov.

Thomas Vinterberg's *The Celebration* mixes farce and tragedy so completely that it challenges us to respond at all. There are moments when a small, choked laugh begins in the audience, and is then instantly stifled, as we realize a scene is not intended to be funny. Or is it? Imagine Eugene O'Neill and Woody Allen collaborating on a screenplay about a family reunion. Now let Luis Buñuel direct it.

The story involves a sixtieth birthday party at which all of a family's corrupt and painful secrets are revealed at last. To the family's country inn in Denmark come the surviving children of Helge (Henning Moritzen) and his wife, Elsa (Birthe Neumann). We meet the eldest son, Christian (Ulrich Thomsen), his younger brother, Michael (Thomas Bo Larsen), and their sister Helene (Paprika Steen). Christian's twin sister has recently committed suicide. Also gathering around the table for the patriarch's birthday are assorted spouses, relations, and friends.

The film opens with a family in turmoil. The drunk and furious Michael careens his car down a country road while blaming his wife for everything. He comes across Christian, walking, and stops to give him a lift (throwing out his wife and children, who must walk the rest of the way). In their room, Michael starts berating his wife again (she has not packed some of his clothing) before they have rough sex; we assume this vaudeville is the centerpiece of their marriage.

At the birthday banquet, Christian raps his spoon against a glass and rises to calmly accuse his father of having raped his children. The gathering tries to ignore these remarks; Helene says they are not true. In the kitchen, the drunken chef gleefully observes that he has been waiting for this day for a long time and dispatches his waitresses to steal everyone's car keys from their rooms, so they won't be able to escape. Christian rises again and accuses his father of essentially murdering the sister who killed herself.

The evening spins down into a long night of revelation and accusation. The father at first tries to ignore his son's performance. The mother demands an apology, only to have Christian remind her she witnessed her husband raping him. Helene's boyfriend, an African-American anthropologist, arrives late and is the target of Michael's drunken racist comments. The family joins in a racist Danish song. A servant accuses a family member of having impregnated her; she had an abortion, but still loves him. And on and on, including fights and scuffles and an interlude when Christian is tied to a tree in the woods.

Vinterberg handles his material so cannily that we must always look for clues to the intended tone. Yes, the family history is ugly and tragic. But the chef, hiding the keys and intercepting calls for taxis, is out of French farce. The fact that the family even stays in the same room is a comic artifice (in farce, you can never just walk away). That nearly everyone is drunk doesn't explain everything, but that many of them are chronic alcoholics may explain more: This is a chapter in a long-running family saga.

Vinterberg shot the film on video, then blew it up to 35mm film. He joined with Lars von Trier *(Breaking the Waves)* and two other Danish directors in signing a document named "Dogma 95," which was unveiled at the 1998 Cannes Film Festival and pledged them all to shoot on location, using only natural sounds and props discovered on the site, using no special effects, using no music, using only handheld cameras. *The Celebration* and Von Trier's *The Idiots* are the first two, and may be the last two, films shot in this style. It would be tiresome if enforced in the long run, but the style does work for this film, and suits it, as a similar style is at the heart of John Cassavetes's work.

It's a tribute to *The Celebration* that the style and the story don't stumble over one another. The script is well planned, the actors are skilled at deploying their emotions, and the long day's journey into night is fraught with wounds that the farcical elements only help to keep open. Comes the dawn, and we can only shake our heads in disbelief when we see the family straggling back into the same room for breakfast.

Celebrity ★ ★ ½

R, 113 m., 1998

Kenneth Branagh (Lee Simon), Judy Davis (Robin Simon), Leonardo DiCaprio (Brandon Darrow), Melanie Griffith (Nicole Oliver), Famke Janssen (Bonnie), Michael Lerner (Dr. Lupus), Joe Mantegna (Tony Gardella), Hank Azaria (David), Charlize Theron (Model), Gretchen Mol (Girlfriend), Winona Ryder (Nola). Directed by Woody Allen and produced by Jean Doumanian. Screenplay by Allen.

Celebrity plays oddly like the loose ends and unused inspirations of other Woody Allen movies; it's sort of a revue format in which a lot of famous people appear on-screen, perform in the sketch Woody devises for them, and disappear. Some of the moments are very funny. More are only smile material, and a few don't work at all. Like all of Allen's films, it's smart and quirky enough that we're not bored, but we're not much delighted, either. All of his films can't be as good as *Everyone Says I Love You*, and this one proves it.

The film stars Kenneth Branagh as—there is only one way to put this—Woody Allen. The character is named Lee Simon, but Branagh has all the Allen vocal mannerisms and the body language of comic uncertainty. He does Allen so carefully, indeed, that you wonder why Allen didn't just play the character himself. Lee Simon is supposed to be a celebrity journalist, and Branagh might have been more useful and amusing if he'd used another real-life legend as his model: Perhaps the indestructible Anthony Hayden-Guest, who has been playing a Lee Simon–like role so long he even inspired a character in *Bonfire of the Vanities*.

Simon is a thirty-fivish man on the make with a precious antique Aston-Martin and the touching belief that his car can help him pick up chicks. The chicks he wants to pick up, he'd have to give the car to, and that would only get his foot in the door. In a flashback, we see him divorcing his wife (Judy Davis) for reasons that he tries to explain in sentences that never quite arrive at a subject or an object.

As the movie opens, he's doing a profile of a movie star played by Melanie Griffith, who takes him on a visit to her childhood home and in her old bedroom performs an act we suspect she rehearsed there many times in her imagination, in the years before stardom. Is it unethical for a journalist to have sex with the person he is interviewing? Yes, but not as unethical as what he does next, which is to pitch her his screenplay. That's getting too personal.

The film is filled with cameos (Donald Trump buying St. Patrick's Cathedral as a tear-down, Isaac Mizrahi as a painter who fears that fame will cut into his success). The best of the self-contained sequences stars Leonardo DiCaprio as a spoiled young movie star who beats up his girlfriend (Gretchen Mol), trashes his hotel room, and offers Lee Simon a leftover groupie when the journalist arrives (once again, to pitch his script).

As in *Deconstructing Harry*, his 1997 film, Allen seems fascinated by the mechanics of sex. Charlize Theron plays a model who informs the writer that she is polymorphously perverse, and has orgasms when touched on any part of her body. Simon's fingers flutter near her like a man about to test a hot stove.

Simon is also bewitched throughout the movie by the reappearances of a bright, pretty young thing played by Winona Ryder, who actually even likes him. They might have had a future together, but the message is that Simon uses women like stepping-stones, landing on one only long enough to launch himself toward the next.

The movie's shot in black and white; Allen is one of the rare and valuable directors who sometimes insists in working in the format that is the soul of cinema. It has a nice, crisp look, and the b + w places the emphasis on the body language and dialogue, instead of allowing too much of incidental atmosphere in. But the screenplay isn't as sharp as the movie's visuals. As the movie careens from one of Simon's quarries to the next, Allen pauses on most scenes only long enough to extract the joke, and the film begins to seem as desperately promiscuous as its hero. The words "The End" no longer appear at the ends of most films, but *Celebrity* ends (and begins) on a note that seems about right: An airplane skywriting the word "HELP!"

Central Station ★ ★ ★
R, 115 m., 1998

Fernanda Montenegro (Dora), Marilia Pera (Irene), Vinicius De Oliveira (Josue), Soia Lira (Ana), Othon Bastos (Cesar), Otavio Augusto (Pedrao), Stela Freitas (Yolanda), Matheus Nachtergaele (Isaias). Directed by Walter Salles and produced by Arthur Cohn and Martine De Clermont-Tonnerre. Screenplay by Joao Emanuel Carneiro and Marcos Bernstein, based on an original idea by Salles.

The tone of life in Rio is established in an early scene in Walter Salles's *Central Station*, as a train pulls into the platform and passengers crawl through the windows to grab seats ahead of the people who enter through the doors. In this dog-eat-dog world, Dora (Fernanda Montenegro) has a little stand in the rail station where she writes letters for people who are illiterate.

A cynic, she destroys most of the letters. One day a mother and son use her services to dictate a letter to the woman's missing husband. Soon after, the mother is struck and killed by a bus. The kid knows one person in Rio: Dora. He approaches her for help, and her response is brief: "Scram!"

The key to thc power of *Central Station* is in the way that word echoes down through most of the film. This is not a heartwarming movie about a woman trying to help a pathetic orphan, but a hard-edged film about a woman who thinks only of her own needs. After various attempts to rid herself of young Josue (Vinicius De Oliveira), she finally sells him to an adoption agency and uses the money to buy herself a new TV set.

There's not a shred of doubt or remorse as she settles down before the new set. But the whole story is known by her friend Irene (Marilia Pera, who played the prostitute who adopts the street kid in *Pixote*). "Those children aren't adopted!" she cries. "They're killed, and their organs are sold!" As if it is a great deal of trouble to go to, Dora now steals Josue back from the "orphanage" and finds herself, against her will and beyond her comprehension, trying to help him find his father, who lives far away in an interior city.

Central Station then settles into the pleasures of a road movie, in which we see modern Brazil through the eyes of the characters: the long-haul trucks that are the lifeline of commerce, the sprawling new housing developments, the hybrid religious ceremonies, the blend of old ways and the twentieth century. Whether they find the father is not really the point; the film is about their journey, and relationship.

The movie's success rests largely on the shoulders of Fernanda Montenegro, an actress who successfully defeats any temptation to allow sentimentality to wreck her relationship with the child. She understands that the film is not really about the boy's search for his father, but about her own reawakening. This process is measured out so carefully that we don't even notice the point at which she crosses over into a gentler person.

The boy, ten-year-old De Oliveira, was discovered by the director in an airport, shining shoes. He asked Walter Salles for the price of a sandwich, and Salles, who had been trying for months to cast this role, looked at him thoughtfully and saw young Josue. Whether he is an actor or not I cannot say. He plays Josue so well the performance is transparent. I hope he avoids the fate of Fernando Ramos da Silva, the young orphan who was picked off the streets to star in *Pixote*, later returned to them, and was murdered. I met De Oliveira at the Toronto Film Festival, where, barbered and in a new suit, he looked like a Rotarian's nephew.

It's strange about a movie like this. The structure intends us to be moved by the conclusion, but the conclusion is in many (not all) ways easy to anticipate. What moved me was the process, the journey, the change in the woman, the subtlety of sequences like the one where she falls for a truck driver who doesn't fall for her. It's in such moments that the film has its magic. The ending can take care of itself.

Character ★ ★ ★ ½
R, 114 m., 1998

Fedja van Huet (Katadreuffe), Jan Decleir (Dreverhaven), Betty Schuurman (Joba [mother]), Victor Low (De Gankelaar), Tamar van den Dop (Lorna Te George), Hans Kesting (Jan Maan), Lou Landre (Retenstein), Bernhard

Droog (Stroomkoning). Directed by Mike van Diem and produced by Laurens Geels. Screenplay by van Diem.

Character oozes with feelings of spite and revenge that grow up between a father and the son he had out of wedlock. It is dark, bitter, and fascinating, as all family feuds are—about hatred so deep that it can only be ended with a knife.

The Dutch winner of this year's Academy Award as Best Foreign Film, it involves the character of Dreverhaven (Jan Decleir), a lone and stony bailiff who exacts stern measures on the poor. One day, and one day only, he enters the room of his housekeeper, Joba (Betty Schuurman). That visit leads to a pregnancy. The man doesn't send his housekeeper into disgrace and abandonment, as we might expect; she freely chooses such a state, preferring it to the prospect of becoming Dreverhaven's wife. "When is our wedding?" the stern man demands of her, from time to time, but she does not answer.

The boy is named Katadreuffe (Fedja van Huet). In school he is taunted as a bastard, and his mother is shouted at in the streets. He grows up with a deep hatred for his father. We learn all of this in flashbacks; the film opens with a confrontation between father and son, and with reasons to suspect that the boy is guilty of his father's murder.

The film is based on a 1938 novel by Ferdinand Bordewijk. It evokes some of the darker episodes of Dickens, and also, in its focus on the grind of poverty and illegitimacy, reflects the twisted stories of family secrets by that grim Victorian, George Gissing. It is essentially the story of a young man growing up and making good, by pluck and intelligence, but all of his success comes out of the desire to spite his father.

"Today, I have been made a lawyer. You no longer exist for me! You have worked against me all my life," the son tells his father in the opening scene. "Or for you," the father replies. For reasons concealed in his own past, he believes that to spare the rod is to spoil the child, and indeed calls in a loan just three days before the son's final examinations, apparently hoping to cause him to fail. "Why don't you leave our boy in peace?" Joba asks Dreverhaven in one of their rare meetings. "I'll strangle him for nine-tenths, and the last tenth will make him strong," the old man replies, carrying Tough Love a shade too far.

The film is set in Rotterdam, in sets and streets suggesting its gloomy turn-of-the century shadows; I was reminded of *M* and other German Expressionist films in which the architecture sneers at the characters. The boy finds work in a law firm, rises to the post of office manager, and even falls in love, with Lorna Te George (Tamar van den Dop). She perhaps likes him, too, but he is so mired in self-abasement that he cannot declare his love, and he bitterly looks on as she keeps company with another man from the office. When he encounters her in a park some years later, he tells her, "I shall never marry anyone else. I have never forgotten you." For a man like him, masochistic denial is preferable to happiness.

The film is filled with sharply seen characters, including Katadreuffe's friend, an odd-looking man with an overshot lower jaw, who tries to feed him common sense. There are scenes of truly Dickensian detail, as when the father evicts a family from quarters where the rent has not been paid—going so far as to carry their dying mother into the streets himself. (He says she's faking it; he has a good eye.)

The opening scenes, which seem to show a murder, provide the frame, as the young man is cross-examined by the police. The closing scenes provide all the answers, in a way, although there is a lot more about old Dreverhaven we would like to know, including how any shreds of goodness and decency can survive in the harsh ground of his soul.

Chasing Amy ★ ★ ★ ½

R, 114 m., 1997

Joey Lauren Adams (Alyssa), Ben Affleck (Holden), Jason Lee (Banky), Dwight Ewell (Hooper), Jason Mewes (Jay). Directed by Kevin Smith and produced by Scott Mosier. Screenplay by Smith.

Chasing Amy is a romantic comedy about people who write comic books for a living—whose most passionate conversations can involve the sex lives of Archie and Jughead. Kevin Smith, who wrote and directed the movie, makes these characters intense and funny, and it's all in the writing.

We meet his Gen X heroes at a comic-book convention, where they're autographing copies of their book *Bluntman and Chronic.* Holden (Ben Affleck) and Banky (Jason Lee) have been best friends for years, live together, and take their art so seriously that when an obnoxious fan says, "An inker is only a tracer," there's a fight. Then Holden meets Alyssa (Joey Lauren Adams), and during a long dart game in a nearby pub they find that their minds are well matched; Holden assumes that where the minds go the bodies should follow, but what he doesn't realize is that Alyssa is a lesbian.

This could be the setup for an empty-headed sexcom, but Smith is more ambitious and subtle. While the surface of his film sparkles with sharp ironic dialogue, deeper issues are forming, and *Chasing Amy* develops into a film of touching insights. Most romantic comedies place phony obstacles in the way of true love, but Smith knows that at some level there's nothing funny about being in love: It's a dead serious business, in which your entire being is at risk. (That's why lovers can be so funny for the rest of us.)

For Kevin Smith, *Chasing Amy* represents a big step ahead into the ranks of the most interesting new directors. Smith is the legendary guerrilla filmmaker from New Jersey who made the 1994 comedy *Clerks* on a budget of $24,000; his heroes, who worked behind the counters of a convenience store and the video store next door, talked endlessly about sex, life, and videotapes, and because Smith was such a gifted creator of dialogue, the movie worked despite its bargain-basement production values.

His next film was *Mallrats* (1995), a disaster (Smith actually apologized for it at the 1996 Independent Spirit Awards). His mistake was to try to direct an action comedy with stunts and special effects, when in fact his real gift is as a writer. Smith's direction is clunky and basic: He tends to arrange his characters, aim the camera, and let them talk. Visual grace is not yet his strong point, but in a movie like *Chasing Amy,* that is absolutely all right, because his strength is the ability to create characters and give them dialogue that's alive and charged.

Like Quentin Tarantino he is willing to follow his characters into the subjects that obsess them, even if they seem to be straying from the plot. Here we get, for example, a hilarious speech at the ComicCon about the racism and white imperialism of "the holy trilogy" *(Star Wars),* delivered by a wonderful character named Hooper (Dwight Ewell)—a gay black man whose militant anger is partly a put-on and partly real pain, masked in irony.

There are also well-written speeches of surprising frankness about sex (the plumbing as well as the glory). "Chicks never tell you what to do," Holden complains. He thinks they should handle sex "like CNN or The Weather Channel—providing constant updates."

The main line of the story involves Holden's discovery that Alyssa is gay, and his even more inconvenient discovery that he loves her anyway—loves her, and her wit and personality and piercing chuckling voice with an intensity that reveals to him the vacuity of all his previous loves. He is desperate. And so is Banky, his best friend, who may be also secretly in love with him.

The movie's sneaky in the way it draws us in. We expect the characters to exist at a certain comic level, and they do, but then important things happen to them (love, friendship, and happiness are all threatened—along with all the adjustments of self-image that are necessary if romance is going to be able to leap across the straight/gay divide). Even the most simple characters can be eloquent when their lives are at issue, and these characters aren't simple. Like the clerks in Smith's first film, they're verbal, passionate, and poetic.

There are touching dialogue scenes between Alyssa and Holden, in which they spill out their secrets. In a lesser movie, that would be that. *Chasing Amy* has more up its sleeve. The closing scenes, which I will not reveal, spring deeper psychological surprises, and there is a three-way meeting between Holden, Alyssa, and Banky that is touching and yet written with the skill of a screwball comedy.

Joey Lauren Adams is a discovery as Alyssa: She has the kind of deep voice and conspiratorial smile that make you think she could be a buddy as well as a lover. Ben Affleck's role is tricky—emotionally, he makes the biggest changes—and he always makes us believe him. Jason Lee's sidekick is good at not showing us all his cards; at the end, when it's important to know how he really feels, he doesn't make it easy for us. And Kevin Smith himself appears as Silent Bob, the character he's played in all three of his films. This time Silent Bob opens up, with a heartfelt parable that explains who Amy was, and why she was being chased.

A Chef in Love ★ ★ ★

PG-13, 95 m., 1997

Pierre Richard (Pascal Ichac), Micheline Presle (Marcelle Ichac), Nino Kirtadze (Cecilia Abachidze), Teimour Kahmhadze (Zigmund Gogoladze), Jean-Yves Gautier, Ramaz Tchkhikvadze (Anton Gogoladze). Directed by Nana Dzhordzhadze and produced by Marc Ruscart. Screenplay by Irakli Kvirikadze and Andre Grall.

When communism comes to the Republic of Georgia, one of its great chefs is philosophical: Marxism will pass away, he observes, but great cuisine will live forever. It is perhaps relevant that the chef making this remark is a Frenchman, who has moved to the Georgian capital of Tbilisi out of love for a woman.

Nana Dzhordzhadze's *A Chef in Love,* which was filmed in Paris and the former Soviet Georgia, paints the chef, named Pascal Ichac, as a great eccentric bon vivant: a man capable of identifying any vintage by its bouquet, of finding a bomb at the opera by his nose alone, of criticizing another chef's recipes by the aromas that float in through an attic window.

In the past he has also been something of an opera singer and, it is rumored, a gigolo on a cruise ship on the Nile.

As we meet Pascal, played by Pierre Richard, he is well into his fifties and looks like a cuddly, fuzzy version of Peter Ustinov. He enters the train compartment of the beautiful Cecilia (Nino Kirtadze), smiles, uncorks a rare vintage, and offers her a glass. It is her favorite wine. He asks for five minutes to prepare something to go along with it. She steps into the corridor for a cigarette. When she returns, he has laid out a feast of hard-cooked eggs, cheese, and fruit, presented on fine china; apparently he assembled it from ingredients in his valise, or perhaps, like all great chefs, he always has a meal in his pocket.

Pascal's story is told in flashbacks, after Cecilia's son, an artist, is given his mother's journal. In it she describes the great love of her life. She was in her twenties, much younger than Pascal when she met him, but she identified immediately with his passion, which was not so much for food as for all the things of life: sex, music, art, living creatures.

For love of Cecilia, he remains in Georgia and opens a restaurant, which thrives until the communist takeover in the early 1920s, when he has to turn it over to the state and run it for the benefit of the new communist bosses. (Cecilia is forced into a union with the piggish local party chief.)

He grows angry and morose, attempts to poison the bosses at a picnic, and is banished to imprisonment in the attic. Never mind; Pascal, sitting unhappily by his garret window, smells what's cooking in the kitchen below, and sends helpful suggestions to the chef (who cannot read—but a young cook can, and the recipes are preserved to become a famous cookbook).

Pascal hates communism not on ideological grounds but because it gets in his way. When he and a party chief get into a bitter exchange, a duel results; after considering guns and knives, they end up throwing bricks at one another. The movie is droll about its forms of violence; when Pascal's enemy wants to murder him, shooting is rejected as too mundane, and the poltroon, having recently read *Hamlet,* decides to pour mercury into his ear.

A Chef in Love was Georgia's entry in the foreign film category of the Oscars, and plays as a hymn, somewhat disjointed, to bon vivants everywhere. It also functions, I imagine, to recall decades when it was difficult to get a great meal in Georgia unless you cooked it yourself (Cecilia takes Pascal on a tour of great Georgian cooking in the prerevolutionary era).

Pierre Richard, best known for *The Tall Blond Man with One Black Shoe,* is convincing here at something that is hard for an actor to do: He really seems to be savoring the tastes and aromas of the foods and wines he loves. On TV food commercials, I'm distracted by the sanitary way the models always eat; food disappears into their mouths and they immediately smile, but they never seem to chew or swallow. In addition to his other joyous qualities, old Pascal is an enthusiastic masticator.

Chicago Cab ★ ★ ★

R, 96 m., 1998

Paul Dillon (Cab Driver), John Cusack (Scary Man), Gillian Anderson (South Side Girl), Laurie Metcalf (Female Ad Exec), Michael Ironside (Al), Moira Harris (Religious Mother). Directed by Mary Cybulski and John Tintori and produced by Paul Dillon and Suzanne De Walt. Screenplay by Will Kern, based on his play *Hellcab.*

Chicago Cab has received reviews complaining that every single one of the taxi driver's passengers is a colorful character with a story. True, the movie seems to be mixing the paint a bit thick—but would the film improve with the substitution of boring passengers who just want to go to the Wrigley Building and leave a nice tip? Drama is always made of the emotional high points.

The film, based on Will Kern's play *Hellcab,* stars Paul Dillon of TV's *Pretender* as a taxi driver whose job makes him confessor to some, target of others, witness to the misery of the city. I was reminded of the Fritz Leiber story about the man who could read minds and went crazy because of all the unhappiness he picked up. The driver works from early in the morning until late at night, North Side, Loop, South Side, O'Hare, his direction and ultimately his destiny determined by who happens to get into his cab.

There are more than thirty different fares (played by such as John Cusack, Laurie Metcalf, Gillian Anderson, and Michael Ironside). The first passengers of the day are churchgoers who prompt their sullen young daughter to assist in saving the driver for Jesus. The last passenger is a quiet black man who listens to the driver's sad story of the rape victim he has just taken home.

In between he races a pregnant woman to the hospital, is tricked by a couple who pretend to have sex, witnesses a drug deal, gives legal advice to a man cheated by a used car lot, gets into what looks like a stickup situation, has a girl say, "I wish you were my boyfriend," and listens silently to some New Yorkers insulting Chicago (he speaks only when they bring up the Bulls, warning them ominously, "Leave Michael out of this").

The driver, whose name is not established, is a weird-looking duck, with a bald head but sideburns. He smokes, drinks coffee, is made obscurely miserable because an arm rest in the backseat has fallen off (he tries to fix it with Elmer's Glue, an excellent product that is nevertheless somehow rarely quite strong enough for the uses you want to put it to).

At O'Hare he gets a snack from the stainless steel food truck. He observes Muslim drivers on the side of the parking area, facing Mecca for their prayers. In a hotel cab stand he gets in a discussion about the ancient topic of giving rides to dangerous-looking black guys. He gives rides to everyone. The most alarming guys he meets are the white kids looking for drugs on the South Side; they leave a girl in the cab, and he drives off with her—saving them both, maybe, from something bad.

There is the seed of a savior in him. A guy drops off his date and then tells the guy all about her: what a slut she is, how he's mistreating her, how he lies to her. "Should I tell her what he said?" the driver asks himself. He does. Then he is furious at himself for handling the situation so badly.

Dillon plays the role properly by giving us very little of this driver: no name, no background, just a few insights when he talks to himself in the empty cab. Essentially he is a witness. I have had friends who drove cabs part-time. "You wouldn't believe some of the stories," they say. When you do it full-time, for years and years, I suppose you have two choices: Become a saint, or tune out. Here is a cab driver who doesn't know which way to turn.

Children of Heaven ★ ★ ★ ★

PG, 87 m., 1999

Amir Naji (Ali's Father), Amir Farrokh Hashemian (Ali), Bahare Seddiqi (Zahra), Nafise Jafar-Mohammadi (Roya), Fereshte Sarabandi (Ali's Mother), Kamal Mir Karimi (Assistant), Behzad Rafiee (Trainer), Dariush Mokhtari (Ali's

Teacher). Directed by Majid Majidi and produced by the Institute for the Intellectual Development of Children and Young Adults. Screenplay by Majidi.

Children of Heaven is very nearly a perfect movie for children, and of course that means adults will like it too. It lacks the cynicism and smart-mouth attitudes of so much American entertainment for kids, and glows with a kind of good-hearted purity. To see this movie is to be reminded of a time when the children in movies were children, and not miniature stand-up comics.

The movie is from Iran. Immediately you think kids would not be interested in such a movie. It has subtitles. Good lord!—kids will have to read them! But its subtitles are easy for eight- or nine-year-olds, who can whisper them to their siblings, and maybe this is their perfect introduction to subtitles. As for Iran: The theme of this movie is so universal there is not a child who will not be wide-eyed with interest and suspense.

The film is about a boy who loses his sister's shoes. He takes them to the cobbler for repairs, and on the way home, when he stops to pick up vegetables for his mother, a blind trash-collector accidentally carries them away. Of course the boy, named Ali, is afraid to tell his parents. Of course his sister, named Zahra, wants to know how she is supposed to go to school without shoes. The children feverishly write notes to each other, right under their parents' noses.

The answer is simple: Zahra will wear Ali's sneakers to school every morning, and then run home so that Ali can put them on for his school in the afternoon. But Zahra cannot always run fast enough, and Ali, who is a good student, gets in trouble for being late to class. And there is a heartbreaking scene where Zahra solemnly regards her own precious lost shoes, now on the feet of the ragpicker's daughter.

I submit that this situation is scarier and more absorbing for children than a movie about Godzilla or other manufactured entertainments. When you're a kid, you know you're not likely to be squished by a giant lizard, but losing something that has been entrusted to you? And getting in trouble at school? That's big time.

Majid Majidi's film has a wonderful scene where Ali and his father bicycle from the almost medieval streets and alleys of the old town to the high-rises and luxury homes where the rich people live. The father hopes for work as a gardener, but he is intimidated by the challenge of speaking into the intercoms on the gates of the wealthy. His son jumps in with offers of pruning, weeding, spraying, and trimming. It is a great triumph.

And then there is a footrace for the poor children of the quarter. The winner gets two weeks in a summer camp and other prizes. Ali doesn't care. He wants to place third, because the prize is a new pair of sneakers, which he can give to his sister. My guess is that the race and its outcome will be as exciting for many kids as anything they've seen at the movies.

Children of Heaven is about a home without unhappiness. About a brother and sister who love one another, instead of fighting. About situations any child can identify with. In this film from Iran, I found a sweetness and innocence that shames the land of Mutant Turtles, Power Rangers, and violent video games. Why do we teach our kids to see through things before they even learn to see them?

Children of the Revolution ★ ★

R, 102 m., 1997

Judy Davis (Joan), Sam Neill (Nine), F. Murray Abraham (Stalin), Richard Roxburgh (Joe), Rachel Griffiths (Anna), Geoffrey Rush (Welch), Russell Kiefel (Barry), John Gaden (Dr. Wilf Wilke). Directed by Peter Duncan and produced by Tristram Miall. Screenplay by Duncan.

There were some die-hard Western communists who never did get the news that Stalin was a murdering tyrant, and his Soviet Union was not the progressive mecca of their dreams, but a sinkhole of repression, tyranny, and racism. They dreamed on, long after the Hitler-Stalin pact and the show trials and all the other signals that their god had failed. Like true believers in all times and places, they made the fatal error of believing that the ends justified the means. Their error was that Stalin was not even in agreement with them about what the ends were.

Children of the Revolution is a satirical comedy about one such true believer in Australia in the late 1940s. Her name is Joan (Judy Davis), she worships Stalin, and she sends him a chatty letter every week. This sets into motion a chain of events that, some twenty years later, brings Australia to within a week of civil war. "The government blamed one man," we're told by the movie's newsreel narration. "He blamed his mother."

Joan's letters find a wide readership. They are read by Australian intelligence agents, Soviet bureaucrats, and finally by Stalin (F. Murray Abraham) himself, who finds them so seductive he invites Joan to the 1952 party congress, and ends up sleeping with her on the last night of his life (the look on her face is priceless when Stalin sneaks an arm around her during a movie screening). Another visitor to her bed during that busy night is a double agent named Nine (Sam Neill). Nine months later, a boy named Joe is born. But is Stalin his father, as Joan insists?

Whoever his biological father is, the man who raises him is Welsh (Geoffrey Rush of *Shine*), a fellow traveler who stands by the fanatic Joan in good times and bad. Joan is played as only Davis could play her, with ferocious intensity and the kind of humorlessness and lack of irony that is needed to believe many forms of fundamentalism.

The fruit of the liaison between Joan and Stalin doesn't fall far from the tree, and when her son, Joe (Richard Roxburgh), grows up, he becomes an agitator who, with more modern causes and methods, is able to bring the government to its fictional crisis.

The film tells this story in many styles. There are newsreels, photo montages, clips from history, and even a musical comedy sequence in which Stalin and his three side men (Khrushchev, Beria, and Malenkov) do a song-and-dance number to "I Get No Kick from Champagne." It also finds more than one acting approach, ranging from Abraham's barely controlled farce as Stalin to Davis's zealotry to Rush's genial patience.

Children of the Revolution is the first film by writer-director Peter Duncan (whose own father was reportedly a lifelong Stalin supporter). It is enormously ambitious—maybe too much so, since it ranges so widely between styles and strategies that it distracts from its own flow. It is specifically Australian in a lot of its material (the Communist Party there was more mainstream and labor oriented and thus respectable than it ever was in the United States), and American audiences, I think, will tend to view it more from the outside, as a curiosity, rather than as a film that speaks to them directly.

Citizen Ruth ★ ★ ★

R, 106 m., 1997

Laura Dern (Ruth Stoops), Swoozie Kurtz (Diane), Kurtwood Smith (Norm Stoney), Mary Kay Place (Gail Stoney), M. C. Gainey (Harlan), Kelly Preston (Rachel), Burt Reynolds (Blain Gibbons), Tippi Hedren (Jessica Weiss), Kenneth Mars (Dr. Charlie), Diane Ladd (Ruth's Mother). Directed by Alexander Payne and produced by Cary Woods and Cathy Konrad. Screenplay by Payne and Jim Taylor.

One of the danger signals of substance abuse, I'm pretty sure, is finding yourself sniffing patio sealant. Ruth Stoops, the heroine of *Citizen Ruth*, gets an even clearer signal: When the arresting cops already know your name, that's a real tip-off you have a problem. Pitiful, bedraggled Ruth (Laura Dern) is a forlorn specimen of hopelessness with more than a dozen arrests for "illegal inhalation." She has just been thrown out by her boyfriend (of one night) and turned away by her brother-in-law, and now she's told she is pregnant.

"You've been found to be an unfit mother four times!" a Tulsa judge informs her. "Uh-uh," Ruth says. "Two times." The judge threatens her with the charge of "felony criminal endangerment of a fetus," but offers to drop the charges if she'll have an abortion. The logic there is difficult to follow, but it's nothing compared to the ideological thicket that Ruth wanders into after her case becomes a national battleground for pro- and antichoice groups.

Citizen Ruth, written and directed by Alexander Payne, is a satire with the reckless courage to take on both sides in the abortion debate. There are no positive characters in the film—certainly not Ruth, whose preferred state is oblivion, and who perks up only when both sides start making cash offers. At a time when almost every film has a "market" in mind, here is a movie with a little something to offend anyone who has a strong opinion on abortion. Who's left to buy tickets? Maybe those dwindling numbers who admire movies for their daring and wit, and do not expect to be congratulated and reinforced by the characters on the screen.

The movie is a gallery of sharp-edged, satiric portraits. Thrown into jail, Ruth finds herself sharing the same cell with hymn-singing "Baby Savers" who have been jailed after a protest at an abortion clinic. She is quickly taken under the wings of Norm and Gail Stoney (Kurtwood Smith and Mary Kay Place), who bring her home to a safe environment (safe, that is, until she finds their son's airplane glue). Gail alternates between praise of life and bitter fights with her teenage daughter, who eventually helps Ruth sneak out of the house to a party.

One of the Baby Savers is Diane (Swoozie Kurtz), who reveals herself as a spy for the prochoice side, and spirits Ruth away to the wilderness retreat she shares with her lesbian lover, Rachel (Kelly Preston), who sings to the Moon. They arrange for Ruth to have an abortion, but by now the Baby Savers have issued a national alert, the network crews are camped out in the parking lot, and the national leaders for both sides have flown into Tulsa to make their stands.

Payne has a good eye for the character traits of zealots who feel the call to run other people's lives. The leader of the choice side, played by Tippi Hedren, is portrayed as so fashionable and sensible that you know it's a cover-up for unspeakable demons lurking beneath. And the leader of the prolifers is played by Burt Reynolds as a sloganeering hypocrite who praises the American family while maintaining a boy toy on his payroll.

There is a point at which this all perhaps grows a little thin; we yearn for someone to cheer for, instead of against. But there is courage in the decision to make Ruth an unredeemed dopehead whose only instinct is to go for the cash. I doubt that the two sides in the debate would actually engage in a bidding war, but that's what satire is for: to take reality and extend it to absurdity.

The movie illuminates the ways in which mainstream films train us to expect formula endings. Most movies are made with the belief that no one in the audience can be expected to entertain more than one idea at a time, at the very most. We are surprised when it develops that there will be no "good side" and "bad side" in the struggle over Ruth, and incredulous when it appears that the movie will not arrive safely in port with a solution to please everyone. Some situations, Payne seems to be arguing, can simply not be settled to everyone's satisfaction. Maybe, for some viewers, that will make this a horror film.

City of Angels ★ ★ ★

PG-13, 116 m., 1998

Nicolas Cage (Seth), Meg Ryan (Dr. Maggie Rice), Dennis Franz (Nathaniel Messinger), Andre Braugher (Cassiel). Directed by Brad Silberling and produced by Dawn Steel and Charles Roven. Screenplay by Dana Stevens.

Angels are big right now in pop entertainment, no doubt because everybody gets one. New Age spirituality is Me-oriented, and gives its followers top billing in the soap operas of their own lives. People like to believe they've had lots of previous incarnations, get messages in their dreams, and are psychic. According to the theory of karma, however, if you were Joan of Arc in a past life and are currently reduced to studying Marianne Williamson paperbacks, you must have made a wrong turn.

When there's a trend toward humility and selflessness, then we'll know we're getting somewhere on the spiritual front. That time is not yet. *City of Angels* hits the crest of the boom in angel movies—and like most of them, it's a love story. Hollywood is interested in priests and nuns only when they break the vow of chastity, and with angels only when they get the hots for humans. Can you imagine a movie where a human renounces sexuality and hopes to become an angel?

Still, as angel movies go, this is one of the better ones, not least because Meg Ryan is so sunny and persuasive as a heart surgeon who falls in love with an angel. This is one of her best performances, as Dr. Maggie Rice, who loses a patient early in the film and then, in despair, finds herself being comforted by an angel named Seth (Nicolas Cage). The amazing thing is that she can see him. Angels are supposed to be invisible and hang around in long black coats, looking over people's shoulders and comparing notes at dawn and dusk.

Seth is deeply moved that he is visible to Maggie. He has wondered for a while (which in his case could be millions of years) what it would be like to have a physical body. "Do you ever wonder what that would be like—touching?" he asks another angel. Maggie has a patient named Nathaniel Messinger (Dennis Franz) who is due for a heart operation, and as she operates on him she tips her hand: "No dying, now, Mr. Messinger—not until you give me Seth's phone number."

She knows Seth is special: "Those eyes. The way he looked right down into me." Soon she has him over for dinner, where he slices his finger, but does not bleed. She feels betrayed, and cuts him again. Still no blood. She slaps him: "You freak! Just get out! Get out!" This is jarringly the wrong note, forced and artificial, but required by modern screenplay formulas, which specify that the loving couple must fight and break up so that later they can get back together again.

There are revelations in the story, involving Mr. Messinger and others, that I will leave you to discover. And a surprise development toward the end that the movie sets up so mechanically that it comes as an anticlimax. It's not a perfect movie, and there are times when Cage seems more soppy and dewy-eyed than necessary. But it has a heart, and Meg Ryan convincingly plays a woman who has met the perfect soul mate (as, indeed, she has).

The movie is based on *Wings of Desire,* the great 1988 film by Wim Wenders. But it's not really a remake. It's more of a formula story that benefits from some of Wenders's imagery (solitary angels standing in high places, solemnly regarding humanity) and his central story idea (in his film, an angel played by Bruno Ganz falls in love with a trapeze artist and chooses to become human, with the guidance of a former angel played by Peter Falk).

The Wenders film is more about spirituality. The decision to fall to Earth comes toward the end. In *City of Angels* the angel's decision to fall is, of course, only the necessary theological prelude to the big scene in front of the fireplace ("Do you feel that? And that?"). To compare the two films is really beside the point, since *Wings of Desire* exists on its own level as a visionary and original film, and *City of Angels* exists squarely in the pop mainstream. Using Dwight Macdonald's invaluable system of cultural classification, *Paradise Lost* would be high cult, *Wings of Desire,* would be midcult, and *City of Angels* would be masscult.

Example of the difference: In *Wings of Desire,* an angel simply says, "I learned amazement last night." In *City of Angels,* Seth says: "I would rather have had one breath of her hair, one kiss from her mouth, one touch of her hand, than eternity without it. One." That's too much icing on the cake. Much more effective would have been simply, "I would rather have had one breath of her hair." Period. And then give the audience the pleasure of mentally completing the implications of that statement. By spelling it all out, the dialogue keeps the emotion on the screen, instead of allowing it to unfold in the viewer's imagination.

What I did appreciate is that *City of Angels* is one of the few angel movies that knows one essential fact about angels: They are not former people. "Angels aren't human. We were never human," observes Seth. This is quite true. Angels are purely spiritual beings who predate the creation of the physical universe. That leaves us with the problem of why Seth is male, and attracted to a female, when angels are without gender. But Maggie doesn't seem to have any complaints there in front of the fireplace.

City of Industry ★ ½

R, 97 m., 1997

Harvey Keitel (Roy Egan), Stephen Dorff (Skip Kovich), Timothy Hutton (Lee Egan), Famke Janssen (Rachel Montana), Wade Dominguez (Jorge Montana), Michael Jai White (Odell), Reno Wilson (Keshaun Brown). Directed by John Irvin and produced by Evzen Kolar and Ken Solarz. Screenplay by Solarz.

City of Industry is a performance in search of a movie. Harvey Keitel comes to play, delivering a fully formed and convincing portrait of a professional criminal who wants revenge—and the loot that's been stolen from him. He stalks through a movie that is otherwise so confused even day and night seem interchangeable. In a key daylight scene, he is wounded and nearly blown up, and yet it's night when he crawls into a drainage pipe and out of sight of nearby police and firemen. How much time has passed? How did he get there? No one saw him?

You don't ask questions like that. The movie has been directed by a seasoned pro, John Irvin *(Turtle Diary, A Month by the Lake)*, but it has awkward shots in it that a film student wouldn't okay. When motel keys are going to be important, there's a big close-up of keys falling out of Keitel's pocket. When Keitel enters a motel room, the camera keeps panning past the door until it ends in a close-up of a propane tank. Think it will explode? And when a woman points out "Uncle Luke," a Chinese gangster, to Keitel, they're parked in a car on the street—but we get an interior tracking shot, which is an impossible point of view.

Why get bogged down in details? Because the details in this movie bog it down. There are too many characters, sketchily introduced; they often get a setup but not a payoff. When the bad guy (Stephen Dorff) wants to confront some dangerous bad guys, for example, he hires a black gang to back him up. The black gang leader is very interested in what's going down; he obviously wants to rip off some of the players. But there's no follow-through. After a time the movie seems to be going through crime-movie exercises; scenes look competent, but don't flow smoothly into the story.

As the film opens, three guys are planning a Palm Springs diamond robbery (the Russian Mafia drops off hot jewels every April). The thieves are played by Wade Dominguez, Dorff, and Timothy Hutton—who calls in his older brother, played by Keitel. The heist planning process is interesting, although we've seen such scenes many times before. The robbery is a success. And then there is a betrayal that comes with sudden brutality, and is very effective. Keitel is left to even the score.

I like him as an actor, and I like him in this movie: taciturn, dogged, tough. He has some brief tender moments with the wife (Famke Janssen) of one of the robbers, but they don't add up to much, because there's so much other ground to cover. I never quite understood the relationships and roles of the Chinese and black gangsters in the film, and other characters—such as Dorff's lawyer—have scenes that are padding. (I liked it, though, when he offers Keitel a phone number and Keitel simply takes the laptop computer it's in.)

Los Angeles and environs have been photographed so often for so long that it takes a gifted location scout to find new locations. The scout on *City of Industry* does too good a job: Every single scene seems set in a new, exotic, colorful, and unlikely locale, until you wonder how much gas these guys burn, racing from junkyards to strip clubs to motels that look like sets for *The Grapes of Wrath*.

The screenplay, by Ken Solarz, has some nice touches. I like Keitel's line "I'm my own police." And a scene after violence is committed and all the neighbors turn out to have guns. And the laptop business. But the movie plays more like an exercise in *noir* atmosphere and violence than like a story; the pieces are sometimes nice, but they don't fit.

A Civil Action ★ ★ ★ ½

PG-13, 118 m., 1999

John Travolta (Jan Schlichtmann), Robert Duvall (Jerome Facher), Tony Shalhoub (Kevin Conway), William H. Macy (James Gordon), Zeljko Ivanek (Bill Crowley), Bruce Norris (William Cheeseman), John Lithgow (Judge Skinner), Kathleen Quinlan (Anne Anderson), David Thornton (Richard Aufiero). Directed by Steven Zaillian and produced by Scott Rudin, Robert Redford, and Rachel Pfeffer. Screenplay by Zaillian based on the book by Jonathan Harr.

A Civil Action is like John Grisham for grownups. Watching it, we realize that Grisham's lawyers are romanticized hotshots living in a cowboy universe with John Wayne values. The real world of the law, this movie argues, has less to do with justice than with strategy, and doesn't necessarily arrive at truth. The law is about who wins, not about who should win.

The movie costars John Travolta and Robert Duvall as the leaders of two opposing legal teams. At issue are the deaths by leukemia of twelve children. Travolta's argument is that the deaths were the result of pollution by two large corporations, W. R. Grace and Beatrice. Duvall, working for Beatrice, argues that neither the pollution nor its results can be proven. He also angles to separate Beatrice from its bedmate, Grace, correctly perceiving that the Grace legal strategy is unpromising.

Beatrice and Grace are real companies, and *A Civil Action* is based on a nonfiction best-seller by Jonathan Harr, which won the National Book Award. But the movie takes fictional liberties, which have been much discussed in the financial press. In particular, the Grace lawyer, William Cheeseman (Bruce Norris), is said not to be a doofus in real life. For the facts, read the book or study the case; the movie is more concerned with how the law works, and how perhaps the last thing you want is a lawyer who is committed heart and soul to your cause. What you want is a superb technician.

Duvall plays Jerome Facher, brilliant and experienced, who hides his knowledge behind a facade of eccentricity. He knows more or less what is going to happen at every stage of the case. He reads the facts, the witnesses, the court, and his opposition. There is a moment at which he offers the plaintiffs a $20 million settlement, and an argument can be made, I think, that in the deepest recesses of his mind he knows it will not be necessary. He makes the offer in the same spirit that Vegas blackjack tables offer "insurance"—he thinks he'll win, but is guarding the downside. His style is indirection; his carefully nurtured idiosyncrasies conceal his hand.

Travolta plays Jan Schlichtmann, the head of a small firm of personal injury attorneys who take on cases they believe they can win. Often their clients are too poor to pay legal fees, but Schlichtmann's firm eats the legal costs itself, hoping for a rich slice of an eventual settlement. Essentially, he's gambling with the firm's money every time he accepts a case. That's why he turns down the delegation of parents who tell about the deaths of their children: He doesn't see enough money in it to justify the risk. (The movie has a hard-boiled discussion of how much various victims are "worth." A white male professional struck down in his prime gives the biggest payoff; a dead child is worth the least of all.)

From the point of view of his financial well-being, Schlichtmann makes two mistakes. First, he decides the parents have a moral case. Second, he begins to care too much about justice for them and loses his strategic bearings. (Of course, all follows from his discovery that the polluters, whom he thought were small, shabby local firms, are actually owned by rich corporations.)

The movie, written and directed by Steven Zaillian, doesn't simplify the issues and make Schlichtmann into a romantic hero. He's more the kind of guy you refer to affectionately as "that poor sap." We hear what he hears: the emotion in the voice of one of the mothers (Kathleen Quinlan) who asks him to take the case because "all we want is somebody to apologize to us." And the heartrending story of how one of the boys died, told by his father (David Thornton) in details so sad that Schlichtmann is very deeply moved—which is, perhaps, not the best thing for his clients.

Zaillian is clear about his movie's approach. This is not a film in which a hero attorney beats up the bad guys in a climactic courtroom scene. The movie doesn't even end with its courtroom scene, but has a wry aftermath. No major characters are painted in black-and-white terms, least of all Duvall's; he is not a man without emotions and sympathies, we sense, but simply a man whose long and wise experience of the law has positioned him above the fray. He's fascinated by the law, by its opportunities and maneuverings, by its realities. Like a chess player, he knows that to win a tournament it is sometimes wise to offer a draw even when you think you can win it.

Some of the film's tension comes not from the battle between good and evil, but from the struggle between Schlichtmann's firm and its creditors. The small firm eventually sinks $1.4 million into the case, the homes of all the partners are mortgaged, and in the background during some scenes their furniture is being removed. William H. Macy plays their accountant, whose function is to announce steady progress toward professional and personal bankruptcy.

This is Zaillian's second film. His first was *Searching for Bobby Fischer* (1993), one of the most absorbing films of recent years, about a child chess prodigy whose great gift might take him to the top of the game—but at what personal price? *A Civil Action* is also about the gulf between skill and justice. In the law as in chess, the better player usually wins. It has nothing to do with which is the better person. The theme of Zaillian's first film, I wrote, was: "What makes us men is that we can think logically. What makes us human is that we sometimes choose not to." That's the message this time too. There's a subtext: When hiring an attorney, go for the logician. ☞

Clay Pigeons ★ ★ ½

R, 104 m., 1998

Joaquin Phoenix (Clay), Janeane Garofalo (Agent Shelby), Vince Vaughn (Lester), Scott Wilson (Sheriff Mooney), Georgina Cates (Amanda), Vince Vieluf (Barney). Directed by David Dobkin and produced by Ridley Scott and Chris Zarpas. Screenplay by Matthew Healy.

Clay Pigeons allows the wheels of its story to spin a little too long. Creation takes two steps. First you put in. Then you take out. Many first-time filmmakers leave in too much, maybe because they don't want to take any chances, maybe because they worked so hard on their film that every shot has become a treasure for them. Within *Clay Pigeons* is a smaller story that might have involved us more, but it's buried by overkill.

The film is one of those macabre comedies where the body count steadily rises while a (possibly) innocent man looks guilty. It's set in a small Montana town where everybody knows everybody else, you can find your friends if you look in the saloon, and the deputy sheriff is named Barney.

Joaquin Phoenix stars as Clay, who has been having an affair with his best friend's wife. The best friend kills himself in an opening scene, setting it up to look like Clay killed him. Terrified, Clay tries to make the death look like a suicide, and this mistake compounds itself until he looks exactly like a serial murderer. His wife, Amanda (Georgina Cates), isn't much help at first, and even less later. A friendly local waitress also comes to an unfortunate end.

A lot of people die in *Clay Pigeons.* If Clay isn't the serial killer, someone certainly is. But to FBI Agent Shelby (Janeane Garofalo), Clay seems like a logical suspect: "You're dating one victim, you're having an affair with another, and you find the body of the third. Kind of a coincidence, wouldn't you say?"

The Garofalo character, obviously inspired by Chief Marge Gunderson (Frances McDormand) in *Fargo,* is one of the best things in the movie. She's smart, direct, sarcastic, a wise guy. She even knows how to handle approaches in bars from tall strangers in ten-gallon hats, although her confidence is shaken somewhat when she discovers, after he leaves, that he was probably the killer.

Another important character is Lester Long (Vince Vaughn), a stranger in town who forces his way into Clay's life and soon seems like the only person who knows all his secrets. Lester has the kind of high-pitched laugh that, when you hear it, makes it seem prudent to stop whatever you're doing and move to another state. And there's Sheriff Mooney (Scott Wilson), who is none too thrilled to have the FBI butting into his jurisdiction, but realizes he needs help every time he observes Deputy Barney (Vince Vieluf), a borderline narcoleptic.

The plot cannot really be described without going into the setups and payoffs of a great many crimes, alibis, suspicions, appearances, and investigations. Director David Dobkin and writer Matthew Healy find the right tone and many individual moments spring alive, but I think they go around the track a couple of extra times.

Once we get the notion that poor Clay is digging himself deeper and deeper, once we understand that the body count will multiply, that's the moment to stop with the digging and the counting. When it comes to the use of repetition in comedy, a curious math takes place. Twice may be funnier than once and three times may be funnier than twice, but four times is about as funny as the first time and then you get into negative numbers.

What I liked were the performances, all of them, not neglecting Scott Wilson's solid work as the sheriff; he correctly understands that his character is not supposed to be funny, but to ground the others. Vince Vaughn, who is in a lot of movies these days, relishes this role and it's fun to watch him relish it. Janeane Garofalo stands there and belts out zingers and is a delight. You don't dislike the movie, but it just unwinds on you.

And at the end the plot abandons all common sense. Isn't jailbreak a crime even if you're innocent? And how is that whole business with the racehorse and the hitchhiker going to work? And is it necessary? And in an area that flat, how far away would police cars have to be before a jumpy serial killer couldn't see them?

Clockwatchers ★ ★ ★ ½

PG-13, 96 m., 1998

Toni Collette (Iris), Parker Posey (Margaret), Lisa Kudrow (Paula), Alanna Ubach (Jane). Directed by Jill Sprecher and produced by Gina Resnick. Screenplay by Jill Sprecher and Karen Sprecher.

Clockwatchers is a wicked, subversive comedy about the hell on earth occupied by temporary office workers. Hired by the day, fired on whims, they're victims of corporate apartheid: They have no rights or benefits and can't even call their desks their own. They're always looking at Polaroids of someone else's family.

This is a rare film about the way people actually live. It's about the new world of security cameras, Muzak, cubicle life, and hoarding office supplies. "Try not to make too many mistakes," a new temp worker is told. "These forms are expensive." When she botches some forms, she throws them out in the ladies' room to hide her crime. The toilet, indeed, is the only sanctuary in a big office: the refuge, the retreat, the confessional. Only when your underwear is off can you find a space to call your own.

Clockwatchers was written by two sisters, Jill and Karen Sprecher, and directed by Jill. I don't have to be psychic to know they've worked as office temps. The Coen, Hughes, and Wachowski brothers make movies about crime and passion, and so do the Sprecher sisters, but their violence is more brutal and direct, like stealing the precious rubber-band ball of Art, the anal-retentive guy in charge of the office supplies.

The movie stars Toni Collette as Iris, the new temp. Frightened and insecure, blinded by the buzzing overhead fixtures like a rabbit in the headlights, she's taken under the wing of Margaret (Parker Posey), a temp who knows the ropes and has a healthy contempt for the office, her bosses, and temp life in general. When she answers someone else's phone, she doesn't take a message, she just leaves the caller on hold until they get bored and hang up: "By the time they find out, you're long gone."

At lunchtime, Margaret leads Iris to the lonely Formica tables in the corner of the cafeteria, where the temps sit huddled together. None of the permanent workers mix with them; it's like they have a disease. Jane (Alanna Ubach) tells Iris: "I used to work in a bank. There was this button on the desk and I kept looking at it every day for a month and finally I just pushed it. It was the alarm. They never tell you anything because they're afraid you'll take their stupid jobs."

Boredom hangs low over the office like a poisonous fog. It's the kind of place where you carve I WAS HERE into the desk, but don't sign your name. Paula (Lisa Kudrow), another temp, is given a business card by a male coworker and it's the same card she's always finding left in the ladies' room, as if the guy's pathetic title and embossed little name would make him sexually irresistible. A new girl is hired, and the temps try to figure out how she got the job as the boss's new permanent assistant. At quitting time, every eye is riveted to the wall clock: They're like third-graders, waiting to be dismissed, so they can go to nearby bars, smoke cigarettes, and be lied to by half-looped junior executives.

Something interesting happens. There is a crime wave. Office supplies and little doodads are missing from people's desks. Who is the thief? Eyes narrow. There's lots of whispering at lunchtime. Security cameras are pointed directly at the desks of the temps: Yeah, like they're going to steal from themselves. One of the girls is fired and gets the last word: "How can you fire me? You don't even know my name!"

I take hope when I see a movie like this, because it means somebody is still listening and watching. Most new movies are about old movies; this one is about the way we live now. *Clockwatchers* is the kind of movie that can change lives by articulating anger; a few of the people who see it are going to make basic changes because of it—they're going to revolt—and ten years from now the Sprecher sisters will get a letter from one of them, thanking them.

There's that, and then there's also the way the movie is so mercilessly funny, because it sees stupidity so clearly. Take Iris's first day on the job, where she's told to sit in a chair and wait, and sits there for hours, until the office manager says, "Why didn't you tell me you were here?" Like it's her fault. Like Iris knew who the stupid office manager was. Like it's not the office manager's job to see if anyone is sitting in the stupid chair. Like at the salary level of a temp, it makes any difference how long she sits there. Like maybe someday, with hard work, good luck, patience, and timing, she can be a big shot like Art, and have her own stupid rubber-band ball.

Commandments ★ ★

R, 87 m., 1997

Aidan Quinn (Seth Warner), Courteney Cox (Rachel Luce), Anthony LaPaglia (Harry Luce), Shirl Bernheim (Sylvia), Pamela Gray (Melissa Murphy). Directed by Daniel Taplitz and produced by Michael Chinich, Joe Medjuck, and Daniel Goldberg. Screenplay by Taplitz.

In the opening scenes of *Commandments*, Seth Warner's wife drowns at the beach, his house is destroyed by a tornado, and he is struck by lightning while threatening suicide.

Seth, played by Aidan Quinn, has rotten luck. Either that, or God is angry with him. But why? With one parent Jewish and the other Catholic, he seeks answers in both religions, crying out in a synagogue: "Why does God play tricks?" The answer is that God does not—or so at least Einstein assured us. But as Seth tells his brother-in-law, Harry: "If your shoestring breaks every day for two years, it's time to check the Bible."

Things get worse. Seth loses his job. He discovers that his dog's leg was burned by the lightning bolt. Why would God pick on a dog? Or, for that matter, on Seth's innocent wife? His brother-in-law, Harry, doesn't much care. Played by Anthony LaPaglia, he considers Seth such a loser that he thinks Seth might be better off ending it all. But Seth has one last weapon in his battle with heaven: "I'm gonna break every one of the Commandments," he vows, "until I get an answer."

One of the problems with *Commandments* is that I was never sure how seriously I should take Seth's problem. Is this a heavy theological story? Not at all. Is it a comedy, distantly related to *Joe vs. the Volcano*? There are times when it tilts in that direction. But a great deal of the story time is given over to romance, mostly involving the love that grows between Seth and Harry's wife, Rachel (Courteney Cox). That Rachel is also the sister of Seth's dead wife is, given this movie, just one more coincidence.

Of course, Seth may be pursuing his course because of a determination to commit adultery while working his way through the Commandments. But it's not really that, because he loves Rachel. (Harry, meanwhile, has a mistress, which is one relationship too many for a movie that is not about relationships.) Perhaps the writer and director, Daniel Taplitz, began with a heavy *Seven*-type story and then decided it couldn't hurt to work in a little comedy and romance.

The sequence that reminded me the most of *Joe vs. the Volcano* was the ending one, with Seth standing in a lighthouse waiting for a hurricane to strike. Nothing can compel me to tell you where this particular gesture leads, but let me say it suggests possibilities so heavy that the rest of the movie looks irreverent by comparison.

Instead of revealing the ending, let's talk theology. Did Seth's wife drown just so God could prove a point to Seth? Hey, isn't that sort of unfair to her? Is God indeed toying with Seth? The movie makes this pretty clear. If he is, why would he be pleased that Seth is violating the Ten Commandments? Could it be that by breaking them, Seth is proving he believes in them, and in God? And this pleases God? But . . . why would God give us the Commandments if the only way to send him a message is by breaking them?

I ask these questions not expecting an answer, but only to suggest how weird they seem, coming at the end of a dark comedy about love affairs and suchlike. This is one strange movie; it's as if *When Harry Met Sally* were directed by Ingmar Bergman.

Con Air ★ ★ ★

R, 115 m., 1997

Nicolas Cage (Cameron Poe), John Cusack (Larkin), John Malkovich (Cyrus the Virus), Steve Buscemi (Garland Greene), Nick Chinlund (Billy Bedlam), Rachel Ticotin (Bishop), Colm Meaney (Malloy), M. C. Gainey (Swamp Thing), Ving Rhames (Diamond Dog), Danny Trejo (Johnny 23), Mykelti Williamson (Baby O). Directed by Simon West and produced by Jerry Bruckheimer. Screenplay by Scott Rosenberg.

Midway in *Con Air*, the Nicolas Cage character observes: "Somehow they managed to get every creep and freak in the universe on this one plane." That's the same thought I was having. The plane—a hijacked flight of dangerous convicts—has so many criminal superstars on it, it's like a weirdo version of those comic books where the superheroes hold a summit conference.

Let's take an inventory. There's the ringleader, Cyrus the Virus (John Malkovich), who cheerfully reports that his last evaluation found him insane. Diamond Dog (Ving Rhames), a black militant who's pretending to be Cyrus's lieutenant until he sees an opening to make his own move. And Johnny 23 (Danny Trejo), so called because of his twenty-three rape victims ("It woulda been Johnny 600 if they knew the whole story").

Plus about ten more creeps—including, of course, Garland Greene (Steve Buscemi), a serial killer with thirty-seven victims, who arrives on board encased in custom-made restraints patterned after Hannibal Lecter's traveling suit. (When Cyrus the Virus sees Greene strapped in a cocoon of leather and steel, he protests, "This is no way to treat a national treasure!" And adds, "Love your work.")

All of these monsters are on board the same flight, a lumbering C-123K troop transport that is taking them to a maximum security prison. Also on board is a good guy: Cameron Poe (Nicolas Cage), an Army Ranger unfairly locked up for eight years for protecting his family from drunken goons. This is his flight home for parole. Sitting next to him is a friend from prison (Mykelti Williamson), a diabetic who must have an insulin shot or die. Among the guards who survive the initial takeover of the plane is Bishop (Rachel Ticotin), who immediately inspires the rapist to change his name to Johnny 24.

That's just the partial roll call of creeps and freaks in the air. On the ground, we meet a good-guy U.S. marshal (John Cusack) and a mad-dog DEA agent (Colm Meaney), whose solution to the problem is to blow the commandeered plane out of the air. This is a big cast, but easy to keep straight, because everyone is typecast and never does anything out of character.

The movie is a solo production by Jerry Bruckheimer, who with his late partner Don Simpson masterminded a series of high-tech special-effects extravaganzas *(Beverly Hills Cop, Top Gun, Days of Thunder, Crimson Tide, The Rock). Con Air* is in the same vein, but with less of the dogged seriousness of many action pictures and more of the self-kidding humor of *The Rock.* This is a movie that knows it is absurd, and does little to deny the obvious.

Malkovich has the charisma to hold the plot together, with another of his dry, intellectual villains. Cage makes the wrong choice, I think, by playing Cameron Poe as a slow-witted Elvis type who is very, very earnest and approaches every task with tunnel vision; it would have been more fun if he'd been less of a hayseed. Cusack is limited in many of his scenes to screaming into a phone, which he does with great conviction. Buscemi is a gifted character actor who wisely avoids imitating Anthony Hopkins's Hannibal Lecter, and plays his serial killer as a soft-spoken, reasonable guy. The movie skirts dangerously close to bad taste in a scene where he has tea with a little girl who, we fear, will become his next victim; humor saves the scene, as the toddler leads him in a sing-along of the last song you'd think he knew.

The movie is essentially a series of quick setups, brisk dialogue, and elaborate action sequences. You may have seen most of the high points in the TV commercials: the car being dragged behind the plane, the crash-landing in Las Vegas, and the obligatory shot of humans somehow outrunning fireballs. Still, assembled by first-time director Simon West, a British music video whiz, it moves smoothly and with visual style and verbal wit. It even continues a recent tradition in Nicolas Cage's career (after *Honeymoon in Vegas* and *Leaving Las Vegas*) of finding new ways to crash-land on the Strip.

In a film filled with strange people and bizarre events, here is the strangest and most bizarre: The closing credits, played over "Sweet Home Alabama," include a montage of all the major characters—smiling. Yes, smiling. Cyrus the Virus and Johnny 23 and all the rest, looking like nice guys in a fast-food ad. Apparently the strategy is to leave the audience on an upbeat note. That would require a very short attention span on the part of the audience, but this may be just the movie to assemble that audience.

Conspiracy Theory ★ ★ ½

R, 129 m., 1997

Mel Gibson (Jerry Fletcher), Julia Roberts (Alice Sutton), Patrick Stewart (Dr. Jonas), Cylk Cozart (Agent Lowry). Directed by Richard Donner and produced by Donner and Joel Silver. Screenplay by Brian Helgeland.

Conspiracy Theory cries out to be a small film—a quixotic little indee production where the daffy dialogue and weird characters could weave their coils of paranoia into great offbeat humor. Unfortunately, the parts of the movie that are truly good are buried beneath the deadening layers of thriller clichés and an unconvincing love story.

I can almost guess how this happened. The original screenplay by Brian Helgeland must have been strange and wonderful. It told the story of a New York cabby who combines everything he hears into one grand unified conspiracy theory. Most of the time he's wacko. Sometimes, like a stopped clock, he's on the money. ("I was right!" he says at one point. "But what was I right about?")

This screenplay no doubt attracted widespread attention in Hollywood because of its originality and brilliance. Then it was packaged with major stars (Mel Gibson and Julia Roberts) and an A-list director (Richard Donner, of *Lethal Weapon*). The movie could essentially have been filmed for a few million dollars, but not with talent like that, so it turned into a megaproduction and was lost.

Almost immediately (I'm still weaving my fantasy here) some industry genius decreed that Gibson and Roberts had to fall in love in the movie "because the audience will want to see that." Oh, yeah? Not if it involves such torturous contrivances that whole shards of the plot are torn off and sent flying like rubber off of truck tires. The same genius, or his clone, then decreed that since there was the money for bloated action sequences, of course there had to be some.

Very few action sequences work. Most of them bring movies to a lurching halt. *Conspiracy Theory* is never more interesting than when Gibson is spinning his bizarre theories, and never more boring than when secret agents are rappelling down ropes from helicopters hovering over New York streets. There have been so many action sequences in so many movies that we have lost the capacity for surprise; unless they work as part of the plot, our eyes glaze over because we know the actors have gone out for lunch and we are looking at stuntmen supervised by the second unit.

Anyway. The Gibson character in *Conspiracy Theory* is a wonderful creation, a guy named Jerry Fletcher who has listened to way too much talk radio. Secrets spin from his fertile imagination and into the incredulous ears of his passengers: The right-wing militias, which say they'll defend us from a UN invasion, *are* UN troops. Vietnam was fought over a bet between Howard Hughes and Aristotle Onassis. They rounded up the fathers of all the Nobel Prize winners to extract and freeze their sperm. Oliver Stone is a disinformation specialist who works to discredit conspiracy theories. NASA plans to assassinate the president with an earthquake triggered by the space shuttle. And there is a reason all the goofballs seem to read *Catcher in the Rye*.

This is great stuff, and Gibson, a gifted comic actor, delivers it with a kind of intense, insane conviction. (He would have been fine in the little indee production, except that the mere presence of a big star in a perfect screenplay tends to alter it, in a Hollywood version of the Heisenberg Uncertainty Principle.) Turns out he has an obsession: a Justice Department agent (Julia Roberts) he fell in love with after saving her from a mugging. He tries to tell her all of his conspiracy theories, and she tries to humor him, until one day it appears he may actually be onto something.

More of the plot I will not reveal. Much of it involves Patrick Stewart as a government psychiatrist who spends much of the movie with an injured nose, although not to the effect of Jack Nicholson in *Chinatown*. What's good about the movie are the gritty scenes of the taxi driver's life (including a little homage to *Taxi Driver* in the form of street drummers in Times Square). If the movie had stayed at ground level—had been a real story about real people—it might have been a lot better, and funnier. All of the energy is in the basic material, and none of it is in a romance that is grafted on like an unneeded limb or superfluous organ.

I have no inside knowledge of the production details. Not a smidgen. I'm going entirely on instinct. But all my instincts tell me that major changes were made to the original material in order to suit "audience expectations" about the stars. If you want to experience the anguish of rewrites dictated by knee-jerk bureaucrats, attentively watch the scenes where the movie tries to explain why this woman and this man could arrive at this relationship. It is always painful to see a movie in flight from its strengths.

Conspirators of Pleasure ★ ★ ★

NO MPAA RATING, 83 m., 1998

Petr Meissel (Peony), Anna Wetlinska (Mrs. Beltinska), Gabriela Wilhelmova (Mrs. Loubalova), Jifi Labus (Kula), Barbora Hrzanova (Mrs. Malkova), Pavel Novy (Beltinsky). Directed by Jan Svankmajer and produced by Jaromir Kallista. Screenplay by Svankmajer.

The opening scene of *Conspirators of Pleasure* shows a man examining the skin magazines in a porno shop and finally selecting one. This will be the most normal moment of sexual behavior in the movie. At home, paging through the magazine, the man's attention is distracted by a large cabinet standing by the wall. The busty girls in the magazine are no competition for whatever it contains. As the man eyes the cabinet's keyhole and nervously licks his lips, we meet some of his neighbors.

His landlady, for example, is involved in stealing straw from a mattress to construct a large dummy. The man who owns the magazine store is building an apparatus that will embrace and caress him while he watches tapes of a pretty newscaster. The newscaster, while she is broadcasting, keeps her feet in a tank so catfish can nibble her toes. Out in the garage, her husband is building devices that will roll up and down his body, alternating nail heads with tickly fluff. Then there is the postwoman, who rolls a loaf of bread into little round balls that she pokes into her nose and ears.

These pastimes reminded me of the films of Luis Buñuel, the great Spanish filmmaker whose characters pleasured themselves in strange ways (a bishop got off by pretending to be a gardener, a man constructed wax dolls and put them into furnaces, and in *Belle de Jour* there was that strange client with his little box; we never saw what was in it, but the women in the brothel wanted nothing to do with it).

Conspirators of Pleasure is a film about lonely people who apply the "do-it-yourself" approach to previously unimagined possibilities. By the end of the film, when the first little man has pulped his porno magazines to construct a papier-mâché chicken head, and is flapping about the garden with wings made of old umbrellas, we realize our notions of kinky behavior are seriously deficient. Whether the movie is serious or funny depends, I suppose, on whether you're the toes or the fish.

This is the third feature film by Jan Svankmajer, a Czech who gets around the problem of subtitles by the simple device of having no dialogue in his movie. There are sound effects and music, but no conversations, because these six people are in isolation chambers of their own making. As they tinker busily in their solitary rooms and garages, constructing devices that will give them pleasure, I thought of the great crushing loneliness that must have descended on creatures like Jeffrey Dahmer, who literally stood outside the ordinary consolations of the human race.

And yet *Conspirators of Pleasure* is not an angry or tragic film. It's too matter-of-fact for that. It's not even overtly sexual, because its eroticism takes place inside the imaginations of its characters. It doesn't have an MPAA rating, but I'd love to see how the ratings board would deal with a film that is entirely about masturbation, but has no explicit nudity, no "language," no contact between two people and no intimate touching. Would they rate it "R" because we can see some breasts in the skin mags at the beginning? Films like this subvert the whole notion of ratings by showing that pornography exists in the unseen places of the individual mind.

Svankmajer up until now has been mostly an animator; his short films are seen all over the world. Here he's used living actors, but treats them like the subjects of animation: caricatures whose thoughts are conveyed in broad physical terms. There is a little stop-action animation in the film, but essentially it's as unadorned and straightforward as porno, with people in their rooms, absorbed in their activities. Its lesson, I suppose, is that in the absence of love one turns to technology, which is a small consolation; the characters seem to derive more pleasure out of constructing their toys than using them.

In his end credits, Svankmajer acknowledges the "technical expertise" of a number of people, including de Sade, Sader-Masoch, Freud, and, of course, Buñuel—whose *Un Chien Andalou,* made with Salvador Dali, must have helped inspire *Conspirators of Pleasure.* Svankmajer calls himself a radical surrealist, and like the original surrealists he gains his effects not by abstract fantasies but by taking a skewed new look at everyday reality. So much of this film is practical: how to keep the fish alive under the bed, or what to do with little bread balls after you've used them (the postwoman mails them to the newscaster to feed the fish). All of this ingenuity reminded me of a college friend, the late novelist Paul Tyner, who was studying ads for electric sexual aids when he hit upon the ultimate perversion: plug them in, fit them together, and watch them.

Contact ★ ★ ★ ½

PG, 150 m., 1997

Jodie Foster (Dr. Eleanor "Ellie" Arroway), Matthew McConaughey (Palmer Joss), James Woods (Michael Kitz), John Hurt (S. R. Hadden), Tom Skerritt (David Drumlin), William Fichtner (Kent Clark), David Morse (Ted Arroway), Angela Bassett (Rachel Constantine), Rob Lowe (Richard Rank). Directed by Robert Zemeckis and produced by Zemeckis and Steve Starkey. Screenplay by James V. Hart and Michael Goldenberg, based on the novel by Carl Sagan.

"Do you think there are people on other planets?"

"I don't know. But if it's just us, it would be an awful waste of space."

—dialogue from *Contact*

You can hear an echo there of the hopeful, curious voice of the late Carl Sagan, who spoke optimistically of "billions of billions of stars," and argued that if life can exist at all (and it can) then it should presumably be found all over the universe. Sagan's novel *Contact* provides the inspiration for Robert Zemeckis's film, which tells the smartest and most absorbing story about extraterrestrial intelligence since *Close Encounters of the Third Kind.*

It also makes an argument that sounds like pure common sense. Because the universe is so awesomely large, it would hardly be practical for alien beings to go zipping around it in spaceships, tracking down hints of intelligent life. Why wouldn't they simply set up an automated program to scan the skies for signals—and then auto-respond with instructions on how another race (ourselves, for example) could contact *them?* That would be faster, easier, cheaper, and less of a waste of resources, since if we're not capable of following the instructions, we're not ready to meet them.

This idea, so simple, so seductive, inspires the intriguing payoff of *Contact,* which stars Jodie Foster as Dr. Ellie Arroway, a radio astronomer who has dedicated her life to the cosmological field of SETI (Search for Extra-Terrestrial Intelligence). She uses a giant radio telescope in Puerto Rico to scan the skies for signals that might originate from intelligent beings. One clue would be that a series of prime numbers, which can be easily transmitted in a universal code, would be the same everywhere, and would stand out from random radio noise.

The movie is about Ellie's search, but it is also about her mind and personality. It's surprising to find a science-fiction film exploring issues like love, death, and the existence of God; science fiction as a literary form has, of course, explored those subjects for years, but SF movies generally tend toward titles like *Independence Day,* which are about actors being attacked by gooey special effects. (Why do we always assume aliens will be bug-eyed and ugly? The next time you look in the mirror, ask yourself how you'd feel if you were a cat, and Earth was visited by something looking like you.)

Ellie's scientific quest is a lonely one. Her superior, Dr. David Drumlin (Tom Skerritt), tells her the SETI field is tantamount to professional suicide. She's needled ("Hi, Ellie. Still waiting for E.T. to call?"), but her obsession runs deep: With her father (David Morse), she shared the excitement of picking up distant stations on a ham radio outfit. He died while she was still young, and she became convinced that somehow, someday, she could contact him. This conviction is complicated by the fact that she does not believe in God or the supernatural; perhaps her SETI is a displaced version of that childhood need.

In Puerto Rico she meets Palmer (Matthew McConaughey), a young man who does believe in God. They have a brief but tender and important love affair, and then, when the dubious Drumlin pulls the plug on her research, she leaves for New Mexico, and an alternate research site. Before they separate, they talk about a paradox: Pondering the immensity and mystery of the universe, you're tempted to explain it with a concept like God, and yet you wonder if "God" isn't a patronizing simplification. Ellie and Palmer disagree about God; as viewers, we are surprised and pleased that the movie lets them debate the subject. Most Hollywood movies are too timid for theology. Question for discussion: Should man's first emissary to an alien race be required to believe in God? And if so, whose?

Ellie's research project has been all but ended when there's a sudden breakthrough: unmistakably intelligent signals from space! Drumlin, in the manner of all bureaucrats everywhere, conveniently forgets his opposition to SETI and smoothly takes the credit. The signals, which include a startling bounce back of a TV image from Earth, provide a schematic diagram for a machine which, apparently, would allow a representative of the human race to travel to the home of the race that sent the signal.

Zemeckis has filled his movie with intriguing characters, played by good actors. There is, for example, old Hadden (John Hurt), a billionaire incorporating elements of Howard Hughes and Armand Hammer. He follows Ellie's search and commands vast resources of his own. And there are two presidential advisers (James Woods and Angela Bassett), who, in the great tradition of movies about aliens, consider the signals to be a possible threat. And there are others, but I will not describe them, in order to leave key secrets intact.

What happens in the last third of the film, indeed, I will not describe. Some of it you can guess. You may be guessing wrong. Zemeckis uses special effects to suggest the climactic events without upstaging them. (Earlier effects, however, that seemingly incorporate President Clinton into the film, are simply distracting.)

Movies like *Contact* help explain why movies like *Independence Day* leave me feeling empty and unsatisfied. When I look up at the sky through a telescope, when I follow the landing of the research vehicle on Mars, when I read about cosmology, I brush against transcendence. The universe is so large and old and beautiful, and our life as an intelligent species is so brief, that all our knowledge is like a tiny hint surrounded by a void. Has another race been around longer and learned more? Where are they? We have been listening for only a few decades. Space and time are so vast. A signal's chances of reaching us at the right time and place are so remote they make a message in a bottle look reliable. But if one came . . .

Contempt ★ ★ ★

NO MPAA RATING, 103 m., 1963 (rereleased 1997)

Brigitte Bardot (Camille Javel), Jack Palance (Jeremiah Prokosch ["Jerry"]), Michel Piccoli (Paul Javel), Giorgia Moll (Francesca Vanini), Fritz Lang (Fritz Lang), Jean-Luc Godard (The Assistant Director), Linda Veras (Siren), Raoul Coutard (Cameraman). Directed by Jean-Luc Godard and produced by Georges de Beauregard, Carlo Ponti, and Joseph E. Levine. Screenplay by Godard, based on Alberto Moravia's novel *A Ghost at Noon.*

Contempt was Jean-Luc Godard's 1963 attempt at a big-budget, big-star production, and more or less satisfied his curiosity. It was not the direction he wanted to move in, and the rest of his career can be seen, in a way, as a reaction to the experience. Not that the film itself is a compromise; you can see the tension between Godard and his backers right there on the screen, and hear it between the lines of the dialogue in this newly restored 1997 print.

The film is about a failed playwright (Michel Piccoli) who is hired by a corrupt American producer (Jack Palance) to work on the script of a movie by a great veteran director (Fritz Lang, playing himself). The playwright is married to a sexy former typist (Brigitte Bardot) that the producer has his eye on. The film is going to be based on *The Odyssey*, but Palance has a *Hercules* ripoff in mind, while Lang wants to make an art film.

Many critics have interpreted *Contempt* as a parallel to *The Odyssey*, with Piccoli as Odysseus, Bardot as Penelope, and Palance as Poseidon, but it is just as tempting to see the frustrated screenwriter as Godard, the woman as Godard's then-wife Anna Karina, and the producer as a cross between Joseph E. Levine and Carlo Ponti, who were both attached to the project. There's a scene where Palance views a rough cut of the movie (which looks like stark, modernist wallpaper) and shouts at Lang: "You cheated me, Fritz! That's not what's in the script!"

As Palance hurls cans of film around the screening room, we may be reminded that the film opened with a curious, extended scene in which Bardot's naked (but not explicitly revealed) body is caressed and praised by Piccoli. Insecure, she asks him about her thighs, her arms, her breasts, and he replies in every case that he gazes upon perfection. This sequence was belatedly photographed after the producers screamed at Godard that he had cheated them by shooting a film starring Bardot and including not one nude shot. In revenge, he gave them acres of skin but no eroticism.

Fritz Lang sails through the movie like an immovable object, at one point telling Palance, "Include me out—as a real producer once said." The others carry the real weight of the story. Early in the film, after the disastrous screening, Palance storms out and then offers Bardot a ride to his Roman villa, leaving his secretary and Piccoli to follow behind. Palance makes a pass at Bardot, who turns him down contemptuously, and is then disturbed when Piccoli doesn't seem to defend her as he should—is he trying to provide his wife to the producer?

That leads to the film's second act, an extended marital argument between Piccoli and Bardot, shot in the disconnected cadences of real life; couples do not often argue logically, because what both sides are really asking for is uncritical acceptance and forgiveness. Then comes the third major location, a sensational villa jutting out high above the Mediterranean, its roof reached by a broad flight of steps that look like the ascent to a Greek temple.

Godard's screenplay, based on the novel *A Ghost at Noon* by Alberto Moravia, contains many moments to be savored by those who have enjoyed Godard's long battle with the film establishment. He has the crass producer constantly misquoting or misusing half-understood snippets of Great Quotations, and at one point shouting: "I like gods. I like them very much. I know exactly how they feel."

Lang's character includes details from his own life (we are told the possibly exaggerated story about how Goebbels offered him the German film industry, and he fled Germany on the midnight train). He also frequently seems to be speaking for Godard, who was forced to shoot in CinemaScope, and has Lang say, "CinemaScope is fine for snakes and coffins, but not for people."

Jack Palance is not well cast as the producer; perhaps he was too much of an outsider himself to play a craven money man. He seems ill at ease in many scenes, unconvinced by his own dialogue. Bardot, whose role is emotionally easier to understand, seems very natural. And Michel Piccoli (in his first role!) is persuasive as a man with few talents and great insecurities; his screenwriter is quite different from the typical Piccoli roles of years to come, when he played men who were confident, smooth, devious.

As for Godard, he stays as always a little aloof. All of his films are, in a way, about filmmaking; he breaks the illusion of the fourth wall in order to communicate directly with the audience, usually in such an enigmatic way that he seems to be satirizing the whole idea of communication. He likes mannered shots that call attention to themselves, and here, faced with the great width of the CinemaScope screen, he has moments when he pans slowly back and forth from one side of the room to the other, using an unbroken take but refusing to place both characters on the screen at the same time.

When widescreen movies are shown on TV these days, they are often subjected to the annoying practice of "pan and scan," in which the sides are chopped off and then the camera moves back and forth to show two people who were originally meant to be seen at once. I can only imagine how the "pan-and-scan" process would look if applied to this movie, in which Godard has built his own panning into the wide-screen compositions. The worst scenario: The movie pans in two directions at once.

Contempt is not one of the great Godard films, for reasons it makes clear. In a way, it's about its own shortcomings. A drama exists at ground level involving the characters, while the film fights between the tendency to elevate them into art (Lang) or vulgarize them into commerce (Palance). It is interesting to see, and has moments of brilliance (the marital argument, the use of the villa steps), but its real importance is as a failed experiment. *Contempt* taught Godard he could not make films like this, and so he included himself out, and went on to make the films he could make.

Cookie's Fortune ★ ★ ★ ★

PG-13, 118 m., 1999

Glenn Close (Camille Dixon), Julianne Moore (Cora Duvall), Liv Tyler (Emma Duvall), Chris O'Donnell (Jason Brown), Charles S. Dutton (Willis Richland), Patricia Neal (Cookie Orcutt), Ned Beatty (Lester Boyle), Niecy Nash (Deputy Wanda), Lyle Lovett (Manny Hood), Donald Moffat (Jack Palmer), Courtney B. Vance (Otis Tucker), Ruby Wilson (Josie Martin). Directed by Robert Altman and produced by Altman and Etchie Stroh. Screenplay by Anne Rapp.

Cookie's Fortune is Robert Altman's sunniest film, a warmhearted comedy that somehow manages to deal with death and murder charges without even containing a real villain. True, the Glenn Close character comes close to villainy by falsifying a death scene, but since she's in the middle of directing the Easter play at her church, maybe it's partly a case of runaway theatrical zeal.

The movie takes place in the small town of Holly Springs, Mississippi, where Altman assembles a large cast of lovable characters. He's a master of stories that interconnect a lot of people *(M*A*S*H, Nashville, The Player, Short Cuts)*, and here one of the pleasures is discovering the hidden connections.

The film begins with a false alarm. A black man named Willis (Charles S. Dutton) wanders out of a bar, seems to break into a home, and studies the guns displayed in a cabinet. An elderly white woman (Patricia Neal) comes downstairs and finds him, and then we discover they're best friends. Neal plays Cookie, a rich widow who misses her husband fiercely. Glenn Close is Camille Dixon, her niece, who before long discovers Cookie's dead body and rearranges the death scene to make it look like a break-in and a murder.

Meanwhile, Altman's camera strolls comfortably around town, introducing us to Cora (Julianne Moore), Camille's dim sister; Emma (Liv Tyler), Cora's daughter, who takes a pass on genteel society and works at the catfish house; and the forces down at the police station, including the veteran officer Lester (Ned Beatty), Jason the doofus rookie (Chris O'Donnell), and Wanda the deputy (Niecy Nash). Some of these people have roles in the Easter play, which is *Salome* (the letterboard in front of the church says it's "by Oscar Wilde and Camille Dixon").

The key dramatic event in the film is the arrest of Willis on suspicion of murder, even though everyone in the town is convinced he could not have committed such a crime. His fingerprints are indeed on the guns in Cookie's house, but no wonder, since he just finished cleaning them.

"He's innocent. You can trust me on that," declares Lester the cop.

"What makes you so sure of that?"

"Because—I fish with him."

Emma also believes he's innocent, and demonstrates her confidence by moving into his jail cell. The cell door is kept open, which is convenient for Emma and Jason the doofus deputy, since they are desperately in love and sneak off behind the Coke machine for rumpy-pumpy whenever possible.

"They read you your rights?" the lawyer (Donald Moffat) asks Willis. "Yeah, and gave me a cup of coffee and an issue of *Field and Stream.*" Also a Scrabble board. Meanwhile, Camille and Cora (who has been sworn to secrecy about the falsified death scene) are beside themselves: They like Willis and are horrified he's under arrest, but to free him would involve incriminating themselves.

Altman and his writer, Anne Rapp, use the crime story as a way to reveal connections of one sort or another between almost everyone in the movie. They also show a small southern town that is not seething with racism, classism, and ignorance, but is in fact a sort of heavenly place where most people know and like one another, and are long accustomed to each other's peculiarities. (There's a lovely scene where the bar owner tries to explain to the cops, without really saying so, that it is Willis's custom to steal a half-pint of Southern Comfort when he's broke, and return it when he's in funds.)

Altman has always been good with sly humor at the edges of his frame. He doesn't only focus on the foreground action, but allows supporting characters to lead their own lives on the edges. Notice in particular the delightful character of Wanda (Niecy Nash), the African-American deputy, who wields a tape recorder with great drama. There's a scene where a state investigator arrives from Jackson to look into the case, and is a handsome black man (Courtney B. Vance). He interviews the blues singer at the bar (Ruby Wilson), while Wanda mans the tape recorder, and both women subtly but shamelessly flirt with him.

Cookie's Fortune is the kind of comedy with a lot of laughs, and even more smiles. The cast blends so smoothly you can believe they all live in the same town. There is a great warmth at the center of the story, in the performance by Charles S. Dutton, who is one of the most likable characters in any Altman film (his scenes with Liv Tyler include some very tricky revelations, which they both handle with perfect simplicity). Glenn Close has the richest comedy in the film, as the meddling, stage-struck director ("The two of you keep forgetting this is ancient Galilee!"). Patricia Neal's role is brief, but crucial and touching. Ned Beatty's sheriff uses fishing as his metaphor for life.

Altman's films are sometimes criticized for being needlessly enigmatic and elliptical, for ending at quixotic moments, for getting too cute with the asides. He does sometimes commit those sins, if sins they are, but in the service of creating movies that are fresh and original. *Cookie's Fortune* has no ragged edges or bothersome detours, and flows from surprise to delight. At the end, when just deserts are handed out, it arrives at a kind of perfection.

Cop Land ★ ★

R, 104 m., 1997

Sylvester Stallone (Freddy Heflin), Harvey Keitel (Ray Donlan), Ray Liotta (Gary "Figs" Figgis), Robert De Niro (Moe Tilden), Peter Berg (Joey Randone), Janeane Garofalo (Cindy Betts), Robert Patrick (Rucker), Michael Rapaport (Murray Babitch), Annabella Sciorra (Liz Randone), Cathy Moriarty (Rose). Directed by James Mangold and produced by Cary Woods, Cathy Konrad, and Ezra Swerdlow. Screenplay by Mangold.

A reader, Rich Gallagher of Fishkill, New York, writes to ask why they remake only the good movies, not bad ones. Good films don't require remaking, he observes, but what about "promising concepts which were poorly executed for one reason or another?"

Mr. Gallagher could have been writing about *Cop Land*, a movie with such a promising concept, yet so poorly executed that it begs to be remade. The characters are all over the map, there are too many unclear story threads, our sympathies are confused, and there's an unconvincing showdown in which the story's lovingly developed ambiguities are lost.

The premise: A group of New York cops take part-time jobs as transit policemen in order to get around the requirement that they live in the city. They buy houses in a New Jersey hamlet named Garrison, just across the river. Here they can run the show. Many of them have obtained mortgages from a mob-connected bank through the good offices of a cop fondly known as Uncle Ray (Harvey Keitel), who is connected.

The town's police force is headed by the plump and half-deaf Sheriff Freddy Heflin

(Sylvester Stallone), who isn't and never will be a "real cop," as Uncle Ray tauntingly reminds him. Also on the force is Cindy Betts (Janeane Garofolo), who pulls over Uncle Ray when he's going 71 in a 25 mph zone, and gets a lecture from him. Ray is so cocky he talks smart to Cindy even though, in the backseat of his car, he's hiding a rookie cop who is wanted for questioning in the deaths of two young men.

As the film opens, the rookie (Michael Rapaport), driving while drunk, thinks he sees a rifle pointed at him by two young black men. Actually, it's not a rifle but The Club—a crucial point so poorly established that many viewers will miss it. The cop fires, the kids are killed, and there's no weapon to be found in their car—especially not after a black ambulance attendant gets into a fight with a white cop he sees trying to plant one. In the confusion, the rookie disappears and Uncle Ray announces he has thrown himself from the bridge.

Already we have enough for a movie, especially after we meet Moe Tilden (Robert De Niro), of the department's Internal Affairs Bureau. But there's more. Another cop, named Figgis (Ray Liotta), nurses an old grudge against Ray. Stallone also has memories; when he was a teenager, he dove into the river to save Liz (Annabella Sciorra), who is now married to a cop named Joey Randone (Peter Berg). Stallone lost the hearing in one ear during that rescue, which is why he's stuck in this small town, settling domestic disturbances—as when the blowzy Rose (Cathy Moriarity) dumps her garbage in front of the Randones' house, because Joey is cheating on her by sleeping with his wife.

The screenplay, by director James Mangold, has the richness and complexity of a novel, but the best movies are more like novellas. All of these characters are seen in such detail that any three of them would make a story. A dozen leave us trying to remember who is who and why. The Stallone character offers the closest thing the movie has to a center, but his sheriff, like some of the other characters, seems to have suffered in the editing. Early in the film, for example, he gets drunk and smashes up a squad car, but then his alcoholism is dropped, and his sadness (because he should have married Liz) is established without being developed.

There are even greater problems with the De Niro character, who has three big scenes without any little scenes to tell us how he got from one point to another. He challenges Stallone to work with him in exposing the crooked cops ("I don't know how you do it, sheriff: all blue and everybody packing!"), and then seems to reject him, and then reverses himself with a line of dialogue that stands out like a sore thumb.

And what about the Keitel character? Keitel has some of the best moments in the movie (especially a barroom speech about separating the men from the boys). But after helping the rookie disappear as a suicide, why does he flaunt him alive at a drunken cop party—especially considering what he wants to do next?

James Mangold wrote and directed *Heavy* (1996), one of the year's best films, a rich character study of a mama's boy and a reckless young waitress. He showed an abundance of talent. And talent is on display, too, in *Cop Land*—in the dialogue, in the way the characters are developed, in the ambition of the story. But clarity is lacking. What is the movie really about? Where is the moral center? Why so many subplots about adulteries and old grudges?

There is a rough balance between how long a movie is, how deep it goes, and how much it can achieve. That balance is not found in *Cop Land*, and the result is too much movie for the running time. Still, all the materials are here for the remake. Two remakes: one about the disappearing rookie cop plot, and the other about the town where all the police live. Maybe even a third one about the garbage war between the cop's wife and his mistress.

The Corruptor ★ ½

R, 111 m., 1999

Chow Yun-Fat (Nick Chen), Mark Wahlberg (Danny Wallace), Ric Young (Henry Lee), Elizabeth Lindsey (Louise Deng), Paul Ben-Victor (Schabacker), Jon Kit Lee (Jack), Andrew Pang (Willy Ung), Brian Cox (Sean Wallace), Kim Chan (Uncle Benny). Directed by James Foley and produced by Dan Halsted. Screenplay by Robert Pucci.

Even when it's transplanted to the streets of New York's Chinatown, as *The Corruptor* is, the Hong Kong action genre has certain obligatory requirements. Low-angle shots of bad guys looming over the camera, for example. And the sound of a metallic whoosh when there's a quick cut from one scene to the next. And what seems like more dialogue during action scenes than before and after them.

The Corruptor touches these bases, and has an icon as its lead: Chow Yun-Fat, who has made almost seventy films and has recently followed Jackie Chan into the American market (*Replacement Killers*, with Mira Sorvino, in 1998). His *Hard Boiled* (1992), directed by the master of the genre, John Woo, is a cult favorite. *The Corruptor* isn't in that league.

Chow Yun-Fat plays Nick Chen, a tough cop in an all-Asian station house in Chinatown. A white cop named Danny (Mark Wahlberg) is assigned to the precinct, and greeted with much suspicion: He will stand out, he won't be trusted, he doesn't understand the Chinese, etc. This is a setup for one of the weariest of all cop formulas, the cop-buddy movie, in which opposites first repel and then attract. Will Nick and Danny be friends by the end of the movie? What do you think?

But there are a couple of fundamental twists I dare not reveal, involving secrets held by both men—a secret, in Danny's case, that makes you wonder how his superiors could possibly have hoped for him to operate effectively in an Asian environment. No matter; the plot chugs along as the cops get involved in a scheme involving the boss of Chinatown, Uncle Benny (Kim Chan, who according to the Internet Movie Database played a character with exactly the same name in *Lethal Weapon 4*—is this trivia, or homage?).

Everybody in Chinatown is more or less on the take, but there are degrees of immorality, and Nick is the kind of cop who tries to be realistic and principled at the same time. As for Danny: Well, I just never believed he was a cop at all. Mark Wahlberg was effective in a much more difficult role in *Boogie Nights*, but he's not an action star and he never feels at home in the role.

There's an opportunity for some kind of love or human interest with another cop in the precinct, played by Elizabeth Lindsey; she's set up as a major character, but given a role so underwritten (or badly edited) that she spends a lot of time just standing in the backgrounds of other people's shots. The problem with relationships is that they involve personalities and dialogue, and there's not much time for those in an action picture.

The director is James Foley, who is obviously not right for this material. It's a shame, actually, that he's even working in the genre, since his gift is with the intense study of human behavior, and his best films include *Glengarry Glen Ross*, *At Close Range*, and *After Dark, My Sweet*. John Woo, who might have brought crackling energy to this material (especially if he nixed the casting of Wahlberg), wouldn't be right for *Glengarry*. So there you are.

Cousin Bette ★ ★ ★

R, 108 m., 1998

Jessica Lange (Cousin Bette), Bob Hoskins (Mayor Crevel), Elisabeth Shue (Jenny Cadine), Hugh Laurie (Baron Hulot), Kelly MacDonald (Hortense), Aden Young (Wenceslas), Geraldine Chaplin (Adeline). Directed by Des McAnuff and produced by Sarah Radclyffe. Screenplay by Lynn Siefert and Susan Tarr, based on the novel by Honoré de Balzac.

Characters motivated by money are always more interesting than characters motivated by love, because you don't know what they'll do next. Tom Wolfe knew that when he wrote *The Bonfire of the Vanities*, still an accurate satire of the way we live now. Maybe that's why writers from India, where marriages are often arranged, are the most interesting new novelists in English.

The Victorians knew how important money was. The plots of Dickens and Trollope wallowed in it, and Henry James created exquisite punishments for his naively romantic Americans caught in the nets of needy Europeans. And now consider *Cousin Bette*, a film based on one of Balzac's best-known novels, in which France of the mid-nineteenth century is unable to supply a single person who is not motivated more or less exclusively by greed. Wolfe said his *Bonfire* was inspired by Balzac, and he must have had this novel in mind.

The title character, played by Jessica Lange with the gravity of a governess in Victorian pornography, is a spinster of about forty. Her life was sacrificed, she believes, because her family had sufficient resources to dress, groom, and train only one of the girls—her cousin (Geraldine Chaplin). Bette was sent to work in the garden, and the lucky cousin, on her deathbed, nostalgically recalls the dirt under Bette's nails. When the lucky cousin dies, Bette fully expects to marry the widower, Baron Hulot (Hugh Laurie). But the baron offers her only a housekeeper's position.

Refusing the humiliating post, Bette returns to her shabby hotel on one of the jumbled back streets of Paris, circa 1846, where the population consists mostly of desperate prostitutes, starving artists, and concierges with arms like hams. Bette is not a woman it is safe to offend. She works as a seamstress in a bawdy theater, where the star is the baron's mistress, Jenny Cadine (Elisabeth Shue). The rich playboys of Paris queue up every night outside Jenny's dressing room, their arms filled with gifts. Baron Hulot does not own her, but rents her, and the rent is coming due. Bette knows exactly how Jenny works, and uses her access as a useful weapon ("You will be the ax—and I will be the hand that wields you!").

Every night, pretending to sleep, Bette watches as Wenceslas (Aden Young), the handsome young Polish artist who lives upstairs, sneaks into her room to steal the cheese from her mousetrap and a swig of wine from her jug. She offers to support him from her savings (as a loan, with interest, of course), and falls in love with him, only to learn that he has fallen in love with Jenny. ("They say," Jenny unwisely tells Bette, "that he lives with a hag. A fierce-eyed dragon who won't let him out of her sight.")

Meanwhile, the baron is bankrupt and in hock to the moneylenders. His son fires the family servants in desperation. Nucingen, a familiar figure from many of Balzac's novels, lends money at ruinous interest. And the baron's daughter Hortense (Kelly MacDonald) unexpectedly weds Wenceslas, who unwisely allows love to temporarily blind him to Jenny's more sophisticated appeals. Also lurking about is the rich lord mayor of Paris, Crevel (Bob Hoskins), who once offered Hortense 200,000 francs for a look at her body, and is now, because of her desperation, offered a 50 percent discount.

All of these people are hypocrites, not least Wenceslas, who designs small metal decorations and poses as a great sculptor. When the baron, now his father-in-law, underwrites the purchase of a huge block of marble, Wenceslas's greatest gift is describing what he plans to do with it.

This is a plot worthy of *Dynasty*, told by the first-time director Des McAnuff with an appreciation for Balzac's droll storytelling; he treats the novel not as great literature but as merciless social satire, and it is perhaps not a coincidence that for his cinematographer he chose Andrzej Sekula *(Pulp Fiction)*, achieving a modern look and pace. The movie is not respectful like a literary adaptation, but wicked with gossip and social satire. ("The nineteenth century as we know it was invented by Balzac," Oscar Wilde said.)

Between 1846, when the movie opens, and 1848, when it reaches a climax, popular unrest breaks out in Paris. Angry proletarians pursue the carriages of the rich down the streets, and mobs tear up cobblestones and build barricades. Balzac's point is that history has dropped an anvil on his spoiled degenerates. But the plot stays resolutely at the level of avarice, and it is fascinating to watch Cousin Bette as she lies to everyone, pulls the strings of her puppets, and distributes justice and revenge like an angry god. By the end, as she smiles upon an infant and the child gurgles back, the movie has earned the monstrous irony of this image.

Crash ★ ★ ★ ½

NC-17, 100 m., 1997

James Spader (James Ballard), Holly Hunter (Dr. Helen Remington), Elias Koteas (Vaughan), Deborah Unger (Catherine Ballard), Rosanna Arquette (Gabrielle), Peter MacNeil (Seagrave). Directed and produced by David Cronenberg. Screenplay by Cronenberg, based on the novel by J. G. Ballard.

If you can imagine the state of mind I'm about to describe, you will understand David Cronenberg's *Crash*. It is that trancelike state when you are drawn to do something you should not do, and have passed through the stages of common sense and inhibition and arrived at critical velocity. You are going to do it.

Such a trance or compulsion is often associated with sex, and is also experienced by shoplifters, gamblers, drug users, stunt men, and others mesmerized by pleasure through risk. All of the key characters in *Crash* live in such a trance; they are hopelessly fascinated by a connection between eroticism and automobile accidents.

Now of course there is no connection between eroticism and automobile accidents. Show me a man who can become aroused while aiming into the oncoming lane at 60 mph, and I will show you a man whose mind is not on the road. Even sadomasochists require a degree of control. The idea of deliberately seeking accidental death in a speeding car is not attractive to anyone; those who seek it want suicide, not ecstasy.

Crash is about characters entranced by a sexual fetish that, in fact, no one has. Cronenberg has made a movie that is pornographic in form, but not in result. Take out the cars, the scars, the crutches, and scabs and wounds, and substitute the usual props of sex films, and you'd have a porno movie. But *Crash* is anything but pornographic: It's about the human mind, about the way we grow enslaved by the particular things that turn us on, and forgive ourselves our trespasses.

When a college president makes dirty phone calls, when a movie star or a TV preacher picks up a hooker in a red-light district, we ask: What in the world were they thinking of? The answer is, they were thinking (a) I want to do this, and (b) I can get away with it. *Crash* is a movie that understands that thinking. One of the characters speaks of "a benevolent psychopathology that beckons toward us." It is a strange and insightful film about human sexual compulsion (*Belle de Jour, Peeping Tom,* and *Damage* are others). By deliberately removing anything that an audience member is likely to find even remotely erotic, Cronenberg has brought a kind of icy, abstract purity to his subject.

The movie begins with a woman pressing her breast against the metal of a shiny new airplane. Then she licks the paint, while her lover licks her. This is Catherine Ballard (Deborah Unger). When her husband, James (James Spader), returns home, they compare notes; both risked being discovered having sex in public places. Notice how they talk to one another: It is a point of pride to be cold and detached. That's not because they don't care. It's because they do. They are fascinated by each other's minds, and by the tastes they share.

Soon after, James is involved in a head-on crash. A man in the other car is propelled through the windshield and into James's car, dead. James is badly injured but alive. His eyes lock into the eyes of Helen (Holly Hunter), the woman in the other car. They find themselves in the same hospital ward, walking with canes and braces, trailing their IV bags behind them. After they're released, they happen to meet in the car pound, where they've gone to visit their smashed cars. "Can I give you a lift?" James asks. "I somehow find myself driving again." Soon they narrowly escape another head-on crash, and then they drive directly to an airport garage and have quick, passionate sex.

What's happening here? Take out the crashes and the injuries, and substitute the usual romantic movie story line, and it would be easy to understand this progression. For the first crash, substitute a chance meeting at a party. Have the husband make a fool of himself. Have them meet later by chance. Have them survive a dangerous experience. Let them feel sudden sexual attraction. No one in the audience would bat an eye if there was then a sex scene. It's not what happens that disturbs us; it's their turn-on that turns us off.

More characters are introduced. Vaughan (Elias Koteas) is a photographer who specializes in restaging celebrity car crashes, like the James Dean crash. "Notice that we use no seat belts, padded suits, or roll bars," he tells his small but exclusive audiences. "We rely only on the skill of our drivers." He lives with Gabrielle (Rosanna Arquette), who walks with braces. He works with a stunt driver (Peter MacNeil). He drives a Lincoln Continental similar to the one JFK was riding in when shot.

Soon James, Catherine, and Helen are involved in his scene. It's not an accident these people have found each other, since they share the same tastes and fetishes. They have sex together in most of the possible pairings, including homosexual; the focus is not on the other person, but on the settings and props. There are no moments of healing sanity because the characters are comatose with lust and fascination. They follow their self-destructive courses because they do not want to stop. If you seek to understand them, ignore their turn-ons and substitute your own.

When *Crash* premiered in May 1996 at the Cannes Film Festival, some people fled the theater. The movie played in Canada and Europe to widespread controversy, inspiring polemics both pro and con. Ted Turner, whose Fine Line distributed the film in America, has said he hates it. Certainly it will repel and disgust many viewers.

It's like a porno movie made by a computer: It downloads gigabytes of information about sex, it discovers our love affair with cars, and it combines them in a mistaken algorithm. The result is challenging, courageous, and original—a dissection of the mechanics of pornography. I admired it, although I cannot say I "liked" it. It goes on a bit too long. Afterward, I found myself wishing a major director would lavish this kind of love and attention on a movie about *my* fetishes.

Critical Care ★ ★ ★

R, 106 m., 1997

James Spader (Dr. Werner Ernst), Kyra Sedgwick (Felicia Potter), Helen Mirren (Stella), Margo Martindale (Connie Potter), Anne Bancroft (Nun), Albert Brooks (Dr. Butz), Jeffrey Wright (Bed 2), Wallace Shawn (Furnaceman). Directed by Sidney Lumet and produced by Steven S. Schwartz and Lumet. Screenplay by Schwartz, based on the book by Richard Dooling.

"I have lettuce in my refrigerator that has a better chance of becoming conscious than this guy," says the young doctor in charge of Bed 5. The patient is in a "persistent vegetative state." One of his daughters wants the hospital to pull the plug. The other daughter wants full life-support measures to be used, especially after it's claimed that her father's trembling hand is using Morse Code to send the message, "If you love me."

Okay, then: If you love him, what do you do? Young Dr. Ernst (James Spader) gets input from old Dr. Butz (Albert Brooks): "What's wrong with Bed 5? He's all paid up and he's got three insurance companies paying off his bills monthly." In other words, keep him alive as long as the money's coming in. But, asks Ernst, should they carry out a procedure to allow the unconscious patient to be fed artificially? Butz is livid: "You think just because someone's going to die soon, we don't need to feed them? I've news for you! We're *all* gonna die! So why should *any* of us eat?"

This kind of collision between ethics and income is at the heart of Sidney Lumet's *Critical Care*, a smart, hard-edged movie about how insurance policies essentially dictate modern medical care. Spader plays Ernst as an exhausted third-year resident who has been a nerd all his life, and is belatedly enjoying an active sex life because the "M.D." after his name has made him attractive to women. Helen Mirren is Nurse Stella, the veteran in charge of the intensive care unit, and Bed 5's two daughters are the sexpot Felicia (Kyra Sedgwick) and the devout Connie (Margo Martindale).

The film is a stimulating mix of medical drama and courtroom showdown, with broad comedy from Brooks, a little sexual blackmail, and a touching subplot involving another terminally ill patient who thinks he is being visited by the devil. Underlining the sense of heightened and limited reality, the ICU in the movie is bathed in white light, like the command deck of a heavenly spaceship, and essentially contains only the two patients and their problems.

The other patient (Jeffrey Wright) has rejected two kidneys and has lost any will to live. He's in pain and despair, and although there is no hope for him, he is being kept alive because the hospital can profitably transplant kidneys into him indefinitely. Nurse Stella sympathizes with him, but he must also deal with the pep talks of the Furnaceman (Wallace Shawn), who tempts him to die, and a good nun (Anne Bancroft), who holds out the hope of reconciliation.

His case is played as a sober counterpoint to the drama in Bed 5, and Mirren is wonderful in her quiet scenes with the dying young man. Spader's Dr. Ernst, meanwhile, is in a tug-of-war between Bed 5's daughters and the alcoholic Dr. Butz ("Just make sure you don't have money for health care and you'll die happy in your own king-sized bed!"). Ernst invites Felicia out to dinner and their relationship progresses, even though he halfheartedly protests that ethics forbid him from discussing her father's case. In a scene cleverly written by Stephen Schwartz, she uses sex to get what she needs.

The devout daughter, Connie, on the other hand, swears her father is communicating with her and will snap out of his coma at any moment. Could either daughter be motivated by the terms of Bed 5's $10 million trust fund? Will Ernst's career be ruined? The movie debates its issues with a sharpness and cynicism not often seen, and steps wrong only once, with Connie's parting line of dialogue, which is an inappropriate clinker.

Of all the characters, I liked Brooks's Dr. Butz the best. He inhabits a cluttered office up under the eaves of the old wing of the hospital, pouring himself drinks out of the office bottle and denying charges that he is a chronic alcoholic. "If I *were* a chronic alcoholic, I'd have, ah . . . whatever you call it." "Short-term memory loss?" asks Ernst.

Cruel Intentions ★ ★ ★

R, 97 m., 1999

Sarah Michelle Gellar (Kathryn Merteuil), Ryan Phillippe (Sebastian Valmont), Reese Witherspoon (Annette Hargrove), Selma Blair (Cecile Caldwell), Louise Fletcher (Helen Rosemond), Joshua Jackson (Blaine Tuttle), Eric Mabius (Greg McConnell), Sean Patrick Thomas (Ronald Clifford). Directed by Roger Kumble and produced by Neal H. Moritz. Screenplay by Kumble.

Teenagers once went to the movies to see adults making love. Now adults go to the movies to see teenagers making love. *Cruel Intentions* is a modern-day version of *Dangerous Liaisons*, with rich kids in a prep school playing roles that were written for jaded French aristocrats in the wicked 1782 novel by Choderlos De Laclos. He created a world of depraved amorality, in which the only goal was to indulge one's selfishness. It's refreshing, after the sponge-brained teenage romances of recent months, to see this movie reflecting that cynicism—up to a point. It crash-lands with an ending of soppy moralizing, but until the end, it's smart and merciless in the tradition of the original story.

The film stars Ryan Phillippe, a slinky schemer in the tradition of James Spader, as Sebastian Valmont, a rich kid who lives in a Manhattan mansion with his stepsister Kathryn Merteuil (Sarah Michelle Gellar). He's known as an unprincipled seducer who "has never uttered a single word without dishonorable intentions." She's a minx who's angered when her current boyfriend dumps her for the sweeter Cecile (Selma Blair), and in revenge she urges Sebastian to conquer Cecile and destroy her reputation.

Agreed, says Sebastian, but soon he finds a greater challenge—the virginal Annette (Reese Witherspoon), daughter of the new headmaster at their expensive school. She's written an article for *Seventeen* magazine praising premarital virginity, and Sebastian bets Kathryn he can deflower her. The wager: If he loses, his stepsister gets his classic sports car. If he wins, he gets his stepsister.

Sebastian pulls heartstrings, tells lies, and employs devious seductive strategies, and the movie is startling in its frank language and forthright approach to sex; it's like a throwback to the 1970s. The plot's Machiavellian emotional strategies remind us of the same story as it was told in Stephen Frears's *Dangerous Liaisons* (1988) and Milos Forman's *Valmont* (1989), but the much younger actors create the uncanny illusion of a high school production of a grown-up play. Are teenagers capable of sexual strategies this devious and sophisticated? I doubt it; few adults are, and even those who qualify may simply lack the energy.

The movie's at its best in the scenes between Gellar and Phillippe, who develop a convincing emotional charge, and whose wickedness seems to work as a sexual stimulant. There's one scene where she persuades him, emotionally and physically, to do what she wants, and we are reminded that slow, subtle eroticism is, after all, possible in the movies—even though recently it has been replaced by calisthenics. Gellar is effective as a bright girl who knows exactly how to use her act as a tramp, and Phillippe seems cold and detached enough to make it interesting when he finally gets skewered by the arrow of true love.

The best parts of the movie allow us to see how good it might all have been, with a little more care. It steps wrong in three ways. The first is with the ending, which lacks the courage to take the story to its logical conclusion, and instead contrives a series of moralistic payoffs that are false and boring. The second is with the treatment of some gay characters; surely kids as sophisticated as those in this story would be less homophobic. The third is with the use of a black character (Sean Patrick Thomas), Cecile's cello instructor, whose race is uneasily employed in awkwardly written scenes.

Still, overall, the film at least has style and wit, and a lot of devious fun with its plot. Compared to the sluggish *Jawbreaker,* it's a wake-up call. I almost hesitate to repeat my usual complaint about movies where twentysomethings play teenagers. Yes, the characters in this movie look too old to be sixteen or seventeen, but on the other hand, if actors are too young to attend R-rated movies, should they be making them? Only kidding.

The Cruise ★ ★ ★

NO MPAA RATING, 76 m., 1998

A documentary directed and produced by Bennett Miller. Featuring Timothy (Speed) Levitch.

"Right now you are six and a half blocks from where Thomas Paine died!" Speed Levitch announces breathlessly. The necks of the tourists on the Gray Line bus swivel uncertainly. Where are they supposed to be looking? "O. Henry lived and wrote near here! You are five blocks from where Dorothy Parker wrestles with alcoholism, and fails!"

It is like taking a virtual bus tour. You are here and the sights are there. Levitch never pauses for breath, rattling ahead in his adenoidal voice: "There are 2.4 million people in Manhattan!" He adds beneath his breath, "I heard 1.7 the other day, but I don't care."

This is Manhattan's most famous tour bus guide, a man for whom the island is not just the backdrop to his needs and dreams, but their very embodiment: "The anger, the inferiority that some of the smaller buildings feel—I feel." Tourists from Omaha, Altoona, and Cincinnati blink their eyes uncertainly as he tells him how close they are at this very moment to the Greenwich Village home of the poet e. e. cummings. He may be moving too fast for them, but maybe not: "I expect the total transformation of their lives the moment they get on the bus."

Timothy (Speed) Levitch is the star and subject of *The Cruise,* a loopy documentary about a man who literally lives by his wits. Levitch is a 1992 college graduate who has lived in Manhattan ever since without ever having a permanent home. He sleeps over at the houses of friends and depends on the kindnesses of strangers. He calls it "couch surfing." He made $9 an hour plus tips from the Gray Line, better than the $7 paid by Big Apple tours, but still he is winsome: "Big Apple was *Spartacus.* Gray Line is *Willy Wonka.*" His tendency to personalize inanimate objects reaches some sort of apex when he emerges from his bus to gaze up at an early skyscraper and suggests that a terra-cotta frieze is the structure's orgasm.

I get letters from people who would like to make a movie. My advice could be, find a subject like Speed Levitch and follow him around with a video camera. That's what Bennett Miller did—directing, producing, and photographing *The Cruise.* Levitch (who has now retired and gives private tours) became a legend in the New York bus tour universe in the mid-1990s; customers, far from being confused by his curious rants, recommended his tours to one another. That makes a kind of sense. You can see buildings anywhere, but Levitch is the kind of sight perhaps only New York could engender.

"I went to double-decker buses to meet and seduce women," he says. It didn't work (maybe because of homelessness, a Goodwill wardrobe, and a flat-footed duckwalk?). Now he sees that "every double-decker loop is a loop toward my death." He's not just a cheerful clown; there's a strange, dark undertow that we sense beneath lines like: "Eleven people have jumped off this bridge and survived. One of my cruising dreams would be to get those people together on a cruise."

Around and around the city he cruises by land, driven mad by the repetition of the spiel, but not as mad as some guides, since he feels free to comment at length on sights the passengers cannot even see. There is something more to him, we feel, and deeper than this colorful showoff. A story not told. Like Tiny Tim, he gives the sense of a man whose only home is his personality. "I was reemerged into my own naïveté," he explains.

D

Dance With Me ★ ★ ★

PG, 126 m., 1998

Vanessa L. Williams (Ruby Sinclair), Chayne (Rafael Infante), Kris Kristofferson (John Burnett), Joan Plowright (Bea Johnson), Rick Valenzuela (Julian Marshall), Jane Krakowski (Patricia), Beth Grant (Lovejoy), William Marquez (Stefano), Harry Groener (Michael). Directed by Randa Haines and produced by Shinya Egawa, Haines, and Lauren Weissman. Screenplay by Daryl Matthews.

Dance With Me is romance and intrigue in a shabby Houston dance studio, where pro dancers are in training for the World Open Dance Championship in Las Vegas. A lot of the plot is standard, but a lot of it isn't, including the relationship between a young man from Cuba (the Puerto Rican singing star Chayanne) and a gifted dancer (Vanessa L. Williams), who says, "I don't want to be in love."

It goes without saying that these two people are destined to fall in love. But the movie sees Ruby, the Williams character, clearly and with surprising truthfulness; she has a depth associated with more serious movies. And there's another convincing character, grizzled old John Burnett (Kris Kristofferson), who runs the studio but would much rather be standing on the end of a Gulf pier fishing.

The movie opens in Cuba, where the young and handsome Rafael Infante (Chayanne) buries his mother and then accepts an invitation to visit her old friend Burnett in Texas. At the bus station he's greeted not by Burnett but by Ruby Sinclair, who is pointedly standoffish. So is Burnett, who gives the newcomer a place to live over his garage, but doesn't warm up to him.

It's thirty days until the Vegas championships, and Ruby is having trouble with her partner. So is Burnett, whose heart is no longer in dancing. Rafael, pleasant and helpful, begins as a handyman and scores his first success by decorating the studio for a party by using every single decoration he can find—Christmas and Halloween stuff included. Before long, he's dancing.

It's clear to the audience from the first scene that Burnett is Rafael's father. But this is not clear to Burnett, or at least he won't admit it. It's also clear that Ruby and Rafael are powerfully attracted to one another, but Ruby has issues, including her child by her former partner Julian (Rick Valenzuela). She doesn't want love, and eventually she decides to rejoin Julian for the championships, and leave Rafael and Houston for good.

The director, Randa Haines *(Children of a Lesser God)*, says she is a fan of ballroom dancing herself, and makes it clear that relationships off and on the floor are two different things. Ruby needs money and success, and dancing is what she's best at. She's been hurt by men and is single-minded. Yes, she's attracted to Rafael, and sometimes her heart melts, but then she pulls away again. Julian can help her win.

Ruby is the most interesting character in the movie. Williams, who, by the way, is a spectacularly good dancer, plays Ruby as a woman struggling to retain control of her life. There's steel and rigidity in her, and that's how she dances too. Watching her do technical exercises, Rafael asks her, "How do you dance without music? Dancing *comes* from the music. That's why you look so stiff." The first time they dance together, he's clumsy, because he doesn't understand her instructions. But "I'm Cuban, and so of course I can dance," he says, and he can. Even when drenched by sprinklers.

Chayanne is famous in Latin music circles, not so well known in the mainstream. He's good-looking and can dance, but, more important, he's got a pleasing personality, and he doesn't overplay the schmaltz. By the end we're invested in wanting Rafael and Ruby to be together, and a movie that has achieved that has done its job.

I liked Kristofferson as a man tired and lonely. And I liked the other dance studio regulars, including Joan Plowright, an unlikely but inspiring casting choice, as a competitor in the seniors division. I also liked the big dance sequences at the end. Rick Valenzuela is a world-class dancing star whose character treats Ruby like his puppet. (He hisses criticisms even during dance numbers.) Their dance style is like a violent quarrel between two people who have long and bitterly hated and loved one another—perfect, of course, for the tango, but also perfect as a contrast to Rafael's looser and more spontaneous style.

Like *Strictly Ballroom* and *Shall We Dance, Dance With Me* uses the dance scenes as a way to sneak musical numbers into a film that is technically not a musical. It sneaks in a lot more, too, and I was surprised by how much humanity Vanessa L. Williams brings to a character that could have been a cliché. This is a movie of predictable pleasures, and then it has those surprises.

Dancing at Lughnasa ★ ★ ½

PG, 94 m., 1998

Meryl Streep (Kate Mundy), Michael Gambon (Father Jack Mundy), Catherine McCormack (Christina Mundy), Kathy Burke (Maggie Mundy), Sophie Thompson (Rose Mundy), Brid Brennan (Agnes Mundy), Rhys Ifans (Gerry Evans), Darrell Johnston (Michael Mundy). Directed by Pat O'Connor and produced by Noel Pearson. Screenplay by Frank McGuinness, based on the play by Brian Friel.

Why did *Dancing at Lughnasa* affect me so much more deeply on the stage than it does on film? Was it the physical presence of the actors? No, I think just the opposite: It was their distance. Up *there* on the stage, they took on allegorical dimensions, while in the close-ups of film they are too present, too close, too specific. The closer you get to these characters, the less you sympathize with their plight and the more you grow impatient with them.

The story, based on an award-winning play by Brian Friel, tells of the five Mundy sisters, who live in a cottage in rural Ireland in the 1930s. One has an out-of-wedlock son, Michael. As the film opens, they receive a visitor: their older brother, Father Jack, who has returned in retirement after years in Africa. He is not quite all there; his eyes wander and he loses the drift. The equatorial sun and the lure of African customs (shown in the opening credits) have worn down his Catholic beliefs, and after inquiring about his young nephew's father and discovering there is none of record, he suggests cheerfully, "I'd like you all to have a love child!"

This does not go down well with Kate Mundy (Meryl Streep), a local schoolteacher, firm and unyielding. It becomes apparent that the five women and the boy have been living in such close quarters for so long that only silence and routine make it bearable. One sister smokes all the time. Rose (Sophie Thompson), simpleminded, moons for a married man. Christina (Catherine McCormack), Michael's mother, waits (too) patiently for periodic visits from her dashing lover, Gerry (Rhys Ifans). He roars up on a motorcycle, charms her, dazzles his son (Darrell Johnston), and then roars off again—to fight against Franco in Spain, he explains.

The story is narrated, years later, by the adult Michael. He sees the surfaces, and we are meant to see beneath them. We see that Rose yearns to lead a life of her own, that Christina can feed for months on the memory of a kiss, that survival for Kate consists of keeping everyone's real feelings under her fearful discipline. The arrival of Father Jack disturbs this delicate balance, ending the past and beginning the present.

Played with sad charm by Michael Gambon in a performance deliberately vague and well-meaning, Father Jack is a man whose mind, long baked by the sun and cured by alcohol, has brought Christian and pagan ideas together into peaceful harmony. And indeed the Africans dancing around their tribal fires in the opening credits are mirrored, in Ireland, by the annual pagan festival of Lughnasa, held up in the hills, also with bonfires. Rose runs off with her fellow for a night of freedom, and we suspect she finds the courage because Father Jack has somehow set her free. He's in the old dramatic convention of the madman who speaks the truth.

At the end of the film, everyone dances. This time it is to the radio and the dancing is more sedate, but the suggestion is that the Mundy sisters have somehow been able to let out their breath at last, to end the fearful, rigid stillness that enveloped their cottage. Michael, the young narrator, remembers that time of the dancing many years later, and it is his memory that drives the story. But it is all memory and no drama. On stage, they dance and they are dancing now. On film, somehow, they are dancing then. It is not enough.

Dangerous Beauty ★ ★ ★ ½

R, 115 m., 1998

Catherine McCormack (Veronica Franco), Rufus Sewell (Marco Venier), Oliver Platt (Maffio), Moira Kelly (Beatrice), Fred Ward (Domenico Venier), Jacqueline Bisset (Paola Franco). Directed by Marshall Herskovitz and produced by Herskovitz, Ed Zwick, Arnon Milchan, and Sarah Caplan. Screenplay by Jeannine Dominy.

"The life you lead, the freedom you have—will you deny my daughters the same chance?" Not the request every mother would address to a prostitute, but *Dangerous Beauty* makes a persuasive case for the life of a courtesan in sixteenth-century Venice. At a time when Europeans are bemused by our naïveté about dalliance in high places, this is, I suppose, the film we should study. It's based on the true story of Veronica Franco, a well-born Venetian beauty who deliberately chose the life of a courtesan because it seemed a better choice than poverty or an arranged marriage to a decayed nobleman.

Veronica, played by Catherine McCormack with cool insight into the ways of men, is a woman who becomes the lover of many because she cannot be the lover of one. She is in love with the curly-headed Marco (Rufus Sewell), and he with her, but they cannot wed; "I must marry," he tells her, "according to my station and my family's will." Veronica knows this is true, and knows, too, that because her father has squandered the family fortune, she is also expected to marry money.

Shall they then become unmarried lovers? Marco persuasively argues, "God made sin that we might know his mercy." But then Veronica, her virginity lost, could never make a good marriage. Her mother (Jacqueline Bisset) has a better idea. "You cannot marry Marco, but you shall have him! You'll become a courtesan—like your mother used to be."

Veronica's eyes widen, but her mother's logic prevails, and the daughter is launched on a training course in grooming, fashion, and deportment. Her mother even shows her a great Venetian library, off limits to women, but not to Veronica ("Courtesans are the most educated women in the world"). For a courtesan, as for an army recruit, the goal is to be all that she can be. And indeed Veronica is soon the most popular and respected fallen woman in Venice, sought by princes, generals, and merchants, and even dandled on the knee of the cardinal.

The film, directed with great zest by Marshall Herskovitz, positions this story somewhere between a romance novel and a biopic. It looks like Merchant-Ivory but plays like *Dynasty.* And it's set in a breathtakingly lovely Venice, where special effects have been used to empty the Grand Canal of motorboats and fill it with regattas and gondolas. No city is more sensuous, more suited to intrigue, more saturated with secrets.

McCormack plays Veronica as a woman not averse to physical pleasure (the morning after her initiation, she smiles dreamily and asks, "Who's next?"). But sex is not really the point with a courtesan. She provides intellectual companionship for her powerful clients; through her connections she can share valuable pillow talk. And there is high entertainment as she uses poetry for verbal duels with noblemen. Her lover Marco, by contrast, is doomed to marriage with a rich girl who, like all wives of the time, is sheltered and illiterate. "Do you like poetry?" he asks her hopefully on their wedding night. "I know the psalms," she replies.

Veronica's great moment comes when the Turkish fleet seizes Venetian territory and prepares an assault on the city itself. Everything depends on the French king: Will he supply ships for the Venetian cause? The king, young and with a reputation for depravity, visits Venice and singles out Veronica for his night's pleasure. The screenplay, by Jeanine Dominey, who brings a woman's realism to matters of the heart, is pointed.

"What do you yearn for, King Henry?" asks Veronica. "Your tears," he says, pressing a knife to her throat. "I don't think so," she says, and a shadow of doubt crosses his face. "Then what do I yearn for?" he asks. She graces him with a cold smile: "Why don't we find out?" Cut to the next morning, as the doge and other nobles nervously await the king's reappearance.

He emerges, settles himself somewhat painfully on a cushion, and says, "You'll get your ships."

Veronica saves the city, but is herself condemned when the plague strikes Venice and the Inquisition blames it on women and heresy. Obviously a woman with so much power must be a witch. In a courtroom scene that I somehow doubt played out quite this way in real life, she defends herself and the life of a courtesan. It is better, she argues, to prostitute herself willingly, for her own gain, than to do so unwillingly in an arranged marriage: "No biblical hell could be worse than a state of perpetual inconsequence."

I am not surprised, as I said, that the screenwriter is a woman. Few movies have been so deliberately told from a woman's point of view. We are informed in all those best-sellers about Mars and Venus, that a man looks for beauty and a woman for security. But a man also looks for autonomy, power, independence, and authority, and a woman in sixteenth-century Venice (and even today) is expected to surrender those attributes to her husband. The woman regains her power through an understanding of the male libido: A man in a state of lust is to all intents and purposes hypnotized. Most movies are made by males, and show women enthralled by men. This movie knows better.

Dangerous Ground ★★

R, 92 m., 1997

Ice Cube (Vusi), Elizabeth Hurley (Karen), Ving Rhames (Muki), Sechaba Morojele (Ernest), Roslyn Morapedi (Vusi's Mother), Thokozani Nkosi (Young Vusi). Directed by Darrell James Roodt and produced by Gillian Gorfil and Roodt. Screenplay by Greg Latter and Roodt.

Dangerous Ground begins with a promising idea and runs away from it as fast as it can. The movie is set in South Africa—where, we learn, young Vusi (Ice Cube) was forced to flee when he was thirteen, after being threatened by the police because of his connection to revolutionaries. Now fourteen years have passed, there is a new South Africa under Mandela, and Vusi has returned to his home in the Transkei for the funeral of his father.

This leads to some amusing moments of culture shock, as when Vusi, as the oldest son, is expected to cut the neck of a calf as a sacrifice for his father. He wants no part of it. "I left as an African. I came back as an American," he explains to his younger brother, a disaffected freedom fighter who has found no role in peacetime. Vusi is also more or less at a loss about what to do with his father's spear, which he has inherited.

All he really wants to do is drive his rental car back to the airport and fly home to San Francisco. But it will not be that simple. First Vusi will have to abandon this interesting story about two cultures, and bury himself in a plot that is more or less identical with dozens of other action movies about drug dealers and violent confrontations.

He is asked by his brother and mother to go to Johannesburg and bring back his brother Stephen, who has left home and lost touch, and is rumored to be associating with the wrong types. Vusi reluctantly agrees, and makes the mistake of driving his rented red BMW into Soweto, the giant African township near Jo'burg, where he is carjacked by a black gang that also takes his jacket and his shirt. "Why you botherin' me?" he asks them. "We supposed to be brothers!" That gets a good laugh.

In the city, he tracks his brother to a high-rise apartment that looks recycled out of *Blade Runner.* Stephen isn't there, but Vusi meets his next-door neighbor, Karen (Elizabeth Hurley), who seems to know a lot about him. They meet again later at the strip club where she works as a "dancer," and he finds out Karen is Stephen's girlfriend. He also discovers they are both into cocaine, and that Stephen's disappearance is linked to $15,000 owed to Muki (Ving Rhames), a local drug lord.

The plot is standard issue, but the details are new and intriguing. We see a lot of the new South Africa out of the corners of our eyes: There are scenes shot in discos and high-rises, and even a trip to Sun City, the gambling mecca that is Africa's Vegas. And there is a pointed scene in which Muki commits a gangland assassination in the presence of a white police officer who is on his payroll.

The plot comes adorned with a strong message, probably the work of the director and cowriter, Darrell James Roodt. He shows aspects of the crime wave in urban South Africa, puts in a scene involving white neo-Nazis, is unflinching about drugs and police corruption, and gives the Ice Cube character a pointed line: "You can't fall in the same trap as the black Americans did in the seventies. They got free, and then they got high."

Ice Cube delivers this and other lines with a bluntness that is supposed to pass for a performance, but there's little sense here that he's playing a character—certainly not the "student of African literature and community volunteer" he's described as. He seems more like a tourist who has wandered into an action picture.

Much better are Ving Rhames and Elizabeth Hurley. Rhames has perfected the South African accent and brings a kind of easy charm to his role as a drug lord; he's a sadistic killer, but charming. (*Pulp Fiction* fans will enjoy the first view of him, which shows the back of his neck, this time without the bandage that caused so much discussion after the Tarantino movie. We see the scar the bandage was hiding.)

Hurley takes her generic role and makes it particular. We get a feel for her—rootless, careless, addicted to cocaine—and her reckless lifestyle. She's ditzy in the right way, and doesn't make the mistake of seeming too much at home in the action scenes (it's right that she'd fire at the ceiling in her big moment of gunplay).

Dangerous Ground seems to be an attempt to make an American-style action picture and sneak some South African stuff in sideways. That's a doomed approach. Hollywood does Hollywood so well that it's a mistake for overseas filmmakers to even try. Canada could have had a much healthier film industry if it hadn't tried to be a little Hollywood, and the films of Australia and England are thriving right now because they are local, particular, and about something other than canned action scenes.

Dante's Peak ★ ★ ½

PG-13, 112 m., 1997

Pierce Brosnan (Harry Dalton), Linda Hamilton (Rachel Wando), Jamie Renee Smith (Lauren Wando), Jeremy Foley (Graham Wando), Elizabeth Hoffman (Ruth), Charles Hallahan (Paul Dreyfus). Directed by Roger Donaldson and produced by Gale Anne Hurd and Joseph M. Singer. Screenplay by Leslie Bohem.

Dante's Peak is constructed about as skillfully as a disaster movie can be, and there were times when I found it working for me, sort of. But hasn't this genre pretty much been played out to the point of exhaustion? Once you know the premise (volcano, tornado, killer bees), you can guess the story line. Starting in this case with a volcano, we know there will be:

• Ominous portents of doom on a seemingly ordinary day, such as people being boiled alive in a hot springs, too many dead trees in the middle of summer, and alarming seismic activity.

• Everyday folks going about their business, in this case the Dante's Peak Pioneer Day Festival, at which the mayor (Linda Hamilton) accepts the town's *Money* magazine award as the "second best place to live in America."

• Arrival of scientists, including (a) hero scientist, played here by Pierce Brosnan, and (b) pooh-pooh scientist, played by Charles Hallahan, whose job is to dismiss the hero scientist's concerns and tell everyone there is no need for alarm.

• Inevitable subplot involving big corporation that plans to sink millions into the area, but may take its investment elsewhere if it hears rumors that Dante's Peak is about to blow.

• Establishment of friendship, leading to love affair, between hero scientist and town mayor, who comes equipped with a full kit of disaster movie accessories, including children, dog, and gray-haired mother-in-law who refuses to come down from her cabin on the mountainside.

• Mounting alarm, as hero scientist finds dead trees, dead squirrels, brown drinking water, and other early warnings of volcanic doom.

• Town meeting called to prepare for evacuation, but interrupted, of course, by a volcanic eruption.

• Elaborate special effects sequences as citizens flee the town while the mountain roars, ash falls from sky, melting snow causes rivers to rage out of control, a dam bursts, bridges collapse, shock waves flatten forests, etc.

• Gripping human drama involving hero scientist, town mayor, children, dog, and granny, and including flight by four-wheel vehicle, two-wheel vehicle, boat, and foot. Ingenious last-minute scheme to outwit volcanic destruction. (Query: Can a utility vehicle actually ford a river with its engine completely under water?)

• And finally the distribution of poetic justice, which means death of those who scoffed at volcano's fury, survival of those who took it seriously.

• A new dawn. Music swells.

Oh, and of course, the Obligatory Unrelated Opening Crisis, which is defined by *Ebert's Little Movie Glossary:* "In an action movie, the spectacular title sequence that never has anything to do with the rest of the story." It involves a close call the hero had four years earlier on the site of another volcano, and the emotional trauma he suffered there, which can only be repaired this time around.

Dante's Peak, written by Leslie Bohem and directed by Roger Donaldson, follows the disaster formula so faithfully that if you walk in while the movie is in progress, you can estimate how long the story has to run. That it is skillful is a tribute to the filmmakers. Roger Donaldson *(Species)* is a good director who pays attention to the human elements even in a fiction machine like *Dante's Peak,* and Gale Anne Hurd, the producer, is a specialist in action films *(Aliens, Alien Nation, The Abyss, Tremors, Terminator 2).* They orchestrate the special effects so that they look and feel real (mostly), and in Brosnan and Hamilton they have actors who play for realism and don't go over the top—never screaming, not even when molten lava sets their truck tires on fire. The sound track is especially effective.

Is it a case, for me, of simply being overfamiliar, right down to my bones, with the ways in which *Dante's Peak* is simply an old movie in new clothing? For a film like this to work, one must be caught up in it. But every time another familiar story element was trotted out (the gun-shy investors, the pooh-pooher, the dog), I was bungeed back to reality.

In one detail I was not disappointed. In my "Movie Answer Man" column there was a discussion of whether a man can outrun an explosive fireball. The conclusion was that it cannot be done in life, but can be done in the movies. A correspondent wrote me with news of a Jaguar that outran a shock wave from Mount St. Helens, while a hapless utility vehicle was fried. This led to much discussion (how far away were the two vehicles? etc.).

In *Dante's Peak,* Pierce Brosnan ominously informs Linda Hamilton, "If the mountain blows, the blast would get here in less than a minute." The mountain blows. We see the shock wave flatten zillions of pine trees, demolish homes and office buildings, etc. Then we see it rolling down the main street of the town, with the heroes trying to outrace it in a truck. I estimate the mountain to be ten miles from the town. If the blast can travel one mile in six seconds, which would be extremely conservative, then it can travel one village block in . . . but never mind. I'd rather think back on the more convincing moments in the movie, as when a volcanologist looks at his computer readout of the mountain's ominous portents and says, "She's just clearing her throat. She hasn't even begun to sing."

Dark City ★ ★ ★ ★

R, 103 m., 1998

Rufus Sewell (John Murdoch), William Hurt (Inspector Bumstead), Kiefer Sutherland (Dr. Daniel Schreber), Jennifer Connelly (Emma Murdoch), Richard O'Brien (Mr. Hand), Ian Richardson (Mr. Book), Bruce Spence (Mr. Wall), Colin Friels (Walenski). Directed by Alex Proyas and produced by Andrew Mason and Proyas. Screenplay by Proyas, Lem Dobbs, and David S. Goyer.

Dark City by Alex Proyas is a great visionary achievement, a film so original and exciting it stirred my imagination like Lang's *Metropolis* or Kubrick's *2001.* If it is true, as the German director Werner Herzog believes, that we live in an age starved of new images, then *Dark City* is a film to nourish us. Not a story so much as an experience, it is a triumph of art direction, set design, cinematography, special effects—and imagination.

Like *Blade Runner,* it imagines a city of the

future. But while *Blade Runner* extended existing trends, *Dark City* leaps into the unknown. Its vast *noir* metropolis seems to exist in an alternative time line, with elements of our present and past combined with visions from a futuristic comic book. Like the first *Batman*, it presents a city of night and shadows, but it goes far beyond *Batman* in a richness of ominous, stylized sets, streets, skylines, and cityscapes. For once a movie city is the equal of any city we could picture in our minds; this is the city *The Fifth Element* teased us with, without coming through.

The story combines science fiction with *film noir*—in more ways than we realize and more surprising ways than I will reveal. Its villains, in their homburgs and flapping overcoats, look like a nightmare inspired by the thugs in *M*, but their pale faces would look more at home in *The Cabinet of Dr. Caligari*—and, frighteningly, one of them is a child. They are the Strangers, shape-changers from another solar system, and we are told they came to Earth when their own world was dying. (They create, in the process, the first space vessel since *Star Wars* that is newly conceived—not a clone of that looming mechanical vision.)

They inhabit a city of rumbling, elevated, streamlined trains, dank flophouses, scurrying crowds, and store windows that owe something to Edward Hopper's *Night Owls*. In this city lives John Murdoch (Rufus Sewell), who awakens in a strange bathtub beneath a swinging ceiling lamp, to blood, fear, and guilt. The telephone rings; it is Dr. Schreber (Kiefer Sutherland), gasping out two or three words at a time, as if the need to speak is all that gives him breath. He warns Murdoch to flee, and indeed three Strangers are at the end of the corridor and coming for him.

The film will be the story of Murdoch's flight into the mean streets, and his gradual discovery of the nature of the city and the Strangers. Like many science-fiction heroes, he has a memory shattered into pieces that do not fit. But he remembers the woman he loves, or loved—his wife, Emma (Jennifer Connelly), who is a torch singer with sad eyes and wounded lips. And he remembers . . . Shell Beach? Where was that? He sees it on a billboard and old longings stir.

There is a detective after him, Inspector Bumstead (William Hurt). Murdoch is wanted in connection with the murders of six prostitutes. Did he kill them? Like the hero of Kafka's *The Trial*, he feels so paranoid he hardly knows. Rufus Sewell plays Murdoch like a man caught in a pinball machine, flipped back into danger every time it looks like the game is over.

The story has familiar elements made new. Even the hard-boiled detective, his eyes shaded by the brim of his fedora, seems less like a figure from *film noir* than like a projection of an alien idea of *noir*. Proyas and his co-screenwriters, Lem Dobbs and David S. Goyer, use dream logic to pursue their hero through the mystery of his own life. Along the way, Murdoch discovers that he alone, among humans, has the power of the Strangers—an ability to use his mind in order to shape the physical universe. (This power is expressed in the film as a sort of transparent shimmering projection aimed from Murdoch's forehead into the world, and as klutzy as that sounds, I found myself enjoying its very audacity: What else would mind power look like?)

Murdoch's problem is that he has no way of knowing if his memories are real, if his past actually happened, if the woman he loves ever existed. Those who offer to help him cannot be trusted. Even his enemies may not be real. The movie teasingly explores the question that babies first ask in peek-a-boo: When I can't see you, are you there? It's through that game that we learn the difference between ourselves and others. But what if *we're* not there, either?

The movie is a glorious marriage of existential dread and slam-bang action. Toward the end, there is a thrilling apocalyptic battle that nearly destroys the city, and I scribbled in my notes: "For once, a sequence where the fire and explosions really work, and don't play just as effects." Proyas and his cinematographer, Dariusz Wolski, capture the kinetic energy of great comic books; their framing and foreshortening and tilt shots and distorting lenses shake the images and splash them on the screen, and it's not "action" but more like action painting.

Proyas was the director of *The Crow* (1994), the visually inspired film that was almost doomed when its star, Brandon Lee, was killed in an accident. I called that film "the best version of a comic book universe I've seen," but *Dark City* is miles beyond it. Proyas's background was in music videos, usually an ominous sign, but not here: His film shows the obsessive concentration on visual detail that's the hallmark of directors who make films that are short and expensive. There's such a wealth on the screen, such an overflowing of imagination and energy, of sets and effects. Often in f/x movies the camera doesn't feel free because it must remain within the confines of what has been created for it to see. Here we feel there's no limit.

Is the film for teenage boys and comic book fans? Not at all, although that's the marketing pitch. It's for anyone who still has a sense of wonder and a feeling for great visual style. This is a film containing ideas and true poignancy, a story that has been all thought out and has surprises right up to the end. It's romantic and exhilarating. Watching it, I thought of the last dozen films I'd seen and realized they were all essentially about people standing around and talking to one another. *Dark City* has been created and imagined as a new visual *place* for us to inhabit. It adds treasure to our notions of what can be imagined. ☞

The Daytrippers ★★

NO MPAA RATING, 87 m., 1997

Hope Davis (Eliza D'Amico), Stanley Tucci (Louis, Eliza's Husband), Parker Posey (Jo Malone, Eliza's Sister), Liev Schreiber (Carl, Jo's Boyfriend), Anne Meara (Rita, Eliza's Mother), Pat McNamara (Jim, Eliza's Father), Campbell Scott (Eddie, the Author), Marcia Gay Harden (Libby). Directed by Greg Mottola and produced by Nancy Tenenbaum and Steven Soderbergh. Screenplay by Mottola.

Greg Mottola's *The Daytrippers* begins with a wife who is cleaning house and finds what seems to be a love note to her husband. She is concerned but not hysterical. She takes the note over to her parents' house, and it's her mother who goes ballistic. Soon the entire family has packed into the family station wagon for a journey into New York to track down the husband and confront him. We are taken along for the ride, which is sour, contrived, and whiny.

The problem is with the mother, Rita (Anne Meara). She's an insufferable scold, and since she's onscreen or nearby for almost the entire film, her presence becomes unbearable. It has been said that you should never marry anyone you are not prepared to take a three-day bus trip with. I wouldn't even get into a cab with Rita.

Her daughter Eliza (Hope Davis), who found the note in the first scene, is a good deal saner. So is Eliza's sister Jo (Parker Posey), who is engaged to Carl (Liev Schreiber). Jo and Carl are visiting for Thanksgiving; Carl likes to quote metaphysical poets at breakfast, and is working on a novel about a man with the head of a dog. These four characters pile into a car driven by the dad, Jim (Pat McNamara), who has been married to Rita for years and can therefore be forgiven for almost anything.

The outcome of this journey is going to be predictable and disappointing. Mottola does his best to make the trip itself enjoyable. The five people, jammed unconvincingly in the station wagon on an implausible mission, talk and bicker and put themselves at the mercy of the mother's whims. They stake out the apartment of the husband's suspected mistress, they try to follow him when he comes out, they go to his office and find he's suspiciously taken a day off, they find themselves invited into the house of a complete stranger, and eventually, that evening, they stake out a book party where he's expected to appear.

The husband (Stanley Tucci, from *Big Night*) is a book editor. The party, like some of the other scenes, plays more like a self-contained opportunity for satire than like part of the overall story. Brief appearances by Campbell Scott (also from *Big Night*) and Marcia Gay Harden leave us wondering if their characters might not have made a more promising film.

I can see what Mottola is trying to do, and I'm happy that he tried. He uses the trip into town as an excuse to string together character bits and the kind of unsprung, liberated dialogue that Tarantino used in *Pulp Fiction* and Kevin Smith has fun with in *Chasing Amy*. His film is intended to be liberated from plot; the device of the mission into town is so broad and obvious we can take it ironically, and just enjoy the strange characters and their colorful speech.

That would work if it were not for the Anne Meara character. And here I must be precise. I do not mean to criticize Meara herself. She is, almost by definition, superb at her assignment here, which is to create an insufferable mother. The film's problem is that she does it so well. She nags and whines and delivers little zingers and pushes the buttons of her loved ones so effectively that *The Daytrippers* could have raised a cheer from the audience simply by dumping her on the roadside.

As for the film's surprise ending: I was a little offended by how pat it was, how it expected us to accept it as the wrap-up of what went before. The movie shows a talent at writing characters and dialogue, but it doesn't really seem to have a purpose for being. The one character we do care deeply about, unfortunately, is the one we can't stand.

Deceiver ★★

R, 102 m., 1998

Chris Penn (Braxton), Ellen Burstyn (Mook), Tim Roth (Wayland), Renee Zellweger (Elizabeth), Michael Rooker (Kennesaw), Rosanna Arquette (Mrs. Kennesaw). Directed by Josh Pate and Jonas Pate and produced by Peter Glatzer. Screenplay by Josh Pate and Jonas Pate.

Deceiver is a Chinese box of a movie, in which we learn less and less about more and more. It's centered in a police interrogation room, where a rich kid undergoes a lie detector test in connection with the murder of a prostitute. Did he do it? At first it seems he did. Then he turns the tables on the two cops running the polygraph exam, and by the end of the film everyone is a suspect.

Tim Roth stars as Wayland, a Princeton grad and the son of a textile magnate, but currently unemployed. There's no doubt he knew the prostitute, named Elizabeth (Renee Zellweger, from *Jerry Maguire*): He even took her to a black-tie party at his parents' home, and got disowned in the process. But did he cut her into pieces and distribute her throughout Charleston, South Carolina?

The cops are Braxton (Chris Penn) and Kennesaw (Michael Rooker). Their methods are a little crude; they seem intent on helping Wayland fail the test with intimidation and hints he isn't doing too well. Wayland responds with all the cockiness and self-assurance of a man who knows he's not so much a suspect as a character in a movie, taunting the cops with inside information about their private lives.

Deceiver has similarities to *Usual Suspects* in the way it coils around its central facts, looking at them first one way and then another. It also has a less obvious parallel with Quentin Tarantino's practice of working arcane knowledge into the dialogue of his characters. Carefully polished little set-pieces are spotted through the film; the action stops for well-informed discussions about Vincent van Gogh, the dangers of absinthe, the symptoms of epilepsy, and the relative intelligence of the two cops.

There wasn't much I could believe. The movie is basically about behavior—about acting, rather than about characters. The three leads and some supporting characters get big scenes and angry speeches, and the plot manufactures big moments of crisis and then slips away from them. It feels more like a play than a movie.

One of the ways it undermines its characters is by upstaging them with the plot. We get several theories about the death of the prostitute, and lots of flashbacks in which Wayland's tortured childhood offers explanations for actions he may or may not have taken. Facts are established, only to be shot down. Having seen the film twice, I am prepared to accept that its paradoxes are all answered and its puzzles solved, although unless you look closely and remember the face of an ambulance driver, you may miss the explanation for one of the big surprises.

The thing is, even after you figure it all out, a movie like this offers few rewards. It's well acted, and you can admire that on a technical level, but the plot is such a puzzle it shuts us out: How can we care about events that the movie itself constantly undercuts and revises? By the time the final twist comes along, it's as if we've seen a clever show in which the only purpose, alas, was to demonstrate the cleverness.

Deconstructing Harry ★ ★ ★ ½

R, 95 m., 1997

Woody Allen (Harry Block), Kirstie Alley (Joan), Richard Benjamin (Ken), Hazelle Goodman (Cookie), Eric Bogosian (Burt), Billy Crystal (Larry), Judy Davis (Lucy), Mariel Hemingway (Beth Kramer), Julie Kavner (Grace), Elisabeth Shue (Fay). Directed by Woody Allen and produced by Jean Doumanian. Screenplay by Allen.

Once a year, like clockwork, Woody Allen writes, directs, and usually stars in exactly the film he feels like making. He works on budgets that make this possible—and just as well, given the mugging he's received from critics who think he shouldn't have made *Deconstructing Harry.*

His new movie is vulgar, smutty, profane, self-hating, self-justifying, self-involved, tasteless, bankrupt, and desperate, I've read. Even the kinder reviews turn sour. Here's a quote from David Edelstein of *Slate:* "The result is more rambunctious—and more fun—than any movie he has made in years. What puzzles me is why it still adds up to something so anemic and coldly distasteful." When a film makes me laugh and then I learn that it's vulgar, I'm reminded of Mel Brooks's defense of *The Producers:* "My film rises below vulgarity." That's the *Deconstructing Harry* defense; there is hardly a criticism that can be thrown at Allen that he hasn't already thrown at himself (or his alter ego) in the film.

This is in many ways his most revealing film, his most painful, and if it also contains more than his usual quotient of big laughs. What was it the man said? "We laugh, that we may not cry."

The film stars Allen as Harry Block, a novelist whose material vaguely suggests Philip Roth. Both names represent aspects of the character, who is blocked, and who is seen by many (and sometimes by himself) as Satan. Harry is under attack. His sister-in-law (Judy Davis) cries out that his new book "is totally about us"—about the two of them, and the affair she thought he would keep a secret. He's told he "can't function in life, only in art." We get the sense that many of the lines assigned to characters were first shouted at Allen himself; there's one line in particular that I'm willing to bet originally came from someone close to him: "This little sewer of an apartment where you take everyone's suffering and turn it into gold."

Harry is portrayed as a user and borrower: He uses people, and then borrows the story of how he used them, and uses that too. The movie cuts between real time and fictionalized episodes from his books, in which Harry's clones and surrogates indulge their appetites when and as they can.

Harry himself is a philandering cheater who's been through three wives and six psychiatrists (the Kirstie Alley character made it into both categories). All of this is done in the blackout style of some of Allen's earlier films; unlike the smoother, more carefully constructed recent films, *Deconstructing Harry* is built revue-style, and there's even a fantasy sequence in hell. As in his early films, Allen includes comic material about Judaism, and there are caricatures and stereotypes that may offend, but to those who would call him a self-hating Jew, Allen has the answer right there on the screen: "You're a self-hating Jew!" Harry is told.

The fact is, he's a self-hater, period. He's critical of every possible aspect of himself. And although he defends some of his excesses as necessary to an artist in the creative process, he doesn't let himself off that hook, either: Harry's art, in the film, is seen as juvenile, manipulative, derivative, vulgar, and sometimes cornball. (That it is also funny is the redeeming grace.)

Allen has borrowed his basic story line from *Wild Strawberries,* the 1957 film by his hero, Ingmar Bergman, about an old professor who revisits scenes and memories from a long life as he returns to his alma mater to be honored. In the Harry Block version, the school expelled him and wants to make amends. But he can't get anyone to go along with him on the trip—not a single relative, friend, ex-lover, or wife is interested. He eventually hires a black hooker named Cookie (Hazelle Goodman) to accompany him; like Mira Sorvino's hooker in *Mighty Aphrodite,* she's useful mostly for her nonsexual functions, such as accepting and liking him. (As the trip progresses, he also picks up a friend, played by Bob Balaban, and then kidnaps his son from school to take him along too.)

The film has a richness of comic bits, of which the most original involves Robin Williams as an actor who is concerned that he's losing his focus—and is (he's out of focus in every scene). There's a visit to hell to see the devil (Billy Crystal, who also plays the friend who has stolen Harry's latest mistress). And a fantasy sequence in which a wife finds that her husband has a few little secrets to share, which build slowly: He was married before. And had children. And killed them all. And ate them. The cannibal husband ends with a plea for understanding: "If I tell you why I did it, do you promise not to noodge me?"

Essentially, this is Allen's plea throughout the film. His private life has spilled untidily into the news in the last couple of years; enshrined as a cultural hero, he is now in the uncomfortable position of feeling like a defendant. He explains, he excuses, he evades, and his critics are not satisfied: They want less, or more, or otherwise. But no single Woody Allen film ever sums up everything, or could, and what is fascinating is to watch him, year after year, making the most personal of films, and hiding himself in plain view.

Deep Blue Sea ★ ★ ★

R, 106 m., 1999

Saffron Burrows (Dr. Susan McAlester), Samuel L. Jackson (Russell Franklin), Thomas Jane (Carter Blake), LL Cool J/James Todd Smith ("Preacher" Dudley), Jacqueline McKenzie (Janice Higgins), Michael Rapaport (Tom Scoggins), Stellan Skarsgard (Jim Whitlock). Directed by Renny Harlin and produced by Akiva Goldsman, Tony Ludwig, and Alan Riche. Screenplay by Duncan Kennedy, Donna Powers, and Wayne Powers.

Sharks, it is said, are all teeth and muscle, and have been doing two things very efficiently for millions of years: moving and eating. *Deep Blue Sea* resembles a shark. It moves ceaselessly, and someone gets eaten from time to time.

The movie is a skillful thriller by Renny Harlin, who made *Die Hard 2* and *Cutthroat Island*, and here assembles a neat package of terror, sharks, and special effects. That isn't as easy as it sounds. After slogging through the predictability of countless would-be action thrillers, I admired the sheer professionalism of this one, which doesn't transcend its genre, but at least honors it.

The premise: A scientist (Saffron Burrows) has devised a way to use the brain tissue of sharks to cultivate a substance that might be useful in fighting Alzheimer's. A big corporation underwrites the research and maintains a deep-sea station with shark corrals and underwater living and research areas. One of the sharks escapes and tries to eat a boat. The head of the corporation (Samuel L. Jackson) pays a visit to the station and meets the other key characters, including a shark wrangler (Thomas Jane), a Bible-quoting cook (LL Cool J), and crew members including Jacqueline McKenzie, Michael Rapaport, Stellan Skarsgard, and Aida Turturro.

Some of these characters turn up on the shark menu, although the timing and manner of their ingestion is often so unexpected that I'll say nothing more. The shark attacks are intercut with a desperate escape plot, after storms and explosions incapacitate the station and the characters are trapped below the waterline in areas threatened by water pressure and sharks.

Common sense, of course, has nothing to do with the screenplay, ingeniously devised by Duncan Kennedy, Donna Powers, and Wayne Powers. Its premise is that the sharks' brains have been increased fivefold, with a corresponding increase in intelligence, so that the sharks can figure out the layout of the station and work together to batter down watertight doors, swim down corridors, etc. The most obvious problem with this premise is that just because a shark is smarter doesn't mean it has more information; the smartest shark in the world would only know how to be a smart shark if it had a way to learn.

But never mind. The sharks exist in *Deep Blue Sea* as the McGuffins, creating situations that require the characters to think fast, fight bravely, improvise their way out of tight spots, dangle between flames and teeth, etc. There's a little perfunctory scientist-bashing, but not much (the Burrows character violates ethical guidelines, but, hey, it's for a good cause—fighting Alzheimer's).

Jackson is more or less the straight man in

the cast. Jane handles most of the action duties, convincingly if, of course, not plausibly (in other words, he looks like he can hold his breath underwater indefinitely even though we know it's impossible). The surprise in the cast is LL Cool J, who has a kind of Cuba Gooding Jr. quality as a cook whose best friend is a parrot, and who hides from the shark in an oven, which the shark cleverly sets to five hundred degrees.

The movie is essentially one well-done action sequence after another. It involves all the usual situations in movies where fierce creatures chase victims through the bowels of a ship/space craft/building (the *Alien* movies, *Deep Rising,* etc). It's just that it does them well. It doesn't linger on the special effects (some of the sharks look like cartoons), but it knows how to use timing, suspense, quick movement, and surprise.

Especially surprise. There is a moment in this movie when something happens that is completely unexpected, and it's over in a flash—a done deal—and the audience laughs in delight because it was so successfully surprised. In a genre where a lot of movies are retreads of the predictable, *Deep Blue Sea* keeps you guessing.

Deep Crimson ★ ★ ★ ½

NO MPAA RATING, 109 m., 1998

Regina Orozco (Coral Fabre), Daniel Gimenez Cacho (Nicolas Estrella), Marisa Paredes (Irene Gallardo), Patricia Reyes Espindola (The Widow Ruelas), Julieta Egurrola (Juanita Norton), Rosa Furman (The Widow Morrison), Veronica Merchant (Rebecca San Pedro), Sherlyn Gonzales (Teresa). Directed by Arturo Ripstein and produced by Miguel Necoechea and Paolo Barbachano. Screenplay by Paz Alicia Garciadiego.

Deep Crimson, macabre and perverse, is based on a true story from the 1940s, about the "Lonely Hearts Killers"—a couple who posed as brother and sister, victimized lonely widows, and then killed them. Their story was told in a 1970 American film, *The Honeymoon Killers,* but now here is Arturo Ripstein with a Mexican version that combines black comedy with horrifying heartlessness. There were walkouts when I saw the film; those who stay will not easily forget it.

The movie opens like a dark comedy by Pedro Almodovar or Luis Buñuel (who Ripstein once worked for as an assistant director). We meet Coral Fabre, played by the opera singer Regina Orozco; she is a sometime embalmer, now caring for an old man and raising two children haphazardly. My diagnosis: hysteria and manic-depression. She answers a lonely hearts' ad from a "Charles Boyer type," and soon meets Nicolas Estrella (Daniel Gimenez Cacho), a vain, bald gigolo who spends hours adjusting his hairpiece before putting on his trench coat, snapping the brim of his fedora, and sailing out to defraud lonely women.

She has sent him a picture of herself when slim. She is fat. "I lose weight when I want to," she tells him. "How lucky to be able to control your body like that!" he says, before trying to flee. She begs him to stay, blaming his distaste on the smell of formaldehyde from her undertaking duties. "I've never been with a gentleman," she weeps. "Do it to me. Just do it—as a favor!" He does, but not as a favor; as she sleeps, he steals the money from her purse and creeps out.

But Coral has seen him from beneath lowered lids. The next day she arrives at Nicolas's apartment with her two children in tow. "I saw you robbing me," she tells him. "Maybe you were charging for excess fat. I came to stay with you. We're made for each other." He demurs, and so she takes decisive action: dumps her kids at an orphanage, enters his apartment when he's not there, reads his phony letters to lonely hearts victims, and when he returns offers him a partnership. They'll pose as brother and sister, and she'll select the victims.

Nicolas, who is as stupid as he is vain, is flattered. ("You gave up your kids for me! Nobody's ever done anything like that before.") Soon they are choosing their victims, but there's a hitch: Coral is not content to simply defraud and rob them. When she eavesdrops as Nicolas makes love to them, or even talks sweet, she grows jealous, and soon they're leaving a trail of corpses behind.

Deep Crimson sinks easily into the swamp of human depravity. Coral and Nicolas are demented even when apart; together, they create an amoral composite personality, a world in which soap opera clichés about love are used to excuse unspeakable sins. Ripstein leads us into this world with the seduction of deadpan black humor, and then pulls out the rug in the final scenes, which are truly horrific. As a study in abnormal psychology, *Deep Crimson* would make his master, Buñuel, proud.

The film has a strong effect on its viewers. When I saw it, there was a scene of harm toward a child that sent many audience members racing for the exits. Others feel betrayed because they laughed along with the earlier scenes, only to be blindsided by the cruelty and dark despair of the conclusion.

One thing that engages some viewers is Coral's weight. It is an unspoken rule of female killers in movies that they be thin. "While Coral's plight calls out for some sympathy from the audience, her loathsome obesity prevents us from commiseration," writes Harvey Karten, an Internet critic. Yet here is Ruthe Stein from the *San Francisco Chronicle*, who cites the slender killers played by Faye Dunaway and Linda Fiorentino and then adds of this one: "Anyone in Hollywood who thinks large women can't be sexy should get a load of her."

This disagreement is revealing. Karten is obviously a candidate for urgent briefings by the Fat Acceptance lobby. Stein may find Coral sexy for politically correct reasons, but Nicolas certainly doesn't. The film isn't about appearances at all, but about the way Coral and Nicolas see what they need to see. She sees not a pathetic, toupee-wearing fraud, but Charles Boyer. He sees not a fat embalmer who has dumped her children, but a woman who would make any sacrifice for him. Their mutual weakness is vanity: She can feel she has Charles Boyer as a lover, and he can feel that she sees Boyer when she looks at him. As long as these mutual fantasies are reinforced, the deaths of a few unfortunate widows can be excused.

Ripstein, not well-known in America, is Mexico's most respected director, and in *Deep Crimson* he creates the kind of dangerous film that Americans made more freely in the 1970s (when *The Honeymoon Killers* got reviews similar to this one's). He is unafraid of offending his audience. He is going for hard truths, and approaching them through humor and a willingness to offend. His purpose is to undercut the way that movies glamorize legendary criminals like Coral and Nicolas. Anyone who thought *Bonnie and Clyde* romanticized its killers is likely to feel that the heroes of *Deep Crimson* get what they have coming, without mercy.

The Deep End of the Ocean ★ ½

PG-13, 108 m., 1999

Michelle Pfeiffer (Beth), Treat Williams (Pat), Whoopi Goldberg (Candy), Jonathan Jackson (Vincent [sixteen]), John Kapelos (George Karras), Cory Buck (Vincent [seven]), Ryan Merriman (Sam). Directed by Ulu Grosbard and produced by Kate Guinzberg and Steve Nicolaides. Screenplay by Stephen Schiff, based on the novel by Jacquelyn Mitchard.

Ulu Grosbard's *The Deep End of the Ocean* is a painfully stolid movie that lumbers past emotional issues like a wrestler in a cafeteria line, putting a little of everything on its plate. It provides big roles for Michelle Pfeiffer and Treat Williams, but doesn't provide them with the screenplay support they need; the result is awkwardness when characters express emotions the audience doesn't share.

(There's no way I can discuss the failure of the movie without revealing details, so if you plan to see it, I'd suggest reading this review later to preserve the surprises.)

Pfeiffer and Williams play the parents of a three-year-old boy who is kidnapped from a hotel lobby during a class reunion. They are befriended by a detective (Whoopi Goldberg), who reveals she is gay, for no other reason than to provide a politically correct line, since her sexuality is utterly irrelevant to the story. Nine years pass, they move to Chicago, and then the boy is found again—mowing their lawn. He was kidnapped by a neurotic classmate of Pfeiffer's, who later married and then committed suicide. So the child has been raised by an adoptive father who of course had no idea he was kidnapped.

The film's most crippling failure is in the treatment of the father, who is played with gentleness and great strength by John Kapelos. The audience knows, but the movie apparently doesn't, that the real drama in the later stages is in the father's story. We suffer with Pfeiffer and Williams as they grieve their lost child and fight over the blame, but after nine years their life has fallen into a rhythm, and it is the other family that is ripped apart when the boy's true identity is revealed.

Consider. You raise a son from infancy in a happy household, only to have him snatched away from you, just like that. (The movie doesn't even supply the usual hearings, social workers, etc.) There is a scene at the other home, with Kapelos protesting his innocence to dozens of cops, and then an awkward scene in which the story of the kidnapping is explained in snappy dialogue. (This scene feels suspiciously as if it were slapped in as a replacement for cuts.)

And then . . . well, the boy is back with his birth family eating pizza. And then there is a scene at night, with an older brother curling up on the floor next to his bed. And then the family goes to church, where the priest welcomes him back to his birth family—with no mention of or reference to the adoptive father, who is sitting in another pew. And then a scene in the Italian restaurant that Williams owns; the kid is recruited for an Italian dance, but prefers a Greek dance he learned from his father.

All of this time, all of these scenes are undermined by our concern for the father. How does he feel? The film eventually allots him one brief but telling speech ("This was my wife and my son. This wasn't some lunatic and the boy she kidnapped. Not to me.") The weight it is given is suggested by Treat Williams's question to his wife after the man's visit: "So, what happened?"

The boy misses his adoptive father and the only home he has ever known, but he's almost too articulate about it ("[My mom] didn't mean to be sick. So why am I being punished?"). Oh, there's a scene where the boy and his new family fight over where he's going to spend Thanksgiving. But we never see the outcome. Where *did* he spend Thanksgiving and how did it go? And the film's ending, when it comes, feels unconvincingly neat. King Solomon could not have divided the child with more skill.

The movie's background details feel shoveled in for effect, instead of growing organically from the story. Consider that Treat Williams is said to run an Italian restaurant. The character talks, acts, and moves like no Italian-American restaurant owner I have ever encountered. He projects the aura of a Kinko's franchisee. There is a scene on a Saturday morning where the guy is in his workshop building *birdhouses,* for cripe's sake. (These are Screenplay Birdhouses—provided by the prop department to give him something to hold in his hands.) Eventually he says, "I've got to go to work." At noon on a Saturday? Any Italian restaurant owner worth his oregano would have been up before dawn, visiting the produce market and supervising the marinara.

Such lapses wouldn't be fatal in a better movie, but *The Deep End of the Ocean* is unconvincing from start to finish. One can see that Pfeiffer's performance would have adorned a better screenplay, and that Jonathan Jackson, as the family's older son, has a convincing screen presence. But the film curiously seems to be long and slow, and yet missing large chunks of the story (it runs 108 minutes, but early press material clocks it at 148). My best guess: It was filmed before it was adequately written.

Deep Impact ★ ★ ½

PG-13, 115 m., 1998

Robert Duvall (Spurgeon Tanner), Tea Leoni (Jenny Lerner), Morgan Freeman (President Beck), Elijah Wood (Leo Biederman), Vanessa Redgrave (Robin Lerner), Maximilian Schell (Jason Lerner), Leelee Sobieski (Sarah Hotchner), James Cromwell (Alan Rittenhouse). Directed by Mimi Leder and produced by Richard D. Zanuck and David Brown. Screenplay by Michael Tolkin and Bruce Joel Rubin.

Early in *Deep Impact* we learn that a comet "the size of Mt. Everest" is on a collision course for Earth. There would seem to be two possible outcomes: (1) The comet hits Earth, destroying it, or (2) the comet does not hit Earth, in which case humanity is spared but the audience is denied the sight of lots of special effects. In the first scenario you don't get the obligatory happy ending, and in the second one everyone leaves feeling cheated.

Most doomsday movies avoid this choice by prudently choosing less than apocalyptic events. A volcano, a twister, or a tidal wave can supply lots of terrifying special effects and still leave a lot of people standing. But *Deep Impact* seems to back itself into a corner, and maybe that's why the producers hired not one but two of the brightest writers in Hollywood to work on the project: Bruce Joel Rubin *(Ghost)* and Michael Tolkin *(The Player)*. Together, they've figured out how to have their cake and eat it too.

How do they do this? I would not dream of revealing their inspiration, although you may be able to figure it out yourself. Meanwhile, you can enjoy the way they create little flashes of wit in the dialogue, which enlivens what is, after all, a formula disaster movie. What's the formula? Assorted archetypal characters are introduced, they're assigned personal problems, and the story cuts between them as the moment of disaster grows closer. I always think it's more interesting if they know from the start that there's a big problem; I get tired of scenes in which they live blissfully unaware of the catastrophe unfolding beneath their feet, or above their heads, or wherever.

Deep Impact begins with the obligatory opening precatastrophe, in this case a runaway semi that mows down a Jeep and kills the astronomer who is bringing news of the approaching comet. (The other movie I saw on the same day, *The Horse Whisperer,* also opened with a runaway semi, and indeed I cannot recall a single movie in which a semi on a two-lane road does not careen out of control.)

Then there's a little ritual media-bashing; Tea Leoni plays a reporter for MSNBC who suspects there's more to the story of a cabinet official's resignation. She accuses him of having an affair with a woman named "Ellie," and he gets to say, "I know you're just a reporter, but you used to be a person." (The approved media response to this is, "Look who's talking! A cabinet member!")

Soon she discovers her error; he is resigning not because of Ellie but because of an E.L.E., which is jargon for "Extinction Level Event." He wants to spend more time with his family, and has stocked a yacht with dozens of cases of vitamin-rich Sustain. He must not have been invited to the briefing where it was explained that all surface life would be destroyed by the comet, or the other briefing about the 1,000-foot-tall tidal wave. My guess is the president wanted him out of the cabinet.

The president, played convincingly by Morgan Freeman, goes on TV to break the bad news to the world, and talks of the *Messiah* Project, which will send a manned U.S.-Russian spacecraft to plant nuclear bombs in the comet and blow it up. We meet the *Messiah* crew members, including old Spurgeon Tanner (Robert Duvall), called out of retirement because he once landed on the Moon and might be able to land on the comet.

The younger crew members resent him, we are told, although dissension onboard is never followed up on. The veteran has a nice line about the youngsters: "They're not scared of dying. They're just scared of looking bad on TV." There's another good line at the high school assembly where the kid (Elijah Wood) who codiscovered the comet is honored. A friend tells him, "You're gonna have a lot more sex starting now. Famous people always get more sex." And I liked a line from late in the movie when one hero tells another, "Look on the bright side. We'll all have high schools named for us."

But the movie as a whole is pretty routine. There's a laborious subplot in which Tea Leoni resents her father (Maximilian Schell) for divorcing her mother (Vanessa Redgrave) and marrying a bimbo, and while Redgrave brings a nice sad quality to her scenes, the rest of the subplot plays out suspiciously like a scheme to place two humans in front of a big special effect. There are also some fairly unconvincing scenes in which millions of people try to flee from a city, and all of them are trapped in gridlock except, of course, for the two who are required by the plot to get somewhere fast.

Whether Earth is saved or doomed or neither, I will leave you to discover for yourself. I personally found it easier to believe that Earth could survive this doomsday scenario than that the *Messiah* spacecraft could fly at thousands of miles an hour through the comet's tail, which contains rocks the size of two-car garages, without serious consequences. On the disaster epic scale, on which *Titanic* gets four stars and *Volcano* gets one and a half, *Deep Impact* gets two and a half—the same as *Dante's Peak*, even though it lacks a dog that gets left behind.

Deep Rising ★ ½

R, 106 m., 1998

Treat Williams (Finnegan), Famke Janssen (Trillian), Anthony Heald (Carlton), Kevin J. O'Connor (Pantucci), Wes Studi (Hanover), Derrick O'Connor (Captain), Jason Flemyng (Mulligan), Cliff Curtis (Mamooli). Directed by Stephen Sommers and produced by Laurence Mark and John Baldecchi. Screenplay by Sommers.

Deep Rising could also have been titled *Eat the Titanic!* It's about a giant squid that attacks a luxurious cruise ship in the South China Sea. Like all movie monsters, the squid has perfect timing and always bursts into the frame just when the characters are least expecting it. And it has an unsavory way of dining. "They eat you?" asks one of the survivors. "No—they drink you."

The mechanics for a movie like this were well established in the *Alien* pictures, and *Deep Rising* clones the same formula: Survivors are trapped inside giant vessel. Creature finds its way around air ducts and sewer pipes, popping out of shaft openings to gobble up minor characters (the first victim is sucked down the toilet).

D'ya think they have meetings out in Hollywood to share the latest twists? I've been seeing the same gimmicks in a lot of different pictures. Evidence: No sooner does the snake in *Anaconda* release a slimy survivor from its innards than the squid in *Deep Rising* does the same thing. No sooner is there an indoor Jet Ski chase in *Hard Rain* than there's one in *Deep Rising*. No sooner does a horrible monster crawl out of the air ducts in *Alien Resurrection* than it does so in *Deep Rising*. And last week I saw *Phantoms*, which was sort of *Deep Rising Meets Alien and Goes West*. In that one, the creature emerged from the depths of the earth rather than the sea, but had the same nasty practice of living behind piles of undigested remains.

An effort has been made by Stephen Sommers, writer-director of *Deep Rising*, to add humor to his story, although not even the presence of Leslie Nielsen could help this picture. The hero, Treat Williams, is a freelance power cruiser skipper who hires his craft out to a gang of vile and reprehensible bad guys, led by Wes Studi. They want to hijack a new casino ship on its maiden voyage. The owner of the ship (Anthony Heald) makes several speeches boasting about how stable it is; it can stay level in the water even during a raging tempest. I wonder if those speeches were inserted after the filmmakers realized how phony their special effects look. Every time we see the ship, it's absolutely immobile in the midst of churning waves.

No matter; the creature from the deep attacks the ship, and by the time Williams delivers the pirates, it seems to be deserted. All except for the evil owner, of course, and also a jewel thief (Famke Janssen) who was locked in the brig and survived the carnage.

A movie like this depends much upon the appearance of the monster, which has been designed by f/x wizard Rob Bottin. There is a vast evil squid head, and lots of tentacles (which seem to have minds of their own, and lots of mouths with many teeth). So vicious is the squid, indeed, that only the cynical will ask how it can survive for long periods out of water, or how and why it emits its piercing howl, which goes reverberating through the air shafts.

There's comic relief from Williams's engine room man, Pantucci (Kevin J. O'Connor), who plays the Donald O'Connor role and is always wisecracking in the face of adversity. And an effective supporting performance by Djimon Hounsou, as one of the more fanatic members of the pirate gang (he played Cinque in *Amistad*, and shows a powerful screen presence once again, although on the whole I'll bet he wishes the giant squid movie had come out *before* the Spielberg film).

Bemusing, how much money and effort goes into the making of a movie like this, and how little thought. It's months of hard work—for what? The movie is essentially an

Alien clone with a fresh paint job. You know something's wrong when a fearsome tentacle rears up out of the water and opens its mouth, and there are lots of little tentacles inside with their own ugly mouths, all filled with nasty teeth, and all you can think is, been there, seen that.

Deja Vu ★ ★ ★ ½

PG-13, 116 m., 1998

Victoria Foyt (Dana), Vanessa Redgrave (Skelly), Stephen Dillane (Sean), Michael Brandon (Alex), Glynis Barber (Claire), Noel Harrison (John Stoner), Anna Massey (Fern Stoner). Directed by Henry Jaglom and produced by John Goldstone. Screenplay by Jaglom and Victoria Foyt.

We all look for love like the love in *Deja Vu.* We hardly ever find it. That's why there are movies. We want a love that spans the generations and conquers time, a love so large that only the supernatural can contain it. Here is a movie about a love like that. It makes *City of Angels* look timid.

The story involves an American woman named Dana (Victoria Foyt) on a buying trip to Jerusalem when she is approached by a mysterious older blonde who engages her in conversation. Soon she is revealing all her secrets: Yes, she is engaged, because "being engaged has become a condition of my life," but after six years and no marriage she is not very happy.

The other woman tells her about the love of her life. It was a wartime romance. She was a French Jewish woman; he was an American GI. They planned to wed. He went home "to tell his girlfriend" and never returned. Eventually she got a letter with a photo of the man's first child.

Perhaps, Dana says, he could not find you. The woman smiles sadly. "He knew where to find me. Life had got hold of us." She pauses. "Nothing seemed so real again. In fact, all my life since then has been like a dream." The woman gives her a piece of jewelry—a clip—and disappears, after mentioning that the clip was a gift from the GI, who kept the other one.

Dana heads toward home. When the Chunnel train stops briefly at Dover, she inexplicably gets off instead of going on to London. Above the white cliffs of Dover, she meets a painter named Sean (Stephen Dillane). "Have we met before?" she asks him. He says, "It feels like one of those moments where if you turn the wrong way you regret it forever." It's love at first sight, but they fight it. She's engaged, after all. But then they meet again, by coincidence, at the house of British friends. She discovers he is married.

Her fiancé is Alex (Michael Brandon). His wife is Claire (Glynis Barber). It becomes clear that Dana and Sean are helplessly in love, and their partners react in disbelief and anger, but with a certain civilized restraint. I must not reveal any more. I must say instead that old songs like "The White Cliffs of Dover" and "We'll Meet Again" and "These Foolish Things" are like time machines that can carry love down through the years and can leap from mind to mind, spreading their foolishness and dreams.

Deja Vu is not a weepy romantic melodrama, but a sophisticated film about smart people. Foyt and Dillane make convincing lovers not because they are swept away, but because they regard what has happened to them and accept it. When they fall in love, there is a lot at risk: jobs, businesses, which country they live in, the people they're committed to. It takes no trouble at all to fall in love when you're twenty and single. But Dana and Sean must look in their hearts and be sure they cannot live without one another.

The film was directed by Henry Jaglom and written by Jaglom and his star, Victoria Foyt, who is also his wife. Ah-ha, you think, guessing the connection, especially since the movie is dedicated "to the love of my life." But there is another connection coiling down through the years. The trademark of Jaglom's film company is a brief moment of time, showing Orson Welles producing a rainbow out of thin air. Jaglom was one of Welles's close confidants and friends.

In *Citizen Kane,* which Welles made in 1941, there occurs my favorite passage of movie dialogue. Old Mr. Bernstein is talking about the peculiarities of time. "A fellow will remember a lot of things you wouldn't think he'd remember," he says. "You take me. One day, back in 1896, I was crossing over to Jersey on the ferry, and as we pulled out, there was another ferry pulling in, and on it there was a girl waiting to get off. A white dress she had on. She was carrying a white parasol. I only saw her for one second. She didn't see me at all, but I'll bet a month hasn't gone by since that I haven't thought of that girl."

Late in *Deja Vu*, a character tells a similar story, about a woman he once met: "A week hasn't gone by since I last saw her that I haven't thought of her. She was the love of my life."

Yes. And can you, dear reader, think of such a moment too? Perfect love is almost always unrealized. It has to be. What makes those memories perfect is that they produce no history. The woman with the white parasol remains always frozen in an old man's memory. She never grows old, is never out of temper, never loses interest in him, never dies. She exists forever as a promise, like the green light at the end of Gatsby's pier.

Only rarely does the universe wheel around to bring two hearts once again into communion. That's what *Deja Vu* is about. And that explains the two most curious characters in it. They are the old couple (Anna Massey and Noel Harrison) who own the house where Dana and Sean meet by accident. They have been married a very long time, and like to read in bed and eat Mars bars at the same time and be happy to be together. At first you wonder what their scenes mean. Then you understand.

The Designated Mourner ★ ★ ★

R, 95 m., 1997

Mike Nichols (Jack), Miranda Richardson (Judy), David de Keyser (Howard). Directed by David Hare and produced by Donna Grey, Mike Nichols, and Hare. Screenplay by Wallace Shawn.

The second time I saw *The Designated Mourner*, I kept my eyes mostly closed, and that was a useful approach. This is not a film so much as a filmed record of an audio performance; the words and the voices carry what is important, and when you open your eyes to look occasionally at the readers, it is like breaking the illusion.

Three people sit behind a table furnished with papers, pencils, cups of water, books. They talk, sometimes to us, rarely to each other, mostly to themselves (or "for the record"). Most of the talking is done by Jack (Mike Nichols), a loquacious journalist who was once married to Judy (Miranda Richardson), the daughter of an intellectual named Howard (David de Keyser). In the unspecified country where they live, a totalitarian regime swept away those who thought too much, finding such men dangerous, and Judy and Howard were among the victims. (This is not the sort of film where it matters that I reveal such details.) Jack is left behind, the "designated mourner for a very special way of life that died."

The film is based on a play by Wallace Shawn, whose works like the screenplay for *My Dinner with André* and the play *Aunt Dan and Lemon* pile up monologues from characters who are looking for something to hang on to. In *The Designated Mourner*, his narrator is an engaging philistine who once agreed with his father-in-law, Howard, that the intellectual life was important—that to understand the poems of John Donne was a valuable achievement. But Jack lost that faith, came to see Howard as an empty vessel, and now seeks to clear his mind of its incessant chatter of secondhand notions, received ideas, and buzzwords. At the end of the play he evokes the ideal of sitting at a café table feeling a gentle evening breeze on his face, and thinking of almost nothing.

Well, is it important to understand the poems of John Donne? I write the question knowing that most people will not be familiar with his poems (although the words "No man is an island" may toll a distant bell). Last night at dinner I found myself next to a woman who talked about the novels of Henry James, which filled me with gratitude, and then about Cynthia Ozick's essays about James, which filled me with amazement—because unless you are lucky enough to live on a university campus, you are likely to do most of your serious reading in solitude.

I feel, stubbornly, that it is important to read Donne and the other masters because they have thought and written at the highest level about what it means to be alive, to be conscious of choices, to consider the approach of death, and to turn those subjects into meditations that are sometimes true, false, cheerful, sad, ironic, bitter, or hopeful. A great writer engages you in a conversation that you are not likely to be able to have with anyone you know.

But we exist under a daily reprieve. We can choose to read John Donne because we live for the moment in a free, stable society that does not make our reading impossible. War, famine, or poverty—the conditions under which most people have always lived—would make reading (not to mention intellectualism) an idle fantasy. *The Designated Mourner* is about a society that does not like readers, and most of its words are spoken by a survivor who stands a little outside and looks wryly at what happened to the members of his circle. He chuckles sometimes at the entire foundation of his idea of himself. His all-important, precious "I" is, he fears, simply a rummage sale of whatever has been shoveled into his memory over the years.

To see this play on a stage would be a pleasure, because then you would be in the same time and space as the actors, and the words would take on the allure of storytelling. To read the play would also be a pleasure, because the scenes being described would take form in your mind. To see this film (directed by David Hare while his stage production was being performed in London with the same actors) is not the best choice. The material suffers by being placed in a frame it is not suited to. It's likely that an audio book of the play or film will be released, and that would be a good way to absorb Shawn's disturbing, introspective, Prufrockian words. I give the film "three stars" as a compromise between its material and the presentation.

At the end, I concluded: It is better to be able to read John Donne than not, but if the tide turns against you, it isn't likely to do you much good. Of course, in a nutshell, that's life.

Desperate Measures ★ ★

R, 100 m., 1998

Michael Keaton (Peter McCabe), Andy Garcia (Frank Connor), Brian Cox (Jeremiah Cassidy), Marcia Gay Harden (Samantha Hawkins), Erik King (Nate Oliver), Efrain Figueroa (Vargus), Joseph Cross (Matthew Connor), Janel Maloney (Sarah Davis). Directed by Barbet Schroeder and produced by Schroeder, Susan Hoffman, Gary Foster, and Lee Rich. Screenplay by David Klass, Henry Bean, and Neal Jimenez.

Desperate Measures opens with the same hook as *Hard Rain:* What looks like a robbery turns out to be an action by the good guys. *Hard Rain* really cheated (hey—they're not robbers; they're armored car drivers!). *Desperate Measures,* which is a better movie, has a better gimmick. A raid is staged on government computers in order to search for the perfect DNA match for a kid who is dying and needs a bone marrow transplant.

Andy Garcia plays a cop named Connor, the father who will do anything to save his son's life. Searching a national database, he discovers that only one man has the proper DNA. He's Peter McCabe (Michael Keaton), a psychopath now in prison after killing four people, including a fellow inmate. Will McCabe agree to become a bone marrow donor? Why should he? Offered the opportunity, he reflects on the alternative: "After all these years of being locked up, I'm given the opportunity to kill again."

But McCabe eventually caves in, after a laundry list of demands including better prison quarters and all the cigarettes he wants. Turns out it's all a trick. Using blueprints available (of course) on the Internet, he plans an elaborate escape from the hospital where he's taken to have the tricky operation. How does he get out of the handcuffs? How does he ward off the effects of anesthesia? It's all here. It's not convincing, but it's here.

All of this is prelude to the movie's real plot, which centers on the fact that McCabe must remain alive in order for his bone marrow to be of any use to little Matthew, the dying kid. McCabe sets people on fire during his escape attempt and uses violence as he flees a police dragnet. And Connor finds himself in the curious position of trying to shield this vicious killer, sometimes with his own body, against fellow policemen who might kill him.

What is the proper morality here? Or, as a police official (Brian Cox) succinctly asks, "How many people are gonna have to die here tonight so that kid of yours can live?" It's a good question, and explored a different way in a more thoughtful movie, it might have generated some genuine drama.

Desperate Measures is, unfortunately, only masquerading as a thoughtful movie that's really about something. At heart, it's an action thriller—a chase picture. It has all the usual implausible or impossible stunts, the highway carnage, the jumps off bridges, the slides down laundry chutes, and other feats that make it more of a video game than a drama.

Too bad, because the actors could have brought class to better material. Michael Keaton, an actor who can convincingly project intelligence, is intriguing as McCabe, a thinker who likes to toy with people he can control. Garcia's dilemma as a cop and a father is handled well in a handful of quiet scenes (especially in conversations with pediatrician Marcia Gay Harden), and his son (Joseph Cross) is a smart kid who asks all the right questions at the wrong times.

But the movie would rather jolly along an action audience than play fair with its material, and so we're treated to the usual, standard, obligatory bankrupt action dreck: kinetic energy on autopilot. Too bad. The director, Barbet Schroeder, has made some good movies *(Barfly, Reversal of Fortune, Single White Female)*. This time he's a hired gun. He could have made a better movie, I imagine, if the producers had wanted him to, but sometimes that's just not the way it works.

Destiny ★ ★ ½

NO MPAA RATING, 135 m., 1999

Nour el-Cherif (Averroes), Laila Eloui (Gypsy Woman), Mahmoud Hemeida (Al Mansour [Caliph]), Safia el-Emary (Averroes's Wife), Mohamed Mounir (The Bard), Khaled el-Nabaoui (Nasser [Crown Prince]), Abdallah Mahmoud (Borhan), Ahmed Fouad Selim (Cheikh Riad). Directed by Youssef Chahine and produced by Humbert Balsan and Gabriel Khoury. Screenplay by Chahine and Khaled Youssef.

Destiny takes place in twelfth-century Spain, but could take place today. It is an odd, brave film, part impassioned melodrama, part musical, taking a broad popular approach to questions of religious belief. It was directed by an Egyptian, financed from France, set in the Spanish province of Andalusia, and photographed in Lebanon and Syria. It's completely off the map for most American moviegoers, which is one of its charms.

The story involves an Arabic philosopher named Averroes, who believed that the Koran was open to interpretation. Yes, he taught, the book is the word of God, but God gave us intelligence so that we might reason about his words and not blindly follow their literal meanings. After all, to assume that the mind of God can be reduced to ordinary human language and contained in mere words is itself a kind of heresy. And those who oppose the interpretation of the Koran are of course imposing their own interpretation upon it.

As the film opens, one of Averroes's followers is being burned at the stake, the bonfire fed by his writings. The burning man calls out to his son to seek out the philosopher, and the main story takes place in Andalusia, where Averroes has gathered a group of disciples who study his books and copy them out by hand. Ah, but that gives a wrong idea of the film, which is not about scholars in their cells, but about politics, sexual passion, jealousy, and romance, and contains several song and dance numbers. Imagine *My Dinner with André* as a musical.

Andalusia is ruled by a caliph who has two sons, one a follower of Averroes, the other a party animal who is lured into the camp of fundamentalists. One feels of these fundamentalists, as one often does about the type in general, that they're driven not so much by what they believe, as by their fear or envy of those who do not agree. The movie argues that a belief that cannot stand up to free debate is not a belief worth holding.

Political intrigue is rife in the area. The caliph supports Averroes, but is opposed by a cult that hopes to overthrow him. Meanwhile, his oldest son is concealing a forbidden love with a gypsy woman, and his trusted adviser is working both sides of the street. A secret project is set in motion, to copy out the writings of Averroes and spirit them far away, in case the tide turns and his books are burned again (a good possibility).

Much of the film's interest comes from historical details. We hear of the great Arabic contributions to mathematics, and we see a fascinating invention, a telescope that uses the magnifying power of water in order to work. We see a society that is part European, part Arabic, in which Islam is as much a political movement as a religious one. And then there is the uncanny way the characters have of looking toward the camera and simply breaking out into song. (I was reminded of Woody Allen's *Everyone Says I Love You,* which was equally direct in the way ordinary people moved from speech to singing.)

There are places in the world where *Destiny,* directed by the veteran Egyptian filmmaker Youssef Chahine, would be controversial—even dangerous. In those places, the music and romance will help find a wider audience for a charged message. The interest in this country is more indirect. The film is naive and simple at times, even clumsy in its musical sequences, and yet lurking beneath its story is a conflict between rationalism and fundamentalism that is as fraught today as it ever was.

As I write these words, Serbs are slaughtering ethnic Albanians and we are bombing Serbs, all because of religious and ethnic differences that date back almost to the period of this film. At the end of *Destiny,* Chahine quotes Averroes: "Ideas have wings. No one can stop their flight." Heartening words. But are they flying or fleeing?

Devil's Advocate ★★½

R, 138 m., 1997

Keanu Reeves (Kevin Lomax), Al Pacino (John Milton), Charlize Theron (Mary Ann Lomax), Jeffrey Jones (Eddie Barzoon), Judith Ivey (Mrs. Lomax), Craig T. Nelson (Alexander Cullen), Connie Nielsen (Christabella), Tamara Tunie (Jackie Heath). Directed by Taylor Hackford and produced by Arnon Milchan, Arnold Kopelson, and Anne Kopelson. Screenplay by Jonathan Lemkin and Tony Gilroy.

Most movies about lawyers involve selling their souls to the devil, but *Devil's Advocate* is the first in which the devil gets more dialogue than the lawyers. The movie chronicles the descent of Kevin Lomax (Keanu Reeves), a small-time legal star from Florida, into the depths of the New York big time. Recruited by a powerful Manhattan law firm, he finds himself defending goat killers and real estate tycoons for a boss named John Milton, who offers him a paradise found.

Milton (Al Pacino) is the devil. That is a secret reserved for the second hour of the film, although the title hints it, the posters and TV commercials reveal it, and by the time it arrives Lomax is the only character who hasn't suspected. Charming, persuasive, with a wise little cackle, Milton sends a recruiter to Florida, where Lomax is an undefeated master of picking juries that do not convict. He wants the young man to join his team, and tempts him not on a mountaintop but on a rooftop.

The scene of the first meeting between Milton and Lomax, on a skyscraper roof, scores a stunning visual impact. The production designer, Bruno Rubeo, has created a spectacular effect: a water garden in the sky, with pool surfaces spilling over the edges of the building, so that water and sky seem to meet without any architectural separation. The two men walk perilously close to the edge, as the director, Taylor Hackford, plays with vertigo to suggest that Lomax is being offered all of Manhattan at his feet—and also the possibility of a great and sudden fall.

The young lawyer is impressed. So, at first, is his wife, Mary Ann (Charlize Theron), who can't believe it when Milton offers them a three-bedroom apartment in a luxurious Fifth Avenue co-op. Only Lomax's Bible-quoting mother (Judith Ivey) has her doubts, quoting scripture about Sodom, Gomorrah, and other keywords that pop into the mind when Manhattan is mentioned. Her advice, indeed, seems increasingly sound as the film progresses.

Lomax becomes obsessed with his job, ignoring his wife and drawing closer to a sexy woman at the office (Connie Nielsen). And the wife, obsessed with having a baby, begins to come apart. She has the film's first supernatural vision, when she sees a demon materialize in the face and body of a helpful neighbor (Tamara Tunie), and soon she's begging to go back to Gainesville.

The satanic character is played by Pacino with relish bordering on glee. Reeves in contrast is sober and serious—the straight man. That's the correct choice for his role, but it leaves Pacino with many of the best lines ("I'm maybe the last humanist. The twentieth century was entirely mine. I'm perking!") *Devil's Advocate* is neither fish nor fowl: It is not a serious film about its subject, nor is it quite a dark comedy, despite some of Pacino's good lines. The epilogue, indeed, cheats in a way I thought had been left behind in grade school. And yet there are splendid moments.

I liked the way Hackford used speeded-up photography, as in *Koyaanisqatsi*, to indicate the passage of time; the fact that Milton's office looks the way Satan's might look if he had a great designer; the nice little throwaways, as when the goat killer (Delroy Lindo) apparently causes the prosecutor to have a coughing fit. The casting is good in small roles, including Heather Matarazzo, from *Welcome to the Dollhouse*, as the victim in an early courtroom scene.

But the movie never fully engaged me; my mind raced ahead of the plot, and the John Grisham stuff clashed with the *Exorcist* stuff. Still, I enjoyed Pacino. Looking less deeply wrinkled than of late, his face smooth with satanic self-contentment, he relishes the details, such as that Milton likes to stand in front of fires and always travels by subway. The phantasmagorical final confrontation between the two men, set to the Sinatra version of "It Happened in Monterey," ranges from melodrama to camp ("You're the anti-Christ!" "Whatever."). It includes an extraordinary special effect of a marble bas-relief that comes to life and melts into a licentious orgy. If the whole film were as good as its production design, we'd really have something here.

The Devil's Own ★ ★ ½

R, 107 m., 1997

Harrison Ford (Tom O'Meara), Brad Pitt (McGuire/Devaney), Margaret Colin (Sheila O'Meara), Rubén Blades (Edwin Diaz), Treat Williams (Billy Burke), George Hearn (Peter Fitzsimmons), Mitchell Ryan (Chief Jim Kelly), Natascha McElhone (Megan Doherty). Directed by Alan J. Pakula and produced by Lawrence Gordon and Robert F. Colesberry. Screenplay by Robert Mark Kamen and Kevin Jarre, based on a story by Jarre.

"It's not an American story. It's an Irish one."
—Brad Pitt in *The Devil's Own*

Ah, but that's just where he's wrong. *The Devil's Own* is an American story, to such a degree that American audiences will be able to watch this movie in total ignorance of the history of Northern Ireland, and be none the wiser at the end. Imagine this: One of the key characters is an Irish Republican Army leader who has killed more than twenty men and goes to America to buy guided missiles—and at no point in the movie, to the best of my recollection, are the words "Catholic" or "Protestant" ever uttered, even though sectarian conflict is at the heart of the Troubles.

This is history lite. In the opening scenes, an eight-year-old boy is having dinner with his family when masked men burst into their cottage and shoot his father dead. Flash forward twenty years, and now Francis McGuire (Brad Pitt) has been cornered in a Belfast hideout. There's a shoot-out with police and British troops, and then he escapes out the back way (with hundreds of men, as the British somehow didn't think of the rear door). We know the father was shot by either British troops or Protestant militants (the movie doesn't bother to say), and we gather McGuire is in the IRA. But the issues involved between the two sides are never mentioned, even obliquely; for all we learn, he's avenging his father's death and that's it.

Soon he's in America, where an Irish-American judge gets him a place to live, in the basement of an honest cop named Tom O'Meara (Harrison Ford). O'Meara knows nothing about the past of the man, now calling himself Rory Devaney. He's just being a good Samaritan. Ask yourself this: How many cops, knowing what they know about the dangers of modern society, would allow a complete stranger with no job to live under the same roof with the cop's wife and daughters?

But don't ask. O'Meara is simply being a nice guy. Soon we learn that Devaney has lots of money for buying guided missiles from a creep named Billy Burke (Treat Williams).

And we learn that O'Meara is a very good cop, honest and unswerving. There are several scenes in which we see him avoiding the use of force and condemning cops who shoot first and ask questions later. When his partner (Rubén Blades) does just that, it forces a crisis of conscience—but it doesn't pay off; it simply sets up the cop's determination, later in the film, to bring in Devaney alive.

Both Pitt and Ford have criticized this film because, they say, it started shooting without a completed screenplay. I can believe that. Consider that Pitt, while nominally the villain, is seen in an attractive light, while a British intelligence operative is seen as a sleazeball, and yet Ford, fearing the sleazeball wants to kill Pitt, dedicates himself to bringing him in alive—so he can be brought to trial by the sleazeball for crimes which the IRA, of course, considers to be justified acts of war. The moral reasoning in the film is so confusing that only by completely sidestepping it can the plot work at all.

And sidestep it does. Harrison Ford and Brad Pitt are enormously appealing and gifted actors, and to the degree that the movie works, it's because of them. Using all the gifts of the actor's craft, they're able to sell scenes that don't make sense and don't add up. Even in a final confrontation, they're so convincing that only later do we ask ourselves, hey, did Devaney really plan to sail across the North Atlantic Ocean in a leaky old tugboat?

The Devil's Own (what does the title mean?) plays better if you don't give it a single thought and just let the knee-jerk cues dictate your emotions. Handsome guy's father is killed, so he fights back (for personal, not political reasons). Nice-guy cop likes Irish kid, but gets frosted when bad guys (British? Irish turncoats?) invade his home looking for kid. Cop wants to arrest kid, yet doesn't want to see him gunned down by British creeps. All criminals deserve their rights, cop believes; fine, except what opinion, if any, does cop have about terrorism or the presumed use of missiles against civilian targets? (Cop never, during entire movie, expresses any opinion about long history of struggle involving British, Northern Irish, and IRA.)

I've got a notion for a quick rewrite: Leave out Ireland altogether and make it a revenge picture. Or deal with Ireland intelligently, as *In the Name of the Father*, *Michael Collins*, and *Cal* have. Either way, the film should make it clear whether it considers the Brad Pitt character to be a hero or villain. My best guess is he's a villain given a moral touch-up because he's also a movie star. He may be a cold-blooded terrorist, but he's our cold-blooded terrorist, and, saints preserve us, isn't he a likable lad?

Dick ★ ★ ★ ½

PG-13, 90 m., 1999

Kirsten Dunst (Betsy Jobs), Michelle Williams (Arlene Lorenzo), Dan Hedaya (Dick), Will Ferrell (Bob Woodward), Bruce McCulloch (Carl Bernstein), Saul Rubinek (Henry Kissinger), Teri Garr (Helen Lorenzo), Dave Foley (Bob Haldeman), Jim Breuer (John Dean), Harry Shearer (G. Gordon Liddy). Directed by Andrew Fleming. Produced by Gale Anne Hurd. Screenplay by Fleming and Sheryl Longin.

Dick is the flip side of *All the President's Men*, explaining at last all of the loose ends of the Watergate scandal—how the duct tape got on the Watergate lock, who Deep Throat really was, and why the 18½-minute gap appeared on the White House tapes. We also learn that Richard M. Nixon resented the fact that his dog didn't follow him around adoringly, like the Kennedy and Johnson dogs; at one point, he snarls, "Checkers—shut up! I'll feed you to the Chinese!"

The movie is a bright and sassy comedy, seeing Watergate entirely through the eyes of its prime movers, who are revealed to be two fifteen-year-old girls. Betsy Jobs (Kirsten Dunst) and Arlene Lorenzo (Michelle Williams) are best friends who live in the Watergate complex, and one night they sneak downstairs to mail a letter to the Bobby Sherman Fan Club; they slap the tape on the door lock, it's discovered by a security guard, and the White House burglars are busted inside Democratic National Headquarters.

Ah, but it doesn't end there. The girls are on a class trip to the White House when they spot a man they'd seen in the Watergate. He's G. Gordon Liddy (Harry Shearer), but they don't know that; they get separated from their group and wander the White House corridors, stumbling upon shredding operations and cash rooms, and overhearing crucial conversations in the Oval Office itself.

President Nixon (Dan Hedaya, very funny) grows concerned over how much they may have heard and puts on a show of false good cheer: "How would you young ladies like to be the White House dog walkers?" Calling every day to walk Checkers, they dimly perceive that all is not as it should be in the Oval Office, and the plot reveals how they became Deep Throat, why John Dean had an attack of conscience, and why their rendition of Olivia Newton-John's "I Love You" appeared on a tape in the desk drawer of Rosemary Woods.

Yes, Arlene, the apple-cheeked one with the merry smile, gets a crush on Nixon. There's a funny dream sequence in which he appears to her riding a white charger on the beach, but even funnier is the classroom scene where, like millions of teenage girls before her, she tries out a married name by writing it in her notebook: "Mrs. Arlene Nixon."

Dick, directed by Andrew Fleming and written by Fleming and Sheryl Longin, finds just the right tone for its merciless satire: not strident, not wacky, but kind of earnest and intent, as the girls, who are not geniuses, blunder onto one incriminating secret after another. Their motivation seems to stem from ordinary teenage attributes, like curiosity, idealism, and romance.

The crusading reporters Woodward and Bernstein (Will Ferrell and Bruce McCulloch), on the other hand, are played more broadly—Woodward as a self-important totem pole, Bernstein as an insecure runt. They're always trying to grab the phone away from each other, and their Watergate coverage, so majestic when seen from the outside, is portrayed as the work of a couple of ambitious reporters on a power trip, believing everything the teenage ditzos tell them. (Of course, everything the girls tell them turns out to be correct.)

Comedy like this depends on timing, invention, and a cheerful cynicism about human nature. It's wiser and more wicked than the gross-out insult humor of many of the summer's other comedies. Consider the scene where the girls accidentally bake cookies with a secret herbal ingredient from their brother's stash and take them to Nixon, who offers one to Leonid Brezhnev. His mood is so altered that Nixon tells them, "You know, girls, I think your cookies just saved the world from nuclear catastrophe."

Dan Hedaya's president looks a little like the real Nixon, and the match of the public persona is uncanny, as he complains to Henry Kissinger (Saul Rubinek) about his enemies, his insecurities, and his dog. He grows bitter as his administration collapses around him, eventually retreating to bourbon and recrimination, while even the faithful Arlene grows disenchanted ("You're prejudiced and you have a potty mouth").

Will the movie play for audiences who don't remember Watergate—for teenage Kirsten Dunst fans? I think so, because it contains all the information the audience really needs to know, although older viewers will enjoy the wealth of cross-references, as when the Plumbers offer Nixon menus of dirty tricks. *Dick* is a sly little comic treasure.

Different for Girls ★ ★ ★

R, 101 m., 1997

Steven Mackintosh (Kim Foyle), Rupert Graves (Paul Prentice), Miriam Margolyes (Pamela), Saskia Reeves (Jean), Charlotte Coleman (Alison), Neil Dudgeon (Neil), Nisha K. Nayar (Angela), Lia Williams (Defense Solicitor). Directed by Richard Spence and produced by John Chapman. Screenplay by Tony Marchant.

The unexamined mystery at the heart of *Different for Girls* is—what, exactly, does Paul see in Kim? Paul is a rowdy motorbike messenger who roars through the streets and punk clubs of London. Kim, whose name was once Karl, is a postoperative transsexual. "I am straight, you know," Paul tells Kim. "So am I," she replies.

They knew each other sixteen years ago at a boarding school, and the opening titles include a flashback to those days. Karl is taunted in the shower by his gay-bashing schoolmates, and Paul gallantly comes to the rescue. When they meet again after a minor traffic accident, Paul recognizes the former Karl almost at once, but Kim—as she now is—at first denies they knew each other.

Of course, they did. But in what way? Was Paul (Rupert Graves) sexually attracted in his school days? Or is he fascinated only now by the unexplored country of gender swapping? He asks Kim (Steven Macintosh) out for lunch, and then causes a scene that cuts the date short (deliberately, Kim senses). He apologizes with flowers and asks her out again, but it's clear he's deeply conflicted: He is attracted to this mannish woman, but reluctant to admit it, to her or to himself.

Different for Girls follows the time-honored conventions of the romantic comedy, in which opposites attract despite obstacles. Paul is macho, he already has a girlfriend, he likes loud music, he gets drunk. Kim wants to blend in and disappear. Even her clothes give that message: She wears the sort of conservative fashions a nun might choose as civilian garb. If it's a mystery what Paul thinks of her, it's a puzzle why she's attracted to him. Immature and reckless, he lands them both in jail one night by exposing himself in public (not as a sexual act, but to make a point during a drunken rant).

The movie's effect depends on the performance by Mackintosh, as Kim. The actor does not look persuasively feminine, and indeed many of the other characters in the movie immediately read Kim as a transvestite. But the point of the movie is not deception, as it was in *The Crying Game*. It is self-discovery. Kim considers herself a woman born into a man's body, and explains herself patiently to Paul: the confusion, the counseling, the gender reassignment surgery, the hormones. As Kim explains the changes in her body, Paul discovers to his horror that he has grown aroused. And here is the interesting question: Is Paul aroused by Kim's description of her breasts and hips, or by the fact that the description comes from someone Paul used to know as a man?

"I always thought you was gay," Paul says. "So did I," Kim says. We believe Kim. But what about Paul, who drops his current girlfriend in a second to circle with fascination around this person he has nothing in common with? If the movie had explored the dynamic of Paul's attraction, it might have been more honest. Instead, it moves sideways into an unnecessary subplot involving Kim's sister (Saskia Reeves) and her husband, an army career officer (Neil Dudgeon), haunted by his infertility. The obvious point is that there is more to being a man (or a woman) than reproduction. But we knew that.

As Kim, Mackintosh's performance finds and holds the right notes of shyness, determination, privacy, and love. Yes, Kim is attracted to Paul—probably because she always was, even in prep school. Attracted not by the swashbuckling, irresponsible lifestyle, but by the good heart that inspired Paul to come to the rescue. Despite her sex change, Kim is less complicated than Paul: What you see is what you get with her, while Paul doesn't know how to present himself or how to give.

Transsexuality is so new as a subject for films that the movie can be excused, I suppose, for thinking it is about Kim. But I wish *Different for Girls* had explored Paul's struggle with his own feelings. Is he attracted to Kim because it gives him an excuse to date a boy who is a girl? Or is he attracted to the good feminine and human qualities Kim definitely has? Or it is simply fascination with Kim's redefinition of herself? The movie ends on a conventional romantic note, leaving all of those questions unasked. Here is one of those rare films where the sequel would be infinitely more intriguing than the original.

The Disappearance of Garcia Lorca ★ ★ ★

R, 109 m., 1997

Esai Morales (Ricardo), Edward James Olmos (Lozano), Andy Garcia (Federico García Lorca), Jeroen Krabbe (Colonel Aguirre), Giancarlo Giannini (Taxi), Miguel Ferrer (Centeno), Marcela Walerstein (Maria Eugenia), Eusebio Lazaro (Vicente Fernandez). Directed by Marcos Zurinaga and produced by Enrique Cerezo and Marcos Zurinaga. Screenplay by Zurinaga, Juan Antonio Ramos, and Neil Cohen, based on the books *The Assassination of Federico Garcia Lorca* and *Federico Garcia Lorca: A Life* by Ian Gibson.

Near the beginning of *The Disappearance of Garcia Lorca*, a teenage boy attends an opening night in Madrid in 1934—a performance of a work by the poet and playwright Federico García Lorca. Twenty years later he recalls,

"That night I learned that poetry could be an act of violence." Backstage, he is introduced to the poet, who asks, "How old are you?" "Fourteen," he replies. "So am I," says the poet, adding, "Remember me."

Not long after, García Lorca is dead, another victim of the Spanish civil war. He had thought perhaps he was too visible to be assassinated by the forces of the fascist rebel Franco, but he was wrong. And ever since there has been a veil of mystery around the questions of how García Lorca was killed, and by whom.

This movie, based on two books by Ian Gibson, is a reconstruction and speculation, told through the eyes of the young boy, Ricardo, who moves with his family to Puerto Rico, and tells his father one day in 1954 that he intends to return to Spain and try to find out what happened. For his father, all of that is in the past and, with Franco still in power, best left there. But the boy, now grown to manhood and played by Esai Morales, returns anyway, and begins to unravel the secrets of the death.

García Lorca, played by Andy Garcia, is seen in the movie as an artist whose very existence is a challenge to the insurgents. What is often forgotten about Spain, because it reverses the usual pattern, is that the elected government was left-wing, and the rebels were fascists; Franco was supported by Hitler and Mussolini, and the air battles in Spain were seen by historians as a dress rehearsal for the Luftwaffe.

To the rebels, the famous poet was a symbol, and his poetry like a red flag at a bullfight. But García Lorca was also well connected, with influence, with powerful friends. There is a scene in the movie where he strides confidently from a house to where some military men are beating his friend; he thinks his prestige will be enough to stop them, but he is wrong, and a fascist goon named Centeno (Miguel Ferrer) slugs him in the stomach. García Lorca does not quite realize even after this event that his society has changed fundamentally, that a new class is taking power, that he is doomed.

Returning to Spain in 1954, Ricardo meets a publisher named Lozano (Edward James Olmos), who is bringing out a handsome edition of García Lorca's works. "But . . . didn't you arrest him?" Ricardo asks. Lozano replies, "You're a brave man, Ricardo. No one else has been brave enough to say that to me." Lozano did sign the arrest order, and was possibly present at the death, along with others who would now rewrite their roles in history.

The lesson apparently is that poets who are alive are a threat to repression, but dead poets can be safely embalmed as national treasures or legends. The film is also about how the secrets of the past still hold their power for revenge, if they are exposed, and in 1954 there are many people still alive who know how and why García Lorca was killed—people whose current lives cannot accommodate that knowledge, so that Ricardo's quest is a threat.

Ricardo enters a Madrid where there are suspicious eyes and ears everywhere, and a taxi driver (Giancarlo Giannini) may be a friend or a spy. Where nothing is simple, and people who thought they had sufficient reason in 1934 to side with the fascists and the Third Reich no longer wish their association to be recalled. The movie is a murder investigation, really, except that Ricardo will also be discovering things about his own origin that he does not suspect.

Do people read García Lorca today? Or poetry in general? Not many, I suppose. I took down my book of his poems and read some of them after seeing the movie, and felt the passion. But García Lorca is perhaps more important today as a symbol than as a poet, and this film is really not so much about him as about memory and history—about how poets are given most of their power not by those who love them, but by those who fear them.

Disturbing Behavior ★ ★

R, 83 m., 1998

James Marsden (Steve Clark), Nick Stahl (Gavin Strick), Katie Holmes (Rachel Wagner), Bruce Greenwood (Dr. Caldicott), Steve Railsback (Officer Cox), William Sadler (Dorian Newberry). Directed by David Nutter and produced by Armyan Bernstein and Jon Shestack. Screenplay by Scott Rosenberg.

Disturbing Behavior is a small-town horror movie with an ironic flip-flop: This time, a sinister local cult takes rebels and delinquents and turns them into clean-cut models of deportment. "You still think this is about blood drives and bake sales?" one of the kids whispers fearfully, as they eavesdrop on a secret meeting where citizens are planning bake sales and blood drives.

The kid is named Gavin, and he's the whistle-blower, the one kid in school who knows what's going on. In the movie's best scene, he gives Steve, the newcomer, a guided tour of the various factions in the lunchroom: the dopers, the brains, the car crowd, and the Blue Ribbons, who wear letter jackets and have trim haircuts and always exhibit exemplary behavior.

It's the Blue Ribbons who are the dangerous ones, Gavin knows. Smoking some weed in the forest by the hydroelectric plant, he witnessed one of them break a girl's neck and shoot a cop—and then saw the cop's partner let the killer go. From his vantage point, Gavin was unable to see the evil red glow in the killer kid's eyes, but obviously, these are dangerous people.

The cult members hate all forms of rebellion. The reason the girl had to die was that she had a tattoo. "Self-mutilation," says her killer, who refuses sex because he has to "conserve his fluids" for the big game, and later utters the very worst line in the movie: "Self-mutilate this, fluid girl!"

Gavin is played by Nick Stahl. James Marsden is Steve, the newcomer, and Katie Holmes (from *Dawson's Creek*) is Rachel, who dresses in black and likes to strike poses on the beds of pickup trucks and is a bad girl who is in great danger of becoming a very good one. Meanwhile, down in the school basement, the janitor (William Sadler) has what Gavin describes as "the village idiot, Quasimodo thing going." But is the janitor quite what he seems?

Teenage horror movies are a popular genre after *Scream* and *Scream 2*, but this one doesn't make it. It's too murky and disorganized. The director, David Nutter, has done some *X-Files* episodes, and is great at suggesting conspiracies but not so good at payoffs. It's like he wants to postpone the answers to the end of the season.

But we catch on fairly quickly that this is, as the advance buzz has it, a teenage version of *The Stepford Wives*. The Blue Ribbons, with their Weekend Enlightenment Seminars, are, as Gavin says, "hypnotized, lobotomized, and brainwashed." And there's the obligatory element of scheming parents who double-cross their kids: They'd rather have a polite zombie than a sullen rebel.

Unlike *Scream 2*, which kids the horror clichés, *Disturbing Behavior* pretends they still hold power. But the movie is light on shocks and not ever scary. It does, however, find a great way to illustrate Pink Floyd's immortal line, "Hey! Teacher! Leave those kids alone!"

Doctor Dolittle ★ ★ ★

PG-13, 90 m., 1998

Eddie Murphy (Dr. John Dolittle), Ossie Davis (Archer Dolittle), Oliver Platt (Dr. Mark Weller), Peter Boyle (Calloway), Richard Schiff (Dr. Gene Reiss), Kristen Wilson (Lisa), Jeffrey Tambor (Dr. Fish), Kyla Pratt (Maya). Directed by Betty Thomas and produced by John Davis, David T. Friendly, and Joseph M. Singer. Screenplay by Nat Mauldin and Larry Levin.

Doctor Dolittle is a gross-out movie, yes, and it's going to be criticized by those who can't believe it got a PG-13 rating. Like Eddie Murphy's previous film, *The Nutty Professor*, it has a lot of jokes about bodily functions. It breaks some new ground, with a scene where the Murphy character gives the kiss of life to a rat, and when a pigeon makes a low-level bombing run at Oliver Platt's nostrils. And of course, there's the scene where the Murphy character, as a little boy, learns from his dog why dogs sniff each other's behinds, and then tries the same tactic in checking out the new school principal.

Is this material a mistake? I don't think so. Kids have a healthy interest in bodily functions, and if you don't believe me, ask Captain Mike, who runs a kiddie playland in Sawyer, Michigan, and gives away an amazing number of Whoopee Cushions as free prizes. Too many adults have a tendency to confuse bad taste with evil influences; it's hard for them to see that the activities in *Doctor Dolittle*, while rude and vulgar, are not violent or antisocial. The movie will not harm anyone, and in the audience I saw it with, lots of parents and kids seemed to be laughing together.

The movie stars Murphy as John Dolittle, who as a child could talk to the animals (there's a gem of an opening scene in which he chats matter-of-factly with his dog, whose voice is by Ellen DeGeneres, about what dogs think about people). The boy grows out of this stage, however, and even goes through an animal-hating phase before he knocks his head in a car accident and regains his inner ear for animals.

By now Murphy is grown up, a famous doctor whose partner (Platt) is in a lather to sell out their medical operation to an HMO. But Murphy gets seriously distracted by his new insights into animals, and on the night of a big business meeting he's more interested in emergency treatment for an ailing tiger from the zoo. There's also trouble with his despairing family, which has him committed to a mental institution.

Murphy is essentially the straight man in the movie; most of the laughs belong to the animals, who are brash and outspoken—especially Rodney the guinea pig, voiced by Chris Rock. Albert Brooks finds a nice long-suffering note as the ailing tiger, and Reni Santoni and John Leguizamo have some nice zingers as the laboratory rats who are brought back to life by Dolittle's first aid: "You want gratitude? Get a hamster." Some of the animals are real. Most of them are creations of the Jim Henson muppet builders. All of them look real enough, and there's some nice physical humor in a scene where Rodney gets drenched, dries itself out under a blower, and then enjoys a quick massage.

Murphy, I think, finds the right strategy in acting opposite this menagerie: He's mostly quiet, calm, not trying too hard for laughs; the overall tone of the movie, despite the gross material, is one of sweetness and gentleness. Sure, a lot of the stuff is in bad taste, but I'll never forget Mel Brooks's defense of one of his movies: "Vulgar? It rises *below* vulgarity."

Donnie Brasco ★ ★ ★ ½

R, 121 m., 1997

Al Pacino (Lefty Ruggiero), Johnny Depp (Joe/Donnie), Michael Madsen (Sonny), Bruno Kirby (Nicky), Anne Heche (Maggie), James Russo (Paulie), Andrew Parks (Hollman). Directed by Mike Newell and produced by Mark Johnson, Barry Levinson, Louis DiGiaimo, and Gail Mutrux. Screenplay by Paul Attanasio, based on the book *Donnie Brasco: My Undercover Life in the Mafia,* by Joseph Pistone and Richard Woodley.

Norman Mailer told us tough guys don't dance, but in the movies it's mostly tough guys who do dance. We're so leery of close emotional bonds between men that the movies are only comfortable showing them if the guys are cops, jocks, soldiers, or Mafioso. Beneath everything else, *Donnie Brasco* is the story of two men who grow to love one another within the framework of a teacher-student relationship. It's not about sex. It's about need.

The movie opens in a New York coffee shop that's a hangout for the mob. A young guy named Donnie (Johnny Depp) comes in and talks disrespectfully to an older guy named Lefty (Al Pacino). Lefty can't believe his ears: "You're calling me a dumbski? You know who you're talkin' to? Lefty from Mulberry Street!" As if that means anything.

Actually, though, it means a lot to Donnie Brasco, whose real name is Joe Pistone, and who is an undercover agent for the FBI. He gradually wins Lefty's trust, and it becomes clear that Lefty badly needs someone to trust; he has cancer, his son is a junkie, and his mob career is going nowhere. Donnie is a good-looking kid who listens well, and Lefty desperately needs to be a mentor. In another world he would have been your favorite high school teacher.

"If I say you're a friend of mine, that means you're connected," Lefty explains to Donnie. "If I say you're a friend of ours, that means you're a made guy. If I introduce you, I'm responsible for you. Anything wrong with you, I go down."

The movie is based on a 1978 book inspired by the real "Donnie Brasco" case (its author is still living in the government protection program). The story plays like a companion to *GoodFellas,* with the same lore, the same fierce Mafia code, the same alternation between sudden violence and weird comedy. (At one point Lefty is summoned to a meeting with his boss and expects to be killed. Instead, he's given a present—a lion, because he likes to watch wild animals on videos.)

The British director Mike Newell, whose biggest hit was *Four Weddings and a Funeral*, might seem like a strange choice for this material, but he's the right one because the movie is not really about violence or action, it's about friendship. We can see immediately why Lefty is drawn to Donnie, but it takes a little longer to see why Donnie begins to like Lefty. After all, a guy risks his life because he trusts you, you can't help feeling like a rat if you're double-crossing him.

Michael Madsen plays the boss Lefty reports to. He's tall, tough, relentless—and scared, too, because when he gets bumped up a notch, the job includes a $50,000 monthly payment to the guy above him. A lot of the time these guys spend time hanging around their social club, playing cards, and complaining that business is bad. In this movie Mafia guys don't get away with anything: With them it's work, work, work, just like with everybody else.

Donnie has some ideas for them, including a club in Florida that he thinks might make them some money. But opening night goes wrong, and although they suspect a stoolie in their midst, what they do not suspect is that a rival mob faction was responsible. Everytime I see a Mafia movie, I wonder how any Mafiosi can still be alive, given the rate of sudden, violent attrition and the willingness to shoot first and find out the rest of the facts later.

The Florida project and the other jobs are a backdrop for the relationship between Donnie and Lefty, which is complicated because the FBI agent has a wife and kids squirreled away in the suburbs, where they go for weeks at a time without hearing from him. He can't even tell them what he does (nor would they believe him). "I pretend I'm a widow," his wife tells him.

Eventually all of the threads, personal and criminal, come down to one moment when Lefty either will or will not act on what he knows, or thinks he knows. As the two men face their moment of truth, we are reminded what fine acting the movie contains. We expect it from Pacino, who is on ground he knows well, and who is poignant and gentle as a man who is "just a spoke in the wheel," a loyal soldier who lives and dies by the rules. For Johnny Depp, *Donnie Brasco* breaks new ground; he seems a little older here, a little wearier, and he makes the transition from stoolie to friend one subtle step at a time.

The violence in this movie is gruesome (a scene involving the disposal of bodies is particularly graphic). But the movie has many human qualities, and contains what will be remembered as one of Pacino's finest scenes. At an important moment in his life, he puts some things in a drawer. He starts to leave, then thinks again, turns back, and leaves the drawer ajar. What this implies and how it plays creates the perfect ending for the film, which fades to black—only to start up again with unnecessary footnotes. No matter; I'll remember that scene. ☞

Don't Look Back ★ ★ ★

NO MPAA RATING, 96 m., 1967 (rereleased 1998)

A documentary directed by D. A. Pennebaker and produced by Albert Grossman, John Court, and Leacock-Pennebaker Inc. With Bob Dylan, Joan Baez, Bob Neuwirth, Donovan, Tito Burns, and Albert Grossman.

What a jerk Bob Dylan was in 1965. What an immature, self-important, inflated, cruel, shallow little creature, lacking in empathy and contemptuous of anyone who was not himself or his lackey. Did we actually once take this twerp as our folk god?

I scribbled down these and other observations as I watched the newly restored print of *Don't Look Back*, the 1967 documentary about Dylan's 1965 concert tour of England. And I was asking myself: Surely I didn't fall for this at the time? I tried to remember the review I wrote when the movie was new. Was I so much under the Dylan spell that I couldn't see his weakness of character?

Take the two scenes, for example, where he mercilessly puts down a couple of hardworking interviewers who are only trying to do their job (i.e., give Dylan more publicity), while a roomful of Dylan yes-men, groupies, and foot-kissers join in the jeers. I was chilled by the possibility that I reacted to these scenes differently the first time around, falling for Dylan's rude and nearly illiterate word games as he pontificates about "truth."

I hurried home and burrowed into my files for the 1967 review of *Don't Look Back*, and was relieved to discover that, even then, I had my senses about me. "Those who consider Dylan a lone, ethical figure standing up against the phonies will discover after seeing this film," I wrote, "that they have lost their hero. Dylan reveals himself, alas, to have clay feet like all the rest of us. He is immature, petty, vindictive, lacking a sense of humor, overly impressed with his own importance and not very bright." Thank God I was not deceived. I gave the movie three stars, and still do, for its alarming insights.

Of course there is the music. Always the music. I'm listening to "Highway 61 Revisited" as I write these words. I like his music, and I like his whiny, nasal delivery of it; it speaks to the eternal misunderstood complainer in all of us. I remember the thrill we all felt as undergraduates when we first heard "Blowin' in the Wind." Of course, at the time we thought *we* were the answer, my friends, but we were young and hadn't seen this movie.

As a musician, Dylan has endured and triumphed. Perhaps he has also grown and matured as a human being, and is today a nice guy with an infectious sense of humor and a certain soft-spoken modesty. Or maybe not. I don't know. What I do know is that D. A. Pennebaker's 1967 film, which invented the rock documentary, is like a time capsule from just that period when Sgt. Pepper was steamrollering Mr. Tambourine Man. "You don't ask the Beatles those questions, do you?" Dylan says to one reporter. To which the only possible answer was, Bob, you just don't know the half of it.

Another irony is that a true folk goddess, Joan Baez, with her remarkable voice, presence, and soul, tags along during the early scenes, barely acknowledged by Dylan. She brings a glow to the film by singing "Love Is a Four-Letter Word" in a hotel room one night, and then disappears from the film, unremarked. My guess is that she'd had enough.

The movie is like a low-rent version of the rock concert documentaries that would follow. Dylan is badgered by a room full of journalists at a press conference—but it's a small room, with only half a dozen reporters. He insults them, lacking the Beatles' saving grace of wit. He's mobbed by fans—hundreds, not thousands. He fills Royal Albert Hall, not Wembley Stadium. He reminds me of that mouse floating down the Chicago River on its back, signaling for the drawbridge to be raised.

Sometimes you simply cannot imagine what he, or the filmmakers, were thinking. "How did you start?" he's asked at a press conference. Cut to a scene in a southern cotton field. Dylan stands in front of a pickup truck with some old black field hands sitting on it. He sings a song. Are we supposed to think he rode the rails and bummed in hobo jungles and felt proletarian solidarity with the workers, like Woody Guthrie, Pete Seeger, or Ramblin' Jack Elliott? I was reminded of Steve Martin in *The Jerk* saying, "I was born a poor black child." The field hands break into grateful applause, as the scene dissolves into a thunderous London concert ovation. Give us a break.

If Dylan sees this rerelease, I hope he cringes. We were all callow once, but it is a curable condition. A guy from *Time* magazine comes to interview him. "I know more about what you do just by looking at you than you'll ever be able to know about me," Dylan tells him, little suspecting how much we know just by looking at him. He suggests that the magazine try printing the truth. And what would that be? "A photo of a tramp vomiting into a sewer, and next to it a picture of Rockefeller," suggests the man described in a recent review as "one of the most significant artists of the second half of the twentieth century." Significance I will grant him. More than we knew.

Double Team ★★

R, 90 m., 1997

Jean-Claude Van Damme (Jack Quinn), Mickey Rourke (Stavros), Dennis Rodman (Yaz), Natacha Lindinger (Katherine), Paul Freeman (Goldsmythe), Jay Benedict (CIA Agent Brandon), Rob Diem (Dieter Staal). Directed by Tsui Hark and produced by Moshe Diamant. Screenplay by Don Jakoby and Paul Mones.

Double Team is one of the most preposterous action films ever made, and I do not mean that as a criticism. It will give you some notion of this movie's strangeness if I tell you that

Dennis Rodman does not play the most peculiar character.

Oh, he's the weirdest *looking*, all right. But consider what Mickey Rourke's villain does: Burning for vengeance on Jean-Claude Van Damme, he captures Van Damme's newborn son and puts the tot in the center of the Roman Coliseum, surrounded by land mines and threatened by a prowling tiger. "If you live, you'll know your son," he shouts. "If not—I'll raise him as my own."

Van Damme plays Jack Quinn, a counterterrorist operative recruited for one last assignment. Scribbling madly in the dark, I got down the highlights of his briefing. If you read closely, you may notice a contradiction between the fourth and sixth sentences: "You're a hunter, Jack. You miss the game. Stavros is bad. And we want him alive. We've got a Delta team prepped and waiting for you at Antwerp. Face it, Jack—you can't retire until he dies."

In Antwerp, Van Damme meets Yaz (Rodman) in an omnisexual club in the red-light district, and Rodman sets him up with weapons from such a formidable workshop that Van Damme calls him "Santa." Rodman: "I may not have reindeer, but I do have the best elves in the business." Stavros (Rourke) is also in Antwerp, and takes his child to an amusement park, where the kid is killed in a shoot-out.

Stavros escapes, and as punishment Van Damme is banished to the Colony, a think tank for those "too valuable to kill—too dangerous to set free." Determined to escape and rejoin his pregnant wife, Van Damme cuts off his thumbprint to fool a security device. His getaway is done via aerial stunts, and indeed all the stunt work and special effects are impressive; the direction is by Tsui Hark of Hong Kong, famous for the *Chinese Ghost Story* films.

The trail leads to Rome. Van Damme is joined by Rodman. They jump from a plane without parachutes and land inside a giant basketball, although I'm none too clear about how it inflated around them. Meanwhile, Stavros kidnaps Van Damme's wife and sets a trap for him involving a bomb disguised as a baby. The movie is moving so fast here that the poor wife has her big childbirth scene reduced to a cameo (someone shouts "Push! Push!" as a battle rages around her).

Rodman analyzes the situation: "It's time to get off the bench. The best defense is a strong offense." Van Damme is desperate to find his wife. Rodman comes to the rescue. He just happens to be on friendly terms with an order of monks whose subterranean database can track down missing persons. This leads to a trip through the Catacombs and a scene where Rodman throws a human skull at a detonator, misses, and says, "Oops! Air ball!" Then come the baby and the tiger.

The movie is a typical international action thriller, with as little dialogue as possible (to make dubbing easier). The structure is simple: setup scene, action, stunts, next setup, etc. Van Damme was better in his last two movies (*Timecop* and *Sudden Death*) because he had more to do: Here he's at the mercy of the jam-packed plot.

And Dennis Rodman? He does a splendid job of playing a character who seems in every respect to be Dennis Rodman. He seems at home on the screen, he's confident, and in action scenes he'll occasionally do a version of the high-spirited hop-skip-and-jump he sometimes does on the court. He looks like he's having fun, and that's crucial for a movie actor. His agent should have told him, though, that if you can't be the hero, be the villain. That's always a better role than the best friend.

Doug's 1st Movie ★ ½

G, 77 m., 1999

Directed by Maurice Joyce and produced by Jim Jinkins, David Campbell, Melanie Grisanti, and Jack Spillum. Screenplay by Ken Scarborough. With the voices of: Thomas McHugh (Doug Funnie, Lincoln), Fred Newman (Skeeter Valentine, Mr. Dink, Porkchop, Ned), Constance Shulman (Patti Mayonnaise), Chris Phillips (Roger Koltz, Boomer, Larry, Mr. Chiminy), Gay Hadley (Guy Graham), Doug Preis (Bill Bluff, Doug's Dad, Secret Agent).

Doug's 1st Movie is a thin and less-than-thrilling feature-length version of a Saturday morning animated series, unseen by me. Chatter on the Web suggests it was originally intended to go straight to video, but was rechanneled into theaters after the startling success of *The Rugrats Movie*. Since Doug originally started on Nickelodeon, where *Rugrats* resides, the decision made sense—or would have if this had been a better movie.

The plot: Skeeter, the best pal of twelve-year-old Doug, finds a polluted pond and is about to take a photo when a nasty trick is played on him by some schoolmates who pretend to be a monster. Then a real monster emerges from the waters behind him.

This creature, which serves as proof that the lake is polluted, is actually such a nice monster that it argues for, not against, pollution. It borrows the name Herman Melville from the cover of the book it's reading *(Moby-Dick)*, and becomes a secret friend of Doug and Skeeter's, in *E.T.* fashion.

The plot thickens: The lake is being polluted by the evil Bill Bluff, a local industrialist. Bluff's spy at the school is Guy Graham, editor of the school paper. Guy is also Doug's rival for the love of Patti Mayonnaise, whom Doug wants to take to the prom. Patti grows convinced that Doug is cheating on her with an exchange student, who is actually the monster in drag.

Meanwhile . . . but is the plot of any importance? I think not. It is the vehicle for some fairly routine animation, and characters who may inspire Saturday morning TV watchers but left me indifferent. They have a kind of joy in stupidity. I did like one sequence in the film, involving the ultimate in virtual reality: a VR experience in which everything is exactly as it is in real life, except more expensive.

Will kids like this movie? Who can say? *Rugrats* it ain't.

Down in the Delta ★ ★ ★ ½

PG-13, 111 m., 1998

Alfre Woodard (Loretta), Al Freeman Jr. (Earl), Mary Alice (Rosa Lynn), Esther Rolle (Annie), Loretta Devine (Zenia), Wesley Snipes (Will), Mpho Koaho (Thomas), Kulani Hassen (Tracy). Directed by Maya Angelou and produced by Rick Rosenberg, Bob Christiansen, Victor McGauley, Wesley Snipes, and Reuben Cannon. Screenplay by Myron Goble.

There is a moment in Maya Angelou's *Down in the Delta* when a Chicago woman applies for a job in a supermarket and cannot pass a math test. Turned down, she leaves the store and buys a bottle. Her feelings of inadequacy and worthlessness come through so painfully that we understand, with a surge of empathy, why her life has grown so complicated: She has experienced versions of this rejection for years, and booze or reefer at least offers a brief oblivion.

The woman is named Loretta, and she is played by Alfre Woodard in a performance that is like an act of sympathy with the character. Loretta lives in the Chicago projects with her mother, Rosa Lynn (Mary Alice), and her two children. Thomas (Mpho Koaho) is bright and hard-driving, taking Polaroids of tourists on Rush Street for $5 to make money. Tracy (Kulani Hassen), the baby, is autistic. For years Rosa Lynn has watched her daughter sleep late, sleep around, get drunk, and keep her life on hold. In an early scene, we see Rosa telephone Loretta to wake her up in the morning. She reminds Loretta to feed the baby. Loretta puts some Coca-Cola in a baby bottle.

Rosa Lynn decides things have to change. She delivers an ultimatum: Either Loretta agrees to take her children and spend the summer in the family home on the Mississippi Delta, or Rosa Lynn calls in the child welfare people to take the kids. Loretta has to agree. Rosa Lynn pawns an 1852 silver candelabra, a family heirloom, to finance the trip, which places Loretta and her kids in the hands of her brother-in-law Earl (Al Freeman Jr.).

Uncle Earl runs a diner and employs a local woman (Loretta Devine) to care for his wife, Annie (Esther Rolle), who has Alzheimer's. He's not crazy about taking in three visitors for the summer—especially since he and his sister Rosa have been arguing over that candelabra for years. Loretta doesn't fit in well at first, and her city son doesn't immediately take to the country. But eventually family feelings and values begin to take hold.

If this sounds perhaps like a morality play, it's because no summary can explain the effect of the details in the film. Woodard's performance as Loretta is good at illustrating her problems without ever making her pathetic. Al Freeman, recently seen in *Once Upon a Time . . . When We Were Colored*, is one of the most convincing and natural of actors. And the atmosphere of the Delta is evoked in side stories involving the closure of a chicken plant and the visit of Earl's son (Wesley Snipes), a lawyer from Atlanta.

Angelou is famous as a writer, but she didn't write this movie. It's based on a screenplay by a Georgian named Myron Goble, which won a contest. It illustrates that a strong story, deeply felt and engendered outside the Hollywood assembly line, is likely to get its effects from observation, instead of by following the lazy outlines of formulas from the screenwriting tutors. Study this film side by side with *Patch Adams,* the Robin Williams vehicle, and you will see the contrast between characters who are alive and those who are puppets.

Angelou's first-time direction stays out of its own way; she doesn't call attention to herself with unnecessary visual touches, but focuses on the business at hand. She and Goble are interested in what might happen in a situation like this, not in how they can manipulate the audience with phony crises. When Annie wanders away from the home, for example, it's handled in the way it might really be handled, instead of being turned into a set-piece.

Year after year, in film after film, I've seen Alfre Woodard at work. She is on that very short list of people who rarely seem to appear in anything unworthy. Films may work or they may not, but you don't sense cynicism in her choices. She looks for roles that look like they need to be played.

Woodard says she was more interested in the "early" Loretta than in the later one. Success has many parents, but failure has none, and the early Loretta, going to buy a bottle, is all alone and has little help. But she's not a bad person. Perhaps she was failed by a school system that didn't take care to teach her. Or by a community with few role models. Or by herself. When you are young, you can carelessly take a path that branches far off from where you thought you were headed. Woodard plays her without turning her into a case study.

I liked the symbolism of the antique candelabra. I won't reveal its history. I will observe that in a poetic and unexpected way, it shows how Loretta's great-great-grandfather buys her out of slavery.

Dr. Akagi ★ ★ ★

NO MPAA RATING, 128 m., 1999

Akira Emoto (Dr. Akagi), Kumiko Aso (Sonoko), Jyuro Kara (Umemoto), Jacques Gamblin (Piet), Masanori Sera (Toriumi). Directed by Shohei Imamura and produced by Hisa Ino and Koji Matsuda. Screenplay by Imamura and Daisuke Tengan.

Dr. Akagi is the kind of family doctor that Spencer Tracy might have played in a 1940s Hollywood film—if Hollywood doctors in those days had lived with prostitutes, befriended morphine addicts, sheltered escaped prisoners of war, and dug up bodies to remove their livers. But I make him sound like a wild man, and in fact he is a gentle, driven soul—more an absentminded professor than a mad scientist.

The doctor (Akira Emoto) is the subject of the new film by Shohei Imamura, the Japanese director who makes films along the fault line between everyday life and outlaw human behavior. "I am interested in the relationship between the lower part of the human body and the lower part of the social structure," he has said. His previous film, *The Eel,* which won the Palme d'Or at the 1997 Cannes festival, was about a wife-murderer who is released from prison and sets up a barbershop in a remote area. Now here is *Dr. Akagi,* set during the last days of World War II.

Because of the war, its hero is the only family doctor for miles around, and in the first shot we see him running to a bedside. "Being a family doctor is all legs," he says. He is known locally as "Dr. Liver," because his diagnosis is invariably the same: hepatitis, treated with an injection of glucose. Sometimes he doubles as a social worker, as when a mother moans to him that her son, a respectable clerk at city hall, has taken up with a prostitute. He is not much shocked, not even when he finds the clerk has embezzled funds to pay the woman. Her name is Sonoko (Kumiko Aso) and she eventually falls in love with Dr. Akagi. How much in love? She was raised in a red-light district, where her mother lectured her, "No freebies!" But for Akagi, it's free—or would be, if he didn't reject her enthusiastic assaults.

He's too busy. He has a theory about why hepatitis cases are spreading so quickly, and experiments with new kinds of microscopes, borrowing an arc lamp from a movie projector to see the little microbes more clearly. Sonoko, peering over his shoulder, asks if there are male and female bacteria, and is shocked to learn there are not: "You mean there is no prostitution in nature?" She moves in and becomes the doctor's housekeeper. His laboratory assistant is another doctor, addicted to drugs. An oddly secular monk joins the household. When a Dutch POW escapes from a torture chamber, Akagi takes him in, too, treating his wounds and letting him help with the research.

Imamura's work reflects on Japanese life as it has changed in his lifetime (he is seventy-two). His best film is *Vengeance Is Mine* (1979), based on the true story of a serial killer who travels the countryside, hunted and hunting. In 1989, he made *Black Rain*, about the aftermath of radioactive fallout in a village near Hiroshima. I will never forget his famous *Ballad of Narayama*, the 1983 Cannes grand prize winner, based on a Japanese legend about a village that takes its old people up onto the mountain to die when they outlive their usefulness.

Dr. Akagi is more matter-of-fact. It is about a busy middle-aged man who treats all manner of illness, physical and mental, while obsessing over hepatitis. At one point he literally does dig up a corpse to dissect a fresh liver (the mourners find it curious that the doctor specifies the abdomen be kept iced after death). There is a war going on all during the movie, and indeed Akagi's son dies, but daily life in the village bumbles along, punctuated only by air raids and announcements of smaller rice rations.

Imamura allows himself poetic touches, sparingly. When the telegram arrives telling Akagi that his son is dead, he shreds it into tiny pieces and throws it into the air; countless more little paper scraps float down like snow, a reminder of how many telegrams the war has inspired. And at the end, Akagi and the former prostitute are out in a boat when an atomic bomb falls. He looks at the mushroom cloud and observes that it resembles a hypertrophied liver.

The Dreamlife of Angels ★ ★ ★ ½

R, 113 m., 1999

Elodie Bouchez (Isa), Natacha Regnier (Marie), Gregoire Colin (Chris), Jo Prestia (Fredo), Patrick Mercado (Charly). Directed by Erick Zonca and produced by Francois Marquis. Screenplay by Zonca and Roger Bohbot.

The French believe that most of the characters in American movies, no matter what their ages, act like teenagers. I believe that the teenagers in most French movies seem old, wise, and sad. There is a lesson here, perhaps that most American movies are about plots, and most French movies are about people.

The Dreamlife of Angels serves as an example. It is about two twenty-year-olds who are already marked by the hard edges of life. They meet, they become friends, and then they find themselves pulled apart by sexuality, which one of them sees as a way to escape a lifetime of hourly wages. This is a movie about a world where young people have to work for a living. Most twenty-year-old Americans in the movies receive invisible monthly support payments from God.

We meet Isa (Elodie Bouchez), a tough little nut with a scar over one eye and a gift of gab. She's a backpacker who cuts photos out of magazines, pastes them to cardboard squares, and peddles them in bars as "tourist views." She doesn't really expect to support herself that way, but it's a device to strike up conversations, and sure enough she meets a guy who offers her a job—as a seamstress in a sweatshop.

At work, she meets Marie (Natacha Regnier). The two women become friends, and Isa moves in with Marie. They hang out in malls and on the streets, smoking, kidding, playing at picking up guys. They aren't hookers; that would take a degree of calculation and planning ability that they lack—and, besides, they still dream of true romance. Isa tells Marie about one guy she met when she was part of a remodeling crew working on his house. They slept together, but when the job was over, she left, and he let her leave. She wonders if maybe she missed a good chance. Unlikely, Marie advises.

Marie steals a jacket and is seen by Chris (Gregoire Colin). He owns a club, and asks them to drop in one night. They already know the bouncers, and Marie has slept with one of them. Soon it comes down to this: Chris has money, Marie has none, and although her friendship with Isa is the most important relationship in her life, she is willing to abandon it in order to share Chris's bed and wealth. Isa, who in the beginning looked like a mental lightweight, has the wisdom and insight to see how this choice will eventually hurt Marie. But Marie will not listen.

The movie understands what few American movies admit: Not everyone can afford the luxury of following their hearts. Marie has already lost the idealism that would let her choose the bouncer (whom she likes) rather than the owner (whom she likes too, but not for the same reasons). The story is played out against the backdrop of Lille, not the first French city you think of when you think of romance. In this movie it is a city of gray streets and tired people, and there is some kind of symbolism in the fact that Marie is house-sitting her apartment for a girl in a coma.

The movie was directed and cowritten by Erick Zonca, a forty-three-year-old Parisian who lived in New York from the age of twenty, worked at odd jobs for ten years, then became the director of TV commercials. He returned to France to make his features; this is his third. He creates an easy familiarity with Isa and Marie. The story is about their conversation, their haphazard progress from day to day; it doesn't have contrived plot points.

I can't easily imagine Isa and Marie in Los Angeles, nor can I imagine an American indie director making this film, which contains no guy-talk in diners, no topless clubs, no drug dealers in bathrobes, no cigars. This year's Critics Week at Cannes has just announced that it was unable to find a single American film it admired enough to program. *The Dreamlife of Angels* shared the Best Actress Award between Bouchez and Regnier last year in the Cannes main competition. There you have it.

Dream With the Fishes ★ ★ ★

R, 96 m., 1997

David Arquette (Terry), Brad Hunt (Nick), Cathy Moriarty (Aunt Elise), Kathryn Erbe (Liz), Patrick McGaw (Don), J. E. Freeman (Joe, Nick's Father), Timi Prulhiere (Michelle), Anita Barone (Mary), Allyce Beasley (Sophia). Directed by Finn Taylor and produced by Johnny Wow and Mitchell Stein. Screenplay by Taylor.

Desperation sometimes brings with it a certain clarity. Early in *Dream With the Fishes,* a character is balanced on a bridge, ready to commit suicide by throwing himself off, when he's interrupted by a stickup man who asks for his wristwatch: "Since you're going to be dead in a few minutes anyway, what use will it be to you?"

The would-be suicide is named Terry (David Arquette). The stickup guy is Nick (Brad Hunt). "Could I have some privacy?" Terry asks. That's ironic, since in the movie's opening scenes we've seen that Terry is a Peeping Tom who spies on his neighbors with binoculars, and his favorite subjects are Nick and his girlfriend Liz (Kathryn Erbe).

From this unlikely Meet Cute, *Dream With the Fishes* generates a free-ranging road and buddy movie that, with its use of drugs and counterculture spirit, could be a seventies production—made when characters could slip through a movie without carrying a lot of plot along with them.

Terry climbs down off the bridge after Nick paints an unpleasant picture ("Hitting the water from this height, it will be like hitting concrete"). Nick makes a better offer: In return for the watch, he'll give Terry enough pills to finish himself off. But the offer is a fraud, the pills are vitamins, and the two opposites gradually, warily, become friends. If this sounds too easy, it doesn't feel that way in Finn Taylor's movie, because the screenplay goes for an edgy, elegiac tone, and we suspect that both men are carrying more secrets than they're willing to reveal.

Motivated by Nick's deteriorating health and a bargain the two of them strike, they embark on a journey. There are adventures in the spirit of the old road movies, an unplanned robbery, and even an acid trip involving a cop who pulls his gun and shoots some doughnuts dead. Their destination is Nick's childhood home, where his father, Joe (J. E. Freeman), slams the door on him. Joe has apparently had enough of his son for one lifetime, and after he finally lets his son into the house we guess the nature of their relationship from a painful shoulder-butting contest.

Freeman is good as the cool, distant father: a hard case himself, and fed up with his son. Allyce Beasley, as Nick's mother, is weary of her son's lifelong screwups, but more loving. Where he finds acceptance and some understanding, however, is with his Aunt Elise (Cathy Moriarty), a former stripper with a blowzy friendliness. Eventually Liz, the apprehensive, tattoo-obsessed girlfriend, catches up with them.

The story provides a deadline in the form of Nick's health. But the surface is as meandering as a 1970s road movie: Colorful characters materialize, do their thing, and shrink in the rear-view mirror. Taylor's screenplay is skillful in the way it presents us with Nick and Terry, who are equally unlikable, and subtly humanizes them, while Kathryn Erbe gradually modulates Liz, Nick's girlfriend, so that beneath her fearsome surface we begin to sense shadows and softness.

Dream With the Fishes is a first film, and shows some of the signs of unchained ambition. Its visual style can be a distraction, beginning with the grainy, saturated look of a music video, and then leveling out into flat realism, then getting fancy again. Although many directors have tried using contrasting visual styles to control the tone of a film (switching between black and white and color is an old technique), what usually happens is that we get sidetracked by the style changes, and the mood is broken. Better, I think, to choose a look for a film and stick with it, unless there are persuasive reasons to experiment.

There is also a plot point, involving the wife Terry says he lost in a car crash, that is resolved a little awkwardly. That strand shows signs of having survived from a first draft, maybe because Taylor needed some quick motivation. His finished film creates enough of an arc for Terry that the wife is not needed. How *Dream With the Fishes* works is that the road-movie and buddy-movie formulas slowly dissolve from around Nick and Terry, who by the end of the movie stand revealed in three dimensions; it's like the cinematic equivalent of what sculptors call the lost-wax method.

Drifting Clouds ★ ★ ★ ½

NO MPAA RATING, 96 m., 1998

Kati Outinen (Ilona), Kari Vaananen (Lauri), Sakari Kuosmanen (Melartin), Shelley Fisher (Pianist), Tero Jartti (Tax Inspector), Aarre Karen (Bank Director). Directed by Aki Kaurismaki and produced by Erkki Astala and Kaurismaki. Screenplay by Kaurismaki.

Aki Kaurismaki is the fortyish Finnish director of strange and quirky comedies, in which little people are crushed by vast economic systems, but they keep on truckin'. In *Drifting Clouds,* a woman loses her job at a bankrupt restaurant, her husband is laid off by the transport system, the TV is repossessed, she pays her savings to an employment agency for another job, she isn't paid, and when her husband tries to collect he gets beaten up. But there's a happy ending.

Kaurismaki has enormous love for these characters. He embraces their comic pathos and rejoices that they do not surrender. It's all done with such subtle irony that critics use words like "minimalist" to describe him—even though his screen is saturated with images and ideas, and true minimalism is more easily seen in something like *Armageddon,* which has half an idea and spreads it thinly over 144 minutes.

The heroine of *Drifting Clouds* is Ilona (Kati Outinen), a wan, sweet blonde with a dour expression, who works as the manager of a failing restaurant. The movie opens with a pianist singing of "the wonderful girl I love," and then there's a long shot of the interior, with customers seated at their tables like mourners at a wake. Lighting is used to highlight Ilona at her perch in the back of the shot, and after she seats a customer, there's a zoom in to her sad, thoughtful face.

There's a crisis in the kitchen. The cook is drunk again, and brandishing a knife. After an offscreen struggle, the headwaiter returns to view with a bleeding wrist. Then Ilona disappears from the screen, there is a loud thud, she returns, and then we see the chef again, disconsolate. Kaurismaki loves to keep the action offscreen and focus on the reaction shots.

After closing, Ilona boards a streetcar and kisses the driver—her husband, Lauri (Kari Vaananen). At home, he covers her eyes to spring a surprise: a new TV set, bought on time. Of course they can't afford it (you can sense that in the haunted way they look at it), but as they sit side by side on a couch that's too small, we feel curious tenderness for them.

The couch is too small because Kaurismaki insists on bargain-basement sets; he wants his characters to always seem a little too large for their rooms and furniture, and the result is cartoonlike. Consider, for example, Ilona's interview with an employment agency; the interviewer's chair squeaks loudly as he confronts her across a desk that seems scaled for a grade-school classroom.

One misfortune follows another. The restaurant closes. The husband loses his job by drawing the wrong card in an office lottery. Ilona gets another job in a restaurant whose owner is a tax cheat. Desperate to keep up appearances, she calls each order loudly into the kitchen before sneaking around a corner to cook it herself. The cook from the former restaurant appears, announcing, "I am on a journey to the end of vodka." And then, improbably, there is a happy ending, which I will not reveal except to observe that it involves a reservation for thirty from the perfectly titled Helsinki Workers' Wrestlers.

Like Godard, Jarmusch, and Mark Rappaport, Kaurismaki pays great attention to the frame around his characters. Their costumes, their props, their sets, and the colors all conspire to make each shot look deliberately composed, as if we're being asked to contemplate people trapped by, and defined by, their environment. Ilona always seems self-conscious, as if she's posing for her photo. There's a shot at a time when things are going badly; she stands next to the bookcases they've bought on credit, and her face remains impassive—but her earrings vibrate, and that's the giveaway that she's trembling.

Kaurismaki himself is a jovial, self-deprecating sort, reportedly hard drinking; he said once that he doesn't move his camera a lot because "that's a nuisance when you have a hangover" (actually, his setups show infinite thought and patience). "I'm just a medium class of director," he told Jonathan Romney of *Sight & Sound* magazine. "I may never make a masterpiece, but if I make many quite good films, together they're something." That statement, which describes many of the most successful directors working today, would never be made by any of them; that Kaurismaki can look at his work so objectively helps to explain why it has such a dry, deadpan appeal.

Drop Dead Gorgeous ★★

PG-13, 97 m., 1999

Kirstie Alley (Gladys Leeman), Ellen Barkin (Annette), Kirsten Dunst (Amber), Denise Richards (Becky), Brittany Murphy (Lisa Swenson), Allison Janney (Loretta), Will Sasso (Hank Vilmes), Amy Adams (Leslie Miller). Directed by Michael Patrick Jann and produced by Gavin Polone and Judy Hofflund. Screenplay by Lona Williams.

Sometimes I wonder how anyone could have thought a screenplay was funny enough to film. The script for *Drop Dead Gorgeous*, on the other hand, must have been a funny read. It's the movie that somehow never achieves takeoff speed. Subtle miscalculations of production and performance are probably responsible; comedy is a fragile rose, eager to wilt.

The movie takes place in Mount Rose, Minnesota, a setting created after long study of *Fargo*. The fiftieth anniversary of the Miss Teen Princess America contest is approaching, and the local chairwoman is former winner Gladys Leeman (Kirstie Alley), whose daughter Becky (Denise Richards) is a leading contender. Her big competition: trailer-park cutie Amber (Kirsten Dunst), whose alcoholic mother, Annette (Ellen Barkin), is burned in a fire and spends much of the movie with a beer can permanently fused to the flesh of her hand.

Now there's an example of how a mental image can be funnier than a real one—how a screenplay can fail to translate. You possibly smiled as you read about Annette's hand being fused to a beer can. I did as I wrote the words. But the image of the charred can embedded in scarred flesh is not funny, and every time it turns up it casts its little pall.

Another example. One of the contestants has put herself on a four-hundred-calorie-a-day diet and is a patient at a recovery center for anorexics. Nevertheless, she's determined to compete in the pageant, and arrives onstage in a wheelchair. Funny as a satirical concept? Yes. Funny as a sight? No, because the concept, not the image, contains the joke.

The movie was written by Lona Williams, who is herself a beauty pageant survivor. She understands the backstage politics of such events, especially at the local level, where almost everyone has a buried agenda. Some of the mothers are using their daughters as surrogate reminders of their own faded beauty. Some of the daughters are compensating for insecurity; they think a crown will affirm their worth. Other daughters are resentful puppets. Some of the older men enjoy the proximity to nubile contestants. Some of the women may too.

I sometimes wonder if anybody involved in beauty pageants at the administrative level is completely without motivations they would rather not discuss. The idea of devoting your life to running an event at which young women are judged on the basis of their beauty and personality—as evaluated in a game show format—gets creepier the more you think about it.

As the title of *Drop Dead Gorgeous* suggests, some of the characters turn up dead or injured. The ferocious intensity of the parents is a reminder of *The Positively True Adventures of the Alleged Texas Cheerleader-Murdering Mom*, a made-for-cable movie that's one of the great buried comic treasures of recent years, with a Holly Hunter performance that would have been Oscar material if the movie had opened in theaters. Both films are savage, but *Cheerleader-Murdering Mom* was rich in human nature, while *Drop Dead Gorgeous* simply manipulates the ideas of satire without connecting to the underlying truth. I believed the Holly Hunter character would do what she did for the reasons she had; I felt the Kirstie Alley character was generated by a screenplay.

There is, however, a lot of funny stuff in *Drop Dead Gorgeous*, and Lona Williams has a future as a comedy writer—maybe in the Dave Barry/Molly Ivins tradition, since her ideas seem more literary than cinematic. I liked the idea of a contestant's dramatic reading being from *Soylent Green*. And the way another contestant kills two birds with one stone in the talent section of the contest by singing "I Love You, Baby" to Jesus. The notion that Mount Rose is famous as the "home of the oldest living Lutheran" (recently deceased) is worthy of Garrison Keillor's Lake Wobegon.

The attempt to link Lutherans with gun nuts is less successful; Becky belongs to the Lutheran Sisterhood Gun Club, but this doesn't ring true because, well, it doesn't fit with the general notion of Lutherans as pretty peaceable folks. For satire to work, it has to contain a kernel of truth. What made *Fargo* brilliant was the way it combined satire with affection and accuracy.

The climax of *Drop Dead Gorgeous* contains a few cheerfully disgusting scenes that qualify it to open in this Summer of Raunch. But once again, the ideas are funnier than the images. Contestants get food poisoning during their trip to the finals, and vomit into the atrium lobby of the host hotel. Funny to read about? You bet. To see? Judge for yourself.

E

The Edge ★ ★ ★

R, 118 m., 1997

Anthony Hopkins (Charles Morse), Alec Baldwin (Robert Green), Elle Macpherson (Mickey Morse), Harold Perrineau (Stephen), L. Q. Jones (Styles), Kathleen Wilhoite (Ginny), David Lindstedt (James), Marc Kiely (Mechanic). Directed by Lee Tamahori and produced by Art Linson. Screenplay by David Mamet.

The Edge is like a wilderness adventure movie written by David Mamet, which is not surprising, since it *was* written by Mamet. It's subtly funny in the way it toys with the clichés of the genre. Too subtle, apparently, for some; I've read a couple of reviews by critics who think director Lee Tamahori *(Once Were Warriors)* misses the point of the Mamet screenplay and plays the material too straight. But if he'd underlined every laugh line and made the humor as broad as *The Naked Gun,* would that have made a better picture? Not at all.

Although Mamet, a poet of hard-boiled city streets, is not usually identified with outdoor action films, *The Edge* in some ways is typical of his work: It's about con games and occult knowledge, double-crosses and conversations at cross-purposes. Its key scenes involve two men stalking each other, and it adds to the irony that they are meanwhile being stalked by a bear. "Most people lost in the wild die of shame," the older character tells the younger. "They didn't do the one thing that could save their lives—thinking."

The setup: Billionaire Charles Morse (Anthony Hopkins) flies his private plane into the Alaskan wilderness so that fashion photographer Robert Green (Alec Baldwin) can photograph Morse's wife, a famous model (Elle Macpherson). Leaving the wife behind at a lodge, the two men and a photographer's assistant fly farther into the bush, and when the plane crashes and the pilot is killed, the three survivors are left to face the wilderness.

At this point we can easily predict the death of the assistant (Harold Perrineau). He's an African-American, and so falls under the BADF action movie rule ("The Brother Always Dies First"). The redeeming factor in this case is that Mamet knows that, and is satirizing the stereotype instead of merely using it. His approach throughout the movie is an amused wink at the conventions he lovingly massages.

Now Charles and Bob are left alone in the dangerous wild. Charles luckily is a very bright man, who just happens to have been reading the book *Lost in the Woods,* and has the kind of mind that absorbs every scrap of information that floats into it. Before the movie is over he will fashion a compass from a paper clip, build a bear trap, make fire from ice, and explain how you can use gunpowder to season meat.

Charles is also smart enough to suspect that Bob has been having an affair with his wife. "So, how you planning to kill me?" he asks. The catch is that each man needs the other to survive, and so a murder, if any, must be postponed or carefully timed.

The movie contains glorious scenery, quixotic Mamet conversations, and of course the obligatory action scenes. Even in generating tension, the movie toys with convention. As a bear pursues them, the men desperately bridge a deep chasm with a log, and hurry to cross it—not sitting down and scooting as any sensible person would, but trying to walk across while balancing themselves, like the Escaping Wallendas. Meanwhile, the bear, which often seems to have its tongue in its cheek, stands on the far edge and shakes the log with both paws.

There are a couple of bear-wrestling matches and a big showdown with the beast, but the movie doesn't lose its mind and go berserk with action in the last half-hour, as most action films seem to. (One of the enduring disappointments for the faithful moviegoer is to see interesting characters established in the first two acts, only to be turned into action puppets in the third.) It is typical of Mamet that he could devise his plot in such a way that the climactic payoff would be not bloodshed, but the simple exchange of a wristwatch.

Footnote: Having successfully negotiated almost its entire 118 minutes, The Edge *shoots itself in the foot. After the emotionally fraught final moments, just as the audience is savoring the implications of what has just happened, the screen fades to black and we immediately get a big credit for "Bart the Bear." Now Bart is one helluva bear (I loved him in the title role of* The Bear*), but this credit in this place is a spectacularly bad idea.*

EDtv ★★½

PG-13, 122 m., 1999

Matthew McConaughey (Ed Pekurny), Jenna Elfman (Shari), Woody Harrelson (Ray Pekurny), Sally Kirkland (Jeanette), Martin Landau (Al), Ellen DeGeneres (Cynthia Topping), Rob Reiner (Whitaker), Dennis Hopper (Hank), Elizabeth Hurley (Jill), Adam Goldberg (John), Viveka Davis (Marcia), Clint Howard (Ken). Directed by Ron Howard and produced by Brian Grazer and Howard. Screenplay by Lowell Ganz and Babaloo Mandel, based on the film *Louis XIX: Le Roi des Ondes.*

Now that two movies have been made about a man living twenty-four hours a day on television, how long until TV actually tries this as a programming idea? *EDtv* arrives less than a year after *The Truman Show,* and although the two films have different approaches (*Truman* is a parable; *EDtv* is an ambitious sitcom), they're both convinced that enormous audiences would watch intently as a man brushes his teeth, clips his nails, and is deceived by a wicked woman.

Is this true? Would they? Much would depend on the nature of the experiment, of course. *The Truman Show* gathered its poignancy from the fact that its hero didn't know he was on TV. *EDtv* is about a man who auditions for the job; as his brother points out, "How many chances do guys like us get?" The two movies offer us a choice: Would you rather be a hidden voyeur, or watch an exhibitionist?

I'd rather be a voyeur. The star of a TV show like this is likely to show me more about human nature if he doesn't know I'm watching. The kind of guy who would agree to having his whole life televised, on the other hand, is essentially just a long-form Jerry Springer guest. Anyone who would agree to such a deal is a loser, painfully needy, or nuts. And since the hero of Ron Howard's *EDtv* isn't really any of those things, the film never quite feels convincing.

The film stars Matthew McConaughey as Ed Pekurny, a Texas charmer who is discovered during auditions by a desperate cable channel. He can talk "regular" or he can talk Texan, he says, demonstrating accents as a TV executive (Ellen DeGeneres) watches, enraptured. Televising Ed's life is her idea; her boss (Rob Reiner) has his doubts at first, until she points out their current ratings are lower than the Gardening Channel ("People would rather watch soil").

Ed is signed by the channel, which also gets releases from the people in his world, including his brother Ray (Woody Harrelson), Ray's girlfriend, Shari (Jenna Elfman), his mother (Sally Kirkland), and his stepfather (Martin Landau). The first hours of the new show are slow-going (including the toenail-clipping demonstration), but things pick up after it's revealed that Ed and Shari are poised to start cheating on Ray ("I just kissed my boyfriend's brother on television!").

The movie strikes an uneasy bargain between being about television, and just being a straightforward romantic comedy. After a few setup scenes, we never have the notion that Ed's *whole* life is being shown on TV; the alleged *cinema verité* approach has an uncanny way of always being there for the right moments, with the right camera angles. And when they're needed for story conflict, new characters arrive; Ed's birth father (Dennis Hopper) appears for some touching confessions, and when a *USA Today* poll shows that viewers are bored with Shari, the producers arrange for a British sex bomb (Elizabeth Hurley) to appear on Ed's viewfinder.

The juiciest character is Ray, played by Woody Harrelson as a man always on the edge of someone else's success. After it's announced on TV that he's a lousy lover, he actually produces a defense witness—a former girlfriend who testifies, "I've had worse." The character I never quite understood was Shari, who becomes totally disillusioned with the idea of having her romance telecast, even though she's so oblivious to the cameras that she dumps Ray and embraces Ed in full view of millions during the first few days.

The movie has a lot of TV lore, including programming meetings presided over by Reiner, whose enthusiasm for EDtv grows as DeGeneres loses hers. The story arc is obvious: TV is bad for invading the privacy of these lives, and we're bad for watching. Still, Ray was right: The brothers had nothing going for them before, and now Ed is rich and famous. If he doesn't have the girl he loves, at least he has Elizabeth Hurley as a consolation prize. The story keeps undercutting its own conviction that TV is evil.

I enjoyed a lot of the movie in a relaxed sort of way; it's not essential or original in the way *The Truman Show* was, and it hasn't done any really hard thinking about the ways we interact with TV. It's a businesslike job, made to seem special at times because of the skill of the actors—especially Martin Landau, who gets a laugh with almost every line as a man who is wryly reconciled to very shaky health ("I'd yell for her, but I'd die"). After it's over, we've laughed some, smiled a little, and cared not really very much.

The Education of Little Tree ★ ★ ★

PG, 117 m., 1998

Joseph Ashton (Little Tree), Graham Greene (Willow John), James Cromwell (Granpa), Tantoo Cardinal (Granma), Mika Boorem (Little Girl), Leni Parker (Martha), Rebecca Dewey (Dolly), William Rowat (Henry). Directed by Richard Friedenberg and produced by Jake Eberts. Screenplay by Friedenberg, based on the novel by Forrest Carter.

The Education of Little Tree is another fine family movie that will no doubt be ignored by the fine families of America. The notion that there is a hungry audience for good family entertainment, nurtured by such dreamers as the critic Michael Medved, is a touching mirage. American families made it a point to avoid *The Secret Garden, The Little Princess, Shiloh,* and even *Rocket Man,* and I fear they'll also shield their offspring from *The Education of Little Tree.* Too bad. If children still exist whose imaginations have not been hammered into pulp by R-rated mayhem like *Starship Troopers,* this film will play as a magical experience.

The film tells the story of a half-Cherokee orphan who eludes the clutches of his prim white aunt and is raised in the wilderness of the Great Smoky Mountains by his grandparents. Granma (Tantoo Cardinal) is Cherokee; Granpa (James Cromwell) was "born white, but learned to see through Cherokee eyes." In a series of vignettes that add up to life's lessons, they teach Little Tree (Joseph Ashton) his school lessons, the poetry of nature, and a lot of common sense.

The film, set in the 1930s, of course sentimentalizes the wisdom of Native Americans—who, after decades in which they could do no right in the movies, now can do no wrong. Even Granpa's occupation—distilling and selling moonshine—is seen as a sort of public service for the local population, who don't have the money for store-bought booze. But for Little Tree, life in his grandparents' small cabin is an idyll: He learns of nature, of the seasons, of dogs and frogs, and the mysteries of life and death. More insights are provided by an Indian neighbor, played by Graham Greene.

The movie has its share of suspense and action, especially when "revenooers" come tramping through the woods looking for the still (the loyal dog Blue Boy holds them at bay while the boy crashes through the undergrowth rescuing a sack of granpa's equipment). And when the grandparents lose custody of the boy because of the moonshine business, there is a sequence set in a place called the Notched Gap Indian School, which is less a school than a reformatory, trying to cure its students of the notion that they are Indians. Little Tree looks through a window at the star that Granma told him to keep in sight, and knows that it looks down on her too. Granpa takes more direct action.

The film is quietly well acted. James Cromwell, as Granpa, proves here, as he did as the farmer in *Babe* and the police chief in *L.A. Confidential,* that despite his unmistakable physical presence he can play characters who are completely different from one another. What I liked here was the way Granpa is allowed to be sweet and light from the start; the movie avoids the usual cliché in which the older man is stiff and unbending, and only gradually yields. There is a touching sequence where we fear deeply for him. Tantoo Cardinal, as Granma, has a presence and conviction that gives freshness to her dialogue, which on the page might have looked rather simplistic. And Joseph Ashton, as Little Tree, is another of those young actors who is fresh and natural on camera; I believed in his character.

The movie arrives with some baggage. It is based on a book by Forrest Carter, which was first identified as autobiographical, and then, after a literary scandal, moved across the page from the *New York Times* nonfiction best-seller list to the "fiction" column. In the process it was revealed that Carter was in fact a man named Asa Carter, who had links to white supremacist groups and wrote speeches for George Wallace in his preenlightened days. What journey Asa made on his way to becoming Forrest might make a good movie, too; in *The Education of Little Tree* he wrote a story that has the elements in it for a strong, unusual, affecting drama. Anyone can find redemption.

I began on a note of pessimism, fearing that families will not embrace this wholesome PG-rated film. That would be a shame. My best guess is that more nine-year-olds will see *Scream 2* than *Little Tree.* The loud, violent, cartoonish entertainment that's pumped into the minds of kids cannot be creating much room for thought and values. It's all sensation. Movies like *Little Tree* are the kinds that families can discuss afterward. There are truths to be found in them. And questions. Somehow the noisy action junk never leaves any questions (except about the future of our civilization).

The Eel ★ ★ ★

NO MPAA RATING, 117 m., 1998

Koji Yakusho (Takuro Yamashita), Misa Shimizu (Keiko Hattori), Fujio Tsuneta (Jiro Nakajima), Mitsuko Baisho (Misako Nakajima), Akira Emoto (Tamotsu Takasaki), Sho Aikawa (Yuji Nozawa), Ken Kobayashi (Masaki Saito), Sabu Kawara (Seitaro Misato). Directed by Shohei Imamura and produced by Hisa Iino. Screenplay by Motofumi Tomikawa, Daisuke Tengan, and Imamura, based on a story by Akira Yoshimura.

The Eel opens with a shocking sequence in which a man stabs his wife to death, and the screen is stained red with blood splashed on the lens. We spend the rest of the film in uneasy anticipation that the bloodshed will be repeated; the fact that the man is capable of such an act lurks quietly beneath the everyday life that follows, and prevents us from ever being sure what tone the movie is finally taking.

The man's name is Yamashita, and he is played by Koji Yakusho, the man who took the ballroom lessons in *Shall We Dance.* He's an office worker as the film opens. Receiving an anonymous letter telling him his wife has taken a lover, he arrives home early, finds them in bed, stabs her, and turns himself in to the police. Eight years pass, he is released from prison, and he settles in a rural backwater close to the Buddhist priest who is his parole officer. He opens a barbershop. One day he saves a young woman from suicide; the priest suggests he give her a job in his shop, and . . .

And we're wrong if we think we know what happens then. The movie doesn't fall into easy generic developments, but stubbornly focuses on the oddness of human nature. Yamashita is not a good candidate for redemption, but neither is he necessarily a dangerous man. The film seems to be about a lot of things (it is filled with colorful local characters, with a subplot about the young woman's problems), but in a way they all merely whirl about the still center, which is the enigma of Yamashita.

Why, for example, did he spend his prison years never speaking, except to an eel? And why does the pet eel remain so important to him? (He almost left it behind in prison, so we suspect it is not this eel so much as the idea of the eel that obsesses him.) He says he wants nothing to do with women, and little enough to do with men; his barbershop is not a center for happy chatter. When the woman comes to work for him, she brings her own damaged past, and when she tries to be friends—bringing him lunch while he fishes—he holds himself aloof. All around are people who are easily read (an angry former fellow inmate, a nutty mother, a man who thinks UFOs are landing), and here is Yamashita, in a zone of his own.

The Eel, which shared the grand prize at Cannes in 1997, is by Shohei Imamura. Born in 1927, he began as an assistant director for the great and poetic director Yasujiro Ozu but has never been attracted to his domestic stories. Instead, Imamura is drawn to the strangeness of the violent; he is interested in people who are not violent as a profession (as criminals are), but whose inner violence leaps out and shows us how wounded they are. His *Vengeance Is Mine* (1979), the story of a serial killer, is not only about the man's crimes but about his utter loneliness. *The Ballad of Narayama* (1983) is about the custom of leaving old people exposed on a mountain to die when they grow too old to live comfortably. It is quietly, unblinkingly cruel, and yet told in terms of domestic details (one old woman does not want to die until she has married off all of her children).

The portrait of everyday Japan in *The Eel* is intriguing; the quiet area where the story is set is filled with people who take a lively interest in each other's business, while all the time seeming to keep their distance. There are conventional plot elements (will the fellow ex-con tell the woman that Yamashita murdered his wife?). There's comic relief from the local oddballs. And yet always thrumming beneath everything else is the possibility that Yamashita is a time bomb, that he may kill again. Or perhaps not. Perhaps the eel could tell us.

The Eighth Day ★★★

NO MPAA RATING, 118 m., 1997

Daniel Auteuil (Harry), Pascal Duquenne (Georges), Miou-Miou (Julie), Isabelle Sadoyan (Georges's Mother), Henri Garcin (Company Director), Michele Maes (Nathalie), Laszlo Harmati (Luis Mariano), Helene Roussel (Julie's Mother), Fabienne Loriaux (Fabienne), Didier De Neck (Fabienne's Husband). Directed by Jaco Van Dormael and produced by Philippe Godeau. Screenplay by Van Dormael.

The Eighth Day teaches a lesson that everybody piously agrees with and nobody practices: We must embrace simplicity and freedom, give ourselves room to breathe, and shake off the shackles of the lockstep world. In the movie, evil is represented by a faceless giant corporation, photographed in cold shades of gray and blue. Goodness is embodied in a character who has Down syndrome and approaches life directly, with great delight. During the course of the story he will teach the lesson of freedom to Harry, a harassed executive.

There is nothing to quarrel with here, but we must be careful before we sign up for freedom. I applaud it, but if I miss too many deadlines while embracing joy and freedom, I will find myself without a job. You, dear reader, can read my review and likewise subscribe to freedom. But if you are like me, reading the paper is a blessed oasis of private time in the morning before you must race out of the house and rejoin the rat race.

I've seen a lot of movies where simple characters teach complex ones how to relax and enjoy life. *Rain Man* is an obvious example. Offhand, I can't recall a movie where a character starts out unfettered and free, and the movie teaches him that he needs to punch a time clock. I guess nobody would buy a ticket to that movie.

The hero of *The Eighth Day* is Georges, played by Pascal Duquenne, a professional actor in Belgium who has Down syndrome. Since the death of his mother, Georges has lived in an institution that looks like a pleasant place. He has a sweetheart there, and some friends, and in his dreams he's comforted by his mother. One day a lot of the patients prepare for visits. Georges has no one to visit, but he packs his bag and sets off across the fields, his destination uncertain.

The movie's other central character is Harry (Daniel Auteuil), whose corporate job is to teach his company's faceless minions how to fake a smile. He is consumed by unreleased anger. His wife (Miou-Miou) has left him, he is under orders not to approach her home, and although his daughters are allowed to visit him, he forgets they're coming. They wait at the train station and then take the next train home, furious.

Harry's life is not worth living. In a touching scene, he addresses a chair as if his wife were sitting in it. He drives out recklessly into the rain, inviting suicide, and kills a big dog that has accompanied Georges. He is at a loss what to do. The police are no help. Eventually he finds himself saddled with Georges, and after they bury the dog they find themselves sharing life together for a few days. Harry wants nothing more than to get rid of Georges. In real life, of course, that would take only a phone call, but this is a movie.

Georges lives in a world where fantasy and reality pass back and forth through the membrane of his perceptions. He takes things literally. He believes that after you cut the grass, you should comfort it. He is visited by a singing Mexican cowboy from a Technicolor musical. When he hears the word "Mongoloid," he imagines a world of Mongols with Chinese hats and pigtails. He responds directly and without affectation to whatever happens. He embraces life. He goes with the flow. Whatever.

You now have everything you need to imagine the movie. It is about Harry's gradual alienation from his corporate prison, and about the lessons Georges can teach him. About how the two men become friends. There is even a scene late in the film where Georges is reunited with some of his former fellow patients, and they commandeer a bus and drive it wildly through the streets; such an adventure is more or less obligatory for a story like this.

Watching *The Eighth Day,* I felt contradictory impulses. On the one hand, I was acutely aware of how conventional the story was. On the other, I was enchanted by the friendship between Harry and Georges. Auteuil is a fine actor, and so is Duquenne, who belongs to a Brussels experimental theatrical troupe and approaches every scene with a combination of complete commitment and utter abandon. These two men shared the Best Acting prize at the 1996 Cannes Film Festival, and indeed it would be impossible to honor one without the other.

What I also liked was the visual freedom that the director, Jaco Van Dormael, brings to the screen. We see the most unexpected sights here: busy little ladybugs, and an ant being trapped inside a vacuum cleaner, and Georges walking on water, and scenes of flying and drifting, clouds and fantasies, dreams and rest. The single most enchanting moment in the film is an overhead shot, looking straight down on the two men after one has said "in a minute," and then for exactly sixty seconds they pause, and wait, and experience a minute, so that we can too.

The Eighth Day could have been a better film. Its message is too easy. It could have dealt more deeply with these characters. One can choose to reject its easy sentimentality. I eventually chose not to. I opened myself to it. Went with the flow. Whatever.

8 Heads in a Duffel Bag ★ ★

R, 97 m., 1997

Joe Pesci (Tommy Spinelli), Andy Comeau (Charlie), Kristy Swanson (Laurie Bennett), Todd Louiso (Steve), George Hamilton (Dick Bennett), Dyan Cannon (Annette Bennett), David Spade (Ernie). Directed by Tom Schulman and produced by Brad Krevoy, Steve Stabler, and John Bertolli. Screenplay by Schulman.

8 Heads in a Duffel Bag sounds, I know, like a miniseries inspired by *Bring Me the Head of Alfredo Garcia.* But the movie's roots are in screwball comedy, and occasionally it does approach the zaniness it yearns for. It stars Joe Pesci as a gangster whose mission is to deliver the heads of eight gangsters to a man in San Diego who will accept them, not unreasonably, as evidence that their owners are dead.

Pesci's duffel bag is switched at an airport with an identical bag owned by Charlie (Andy Comeau), a medical student headed for a Mexican vacation with his fiancée. He has enough problems. His beloved, named Laurie (Kristy Swanson), is no longer sure she wants to marry him. Under the influence of her alcoholic mother (Dyan Cannon) and deeply tanned father (George Hamilton), she has changed. "Look at you!" Charlie cries. "Six months at home and you've mutated from a fun-loving free spirit into . . . into . . . Nancy Reagan!"

Spinelli, the Pesci character, has twenty-four hours to find those heads. Using clues in Charlie's bag, he visits the kid's fraternity house and tortures two of his frat brothers (David Spade and Todd Louiso) to find out Charlie's vacation plans. I've seen a lot of torture methods in the movies, but never one as ingenious as this: He makes them put on their stethoscopes, and then bangs the little metal discs together. They talk.

Meanwhile, in Mexico, Charlie has discovered the heads in his bag. So has the resort's pet dog, who sniffs out the secret and would have gotten more laughs if they'd cast a truly funny dog, like a Chihuahua. Spinelli and the fraternity brothers fly to Mexico for the climax, which involves at one point as many as fourteen heads, I believe, along with much debate about whether it's murder if you thaw out a cryogenically frozen person.

Joe Pesci is the best thing in the movie; he's funny every moment he's on the screen. None of the other characters is fully realized, and the two most promising—played by Hamilton and Cannon—aren't on-screen enough. Andy Comeau, as Charlie, doesn't generate the madness the role requires. He seems merely frenzied when he needs to seem crazed. For screwball comedy to work, there has to be a frightening intensity in the characters. The plots are always threatening to spin out of control, and their single-minded urgency is needed to keep the story grounded. Everyone here, except Pesci, is just a little too comfortable.

Pesci has a lot of scenes that strike just the right note, as when he gets into a fight with a flight attendant over whether he can put his oversize bag into the overhead compartment. Consider his dilemma: He's desperate because the heads need to be in San Diego. He's trapped because if he protests too much they'll throw him off the plane. Anger and ferocity lurk just beneath the surface, but he can't explode or he'll get in trouble with the airline. Pesci finds a great actor's solution to the scene: He's not fighting with the attendant, he's fighting with himself. (Jim Carrey did the same sort of thing in *Liar Liar.*)

He has other good scenes, including one in which George Hamilton's mother gets on his nerves, and he sends her on a quick tour of the Mexican mountains. But the others in the cast aren't at his level, and scenes that should be funnier (as when a blind laundress pops a head in the dryer) lack focus and a payoff. We also get an unnecessary Mexican youth gang, which surrounds Charlie and laughs maniacally while calling him a gringo, simply because every single time a gringo gets lost in Mexico it is written in the clouds that he must be surrounded and laughed at maniacally. (Did this cliché start with Alfonso Bedoya in *The Treasure of the Sierra Madre,* or is it even older?)

8 Heads in a Duffel Bag, written and directed by Tom Schulman, takes a lot of chances, and if they'd all worked it might have been a great comedy—its combination of Mafia logic and grotesque humor might have propelled it toward the success of a triumph like *Bound.* But it doesn't scale those heights. It stops at the foothills, and only Pesci continues, climbing on alone.

8MM ★ ★ ★

R, 123 m., 1999

Nicolas Cage (Tom Welles), Joaquin Phoenix (Max California), James Gandolfini (Eddie Poole), Peter Stormare (Dino Velvet), Anthony Heald (Longdale), Chris Bauer (Machine), Catherine Keener (Amy Welles), Amy Morton (Mrs. Mathews). Directed by Joel Schumacher and produced by Gavin Polone, Judy Hofflund, and Schumacher. Screenplay by Andrew Kevin Walker.

Joel Schumacher's *8MM* is a dark, dank journey into the underworld of snuff films undertaken by a private investigator who is appalled and changed by what he finds. It deals with the materials of violent exploitation films, but in a nonpornographic way; it would rather horrify than thrill. The writer is Andrew Kevin Walker, who wrote *Seven,* and once again creates a character who looks at evil and asks (indeed, screams) "Why?"

The answer comes almost at the end of the film, from its most vicious character: "The things I do—I do them because I like them. Because I want to." There is no comfort there, and the final shots, of an exchange of smiles, are ironic; Walker accepts that pure evil can exist, and that there are people who are simply bad; one of his killers even taunts the hero: "I wasn't beaten as a child. I didn't hate my parents."

The movie stars Nicolas Cage as an enigmatic family man named Tom Welles, who works as a private investigator and comes home to a good marriage with his wife (Catherine Keener) and baby. He specializes in top-level clients and total discretion. He's hired by the lawyer for a rich widow who has found what appears to be a snuff film in the safe of her late husband; she wants reassurance that the girl in the film didn't really die, and Welles tells her snuff films are "basically an urban legend—makeup, special effects, you know."

The film follows Welles as he identifies the young woman in the film, meets her mother, follows her movements, and eventually descends into the world of vicious pornographers for hire, who create films to order for a twisted clientele. Joel Schumacher has an affinity for dark atmosphere (he made *The Lost Boys, Flatliners,* and two of the Batman pictures). Here, with Mychael Danna's mournful music and Robert Elswit's squinting camera, he creates a sense of foreboding even in an opening shot of passengers walking through an airport.

The purpose of the film is to take a fairly ordinary character and bring him into such a disturbing confrontation with evil that he is driven to kill someone. Tom Welles, we learn, went to a good school on an academic scholarship, but although his peers "went into law and finance," the rich widow's attorney muses, "you chose surveillance." Yes, says Welles: "I thought it was the future." Mostly his work consists of tailing adulterers, but this case is different. He meets and talks with the mother of the girl in the film, traces her journey to Hollywood, and then enlists a guide to help him explore the hidden world of the sex business.

This is Max California (Joaquin Phoenix), who once aimed high but now works in porno retail; the film suggests that the Los Angeles economy takes hopeful young job-seekers and channels them directly into the sex trades. Through Max, Welles meets Eddie Poole (James Gandolfini), the kind of guy who means it when he says he can get you whatever you're looking for. And through Eddie, they meet Dino Velvet, a vicious porn director played by Peter Stormare—who was the killer who said almost nothing in *Fargo,* and here creates a frightening set of weirdo verbal affectations. The star of some of his films is Machine (Chris Bauer), who doesn't like to remove his mask.

We expect Welles to get into danger with these men, and he does, but *8MM* doesn't treat the trouble simply as an occasion for action scenes. There is a moment here when Welles has the opportunity to get revenge, but lacks the will (he is not a killer), and he actually telephones a victim and asks to be talked into it. I haven't seen that before in a movie, and it raises moral questions that the audience has to deal with, one way or another.

I know some audience members will be appalled by this film, as many were by *Seven.* It is a very hard R that would doubtless have been NC-17 if it had come from an indie instead of a big studio with clout. But it is a real film. Not a slick exploitation exercise with all the trappings of depravity but none of the consequences. Not a film where moral issues are forgotten in the excitement of an action climax. Yes, the hero is an ordinary man who finds himself able to handle violent situations, but that's not the movie's point. The last two words of the screenplay are "save me," and by the time they're said, we know what they mean. ☞

Election ★ ★ ★ ½

R, 104 m., 1999

Matthew Broderick (Jim McAllister), Reese Witherspoon (Tracy Flick), Chris Klein (Paul Metzler), Phil Reeves (Walt Hendricks), Mark Harelik (Dave Novotny), Delaney Driscoll (Linda Novotny), Jessica Campbell (Tammy), Molly Hagan (Diane McAllister), Colleen Camp (Judith R. Flick). Directed by Alexander Payne and produced by Albert Berger, Ron Yerxa, David Gale, and Keith Samples. Screenplay by Payne and Jim Taylor, based on the novel by Tom Perrotta.

I remember students like Tracy Flick, the know-it-all who always has her hand in the air while the teacher desperately looks for someone else to call on. In fact, I *was* a student like Tracy Flick. "A legend in his own mind," they wrote under my photo in the Urbana High School yearbook. I remember informing an English teacher that I didn't know why we were wasting time on the short stories of Eudora Welty when I could write better ones myself.

Tracy is smarter than that, and would never occupy such an exposed position. She's the subject of Alexander Payne's *Election,* a wicked satire about an election for student government president, a post Tracy wants to win to go along with her collection of every other prize in school. What sets this film aside from all the other recent high school movies is that it doesn't limit itself to the worldview of teenagers, but sees Tracy mostly through the eyes of a teacher who has had more than enough of her.

Tracy is embodied by Reese Witherspoon, an actress I've admired since she had her first kiss in *The Man in the Moon* (1991), and who moved up to adult roles in *Freeway* (1997), a harrowing retelling of "Little Red Riding Hood" with Kiefer Sutherland as the wolf. She was a virginal headmaster's daughter in *Cruel Intentions,* which opened last month, but she hits her full stride in *Election* as an aggressive, manipulative vixen who informs a teacher she hopes they can work together "harmoniously" in the coming school year.

The teacher is Jim McAllister (Matthew Broderick), the kind of man who turns up for an adulterous liaison and succeeds only in getting a bee sting on his eyelid. He thinks he knows what she means about "harmoniously," since last year she seduced a faculty member who was one of his best friends. Much as McAllister detests her, he also lusts after her; talking another student into running against her is his version of a cold shower. His recruit is a slow-witted jock named Paul (Chris Klein), and the race gets complicated when Paul's lesbian sister, Tammy (Jessica Campbell), jumps into the race on a platform of dismantling the student government "so we'll never have to sit through one of these stupid elections again."

Election is not really about high school, but about personality types. If the John Travolta character in *Primary Colors* reminded me of Bill Clinton, Tracy Flick puts me in mind of Elizabeth Dole: a person who always seems to be setting you a logical puzzle for which she is the answer. What is Tracy Flick's platform? That she should win simply because she is the school's (self-)designated winner. When a candidate turns up on election day having baked 480 customized cupcakes for the voters, doesn't she seem kind of inevitable?

For Jim McAllister, the Tracy Flicks have to be stopped before they do damage to themselves and others. She is always perfectly dressed and groomed, and is usually able to conceal her hot temper behind a facade of maddening cheerfulness. But she is ruthless. She reminds me of a saying attributed to David Merrick: "It is not enough for me to win. My enemies must lose."

The story, based on a novel by Tom Perrotta, shows McAllister as a dedicated teacher who is simply steamrollered by Tracy Flick. He narrates the film in a tone balanced between wonder and horror, and Broderick's performance does a good job of keeping that balance. Whatever else, he is fascinated by the phenomenon of Tracy Flick. We're inevitably reminded of Sammy Glick, the hero of Budd Schulberg's Hollywood classic *What Makes Sammy Run?* who had his eye on the prize and his feet on the shoulders of the little people he climbed over on his way to the top. *Election* makes the useful observation that although troublemakers cause problems for teachers, it's the compulsive overachievers who can drive them mad.

Alexander Payne is a director whose satire is omnidirectional. He doesn't choose an easy target and march on it. He stands in the middle of his story and attacks in all directions. His first film was *Citizen Ruth* (1996), starring Laura Dern as a pregnant, glue-sniffing young woman who was a moronic loser, but inspired a focus for a court battle between pro-choice and antiabortion forces. What was astonishing about his film (and probably damaged it at the box office) was that he didn't choose sides, but satirized both sides with cheerful open-mindedness.

Now here is a movie that is not simply about an obnoxious student, but also about an imperfect teacher, a lockstep administration, and a student body that is mostly just marking time until it can go out into the world and occupy valuable space. The movie is not mean-spirited about any of its characters; I kind of liked Tracy Flick some of the time, and even felt a little sorry for her. Payne doesn't enjoy easy targets and cheap shots. What he's aiming for, I think, is a parable for elections in general—in which the voters have to choose from among the kinds of people who have been running for office ever since high school.

Elizabeth ★ ★ ★ ½

R, 124 m., 1998

Cate Blanchett (Elizabeth I), Geoffrey Rush (Sir Francis Walsingham), Christopher Eccleston (Duke of Norfolk), Joseph Fiennes (Robert Dudley, Earl of Leicester), Richard Attenborough (Sir William Cecil), Fanny Ardant (Mary of Guise), John Gielgud (The Pope), Kathy Burke (Queen Mary Tudor), Vincent Cassel (Duke of Anjou). Directed by Shekhar Kapur and produced by Alison Owen. Screenplay by Michael Hirst.

The England of the first Elizabeth is a dark and sensuous place; the court lives intimately with treachery, and cloaks itself in shadows and rude luxury. As seen through the fresh eyes of an Indian director, Shekhar Kapur, *Elizabeth* is not a light *Masterpiece Theater* production, but one steeped in rich, saturated colors and emotions. The texture of the film is enough to recommend it, even apart from the story.

Cate Blanchett stars as Elizabeth I, who in 1558, at the age of twenty-five, took the throne of a Catholic country, declared it Protestant, fought off assassination by the French, the Spanish, her rivals, and the pope, and ruled for forty-five years. She succeeded, the film demonstrates, by learning on the job, growing from a naive girl to a willful strategist who picked her advisers well, and ignored them when they urgently advised her to marry: "I will have one mistress here! And no master!"

She was known as the Virgin Queen. Virginity for her, as for so many, was something she grew into. As the film opens, she frolics with her lover, Robert Dudley (Joseph Fiennes), and her ardor only subsides as she realizes no man loves the queen of England only for herself. She is contemptuous of such other suitors as the duke of Anjou (Vincent Cassel), who sees marriage as a social move and is surprised while frolicking in a frock. And her eyes narrow as she listens to proposals couriered in by various rulers who want to marry her as a sort of mergers-and-acquisitions deal.

The screenplay provides a series of hard-edged conversations in which Elizabeth's enemies conspire against her and her friends urgently counsel her, while she teaches herself to tell true allies from false ones. She is much helped in the beginning by white-bearded old Sir William Cecil (Richard Attenborough), although there comes a time when he must be put to pasture, and Attenborough's character accepts this news with humility that is truly touching.

Then the lurking, sinister Sir Francis Walsingham (Geoffrey Rush) moves to her side, and brilliantly helps guide her to triumph. He's instrumental to the plot, even though his role is at first murky. After Elizabeth's archrival Mary of Guise (Fanny Ardant) sends her a poisoned dress, which luckily claims the life of another, it is Sir Francis who adroitly convinces Mary he will betray Elizabeth. Francis and Mary spend a night together, and in the morning Mary is dead. It didn't happen like that in history, but it should have.

The movie, indeed, compresses and rewrites history at its own convenience, which is the rule anyway with English historical romances. What it gets right is the performance by Cate Blanchett, who was so good as the poker-playing glass manufacturer in *Oscar and Lucinda* (1997) and here uncannily comes to resemble the great monarch. She is saucy and heedless at the first, headstrong when she shouldn't be, but smart and able to learn. By the end she has outsmarted everyone and become one of the rare early female heads of state to rule successfully without an alliance with a man.

Shekhar Kapur, who directed *The Bandit Queen* (1995), about a fierce modern Indian Robin Hood, here clothes Elizabeth, her court, and her architecture in the colors and texture of medieval India. The film is largely set in vast, echoing halls, their pillars reaching up into the shadows. He is attentive to the rustle of dresses and the clank of armor, gives us a barge on the Thames like a houseboat on a lake in Kashmir. Action is glimpsed through iron filigree screens, dresses are rich with embroidery, hairstyles are ornately elaborate, and yet there is the feeling that just out of sight of these riches are the rats in the kitchen and the slop pots in the halls. This is not the Ye Olde approach, but a society still inventing gentility; sex is so linked with politics that old Sir William demands to inspect Elizabeth's sheets every morning to keep tabs on possibly alarming developments in her private life.

At the end of the film, Elizabeth announces, "I have become a virgin." And so she remained, ruling over and in some sense creating the England that gave us Shakespeare. Think what a play he might have written about her if commoners had been allowed to create characters out of reigning monarchs. No doubt he retired in sheer frustration.

The Emperor's Shadow ★★★

NO MPAA RATING, 116 m., 1999

Ge You (Composer Gao Jianli), Jiang Wen (Emperor Ying Sheng), Xu Qing (His Daughter, Yueyang). Directed by Zhou Xiaowen and produced by Tong Gang, Hu Yuesheng, and Cai Huansong. Screenplay by Lu Wei. In Mandarin with English subtitles.

The Emperor's Shadow tells the story of two boys raised at the same breast as foster brothers. One becomes emperor—the founder of China's Qin dynasty, circa 200 B.C. The other becomes his court composer, more or less over his own dead body. The film, which has caused some alarm in China because it may be read as an argument against government interference in the arts, is filmed as a large-scale costume epic, with countless extras, rivers running with blood, and dramatic readings of lines like, "You are the only man with the right to call me brother."

Once you accept the likelihood that no subtle emotional nuances are going to be examined in the course of the film, it's absorbing. The same story told today might seem a tad melodramatic, but the magnificent settings and the exotic world of the Chinese court inspire a certain awe. The director, Zhou Xiaowen, has possibly studied such Japanese epics as *Ran* and *Kagemusha*, and uses the Kurosawa-style telephoto lens to compress armies of men into faceless patterns moving on a plain; our first sight of imperial style comes when horses draw up with the emperor's carriage, which is about the same size and design as the location office on a construction site.

The emperor is named Ying Sheng (Jiang Wen). Although his predecessor ordered, "After my death, execute anyone who supports musicians," Ying is a music lover, and that causes a lifetime of agony for the composer Gao Jianli (Ge You), who lives in a neighboring province and wants to be left alone to pluck his gin (an instrument that looks like the ancestor of Chet Atkins's flatbed steel guitar).

Ying conquers Gao's province, has the composer hauled before him, and orders him to compose an anthem. His first effort ("10,000 men must suffer so that one may reach heaven") strikes the emperor as just possibly a veiled criticism of his reign. When Gao demurs at his request for a rewrite, Ying starts beheading slaves, which seems to confirm the accuracy of the first version, but eventually persuades Gao.

Meanwhile, Gao has fallen in love with Yueyang (Ying Zheng), the emperor's daughter, whose legs are paralyzed. Her form of locomotion is to be passed from arm to arm by the (remaining) slaves, her head above the crowd like a Super Bowl hero. Yueyang has been betrothed to a famous general, but likes Gao, and they make love, after which she discovers she can walk. Gao asks Ying if he can marry Yueyang, but Ying refuses. Still, moved by the miracle, he tries to be reasonable: "Look, her general will certainly die in battle within the next five years, and after a year of mourning, she can marry you. Can't you wait?"

The interesting dynamic in the film is that Ying, an absolute ruler who can enforce his will on anyone, is utterly baffled by Gao's independent spirit. Their arguments sometimes sound more like sibling quarrels than master and servant. Ying is forever ordering fearsome punishments against Gao and then repenting, sometimes too late (he doesn't mind having the musician blinded by the fumes of horse urine thrown into a coal fire, but is outraged to discover that it hurts).

The movie is not subtle or especially insightful, but it is intrinsically interesting (when have you seen these characters or situations before?), and sumptuously mounted and photographed. One of its closing images, of Ying mounting a pyramid, provides the closest thing to a message: It's lonely at the top. (On the other hand, as Mel Brooks reminds us, "It's *good* to be the king.") The end titles provide information about the Qin dynasty that adds a nice wry zinger.

The Empire Strikes Back ★★★★
PG, 127 m., 1980 (rereleased 1997)

Mark Hamill (Luke Skywalker), Harrison Ford (Han Solo), Carrie Fisher (Princess Leia), Billy Dee Williams (Lando Calrissian), Anthony Daniels (C-3PO), Frank Oz (Yoda), David Prowse (Darth Vader), James Earl Jones (Vader's Voice), Alec Guinness (Ben [Obi-Wan] Kenobi). Directed by Irvin Kershner and produced by Gary Kurtz. Screenplay by Leigh Brackett and Lawrence Kasdan, based on a story by George Lucas.

The Empire Strikes Back is the best of three *Star Wars* films, and the most thought-provoking. After the space opera cheerfulness of the original film, this one plunges into darkness and even despair, and surrenders more completely to the underlying mystery of the story. It is because of the emotions stirred in *Empire* that the entire series takes on a mythic quality that resonates back to the first and ahead to the third. This is the heart.

The film was made in 1980 with full knowledge that *Star Wars* had become the most successful film of all time. If corners were cut in the original budget, no cost was spared in this one, and it is a visual extravaganza from beginning to end, one of the most visionary and inventive of all films.

Entirely apart from the story and the plot, the film is worth seeing simply for its sights. Not for the scenes of space battle, which are more or less standard (there's nothing here to match the hurtling chase through the high walls of the Death Star). But for such sights as the lumbering, elephantlike Imperial Walkers (was ever a weapon more impractical?). Or for the Cloud City, on its spire high in the sky. Or for the face of a creature named Yoda, whose expressions are as convincing as a human's, and as subtle. Or for the dizzying, vertiginous heights that Luke Skywalker dangles over, after nearly plunging to his death.

There is a generosity in the production design of *The Empire Strikes Back.* There are not only the amazing sights before us, but plenty more in the corners of the screen, or everywhere the camera turns. The whole world of this story has been devised and constructed in such a way that we're not particularly aware of sets or effects—there's so *much* of this world that it all seems seamless. Consider, for example, an early scene where an Empire "probe droid" is fired upon on the ice planet Hoth. It explodes. We've seen that lots of times. But then hot pieces of it shower down on the snow in the foreground, in soft, wet plops. That's the kind of detail that George Lucas and his team live for.

There is another moment. Yoda has just sent Luke Skywalker into a dark part of the forest to confront his destiny. Luke says a brave farewell. There is a cut to R2-D2, whirling and beeping. And then a cut back to Yoda, whose face reflects a series of emotions: concern, sadness, a hint of pride. You know intellectually that Yoda is a creature made by Frank Oz in a Muppet shop. But Oz and Lucas were not content to make Yoda realistic. They wanted to make him a good actor too. And they did; in his range of wisdom and emotion, Yoda may actually give the best performance in the movie.

The worst, I'm afraid, is Chewbacca's. This character was thrown into the first film as window dressing, was never thought through, and as a result has been saddled with one facial expression and one mournful yelp. Much more could have been done. How can you be a space pilot and not be able to communicate in any meaningful way? Does Han Solo really understand Chew's monotonous noises? Do they have long chats sometimes?

Never mind. The second movie's story continues the saga set up in the first film. The Death Star has been destroyed, but Vader, of course, escaped, and now commands the Empire forces in their ascendancy against the rebels. Our heroes have a secret base on Hoth, but flee it after the Empire attack, and then the key characters split up for parallel stories. Luke and R2-D2 crash-land on the planet Dagobah and Luke is tutored there by Yoda in the ways of the Jedi and the power of the Force. Princess Leia, Han Solo, Chewbacca, and C-3PO evade Empire capture by hiding their ship in plain sight, and then flee to the Cloud City ruled by Lando (Billy Dee Williams), an old pal of Han's and (we learn) the original owner of the Millennium Falcon, before an unlucky card game.

There are a couple of amusing subplots,

one involving Han's easily wounded male ego, another about Vader's knack of issuing sudden and fatal demotions. Then comes the defining moment of the series. Can there be a person alive who does not know (read no further if you are that person) that Luke discovers Darth Vader is his father? But that is not the moment. It comes after their protracted (and somewhat disorganized) laser-sword fight, when Luke chooses to fall to his death rather than live to be the son of Vader.

He doesn't die, of course (there is a third movie to be made); he's saved by some sort of chute I still don't understand, only to dangle beneath the Cloud City until his rescue, and a conclusion that only by sheer effort of will doesn't have the words "To be continued" superimposed over it.

Perhaps because so much more time and money was spent on *The Empire Strikes Back* in the first place, not much has been changed in this restored and spruced-up 1997 rerelease. I do not recall the first film in exact detail, but learn from the *Star Wars* Web pages that the look of the Cloud City has been extended and enhanced, and there is more of the Wampa ice creature than before. I have no doubt there are many improvements on the sound track, but I would have to be a dog to hear them.

In the glory days of science fiction, critics wrote about the "sense of wonder." That's what *The Empire Strikes Back* creates in us. Like a lot of traditional science fiction, it isn't psychologically complex or even very interested in personalities (aside from some obvious character traits). That's because the characters are not themselves—they are us. We are looking out through their eyes, instead of into them, as we would in more serious drama. We are on a quest, on a journey, on a mythological expedition. The story elements in the *Star Wars* trilogy are as deep and universal as storytelling itself. Watching these movies, we're in a receptive state like that of a child—our eyes and ears are open, we're paying attention, and we are amazed.

Encounter in the Third Dimension ★ ★

NO MPAA RATING, 45 m., 1999

Stuart Pankin (Professor), Stuart Pankin (Voice of M.A.X.), Cassandra Peterson (Elvira, Mistress of the Dark), Harry Shearer (Narrator), Andrea Thompson (Ruth in the Booth). Directed by Ben Stassen and produced by Charlotte Clay Huggins. Screenplay by Kurt Frey and Stassen.

Encounter in the Third Dimension resembles several other giant-screen IMAX releases in being interesting primarily because of the size of the screen. The movie packages a lot of information about 3-D movies into a goofy story about a scientist who wants to demonstrate his latest 3-D invention.

The story is pretty lame, and the info is familiar. Is there likely to be anyone in the audience who isn't familiar with the 3-D effect of the Stereopticon? (Children know it as the familiar ViewMaster.)

Still, no doubt about it, the 3-D effect in IMAX and its cousin, Omnimax, is the best I've seen. That's because of the huge screen, which covers peripheral vision, and the oversize projectors that pump out a lot of brightness. The glasses, which resemble science-fiction headsets, contain shutters that separate the images for each eye. The result is truly three-dimensional, all right. There was an undersea IMAX film shot in 3-D that I really enjoyed.

But the underlying problem with 3-D remains exactly the same as when *Bwana Devil* and *House of Wax* first hit the screen in the 1950s: It's unnecessary most of the time, and distracting the rest of the time. The ordinary 2-D illusion of movies has long been accepted all over the world as an acceptable illusion of reality. The 3-D illusion seems used mostly to throw things at the audience. That gets old after a while. If the purpose of a movie's story is to absorb us, every exaggerated 3-D effect breaks our reverie and calls attention to the technique itself.

In *Encounter in the Third Dimension,* we meet a professor (Stuart Pankin) who hopes to unveil his new gimmick, Real-O-Vision. He has enlisted Elvira ("Mistress of the Dark," the credits remind us) to sing a song in this new process, but she keeps getting interrupted as the machinery breaks down, and so the professor dispatches a flying robot named M.A.X. (voice also by Pankin) to entertain us while he works on his invention.

The primary function of M.A.X., it goes

without saying, is to zoom toward the audience and hang in midair, seemingly inches from our faces. Dr. Johnson once said of a dog standing on its hind legs: "It is not done well, but one is surprised to find it done at all." Watching M.A.X. whizzing about, I reflected that it was done well, but, alas, I did not want it done at all.

The End of Violence ★★

R, 122 m., 1997

Andie MacDowell (Paige), Bill Pullman (Mike), Gabriel Byrne (Ray), Traci Lind (Cat), Loren Dean (Detective Doc Block). Directed by Wim Wenders and produced by Deepak Nayar, Wenders, and Nicholas Klein. Screenplay by Klein.

Some of the key scenes in Wim Wenders's *The End of Violence* involve a man who sits high above Los Angeles in the Griffith Park observatory, spying on the city through a network of secret TV cameras. Of course, he doesn't need to be high (he can sit anywhere and watch the screens), but the detail is significant; Wenders may be evoking an echo of *Wings of Desire* (1988), the great film in which he imagined lonely angels in Berlin, looking down at the lives of men.

Wenders revisited that image to much less effect in *Faraway . . . So Close* (1993), and now here it is again, with the mysterious observer (Gabriel Byrne) free to watch but powerless to intercede, and not always sure what he is seeing. One of the things he sees is the violent abduction of a Hollywood producer (Bill Pullman), who is kidnapped by paid thugs, for reasons that will gradually become clear. These two character threads—the producer and the voyeur—will continue through the film, but there is a lot of other stuff, not all of it necessary. Wenders has always liked to make very long films, and at 122 minutes, *The End of Violence* may not be long enough to do justice to all of his ideas.

The movie in its present form, although reedited since an unsuccessful screening at Cannes, is essentially a mess. Films work best when audiences are absorbed by the flow. Although there is pleasure in trying to untangle puzzles and mysteries, that's not what we get here; instead, like archaeologists, we're given incomplete shards of a work and asked to imagine the whole.

Many of the scenes involving the Pullman character are, however, sharp-edged and on target. We see him first sitting on the lawn of his expensive home, dealing with the world through telephones, computers, and fax machines. When his wife (Andie MacDowell), who is in the same house, wants to talk to him, she calls him. "I'm leaving you," she says. "I'll get right back to you," he says, putting her on hold and then forgetting all about her as he hurries to the hospital room of an injured stunt woman.

This blinkered Hollywood mentality is illuminated again, hilariously, after the producer is kidnapped and tries to buy his own freedom. "I wanna give you a million dollars," he says. "In points." They aren't buying. Eventually Pullman finds himself free and under the protection of the Mexican family that tends his lawn. He lets his beard grow, puts on gardener's clothes, and avoids a citywide manhunt because by becoming Mexican, he has made himself invisible.

There is more. A subplot involves a secret government plan to use the surveillance cameras to control crime and violence in Los Angeles, and Byrne, sad-faced and thoughtfully musing as only he can be, tries to piece together what he knows about his job, and what he guesses. Everything comes together, somewhat unconvincingly, at the end.

Wim Wenders is a gifted and poetic filmmaker whose reach sometimes exceeds his grasp. It helps when he has some kind of clear narrative thread to organize his material—as he did in *Kings of the Road* (1976), where two men confront their problems within the conventions of a road movie, or *Paris, Texas* (1984), with Harry Dean Stanton as an amnesiac trying to piece together the pieces of his life. Those films had goals, as did the search for the sharing of loneliness in *Wings of Desire.*

The End of Violence, on the other hand, doesn't seem sure what it is about, or how it is about it. There is an abundance of ideas here, but they're starting points, not destinations. Wenders is able to invest individual scenes with a feeling of urgency and importance, but at the end there is a certain emptiness, a feeling that the movie has not really been pulled together.

Endurance ★ ★ ★

G, 83 m., 1999

Himself (Haile Gebrselassie), Bekele Gebrselassie (Haile's Father), Shawananness Gebrselassie (Haile's Mother), Yonas Zergaw (Young Haile), Assefa Gebrselassie (Haile's Brother), Alem Tellahun (Haile's Wife), Tizazu Mashresha (Haile's Police Trainer). Directed by Leslie Woodhead and produced by Edward R. Pressman, Terrence Malick, and Max Palevsky. Screenplay by Woodhead.

The sound of the runner's breathing is like a percussion instrument made of wind. Each exhalation is a thrum of effort. He runs as if he has been running since time immemorial. His name is Haile Gebrselassie, and after he set a new record at the Atlanta Olympics in 1996, *Runner's World* magazine described him as "the greatest distance runner of all time."

Endurance is a film about Gebrselassie, his early life on an Ethiopian farm, his training, his shy courtship, and his Olympic triumph. It is not a documentary, exactly; scenes are written and staged, and actors play him at younger ages. But it is drawn from his life. His father, brother, and wife play themselves, and the footage of his triumph at Atlanta is real. So, I think, is the sound of his breathing.

The runner was raised in a rural area, where his father wanted him to stay and work on the farm. But in 1980, when the Ethiopian runner Miruts Yifter won the 10,000-meter race at the Moscow Olympics running barefoot, young Haile, like all of his countrymen, was stirred to hear the Ethiopian national anthem played after his victory. He determined to become a runner, and we see him as a boy (played by his nephew, Yonas Zergaw), running everywhere on the farm where his family of twelve lived in a mud hut.

Gebrselassie himself takes over the role as a teenager, and there is a scene where he and his father stand on a hilltop, the landscape unfolding below them, as he explains his plans to go to Addis Ababa to go into serious training for the Olympics. His father prefers him to stay on the farm. There is a stilted, formal quality to their conversation that oddly enough gives it more force: We are not seeing actors, but the real people somewhat self-consciously re-creating a conversation they actually had.

The British director, Leslie Woodhead, uses title cards to separate the sections of his film and provide information about Gebrselassie. "Finished 99th in first marathon," we read, and then a little later, "Two years of hard training." As we see marathon runners winding their way through the city streets: "A thousand others with the same dream." Gebrselassie doesn't fit the stereotype of the long-distance runner, tall and long-limbed. He is compact, wiry, muscular. The secret of his greatness, we gather, is that he ran and ran, longer and harder than anyone else, until in his big race he was simply the best prepared.

There are glimpses of his personal life. A shy date with a girl named Alem (who plays herself, and became his wife). One has coffee, the other a Fanta orange drink. Later, he has a heart-to-heart talk with her about his father's disappointment. The father's feelings are understandable: He has lost a strong son to help on the farm, so that the boy can move to the city and . . . run?

The footage of the race itself is never less than thrilling, as such races always are; the close-up lens lets us see the pain of the runners, who by the end are relying mostly on will and endurance. John Powell's music is not exhilarating boilerplate, as scores often are during films about athletics. Instead, it is brooding, introspective, almost sad, suggesting how the runners must look within themselves and endure their burning lungs in a race of such length and difficulty. There is a lot of time to be by yourself in a 10,000-meter race.

I learn from the *Variety* review of the film that the filmmakers had the eight leading contenders under contract, so that they were almost assured of being able to tell the story of the winner. Fair enough, but in Haile Gebrselassie they surely got the most interesting of subjects, a runner whose triumph must be explained almost entirely from within his own determination. He didn't come from a background of training, coaching, and determination, but from the rural hills, where we see him running to school, running to the water well, running to the fields, always with that stoic thrumming of his breath.

Enemy of the State ★★★

R, 128 m., 1998

Will Smith (Robert Dean), Gene Hackman (Brill), Jon Voight (Reynolds), Lisa Bonet (Rachel Banks), Regina King (Carla Dean), Loren Dean (Hicks), Jason Robards (Hammersly). Directed by Tony Scott and produced by Jerry Bruckheimer. Screenplay by David Marconi.

Enemy of the State uses the thriller genre to attack what it calls "the surveillance society," an America in which underground computers at Fort Meade monitor our phone calls for trigger words like "bomb," "president," and "Allah." It stars Will Smith as a Washington, D.C., lawyer whose life is dismantled bit by bit (and byte by byte) because he possesses proof that a congressman was murdered for opposing a bill that would make government snooping easier.

For much of the movie, the lawyer doesn't even know he has the evidence, a videotape showing the congressman's suicide being faked while a high government official looks on. The official, named Reynolds and played by Jon Voight with glasses and a haircut that make him uncannily resemble Robert McNamara, directs a vendetta against the lawyer that includes planting sexual gossip in the paper, canceling his credit cards, getting him fired, and eventually even trying to frame him for the murder.

Paranoid? Exaggerated? No doubt, although the movie reminded me of that scary recent Anthony Lewis column in the *New York Times* about Julie Hiatt Steele, an innocent bystander in the Kenneth Starr investigation who had her tax returns audited, her neighbors and employers questioned, and her adoption of a war orphan threatened—all because she testified that Kathleen Willey asked her to lie about a meeting with President Clinton.

It's not the government that is the enemy, this movie argues, so much as bureaucrats and demagogues who use the power of the government to gain their own ends and cover their own tracks. Voight's character is really acting on his own behalf: He wants a communications bill passed because it will make his job easier (and perhaps make him richer). He has the congressman (Jason Robards) killed because he's the key opponent of the bill. Everything else follows from the cover-up of the murder.

The movie was directed by Tony Scott (*Top Gun*), who films technology the way the *National Geographic* films wetlands. As the Will Smith character dodges around Washington, trying to figure out who's after him and why, the story is told with footage from spy satellites, surveillance cameras, listening devices, bugs, wiretaps, and database searches. The first time I saw a movie where a satellite was able to zoom in on a car license plate, I snickered. Recently I was able to log onto a Website (www.terraserver.microsoft.com/) and see the roof of my house—or yours. If Microsoft gives that away for free, I believe the National Security Agency can read license plates.

The fugitive lawyer's only friend is a shadowy underground figure named Brill (Gene Hackman), who was a U.S. spy until 1980, and since then has lived an invisible life as a hired gun in the outlands of intelligence and communications. His headquarters: a high-tech hideaway in an old warehouse building, with his equipment fenced in by copper mesh to stop the snoopers. (There is an echo here of Francis Coppola's 1974 film *The Conversation*, which also starred Hackman as a paranoid high-tech eavesdropper; the workplaces in the two movies resemble each other—deliberately, I assume.)

It's Brill who briefs the lawyer on what the government can do. I don't believe him when he says the feds have computers at Fort Meade monitoring our phone calls; I read that as a screenwriter's invention. But I do believe the government can listen to any phone call it wants to, and does so much more often than the law suggests it should.

The movie is fast-paced, centered around two big chase scenes, and ends in a clever double-cross that leads to a big shoot-out. In its action and violence it shows us how the movies have changed since 1974; *The Conversation* is a similar story that depended only on its intelligence and paranoia for appeal. *Enemy of the State* shoehorns in brief scenes between the lawyer and his wife (Regina King) and former girlfriend (Lisa Bonet), but is in too much of a hurry to be much of a people picture. And the standoff at the end edges perilously close to the ridiculous for a movie that's tried so hard to be plausible.

But by and large the movie works. Smith is credible as a good lawyer who is blindsided by the misused power of the state. Gene Hackman, with a bristly haircut and horn-rimmed nerd glasses, seems utterly confident of everything he says. Jon Voight's bureaucrat seems convinced that his job somehow places him above the law. "We are at war twenty-four hours a day," he barks out near the beginning of the film. It was Pogo who said, "We have met the enemy, and he is us." ☞

Entrapment ★ ★ ★

PG-13, 113 m., 1999

Sean Connery (Mac), Catherine Zeta-Jones (Gin), Ving Rhames (Thibadeaux), Will Patton (Cruz), Maury Chaykin (Conrad Greene), Kevin McNally (Haas), Terry O'Neill (Quinn), Madhav Sharma (Security Chief). Directed by Jon Amiel and produced by Sean Connery, Michael Hertzberg, and Rhonda Tollefson. Screenplay by Ron Bass and William Broyles.

Entrapment is the very embodiment of a star vehicle: a movie with a preposterous plot, exotic locations, absurd action sequences, and so much chemistry between attractive actors that we don't care. It stars Sean Connery and Catherine Zeta-Jones in a caper that reminded me of *To Catch a Thief, Charade, Topkapi,* and the stunt sequences in Bond pictures. I didn't believe a second of it, and I didn't care that I didn't.

The film is about thieves. Connery plays a man named Mac, who is getting along in years but is still respected as the most resourceful master thief in the world. Jones plays Gin, who in the early scenes is established as an insurance investigator who sets an elaborate trap for Mac. I will be revealing little about the plot if I say that neither of these people is precisely as they seem.

Watching the film, I imagined the trailer. Not the movie's real trailer, which I haven't seen, but one of those great 1950s trailers where big words in fancy typefaces come spinning out of the screen, asking us to Thrill! to risks atop the world's tallest building, and Gasp! at a daring bank robbery, and Cheer! as towering adventure takes us from New York to Scotland to Malaysia.

A trailer like that would only be telling the simple truth. It would also perhaps include a few tantalizing shots of Zeta-Jones lifting her leather-clad legs in an athletic ballet designed to avoid the invisible beams of security systems. And shots of a thief hanging upside down from a seventy-story building. And an audacious raid through an underwater tunnel. And a priceless Rembrandt. And a way to steal $8 billion because of the Y2K bug. And so on.

It works because it is made stylishly, because Connery and Zeta-Jones are enormously attractive actors, and because of the romantic tension between them. I got a letter the other day complaining about the age differences between the male and female leads in several recent pictures—and, to be sure, Connery at sixty-nine and Zeta-Jones at twenty-nine remember different wars. But the movie cannily establishes ground rules (Mac lectures that thievery is a business that permits no personal relationships), and so instead of questioning why they're erotically involved, we wish they would be.

The plot, by Ron Bass and William Broyles, is put together like a Swiss watch that keeps changing time zones: It is accurate and misleading at once. The film consists of one elaborate caper sequence after another, and it rivals the Bond films in its climactic action sequence, which has Mac and Gin hanging from a string of holiday bulbs beneath the walkway linking the two towers of the Petronas Twin Towers in Kuala Lumpur. The stunt and f/x work here do a good job of convincing us that human beings are actually dangling precariously seventy stories in the air, and I for one am convinced that Zeta-Jones personally performs an earlier stunt, in which she treats an old wooden beam in Mac's Scottish castle as if it were a parallel bar at the Olympics. Most of the movie's action is just that—action—and not extreme violence.

Watching Connery negotiate the nonsense of the plot is an education in acting: He treats every situation as if it is plausible but not that big of a deal, and that sets the right tone. He avoids the smile in the voice that would give away the silliness of the plot. When he says, "I'm never late. If I'm late, it's because I'm dead," we reflect that some actors can get away with lines like that and others can't, and Connery is the leader of the first group.

As for Catherine Zeta-Jones, I can only reflect, as I did while watching her in *The Mask of Zorro,* that while beautiful women are a dime a dozen in the movies, those with fire, flash, and humor are a good deal more scarce. Taking her cue perhaps from Connery, she also plays a preposterous role absolutely straight. The costars and Jon Amiel, the director, respect the movie tradition they're working in, instead of condescending to it. There are scenes in this film when astounding revelations are made, and although I didn't believe them, I accepted them, which is more difficult and enjoyable. ☞

Event Horizon ★ ★

R, 97 m., 1997

Laurence Fishburne (Captain Miller), Sam Neill (Weir), Kathleen Quinlan (Peters), Joely Richardson (Stark), Richard T. Jones (Cooper), Jack Noseworthy (Justin), Jason Isaacs (D.J.), Sean Pertwee (Smith). Directed by Paul Anderson and produced by Lawrence Gordon, Lloyd Levin, and Jeremy Bolt. Screenplay by Philip Eisner.

The year is 2047. A rescue mission has been dispatched to the vicinity of Neptune, where seven years earlier a deep space research vessel named *Event Horizon* disappeared. As the rescue ship *Lewis and Clark* approaches, its sensors indicate the temperature on board the other ship is very cold. No human life signs are detected. Yet there are signs of life all through the ship—some other form of life.

Event Horizon opens with a lot of class. It has the detailed space vessels moving majestically against the background of stars, it has the deep rumble of the powerful drives, it has sets displaying persuasive technology, and it even has those barely audible, squeaky, chattering voicelike noises that we remember from *2001,* which give you the creepy feeling that little aliens are talking about you.

I love movies like this. I got up and moved closer to the screen, volunteering to be drawn in. I appreciate the anachronistic details: Everybody on board the rescue ship smokes, for example, which is unlikely in 2047 on a deep space mission where, later, the CO^2 air scrubbers will play a crucial role. And the captain (Laurence Fishburne) wears a leather bomber jacket, indicating that J. Peterman is still in business half a century from now. I liked all of that stuff, but there wasn't much substance beneath it.

What happened to the ship named *Event Horizon*? Dr. Weir (Sam Neill) may know. He designed the ship's gravity drive, which looks uncannily like a smaller version of the machine in *Contact,* with three metal rings whirling around a central core. The drive apparently creates a black hole and then slips the ship through it, so that it can travel vast distances in a second.

Dr. Weir performs the obligatory freshman-level explanation of this procedure, taking a piece of paper and showing you how far it is from one edge to the other, and then folding it in half so that the two edges touch, and explaining how that happens when space curves. The crew members nod, listening attentively. They're a highly trained space crew, on a mission where space and time are bread and butter, yet they apparently know less about quantum theory than the readers of this review. It's back to Physics 101 for them.

So, okay, where did the ship go for seven years, and what happened while it was there? Why is the original crew all dead? Unfortunately, *Event Horizon* is not the movie to answer these questions. It's all style, climax, and special effects. The rules change with every scene.

For example, early in the film the *Lewis and Clark* approaches the *Event Horizon* through what I guess is the stormy atmosphere of Neptune, with lots of thunder, lightning, and turbulence. But once those effects are exploited, the rest of the movie takes place in the calm of space. And although we are treated to very nice shots of Neptune, the crew members never look at the planet in awe, or react to the wondrous sight; like the actors standing next to the open airplane door in *Air Force One,* they're so intent on their dialogue that they're oblivious to their surroundings.

The obvious inspiration for *Event Horizon* is a much better film, Andrei Tarkovsky's *Solaris* (1972), where a space station orbits a vast planet. The planet in that film is apparently alive, and creates hallucinations in the minds of the orbiters, making them think they're back on Earth with their families. Same thing happens in *Event Horizon*, where the crew members hallucinate about family members they miss, love, or feel guilty about. But while Tarkovsky was combining the subconscious with the Gaia hypothesis, *Event Horizon* uses the flashbacks mostly for shocks and false alarms (hey, that's not really your daughter under the plastic tent in the equipment room!).

Because sensors picked up signs of life all over the ship, we assume it has been inhabited by a life form from wherever the ship traveled. But this possibility is never resolved. One of the crew members approaches the gravity drive, which turns into something resembling liquid mercury, and he slips through it and later returns, babbling, "It shows you things—horrible things—the dark inside me from the other place. I won't go back there!"

Perhaps Dr. Weir has the answers. But then again, perhaps not. Without revealing too much of the ending, let me say that Weir presumably knows as little from personal experience about what lies on the other side of the gravity drive as anyone else in the movie. He has not been there. That makes one of his most dramatic statements, late in the film, inexplicable. But then perhaps it doesn't matter. The screenplay creates a sense of foreboding and afterboding, but no actual boding.

It is observed darkly at one point that the gravity drive is a case of man pushing too far into realms where he should not go. There is an accusation that someone has "broken the laws of physics," and from the way it's said, you'd assume that offenders will be subject to fines or imprisonment. Of course there are no "laws" of physics—only observations about the way things seem to be. What you "break," if you break anything, is not a law but simply an obsolete belief, now replaced by one that works better. Deeply buried in *Event Horizon* is a suspicion of knowledge. Maybe that's why its characters have so little of it.

Ever After ★ ★ ★

PG-13, 121 m., 1998

Drew Barrymore (Danielle), Anjelica Huston (Rodmilla), Dougray Scott (Prince Henry), Patrick Godfrey (Leonardo), Megan Dodds (Marguerite), Melanie Lynskey (Jacqueline), Timothy West (King Francis), Judy Parfitt (Queen Marie), Jeanne Moreau (Old Woman), Jeroen Krabbe (Auguste). Directed by Andy Tennant and produced by Mireille Soria and Tracey Trench. Screenplay by Susannah Grant, Tennant, and Rick Parks.

Ever After opens with an old lady offering to tell the true story of "the little cinder girl," who was, she says, a real person long before she was immortalized by the Brothers Grimm in the Cinderella myth: "Her name was Danielle. And this . . . was her glass slipper."

The movie that follows is one of surprises, not least that the old tale still has life and passion in it. I went to the screening expecting some sort of soppy children's picture, and found myself in a costume romance with some of the same energy and zest as *The Mask of Zorro*. And I was reminded again that Drew Barrymore can hold the screen and involve us in her characters.

The movie takes place in sixteenth-century Europe, although it is a Europe more like a theme park than a real place, and that accounts for Danielle's remarkable ability to encounter the rich and famous—not only Prince Henry of France, but even Leonardo da Vinci, who functions as sort of a fairy godfather. It's a Europe of remarkable beauty (magnificent castles and châteaus are used as locations), in which a young girl with spunk and luck has a chance even against a wicked stepmother.

Not that the stepmother is merely wicked. *Ever After* brings a human dimension to the story, which begins with Danielle living happily with her father (Jeroen Krabbe). He springs a surprise: He is to marry Rodmilla (Anjelica Huston), who will bring her daughters, Jacqueline and Marguerite (Melanie Lynskey and Megan Dodds), to live with them. Soon after the marriage, alas, the father drops from his horse, dead, and life changes abruptly for Danielle.

"To be raised by a man!" exclaims Rodmilla. "No wonder you're built for hard labor." She puts Danielle to work as the family maid—swabbing floors, cooking and doing the dishes, tending the barnyard. Meanwhile, she grooms the beautiful Jacqueline for marriage in high places.

But Rodmilla sometimes allows herself a certain sympathy for Danielle; it's not that she's cruel to the girl, so much as that she must look out for her own daughters. The older woman has had problems of her own. "Did you love my father?" Danielle asks her. Rodmilla conceals much in her answer: "I barely knew him. Now, go away—I'm tired."

Danielle's entry into the life of Prince Henry is handled through a series of coincidental encounters after a Meet Cute in which she bops him with an apple. And there is a false crisis after Danielle pretends to be a countess (but only to help a friend) and Henry falls in love with her. She is afraid that when her masquerade is exposed, he will scorn her, and she is very nearly right, but Danielle's attitude toward her dilemma is closer to modern feminism than to the cheerful sexism of the Brothers Grimm.

Henry is played by Dougray Scott with a certain complexity; he is not simply a shining knight. His parents, the king and queen of France, are, however, improbably benign, and lack the ruthlessness one might expect from historical figures. They're more like Madame Harriet and Monsieur Ozzie. Further intrigue comes from the fact that Marguerite, the younger and darker of Rodmilla's two daughters, is not at all a bad sort herself.

Drew Barrymore has been in the movies for nineteen years now (she was in *Altered States* when she was four, and starred in *E.T.* at the age of seven). I seem to have known of her for decades, and she's still only twenty-three. Child stars have a hard time of it, convincing us to forget their cherubic little faces, and there is usually a period of trouble along the way. Now her adult career is safely launched.

Barrymore has had no big hits as an adult (well, *Batman Forever,* but it wasn't exactly her picture). But she has put together a series of sound, interesting performances: as a runaway teenager on a shooting spree in *Guncrazy* (1992), as a druggie's abused girlfriend in *Boys on the Side* (1995), as an unstable teenager in love in *Mad Love* (1995, still her best film), and as the waitress who falls in love with *The Wedding Singer* (1998—not a good movie, but she was okay). Here, as the little cinder girl, she is able at last to put aside her bedraggled losers and flower as a fresh young beauty, and she brings poignancy and fire to the role.

Ever After has been directed by Andy Tennant, whose *Fools Rush In* (1997) was also a Cinderella story of sorts, about a rich developer (Matthew Perry) who falls in love with a poor little Mexican-American camera girl (Salma Hayek) at Caesars Palace in Vegas. I liked that movie for its human comedy and romantic energy, and the same qualities are abundant in *Ever After*—along with lush scenery, astounding locations, and luxuriant costumes. Also Leonardo da Vinci, who functions like a cross between a wise old saint and the kind of artist who sketches the guests at a wedding.

Everyone Says I Love You ★★★★

R, 101 m., 1997

Alan Alda (Bob), Woody Allen (Joe), Drew Barrymore (Skylar), Goldie Hawn (Steffi), Julia Roberts (Von), Tim Roth (Charles Ferry), Lukas Haas (Scott), Gaby Hoffmann (Lane), Natasha Lyonne (D.J.), Edward Norton (Holden), Natalie Portman (Laura), David Ogden Stiers (Holden's Father). Directed by Woody Allen and produced by Jean Doumanian and Robert Greenhut. Screenplay by Allen.

Sometimes, when I am very happy, I sing to myself. Sometimes, when they are very happy, so do the characters in *Everyone Says I Love You,* Woody Allen's magical new musical comedy. I can't sing. Neither can some of Allen's characters. Why should that stop them? Who wants to go through life not ever singing?

Here is a movie that had me with a goofy grin plastered on my face for most of its length. A movie that remembers the innocence of the old Hollywood musicals and combines it with one of Allen's funniest and most labyrinthine plots, in which complicated New Yorkers try to recapture the simplicity of first love. It would take a heart of stone to resist this movie.

Allen's most inspired decision was to allow all of his actors to sing for themselves, in their own voices (all of them except for Drew Barrymore, who just plain can't sing). Some of them are accomplished (Alan Alda, Goldie Hawn, Edward Norton). The rest could hold their own at a piano bar. Allen knows that the musical numbers are not about performance or technical quality or vocal range; they're about feeling.

"Cuddle Up a Little Closer." "My Baby Don't Care for Pearls." "Looking at You." "I'm Through With Love." "I'm a Dreamer." "Makin' Whoopee." "Enjoy Yourself, It's Later Than You Think." These are songs that perhaps suffer a little when they're sung too well (just as trained opera singers always overdo it in musical comedy). They're for ordinary, happy voices, and from the first moment of the film, when Edward Norton turns to Drew Barrymore and sings "Just You, Just Me," the movie finds a freshness and charm that never ends.

The story involves a lot of Allen's familiar elements. His character, named Joe, is unlucky in love; he's a writer who lives in Paris, where his French girlfriend Giselle has just dumped him. He contemplates suicide, and debates the wisdom of taking the Concorde to New York before killing himself (with the time gain, he could get an extra three hours of stuff done and still be dead on schedule).

He returns to New York to be comforted by his best friends, who are his first wife, Steffi (Goldie Hawn), and her current husband, Bob (Alan Alda). The extended family is a yours, mine, and ours situation. D.J. (Natasha Lyonne) is Joe's daughter with Steffi. She serves as the narrator. Then there are Skylar (Drew Barrymore), who has just gotten engaged; Scott (Lukas Haas), who has the family concerned with his newfound conservatism; and his sisters Lane (Gaby Hoffman) and Laura (Natalie Portman), who are just discovering boys and have unfortunately discovered the same one.

The plot is simultaneously featherweight and profound, like a lot of Allen's movies: Big questions are raised and then dispatched with a one-liner, only to keep eating away at the hero until an eventually happy ending. Most of the questions have to do, of course, with unwise or inappropriate romances.

Joe decides to get away from it all by taking his daughter D.J. to Venice. Here we get one of the movie's loveliest moments, Allen singing "I'm Through With Love" on a balcony overlooking the Grand Canal. Of course he is not; soon after, he sees the enticing Von (Julia Roberts) in Venice, and falls in love at first sight. Amazingly, D.J. is able to supply him with useful insights into this mystery woman. D.J.'s best friend's mother is Von's psychiatrist, and the kids have eavesdropped on therapy sessions, so D.J. knows Von's likes (Tintoretto) and dislikes (her current husband), and coaches her father. This is, of course, dishonest and unethical, and delicious.

Joe's inside knowledge makes him irresistible to Roberts, although their romance is doomed from the start. Meanwhile, D.J. falls in love with a gondolier and announces an impending marriage. Back in New York, Holden (Edward Norton) has bought an engagement ring for Skylar (while the salesmen at Harry Winston's celebrate in a song and dance). Also meanwhile, Steffi, a liberal who wears her heart on her sleeve, arranges the release of a prisoner (Tim Roth) she thinks has been unfairly treated, and he steals Skylar's heart, for a time, anyway—and also contributes to an unusual dinner party.

Oh, there's more. Including the scene where Skylar accidentally swallows her $8,000 engagement ring and is told by the doctor examining the X rays, "I could have got it for you for $6,000." And a miraculous cure for Scott's conservatism. And a fanciful song-and-dance scene involving some ghosts in a funeral home. And the absolutely wonderful long closing sequence, which begins at a New Year's Eve party in Paris where everyone is dressed like Groucho Marx.

Steffi's family is visiting Paris, and at dawn she and Joe walk off alone to the café where their romance started many years ago. Was their divorce a mistake? Should Steffi dump Bob and come back to Joe? At dawn in a romantic café in Paris all sorts of seductive ideas can occur, but the movie segues away from hard decisions and into a dance number involving Allen and Hawn on the banks of the Seine, Goldie floating effortlessly in a scene that combines real magic with the magic of the heart.

Watching that scene, I thought that perhaps *Everyone Says I Love You* is the best film Woody Allen has ever made. Not the most profound, or the most daring, or the most successful in every one of its details—but simply the best, because he finds the right note for every scene, and dances on a tightrope between comedy and romance, between truth and denial, between what we hope and what we know.

Not many musicals are made these days. They're hard to do, and the fashion for them has passed. This one remembers the musicals of the 1930s, the innocent ones starring Astaire and Rogers, or Powell and Keeler, and to that freshness it adds a sharper, contemporary wit. Allen knows that what modern musicals are missing is not the overkill of multimillion-dollar production numbers, or the weight of hit songs from the charts, but the feeling that some things simply cannot be said in words and require songs to say them. He is right. Attempt this experiment: Try to say "Cuddle up a little closer, baby mine" without singing. Can't be done. Should rarely be attempted.

Eve's Bayou ★★★★

R, 109 m., 1997

Jurnee Smollett (Eve Batiste), Meagan Good (Cisely Batiste), Samuel L. Jackson (Louis Batiste), Lynn Whitfield (Roz Batiste), Debbi Morgan (Mozelle Batiste Delacroix), Jake Smollett (Poe Batiste), Ethel Ayler (Gran Mere), Diahann Carroll (Elzora), Vondie Curtis Hall (Julian Grayraven). Directed by Kasi Lemmons and produced by Caldecot Chubb and Samuel L. Jackson. Screenplay by Lemmons.

"Memory is a selection of images, some elusive, others printed indelibly on the brain. The summer I killed my father, I was ten years old."

With those opening words, *Eve's Bayou* coils back into the past, into the memories of a child who grew up in a family both gifted and flawed, and tried to find her own way to the truth. The words explain the method of the film. This will not be a simpleminded story that breathlessly races from A to B. It is a selection of memories, filtered through the eyes of a young girl who doesn't understand everything she sees—and filtered, too, through the eyes of her older sister, and through the eyes of an aunt who can foretell everyone's future except for her own.

As these images unfold, we are drawn into the same process Eve has gone through: We, too, are trying to understand what happened in that summer of 1962, when Eve's handsome, dashing father—a doctor and womanizer—took one chance too many. And we want to understand what happened late one night between the father and Eve's older sister, in a moment that was over before it began. We want to know because the film makes it perfectly possible that there is more than one explanation; *Eve's Bayou* studies the way that dangerous emotions can build up until something happens that no one is responsible for and that can never be taken back.

All of these moments unfold in a film of astonishing maturity and confidence; *Eve's Bayou,* one of the very best films of the year, is the debut of its writer and director, Kasi Lemmons. She sets her story in Southern Gothic country, in the bayous and old Louisiana traditions that Tennessee Williams might have been familiar with, but in tone and style she earns comparison with the family dramas of Ingmar Bergman. That Lemmons can make a film this good on the first try is like a rebuke to established filmmakers.

The story is told through the eyes of Eve Batiste, played with fierce truthfulness by Jurnee Smollett. Her family is descended from a slave, also named Eve, who saved her master's life and was rewarded with her freedom and with sixteen children. In 1962, the Batistes are the premiere family in their district, living in a big old mansion surrounded by rivers and swampland. Eve's father, Louis (Samuel L. Jackson), is the local doctor. Her mother, Roz (Lynn Whitfield), is "the most beautiful woman I ever have seen." Her sister, Cisely (Meagan Good), is on the brink of adolescence, and the apple of her father's eye; Eve watches unhappily at a party and afterwards asks her father, "Daddy, why don't you ever dance with me?" Living with them is an aunt, Mozelle (Debbi Morgan), who has lost three husbands, "is not unfamiliar with the inside of a mental hospital," and has the gift of telling fortunes.

Dr. Batiste is often away from home on house calls—some of them legitimate, some excuses for his philandering. He is a weak but not a bad man, and not lacking in insight: "To a certain type of woman, I am a hero," he says. "I need to be a hero." On the night that her father did not dance with her, Eve steals away to a barn and falls asleep, only to awaken and see her father apparently making love with another man's wife. Eve tells Cisely, who says she was mistaken, and the doubt over this incident will echo later, on another night when much depends on whether Cisely was mistaken.

Lemmons surrounds her characters with a rich setting. There is a marketplace, dominated by the stalls of farmers and fishermen, and by the presence of a voodoo woman (Diahann Carroll) whose magic may or may not be real. Certainly Aunt Mozelle's gift is real; her prophecies have a terrifying accuracy, as when she tells a woman her missing son will be found in a Detroit hospital on Tuesday. But Mozelle cannot foresee her own life: "I looked at each of my husbands," she says, "and never saw a thing." All three died. So when a handsome painter (Vondie Curtis Hall) comes into the neighborhood and Mozelle knows she has found true love at last, she is afraid to marry him, because it has been prophesied that any man who marries her will die.

The film has been photographed by Amy Vincent in shadows and rich textures, where even a sunny day contains dark undertones; surely she looked at the Bergman films photographed by Sven Nykvist in preparing her approach. There is a scene of pure magic as Mozelle tells Eve the story of the death of one of her husbands, who was shot by her lover; the woman and the girl stand before a mirror, regarding the scene from the past, and then Mozelle slips out of the shot and reappears in the past.

There is also great visual precision in the scenes involving the confused night when the doctor comes home drunk, and Cisely goes downstairs to comfort him. What happened? We get two accounts and we see two versions, and the film is far too complex and thoughtful to try to reduce the episode to a simple formula like sexual abuse; what happens lasts only a second, and is charged with many possibilities for misinterpretation, all of them prepared for by what has gone before.

Eve's Bayou resonates in the memory. It called me back for a second and third viewing. It is a reminder that sometimes films can venture into the realms of poetry and dreams.

Evita ★ ★ ★ ½

PG, 134 m., 1997

Madonna (Eva Peron), Antonio Banderas (Che), Jonathan Pryce (Juan Peron), Jimmy Nail (Agustin Magaldi), Victoria Sus (Dona Juana), Julian Littman (Brother Juan), Olga Merediz (Blanca), Laura Pallas (Elisa), Julia Worsley (Erminda). Directed by Alan Parker and produced by Robert Stigwood, Parker, and Andrew G. Vajna. Screenplay by Parker and Oliver Stone, based on the musical *Evita,* with music by Andrew Lloyd Webber and lyrics by Tim Rice.

Evita allows the audience to identify with a heroine who achieves greatness by—well, golly, by being who she is. It celebrates the life of a woman who begins as a quasi-prostitute, marries a powerful man, locks him out of her bedroom, and inspires the idolatry of the masses by spending enormous sums on herself. When she sings: "They need to adore me—to Christian Dior me," she's right on the money.

I begin on this note not to criticize the new musical *Evita* (which I enjoyed very much), but to bring a touch of reality to the character of Eva Peron, who, essentially, was famous because she was so very well known. Her fame continued after her death, as her skillfully embalmed body went on to a long-running career of its own, displayed before multitudes, spirited to Europe, fought over, prayed over, and finally sealed beneath slabs of steel in an Argentine cemetery. Eva Peron lived only until thirty-three, but she went out with a long curtain call.

She was not an obvious subject for a musical. Andrew Lloyd Webber and Tim Rice, who wrote the stage version of *Evita* and whose songs are wall-to-wall in the movie, must have known that; why else did they provide a key character named Che Guevera (onstage) and Che (onscreen), to ask embarrassing questions? "You let down your people, Evita," he sings. She let down the poor, shirtless ones by providing a glamorous facade for a fascist dictatorship, by salting away charity funds, and by distracting from her husband's tacit protection of Nazi war criminals.

Why, then, were Webber and Rice so right in choosing Eva Peron as their heroine? My guess is that they perfectly anticipated *Evita*'s core audience—affluent, middle-aged, and female. The musical celebrates Eva Peron's narcissism, her furs and diamonds, her firm management of her man. Given such enticements, what audience is going to quibble about ideology?

For years I have wondered, during "Don't Cry for Me, Argentina," why we were not to cry. Now I understand: We need not cry because (a) Evita got everything out of life she dreamed of, and (b) Argentina should cry for itself. Even poor Juan Peron should shed a tear or two; he is relegated in the movie to the status of a "walker," a presentable man who adorns the arm of a rich and powerful woman as a human fashion accessory.

All of these thoughts, as I watched Alan Parker's *Evita,* did not in the least prevent me from having a good time. I suspect Parker has as many questions about his heroine as I do, and I am sure that Che (Antonio Banderas) and Juan Peron (Jonathan Pryce) do—not to mention Oliver Stone, coauthor of the screenplay. Only Evita herself, magnificently embodied by Madonna, rises above the quibbles, as she should; if there is one thing a great Evita should lack, it is any trace of self-doubt. Here we have a celebration of a legendary woman (for those who take the film superficially), and a moral tale of a misspent life (for those who see more clearly).

Certainly Alan Parker is a good director for this material. He has made more musicals than his contemporaries, not only *Bugsy Malone, Fame,* and *The Commitments,* but especially *Pink Floyd—The Wall,* one of the great modern musicals, where he uses similar images of marching automatons. Working with exteriors in Argentina and Hungary and richly detailed interior sets, he stages Evita's life as a soap opera version of *Triumph of the Will,* with goose-stepping troops beating out the cadence of her rise to glory.

The movie is almost entirely music; the fugitive lines of spoken dialogue sound sheepish. Madonna, who took voice lessons to extend her range, easily masters the musical material. As important, she is convincing as Evita—from the painful early scene where, as an unacknowledged child, she tries to force entry into her father's funeral, to later scenes where the poor rural girl converts herself into a nightclub singer, radio star, desirable mistress, and political leader.

There is a certain opaque quality in Madonna's Evita; what you see is not exactly what you get. The Che character zeroes in on this, questioning her motives, doubting her ideals, pointing out contradictions and evasions. Yet for Evita there are no inconsistencies, because everything she does is at the service of her image. It is only if you believe she is at the service of the poor that you being to wonder. Listen closely as she sings:

For I am ordinary, unimportant
And undeserving
Of such attention
Unless we all are
I think we all are
So share my glory.

The poor, in other words, deserve what Evita has, so her program consists of her having it and the poor being happy for her. After all, if she didn't have it, she'd be poor too. In other words: The lottery is wonderful, just as long as I win it.

Banderas, as Che, sees through this; his performance is one of the triumphs of the movie. He sings well, he has a commanding screen presence, and he finds a middle ground between condemnation and giving the devil her due. He is "of the people" enough to feel their passion for Evita, and enough of a revolutionary to distrust his feelings.

Jonathan Pryce, as the dictator, remains more difficult to read. He is grateful for the success Evita brings him (her broadcasts free him from prison, her campaigns win his elections, her fame legitimatizes his regime). But there is a quiet little scene where he knocks on her locked bedroom door and then shuffles back to his own room, and that scene speaks volumes for the haunted look in his eyes.

The music, like most of the Webber/Rice scores, is repetitive to the point of brainwashing. It's as if they come up with one good song and go directly into rehearsals. The reason their songs become hits is that you've heard them a dozen times by the end of the show. But Parker's visuals enliven the music, and Madonna and Banderas bring it passion. By the end of the film we feel like we've had our money's worth, and we're sure Evita has.

Excess Baggage ★ ★ ★

PG-13, 98 m., 1997

Alicia Silverstone (Emily), Benicio Del Toro (Vincent), Christopher Walken (Ray), Jack Thompson (Alexander), Harry Connick Jr. (Greg), Nicholas Turturro (Stick), Michael Bowen (Gus), Robert Wisden (Detective Sims). Directed by Marco Brambilla and produced by Bill Borden and Carolyn Kessler. Screenplay by Max D. Adams, Dick Clement, and Ian La Frenais.

Alicia Silverstone, she of the blond locks and quick intelligence, was perfectly cast in *Clueless* as a popular girl who tries to pull all the strings, and gets a few of her own pulled in return. She was such a hit in the film that she formed her own production company while still in her teens, and there were cover stories hailing her as the next . . . I dunno . . . Winona Ryder? Grace Kelly?

She was wonderful in that film, but could she pick another hit? Certainly her agents advised her to take the role of Robin's girlfriend in *Batman and Robin,* where she looked unconvincing, uncomfortable, and a size larger than the costume. Now she is back in a starring role in *Excess Baggage,* a film she coproduced. She's okay in it, but no better than okay. Benicio Del Toro steals it with his performance as a car thief who becomes an unwilling kidnapper.

Silverstone plays Emily, a rich kid who fakes her own kidnapping in order to attract her father's attention. She locks herself in the trunk of her own car, expecting to be rescued quickly, but her plans go wrong when Del Toro's thief, named Vincent, steals the car. At his chop shop, he is amazed to find her in the trunk, and even more amazed when she refuses to be intimidated.

There's a shade of *The Ransom of Red Chief* here, as the kidnapping victim turns into more trouble than she's worth. Vincent's partner, Greg, played by Harry Connick Jr., is possibly smarter and certainly unwilling to get anywhere near a kidnapping, although his situation grows more difficult after they succeed in misplacing $200,000 in mob money.

The architecture of the plot will be familiar. We have Jack Thompson as the wealthy, distant father named Alexander, Christopher Walken as Uncle Ray, Alexander's Mr. Fixit, and handy MacGuffins like the mob money that obviously exist only as tools for the plot. One inspiration may have been enough for this movie; why not set up the phony kidnapping and the carjacking and then play out the plot based on the personalities of the characters, instead of penciling in all the clichés? (At one point, Emily is unhappy with Vincent in a rural diner and stages a scene indicating he has mistreated her, and three very big and ominous guys stand up slowly to come and settle Vincent's hash and defend the little lady. I'm thinking, no diner in a movie is complete without those three guys.)

Despite the elements I could have done without, the movie is often very funny, and a lot of the credit goes to Benicio Del Toro, who creates a slow-talking, lumbrous character who's quite unlike his image in *The Usual Suspects.* Here he has a dash of Brad Pitt and a touch of city-style cornpone; he's one of those guys who cultivates a personal style as a way of giving himself time to think.

The plot creates some fairly involved reasons why Emily and Vincent have to hit the road together, and why Alexander and Uncle Ray never quite figure out what they're up against. Many scenes are based on misunderstandings, and Del Toro grows funnier as he grows more ingenious and desperate in trying to think his way out of a situation he only vaguely comprehends. And Silverstone, as I said, is okay, although she's still coasting here on the success of *Clueless.* Maybe that movie was so entertaining that no follow-up could satisfy us; maybe next time she'll find the perfect role again. *Hint:* It will probably not be in any script containing the words "mob," "kidnapping," "ransom," and "millionaire."

eXistenZ ★ ★ ★

R, 97 m., 1999

Jennifer Jason Leigh (Allegra Geller), Jude Law (Ted Pikul), Willem Dafoe (Gas), Ian Holm (Kiri Vinokur), Don McKellar (Yevgeny Nourish), Callum Keith Rennie (Hugo Carlaw), Sarah Polley (Merle), Christopher Eccleston (Levi). Directed by David Cronenberg and produced by Robert Lantos, Andras Hamori, and Cronenberg. Screenplay by Cronenberg.

Guys are always using the same lame excuses. First Ted licks Allegra's bio-port. Then he says, "That wasn't me—it was my game character!" Allegra is the world's leading designer of virtual reality games. Her newest game is named eXistenZ, and the bio-port plugs directly into the lower spine and connects to the game's control pod via an "umbrycord." When you're hooked up, you can't tell the game from reality. Not even if you designed the game.

eXistenZ is the new film from David Cronenberg, the Canadian director who must be a thorn in the side of the MPAA ratings board. He's always filming activities that look like sex, but don't employ any of the appurtenances associated with that pastime. In his previous film, *Crash,* the characters exhibited an unhealthy interest in wounds. This time it's bio-ports. And what about those "MetaFlesh Game Pods," input devices that combine the attributes of a joystick, a touch pad, and a kidney? They pulse with a life of their own, and Allegra holds hers as if it's a baby, or a battery-powered shiatsu machine.

eXistenZ arrived a few weeks after *The Matrix,* another science-fiction movie about characters who find themselves inside a universe created by virtual reality. *The Matrix* is mainstream sci-fi, but *eXistenZ,* written by Cronenberg, is much stranger; it creates a world where organic and inorganic are not separate states, but kind of chummy. Consider the scene where an oil-stained grease monkey implants a bio-port in the hero, using a piece of equipment that seems designed to give a lube job to a PeterBilt.

Jennifer Jason Leigh, that fearless adventurer in extreme roles, plays Allegra, whose new game is being marketed by Antenna Research. Jude Law is Ted, the company's marketing trainee. She barely misses being killed during a demonstration of eXistenZ, when an assassin slips past the metal detectors at the door with a gun made of flesh and blood. Ted helps her escape, and later, when he cuts the bullet out of her shoulder, he discovers it's not a bullet but a . . . hmmm, this is interesting . . . a human tooth. She decides Ted needs his own bio-port, and looks for a "country gas station." When she finds one (with a sign that says Country Gas Station) we assume they're inside the game, which is why she knows the station's name: She wrote it, and maybe also created its owner, named Gas (Willem Dafoe).

She knows her way around this world, and isn't surprised when they're told, "Look for a Chinese restaurant in the forest—and order the special." The owner rattles off the chef's daily selection, explaining that "mutant reptiles and amphibians produce previously unknown taste sensations." But Ted insists on *the* daily special and gets a dish that's really bony. No wonder. The bones click together into a gun. And soon they visit the Trout Farm, where organic game pods are grown, and come up against Kiri Vinokur (Ian Holm), owner of Cortical Systematics, a rival game firm.

Cronenberg's film is as loaded with special effects as *The Matrix,* but they're on a different scale. Many of his best effects are gooey, indescribable organic things, and some of the most memorable scenes involve characters eating things that surgeons handle with gloves on. He places his characters in a backwoods world that looks like it was ordered over the phone from L.L. Bean. Then he frames them with visuals where half the screen is a flat foreground that seems to push them toward us, while the other half is a diagonal sliding off alarmingly into the background.

eXistenZ is likely to appeal especially to computer game players, since it's familiar with that world and speculates on its future development. Allegra explains to Ted such phenomena as "genuine game urges"—"something your game character was born to do." She regards her programming handiwork with musings like, "I've devoted five of my most passionate years to this strange little creature." At one point she's alarmed to discover, "I'm locked outside my own $38 million game!" And without the password, it looks like neither she nor anyone else can get back inside. What? You mean she didn't back up her disk?

Eye of God ★ ★ ★

R, 84 m., 1998

Martha Plimpton (Ainsley Dupree), Kevin Anderson (Jack), Hal Holbrook (Sheriff Rogers), Nick Stahl (Tommy Spencer), Mary Kay Place (Clair Spencer), Chris Freihofer (Les Hector), Woody Watson (Glen Briggs), Richard Jenkins (Parole Officer). Directed by Tim Blake Nelson and produced by Michael Nelson and Wendy Ettinger. Screenplay by Tim Blake Nelson.

Rural Oklahoma. Town named Kingfisher. Ainsley sits in the convenience store by the road, watching strangers on their way through. She works in a hamburger shop. She's lonely. Through a magazine, she gets into correspondence with a prisoner, and when he gets out he comes to see her. They get married.

This time and place are evoked with quiet, atmospheric shots in Tim Blake Nelson's *Eye of God,* a film in which dreams seem to yearn toward a place where they can grow. Kingfisher is a boring place which is a boring drive from other places just as boring. Ainsley (Martha Plimpton) likes people and would like to know more of them, but her opportunities are limited and her desperation makes her see the ex-convict as salvation.

Well, he looks wholesome enough. Jack (Kevin Anderson) is straightforward and sincere, looks her in the eye, tells her how he found Jesus in prison. At first their marriage looks like it will work. Then his controlling side takes over. He doesn't want her working. Doesn't want her hanging out at the truck stop. Doesn't want her to leave the house, indeed, except to go to church with him on Sunday. It's ironic: Her life was empty and barren before, and by marrying him, she's losing what little variety she was able to find.

The film tells this story in flashes of action, intercut with another story involving a local fourteen-year-old named Tommy (Nick Stahl) whose mother gassed herself. Now he lives with an aunt who can't control him. He's trapped in the town too. *Eye of God* works in a fractured style, telling both films out of chronological order, cutting between them in a way that's disorienting at first, as it's meant to be.

Perhaps there's a clue to the editing in the title. The eyes of god exist outside time and don't need to see stories in chronological order, because they know the beginning, middle, and end before the story begins or the characters even exist. *Eye of God* sees its story in the same way: as events that are so interlocked by fate that, in a way, they don't have to happen one after another because they will all happen eventually.

Continuity of sorts is supplied by the sheriff (Hal Holbrook), who provides a narration of sorts, beginning with the story of Abraham and Isaac: How did the son feel as he saw his father poised to kill him? He finds Tommy wandering by the roadside, covered with blood, in one of the first shots of the film. It's not his blood, but whose is it? He doesn't seem able to talk.

Another outside observer is Jack's parole officer (Richard Jenkins), who tells Ainsley something she should have known before she got married: Jack was in prison for beating a woman nearly to death—a woman who was carrying his child, as, before long, Ainsley is.

Martha Plimpton's performance is the center of the movie, quiet and strong. She plays a capable woman for whom life has not supplied a role. I've often seen her playing bright, glib city girls (that was her first big role, in *Shy People*). As Ainsley, she isn't tragically shy and lonely; it's more that she's waiting patiently for her life to begin, with less and less evidence that it's about to.

The villain in the film is not exactly Jack. Like an animal, he behaves according to his nature, and the way to deal with him is to stay away from him. The movie is more about Ainsley's luck than Jack's behavior. Somebody always marries these jerks, but you gotta hope it's not you.

Eyes Wide Shut ★ ★ ★ ½

R, 159 m., 1999

Tom Cruise (Dr. William Harford), Nicole Kidman (Alice Harford), Sydney Pollack (Victor Ziegler), Marie Richardson (Marion), Rade Sherbedgia (Milich), Thomas Gibson (Carl), Vinessa Shaw (Domino), Todd Field (Nick Nightingale), Alan Cumming (Desk Clerk), Leelee Sobieski (Milich's daugher), Carmela Marner (Waitress). Produced and directed by Stanley Kubrick. Screenplay by Kubrick and Frederic Raphael. Inspired by *Traumnovelle*, a novel by Arthur Schnitzler.

Stanley Kubrick's *Eyes Wide Shut* is like an erotic daydream about chances missed and opportunities avoided. For its hero, who spends two nights wandering in the sexual underworld, it's all foreplay. He never actually has sex, but he dances close and holds his hand in the flame. Why does he do this? The easy answer is that his wife has made him jealous. Another possibility is that the story she tells inflames his rather torpid imagination.

The film has the structure of a thriller, with the possibility that conspiracies and murders have taken place. It also resembles a nightmare; a series of strange characters drift in and out of focus, puzzling the hero with unexplained details of their lives. The reconciliation at the end of the film is the one scene that doesn't work; a film that intrigues us because of its loose ends shouldn't try to tidy up.

Tom Cruise and Nicole Kidman star as Dr. Bill and Alice Harford, a married couple who move in rich Manhattan society. In a long, languorous opening sequence, they attend a society ball where a tall Hungarian, a parody of a suave seducer, tries to honey-talk Alice ("Did you ever read the Latin poet Ovid on the art of love?"). Meanwhile, Bill gets a come-on from two aggressive women, before being called to the upstairs bathroom, where Victor, the millionaire who is giving the party (Sydney Pollack), has an overdosed hooker who needs a doctor's help.

At the party, Bill meets an old friend from medical school, now a pianist. The next night, at home, Alice and Bill get stoned on pot (apparently very good pot, considering how zonked they seem) and she describes a fantasy she had about a young naval officer she saw last summer on Cape Cod: "At no time was he ever out of my mind. And I thought if he wanted me, only for one night, I was ready to give up everything."

There is a fight. Bill leaves the house and wanders the streets, his mind inflamed by images of Alice making love with the officer. And now begins his long adventure, which has parallels with Joyce's "Nighttown" section of *Ulysses* and Scorsese's *After Hours*, as one sexual situation after another swims into view. The film has two running jokes, both quiet ones: Almost everyone who sees Bill, both male and female, reacts to him sexually. And he is forever identifying himself as a doctor, as if to reassure himself that he exists at all.

Kubrick's great achievement in the film is to find and hold an odd, unsettling, sometimes erotic tone for the doctor's strange encounters. Shooting in a grainy high-contrast style, using lots of backlighting, underlighting, and strong primary colors, setting the film at Christmas to take advantage of the holiday lights, he makes it all a little garish, like an urban sideshow. Dr. Bill is not really the protagonist but the acted-upon, careening from one situation to another, out of his depth.

Kubrick pays special attention to each individual scene. He makes a deliberate choice, I think, not to roll them together into an ongoing story, but to make each one a destination—to give each encounter the intensity of a dream in which *this* moment is clear but it's hard to remember where we've come from or guess what comes next.

The film pays extraordinary attention to the supporting actors, even cheating camera angles to give them the emphasis on two-shots; in several scenes, Cruise is like the straight man. Sydney Pollack is the key supporting player, as a confident, sinister man of the world, living in old-style luxury, deep-voiced, experienced, decadent. Todd Field plays Nick, the society piano player who sets up Bill's visit to a secret orgy. And there is also a wonderful role for Vinessa Shaw as a hooker who picks up Dr. Bill and shares some surprisingly sweet time with him.

The movie's funniest scene takes place in a hotel where Bill questions a desk clerk, played by Alan Cumming as a cheerful queen who makes it pretty clear he's interested. Rade Sherbedgia, a gravel-voiced, bearded patriarch, plays a costume dealer who may also be retailing the favors of his young daughter. Carmela Marner is a waitress who seems to have learned her trade by watching sitcoms. And Marie Richardson is the daughter of a dead man, who wants to seduce Dr. Bill almost literally on her father's deathbed.

All of these scenes have their own focus and intensity; each sequence has its own dramatic arc. They all lead up to and away from the extraordinary orgy sequence in a country estate, where Dr. Bill gate-crashes and wanders among scenes of Sadeian sexual ritual and writhings worthy of Bosch. The masked figure who rules over the proceedings has ominous presence, as does the masked woman who warns Dr. Bill he is in danger. This sequence has hypnotic intensity.

The orgy, alas, has famously undergone digital alterations to obscure some of the more energetic rumpy-pumpy. A shame. The events in question are seen at a certain distance, without visible genitalia, and are more atmosphere than action, but to get the R rating the studio has had to block them with digitally generated figures (two nude women arm in arm, and some cloaked men).

In rough draft form, this masking evoked Austin Powers's famous genital hide-and-seek sequence. Later I saw the polished version of the technique and will say it is done well, even though it should not have been done at all. The joke is that *Eyes Wide Shut* is an adult film in every atom of its being. With or without those digital effects, it is inappropriate for younger viewers. It's symbolic of the moral hypocrisy of the rating system that it would force a great director to compromise his vision, while by the same process making his adult film more accessible to young viewers.

Kubrick died in March. It is hard to believe he would have accepted the digital hocus-pocus. *Eyes Wide Shut* should have been released as he made it, either "unrated" or NC-17. For adult audiences, it creates a mesmerizing daydream of sexual fantasy. The final scene, in the toy store, strikes me as conventional moralizing—an obligatory happy resolution of all problems—but the deep mystery of the film remains. To begin with, can Dr. Bill believe Victor's version of the events of the past few days? I would have enjoyed a final shot in a hospital corridor, with Dr. Bill doing a double take as a gurney wheels past carrying the corpse of the piano player. ☞

F

Face/Off ★ ★ ★

R, 140 m., 1997

John Travolta (Sean Archer), Nicolas Cage (Castor Troy), Joan Allen (Eve Archer), Gina Gershon (Sasha Hassler), Alessandro Nivola (Pollux Troy), Dominique Swain (Jamie Archer), Nick Cassavetes (Dietrich Hassler), Harve Presnell (Victor Lazzaro). Directed by John Woo and produced by David Permut, Barrie Osborne, Terence Chang, and Christopher Godsick. Screenplay by Mike Werb and Michael Colleary.

There is a moment in *Face/Off* when Sean Archer (John Travolta), a member of a secret FBI antiterrorist team, confronts the comatose body of Castor Troy (Nicolas Cage), his archenemy, in the hospital. "You're keeping him alive?" he asks incredulously. "Relax," says a medical technician. "He's a turnip." To prove it, she puts out her cigarette on Troy's arm. Troy won't feel a thing when his face is surgically removed in order to be transplanted to Archer's skull, so the FBI man can enter prison disguised as Troy and get information about a deadly biological bomb.

That exchange of faces and identities is the inspiration for *Face/Off*, the new John Woo action thriller that contains enough plot for an entire series. It's a gimme, for example, that as gravely injured as he may be, Troy will snap out of his coma and force a doctor to transplant Archer's face onto his own bloody skull—so that the lawman and the outlaw end up looking exactly like each other.

This is an actor's dream, and Travolta and Cage make the most of it. They spend most of the movie acting as if they're in each other's bodies—Travolta acting like Cage and vice versa. Through the plot device of a microchip implanted in his larynx, Travolta is allegedly able to sound more like Cage—enough, maybe, to fool the terrorist's paranoid brother, who is in prison and knows the secret of the biological weapon.

The movie is above all an action thriller. John Woo, whose previous American films include *Broken Arrow* with Travolta, likes spectacular stunts in unlikely settings, and the movie includes chases involving an airplane (which crashes into a hangar) and speedboats (which crash into piers and each other). There are also weird settings, including the high-security prison where the inmates wear magnetized boots that allow security to keep track of every footstep.

The high-tech stuff is flawlessly done, but the intriguing elements of the movie involve the performances. Travolta and Cage do not use dubbed voices, and don't try to imitate each other's speaking voices precisely when "occupying" each other's bodies. Instead, knowing that the sound of a voice is created to some degree by the larynx of his host body, they provide suggestions of each other's speech and vocal patterns, along with subtle physical characteristics. The movie's premise is that only the faces change—so each actor also finds ways to suggest that he is not the original inhabitant of his body. (Troy as Archer at one point refers unhappily to Archer's "ridiculous chin," and the fact that it's Travolta playing Cage criticizing Travolta is typical of the spins they put on the situation.)

For the Archer character, who begins inside Travolta's body and then spends most of the movie inside Cage's, the challenge is to fool a convict brother so suspicious that even when faced with the face of his own brother, he's cautious. For Troy, it's even trickier: He goes home to Archer's family, including his wife (Joan Allen) and confused teenage daughter (Dominique Swain), and has to convince them he's the husband and father they know. The wife in particular is surprised by the renewed ardor of a husband whose thoughts, for years, have been on revenge rather than romance. (Meanwhile, Archer as Troy is confronted by Troy's girlfriend, played by Gina Gershon.)

Woo, who became famous for his Hong Kong action pictures before hiring on in Hollywood, is a director overflowing with invention. He works here with an original screenplay by Mike Werb and Michael Colleary, which explores the strange implications of the face swap. One of the issues they touch on involves how much our appearance shapes our personality: If sweet, shaggy John Travolta looked like angular, sardonic Nicolas Cage, would he act any differently?

The summers of 1996 and 1997 were dominated by big-budget special-effects extravaganzas. Interesting that Cage was in three of them: *The Rock, Con Air,* and now *Face/Off.* He brings a quirkiness to the material that's useful. Given the undeniable fact that the plot of *Face/Off* is utterly absurd, it would be strange to see a traditional action hero playing it straight. Cage adds a spin. And here I was about to write: "For example, when he first sees Travolta's teenage daughter, he quips, 'The plot thickens.'" But, of course, it is *Travolta* who sees Travolta's teenage daughter, because it is Travolta playing the Cage character. You see what thickets this plot constructs; it's as if Travolta adds the spin courtesy of Cage's personality, while Cage mellows in the direction of Travolta. Better to conclude that the two actors, working together, have devised a very entertaining way of being each other while being themselves.

This business of exchanged identities is, of course, not new to drama. Shakespeare enjoyed having characters play each other (see *Twelfth Night*), and in Chinese and Japanese plays it's common for masks to be used to suggest identity swaps. Here, using big movie stars and asking them to play each other, Woo and his writers find a terrific counterpoint to the action scenes: All through the movie, you find yourself reinterpreting every scene as you realize the "other" character is "really" playing it.

FairyTale: A True Story ★ ★ ★

PG, 99 m., 1997

Florence Hoath (Elsie Wright), Elizabeth Earl (Frances Griffiths), Paul McGann (Arthur Wright), Phoebe Nicholls (Polly Wright), Peter O'Toole (Sir Arthur Conan Doyle), Harvey Keitel (Harry Houdini). Directed by Charles Sturridge and produced by Wendy Finerman and Bruce Davey. Screenplay by Ernie Contreras, based on a story by Albert Ash, Tom McLoughlin, and Contreras.

In 1917, two young English girls produced photographs that showed fairies. The photographs were published in a national magazine by Sir Arthur Conan Doyle, creator of Sherlock Holmes and an ardent spiritualist, and he vouched for their authenticity. The "Cottingley fairies" created an international sensation, though there were many doubters. Many years later, when they were old ladies, the girls confessed that the photos were a hoax.

That much is true. *FairyTale: A True Story* fudges so much of it that it should not really claim to be true at all. Not that it really matters. The movie works as a fantasy, and as a story of little girls who fascinate two of the most famous men of the age—Conan Doyle and the magician Harry Houdini, an outspoken debunker of all forms of spiritualism.

Early in the film we see a performance of *Peter Pan* that sets the stage, I think, for the movie's confusion between fantasy and reality. There is a point in the play where the children in the audience are asked, "Do you believe in fairies?" They all shout "yes!" and then the coast is clear for fairies to appear. There is the implication that if they shouted "no!" there would be no fairies, although no audience has been bold enough to test this.

In the movie, too, the fairies appear to those who believe in them. Are they real? Yes, Virginia. The film centers on twelve-year-old Elsie Wright (Florence Hoath) and eight-year-old Frances Griffiths (Elizabeth Earl), who has come to live with her cousin; her father is "missing" in the war in France, and she thinks she knows what that means. Elsie has also had a loss; her brother died not long ago. So both children are primed for belief in the other world, and one day they take a camera into the garden and return with film which, when developed, shows fairies.

Elsie's mother (Phoebe Nicholls), a member of the Theosophical Society, takes the photos to a society official, and soon they find their way into the hands of Conan Doyle (Peter O'Toole), who declares them the real thing, and finds an expert who declares them "as genuine as the king's beard." Harry Houdini (Harvey Keitel) is not convinced, and after escaping from the Chinese water torture tank, he joins Doyle in a visit to the girls' rural home.

Doyle publishes the photos, a journalist

tracks down the location where they were taken, and soon the meadows are being trampled by nutcases brandishing cameras and butterfly nets. Meanwhile, Frances continues to worry about her missing father, and the girls gain consolation from the fairies.

Yes, there are fairies. We see them. We see them even when there are no humans around, which I suppose is a sign either that (a) they really exist, or (b) "we believe in fairies!" The fairies are sprites dressed like Arthur Rackham illustrations for children's books, and they flit about being fairylike. (It is often the case that fairies and elves, etc., are so busy expressing their fairyness and elvehood that they never have time to be anything else—like interesting characters, for example.)

The movie is absorbing from scene to scene, and has charm, but it is a little confusing. Not many children, for example, will leave the theater being quite sure who Houdini and Doyle are. And not many adults will know exactly where Houdini stands on the issue of fairies. There's a scene where he skulks around in the family darkroom, looking for evidence. And another where he speaks to the children as one trickster to another, telling them he never reveals secrets, and they shouldn't either.

"I see no fraud here," the movie Houdini says. This is a line that would have the real Houdini doing back flips in his grave. Houdini dedicated the last decades of his life to revealing the tricks of mediums and spiritualists, and would of course have seen fraud. Even *we* can see fraud; although an expert says the photos could have been faked "by an operator of consummate skill," they were in fact (stop reading if you don't want to know) faked by the little girls. They simply put cutouts of drawings from a children's book in front of the camera—as any but the most gullible can see. Examine the originals for yourself on the Web at www.parascope.com/articles/0397/ghost08.htm.

I wish *FairyTale* had been clearer in its intentions. There are scenes in the movie suggesting the girls were sneaky deceivers, and others suggesting the fairies were real. What are we to assume? That Elsie and Frances committed fraud in an area that coincidentally was inhabited by fairies? Children are not likely to be concerned with these questions, and will view the movie, I suspect, as being about kids who know stuff is real even though adults don't get it.

Fallen ★ ★ ½

R, 120 m., 1998

Denzel Washington (John Hobbes), John Goodman (Jonesy), Donald Sutherland (Lieutenant Stanton), Embeth Davidtz (Gretta Milano), James Gandolfini (Lou), Elias Koteas (Edgar Reese). Directed by Gregory Hoblit and produced by Charles Roven and Dawn Steel. Screenplay by Nicholas Kazan.

Fallen is the kind of horror story I most enjoy, set in ordinary and realistic circumstances, with a villain who lives mostly in our minds. Movies like this play with our apprehensions, instead of slamming us with freaky special effects. By suggesting that the evil resides in the real world, they make everything scary; one of the movie's best moments is supplied by a pop machine.

Denzel Washington stars as John Hobbes, a detective who works with his partner, good old Jonesy (John Goodman), on murder cases. The film opens with a flashback ("I want to tell you about the time I almost died"), and then cuts to Death Row, where a vicious killer (Elias Koteas) faces the gas chamber. Hobbes is among the witnesses as the poison capsule drops, and the killer uses his dying breath to sing "Time Is on My Side." And then, this is curious, there is a POV shot from above the dead man's head, and we wonder whose point of view it could possibly be.

Having established the possibility of the supernatural, *Fallen* is at pains to center Hobbes firmly in a real world. The screenplay, by Oscar nominee Nicholas Kazan *(Reversal of Fortune)*, shows us Hobbes at home (he lives with his brother and nephew) and at work (Jonsey is a good pal, but a lieutenant played by Donald Sutherland seems to know more than he says). The story develops along the lines of a police procedural, with the cops investigating some strange murders, including a corpse left in a bathtub while the killer apparently enjoyed a leisurely breakfast.

Hobbes notices an incredible coincidence:

The dead man in the bathtub is the same man who walked past him last night, drawing his attention by his singular manner. Now that's strange. And strange, too, are other developments, including the verdict of a linguist that the gas chamber victim's words, on a videotape, were spoken in ancient Aramaic, a language he had no way of knowing.

There is a connection between all these threads, which we discover along with Hobbes. (The audience, indeed, discovers it before Hobbes—but we have the advantage, because we know he's in a horror movie and he doesn't.) Among the characters Hobbes encounters on his search for missing threads, the most interesting is the daughter (Embeth Davidtz) of a cop who committed suicide after being accused of the kinds of offenses that Hobbes himself now seems to face. "If you value your life, if there's even one human being you care about," she tells him, "walk away from this case." Did her father leave a warning behind? What is the meaning of the word *Alazel*, scrawled on the wall of the basement where he killed himself?

Denzel Washington is convincing as a cop, but perhaps not the best choice for the role of Hobbes, which requires more of a *noir* personality. There's something essentially hopeful and sunny about Washington, and the best *noir* heroes encounter grim news as if they were expecting it. There should be, at the core of the protagonist in any *noir* story, guilt and shame, as if they feel they deserve what's happening to them. Washington plays Hobbes more like a conventional hero, and doesn't internalize the evil.

As for the rest of the characters, perhaps they are as they seem, perhaps not, at any given time. The evil presence in the film moves from person to person, and there is a chase scene in a crowd that is eerily effective, because there's no way to tell who the pursuer is. See the film, and you'll understand.

Fallen was directed by Gregory Hoblit, who also made *Primal Fear* (1996). Both films contain characters who are not as they seem, and leads who are blindsided by them. *Fallen* reaches further, but doesn't achieve as much; the idea is better than the execution, and by the end, the surprises become too mechanical and inevitable. Still, for an hour *Fallen* develops quietly and convincingly, and it never slips down into easy shock tactics. Kazan writes plausible, literate dialogue and Hoblit creates a realistic world, so that the horror never seems, as it does in less ambitious thrillers, to feel at home.

Fallen Angels ★ ★ ★

NO MPAA RATING, 96 m., 1998

Leon Lai (Wong Chi-Ming, the killer), Takeshi Kaneshiro (He Zhiwu), Charlie Young (Cherry), Michele Reis (The Agent), Karen Mok (Baby), Toru Saito (Sato, the manager), Chen Wanlei (Father), Kong To-Hoi (Ah-Hoi). Directed by Wong Kar-Wai and produced by Kar-Wai and Jeff Lau. Screenplay by Kar-Wai.

Fallen Angels is the latest work from the Hong Kong wild man Wong Kar-Wai, whose films give the same effect as leafing through hip photo magazines very quickly. It's a riff on some of the same material as his *Chungking Express* (1996), about which I wrote, "You enjoy it because of what you know about film, not because of what it knows about life."

I felt transported back to the 1960s films of Godard. I was watching a film that was not afraid of its audience. Almost all films, even the best ones, are made with a certain anxiety about what the audience will think: Will it like it? Get it? Be bored by it? Wong Kar-Wai, like Godard, is oblivious to such questions and plunges into his weird, hyper style without a moment's hesitation.

To describe the plot is to miss the point. *Fallen Angels* takes the materials of the plot—the characters and what they do—and assembles them like a photo montage. At the end, you have impressions, not conclusions. His influences aren't other filmmakers, but still photographers and video artists—the kinds of artists who do to images what rap artists are doing to music when they move the vinyl back and forth under the needle.

The people in his films are not characters but ingredients, or subjects. They include a hit man and his female "manager," who share separate dayparts in a hotel room that seems only precariously separate from the train tracks outside. (She scrubs the place down before her shift, kneeling on the floor in her leather minidress and mesh stockings.) There is also a man who stopped speaking after eating a can of outdated pineapple slices (pineapple sell-by dates were also a theme in *Chungking Express*). He makes a living by "reopening" stores that are closed for the night, and has an uncertain relationship with a young woman who acts out her emotions theatrically. There is another woman wandering about in a blond wig, for no better purpose, I suspect, than that *Chungking Express* also contained such a character.

Does it matter what these people do? Not much. It is the texture of their lives that Wong is interested in, not the outcome. He records the frenetic, manic pace of the city, exaggerating everything with wide-angle lenses, handheld cameras, quick cutting, slow motion, fast motion, freeze frames, black and white, tilt shots, color filters, neon-sign lighting, and occasionally a camera that pauses, exhausted, and just stares.

That exhausted camera supplies the movie's best moment. The hit man (Leon Lai) has just wiped out a roomful of gamblers. He runs into the street and boards a commuter train. The man behind him is—good God!—a junior high school classmate, now an insurance salesman. The classmate chatters about insurance policies and his own impending marriage, handing the killer an invitation ("fill in your name"). The camera framing holds the killer in left foreground, his face frozen into a rictus of unease and dislike, his eyes turned away, as the classmate rattles on and on.

Finally the classmate asks for the hit man's card, which he supplies ("Ah! You have your own business!"). Then he asks to see a photo of his wife. The hit man supplies a photo of a black woman and a child. On the sound track, narration tells us he paid the woman five dollars to pose with him, and bought the kid an ice cream. The scene is telling us, I think, that in this society even a hit man feels obligated to be able to produce a business card and family photos on request.

A structure emerges uneasily from the film's unceasing movement. We watch the "midnight shopper" as he visits his old father and videotapes him cooking a steak. We see an inflatable doll being slammed in a refrigerator door. We see all-night cafés and hurtling traffic and a man riding a dead pig.

It's kind of exhausting and kind of exhilarating. It will appeal to the kinds of people you see in the Japanese animation section of the video store, with their sleeves cut off so you can see their tattoos. And to those who subscribe to more than three film magazines. And to members of garage bands. And to art students. It's not for your average moviegoers—unless, of course, they want to see something new.

Family Name ★ ★ ★

NO MPAA RATING, 89 m., 1998

A documentary directed by Macky Alston and produced by Selina Lewis. Screenplay by Alston and Kay Gayner.

Family Name tells a story that could have been written by Faulkner. It coils back through the secrets of the South to find if there is a connection between two large families with the uncommon name of Alston. One family is white, the other black. As the film opens, both are having their family reunions only a week and a few miles apart in North Carolina. Neither family knows about the other reunion.

"When I was growing up in Durham," remembers Macky Alston, who is white, "I noticed that many of my black schoolmates had the same last name that I did." When Macky is thirty, living in New York, he decides to make a documentary about what that might mean. He finds two other Alston families, both black, living not far away, and his investigation begins with them and then moves south.

Slavery is the great shame of the nation, and like all shameful things it is not much talked about within families touched by it. The Alstons, Macky finds, "were one of the largest slaveholding families in the state." But the time itself is on the edge of living memory. His father's grandfather owned slaves. There are two very old sisters, light-skinned enough to pass as white, whose family name is also Alston, and who remember their grandparents, who were slaves.

Are the Alstons related by blood? "In slave time," one of the black Alstons tells him, "they knew everything that happened, and they never talked about it." Whose children were whose, even across racial lines, was known but not recorded, and the tombstones of old family cemeteries contain tantalizing hints but never the facts.

Family Name, which begins like a family album, develops into a fascinating detective story as Macky follows leads. He discovers old courthouse records, visits cemeteries, finds documents in unexpected places. He begins to focus on a great-great-great-great-granduncle named Chatham Jack, who may have had mixed children, and who in his old age, it was said, always "kept a couple of little black children around to sit on his feet when they got cold." Is Jack's blood in both branches of the Alston family?

Tracing descendants down through the years, Macky finds black Alstons of distinction. One, Spinky Alston, was a well-known painter during the Harlem Renaissance. His father, Primus, was a light-skinned man—and not a slave. Was Primus descended from Chatham Jack? Amazingly, Macky finds that Spinky's sister, Rousmaniere, is still alive. But what does she remember?

Another African-American branch includes a professional storyteller named Charlotte, whose ex-husband, Fred, is a classical musician. Coincidentally, Fred and their son Jeff are also interested in traveling south to explore their roots. In living rooms and on front porches, in old baptismal records and birth certificates and wills, there are possibilities and conjectures but no facts. Macky tries to narrow down the possibilities—to see if only one scenario will fit his findings.

But there is much more going on here. For one thing, Macky is gay, and this fact has been withheld from his own grandmother. So in his own life he has experienced the way that secrets work. Must he tell her? And Macky's parents? What secrets do they hide? The trails seem to grow warmer, and a chance remark by an ancient survivor might provide the crucial clue. By the end of the film, we sit in astonishment at the unexpected turn the story has taken. *Family Name* begins by seeking the secrets of a family, and the secrets it discovers cause us to question the very definition of a family. If blood is thicker than water, then perhaps love is thicker even than blood.

Fast, Cheap & Out of Control ★ ★ ★ ★

PG, 82 m., 1997

Dave Hoover (Animal Trainer), George Mendonca (Topiary Gardner), Ray Mendez (Mole-Rat Specialist), Rodney Brooks (Robot Scientist). Directed by Errol Morris and produced by Morris, Julia Sheehan, Mark Lipson, and Kathy Trustman.

Life is a little like lion taming, wouldn't you say? Here we are in the cage of life, armed only with a chair and a whip, trying to outsmart the teeth and the claws. If we are smart enough or know the right lore, sometimes we survive, and are applauded.

Errol Morris's magical film *Fast, Cheap & Out of Control* is about four people who are playing the game more strangely than the rest of us. They have the same goal: to control the world in a way that makes them happy. There is a lion tamer, a man who designs robots, a gardener who trims shrubs so they look like animals, and a man who is an expert on the private life of the naked mole rat.

Morris weaves their dreams together with music and images, into a meditation. To watch the movie is to reflect that no matter how hard we work, our lives are but a passing show. Maybe Rodney Brooks, the robot scientist from MIT, has the right idea: We should develop intelligent robots that can repair themselves, and send them out into the universe as our proxies. Instead of a few incredibly expensive manned space missions, why not send up thousands of robots that are fast, cheap, and out of control—and trust that some of them will work?

Consider the lifework of George Mendonca, who is a topiary gardener, and must sometimes reflect that he has spent fifty years or more practicing an art that most people cannot even name. What is a topiary? A shrub that has been trained, clipped, and trimmed in such a way that it looks like a giraffe, or a bear, or a geometric shape. That is not in the nature of shrubs, and Mendonca, who is in his seventies, reflects that a good storm could blow his garden away, and that the moment he stops clipping, nature will go to work undoing his art. There is a beautiful slow-motion shot of him in the rain, at night, walking past his creations as if he, too, were a topiary waiting to be overcome by nature.

And consider Ray Mendez. Here is a happy man. When he first learned of the discovery of the naked mole rat, he felt the joy of a lottery winner. There are not supposed to be mammals like this. They have no hair and no sweat glands because they live always in a controlled environment—their tunnels beneath the African savanna, where they organize themselves like insects. Mendez lives with mole rats in his office, and creates museum environments for them. That means he has to ask himself a question no scientist before him has ever asked: What makes a mole rat happy? So that they can tell the members of one colony from another, they roll cheerfully in their communal feces—but where do they like to do that? In a room at the end of a tunnel system or in the middle? Like the architect of a luxury hotel, Mendez wants his guests to feel comfortable.

Dave Hoover is a lion tamer. He goes into a cage with animals whose nature it is to eat him. He outsmarts them. He explains why animal trainers use chairs: Not to hold off a savage beast, but to confuse it. "Lions are very single-minded. When you point the four legs of a chair at them, they get confused. They don't know where to look, and they lose their train of thought."

Hoover has lived his life in the shadow of a man he readily acknowledges as his superior: Clyde Beatty, the famous animal trainer who also starred in movie serials and radio programs. "There will never be another Clyde Beatty," he says, as we watch images from *Darkest Africa,* a serial in which Beatty and a little fat kid in a loincloth do battle in a hidden city with soldiers who wear large cardboard wings. It is clear that Beatty captured Hoover's imagination at an early age—that Hoover is a lion tamer because Beatty was, so that, in a way, Hoover is carrying out Beatty's programming just as Rodney Brooks's robots are following instructions, and the mole rats are crapping where Ray Mendez wants them to.

Morris's film assembles these images not so much as a documentary might, but according to musical principles: Caleb Sampson's score creates a haunting, otherworldly, elegiac mood that makes all of the characters seem noble and a little sad. The photography uses a lot of styles and textures, from 35mm to Super 8, from film to the handheld feel of home video. The cinematographer is Robert Richardson, who achieved a similar effect for Oliver Stone in *JFK* and *Natural Born Killers.* (Morris adds the year's most memorable end credit: "Mole Photography Sewercam by Roto Rooter.")

Errol Morris has long since moved out of the field of traditional documentary. Like his subjects, he is arranging the materials of life according to his own notions. They control shrubs, lions, robots and rats, and he controls them. *Fast, Cheap & Out of Control* doesn't fade from the mind the way so many assembly-line thrillers do. Its images lodge in the memory. To paraphrase the old British beer ad, Errol Morris refreshes the parts the others do not reach.

Father's Day ★

PG-13, 102 m., 1997

Robin Williams (Dale Putley), Billy Crystal (Jack Lawrence), Julia Louis-Dreyfus (Carrie), Nastassja Kinski (Colleen), Charlie Hofheimer (Scott). Directed by Ivan Reitman and produced by Reitman and Joel Silver. Screenplay by Lowell Ganz and Babaloo Mandel, based on the film titled *Les Comperes* by Francis Veber.

Father's Day is a brainless feature-length sitcom with too much sit and no com. It stars two of the brighter talents in American movies, Robin Williams and Billy Crystal, in a screenplay cleverly designed to obscure their strengths while showcasing their weaknesses.

The story is recycled out of a 1983 French film named *Les Comperes,* as part of a trend in which Hollywood buys French comedies and experiments on them to see if they can be made in English with all of the humor taken out. The discussion about this one seems to have been limited to who got to play the Gérard Depardieu role.

Billy Crystal won, I think. At least he's the one who is a master of the sudden, violent head-butt, which is supposed to be amusing because he's a high-powered lawyer and so nobody expects him to be good at head-butting. As the movie opens, he gets an unexpected visit from a woman (Nastassja Kinski) he knew seventeen years ago. She's now happily married, but needs to tell him something: They had a son, the son has disappeared, she's desperate, and she needs his help in finding him.

Robin Williams plays an unsuccessful performance artist from San Francisco who is at the point of suicide when his phone rings. It's Kinski, with the same story: Seventeen years ago, they had a son, who is now missing, etc. She tells both men to be on the safe side, in case one doesn't want to help. But both men are moved by her story, and by the photograph she supplies of a lad who looks born to frequent the parking lots of convenience stores.

At this point, it is inconceivable that the following events will not transpire: (1) The two men will discover they're both on the same mission. (2) They'll team up, each one secretly convinced he's the real father. (3) They'll find the son, who doesn't want to be saved. (4) They'll get involved in zany, madcap adventures while saving him, preferably in San Francisco, Reno, and places like that. (5) The married one (Crystal) will lie to his wife about what he's doing, and she'll get suspicious and misread the whole situation.

Will the movie get all smooshy at the end, with the kind of cheap sentimentality comedians are suckers for, because they all secretly think they embody a little of Chaplin? You betcha. This movie could have been written by a computer. That it was recycled from the French, by the team of Lowell Ganz and Babaloo Mandel is astonishing, given the superior quality of their collaborations like *Parenthood* and *City Slickers.*

Williams and Crystal are pretty bad. You can always tell a lazy Robin Williams movie by the unavoidable scene in which he does a lot of different voices and characters. This time, nervous about meeting his son, he tries out various roles in front of a mirror. All right, already. We know he can do this. We've seen him do it in a dozen movies and on a hundred talk shows. He's getting to be like the goofy uncle who knows one corny parlor trick and insists on performing it at every family gathering. Crystal is more in character most of the time—more committed to the shreds of narrative that lurk beneath the movie's inane surface.

The kid, played by Charlie Hofheimer, is another weak point. He's not much of an actor—not here, anyway, in material that would have defeated anybody—but the movie doesn't even try to make his character interesting. That would upstage the stars, I guess. An indication of the movie's lack of ambition is its decision to surround the runaway with clichés: His girlfriend has run off with a rock singer, he follows her, Crystal and Williams follow him into the mosh pits of rock concerts and to the band's engagement in Reno, etc. There's even a gratuitous drug dealer, hauled into the plot so he can threaten the kid about a missing $5,000. Would it have been too much to motivate the kid with something besides sex, drugs, and rock 'n' roll? Do we need a drug dealer in this innocuous material?

And what about poor Julia Louis-Dreyfus? She has the thankless role of Crystal's wife. When Crystal and Williams drag the kid into a hotel room for a shower, she misunderstands everything she hears on the phone and thinks her husband is showering with strange men and boys. Later she turns up while he's telephoning her, and he talks into the phone, not realizing her answers are coming from right behind him. This will be hilarious to anyone who doesn't know how telephones work.

The people connected with this movie are among the brighter talents in Hollywood. Ivan Reitman is the director; Ganz and Mandel have a great track record; Williams and Crystal are so good they could improvise a better movie than this. Here's a promising starting point: Two comics get stuck in doomed remake of French comedy and try to fight their way free.

Fear and Loathing in Las Vegas ★

R, 128 m., 1998

Johnny Depp (Raoul Duke), Benicio Del Toro (Dr. Gonzo), Ellen Barkin (Waitress), Gary Busey (Highway Patrolman), Cameron Diaz (Blond TV Reporter), Lyle Lovett (Musician at Matrix Club), Flea (Musician). Directed by Terry Gilliam and produced by Laila Nabulsi, Patrick

Cassavetti, and Stephen Nemeth. Screenplay by Gilliam, Tony Grisoni, Tod Davies, and Alex Cox, based on the book by Hunter S. Thompson.

Hunter S. Thompson's *Fear and Loathing in Las Vegas* is a funny book by a gifted writer, who seems gifted and funny no longer. He coined the term "gonzo journalism" to describe his guerrilla approach to reporting, which consisted of getting stoned out of his mind, hurling himself at a story, and recording it in frenzied hyperbole.

Thompson's early book on the Hells Angels described motorcyclists who liked to ride as close to the line as they could without losing control. At some point after writing that book, and books on Vegas and the 1972 presidential campaign, Thompson apparently crossed his own personal line. His work became increasingly incoherent and meandering, and reports from his refuge in Woody Creek, Colorado, depicted a man lost in the gloom of his pleasures.

Ah, but he was funny before he flamed out. *Fear and Loathing in Las Vegas* is a film based on the book of the same name, a stream-of-altered-consciousness report of his trip to Vegas with his allegedly Samoan attorney. In the trunk of their car they carried an inventory of grass, mescaline, acid, cocaine, uppers, booze, and ether.

That ether, it's a wicked high. Hurtling through the desert in a gas-guzzling convertible, they hallucinated attacks by giant bats, and "speaking as your attorney," the lawyer advised him on drug ingestion.

The relationship of Thompson and his attorney was the basis of *Where the Buffalo Roam,* an unsuccessful 1980 movie starring Bill Murray as the writer and Peter Boyle as his attorney. Now comes *Fear and Loathing in Las Vegas,* with Johnny Depp and Benicio Del Toro. The hero here is named Duke, which was his name in the original Thompson book and is also the name of the Thompson clone in the *Doonesbury* comic strip. The attorney is Dr. Gonzo. Both Duke and the Doctor are one-dimensional walking chemistry sets, lacking the perspective on themselves that they have in both the book and the strip.

The result is a horrible mess of a movie, without shape, trajectory, or purpose—a one-joke movie, if it had one joke. The two characters wander witlessly past the bizarre backdrops of Las Vegas (some real, some hallucinated, all interchangeable) while zonked out of their minds. Humor depends on attitude. Beyond a certain point, you don't have an attitude; you simply inhabit a state. I've heard a lot of funny jokes about drunks and druggies, but these guys are stoned beyond comprehension, to the point where most of their dialogue could be paraphrased as "eh?"

The story: Thompson has been sent to Vegas to cover the Mint 400, a desert motorcycle race, and stays to report on a convention of district attorneys. Both of these events are dimly visible in the background; the foreground is occupied by Duke and Gonzo, staggering through increasingly hazy days. One of Duke's most incisive interviews is with the maid who arrives to clean the room he's trashed: "You must know what's going on in this hotel! What do you think's going on?"

Johnny Depp has been a gifted and inventive actor in films like *Benny and Joon* and *Ed Wood.* Here he's given a character with no nuances, a man whose only variable is the current degree he's out of it. He plays Duke in disguise, behind strange hats, big shades, and the ever-present cigarette holder. The decision to *always* use the cigarette holder was no doubt inspired by the Duke character in the comic strip, who invariably has one—but a prop in a comic is not the same thing as a prop in a movie, and here it becomes not only an affectation but a handicap: Duke isn't easy to understand at the best of times, and talking through clenched teeth doesn't help. That may explain the narration, in which Duke comments on events that are apparently incomprehensible to himself on screen.

The movie goes on and on, repeating the same setup and the same payoff: Duke and Gonzo take drugs, stagger into new situations, blunder, fall about, wreak havoc, and retreat to their hotel suite. The movie itself has an alcoholic and addict mind-set, in which there is no ability to step outside the need to use and the attempt to function. If you encountered characters like these on an elevator, you'd push a button and get off at the next floor. Here the elevator is trapped between floors for 128 minutes.

The movie's original director was Alex Cox,

whose brilliant *Sid & Nancy* showed insight into the world of addiction. Maybe too much insight—he was replaced by Terry Gilliam *(Brazil, Time Bandits),* whose input is hard to gauge; this is not his proudest moment. Who was the driving force behind the project? Maybe Depp, who doesn't look unlike the young Hunter Thompson but can't communicate the genius beneath the madness.

Thompson may have plowed through Vegas like a madman, but he wrote about his experiences later, in a state which, for him, approached sobriety. You have to stand outside the chaos to see its humor, which is why people remembering the funny things they did when they were drunk are always funnier than drunks doing them.

As for Depp, what was he thinking when he made this movie? He was once in trouble for trashing a New York hotel room, just like the heroes of *Fear and Loathing in Las Vegas.* What was that? Research? After River Phoenix died of an overdose outside Depp's club, you wouldn't think Depp would see much humor in this story—but then, of course, there *isn't* much humor in this story.

Female Perversions ★ ★ ★ ½

R, 119 m., 1997

Tilda Swinton (Eve Stephens), Amy Madigan (Madelyn Stephens), Karen Sillas (Renee), Frances Fisher (Annunciata), Laila Robins (Emma), Paulina Porizkova (Langley Flynn), Clancy Brown (John), Dale Shuger (Ed). Directed by Susan Streitfeld and produced by Mindy Affrime. Screenplay by Julie Hebert and Streitfeld, based on the book by Dr. Louise J. Kaplan.

There is a scene early in *Female Perversions* where a woman attorney is summarizing her case in a courtroom. Her body language indicates her aggressive intelligence: She uses abrupt, decisive movements. Her language is crisp and definitive. As she talks, the camera uses close-ups to indicate what the judge and the male attorneys are noticing: the neckline of the white blouse beneath her business suit, the slit in her skirt, her high-heeled shoes.

Is this a scene illustrating male chauvinist piggism? Not at all. The attorney is precisely aware of the impression she is making. She is a gender warrior who is fiercely ambitious (she's in line for a judgeship) and fiercely competitive (she throws away a lipstick when she sees another woman using the same shade). The woman, whose name is Eve (Tilda Swinton), is rising in the legal world and succeeding at romance, too—she has a relationship with a male executive that involves twisted sex in his office with the door unlocked.

All of her accomplishments are driving her mad. And *Female Perversions,* uneven and sometimes infuriating, is one of the most provocative films I've seen about the complications of being female in the modern world. It opens with a quote by the feminist scholar Louise J. Kaplan, who says that the roles women are required to play in our society are in themselves a form of perversion. And throughout the movie we see graffiti scrawled on billboards and benches, saying things like, "Perversion scenarios are about desperate need."

They are in Eve's case. Sex for her is a form of hunger, and she is less interested in the other person than in the sudden, savage gratification of her needs (which include the need to dominate, to be desired, to be admired). While continuing her relationship with the male executive, she picks up a woman psychiatrist (Karen Sillas) in an elevator, and they become lovers, too—until the other woman calls it off, saying she moved towns precisely to get out of "this kind" of a relationship.

Eve is on the edge of disintegrating. She hears voices criticizing her appearance, her sexuality, her clothing, and makeup. She fantasizes that she is being tormented by looming male figures. There are imaginary scenes with a rope, which is sometimes phallic, sometimes suggests bondage, sometimes seems to be a lifeline. There are also fantasy scenes in which a vast Earth Mother type exhorts Eve to express her inner femaleness, or whatever. The fantasy scenes in general seem unnecessary; the movie could have stayed with realism.

But the central story is compelling. Eve's sister Madelyn (Amy Madigan) lives in a semirural town, and is finishing her Ph.D. thesis (on a small Mexican village where the women rule—"and as a result get fat, which is what happens in a matriarchy"). Eve dresses in power business suits; Madelyn dresses in shirts and jeans, and has a shoplifting problem. Eve, concerned that a scandal might derail her judgeship, goes to defend Madelyn and finds that she is probably guilty—and has been shoplifting for a long time.

"It's erotic," Madelyn tells Eve. She does it because she finds fulfillment and release. The danger of being caught is part of it. Eve lectures and berates her, but of course Eve's own turn-ons include the danger of being caught while having sex in her lover's office. Is there any difference? Yes: Eve has more to lose.

Madelyn's friends in the small town include a woman who runs a bridal store (Laila Robins); a stripper (Frances Fisher); and a young adolescent tomboy named Ed (Dale Shuger), who loathes her body because of menstruation and is into self-mutilation. The scenes in their household have a quirky fascination of their own; sort of a *Bagdad Cafe* atmosphere. These characters represent an obvious attempt to get still more female role models into the film (and I must not overlook Paulina Porizkova, who plays the lawyer poised to get Eve's old job if she becomes a judge).

The film might have been better served by scaling back to more obvious material about women's roles and absorbing its ideology into the story of Eve and Madelyn. But it's aggressively thought-provoking all the same. It sees so clearly how confused Eve is, how she plays her various roles so well and yet cannot allow them to fit together or make her happy.

The film was directed and cowritten by Susan Streitfeld, who was a high-powered agent (her clients have included Daniel Day-Lewis, Jennifer Jason Leigh, Juliette Binoche, and Joanne Whalley). She knows the business world firsthand. The Kaplan book that inspired the film is theory, not fiction; the story comes from Streitfeld and Julie Hebert, and has a raw power that is impossible to dismiss. Tilda Swinton, who played the androgynous title character in *Orlando*, creates a character perfectly poised between perfection and madness, and Amy Madigan, always persuasive, plays a character who has her problems all more or less figured out, and finds that's not much help. This is the kind of movie you can't stop thinking about.

Fetishes ★ ★ ★

NO MPAA RATING, 90 m., 1997

A documentary directed by Nick Broomfield and produced by Broomfield and Michelle D'Acosta.

Howard Stern has his moments of insight, and one came while he was discussing the murder of Mistress Hilda, a fifty-eight-year-old French-born dominatrix whose body was found in her New York apartment surrounded by whips, chains, and the other tools of her craft. It's often said, Stern observed, that the clients of S&M parlors are powerful men. "It's the wimps and the weaklings who are the rapists," he added.

It makes a certain amount of sense. Some men, deprived of a sense of power, compensate by assaulting the weaker. Others, uncomfortable because they have so much power, pay to have someone take command. Certainly the second part of that scenario is borne out by *Fetishes*, a documentary by Nick Broomfield that is fascinating, horrifying, funny, and sad.

Broomfield is the BBC documentarian who specializes in films about sex for cash. Early in his career he made a doc about a Nevada brothel, and two years ago he made *Heidi Fleiss: Hollywood Madam*, a version of that famous case in which Fleiss emerges more sinned against than sinning. *Heidi Fleiss* was one of the year's best films, an unblinking portrait of the manipulation of one person by another. *Fetishes* is not as powerful a film because it lacks the drama of a woman going to jail while the deeper corruption of her lover goes unpunished. But it provides an unblinking portrait of the S&M world that is joked about on late-night talk shows but rarely seen—certainly not in this detail.

Broomfield, who travels light, works with a cameraman and acts as his own sound man. He enters a situation and records it while it is happening, making no attempt to conceal his mike and camera. He spent two months in Pandora's Box, described as an upscale Manhattan S&M brothel where the clients pay up to $1,000 to have the dominatrixes enact elaborate physical and mental fantasies for them.

Is "brothel" the right word? The women insist they never, ever have sex with their clients. The woman in charge is Mistress Raven, who must have a snapshot of Cher tacked up next to her vanity mirror. She is intelligent, articulate, thoughtful. She explains the rationale behind her operation. Then we see her and the other women at work on their clients.

Surprisingly, some of the men are willing to be shown on screen, and although many are masked or concealed, it is probably possible to identify some of them. Why are they so reckless? Perhaps it's part of the thrill of humiliation. They submit to physical and psychological torture here, and some of the most painful sequences involve racial humiliation: a Jew who pays to have a woman play a Nazi, an African-American who wants to be treated like a slave, a white cop who wants to be treated like a black criminal.

Other fantasies are (more? less?) conventional. A stockbroker wears an expensive rubber suit that is airtight, except for a breathing tube that is controlled by his mistress. A man licks a woman's shoes. There are even women who pay to be submissive. Various domestic and toilet scenarios are enacted. There are some whips and chains, although most of the sessions deal more with the mind, or restraint, than with actual physical punishment.

Why do these men pay for such experiences? Mistress Raven and the other women have their theories. The men feel under unbearable pressure of various kinds: professional, personal, sexual. It is a vast relief for them to hand over control, to embrace the blamelessness of the victim. Raven notes with amusement an obvious paradox: It is the client, not the dominatrix, who has the real power, because he pays the money and writes the script, and both he and the woman do exactly what he desires.

There is a subtext to the movie, which emerges subtly. What Raven and her women do is hard work. Transference takes place. The men arrive with tensions and compulsions, responsibilities and hang-ups, and leave them at Pandora's Box—on the shoulders, or the psyches, of the women. At the end of the day, Raven says, she's exhausted, worn down by the weight of the gloom and guilt she has taken on board. She doesn't know how much longer she can stand it. One wonders if after a hard day's work she yearns for someone else to take her reins.

Fierce Creatures ★ ★ 1/2

PG-13, 93 m., 1997

John Cleese (Rollo Lee), Jamie Lee Curtis (Willa Weston), Kevin Kline (Vince McCain), Kevin Kline (Rod McCain), Michael Palin (Bugsy Malone), Ronnie Corbett (Reggie Sealions), Carey Lowell (Cub Felines), Robert Lindsay (Sydney Small Mammals). Directed by Robert Young and Fred Schepisi and produced by Michael Shamberg and John Cleese. Screenplay by Cleese and Iain Johnstone.

Having worked under the proprietorship of the media baron Rupert Murdoch, I was receptive to the satirical version of him presented in *Fierce Creatures*, where a Murdochian tycoon wonders if he could buy the satellite TV rights to all of the executions in China. Nor did I blink at a scene where a new employee turns up to program his station, only to learn he has sold it that very morning. At that level, corporations change hands faster than the rest of us unload used cars.

The Murdoch figure in *Fierce Creatures*, named McCain (Kevin Kline), is a blustering bully who demands that all of his properties return an annual profit of at least 20 percent. That includes a zoo he has recently acquired, more or less by accident, in England. He assigns a man named Rollo Lee (John Cleese) to run the zoo, and Lee immediately orders that it will feature only dangerous animals—since they're the best at boosting ticket sales. All other animals must be shot.

This is a funny idea, especially when filtered through the apoplectic character Cleese created on *Fawlty Towers* and essentially repeats here. Autocratic, shortsighted, and short-tempered, Rollo orders his staff to start shooting the harmless animals, and when they balk he determines to do it himself.

The staff, a grab bag of eccentric animal lovers, unsuccessfully try to convince him all of the animals are dangerous. ("The meercat is known as the piranha of the desert! It can strip a corpse clean in three minutes!") Although Rollo's executions do not proceed precisely on schedule, a greater threat to his reign is presented by the arrival of old McCain's son Vince (Kline, in a dual role) and Willa Weston (Jamie Lee Curtis), the deposed programmer. Vince desperately hopes to take over the zoo and increase its profits in order to prove himself to his cruel and distant father. Willa wants a share of the glory, and both Vince and Rollo want a share of her generous charms, displayed in the kind of wardrobe that might result if women's business suits were designed by Frederick's of Hollywood.

Kline, Cleese, Curtis, and Michael Palin (as a hapless animal lover) are reassembled here for the first time since the brilliant comedy *A Fish Called Wanda* (1988). Few movies can hope to be that funny. *Fierce Creatures* is not. It lacks the hair-trigger timing, the headlong rush into comic illogic that made *Wanda* so special. But it does have a charm of its own, and moments of wicked inspiration (regarding the problem of shooting the harmless animals: "It's a pity this isn't Texas; we could charge people to do it for us").

One of the problems may be the dual role by Kevin Kline. Although multiple roles sometimes work (as in Eddie Murphy's family dinner scene in *The Nutty Professor*), they're more often a distraction. Part of my mind is forever trying to see through the trick. I'm observing that they're usually not in the same frame at the same time—and when they are, I'm thinking about how it was done. That brief lack of focus is deadly to the concentration needed for perfect comic timing.

There's also a subtle failure of timing in some of the slapstick sequences, as when a dead body is being dealt with toward the end. Slapstick doesn't consist merely of rushing around frantically; it has a clockwork logic, in which every element must be in position at precisely the right moment. This is so hard to do that it's a miracle when it works; it involves almost musical cadences. *Fierce Creatures* doesn't quite click.

Still, I'm fond of the movie. I like its use of lust and greed, always the most dependable elements of comedy, and I like the way Jamie Lee Curtis demonstrates how a low-cut dress can shift the balance of power in almost any room.

The Fifth Element ★ ★ ★

PG-13, 127 m., 1997

Bruce Willis (Korben Dallas), Gary Oldman (Zorg), Ian Holm (Cornelius), Milla Jovovich (Leeloo), Chris Tucker (Ruby Rhod), Luke Perry (Billy), Brion James (General Munro), Tommy "Tiny" Lister Jr. (President Lindberg). Directed by Luc Besson and produced by Patrice Ledoux. Screenplay by Besson and Robert Mark Kamen.

The Fifth Element is one of the great goofy movies—a film so preposterous I wasn't surprised to discover it was written by a teenage boy. That boy grew up to become Luc Besson, director of good smaller movies and bizarre big ones, and here he's spent $90 million to create sights so remarkable they really ought to be seen.

That's not to say this is a good movie, exactly. It's more of a jumble that includes greatness. Like *Metropolis* or *Blade Runner*, it offers such extraordinary visions that you put your criticisms on hold and are simply grateful to see them. If Besson had been able to link those sights with a more disciplined story and more ruthless editing, he might have really had something.

The movie begins in "Egypt, 1914," that birthplace not only of civilizations but of countless horror and occult films. Inside an ancient tomb, scientists gather at the site of an event that took place (we learn) centuries earlier. Four crucial stones, representing the four elements, had been kept here until a spaceship, looking something like a hairy aerodynamic pineapple, arrived to take them away, one of its alien beings intoning in an electronically lowered voice, "Priest, you have served us well. But war is coming. The stones are not safe on Earth anymore."

Deep portentous opening omens almost invariably degenerate into action sequences. But *The Fifth Element* cuts quickly to another extraordinary scene, New York City in the mid-twenty-third century. The futuristic metropolis, constructed at enormous cost with big, detailed models and effects, is wondrous to behold. It looks like Flash Gordon crossed with those old *Popular Mechanics* covers about the flying automobiles of the future. Towers climb to the skies, but living conditions are grungy, and most people live in tiny modular cells where all the comforts of home are within arm's reach.

Meanwhile, Earth is threatened by a giant pulsating fiery object that is racing toward the planet at terrific speed. "All we know is it just keeps getting bigger," one scientist reports. Ian Holm plays an astrophysicist who significantly observes, "It is evil—evil begets evil."

What is this object? What rough aliens are slouching toward Earth in its wake? And how to stop it? Man's hopes may lie with Leeloo (Milla Jovovich), cloned from a single unworldly cell, who comes into existence with flaming red hair already dark at the roots (those cells remember everything). Leeloo is clad in a garment that looks improvised from Ace bandages but gets no complaints from me (the costumes are by Jean-Paul Gaultier, whose favorite strategy as a designer is to start by covering the strategic places and then stop).

Military-industrial types want to employ Leeloo for their own ends; they observe her from behind unbreakable glass. She breaks the glass, grabs a general's privates, and dives through what looks like a wall of golden crumpled aluminum foil, racing outside to a ledge high in the clouds. She leaps, but is saved from dashing her genes out on the pavements far below by crashing through the roof of a taxi driven by Korben Dallas (Bruce Willis), who seems to have been ported directly here from the cab in *Pulp Fiction.*

Leeloo holds unimaginable powers, but she needs help, and Korben befriends her. Soon the future of the universe is in their hands as the movie unfolds the rest of the story. The "fifth element" of the title, we learn, is the life force itself—that which animates the inanimate (the other four elements are earth, air, fire, and water). Leeloo represents this element. Arrayed against her is a vast antilife force, a sort of black hole of death. Every 5,000 years, a portal opens between the universes where these two forces live; the evil force can slip through unless the five elements are correctly deployed against it. The pulsating fireball in space is the physical manifestation of the dark force.

Involved with mankind in this approaching battle are two alien races: the Mondoshawan, who live inside great clunky armored suits (that was their hairy pineapple) and the Mangalores, whose faces can be pictured by crossing a bulldog, a catfish, and an alderman. The Mangalores are in the hire of the sinister Zorg (Gary Oldman), who supports the evil force despite the fact that (as nearly as I can figure) it would destroy him along with everything else.

Now if this doesn't sound like a story dreamed up by a teenager, nothing does. The *Star Wars* movies look deep, even philosophical, in comparison, but never mind: We are watching *The Fifth Element* not to think, but to be delighted. Besson gives us one great visual conceit after another. A concert, for example, starring a towering alien diva whose skin shines with a ghostly blue light, and who has weird ropes of sinew coming out of her skull. And a space station that seems to be a sort of intergalactic Vegas, in which a disc jockey (Chris Tucker) prances about hosting an endless TV show. And spaceship interiors that succeed in breaking the *Star Wars/Trek* mold and imagining how an alien race might design its command deck.

The movie is a triumph of technical credits; the cinematographer is Thierry Arbogast, the production designer is Dan Weil, and the special effects are by Digital Domain, which created the futuristic Mars in *Total Recall.* And remember that Besson conceived of these sights, and had the audacity to believe his strange visions could make a movie.

For that I am grateful. I would not have missed seeing this film, and I recommend it for its richness of imagery. But at 127 minutes, which seems a reasonable length, it plays long. There is way too much of the tiresome disc jockey character late in the movie when the plot should be focused on business. Sequences are allowed to drag on, perhaps because so much work and expense went into creating them. The editor, Sylvie Landra, is ultimately responsible for the pacing, but no doubt Besson hovered over her shoulder, in love with what he had wrought. A fierce trimming would preserve what makes *The Fifth Element* remarkable, and remove what makes it redundant. There's great stuff here, and the movie should get out of its own way.

Fire ★ ★ ★

NO MPAA RATING, 104 m., 1997

Shabana Azmi (Radha), Nandita Das (Sita), Ranjit Chowdhry (Mundu [servant]), Kulbushan Kharbanda (Ashok), Jaaved Jaaferi (Jatin), Kushal Rekhi (Biji), Alice Poon (Julie). Directed by Deepa Mehta and produced by Bobby Bedi and Mehta. Screenplay by Mehta.

Deepa Mehta's *Fire* arrives advertised as the first Indian film about lesbianism. Among other recent Indian productions (according to the *Hindu,* the national newspaper) are films about tranvestism, eunuchs, sadomasochism, and male homosexuality. Along with Mira Nair's *Kama Sutra, Fire* seems to be part of a new freedom in films from the subcontinent.

Both of these films, directed by women, resent a social system in which many women have no rights. Neither is an angry polemic; the directors cloak their anger in melodrama, in romance, in beautiful photography, and in the sort of gentle sexuality that is often more erotic than explicit scenes, if only because it allows us to watch the story without becoming distracted by the documentary details.

Fire is about a beautiful young woman named Sita (Nandita Das), who marries into a New Delhi family that runs a sundries and video store. The entire family lives above the store: her husband, Jatin (Jaaved Jaaferi); her brother-in-law, Ashok (Kulbushan Kharbanda); his wife, Radha (Shabana Azmi); the ancient matriarch, Biji (Kushal Rekhi); and Mundu (Ranjit Chowdhry), the servant, who watches over the old woman during the day. Mundu's favorite pastime is masturbating enthusiastically to videos he sneaks upstairs from the store; a stroke has rendered Biji speechless, but she has a little bell that she rings furiously at him.

It is an arranged marriage between Sita and Jatin, insisted on by Ashok because the family needs children and his wife can give him none. ("Sorry, no eggs in ovary," the doctor explains.) Jatin, a modern young man with few serious beliefs, religious or otherwise, has gone along with the marriage but flaunts his mistress, Julie (Alice Poon), a Chinese woman. When Sita discovers Julie's photo in her husband's wallet, he is less than apologetic: "Julie is so smart, so special, so pretty—you should meet her!"

It is only a matter of time until the two wives, Sita and Radha, are sharing their unhappiness while looking out over the city from a rooftop veranda. Radha is alienated from her husband—who, depressed by her sterility, follows the teachings of a swami who advises chastity. Sita is devastated that her husband does not love her. One day, simply and directly, she kisses the older woman, and the next day the older woman dresses her hair, and soon they are in each other's arms, I think, although the sex scenes are shot in shadows so deep that censors will be more baffled than offended.

It is, of course, the Indian context that gives this innocent story its resonance. Lesbianism is so outside the experience of these Hindus, we learn, that their language even lacks a word for it. The men are not so much threatened as confused. Sita and Radha see more clearly: Their lives have been made empty, pointless, and frustrating by husbands who see them as breeding stock or unpaid employees.

The film has a seductive resonance. Women do a better job of creating art about sex, I think, because they view it in terms of personalities and situations, while men are distracted by techniques and results. The two women are very beautiful, gentle, and sad together, and the movie is all but stolen by Chowdhry, as the servant who lurks constantly in the background providing, with his very body language, a comic running commentary.

Fireworks ★ ★ ★

NO MPAA RATING, 103 m., 1998

Takeshi Kitano (Yoshitaka Nishi), Kayoko Kishimoto (Miyuki [Nishi's wife]), Ren Osugi (Horibe), Susumu Terajima (Nakamura), Tetsu Watanabe (Junkyard Owner), Hakuryu (Yakuza Hitman), Yasuei Yakushiji (Criminal).

Directed by Takeshi Kitano and produced by Masayuki Mori, Yasushi Tsuge, and Takio Yoshida. Screenplay by Kitano.

It has been said that Western art is the art of putting in, and Oriental art is the art of leaving out. The Japanese film *Fireworks* is like a Charles Bronson *Death Wish* movie so drained of story, cliché, convention, and plot that nothing is left except pure form and impulse. Not a frame, not a word, is excess. Takeshi Kitano, who made it, must be very serene or very angry; only extreme states allow such a narrow focus.

Kitano, who wrote, directed, and edited the film, stars in it as Nishi, a man whose only two emotional states are agony and ecstasy. As the film opens, he is a policeman whose young daughter died not long ago; now his wife is dying of leukemia. During a stakeout, his partner Horibe (Ron Osugi) suggests he go visit his wife in the hospital. He does, and while he is gone another cop is killed and Horibe is so badly wounded that he will spend his life in a wheelchair.

A cop movie would have dwelled on the action. *Fireworks* reveals what happened only gradually, and at first we even misunderstand the source of the bullets. The movie is not about action, but about consequences and states of mind. Nishi leaves the police force, and we learn, abruptly, that he is deep in debt to yakuza loan sharks. How? Why? Unimportant. All of those scenes that other films find so urgent are swept away here. When punk yakuza collectors arrive in a noodle shop to try to get money from Nishi, he stabs one in the eyeball with a chopstick so suddenly and in a shot so brief that we can hardly believe our eyes.

Nishi cares deeply for his wife, Miyuki (Kayoko Kishimoto), and wants to spend time with her. He robs a bank to raise the necessary cash. They do childish things together, like playing with the kite of a girl they meet on the beach. Sometimes they dissolve in laughter. But when a stranger laughs at Miyuki for trying to water dead flowers, Nishi brutally beats him. And when more collectors arrive from the yakuza, Nishi explodes again.

The pattern of the movie is: ordinary casual life, punctuated by sharp, clinical episodes of violence. Nishi hardly speaks (there is little dialogue in the film), and his face shows almost no expression (reportedly because of injuries to Kitano in a motorcycle crash). He is like a blank slate that absorbs the events in the film without giving any sign that he has registered them. When he attacks, he gives no warning; the wrong trigger word releases his rage.

Nishi is therefore, I suppose, psychotic, a dangerous madman. To read his behavior any other way, as "protecting his wife," say, would be childish. Sane people do not behave like this. And his wife, who hardly says six words in the movie, and who seems unaffected by his brutal behavior, shares the family madness. But that isn't really the point: This is not a clinical study, but a distillation of attitudes. In Kitano's bipolar universe, you are happy when the world leaves you alone, and when it doesn't, you strike back.

Against this swing of yin and yang there is a steadying character: Horibe, the man in the wheelchair. He paints naive and yet colorful and disturbing pictures of people with the faces of flowers. At one point his wheelchair is at the edge of the sea, and we anticipate suicide as the tide washes in, but he is a man who has found some accommodation with life, and will endure. Nishi, on the other hand, has adopted such an inflexible and uncompromising attitude toward the world that it will, we feel, sooner or later destroy him.

The film is an odd viewing experience. It lacks all of the narrative cushions and handholding that we have come to expect. It doesn't explain, because an explanation, after all, is simply something arbitrary the story has invented. *Fireworks* is a demonstration of what a story like this is *really* about, fundamentally, after you cut out the background noise.

Flubber ★

PG, 92 m., 1997

Robin Williams (Professor Phillip Brainard), Marcia Gay Harden (Sara Jean Reynolds), Christopher McDonald (Wilson Croft), Wil Wheaton (Bennett Hoenicker), Raymond Barry (Chester Hoenicker), Clancy Brown (Smith), Ted Levine (Wesson), Edie McClurg (Martha George), Jodi Benson (Weebo's Voice).

Directed by Les Mayfield and produced by John Hughes and Ricardo Mestres. Screenplay by Hughes and Bill Walsh.

How absentminded do you have to be before they begin clinical testing? This question may occur to the more cynical members of *Flubber's* audience, as the movie's hero succeeds in forgetting his wedding day for the third time in a row. In this remake of the 1961 hit, Robin Williams plays the absentminded professor who accidentally invents flubber ("Flying rubber! Flubber!") and saves his college, his career, and his romance.

Flubber is a substance that somehow magnifies energy, bouncing faster and higher than it should. Barely drop it, and it rebounds crazily off the walls. *Flubber* the movie seems to be made out of antiflubber; you drop it, and it stays on the floor. Although the movie may appeal to kids in the lower grades, it's pretty slow, flat, and dumb.

Williams stars as Professor Phillip Brainard, who must be related somehow to Professor Ned Brainard, the role originally played by Fred MacMurray in *The Absent-Minded Professor* and *Son of Flubber* (1963). He tinkers in his basement laboratory, creating marvelous inventions that are usually stolen by the scheming Wilson Croft (Christopher McDonald), who now wants to steal flubber—and Brainard's fiancée. She's Sara Jean Reynolds (Marcia Gay Harden), president of the university where Brainard teaches. It's a school about to go bankrupt.

Maybe Brainard keeps forgetting his wedding day because he already has all the woman a techhead like him could possibly want. He's accompanied everywhere by a levitating electronic sidekick named Weebo (voice by Jodi Benson), who has a seductive, womanly tone and a pop-up screen that illustrates her comments with clips from old TV shows. She's kind of like a cross between phone sex and an e-mate.

Weebo advises and encourages the professor, and keeps his appointment calendar. The movie makes much of how the patent on flubber might save the university, while overlooking the obvious fact that Weebo is the sort of personal digital assistant that would sell millions of units in the first year.

No matter. There's a villain on the scene—the scheming millionaire Chester Hoenicker (Raymond Barry), whose son Bennett (Wil Wheaton) just failed Brainard's class. Chester dispatches two goons named Smith and Wesson (Clancy Brown and Ted Levine) to spy on Brainard, and they observe his great new flying rubber just before flubber-covered golf and bowling balls bounce off their heads. (These two prowlers are clones of the bad guys in the *Home Alone* movies, also scripted by *Flubber* writer John Hughes.)

All of this is pretty slow going. Williams plays Brainard straight and steady, with a few whimsical asides, and the special effects team has fun with flubber, making it into a malleable green substance that can take any shape, and at one point forms itself into a song-and-dance number. There's also a flubberized basketball game, and a flubber-powered automobile, which Brainard pilots through the sky without, somehow, creating the magical effect you'd expect.

The suspense hinges on whether he can save flubber from Croft, fight off Smith and Wesson, marry the girl, and save the university. Call me perverse, but just once, just for the sheer novelty value, I'd like one of these movies to end with the hero losing the rights to his invention, while the bad guy marries the girl and the school goes belly-up.

Follow Me Home ★ ★ ★

NO MPAA RATING, 102 m., 1998

Alfre Woodard (Evey), Benjamin Bratt (Abel), Jesse Borrego (Tudee), Steve Reevis (Freddy), Calvin Levels (Kaz), Tom Bower (Larry), John Allen Nelson (Perry). Directed by Peter Bratt and produced by Bratt, Irene Romero, and Alan Renshaw. Screenplay by Bratt.

After *Follow Me Home* was turned down by every mainstream distributor in America, a new distribution plan was conceived: It would be booked one theater at a time around the country, with a discussion scheduled after almost every screening. For the last year this difficult, challenging film has found audiences in that way. There is a lot to discuss afterward.

The film is about four graffiti mural artists who pile into a van and head cross-country from Los Angeles to Washington with a plan to cover the White House with their paintings. In an age when Cristo wraps up buildings, this is perhaps not as far-fetched as it sounds, although I imagine they'll have trouble getting a National Endowment grant through Congress.

The artists include an African-American, an American Indian, and two Chicanos; on their odyssey most of the people they meet are white weirdos. One is reminded of the ominous rednecks encountered by the hippie motorcyclists in *Easy Rider.* The whites are stereotyped in broad, unfair strokes, but then the movie throws you off balance by throwing in one decent white guy and one redeemable one, and by making one of the painters into a fulminating cauldron of prejudice. By the end, you realize *Follow Me Home* isn't making a tidy statement about anything, but is challenging the audience to make up its own mind: to view racial attitudes and decide where they come from and what lies beneath them.

The writer-director, Peter Bratt, might almost have taken *Easy Rider* as his model—the parts that work, and the other parts too. Some of his dialogue scenes are too long and disorganized, but then suddenly everything snaps together in a scene of real power.

Consider, for example, a scene in a diner where a waitress feels she's been mistreated by one of the men (she is right). The owner comes out, lays a shotgun on the table, and delivers a lecture about their right to free speech and his right to bear arms. What is this scene about? A racist gun owner? Not necessarily, or entirely. The four men in the booth have different ways of seeing the situation, and the scene is about styles of intimidation.

Along the road, the men encounter whites wearing various costumes. There's a white guy who dresses like an Indian; they steal his antique tomahawk. Later, they encounter three white guys dressed in uniform for a U.S. Cavalry reenactment. Are they so inflamed they mistake the men of color for savage redskins? The development and outcome of this scene is hard to believe, but since it builds into magic realism, belief isn't the point. It's about a battle between two myths: the white myth of taming the West, and the black/Indian myth of soul power.

A key character in the film, encountered midway, is an African-American woman played by Alfre Woodard. She takes a lift from the guys, and gets angry when one of them can think of no words for a woman except "whore" and "bitch." Her powerful speech ("Look at me! I am a woman!") quiets him, and later woman power saves them all.

The personal styles of the four painters are all different. The black guy (Calvin Levels) is an intellectual, vegetarian, and pacifist, who uses terms like "patriarchal theocracy." The Indian guy (Steve Reevis) is a recovering alcoholic (a little stereotyping there?). The leader of the expedition, Tudee (Jesse Borrego), is the idealist whose vision brought them together. His cousin Abel (Benjamin Bratt) is angry at everyone, especially women. Are they a cross section? No, just a collection.

Watching the film, I resented the broad caricatures of whites. Then I reflected that broad caricatures of blacks were a feature of movies for decades and decades; just their luck that when a generation of black filmmakers arrives, stereotyping has gone out of style. I don't think Bratt is a racist, however: He's an instigator. He's putting highly charged material on the screen and standing back to see what happens. Most movies are too timid to deal in such controversy.

Follow Me Home is being shown in just the right way. It needs that discussion afterward. It doesn't come as a package that you can wrap up and take home. It's open-ended. It shows how films can cut, probe, and wound. It can awaken a sense of fair play in the audience. And in its fantasy and symbolism, it evokes a mystery level, beneath explanation. Most movies are over when they're over. This one is only beginning.

Fools Rush In ★ ★ ★

PG-13, 106 m., 1997

Matthew Perry (Alex Whitman), Salma Hayek (Isabel Fuentes), Jon Tenney (Jeff), Carlos Gomez (Chuy), Tomas Milian (Tomas), Siobhan Fallon (Lanie), John Bennett Perry (Richard), Jill Clayburgh (Nan). Directed by Andy Tennant and produced by Doug Draizin. Screenplay by Katherine Reback.

In actual fact, of course, angels rush in where fools fear to tread. And that's what happens to Alex Whitman, a fairly unexciting builder of nightclubs, when Isabel Fuentes comes into his life. Alex comes from Manhattan, where he leads the kind of WASP life that requires Jill Clayburgh as his mother. He's in Las Vegas to supervise the construction of a new club when he crosses paths with Isabel, a Mexican-American camera girl at Caesar's, who believes in fate: "There is a reason behind all logic to bring us to the exact same time and place."

The reason, which may be the oldest one in the world, leads them to the same bed for a one-night stand, which both insist they "never" do. But then Isabel disappears for three months, returning unexpectedly one day for a visit during which she asks for saltines (always an ominous sign) before telling Alex she is pregnant.

Fools Rush In is a sweet, entertaining retread of an ancient formula, in which opposites attract despite all the forces arrayed to push them apart. Alex (Matthew Perry of *Friends*), who has been fleeing from the same marriage-minded girl "since first grade," decides that Isabel is "everything I never knew I always wanted." Isabel, who also has a suitor in pursuit, knows only that Alex is the man she loves.

Of course there will be roadblocks to their union, although most of them occur after they're married (they get hitched almost immediately in a wedding chapel on the Strip, with an Elvis impersonator as witness). Isabel tearfully decides the marriage cannot work, and tells him, "I ask only that you meet my parents—so when the baby comes they can at least say they met you." She invites him over for dinner, which consists of a backyard barbecue for about one hundred guests, complete with a mariachi band. Alex tries to get in the spirit, despite ominous glares by suspicious male relatives who suspect (correctly) his designs on her.

Much of the rest of the movie consists of misunderstandings that threaten to destroy their potential happiness. There is a movie convention that whenever a lover sees a loved one from afar in a situation that can be wrongly interpreted, it is always interpreted in exactly the wrong way, with no questions asked. That leads to Isabel disappearing on occasion ("we are too different and always will be"), and Alex disappearing on other occasions (she wants to live in Vegas and finish her book of desert photography, he has to work in New York, he lies, she feels betrayed, etc.). "To you," she shouts, "a family is something you put up with on national holidays."

They fight about everything. Even religion. Are they really married after the farce at the wedding chapel? Not according to her parents, who want a Catholic ceremony, or his parents, who are Protestant. ("Presbyterian is not a religion!" she cries.) When she wants him to give up his New York job, he counterattacks: "This is something I waited my whole life for, and I'm not giving it up because I put a $5 ring on your finger in front of Elvis."

All of this manipulation comes with the territory. What makes *Fools Rush In* entertaining is the energy of the performances—especially Salma Hayek's. Until now she's mostly been seen as the partner of gunslingers in action thrillers *(Desperado, From Dusk to Dawn)*; here she reveals a comic zestfulness that reminds me of Maria Conchita Alonso. She's one of those women who is sexier in motion than in repose, sexier talking than listening, and should stay away from merely decorative roles.

I also liked the way her parents were portrayed. Tomas Milian is all bluster and ultimatums, but with a tender heart. For some reason the studio's publicity material does not supply the name of the actress playing her mother, even though this is one of the key performances in the movie, and played with a combination of great romance and pragmatism (yes, she agrees, her daughter wants to stay in Vegas near her family—"but your husband has a family to support"). Clayburgh and John Bennett Perry, as his parents, are more narrowly drawn, but that's because of the angle of the movie. (Someday we will get excitable WASPs and dour Mexicans, but not yet.)

By the end, by the time of the obligatory childbirth scene, I was surprised how involved I'd become. Yes, the movie is a cornball romance. Yes, the plot manufactures a lot of standard plot twists. But there is also a level of observation and human comedy here; the movie sees how its two cultures are different and yet share so many of the same values, and in Perry and Hayek it finds a chemistry that isn't immediately apparent. That's a nice touch. Most movies about opposites who attract do not really start out with opposites. (Consider the obviously perfectly compatible Michelle Pfeiffer and George Clooney in *One Fine Day.*) In *Fools Rush In,* they are opposite, they do attract, and somehow in the middle of the formula comedy there is the touch of truth.

Forces of Nature ★

PG-13, 103 m., 1999

Sandra Bullock (Sarah), Ben Affleck (Ben), Maura Tierney (Bridget), Steve Zahn (Alan), Blythe Danner (Virginia Cahill), Ronny Cox (Hadley Cahill), David Strickland (Steve), Meredith Scott Lynn (Debbie). Directed by Bronwen Hughes and produced by Susan Arnold, Ian Bryce, and Donna Roth. Screenplay by Marc Lawrence.

So I'm sitting there, looking in disbelief at the ending of *Forces of Nature,* and asking myself—if this is how the movie ends, *then what was it about?* We spend two endless hours slogging through a series of natural and man-made disasters with Sandra Bullock and Ben Affleck, and then . . . that's it?

Bronwen Hughes's *Forces of Nature* is a romantic shaggy dog story, a movie that leads us down the garden path of romance, only to abandon us by the compost heap of uplifting endings. And it's not even clever enough to give us the right happy ending. It gives us the *wrong* happy ending.

By then, of course, any ending is good news. The movie is a dead zone of boring conversations, contrived emergencies, unbelievable characters, and lame storytelling. Even then it might have worked at times if it had generated the slightest chemistry between Ben Affleck and Sandra Bullock, but it doesn't. She remains winsome and fetching, but he acts like he's chaperoning his best friend's sister as a favor.

The movie combines at least five formulas, and probably more: the Meet Cute, the Road Movie, the Odd Couple, Opposites Attract, and Getting to Know Yourself. It also cuts back and forth between a journey and the preparations for a marriage, and it tries to keep two sets of parents in play. With so much happening it's surprising that the movie finds a way to be boring, but it does, by cross-cutting between one leaden scene and another.

Affleck stars as an ad man who is flying from New York to Savannah, Georgia, for his wedding. On the plane, he's strapped in next to Bullock, who has held a lot of jobs in her time: flight attendant, wedding photographer, exotic dancer, auto show hostess. The flight crashes on takeoff, and they end up driving to Georgia together amid weather reports of an approaching hurricane.

Of course, circumstances conspire to make him pretend to be a doctor, and them to pretend they're married, and a motel to put them in the same room, and his best man to see him with this strange woman even though he tries to hide by holding his breath in a swimming pool, and so on. Rarely does the artificial contrivance of a bad screenplay reveal itself so starkly on the screen. And when the contrivances stop the revelations begin, and we learn sad things about Bullock's past that feel exactly as if Marc Lawrence, the writer, supplied them at random.

They have a lot of adventures. Arrests, crashes, trees falling on their car, hospitalizations. They take a train for a while (standing on top of one of the cars in a shamelessly pandering shot). And they take a bus (with condo-shopping oldsters). And a Spinning Sombrero ride. At one point they both find themselves performing onstage in a strip club—not quite the kind of club you have in mind. This scene would seem to be foolproof comedy, but the timing is off and it sinks.

Despite my opening comments, I have not actually revealed the ending of the movie, and I won't, although I will express outrage about it. This movie hasn't paid enough dues to get away with such a smarmy payoff. I will say, however, that if the weatherman has been warning for three days that a hurricane is headed thisaway, and the skies are black and the wind is high and it's raining, few people in formal dress for a wedding would stand out in the yard while umbrellas, tables, and trees are flying past. And if they did, their hair would blow around a little, don't you think?

For Richer or Poorer ★ ★

PG-13, 119 m., 1997

Tim Allen (Brad Sexton), Kirstie Alley (Caroline Sexton), Jay O. Sanders (Samuel Yoder), Michael Lerner (Phil Kleinman), Wayne Knight (Bob Lachman), Larry Miller (Derek Lester), Miguel A. Nunez Jr. (Frank Hall), Megan Cavanagh (Levinia Yoder). Directed by Bryan Spicer and produced by Sid Sheinberg, Bill Sheinberg, and Jon Sheinberg. Screenplay by Jana Howington and Steve Lukanic.

Kirstie Alley and Tim Allen are warm and appealing, and good with the zingers after years of practice on sitcoms. Watching them work in *For Richer or Poorer,* I admired their sheer professionalism. The plot is a yawner, another one of those "fish out of water" formula jobs complete with car chases and jokes about cow manure. But they succeed somehow in bringing a certain charm to their scenes, and they never miss with a laugh line.

Allen plays a Trumpian real estate magnate (how I love the word "magnate"), who is celebrating his tenth wedding anniversary by unveiling his latest scheme for a theme park: "Holyland—inspired by God himself." Alley, his wife, works the crowd for investors, but is fed up with the marriage and wants out. Before they get a chance to file for divorce, however, they find themselves in deep doo-doo with the IRS; Allen's accountant has stolen $5 million and made it look like a tax fraud.

These developments naturally make a car chase necessary, and after Alley coincidentally jumps into the back of the Yellow Cab that Allen has stolen, they head for the back roads and end up in Intercourse, Pennsylvania (joke), the center of an Amish community. They need to hide out somewhere, and Allen has studied the movie *Witness,* so they pass themselves off as long-lost Amish cousins from Missouri and move in with a farm family headed by Jay O. Sanders.

What happens during their stay on the farm can be imagined, in broad outline, by anyone who cares to give it a moment's thought, or perhaps less. The city slickers are put to work on farm chores ("Look, honey—it's 4:45 A.M.! We must have overslept!"). Allen is assigned to train a gigantic horse, and Alley tries to fake needlepoint lessons. All routine.

What does work are (a) their personal charm, which invests a lot of these assembly-line scenes with cheerful enthusiasm, and (b) one-liners in the screenplay by Jana Howington and Steve Lukanic. Trying to explain why he doesn't have an Amish beard, Allen stumbles and Alley volunteers: "Lice!" Allen says it was a very brief infestation. "Minute lice," says Alley. I laughed. I also liked Alley's bright idea that the Amish try dressing in a color other than black, and the fashion show she stages for the elders.

But the movie isn't convinced that it's really about its story. It doesn't stay within the logic of the characters. People change their basic natures for a laugh. (Example: The old hatchet-wielding grandfather who wakes them every morning, and then unconvincingly lets them sleep late one day.) There's a romance between two of the local young people, who are seen so one-dimensionally, often at a distance, that they might as well wear name cards saying "Soppy romantic subplot." And the IRS agents who chase the couple, led by the usually reliable Larry Miller, are made into shallow buffoons and kept that way.

And yet there were laughs. Enough of them that I resented it when the movie got soft-hearted and sentimental at the end. I like a comedy that goes for the jugular and takes no prisoners. If you must see a comedy involving the Amish, I recommend *Kingpin.* It's in terrible taste, but that's part of the fun. *For Richer or Poorer,* on the other hand, has an attack of sincerity just when it needs it the least.

For Roseanna ★ ★ ★

PG-13, 99 m., 1997

Jean Reno (Marcello), Mercedes Ruehl (Roseanna), Polly Walker (Cecilia), Mark Frankel (Antonio), Giuseppe Cederna (Father Bramilla), Renato Scarpa (Dr. Benvenuto), Luigi Diberti (Capestro), Roberto Della Casa (Rossi). Directed by Paul Weiland and produced by Paul Trijbits, Alison Owen, and Dario Poloni. Screenplay by Saul Turteltaub.

Death inspires a certain logic that can seem very funny if seen from a safe distance. *For*

Roseanna tells the story of a woman who believes she has weeks, if not days, to live, and of her loving husband, who wants to observe her dying wish—to be buried in the village cemetery with their child. It is not a simple matter; since the tightrope walker fell from the rope, there are only three graves left.

The village is in Italy—a movie Italy where everyone speaks English with an Italian accent. The international cast populates a picturesque location just around the corner, I imagine, from the location of *Enchanted April.* Every time I see a movie like this, I find myself thinking, to hell with the movie, I want to go there on vacation.

The dutiful husband is named Marcello (Jean Reno), as well he might be, since this is the kind of role Marcello Mastroianni could have performed in his sleep. He's a friendly but worried trattoria owner whose fear that the cemetery will fill up leads him to a desperate death-prevention campaign in which he directs traffic in the town square, grabs cigarettes out of the mouths of smokers, and even lies that a coma victim in the hospital has regained consciousness and asked for the soccer scores.

Reno, who played a cold, skilled killer in *The Professional,* is here a warm everyman, besotted with love. His wife, Roseanna, is played by Mercedes Ruehl, who may be surprised to find herself as a housewife in Italy but rises to the occasion. She doesn't appear terribly ill; perhaps she suffers from Ali MacGraw's Disease, first identified in *Love Story,* where the only symptom is that the patient grows more beautiful until finally dying.

Her heart is weak. She wants to stage-manage from the grave, and is obsessed with making plans for those who will have to carry on without her. Her husband, for example, should marry her sister Cecilia (Polly Walker). Fine, except that they don't much like each other, and besides, Cecilia falls in love with Antonio (Mark Frankel), the nephew of the rich landowner Capestro (Luigi Diberti), who has caused all the trouble in the first place by refusing to sell the village more land to expand the cemetery. Why is Capestro such a killjoy? Because he and Marcello have been enemies for years. It may have something to do with an old feud over a bicycle race, but there are also deeper currents and old loves that have not died.

We now have all the pieces in place for a good-hearted farce, in which lovers will be split up and united, misunderstandings will nearly lead to tragedy, and death will be feared, avoided, and confronted. There's enough going on that we hardly need the escaped kidnapper, although his final act of vengeance against the man who wronged him does show a certain ingenuity.

For Roseanna isn't of much consequence, perhaps, and the gears of the plot are occasionally visible as they turn. But it's a small, sweet film that never tries for more than it's sure of, and the actors find it such a relief to be playing such good-hearted characters that we can almost feel it. Of course, we're sure that with a setup like this the movie must have a sad ending. That only adds to the fun.

Four Days in September ★ ★

R, 113 m., 1998

Alan Arkin (Charles Burke Elbrick), Pedro Cardoso (Fernando/Paulo), Fernanda Torres (Maria), Luiz Fernando Guimaraes (Marcao), Claudia Abreu (Renee), Nelson Dantas (Toledo), Matheus Nachtergaele (Jonas), Marco Ricca (Henrique). Directed by Bruno Barreto and produced by Lucy Barreto. Screenplay by Leopoldo Serran.

A quiet sadness hovers over *Four Days in September,* the story of young Brazilian revolutionaries who are described even by a government torturer as "innocent kids with big dreams." Based on a memoir by one of a group who kidnapped the American ambassador in 1969, the film examines the way that naive idealists took on more than they could handle.

The movie opens with newsreel footage of demonstrations against a military junta that overthrew the democratic government of Brazil, suspended freedoms, and ran a reign of terror. After the free press was shut down, a group of students decided that kidnapping the ambassador would be one way to get attention for their demands to release political prisoners.

In most movies about political terrorists,

the characters are hard-edged and desperate, and the planning is incisive. Not here. The October 8 Revolutionary Movement uses the time-tested system of being sure no one in a cell knows the names of the others (that's also a way of concealing how few cells there may be). But two of the members conceal their friendship, and when one is captured by the police, it doesn't take long to make him talk.

Meanwhile, Paulo (Pedro Cardoso), the most intelligent and uncertain of the kidnappers, forms a bond with the kidnapped American (Alan Arkin). Guarding him for long hours, Paulo feels a certain gentleness toward the older man, who maintains his own dignity. Since Paulo may be called on to shoot the ambassador, this leads to an impossible situation.

The movie cuts between the kidnappers and the police, showing both sides more or less aware of the other's moves. Indeed, there's an amateurish air about the whole situation. As the terrorists wait to intercept the ambassador's Cadillac, a woman looking out her window finds them suspicious and tries to warn the police, who ignore her. And, incredibly, after two cops knock on the gang's hideout, Paulo is able to follow them back to headquarters and eavesdrop at a window to find out how much they know.

These are not brilliant revolutionaries. They're found by the cops because of their large orders of take-out food ("If only they had learned to cook!" a cop says), and at one point, as they wait uneasily inside the house where they're holding the ambassador, the sound track is filled with the same mournful passage from Mascagni's "Cavalleria Rusticana" that opens Scorsese's *Raging Bull.* The tone is not one of determination, but of regret.

I suppose the purpose of the film is to humanize both sides. It succeeds only to a degree. We can sense what the film wants to say better than the film can say it. Political terrorism may be justified in some situations (when it's your revolution, you call it heroism), but these callow students are in over their heads. And making the police and torturers into more human characters doesn't excuse them. Although the kidnapping did result in the release of some political prisoners, it's unclear whether it sped the day of Brazil's return to democracy. And for the participants, in retrospect, it may have been an unwise strategy.

Four Days in September was directed by Bruno Barreto, best known in America for *Dona Flor and Her Two Husbands.* Its screenplay, by Leopoldo Serran, is based on the book by Fernando Gabeira (who took the revolutionary name Paulo). He is now an elected official, and we sense a mixture of pride and regret in his memories. Films of the 1960s *(Z, The Battle of Algiers)* were sure of their sympathies. Costa-Gavras's *State of Siege* (1973), about the kidnapping and killing of an American official in Uruguay, was uncompromising in its portrait of U.S. interference in another country's politics.

It was also more clear in its consideration of the choice facing the kidnappers, who stood to lose whether they killed the official or not. This film is more muddled, and by the end we are not quite sure what we feel—or, in the final scene, what the young revolutionaries feel, either. The point of view is that of a middle-aged man who no longer quite understands why, as a youth, he was so sure of things that now seem so puzzling.

4 Little Girls ★ ★ ★ ★

NO MPAA RATING, 102 m., 1997

A documentary directed by Spike Lee and produced by Lee and Sam Pollard.

Spike Lee's *4 Little Girls* tells the story of the infamous Birmingham church bombing of September 15, 1963, when the lives of an eleven-year-old and three fourteen-year-olds, members of the choir, were ended by the explosion. More than any other event, that was the catalyst for the civil rights movement, the moment when all of America could look away no longer from the face of racism. "It was the awakening," says Walter Cronkite in the film.

The little girls had gone to church early for choir practice, and we can imagine them, dressed in their Sunday best, meeting their friends in the room destroyed by the bomb. We can fashion the picture in our minds because Lee has, in a way, brought them back to life through photographs, through old home movies, and especially through the memories of their families and friends.

By coincidence, I was listening to the radio not long after seeing *4 Little Girls,* and I heard a report from Charlayne Hunter-Gault. In 1961, when she was nineteen, she was the first black woman to desegregate the University of Georgia. Today she is an NPR correspondent. That is what happened to her. In 1963, Carole Robertson was fourteen, and her Girl Scout sash was filled with merit badges. Because she was killed that day, we will never know what would have happened in her life.

That thought keeps returning: The four little girls never got to grow up. Not only were their lives stolen, but their contributions to ours. I have a hunch that Denise McNair, who was eleven when she died, would have made her mark. In home videos, she comes across as poised and observant, filled with charisma. Among the many participants in the film, two of the most striking are her parents, Chris and Maxine McNair, who remember a special child.

Chris McNair talks of a day when he took Denise to downtown Birmingham, and the smell of onions frying at a store's lunch counter made her hungry. "That night I knew I had to tell her she couldn't have that sandwich because she was black," he recalls. "That couldn't have been any less painful than seeing her with a rock smashed into her head."

Lee's film re-creates the day of the bombing through newsreel footage, photographs, and eyewitness reports. He places it within a larger context of the southern civil rights movement, the sit-ins and the arrests, the marches, the songs, and the killings.

Birmingham was a tough case. Police commissioner Bull Connor is seen directing the resistance to marchers and traveling in an armored vehicle—painted white, of course. Governor George Wallace makes his famous vow to stand in the schoolhouse door and personally bar any black students from entering. Though they could not know it, their resistance was futile after September 15, 1963, because the hatred exposed by the bomb pulled all of their rhetoric and all of their rationalizations out from under them.

Spike Lee says he has wanted to make this film since 1983, when he read a *New York Times Magazine* article by Howell Raines about the bombing. "He wrote me asking permission back then," Chris McNair told me in an interview. "That was before he had made any of his films." It is perhaps good that Lee waited, because he is more of a filmmaker now, and events have supplied him a denouement in the conviction of a man named Robert Chambliss ("Dynamite Bob") as the bomber. He was, said Raines, who met quite a few, "the most pathological racist I've ever encountered."

The other two victims were Addie Mae Collins and Cynthia Wesley, both fourteen. In shots that are almost unbearable, we see the bodies of the victims in the morgue. Why does Lee show them? To look full into the face of what was done, I think. To show racism's handiwork. There is a memory in the film of a big, burly, white Birmingham policeman who in the aftermath of the bombing tells a black minister, "I really didn't believe they would go this far."

The man was a Klansman, the movie says, but in using the word "they" he unconsciously separates himself from his fellows. He wants to dissociate himself from the crime. So did others. Before long even George Wallace was apologizing for his behavior and trying to define himself in a different light. There is a scene in the film where the former governor, now old and infirm, describes his black personal assistant, Eddie Holcey, as his best friend. "I couldn't live without him," Wallace says, dragging Holcey in front of the camera, insensitive to the feelings of the man he is tugging over for display. Why is that scene there? It's sort of associated with the morgue photos, I think. There is mostly sadness and regret at the surface in *4 Little Girls,* but there is anger in the depths, as there should be.

Freeway ★ ★ ★ ½

R, 102 m., 1997

Kiefer Sutherland (Bob Wolverton), Reese Witherspoon (Vanessa Lutz), Amanda Plummer (Ramona Lutz), Michael T. Weiss (Larry [Stepdad]), Brooke Shields (Mimi Wolverton), Wolfgang Bodison (Detective Breer), Dan Hedaya (Detective Wallace), Bokeem Woodbine (Chopper). Directed by Matthew Bright and produced by Brad Wyman and Chris Hanley. Screenplay by Bright.

If Little Red Riding Hood were alive today, she would find that the wolves are bigger and badder, and she'd need to be a lot more resourceful to stay alive. That is the lesson (if it has a lesson) of *Freeway,* a dark comic excursion into deranged pathology. The movie retells the Grimm fairy tale in a world of poor white trash, sexual abuse, drug addiction, and the "I-5 Killer," who prowls the freeways in search of victims.

Written and directed by Matthew Bright, who wrote the teenagers-in-trouble saga *Guncrazy,* it plays like a cross between the deadpan docudrama of *Henry: Portrait of a Serial Killer* and the berserk revenge fantasy of *Switchblade Sisters.* It seems aimed at people who loved *Pulp Fiction* and have strong stomachs. Like it or hate it (or both), you have to admire its skill, and the over-the-top virtuosity of Reese Witherspoon and Kiefer Sutherland as the girl and the wolf.

The opening scenes play like updated Dickens, in which warped outlaws inhabit a lair. The heroine, Vanessa (Witherspoon), is struggling, at fifteen, to sound out such sentences as "The cat drinks milk." After school she meets her mother, Ramona (Amanda Plummer), on the corner where her mom works as a hooker. They return home to Ramona's current husband, Larry (Michael T. Weiss), a stepdad who complains: "Hey, me and your momma both spent the whole day in line getting rent vouchers, and we could use a little consideration."

The Lutz family idyll is interrupted by a narcotics raid. The cops share a little family history: "There's some bad blood between her mom and grandma, on account of she threw a chemical on her face or something." The parents are taken to jail, and a youth officer is assigned to take Vanessa to a youth home; thinking quickly, she handcuffs the officer to the bed, steals her car, and hits the road—on her way to grandmother's house, of course. She packs a handgun given her by her boyfriend.

After a car fire, she's befriended by Bob Wolverton (Sutherland), who has all the right moves to sound like a helpful child psychiatrist. Vanessa confides in him ("It looks like my stepfather's next parole officer ain't even been born yet") and opens her cheap wallet to show him a snapshot of her real father (the photo is of Richard Speck). Bob treats her to dinner and an attempted sexual assault, and chops off her ponytail before she asks if Jesus is his savior, empties the handgun into him, and throws up. She sees a shooting star, a sign from heaven that she did the right thing, and after imprisonment and escape she crosses the border into Mexico, where she works as a hooker in Tijuana until she's arrested.

Am I giving away too much of the plot? Not at all. There's a lot more. And *Freeway* isn't about what happens so much as about Bright's angle on the material; this is like a story based on the most disquieting and disgusting experiences of the most hapless guests on the sleaziest daytime talk shows.

Sutherland, who has played great villains before, outdoes himself this time. Turns out he was not killed by the gunshot wounds, but only wounded in all the most inconvenient places. The doctors patch him together into a Halloween monster whose face was shot away, who speaks through a hole in his throat, and whose other infirmities and amputations are too distressing to catalog. Backed by his all-American wife, Mimi (Brooke Shields—yes, Brooke Shields), he appears on television to lead a campaign against coddling such human garbage as Vanessa. Of course, Mimi does not know Bob is the I-5 Killer.

Occasionally an unsuspecting innocent will stumble into a movie like this and send me an anguished postcard, asking how I could possibly give a favorable review to such trash. My stock response is Ebert's Law, which reads: "A movie is not about what it is about. It is about how it is about it." *Freeway* is a hard-edged satire of those sensational true-crime reports that excite the prurient with detailed re-creations of unspeakable events. We have a great appetite in this country for books, TV shows, and movies about serial killers, perverted hermits, mad bombers, and pathological torturers—just so long as their deeds are cloaked in moralistic judgments. We pant over the pages before closing the book and repeating, with Richard Nixon, "But . . . that would be wrong."

Freeway illuminates our secret appetites. Like all good satire, it starts where the others end. And its actors wisely never ever act as if they're in on the joke. Reese Witherspoon (who had her heartbreaking first kiss in the wonderful movie *Man in the Moon*) is as focused and tightly wound here as a young Jodie Foster; she plays every scene as if it's absolutely real. Sutherland plays his early scenes with the complete confidence of a man walking in the trance of his obsession. His bizarre wounds make him a figure of parody in the later scenes, but he plays them, too, with complete conviction. All the way up to the end—which is, shall we say, not only predictable but obligatory.

Free Willy 3: The Rescue ★ ★ ★

PG, 89 m., 1997

Jason James Richter (Jesse), August Schellenberg (Randolph Johnson), Annie Corley (Drew), Vincent Berry (Max Wesley), Patrick Kilpatrick (John Wesley). Directed by Sam Pillsbury and produced by Jennie Lew Tugend. Screenplay by John Mattson.

Willy the whale spends most of his time at sea and underwater in *Free Willy 3: The Rescue*, and I liked him that way—as a whale rather than a toy. The movie is more interested in its human characters and in the issue of whale hunting than in whether Willy knows how to shake its head for "yes" and "no." There is a majesty to whales that the second *Willy* movie trivialized. Part three returns to some of the human elements that made the first movie so good.

As the film opens, Jesse (Jason James Richter) has signed on for the summer as an intern aboard a whale study vessel whose crew includes Randolph (August Schellenberg), his wise old friend from the earlier movies, and the oceanographer Drew (Annie Corley). Jesse rigs the onboard sound system to play a harmonica tune he knows will attract Willy, who is now free, gamboling in the waves of the Pacific Northwest and about to become a father.

Jesse has grown up (people keep asking him how old he is), and the movie supplies a new kid for the story: Max (Vincent Berry), still in grade school. He's thrilled when he learns that his dad (Patrick Kilpatrick) will take him along on his fishing boat—but saddened when he sees that the boat is secretly, and illegally, harpooning whales.

Max's dad, named John Wesley, is not a bad man, although he is doing a bad thing. He's a loving father who promises his son, "I'll teach you everything I know." And he speaks sadly of the days when hunting whales meant bringing light to the world—back when whale oil was used for lamps. Today, fetching $200 a pound, whale meat is secretly exported to Japan for sushi, but hunting them "means the right to earn a living."

Max, wide-eyed and silent, keeps his peace. But then he meets Jesse, and the two boys have a moonlight meeting on board the fishing ship during which Jesse simply and eloquently tells Max why it's wrong to hunt whales. Later, Max has a conversation on morality with his dad, who is hard-pressed to defend what he does.

Meanwhile, the research vessel is tagging Orca whales with little suction-cup devices that I, for one, doubt would last five minutes before being torn off by water pressure. The evil whalers have nabbed Jesse's signal and are using it to lure Willy to his doom. And Max falls overboard and in a magical moment finds himself eyeball-to-eyeball with Willy, who saves him (although this is not the "rescue" of the title).

Free Willy 3: The Rescue is filled with sparkling nature cinematography by Tobias Schliessler, and looks great. I assume some of the shots are special effects and that not all of the whales are real, but it's all done so seamlessly that it's convincing. And although the movie has elements of real-life adventure that are improbable, it's essentially grounded in real life. Smart kids will enjoy it.

There was publicity after the first movie revealing that the Orca used in the film had later been transferred to an aquarium and was anything but free. This film ends with a phone number offering more information on that and other whales. And the movie itself is more realistic and serious; the whales here are inspirations for kids, instead of pets. Will there be a *Free Willy 4*? Perhaps; Max has some growing up to do. What's interesting is that the series has grown up too.

Friends & Lovers ½★

NO MPAA RATING, 102 m., 1999

Stephen Baldwin (Jon), Danny Nucci (David), George Newbern (Ian), Alison Eastwood (Lisa), Claudia Schiffer (Carla), Suzanne Cryer (Jane), David Rasche (Richard), Neill Barry (Keaton), Robert Downey Jr. (Hans). Directed by George Haas and produced by Josi W. Konski. Screenplay by Haas.

I don't want to review *Friends & Lovers;* I want to flunk it. This movie is not merely bad, but incompetent. I get tapes in the mail from tenth-graders that are better made than this.

Recently I hosted the first Overlooked Film Festival at the University of Illinois, for films that have been unfairly overlooked. If I ever do a festival of films that deserve to be overlooked, here is my opening night selection. The only possible explanation for the film being released is that there are stars in the cast (Stephen Baldwin, Claudia Schiffer, Alison Eastwood, Robert Downey Jr). They should sue their agents.

The story involves a group of friends spending the holidays in a Park City ski chalet. They're involved in what an adolescent might think were adult relationships. Much time is spent in meaningless small talk. We also get the ultimate sign of writer desperation: characters introducing themselves to each other.

If I were marking this as a paper, I would note:

—Director George Haas often lines up actors so they awkwardly face the camera and have to talk sideways to one another.

—Much of the dialogue is handled by cutting to each character as he speaks. This is jarring because it reveals that the movie knows when each character will speak. Professional movies overlap sound and image so that dialogue begins offscreen, before a cut to the speaker.

—The characters frequently propose toasts, as if the movie is a social occasion.

—Pregnant girl looks like she has a pillow stuffed down her dress. Self-consciously holds her belly with both hands in many scenes.

—Dad puts tin can in microwave. Can explodes, and whole chalet is plunged into darkness. I am not surprised that a character in this movie would be stupid enough to microwave an unopened can, but why would the explosion blow every fuse?

—Characters gossip that one character has a big penis. Everyone strips for the Jacuzzi. Movie supplies close-up of penis. Since this is the first nudity of any kind in the movie, audience is jolted. In a light comedy, a close-up of a penis strikes a jarring note. An amazed reaction shot might work, but represents a level of sophistication beyond the reach of this film.

—The general preoccupation with sex and size reminds me of conversations I had when I was eleven. One guy says a female character has two-inch nipples. No one questions this theory. I say two-inch nipples are extremely rare among bipeds.

—Dad says, "My generation thought that working was the best way to support a family." Dad doesn't even know what generation he belongs to. Dad is in his fifties, so is a member of the sixties generation. He is thinking of his parents' generation.

—All dialogue on ski slopes involves ludicrous echoing effects. Yes, a yodel will echo in the Alps. No, conversational levels will not echo in Utah.

—David seems to be a virgin. Friend asks, "You have never done the dirty deed?" David asks, "How exactly would you define that?" Friend makes circle with thumb and finger, sticks another finger through it. Most twenty-something movie characters have advanced beyond this stage.

—Automobile scenes are inept. One "crash" is obviously faked to avoid damaging either vehicle. In a scene that cuts between girl walking by road while a guy drives beside her and talks through open window, the girl is walking at a slower rate of speed than car.

I have often asked myself, "What would it look like if the characters in a movie were animatronic puppets created by aliens with an imperfect mastery of human behavior?" Now I know.

Frogs for Snakes no stars

R, 98 m., 1999

Barbara Hershey (Eva), Robbie Coltrane (Al), Harry Hamlin (Klench), Ian Hart (Quint), David Deblinger (UB), John Leguizamo (Zip), Ron

Perlman (Gascone), Lisa Marie (Myrna), Debi Mazar (Simone). Directed by Amos Poe and produced by Phyllis Freed Kaufman. Screenplay by Poe.

Amos Poe's *Frogs for Snakes* is not a film so much as a filmed idea. That could be interesting, but alas, it is a very bad idea. The film is about a group of Manhattan actors who support themselves between roles by acting as gangsters and hit men, and as the film opens they turn their guns on one another. This is a movie that gives new meaning to the notion of being willing to kill for a role.

Barbara Hershey stars, as a waitress and debt collector who used to be married to crime kingpin Al (Robbie Coltrane), who doubles as a theater producer and is preparing a production of Mamet's *American Buffalo.* She and several other characters spend much of their time hanging out in a diner and talking about absent friends. So much time is spent in the diner, indeed, that *Frogs for Snakes* begins to resemble a one-set play, until there are excursions to pool halls, apartments, and even a theater.

Sample dialogue from a pool hall:

"What are you doing here?"

"We heard you were doing *True West.*"

"Well, you heard wrong. We're doing *American Buffalo.*"

(Shoots him)

Not a single one of the characters is even slightly convincing as anything other than an artificial theatrical construction. Is that the point? I haven't a clue. Much of their dialogue is lifted intact from other movies, sometimes inappropriately (Lisa Marie plays a buxom sex bomb who recites Harry Lime's speech about cuckoo clocks from *The Third Man*). Other speeches come from *Night and the City, Sex, Drugs and Rock 'n' Roll, The Hustler, The Apartment, Repo Man, I Am a Fugitive from a Chain Gang,* and several more. (The film ends by crediting the screenplays, just as most films end with a scroll of the songs on the sound track.)

"Today they write dialogue about cheeseburgers and big special effects," one of the characters says, contrasting the quoted classics with *Pulp Fiction.* Yes, but Tarantino's cheeseburger dialogue is wonderful comic writing, with an evil undercurrent as the hit men talk while approaching a dangerous meeting; no dialogue in this movie tries anything a fraction as ambitious, or risks anything.

Seeing the cast of familiar actors (not only Hershey and Coltrane but Harry Hamlin, Ian Hart, Debi Mazar, John Leguizamo, and Ron Perlman), I was reminded of *Mad Dog Time* (1996), another movie in which well-known actors engaged in laughable dialogue while shooting one another. Of that one, I wrote: "*Mad Dog Time* is the first movie I have seen that does not improve on the sight of a blank screen viewed for the same length of time." Now comes *Frogs for Snakes,* the first movie I have seen that does not improve on the sight of *Mad Dog Time.*

The Full Monty ★ ★ ★

R, 95 m., 1997

Robert Carlyle (Gaz), Tom Wilkinson (Gerald), Mark Addy (Dave), Steve Huison (Lomper), Paul Barber (Horse), Hugo Speer (Guy), Lesley Sharp (Jean), Emily Woof (Mandy), Deirdre Costello (Linda). Directed by Peter Cattaneo and produced by Uberto Pasolini. Screenplay by Simon Beaufoy.

"A few more years and men won't exist," mourns one of the unemployed workers in *The Full Monty.* Sheffield was once a thriving British manufacturing town known for its steel, but now its mills are closed and the men hang about all day in the gloomy job center, where there are no jobs to be found. Their remaining functions in life seem limited to drinking, getting into mischief, and avoiding child support payments they can't afford.

From this grim working-class prospect, *The Full Monty* creates a lovable comedy, as the men decide to go where the work is. The Chippendale dancers have recently entertained a full house at a local club, including most of the wives, mothers, daughters, sisters, and girlfriends of the unemployed workers. If the Chippendales can make hundreds or thousands of pounds by stripping down to their Speedos, why can't some local blokes make a few quid by going all the way—the "full monty"?

They're led by Gaz, a determined, inventive

man played by Robert Carlyle (he was the alarming Begbie in *Trainspotting*). For dance lessons they turn in desperation to their former foreman, Gerald (Tom Wilkinson). He's always lorded it over them, but is now reduced to haunting the jobs center and trying to keep it a secret from his wife that he's out of work: He's too proud to tell her, and one of the movie's best scenes is when he lets down his guard and confesses his financial desperation.

Can he teach them to dance? Sort of, and some of the funniest scenes come during auditions and rehearsals. Their troupe, as it forms, includes Guy (Hugo Speer), who can't dance but will be the star when the Speedos come off; Lomper (Steve Huison), who is young and suicidal; and Horse (Paul Barber), a middle-aged black man with a bad hip, who explains, "me break-dancing days is probably over, but there's always the funky chicken."

The director, Peter Cattaneo, takes material that would be at home in a sex comedy, and gives it gravity because of the desperation of the characters; we glimpse the home life of these men, who have literally been put on the shelf, and we see the wound to their pride. *The Full Monty* belongs in the recent tradition of bittersweet films from Britain that depict working-class life: movies like *The Snapper* and *The Van,* based on Roddy Doyle books; *Raining Stones,* about an unemployed man desperate to buy his daughter's communion dress; and *Brassed Off,* which was also about an industry shutting down and leaving its community stranded.

Robert Carlyle might seem like a strange choice to play Gaz, if you remember him only from *Trainspotting,* but one of his first roles was in Ken Loach's *Riff-Raff,* which took place mostly on a construction site where the workers, itinerants, lived off the land. He has a daring here, as if he's walking on a wire and won't fall if he doesn't look down. He doesn't know himself if his plan has been inspired by courage or bravado.

The Full Monty is about more than inventiveness in the face of unemployment: It's about ordinary blokes insisting that their women regard them as men—job or no job. If they're reduced to stripping to pay the bills, well, a lot of women know all about that. This is the undertone, and yet the movie develops a broad, healthy band of humor; it's bawdy, but also gentle and good-hearted, and I felt affection for the characters.

The film's last shot is not hard to guess, although less explicit than some audiences will expect. It was applauded at the screening I attended, but I wish there had been another scene afterward. It's not what you do, it's how you feel about it, and I wanted to see a payoff (triumph, maybe, or more likely relief) on the faces of the men.

G

Gabbeh ★ ★ ★

NO MPAA RATING, 75 m., 1997

Shaghayegh Djodat (Gabbeh), Abbas Sayahi (The Uncle), Hossein Moharami (The Old Man), Roghieh Moharami (The Old Woman). Directed by Mohsen Makhmalbaf and produced by Khalil Doroudchi and Khalil Mahmoudi. Screenplay by Makhmalbaf.

Gabbeh is a fable, clear on the surface, tangled in the shadows, told by a Persian carpet. As the film opens, an old couple in Iran pause by a stream to wash their rug, or "gabbeh," and we see that it is decorated with a portrait of a young woman and a man on horseback. "Who are you?" the old woman asks the girl on the rug, and the girl steps out of the rug and answers her question.

She is Gabbeh. She lived with her nomadic people in the desert, and was in love with the young horseman. But it was decreed that she could not marry until her uncle did—and, at fifty-seven, he was still single. Meanwhile, the horseman followed her through the desert, and at night, as Gabbeh sat with her family around the fire, she heard him making wild wolf cries at the moon.

Gabbeh is the thirteenth film directed by Mohsen Makhmalbaf, but the first I have seen. He was imprisoned as a youth in the Shah's Iran for his fundamentalist Islamic beliefs, but this is not the film of an unyielding person. By choosing Gabbeh to tell her own story, he sides with her, and therefore against tradition. It is all very well to wait until the old uncle marries, but in the meantime there is the call of the heart in the blood of the young. I am reminded of a talk show I saw once featuring Louis Farrakhan, who voiced his opposition to interracial romance, but then sighed and spread his hands palms upward, and said, "But the young people—what can you say to them?"

The young people depicted on the rug may have a connection with the present day, but that is a secret for the film to reveal. More to the point is its visual richness. Makhmalbaf uses not only the glories of nature—the desert landscape and sky—but also man's own use of color, and there is a scene where the old uncle talks of color, and the colors magically appear as he names them. In other scenes, we see the wildflowers from which the dyes come, to color the threads of the rug.

There is no shyness here about bold primary colors, and I was reminded of Zhang Yimou's *Ju Dou* (1989), with its scenes set in a workshop where bolts of cloth are dipped into vats of bright colors. There is a kind of voluptuousness that comes with seeing color boldly splashed across the screen, and we are reminded that modern art direction, with its prudently controlled palates, may be too timid or "tasteful" to give us that pleasure.

Is there a message here about the society where the film is set? Probably there is more of an attitude, a feeling that universal human desires cannot be denied. Certainly one can imagine a film asking us to sympathize with the fifty-seven-year-old uncle, whose life has been made a misery because of his niece's desire for romance. Love is the preoccupation of the young for no doubt sound Darwinian reasons.

Gabbeh is a simple film. There is hardly more to say about it than I have said. Yet it remains in the memory in a way that more thickly plotted films do not. It teaches a lesson: that there can be more to a movie than episodes and events, that a film can stand back from the micromanagement of small bits of time, and show us the sweep of a life and the long, slow seasons of a heart. Movies like this work like meditation or music, to nudge us toward the important.

The Game ★ ★ ★ ½

R, 128 m., 1997

Michael Douglas (Nicholas van Orton), Sean Penn (Conrad van Orton), Deborah Kara Unger (Christine), James Rebhorn (Jim Feingold), Carroll Baker (Ilsa), Peter Donat (Sam Sutherland), Armin Mueller-Stahl (Anson Baer). Directed by David Fincher and produced by Steve Golin and Cean Chaffin. Screenplay by John Brancato and Michael Ferris.

The opening scenes of *The Game* show Michael Douglas as a rich man in obsessive control of his life. The movie seems to be about how he is reduced to humility and humanity—or maybe that's just a trick on him. The movie is like a control freak's worst nightmare. The Douglas character, named Nicholas van Orton, is surrounded by employees who are almost paralyzed by his rigid demands on them. "I have an Elizabeth on line three," says one secretary, and then a second adds, "Your wife, sir."

"I know," he says coldly. We have the feeling that if the second secretary had not spoken, he would have replied, "Elizabeth who?" His underlings are in no-win situations. It is, in fact, his ex-wife; at age forty-eight, van Orton lives alone in the vast mansion where his father committed suicide at the same age. His birthday evening consists of eating a cheeseburger served on a silver tray and watching CNN.

Van Orton's younger brother Conrad (Sean Penn) visits him and announces a birthday present: The Game, which is "sort of an experiential Book of the Month Club." Operated by a shadowy outfit named Consumer Recreation Services, The Game never quite declares its rules or objectives, but soon van Orton finds himself in its grasp, and his orderly life has become unmanageable. "It will make your life fun again," he is promised, but that's not quite how he sees it, as a functionary (James Rebhorn) leads him through the sign-up process.

Soon everything starts to fall apart. His pen leaks. His briefcase won't open. Food is spilled on him in a restaurant. He is trapped in an elevator. The level of chaos rises. He finds himself blackmailed, his bank accounts are emptied, he wanders like a homeless man, he is left for dead in Mexico, he is trapped inside a cab sinking in a bay.

Of course, many of the physical details of what happens to him are implausible or even impossible, but so what? The events are believable in the sense that events can be believed in a nightmare: You can hardly worry about how a horror has been engineered when you're trapped inside it.

The mounting campaign of conspiratorial persecution is greeted by van Orton with his usual style of cold contempt and detachment: He knows all the angles, he thinks, and has foreseen all the pitfalls, and can predict all the permutations. But he finds he is totally wrong. Even those few people he thinks he can trust (including a waitress played by Deborah Kara Unger—or is she a waitress?) may be double agents. There is even the possibility that The Game is a front for a well-planned conspiracy to steal his millions. Michael Douglas, who is superb at playing men of power (remember his Gordon Gekko in *Wall Street*) is reduced to a stumbling, desperate man on the run (remember his unemployed engineer in *Falling Down*).

The Game, written by John Brancato and Michael Ferris, is David Fincher's first film since *Seven*, and projects the same sense of events being controlled by invisible manipulation. This time, though, there's an additional element: Van Orton is being broken down and reassembled like the victim of some cosmic EST program. And it is unclear, to him and to us, whether The Game is on the level, or a fraud, or perhaps spinning out of control.

The movie's thriller elements are given an additional gloss by the skill of the technical credits and the wicked wit of the dialogue. When van Orton's brother asks, "Don't you think of me any more?" he shoots back, "Not since family week at rehab." And when his ex-wife asks if he had a nice birthday, he answers, "Does Rose Kennedy have a black dress?"

The film's dark look, its preference for shadows, recalls *Seven* and also Fincher's *Alien 3*. The big screen reveals secrets and details in dark corners; on video, they may disappear into the murk. Like *Seven*, the plotting is ingenious and intelligent, and although we think we know the arc of the film (egotist is reduced to greater humility and understanding of himself), the film doesn't progress in a docile, predictable way; for one thing, there is the real possibility that The Game is not an ego-reduction program, but a death plot.

Douglas is the right actor for the role. He can play smart, he can play cold, and he can play angry. He is also subtle enough that he never arrives at an emotional plateau before the film does, and never overplays his process of inner change. Indeed, one of the refreshing things about the film is that it stays true to its paranoid vision right up until what seems like the very end—and then beyond it, so that by the time the real ending arrives, it's not the payoff and release so much as a final macabre twist of the knife.

Gamera: Guardian of the Universe

★★★

NO MPAA RATING, 96 m., 1997

Tsuyoski Ihara (Yoshinari Yonemori), Akira Onodera (Naoya Kusanagi), Ayoko Fujitani (Asagi Kusanagi), Shinobu Nakayama (Matumi Nagamine). Directed by Shusuke Kaneko and produced by Yasuyoshi Tokuma. Screenplay by Kazunori Ito.

Gamera: Guardian of the Universe is precisely the kind of movie that I enjoy despite all rational reasoning. How, you may ask, can I possibly prefer this Japanese monster film about a jet-powered turtle to a megabudget solemnity like *Air Force One*? It has laughable acting, a ludicrous plot, second-rate special effects, and dialogue like, "Someday, I'll show you around monster-free Tokyo!" The answer, I think, is that *Gamera* is more fun.

There's a learning process that moviegoers go through. They begin in childhood without sophistication or much taste, and like *Gamera* more than *Air Force One* because flying turtles are obviously more entertaining than U.S. presidents. Then they grow older and develop "taste," and prefer *Air Force One*, which is better made and has big stars and a more plausible plot. (Isn't it more believable, after all, that a president could single-handedly wipe out a planeload of terrorists than that a giant turtle could spit gobs of flame?) Then, if they continue to grow older and wiser, they complete the circle and return to *Gamera* again, realizing that while both movies are preposterous, the turtle movie has the charm of utter goofiness and, in an age of flawless special effects, it is somehow more fun to watch flawed ones.

Gamera is not a good movie, but it is a good moviegoing experience. I am reminded of Pauline Kael's wise observation: The movies are so seldom great art that we should not go unless we can appreciate great trash. I am satiated, for the time being, by terrorists and fireballs and bomb threats and special effects, and my eyes yearn for new sights, such as a giant radioactive bat trapped inside a baseball dome and emitting green rays. (There is even a voluptuous pleasure to be derived from simply typing the *words* "emitting green rays.") Please, mister, show me something new.

Gamera has starred in nine films in thirty-two years, but has never attained the stardom of Godzilla, perhaps because of speciesism, which prejudices us to prefer dinosaurs to turtles. Gamera lives for much of the time beneath the ocean (or, as the movie refers to it, "The Pacific-Ocean of Death!"), where he shows up on radar screens as a giant atoll. But when Gamera is needed, the atoll begins to glow, and (I can't stop myself) emits rays. And then Gamera flies through the skies, powered by jet outlets on its underside.

Now, then. Considering that Gamera never needs to refuel, we must assume he is organic and not mechanical. Therefore, the jet blasts come not from burning petrol, but from the by-products of organic material. This is not a matter of shame for the Japanese, who are more frank about bodily processes, and even have a best-selling children's book named *The Gas We Pass*. Yes, Gamera is powered by farts.

The plot. A 10,000-year-old bat named Gyaos has aroused itself from slumber and attacks Tokyo. Scientists use floodlights to lure it into a baseball stadium, where they stand in the dugout shouting lines like, "Take your posts!" But only Gamera is a match for Gyaos, and soon the two flying creatures are engaged in a fierce battle that extends even to outer space. (How does a bat fly in space? Don't ask me. I still don't know how Gyaos flies in the air, since it has no moving wings.)

I have referred to Gyaos as a bat, but at one point, after being severely pummeled by Gamera, it drops several eggs the size of minivans on the streets of Tokyo. Bats are mammals and do not lay eggs, I think, so perhaps (a) Gyaos is a bird, (b) bats do lay eggs, or (c) those are turtle eggs, and the movie is about Mrs. Gamera.

There is, strictly speaking, no need for human characters in *Gamera: Guardian of the Universe*, since the creatures are self-contained in their age-old enmity. But the movie does provide us with four observers, including Asagi (Ayoko Fujitani), a teenage girl who seems able to read Gamera's mind, and carries a glowing stone that helps her do that, I think. Late in the film, there is a big close-up of the girl's eyes, and then Gamera's eyes, and then a blob of energized spirit is exchanged somehow, and Gamera is able to live to fight again another day. Studying the film's press releases, I discover that Ayoko Fujitani is Steven Seagal's daughter, and I punch my fist into the air, and cry "Yesssss!"

Gang Related ★ ★ ★

R, 111 m., 1997

James Belushi (Divinci), Tupac Shakur (Rodriguez), Lela Rochon (Cynthia), Dennis Quaid (William ["Joe"]), James Earl Jones (Arthur Baylor), David Paymer (Elliot Goff), Wendy Crewson (Helen Eden), Gary Cole (Richard Simms). Directed by Jim Kouf and produced by John Bertolli, Brad Krevoy, and Steven Stabler. Screenplay by Kouf.

The two cops in *Gang Related* are like that vaudeville act where the guy tried to keep the plates spinning on the poles. They've made a bad mistake and are desperately trying to conceal it, but their cover-up keeps coming to pieces—they're forced into improvisations and intimidations while the truth seems to march inexorably straight at them.

The movie, which stars Jim Belushi and the late Tupac Shakur as the cops, is a skillful police procedural all the way up until the end, which doesn't quite work. It doesn't cheat with lazy action or chase scenes; the writer-director, Jim Kouf, knows he has a good story to tell and he tells it. And he employs a large and skilled supporting cast; most modern movies, having paid their stars big salaries, keep them onscreen all the time, but *Gang Related* is more like a classic Warner Bros. *film noir* with a lot of colorful speaking roles.

Belushi and Shakur are Divinci and Rodriguez, police partners who operate a scam in which they sell drugs, collect the money, and kill the buyers—thus ridding the city of scum and making themselves rich at the same time. When the movie opens, they've offed ten dealers, but their luck turns bad with their eleventh victim, who is an undercover agent for the DEA.

Because they "investigated" the man's shooting death in the first place, they're assigned to find his killer. And they start shopping for someone to frame—finally settling on a wet-brained homeless man called Joe (Dennis Quaid), who doesn't remember much, and agrees to confess in return for a drink. Divinci is also able to persuade him he actually did commit the murders. It looks like a neat package, but this witness will bring nothing but trouble.

These events are told against a rich backdrop formed by many other characters, including a stripper (Lela Rochon) who sometimes sleeps with Divinci, and who he asks to be a witness against "Joe." And there are others—police captains, federal agents, bail bondsmen, and finally a spirited prosecutor (Wendy Crewson), a public defender (David Paymer), and a famous lawyer (James Earl Jones) who is a surprise entry into the case. Dennis Quaid, unrecognizable at first, does a quietly effective job of disappearing into the role of a shattered man (although his last scene is highly unlikely). The only doubtful casting decision is Rochon as the stripper; she seems too much like a classy ingenue. The movie would have benefited from an older, more streetwise actress (that would also make the romance with the cop more plausible).

For most of the film, I sat in quiet amazement: I was witnessing a complex, well crafted, clearly told story, in a screenplay that moved well and had dialogue that sounded colorful without resembling a Quentin Tarantino clone. Modern screenplays are often so tired in their conventions, using action to replace characters and events. The fascination of *Gang Related* is in the way we understand exactly what the two cops are trying to do, and what they're up against. Even the courtroom scenes aren't recycled clichés but use the personalities of the players to develop genuine tension—they're like a reminder of what a charged silence can feel like.

It is refreshing that the film has no heroes. It's a story about flawed people. Like a novel by Georges Simenon, it is fascinated by criminal psychology and wants to see how certain types function under great stress. It gives the audience credit for being interested in human nature; we don't need a conventional hero to identify with because we identify with the guilt, desperation, and greed of these two cops. We are incapable of doing what they did, but not incapable of feeling what they feel.

Belushi and Shakur work well together; the film, dedicated to the murdered rap artist, is proof (along with *Gridlock'd* earlier this year) that he had an authentic talent. Instead of forcing the two characters into molds, Kouf lets them develop: Belushi's Divinci is not a shallow villain, but a truly amoral man who gives little pep talks to his dubious partner. Shakur's Rodriguez is a problem gambler with a juice enforcer after him, and he struggles with a troublesome conscience. They have a funny, scary scene together where Belushi asks, "Okay—what's the worst-case scenario?" as they're already facing the worst possible case.

I was not persuaded by the film's ending. It's too much of a shaggy dog story; this material deserves more than an ironic twist and a blackout. The film is otherwise so well crafted that I am tempted to wonder if the ending was imposed on Kouf by a lockstep studio executive. I can imagine any number of endings that could have emerged organically from the material, but this one couldn't, and doesn't.

I have a little meter that runs in my mind during a movie, with an imaginary needle that points at a number of stars between one and four. *Gang Related* wavered high for most of its running time, and only settled down to "three" because of the unsatisfying closing scenes. It's one of the best pure police procedurals I've seen in a long time.

Gattaca ★ ★ ★ ½

PG-13, 112 m., 1997

Ethan Hawke (Vincent/Jerome), Uma Thurman (Irene), Jude Law (Jerome/Eugene), Alan Arkin (Detective Hugo), Loren Dean (Anton), Gore Vidal (Director Josef), Xander Berkeley (Lamar), Tony Shalhoub (German), Elias Koteas (Antonio). Directed by Andrew Niccol and produced by Danny DeVito, Michael Shamberg, and Stacey Sher. Screenplay by Niccol.

What is genetic engineering, after all, but preemptive plastic surgery? Make the child perfect in the test tube and save money later. Throw in perfect health, a high IQ, and a long life span, and you have the brave new world of *Gattaca*, in which the bioformed have inherited Earth, and babies who are born naturally get to be menial laborers.

This is one of the smartest and most provocative of science-fiction films, a thriller with ideas. Its hero is a man who challenges the system. Vincent (Ethan Hawke) was born in the old-fashioned way, and his genetic tests show he has bad eyesight, heart problems, and a life expectancy of about thirty years. He is an "In-Valid," and works as a cleaner in a space center.

Vincent does not accept his fate. He never has. As a child, he had swimming contests with his brother, Anton (Loren Dean), who has all the right scores but needs to be saved from drowning. Now Vincent dreams of becoming a crew member on an expedition to one of the moons of Saturn. Using an illegal DNA broker, he makes a deal with a man named Jerome (Jude Law), who has the right genes but was paralyzed in an accident. Jerome will provide him with blood and urine samples and an identity. In a sense, they'll both go into space.

Gattaca is the remarkable debut of a writer-director from New Zealand, Andrew Niccol, whose film is smart and thrilling—a tricky combination—and also visually exciting. His most important set is a vast office where genetically superior computer programmers come to work every day, filing into their long rows of desks like the office slaves in King Vidor's *The Crowd* and Orson Welles's *The Trial.* (Why are "perfect" human societies so often depicted by ranks of automatons? Is it because human nature resides in our flaws?) Vincent, as "Jerome," gets a job as a programmer, supplies false genetic samples, and becomes a finalist for the space shot.

The tension comes in two ways. First, there's the danger that Vincent will be detected; the area is swept daily, and even an eyelash can betray him. Second, there's a murder; a director of the center, who questions the wisdom of the upcoming shot, is found dead, and a detective (Alan Arkin) starts combing the personnel for suspects. Will a computer search sooner or later put together Vincent, the former janitor, with "Jerome," the new programmer?

Vincent becomes friendly with Irene (Uma Thurman), who works in the center but has been passed over for a space shot because of low scores in some areas. They are attracted to one another, but romance in this world can be dangerous; after kissing a man, a woman is likely to have his saliva swabbed from her mouth so she can test his prospects. Other supporting characters include Gore Vidal as a mission supervisor and Tony Shalhoub as the broker ("You could go anywhere with this guy's helix under your arm").

Hawke is a good choice for the lead, combining the restless dreams of a "Godchild" with the plausible exterior of a lab baby. The best scenes in the movie involve his relationship with the real Jerome, played by Law as smart, bitter, and delighted to be sticking it to the system that has grounded him. (He may be paralyzed from the waist down, but after all, as the movie observes, you don't need to walk in space.) His drama parallels Vincent's, because if either one is caught they'll both go down together.

Science fiction in the movies has recently specialized in invasions by aliens, but the best of the genre deals with ideas. At a time when we read about cloned sheep and tomatoes crossed with fish, the science in *Gattaca* is theoretically possible. When parents can order "perfect" babies, will they? Would you take your chances on a throw of the genetic dice, or order up the make and model you wanted? How many people are prepared to buy a car at random from the universe of all available cars? That's how many, I suspect, would opt to have natural children.

Everybody will live longer, look better, and be healthier in the Gattacan world. But will it be as much fun? Will parents order children who are rebellious, ungainly, eccentric, creative, or a lot smarter than their parents are? There's a concert pianist in *Gattaca* who has twelve fingers. Don't you sometimes have the feeling you were born just in time? ☞

The General ★ ★ ★ ½

R, 129 m., 1999

Brendan Gleeson (Martin Cahill), Jon Voight (Inspector Ned Kenny), Adrian Dunbar (Noel Curley), Sean McGinley (Gary), Maria Doyle Kennedy (Frances), Angeline Ball (Tina), Eanna McLiam (Jimmy), Tom Murphy (Willie Byrne). Directed by and produced John Boorman. Screenplay by Boorman.

There is a certain honor in sticking to your guns, even if they are the wrong guns. Martin Cahill, the subject of John Boorman's *The General,* was for many years the most famous professional criminal in Ireland, a man who copied Robin Hood, up to a point: He stole from the rich and gave to himself. He was as stubborn a man as ever was born, and so clever that even though he was a villain, he inspired grudging admiration even from the police. He was shot dead in 1994 by the IRA, after getting involved in politics, the one thing in Ireland more dangerous than crime.

Boorman, whose films have ranged from *Deliverance* to *Excaliber,* had one close brush with Cahill, who broke into his house and stole the gold record he was awarded for "Dueling Banjos." The movie includes that episode; when Cahill gets the record home and finds it is not really made of gold, it confirms his low regard for straight society. Most of the time he was more lucky; his lifetime haul is estimated at $60 million.

Cahill is played in *The General* by Brendan Gleeson, an expert Irish actor (he was Hamish, Mel Gibson's sidekick, in *Braveheart*) who succeeds in doing two things not easy for an actor: He creates the illusion that we are looking at Cahill himself, and he makes us admit we like him even despite his vicious streak. Gleeson and Boorman, who wrote his own screenplay, look unblinkingly at horrors, and then find the other side of the coin.

Consider, for example, a scene where Cahill suspects a longtime partner of ratting to the cops. To get a confession out of him, he nails him to a snooker table. The man protests his innocence. Finally Cahill pulls out the nails, observing, "No one can stand that much pain without talking." Then he personally takes him to the hospital, reassuring him, "You came through with flying colors." Look on the positive side: Cahill at least has the integrity to pound the nails himself and not leave it to a flunky. And he's man enough to admit his mistake.

Cahill is, in fact, a charming rogue, able to

bestir shreds of admiration even in the heart of his archenemy, police inspector Ned Kenny (Jon Voight). He embodies a certain style in his planning. Trying to buy a house, for example, he is told the agent cannot accept cash. So he takes 80,000 pounds to the bank and purchases a bank draft. He puts the draft in his pocket and walks across the street to the police station, where he is in conversation with Inspector Kenny at the very moment when, wouldn't you know, two masked men approach the very same teller and rob her of all the money in her drawer.

The General opens with Cahill as a young boy, stealing from a local merchant and being sent to reform school (where he socks a would-be molester). As an adult, he was a man who attracted enormous publicity even while obsessively guarding his privacy (he hides his face inside hooded sweatshirts, and invariably holds a hand over his face, peering out from between the fingers). His jobs included knocking over Dublin's largest jewelers, and stealing Old Masters from an Irish country house. In both cases, he uses a devious plan rather than a frontal assault.

Boorman finds subtle humor in Cahill's domestic arrangements; he was married to one woman (Maria Doyle Kennedy) but also shared his bed with her sister (Angeline Ball) and had children by both—apparently a satisfactory arrangement, perhaps because if you were going to be Cahill's sister-in-law you were in bed with him anyway, in one way or another. With his son he shares a delight in pigeons, and one of the low blows struck him by the Dublin police involves setting a ferret loose to kill his prized birds.

Cahill was not a political man, and the way he runs afoul of the IRA is presented in the movie as a lapse of strategy: He did a deal he shouldn't have. In real life, I learn, Cahill's problems came when he interfered in the IRA's drug trade, but such an inference is no doubt still too hot a potato for a director who hopes to film again in Ireland.

Boorman's film is shot in wide-screen black and white, and as it often does, black and white emphasizes the characters and the story, instead of setting them awash in atmosphere. And Boorman's narrative style has a nice offhand feel about it. Instead of explaining everything in neat little simpleminded setups, he lets us discover for ourselves that Cahill is living with both women. As the general unfolds his devious criminal schemes, we see them as they develop, instead of getting those clichéd crime movie chalk talks.

Part of Cahill's charm comes in the way he insists that crime is not his vice, but his occupation. After his neighborhood is torn down by city planners (over his stubborn protests), he demands to be relocated to "a nice neighborhood." A public official sneers: "Wouldn't you sooner live closer to your own kind?" Cahill replies, "No, I'd sooner live closer to my work." ☞

The General's Daughter ★ ★ ½

R, 115 m., 1999

John Travolta (Paul Brenner), Madeleine Stowe (Sarah Sunhill), James Cromwell (General Joe Campbell), Timothy Hutton (Colonel William Kent), James Woods (Colonel Robert Moore), Clarence Williams III (Colonel Fowler), Leslie Stefanson (Captain Elisabeth Campbell), Daniel Van Bargen (Chief Yardley). Directed by Simon West and produced by Mace Neufeld. Screenplay by William Goldman and Christopher Bertolini, based on the novel by Nelson DeMille.

"Elisabeth once told me she was conducting a field investigation in psychological warfare, and the enemy was Daddy."

So speaks one of the friends of the late Captain Elisabeth Campbell, whose bizarre death is the centerpiece of *The General's Daughter.* Her army job is to teach "psychological operations"—or, as she explains to a guy whose tire she helps to change, to mess with people's minds. Nobody's mind has been messed with more than her own.

The friendly guy is Warrant Officer Paul Brenner, played by John Travolta—first as a slow-talking redneck, and then, after he drops the undercover masquerade, as an aggressive army cop. He meets Elisabeth Campbell (Leslie Stefanson) just that once before her naked corpse is found staked spread-eagled to the ground, having been strangled. And if you blinked at that description of her dead body, well, so did I. The circumstances of the victim's death are so bizarre and unlikely that they derail most of the scenes they involve.

The General's Daughter is a well-made thriller with a lot of good acting, but the death of Elisabeth Campbell is so unnecessarily graphic and gruesome that by the end I felt sort of unclean. If this had been a documentary, or even a fiction film with serious intentions, I would have accepted it. But does entertainment have to go this far just to shake us up?

The movie is based on a page-turner by Nelson DeMille, adapted for the screen by William Goldman and Christopher Bertolini, who along the way provide a dialogue scene for Travolta and James Woods that's sharp-edged and crisply delivered; one-on-one, they fence with words and the theater grows as quiet as if it were a sex scene. Simon West, the director, creates a gloomy southern Gothic atmosphere for his film, which is set at an "urban warfare center," an army base that includes mock-ups of civilian architecture, and an antebellum mansion for the general to occupy.

The general (James Cromwell) seems to have lived there quite some time, judging by the furnishings, which make the interiors look like pages from *Architectural Digest.* General Campbell occupies rooms filled with wood, leather, brass, crystal, weapons, and flags, and is doted on by his loyal aide-de-camp, Colonel Fowler (Clarence Williams III). Campbell is a war hero now considered vice-presidential timber, although of course the messy murder of his daughter may put an end to that, especially if he had anything to do with it.

He is not the only suspect. With the efficiency of all good police procedurals, every single main character is a suspect, except for those deployed for local color and comic effect (and you can never be sure about them). Travolta's warrant officer is assigned to the case and partnered with another army cop, Sarah Sunhill (Madeleine Stowe); they had an affair once in Brussels, which gives them something to talk about—just as well, since the primary function of her character is to wait around in hopes that the screenplay will hurl her into a dangerous and threatening situation.

They quiz Captain Moore (Woods), who describes himself as Elisabeth's mentor in psychological warfare, and Colonel Kent (Timothy Hutton), the provost marshal, who seems awfully nosy if he has nothing to hide. The local police chief insulted Travolta while he was undercover, and now Travolta insults him back, and finds out that the chief's son and deputy was dating the dead woman.

He had a lot of company. Travolta finds a secret room in the woman's basement that contains S&M props and equipment, an automatic video system, and lots of incriminating tapes. The sweet blonde who changed Travolta's tire apparently spent her evenings tightening more than lugs. Travolta finds out from the tapes (and from gossip universally offered) that the general's daughter had apparently slept with more or less everyone on the general's staff.

We know from long experience with other thrillers that present problems always have their explanations in lurid flashbacks. Travolta discovers that something unspeakable happened to Captain Campbell during her third year at West Point. What that is, and how it leads to the death of the general's daughter, I leave to you to discover. The explanation does not speak highly for the psych courses at the Point, however, since Elisabeth apparently learned that the way to exorcise a traumatic memory is to reenact the events that produced it.

The General's Daughter is, as I have said, a well-made film. It is populated by edgy performances, and we get a real feeling for the characters played by Woods, as a career man with a secret to hide, Cromwell, as an unbending officer and father, and Williams, as a man who hero-worships the general to a fault. Travolta demonstrates again, as he did in *A Civil Action* and *Primary Colors,* that he has developed into a fine actor.

I also admired the darkly atmospheric look of the film, and the way it sustains its creepy mood. But I cringed when the death of the general's daughter was played out. Did the details have to be so graphic? Did we need to linger on the sight of a terrified woman? Did the filmmakers hesitate before supplying actual shots of her being strangled? Can anything be left to the imagination? I believe that any subject matter is legitimate for artistic purposes, but this isn't art. It's a thriller that could have spared us the details of that woman's horrible death. ☞

George of the Jungle ★ ★ ★

PG, 92 m., 1997

Brendan Fraser (George), Leslie Mann (Ursula Stanhope), Thomas Haden Church (Lyle Van de Groot), Richard Roundtree (Kwame), Greg Cruttwell (Max), Abraham Benrubi (Thor), Holland Taylor (Beatrice Stanhope), Kelly Miller (Betsy). Directed by Sam Weisman and produced by David Hoberman, Jordan Kerner, and Jon Avnet. Screenplay by Dana Olsen and Audrey Wells, based on characters developed by Jay Ward.

It was a strange experience, watching *George of the Jungle.* The movie would meander along, not going very much of anywhere, and then—pow!—there'd be an enormous laugh. More meandering, and then pow! again. Instead of spreading the laughter out and making a movie that was moderately funny from beginning to end, they concentrated the laughs, and made a movie that is sort of funny some of the time, and then occasionally hilarious.

Consider, for example, the character of Shep, the elephant. Shep looks like an elephant and is played by an elephant (named Tai), but Shep thinks it's a dog. George of the Jungle has trained him that way. When Shep first came bounding through the jungle and slid to a halt and sat on its haunches, barking and panting and wagging its tail, I was blindsided by laughter. And when George demonstrated Shep's ability to fetch by throwing a stick (actually a log), the joke only got funnier.

Then there's an Ape, named Ape, whose voice is dubbed by John Cleese, and who sounds and behaves exactly like George's British butler. I liked the way he looks down his glasses at people, and explains situations in a reserved and very proper tone, like Jeeves might. He's the funniest ape since those gorillas who drank the martinis in *Congo.*

George himself is pretty funny too. He's played by Brendan Fraser, who has bulked up and perfected a facial expression that can best be described as sheeplike goodwill. George has approximately the IQ of his namesake on Jay Ward's famous TV cartoon series, and makes the same mistakes, swinging on vines and crashing into trees.

The movie, which is live action and tries for the look and feel of a cartoon, involves a rich American girl named Ursula Stanhope (Leslie Mann) who goes on an expedition in the jungle, hears of a mysterious white ape, meets George, falls for him, and spends the rest of the movie trying to get out of her engagement to the society snob Lyle Van de Groot (Thomas Haden Church).

George meanwhile knows nothing of the ways of women, doesn't realize she likes him, and turns desperately to Ape for tips on how to woo her. Ape suggests baring his fangs, uprooting grass, beating his chest, and all the other usually dependable approaches, but when they don't work, he's adaptable: He gives his young master a copy of *Coffee, Tea or Me?* and says it contains all of the answers.

The screenplay by Dana Olsen and Audrey Wells makes some obligatory stops (we know more or less what will happen at the society functions in San Francisco, and we guess the fate of the wedding cake), but the movie is good-natured, slightly vulgar (in a mild Jim Carrey way) and well played by actors who are certainly good sports. Among the other cast members are Richard Roundtree, many years down the road from *Shaft in Africa,* as Kwame, an African leader, and Greg Cruttwell and Abraham Benrubi as two expedition members with vile plans of their own.

Is *George of the Jungle* a great movie? No.

But it was well positioned for the silly season, when we'd had just about all of the terrorist explosions we needed for one summer. I recommend a spin-off: a Saturday morning cartoon series about an elephant who thinks he's a dog. Think of all the things a dog could do if he had a trunk, and you'll get the idea.

Get Real ★ ★ ★

R, 110 m., 1999

Ben Silverstone (Steven Carter), Brad Gorton (John Dixon), Charlotte Brittain (Linda), Stacy A. Hart (Jessica), Kate McEnery (Wendy), Patrick Nielsen (Mark), Tim Harris (Kevin), James D.

White (Dave). Directed by Simon Shore and produced by Stephen Taylor. Screenplay by Patrick Wilde, based on the play *What's Wrong with Angry?* by Wilde.

Get Real tells the story of a teenage boy who has become sexually active at sixteen. That is, of course, the fodder for countless teenage sexcoms, in which the young heroes raid the brothels of Tijuana, are seduced by their French governesses, or have affairs with their teachers. The difference is that the hero in *Get Real* is gay, and so no doubt some critics will be offended by the film's assumptions.

I am thinking, for example, of a columnist for my own newspaper who doesn't think gays should be allowed into the Boy Scouts. His opposition to abortion clinics is matched only by his outrage at the birth control information supplied on a Planned Parenthood Web page; the logical result of his arguments is teenage childbearing. While it may be true that in his ideal world everyone is straight and they never have sex until they have been united by clergy, the real world is filled with young people who must deal every day with strong emotional and sexual feelings. Some of them have sex. This is a fact of life.

Such a person is Steven Carter (Ben Silverstone), the young British student who is the subject of *Get Real.* He has known he was gay since he was eleven. He keeps it a secret because in his school, you can be beaten for being gay. He's picked on anyway by insecure kids who deal with their own sexual anxiety by punishing it in others. The cards are stacked against him, he tells a girl who's his best friend: "I don't smoke or play football, and I have an IQ over 25."

One day Steven visits a local park where gays are known to meet, and is surprised to find that John Dixon (Brad Gorton), an athletic hero at his school, is hanging out there, too—and apparently for the same reason. John is far from out of the closet. He's attracted to Steven, and then runs away, and then comes creeping curiously back, and then denies his feelings. There is a heartbreaking scene (after they have become lovers) where he beats up Steven in the locker room, just to keep his cover in front of a gang of gay-bashers.

The movie deals with this material in a straightforward way, but is not sexually graphic and it somehow finds humor and warmth even while it shows Steven's lonely, secretive existence. In its general outlines, it's a typical teenage comedy like the ones that have been opening every weekend all spring, where the shy outsider is surprised to attract the most popular boy in class. This time the outsider is not played by Drew Barrymore, Rachel Leigh Cook, or Reese Witherspoon. And when Steven and John go to the school dance, they both dance with girls, while their eyes meet in hopeless longing.

Much of the humor in the film comes from Linda (Charlotte Brittain), Steven's plump best friend and for a long time the only one who knows he is gay. She acts as a confidante and cover, and even obligingly faints at a wedding when he needs to make a quick getaway. He's known her since the early days when everything he knew about sex was learned from his dad's hidden porno tapes ("I thought babies were made when two women tie a man to a bed and cover his willy with ice cream").

There is also Jessica (Stacy A. Hart), an editor on the school magazine, who likes Steven a lot and wants to be his girlfriend. He would like to tell her the truth, but nobody guesses it, certainly not his parents, and he lacks the courage. Then the relationship with John helps him to see his life more clearly, to grow tired of lying, and he writes an anonymous article for the magazine that is not (as he must have known) destined to remain anonymous for long.

The film takes a bit long to arrive at its obligatory points, and Steven's brave decision at the end is probably unlikely—he acts not as a high school boy probably would, but as a screenwriter requires him to. But the movie is sound in all the right ways; it argues that we are as we are, and the best thing to do is accept that. I doubt if movies have much influence on behavior, but I hope they can help us empathize with those who are not like us. There were stories that the Colorado shooters were taunted (inaccurately, apparently) for being gay. Movies like *Get Real* might help homophobic teenagers and adults become more accepting of differences. Certainly this film has deeper values than the mainstream teenage comedies that retail aggressive materialism, soft-core sex, and shallow ideas about "popularity."

G.I. Jane ★ ★ ★ ½

R, 125 m., 1997

Demi Moore (Lieutenant Jordan O'Neil), Viggo Mortensen (Master Chief Urgayle), Anne Bancroft (Senator DeHaven), Jason Beghe (Royce), Scott Wilson (C. O. Salem), Lucinda Jenney (Blondell), Morris Chestnut (McCool), Josh Hopkins (Flea), James Caviezel (Slovnik). Directed by Ridley Scott and produced by Roger Birnbaum and Suzanne Todd. Screenplay by Danielle Alexandra and David Twohy.

"I'm not interested in being some poster girl for women's rights," says Lt. Jordan O'Neil, played by Demi Moore in *G.I. Jane.* She just wants to prove a woman can survive Navy SEAL training so rigorous that 60 percent of the men don't make it. Her protest loses a little of its ring if you drive down Sunset Boulevard in Los Angeles, as I did the other night, and see Demi Moore in a crewcut, glaring out fiercely from the side of an entire office building on one of the largest movie posters in history. Well, the lieutenant is talking for herself, not Moore.

Jordan O'Neil is a navy veteran who resents not being allowed into combat during the Gulf War. Now there's a move under way for full female equality in the fighting forces. Its leader, Senator DeHaven (Anne Bancroft), wants no more coddling: "If women measure up, we'll get 100 percent integration." O'Neil is selected as a promising candidate, and reports for SEAL training after a farewell bubble bath with her lover, a fellow navy officer named Royce (Jason Beghe).

Now come the scenes from the movie that stay in the memory, as O'Neil joins a group of trainees in a regime of great rigor and uncompromising discomfort. The shivering, soaking-wet, would-be SEALS stand endlessly while holding landing rafts over their heads, they negotiate obstacle courses, they march and run and crawl, they are covered with wet, cold mud, and then they do it all over again.

There is a bell next to the parade ground. Ring it, and you can go home. "I always look for one quitter on the first day," barks Master Chief Urgayle (Viggo Mortensen), "and that day doesn't stop until I get it." He gets it, but not from O'Neil.

Urgayle is an intriguing character, played by Mortensen to suggest depths and complications. In an early scene he is discovered reading a novel by J. M. Coetzee, the dissident South African who is not on the navy's recommended reading list, and in an early scene he quotes a famous poem by D. H. Lawrence, both for its imagery (of a bird's unattended death) and in order to freak out the trainees by suggesting a streak of subtle madness.

The training sequences are as they have to be: incredible rigors, survived by O'Neil. They are good cinema because Ridley Scott, the director, brings a documentary attention to them, and because Demi Moore, having bitten off a great deal here, proves she can chew it. The wrong casting in her role could have tilted the movie toward *Private Benjamin,* but Moore is serious, focused, and effective.

Several of the supporting roles are well acted and carefully written (by Danielle Alexandra and David Twohy). Anne Bancroft is brisk, smart, and effective as the powerful U.S. senator. And consider Salem, the commanding officer, played by Scott Wilson. In an older movie he would have been presented as an unreconstructed sexist. This movie is smart enough to know that modern officers have been briefed on the proper treatment of female officers, and that whatever their private views they know enough about military regulations and the possibility of disciplinary hearings that they try to go by the book.

Salem makes some seemingly helpful remarks about menstruation that are not quite called for (by the time a navy woman gets to SEAL training, she has undoubtedly mastered the management of her period). But neither he nor Master Chief Urgayle are the enemy: They are meant to represent the likely realities a woman might face, not artificial movie villains.

There is a villain in the film. I will not reveal the details, although after the film is over you may find yourself asking, as I did, whether the villainous acts were inspired more by politics and corruption, or by the demands of the plot.

The plot also rears its head rather noticeably in the closing scenes, when the SEAL group finds itself in a situation much more likely to occur in a movie than in life. There is a battle sequence that is choreographed somewhat uncertainly by Scott, so that we cannot quite understand where everyone is or what is possible, and as a result the SEALS come across as not particularly competent. But by now we're into movie payoff time, where the documentary conviction of the earlier scenes must give way to audience satisfaction.

Demi Moore remains one of the most venturesome of current stars, and although her films do not always succeed, she shows imagination in her choice of projects. It is also intriguing to watch her work with the image of her body. The famous pregnant photos on the cover of *Vanity Fair* can be placed beside her stripper in *Striptease*, her executive in *Disclosure*, and the woman in *Indecent Proposal*, who has to decide what a million dollars might purchase; all of these women, and now O'Neil, test the tension between a woman's body and a woman's ambition and will. *G.I. Jane* does it most obviously, and effectively.

The Gingerbread Man ★ ★ ★

R, 115 m., 1998

Kenneth Branagh (Rick Magruder), Embeth Davidtz (Mallory Doss), Robert Downey Jr. (Clyde Pell), Daryl Hannah (Lois Harlan), Tom Berenger (Pete Randle), Famke Janssen (Leeanne), Mae Whitman (Libby), Jesse James (Jeff), Robert Duvall (Dixon Doss). Directed by Robert Altman and produced by Jeremy Tannenbaum. Screenplay by Al Hayes, based on an original story by John Grisham.

The ominous approach of Hurricane Geraldo drenches the opening scenes of Robert Altman's *The Gingerbread Man* in sheets of rain and darkness at noon. John Grisham, who wrote the story, named the hurricane well, for like a week's episodes of the television program, the movie features divorce, adultery, kooky fringe groups, kidnapped children, hotshot lawyers, drug addiction, and family tragedy. That it seems a step up from sensationalism is because Grisham has a sure sense of time and place, and Altman and his actors invest the material with a kind of lurid sincerity.

As the film opens, a lawyer named Magruder (Kenneth Branagh, Georgia accent well in hand) has won a big case and driven back to his Savannah law offices for a celebration. Awaiting him in Georgia are his faithful assistant Lois (Daryl Hannah), his faithless estranged wife, Leeanne (Famke Janssen), and his office staff, not excepting the muddled private investigator Clyde (Robert Downey Jr.). After a catered office party at which he drinks too much, Magruder leaves for his car, only to find a woman outside in the rain, screaming after her own departing car. This is Mallory Doss (Embeth Davidtz), who was a waitress at the party, and now believes her car to be stolen.

Magruder offers her his cell phone and then a ride home, where, to their amazement, they find her stolen car. Her door is unlocked, the lights are on, a TV is playing, and she hints darkly that this sort of thing has happened before. It may be the work of her father, who belongs to a "group." Weeping and lashing out at her absent parent, Mallory absentmindedly undresses in front of Magruder, and as thunder and lightning tear through the sky they engage in what is categorically and unequivocally a sexual relationship.

Neat touch in the morning: Magruder prods Mallory's prone body and, getting no response, dresses and leaves, while we wonder if she's dead and he will be framed with the crime. Not at all. A much more complex plot is afoot, and only after the movie is over do we think back through the plot, trying to figure out what the characters planned in advance, and what was improvised on the spot.

Grisham's story line resembles one of those Ross Macdonald novels from thirty years ago, in which old sins beget new ones, and the sins of the fathers are visited on the children. Altman's contribution is to tell the story in a fresh and spontaneous way, to use Branagh's quickness as an actor to make scenes seem fresh. Consider the scene where Magruder, tired and hung over, returns to his office the next morning, marches grimly past his staff toward his office, and asks for "Some of that . . . you know." As his door closes, one secretary turns to another: "Coffee." It's just right: Hangovers cause sufferers to lose track of common words, and office workers complete the boss's thoughts. Lois, the Hannah character, is especially effective in the way she cares for a boss who should, if he had an ounce of sense, accept her safe harbor instead of seeking out danger.

Grisham's works are filled with neo-Nazis, but when we meet Mallory's dad he's hard to classify. Dixon Doss (Robert Duvall) is a stringy, unlovely coot, and his "group" seems to be made up of unwashed and unbarbered old codgers, who hang around ominously in a clubhouse that looks like it needs the Orkin man. In a cartoon they'd have flies buzzing about their heads. In a perhaps unintentional touch of humor, the codgers can be mobilized instantly to speed out on sinister missions for old Doss; they're like the Legion of Justice crossed with Klan pensioners.

Magruder has lots on his hands. He feels protective toward Mallory and assigns Clyde (Downey) to her case; Clyde's method of stumbling over evidence is to stumble all the time and hope some evidence turns up. Magruder's almost ex-wife, who is dating his divorce lawyer, is in a struggle with him over custody, and Magruder finds it necessary to snatch his kids from their school, after which the kids are snatched again, from a hideaway motel, by persons unknown, while the winds pick up and walls of rain lash Savannah.

It's all atmospheric, quirky, and entertaining: the kind of neo-*noir* in which old-fashioned characters have updated problems. There is something about the South that seems to breed eccentric characters in the minds of writers and directors; the women there are more lush and conniving, the men heroic and yet temptable, and the villains Shakespearean in their depravity. Duvall, who can be a subtle and controlled actor (see *The Apostle*), can also sink his fangs into a role like this one and shake it by its neck until dead. And then there's Tom Berenger as Mallory's former husband, who seems to have nothing to do with the case, although students of the Law of Economy of Characters will know that no unnecessary characters are ever inserted into a movie—certainly not name players like Berenger.

From Robert Altman we expect a certain improvisational freedom, a plot that finds its way down unexpected channels and depends on coincidence and serendipity. Here he seems content to follow the tightly plotted maze mapped out by Grisham; the Altman touches are more in dialogue and personal style than in construction. He gives the actors freedom to move around in their roles. Instead of the tunnel vision of most Grisham movies, in which every line of dialogue relentlessly hammers down the next plot development, *The Gingerbread Man* has space for quirky behavior, kidding around, and murky atmosphere. The hurricane is not just window dressing, but an effective touch: It adds a subtle pressure beneath the surface, lending tension to ordinary scenes with its promise of violence to come.

Go ★★★

R, 100 m., 1999

Katie Holmes (Claire Montgomery), Sarah Polley (Ronna Martin), William Fichtner (Burke), Desmond Askew (Simon Baines), Taye Diggs (Marcus), Scott Wolf (Adam), Jay Mohr (Zack), Timothy Olyphant (Todd Gaines), Jane Krakowski (Irene). Directed by Doug Liman and produced by Paul Rosenberg, Mickey Liddell, and Matt Freeman. Screenplay by John August.

Sooner or later the statute of limitations has to run out on comparisons between new movies and *Pulp Fiction*. Quentin Tarantino's 1994 film mesmerized the Sundance generation, who have been doing riffs ever since on its interlocking time lines, its quirky sex and violence, its pop culture expertise, its familiarity with drugs, its squirmy comedy, its black-white friendships, its ironic profundity, and its revelations in all-night diners. Those who haven't seen it must wonder why it's cited in so many movie reviews; has no other movie been made in the interim?

Well, no, not one that staked out the territory so firmly. Consider, for example, Doug Liman's *Go*. This is an entertaining, clever black comedy that takes place entirely in Tarantino-land. Liman is a talented director who works as his own cinematographer and finds a nice off-center humor. His *Swingers* (1996) was an accomplished debut film, and here, with a screenplay by John August, he does more, and better, and yet the shadow of QT falls on many scenes.

When his characters deliberately create a flesh wound with a gunshot, for example, the setup and payoff reminds us of the needle plunging into the heart in *Pulp Fiction* (and of the deliberate blade wound in *Gridlock'd*). And when two of his characters sit in a diner and have a conversation about the comic strip *Family Circus,* we think of Uma Thurman and John Travolta sharing pop lore over their milk shakes in *PF.* We're also reminded of *Pulp* in scenes involving a laconic drug dealer, a crisis involving body disposal, an unintended drug overdose, the way its story lines branch off and then join up again, and even in an unusual character name, Zack.

Tarantino has created a generation of footnoters and cross-referencers. I'm not saying *Go* couldn't have been made without the example of *Pulp Fiction,* but it can't be seen without thinking of it. What it adds is a grittier feel; Liman's characters are closer to ground level.

The story begins in a supermarket, where Ronna the checkout girl (Sarah Polley) takes a shift for her friend Simon (Desmond Askew), a part-time drug dealer who wants to go to Vegas. She needs rent money. When two customers named Adam and Zack (Scott Wolf and Jay Mohr) want to score some ecstasy, she goes to Simon's usual dealer (Timothy Olyphant) to get twenty hits. Olyphant, lounging bare-chested in his apartment hideaway, stroking his girlfriend and his cat, working the phone, supplies the legal expertise such stories always require: "Twenty hits! The magic number where intent to sell becomes trafficking."

Without revealing too much of the plot, which depends on surprises and connections, I can say that the other main stories involve (1) Simon's adventures in Las Vegas, where he and his black friend Marcus (Taye Diggs) get into big trouble with the owners of a topless bar, and (2) the relationship between Adam, Zack, and a cop named Burke (William Fichtner), who invites the two men over to Christmas dinner with his wife (Jane Krakowski). This couple is extremely open to sexual adventures with strangers, but turns out to have another even stronger obsession; there is nothing like a pyramid scheme to bring out fanaticism.

Trouble in Vegas leads to more trouble in Los Angeles, where the stories of the checkout clerk and the two young men also meet again, unexpectedly. The plot, of course, is a complete contrivance, but Liman and August have a lot of fun with the details, including a "Macarena" dance in an unlikely setting, a telepathic cat, and a scene with echoes of *Blood Simple,* in which some characters try to leave a hotel room while others are trying to break in.

Go has energy and wit, and the performances are right for the material—especially Sarah Polley, who thinks fast and survives harrowing experiences, and Fichtner, the cop who is so remarkably open to new experiences. The movie is ruthless in its attitude toward the apparently dead or dying, but then grisly indifference is central to the self-centered values without which these characters would have no values at all. Liman shows here, as he did in *Swingers,* that he has a good eye and can create screwy characters. Can he break out of QT-land?

The Godfather ★★★★

R, 175 m., 1972 (rereleased 1997)

Marlon Brando (Vito Corleone), Al Pacino (Michael Corleone), James Caan (Sonny Corleone), Richard S. Castellano (Clemenza), Robert Duvall (Tom Hagen), Sterling Hayden (McCluskey), John Marley (Jack Woltz), Richard Conte (Barzini), Al Lettieri (Sollozzo), Diane Keaton (Kay Adams), Abe Vigoda (Tessio), Talia Shire (Connie), Gianni Russo (Carlo Rizzi), John Cazale (Fredo Corleone), Rudy Bond (Cuneo), Al Martino (Johnny Fontane), Morgana King (Mamma Corleone), Lenny Montana (Luca Brasi), John Martino (Paulie Gatto), Alex Rocco (Moe Greene), Tony Giorgio (Bruno Tattaglia). Directed by Francis Ford Coppola and produced by Albert S. Ruddy. Screenplay by Coppola and Mario Puzo, based on Puzo's novel.

The Godfather is told entirely within a closed world. That's why we sympathize with characters who are essentially evil. The story by Mario Puzo and Francis Ford Coppola is a brilliant conjuring act, inviting us to consider the Mafia entirely on its own terms. Don Vito Corleone (Marlon Brando) emerges as a sympathetic and even admirable character; during the entire film, this lifelong professional criminal does nothing that we can really disapprove of.

During the movie we see not a single actual civilian victim of organized crime. No women trapped into prostitution. No lives wrecked by gambling. No victims of theft, fraud, or protection rackets. The only police officer with a significant speaking role is corrupt.

The story views the Mafia from the inside. That is its secret, its charm, its spell; in a way it has shared the public perception of the Mafia ever since. The real world is replaced by an authoritarian patriarchy where power and justice flow from the godfather, and the only villains are traitors. There is one commandment, spoken by Michael (Al Pacino): "Don't ever take sides against the family."

It is significant that the first shot is inside a dark, shuttered room. It is the wedding day of Vito Corleone's daughter, and on such a day a Sicilian must grant any reasonable request. A man has come to ask for punishment for his daughter's rapist. Don Vito asks why he did not come to him immediately.

"I went to the police, like a good American," the man says. The godfather's reply will underpin the entire movie: "Why did you go to the police? Why didn't you come to me first? What have I ever done to make you treat me so disrespectfully? If you'd come to me in friendship, then this scum that ruined your daughter would be suffering this very day. And, if by chance, an honest man like yourself should make enemies . . . then they would become my enemies. And then they would fear you."

As the day continues, there are two more séances in the godfather's darkened study, intercut with scenes from the wedding outside. By the end of the wedding sequence, most of the main characters will have been introduced, and we will know essential things about their personalities. It is a virtuoso stretch of filmmaking: Coppola brings his large cast onstage so artfully that we are drawn at once into the godfather's world.

The screenplay of *The Godfather* follows no formulas except for the classic structure in which power passes between the generations. The writing is subtly constructed to set up events later in the film. Notice how the request by Johnny Fontane, the failing singer, pays off in the Hollywood scenes; how his tears set up the shocking moment when a mogul wakes up in bed with what is left of his racehorse. Notice how the undertaker is told, "some day, and that day may never come, I will ask a favor of you . . ." and how when the day comes the favor is not violence (as in a conventional movie), but Don Vito's desire to spare his wife the sight of his son's maimed body. And notice how a woman's "mistaken" phone call sets up the trap in which Sonny (James Caan) is murdered: It's done so neatly that you have to think back through the events to figure it out.

Now here is a trivia question: What is the name of Vito's wife? She exists in the movie as an insignificant shadow, a plump Sicilian grandmother who poses with her husband in wedding pictures, but plays no role in the events that take place in his study. There is little room for women in *The Godfather.* Sonny uses and discards them, and ignores his wife. Connie (Talia Shire), the don's daughter, is so disregarded her husband is not allowed into the family business. He is thrown a bone—"a living"—and later, when he is killed, Michael coldly lies to his sister about what happened.

The irony of the title is that it eventually comes to refer to the son, not the father. As the film opens, Michael is not part of the family business, and plans to marry a WASP, Kay Adams (Diane Keaton). His turning point comes when he saves his father's life by moving his hospital bed, and whispers to the unconscious man: "I'm with you now."

After he shoots the corrupt cop, Michael hides in Sicily, where he falls in love with and marries Appolonia (Simonetta Stefanelli). They do not speak the same language; small handicap for a Mafia wife. He undoubtedly loves Appolonia, as he loved Kay, but what is he thinking here? That he can no longer marry Kay because he has chosen a Mafia life? After Appolonia's death and his return to America, he seeks out Kay and eventually they marry. Did he tell her about Appolonia? Such details are unimportant to the story.

What is important is loyalty to the family. Much is said in the movie about trusting a man's word, but honesty is nothing compared to loyalty. Michael doesn't even trust Tom Hagen (Robert Duvall) with the secret that he plans to murder the heads of the other families. The famous "baptism massacre" is tough, virtuoso filmmaking: The baptism provides him with an airtight alibi, and he becomes a godfather in both senses at the same time.

Vito Corleone is the moral center of the film. He is old, wise, and opposed to dealing in drugs. He understands that society is not alarmed by "liquor, gambling . . . even women." But drugs are a dirty business to Don Vito, and one of the movie's best scenes is the Mafia summit in which he argues his point. The implication is that in the godfather's world there would be no drugs, only "victimless crimes," and justice would be dispatched evenly and swiftly.

My argument is taking this form because I want to point out how cleverly Coppola structures his film to create sympathy for his heroes. The Mafia is not a benevolent and protective organization, and the Corleone family is only marginally better than the others. Yet when the old man falls dead among his tomato plants, we feel that a giant has passed.

Gordon Willis's cinematography is celebrated for its darkness; it is rich, atmospheric, expressive. You cannot appreciate this on television because the picture is artificially brightened. Coppola populates his dark interior spaces with remarkable faces. The front line—Brando, Pacino, Caan, Duvall—are attractive in one way or another, but the actors who play their associates are chosen for their fleshy, thickly lined faces—for huge jaws and deeply set eyes. Look at Abe Vigoda as Tessio, the fearsome enforcer. The first time we see him, he's dancing with a child at the wedding, her satin pumps balanced on his shoes. The sun shines that day, but never again: He is developed as a hulking presence who implies the possibility of violent revenge. Only at the end is he brightly lit again, to make him look vulnerable as he begs for his life.

The Brando performance is justly famous and often imitated. We know all about his puffy cheeks, and his use of props like the kitten in the opening scene. Those are actor's devices. Brando uses them but does not depend on them: He embodies the character so convincingly that at the end, when he warns his son two or three times that "the man who comes to you to set up a meeting—that's the traitor," we are not thinking of acting at all. We are thinking that the don is growing old and repeating himself, but we are also thinking that he is probably absolutely right.

Pacino plays Michael close to his vest; he has learned from his father never to talk in front of outsiders, never to trust anyone unnecessarily, to take advice but keep his own counsel. All of the other roles are so successfully filled that a strange thing happened as I watched this restored 1997 version: Familiar as I am with Robert Duvall, when he first appeared on the screen I found myself thinking, "There's Tom Hagen."

Coppola went to Italy to find Nino Rota, composer of many Fellini films, to score the picture. Hearing the sadness and nostalgia of the movie's main theme, I realized what the music was telling us: Things would have turned out better if we had only listened to the godfather.

God Said, 'Ha!' ★ ★ ★ ½

PG-13, 85 m., 1999

Directed and performed by Julia Sweeney and produced by Rana Joy Glickman. Screenplay by Sweeney, based on the stage play directed by Greg Kachel.

There is a kind of luminous quality in the way Julia Sweeney talks about her life and family in *God Said, 'Ha!'* She wanders the stage for an hour and a half, talking about a year in her life when her brother, Mike, was dying of cancer. This is a sad subject, painful to her, and yet she makes humor of it. She is a comedian, and, like the hero of *Life Is Beautiful,* she deals with life with the gifts at her command.

What she weaves out of her memories is a funny love poem to Mike and her parents—who all moved into her small house for the duration of the crisis. She sees their human weaknesses, she smiles at their goofy logic, she lets their habits get on her nerves, but above all she embraces them. And when, midway through the year, even more bad news descends upon her, she is able to transform that, too, into truth and fond humor.

Sweeney may be familiar to you as a former cast member of *Saturday Night Live.* Her androgynous character "Pat" was a regular on the show, and later appeared in a movie. She began in show business as an accountant, keeping the books for *Rainman*, and edged into performance through local comedy clubs. After the *SNL* gig was over, she moved to Los Angeles, looking for work in movies and sitcoms, and bought her own house. Soon she was sharing it with her parents and Mike, and "the lines started to cross about whose house it really was."

Mike had lymphoma. He got worse and then he got better and then he got even worse, and then he got a little bit better—she charts the progress of an implacable foe. But there is laughter, too, especially from Mike, who found wry material in the doctor's decision to administer chemotherapy by inserting a permanent "shunt" into his body: Should it be called a faucet? A spigot? Where should it go? The possibilities were endless.

Sweeney's parents come across as nice people who, in their well-meaning attempts to stay out of the way, are usually in the way. When a light goes out in the bathroom, her mother reports, "I found a bulb—but I didn't know if there was some special way to screw it in."

During Mike's illness, Sweeney began talking about what she was going through as part of her act. "It must be hard," Mike joked, "you being an actress, and me in the cancer spotlight." It was hard for Mike, too—who now spent much of his time in a bed in her living room, and who as a child so valued his privacy that he installed a doorbell on his bedroom door.

Sweeney and other family members would take him to the UCLA Medical Center several times a week for chemotherapy, and as they met patients with many kinds of cancer, they began to muse on why cancer only seemed to strike vital organs. "Why can't there be cancer of the fat?" she wondered, only to find out that there was—and that you don't want it, either.

Watching *God Said, 'Ha!'*, I wished that I could show it to people who wondered why I didn't approve of *Patch Adams*. This film has a dignity, an underlying taste, in the way it deals with subjects like cancer and dying. It doesn't simply use the subjects as an occasion for manipulative sentiment. At the end of the film, we feel we've been through a lot with Julia and Mike Sweeney and their family. We're sad, but we're smiling. I was thinking: Life's like that.

Gods and Monsters ★ ★ ★

NO MPAA RATING, 105 m., 1998

Ian McKellen (James Whale), Brendan Fraser (Clayton Boone), Lynn Redgrave (Whale's Housekeeper), Lolita Davidovich (Boone's Girlfriend). Directed by Bill Condon and produced by Paul Colichman, Gregg Fienberg, and Mark R. Harris. Screenplay by Condon, based on the novel *Father of Frankenstein*, by Christopher Bram.

The yard man looks a little like Frankenstein's monster, with his hulky body and flat-top haircut. Of course, he's more handsome. The old man sizes him up, invites him to tea, is friendly: "Feel free to use the pool. We're quite informal here—no need to use a bathing suit." We are listening to the last hopeful sigh of a dying romantic, an aging homosexual who is still cheered by the presence of beauty.

Gods and Monsters is a speculation about the last days of the director James Whale, who was open about his sexuality in an era when most homosexuals in Hollywood stayed prudently in the closet. Whale (1889–1957) directed some twenty-one films, but is best remembered for seven made between 1931 and 1939: *Frankenstein, The Old Dark House, The Invisible Man, Bride of Frankenstein, Show Boat, The Great Garrick,* and *The Man in the Iron Mask.* At the time of his death he had not made a movie in sixteen years, but still lived comfortably, dabbling at a little painting and a little lusting.

He made some good movies (*Frankenstein* placed eighty-seventh on the AFI's list of great American films, although *Bride of Frankenstein* is by far the better of the two pictures). He began as an actor, lost his first love in World War I, and joined the exodus to Hollywood, where he made a lot of money and never quite realized his potential. He must have seemed an attractive challenge to Ian McKellen, the gifted British Shakespearean who in this film and *Apt Pupil* is belatedly flourishing in the movies after much distinction on the stage.

McKellen playing Whale makes sense, but is it ideal casting to use Brendan Fraser *(George of the Jungle)* as Clayton Boone, the young man who comes to cut the grass? Fraser is subtle and attuned to the role, but doesn't project strong sexuality; shouldn't the yard man be not simply attractive but potentially exciting to the old man? We never ever believe there's a possibility that anything physical will occur between them—and we should, I think.

Of course, Whale's ambitions in that direction are mostly daydreams, and finally he's more interested in simply regarding the young man. He asks Clayton to be his artist's model, a request that essentially translates as, "Will you take off your clothes and stand there while I look at you?"

Clayton is slow to understand that Whale is gay. Well, in 1957 a lot of people might not have understood. When he figures it out, he isn't angered, and there's no painful and predictable scene of violence. Instead, the film proceeds on a bittersweet course in which a young and not terribly bright man grows to like an old and very intelligent man, and to pity him a little. The film is a biopic leading toward a graceful elegy.

Similar material was dealt with earlier this year in *Love and Death on Long Island,* starring John Hurt as an aging British writer who develops a crush on an American teen heartthrob (Jason Priestley). That was a funnier movie, and also more elusive, since the Hurt character is not an active homosexual (indeed, hardly seems sexual at all) and barely understands the nature of his own obsession. Levels of irony were possible. In *Gods and Monsters,* on the other hand, both the director and the yard man are pretty much kept at the service of the film's sentimental vision.

Directed by Bill Condon, who based his screenplay on the novel *Father of Frankenstein* by Christopher Bram, the movie has flashbacks to the making of Whale's classics, scenes where Clayton and his girlfriend (Lolita Davidovich) watch some of them, and memories of the pool parties that the closeted director George Cukor held every Sunday at his mansion above Sunset. (I once interviewed Cukor at the very poolside. A venerable and beloved figure in a liberated age, he was still prudent about his revelations; he remembered Katharine Hepburn swimming in the pool, but of course there was no whisper about the Sunday skinny-dips.)

In *Gods and Monsters,* Whale knows his health is failing. He lives alone except for a cheerless housekeeper (Lynn Redgrave, very good) who lectures him on bad behavior and tells him he will go to hell. She sizes up Clayton and knows the whole story instantly—has no doubt seen the same scenario enacted many times. But this time, because Clayton feels empathy and because Whale feels the chill of approaching death, the seduction strategies are pro forma. What the man most needs to do is talk, and Clayton lets him, as he slips between the present and his vivid memories.

Gods and Monsters is not a deep or powerful film, but it is a good-hearted one, in which we sense the depth of early loss that helped to shape Whale's protective style, and the California openness that allows Clayton Boone to care for a man he has nothing in common with. The film includes a clip from *Bride of Frankenstein* of a toast to "gods and monsters." By creating a wife for Frankenstein's monster out of base materials, Dr. Praetorious of course was the god. Now James Whale finds he no longer has the strength or the impulse to create a lover for himself. At the end there are neither gods nor monsters, only memories.

Godzilla ★ ½

PG-13, 138 m., 1998

Matthew Broderick (Dr. Niko Tatopoulos), Jean Reno (Philippe Roche), Maria Pitillo (Audrey Timmonds), Hank Azaria (Victor [Animal] Palotti), Kevin Dunn (Colonel Hicks), Michael Lerner (Mayor Ebert), Harry Shearer (Charles Caiman), Arabella Field (Lucy Palotti), Vicki Lewis (Dr. Elsie Chapman), Doug Savant (Sergeant O'Neal), Malcolm Danare (Dr. Mendel Craven). Directed by Roland Emmerich and produced by Dean Devlin. Screenplay by Devlin and Emmerich, based on the character Godzilla in films by Toho Co. Ltd.

CANNES, France—Going to see *Godzilla* at the Palais of the Cannes Film Festival is like attending a satanic ritual in St. Peter's Basilica. It's a rebuke to the faith that the building represents. Cannes touchingly adheres to a belief that film can be intelligent, moving, and grand. *Godzilla* is a big, ugly, ungainly device designed to give teenagers the impression they are seeing a movie. It was the festival's closing film, coming at the end like the horses in a parade, perhaps for the same reason.

It rains all through *Godzilla,* and it's usually night. Well, of course it is: That makes the special effects easier to obscure. If you never get a clear look at the monster, you can't see how shoddy it is. Steven Spielberg opened *Jurassic Park* by giving us a good, long look at the dinosaurs in full sunlight, and our imaginations leapt up. *Godzilla* hops out of sight like a camera-shy kangaroo.

The makers of the film, director Roland Emmerich and writer Dean Devlin, follow the timeless outlines of many other movies about Godzilla, Rodan, Mothra, Gamera, and their radioactive kin. There are ominous attacks on ships at sea, alarming blips on radar screens, and a scientist who speculates that nuclear tests may have spawned a mutant creature. A cast of stereotyped stock characters is introduced and made to say lines like, "I don't understand—how could something so big just disappear?" Or, "Many people have had their lives changed forever!" And then there are the big special effects sequences, as Godzilla terrorizes New York.

One must carefully repress intelligent thought while watching such a film. The movie makes no sense at all except as a careless pastiche of its betters (and, yes, the Japanese *Godzilla* movies are, in their way, better—if only because they embrace dreck instead of condescending to it). You have to absorb such a film, not consider it. But my brain rebelled and insisted on applying logic where it was not welcome.

How, for example, does a 300-foot-tall creature fit inside a subway tunnel? How come it's sometimes only as tall as the tunnel, and at other times taller than high-rise office buildings? How big is it, anyway? Why can it breathe fire but hardly ever makes use of this ability? Why, when the heroes hide inside the Park Avenue tunnel, is this tunnel too small for Godzilla to enter, even though it is larger than a subway tunnel? And why doesn't Godzilla just snort some flames down there and broil them?

Most monster movies have at least one bleeding-heart environmentalist to argue the case of the monstrous beast, but here we get only Niko Tatopoulos (Matthew Broderick), an expert on the mutant earthworms of Chernobyl, who seems less like a scientist than like a placeholder waiting for a rewrite ("insert more interesting character here"). It is he who intuits that Godzilla is a female. (You would think that if a 300-foot monster were male, that would be hard to miss, but never mind.) The military in all movies about monsters and aliens from outer space always automatically attempts to kill them, and here they fire lots of wimpy missiles and torpedoes at Godzilla, which have so little effect we wonder how our tax dollars are being spent. (Just once, I'd like a movie where they train Godzilla to do useful tasks, like pulling a coaxial cable across the ocean floor, or pushing stuck trains out of tunnels.)

In addition to the trigger-happy Americans, there is a French force, too, led by Jean Reno, a good actor who plays this role as if he got on the plane shouting, "I'm going to Disneyland!" All humans in monster movies have simpleminded little character traits, and Reno's obsession is with getting a decent cup of coffee. Other characters include a TV newswoman (Maria Pitillo) who used to be the worm man's girlfriend, a determined cameraman (Hank Azaria), a grim-jawed military leader (Kevin Dunn), and a simpering anchorman (Harry Shearer). None of these characters emerges as anything more than a source of obligatory dialogue.

Oh, and then there are New York's Mayor Ebert (gamely played by Michael Lerner) and his adviser, Gene (Lorry Goldman). The mayor, of course, makes every possible wrong decision (he is against evacuating Manhattan, etc.), and the adviser eventually gives thumbs-down to his reelection campaign. These characters are a reaction by Emmerich and Devlin to negative Siskel and Ebert reviews of their earlier movies *(Stargate, Independence Day),* but they let us off lightly; I fully expected to be squished like a bug by Godzilla. Now that I've inspired a character in a Godzilla movie, all I really still desire is for several Ingmar Bergman characters to sit in a circle and read my reviews to one another in hushed tones.

There is a way to make material like *Godzilla* work. It can be campy fun, like the recent *Gamera, Guardian of the Universe.* Or hallucinatory, like *Infra-Man.* Or awesome, like *Jurassic Park.* Or it can tap a certain elemental dread, like the original *King Kong.* But all of those approaches demand a certain sympathy with the material, a zest that rises to the occasion.

In Howard Hawks's *The Thing,* there is a great scene where scientists in the Arctic spread out to trace the outlines of something mysterious that is buried in the ice, and the camera slowly pulls back to reveal that it is circular—a saucer. In *Godzilla,* the worm expert is standing in a deep depression, and the camera pulls back to reveal that he is standing in a footprint—which he would obviously already have known. There might be a way to reveal the astonishing footprint to the character and the audience at the same time, but that would involve a sense of style and timing, and some thought about the function of the scene.

There is nothing wrong with making a *Godzilla* movie and nothing wrong with special effects. But don't the filmmakers have some obligation to provide pop entertainment that at least lifts the spirits? There is real feeling in King Kong fighting off the planes that attack him, or the pathos of the monster in *Bride of Frankenstein,* who was so misunderstood. There is a true sense of wonder in *Jurassic Park.*

Godzilla, by contrast, offers nothing but soulless technique: A big lizard is created by special effects, wreaks havoc, and is destroyed. What a coldhearted, mechanistic vision, so starved for emotion or wit. The primary audience for *Godzilla* is children and teenagers, and the filmmakers have given them a sterile exercise when they hunger for dreams.

Going All the Way ★★★

R, 110 m., 1997

Jeremy Davies (Sonny Burns), Ben Affleck (Gunner Casselman), Amy Locane (Buddy Porter), Rose McGowan (Gale Ann Thayer), Rachel Weisz (Marty Pilcher), John Lordan (Elwood Burns), Jill Clayburgh (Alma Burns), Lesley Ann Warren (Nina Casselman). Directed by Mark Pellington and produced by Tom Gorai and Sigurjon Sighvatsson. Screenplay by Dan Wakefield, based on his novel.

One problem with a lot of coming-of-age movies is that the characters seem too old and confident for their problems. Even the Dustin Hoffman character in *The Graduate* seems a little too ironically plugged in, as if he's aware of the movie's subtext. But the characters in *Going All the Way* ring true: They're callow and limited, their motivation is centered on their genitals, and yet they burn with idealism, with fevered fantasies of their own eventual triumph.

The movie, based on Dan Wakefield's novel, is set in Indianapolis soon after the Korean War. Two recently discharged veterans meet on the train home: Sonny Burns (Jeremy Davies), a shy, secretive bundle of insecurity, and Gunner Casselman (Ben Affleck), the golden-boy type. Gunner was a high school sports hero and Sonny was an overlooked nerd; Sonny fully expects Gunner to ignore him, but Gunner amazingly seeks him out, and they become friends.

What happened? Gunner obviously went through a spiritual awakening while stationed overseas ("I never really thought about anything until I got to Japan," he confides, and "Those Zen riddles really made me think"). He seeks out Sonny, no doubt, because he assumes the class nerd was thinking deep thoughts while Gunner was scoring touchdowns. Sonny was actually spending much of his time masturbating, but no matter; soon the two friends are discussing *The Catcher in the Rye,* and Gunner, reading *The Lonely Crowd,* decides he's "inner-directed."

Sonny thinks of little but women. He has a loyal high school girlfriend named, ominously, Buddy (Amy Locane). She's reliable, cheerful, friendly, and sexually available (too available for the 1950s period, I think). Sonny's mother (Jill Clayburgh) enthusiastically promotes marriage, while his father (John Lordan) speaks approvingly of the excellent pension plan at Eli Lilly.

But Sonny doesn't want to get married or go to work for the local pharmaceutical corporation. He wants to wrap his arms around a woman who can fuel his skin magazine–inspired fantasies—like Gunner's sexpot mom (Lesley Ann Warren), for example, or Gayle Ann Thayer (Rose McGowan), the best friend of Gunner's sexy new Jewish girlfriend Marty

Pilcher (Rachel Weisz). Gunner's mother, who obviously has incestuous feelings for her son, is jealous of Marty and feeds her son vile anti-Semitic fantasies, but Gunner is his own man and chooses his own course in life.

Not so with Sonny, who is impotent with the women he desires and finds Buddy boring even though, therefore, he can perform with her. During the course of a long summer, it becomes clear to Gunner and Sonny that their future lies outside Indianapolis—lies, instead, amid the gleaming towers of Manhattan, where they will find glory, fame, and lotsa women.

Going All the Way is a deeper, more clever film than it first seems. Much of its strength depends on the imploding performance of Jeremy Davies, who swallows his words, ducks his head, squirms away from parental domination, and vaguely knows he must escape home for his own survival. (It says everything that he still has baseball trading cards tacked to the headboard of his bed, and hides his skin magazines in the boxes of his childhood board games.) I'm a decade younger than the characters in this movie, but I grew up in a time and place not far from the film's psychic setting. I recognized much. And here I am, amid the gleaming towers of Chicago.

Good Burger ★ ★

PG, 94 m., 1997

Kel Mitchell (Ed), Kenan Thompson (Dexter Reed), Sinbad (Mr. Wheat), Abe Vigoda (Otis), Shar Jackson (Monique), Dan Schneider (Mr. Bailey), Jan Schwieterman (Kurt Bozwell), Ron Lester (Spatch). Directed by Brian Robbins and produced by Mike Tollin, Robbins, Heath Seifert, and Kevin Kopelow. Screenplay by Dan Schneider and Kopelow.

Good Burger was not made for me, and if I say I didn't much enjoy it, that wouldn't be useful information. The movie was made for daytime viewers of Nickelodeon, and it's a spin-off from a character first seen in the cable channel's *All That* comedy series—Ed, a fast-food worker whose life and dreams are dominated by his love for his work, and whose catchphrase, "Welcome to Good Burger," is as well known to kids as "Where's the beef?" is at the other end of the age spectrum. The movie's stars, Kel Mitchell and Kenan Thompson, also appear on another Nickelodeon series, *Kenan and Kel*.

Good Burger is a small, independent burger stand in the middle of a vague urban landscape (I'm not even sure what state it's supposed to be in—California, probably). Ed (Mitchell) is the counter guy, and he's made the position behind the cash register into his personal sacred ground; when he's late to work the whole operation is paralyzed. As the movie opens, he gets a new coworker named Dexter (Thompson), who desperately needs to earn money because he was driving without a license and crashed into a car much beloved by his teacher, Mr. Wheat (Sinbad).

Dexter was not born to work at the fast-food trade, but he and Ed become good friends, and some of Ed's spirit rubs off. Then a crisis strikes: A gargantuan Mondo Burger stand is opened right across the street. With its towers and searchlights, it looks vaguely like the 20th Century-Fox logo, and it's managed by a neo-Nazi named Kurt (Jan Schwieterman), who predicts Good Burger will soon be history.

The plot involves Ed saving the Good Burger stand by inventing a secret sauce, and Kurt scheming to get his hands on it; meanwhile Ed and Dexter become pals with Otis (Abe Vigoda), arguably the world's oldest fast-food employee, who through a series of mishaps must be rescued from the Demented Hills Asylum. There's also a sweet little romantic subplot involving Monique (Shar Jackson), who has a crush on Ed—to no avail, since burgers are his life. Among the supporting characters is Spatch (Ron Lester), who likes to squash flies on his forehead.

Kel Mitchell, as Ed, provides the heart of the movie, creating an asexual otherworldly character who is protected by his strangeness. Asked "How does ten bucks sound to you?" he crumples the bill next to his ear to find out. Asked "You know what would look great on these corn dogs?" he replies, "A turtleneck?" He wears his Good Burger hat at all times, even in the shower, and at one point thinks it makes him look like a nurse. It's impossible not to like him.

But to understand this movie on its intended level, it's necessary, I think, to be between four and eleven years old and know about the characters from TV. The movie is innocent, good-hearted, colorful, and energetic, but it doesn't have the kind of sophistication that allowed the Pee-wee Herman movies to break out of their primary kiddie audiences and appeal to adult viewers. It's a kid movie, plain and simple. It didn't do much for me, but I am prepared to predict that its target audience will have a good time. I'm giving it two stars. If I were eight, I might give it more.

Goodbye, Lover ★

R, 102 m., 1999

Patricia Arquette (Sandra), Dermot Mulroney (Jake), Don Johnson (Ben), Mary-Louise Parker (Peggy), Ellen DeGeneres (Detective Rita Pompano), Ray McKinnon (Detective Rollins). Directed by Roland Joffe and produced by Arnon Milchan. Screenplay by Ron Peer, Joel Cohen, and Alec Sokolow.

I've just transcribed no less than eleven pages of notes I scribbled during *Goodbye, Lover,* and my mind boggles. The plot is so labyrinthine that I'd completely forgotten the serial killer named The Doctor, who murders young women by injecting curare into their veins with a syringe. When a character like The Doctor is an insignificant supporting character, a movie's plate is a little too full, don't you think?

Goodbye, Lover is not so much a story as some kind of a board game, with too many pieces and not enough rules. The characters careen through the requirements of the plot, which has so many double-reverses that the real danger isn't murder, it's being disemboweled by G-forces. There's no way to care about the characters, because their fates are arbitrary—determined not by character, not by personality, but by the jigsaw puzzle constructed by the screenwriters (there are three of them—which, for this material, represents a skeleton crew).

And yet the film does have a certain audacity. It contains a character played by Patricia Arquette who is the most enthusiastic sexual being since Emmanuelle, and another, played by Don Johnson, who just plain gets tuckered out by her demands. (At one point, they've taken the collection in church and are walking down the aisle with the offering, and she's whispering that he should meet her for sex tomorrow, or else.) There's also a droll supporting role for Ellen DeGeneres, as a police detective who keeps picking on her partner, a Mormon man who doesn't, I hope, understand most of her jokes. One of her key clues comes with the discovery of a *Sound of Music* tape, which arouses her suspicions: "I don't trust anybody over the age of ten who listens to 'The Sound of Music.'"

The movie opens with phone sex and never looks back. We meet Sandra (Arquette), a Realtor who memorizes Tony Robbins self-help tapes, treasures *The Sound of Music* as her favorite movie, and likes to whisper, "I'm not wearing any underwear." She is having an affair with Ben (Johnson), and at one point handcuffs him with some sex toys she finds in a house she's selling. When the clients return unexpectedly, poor Ben barely has time to release himself and hide the cuffs in his pants pocket. (The Foley artists, concerned that we may have missed the point, cause the cuffs to rattle deafeningly, as if Ben had a tambourine concealed in his underwear.)

Sandra is married to Jake (Dermot Mulroney), who is Ben's brother. Ben is the straight arrow who runs an ad agency, and Jake is the unkempt alcoholic who nevertheless is a brilliant copywriter. Why is Sandra cheating on Jake? The answer is not only more complicated than you might think—it's not even the real answer. This is one of those plots where you might want to take a night school class about double-indemnity clauses in insurance policies before you even think about buying a ticket.

My space is limited, but I must also mention the GOP senator who is caught with a transvestite hustler; the struggle on the condo balcony; the motorcycle-car chase; the sex scene in a church's organ loft; the black leather mask; the Vegas wedding chapel ploy; Mike, the professional killer (not to be confused with The Doctor); and Peggy, Ben's secretary, who is played by Mary-Louise Parker as the kind of woman who would be a nymphomaniac in any other movie, but compared to Sandra is relatively abstentious.

There is a part of me that knows this movie is very, very bad. And another part of me that takes a guilty pleasure in it. Too bad I saw it at a critic's screening, where professional courtesy requires a certain decorum. This is the kind of movie that might be materially improved by frequent hoots of derision. All bad movies have good twins, and the good version of *Goodbye, Lover* is *The Hot Spot* (1990), which also starred Don Johnson, along with Virginia Madsen and Jennifer Connelly, in a thriller that was equally lurid but less hyperkinetic. *Goodbye, Lover* is so overwrought it reminds me of the limerick about that couple from Khartoum, who argued all night, about who had the right, to do what, and with which, and to whom.

Good Will Hunting ★★★

R, 125 m., 1997

Matt Damon (Will), Robin Williams (Sean McGuire), Ben Affleck (Chuckie), Minnie Driver (Skylar), Stellan Skarsgard (Lambeau), John Mighton (Tom), Rachel Majowski (Krystyn), Colleen McCauley (Cathy), Casey Affleck (Morgan), Cole Hauser (Billy). Directed by Gus Van Sant Jr. and produced by Lawrence Bender. Screenplay by Matt Damon and Ben Affleck.

It must be heartbreaking to be able to appreciate true genius, and yet fall just short of it yourself. A man can spend his entire life studying to be a mathematician—and yet watch helplessly while a high school dropout, a janitor, scribbles down the answers to questions the professor is baffled by. It's also heartbreaking when genius won't recognize itself, and that's the most baffling problem of all in *Good Will Hunting*, the smart, involving story of a working-class kid from Boston.

The film stars Matt Damon as a janitor at MIT, who likes to party and hang around the old neighborhood, and whose reading consists of downloading the contents of whole libraries into his photographic memory. Stellan Skarsgard (the husband in *Breaking the Waves*) plays Lambeau, the professor, who offers a prize to any student who can solve a difficult problem. The next morning, the answer is written on a blackboard standing in the hall.

Who claims credit? None of the students do. A few days later, Lambeau catches Will Hunting (Damon) at the board, and realizes he's the author—a natural mathematical genius who can intuitively see through the thorniest problems. Lambeau wants to help Will, to get him into school, maybe, or collaborate with him—but before that can take place, Will and some buddies are cruising the old neighborhood and beat up a guy. Will also hammers on the cops a little and is jailed.

He's a tough nut. He sees nothing wrong with spending his whole life hanging out with his friends, quaffing a few beers, holding down a blue-collar job. He sees romance in being an honest bricklayer, but none in being a professor of mathematics—maybe because bricklaying is work, and, for him, math isn't.

Good Will Hunting is the story of how this kid's life edges toward self-destruction, and how four people try to haul him back. One is Lambeau, who gets probation for Will with a promise that he'll find him help and counseling. One is Sean McGuire (Robin Williams), Lambeau's college roommate, now a junior college professor who has messed up his own life, but is a gifted counselor. One is Skylar (Minnie Driver), a British student at Harvard who falls in love with Will and tries to help him. And one is Chuckie (Ben Affleck), Will's friend since childhood, who tells him: "You're sitting on a winning lottery ticket. It would be an insult to us if you're still around here in twenty years."

True, but Will doesn't see it that way. His reluctance to embrace the opportunity at MIT is based partly on class pride (it would be betraying his buddies and the old neighborhood) and partly on old psychic wounds. And it is only through breaking through to those scars and sharing some of his own that McGuire, the counselor, is able to help him. Robin Williams gives one of his best performances as McGuire, especially in a scene where he finally gets the kid to repeat, "It's not my fault."

Good Will Hunting perhaps found some of

its inspiration in the lives of its makers. The movie was cowritten by Damon and Affleck, who did grow up in Boston, who are childhood friends, and who both took youthful natural talents and used them to find success as actors. It's tempting to find parallels between their lives and the characters—and tempting, too, to watch the scenes between Damon and Driver with the knowledge that they fell in love while making the movie.

The Will Hunting character is so much in the foreground that it's easy to miss a parallel relationship: Lambeau and McGuire are also old friends, who have fought because of old angers and insecurities. In a sense, by bringing the troubled counselor and the troublesome janitor together, the professor helps to heal both of them.

The film has a good ear for the way these characters might really talk. It was directed by Gus Van Sant *(Drugstore Cowboy, To Die For)*, who sometimes seems to have perfect pitch when it comes to dialogue; look at the scene where Matt and Skylar break up and say hurtful things, and see how clear he makes it that Matt is pushing her away because he doesn't think he deserves her.

The outcome of the movie is fairly predictable; so is the whole story, really. It's the individual moments, not the payoff, that makes it so effective. *Good Will Hunting* has been rather inexplicably compared to *Rainman*, although *Rainman* was about an autistic character who cannot and does not change, and *Good Will Hunting* is about a genius who can change, and grow, if he chooses to. True, they can both do quick math in their heads. But Will Hunting is not an idiot savant or some kind of lovable curiosity; he's a smart man who knows he's smart but pulls back from challenges because he was beaten down once too often as a child.

I'm writing this review just after hearing remarks by friends of the late comedian Chris Farley, by friends who tried to help him and failed. *Good Will Hunting* knows how that goes. Here is a character who has four friends who all love him and want to help him, and he's threatened by their help because it means abandoning all of his old, sick, dysfunctional defense mechanisms. As Louis Armstrong once said, "There's some folks, that, if they don't know, you can't tell 'em." This movie is about whether Will is one of those folks.

The Governess ★ ★ ★

R, 114 m., 1998

Minnie Driver (Rosina da Silva), Tom Wilkinson (Charles Cavendish), Florence Hoath (Clementina), Jonathan Rhys Meyers (Henry), Harriet Walter (Mrs. Cavendish), Arlene Cockburn (Lily Milk). Directed by Sandra Goldbacher and produced by Sarah Curtis. Screenplay by Goldbacher.

The Governess could be an illustration of the ideas in Virginia Woolf's *A Room of One's Own*, in which she marvels at how necessary it is for men to have women to feel superior to. The film tells the story of an educated, spirited Jewish girl from London who, in the 1840s, finds work as a governess on a remote Scottish island to support her family. She enters a household where she is clearly the intellectual equal of the father, and that is more than he can take—although he gives it a good try.

Minnie Driver, grave and thoughtful between moments of high spirits and passion, plays Rosina, who grew up in a Sephardic Jewish community in London. Her family life is richly cultured, but almost entirely cut off from the gentile world around her, and anti-Semitism is a fact of life. When her father dies, she hopes to help her mother and sister, but there are few professions open to her; it was a truism much beloved of Victorian novelists that a single woman in her position had three choices: marriage, domestic service, or prostitution.

She takes the middle choice, and to sidestep discrimination renames herself Mary Blackchurch, a Protestant whose part-Italian ancestry explains her olive skin. She is hired by the Cavendish family of Scotland as a governess for their unpleasant little girl Clementina. The father (Tom Wilkinson) is a man obsessed with the new science of photography, and spends long hours in his studio and darkroom, as indeed anyone married to his ignorant and controlling wife (Harriet Walter) would have great inspiration to do. There is also a teenage boy, Henry (Jonathan Rhys Meyers), who falls instantly into lust for "Mary," perhaps the first attractive girl he has seen.

The governess is fascinated by Cavendish's photography—both the artistic side and the technical problem of fixing images so they do not fade. She spends long hours in his company and they are drawn together, she by a healthy interest in a smart and virile man, he struggling with the mossy ropes of Protestant guilt. Photography is the instrument of their mutual seduction; she insists on posing for him, her image on the negative a way of forcing him to see her as a woman and not just a servant.

The film was written and directed by Sarah Goldbacher, who is, I understand, the child of an Italian Jewish father and a mother born on the very island where the film was shot. Although she sets the story at an earlier time in which all tensions and questions would have been heightened, there is no doubt some autobiography here, especially in her character's determination to remain privately true to her Jewish heritage. Her affair with Cavendish is given additional irony by the likelihood that he would scorn her if he knew she was Jewish.

Minnie Driver is an actress who creates the illusion of eroticism, not through appearance but through behavior. She is of course physically attractive, but that isn't the point: Her characters have a way of focusing on men, on paying them observant attention that causes them to grow a little squirmy, and that's a sexy phenomenon. Many male actors feel that their task in romantic scenes is to seem powerful, attractive, and in charge, when in fact those are precisely the qualities that obscure what effect, if any, the woman has on them. Tom Wilkinson (the proud foreman in *The Full Monty* and the outraged Marquese of Queensbury in *Wilde*) shows Cavendish attracted to this young woman despite his own best efforts, and that is ever so much more erotic than a confident seduction.

Photography provides the counterpoint: Their dance of attraction begins at arm's length through the pictures they take of one another. The claustrophobic, isolated Victorian household is a stage on which every nuance, however small, is noticed. And there are rich underlying ironies, not least that by denying their assigned places in society (he as a husband, she as a Jew), they are able for a time to function freely just as two people happy to be together in mind and body.

Gravesend ★★

R, 85 m., 1997

Tony Tucci (Zane), Michael Parducci (Ray), Tom Malloy (Chicken), Tom Brandise (Mikey), Macky Aquilino (Jo-Jo). Directed and produced by Salvatore Stabile. Screenplay by Stabile.

"I'm proud of where I came from," the narrator of *Gravesend* tells us near the end of the film. Since he has shown us not one single thing to be proud of, I can only assume he's setting us up for the sequel. The movie's characters are stupid and brutish, and spend their nights getting into fights every fifteen minutes, possibly because they can think of nothing else to do.

Gravesend, we learn, is a Brooklyn neighborhood, little known because its residents "usually claim to be from Bensonhurst or Coney Island." I have no doubt that many of its streets and people are delightful, but such delights have been denied us by the writer-director of the film, Salvatore Stabile, who wants to share a memory of the night that four of his buddies somehow wound up with three bodies in the trunk of their car, and that was only for starters.

There are possibilities for humor here, and rich characters. I am reminded of movies like *New Jersey Drive, Straight Out of Brooklyn, Spike of Bensonhurst,* and *True Love.* But the lives of these four friends are lived at a monotonous level; they lack the words and perhaps the concepts for pastimes more challenging than drinking, smoking dope, holding aimless arguments, and getting into meaningless fights. Even *this* material could be made amusing, but not here, where the characters seem to circle in loops of their own devising.

And yet *Gravesend* has good things to be said about it, and the most astonishing is that it was made for a reported $5,000, which is $3,000 less than the previous record holder,

Robert Rodriguez, spent on *El Mariachi.* Stabile made the film when he was nineteen, found backers to put up postproduction cash, and impressed so many people with his raw talent that *Gravesend* is "An Oliver Stone Presentation" and the director, now twenty-two, has two projects under contract with Steven Spielberg.

Stabile probably has good films in him. *Gravesend,* made with limited resources, shows that. It also gives hints of the ways he'll be able to find humor in tough characters. The most entertaining performance in the movie is by Macky Aquilino, as Jo-Jo the junkie, a janitor and drug dealer who the four friends ask for a favor: They need to dispose of a body. His price, after negotiation: "$500, and a thumb."

Cars with bodies in their trunks tend to attract trouble in the movies, and Stabile has fun with a tow-truck operator and a cop, who both want to get their hands on the car. He also writes in a lot of unsuccessful Tarantinoesque dialogue, including arguments about math problems and lottery odds, and whether Walter Cronkite or Hugh Downs is the host of *20/20.* There are flashes of life here, a feeling of immediacy in the camera style, a lot of energy—and promise. But not yet the movie he's probably capable of; I have a feeling anyone with the wit to make a movie for $5,000 can write characters more worth knowing than these.

Grease ★ ★ ★

PG, 112 m., 1978 (rereleased 1998)

John Travolta (Danny), Olivia Newton-John (Sandy), Stockard Channing (Rizzo), Jeff Conaway (Kenickie), Barry Pearl (Doody), Michael Tucci (Sonny), Kelly Ward (Putzie), Didi Conn (Frenchy). Directed by Randal Kleiser and produced by Robert Stigwood and Allan Carr. Screenplay by Bronte Woodard, based on the original musical by Jim Jacobs and Warren Casey.

Grease, a 1970s celebration of nostalgia for the 1950s, is now being resurrected as 1970s nostalgia. But no revival, however joyously promoted, can conceal the fact that this is just an average musical, pleasant and upbeat and plastic.

The musical is being revived not because it is invaluable, but because it contains an invaluable cultural icon: the singing, dancing performance of John Travolta. It is now clear that, slumps or not, comebacks or not, Travolta is an important and enduring movie star whose presence can redeem even a compromised *Grease.* This is not one of his great films, and lacks the electricity of *Saturday Night Fever* or the quirky genius of *Pulp Fiction,* but it has charm. If Travolta lacks the voltage of Elvis Presley (his obvious role model for this film), at least he's in the same ballpark, and Elvis didn't make such great movies, either.

The story, smoothed out and set in southern California, involves a greaser named Danny (Travolta) who has a sweet summertime romance with Sandy, an Australian girl (Olivia Newton-John; making her character Australian was easier than coaching her American accent). When summer ends, they part forever, they think, only to find themselves at the same school, where Danny's tough-guy image makes it hard for him to acknowledge the squeaky-clean Sandy.

The film re-creates a 1950s that exists mostly in idyllic memory (for an alternative version, see *Rebel Without a Cause*). There are hot rods, malt shops, school dances, songs from the original Jim Jacobs and Warren Casey musical, and new songs, written to fit the characters. It's fun, yes, but it doesn't lift off the screen; the only element that bears comparison with the musicals of the Golden Age is Travolta's performance, although in the 1950s at MGM he would have been best friend, not star.

One problem I always have watching the movie is that all the students look too old. They're supposed to be sixteen or seventeen, I guess, but they look in their late twenties, and don't seem comfortable as teenagers. One of my favorite performances is by Stockard Channing, as Rizzo, the tough girl who forges ahead heedlessly after the condom breaks. She's fun, but were there sixteen-year-old girls like that in the 1950s? Call me a dreamer, but I don't think so.

The movie's worth seeing for nostalgia, or for a look at vintage Travolta, but its underlying problem is that it sees the material as silly camp: It neuters it. Romance and breaking up are matters of life and death for teenagers, and a crisis of self-esteem can be a crushing burden. *Grease* doesn't seem to remember that. *Saturday Night Fever* does.

Great Expectations ★ ★ ★

R, 111 m., 1998

Ethan Hawke (Finnegan Bell), Gwyneth Paltrow (Estella), Anne Bancroft (Ms. Dinsmoor), Hank Azaria (Walter Plane), Chris Cooper (Joe), Robert De Niro (Prisoner/Lustig), Josh Mostel (Jerry Ragno). Directed by Alfonso Cuaron and produced by Art Linson. Screenplay by Mitch Glazer, based on a novel by Charles Dickens.

This is not, says Finn, the way the story really happened, but the way he remembers it. That is how everyone tells the stories that matter to them: Through their own eyes, rewritten by their own memories, with bold underscores for the parts that hurt. Finn's story is the life of a poor boy who falls in love with a rich girl who has been trained since childhood to break the hearts of men.

This tale has been borrowed from Charles Dickens's *Great Expectations,* where it is told in less lurid images and language, to be sure, but with the same sense of an innocent boy being lured into the lair of two dangerous women. That the women are lonely, sad, and good at heart makes it bittersweet. "What is it like not to feel anything?" Finn shouts at Estella after she has abandoned him. Of course, if you cannot feel anything, that is exactly the question you cannot answer.

The story has been updated by director Alfonso Cuaron, who moves it from Victorian England to a crumbling neo-Gothic mansion in Florida. It stars Ethan Hawke as Finn (Pip in the book), and Gwyneth Paltrow as Estella, the beautiful niece of the eccentric millionairess Ms. Dinsmoor (Anne Bancroft). Their paths cross in one of those backwaters of Florida that have been immortalized by writers like Elmore Leonard and John D. MacDonald, where creeping condos from the north have not yet dislodged small fishing shacks and the huge masonry pile of Paradiso Perduto, which once was a glittering showplace but is now engulfed in trees and creepers, and falling into decay.

Finn lives with his sister Maggie and "her man," Joe (Chris Cooper), who raises him after Maggie disappears. One day he is seen by Ms. Dinsmoor, who invites him to Paradiso Perduto to play with her niece. The two children are about ten. Finn is a gifted artist, and as he sketches the young girl, the old crone perceives that he will eventually fall in love with the girl, and sees her chance for revenge against men.

The original of Ms. Dinsmoor is, of course, Dickens's Miss Havisham, one of the most colorful and pathetic characters in Dickens, who was left stranded on her wedding day by a faithless lover. This version of *Great Expectations* spares us the sight of her wedding cake, covered in cobwebs after the decades (in Florida, tiny visitors would make short work of that feast). But it succeeds in making Ms. Dinsmore equally sad and venomous, and Anne Bancroft's performance is interesting: Despite the weird eye makeup and the cigarettes, despite the flamboyant clothing, she is human, and not without humor. "That's the biggest cat I've ever seen," Finn says on his first visit. "What do you feed it?" She waits for a beat. "Other cats," she says.

Paradiso Perduto and its inhabitants reminded me of *Grey Gardens,* the 1976 documentary about two relatives of Jackie Onassis, who lived in a decaying mansion in East Hampton with countless cats. There is the same sense of defiance: If I was once young, rich, and beautiful, these women say to the world, see what you have made of me! Cuaron, whose previous film was *The Little Princess,* brings a touch of magic realism to the setting, with weeping willows, skies filled with seabirds, and a scene where Finn and Estella dance to "Besame Mucho" while Ms. Dinsmore looks on, cold-eyed.

Time passes. The young actors who played Finn and Estella are replaced by Hawke and Paltrow, who meet again at the mansion after several years, and share a sudden kiss at a water fountain, which is cut between backlit shots from moving cameras so that it seems more orgiastic than most sex scenes. After this romantic spark Estella again dances away, and the story continues some years later in New

York, where a mysterious benefactor offers to bankroll Finn's show at an important gallery, and Estella again appears on the scene, this time with a hapless fiancé/victim named Walter in tow.

Great Expectations begins as a great movie (I was spellbound by the first thirty minutes), but ends as only a good one, and I think that's because the screenplay, by Mitch Glazer, too closely follows the romantic line. Dickens, who of course had more time and space to move around in, made it the story of a young man's coming of age, and the colorful characters he encountered—from the escaped prisoner of the opening scenes (played here by Robert De Niro) to good old, proud old Joe. The moment this movie declares itself as being mostly about affairs of the heart, it limits its potential.

And yet the film is a successful translation of the basic material from one period and approach to another. Especially in the early Florida scenes, it seems timeless. Hawke and Paltrow project that uneasy alertness of two people who know they like one another and suspect they'll regret it. But the subplot involving the escaped prisoner doesn't really pay off (it feels more like a bone thrown to Dickens than a necessity of the plot). And I am not quite sure that any good artist can create only when he's in sync with the girl of his dreams: Some artists paint best when their hearts are broken, and most artists paint no matter what, because they have to.

Great Expectations doesn't finish at the same high level that it begins (if it did, it would be one of the year's best films), but it's visually enchanted; the cinematographer, Emmanuel Lubezki, uses lighting and backlighting like a painter. And the characters have more depth and feeling than we might expect in what is, underneath everything, a fantasy. There's great joy in a scene where Finn sweeps Estella out of a restaurant and asks her to dance. And sadness later as she observes that Ms. Dinsmore's obsessions have become her own.

Gridlock'd ★ ★ ★

R, 91 m., 1997

Tim Roth (Stretch), Tupac Shakur (Spoon), Thandie Newton (Cookie), Charles Fleischer (Mr. Woodson), Howard Hesseman (Blind Man), Elizabeth Pena (ER Nurse), James Pickens Jr. (Supervisor), John Sayles (Cop 1), Eric Payne (Cop 2), Tom Towles (D-Reper's Henchman), Tom Wright (Koolaid). Directed by Vondie Curtis Hall and produced by Damian Jones, Paul Webster, and Erica Huggins. Screenplay by Hall.

It is possible to imagine *Gridlock'd* as a movie of despair and desperation, but that would involve imagining it without Tupac Shakur and Tim Roth, who illuminate it with a gritty, goofy comic spirit. This is grim material, but surprisingly entertaining, and it is more cause to mourn the death of Shakur, who gives his best performance as Spoon, a musician who wants to get off drugs.

Spoon and his friend Stretch (Roth) arrive at this decision after rushing Spoon's girlfriend, Cookie (Thandie Newton), to an emergency room, comatose after a drug overdose. The three of them have a jazz trio. Ironically, she's the clean liver, always eating veggieburgers and preaching against smoking. While Cookie hovers in critical condition, Spoon and Stretch spend a very long day trying to find a rehab program they can turn themselves in to.

The heart of the movie is their banter, the grungy dialogue that puts an ironic spin on their anger and fear. Tim Roth is a natural actor, relaxed in his roles, with a kind of quixotic bemusement at life's absurdities. Shakur matches that and adds an earnestness: In their friendship, Spoon is the leader and thinker, and Stretch is the sidekick who will go along with whatever's suggested. It's Spoon who decides to kick, telling his friend (in a line that now has dark undertones), "Lately I feel like my luck's been running out."

Writer-director Vondie Curtis Hall, making his directing debut after a TV acting career on *Chicago Hope* and other shows, combines the hard-edged, in-your-face realism of street life with a conventional story that depends on stock characters: evil drug dealers, modern Keystone Kops, colorful eccentrics. The movie isn't as powerful as it could have been, but it's probably more fun: This is basically a comedy, even if sometimes you ask yourself why you're laughing.

That's especially true in a scene that moviegoers will be quoting for years. Spoon, desperate to get into an emergency room and begin detox, convinces Stretch to stab him. As the two friends discuss how to do it (and try to remember which side of the body the liver is on), there are echoes of the overdose sequence in *Pulp Fiction.* What Tarantino demonstrated is that with the right dialogue and actors you can make anything funny.

The daylong duel with the drug dealers and the encounters with suspicious cops work like comic punctuation. In between is the real life of the movie: the friendship of the two men and their quest to get into rehab. They circle endlessly through a series of Detroit social welfare agencies that could have been designed by Kafka: They find they can't get medicards without being on welfare, can't get into detox without filling out forms and waiting ten days, can't get into a rehab center because it's for alkys only, can't get the right forms because an office has moved, can't turn in the forms because an office is about to close. If this movie reflects real life in Detroit, it's as if the city deliberately plots to keep addicts away from help.

In movies about stupid bureaucracies, the heroes inevitably blow up and start screaming at the functionaries behind the counters. Hall's script wickedly turns the tables: The clerks shout at Spoon and Stretch. Elizabeth Pena plays an ER nurse who maddeningly makes them fill out forms while Cookie seems to be dying. When Spoon screams at her, she screams back, in a monologue that expresses all of her exhaustion and frustration. Later, at a welfare center, an overworked clerk shouts back: "Yeah, we all been waiting for the day you come through that door and tell us you're ready not to be a drug fiend. After five, ten years, you decide this is the day, and the world stops for you?"

This material is so good I wish we'd had more of it. Maybe Hall, aiming for a wider audience, hedged his bets by putting in scenes where the heroes, the drug dealers, and the cops chase each other on foot and in cars around downtown Detroit. Those scenes aren't plausible and they're not about anything.

Much better are the moments when the two friends sit, exhausted, under a mural of the great outdoors, and talk about how they simply lack the energy to keep on using drugs. Or when Spoon remembers his first taste of cocaine in high school: "I didn't even know what it was. Everybody else was throwin' up. But for me it was like going to the Moon." Or when they watch daytime TV and do a running commentary. Or when they're almost nabbed for a murder they didn't commit.

Still, maybe Hall made the smart bet by positioning this story halfway between real life and a crime comedy. The world of these streets and tenements and hospitals and alleys is strung out and despairing, and the human comedy redeems it. By the time a guy is trying to help his friend by stabbing him, we understand well enough what drugs will lead you to. For the premiere audience at the Sundance Film Festival, *Gridlock'd* played like a comedy, with big laughter. Too bad Tupac couldn't be there.

Grosse Pointe Blank ★ ★ ½

R, 106 m., 1997

John Cusack (Martin Q. Blank), Minnie Driver (Debi Newberry), Alan Arkin (Dr. Oatman), Dan Aykroyd (Mr. Grocer), Joan Cusack (Marcella), Jeremy Piven (Paul Spericki), Hank Azaria (Lardner), Barbara Harris (Mary Blank). Directed by George Armitage and produced by Susan Arnold, Donna Arkoff Roth, and Roger Birnbaum. Screenplay by Tom Jankiewicz, D. V. DeVincentis, Steve Pink,and John Cusack, based on a story by Jankiewicz.

John Cusack is one of those rare actors who can convincingly look as if he is thinking about words of many syllables. He seems smart, and that's crucial for the character he plays in *Grosse Pointe Blank,* because like so many really smart people this one is clueless about matters of the heart. Cusack plays Martin Q. Blank, a professional assassin who is more articulate while discussing his kills with a shrink than while explaining to his high school sweetheart why he stood her up at the prom.

As the movie opens, he's preparing to do a job with a high-powered rifle, while simultaneously discussing his busy schedule with his office manager (played by his sister, Joan Cusack). She thinks he should attend his tenth high school reunion in the Detroit suburb of Grosse Pointe, Michigan. He thinks not. He misses on the assassination attempt, however, and that leads to an interesting coincidence: He can redeem himself by pulling a job in Detroit—killing two birds, so to speak, with one stone.

He discusses his plight with his psychiatrist (Alan Arkin), a man alarmed to learn he has a hit man for a client. "I don't think what a person does for a living is necessarily who he is," Blank observes reassuringly, but the shrink gives the impression of a man constantly holding himself in readiness to take a bullet.

Cusack plays Blank as a man who entered his chosen profession with good skills and high spirits, but is now beginning to entertain doubts about its wisdom as a lifelong career. He has no qualms about killing people (someone has to do it, and as a character in the film observes, it's a "growth industry"). But for him, it's getting to be the same old same old. Against his better judgment, he caves in and heads for Michigan.

Grosse Pointe may hold the key to why Martin's life seems on hold. Unfinished business waits for him there: a woman named Debi (Minnie Driver), whom he loved in high school, but stood up at the senior prom. Tooling through town in a rented car, he hears her voice on the radio and is soon peering through the window of the local radio station. She's a DJ, who smoothly segues into asking her listeners how she should feel when her prom date turns up ten years late.

Another major player in Martin's life is Mr. Grocer (Dan Aykroyd), also a professional assassin, who wants Martin to join a union he is forming: "We could be working together again, for chrissakes! Making big money! Killing important people!" He is also in Grosse Pointe, possibly on the same assignment, and soon Blank and Grocer are seated uneasily across from one another at a diner, both armed and both dangerous, mostly to one another.

The film takes the form but not the feel of a comic thriller. It's quirkier than that. The underlying plot, which also involves Martin being shadowed by assorted mysterious types who want to kill him, is not original. But the screenplay, by Cusack, Tom Jankiewicz, and others, uses that story as a backdrop for Martin Blank's wry behavior. It's not often that a film about professional killers has a high school reunion dance as its centerpiece, and rarer still that the hero kills someone during the dance and disposes of the body in the school boiler.

I enjoyed the exchanges between Cusack and Driver, as the couple on a long-delayed date. Affection still smolders between them, and it was sexy the way Driver casually put an arm around Cusack's shoulders, her hand resting possessively on the back of his neck. I liked the dialogue, too, and the assortment of classmates they encounter; have you ever noticed that whatever odd qualities your friends had in school seem to grow as the years go by?

Despite these qualities, the movie for me is a near miss. One of the problems is the conclusion, in which things are resolved with an elaborate action sequence. This sequence may have been intended ironically, but the gunshots are just as loud as if they were sincere. Too many movies end like video games, with characters popping up and shooting each other. *Grosse Pointe Blank*, which takes such a detached view toward killing and has such an articulate hero, could have done better.

Guantanamera ★ ★ ★

NO MPAA RATING, 104 m., 1997

Carlos Cruz (Adolfo), Mirtha Ibarra (Georgina), Raul Eguren (Candido), Jorge Perugorria (Mariano), Pedro Fernandez (Ramon), Luis Alberto Garcia Novoa (Tony), Conchita Brando (Aunt Yoyita), Suset Perez Malberti (Iku). Directed by Tomas Gutierrez Alea and Juan Carlos Tabio and produced by Gerardo Herrer. Screenplay by Eliseo Alberto Diego, Alea, and Tabio.

Cuba may languish under a bankrupt and dour political system, but it is after all a Caribbean island—filled with life, color, and invention. *Guantanamera* celebrates Cuban paradoxes in a cheeky little comedy about two romances that endure through the years.

This is the last film by Tomas Gutierrez Alea, the sly satirist who insisted he was a loyal Cuban even while making comedies indicating there was a great deal in his native land that he found overripe for improvement. He died while making it; the direction was taken over by his collaborator, the writer Juan Carlos Tabio, and it stars his widow, Mirtha Ibarra.

The film's target is mindless, pigheaded bureaucracy. The weapons it brings to bear against it are romance, sexuality, and irreverence. The film opens in the small town of Guantanamera, where Yoyita, a famous singer (Conchita Brando) has returned to a heroine's welcome after fifty years in Havana. She is reunited with Candido (Raul Eguren), the lover of her youth, and as they gaze upon each other their old love is rekindled—placing too great a stress on poor Yoyita's heart.

The dead singer is the aunt of Georgina (Ibarra), the long-suffering wife of a local bureaucrat named Adolfo (Carlos Cruz). He is a humorless tyrant with a mad scheme for transporting corpses. Instead of putting a dead body into a hearse at this end and taking it out at the other, he believes the body should be transferred to a different vehicle at every provincial border, spreading the petrol costs around. Elementary math suggests that everyone would end up with essentially the same gas bill, but no matter—Adolfo is a zealot backed by the power of his office.

Adolfo, Georgina, and the grieving old Candido set off on a journey to return the body to the family plot, and that provides *Guantanamera* with the excuse for a road comedy that also documents in zestful detail how sanity survives in the everyday life of today's Cuba. As they hit the road, we meet two truck drivers, the womanizing Mariano (Jorge Perugorria) and the devout Ramon (Pedro Fernandez). They pilot a big vehicle over ill-kept rural roads, providing not only a delivery service but also a sort of lifeline; hitchhikers jump on and off, messages are sent, gossip is exchanged, and Mariano has a lover in every hamlet (some of them as devious as he is).

The truck drivers and the mourners encounter one another, and we learn that Mariano was once Georgina's student, when she was a university teacher. She touched his idealism, he inspired her hope, and now circumstances conspire to draw them back into one another's arms—although there are obstacles, such as the buffoon Adolfo, and Mariano's taste for women who are younger and juicer than the sexy but mature Georgina.

There is fascination everywhere in the frames of *Guantanamera.* In the sides and backgrounds of his shots, Alea has made an unwitting (or perhaps a very witting) documentary. We see a poor economy where black markets flourish, where every yard is home to vegetables and chickens, where shops want U.S. dollars instead of Cuban currency, where meaningless paperwork slows every transaction to a crawl—and provides a constant temptation for bribery.

Let's indulge in some idle speculation—a little harmless decoding. Adolfo represents, perhaps, the crushing weight of the socialist bureaucracy. Mariano and Georgina, when they were younger, represented the hope of workers and intellectuals; now, in middle age, they wonder if they can recapture their exhausted idealism. On the road, they are surrounded by the vitality and humor of everyday Cuba. There is hope—if only the country can break loose from its obsession with finding new ways to cart around the cadavers of its past.

H

Habit ★★★

NO MPAA RATING, 112 m., 1997

Larry Fessenden (Sam), Meredith Snaider (Anna), Aaron Beall (Nick), Patricia Coleman (Rae), Heather Woodbury (Liza), Jesse Hartman (Lenny), Marcus A. Miranda (Segundo), Herb Rogers (Slimman), Hart Fessenden (Sam's Dad), Lon Waterford (Mr. Lyons). Written, directed, and edited by Larry Fessenden and produced by Dayton Taylor.

Are we all agreed—all of us except for Anne Rice—that there is no such thing as a vampire? Yes? And yet the children of the darkness prey on our imaginations, and there is something inexplicably erotic about vampirism. *Habit,* a sad and haunting film by Larry Fessenden, is a modern vampire story, or maybe it's not. Maybe, in a way, the hero is drinking his own blood.

Fessenden stars as Sam, an alcoholic whose life is in disrepair. He spends every waking moment drinking, suggesting a drink, or recovering from a drink. His life reflects the discontinuous reality of the advanced alcoholic for whom life is like being in a room where the lights go on and off unexpectedly. He more or less lives in a bar in Greenwich Village, although he has an explanation: "I'm the manager four days a week."

Sam's girlfriend, Liza (Heather Woodbury), has moved out. She's still friendly, but has grown tired of waiting for him to decide to do something about his drinking. His best friend is Nick (Aaron Beall), who wanders around town in a long overcoat, clutching a bottle inside a paper bag and affecting theatrical speech.

One night at a party, very drunk, Sam finds himself talking to an attractive brunette named Anna (Meredith Snaider). She's one of those women who look at you so attentively you feel self-conscious. Anna looks too attractive for Sam, who is missing some front teeth, needs a shave, and is slurring his words. But one thing leads to another, and eventually he finds himself having sex at her hands and waking up in a park in the morning with a bloody lip.

He keeps losing track of Anna, but no matter: She has a way of turning up. Sex with her is great ("It's like having hot milk run through your veins"), but he keeps finding little bites and cuts here and there on his body. And he keeps on drinking. "I'm just not feeling right," he complains. Nick blithely explains that Sam's poor health may be because of "a change in the weather."

Now then. Is Anna a vampire? Or not? Fessenden's movie is a sly exercise in ambiguity. More than one explanation fits all of the events in the film, even those we see with our own eyes. Of all the recent vampire movies *(Interview With the Vampire, The Addiction, Nadja),* this one is the only one to suggest that the powerful symbolism of vampirism could create results even in the absence of causes. You could be killed by vampires even if they do not exist.

The movie is done in a flat, realistic tone that is perfectly suited to the material. Fessenden, Snaider, Beall, and Patricia Coleman (as Nick's girlfriend) are all naturalistic actors who find a convincing everyday tone; Snaider is particularly good at controlling a role that was almost doomed to be overacted. And Woodbury, as the ex-girlfriend, supplies the right note of cool, detached sanity.

I have received a lot of mail from those who feel I need to have David Lynch's *Lost Highway* explained to me. Their explanations are invariably detailed and serenely confident, even though none of them agree. One correspondent, who has obviously never read a single one of my reviews except for *Lost Highway,* lectured me that I should be more open to the experimental and not limit myself to praising formula films. I wrote to him privately in colorful detail; publicly, to him and his kind, I recommend *Habit,* which in the subtlety of its ambiguity reveals *Lost Highway* as an exercise in search of a purpose.

Fessenden, who wrote, directed, acted, and edited this film, is a talent to watch. That he is able to see himself with such objectivity is almost frightening; there is not a shred of ego in his performance. Wandering about the streets, coat flapping open, aimless, sad, drinking without even remembering why, his Sam is an ideal vampire's victim, because he takes so long to catch on. But then, of course, perhaps that's because there is no such thing as a vampire.

Halloween: H2O ★★

R, 92 m., 1998

Jamie Lee Curtis (Laurie/Keri), Michelle Williams (Molly Cartwell), Josh Hartnett (John Tate), Adam Arkin (Will Brennan), Jodi Lyn O'Keefe (Sarah), LL Cool J (Ronnie Jones), Adam Hann-Byrd (Charlie), Joseph Gordon-Levitt (Jimmy Howell), Janet Leigh (Norma), Chris Durand (The Shape). Directed by Steve Miner and produced by John Carpenter, Paul Freeman, and Debra Hill. Screenplay by Robert Zappia and Matt Greenberg.

Notes jotted down while watching *Halloween H2O*:

—Medical science should study Michael Myers, the monster who has made the last two decades a living hell for Laurie Strode. Here is a man who feels no pain. He can take a licking and keep on slicing. In the latest *Halloween* movie he absorbs a blow from an ax, several knife slashes, a rock pounded on the skull, a fall down a steep hillside, and being crushed against a tree by a truck. Whatever he's got, mankind needs it.

—How does Michael Myers support himself in the long years between his slashing outbreaks? I picture him working in a fast-food joint. "He never spoke much, but boy, could he dice those onions!"

—I have often wondered why we hate mimes so much. Many people have such an irrational dislike for them that they will cross the street rather than watch some guy in whiteface pretending to sew his hands together. Examining Michael Myers's makeup in *Halloween H2O,* I realized he looks so much like Marcel Marceau as to make no difference. Maybe he is a mime when he's not slashing. Maybe what drove him mad was years and years of trying to make a living in malls while little kids kicked him to see if he was real. This would also explain his ability to seem to walk while somehow staying in the same place.

—I happen to know Jamie Lee Curtis is one of the smartest people in Hollywood. I cannot wait for the chapter on horror movies in her autobiography.

—There is a scene in the movie where a kid drops a corkscrew down a garbage disposal. Then the camera goes *inside* the garbage disposal to watch while he fishes around for it. Then the camera cuts to the electric switch on the wall, which would turn the disposal on. I am thinking, if this kid doesn't lose his hand, I want my money back.

—Michael Myers may also have skills as an electrician. All of the lights and appliances in every structure in this movie go on or off whenever the plot requires them to. I can imagine Myers down in the basement by the fuse box, thinking, "Gotta slash somebody. But first . . . geez, whoever filled in the chart on the inside of this fuse box had lousy handwriting! I can't tell the garage door from the garbage disposal!"

—I think Jamie Lee Curtis shouts, "Do as I say!" twice in the movie. I could be low by one.

—Yes, the movie contains the line "They never found a body."

—Michael Myers, described in the credits as "The Shape," is played by Chris Durand. There is hope. Steve McQueen started his career in (but not as) *The Blob.*

—Half of the movie takes place in an exclusive private school, yet there is not a single shower scene.

—Speaking of shower scenes: Janet Leigh, Jamie Lee's mother, turns up in a cameo role here, and she started me thinking about what a rotten crock it is that they're remaking *Psycho.* I imagined Miss Leigh telling her friends, "They wanted me to do a cameo in the remake of *Psycho,* but I said, 'Hell, I'd do *Halloween H2O* before I'd lower myself to that.'"

Hamlet ★★★★

PG-13, 238 m., 1997

Kenneth Branagh (Hamlet), Derek Jacobi (Claudius), Julie Christie (Gertrude), Kate Winslet (Ophelia), Richard Briers (Polonius), Charlton Heston (Player King), Nicholas Farrell (Horatio), Michael Maloney (Laertes), Timothy Spall (Rosencrantz), Reece Dinsdale (Guildenstern), Billy Crystal (First Gravedigger), Gérard Depardieu (Reynaldo), Richard Attenborough (English Ambassador), John

Gielgud (Priam), Robin Williams (Osric), Rosemary Harris (Player Queen), Judi Dench (Hecuba), Jack Lemmon (Marcellus), Brian Blessed (Ghost), John Mills (Old Norway). Directed by Kenneth Branagh and produced by David Barron. Screenplay adapted by Branagh from the play by William Shakespeare.

There is early in Kenneth Branagh's *Hamlet* a wedding celebration, the Danish court rejoicing at the union of Claudius and Gertrude. The camera watches, and then pans to the right to reveal the solitary figure of Hamlet, clad in black. It always creates a little shock in the movies when the foreground is unexpectedly occupied. We realize the subject of the scene is not the wedding, but Hamlet's experience of it. And we enjoy Branagh's visual showmanship: In all of his films, he reveals his joy in theatrical gestures.

His *Hamlet* is long but not slow, deep but not difficult, and it vibrates with the relief of actors who have great things to say and the right ways to say them. And in the 70mm version, it has a visual clarity that is breathtaking. It is the first uncut film version of Shakespeare's most challenging tragedy, the first 70mm film since *Far and Away* in 1992, and at 238 minutes the second-longest major Hollywood production (one minute shorter than *Cleopatra*). Branagh's Hamlet lacks the narcissistic intensity of Laurence Olivier's (in the 1948 Academy Award winner), but the film as a whole is better, placing Hamlet in the larger context of royal politics and making him less a subject for pity.

The story provides a melodramatic stage for inner agonies. Hamlet (Branagh), the prince of Denmark, mourns the untimely death of his father. His mother, Gertrude, rushes with unseemly speed into marriage with Claudius, her husband's brother. Something is rotten in the state of Denmark. And then the ghost of Hamlet's father appears and says he was poisoned by Claudius.

What must Hamlet do? He desires the death of Claudius but lacks the impulse to action. He despises himself for his passivity. In tormenting himself he drives his mother to despair, kills Polonius by accident, speeds the kingdom to chaos, and his love, Ophelia, to madness.

What is intriguing about *Hamlet* is the ambiguity of everyone's motives. Tom Stoppard's *Rosenkrantz and Guildenstern Are Dead* famously filtered all the action through the eyes of Hamlet's treacherous school friends. But how does it all look to Gertrude? To Claudius? To the heartbroken Ophelia? The great benefit of this full-length version is that these other characters become more understandable.

The role of Claudius (Derek Jacobi) is especially enriched: In shorter versions, he is the scowling usurper who functions only as villain. Here, with lines and scenes restored, he seems more balanced and powerful. He might have made a plausible king of Denmark, had things turned out differently. Yes, he killed his brother, but regicide was not unknown in the twelfth century, and perhaps the old king was ripe for replacement; this production shows Gertrude (Julie Christie) as lustfully in love with Claudius. By restoring the original scope of Claudius's role, Branagh emphasizes court and political intrigue instead of enclosing the material in a Freudian hothouse.

The movie's very sets emphasize the role of the throne as the center of the kingdom. Branagh uses costumes to suggest the nineteenth century, and shoots his exteriors at Blenheim Castle, seat of the Duke of Marlborough and Winston Churchill's childhood home. The interior sets, designed by Tim Harvey and Desmond Crowe, feature a throne room surrounded by mirrored walls, overlooked by a gallery, and divided by an elevated walkway. The set puts much of the action onstage (members of the court are constantly observing) and allows for intrigue (some of the mirrors are two-way, and lead to concealed chambers and corridors).

In this very public arena Hamlet agonizes, and is observed. Branagh uses rapid cuts to show others reacting to his words and meanings. And he finds new ways to stage familiar scenes, renewing the material. Hamlet's most famous soliloquy ("To be, or not to be . . .") is delivered into a mirror, so that his own indecision is thrust back at him. When he torments Ophelia, a most private moment, we spy on them from the other side of a two-way mirror; he crushes her cheek against the glass and her frightened breath clouds it. When he comes upon Claudius at his prayers and can kill him, many productions imagine Hamlet lurking behind a pillar in a chapel. Branagh is more intimate, showing a dagger blade insinuating itself through the mesh of a confessional.

One of the surprises of this uncut *Hamlet* is the crucial role of the play within the play. Many productions reduce the visiting troupe of actors to walk-ons; they provide a hook for Hamlet's advice to the players, and merely suggest the performance that Hamlet hopes will startle Claudius into betraying himself. Here, with Charlton Heston magnificently assured as the Player King, we listen to the actual lines of his play (which shorter versions often relegate to dumb-show at the back of the stage). We see how ingeniously and cleverly they tweak the conscience of the king, and we see Claudius's pained reactions. The episode becomes a turning point; Claudius realizes that Hamlet is on to him.

As for Hamlet, Branagh (like Mel Gibson in the 1990 film) has no interest in playing him as an apologetic mope. Branagh is an actor of exuberant physical gifts and energy (when the time comes, his King Lear will bound about the heath). Consider the scene beginning, "Oh, what a rogue and peasant slave am I . . . ," in which Hamlet bitterly regrets his inaction. The lines are delivered not in bewilderment but in mounting anger, and it is to Branagh's credit that he pulls out all the stops; a quieter Hamlet would make a tamer *Hamlet.*

Kate Winslet is touchingly vulnerable as Ophelia, red-nosed and snuffling, her world crumbling about her. Richard Briers makes Polonius not so much a foolish old man as an adviser out of his depth. Of the familiar faces, the surprise is Heston: How many great performances have we lost while he visited the Planet of the Apes? Billy Crystal is a surprise, but effective, as the gravedigger. But Robin Williams, Jack Lemmon, and Gérard Depardieu are distractions, their performances not overcoming our shocks of recognition.

At the end of this *Hamlet,* I felt at last as if I was getting a handle on the play (I never expect to fully understand it). It has been a long journey. I read it in high school, underlining the famous lines. I saw the Richard Burton film version, and later Olivier's. I studied it in graduate school. I have seen it on stage in England and America (most memorably in Aidan Quinn's punk version, when he sprayed graffiti on the wall: "2B=?"). Zeffirelli's version with Gibson came in 1990. I learned from them all.

One of the tasks of a lifetime is to become familiar with the great plays of Shakespeare. *Hamlet* is the most opaque. Branagh's version moved me, entertained me, and made me feel for the first time at home in that doomed royal court. I may not be able to explain *Hamlet,* but at last I have a better idea than Rosencrantz and Guildenstern.

The Hanging Garden ★ ★ ★

R, 98 m., 1998

Chris Leavins (Sweet William), Troy Veinotte (Teenage Sweet William), Kerry Fox (Rosemary), Sarah Polley (Teenage Rosemary), Seana McKenna (Iris), Peter MacNeill (Whiskey Mac), Joe S. Keller (Fletcher), Joan Orenstein (Grace). Directed by Thom Fitzgerald and produced by Louise Garfield, Arnie Gelbart, and Fitzgerald. Screenplay by Fitzgerald.

There is a character named William who appears in *The Hanging Garden* at three different ages: as an eight-year-old who is terrified of his father; as a fat fifteen-year-old; and as a twenty-five-year-old, now thin, who has returned for his sister's wedding. The peculiar thing is that the characters sometimes appear on the screen at the same time, and the dead body of the fifteen-year-old hangs from a tree during many of the scenes.

Well, why not? It may be magic realism, but isn't it also the simple truth? Don't the ghosts of our former selves attend family events right along with our current manifestations? Don't parents still sometimes relate to us as if we were children, don't siblings still carry old resentments, aren't old friends still stuck on who we used to be? And don't we sometimes resurrect old personas and dust them off for a return engagement? Aren't all of those selves stored away inside somewhere?

The movie opens on a wedding day. Rosemary (Kerry Fox, from *An Angel at My Table*), who has already started drinking, struggles with her wedding dress and vows she won't show herself until her brother arrives. Her brother, Sweet William (Chris Leavins), does eventually arrive, late, and is about 150 pounds too light to fit into the tux his mother has rented for him. He was fat when he left home. Now he is thin, and gay. We learn that his first homosexual experience was with Fletcher (Joe S. Keller), the very person Rosemary is planning to marry.

The family also includes Whiskey Mac (Peter MacNeill), the alcoholic patriarch, and Iris (Seana McKenna), the mother, who seems like a rock of stability. It's no accident that all the family members are named for flowers; Whiskey Mac poured all of his love and care into his garden, while brutalizing his family. His treatment of his overweight, gay son led the boy to hang himself in one version of reality, and to run away in another, so that when the twenty-five-year-old returns home the body of the fifteen-year-old is still hanging in the garden.

But I am not capturing the tone of the movie, which is not as macabre and gloomy as this makes it sound, but filled with eccentricity. The family members, who live in Canada's Maritime provinces, have survived by becoming defiantly individual. This is going to be one of those weddings where the guests look on in amazement.

The writer-director, Thom Fitzgerald, moves easily through time, and we meet the teenage version of Sweet William (Troy Veinotte) and Rosemary (Sarah Polley, from *The Sweet Hereafter*) as they form a bond against their father. Fitzgerald never pauses to explain his time-shifts and overlaps, and doesn't need to. Somehow we understand why a 300-pound body could be left hanging from a tree for ten years. It isn't really there, although in another sense, of course, it is.

Like many movies about dysfunctional families, *The Hanging Garden* involves more dysfunction than is perhaps necessary. There is the grandmother, who is senile but still has good enough timing to shout "I do!" out the window at the crucial moment in the marriage. And the tomboy little sister, Violet, who bitterly resents having to be the flower girl. And for all the secrets I have suggested, there are others that will surprise you even at the end—including a great big one that I doubt really proves anything.

The heart of the movie is its insight into the way families are haunted by their own history. How the memory of early unhappiness colors later relationships, and how Sweet William's persecution at the hands of his father hangs in the air as visibly as the corpse in the garden.

The movie is Canadian, and joins a list of other recent Canadian films about dread secrets, including *Exotica*, *The Sweet Hereafter*, and *Kissed*. Although there's a tendency to lump Canadian and American films together into the same cultural pool, the personal, independent films from Canada have a distinctive flavor. If Americans are in your face, Canadians are more reticent. If a lot of American movies are about wackos who turn out to share conventional values at the core, Canadian characters tend to be normal and pleasant on the surface, and keep their darker thoughts to themselves. I don't know which I prefer, but I know the Canadians usually supply more surprises.

Happiness ★ ★ ★

NO MPAA RATING, 140 m., 1998

Jane Adams (Joy Jordan), Lara Flynn Boyle (Helen Jordan), Cynthia Stevenson (Trish Maplewood), Dylan Baker (Bill Maplewood), Philip Seymour Hoffman (Allen), Camryn Manheim (Kristina), Louise Lasser (Mona Jordan), Ben Gazzara (Lenny Jordan), Rufus Read (Billy Maplewood), Jared Harris (Vlad), Jon Lovitz (Andy Kornbluth), Elizabeth Ashley (Diane Freed), Marla Maples (Ann Chambeau). Directed by Todd Solondz and produced by Ted Hope and Christine Vachon. Screenplay by Solondz.

Todd Solondz's *Happiness* is a film that perplexes its viewers, even those who admire it, because it challenges the ways we attempt to respond to it. Is it a portrait of desperate human sadness? Then why are we laughing? Is it an ironic comedy? Then why its tenderness with these lonely people? Is it about depravity? Yes, but why does it make us suspect, uneasily, that the depraved are only seeking what we all seek, but with a lack of ordinary moral vision?

In a film that looks into the abyss of human

despair, there is the horrifying suggestion that these characters may *not* be grotesque exceptions, but may in fact be part of the stream of humanity. Whenever a serial killer or a sex predator is arrested, we turn to the paper to find his neighbors saying that the monster "seemed just like anyone else."

Happiness is a movie about closed doors—apartment doors, bedroom doors, and the doors of the unconscious. It moves back and forth between several stories, which often link up. It shows us people who want to be loved, and who never will be—because of their emotional incompetence and arrested development. There are lots of people who do find love and fulfillment, but they are not in this movie.

We meet Joy (Jane Adams), who has just broken up with the loser she's been dating (Jon Lovitz). He gives her a present, an engraved reproduction ashtray he got through mail order, but after she thanks him ("It almost makes me want to learn to smoke"), he viciously grabs it back: "This is for the girl who loves me for who I am."

We meet Allen (Philip Seymour Hoffman), who describes pornographic sexual fantasies to his psychiatrist (Dylan Baker) and then concludes that he will never realize them because he is too boring. The psychiatrist, named Bill, is indeed bored. Later he buys a teen-idol magazine and masturbates while looking at the photos.

We meet Joy's two sisters, Trish (Cynthia Stevenson) and Helen (Lara Flynn Boyle). Trish is a chirpy housewife, who is married to Bill the psychiatrist but knows nothing of his pedophilia. Helen is a poet who drops names ("Salman is on the line") and describes the countless men who lust for her. The parents of the three sisters, Mona and Lenny (Louise Lasser and Ben Gazzara), have been married for years, but now Lenny wants to leave. Not to fool around. Just to be alone.

We meet Kristina (Camryn Manheim), a fat girl who lives down the hall from the solitary Allen, and knocks on his door to announce that Pedro, the doorman, has been murdered. (His body has been dismembered and put in plastic bags: "Everyone uses Baggies. That's why we can relate to this crime.") Allen doesn't want to know. He leafs through porno magazines, gets drunk, and makes obscene phone calls. One of his calls goes to the woman he fantasizes about. It is Helen, the "popular" sister, who enjoys his heavy breathing and calls him back.

We get the sense of warehouses of strangers—of people stacked into the sky in lonely apartments, each one hiding secrets. We watch in sadness and unease as Bill the shrink attends his son Billy's Little League game and becomes enraptured by one of his teammates. When the other boy has a "sleepover" with Billy, Bill drugs his family and molests the young boy (not on-screen).

Later, there is a heartbreaking conversation between Billy and his father. (Billy is isolated in close-up and we assume the young actor is reading the lines without knowing what the older actor is saying.) Their talk lingers in uneasy memory. The boy has been told at school that his father is a molester. He asks his dad if it is true. His father says it is. In a scene of pain and sadness, the boy asks more questions and the father answers simply, briefly, and completely honestly. A friend who saw the movie told me, "Instead of lying, he kept telling him the truth, regardless of how hard that was for both of them. The honesty may be the one thing that saves the son from the immense damage done by the father." Well, I hope so.

Happiness belongs to the emerging genre of the New Geek Cinema, films that occupy the shadowland between tragedy and irony. Todd Solondz also made *Welcome to the Dollhouse* (1996), about an unpopular eleven-year-old girl who defiantly improvises survival tactics. *Happiness* is harder to take, and yet equally attentive to the suffering of characters who see themselves outside the mainstream—geeks, if you will, whose self-images are formed by the conviction that the more people know about them, the less people will like them.

Why see the film? *Happiness* is *about* its unhappy characters in a way that helps us see them a little more clearly, to feel sorry for them, and at the same time to see how closely tragedy and farce come together in the messiness of sexuality. Does *Happiness* exploit its controversial subjects? Finally, no: It sees them as symptoms of desperation and sadness. It is more exploitative to create a child molester as a convenient villain, as many movies do; by disregarding his humanity and seeing him as an object, such movies do the same thing that a molester does.

These are the kinds of thoughts *Happiness* inspires. It is not a film for most people. It is certainly for adults only. But it shows Todd Solondz as a filmmaker who deserves attention, who hears the unhappiness in the air and seeks its sources. ☞

Hard Eight ★ ★ ★ ½

R, 93 m., 1997

Philip Baker Hall (Sydney), John C. Reilly (John), Gwyneth Paltrow (Clementine), Samuel L. Jackson (Jimmy). Directed by Paul Thomas Anderson and produced by Robert Jones and John Lyons. Screenplay by Anderson.

The man's face is sad and lined, and he lights cigarettes as if he's been living in casinos for centuries. He has a deep, precise voice: We get a quick impression that he knows what he thinks, and says what he believes. His name is Sydney, and he has found an unshaven young bum dozing against the wall of a coffee shop and offered him a cup of coffee and a cigarette.

Why? The answer to that question is the engine behind the first half of *Hard Eight.* I am not sure it is ever fully answered, or needs to be. Sydney (Philip Baker Hall) is a man who has been gambling for a long time, and knows a lot about the subject, and shares his knowledge with the kid because—well, maybe just because he has it to share.

The kid is named John (John C. Reilly). He needs $6,000 to bury his mother, and has lost everything. Step by step, Sydney teaches him some ropes. How to start with $150 and recycle it through the casino cashier cages until he seems to have spent $2,000 in the casino and is given a free room. This opening sequence is quietly fascinating: I like movies that show me precisely how to get away with something. At the end of the process, it's funny how John, now that he's in his own room, becomes the genial host. "Free movies on TV?" he asks Sydney. "Drink from the mini-bar?"

Two years pass. Sydney and John are still friends, John dressing like Sydney and even ordering the same drinks. We begin to understand more about the older man. He is a gentleman, with a deep courtesy. He watches the waitress Clementine (Gwyneth Paltrow) flirt with a table of drunks, asks her if she "has" to do that to keep her job, and says, "You don't have to do that with me."

John and Clementine become a couple, even though it's clear Clemmie does some hooking on the side. John also makes a friend of an ominous man named Jimmy (Samuel L. Jackson), whom Sydney doesn't trust. "What do you do?" Sydney asks him. "I do some consulting, security, help out on busy nights," Jimmy says. "Parking lot?" says Sydney. "No, I'm inside," Jimmy says, but Sydney's shot has found its target.

By this point in the film, its writer-director, Paul Thomas Anderson, has us so hooked that we're watching for the sheer pleasure of the dialogue and the acting. Anderson has a good ear. Sydney says precisely what he means. John's statements are based more on hope than reality. Clementine says what she thinks people want to hear. Jimmy likes to say things that are probably not true, and then look at you to see if you'll challenge him. All of them live in the twenty-four-hour days of Reno, where gambling is like a drumbeat in the back of everything they do.

There turns out to be a kind of a plot (a customer doesn't pay Clementine $300, and John gets violent and then calls Sydney to help him out of a mess). There is even a secret from the past, although not the one we expect. But the movie isn't about a plot. It's about these specific people in this place and time, and that's why it's so good: It listens and sees. It observes, and in that it takes its lead from Sydney, who is a student of human nature and plays the cards of life very, very close to his vest.

Philip Baker Hall has been in the movies since 1975, and has been on a lot of TV shows, even *Seinfeld.* He's familiar, in a way: He looks middle-aged and a little sad. And grown-up. Many Americans linger in adolescence, but Hall is the kind of man who puts on a tie before he leaves the house. In 1984, he gave one of the great performances in American movies, in a one-man show, playing Richard Nixon in Robert Altman's *Secret Honor.* Here is another great performance. He is a man who has been around, who knows casinos and gambling, who finds himself attached to three people he could easily have avoided, who thinks before he acts.

Movies like *Hard Eight* remind me of what original, compelling characters the movies can sometimes give us. Like David Mamet's *House of Games* or Mike Figgis's *Leaving Las Vegas,* or the documentary *Crumb,* they pay attention to the people who inhabit city nights according to their own rules, who have learned from experience, and don't like to make the same mistake twice. At one point, when Clementine asks him a question, Sydney says, "You shouldn't ask a question like that unless you know the answer." It's not so much what he says as how he says it.

Hard Rain ★

R, 98 m., 1998

Morgan Freeman (Jim), Christian Slater (Tom), Randy Quaid (Sheriff), Minnie Driver (Karen), Ed Asner (Charlie), Michael Goorjian (Kenny), Dann Florek (Mr. Mehlor), Ricky Harris (Ray). Directed by Mikael Salomon and produced by Mark Gordon, Gary Levinsohn, and Ian Bryce. Screenplay by Graham Yost.

Hard Rain is one of those movies that never convince you their stories are really happening. From beginning to end, I was acutely aware of actors being paid to stand in cold water. Suspension of my disbelief in this case would have required psychotropic medications.

Oh, the film is well made from a technical viewpoint. The opening shot is a humdinger, starting out with a vast flood plain, zooming above houses surrounded by water, and then ending with a close-up of a cop's narrowing eyes. But even then, I was trying to spot the effects—to catch how they created the flood effect, and how they got from the flood to the eyes.

Funny how some movies will seduce you into their stories while others remain at arm's length. *Titanic* was just as artificial and effects-driven as *Hard Rain,* and yet I was spellbound. Maybe it was because the people on the doomed ship had no choice: The *Titanic* was sinking, and that was that.

In *Hard Rain,* there is a bad guy (Morgan Freeman) who *has* a choice. He wants to steal some money, but all during the film I kept wondering why he didn't just give up and head for dry ground. How much of this ordeal was he foolish enough to put up with? Water, cold, rain, electrocutions, murders, shotguns, jet ski attacks, drownings, betrayals, collisions, leaky boats, stupid and incompetent partners, and your fingertips shrivel up: Is it worth it?

The film opens in a town being evacuated because of rising flood waters. There's a sequence involving a bank. At first we think we're witnessing a robbery, and then we realize we are witnessing a pickup by an armored car. What's the point? Since the bankers don't think they're being robbed and the armored truck drivers don't think they're robbing them, the sequence means only that the director has gone to great difficulty to fool us. Why? So we can slap our palms against our brows and admit we were big stupes?

By the time we finally arrived at the story, I was essentially watching a documentary about wet actors at work. Christian Slater stars as one of the armored truck crew. Randy Quaid is the ambiguous sheriff. Morgan Freeman is the leader of the would-be thieves, who have commandeered a power boat. Ah, but, I hear you asking, why was it so important for the armored car to move the cash out of the bank before the flood? So Freeman's gang could steal it, of course. Otherwise, if it got wet, hey, what's the Federal Reserve for?

Minnie Driver plays a local woman who teams up with Slater so that they can fall in love while saving each other from drowning. First Slater is in a jail cell that's about to flood, and then Driver is handcuffed to a staircase that's about to flood, and both times I was thinking what rotten luck it was that *Hard Rain* came so soon after the scene in *Titanic* where Kate Winslet saved Leonardo DiCaprio from drowning after he was handcuffed on the sinking ship. It's bad news when a big action scene plays like a demonstration of recent generic techniques.

Meanwhile, Morgan Freeman's character is too darned nice. He keeps trying to avoid violence while still trying to steal the money. This plot requires a mad dog like Dennis Hopper. Freeman's character specializes in popping up suddenly from the edge of the screen and scaring the other characters, even though it is probably pretty hard to sneak up on somebody in a powerboat. Freeman is good at looking wise and insightful, but the wiser and more insightful he looked, the more I wanted him to check into a motel and order himself some hot chocolate.

Hard Rain must have been awesomely difficult to make. Water is hard to film around, and here were whole city streets awash, at night and in the rain. The director is Mikael Salomon, a former cameraman, who along with cinematographer Peter Menzies Jr. does a good job of making everything look convincingly wet. And they stage a jet ski chase through school corridors that's an impressive action sequence, unlikely though it may be.

I was in Los Angeles the weekend *Hard Rain* had its preview, and went to talk to the cast. I found myself asking: Wasn't there a danger of electrocution when you were standing for weeks in all that water with electrical cables everywhere? That's not the sort of question you even think about if the story is working. Hey, how about this for a story idea? An actor signs up for a movie about a flood, little realizing that a celebrity stalker, who hates him, has been hired as an electrician on the same picture.

The Harmonists ★ ★ ★

R, 115 m., 1999

Ben Becker (Robert Biberti), Heino Ferch (Roman Cycowski), Ulrich Noethen (Harry Frommermann), Heinrich Schafmeister (Erich A. Collin), Max Tidof (Ari Leschnikoff), Kai Wiesinger (Erwin Bootz), Meret Becker (Erna Eggstein), Katja Riemann (Mary Cycowski). Directed by Joseph Vilsmaier and produced by Reinhard Kloos, Hanno Huth, and Danny Krausz. Screenplay by Klaus Richter.

The Harmonists tells the story of the rise and fall of a vocal group that was wildly popular in Germany before it was disbanded in 1934 as part of the mounting persecution of Jews. The Comedian Harmonists, who did comic and romantic songs in intricate harmony, were popular and beloved. Even members of the Nazi hierarchy were among their fans. But eventually they were forbidden to sing songs by Jewish composers—and finally, because three of their members were Jewish, they were banned from performing in public.

Given the suffering created by the Nazis, the fate of the Harmonists ranks low on the scale. But as one of the countless little stories that add up to the plague of Nazism, they deserve an entry in the chronicle of despair. And it is revealing how, like many of their countrymen both Jewish and gentile, they were blind until the last moment to the actual intentions of the Nazis. There is a moment in the film when the Harmonists are performing in New York and consider staying in America. But they do not. The handwriting was on the wall, but it was not yet sufficiently clear.

The arc of the film leads from early cheerfulness to eventual defeat, but for much of the time *The Harmonists* plays like a standard showbiz biopic. We meet the founder of the group, Harry Frommermann (Ulrich Noethen), who in 1927 hears a record by a black American jazz group named the Revellers. Entranced by the beauty of their close harmony, he determines to start a German group that would sing in the same style. It's slow-going at first, but after the brash, confident Robert Biberti (Ben Becker) joins him, they find the other recruits and end up with five singers and a piano player.

The first agent they audition for tells them their music sounds "funereal." That night, the pianist plays around with a faster tempo, and they find their style. I've never heard the Revellers, but the Harmonists remind me of the Mills Brothers, and they do something the Mills Brothers also did: They use their voices, hands, and breath control to imitate the sound of musical instruments. There's an instrumental solo in the film done entirely without instruments.

As the six men work and travel together, tensions of course develop, and the most delicate involves the fact that Harry and Robert are both in love with the same woman, a comely music store clerk named Erna (Meret Becker). She likes Harry (indeed, she makes sure she's up on a ladder with a little of her slip and a lot of her leg showing when he enters the store). He likes her, too, enough to propose marriage even though he's Jewish and she isn't. (He visits his parents' grave to tell them, "God will forgive me—after all; it's his job.")

But Harry is a complicated man—distracted, driven, inattentive, forgetful, maddening. Robert, on the other hand, is as solid as a Teutonic rock, and looks a little like Mencken with the stogie he keeps planted in his mouth. Robert is not Jewish, but he's not a Nazi, either, and his decency helps hold the Harmonists together.

There are a lot of entertaining musical numbers in the film, and an ominous low-key, background treatment of the way that Nazism and anti-Semitism change the fabric of German society even while many of the characters are busy denying it. (When ugly slogans are painted on the window of the music store, the grandmotherly owner says it's "just kids.")

Eventually the situation can no longer be ignored. There's an electrifying scene just before the group sails for New York; a high Nazi official asks them to perform at his home, which they do, but when he requests a German folk song with Nazi associations, Harry says he "just cannot sing it." Their fate as a group is sealed at that moment, although it would have been sealed sooner or later anyway. Roman Cycowski (Heino Ferch), another Jewish member, announces eventually, "No power on Earth can force me to sing in this country again."

After they break up, the three Jewish Harmonists regroup outside Germany, and the three Germans start a new group at home. But what made them special fades away, and their music somehow seems like a reproach to the rising tide of war. An epilogue reveals what eventually happened to all the Harmonists. One moved to California and became the oldest active cantor in America. Others did not end so happily.

Hav Plenty ★ ½

R, 92 m., 1998

Christopher Scott Cherot (Lee Plenty), Chenoa Maxwell (Havilland Savage), Hill Harper (Michael Simmons), Tammi Katherine Jones (Caroline Gooden), Robinne Lee (Leigh Darling), Reginald James (Felix Darling). Directed by Christopher Scott Cherot and produced by Cherot and Robyn M. Greene. Screenplay by Cherot.

I've grown immune to the information that a movie is "a true story," but when a movie begins with that promise *and* a quote from the Bible, I get an uneasy feeling. And when it starts with a "true story," a Bible quote *and* clips from home movies, *and* photos of several main characters, I wonder if I'm watching a movie or a research project. Amateur writers love to precede their own prose with quotations. I don't know whether they think it's a warm-up or a good luck charm.

Hav Plenty is basically an amateur movie, with some of the good things and many of the bad that go along with first-time efforts. Set in a comfortable milieu of affluent African-Americans, it's ostensibly the autobiographical story of its writer-director, Christopher Scott Cherot, who plays a homeless writer named Lee Plenty. As the movie opens, he's cat-sitting for a woman named Havilland Savage (Chenoa Maxwell), who has just broken up with a famous musician. She's with her family in Washington, D.C., for New Year's Eve, and invites him to come down and join them, and he does. (So much for the cat.) At the end of the movie, there's a thank-you to "the real Havilland Savage," and I gather most of the things in the movie actually happened, in one way or another. How else to account for an episode involving the offscreen explosion of a toilet?

Cherot plays Lee Plenty as a smart young man of maddening passivity. The plot essentially consists of scenes in which Havilland's best friend Caroline throws herself at Plenty, who rebuffs her. Then Havilland's sister, who has only been married for a month, throws herself at Plenty, but he rebuffs her too. Then Havilland herself throws herself at Plenty, and he does his best to rebuff her. Although we see the beginning of a sex scene, he eventually eludes her too. The movie ends with a scene at a film festival at which Plenty speaks after the premiere of a film that is a great deal like this one.

As a young man I would have been quite capable of writing and starring in a movie in which three beautiful women threw themselves at me. I would have considered this so logical that I would not have bothered, as Cherot does not bother, to write myself any dialogue establishing myself as intelligent, charming, seductive, etc. I would assume that the audience could take one look at me and simply intuit that I had all of those qualities. So I can accept that the homeless Lee Plenty character is irresistible, even to a newlywed and to a beautiful, rich ex-fiancée of a big star. What I cannot accept is that he fights them all off with vague excuses and evasions. "He's not gay," the women assure each other. That I believe. But either he's asexual, or exhibiting the symptoms of chronic fatigue syndrome.

Hav Plenty is not a film without charm, but, boy, does it need to tighten the screws on its screenplay. The movie's dialogue is mostly strained, artificial small talk, delivered unevenly by the actors, who at times seem limited to one take (how else to account for fluffed lines?). There are big setups without payoffs, as when Hav's grandmother insists, "You're going to marry him!" And nightmare dream sequences without motivation or purpose. And awkward scenes like the one where the newlywed sister tells her husband that something went on between her and Plenty. The husband enters the room, removes his jacket to reveal bulging muscles, and socks poor Plenty in the stomach. This scene illustrates two of my favorite obligatory cliches: (1) The husband is told only enough of the story to draw exactly the wrong conclusion, and (2) all muscular characters in movies always take off outer garments to reveal their muscles before hitting someone.

Hav Plenty is basically a three-actress movie; Cherot, as the male lead, is so vague and passive he barely has a personality (listen to his rambling explanations about why he "doesn't date"). All three actresses (Chenoa Maxwell as Hav, Tammi Katherine Jones as Hav's best friend, and Robinne Lee as the married sister) have strong energy and look good on the screen. With better direction and more takes, I suspect they'd seem more accomplished in their performances. But *Hav Plenty* is more of a first draft than a finished product.

He Got Game ★ ★ ★ ½

R, 131 m., 1998

Denzel Washington (Jake Shuttlesworth), Ray Allen (Jesus Shuttlesworth), Milla Jovovich (Dakota Burns), Rosario Dawson (Lala Bonilla), Hill Harper (Coleman "Booger" Sykes), Zelda Harris (Mary Shuttlesworth), Ned Beatty (Warden Wyatt), Jim Brown (Spivey). Directed by Spike Lee and produced by Jon Kilik and Lee. Screenplay by Lee.

Spike Lee brings the spirit of a poet to his films about everyday reality. *He Got Game*, the story of the pressures on the nation's best high school basketball player, could have been a gritty docudrama, but it's really more of a heartbreaker about a father and his son.

Lee uses visual imagination to lift his material into the realms of hopes and dreams. Consider his opening sequence, where he wants to establish the power of basketball as a sport and an obsession. He could have given us a montage of hot NBA action, but no: He uses the music of Aaron Copland to score a series of scenes in which American kids—boys, girls, rich, poor, black, white, in school and on playgrounds—play the game. All it needs is a ball and a hoop; compared to this simplicity, Jerry Seinfeld observes, when we attend other sports we're cheering laundry.

This opening evocation is matched by the closing shots of *He Got Game*, in which Lee goes beyond reality to find the perfect way to end his film: His final image is simple and very daring, and goes beyond words or plot to summarize the heart of the story. Seeing his films, I am saddened by how many filmmakers allow themselves to fall into the lazy rhythms of TV, where groups of people exchange dialogue. Movies are not just conversations on film; they can give us images that transform.

He Got Game is Lee's best film since *Malcolm X* (1982). It stars Denzel Washington as Jake, a man in prison for the manslaughter of his wife (we learn in a flashback that the event was a lot more complicated than that). His son, Jesus (Ray Allen), is the nation's top prospect. The state governor makes Jake an offer: He'll release him for a week, and if he can talk his son into signing a letter of intent to attend Big State University, the governor will reduce Jake's sentence.

The son is not happy to see Jake ("I don't have a father. Why is there a stranger in the house?"). He still harbors deep resentment, although his sister, Mary (Zelda Harris), has understood and forgiven. Jesus (named not after Christ but after a basketball player) is under incredible pressure. Recruiting offers arrive daily from colleges, and even his girlfriend Lala (Rosario Dawson) is involved; aware that she's likely to be dropped when Jesus goes on to stardom, she's working with a sports agent who wants the kid to turn pro ("He's a friend of the family," she keeps saying, as if her family would just happen to have a high-powered agent as a pal).

Spike Lee's connections with pro ball have no doubt given him a lot of insight into what talented high school players go through. There's a scene in *Hoop Dreams* where he exhorts all-stars at a summer basketball camp to be aware of how they're being used. In *He Got Game,* the temptations come thick and fast: job offers, a new Lexus, $10,000 from his own coach, even a couple of busty "students" who greet him in a dorm room with their own recruiting techniques.

Jake, on the other hand, faces bleak prospects. He moves into a flophouse next door to a hooker (Milla Jovovich) who is beaten by her pimp. Gradually they become friends, and he tries to help her. He also tries to reach his son, and it's interesting the way Lee and Washington let Jake use silence, tact, and patience in the process. Jake doesn't try a frontal assault, maybe because he knows his son too well. Finally it all comes down to a one-on-one confrontation in which the son is given the opportunity to understand and even pity his father.

This is not so much a movie about sports as about capitalism. It doesn't end, as the formula requires, with a big game. In fact, it never creates artificial drama with game sequences, even though Ray Allen, who plays for the Milwaukee Bucks, is that rarity, an athlete who can act. It's about the real stakes, which involve money more than final scores, and showmanship as much as athletics.

For many years in America, sports and big business have shared the same rules and strategies. One reason so many powerful people are seen in the stands at NBA games is that the modern game objectifies the same kind of warfare that takes place in high finance; while "fans" think it's all about sportsmanship and winning, the insiders are thinking in corporate and marketing metaphors.

He Got Game sees this clearly and unsentimentally (the sentiment is reserved for the father and son). There is a scene on a bench between Jesus and his girlfriend in which she states, directly and honestly, what her motivations are, and they are the same motivations that shape all of professional sports: It's not going to last forever, so you have to look out for yourself and make all the money you can. Of course, Spike Lee still cheers for the Knicks, and I cheer for the Bulls, but it's good to know what you're cheering for. At the end of *He Got Game,* the father and son win, but so does the system. ☞

Henry Fool ★ ★ ½

R, 138 m., 1998

Thomas Jay Ryan (Henry Fool), James Urbaniak (Simon Grim), Parker Posey (Fay), Maria Porter (Mary), James Saito (Deng), Kevin Corrigan (Warren). Directed and produced by Hal Hartley. Screenplay by Hartley.

Simon is a garbage man who approaches the world at an angle. Literally. In Hal Hartley's new film *Henry Fool,* Simon is almost always shot with his head tilted down and cocked to one side, with the rims of his glasses positioned right above his eyes, which regard us sideways. He is a man so beaten down by life that he cannot look at anything straight on. Then Henry arrives to save him.

Simon Grim (James Urbaniak) has just been savagely beaten by a motorcyclist and his girlfriend. Like everyone else in the neighborhood, they treat Simon like a punching bag. Henry Fool (Thomas Jay Ryan) is a homeless drifter with a deep, wise voice. He moves into Simon's basement, where the flames from the furnace reinforce his Satanic undertones. His mission is to lift Simon to his feet, apparently, and instill a sense of mission in him.

Simon's family includes his mother, Mary (Maria Porter), who is on a lot of pills, and a chain-smoking sister named Fay (Parker Posey), who is an idle slattern quickly attracted to Henry. But Henry makes an unexpected choice and confesses to Simon: "I made love to your mother half an hour ago, and I'm beginning to think it wasn't such a good idea, because it makes Fay jealous." Simon looks at this statement as he looks at everything, askance.

Henry is working on his "Confessions," a vast opus. He claims to have connections at a publishing house. He gives Simon a journal with large blank pages and encourages him to write down everything that happens to him. Simon's thoughts flow out effortlessly in iambic pentameter, and when they are posted on the Web they make him world famous. Meanwhile, nobody much likes Henry's confessions, and it turns out his connection to the publisher is as a janitor, not an editor. There is also the matter of his conviction for child molestation.

What are we to make of all this? That is always the question with a Hal Hartley film, and I wish I were more sure of the answer. He works in a style of his own devising, he has an image of the world that is developing in a series of films, he seems to regard his characters in the same way Simon regards the world—obliquely, quizzically, without commitment. Sometimes he has a character do something odd and unexpected, and you think of a chess player making an unorthodox move just to make the game a little more interesting.

I wonder if the fault is in myself. I don't think this is a bad film, but after seeing it twice I'm unable to respond to it in any clear way. Things happen, and I don't know what they mean, and I have a feeling that in Hartley's view they need not mean anything. Henry Fool lives in the basement and is illuminated by flames, but is not Mephistopheles; he is finally revealed as not as bright as he seems. Simon writes a famous poem but develops, not into a genius or into a savior, but simply into the semblance of a reasonable, successful man. Mary and Fay both go into orbit around Henry, but to what consequence?

Hartley is a gifted filmmaker (this time he wrote, produced, directed, and composed), and he has a precise visual style that develops themes over a series of scenes (notice the gradual shift in the relative balance of the body language between Simon and Henry). He has actors who evoke more than they reveal, although with the Henry Fool character I was never able to fit the child molestation into anything else, and wondered if Hartley added it capriciously. And what about the protracted, studiously graphic scenes of vomiting and defecation? What are they for? They break the frame of the picture. They're like fingers in the eyeballs of the film's style.

You watch, you are absorbed, and from scene to scene *Henry Fool* seems to be adding up, but then your hand closes on air. I am left unsure of my response—of any response. I want to see Hartley's next film. I always do. I sense he is headed somewhere, and perhaps his next work will provide the key allowing me to enter this one.

Hercules ★ ★ ★ ½

G, 93 m., 1997

With the voices of: Tate Donovan (Hercules [Herc]), Susan Egan (Megara [Meg]), James Woods (Hades), Rip Torn (Zeus), Danny DeVito (Philoctetes [Phil]), Samantha Eggar (Hera), Bobcat Goldthwait (Pain), Matt Frewer (Panic), Paul Shaffer (Hermes). Directed by John Musker and Ron Clements and produced by Musker, Clements, and Alice Dewey. Screenplay by Musker, Clements, Bob Shaw, Don McEnery, and Irene Mecchi.

The wonder is that it took Disney so long to get to the gods of Greek mythology. *Hercules* jumps into the ancient legends feetfirst, cheerfully tossing out what won't fit and combining what's left into a new look and a lighthearted style.

Starting with a day-glo Olympian city in the clouds, and using characters based on the drawing style of the British illustrator Gerald Scarfe, this new animated feature has something old (mythology), something new (a Pegasus equipped with helicopter blades), something borrowed (a gospel singing group) and something blue (the flaming hair of Hades, which turns red when he gets mad—it works like a mood ring).

Hercules, known as Herc, is a rather different character here than in the pages of *Bullfinch's Mythology.* There, you may recall, he murdered his wife and children. Here he's a big, cute hunk who's so clumsy he knocks over temples by accident, but you gotta love the guy.

In fact, as film critic Jack Matthews has pointed out, the Disney storytellers have merged the Hercules of myth with the modern-day superhero Superman: In both *Hercules* and the Superman story, the hero has other-worldly origins, is separated from his parents, is adopted by humble earthlings, and feels like a weirdo as a kid before finally finding his true strength and calling.

It's getting to be an in-joke, how Disney shapes the story in every new animated feature to match its time-tested underlying formula. The hero is essentially an orphan. There is a colorful villain who schemes against him. There are two twirpy little characters who do a double act (in *The Lion King* they were the friendly Timon and Pumbaa; here they're the scheming Pain and Panic). There are trusted sidekicks and advisers (not only the faithful Pegasus, but also a little satyr named Phil who signs up as a personal trainer). And there's a sexy dame who winds up in the hero's arms, although not without difficulties.

Is Disney repeating a formula? No more than mythology always repeats itself; as Joseph Campbell taught George Lucas, many of the eternal human myths have the same buried structures, and Disney's annual animated features are the myths of our time.

Although I thought 1996's *Hunchback of Notre Dame* was a more original and challenging film, *Hercules* is lighter, brighter, and more cheerful, with more for kids to identify with. Certainly they can care about Herc (voice by Tate Donovan), child of a god and a human, who must leave his father, Zeus (Rip Torn), in heaven and toil among the mortals to earn his ticket back to paradise. Herc stumbles through adolescence as the clumsy "Jerkules" before a statue of his father comes to life and reads him the rules. His tutor will be the satyr Philoctetes (Danny DeVito), who, like all the best movie trainers, advises his student to do as he says and not as he does.

Playing on the other team is Hades, Lord of the Underworld, voiced by James Woods with diabolical glee and something of the same verbal inventiveness that Robin Williams brought to *Aladdin* (Hades to Fate: "You look like a fate worse than death"). Hades is assisted by the two little form-shifting sidekicks Pain and Panic (Bobcat Goldthwait and Matt Frewer), who are able to disguise themselves in many different shapes while meddling with Herc's well-being. Another one of Hades' weapons is the curvaceous Megara (Susan Egan), known as Meg, who is assigned to seduce Herc but ends up falling in love with the lug.

The movie has been directed by John Musker and Ron Clements, who inaugurated the modern era of Disney animation with the inspired *Little Mermaid* (1989) and also made *Aladdin* (1992). The look of their animation has a new freshness because of the style of Gerald Scarfe, famous in the United Kingdom for his sharp-penned caricatures of politicians and celebrities; the characters here are edgier and less rounded than your usual Disney heroes (although the cuddly Pegasus is in the traditional mode). The color palate, too, makes less use of basic colors and stirs in more luminous shades, giving the picture a subtly different look that suggests it is different in geography and history from most Disney pictures.

What *The Little Mermaid* began and all of the subsequent Disney animation features have continued is a sly combination of broad strokes for children and in-jokes and satire for adults. It's hard to explain, for example, why a black female gospel quintet would be singing the legend of Hercules in the opening sequence (returning later to add more details), but the songs (by Alan Menken and David Zippel) are fun, and probably more entertaining than the expected Greek chorus. Other throwaways: lines like "get ready to rumble"; images like Pegasus outfitted by Phil like an LAPD helicopter; Herc's promotion of his own prehistoric exercise video; an arch saying "OVER 500,000,000 SERVED"; Hades offering two burning thumbs "way up for our leading lady"; Hermes (Paul Shaffer) observing the preening gods and quipping, "I haven't seen so much love in one room since Narcissus looked at himself"; and quick little sight gags like a spider hanging from the nose of Fate, who disposes of it in a spectacularly unappetizing way.

Will children like this subject matter, or will they find Greek myth unfamiliar? I think they'll love it. And in an age when kids get their heroes from TV instead of books, is Hercules any more unfamiliar than Pocahontas (or Aladdin or the Hunchback, for that matter)? A riffle through *Bullfinch's Mythology* suggests dozens more Disney plots, all safely out of copyright. Next: *Ulysses*?

Hideous Kinky ★ ★ ★

R, 99 m., 1999

Kate Winslet (Julia), Said Taghmaoui (Bilal), Bella Riza (Bea), Carrie Mullan (Lucy), Pierre Clementi (Santoni), Abigail Cruttenden (Charlotte), Ahmed Boulane (Ben Said), Sira Stampe (Eva). Directed by Gillies MacKinnon and produced by Ann Scott. Screenplay by Billy MacKinnon, based on the novel by Esther Freud.

In the 1970s there were movies about the carefree lives of hippies and flower people, and on the screen you could see their children, long-haired, sunburned, and barefoot, solemn witnesses at rock concerts and magical mystery tours. Remember the commune in *Easy Rider*.

Now it is the 1990s and those children have grown up to make their own movies and tell their side of the story. *A Soldier's Daughter Never Cries* (1998) was based on an autobiographical novel by Kaylie Jones, whose novelist father, James, raised his family in bohemian freedom as exiles in Paris. Now here is *Hideous Kinky*, based on an autobiographical novel by Esther Freud, whose father is the British painter Lucien Freud. I'm not sure how much of the story is based on fact, but presumably the feelings are accurately reflected, as when a child tells her hippie mother: "I don't need another adventure, Mom! I need to go to school. I want a satchel!"

The film stars Kate Winslet, in an about-face after *Titanic*, as a thirtyish British mom named Julia, who has journeyed to Marrakech in 1972 with her two young daughters, Bea (Bella Riza) and Lucy (Carrie Mullan). She is seeking the truth, she says, or perhaps she is making a grand gesture against her husband, a London poet whom she caught cheating. Well, actually, he's not officially her husband, although he is the father of the children, and is sending them packages and checks from time to time, although sometimes they get packages intended for his other family, and the bank doesn't often receive the checks.

Julia is not a bad woman—just reckless, naive, foolishly trusting, and seeking truth in the wrong places, times, and ways. She doesn't do drugs to speak of, drinks little, wants to study Sufi philosophy. Her children, like most children, are profoundly conservative in the face of anarchy. They want a home, school, "real shirts." They're tired of Julia's quest, and ask, "Mom, when can we have rice pudding again?" The movie's tension comes from our own uneasiness about the mother, who with the best intentions seems to be blundering into trouble.

The film, directed by Gillies MacKinnon, fills its canvas with details about expatriate life in the time of flower power. Moroccan music blends with psychedelic rock, and they meet a teacher from the School of the Annihilation of the Ego. The expatriate American novelist Paul Bowles is presumably lurking about somewhere, writing his novel *The Sheltering Sky*, which is about characters not unlike these. One day in the bazaar the family encounters Bilal (Said Taghmaoui), a street performer who possibly has some disagreements with the police, but is humorous and friendly, and is soon Julia's lover.

Bilal is not a bad man, either. *Hideous Kinky* is not a melodrama or a thriller, and doesn't need villains; it's the record of a time when idealism led good-hearted seekers into danger. Some of the time Julia doesn't have enough food for her children, or a place for them to stay, and her idea for raising money is pathetic: She has them all making dolls to sell in the marketplace. Their trip to the desert leads to a nearly fatal ride with a sleepy truck driver, and to an uneasy meeting with a woman who may or may not be Bilal's wife.

In Marrakech, invitations come easily. They meet a Frenchman (Pierre Clementi, who played young hippies himself in the 1960s and 1970s) who invites them to his house: "I have lots of rooms." There they get involved in a strange ménage. Later, incredibly, Julia leaves Bea with them for safekeeping, only to discover that the household has broken up and her child has disappeared. She finds Bea in the keeping of an earnest Christian woman who runs an orphanage and doesn't seem inclined to surrender the child. "It's what Bea always wanted," she tells Julia. "To be an orphan?" "To be normal."

The movie is episodic and sometimes repetitive; dramatic scenes alternate with music and local color, and then the process repeats itself. What makes it work is Winslet's performance, as a sincere, good person, not terrifically smart, who doggedly pursues her dream and drags along her unwilling children. Parents, even flower-child moms, always think they know what's best for their kids. Maybe they do. Look at it this way: To the degree that this story really is autobiographical, Julia raised a daughter who wrote a novel and had it made into a movie. Bea might not have turned out quite so splendidly by eating rice pudding and carrying a satchel to school.

High Art ★ ★ ★ ½

R, 101 m., 1998

Ally Sheedy (Lucy Berliner), Radha Mitchell (Syd), Patricia Clarkson (Greta), Gabriel Mann (James, Syd's Boyfriend), Bill Sage (Arnie), Anh Duong (Dominique [The Editor]), Tammy Grimes (Vera, Lucy's Mother), David Thornton (Harry, Syd's Boss). Directed by Lisa Cholodenko and produced by Dolly Hall, Jeff Levy-Hinte, and Susan A. Stover. Screenplay by Cholodenko.

To explain the special strength of *High Art,* it is necessary to begin with the people who live in the apartment above Syd and James. There's a shifting population in the upstairs flat, since drugs are involved, but the permanent inhabitants are Lucy, who was a famous photographer ten years ago; Greta, who once starred in Fassbinder films; and Arnie, an unfocused layabout who's along for the ride and the heroin.

Syd has just been made an associate editor of a New York photo magazine—the kind with big pages, where you have to read the small print to tell the features from the ads. She goes upstairs because there's a leak coming through the ceiling, and walks into the sad, closed, claustrophobic life of the heroin users. And now here is my point: Those people really seem to be living there. They suggest a past, a present, a history, a pattern that has been going on for years. Their apartment, and how they live in it, is as convincing as a documentary could make it.

In other words, they aren't "characters." They don't feel like actors waiting for the camera to roll. And by giving them texture and complexity, writer-director Lisa Cholodenko has the key to her whole movie. The couple downstairs, Syd (Radha Mitchell) and her boyfriend, James (Gabriel Mann), are conventional movie characters—Manhattan yuppies. It's not that they seem false in the movie; it's that their lives are borrowed from media. Then Syd senses something upstairs that stirs her.

To begin with, she sees some photographs taken by Lucy (Ally Sheedy). They're good. She tells her so. "I haven't been deconstructed in a long time," Lucy says. Lucy is thin, a chain-smoker, projecting a kind of masochistic devotion to the older Greta (Patricia Clarkson). Both are deeply into drugs. Greta seems to drift between lassitude and oblivion; she's like a Fassbinder movie so drained of life it doesn't move anymore. She falls asleep during sex with Lucy. She nods off in a restaurant, and the waiter tells Lucy: "You know this restaurant has a policy about sleeping in here."

Syd is on the make. She wants to move up at her magazine. Her editor, the often hungover Dominique (Anh Duong), started as a receptionist at *Interview*—so all things are possible. Syd pitches Lucy's photos to Dominique. "She was so belligerent when she left New York," Dominique muses. They set up a luncheon. "I made it impossible for myself to continue," Lucy explains about her dead career. "I stopped showing up."

Dominique asks Lucy to do a shoot for the magazine. Lucy insists on Syd being her editor. Gradually, by almost imperceptible degrees, the two women are drawn toward one another. Greta sees what is happening, but her hold on Lucy is strong: a triangulation of drugs, exploited guilt, and domination. She knows what buttons to push.

High Art is masterful in the little details. It knows how these people might talk, how they might respond. It knows that Lucy, Greta, and the almost otherworldly Arnie might use heroin and then play Scrabble. It is so boring, being high in an empty life. The movie knows how career ambition and office politics can work together to motivate Syd: She wants Lucy to get the job because she's falling for Lucy, but also because she knows Lucy is her ticket to a promotion at the magazine.

Finally, at what seems like the emotionally inevitable moment, Syd and Lucy sleep together. This is one of the most observant sex scenes I have seen, involving a lot of worried, insecure dialogue; Syd feels awkward and inadequate, and wants reassurance, and Lucy provides it from long experience, mixed with a sudden rediscovery of the new. They talk a lot. Lucy is like ground control, talking a new pilot through her first landing.

The movie is wise about drug addiction. There are well-written scenes between Lucy and her mother (Tammy Grimes), who keeps her distance from her daughter. Lucy looks at her life and decides, "I can't do this anymore." She tries to open up with her mother: "I have a love issue and a drug problem." Her mother closes her off: "I can't help you with that." Lucy is tired of Greta, tired of drugs, tired of not working, tired of boredom. Greta's final, best weapon is heroin: Can she keep Lucy with that? Or will Lucy be able to see that Greta is only the human face of her addiction?

High Art is so perceptive and mature it makes similar films seem flippant. The performances are on just the right note, scene after scene, for what needs to be done. The reviews keep mentioning that Ally Sheedy has outgrown her Brat Pack days. Well, of course she has. (She'd done that by the time of *Heart of Dixie,* in 1989.) Patricia Clarkson succeeds in creating a complete, complex character without ever overplaying the stoned behavior (she's like Fassbinder's Petra von Kant on heroin instead of booze). Radha Mitchell is successful at suggesting the interaction of several motives: love, lust, curiosity, ambition, admiration. And the movie's ending does not cheat. Just the opposite.

Hilary and Jackie ★ ★ ★ ½

R, 121 m., 1998

Emily Watson (Jacqueline du Pre), Rachel Griffiths (Hilary du Pre), David Morrissey (Kiffer Finzi), James Frain (Daniel Barenboim), Charles Dance (Derek du Pre), Celia Imrie (Iris du Pre), Rupert Penry-Jones (Piers du Pre), Bill Paterson (Jackie's Cello Teacher). Directed by Anand Tucker and produced by Andy Paterson and Nicolas Kent. Screenplay by Frank Cottrell-Boyce, based on the book *A Genius in the Family* by Hilary and Piers Du Pre.

Jackie to Hilary: "The truth is, you're not special."

Hilary to Jackie: "If you think that being an ordinary person is any easier than being an extraordinary one, you're wrong. If you didn't have that cello to prop you up, you'd be nothing."

And yet the two sisters love each other with a fierceness that stands beside their lifelong rivalry. *Hilary and Jackie* is the story of two gifted musicians, who in a way were always playing for (or against) each other, and how one of them was struck down by disease. "I have a fatal illness," Jackie says, "but the good news is, I have a very mild case."

Jacqueline du Pre (Emily Watson) was one of the most gifted cellists of her time, and her brilliant marriage to the pianist and conductor Daniel Barenboim was a celebrated musical and romantic liaison. Hilary du Pre (Rachel Griffiths), her older sister, played the flute and might perhaps have been as gifted as her sister. But that we will never know, because a music teacher beat down her talent and crushed her spirit. Perhaps she had a happier life as a result.

Hilary and Jackie is an extraordinary film about riding the tiger of genius, and how that cuts through conventional rules and invests the rider with special license. That Jackie's long illness and too-young death was tragic there is no doubt, but she played such beautiful music that it is our tragedy as well as hers. And yet to those close to the story, there is always another side and more personal feelings. *Hilary and Jackie,* directed by Anand Tucker, is based on a memoir written by Hilary and her brother, Piers du Pre, and it is unusually knowing for a biopic.

It opens with a long section seen from Hilary's point of view. We see the two young sisters playing at the beach and practicing their instruments. Hilary is the talented one, applauded at family gatherings, while Jackie smolders ignored in the corner. But when Hilary is asked to play on a BBC children's concert, she won't go without Jackie. And when Jackie is not very good, they're told by their mother: "If you want to be together, you've got to be as good as each other."

That line of instruction may have been the turning point in Jacqueline du Pre's musical career, inspiring her to practice obsessively until she was not only as good as Hilary, but better. It was her fortune to find teachers who supported her, while Hilary was driven off the stage by pressures mostly engendered by her teacher. Both young women moved freely while playing; Jackie's onstage enthusiasm helped make her famous, but Hilary was ordered to stand still: "It is impossible to produce a proper tone without proper deportment."

She freezes during an audition and abandons any hope of a concert career. Luckily, she finds a man who believes in her: Kiffer Finzi (David Morrissey). Jackie also finds love with "Danny" (James Frain), and they are happy, but there comes a time when Jackie walks off a concert stage and goes to Hilary's farm and demands to be allowed to make love to her husband: "You don't mind, do you, Sis?"

Her arrival, her demand, and her behavior ("bonkers") are all seen from Hilary's point of view. Then the film's next section, seen through Jackie's eyes, details the early warning signs of multiple sclerosis. The film follows through to the unhappy end, showing the destruction of a career, a personality, and a life. It stays tactfully at arm's-length in the way it handles Jacqueline's troubled relationship with Barenboim, and looks mostly through Hilary's eyes as the sad story unfolds.

A film like this lives in its performances. Emily Watson is fiery and strong willed as Jackie; we see the fierce stubbornness of her character in *Breaking the Waves* now wedded to talent and neurosis. The key performance, however, is Rachel Griffiths's, as Hilary, the witness, the person who senses on an almost telepathic level what her sister thinks and feels. Griffiths, not yet well known, is able to convey penetrating intelligence in a look; in a film named *My Son the Fanatic,* she plays a prostitute whose sense of herself and her occupation is almost scarily perceptive.

The film has details that only a family member could supply, such as the few but significant scenes involving the parents: the mother who engenders competition, the father (Charles Dance) who doesn't want his girls living near Soho for fear they will be snatched for the white slave trade. Although the brother, Piers, is coauthor of the book, he has hardly any dialogue in the movie; it is the sisters' story.

The movie makes no attempt to soften the material or make it comforting through the clichés of melodrama; it is instructive to see it side by side with *At First Sight.* One takes true experience and masks it with scenes that could literally be in any romantic melodrama; *Hilary and Jackie* feels as if every scene was newly drawn out of the sharp memories of actual lifetimes.

There is, of course, a lot of music in the film, and the sound track will be good to have; but it is not a film about performances, it is a film about performing: about how physically and emotionally difficult it is to travel from city to city, adored by strangers, far from friends, and find every night the ability to play the cello as well as it can be played. "Would you still love me if I couldn't play?" Jacqueline asks her husband. "You wouldn't be you if you didn't play," he replies, and that is the simple truth made clear by this film. We are what we do.

The Hi-Lo Country ★★

R, 114 m., 1999

Billy Crudup (Pete Calder), Woody Harrelson (Big Boy Matson), Patricia Arquette (Mona), Penelope Cruz (Josepha O'Neil), Sam Elliott (Jim Ed Love), Cole Hauser (Little Boy Matson), James Gammon (Hoover Young), Lane Smith (Steve Shaw), Katy Jurado (Meesa), Don Walser (Singer). Directed by Stephen Frears and produced by Barbara De Fina, Martin Scorsese, Eric Fellner, and Tim Bevan. Screenplay by Walon Green.

When poker players want to make the game a little more interesting, they either raise the stakes or declare a wild card. Woody Harrelson has the same effect on a movie. He has a reckless, risky air; he walks into a scene and you can't be sure what he'll do. He plays characters who are a challenge to their friends, let alone their enemies.

In Stephen Frears's *The Hi-Lo Country,* Harrelson has an energy the rest of the film lacks. He plays a variation on that old theme, the Last of the Cowboys, but does it with a modern irony. Watching his character tame unruly horses and strut into bars, I was reminded of a line from a completely different kind of movie, *A New Leaf,* where the aging playboy is told, "You are carrying on in your own lifetime a way of life that was dead before you were born."

Harrelson plays Big Boy Matson, a man's man in the arid Hi-Lo country of New Mexico. He's seen through the eyes of the film's narrator and nominal hero, Pete Calder (Billy Crudup), who returns to the area after serving in World War II and plans to raise cattle. He's advised against it by the rich local rancher Jim Ed Love (Sam Elliott), who says the days of the independent herds are over and gone. "People still drive cattle to railheads," Pete tells him. "Only in the movies," Jim Ed says.

The movie evokes the open space of New Mexico with a bright, dusty grandeur; Oliver Stapleton's camera places the characters in a wide-screen landscape of weathered buildings, lonesome windmills, and distant mountains. There do not seem to be enough people around; the inhabitants of the small town live in each other's pockets, and there are no secrets.

One secret that would be hard to keep is the allure of Mona (Patricia Arquette), a local man's wife who dances on Saturday nights at the tavern as if she might go home with the next man who takes her out on the floor. Mona likes Pete. Indeed, the first time she sees him after the war, at the tavern, she all but propositions him: "Am I keepin' you from something? Or someone? You look good, Pete. Real good." Pete dances with her, and confides in a voice-over, "She was right. I was lookin' for someone. She came up against me like silver foil, all fragrance and warm pressure."

That's not the sort of line a New Mexico cowboy is likely to use in 1946, but there's a kind of distance between the hard-boiled life of the Hi-Lo country and the poetry of the film, which wants the characters steeped in nostalgia and standing for a vanishing way of life. The screenplay is by Walon Green, who also wrote *The Wild Bunch,* which was more hard-boiled about nostalgia.

Mona's problem is, as good as Pete looks to her, Big Boy looks better. That's who she really loves, and who really loves her. But Big Boy is untamed, just like Old Sorrel, the unruly horse he bought from Pete. And Big Boy is incautious in his remarks. Even though Mona is married to a man with friends who have guns, Big Boy makes reckless announcements for the whole bar to hear, like "A good woman's like a good horse—she's got bottom. Mona's gonna make me a partner to go along with Old Sorrel."

The romantic lines grow even more tangled because there is, as there always is in a Western, a Good Woman who steadfastly stands by the hero even while he hangs out with the boys and the bad girls. This is Josepha (Penelope Cruz), a Mexican-American Pete was seeing before the war. She loves Pete, and Pete says he loves her (he lies), and she knows about Mona: "She's a cheap ex-prostitute and a phony."

Mona may be, but she's sincere in her love for Big Boy, and in one way or another that drives most of the plot. The underlying psychology of the film is in the tradition of those Freudian Westerns of the 1950s, in which a man was a man but a gun was sometimes not simply a gun. There's a buried attraction between Big Boy and Pete, who not only sleep with the same woman (and know they do) but engage in roughhouse and camaraderie in a way that suggests that no woman is ever going to be as important to them as a good buddy (or a horse). Jim Ed Love, of course, represents patriarchal authority: He stands for wisdom, experience, and money, and for telling boys to stop that fooling around and grow up.

Stephen Frears is an Irish director who therefore grew up steeped in the lore of the American West (country-and-western music is more popular in Irish pubs than in some states of the union). He's seen a lot of revisionist modern Westerns (especially *Giant*), and he gets the right look and feel for his film. But I think he brings a little too much taste and restraint to it. If he'd turned up the heat under the other characters, they could have matched Big Boy's energy, and the movie could have involved us in the way a good Western can.

Instead, *The Hi-Lo Country* is reserved and even elegiac. It's about itself, rather than about its story. The voice-over narration insists on that: It stands outside and above the story, and elevates it with self-conscious prose. By the end, we could be looking at Greek tragedy. Maybe that's the idea. But Harrelson suggests another way the movie could have gone. With his heedless energy and his sense of complete relaxation before the camera (he glides through scenes as easily as a Cary Grant), he shows how the movie might have been better off staying at ground level and forgetting about the mythological cloud's-eye view.

Note: Two small scenes deserve special mention. One involves the legendary Mexican-American actress Katy Jurado, as a fortune-teller. When the boys visit her, she's asked if "all of us who are here will be alive and prosperous next year." They get their money's worth: "No." The other showstopper is a C&W singer named Don Walser, whose high, sweet voice provides a moment when the movie forgets everything and just listens to him.

Holy Man ★ ★

PG, 113 m., 1998

Eddie Murphy ("G"), Jeff Goldblum (Ricky), Kelly Preston (Kate), Robert Loggia (McBainbridge), Jon Cryer (Barry), Eric McCormack (Scoot Hawkes), Sam Kitchin (Director), Robert Small (Assistant Director). Directed by Stephen Herek and produced by Roger Birnbaum and Herek. Screenplay by Tom Schulman.

Holy Man is a love story about two people with no apparent chemistry, whose lives are changed by a stranger who remains an uninteresting enigma. No wonder it just sits there on the screen. This screenplay was in no shape to be filmed; perhaps the filmmakers assumed that the mere presence of Eddie Murphy would repair its wrongs and give them a big opening weekend.

Murphy is a charismatic star in the right material. Give him *The Nutty Professor* and he sparkles. Put him in a half-digested formula, and he sinks as quickly as a mortal would. Examine his flops and you can almost hear the executives reassuring each other, "We don't need a rewrite; we have Eddie!"

In *Holy Man*, Murphy plays a man in Indian garb who wanders through life on his "pilgrimage" while reciting platitudes recycled from twelve-step programs. His story is counterpoint to a romance between two executives for a TV shopping network, whose relationship rigidly follows the conventional outline: They dislike each other on sight, they become rivals at work, then mutual respect flowers in a difficult situation, they fall in love, and then (of course) she is disillusioned when he sells out, and then (of course) he does what he knows is right, and she comes flying back into his arms. It helps if the final embrace can be broadcast on live TV.

The Murphy character, named simply "G," materializes while walking down the median strip of a Miami expressway. He spots TV executives Ricky and Kate (Jeff Goldblum and Kelly Preston) with a flat tire, and offers to help them. He looks like a loony. Then he walks calmly across four lanes of the expressway while every speeding car misses him. (The flaw in this computer-assisted effect is that none of the oncoming cars slows down or swerves.)

"G" becomes a part of their lives. He has no history, no story, no philosophy except for boilerplate advice like "Be careful what you wish for—you may get it." Opportunities for satire are lost because "G" is presented not only as a straight holy man, but as a boring one.

At a party of TV executives at Ricky's house, he confronts an obnoxious guest, borrows his Rolex, wraps it in a hanky and pounds it with a shoe. Then the Rolex disappears. "Give me back my goddamn watch!" shouts the guest, only to find it has been returned to his arm. Proof that "G" has miraculous powers? Only if you have not seen this trick done by countless magicians. (Ah, but did "G" perhaps perform it by miraculous means? If he did, I have advice for him: It's counterproductive to perform miracles that duplicate magic tricks.)

Ricky and Kate work for a TV shopping

network run by Robert Loggia. The movie, credulous and soppy in its story of "G" and the romance, tries uneasily to convert itself into sketch comedy in portraying the network. We see a lot of celebs hawking their wares ("The James Brown Soul Survival System," etc.). Then "G" wanders onto a live set and begins to speak the truth, and sales shoot up. He quickly becomes a superstar salesman and gets his own show, inevitably named *The G Spot*.

Holy Man's director, Stephen Herek, and his editor, Trudy Ship, fall into a tiresome editing pattern in showing "G" on the air. First "G" says something. Then we cut to counterpoint from the control booth. Then "G." Then the booth. There's editing Ping-Pong for seven or eight rounds, and the same formula is repeated every time "G" goes on the air. This is fatal to comedy, which must seem spontaneously generated and not timed according to a system imposed from above.

Goldblum and Preston don't convince us they're really in love, although perhaps sincerity is impossible to find in this story. Robert Loggia supplies the standard apoplectic executive without the quirks and eccentricities that would have elevated the character above the cookie-cutter level.

And as for Murphy, the movie seems to think its task was completed when it put Eddie in a holy man uniform. Consider his lengthiest parable. He was walking along the beach, he says, when he saw thousands of starfish washed ashore. Then he saw a girl throwing as many as she could back into the sea. "You are wasting your time," the holy man tells her, "because there are just too many starfish." The girl holds up the starfish she is holding. "To this one," she says, "it makes a difference."

You've heard it a thousand times. So have I. Let's deconstruct it. The first error is for "G" to claim the story happened to him. It is such an ancient parable that he is obviously lying. Second error: The girl teaches him the lesson. As a self-respecting guru, he should be throwing in the starfish and explaining it to her. Third error: The movie has him tell the story to listeners whose mouths gape open in astonishment at his wisdom. A smart screenplay would have had someone interrupt him: "Yeah, yeah, I know—it makes a difference to *this* starfish! Everybody's heard that story." If "G" has a comeback to that line, then he's a guru and not just another underwritten character.

Home Alone 3 ★ ★ ★

PG, 103 m., 1997

Alex D. Linz (Alex), Olek Krupa (Beaupre), Rya Kihlstedt (Alice), Lenny Von Dohlen (Jernigan), David Thornton (Unger), Haviland Morris (Karen), Kevin Kilner (Jack), Marian Seldes (Mrs. Hess). Directed by Raja Gosnell and produced by John Hughes and Hilton Green. Screenplay by Hughes.

"Call me hard-hearted, call me cynical, but please don't call me if they make *Home Alone 3*."

These words, from my review of *Home Alone 2*, now have to be eaten. To my astonishment, I liked the third *Home Alone* movie better than the first two; I'm even going so far as to recommend it, although not to grownups unless they are having a very silly day. This movie follows the exact formula of the first two, but is funnier and gentler, has a real charmer for a hero, and provides splendid wish-fulfillment and escapism for kids in, say, the lower grades.

There is even a better rationale for why the hero is left home alone. Played by a winning newcomer named Alex D. Linz, who seems almost too small for a middle initial, the kid gets the chicken pox. His dad is out of town on business, his mom has an emergency at the office, and his brother and sister are at school. So he's left home alone with a beeper number, a fax number, a cell phone number, the number of Mrs. Hess across the street, and dialing "911" as a fallback position.

The subplot has already been set into motion. An international spy ring has stolen a computer chip, and because of an exchange of identical bags at the San Francisco airport, the toy truck containing the chip has ended up at Mrs. Hess's house. Four spies fly to Chicago on the same plane with Mrs. Hess, and have four hours on board to search for the bag, but somehow they fail to find it, and end up deciding to burglarize every house on little Alex's block.

This is going to a lot of extra trouble, in my opinion. They use walkie-talkies, computer programs, surveillance vans, a fake baby buggy and other props in order to be as inefficient and conspicuous as possible, and of course Alex, using his telescope from an attic window, spots them. (Why they never spot Alex up there is the kind of question you're not supposed to ask.)

After he calls the cops twice but no burglars are found, Alex realizes it's up to him. He rigs a lot of elaborate booby traps, just like in the first two movies, and the last forty-five minutes of the film consist of nonstop pratfalls as the bad guys fall for every last trap. As I observed in my review of *Home Alone*, these are the kinds of traps that any eight-year-old could devise if he had a budget of tens of thousands of dollars and the assistance of a crew of movie special effects people.

So, okay. I know the formula, and so does the movie (written, like the first two, by John Hughes). Forewarned and forearmed as I was, why did I actually like *Home Alone 3*? It was partly because of little Alex Linz, who has a genuinely sweet smile on his face as he watches his traps demolish the bad guys. I don't know if he'll have a career like his predecessor, Macaulay Culkin (for his sake, I sort of hope not), but he has the same glint in his eye.

And the booby traps, while painful, are funnier this time. Sure, people fall down dumbwaiters and through floors, and get hit on the head with dumbbells and flower pots, and end up in the frozen swimming pool, but the direction by Raja Gosnell somehow sidesteps the painfulness and makes it okay. The stunts at the end are more pure slapstick and less special effects. And the result is either more entertaining than in the first two films, or I was having a very silly day.

Home Fries ★ ★ ★

PG-13, 92 m., 1998

Drew Barrymore (Sally), Catherine O'Hara (Mrs. Lever), Luke Wilson (Dorian), Jake Busey (Angus), Shelley Duvall (Mrs. Jackson), Kim Robillard (Billy), Daryl Mitchell (Roy), Lanny Flaherty (Red). Directed by Dean Parisot and produced by Mark Johnson, Barry Levinson, Lawrence Kasdan, and Charles Newirth. Screenplay by Vince Gilligan.

Home Fries is the kind of movie where a man is frightened to death by a helicopter, dies sitting bolt upright on a park bench, and one of his killers wants to pose with him. What kind of movie does that make it? I'm not sure. It has elements of sweet romance and elements of macabre humor, and divides its characters between the two—except for a performance by Catherine O'Hara that seems serenely astride both worlds.

The movie stars Drew Barrymore, perky and plucky, as Sally, a drive-thru clerk at the Burger-Matic. We see her in the opening scene, serving a vanilla shake to a middle-aged man who whispers that he has finally told his wife he was having an affair. "Did you tell her about this?" asks Sally, standing up tall so the creep can see how pregnant she is. He offers her a ride home and hints at other pastimes. "I don't need a ride home," she snaps. "I need a father for my baby."

It is all going to get a lot more complicated. Later that night, the man will be frightened to death. We'll meet the two helicopter pilots: Dorian (Luke Wilson) and Angus (Jake Busey). The police will break the news to the man's widow, Mrs. Lever (O'Hara). And then (spoiler warning) we discover that Dorian and Angus are her sons by an earlier marriage, that the dead man was her current husband, and that she encouraged them to scare him.

The sons have reason to suspect that their radio conversations in the helicopter were overheard by Sally on her Burger-Matic headphones, so Dorian gets a job in the drive-in to spy on her, and falls in love with her, little realizing that he is the killer of the father of her unborn child. Are you following this? They begin to fall in love, but as the full implications of their romance start to emerge, Sally tells Dorian, "You can't be the father and the brother at the same time. That's the kind of thing that messes kids up."

The movie requires Barrymore and Wilson to play their characters straight most of the time, while Catherine O'Hara mixes sweetness with irony and Jake Busey chews the scenery with those marvelous teeth. Seeing the movie for the first time at the Toronto Film Festival in September, I found parts of it amusing but doubted the whole. I wanted to see it again before writing this review, and was surprised to find I liked it better the second time. I suspect the barrage of twists and revelations was off-putting at Toronto, distracting from the wit in O'Hara's performance and the sweetness in Barrymore's. The first time, you think the movie is about the plot, and the second time you realize it's about the characters.

This is one of O'Hara's best screen performances. The former Second City star is sweetness and reason as she manipulates her two luggy sons and brazenly acts her way through meetings with the cops and her late husband's young lover. She is so calm, so cool, she implies scary depths that she never has to reveal.

Barrymore, who is emerging this year as a versatile star (there's a big distance between this and *Ever After*), is wise to play Sally on a more or less realistic level, focusing on her pregnancy and newfound romance, and remaining oblivious (when possible) to the web of intrigue around her. She avoids the actor's mistake of knowing more about the screenplay than her character would know.

The movie is the feature debut of Dean Parisot, based on a screenplay that I gather Vince Gilligan found in his bottom drawer after *The X-Files* made him bankable. It might have seemed fresher ten years ago, before this kind of ironic labyrinthine plotting became common, but he has a sharp eye for characters, and introduces Sally's parents (Shelley Duvall and Lanny Flaherty) during an apparent fast-food hostage crisis that dissolves into a marital spat before our eyes.

Home Fries is not a great movie, and as much as I finally enjoyed it, I'm not sure it's worth seeing two times just to get into the rhythm. More character and less plot might have been a good idea. But the actors are tickled by their characters and have fun with them, and so I did too.

And I liked the wicked human comedy in scenes like the one where the blustering, dopey Angus (Busey) asks O'Hara, "Mom, what'd you mean when you said Dorian was your favorite?"

"Oh, Angus," she says, with fondness and exasperation, "I love you both. A difference of this much." She holds her thumb and forefinger two inches apart, knowing that when your mother likes your brother more, an inch is as good as a mile.

Hoodlum ★★★

R, 130 m., 1997

Laurence Fishburne (Bumpy Johnson), Tim Roth (Dutch Schultz), Vanessa L. Williams (Francine Hughes), Andy Garcia (Lucky Luciano), Cicely Tyson (Stephanie St. Clair), Chi McBride (Illinois Gordon), Clarence Williams III (Bub Hewlett), William Atherton (Thomas E. Dewey). Directed by Bill Duke and produced by Frank Mancuso Jr. Screenplay by Chris Brancato.

The business of crime is as much business as crime, as Scorsese demonstrated in *Casino* by centering his story on a gangster who was essentially an accountant and oddsmaker. Now Bill Duke's *Hoodlum* looks into the way the Mafia muscled into the black-run policy racket in Harlem in the 1930s; this is a "gangster movie" in a sense, but it is also about free enterprise, and about how, as the hero says when asked why he didn't go into medicine or law, "I'm a colored man, and white folks left me crime."

Of course, that is not quite the whole story, but by the time Bumpy Johnson (Laurence Fishburne) says it, it's true of him: He's a smart ex-con, returned to the streets of Harlem during its prewar renaissance, when music, arts, and commerce flourished along with the numbers game. He hooks up with old friends, including Illinois Gordon (Chi McBride), who masks his feelings with jokes and introduces him to a social worker, Francine Hughes (Vanessa Williams). Francine sees the good in Bumpy, and encourages him to make something of himself, but Bumpy defends his career choice: "The numbers provide jobs for over 2,000 colored folks right here in Harlem alone. It's the only homegrown business we got."

The game is run by Stephanie St. Clair (Cicely Tyson), known as the Queen of Numbers. She's from the islands, elegant, competitive. She takes on Bumpy as her lieutenant. The mob has up until now let Harlem run its own rackets, but Dutch Schultz (Tim Roth) moves in, trying to take over the numbers. His nominal boss is the powerful Lucky Luciano (Andy Garcia), who disapproves of Schultz because of the way he dresses ("You got mustard on your suit"), and is inclined to stand back and see what happens. He doesn't mind if Schultz takes over Harlem, but is prepared to do business with the Queen and Bumpy if that's the way things work out.

One thing that has kept the Mafia from attaining more power in America is that it has a tendency to murder its most ambitious members; the guys who keep a low profile may survive, but are not leadership material. Imagine a modern corporation run along the same lines. Bumpy is the farsighted strategist who sees that it's better to talk than fight; Dutch is the thug who itches to start shooting.

This is Bill Duke's second period film set in Harlem, after *A Rage in Harlem* (1991). He likes the clothes, the cars, the intrigue. (In both films, interestingly, he didn't film in Harlem, finding better period locations in Cincinnati for *Rage* and in Chicago for *Hoodlum.*) He builds up to some effective set-pieces, including a massacre that interrupts a trip to the opera; in the payoff, Bumpy and the Queen listen to an aria while he has blood on his shirt.

The film's argument is that the policy racket, like many legitimate homegrown black businesses, was appropriated by whites when it became too powerful. The streets of inner-city America are lined with shuttered storefronts while their former customers line up at Wal-Mart. And, yes, there is an element of racism involved: When I was growing up in Champaign-Urbana in the 1940s and 1950s, the richest black man in town was said to be Wardell Jackson, the reputed local numbers czar. Whites had no problem with the numbers (some played), but they couldn't stop talking about how a black man could make all that money.

Duke and his screenwriter, Chris Brancato, don't make *Hoodlum* into a violent action film, although it has its bloody shoot-outs, but into more of a character study. Schultz is painted as a crude braggart, Lucky Luciano is suave and insightful, and the most intriguing figure among the white characters is crime-fighter Thomas Dewey, who ran for president in 1948 as a reformer, but is portrayed here, in scenes sure to be questioned in many quarters, as a corrupt grafter. (Schultz observes that he is paying off Dewey at the same time the famed prosecutor is getting headlines for trying to put him in jail.)

Bumpy Johnson is played by Fishburne as someone who could have had a legit career, and he's torn when Francine, the social worker, cools toward him because of his occupation. Illinois Gordon, his best friend, also asks hard and idealistic questions, especially after a funeral. By creating these two characters, the screenplay gives Bumpy somewhere to turn and someone to talk to, so he isn't limited to action scenes. As Stephanie St. Clair, Cicely Tyson models her character on real women of the period, who were tough, independent, and used men without caving in to them.

Hoodlum is being marketed as a violent action picture, and in a sense it is. But Duke has made a historical drama as much as a thriller, and his characters reflect a time when Harlem seemed poised on the brink of better things, and the despair of the postwar years was not easily seen on its prosperous streets. Was the policy game all that bad? Sure, the odds were stiff, but a couple of times a week, someone had to win. These days, it's called the lottery.

Hope Floats ★ ★

PG-13, 114 m., 1998

Sandra Bullock (Birdee Pruitt), Harry Connick Jr. (Justin Matisse), Gena Rowlands (Ramona Calvert), Mae Whitman (Bernice Pruitt), Michael Pare (Bill Pruitt), Cameron Finley (Travis), Kathy Najimy (Toni Post). Directed by Forest Whitaker and produced by Lynda Obst. Screenplay by Steven Rogers.

Hope Floats begins with a talk show where a woman learns that her husband and her best friend are having an affair. Devastated, she flees from Chicago with her young daughter, and moves back in with her mother in Smithville, Texas. Everybody in Smithville (and the world), of course, witnessed her public humiliation. "Why did you go on that show in the first place?" her mother asks. "Because I wanted a free makeover," she says. "Well, you got one."

The victim's name is Birdee Pruitt (Sandra

Bullock), and she was three-time Queen of Corn in Smithville. But she doesn't type and she doesn't compute, and her catty former classmate, who runs the local employment agency, tells her, "I don't see a listing here for prom queen." Birdee finally gets a job in a photo developing lab, where the owner asks her to make extra prints of any "interesting" snapshots.

This material could obviously lead in a lot of different directions. It seems most promising as comedy or satire, but no: *Hope Floats* is a turgid melodrama with the emotional range of a sympathy card.

Consider the cast of characters in Smithville. Birdee is played by Bullock as bewildered by her husband's betrayal (even though he's such a pig that she must have had hints over the years). Birdee's mother, Ramona (Gena Rowlands), is a salt-of-the-earth type who's able to live in a rambling Victorian mansion *and* keep her husband in a luxurious retirement home, despite having no apparent income. Birdee's daughter, Bernice (Mae Whitman), is a little drip who keeps whining that she wants to live with Daddy, despite overwhelming evidence that Daddy is a cretin. And then there's Justin (Harry Connick Jr.), the old boyfriend Birdee left behind, who's still in love with her and spends his free time restoring big old homes. (There is no more reliable indicator of a male character's domestic intentions than when he invites the woman of his dreams to touch his newly installed pine.)

Hope Floats is one of those screenplays where everything that will happen is instantly obvious, and yet the characters are forced to occupy a state of oblivion, acting as if it's all a mystery to them. It is obvious that Birdee's first husband is a worthless creep. And that Justin and Birdee will fall in love once again. And that Bernice will not go home to live with Daddy and his new girlfriend. And that the creeps who are still jealous of the onetime Corn Queen will get their comeuppance. The only real mystery in the movie is how Birdee keeps her job at Snappy Snaps despite apparently ruining every roll of film she attempts to process (the only photo she successfully develops during the entire movie is apparently done by magic realism).

I grow restless when I sense a screenplay following a schedule so faithfully that it's like a train conductor with a stopwatch. Consider, for example, the evening of tender romance and passion between Birdee and Justin. What comes next? A fight, of course. There's a grim dinner scene at which everyone stares unhappily at their plates, no doubt thinking they would be having a wonderful time—if only the screenwriter hadn't required an obligatory emotional slump between the false dawn and the real dawn.

I watch these formulas unfold, and I reflect that the gurus who teach those Hollywood screenwriting classes have a lot to answer for. They claim their formulas are based on analysis of successful movies. But since so many movies have been written according to their formulas, there's a kind of self-fulfilling prophecy going on here. Isn't it at least theoretically possible that after a man and a woman spend an evening in glorious romantic bliss, they could still be glowing the next day?

Hope Floats was written by Steven Rogers and directed by Forest Whitaker *(Waiting to Exhale)*. It shows evidence of still containing shreds of earlier drafts. At one point, for example, Birdee accuses her mother of embarrassing her as a child with her "roadkill hat and freshly skinned purse." Well, it's a good line, and it suggests that Gena Rowlands will be developed as one of the ditzy eccentrics she plays so well. But actually she's pretty sensible in this movie, and the line doesn't seem to apply.

There's also the problem that the sweet romantic stuff coexists uneasily with harsher scenes, as when little Bernice discovers her daddy doesn't want her to move back in with him. The whole TV talk show setup, indeed, deals the movie a blow from which it never recovers: No film that starts so weirdly should develop so conventionally. Sandra Bullock seems to sense that in her performance; her character wanders through the whole movie like a person who senses that no matter what Harry Connick thinks, she will always be known as the Corn Queen who got dumped on TV.

The Horse Whisperer ★ ★ ★

PG-13, 160 m., 1998

Robert Redford (Tom Booker), Kristin Scott Thomas (Annie MacLean), Scarlett Johansson (Grace MacLean), Sam Neill (Robert MacLean), Dianne Wiest (Diane Booker), Chris Cooper (Frank Booker), Cherry Jones (Liz Hammond), Ty Hillman (Joe Booker). Directed by Robert Redford and produced by Redford and Patrick Markey. Screenplay by Eric Roth and Richard LaGravenese, based on the novel by Nicholas Evans.

The Horse Whisperer is about a man of great patience faced with a woman, a child, and a horse in great need of it. It evokes the healing serenity of the wide-open spaces, and while I suspect that an unhappy New Yorker who moves to Montana is likely to become an unhappy Montanan, I concede that the myth is comforting. In films going back to *Jeremiah Johnson,* Robert Redford has shown that he has a real feeling for the West—he's not a movie tourist—and there is a magnificence in his treatment here that dignifies what is essentially a soap opera.

The story, from the best-selling novel by Nicholas Evans, involves a riding accident that leaves a horse named Pilgrim crippled, and a girl named Grace (Scarlett Johansson) so badly injured that part of her leg must be amputated. The girl's parents are high-powered Manhattanites: The father (Sam Neill) is a lawyer, and the mother, Annie (Kristin Scott Thomas), is clearly modeled on editor Tina Brown.

Their farm workers believe the horse should be put down (it's fearful and skittish), but Annie reads about a famed "horse whisperer" named Tom Booker who heals troubled animals. Booker (Redford) turns her down over the phone, but she's a type-A compulsive who decides to drive both the horse and her daughter to Montana and confront him directly. Her daughter fears "no one will ever want me" with only one leg; if the horse heals, Annie thinks, maybe Grace will heal too.

That's the setup. The heart of the film is in Big Sky country, where Tom Booker runs a cattle ranch with his brother Frank (Chris Cooper) and Frank's wife, Diane (Dianne Wiest). Tom was married once; it was love at first sight, but it didn't last because his city-born wife found the ranch had "too much space for her." Now he's famed for using patience and a gentle touch with difficult horses.

How does horse whispering work? As nearly as I could tell, Tom stares at the horse until the horse gets the idea. Eventually the horse succumbs to its need for love and acceptance. These methods work equally well with women, as both Grace and Annie discover; the girl's anger dissolves, and her mother, a brittle workaholic, finds her hyper personality dissolving in the mountain air—as she falls in love with Tom.

To describe the plot in this way makes it sound cornier than it feels. The elements are borrowed from elsewhere; there's a touch of *The Bridges of Madison County* in the married woman's love for a man who represents freedom, and a touch of *My Friend Flicka* and its sequel, *Thunderhead,* in the treatment of a rebellious horse.

But Redford, as director and star, relates to the underlying themes of the story, which is about city versus country, and responsibility versus passion. The very lifestyle of Redford's ranch is a character in the movie; his plump, cheerful sister-in-law is a contented contrast to Annie, the rail-thin New Yorker who tries to control everything (fretting about her daughter's hospital care, she vows, "I'm going to get to know all the nurses' names"). There are big meals, long hours, and head-clearing rides on the range.

This life has imbued Tom Booker with an empathy that allows him to identify with pain, and for me the best scenes in the movie involved his careful touch with Grace. She's sullen and withdrawn at first, but he insists that Pilgrim will be ridden again—and Grace will ride him. He handles her with respect, and there's a nice moment when he asks her to drive the ranch pickup. She can't drive, she says. "No time like the present to start," he says.

The scenes between Tom and Annie are more problematic. Both adults begin to see the other as the ideal mate they've always been looking for. Love grows between them in unspoken words and quick glances, and eventually it appears that Annie is destined to leave her husband and stay on the ranch with the Bookers. She has fallen so much under the spell of the West that when she's fired from her magazine job, she hardly seems to notice. And Tom sees in her what he needs to see in a woman—what he saw in his wife, until she left.

"This is me," Tom tells her, looking around at the ranch. "This is where I belong. Could you live here?" Yes, says Annie, she could. Maybe that's because she sees the West in terms of a Redford film. Before she burns her bridges, I'd advise her to see *City Slickers.* I never felt much chemistry between Scott Thomas and Redford; their characters are in love with the idea of one another, not with each other's bodies and souls. And so Redford and his writers, Eric Roth and Richard LaGravenese, were correct to supply their story with a different ending than Nicholas Evans's climax.

What works is the beauty of the western country, the tactful way Tom deals with Grace, and the touching scenes in which the damaged horse is healed. The story moves a little too slowly, but it respects its characters, and even the lawyer from New York, when he finally arrives out west, turns out to be a person of insight and intelligence (his confession to his wife is really more touching than anything Tom says to her). *The Horse Whisperer* treads on the brink of contrivance, but the honesty of its feelings pulls it through.

Hotel de Love ★ ★ ½

R, 96 m., 1997

Aden Young (Rick Dunne), Saffron Burrows (Melissa Morrison), Simon Bossell (Stephen Dunne), Pippa Grandison (Alison Leigh), Ray Barrett (Jack Dunne), Julia Blake (Edith Dunne), Peter O'Brien (Norman), Belinda McClory (Janet). Directed by Craig Rosenberg and produced by Michael Lake and David Parker. Screenplay by Rosenberg.

"I fell in love even before I saw her," Stephen, the hero of *Hotel de Love,* tells us. He walked into a party when he was a teenager, felt love, turned and saw Melissa, and that was that. Unfortunately, while walking across the room toward her, he was interrupted for a moment and his twin, Rick, started chatting her up. That was that. Melissa and Rick dated until Melissa moved on with her life, and then years passed like a heartbeat.

These days Stephen (Simon Bossell) sells stocks, and Rick (Aden Young) manages the Hotel de Love, an establishment for which "tacky" would be high praise. It's a honeymoon hotel in which every room illustrates a different theme: one is for soccer fans, one looks like a tropical rain forest, one seems to be a cave. The hotel even has a tiny waterfall named Niagara Smalls.

One day Melissa (Saffron Burrows) returns and checks into the hotel, radiant. She plans to marry the fairly uninteresting Norman (Peter O'Brien). Neither Stephen nor Rick approve of this plan, although Rick has never known that his twin also loved Melissa.

Stephen is not a young man of great self-confidence. He has small twitches, so fast you almost miss them, and a way of bottling up his emotions until they come popping out in a rush. "I love you!" he blurts to Melissa at the door of her room before running away. He turns up so often for such lightning declarations that she eventually calls them "drive-by 'I-love-yous.'" What, he wonders, does Melissa possibly see in Norman the human coat hanger? "Norman and I discuss ideas and philosophies," she explains. "That is not love," Stephen says. "That is a book group."

Hotel de Love is an Australian film in the current tradition of such films, which means that everyone seems secretly peculiar while trying to appear friendly and normal. Australian movies make a particular specialty of dad and mum, who seem to have spent years perfecting a dysfunctional mutual symbiosis. Jack and Edith Dunne, the parents of the twins, have also checked into the hotel—to renew their vows or kill each other in the attempt, it would appear.

The key player in this drama, although at first we don't realize it, is Alison (Pippa Grandison), a palmist and fortune-teller who is Rick's girlfriend as the movie opens and eventually becomes Stephen's friend. She's a dark, lively brunette, who befriends poor Stephen as he carries his hopeless torch for Melissa. Of course, Stephen is destined to eventually notice that true love is right there under his nose, but that will require a lot of deep thought, not to mention the movie's prologue and epilogue, to accomplish.

Hotel de Love is a pleasant and sometimes funny film, without being completely satisfying. It is too twee. Too many lines are said for their cuteness, too many exchanges sound like a comedy routine, and the movie works too earnestly at being daffy. Melissa never convinces me she deserves ten years of anybody's obsession, while Alison is worth a good fifteen. I also grew impatient at a subplot involving anonymous love poems. The one character I wanted more of was the hotel's owner, who plays cocktail piano in the lobby and has a song for every occasion—including ones the characters don't quite realize they are having.

The House of Yes ★ ★ ½

R, 86 m., 1997

Parker Posey (Jackie-O), Josh Hamilton (Marty), Tori Spelling (Lesly), Freddie Prinze Jr. (Anthony), Genevieve Bujold (Mrs. Pascal), Rachael Leigh Cook (Young Jackie-O), David Love (Voice of Young Marty). Directed by Mark Waters and produced by Beau Flynn and Stefan Simchowitz. Adapted for the screen by Waters, based on the stage play by Wendy MacLeod.

"It's just . . . that we've never had a guest before." Not what you want to hear when you're the guest. On a stormy Thanksgiving night in 1983, in a Virginia suburb, Marty Pascal brings home his fiancée to meet his family. They include his twin sister, who calls herself Jackie-O; his kid brother, Anthony (who reveals she's their first guest); and his mother, who tells her children, "I look at you people and wonder, how did you ever fit in my womb?"

The House of Yes exists somewhere between *Long Day's Journey into Night* and *The Addams Family*, as the story of a damaged family that has somehow struggled along until the introduction of a stranger brings all of its secrets crawling into the light. As the story opens, Jackie-O (Parker Posey) is disturbed to learn from Anthony (Freddie Prinze Jr.) that their brother, Marty (Josh Hamilton), is bringing a friend home for the holiday. She is even more ominously alarmed when Marty introduces Lesly (Tori Spelling) and announces that they are engaged.

Few actresses can smolder from beneath lowered brows more dramatically than Parker Posey, and she receives this news with ill-concealed dismay. Her mother, Mrs. Pascal (Genevieve Bujold), does little to reassure their guest: "Jackie and Marty belong to each other. Jackie's hand was holding Marty's penis when they came out of the womb." Anthony, who loses no time visiting Lesly in the guest room, has hopes of talking her out of his brother and into sleeping with him. Outside, the storm rages.

The film's opening scenes intercut actual TV footage of Jacqueline Kennedy's tour of the White House with Jackie-O's parallel tour of her family's home. The real Mrs. Kennedy is surprisingly simpering in the old footage; her memory is not well served by repeating the broadcast. Jackie-O, whose wardrobe copies Mrs. Kennedy's, later turns up in the same pink dress and pillbox hat that the president's wife wore on the fatal trip to Dallas. She reveals that she and her brother often play a game reenacting the shooting, with ketchup and pasta as props for blood and brains.

It's clear fairly soon that Marty and Lesly will never be married and may indeed not last the night. After Anthony's visit to Lesly's room, Jackie-O goes up for a chat ("Where's the wildest place you've ever made love?"). Marty tells the family he met Lesly behind the counter at a Donut King store ("She smells like powdered sugar"). As played well by Tori Spelling, she reads the situation quickly and responds appropriately, by trying to get the hell out of the house. The best exchange between Lesly and Jackie-O comes when the sister says, "Pretend he's not my brother," and Lesly answers quickly, "I do."

The arc of the movie is not hard to predict. The dialogue, adapted by director Mark Waters from Wendy MacLeod's stage play, is smart and terse, with a lot of back-and-forth word play, most of it driven by Jackie-O, who is played by Posey as smart, dark, and fresh out of an institution. When the film was over I was not particularly pleased that I had seen it; it was mostly behavior and contrivance. While it was running, I was not bored.

How Stella Got Her Groove Back ★ ★ ½

R, 116 m., 1998

Angela Bassett (Stella), Whoopi Goldberg (Delilah), Taye Diggs (Winston), Regina King (Vanessa), Suzzanne Douglas (Angela), Michael J. Pagan (Quincy). Directed by Kevin Rodney Sullivan and produced by Deborah Schindler. Screenplay by Ron Bass and Terry McMillan.

How Stella Got Her Groove Back tries its best to turn a paperback romance into a relationship worth making a movie about, but fails. At the end of the movie we're prepared to concede that Stella may indeed have her groove back, but at a considerable price, and maybe not for long. If a romantic couple feels wrong to the audience, no plot gymnastics can convince us.

The movie stars Angela Bassett as Stella, a divorced mom and high-powered San Francisco trader who, as the movie opens, is promising a client a guaranteed 65 percent return on some Russian bonds. Her personal life is lonely, and her sisters advise her to find a man. I'm thinking—if those returns are real, the man will find you.

Stella's best friend, Delilah (Whoopi Goldberg), lays down the law: It's time for them to fly to Jamaica for some R&R. Her first morning, Stella finds herself at breakfast with an improbably handsome young man (Taye Diggs) who introduces himself as Winston Shakespeare. Delilah has lined up a couple of football players for them to party with, but Winston keeps coming around and being sincere and catching at corners of her heart, until Stella realizes she has a problem on her hands: There is the danger they will actually fall in love.

But she is forty and he is twenty and, as Winston's mother says when Stella eventually meets her, "You ought to be ashamed of yourself!" That's about all Winston's mother says. She's trundled onstage for her obligatory line and disappears, along with Winston's father, who doesn't even get a line. At least we got to see what a nice home Winston was raised in. The movie doesn't really care about the parents; it just needs them for a plot point. In a different kind of movie, the parents would have been dealt with, not just put on exhibit.

Meanwhile (spoiler coming up), Delilah is revealed as dying of cancer. It's one of those deaths that makes you cringe, because its only function in the plot is to provide a deathbed scene and a funeral scene (at which, yes, inevitably, Winston arrives late and stands silhouetted in the church doorway just as Stella is delivering her remarks. Has the key person at such a movie event ever arrived on time?). Goldberg and Bassett are fine actors, and the deathbed scene is indeed effective—funny and then sad. But that doesn't make it necessary. (During the course of the film, Stella also goes though two major changes involving employment, both of which seem unnecessary except to establish her professional status.)

Winston moves in with Stella while they test their relationship and the age gap between them. I had problems with those passages because, frankly, I couldn't find any genuine common ground for the two of them, except for physical passion, which can be wonderfully entertaining, yes, but is not invariably the best reason to get married. Stella sometimes has similar doubts, and has a good line: "He's never done anything, he's never been anyplace, he hasn't even had his heart broken. This morning I found Cocoa Puffs in the bed."

Is a twenty-year age difference surmountable? Sure, but maybe not when the man is still unformed (he says he wants to be a doctor). What about Stella? Will she return to her first love, woodworking? In ten years, young Dr. Shakespeare will be introducing his fifty-year-old wife, the cabinetmaker. Maybe she'd be better off looking for somebody like Marvin, the handyman in *Waiting to Exhale*.

Both that movie and this one are based on novels by Terry McMillan, with screenplays by Ron Bass. This time, though, the material is thinner and less convincing, and the movie is slow moving as Stella and Winston go through the routine of fighting and making up until we want to advise them: Look, try shacking up for a year or two and see how things work out.

Angela Bassett is an actress with aggressive intelligence, and when she plays a capable, smart woman, she can be fascinating. See her in *Malcolm X*, *What's Love Got to Do With It*, and *Strange Days*. The problem with *Stella* is that she has been given a woman who the screenplay *says* is smart, but whose intelligence doesn't come into play; if it did, Stella's relationship with Winston would be either briefer or much more complex. Instead, it's been smoothed down into manufactured suspense about whether these two nice people will find true love.

That's where I began. If a couple feels right to an audience, then we cheer for their romance and allow ourselves to care—if only for the length of a silly movie. In *The Parent Trap,* a silly movie if ever there was one, there's genuine chemistry between Dennis Quaid and Natasha Richardson, and so in a dumb way we're cheered by their happiness. In *Stella Got Her Groove Back,* I never felt Stella and Winston were on the same wavelength, that they could share their lives, that it would be a good idea for them to try. Oh, I believed Winston was blinded by her. But I couldn't believe in Stella's feelings. Even at the end, as they embrace, I was giving them three weeks, tops.

Hurlyburly ★ ★ ★

R, 122 m., 1998

Sean Penn (Eddie), Kevin Spacey (Mickey), Robin Wright Penn (Darlene), Chazz Palminteri (Phil), Garry Shandling (Artie), Anna Paquin (Donna), Meg Ryan (Bonnie). Directed by Anthony Drazan and produced by Drazan, Richard N. Gladstein, and David S. Hamburger. Screenplay by David Rabe.

First witch: *When shall we three meet again? In thunder, lightning, or in rain?*
Second witch: *When the hurlyburly's done, When the battle's lost and won.*

—Macbeth

The philosopher William James thought that addiction expressed a yearning for the divine. While the characters in *Hurlyburly* have probably never heard of him (or Henry James or Harry James, for that matter—maybe no James but Etta), there is a real sense that Eddie, the most perpetually stoned character, is using drugs to escape from his hell on Earth. His hell has been created by the drugs he employs to escape it, an irony too simple for a mind that hurls challenges at the universe.

Eddie (Sean Penn) is a Hollywood casting agent who must be doing okay, judging by the house he has up in the Hollywood Hills. His roommate for the time being is Mickey (Kevin Spacey), who is on leave from wife and kids and bemused by the menagerie in Eddie's living room. Phil (Chazz Palminteri) is a frequent visitor, an actor with a sinister emotional underside. He turns up from time to time, and so does Artie (Garry Shandling), who materializes with a "CARE package"—an underage drifter (Anna Paquin) who is ready to trade sex for just about anything.

The major presence in Eddie's life is Darlene (Robin Wright Penn), his girlfriend, who likes him but has her eyes open and sees that Eddie is so far gone into cocaine that she'd better start looking around for another port in the storm. Mickey, maybe? And then there's a stripper named Bonnie (Meg Ryan), who sometimes goes out with Phil. Some of these gender couplings are entirely sex-based, while others append the illusion of meaning; Eddie, for example, is convinced he loves Darlene, although his love is expressed less by communicating with Darlene than by monologues about her that he delivers to his own drug-crazed brain.

The movie follows the loop-the-loops of habitual drug users. The rhythm of a day takes its shape from the availability of drugs and the degree and timing of usage. This is an important insight, because in David Rabe's perceptive screenplay there is no attempt to fashion the usual sort of dramatic give and take. Among characters who are in control of their lives, a dramatic piece takes form based on what they do and say. Among characters who are heavy into drugs, more depends on what is done and said to them.

There is a convention that booze and drugs bring truth. "In vino veritas," the Romans said, and Eugene O'Neill wrote his best plays about boozers who pursued truth into the night. Eddie, the Sean Penn character, is a bruised romantic with a good mind, who is as unhappy as a person can be, and in a remarkable scene uses cocaine to take him to a place of raw emotional pain. It is a remarkable performance.

The others talk, talk, talk. The most amusing is Spacey, who likes to hold himself a little aloof from a scene, as if he were the teacher. His sardonic intelligence aims a zinger here and there; we get the sense that he's only visiting, while the others live in this purgatory. We see that ordinary human judgment has been eroded by cocaine, that people use sex as a way of paying for it (or as a way of having something they can pay for), that if you tape-recorded the talk in this living room for a year it would all just go around and around and around.

There are times, indeed, when *Hurlyburly* feels like a year on a merry-go-round. There are brief excursions to the outside world, but the attention of the characters is always focused on the source of the drugs. They must, essentially, renew contact with the life in this room at regular intervals, or detox, or die, or kill themselves. Drugs make them talk but give them nothing to say. Eddie senses that. He wants to break out. He's digging himself in deeper, but at least his instinct is sound.

Hurricane Streets ★ ★

R, 88 m., 1998

Brendan Sexton III (Marcus), Isidra Vega (Melena), Carlo Alban (Benny), David Roland Frank (Chip), Antoine McLean (Harold), Lynn Cohen (Lucy), Damian Corrente (Justin), L. M. Kit Carson (Mack), Jose Zuniga (Kramer). Directed by Morgan J. Freeman and produced by Galt Niederhoffer, Gill Holland, and Freeman.

Hurricane Streets takes place on the Lower East Side of New York, where its five characters, all fourteen or fifteen, commute to their crimes on bicycles. They're petty thieves who hang out in a secret clubroom and earn spending money by shoplifting CDs and athletic shoes, which they sell at a discount on playgrounds. It's only a matter of time until they graduate to more serious and dangerous things (indeed, it's a little hard to believe, in today's world, that they're not already drug couriers).

The group is racially mixed. The story mostly concerns a white kid, Marcus (Brendan Sexton III), whose mother is in prison and whose grandmother is raising him, after a fashion (she owns a bar, and that's where she holds his birthday party). Marcus dreams of someday moving to New Mexico with his mother, after she gets out on probation, but he doesn't have all the information about when that will be. Meanwhile, he meets a Latina girl named Melena (Isidra Vega) and dates her despite the opposition of her father.

The kids are on the brink of big trouble. The cops know who they are and what they're doing. They're ready to graduate to auto theft and burglary, and their days of stealing food from convenience stores are soon going to resemble a time of innocence. Their story may sound similar to *Kids, Fresh, Straight Out of Brooklyn,* and other films about tough street kids, but *Hurricane Streets* is mild by comparison—more of a love story than a sociological drama. The kids seem relatively harmless and normal, and the plot depends not on impending tragedy but on unlikely coincidences, including one that leads to a very unlikely death.

If you saw *Welcome to the Dollhouse,* the wonderful film about a junior high school girl in the midst of unpopular geekhood, you may remember Brendan Sexton III, the actor who plays Marcus here. In that film he tormented the heroine; that was his way of showing affection, and when he makes a date to "rape" her, she shows up for it—although clearly neither one knows exactly what to do then. Here he's an unlikely hero, a sad sack who drifts through a fairly clueless existence with little of the intelligence that made the characters in *Fresh* and those other films so interesting. His story is sad, yes, but he is not very compelling as its hero.

There was a time, I suppose, when *Hurricane Streets* would have been seen as a harrowing slice of life. So many better films have told the stories of alienated young street kids, alas, that this one seems relatively superficial. The dialogue sounds written, not said, and the twists in the plot are unconvincing (the characters are always able to turn up where and when they're needed).

Hurricane Streets won the Best Director and Best Cinematography at the 1997 Sundance Film Festival. And the "Audience Award." That means the audience preferred it to *In the Company of Men, Chasing Amy, Kissed, Suburbia,* and *love jones.* Strange.

Hush ★ ★

PG-13, 95 m., 1998

Jessica Lange (Martha), Gwyneth Paltrow (Helen), Johnathon Schaech (Jackson), Nina

Foch (Alice Baring), Debi Mazar (Lisa), Kaiulani Lee (Sister O'Shaughnessy), David Thornton (Gavin), Hal Holbrook (Dr. Hill). Directed by Jonathan Darby and produced by Douglas Wick. Screenplay by Darby and Jane Rusconi.

Hush is the kind of movie where you walk in, watch the first ten minutes, know exactly where it's going, and hope devoutly that you're wrong. It's one of those Devouring Woman movies where the villainess never plays a scene without a drink and a cigarette, and the hero is inattentive to the victim to the point of dementia.

Gwyneth Paltrow stars as Helen, a New York career woman who's in love with Jackson (Johnathon Schaech). He takes her home to Virginia to meet his mother, Martha (Jessica Lange), and see the family spread, named Kilronan—a famous horse farm with a main house that looks like Thomas Jefferson either designed it or meant to. The house is large, elaborately decorated, and eerie, but then we knew it would be eerie because the music over the opening titles is "Hush, Little Baby," and that's a song used only in horror films.

Martha is a controlling woman, possessive about her beloved son. She prepares separate bedrooms for them. "It's a Catholic thing," Jackson explains, but when Martha accidentally finds the naked Helen in her son's bed she doesn't seem very perturbed, and I suspect the Catholic theme is there only because Hollywood traditionally depends on the church for props and atmosphere whenever true evil needs to be evoked.

It's a big house, with no servants. "She can't keep 'em," sniffs feisty old Alice (Nina Foch), Jackson's paternal grandmother, who lives in a nursing home and is prepared to talk to anyone, anytime, about Martha's devious ways. The youngsters are deep into lust, which seizes them at inopportune moments, so that they make love on the floor of the entry hall one night, while Martha observes from a shadowed landing.

Is Martha jealous of Helen's sexual relationship with her son? Not at all. She's a horse woman. "Started as a stable girl," Alice tells Helen, supplying a graphic explanation of the ways in which a woman like Martha not only breeds horses in the figurative sense, but is right there in the middle of the fray when a mare needs calming or a stallion needs guidance. Martha devises a way to inspire the young couple to leave New York and move to Kilronan, and we gather she hopes to breed a male heir to Kilronan by Jackson, out of Helen. Once she has one, of course, Helen may become unnecessary.

The general outlines of this scheme are visible early in the film, and the details grow more graphic, right up until a "push! push!" childbirth scene that is given a whole new spin. What's frustrating is that little of the evildoing would be possible if Jackson behaved at any moment like a normal, intelligent person. He consistently does the wrong thing just because the film needs him to.

The plot lumbers on its way to setting up the finale. Martha deviously tells Helen one thing and Jackson another, and we can hear the screenplay creaking in her dialogue. She spreads rumors that could be corrected in an instant if anyone bothered. The old family doctor (Hal Holbrook) is called upon for specialized information that is so transparently dangerous that the audience snickers.

And then credulity breaks down totally. I will step carefully here, to preserve some secrets. I was amazed by the sequence of events after Jackson leaves the big horse race and speeds home to the rescue, only to never go near his possibly dying wife. I was astonished by her miraculous recovery, so that she could preside over a denouement that's not only wildly implausible but probably medically impossible.

The film's most intriguing element is the performance by Jessica Lange, who by *not* going over the top provides Martha with a little pathos to leaven the psychopathology. That side of her doesn't seem consistent with her demented behavior at a crucial moment, but then consistency is not the film's strong point.

Hype! ★ ★ ★

NO MPAA RATING, 84 m., 1997

A documentary film featuring The Mono Men, The Walkabouts, Pearl Jam, Soundgarden, and others. Directed by Doug Pray and produced by Steven Helvey.

"There's so much rain in Seattle," a pioneer of grunge rock observes, "that it was logical to go down to the basement." Grunge began with basement and garage bands playing in local clubs, and became a media event just when it was ripe for the *Spinal Tap* treatment. The popularity of Nirvana and the suicide of its lead singer Kurt Cobain gave it notoriety; *Rolling Stone* ran a fashion layout on flannel shirts, Joan Rivers posed in grunge outfits for *Vanity Fair,* and a local publicist made up a phony glossary of Grunge Speak that the *New York Times* fell for lock, stock, and barrel.

A smart, ironic documentary named *Hype!* charts the rise of grunge and its enormous impact on the Seattle scene (at the height of the phenomenon, *Spin* magazine was gushing, "Seattle is to the rock and roll world what Bethlehem is to Christianity"). Local types are more sardonic. Art Chantry, who designed grunge posters and album covers, observes: "A lot of occult stuff takes place here. The first flying saucers were sighted in the Pacific Northwest. This is the serial killer capital of the world. The Manson family used to vacation up this way."

What grunge did in the mid-eighties was take heavy metal, punk, and old-time rock 'n' roll and put it together into a sound that was looser and more fun than a lot of the music on the national scene. A local label named Sub-Pop, realistically observing that none of the Seattle bands were known outside town, promoted its label instead of its bands. Sub-Pop flew a British journalist into town, he toured the clubs, and wrote an influential article for the UK music magazine *Melody Maker,* and soon, the movie says, "bands that had never played live professionally were being signed up by labels."

Hype! doesn't put down the music; it likes grunge but is amused by the way publicity and image took over, turning a local movement into a commodity. Bands like Pearl Jam, Soundgarden, Mudhoney, and Nirvana are seen performing, but there's also early video footage of obscure club bands, including one where a drummer falls onto a guitarist and the band keeps playing. Nothing stopped a performance, photographer Charles Peterson remembers; audiences and band members would drink together, often during a performance, and fans came to party, not criticize (he contrasts Seattle crowds with sniffy New Yorkers saying, "I think they just missed a note").

By the end, in the early 1990s, "Pearl Jam" was the answer to a question on *Jeopardy!,* and Kurt Cobain's Nirvana was one of the hottest bands in the country. Then Cobain, who had a history of drug problems, killed himself. In such cases it is always said that the publicity and the pressure got to him, but actually, of course, the drugs got to him. There is touching footage of a candlelight vigil at the Space Needle in his honor—and in a way his story is still playing out through his wife, Courtney Love, who got her own act together, emerged as a powerful actress in *The People vs. Larry Flynt,* and may be the most important figure produced by the period, if not by the music. (See *Kurt & Courtney.*)

Pearl Jam's Eddie Vedder is probably the key musical figure from grunge, and in *Hype!* he comes across as intelligent and thoughtful. While acknowledging that the grunge phenomenon was dissipated by its fame (it was most at home in small local clubs), he sounds like the survivor of a war or a shipwreck: "It will be a tragedy if we don't do something with this." But, of course, they did.

Hype! has been directed by Doug Pray and photographed by Robert Bennett, who give you a real sense of the music and its excitement, while at the same time keeping a certain distance as journalists. They find funny, articulate local observers—producers, journalists, musicians, fans, publicists—who lived through the scene and kept it in perspective. Producer Steve Helvey says the whole thing reminds him of Baby Huey, waddling around making delightful discoveries: The record labels waddled to Austin, Texas, and Athens, Georgia, and then they waddled to Seattle and waddled on to Minneapolis: "We were just like part of that process."

I

The Ice Storm ★ ★ ★ ★

R, 112 m., 1997

Kevin Kline (Ben Hood), Joan Allen (Elena Hood), Henry Czerny (George Clair), Sigourney Weaver (Janey Carver), Jamey Sheridan (Jim Carver), Christina Ricci (Wendy Hood), Tobey Maguire (Paul Hood), Elijah Wood (Mikey Carver), Adam Hann-Byrd (Sandy Carver), David Krumholtz (Francis Davenport), Michael Cumpsty (Reverend Philip Edwards). Directed by Ang Lee and produced by Ted Hope, James Schamus, and Lee. Screenplay by Schamus, based on the novel by Rick Moody.

The Ice Storm takes place as an early winter storm descends on Connecticut, casting over Thanksgiving a shroud of impending doom. In a wooded suburb, affluent adults stir restlessly in their split-level homes, depressed not only by their lives but by their entertainments and even by their sins. Their teenage children have started experimenting with the same forms of escape: booze, pot, and sex.

The Hood family is held together by quiet desperation. Ben (Kevin Kline) is having an affair with a neighbor (Sigourney Weaver). His wife, Elena (Joan Allen), is a shoplifter who is being hit on by a longhaired minister. The children sip wine in the kitchen. Young Wendy Hood's grace before Thanksgiving dinner is to the point: "Thanks for letting us white people kill all the Indians and steal all their stuff." Ben and Elena observe later, "The only big fight we've had in years is about whether to go back into couples therapy."

The film, based on a novel by Rick Moody, has been directed by Ang Lee, whose previous credit was an adaptation of Jane Austen's *Sense and Sensibility.* Both films are about families observing protocol and exchanging visits. Only the rules have changed. When Ben Hood visits Janey Carver (Weaver) for an adulterous liaison, he wanders into Janey's rec room to find his own daughter, Wendy (Christina Ricci), experimenting with Janey's son Mikey (Elijah Wood). Wendy, who is fourteen, has also conducted an exploratory session with Mikey's kid brother, Sandy. The father asks his daughter what she's doing there. She could as easily have asked him.

The early 1970s were a time when the social revolution of the 1960s had seeped down, or up, into the yuppie classes, who wanted to be "with it" and supplemented their martinis with reefers. The sexual revolution is in full swing for the characters in this movie, leading to Ben Hood's lecture to his son on the facts of life: "Masturbating in the shower wastes water and electricity." When Janey Carver finds her son and the Hood girl playing "I'll show you mine if you'll show me yours," her response is a bizarre speech on Margaret Mead's book about coming of age in Samoa.

The literate, subtle screenplay by James Schamus cuts between the children and their parents, finding parallels. Paul takes the train into the city to visit the apartment of the girl he likes; he sneaks sleeping pills into the drink of his rival to put him out of the picture, but she, of course, wants a pill of her own, and passes out. Meanwhile in New Caanan, the adults are attending a "key party," which turns into a sort of race: Can they swap their wives before they pass out? Elena Hood even finds Philip, the longhaired minister (Michael Cumpsty), there. "Sometimes the shepherd needs the comfort of the sheep," he explains tolerantly. She answers: "I'm going to try hard not to understand the implications of that."

There is a sense of gathering tragedy, symbolized in one scene where a child balances on an icy diving board over an empty pool. When disaster does strike, it releases helpless tears for one of the characters; we reflect on how very many things he has to cry about. Despite its mordant undertones, the film is often satirical and frequently very funny, and quietly observant in its performances, as when the Weaver character takes all she can of Kline's musings about his dislike of golf, and finally tells her lover: "You're boring me. I have a husband. I don't feel the need for another."

They all feel the need for something. What we sense after the film is that the natural sources of pleasure have been replaced with higher-octane substitutes, which have burnt out the ability to feel joy. Going through the motions of what once gave them escape, they feel curiously trapped.

An Ideal Husband ★ ★ ★

PG-13, 97 m., 1999

Cate Blanchett (Gertrude Chiltern), Minnie Driver (Mabel Chiltern), Rupert Everett (Lord Goring), Julianne Moore (Mrs. Cheveley), Jeremy Northam (Sir Robert Chiltern), John Wood (Lord Caversham), Lindsay Duncan (Lady Markby), Peter Vaughan (Phipps). Directed by Oliver Parker and produced by Barnaby Thompson, Uri Fruchtmann, and Bruce Davey. Screenplay by Parker, based on the play by Oscar Wilde.

A play like Oscar Wilde's *An Ideal Husband* works because it takes place in a society bound by inflexible rules and social inhibitions. Here is a story in which a marriage, a romance, a fortune, and government policy all rest on such foundations as a man's obligation to act like a gentleman. (Of course, he doesn't need to *be* a gentleman—that's where the story comes in.)

In the play, an incriminating letter is sent in the belief that it will never be revealed. Suspicions are aroused, but they don't inspire questions—because they involve matters it would be unseemly to ask a gentleman about. As long as everyone plays by the rules in public, they can be broken in private. But then an entire society is threatened by the willingness of one character to act as she should not.

The play tells the story of Sir Robert Chiltern (Jeremy Northam), a rising parliamentary star who has been a paragon of honesty all of his career—except right at the first, when he shopped some secret government information to a baron, who paid him handsomely. Sir Robert is adored by his wife (Cate Blanchett), whose high standards would not permit her to be married to a cheat and liar. An old acquaintance of theirs reappears in London: Mrs. Cheveley (Julianne Moore), who was once married to the baron and possesses the letter in which Chiltern leaked the information. She blackmails him. Either he will change his position on an upcoming piece of legislation, thus protecting her investments, or she will reveal him as a fraud.

It is even more complicated than that. Chiltern's best friend is Lord Goring (Rupert Everett), a rich and idle bachelor. Chiltern begs him to subtly prepare Lady Chiltern for bad news: to help her understand, in a general way, how a chap could do a bad thing and then lead a spotless life ever since. In the course of the plot machinations, romance appears: Goring falls in love with Chiltern's younger sister Mabel (Minnie Driver), and Mrs. Cheveley decides that Goring would be a splendid choice for her own third husband.

Would a man marry a woman he did not love simply to protect a friend or keep a confidence? Today that would be unlikely, but for the original audiences of *An Ideal Husband* it was plausible enough to keep the entire plot suspended over an abyss of misunderstandings.

In another sense, of course, neither Wilde nor his audience cared a fig about the letter, the bribe, the blackmail, or the romance. They were all just cogs in a complicated windup mechanism to keep several charming people on stage for three hours, and provide them with an excuse for saying witty things (this is the play where Goring observes, "To love oneself is the beginning of a lifelong romance"). I do not know if the British upper classes of a century ago were actually capable of standing handsomely in drawing rooms while trading elegant epigrams, and I suspect many of them were not, but I don't care—just so they do it on the stage.

An Ideal Husband works because Wilde created an expert mechanism (kind of slow-motion, serious screwball comedy) for manipulating the plot and characters. But of course the actors are indispensable: They have to make characters plausible while negotiating a plot of pure contrivance, and they have to be charming even while lying, scheming, and blackmailing. The two leading men, Northam and Everett, are smooth and charming—Northam's Sir Robert more realistic and serious about his life, Everett's Lord Goring like a Wildean visitor from outside the plot, who sees everything clearly, is amused, and hardly believes it when Mrs. Cheveley almost snares him in her net.

Women in the plays of a century ago were technically powerless; they lived through their husbands, and spent much of their time speculating on what the men were really up to or waiting for news. At the same time, the plays were really about them, and everything the men did was designed to win their love, admiration, or forgiveness. It is important that we believe Lady Chiltern (Blanchett) loves her husband but loves his upright character even more, and will leave him if she discovers his sins. And important to believe that Mabel (Driver), Sir Robert's sister, could fall in love with Goring in an instant. Well, of course she could. Modern critics who complain they fall in love too suddenly have forgotten that she would have spent months or years making up her mind about every eligible man in her universe.

As we leave the twentieth century there seems to be a powerful nostalgia for the British nineteenth. Every year brings three or four of these literate comedies (or melodramas) set in London. Life was more exciting when you were the entertainment in your own living room and didn't have to watch it on TV.

Idle Hands ★ ★ ½

R, 92 m., 1999

Devon Sawa (Anton), Seth Green (Mick), Elden Henson (Pnub), Jessica Alba (Molly), Christopher Hart (The Hand), Vivica A. Fox (Debi), Jack Noseworthy (Randy), Katie Wright (Tanya). Directed by Rodman Flender and produced by Suzanne Todd, Jennifer Todd, Andrew Licht, and Jeffrey A. Mueller. Screenplay by Terri Hughes and Ron Milbauer.

Idle Hands samples other teen horror movies like a video DJ with a tape deck, exhibiting high spirits and a crazed comic energy. It doesn't quite work, but it goes down swinging—with a disembodied hand. The hand, which has a mind of its own, is chopped off the arm of a teenage kid who is the victim of some kind of weird Halloween demonic possession.

The film involves the adventures of Anton (Devon Sawa), a pothead so addled he doesn't notice for a few days that his parents are dead—the victims of an evil power that writes, "I'm under the bed," on the ceiling of their bedroom, and is. Anton's chief occupations are getting high and hanging out with his friends Mick and Pnub, who live in a nearby basement. The three of them are dropouts from all possible societies, and their world is like a cross between *SLC Punk* and *Evil Dead 2*. (If neither one of those titles rings a bell, the movie undoubtedly won't, either.)

The possessed killer hand is, of course, lifted from *Evil Dead 2*, but it wasn't original there, and has its origins in such films as *The Hand* and *The Beast with Five Fingers*. Rodman Flender, who directed this film, has fun with it in a scene where Anton is on a date with the babe of his dreams, Molly (Jessica Alba), and tries to fight down the hand as it tries to throttle her. Finally, he ties it to the bed. Molly, who is not very observant, translates this as kinky.

Anton finally rids himself of the hand (it's chopped off in the kitchen, with the wound cauterized by an iron). His pals Mick (Seth Green) and Pnub (Elden Henson, from *The Mighty*) have worse luck. Mick is taken out by a beer bottle, which remains embedded in his skull for the rest of the movie. Pnub loses his head altogether, and carries it in his hands until Anton figures out how to mount it on his shoulders using a barbecue fork. Don't ask. Both of them continue through the entire film as the living dead.

Vivica A. Fox plays the demonbuster, tracking down alarming manifestations and delivering the single best line of dialogue: "Well, my work here is done. Time for the ritualistic sex." The plot involves her pursuit only absentmindedly, however, since most of the big scenes involve comic gore: disembodied eyeballs, unusual biological processes, body parts discovered in unexpected ways, etc. There's no really convincing comic inspiration behind the f/x scenes, however, and although we might laugh at some of the goofiness, a movie like this works best when the effects are a means, not an end.

The movie has energy and is probably going to attract a young audience, especially on video, since the R rating will keep away some viewers in its target audience, which is junior high school boys. After the Colorado tragedy, some commentators have wondered if movies like this aren't partly responsible. I don't think we have to worry about *Idle Hands*. Kids understand this kind of macabre comedy, which is in the ancient horror spoof tradition, and don't take it seriously; any viewer capable of being influenced by such silly gags would have to be deeply disturbed already. The only thing this movie is likely to inspire a kid to do is study *Fangoria* magazine to find out how the special effects were achieved.

I Know What You Did Last Summer ★

R, 100 m., 1997

Jennifer Love Hewitt (Julie James), Sarah Michelle Gellar (Helen Shivers), Ryan Phillippe (Barry Cox), Freddie Prinze Jr. (Ray Bronson), Muse Watson (Fisherman), Bridgette Wilson (Elsa Shivers), Anne Heche (Melissa Egan), Johnny Galecki (Max). Directed by Jim Gillespie and produced by Neal H. Moritz, Erik Feig, and Stokely Chaffin. Screenplay by Kevin Williamson.

The best shot in this film is the first one. Not a good sign. *I Know What You Did Last Summer* begins dramatically, with the camera swooping high above a dark and stormy sea, and then circling until it reveals a lonely figure sitting on a cliff overlooking the surf. The shot leads us to anticipate dread, horror, and atmospheric gloominess, but, alas, it is not to be.

Like so many horror films, this one is set on a national holiday—the Fourth of July. (Christmas and Graduation Day are also popular, although Thanksgiving now seems reserved for movies about dysfunctional families.) In a small North Carolina town, a beauty pageant ends with Helen (Sarah Michelle Gellar) being crowned the Croaker Queen. (The reference is to a fish, but the pun is intended, I fear.) Blinking back tears of joy, she announces her plans: "Through art, I shall serve my country."

We meet her friends: her obnoxious, rich boyfriend, Barry (Ryan Phillippe); her brainy best friend, Julie (Jennifer Love Hewitt); and Julie's boyfriend, Ray (Freddie Prinze Jr.). Barry is a jerk who likes to get in fights and drive while drunk ("Can you say 'alcoholic'?" Julie asks him). They build a bonfire on the beach and debate the old urban legend about the teenage couple who found the bloody hook embedded in their car door. And then, on the way home, they strike a shadowy figure walking in the road.

In a panic, they dump him into the sea, even though he is not quite dead at the time. They're afraid to go to the police and risk reckless manslaughter charges. ("This is your future, Julie," Barry screams at her.) Helen then goes off to New York for her showbiz career, and Julie heads for college, but by the next summer they're back home again, pale, chastened, and racked by guilt.

That's when one of them gets a note that says, "I know what you did last summer." As they panic and try to find out who sent it—who knows what they did—the movie loses what marginal tension it has developed, and unwinds in a tedious series of obligatory scenes in which nonessential characters are murdered with a bloody hook wielded by the Fisherman, a macabre figure in a long slicker and a rubber rain hat.

"This is a fishing village," one of the friends says. "Everybody has a slicker." Yes, but not everybody wears it ashore, along with the hat, during steamy July weather. Only the Fisherman does. And since the movie doesn't play fair with its Fisherman clues, we're left with one of those infuriating endings in which (danger! plot spoiler ahead!) the murders were committed by none of the above.

The ads make much of the fact that *I Know What You Did Last Summer* is from "the creators of *Scream*." That means both scripts are by Kevin Williamson. My bet is that he hauled this one out of the bottom drawer after *Scream* passed the $100 million mark. The neat thing about *Scream* was that the characters had seen a lot of horror films, were familiar with all the conventions, and knew they were in a horror-type situation. In *I Know*, there's one moment like that (as the two women approached an ominous house, they observe ominously, "Jodie Foster tried this . . ."). But for the rest of the movie they're blissfully unaware of the dangers of running upstairs when pursued, walking around at night alone, trying to investigate the situation themselves, going onto seemingly empty fishing boats, etc.

After the screening was over and the lights went up, I observed a couple of my colleagues in deep and earnest conversation, trying to resolve twists in the plot. They were applying more thought to the movie than the makers did. A critic's mind is a terrible thing to waste.

I'll Be Home for Christmas ★

PG, 86 m., 1998

Jonathan Taylor Thomas (Jake), Jessica Biel (Allie), Adam Lavorgna (Eddie), Gary Cole (Jake's Dad), Eve Gordon (Carolyn), Lauran Maltby (Tracey), Andrew Lauer (Nolan), Sean O'Bryan (Max). Directed by Arlene Sanford and produced by David Hoberman and Tracey Trench. Screenplay by Harris Goldberg and Tom Nursall.

Pleasantville is a movie about a bland 1950s world in which lives go around in circles until time travelers break in with the virus of change. Some writers have attacked the movie, arguing that things were better in the 1950s than they are now. They might enjoy *I'll Be Home for Christmas,* an exercise in cinematic Ovaltine.

The movie takes place in the present, I guess, but it feels like a 1950s sitcom. The characters have much in common with old (not new) Archie and Jughead comics. The sound track includes Gene Autry tunes, not selected for ironic purposes. It's the kind of movie that just misses a G rating and gets slapped with a PG for rudeness.

Oh, it'll have its fans. The star is Jonathan Taylor Thomas, from TV's *Home Improvement,* who is an immensely likable actor. But even his easy grin seems to weary a little by the later stretches of the film, which is unrelentingly corny.

The plot: Thomas plays Jake, a student at Palisades University, a campus on the Pacific Coast that, in this film, looks like a high school where Our Miss Brooks would still be on the faculty. His dad has sent him a ticket to fly home to Larchmont for Christmas, but his devious plan is to cash it in for two tickets to a beach resort, and convince his girlfriend Allie (Jessica Biel) to go along. Then Jake's dad bribes him with a restored '57 Porsche if he'll come home for Christmas.

Jake's rival for Allie's affections is Eddie (Adam Lavorgna), but this is the kind of movie where Allie is such a nice girl she doesn't even consider Eddie—no, not even when she drives cross-country with him, which she does because she is convinced Jake has stood her up. Jake was actually the victim of a practical joke, in which Eddie and his pals dressed him in a Santa suit and dumped him in the desert, where turkey vultures eye him beadily, ho, ho.

Jake wears the Santa suit for the rest of the movie, as he desperately tries to get home to Larchmont, rescue Allie from Eddie, etc. As you can imagine, the Santa costume inspires countless wheezy attempts at humor. It even gets him entered in a Santa 5K Charity Run, where all the contestants are dressed as Santa. (In a heartrending finale, he beats the loyal mayor, but still allows the mayor to donate the cash prize to buy turkeys for those without a bird on the table for the holidays.) Of course, Jake steals a sleigh for the big climax.

There is possibly an audience for this movie, but I have the oddest feeling that on opening night the people in the theater will all be in black and white. See *Pleasantville* if you wonder what I mean. In fact, see *Pleasantville* anyway. *I'll Be Home for Christmas* will appeal to people who don't care if nothing good happens in a movie, just so long as nothing bad happens in it.

I'm Not Rappaport ★ ★ ½

PG-13, 135 m., 1997

Walter Matthau (Nat Moyer), Ossie Davis (Midge Carter), Amy Irving (Clara Gelber), Martha Plimpton (Laurie Campbell), Craig T. Nelson (The Cowboy), Boyd Gaines (Pete Danforth), Guillermo Diaz (J.C.), Elina Lowensohn (Clara Lemlich), Ron Rifkin (Feigenbaum), Marin Hinkle (Hannah). Directed by Herb Gardner and produced by John Penotti and John Starke. Screenplayby Gardner, based on his play.

If *I'm Not Rappaport* had been a little more like *My Dinner With André* and a little less like *Grumpy Old Men,* I would have liked it more. It's impossible to *dislike* the film; it stars two immensely warm performers, Walter Matthau and Ossie Davis, in an extended riff on two guys sitting on a park bench. But if they'd stayed on the bench and just talked—talked for two solid hours—it might have been more successful. Instead, writer-director Herb Gardner loses faith in his original impulse and adds plot—way too much plot—to force the movie into more conventional channels.

Imagine an old Jewish left-winger and an old African-American janitor, both about eighty, both articulate and with senses of humor, sitting on a bench and free-associating about where life has taken them and what they learned on the journey. There are scenes like that in *I'm Not Rappaport,* and they're the heart of the movie, as they were of Gardner's 1986 Tony-winning play. When Nat (Matthau) and Midge (Davis) talk, it's like verbal music. We could listen all night.

Now add: A tenant committee that wants to take away Midge's job. A daughter who wants Nat committed to an old folks' home. A lonely girl who's trying to get off drugs. A sinister drug dealer who considers the park his turf. A mugger. And Nat leading the shoppers in a grocery store on a strike against higher prices. Every time one of these developments appears on the screen, it feels yanked in by the scruff of its neck. I could believe, at least, the attempt to retire old Midge (his building is going co-op, etc.), but when Nat impersonates a Mafia don in an attempt to scare off the drug dealer, it's sitcom time: Why contrive material like this when the fundamental idea is so promising?

Matthau has by now ripened into the most engaging old guy in the movies; he's had a long time to do that, since it is hard to remember a movie in which he seemed particularly young. Davis, whose background is on the stage and in less frequent films, is a little more complicated: He's not an "old guy" but a particular character who lets you know he's seen a lot and drawn his conclusions. Here and in Spike Lee's *Get on the Bus,* he has an almost oracular authority.

Together, sitting on the bench, their characters use conversational material they've been rehearsing for years. "You listen to me," Nat says. "I was dead once. I know things." Midge tells Danforth, the head of the tenant's committee: "You givin' me bad guy news, tryin' to look like a good guy doin' it." Nat lives in his fantasies and pretends to be several different people (a Cuban, a gangster, the head of a consumer agency). Midge steadfastly holds to his identity as the only man alive who can get his building's boiler to work. They're wonderful together, and when they use the park band shell to try out their version of the vaudeville act with the punch line "I'm not Rappaport," there is an effortless grace at work.

The other actors in the film are good at what they do, but I wish it had not been done. Martha Plimpton is the art student, fresh out of rehab. Amy Irving is touching as the daughter who wonders if Nat should live on his own any longer. Guillermo Diaz is menacing as a mugger, and Craig T. Nelson, as Cowboy, the drug dealer, plays a man who ruthlessly defends his business. But all of these people and the plot twists they inspire are simply not necessary.

Two old guys, sitting on a bench, talking for two hours. That's my rewrite.

The Impostors ★ ★

R, 102 m., 1998

Oliver Platt (Maurice), Stanley Tucci (Arthur), Lili Taylor (Lily), Campbell Scott (Meistrich), Alfred Molina (Jeremy Burtom), Steve Buscemi (Happy Franks), Isabella Rossellini (Ex-Queen), Billy Connolly (Sparks), Tony Shalhoub (First Mate), Hope Davis (Emily). Directed by Stanley Tucci and produced by Beth Alexander and Tucci. Screenplay by Tucci.

I'll bet when Stanley Tucci has a party he invites all of his friends over. His movies reflect a personality that opens wide and embraces the crowd. He likes big casts and complicated plots that involve them in interlocking intrigues. When that works, as it did in *Big Night* (1996), his movie about a doomed Italian restaurant, the result was a comic masterpiece—and one with a real feeling for people. When it doesn't, as in *The Impostors,* it's more like a traffic jam.

The movie stars Tucci and Oliver Platt as Arthur and Maurice, best friends and fellow actors, who are out of work and starving. They're a little like Laurel and Hardy. They bunk together in a single room, and stage impromptu scenes in public. But nobody hires them, and Arthur says quietly, "I'm going to die if I don't get work."

The opening sequence, which is the movie's best, is played as silent film, and the silent spirit permeates the whole work. Maurice and

Arthur attend a performance of *Hamlet* starring the inept Jeremy Burtom (Alfred Molina), insult him in a bar, flee from his wrath, and end up stowing away on the very ocean liner that he has booked passage on.

What to do? Burtom spots them and raises the alarm, and the chase is directed by Meistrich (Campbell Scott), a Nazi steward with tight lips and patent leather hair. Meistrich is in love with Lily (Lili Taylor), the social director, but she despises him and helps protect the stowaways, in a plot that also involves a first mate (Tony Shalhoub) who is a mad bomber, a tennis pro (Billy Connolly) who is flamboyantly gay, an ex-queen (Isabella Rossellini) in exile, a lounge singer (Steve Buscemi) who is suicidal, and all sorts of other passengers.

The movie has lots of long corridors and lots of doors that characters are forever popping into and out of; in that respect it mirrors screwball comedies like Bogdanovich's *What's Up, Doc?* The ocean liner reminds us of the Marx Brothers in *A Night at the Opera,* and Preston Sturges's great *The Lady Eve.* But the energy level in *The Impostors* is too laid-back for screwball. The movie is gentle and whimsical, not manic, and there are times when Tucci seems to be chewing more than he has bit off.

I liked the way the two lead characters, Maurice and Arthur, share a deep friendship and finish each other's sentences. I liked the way Lily, the social director, feels an instant sympathy for them. But the mad bomber plot and the other intrigues require characters at a boil, and everyone in this movie just sort of simmers sweetly.

There are laughs, but they are quiet chuckles. I found myself smiling a lot. I felt fond of the characters. There is the same warmth that permeated *Big Night.* But there is also the same impulse to bring people on board who don't seem to have a reason for being in the plot. Rossellini's sad queen, for example, signifies a great deal but reveals little; her character feels more like Tucci said he'd write a role for her than like the character needed to exist and she was the perfect person to play it.

There are movies that work, and then movies like *The Impostors* that don't really work but are pleasant all the same. There was nothing I actively disliked about the film. But my affection was more polite than impassioned. If this had been a first draft, I would have advised throwing some characters overboard and turning up the heat under the others.

In and Out ★ ★ ★

PG-13, 92 m., 1997

Kevin Kline (Howard), Joan Cusack (Emily), Tom Selleck (Peter Malloy), Debbie Reynolds (Berniece), Wilford Brimley (Frank), Matt Dillon (Cameron), Bob Newhart (Mr. Halliwell), Gregory Jbara (Walter), Shalom Harlow (Sonya). Directed by Frank Oz and produced by Scott Rudin. Screenplay by Paul Rudnick.

You're a high school English teacher in a small Indiana town, watching the Academy Awards with your fiancée, when one of your former students wins the Oscar. He won for playing a gay soldier, and in his acceptance speech, he thanks a lot of people, including you, his teacher—"who," he volunteers, "is gay."

This comes as news to the fiancée. Also to the teacher, named Howard (Kevin Kline). Also to his father (Wilford Brimley) in the same town, who tells his wife: "We used to mow our lawn. No more!" Also to the high school principal (Bob Newhart), who will eventually try to fire Howard. Also to the players on the football team that Howard coaches, although one of them says there are two places where it's okay to be gay: "Prison and space, where they kind of float into each other while they're weightless."

In and Out is a lighthearted, PG-13–rated comedy about homosexuality, so innocuous you can easily imagine it spinning off into a sitcom. Its opening moments were inspired by the moment on the Oscarcast when Tom Hanks won as best actor for *Philadelphia,* and thanked his own gay high school drama teacher. The story goes that producer Scott Rudin, watching the broadcast, imagined a different outcome to the story, and pitched it to screenwriter Paul Rudnick, who under the pen name Libby Gelman-Waxner writes a funny column for *Premiere* magazine.

The result is one of the jollier comedies of the year, a movie so mainstream that you can almost watch it backing away from confrontation, a film aimed primarily at a middle-American heterosexual audience. Thirty years ago this movie would have been controversial. Now it's simply funny.

Kevin Kline is almost always a dependable comic actor, an everyman who tries to keep his dignity while his life falls apart. Here he's well matched with Joan Cusack, as Emily, the fiancée, who has lost dozens or hundreds of pounds under the inspiration of Richard Simmons, in order to slim down for marriage to Howard; she's had a crush on him for years. Now, on the eve of the wedding, her whole world has come crashing down, and even the parish priest is astonished that during a three-year courtship she has never once slept with her intended.

Howard tries to fix that. "But I'm *not* gay!" he thunders, crashing into her bedroom in a belated display of macho lust. One of the plot mysteries is why the former star pupil (a witty, wry performance by Matt Dillon) would have said so on national TV. No matter; Howard becomes the center of a media blitz, and a celebrity gossip journalist played by Tom Selleck arrives in town to host a TV special documenting the real story.

Selleck's character is gay—and cheerfully prepared to assure everyone of that fact. He also assumes Howard is gay, despite his protestations. So does the high school principal, whom Newhart plays as a man so inhibited that when he speaks, everything of importance is implied by long, agonized pauses.

In and Out is a lot of fun, an audience-pleaser that creates characters that only become more likable the more the plot digs in. Rudnick is a gifted screenwriter whose 1995 *Jeffrey* was not as relaxed about sexuality as this film is. The director and sometime Muppeteer Frank Oz *(Little Shop of Horrors)* knows that while the predictable is the death of comedy, its closest relative, the inevitable, is essential.

Only the ending bogs down. There's a scene in the high school auditorium that could have been recycled directly from a Frank Capra movie, and without giving it away, I will say that it is too long, too lugubrious, and too cloyingly uplifting. On the other hand, the movie takes a cheap shot at Barbra Streisand that's so funny it will probably make even her laugh, and in a year when good comedies seem as hard to make as ever, *In and Out* is one of the best.

In Dreams ★ ½

R, 100 m., 1999

Annette Bening (Claire Cooper), Robert Downey Jr. (Vivian), Aidan Quinn (Paul Cooper), Stephen Rea (Dr. Silverman), Paul Guilfoyle (Detective Jack Kay), Dennis Boutsikaris (Dr. Stevens), Katie Sagona (Rebecca Cooper), Krystal Benn (Ruby). Directed by Neil Jordan and produced by Stephen Woolley and Redmond Morris. Screenplay by Bruce Robinson and Jordan, based on the novel *Doll's Eyes,* by Bari Wood.

In Dreams is the silliest thriller in many a moon, and the only one in which the heroine is endangered by apples. She also survives three falls from very high places (two into a lake, one onto apples), escapes from a hospital and a madhouse, has the most clever dog since Lassie, and causes a traffic pileup involving a truck and a dozen cars. With that much plot, does this movie really need the drowned ghost town, the husband's affair with an Australian woman, the flashbacks to the dominatrix mom, and the garbage disposal that spews apple juice?

All of this goofiness is delivered with style and care by a first-rate team; this is a well-made bad movie. The heroine, named Claire, is portrayed by Annette Bening as a woman in torment. She begins to dream of horrible things, and realizes an evil killer is causing her nightmares ("He's inside my head!"). Her husband (Aidan Quinn) goes to the cops with her premonitions, but gets the brush-off. A frequent dream involves harm to a child; it turns out to be her own.

Eventually she falls into the hands of a psychiatrist (Stephen Rea) who is wise, kindly, and patient, and locks her up in two cruel institutions. One has a padded cell and is guarded by a Nurse Ratchet clone. The other looks like the original snake pit crossed with a dorm at summer camp. The psychiatrist isn't even the villain.

In Dreams is the kind of movie where children's nursery rhymes and sayings are underscored like evil omens. "Mirror, mirror, on the wall . . ." we hear, while the sound track vibrates with menace, and a mother, a daughter, and their dog walk on the banks of a reservoir that was, we learn, created in 1965 by flooding a village that still lurks beneath the waters, a ghost town. Scuba divers explore it, and we see that the napkin dispensers are still on the counters in the diner, while holy statues float around the church.

Was the villain (Robert Downey Jr.) drowned in this town? It's not that simple. The explanation of this movie contains more puzzles than the plot itself. Let's say we grant the premise that the villain can indeed project his dreams into the mind of poor Claire. In addition to being clairvoyant, is he also telekinetic? Can he make children's swings move on their own, and turn on boom boxes at a distance, and project words onto a computer screen, and control garbage disposals?

And does he control the family dog, which has an uncanny ability to find its masters anywhere, anytime? (This is such a clever dog it should know better than to lure Claire into the middle of that highway—unless, of course, its dreams are also under remote control.) And what does the buried village have to do with anything? And although the killer was abused as a child by his mother, whose high heels supply a central image, what does that have to do with the nursery rhyme about how "My father was a dollar"?

I dunno. The movie was directed by Neil Jordan, who has done a whole lot better *(Mona Lisa, The Crying Game, Interview With the Vampire).* Here he navigates uncertainly through a script that is far too large for its container. Whole subplots could have been dumped; why even bother with the other woman in Australia? Although the drowned village supplies some vivid images, wasn't it a huge expense just for some atmosphere? And how many viewers will be able to follow the time-shifted parallels as Claire's escape from a hospital is intercut with the killer's?

In *my* dreams, I'm picturing Tony Lawson's first day on the job. He was the editor of this picture. His survey of the unassembled footage must have been a real horror story.

In Love and War ★ ★

PG-13, 115 m., 1997

Sandra Bullock (Agnes Von Kurowsky), Chris O'Donnell (Ernest Hemingway), Mackenzie Astin (Henry Villard), Emilio Bonucci (Domenico Caracciolo), Ingrid Lacey (Elsie "Mac" MacDonald), Margot Steinberg (Mabel "Rosie" Rose), Colin Stinton (Tom Burnside), Ian Kelly (Jimmy McBride). Directed by Richard Attenborough and produced by Dimitri Villard and Attenborough. Screenplay by Allan Scott, Clancy Sigal, and Anna Hamilton Phelan.

Ernest Hemingway went to the First World War like a kid going to summer camp. It sounded like a lot of fun; he wouldn't have missed it for the world. Early in *In Love and War,* he gets his fun and his war all boiled down into a few minutes. He arrives at the front lines, is thrilled by first sight of the enemy, and then a shell strikes nearby and he is surrounded by mud and body parts.

A wounded man screams for help, Hemingway races to carry him to safety and is shot in the leg. In a field hospital, amputation looks like the best bet, but Hemingway says he would rather be dead than lose a leg. He tells this to a nurse named Agnes, who convinces the doctor to spare his leg. During his long convalescence, they fall in love.

Although Hemingway's love affairs were well charted during a long and publicized life, the specifics of this one escaped notice until Agnes von Kurowsky died in the 1980s, and a cache of love letters to Hemingway came to light. He was eighteen. She was twenty-six. In his mind, it was all planned that she would follow him back to the States and they would marry and live in his father's cabin in the woods and she'd "be making the old place spic and span, while I write great words."

This prospect on reflection did not appeal to von Kurowsky, who wrote him breaking off their engagement. She later married a doctor she met in the war. If Hemingway's biographers did not know of this early romance, Hemingway himself certainly remembered it, and wrote about it in *A Very Short Story,* which takes less than two pages to express his bitterness. Describing what is obviously the same event—the nurse caring for his wound, the wartime love affair—he ends with a few terse sentences about receiving a letter in which she says it was boy-girl love, not man-woman love. A few days later, he says, he got VD from a woman he met in the Loop and took on a cab ride through Lincoln Park. End of story.

Not, as they say, a pretty picture, but Richard Attenborough's *In Love and War* doesn't use the Hemingway angle and indeed could be about someone else altogether. There is little feeling here for the man and writer Hemingway would become, and the movie is essentially the story of a romance between a naive kid and a woman who liked him—maybe even loved him—but was too wise to risk her life on his promises of future glory.

Chris O'Donnell plays Hemingway and Sandra Bullock is Agnes von Kurowsky. Their relationship seems more sentimental than passionate; to recycle a Hemingway phrase that perhaps became more notorious than he would have liked, the earth does not shake. It is hard enough to make a movie about a love affair without a future, and harder still when the audience agrees that maybe it doesn't need a future. Eight years is a big age difference, especially between eighteen and twenty-six, and although great love can certainly transcend it, this is not great love.

There are some problems, also, with the way the love affair is depicted. The movie chooses not to deal with two realities that might have made it more interesting: Hemingway at eighteen was probably sexually inexperienced, and sex before marriage in 1918 was not treated as casually as it is today. The screenplay by Allan Scott, Clancy Sigal, and Anna Hamilton Phelan chooses not to reflect those conditions, and so when Ernest and Agnes make love for the first time in the little pensione down by the railroad station, it is a conventional movie scene, not one specific to these characters.

"I wanted this to be the most beautiful place on God's earth," he says, realizing the pensione is little other than a brothel. "Then close your eyes," she says. Hemingway would have been reaching for his blue pencil. Then again, maybe not, as the earth shook.

I am always suspicious of stories that take on significance because of events that happen after they're over (". . . and that little boy grew up to be—George Washington!"). *In Love and War* is not much interested in Ernest Hemingway's subsequent life and career, and even in its treatment of this early period it doesn't deal with such themes as his macho posturing, his need to prove himself, his grandiosity. Hemingway creates a more interesting (and self-revealing) character in his own stories of the war.

As for Agnes von Kurowsky, she comes across in the Bullock performance as sweet, competent, and loving. She must have reflected, after Hemingway was shipped home, on her choices between marrying a wealthy doctor, or keeping things "spic and span" for a kid trying to become a novelist while living in his dad's cabin. And as she read about Hemingway in the papers, did she sometimes regret the decision she had made? Not if she read the same stories the rest of us have.

Inside/Out ★ ★ ½

NO MPAA RATING, 115 m., 1999

Berangere Allaux (Monica), Tom Gilroy (Priest), Stefania Rocca (Organist), Frederic Pierrot (Jean), Steven Watkin (Roger). Directed by Rob Tregenza and produced by Gill Holland. Screenplay by Tregenza.

It happens that within two days I've seen a 52-minute film that seemed bursting with content, and now a 115-minute film that inspires admiration, but also restlessness. The shorter film *(See the Sea)*, played just long enough to deliver its horrifying punch line. The longer one *(Inside/Out)* has no punch line, and indeed not much of a plot; it's about the arid passage of time in a mental hospital. A director approaching such a subject can either suggest the emptiness and ennui, or attempt to reproduce it. Rob Tregenza, who wrote, directed, photographed, and edited *Inside/Out*, chooses the second approach.

His film takes place in the late 1950s, in a cold and lifeless autumn or early spring, in a mental hospital of whitewashed walls and barren interiors. The institution isn't on the cutting edge of treatment; it's more like a holding cell for patients, a waiting room before death. The patients wander the grounds, sometimes try to run away, line up for their pills, are angry or morose, mill about aimlessly at a dance, attend religious services, and stand stock-still as if lost in thought.

Their actions are watched by Tregenza on the Cinemascope screen, the widest gauge available. The film covers an enormous expanse of screen, and is often photographed in long shots, so that the characters seem isolated within vast, empty spaces. In one sequence two men shoot some baskets (one is completely uninvolved), and in the background there is a man dressed in black who simply stands, swaying slightly, the whole time.

One point of the wide screen may be to emphasize how little contact these people have with one another. They're looked over by nuns (Episcopalian, I gather) who give them their pills, issue instructions ("No sitting on the tables!"), and enforce standards (a female character undresses and tries to snuggle up to another inmate, only to be yanked away by a nun hissing, "You little whore!"). The lives of the people on the screen—patients and caretakers—seem bereft of happiness.

Dialogue is heard only in snatches. There are no word-driven relationships. Visuals make the point. The institution's priest works in a plain little chapel that reminded me of the church in Bergman's *Winter Light,* in the feeling that it was a place little frequented by God.

Some of the scenes have the same kind of deadpan visual punning we find, in another tone, in the films of Jacques Tati. Two men struggle on a train track, and we hear the whistle and roar of the approaching train—which arrives, passes, and disappears, invisibly. In an opening shot, two patients run across the crest of a hill, we hear dogs barking, and they reappear chased by the dogs—and by figures on horseback. It is a hunt.

Tregenza's handling of a "party" scene makes full use of his wide-screen camera. In a barren, low-ceilinged room, too big for the people in it, volunteers arrange clusters of balloons. Crepe paper hangs thinly from beams. An inept rock band sets up. Patients mill about endlessly (one darts across screen and up some stairs). The band starts playing and is accompanied by a patient who rhythmically bangs a folding chair open and closed. Finally, incongruously, a harpist begins to play, and the camera circles the room, which is stilled by the quiet music.

I admired *Inside/Out* in its moments, in individual scenes. I would recommend the party scene to film students, who could learn from it. But I was kept outside the film by the distanced, closed-off characters. That's the idea, I know—but Tregenza succeeds all too well with it. Seeing the movie is like paying dues to his vision. We are witnesses that he accomplished what he set out to do. He does it in his own time and space. He's as little interested in us as his characters would be. We're like guests on visiting day, sitting restlessly on chairs along the side of the room. If anyone asked us, we'd say we were having a good time. But we're thinking restlessly of how long we have to stay, and where we can go next.

Insomnia ★ ★ ★ ½

NO MPAA RATING, 97 m., 1998

Stellan Skarsgard (Jonas Engstrom), Sverre Anker Ousdal (Erik Vik), Maria Bonnevie (Ane), Bjorn Floberg (Jon Holt), Gisken Armand (Hilde Hagen), Marianne O. Ulrichsen (Froya). Directed by Erik Skjoldbjaerg and produced by Anne Frilseth. Screenplay by Nikolaj Frobenius and Skjoldbjaerg. In Norwegian with English subtitles.

In northern Norway in the summer, the night is a brief finger of dusk drawn between the day and the dawn. In his hotel room, Jonas the chief investigator struggles for sleep. He tugs at the blackout curtains, but the sunlight streams in at 2 A.M. and he is haunted by unease. He is a veteran Swedish policeman in exile, working out of Oslo after, in a previous case, being discovered in "intimate conversation" with a witness.

His record is not clean, but he is considered a brilliant investigator, and now he is hunting for a killer who leaves no traces—who even washed the hair of his victim, an attractive young woman. After Jonas discovers the woman's knapsack in a shed on the beach, he sets a trap for the killer. He announces on TV that the knapsack is the key to the investigation, trusting that the killer will return to retrieve it.

And so the killer does—falling into Jonas's ambush. But there is a way out of the shed that the police do not know about, and the killer flees. Chasing him in a thick, muggy morning fog, Jonas sees a figure raise a gun, and shoots. Then he discovers he has killed his own colleague.

Jonas is played by Skellan Skarsgard, the tall, thoughtful Scandinavian who first drew attention as the oil-rig worker in *Breaking the Waves* and the math professor in *Good Will Hunting.* Here he looks thinner, haunted, unsure of himself. Working under the protective blanket of fog, he fakes evidence to make it look as if the other policeman was shot by the escaping killer.

So now we have a police procedural turned in upon itself. Jonas is leading the investigation while at the same time struggling with the guilty knowledge of his cover-up. His queries take him to a writer named Holt, very full of himself, who had a relationship with the dead woman. And to the woman's best friend Froya, whom he is attracted to. He takes her for a drive, and slips his hand between her legs; will this be another intimate conversation with a witness?

His key adversary is a fellow police officer, Ane (Maria Bonnevie). He is able to distract the other cops with routine and exhortation, but Ane doesn't just look, she sees. She senses there is something off about Jonas after the death of the other cop: a certain wariness, a way of changing the subject. Some of her questions do not get good answers. She looks him in the face, and he doesn't like that.

The movie is not a thriller or an action picture, but a psychological study. *Crime and Punishment* comes to mind, with its theme of a man who believes he stands outside the rules that apply to other people. It is not that Jonas is a murderer—he made an honest mistake—but that he does not see himself as an honest man and cannot trust that others would believe him.

It's easy to make movies with external action, chases, and shoot-outs. It is much harder to make a film in which many of the important events take place inside the minds of the characters. Much depends simply on where the actors are arranged in the frame, so that we can see one face and not another. Jonas is sleepless and anguished. Ane is nagged by doubts she cannot silence.

The look of the film is almost a character in itself. The director, Erik Skjoldbjaerg, looks for grays and browns, dark greens and a washed-out drabness. The midnight sun casts an unremitting bright light, like the eye of God that will not blink. There is no place to hide, not even in sleep. And all the time, of course, there is the killer, who is the real villain, but figures for Jonas more like a distraction from his shame.

Instinct ★ ½

R, 124 m., 1999

Anthony Hopkins (Ethan Powell), Cuba Gooding Jr. (Theo Caulder), Donald Sutherland (Ben Hillard), Maura Tierney (Lyn Powell), George Dzundza (Dr. John Murray), John Ashton (Guard Dacks), John Aylward (Warden Keefer), Thomas Q. Morris (Pete). Directed by Jon Turteltaub and produced by Michael Taylor and Barbara Boyle. Screenplay by Gerald Di Pego, suggested by the novel *Ishmael* by Daniel Quinn.

If there's anything worse than a movie hammered together out of pieces of bad screenplays, it's a movie made from the scraps of good ones. At least with the trash we don't have to suffer through the noble intentions. *Instinct* is a film with not one but four worthy themes. It has pious good thoughts about all of them, but undermines them by slapping on obligatory plot requirements, thick. Nothing happens in this movie that has not been sanctioned by long usage in better films.

This is a film about (1) why Man should learn to live in harmony with Nature; (2) how prison reform is necessary; (3) how fathers can learn to love their children; (4) why it is wrong to imprison animals in zoos. The film doesn't free the beasts from their cages, but it's able to resolve the other three issues—unconvincingly, in a rush of hokey final scenes.

Instinct, directed by John Turteltaub *(Phenomenon),* is all echoes. It gives us Anthony

Hopkins playing a toned-down version of Hannibal Lector, Cuba Gooding Jr., reprising his nice-guy professional from *As Good As It Gets,* Donald Sutherland once again as the wise and weary sage, and John Ashton (you'll recognize him) as a man who is hateful for no better reason than that the plot so desperately needs him to be.

Oh, and the settings are borrowed from *Gorillas in the Mist* and *One Flew Over the Cuckoo's Nest.*

The movie's just so darned uplifting and clunky as it shifts from one of its big themes to another while groaning under the weight of heartfelt speeches. The photography labors to make it look big and important, and the music wants to be sad and uplifting at the same time, as if to say it's a cruel world but that's not entirely our fault.

Hopkins stars as Ethan Powell, an anthropologist who went missing in 1994 in an African jungle and surfaced two years later while murdering two rangers and injuring three others. After a year in chains, he's returned to the United States and locked up in a brutal psycho ward. His interrogation is set to be conducted by an eminent psychiatrist (Donald Sutherland), who instead assigns his famous prisoner to Theo Caulder (Gooding), a student just completing his final year of residency. Why give this juicy patient to a kid who admits he wants to write a best-seller about him? Because Cuba Gooding is the star of the movie, that's why, and Donald Sutherland, who cannot utter a word that doesn't sound like God's truth, always has to play the expert who waits in an oak-paneled study, passing around epigrams and brandy.

Powell's hair and beard make him look like the wild man of Borneo—with reason, since he lived with a family of gorillas in the jungle. He has been mute since the murders, but Caulder thinks he can get him to talk—and can he ever. Hopkins faces one of his greatest acting challenges, portraying a character who must seem reluctant to utter a single word while nevertheless issuing regular philosophical lectures. "I lived as humans lived 10,000 years ago," he explains. "Humans knew how to live then." Even 10,000 years ago, don't you suppose humans were giving gorillas lots of room?

Caulder believes that if he can get Powell to talk about what he did, and why, he can "get him out of there." No matter that Powell *did* kill two men; to understand is to forgive. In his struggle to comprehend his patient, Caulder meets Powell's bitter daughter (Maura Tierney, in a good performance). She is angry with her father. Her father doesn't want to talk about her. "Leave it," he snaps, menacingly. What dire issues stand between them? The movie disappoints us with a reconciliation that plays like a happy ending on the Family Channel. One should always have time for one's children, Powell learned (from the gorillas).

The prison is a snake pit of brutality, run by cruel guards and presided over by a sadistic warden and a weak psychiatrist. Each man is supposed to get thirty minutes a day outdoors. Because this is too much trouble, the guards hand out cards, and the man with the ace of diamonds gets to go outside. The toughest prisoner beats up anyone who won't give him the card. Dr. Caulder sees that this is wrong, and institutes a fair lottery, over the objections of the sadistic guards, but with the prisoners chanting their support. The entire business of the ace of diamonds, which occupies perhaps twenty minutes, is agonizingly obvious, contrived, and manipulative; the prison population, colorful weirdos of the *Cuckoo's Nest* variety, responds with enthusiastic overacting.

Ethan Powell, of course, sees through the entire system. Superhumanly strong and violent, he puts Caulder through a brief but painful education in the laws of the wild. What he is able to do at the end of the film, and where he is finally able to do it, I leave you to explain, since the film certainly cannot. I also have the gravest doubts about the thank-you note from Powell, which reads not like something that would be written by a man who had lived with the gorillas and killed two men, but by a marketing expert concerned that audiences feel real good when they leave the theater.

In the Company of Men ★ ★ ★ ★

R, 93 m., 1997

Aaron Eckhart (Chad), Stacy Edwards (Christine), Matt Malloy (Howard), Michael Martin (Coworker 1), Mark Rector (John), Chris

Hayes (Coworker 2), Jason Dixie (Intern), Emily Cline (Suzanne). Directed by Neil LaBute and produced by Mark Archer and Stephen Pevner. Screenplay by LaBute.

Now here is true evil: cold, unblinking, reptilian. The character Chad in *In the Company of Men* makes the terrorists of the summer thrillers look like boys throwing mud pies. And for every Chad there is a Howard, a weaker man, ready to go along, lacking the courage to disagree and half intoxicated by the stronger will of the other man. People like this are not so uncommon. Look around you.

The movie takes place in the familiar habitats of the modern corporate male: hotel corridors, airport "courtesy lounges," corporate cubicles, and meeting rooms. The men's room is an invaluable refuge for private conversations. We never find out what the corporation makes, but what does it matter? Modern business administration techniques have made the corporate environment so interchangeable that an executive from Pepsi, say, can transfer seamlessly to Apple and apply the same "management philosophy" without missing a beat.

Chad (Aaron Eckhart) and Howard (Matt Malloy) have been assigned for six weeks to a regional office of their company. Waiting for their flight, they talk. Chad is unhappy and angry because he's been dumped by his girlfriend ("The whole fade-out thing"). He proposes a plan: "Say we were to find some girl vulnerable as hell . . ." In their new location, they'll select a young woman who doesn't look like she has much of a social life. They'll both shower her with attention—flowers, dinner dates—until she's dizzy, and then, "out comes the rug, both of us dropping her!"

Chad explains this plan with the blinkered, formal language of a man whose recreational reading consists of best-selling primers on excellence and wealth. "Life is for the taking—is it not?" he asks. And, "Is that not ideal? To restore a little dignity to our lives?" He hammers his plan home in a men's room, while Howard, invisible behind a cubicle door, says he guesses he agrees.

The "girl" they choose for their target turns out to be deaf—a bonus. Her name is Christine (Stacy Edwards). She is pleasant, pretty, articulate; it is easy to understand everything she says, but Chad is cruel as he describes her to Howard: "She's got one of those voices like Flipper. You should hear her going at it, working to put the simplest sounds together." Chad makes a specialty of verbal brutality. Christine is not overwhelmed to be dating two men at once, but she finds it pleasant, and eventually she begins to really like Chad.

In the Company of Men, written and directed by Neil LaBute, is a continuing series of revelations, because it isn't simply about this sick joke. Indeed, if the movie were only about what Chad and Howard do to Christine and how she reacts, it would be too easy, a one-note attack on these men as sadistic predators. The movie deals with much more and it cuts deeper, and by the end we see it's about a whole system of values in which men as well as women are victims, and monstrous selfishness is held up as the greatest good.

Environments like the one in this film are poisonous, and many people have to try to survive in them. Men like Chad and Howard are dying inside. Personal advancement is the only meaningful goal. Women and minorities are seen by white males as unfairly advantaged. White males are seen as unfairly advantaged by everyone else.

There is an incredibly painful scene in *In the Company of Men* where Chad tells a young black trainee, "They asked me to recommend someone for the management training program," and then requires the man to humiliate himself in order to show that he qualifies. At first you see the scene as racist. Then you realize Chad and the trainee are both victims of the corporate culture they occupy, in which the power struggle is the only reality. Something forces both of them to stay in the room during that ugly scene, and it is job insecurity.

On a more human level, the story becomes poignant. Both Howard and Chad date Christine. There is an unexpected emotional development. I will not reveal too much. We arrive at the point where we thought the story was leading us, and it keeps on going. There is another chapter. We find a level beneath the other levels. The game was more Machiavellian than we imagined. We thought we were witnessing evil, but now we look on its true face.

What is remarkable is how realistic the

story is. We see a character who is depraved, selfish, and evil, and he is not a bizarre eccentric, but a product of the system. It is not uncommon to know personally of behavior not unlike Chad's. Most of us, of course, are a little more like Howard, but that is small consolation. "Can't you see?" Howard says. "I'm the good guy!" In other words, I am not as bad as the bad guy, although I am certainly weaker.

Christine survives, because she knows who she is. She is deaf, but less disabled than Howard and Chad, because she can hear on frequencies that their minds and imaginations do not experience. *In the Company of Men* is the kind of bold, uncompromising film that insists on being thought about afterward—talked about, argued about, hated if necessary, but not ignored. "How does it feel right now, deep down inside?" one of the characters asks. The movie asks us the same question.

Intimate Relations ★★

R, 105 m., 1997

Rupert Graves (Harold Guppy), Julie Walters (Marjorie Beasley), Matthew Walker (Stanley Beasley), Laura Sadler (Joyce). Directed by Philip Goodhew and produced by Angela Hart, Lisa Hope, and John Slan. Screenplay by Goodhew.

"I'd rather be dead than brazen," Mrs. Beasley tells her husband when he pleads for "relief" in *Intimate Relations.* We already suspect that she might have the opportunity to be both. The film peeks behind the respectable lace curtains of a British village where Marjorie Beasley is a landlady, her husband, Stanley, is a one-legged war veteran, and their teenage daughter, Joyce, is too smart for her own good.

Into their uneasy idyll one day comes the hapless Harold Guppy (Rupert Graves), who is looking for a room to rent. "Call me 'Mom,'" Mrs. Beasley (Julie Walters) tells him firmly. Conducting a tour of the house, she is quite clear about the sleeping arrangements: "Mr. Beasley and I keep separate rooms for medical purposes."

Harold is a bit of a case study himself. Until recently in the merchant marine, he has some shady skeletons in his closet, but seems friendly enough, and enjoys the reasonable rent, good food, and all-around hospitality, especially from "Mom," who embraces him hungrily in the hallways and creeps silently into his room at night.

But not quite silently enough, because Joyce (Laura Sadler) pops in right after her, and demands to join them in bed. "It's my birthday," she explains. "That's not decent!" Harold protests. "I'm her mother," Marjorie says, concerned that Joyce might betray them to Mr. Beasley (Matthew Walker), who by this hour of the night is usually deep in an alcohol-induced snooze.

Intimate Relations tells a story that resembles in some respects pornography, although it suggests that if one ever did find oneself in such a situation it would be a great deal more bother than it was worth. Mother and daughter alternate visits to the handsome young Mr. Guppy, Dad begins to harbor dark suspicions, and "Mom" panics when it appears that Harold may be prepared to escape into the army.

Intimate Relations is about the same sort of repressed sexual goofiness that found an outlet in *Heavenly Creatures,* the New Zealand film about the two close friends who committed murder together, or *The Young Poisoner's Handbook,* about the earnest young man whose chemistry experiments went entirely too far. Its deadpan humor is entertaining, up to a point, but that point is passed before the movie is quite at its halfway point, and then we're left watching increasingly desperate people who are trapped by each other's madness. At the end I was not sure quite what it was all about, and neither, I am sure, was Mr. Guppy.

Inventing the Abbotts ★★

R, 120 m., 1997

Joaquin Phoenix (Doug Holt), Billy Crudup (Jacey Holt), Will Patton (Lloyd Abbott), Kathy Baker (Helen Holt), Jennifer Connelly (Eleanor Abbott), Michael Sutton (Steve), Liv Tyler (Pamela Abbott), Joanna Going (Alice Abbott). Directed by Pat O'Connor and produced by Ron Howard, Brian Grazer, and Janet Meyers. Screenplay by Ken Hixon, based on the story by Sue Miller.

Inventing the Abbotts is a film that seems to have been made in a time machine. Not only the picture's story but also its values and style are inspired by the 1950s. It's like a subtler, more class-conscious *Peyton Place,* and if the same movie had been made forty years ago with Natalie Wood, Sandra Dee, Troy Donahue, and Ricky Nelson, it could have used more or less the same screenplay (minus the four-letter words).

The film seems indirectly inspired by Welles's *Magnificent Ambersons.* It's about the Abbotts, a rich family whose parties and wealth dominate a small Midwestern town, and about a local working-class boy who has made the family his "addiction." He eventually conquers all three of the Abbott girls, while his younger brother lusts after one and loves another, but lacks his courage.

The movie is narrated by the younger brother, Doug Holt (Joaquin Phoenix). He tends to repeat himself, finding countless different ways to say that his upwardly mobile brother Jacey Holt (Billy Crudup) has always been more confident and successful—especially around the Abbott girls. The oldest is Alice (Joanna Going), the official "nice girl," who gets pregnant, gets married, gets divorced, and gets Jacey, in that order. The middle is Eleanor Abbott (Jennifer Connelly), the official "bad girl," who gets sent away to stewardess school for her exploits. The youngest is Pam (Liv Tyler), and she's also the nicest, and the one Doug really likes, although he also lusts after Eleanor.

To understand the three Abbott girls and the two Holt brothers it helps to understand their world. They live in Haley, Illinois, a town of maybe 20,000, dominated by a steel desk factory owned by Mr. Abbott (Will Patton). Years ago, Mr. Abbott and the boys' father were friends. But then Abbott allegedly cheated Holt out of a valuable patent for sliding desk drawers, and then Holt died when he drove his DeSoto roadster onto a frozen lake on a stupid $20 bet. Soon after, rumors raced through town that Mr. Abbott was spending way too much time consoling the new widow Holt (Kathy Baker).

This is the kind of material that might have graced a mid-1950s Universal-International weeper—maybe one adapted from a John O'Hara best-seller filled with descriptions of country clubs. Even then it would have had more energy. *Inventing the Abbotts* seems slow and almost morose, and the director, Pat O'Connor, shows none of the cheerful love of human nature that enlivened his *Circle of Friends* (1995), the smart and touching picture about young love in 1950s Ireland.

The picture is haunted by a story problem: It isn't about anything but itself. There's no sense of life going on in the corners of the frame. The characters, completely preoccupied by the twists of the plot, have no other interests. Mr. Abbott is one of those 1950s dads whose sole functions in life are to drive gas guzzlers, stand behind a big desk, smoke a lot of cigarettes, and tell teenage guys to stay away from his daughters. Kathy Baker is more dimensional as Mrs. Holt—she has some touching scenes—but her life, too, has been completely defined by what happened with the Abbotts in the past, what is happening with the Abbotts now, and what, I fear, will happen with the Abbotts in the future.

The film's art direction is uncanny. It doesn't look like a period picture; it looks like a movie that was actually shot in 1955. Looking at the old cars and the storefronts and the front yards and the clothes, I was reminded of *Young at Heart* or *A Summer Place.* The actors do their best, and are sometimes quite appealing, but the story is so lugubrious there's nowhere they can go with it. And it's a shame the most interesting Abbott girl (the Jennifer Connelly character) is shipped out of town just after she delivers the movie's best line.

I Still Know What You Did Last Summer ★

R, 96 m., 1998

Jennifer Love Hewitt (Julie James), Freddie Prinze Jr. (Ray Bronson), Brandy (Karla Wilson), Mekhi Phifer (Tyrell), Muse Watson (Ben/Fisherman), Bill Cobbs (Estes), Matthew Settle (Will Benson), Jeffrey Combs (Mr. Brooks). Directed by Danny Cannon and produced by Neal H. Moritz, Erik Feig, Stokely Chaffin, and William S. Beasley. Screenplay by Trey Callaway.

I Still Know What You Did Last Summer assembles the building blocks of idiot-proof slasher movies: stings, Snicker-Snacks, false alarms, and POV bait-and-switches. We'll get back to those. The movie's R rating mentions "intense terror, violence, and gore," but only its publicist could consider it intense or terrifying. Gore it has.

The movie stars Jennifer Love Hewitt as Julie, survivor of the original *I Know What You Did Last Summer*, as a college student haunted by nightmares of what she did, in fact, the summer before last (last summer was actually the summer when the slasher knew what she did the previous summer, if you follow me). The pop star Brandy plays her roommate, Karla.

Together with their dates Will (Matthew Settle) and Tyrell (Mekhi Phifer), they go to the Bahamas after winning a radio contest by incorrectly naming Rio as the capital of Brazil. It wouldn't have helped to know that the correct answer is Brasilia, since they could have answered Schaumburg and still won: The contest is a hoax by the Fisherman, a spectral presence who dresses like the Groton's Fisherman and impales his victims with fishhooks. He wants to get them to the Bahamas for the obvious reason that the plot requires a seaside setting (the Fisherman would look oddly dressed anywhere else, and indeed one wonders how many victims he will have to claim before an APB is put out for a guy in a slicker with a fishhook).

Ominous signs have been portending even before they get to the Bahamas. After all those nightmares, Julie is so jumpy that the least little thing disturbs her. For example, the silly girl gets scared when her roommate creaks open the door, enters in the dark, makes assorted stealthy scary sounds, runs across a hallway in the background, and hides in the closet while allowing the clothing to rustle alarmingly. Julie grabs a knife from the kitchen, and that's when we get the first Snicker-Snack, which is the Movie Glossary term for the sound a blade makes in a movie whenever it is seen. (Blades can make this sound, which resembles a knife being drawn quickly across a steel surface, when they are touching absolutely nothing.)

Anyway, Julie darn near stabs Karla to death, when, hey, all Karla wanted to do was borrow a dress. This is the first of many false alarms, which are setups that look like danger but turn out to have an innocent explanation. They are usually followed by moments of real violence, in which we get a sting, which is the technical term for the loud, discordant, frightening chord that plays when the victim is confronted by sudden violence.

Now you'd think that Karla the roommate would figure out that since Julie has been living for two years with terrifying nightmares, and since most of her friends and neighbors have been filleted by the Fisherman, it would be unwise to sneak into her apartment in the dark, make suspicious noises, and hide in the closet. Roommates do not think like this in slasher movies.

The other standby is the POV bait-and-switch. This involves the manipulation of the camera to create a point of view that shows (a) what the character sees but we can't, (b) what we see but the character can't, or (c) what neither of us can see, since the camera is stalking the unwitting victim. It is an unwritten rule of slasher movies that killers are invisible until they actually leap into frame; if we can't see them, neither can the hero, even though the killer occupies space that should be visible from the hero's POV.

Now that we've analyzed the tawdry tricks the movie uses to pound the audience like a Playskool workbench, is there anything else to be said about *I Still Know What You Did Last Summer*? Not really. It contains no characters of any interest, no dialogue worth hearing, no originality of conception, no ambition other than to pocket the dollars of anyone unlucky enough to go to a movie named *I Still Know What You Did Last Summer.* When a movie begins, I imagine an empty room in my mind that is about to be filled. This movie left the room furnished only with dust and a few dead flies.

I Went Down ★★★

R, 107 m., 1998

Brendan Gleeson (Bunny), Peter McDonald (Git), Tony Doyle (Tom French), Antoine Byrne

(Sabrina), David Wilmot (Anto), Peter Caffrey (Frank Grogan), Rachel Brady (Young Woman). Directed by Paddy Breathnach and produced by Robert Walpole and Mark Shivas. Screenplay by Conor McPherson.

I was forbidden several years ago by a politically correct editor to write that the Irish "have the gift of gab." That was an unpermissable ethnic generalization, and probably racist, either by inclusion or exclusion, I forget which. I am reminded of that prohibition every time I review a new movie from Ireland, because so many of these movies are fueled with the music of speech, with the verbal poetry of a nation that until very recent times amused itself primarily by talking, singing, and reciting to one another. (Now that television has taken over I expect them to gradually subside like the rest of us into distracted mutterings the length of commercials.)

Paddy Breathnach's *I Went Down* is a crime movie in which the dialogue is a great deal more important than anything else. It takes the form of a road movie and the materials of gangster movies (do real gangsters learn how to act by watching movies?), but what happens is beside the point. It's what they say while it's happening that makes the movie so entertaining. Consider, for example, this observation of a kidnapped gangster: "Did you ever make love to a gangster's wife? It's like making love with the angel of (bleeping) death looking over your shoulder. Jeezsus, you just can't enjoy yourself."

The movie opens with Git (Peter McDonald) getting out of prison. He learns from his girlfriend that she has taken up with his friend Anto (David Wilmot), and when he goes to a pub looking for Anto, he ends up saving him from having his fingers smashed by the henchmen of Tom French, the local gang boss (Tony Doyle). Git pretty well smashes up French's men, and of course that is something he cannot hope to get away with. The usual punishment might be death or maiming, but French makes him an offer: He'll forgive him, and release Anto, if Git will go to Cork and collect some money for him. To keep an eye on him, French sends along the large and weathered Bunny (Brendan Gleeson).

Gleeson, who gave the best performance I saw at the 1998 Cannes Film Festival (in John Boormann's *The General*), is a rumpled giant, who as Bunny has problems with asthma and thinks he is getting too old for the workload of a gangster. He is a veteran without being an expert, as Git discovers early on when Bunny steals a car and then gets into a tricky situation at a gas station because he doesn't have the key to the gas cap.

The movie unfolds with a series of colorful characters, including Frank Grogan (Peter Caffrey), the villain in Cork. There is also an interlude with a young local girl Git meets on the way and spends a confessional night with. Ireland is small enough that you can drive across it in a day, but somehow it is such an intensely local place that such a journey seems almost epic, and every town and village is like a rich repository of densely packed local legends.

Despite the good supporting characters, the movie is basically a two-hander between McDonald and Gleeson (whose character likes to arrange everything in lists of threes). They talk, and as they talk they get to know one another, and as their personal colors emerge a friendship develops. The friendship is inconvenient, under the circumstances, but there you have it.

And when the inevitable violent showdown arrives, Breathnach makes an interesting decision: Instead of prolonging it with lots of clever shots and exploding body parts, he stylizes it—putting distance between the visuals and the action, so that *I Went Down* doesn't insult the audience it has carefully cultivated. I hate it when a movie treats the audience as if it's intelligent and alert to good dialogue, and then slaps on a bonehead ending. Much nicer this way. In Ireland, it's not so much what happens that matters, anyway, as what kind of a story you can turn it into.

J

The Jackal ★ ½

R, 119 m., 1997

Bruce Willis (The Jackal), Richard Gere (Declan Mulqueen), Sidney Poitier (Preston), Diane Venora (Valentina Koslova), Mathilda May (Isabella). Directed by Michael Caton-Jones and produced by James Jacks, Sean Daniel, and Kevin Jarre. Screenplay by Jarre and Chuck Pfarrer, based on *The Day of the Jackal* by Kenneth Ross.

The Jackal is a glum, curiously flat thriller about a man who goes to a great deal of trouble in order to create a crime that anyone in the audience could commit more quickly and efficiently. An example: Can you think, faithful reader, of an easier way to sneak from Canada into the United States than by buying a sailboat and entering it in the Mackinaw-to-Chicago race? Surely there must be an entry point somewhere along the famous 3,000-mile border that would attract less attention than the finish line of a regatta.

To be sure, the Jackal (for it is he) has the money to buy the boat. He is charging $70 million to assassinate the head of the FBI—half now, half payable on completion. He's hired by the head of the Russian Mafia, who, like many a foreigner with extra change in his pocket, doesn't realize he is being overcharged. There are guys right here in town, so I have heard, who would do a whack for ten grand and be happy to have the business.

The Jackal is based on the screenplay of Fred Zinnemann's 1973 classic *The Day of the Jackal*. That was a film that impressed us with the depth of its expertise: We felt it knew exactly what it was talking about. *The Jackal*, on the other hand, impressed me with its absurdity. There was scarcely a second I could take seriously.

Examples: In the Washington, D.C., subway system, the Jackal jumps across the tracks in front of a train to elude his pursuers. The train stops, exchanges passengers, and pulls out of the station. Is it just possible, do you suppose, that in real life after a man jumps across the tracks, the train halts until the situation is sorted out?

Or, how about the scene where the Jackal parks his van in a garage and paints the hatch handle with a deadly poison? One of his enemies touches the handle, convulses, and dies an agonizing death. Is that a good way to avoid attention? By being sure there's a corpse on the ground next to your van?

Or, how about the scene early in the film where a fight breaks out on cue, and then stops immediately after a gunshot is fired? Bad handling of the extras here by the assistant director: Everybody in a bar doesn't start or stop fighting at once. Even in the movies there are always a few guys who delay before joining in, or want to land one last punch at the end. These barflies are as choreographed as dancing Cossacks.

The Jackal is played by Bruce Willis as a skilled professional killer who hires a man to build him a remote-controlled precision gun mount. The man unwisely asks the kind of questions that, in his business, are guaranteed to get you killed. Hint: If you should find yourself doing business with a man who wants to pay cash for a device to hold, move, and aim a rifle capable of firing 100 explosive rounds before the first one hits its target—hey, don't go into a lot of speculation about what he may be planning to do with it.

On the Jackal's trail is the deputy head of the FBI (Sidney Poitier), who enlists the help of an IRA terrorist (Richard Gere). The IRA man is a federal prisoner, released into Poitier's custody to lead them to his lover, a Basque terrorist (Mathilda May), who knows what the Jackal looks like. The other major character is a Russian-born agent named Valentina (Diane Venora), whose character trait (singular) is that she lights a cigarette every time she is not already smoking one. I kept waiting for her to be killed, so that a last puff of smoke could drift from her dying lips as her fingers relaxed their grip on her lighter.

There was never a moment in *The Jackal* where I had the slightest confidence in the expertise of the characters. The Jackal strikes me as the kind of overachiever who, assigned to kill a mosquito, would purchase contraband insecticides from Iraq and bring them into the United States by hot-air balloon, distilling his drinking water from clouds and shooting birds for food.

Without giving away too much of the plot, I would like to register one dissent on the grounds of taste. There is a scene making a target out of a character clearly intended to be Hillary Clinton (hints: She is blond, fiftyish, the wife of the president, and is dedicating the New Hope Children's Hospital). The next time Bruce Willis or Richard Gere complains about the invasion of their privacy by the media, I hope someone remembers to ask them why their movie needed to show the first lady under fire.

Jack Frost ★

PG, 95 m., 1998

Michael Keaton (Jack Frost), Kelly Preston (Gabby Frost), Joseph Cross (Charlie Frost), Mark Addy (Mac MacArthur). Directed by Troy Miller and produced by Mark Canton and Irving Azoff. Screenplay by Mark Steven Johnson, Steve Bloom, Jonathan Roberts, and Jeff Cesario.

Jack Frost is the kind of movie that makes you want to take the temperature, if not feel for the pulse, of the filmmakers. What possessed *anyone* to think this was a plausible idea for a movie? It's a bad film, yes, but that's not the real problem. *Jack Frost* could have been co-directed by Orson Welles and Steven Spielberg and still be unwatchable because of that damned snowman.

The snowman gave me the creeps. Never have I disliked a movie character more. They say state-of-the-art special effects can create the illusion of anything on the screen, and now we have proof: It's possible for the Jim Henson folks *and* Industrial Light and Magic to put their heads together and come up with the most repulsive single creature in the history of special effects, and I am not forgetting the Chucky doll or the desert intestine from *Star Wars.*

To see the snowman is to dislike the snowman. It doesn't look like a snowman, anyway. It looks like a cheap snowman suit. When it moves, it doesn't exactly glide—it walks, but without feet, like it's creeping on its torso. It has anorexic tree limbs for arms, which spin through 360 degrees when it's throwing snowballs. It has a big, wide mouth that moves as if masticating Gummi Bears. And it's this kid's dad.

Yes, little Charlie (Joseph Cross) has been without a father for a year since his dad (Michael Keaton) was killed—on Christmas Day, of course. A year later, Charlie plays his father's magic harmonica ("If you ever need me . . .") and his father turns up as the snowman.

Think about that. It is an *astounding fact.* The snowman on Charlie's front lawn is a living, moving creature inhabited by the personality of his father. It is a reflection of the lame-brained screenplay that despite having a sentient snowman, the movie casts about for plot fillers, including a school bully, a chase scene, snowball fights, a hockey team, an old family friend to talk to mom—you know, stuff to keep up the interest between those boring scenes when *the snowman is TALKING.*

What do you ask a snowman inhabited by your father? After all, Dad's been dead a year. What's it like on the other side? Is there a heaven? Big Bang or steady state? When will the NBA strike end? Elvis—dead? What's it like standing out on the lawn in the cold all night? Ever meet any angels? Has anybody else ever come back as a snowman? Do you have to eat? If you do, then what? Any good reporter could talk to that snowman for five minutes and come back with some great quotes.

But Charlie, self-centered little movie child, is more concerned with how Jack Frost (his father's real name) can help *him.* His dad has been dead for a year and comes back as a snowman, and all he can think of is using the snowman to defeat the school bully in a snowball fight. Also, the kid tries to keep Dad from melting. (What kind of a half-track miracle is it if a snowman can talk, but it can't keep from melting?) Does the snowman have any advice for his son? Here is a typical conversation:

Jack Frost: *You da man!*

Charlie: *No, YOU da man!*

Jack: *No, I da SNOWMAN!*

Eventually the snowman has to leave again—a fairly abrupt development announced with the cursory line, "It's time for me to go . . . get on with your life." By this time the snowman's secret is known not only to his son but to his wife (Kelly Preston), who takes a phone call from her dead husband with what, under the circumstances, can only be described as extreme aplomb. At the end, the human Jack Frost materializes again, inside swirling fake snow, and tells his wife and son, "If you ever need me, I'm right here." And Charlie doesn't even ask, "What about on a hot day?"

Jackie Brown ★ ★ ★ ★

R, 154 m., 1997

Pam Grier (Jackie Brown), Samuel L. Jackson (Ordell Robbie), Robert Forster (Max Cherry), Bridget Fonda (Melanie), Michael Keaton (Ray Nicolette), Robert De Niro (Louis Gara), Michael Bowen (Mark Dargus), Chris Tucker (Beaumont Livingston), Lisa Gay Hamilton (Sheronda), Tommy "Tiny" Lister Jr. (Winston), Hattie Winston (Simone), Aimee Graham (Billingsley Sales Girl). Directed by Quentin Tarantino and produced by Lawrence Bender, Richard N. Gladstein, Paul Hellerman, Elmore Leonard, Bob Weinstein, and Harvey Weinstein. Screenplay by Tarantino, adapted from the novel *Rum Punch* by Elmore Leonard.

I like the moment when the veins pop out on Ordell's forehead. It's a quiet moment in the front seat of a van, he's sitting there next to Louis, he's just heard that he's lost his retirement fund of $500,000, and he's thinking hard. Quentin Tarantino lets him think. Just holds the shot, nothing happening. Then Ordell looks up and says, "It's Jackie Brown."

He's absolutely right. She's stolen his money. In the movies, people like him hardly ever need to think. The director has done all their thinking for them. One of the pleasures of *Jackie Brown*, Tarantino's new film based on a novel by Elmore Leonard, is that everybody in the movie is smart. Whoever is smartest will live.

Jackie (Pam Grier) knows she needs to pull off a flawless scam or she'll be dead. Ordell (Samuel L. Jackson) will pop her, just like that guy they found in the trunk of the car. So she thinks hard, and so do her bail bondsman (Robert Forster) and the ATF agent (Michael Keaton). Everyone has a pretty good idea of exactly what's happening: They just can't figure it out fast enough to stay ahead of Jackie. The final scenes unfold in a cloud of delight, as the audience watches all of the threads come together.

This is the movie that proves Tarantino is the real thing, and not just a two-film wonder boy. It's not a retread of *Reservoir Dogs* or *Pulp Fiction* but a new film in a new style, and it evokes the particular magic of Elmore Leonard—who elevates the crime novel to a form of sociological comedy. There is a scene here that involves the ex-con Louis (Robert De Niro) and Ordell's druggie mistress (Bridget Fonda) discussing a photograph pinned to the wall, and it's so perfectly written, timed, and played that I applauded it.

Tarantino has a lot of scenes that good in this movie. The scene where one character lures another to his death by tempting him with chicken and waffles. The scene where a nagging woman makes one suggestion too many. The scene where a man comes around in the morning to get back the gun a woman borrowed the night before. The moment when Jackie Brown uses one line of dialogue, perfectly timed, to solve all of her problems.

This movie is about texture, not plot. It has a plot, all right, but not as the whole purpose of the film. Jackie Brown, forty-four years old, is an attendant on the worst airline in North America and supplements her meager salary by smuggling cash from Mexico to Los Angeles for Ordell, who is a gun dealer. Beaumont (Chris Tucker), one of Ordell's hirelings, gets busted by an ATF agent (Keaton) and a local cop (Michael Bowen). So they know Jackie is coming in with $50,000 of Ordell's money, and bust her.

Ordell has Jackie bailed out by Max Cherry (Robert Forster), a bondsman who falls in love the moment he sees her, but keeps that knowledge to himself. Jackie knows Ordell will kill her before she can cut a deal with the law. Maybe she could kill Ordell first, but she's not a killer, and besides, she has a better idea. The unfolding of this idea, which involves a lot of improvisation, occupies the rest of the movie.

At the heart of the story is the affection that grows between Jackie and Max. In a lesser thriller, there would be a sex scene. Tarantino reasonably believes that during a period when everyone's in danger and no one's leveling about their real motives, such an episode would be unlikely.

Max silently guesses part of what Jackie is up to, and provides a little crucial help. Jackie takes the help without quite acknowledging it. And their attraction stays on an unspoken level, which makes it all the more intriguing.

In *Jackie Brown,* as in *Pulp Fiction,* we get the sense that the characters live in spacious worlds and know a lot of people (in most thrillers the characters only know one another). Ordell has women stashed all over southern California, including a dim runaway from the South who he keeps in Glenwood, which he has told her is Hollywood. Max Cherry has a partner (Tiny Lister) who is referred to long before he goes into action.

The sides of the film's canvas are free to expand when it's necessary. If Tarantino's strengths are dialogue and plotting, his gift is casting. Pam Grier, the goddess of 1970s tough-girl pictures, here finds just the right note for Jackie Brown; she's tired and desperate. Robert Forster has the role of a career as the bail bondsman, matter-of-fact about his job and the law; he's a plausible professional, not a plot stooge.

Jackson, as Ordell, does a harder, colder version of his hit man in *Pulp Fiction,* and once again uses the word "nigger" like an obsession or a mantra (that gets a little old). De Niro, still in a longtime convict's prison trance, plays Louis as ingratiatingly stupid. Bridget Fonda's performance is so good it's almost invisible; her character's lassitude and contempt coexist with the need to be high all the time.

A lot of crime films play like they were written by crossword puzzle fans who fill in the easy words and then call the hotline for the solution. (The solution is always: Abandon the characters and end with a chase and a shootout.) Tarantino leaves the hardest questions for last, hides his moves, conceals his strategies in plain view, and gives his characters dialogue that is alive, authentic, and spontaneous. You savor every moment of *Jackie Brown.* Those who say it is too long have developed cinematic attention deficit disorder. I wanted these characters to live, talk, deceive, and scheme for hours and hours.

Jackie Chan's First Strike ★ ★ ★

PG-13, 88 m., 1997

Jackie Chan (Jackie), Jackson Lou (Tsui), Chen Chun Wu (Annie), Bill Tung (Uncle Bill), Jouri Petrov (Colonel Yegorov), Grishajeva Nonna (Natasha). Directed by Stanley Tong and produced by Barbie Tung. Screenplay by Stanley Tong, Nick Tramontane, Greg Mellott, and Elliot Tong.

Here is crucial dialogue from early in *Jackie Chan's First Strike:* "It's me! I found new suspect!"

"Who is he?"

"I don't know!"

Right there you have the beauty of the Jackie Chan movies. He always finds the suspect. And he never quite knows what he's doing. In its exotic locations and elaborate stunts, this could be a James Bond movie, if Bond were a cheerful Hong Kong cop who bumbles into the middle of the action by accident and fights his way out in sheer desperation.

Chan is said to be the world's top action star—except in the United States, which has resisted most of his forty-plus pictures. Now he is engaged in a campaign to conquer this last frontier; in 1996 we got *Rumble in the Bronx* and *Supercop,* and in 1997 we got *Jackie Chan's First Strike* and *Thunderbolt.* All are dubbed in English, mostly by Chan and the other actors themselves.

What makes him popular is not just his stunts (he is famous for doing them all himself) but his attitude to them: After a downhill ski chase in his shirtsleeves, his teeth chatter. When he's submerged in an icy lake, he desperately rubs his hands together for warmth. He wants our sympathy. And there is a sporting innocence in the action: Chan never uses a gun, there is no gore and not much blood, and he'd rather knock someone out than kill him.

The plot of *Jackie Chan's First Strike* is surrealistic. Chan plays a Hong Kong cop named Jackie, who is assigned to follow the mysterious Natasha on a flight to the Ukraine (he carefully makes a note every time she goes to the airplane toilet). In the snow-covered Ukraine, he stumbles into a plot involving conspirators who want to steal the warhead of a nuclear missile.

Chan follows them into a forbidden military area. He sees a warning sign and shouts to his superiors over his cell phone, "It says trespassers will be shot!" "That's just for kids," his boss assures him. Then we get the downhill ski sequences, including one in which Jackie skis off the side of a hill and grabs the runners of a helicopter. To be sure, it's not a very big hill and the helicopter is pretty close—but then we reflect that this is a real stunt, not a special effect, and we're impressed by Chan's skill and determination to entertain.

The "new KGB" surfaces, explains that the nuclear warhead is now in Australia, and that they are cooperating with the Hong Kong police. They will dispatch Jackie to Brisbane—by submarine, which seems a rather slow way to get there. In Australia, Chan meets Annie (Chen Chun Wu), whose job is to enter an oceanarium tank to feed the sharks, and whose brother has stolen the warhead, which she hides for him in the shark tank.

This situation, of course, requires Chan to spend a lot of time just barely escaping being eaten by sharks, while snatching breaths of oxygen from his enemies' scuba tanks. At one point my notes read: "New Russian Mafia terrorists fire rocket grenade at Chinese funeral in Brisbane," which will give you the general idea, if you can also imagine the scene where a guy forces Jackie to strip while singing "I Will Follow You," and then dresses him in a clown suit, after which Jackie tries to operate a cellular phone while wearing porpoise flippers. A little later, Jackie incapacitates a foe by flipping him into a tank filled with "toxic sea creatures," which attach themselves to his body like mean little pincushions.

Jackie Chan is an acquired taste. His movies don't have the polish of big-budget Hollywood extravaganzas, the dialogue sounds like cartoon captions, and as the plot careens from Hong Kong to the Ukraine to Australia we realize that it was probably written specifically to sell well in Russia and Down Under. But Chan himself is a graceful and skilled physical actor, immensely likable, and there's a kind of Boy Scout innocence in the action that's refreshing after all the doom-mongering, blood-soaked Hollywood action movies. It's as if the movie has been made of, by, and for thirteen-year-old boys, and while you watch it you feel like one.

Jawbreaker ★ ½

R, 91 m., 1999

Rose McGowan (Courtney), Rebecca Gayheart (Julie), Julie Benz (Marcie), Judy Evans Greer (Fern Mayo), Chad Christ (Zach), Charlotte Roldan (Liz Purr), Pam Grier (Detective Vera Cruz), Ethan Erickson (Dane Sanders). Directed by Darren Stein and produced by Stacy Kramer and Lisa Tornel. Screenplay by Stein.

I knew high school comedies were desperate for new ideas, but *Jawbreaker* is the first one I've seen where the bad girl is stoned with corsages. The movie is a slick production of a lame script, which kills time for most of its middle hour. If anyone in the plot had the slightest intelligence, the story would implode.

The film opens with an accidental death. The "Fearless Four" are the coolest girls in Reagan High School (and no wonder, since they look well into their twenties). One morning three of them surprise their friend Liz by sticking a jawbreaker into her mouth, taping it shut, and locking her in a car trunk for a ride to a restaurant where they plan a birthday breakfast. Liz chokes to death.

What to do? Cover it up, of course. The ringleader is Courtney (Rose McGowan), a rhymes-with-witch who fakes a phone call from Liz's mother, saying she'll be absent from school. Then she has her pals Julie (Rebecca Gayheart) and Marcie (Julie Benz) help her carry the corpse back to Liz's bed, where they fake a rape scene. Meanwhile, a school wallflower named Fern Mayo (Judy Evans Greer) delivers Liz's homework to her house, overhears the girls talking, and learns of their crime.

What to do? Part II. Make Fern one of them, of course, by giving her a beauty makeover, a new name (Vylette), and instructions on how to be a babe ("Never, ever, eat at lunch—period!"). Vylette, of course, turns out to be even more spiteful than the other girls, and indeed one of the original team, Julie (Rebecca Gayheart), drops out of the clique because she's disgusted with the whole deception.

Once poor Liz is dead and the cover-up begins, the film has to delay the obvious resolution of the situation in order to sketch in two tired subplots: Julie's romance with the star drama student (Chad Christ) and Fern/Vylette's transformation into a monster. Julie could end it all by speaking out, but she delays, because that would not be convenient for the plot.

Another problem. A local detective is investigating the death. She's played by Pam Grier, so cloaked in vast black garments and long hair that she seems to be peeking out from behind the wardrobe department. She has a scene where she's strong and angry, and then the movie forgets that personality trait and makes her into a stooge who listens to unbelievable stories. She arrests a man as a suspect in the case, disregarding a crucial clue: The school received that call from Liz's "mother," and since Liz's real mother didn't make it, it must have come from a female who knew what school Liz went to. Thus, probably not a random male rapist.

And on and on. The movie's fugitive pleasure is Rebecca Gayheart as the good girl; she is wonderfully photogenic, we reflect, as she and the rest of the cast founder in amateur-night dialogue and a plot that desperately stretches its thin material and still barely struggles to the ninety-one-minute mark—and that's counting end credits and various songs including, inexplicably, Frank Sinatra's "Young at Heart."

John Carpenter's Vampires ★ ★

R, 107 m., 1998

James Woods (Jack Crow), Daniel Baldwin (Montoya), Sheryl Lee (Katrina), Thomas Ian Griffith (Valek), Maximilian Schell (Cardinal Alba), Tim Guinee (Father Adam Guiteau), Mark Boone Jr. (Catlin), Gregory Sierra (Father Giovanni). Directed by John Carpenter and produced by Sandy King. Screenplay by Don Jakoby, based on the novel *Vampire$*, by John Steakley.

When it comes to fighting vampires and performing exorcisms, the Catholic Church has the heavy artillery. Your other religions are good for everyday theological tasks, like steering their members into heaven, but when the undead lunge up out of their graves, you want a priest on the case. As a product of Catholic schools, I take a certain pride in this preeminence.

Oh, I'm aware that Rome takes a dim view of sensationalist superstition. The pope wrote an encyclical about New Age tomfoolery just last week. But *John Carpenter's Vampires* gets its imprimatur from the Hollywood Catholic Church, a schism that broke off about the time the priest climbed the stairs to Linda Blair's bedroom in *The Exorcist.* This is the kind of movie where the vampire killers hang rosaries from their rearview mirrors, and are blessed by a priest before they harpoon the vile creatures and drag them into the sunlight for spontaneous combustion.

The movie stars James Woods as Jack Crow, hard-bitten vampire hunter, whose family was destroyed by vampires. He's always fun to watch, with the dark glasses, the little cigar, and the sneer. He's informed by a cleric after the first raid: "I've notified Rome. They're wiring your payment to the Monterey account." Yes, the Church, which once relied on prayer, holy water, and crucifixes, now employs mercenaries to kill vampires. First the lay teachers in the parochial schools, now this.

Crow's partner is Montoya (Daniel Baldwin, jowliest of the Baldwin boys). They use a steel cable attached to a winch on a Jeep to drag the vampires into the sunlight, where they ignite in a way that looks uncannily as if they had roman candles in their pants pockets.

After the big raid in the opening sequence, they line up the skulls of their victims on the hood of their Jeep. One is missing: the Master. The vampire killers celebrate at a local motel with a wild party, but then Valek (Thomas Ian Griffith), the Master, attacks and wipes out all but Crow, Montoya, and a hooker named Katrina (Sheryl Lee). True, she's been bitten by Valek, but Crow explains that since masters communicate telepathically with their conquests, he can use her as a kind of ESP surveillance camera until she "turns."

There's a lot of Catholicism. We meet a cardinal (Maximilian Schell) who apparently supervises Rome's vampire squad. And an innocent priest in a Spanish mission that harbors the Black Cross that Valek covets. Why does he need it? It was used centuries ago in an attempted exorcism that used an "ancient forbidden form of ritual" that led to an "inverse exorcism," which means that instead of driving the evil spirit from the body and leaving the person behind, the person is cast out and the spirit retains rights of tenancy.

It is inevitable that Montoya and Katrina will be drawn to each other. She has wonderful qualities, including the ability to wear the same costume throughout the movie, survive a vampire massacre and a pickup truck crash in it, and still have it look perky the next day, with a neckline that displays the precise 2.2 inches of cleavage that Carpenter's heroines always display, as if just that much and no more or less comforts his libido.

One detail puzzled me. One of the characters is bitten by a vampire, takes out his butane lighter, and cauterizes the wound by holding his flesh above the flame. Yet later the film suggests that he may be infected after all. My thought: Either cauterizing a fresh vampire wound works or it doesn't. If it doesn't, it's not the sort of thing you do for fun.

The movie has a certain mordant humor and some macho dialogue that's funny. Woods manfully keeps a straight face through goofy situations where many another actor would have signaled us with a wink. But the movie is not scary, and the plot is just one gory showdown after another. I was disappointed to find that the traditional spiritual weapons against vampires no longer seem to work. But maybe it's just that Jack Crow's theology is rusty. At the end of the movie, bidding farewell to a couple of vampires he sort of likes, he tells them, *Vaya con dios!* Not a tactful thing to say to a vampire.

johns ★ ★ ★

R, 96 m., 1997

Lukas Haas (Donner), David Arquette (John), Arliss Howard (John Cardoza), Keith David (Homeless John), Christopher Gartin (Crazy Eli), Josh Schaefer (David), Wilson Cruz (Mikey), Terrence Dashon Howard (Jimmy the Warlock), Elliott Gould (Manny). Directed by Scott Silver and produced by Beau Flynn and Stefan Simchowitz. Screenplay by Silver.

johns, a movie about male prostitutes in Los Angeles, has a moment that offers a key to the film: Tourists offer a hustler $20 to pose in a snapshot with them. They want to show the folks back home that they've not only seen the sights, they've met the locals.

There was a time when most people didn't know men sold sex, and didn't want to know. Now the cruising underworld is the stuff of movies, songs, novels, and fashion ads that are easy to decode. *johns* dramatizes the lifestyle at the same time it tells a cautionary tale: "Young man! Stay off of the streets!" (Sing to the tune of "YMCA.") The audience, like the tourists, gets to meet the locals while keeping a safe distance. That's because the hustling world is sentimentalized here, filtered through a lens of romanticism.

The movie stars Lukas Haas and David Arquette as Donner and John, who work Santa Monica Boulevard, nurtured by their dreams: John wants to spend his twenty-first birthday in a luxury hotel room, and Donner wants them both to take the bus to Branson, Missouri. Donner is gay and loves John; John says he's straight and working only for the money, and he does have a girlfriend, although the relationship is fleeting and chancy.

The film's symbolism is established early, when we learn that John's birthday is Christmas Day. He wears a stolen Santa hat for much of the film, and in an encounter with a violent client he picks up the marks of a crown of thorns. More symbolism: Three characters in the movie are named John, and all of the clients, of course, are called "johns," perhaps indicating that everyone is in the same boat. (Donner's name reminds me of the notorious Donner Party, suggesting still more parallels.)

Christ symbolism makes me apprehensive in a movie; it tips the ending, and besides, most Christ-figures die for their own sins, not for ours. But *johns* overcomes the undergraduate symbol-mongering of its screenplay with a story that comes to life in spite of itself, maybe because the actors are so good, or maybe because the writer-director, Scott Silver, has documentary roots that correct for his overwriting.

Silver does a good job of capturing the unsprung rhythm of the street. Although one of the characters is always asking what time it is, that never really matters; time is what he sells, not what he passes. The characters form a loose-knit community at the mercy of strangers in cars. They may spend hours together and then not see each other for a week. We meet some of the street regulars: Crazy Eli (Christopher Gartin), for example, who spouts wild theories, and Homeless John (Keith David), who turns up from time to time like John the Baptist, with support and encouragement.

Working from stories he got from real life, Silver shows his heroes encountering a series of johns: one turns suddenly violent, one (well-played by Elliott Gould) is a kindhearted guy who sneaks in some action while his family is out shopping, one is an old man with peculiar tastes who wants to know "who in the Sam Hill" Donner thinks he is.

There is some underlying urgency: John has stolen $300 that belongs to a drug dealer (Terrence Dashon Howard), and now the dealer and his bodyguard are looking for him. He wants to use the $300 for his hotel room. Will he get his dream before the dealer gets the money? There is an ominous sign: His "lucky sneakers" are stolen at the beginning of the movie. Nothing bad could happen to him while he was wearing them, but now . . .

David Arquette and Lukas Haas find the right note for their characters: They have plans and dreams, but vague ones, and they're often sort of detached, maybe because their lives are on hold in between johns. They have fallen into a lifestyle that offers them up during every waking moment for any passing stranger. They do it for money, but it pays so badly they can't save up enough to stop. What the johns are really paying them for is not sex, but availability: to remain homeless and permanently on call.

Jungle 2 Jungle ★

PG, 111 m., 1997

Tim Allen (Michael), Sam Huntington (Mimi), JoBeth Williams (Patricia), Lolita Davidovich (Charlotte), Martin Short (Richard), Valerie Mahaffey (Jan), LeeLee Sobieski (Karen), Frankie Galasso (Andrew). Directed by John Pasquin and produced by Brian Reilly. Screenplay by Bruce A. Evans and Raynold Gideon.

There is a scene early in *Jungle 2 Jungle* that indicates how brainless the movie is. Before I explore its delights, I must make you familiar with the premise. A Manhattan commodities broker journeys up the Amazon to obtain a divorce from the wife he has not seen in many years. She works now among the Indians. The broker is astonished to find that he has a son, who has been raised by his estranged wife in the jungle. The son now wants to return to New York with his father because he has promised the tribal chief he will bring back the fire from the torch atop the Statue of Liberty.

Now, as we rejoin our story, the broker (Tim Allen) and his son (Sam Huntington) arrive at Kennedy Airport, and here is the brainless part: The boy, who is about thirteen, is still dressed for the jungle. He wears only a loincloth and some feathers and suchlike; no shirt or shoes. If memory serves, he carries his deadly dart blowgun, which is the sort of thing you're not allowed to have on an aircraft, but never mind: Did either of this child's parents stop to consider that perhaps the lad should have jeans and a sweatshirt for a 3,000-mile air journey? Such garments are available in Brazil. I know; I've been there. I flew upstream in a plane with pontoons and landed on the Amazon above Belem without seeing a single person in a loincloth, although I saw many Michael Jordan T-shirts.

But no, the parents didn't stop to think, and that is because they *don't think*. Why don't they think? Because no one is allowed to think in this movie. Not one single event in the entire plot can possibly take place unless every character in the cast has brains made of Bac-O-Bits.

The plot of *Jungle 2 Jungle* has been removed from a French film called *Little Indian, Big City*. The operation was a failure and the patient dies. The only reason I am rating this movie at one star while *Little Indian, Big City* got no stars is that *Jungle 2 Jungle* is too mediocre to deserve no stars. It doesn't achieve truly awful badness, but is sort of a black hole for the attention span, sending us spiraling down into nothingness.

Most of the comic moments come from the "fish out of water" premise, or "FOW," as Hollywood abbreviates it (you know your plot's not original when it has its own acronym).

The kid has been raised in the jungle, and now, in the city, he tries to adapt. There are many jokes involving his pet tarantula, which he has brought along with him, and his darts, which Allen uses to accidentally put his fiancée's cat to sleep.

The fiancée is played by Lolita Davidovich, who is supposed to be a successful businesswoman, but dresses as if she aspires to become a lap dancer. The joke is that she doesn't like the idea of her future husband having a jungle boy. Additional jokes involve Martin Short, who plays Allen's associate and has stolen Jim Jarmusch's hairstyle although not his wit. There are also some Russian Mafia guys, who march in and out like landlords in a Three Stooges comedy.

Little Indian, Big City (1996) got many if not most of the year's worst reviews, but when I heard it was being remade with Tim Allen, I must confess I had some hope: Surely they would see how bad the premise was and repair it? Not a chance. This movie has not learned from the mistakes of others, and like a lemming follows *Little Indian* over the cliff and into the sea.

Junk Mail ★ ★ ★

NO MPAA RATING, 83 m., 1998

Robert Skjaerstad (Roy), Andrine Saether (Line), Per Egil Aske (Georg), Eli Anne Linnestad (Betsy). Directed by Pal Sletaune and produced by Petter Boe and Dag Nordahl. Screenplay by Jonny Halberg and Pal Sletaune. In Norwegian with English subtitles.

Roy is not someone you would want to know. Or stand very close to. Or get your mail from. He brings new aromas to the concept of grunge. He is a mailman in Oslo who reads any letters that look interesting, and then delivers them smeared with cold spaghetti that he eats out of cans. He dumps junk mail into a cave by the railroad tracks. He's so low on the mailman evolutionary chain that even if you crossed him with Kevin Costner in *The Postman,* the result would frighten dogs.

Roy stumbles into the life of Line, a hearing-impaired woman who lives on his route. One day she forgets and leaves her house keys in the lock of her mailbox. He lets himself in, sniffs around, tastes some of her food, looks through her drawers and hears a message from "Georg" on her answering machine: "We did it together. You were as much a part of it as I was."

On another day he returns, falls asleep, and hides under the bed when she comes home early. Hearing nothing after a while, he finds her underwater in the bathtub. He saves her from suicide, calls an ambulance, and escapes. In a nightclub, he meets a blowzy, bosomy blonde in leopard-skin pants, who is long past her sell-by date. He takes her back to Line's apartment, knowing of course that it will be unoccupied. The blonde gets drunk, vomits, and throws things around.

I've been hearing about *Junk Mail* ever since the 1997 Sundance festival. People would mention it with that little smile that suggests a lot is being left unsaid. It's a film about a voyeur, and it appeals to the voyeur in us: We don't like Roy or approve of him, but we watch fascinated because he lives so casually outside the rules. He's the kind of guy who will steal candy from a patient in a coma.

Every once in a while I recommend a film and get an indignant postcard from someone informing me the characters were *disgusting.* I invariably agree. Roy, for example, is disgusting. So is Line (she and Georg mugged a security guard, who is the man in the coma). So is Georg. So is the leopard-skin blonde. In Norway, a land we think of as wholesome and enlightened, it is almost a relief to discover they still have room for a few token outcasts.

But why, oh why, the postcard always continues, should we pay our good money to see a film about *such disgusting people?* The postcards never have a return address, or I would write back arguing that my review described the film accurately, so why did they go? I might even cite Ebert's Law, which teaches us: "A film is not about what it is about. It is about how it is about it." Films about disgusting people can be amusing and interesting, or they can be worthless. But they are not bad simply because of their subject matter. Subjects are neutral. Style is all.

Consider, for example, that Roy does not kill anyone. What are his worst crimes? He is a bad mailman. He eats cold spaghetti out of a can. He needs a bath and a shave. He shouldn't sneak into that poor woman's apartment, although at least he saves her from suicide instead of simply sneaking out again. Compare Roy with—oh, I dunno, how about Art, the FBI guy played by Bruce Willis in *Mercury Rising*? Art also needs a bath and a shave. He kills countless people, speeds dangerously down the streets of Chicago, is associated with explosions and fires, and participates in a shoot-out at an old folks' home. He is a much more alarming specimen than Roy, even if he is the good guy—and yet no one sent me a postcard describing him as *disgusting.*

Why not? It is not because of the behavior or the values, but because of the hygiene. Roy is not attractive, muscular, and well coordinated. He is a scuzzy loser. If he were in a cartoon, flies would be buzzing around his head. And yet we are more likely to meet Roy than Art, because Roy exists in the world and Art exists only in a cinematic machine called a thriller. Roy wants love too. He asks Line out for a cup of coffee. He shares a few meager secrets about his existence with her. And at the end, when the bad guys come, he tries to protect her, just as Art tries to protect Stacy and the cute little autistic kid in *Mercury Rising.* What more can a hero do?

Junk Mail is a first film by Pal Sletaune, who has plunged headfirst into a world of rain, mud, desolate cityscapes, sickly greens, depressing blues, and sad struggling people. His mailman is not admirable, but he is understandable. And at least he doesn't have a hole in the back of his head, so that a director can stick in a key and wind him up.

K

Kama Sutra ★ ★

NO MPAA RATING, 114 m., 1997

Indira Varma (Maya), Sarita Choudhury (Tara), Ramon Tikaram (Jai Kumar), Naveen Andrews (Raj Singh), Rekha (Rasa Devi), Khalik Tyabji (Biki), Arundhati Rao (Annabi), Surabhi Bhansali (Young Maya). Directed by Mira Nair and produced by Nair and Lydia Dean Pilcher. Screenplay by Helena Kriel and Nair.

Kama Sutra is a lush, voluptuous tale told in sixteenth-century India, about two young women who grow up to pleasure a king—one as his wife, the other as his courtesan. To find a film like this from the 1960s, made by a man, would be one thing; to find it made in 1997 by Mira Nair is more startling. Nothing in her previous work (the great film *Salaam Bombay!* and two good films, *Mississippi Masala* and *The Perez Family*) prepared me for this exercise in exotic eroticism.

The heroine of the story is a servant girl named Maya (Indira Varma), who has always lived in the shadow of her childhood friend, the well-born Princess Tara (Sarita Choudhury, from *Mississippi Masala*). When Tara is betrothed to the king, Raj Singh (Naveen Andrews), Maya slips into his chamber on the night before the wedding and seduces him. The next day she taunts her rival: "All my life I have lived with your used things. Now something I have used is yours forever."

Maya is exiled from the village by the bitter Tara and drifts from town to town until she falls beneath the gaze of a sculptor (Ramon Tikaram). She becomes his lover and model, until he decides she cannot be both at the same time, and unwisely (in my opinion) prefers her as his model. She then meets a wise older woman (Rekha) who runs a school for courtesans based on the ancient book *Kama Sutra,* or *Lessons in Love.*

This book is known in the West mostly for its exhaustive (and exhausting) lists of sexual positions, and for its carefully delineated caressing techniques. (Concerning the pressing of the nails against the body, for example, I have always much preferred the subtle "leaf of the blue lotus" technique to the more abrupt "jump of a hare.") But there is much in the book beyond technique: It is a work of art, dance, and philosophy, and Maya proves a good student, telling her teacher: "I want to learn the rules of love and how to use them. And if I can't use them on the one I love, I will use them on the ones I don't."

She does indeed become accomplished as a courtesan, and eventually drifts back into the orbit of the royal court; the king takes her as his lover, and then there are boudoir intrigues involving the sculptor, whom Maya still loves. Nair has prepared the screenplay with great attention to the mores of the time (doctors arrived in the chambers of women covered with a cloth, for example, which provides the means for a lover's escape just in the nick of time).

The movie's story is really just the occasion for the scenes of eroticism, but it must be said that those scenes have a beauty and solemnity that is quietly impressive. And the two actresses are great beauties; Varma, with her lithe model's figure, is the more conventional, but there is much to be said for Choudhury's full lips and deep eyes, and the cinematography by Declan Quinn places them in painterly compositions that have a sensuous quality of their own.

The problem, in the end, is that *Kama Sutra* really adds up to very little. The story is contrived and unconvincing, the psychology is shallow, and moments of truth are passed over for moments of beauty. The film is entrancing to regard, but I expected more from Mira Nair, and I was disappointed. She is better than this work.

Kicked in the Head ★ ½

R, 90 m., 1997

Kevin Corrigan (Redmond), Linda Fiorentino (Megan), Michael Rapaport (Stretch), James Woods (Uncle Sam), Burt Young (Jack), Lili Taylor (Happy), Olek Krupa (Borko). Directed by Matthew Harrison and produced by Barbara De Fina. Screenplay by Kevin Corrigan and Harrison.

Kicked in the Head is one of those movies where you wish the story were about the supporting characters. There are three of them worthy of features of their own: Uncle Sam (James Woods), the hero's con man relative, Megan (Linda Fiorentino), an airline attendant who has an enigmatic one-night stand with the hero, and Stretch (Michael Rapaport), a self-styled beer distribution czar.

In a generally underwritten (and yet too talky) movie, these New Yorkers are so intriguing we want to know more about them. Unfortunately, the movie isn't about them. It involves some time in the life of Redmond (Kevin Corrigan), an aimless young man who spends a lot of his time writing bad poetry about the meaning of life.

The plot, such as it is, involves Uncle Sam sending Redmond to drop off some cocaine at an elevated stop. Cocaine is, of course, the handiest MacGuffin of our time; introduce it into a plot, and you don't have to explain motivations. The dope drop turns into a gun battle in which countless shots are fired but nobody is hit, and then Redmond embarks on an odyssey that takes him into the orbits of Stretch (who runs Stretch's Beer-o-Rama) and Jack (Burt Young), the guy who gave Uncle Sam the cocaine. (Young's character has a great line, even though it is not remotely plausible: "I like organized—with a 'g,' like in 'phlegm.'")

The nearest thing to a sustained relationship takes place between Redmond and Fiorentino, as a woman he sees crying on a train, and hopes to console. Fiorentino plays the character as a milder version of her maneater in *The Last Seduction.* Wary, wounded, and cynical, she sleeps with Redmond for reasons having little to do with the plot and much to do, perhaps, with Kevin Corrigan, who cowrote the screenplay, wanting to give himself a good scene.

Well, there is a good scene (at an airline bar), but when Fiorentino exits, the interest leaves too, because we care about her, not him That's true all through the movie, as the colorless Redmond plays straight man to Stretch (Rapaport does some hilarious riffs on the glories of beer distribution), Woods ("This is my dentist's car. He asked me to watch it for him"), and Burt Young's Russian hit man (who carefully looks up menacing threats in his phrase book).

I've seen the film twice, and there's one scene that played differently the two times. It's a long dialogue exchange between Redmond and Stretch at the beer depot. It's clear the scene is semi-improvised, and there were times when Rapaport seemed to be smiling inappropriately, going out of character to let us see the actor playing with the process. That bothered me the first time, but not the second, because by then I knew the characters weren't as interesting as the actors struggling with the material.

The King and I ★ ★

G, 90 m., 1999

With the voices of: Miranda Richardson (Anna Leonowens), Christiane Noll (Anna's Songs), Martin Vidnovic (King of Siam), Ian Richardson (The Kralahome), Darrell Hammond (Master Little), Allen D. Hong (Prince Chululongkorn), David Burnham (Prince's Songs), Armi Arabe (Tuptim), Tracy Venner Warren (Tuptim's Songs), Adam Wylie (Louis Leonowens). Directed by Richard Rich and produced by James G. Robinson, Arthur Rankin, and Peter Bakalian. Screenplay by Bakalian, Jacqueline Feather, and David Seidler, adapted from the musical by Richard Rodgers and Oscar Hammerstein II.

It makes perfect sense to animate Broadway musicals. The songs are already market-tested, the titles are presold, and there's only one hitch: Their stories appeal mostly to adults, while most feature-length cartoons are aimed at children. It need not be so. In Japan, adults buy more tickets to animation than children do—and as a result, feature cartoons, with their glorious freedom over space and logic, represent up to a fourth of ticket sales.

But here animation is mostly linked with bold heroes, cute little animals, and colorful sidekicks. And one of the problems with *The King and I,* which has been animated by Richard Rich for Warner Bros., is that the story is not intrinsically interesting to kids. The Rodgers and Hammerstein classic is mostly concerned with a romance between a British schoolteacher and the king of Siam; a parallel romance takes place between the prince and a servant girl. Both romances involve defiance of class and convention, and kids aren't much tuned in to that.

To be sure, this animated *The King and I* adds some characters designed for children. There's the roly-poly Master Little, assistant to the evil prime minister. He's flossing his teeth the first time we see him, and then it's a running gag that he keeps getting them knocked out. Alas, he has so many teeth that the gag runs out before the teeth do. The movie also has a fire-breathing dragon, a hot-air balloon adventure, fireworks, a black panther, and a lot of royal children. But still it lacks the energy of a kid's movie, and the story's barriers to romance aren't that interesting to younger viewers.

You know the story. Anna, a British teacher, is hired by the king to come to Siam and educate his children. His evil minister, the Kralahome, plots to make Anna believe the king is a tyrant, so that the British will overthrow him and replace him with—the Kralahome, of course. Anna arrives in Siam with her ten-year-old son, Louis (and a monkey named Moonshee that I don't recall from the original), and after various misunderstandings falls in love with the king. The British indeed arrive to replace him (interesting how in those days the British had a divine right to replace other people's leaders—sort of like the CIA a century later). But after various adventures, etc., there's a happy ending.

If the tooth gag grows old, so, for my money, do the running gags from the original, about how nobody's head is supposed to be higher than the king's, and about how the king constantly repeats "et cetera." Those aren't character touches, but formula stagecraft.

It is good to hear the songs, including "Whistle a Happy Tune," "Hello, Young Lovers," "Getting to Know You," and "Shall We Dance." But the movie seemed kind of stuffy. Although I would not presume to speak for the audience at the kiddie morning screening I attended, they didn't seem to express the kind of noisy, spontaneous delight I've seen at similar movies.

Yet I applaud the experiment. I'd love to see animated versions of *My Fair Lady* and *Oklahoma,* for example—and animation is obviously the right technique for *Cats.* The challenge is to make adaptations that are intended for adults, and then attract adults to the theaters. Go into any video store and you will find long shelves of Japanese animation aimed at grown-ups. The tapes rent like crazy. Now to find a way of porting that audience over to the movie box office.

The King of Masks ★★★

NO MPAA RATING, 101 m., 1999

Zhu Xu (Bian Lian Wang), Zhou Ren-Ying (Doggie), Zhang Riuyang (Tien Che), Zhao Zhigang (Liang Sao Lang). Directed and produced by Wu Tianming. Screenplay by Wei Minglung.

In a remote area of China, in the 1930s, we meet an old street performer. His profession is humble but his secrets are a great prize. One day a famous female impersonator from the Sichuan opera sees him performing, gives him a big coin, invites him to tea, and offers him a job in his troupe. But the old man, whose name is Wang, refuses this offer because it is a tradition in his family that the secrets are passed only from father to son.

Alas, Wang (played by Zhu Xu with touching appeal) has no son. And at his age, traveling the rivers in his little houseboat from one town to another, it is unlikely he will ever have one. The female impersonator begs him: "Do not die without an heir, or your magic will die too." Wang takes this advice to heart. It is a time of floods and homelessness, and in the next city there is a baby market where desperate parents look for homes for their hungry children—and cash. Wang is about to leave when an urchin cries out "Grandpa!" and captures his heart. He pays $10 for the eight-year-old, returns with him to his boat, and nicknames him Doggie. Together they will study the ancient art of silk masks, by which a man's face can take on a new and startling visage in the flash of a second.

That's the setup for *The King of Masks,* a new Chinese film of simplicity, beauty, and surprising emotional power. Like *Central Station,* it tells the story of a journey involving an old curmudgeon and a young child in search of a father. The difference is that the curmudgeon can become the father, if he chooses. And another one: Doggie is not a little boy, but a little girl.

Girls are not highly valued in China. When he discovers the deception, Wang feels cheated and wants to send Doggie away, but Doggie tearfully explains that she pretended to be a boy because she had been sold seven times already: The man who sold her was not her father, but a man who beat her. She promises to scrub the deck, do the cooking, and be a good doggie. The little girl, played with utter simplicity and solemnity by Zhou Ren-Ying, has already touched the old man's heart and he allows her to stay.

The King of Masks benefits by the survival of ancient ways into modern times. Today a street performer might be scorned, but in the 1930s he was seen as a member of an elite fraternity. Wang has a certain fame in the cities where he appears, and gains respect from his colleagues—even the female impersonator who is a great opera star, doted on by army generals. (The character, Liang, who dresses elegantly and travels in state, is played by the opera star Zhao Zhigang; we recall the tradition of female impersonators in Chinese opera from *Farewell, My Concubine.*)

Wang's life is happy, but he frets for a son and visits Buddhist temples (where Doggie plays happily among the toes of vast statues hewn from the hillside). One day Doggie comes upon a homeless little boy, and brings him home as a prize for old Wang, who is overjoyed. But the boy comes attached to great complications, and soon only Doggie can save Wang from imprisonment.

The King of Masks was directed by Wu Tianming, who as a studio head in the 1980s helped bring the Fifth Generation of Chinese filmmakers to prominence. After Tiananmen Square he moved to the United States, and returned only in 1995. This is his first film after his homecoming, and although it has no overt political message, perhaps it is no accident that its hero is a stubborn old artist who clings to his secrets.

Like so many recent Chinese films, it benefits enormously from the beauty of the setting, the costumes, and the customs. It's poignant to realize that a society of such unique beauty existed so recently. The river life of Wang and Doggie may be at the poverty level, but it has a quality that no modern rich man can afford. The story contains elements of fable (the changeling, ancient secrets), but gains weight because we know that to Wang it makes a great difference whether Doggie is a boy or a girl. And Doggie's heroics at the end seem like melodrama until we reflect that, trained by a street artist, she would have known what she was doing.

Note: The King of Masks *is being marketed as an art film for grown-ups. But as I watched it, I realized it would be an absorbing experience for bright children. Yes, there are subtitles, but no words a good reader wouldn't know. And the focus on the eight-year-old girl (not to mention Wang's beloved pet monkey) make this a magical film for third-graders and up. If you know the right child, this is the right film.*

Kissed ★★★

NO MPAA RATING, 78 m., 1997

Molly Parker (Sandra Larson), Peter Outerbridge (Matt), Jay Brazeau (Mr. Wallis), Natasha Morley (Young Sandra). Directed by Lynne Stopkewich and produced by Dean English and Stopkewich. Screenplay by Stopkewich and Angus Fraser, based on the story "We So Seldom Look on Love" by Barbara Gowdy.

"When life turns into death, I've seen bodies shining like stars," says Sandra, who tells her story in *Kissed.* "Each of them has its own wisdom, innocence, happiness, grief. I see it."

From early childhood, Sandra has been obsessed with dead things. She and a playmate would find dead birds and bury them, but then, "after dark I'd go back and give them a proper burial." In a ritual by flashlight, she rubs her body with the dead bird in what she calls "the anointment."

In her late teens, working for a florist, she makes a delivery to a funeral home, absorbs the atmosphere, and states simply, "I'd like to work here." The mortician is happy to show her around. Opening the door to the embalming room, he says with plump satisfaction, "This is where it all happens." Soon she is working there.

Kissed is about a necrophile, but in its approach it could be about spirituality or transcendence. Sandra, played with a grave intensity by Molly Parker, does things that are depraved by normal standards, but in her mind she is performing something like a sacrament. The dead are so lonely. When she comforts them with a farewell touch from the living, the room fills with light, and an angelic choir sings in orgasmic female voices.

Kissed was, needless to say, one of the most controversial films at the Toronto and Sundance film festivals. Mostly people talked about how Lynne Stopkewich, its writer and director, had gotten away with it. One would think there was no way to film this material without disgusting the audience—or, worse, making it laugh at the wrong times. Stopkewich does not disgust, and when there are laughs, she intends them (there is a quiet mordant humor trickling through the film). What is amazing, at the end, is that we feel some sympathy for Sandra, some understanding.

Humans seem to be hard-wired at an early age into whatever sexuality they eventually profess. There is little choice in the matter. Most are lucky enough to fall within the mainstream, but for those who are attracted to obscure fetishes, it is a question of acknowledging their nature, or denying themselves sexual fulfillment. Of course some compulsions are harmful to others, and society rightly outlaws them; but the convenience of necrophilia, as the joke goes, is that it requires only one consenting adult.

In the case of Sandra, her sexuality seems to be bound up with her spirituality. She feels pity for the dead bodies in her care. Stopkewich makes it clear that sex does take place, but like many women directors she is less interested in the mechanics than in the emotion; the movie is not explicit in its sexuality, although there is a scene about embalming techniques that is more detailed than most of the audience will require. In Sandra's mind, she is helping the dead to cross over in a flood of light to a happier place: Her bliss gives them the final push.

Then Sandra, who has never dated in a conventional way, meets a young man in a coffee shop. His name is Matt (Peter Outerbridge). She is stunningly frank with him. "Why would you want to be an embalmer?" he asks. "Because of the bodies," she says. "I make love to them." He is fascinated. Soon she finds a notebook he is keeping, a sexual journal cross-indexed with obituaries from the local paper.

"It's not about facts and figures!" she says. "It's about crossing over."

"I have to do it," he vows.

"I *need* to do it," she tells him. "It's not something you force yourself to do."

If Sandra's obsession is occult and unnatural, Matt's is much more common: His male pride becomes involved in pleasing the woman he loves, and he finds himself in competition with the dead. Jealousy—and jealousy's accomplice, love—drive him. But how can he possibly compare to his rivals?

Kissed is a first film by Stopkewich, who is thirty-two and lives in Vancouver. Talking about the film at Sundance, she said she read the original story, "We So Seldom Look on Love," by Barbara Gowdy, in a book of erotica for women.

"It haunted me. Sandra is in charge of her sexuality. Although she is a fringe dweller, she achieves something we all search for. We're all looking for transcendence." Oddly enough, this is a feeling the movie largely succeeds in conveying, although there is perhaps an insight in something else Stopkewich said: "At the end of the shoot, every single person working on the film said they would choose cremation."

Kissing a Fool ★
R, 105 m., 1998

David Schwimmer (Max Abbott), Jason Lee (Jay Murphy), Mili Avital (Samantha Andrews), Bonnie Hunt (Linda), Vanessa Angel (Natasha), Kari Wuhrer (Dara), Frank Medrano (Cliff Randal), Bitty Schram (Vicki Pelam). Directed by Doug Ellin and produced by Tag Mendillo, Andrew Form, and Rick Lashbrook. Screenplay by James Frey and Ellin.

One of the requirements of TV sitcoms is that the characters live in each other's pockets. They pop into their friends' apartments at any time of day or night, and every development becomes the subject of a group discussion. That works fine on *Seinfeld,* but on the big screen it looks contrived. Consider, for example, the new comedy *Kissing a Fool* in which none of the characters behave at any moment like any human being we have ever met.

The movie involves situations that wouldn't even exist if it were not for the tortuous contortions of the plot. Jay (Jason Lee) introduces his best friend, Max (David Schwimmer), to Sam (Mili Avital), the woman who is editing his book—even though Jay loves Sam himself. Why does he do this? Otherwise there wouldn't be a role for Max, who is such a hapless shmoe that the only reason Sam dates him is because the plot requires her to. It's crashingly obvious to everyone in the audience, but not to anyone in the movie, that Jay and Sam will eventually realize that they are really in love with one another. When we're that much smarter than the characters, you have to wonder why they aren't buying tickets to watch us.

The film begins at a wedding, with a kiss between two newlyweds. Because the shot is obviously and laboriously contrived to conceal the face of one of the newlyweds, we in the audience of course know immediately that there is a reason for this. Could it be that the two people who are getting married are not the two people the movie will spend the next ninety minutes pretending are going to get married?

At the wedding, we meet Linda (Bonnie Hunt), who runs the publishing company where Sam is editing Jay's book. Linda is the film's narrator. She tells two obnoxious guests at the wedding the whole story of how the newlyweds wound up at the altar. She tells this story without ever once using both of their names, and as she picks her way through a minefield of synonyms and vague adverbial evasions, we get downright restless. Obviously, she's concealing something. And we know what it is, so who's she kidding?

Why is this story, pea-brained to begin with, filtered through the annoying device of a narration? Maybe because the filmmakers thought we would be delighted at the wonderful surprise they are concealing for the last shot. I wonder: Do they know anyone that dumb in their own lives, or do they just think the rest of us are clueless?

Sitcoms like to supply their characters with physical props, and so poor Bonnie Hunt is required to hold a cigarette in every single scene she appears in. And not any cigarette. A freshly lit one, in her right hand, held in the air roughly parallel to her ear. I hope they had a masseuse to give her shoulder rubs between takes. Ms. Hunt, who I hope is suing her agent, does what she can with a character whose IQ is higher than those of the other three characters combined.

Max, the Schwimmer character, plays a WGN sportscaster who thinks Australia is in Europe. Sam and Jay immediately compare notes about charming little trattorias in Florence. Max is obviously not the right choice for this woman, but the movie explains their attraction as first love—a love so strong that Max is actually moved to take his toothpick (sitcom prop) out of his mouth when he sees her.

We are then made to endure a lame contrivance in which Max grows fearful that Sam will not remain faithful to him, and so enlists Jay to attempt to seduce her—as a test. Not since Restoration comedy has this plot device been original, but in *Kissing a Fool* it is taken so seriously that it leads to moments of heartfelt dismay, carefully cued by the sound track, and one of those "darkness before the dawn" sequences in which it appears, for a teeth-gnashing instant, that the right people will not end up together. One character, in dismay, goes into a bar and orders four vodkas at once; the movie doesn't even know how drinkers drink.

If James Frey and the director Doug Ellin, who wrote this screenplay, didn't have an outline from a script workshop tacked to the wall in front of them, then they deserve an Oscar for discovering, all by themselves, a basic story formula that was old, tired, and moronic long before they were born.

I like the title, though. *Kissing a Fool.* They got that right.

Kiss Me, Guido ★★

R, 99 m., 1997

Nick Scotti (Frankie), Anthony Barrile (Warren), Anthony DeSando (Pino), Craig Chester (Terry), Dominick Lombardozzi (Joey Chips), Molly Price (Landlady), Christopher Lawford (Dakota), David Deblinger (Actor With No Name). Directed by Tony Vitale and produced by Ira

Deutchman and Christine Vachon. Screenplay by Vitale.

If you can believe that an aspiring actor who studies De Niro movies doesn't know what "GWM" means in a singles ad, then you can believe just about everything in *Kiss Me, Guido,* a movie that gives you lots to believe. It's a mistaken-identity comedy about a straight guy from the Bronx who answers an ad in an alternative weekly and ends up with a gay roommate in the Village.

"Guy With Money, right?" asks Frankie (Nick Scotti), who hangs around the family pizzeria in the Bronx but dreams of someday becoming an actor. His brother Pino (Anthony DeSando) is not much help; while Frankie was studying De Niro, Pino was obviously studying Travolta and Stallone, and yearns for disco to make a comeback and provide him with the stage on which he was intended to strut.

Kiss Me, Guido is a movie with a lot of funny one-liners, but no place to go with them. Like a thirty-minute sitcom, it acts like you already know all the characters and are just happy to have fresh dialogue. It's as if all of the deeper issues have been settled in previous episodes. And yet, also like a sitcom, it's kind of fun as it slides past. Here is a movie that was born to play on television.

Frankie and Warren (Anthony Barrile), his gay roommate-to-be, are both walking wounded: They've recently been unlucky in love. That would give them something in common, except that Frankie is so naive he doesn't even figure out what "GWM" means after he's watching a Julie Andrews movie with one. Not even Warren's chummy peroxided friend Terry (Craig Chester) rings any bells.

The plot device involves a play that Warren is scheduled to star in. He twists an ankle, and through reasoning that is entirely plot-driven, Frankie is picked to substitute for him—in a play about gay lovers, written and directed by Warren's ex-roommate (Christopher Lawford). But . . . can Frankie actually bring himself to kiss another man, as the role requires? Hey, didn't the great Al Pacino himself do that in *Dog Day Afternoon*?

The performances have energy and charm; the movie may be a launching pad for the careers of several actors, especially Scotti and DeSando, who has some funny moves as the Italian stallion brother. If only it had been written a little smarter. There's a scene early in the film where Frankie and Warren talk for the first time on the phone, and their dialogue is all at cross-purposes; everything is misunderstood. Dialogue like that always depresses me, because it's so artificial: You have to be almost as smart to get everything wrong as to get everything right.

I wish that Tony Vitale, the writer and director, had taken a long look at his screenplay and said, "Okay, let's assume he *knows* what 'GWM' means. What would happen then?"

Kiss or Kill ★ ★ ★

R, 96 m., 1997

Frances O'Connor (Nikki), Matt Day (Al), Chris Haywood (Hummer), Barry Otto (Adler Jones), Andrew S. Gilbert (Crean), Barry Langrishe (Zipper Doyle), Max Cullen (Stan). Directed by Bill Bennett and produced by Bill Bennett and Jennifer Bennett. Screenplay by Bill Bennett.

There has never been a movie where a middle-aged couple go on the run, pursued by teenage cops. This is the sort of thing that's so obvious it never occurs to anybody. All lovers on the run are young. All cops are older. That's because road movies are to late adolescence what monster movies are to kids: a way of exorcising unease.

Little kids identify with monsters because, like Godzilla, they feel uncoordinated and misunderstood. Moviegoers in their teens and twenties identify with road movies because, like their fugitive heroes, they feel a deep need to leave home, to flee adult regimentation, to exist outside organized society, to make their own rules. The genre requires them to commit crimes before going on the lam, but that's just a technicality—required in order to explain why the cops are chasing them.

Kiss or Kill is a rare revisionist road movie. It breaks with the genre in three key ways. (1) Although Nikki and Al, the young lovers, are indeed criminal, they spend most of the movie suspecting each other of their crimes. (2) The rebels and nonconformists they meet on the road are all middle-aged or old. (3) The cops are wry practical jokesters—the coolest characters in the movie. I've seen countless road movies, but this one felt different, as if it had an unbalanced flywheel.

The movie takes place in Australia, which in the American imagination is becoming a place like Texas, inhabited by freewheeling eccentrics with too much space on their hands. It opens with a genuinely shocking moment, which I will not reveal, that helps explain why Nikki (Frances O'Connor) grows up with a twisted view of life. As an adult, she teams up with her boyfriend, Al (Matt Day), to pull a scam: She picks up businessmen in bars, returns to their hotels with them, slips pills into their drinks, and then lets Al into the room. They steal whatever they can. Because the businessmen are married, they usually don't call the cops.

So, how many pills did Nikki put into the drink of her latest victim? This is important because the man is unexpectedly dead. Nikki and Al find a video in his briefcase, exposing Zipper Doyle (Barry Langrishe), a local sports hero, as a pedophile. She unwisely calls Zipper's office and makes shrill threats into the answering machine. Nikki and Al go on the run, heading from Adelaide to Perth across the well-named Nullarbor Plain, a reach of the outback where every motel is a shout of defiance against the void.

Nikki and Al do not trust each other very much; maybe Nikki will never trust anybody. Al wonders if she deliberately killed the businessman. Soon Nikki wonders how a motel owner died. Pursued by two cops and the venomous Zipper Doyle, they leave a trail of bodies and robberies behind them—but the crimes take place offscreen, and in a series of getaway cars, they stew in paranoia and suspicion, and we're left to guess which of them (if either) committed the crimes.

Like all road movies, this one serves as a clothesline for colorful characters. There's a drunken motel manager (Max Cullen) who mutters darkly about "unphantomable tunnels under the desert." And a couple who live on an abandoned nuclear test site ("it's very private here") and make handmade jewelry. And the two detectives (Chris Haywood and Andrew S. Gilbert) who have a long, deceptive conversation in a coffee shop that could have been written by David Mamet.

The endings of road movies are usually their least satisfactory elements. There are two possibilities for the characters: die a spectacular death, or get a daytime job. The first choice is preferable, I suppose. Can you imagine Bonnie and Clyde on parole, doing spin-control on Barbara Walters and Larry King? Thelma and Louise, maybe.

Kiss the Girls ★ ★ ★ ½

R, 117 m., 1997

Morgan Freeman (Alex Cross), Ashley Judd (Kate McTiernan), Cary Elwes (Nick Ruskin), Alex McArthur (Sikes), Tony Goldwyn (Will Rudolph), Jay O. Sanders (Kyle Craig), Bill Nunn (Sampson), Gina Ravera (Naomi Cross), Brian Cox (Chief Hatfield). Directed by Gary Fleder and produced by David Brown and Joe Wizan. Screenplay by David Klass, based on the novel by James Patterson.

"Is there a better actor in America than Morgan Freeman?" Pauline Kael once asked, to which one could add, is there one with more authority?

Freeman has a rare presence on the screen, a specific gravity that persuades us. He never seems to be making things up. He never seems shallow, facile, or unconvinced, and even in unsuccessful films like *Chain Reaction* (1996), he doesn't go down with the ship: You feel he's authentic even as the film sinks around him.

In *Kiss the Girls,* Freeman's performance is more central than his work in the movie this one is clearly inspired by, *Seven* (1995). He is the lead, at the center of the story, and that gives it a focus that the buddy aspects of *Seven* lacked. Once again he plays a policeman on the trail of a kinky serial killer, and once again the shadows are deep and the antagonist is brilliant and the crimes are supposed to send some kind of a twisted message. But the movie's not a retread; it's original work, based on a novel by James Patterson, about a criminal who (the Freeman character intuits) is not killing his victims, but collecting them.

Freeman plays Alex Cross, a forensic psychologist with the Washington, D.C., police, who becomes involves in a series of kidnappings in Durham, North Carolina, when his own niece (Gina Ravera) is abducted. He flies to Durham and calls on the police department, where he's kept waiting for hours until he finally bursts into the office of the chief. (In a movie that is generally convincing, this scene played like boilerplate.) The kidnap targets are being taken by a man who signs himself "Casanova," and one of his victims is found dead—tied to a tree and "left for the critters to find."

Cross wonders why there aren't more bodies, and theorizes that Casanova is a collector who kills only when he feels he must. The other victims, including his niece, must still be alive somewhere. His theory is proven when a local doctor named Kate (Ashley Judd) is abducted but escapes after making contact with several other captives in some kind of subterranean warren of cells.

The cop and the doctor become a team during the rest of the movie, working together as the trail leads to the West Coast, and unraveling surprises that it is not my task to reveal. David Klass, the screenwriter, gives Freeman and Judd more specific dialogue than is usual in thrillers; they sound like they might actually be talking with one another and not simply advancing plot points. And what Freeman brings to all of his scenes is a very particular attentiveness. He doesn't merely listen; he seems to weigh what is told him, to evaluate it. That quality creates an amusing result sometimes in his movies, when other actors will tell him something and then (you can clearly sense) look to see if he buys it.

Ashley Judd's debut, *Ruby in Paradise*, established her among the most convincing actresses of her generation, and *Normal Life* (1996), disgracefully relegated to video by a clueless studio, was one of the year's best films. She can't always transcend genre material (what was she doing in *A Time to Kill*?), but when it's well written and directed with care, as it is here, we find we care about her even in a scene of revelation toward the end that could have been handled more subtly.

Kiss the Girls was directed by Gary Fleder, whose first feature, *Things to Do in Denver When You're Dead* (1996), showed talent but a little too much contrivance. Here he's more disciplined and controlled, with a story where the shadows and nuances are as scary as anything else. Fleder has said that he and his cinematographer, Aaron Schneider, studied the work of Gordon *(Prince of Darkness)* Willis, whose photography for *The Godfather* and other pictures often uses a few overhead key lights on crucial elements and leaves the rest in darkness. Here (as in *Seven*) we get a consistent sense of not being able to see everything we think we want to.

When the film is over and we know all of its secrets, here's one we'd like to know more about: What exactly is the dynamic of the relationship between the two most twisted members of the cast? But being left with such a question is much more satisfactory than being given the answer in shorthand Freudian terms. What we're also left with is the real sense of having met two very particular people in the leads. Freeman and Judd are so good you almost wish they'd decided not to make a thriller at all—had simply found a way to construct a drama exploring their personalities.

Kolya ★ ★ ★ ½

PG-13, 105 m., 1997

Zdenek Sverak (Louka), Andrej Chalimon (Kolya), Libuse Safrankova (Klara), Ondrez Vetchy (Mr. Broz), Stella Zazvorkova (Mother), Ladislav Smoljak (Mr. Houdek), Irena Livanova (Nadezda), Lilian Mankina (Aunt Tamara). Directed by Jan Sverak and produced by Eric Abraham and Jan Sverak. Screenplay by Zdenek Sverak.

In Prague in 1988, Russian trucks rumble through the streets and Czechs make an accommodation with their masters, or pay a price. Louka pays a price. Because in a moment of unwise wit he wrote a flippant answer on an official form, he has been bounced out of the philharmonic and now scrapes by playing his cello at funerals and repairing tombstones.

Life has consolations. A parade of young women visits his "tower," an apartment at the top of a rickety old building. At fifty-five, Louka (Zdenek Sverak) looks enough like Sean Connery to make hearts flutter, and he has the same sardonic charm. But he is broke and needs a car, and so he listens when his grave digger pal makes an offer. The pal's Soviet niece must get married or she'll be sent back to Russia, where she does not want to go. The niece and her chain-smoking aunt will pay Louka to go through a phony marriage.

Against his better judgment, he does. Then the niece skips to West Germany to join a former boyfriend, leaving behind her five-year-old son, Kolya (Andrej Chalimon). The aunt dies, and Louka is stuck with the kid. This puts a severe cramp in his love life (the kid is delivered in the middle of a would-be seduction), and besides, he knows nothing about kids, and this one speaks only Russian, a language Louka has on principle refused to learn.

The outlines of this story are conventional and sentimental (is there any doubt he will come to love the child?). What makes *Kolya* special is the way it paints the details. Like the films of the Czech New Wave in the late 1960s, it has a cheerful, irreverent humor, and an eye for the absurdities of human behavior. Consider Louka's old mother, who refuses to care for the child because she will not have a Russian in the house, and watch the scene where Russian army trucks stop outside her cottage and the kid hears his native language and runs out happily to talk to the soldiers.

Consider, too, the bureaucracy, faithful to the Soviets. Louka is subjected to a grilling by a hard-nosed official who suspects, correctly, that the marriage was a sham, but the tone of the interview is much altered because Kolya refuses to stay outside and draws pictures all during the interrogation; his evident love for his "stepfather" is a confusing factor.

Quirky details are chosen to show the gradual coming together of Louka and Kolya. The cellist drags the kid to the funerals where he plays, and the kid watches open-eyed as the musicians play and the soloist sings. It is perhaps not surprising that his first words of Czech are the 23rd Psalm. But look at Louka's face when he realizes the kid is using a puppet theater to stage a cremation.

There are many women in Louka's life, but one becomes special: Klara, played by Libuse Safrankova. He ropes her in to helping him care for the child, and eventually something fairly wonderful happens, and at fifty-five Louka finds a way to break out of the trap of his routine. His new freedom is shown against a backdrop of the end of the Cold War, as the Berlin Wall drops, the Russians leave town, and joyous Czechs take to the streets, chanting "It's finally over!" Louka is placed in the center of the celebrants, where he sees, of course, his former bureaucratic interrogator now part of the joyous crowd.

Kolya was written by its star, Zdenek Sverak, and directed by his son, Jan. It is a work of love, beautifully photographed by Vladimir Smutny in rich deep reds and browns, with steam rising from soup and the little boy looking wistfully at the pigeons on the other side of the tower window. It is said that American audiences are going to fewer foreign films these days. Missing a film like *Kolya,* winner of a 1997 Golden Globe, would not be a price I would be willing to pay.

Krippendorf's Tribe ★ ★

PG-13, 94 m., 1998

Richard Dreyfuss (James Krippendorf), Jenna Elfman (Veronica), Natasha Lyonne (Shelly), Gregory Smith (Mickey), Carl Michael Lindner (Edmund), Lily Tomlin (Ruth Allen). Directed by Todd Holland and produced by Larry Brezner. Screenplay by Charlie Peters, based on the book by Frank Parkin.

Is it possible to recommend a whole comedy on the basis of one scene that made you laugh almost uncontrollably? I fear not. And yet *Krippendorf's Tribe* has such a scene, and many comedies have none. I was reminded of the dead parakeet that had its head taped back on in *Dumb and Dumber.* A scene like that can redeem a lot of downtime.

The scene in *Krippendorf's Tribe* involves the backyard fakery of a primitive circumcision ritual. But I am getting ahead of the story. The movie stars Richard Dreyfuss as James Krippendorf, an anthropologist who has gone to New Guinea, utterly failed to find a lost tribe, and returned to his campus, having spent all of his grant money. Now it is time to produce results, of which he has none.

Krippendorf has two small sons and a teenage daughter; his wife died in New Guinea, but she's handled so remotely in the film that I wonder why they bothered with her. No matter. Back home, Krippendorf has descended into sloth and despond, and pads about the house aimlessly. Then an enthusiastic colleague named Veronica, played with zest and wit by Jenna Elfman, pounds on his door with a reminder that he is to lecture on his findings that very night.

Krippendorf's lack of any findings takes on a whole new meaning when his department head informs him that another colleague will do prison time for misappropriating grant money. Terrified, Krippendorf improvises a lecture in which he claims to have found a lost tribe. He even produces one of its artifacts—a sexual aid, he claims, although sharp eyes might recognize it as a toy space shuttle, belonging to one of his sons who left it in the oven.

Krippendorf has promised home movies of the lost tribe, which, in desperation, he has named the Shelmikedmu, after his children Shelly, Mike, and Edmund. At home, he fakes the footage, dressing his children up like New Guinea tribesmen and intercutting their romps in the backyard with actual footage from his trip. It's at about this point that he hits on the inspiration of the circumcision ritual, which his two boys enter into with such zeal that the scene takes on a comic life of its own.

The movie as a whole isn't that funny. It introduces characters and doesn't really develop them. Lily Tomlin, for example, is Krippendorf's rival. She is given various props, including a pet monkey and an adoring female admirer, and then packed off to New Guinea, where the movie seems to forget her between brief remote appearances. David Ogden Stiers is likewise misused as a video producer who is brought onstage and then never really used. I did like Jenna Elfman's work as Veronica, who towers over Dreyfuss and eventually becomes an accomplice in the deception. Comic momentum threatens to build up during a late scene at a banquet, where the university's aged benefactor unexpectedly discovers the secret of the fraud. But the movie can't find that effortless zaniness that good screwball comedy requires. Dreyfuss and Elfman change into and out of a tribal disguise, and we can see how it's meant to be funny, but it isn't. *Krippendorf's Tribe* contains that one scene that reminds us of what great comedy can play like, and other scenes that don't benefit from the reminder.

Kundun ★ ★ ★

PG-13, 128 m., 1997

Tenzin Yeshi Paichang (Dalai Lama, age two), Tulku Jamyang Kunga Tenzin (Dalai Lama, age five), Gyurme Tethong (Dalai Lama, age twelve), Tenzin Thuthob Tsarong (Adult Dali Lama), Tencho Gyalpo (Dalai Lama's Mother), Tsewang Migyur Khangsar (Dalai Lama's Father), Lobsang Samten (Master of the Kitchen), Sonam Phuntsok (Reting Rinpoch). Directed by Martin Scorsese and produced by Barbara De Fina. Screenplay by Melissa Mathison.

At a midpoint in Martin Scorsese's *Kundun,* the fourteenth Dalai Lama reads a letter from the thirteenth, prophesying that religion in Tibet will be destroyed by China—that he and his followers may have to wander helplessly like beggars. He says, "What can I do? I'm only a boy." His adviser says, "You are the man who wrote this letter. You must know what to do."

This literal faith in reincarnation, in the belief that the child at the beginning of *Kundun* is the same man who died four years before the child was born, sets the film's underlying tone. *Kundun* is structured as the life of the fourteenth Dalai Lama, but he is simply a vessel for a larger life or spirit, continuing through centuries. That is the film's strength, and its curse. It provides a deep spirituality, but denies the Dalai Lama humanity; he is permitted certain little human touches, but is essentially an icon, not a man.

Kundun is like one of the popularized lives of the saints that Scorsese must have studied as a boy in Catholic grade school. I studied the same lives, which reduced the saints to a series of anecdotes. At the end of a typical episode, the saint says something wise, pointing out the lesson, and his listeners fall back in amazement and gratitude. The saint seems to stand above time, already knowing the answers and the outcome, consciously shaping his life as a series of parables.

In *Kundun,* there is rarely the sense that a

living, breathing, and (dare I say?) fallible human inhabits the body of the Dalai Lama. Unlike Scorsese's portrait of Jesus in *The Last Temptation of Christ,* this is not a man striving for perfection, but perfection in the shape of a man. Although the film is wiser and more beautiful than Jean-Jacques Annaud's recent *Seven Years in Tibet,* it lacks that film's more practical grounding; Scorsese and his writer, Melissa Mathison, are bedazzled by the Dalai Lama.

Once we understand that *Kundun* will not be a drama involving a plausible human character, we are freed to see the film as it is: An act of devotion, an act even of spiritual desperation, flung into the eyes of twentieth-century materialism. The film's visuals and music are rich and inspiring, and like a Mass by Bach or a Renaissance church painting, it exists as an aid to worship: It wants to enhance, not question.

That this film should come from Scorsese, master of the mean streets, chronicler of wise guys and lowlifes, is not really surprising, since so many of his films have a spiritual component, and so many of his characters know they live in sin and feel guilty about it. There is a strong impulse toward the spiritual in Scorsese, who once studied to be a priest, and *Kundun* is his bid to be born again.

The film opens in Tibet in 1937, four years after the death of the thirteenth Dalai Lama, as monks find a young boy who they sense may be their reincarnated leader. In one of the film's most charming scenes, they place the child in front of an array of objects, some belonging to the thirteenth, some not, and he picks out the right ones, childishly saying, "Mine! Mine! Mine!"

Two years later, the monks come to take the child to live with them and take his place in history. Roger Deakins's photography sees this scene and others with the voluptuous colors of a religious painting; the child peers out at his visitors through the loose weave of a scarf, and sits under a monk's red cloak as the man tells him, "You have chosen to be born again."

At his summer palace, he sees dogs, peacocks, deer, and fish. He is given a movie projector, on which a few years later he sees the awful vision of Hiroshima. Soon the Chinese are invading Tibet, and he is faced with the challenge of defending his homeland while practicing the tenets of nonviolence. There is a meeting with Chairman Mao at which the Dalai Lama hears that religion is dead and can no longer look in the eyes of a man who says such a thing. He focuses instead on Mao's polished Western shoes, which seem to symbolize the loss of older ways and values.

The film is made of episodes, not a plot. It is like illustrations bound into the book of a life. Most of the actors, I understand, are real Tibetan Buddhists, and their serenity in many scenes casts a spell. The sets, the fabrics and floor and wall coverings, the richness of metals and colors, all place them within a tabernacle of their faith. But at the end I felt curiously unfulfilled; the thing about a faith built on reincarnation is that we are always looking only at a tiny part of it, and the destiny of an individual is froth on the wave of history. Those values are better for religion than for cinema, which hungers for story and character.

I admire *Kundun* for being so unreservedly committed to its vision, for being willing to cut loose from audience expectations and follow its heart. I admire it for its visual elegance. And yet this is the first Scorsese film that, to be honest, I would not want to see again and again. Scorsese seems to be searching here for something that is not in his nature and never will be. During *The Last Temptation of Christ,* I believe Scorsese knew exactly how his character felt at all moments. During *Kundun,* I sense him asking himself, "Who is this man?"

Kurt & Courtney ★★★

NO MPAA RATING, 99 m., 1998

A documentary directed by Nick Broomfield and produced by Tine Van Den Brande and Michael D'Acosta.

Nick Broomfield does not like Courtney Love. Neither do some of the other people in her life. In Broomfield's rambling, disorganized, fascinating new documentary named *Kurt & Courtney,* Love's father teases us with the possibility that she could have killed her rock star husband, Kurt Cobain. An old boyfriend screams his dislike into the camera. A nanny remembers there was "way too much talk about Kurt's will." A deranged punk musician says, "She offered me fifty grand to whack Kurt Cobain." A private eye thinks he was hired as part of a cover-up.

Broomfield is a one-man band, a BBC film-maker who travels light and specializes in the American sex 'n' violence scene. After an exposé of the evil influences on Hollywood madam Heidi Fleiss, and an excursion into a Manhattan S&M parlor *(Fetishes)*, he takes his show to the Pacific Northwest to examine the unhappy life and mysterious death of Cobain—the lead singer of the grunge rock band Nirvana, apparently dead by his own hand.

Did Cobain really kill himself? No fingerprints were found on his shotgun, we're told, and the movie claims his body contained so many drugs it was unlikely he could have pulled the trigger. Broomfield's film opens with Love as a suspect, only to decide she was probably not involved, and the movie ends in murky speculation without drawing any conclusions. It's not so much about a murder investigation as about two people who won fame and fortune that only one was able to handle. Cobain probably did kill himself, but it was a defeat as much as a decision; he could no longer endure his success, his drug addiction, and his demanding wife.

When Courtney met Kurt, we learn, Cobain was already a star; she was lead singer in a second-tier local band. In 1992, in her words, "We bonded pharmaceutically over drugs." In the words of a friend, she came into his life and in a three-year period took over everything. Then, as Kurt descended, lost into drugs, she got her own act together, and after his death in 1994 she won a Golden Globe nomination for *The People vs. Larry Flynt* and, in the doc's closing scenes, is a presenter of a "freedom of information" banquet of the L.A. chapter of the ACLU. As she takes the stage, it is impossible not to think uneasily of *A Star Is Born.*

Broomfield is not objective. He's in the foreground, narrating everything. The real subject of his films is what he goes through to shoot them. We learn that Courtney refused permission to use her music or Kurt's (no kidding), and he tells us what songs he "would have used" over certain scenes. He hires paparazzi to stalk Love into a recording studio, and at the end, at the ACLU event, he barges onto the stage, grabs the microphone, and accuses her (accurately) of making implied death threats against journalists. One gathers that the ACLU, focusing on the message of *The People vs. Larry Flynt* and desiring a high-profile star for their benefit, invited Love a little prematurely.

In all of Broomfield's films, you meet people you can hardly believe exist. El Duce, for example, the punker who claims Love offered him money to kill Cobain, is a character out of Fellini, or hell. At the end of the movie, we are not surprised to learn he died after stumbling into the path of a train, but we are astonished to learn he was in his mid-thirties; he looks like a well-worn fifty-year-old bouncer. Love's father, a former manager for the Grateful Dead, has written two books about Kurt's death, both of them unflattering to his daughter, and speaks of buying pit bulls "to put peace into our house." Assorted old friends, flames, and hangers-on make appearances that seem inspired by the characters in Andy Warhol's *Chelsea Hotel.* Only Kurt's Aunt Mary, who plays tapes of him singing joyously as a child, seems normal.

Why did Kurt Cobain die? Because of his drug use, obviously, from which everything else descended, including his relationship with Courtney. He was filled with deep insecurities that made him unable to cope with the adulation of his fans; he was far too weak for Love's dominating personality; drugs and booze led to chronic stomach pain, and when he climbed over the wall of his last rehab center, he was fleeing to his death.

We learn from one of his old girlfriends that Cobain was acutely sensitive to how scrawny he was. We see a skeletal self-portrait. "He wore lots and lots of layers of clothing to make himself look heavier," she says. It is one of the film's many ironies that the grunge rock fashion statement, with its flannel shirts beloved by millions, may have come about because Kurt Cobain was a skinny kid.

L

La Ceremonie ★ ★ ★

NO MPAA RATING, 111 m., 1997

Sandrine Bonnaire (Sophie), Isabelle Huppert (Jeanne), Jacqueline Bisset (Catherine), Jean-Pierre Cassel (Georges), Virginie Ledoyen (Melinda), Valentin Merlet (Gilles). Directed by Claude Chabrol and produced by Marin Karmitz. Screenplay by Chabrol and Caroline Eliacheff, based on the novel *A Judgement in Stone* by Ruth Rendell.

French gangsters had a word for the events leading up to death by guillotine. They called it "la ceremonie." Claude Chabrol's icy, ruthless new film is also about ceremony—about the patterns of life that divide a rich French family and their strange new housekeeper. Unlike most ceremonies, it ends with an unexpected outcome.

The film opens with Catherine, a pleasant, cultured French art dealer of a certain age (Jacqueline Bisset) interviewing a new housekeeper named Sophie (Sandrine Bonnaire). She explains the job: She lives with her husband and children in an isolated rural district, but Sophie will be free to visit the town from time to time. Sophie agrees, and presents a letter of recommendation from her previous employer. There is something subtly wrong about the way Sophie does this; we feel it but don't understand it.

We meet the rest of the family: the father, Georges (Jean-Pierre Cassel), the attractive twentyish daughter Melinda (Virginie Ledoyen), the younger son Gilles (Valentin Merlet). They live in an elegant but not ostentatious country house, furnished in good taste, with many books and artworks; the wintry classical music on the sound track sets the mood.

Sophie is an excellent housekeeper, but not much company. She stays to herself in her room, staring impassively at the TV. The family agrees, "So far, she's been wonderful." They offer to let her drive the car into town, but she cannot drive. They offer driving lessons, but she says she cannot see well. They offer an eye exam, but she avoids the appointment and buys some cheap ready-made glasses as a cover. One day when the husband calls home asking about a file on his desk, Sophie hangs up the phone and pretends they were disconnected.

We guess her secret before the family does. One day in town she buys some chocolates and presents a 100-franc note. "Do you have any change?" asks the clerk. "No," says Sophie. "Yes you do!" says the clerk, rudely snatching her purse and counting out the coins. (The scene helps establish the film's view of class; the bourgeoisie shopkeeper would do that with a servant girl, but never with a middle-class customer.) By now we know Sophie cannot read or count; she is illiterate or dyslexic.

Sophie makes a friend in the village who can read all too well: the postmistress, Jeanne (Isabelle Huppert), who opens all of Georges's mail. He hates her. She returns the feeling. Sophie and Jeanne become fast friends and learn things about one another. Jeanne was once charged with killing her retarded child, but explains to Sophie, "It's not true . . . she killed herself . . . there's no proof." Jeanne teases Sophie: "I know something about you." She produces a newspaper clipping linking Sophie to a fire that killed fifteen people. Once again, there was no proof. The two girls hug each other with delight and collapse on the bed, giggling like conspirators. It is the scariest moment in the movie.

Now all of the elements are in place: Sophie's deep vulnerability, Jeanne's ability to instigate, the growing resentment of the girls toward the family. Only the family seems oblivious; life for them seems so refined and orderly as they settle down for an evening of watching Mozart on television.

Claude Chabrol has made about fifty films since 1958, when he was one of the figures in the French New Wave. Most of them involve crime, all of them involve pathological or obsessive behavior, and the number of them worth seeing is impressive. *La Ceremonie,* he has said, is a Marxist film about class struggle, but perhaps it is more of a Freudian film, about the scarcely repressed sexuality of Jeanne and Sophie, and the ways it is expressed against a family that represents for both of them a hated authority.

Watching the film, you think maybe you

know where it's headed. Or maybe not. Not every ceremony ends in the way we anticipate. (Who would guess, never having attended a Mass, that flesh and blood are consumed—and not just symbolically, according to believers?) Certainly from the family's point of view their opera has an unexpected outcome. The actors include old hands who have worked with Chabrol before (Huppert was unforgettable in his *Violette Noziere*) and strike the right note: No one in this movie should act as if he knows how it ends. And no one does.

L.A. Confidential ★ ★ ★ ★

R, 138 m., 1997

Kevin Spacey (Jack Vincennes), Russell Crowe (Bud White), Guy Pearce (Ed Exley), James Cromwell (Dudley Smith), Kim Basinger (Lynn Bracken), David Strathairn (Pierce Patchett), Ron Rifkin (D.A. Ellis Loew), Danny DeVito (Sid Hudgens). Directed by Curtis Hanson and produced by Arnon Milchan, Hanson, and Michael Nathanson. Screenplay by Brian Helgeland and Hanson, based on the novel by James Ellroy.

Confidential was a key magazine of the 1950s, a monthly that sold millions of copies with its seamy exposés of celebrity drugs and sex. I found it in my dad's night table and read it breathlessly, the stories of reefer parties, multiple divorces, wife-swapping, and "leading men" who liked to wear frilly undergarments. The magazine sank in a sea of lawsuits, but it created a genre; the trash tabloids are its direct descendents.

Watching *L.A. Confidential*, I felt some of the same insider thrill that *Confidential* provided: The movie, like the magazine, is based on the belief that there are a million stories in the city, and all of them will raise your eyebrows and curl your hair. The opening is breathlessly narrated by a character named Sid Hudgens (Danny DeVito), who publishes *Hush-Hush* magazine and bribes a cop named Jack Vincennes (Kevin Spacey) to set up celebrity arrests; Jack is photographed with his luckless victims, and is famous as the guy who caught Robert Mitchum smoking marijuana.

It's Christmas Eve 1953, and Bing Crosby is crooning on the radio as cops pick up cartons of free booze to fuel their holiday parties. We meet three officers who, in their way, represent the choices ahead for the LAPD. Vincennes, star-struck, lives for his job as technical adviser to *Badge of Honor*, a *Dragnet*-style show. Bud White (Russell Crowe) is an aggressive young cop who is willing to accommodate the department's relaxed ethics. Ed Exley (Guy Pearce) is a straight arrow, his rimless glasses making him look a little like a tough accountant—one who works for the FBI, maybe.

Ed is an ambitious careerist who wants to do everything by the book. His captain, Dudley Smith (James Cromwell), kindly explains that an officer must be prepared to lie, cheat, and steal—all in the name, of course, of being sure the guilty go to jail. Captain Smith likes to call his men "good lads," and seems so wise we can almost believe him as he administers little quizzes and explains that advancement depends on being prepared to give the "right answers."

L.A. Confidential is immersed in the atmosphere and lore of *film noir*, but it doesn't seem like a period picture—it believes its *noir* values and isn't just using them for decoration. It's based on a novel by James Ellroy, that lanky, sardonic poet of Los Angeles sleaze. Its director, Curtis Hanson *(Bad Influence, The Hand That Rocks the Cradle)*, weaves a labyrinthine plot, but the twists are always clear because the characters are so sharply drawn; we don't know who's guilty or innocent, but we know who should be.

The plot involves a series of crimes that take place in the early days of the new year. Associates of Mickey Cohen, the L.A. mob boss, become victims of gangland-style executions. A decomposing body is found in a basement. There's a massacre at an all-night coffee shop; one of the victims is a crooked cop, and three black youths are immediately collared as suspects, although there's evidence that police may have been behind the crime.

We meet a millionaire pornographer named Pierce Patchett (David Strathairn). He runs a high-class call girl operation in which aspiring young actresses are given plastic surgery to make them resemble movie stars; one of them is Lynn Bracken (Kim Basinger), who has been "cut" to look like Veronica Lake. Bud White, the Crowe character, tracks her down, thinking she'll have info about the decomposing corpse, and they fall almost helplessly in love ("You're the first man in months who hasn't told me I look just like Veronica Lake").

At this point, perhaps an hour into the movie, I felt inside a Raymond Chandler novel: not only because of the atmosphere and the dialogue, but also because there seemed to be no way all of these characters and events could be drawn together into a plot that made sense. Not that I would have cared; I enjoy *film noir* for the journey as much as the destination.

But Hanson and his cowriter, Brian Helgeland, do pull the strands together, and along the way there's an unlikely alliance between two cops who begin as enemies. The film's assumption is that although there's small harm in free booze and a little graft, there are some things a police officer simply cannot do and look himself in the mirror in the morning.

The film is steeped in L.A. lore; Ellroy is a student of the city's mean streets. It captures the town just at that postwar moment when it was beginning to become self-conscious about its myth. Joseph Wambaugh writes in one of his books that he is constantly amazed by the hidden threads that connect the high to the low, the royalty to the vermin, in Los Angeles—where a hooker is only a role from stardom, and vice, as they say, versa.

One of the best scenes takes place in the Formosa Cafe, a restaurant much frequented in the 1940s by unlikely boothfellows. Cops turn up to question Johnny Stompanato, a hood who may know something about the Cohen killings. His date gives them some lip. "A hooker cut to look like Lana Turner is still a hooker," one of them tells her, but Jack Vincennes knows better: "She is Lana Turner," he says with vast amusement.

One of the reasons *L.A. Confidential* is so good, why it deserves to be mentioned with *Chinatown,* is that it's not just plot and atmosphere. There are convincing characters here, not least Kim Basinger's hooker, whose quiet line, "I thought I was helping you," is one of the movie's most revealing moments. Russell Crowe *(Proof)* and Guy Pearce *(The Adventures of Priscilla, Queen of the Desert)* are two Australian actors who here move convincingly into star-making roles, and Kevin Spacey uses perfect timing to suggest his character's ability to move between two worlds while betraying both (he has a wonderful scene where he refuses to cooperate with a department investigation—until they threaten his job on the TV show).

Behind everything, setting the moral tone and pulling a lot of the plot threads, is the angular captain, seemingly so helpful. James Cromwell, who was the kindly farmer in *Babe,* has the same benevolent smile in this role, but the eyes are cold, and in his values can be seen, perhaps, the road ahead to Rodney King. *L.A. Confidential* is seductive and beautiful, cynical and twisted, and one of the best films of the year.

La Cucaracha ★★★

R, 94 m., 1999

Eric Roberts (Walter), Tara Crespo (Lourdes), Alejandro Patino (Fruit Vendor), Joaquim de Almeida (Jose Guerras). Directed by Jack Perez and produced by Michael A. Candela and Richard Mann. Screenplay by James McManus.

One moment Walter is sleeping the sleep of the damned. The next moment his eyes snap open, he sits bolt upright, and runs in terror out of his shack, running through the sagebrush to the nearest cantina, where he gasps out an order for cerveza. Lots of cerveza. Eventually he is passed out at his table, sleeping now the sleep of a man who keeps terror at bay with drunkenness.

The title of *La Cucaracha* is possibly inspired by Walter, who like a cockroach hides in cracks and crannies and lives on the crumbs he picks up in bars. Once he was a would-be novelist, and sometimes he writes (or hallucinates that he writes) letters back home about how he cannot write his novel. He claims he is hiding out in Santiago, Mexico, because he killed a man. Unlikely. Like the consul who is the hero of Malcolm Lowry's great novel *Under the Volcano,* reality and fantasy both look the same to him.

Walter is played by Eric Roberts, often an intense and passionate actor, rarely more so than here, where with a bandage holding his broken glasses together, he peers out at a world that terrifies him. He is at the end of his rope, so strung out on booze that sobriety is only an invitation for the DTs. How does a man arrive at such a dead end, so far from home? By accident, bad habits, and rotten luck.

There is a beautiful woman in the town. He yearns for her. He stands in the night and watches her inside her house. He has nothing to offer her. A stranger approaches him in the bar with an offer of $100,000 if he will kill a man. A man, he is told, who is a child killer. He is not sure he can kill, but he is sure he needs $100,000. Soon he is holding a gun on the man he has been paid to kill. He does not pull the trigger.

"If you were worth the money they paid you, I would be dead five minutes ago," the man tells him. "Please—do what you came for." He hesitates. Now the man says: "The man who really killed the boy was the man who hired you. He could not stand the idea that his son was a homosexual."

Does he pull the trigger? The beauty of *La Cucaracha* is that it doesn't matter. This is a movie gloriously free of plot, and all the boring obligatory twists and turns that plot drags along with it. It is a character study about a man in peril. It was directed by Jack Perez and written by James McManus, who at one point includes dialogue mentioning Hemingway, Lowry, and Graham Greene—who wrote about men at the end of the line, drunken writers and whiskey priests. Walter is in that tradition.

The movie won the Austin Film Festival in 1998 and then disappeared until its current limited release. Perez's two earlier credits are *The Big Empty* (1997), which despite its promising title apparently never opened anywhere, and *America's Deadliest Home Video,* which went straight to same.

Now comes this intriguing, stylish little film. In superficial ways it's like *El Mariachi,* the film that made Robert Rodriguez's reputation, except that it lacks a strong marketing push, is not as cheaply made, and is more interested in character than action. It also has a wicked strain of humor, leading to such lines as, "If it's any consolation, this money will now be spent to build a pediatric ward in Santiago hospital."

It must have required a certain courage for Eric Roberts to take a role like this. It's not a prestigious job for a former Oscar nominee. But it's a juicy role for an actor whose career has meandered recently (what was he doing in *Best of the Best 2*?). His performance evokes some of the same desperation and determination as Warren Oates's work in Peckinpah's great *Bring Me the Head of Alfredo Garcia.* He's willing to go over the top with it—and yet his performance is not the manic hyperactivity we sometimes see from him; he finds a sadder, more controlled note.

The movie is not for everybody. Some people will no doubt find it silly, or yearn for the consolations of formula and genre. But the more you're into nuance and atmosphere, the more you appreciate a movie that evokes instead of explains, the more you might like it.

The Land Girls ★ ★ ½

R, 112 m., 1998

Catherine McCormack (Stella), Rachel Weisz (Ag), Anna Friel (Prue), Steven Mackintosh (Joe Lawrence), Tom Georgeson (Mr. Lawrence), Maureen O'Brien (Mrs. Lawrence), Gerald Down (Ratty). Directed by David Leland and produced by Simon Relph. Screenplay by Keith Dewhurst and Leland, based on the novel *Land Girls* by Angela Huth.

The Land Girls tells the story of the Land Army, the volunteer force of civilians raised in England during World War II to take the place of farmworkers who enlisted in the armed forces. The movie takes place during a green, wet winter on a beautiful farm in Dorset, where three "land girls" from the city are sent to become farm laborers.

Their lessons begin, predictably, with the challenge of milking cows. Mr. Lawrence (Tom Georgeson), the farmer, is unimpressed: "It's not an army—it's just an excuse for a lark!" But the girls learn quickly and work hard, and in one way or another all three are attracted to Joe Lawrence (Steven Mackintosh), the farmer's son.

Prue (Anna Friel), who before the war was a hairdresser, is the boldest of the girls, and tells Agatha (Rachel Weisz), who is a Cambridge graduate but still a virgin at twenty-six, she should seize her opportunity with Joe. "Fornication? With him? He's unspeakable!" "So what?" Ag thinks it over and approaches Joe in all seriousness: "I'll come straight to the point. Would you mind giving me a go?"

Joe would not. He is more seriously attracted, however, to Stella (Catherine McCormack from *Dangerous Beauty*), who is engaged to a pilot. She tries to remain loyal to her man, but Joe has an appeal that's apparently irresistible to the women in the movie, although less compelling to the audience.

What happens to the characters is more or less predictable (we guess there will be some setbacks, some wartime tragedies, some angry partners, and weepy reunions). What I liked about the movie—what I preferred to the romances and relationships, indeed—was the look of the film, its sensual evocation of the British countryside in winter.

The cinematographer, Henry Braham, uses a saturated, high-contrast color style that makes the woods look dark and damp and the grass wet, cold, and green. The vast skies are that lonely and yet reassuring shade that watercolorists call Payne's gray. Farmer Lawrence loves his land, which he tramps morning and night in the company of his dog, Jack. His wife (Maureen O'Brien) loves it just as much, and acts as a quiet influence on his temper.

In one of the best sequences in the movie, Farmer Lawrence tells a government official he will not plow his east meadow, no matter how much the land is needed for wartime crops. "You should see this field in the spring," he tells Stella. "It's beautiful—just beautiful." He remembers courting his wife there. But Stella, stung in love and by what she perceives as the farmer's dislike, fires up the tractor one morning and plows it. This act of rebellion is what wins the farmer's respect.

I'll remember that scene, and another one where the land girls wait for the mailman to arrive, and one of them balances on a rail of the farm gate, like a figurehead in the mist. More than with most movies, I felt the reality of the rural setting, the earth beneath the grass, the closeness of the animals to their masters. But the story itself seemed thin in comparison: flirtations, broken hearts, bittersweet regret, all pretty routine.

The Last Days ★ ★ ★ ½

NO MPAA RATING, 88 m., 1999

A documentary directed by James Moll and produced by June Beallor and Ken Lipper for Steven Spielberg's Survivors of the Shoah Visual History Foundation. Featuring U.S. representative Tom Lantos, Alice Lok Cahana, Renee Firestone, Bill Basch, and Irene Zisblatt.

The Holocaust is so overwhelming that it threatens literally to become unthinkable—to become an abstraction of evil. *The Last Days* and other documentaries make it real by telling some of the countless small stories that make up the larger ones. To say that 6 million died is one thing. To listen to a woman's memories of her girlhood, when she hid from her father in a Nazi death camp because she wanted to spare them both the sight of each other—and how their eyes nevertheless met for a last time as he was marched to his death—is another thing altogether.

Steven Spielberg's Survivors of the Shoah Visual History Foundation is engaged in making a record of as many such memories as can be recorded from those who saw the tragedy with their own eyes. The eventual goal is 50,000 taped interviews. *The Last Days* features five of those survivors and others, telling their own stories. It focuses on the last year of the war, when Hitler, already defeated and with his resources running out, revealed the depth of his race hate by diverting men and supplies to the task of exterminating Hungary's Jews. At that late point, muses one of the witnesses in this film, couldn't the Nazis have just stopped? Used their resources where they were needed for the war effort? Even gotten some "brownie points" by ending the death camps?

No, because for the fanatic it is the fixed idea, not the daily reality, that obsesses the mind. Those apologists like the British historian David Irving, who argue that Hitler was not personally aware of many details of the Holocaust, are hard pressed to explain why his military mind could approve using the dwindling resources of a bankrupt army to kill still more innocent civilians.

In Spielberg's *Schindler's List* there are the famous shots of the little girl in the red coat (in a film otherwise shot in black and white). Her coat acts as a marker, allowing us to follow the fate of one among millions. *The Last Days*, directed by James Moll, is in a way all about red coats—about a handful of survivors, and what happened to them.

One describes the Nazis' brutality toward children, and says, "That's when I stopped talking to God." Another, Renee Firestone, confronts the evasive Dr. Hans Munch, who was acquitted in war crimes trials; his defense was that he spared the lives of some prisoners by conducting harmless medical experiments on them. But Firestone believes he was responsible for the death of her sister, Klara, and when he grows vague in his answers, she grows angry. Anyone who worked in a death camp has much to be vague about.

There is another passage where a woman, now around seventy, remembers instructions to Hungarian Jews to gather up their belongings for a trip by train. She took along a precious bathing suit, one she looked forward to wearing at the pool as any teenage girl might, and as she describes the fate of that suit, and of herself and her family, we hear a lifelong regret: In a moment, she was denied the kind of silly, carefree time a teenage girl deserves.

There is a final passage of joy that affected me with the same kind of emotional uplift as the closing scenes in *Schindler's List.* We have met during the film the only Holocaust survivor to be elected to the U.S. Congress—Representative Tom Lantos, whose wife is also a survivor. Both lost all of the members of their families. But they had two daughters, who came to them with the promise of a gift: They would have a lot of children. And then there is a shot of the Lantos family and its seventeen grandchildren.

That scene provides release after a harrowing journey. The movie contains footage of the survivors as they looked on the day their camps were liberated by the Allies—walking skeletons, whose eyes bear mute witness to horror. And the film has angry memories of an aftermath. One witness, an American soldier, describes shooting an unarmed German dead in cold blood, after being spat at. The film doesn't follow up on the implications of that, and because we can understand his rage, perhaps we let it go. But I feel the film should have either left out that memory or dealt with it. The soldier was wrong for the same reason the Holocaust was wrong.

The Holocaust is the most tragic and deadly outburst of the once useful, now dangerous, human trait of tribalism, in which we are right and you are wrong because we are we and you are not. In recent years in Serbia, in Africa, in Cambodia, in Northern Ireland, the epidemic is alive and well. Just the other day in Israel, Orthodox Jewish students booed and insulted visiting Reform rabbis who hoped to pray at the Western Wall, and the *New York Times* reported that some of the attackers "screamed that the rabbis should 'go back to Germany,' to be exterminated, one explained later." Any belief that does not allow others the right to believe something else is based more on fear than on faith. If that is not the lesson of the Holocaust, then what has been learned?

The Last Days of Disco ★ ★ ★ ½

R, 112 m., 1998

Chloe Sevigny (Alice), Kate Beckinsale (Charlotte), Chris Eigeman (Des), MacKenzie Astin (Jimmy), Matt Keeslar (Josh), Robert Sean Leonard (Tom), Jennifer Beals (Nina), Matthew Ross (Dan). Directed by Whit Stillman and produced by Edmon Roch and Cecilia Kate Roque. Screenplay by Stillman.

The Last Days of Disco is about people who *would* like to belong to the kinds of clubs that would accept them as members. It takes place in "the very early 1980s" in Manhattan, where a group of young, good-looking Ivy League graduates dance the night away in discos.

Unlike the characters in *Saturday Night Fever,* who were basically just looking for a good time, these upwardly mobile characters are alert to the markers of social status. *New York* magazine is their textbook, and being admitted to the right clubs is the passing grade.

The movie is the latest sociological romance by Whit Stillman *(Metropolitan, Barcelona),* who nails his characters with perfectly heard dialogue and laconic satire. His characters went to good schools, have good jobs, and think they're smarter than they are. "Alice, one of the things I've noticed is that people hate being criticized," says Charlotte, who seems quietly proud of this wisdom. They are capable of keeping a straight face while describing themselves as "adherents to the disco movement."

Alice (Chloe Sevigny, from *Kids*) is the smartest member of the crowd, and definitely the nicest. She has values. Her best friend, Charlotte (Kate Beckinsale), only has goals: to meet the right guys, to be popular, to do exactly what she imagines someone in her position should be doing. Both girls are regulars at a fashionable disco. Charlotte is forever giving poor Alice advice about what to say and how to behave; she says guys like it when a girl uses the word "sexy," and a few nights later, when a guy tells Alice he collects first editions of Scrooge McDuck comic books, she faithfully observes that she has always found Uncle Scrooge sexy.

As the movie opens, a junior ad executive named Jimmy Steinway (MacKenzie Astin) has just failed to get his boss into the club (he was wearing a brown suit). Jimmy goes in anyway. Alice and Charlotte, working as a team (Charlotte is the coach), forcibly introduce themselves. During the opening scenes we meet other regulars, including Des (Christopher Eigeman), the floor manager, who gets rid of girls by claiming to be gay, and who has his doubts about the club's management ("To me, shipping cash to Switzerland in canvas bags doesn't sound legal"). Other regulars include Josh (Matthew Keeslar), who casually mentions that he's an assistant district attorney, and Tom (Robert Sean Leonard), who has a theory that "the environmental movement was spawned by the rerelease of *Bambi* in the late 1950s."

During the movie these people will date each other with various degrees of intensity. Charlotte's approach is to take no hostages; she invites the D.A. to dinner at a time when she doesn't even have an apartment, and then rents one. A real-estate agent explains the concept of a "railroad flat" to her (you have to walk through both bedrooms and the kitchen to get to the bathroom, but the flat has two hall doors, so the best way to get from the front to the back is to walk down the hall).

If Scott Fitzgerald were to return to life, he would feel at home in a Whit Stillman movie. Stillman listens to how people talk and knows what it reveals about them. His characters have been supplied by their Ivy League schools with the techniques but not the subjects of intelligent conversation, and so they discuss *Lady and the Tramp* with the kind of self-congratulatory earnestness that French students would reserve for Marx and Freud. (Their analysis of the movie is at least as funny as the Quentin Tarantino character's famous deconstruction of *Top Gun* in the movie *Sleep With Me.*)

Stillman has the patience to circle a punch line instead of leaping straight for it. He'll establish something in an early scene and then keep nibbling away until it delivers. The guy who dumps girls by claiming to be gay, for example, eventually explains that he always thought he was straight until, one day, he felt "something different" while watching Jim Fowler on *Wild Kingdom.*

The movie has barely enough plot to hold it together; it involves drugs and money laundering, but it's typical of Stillman that most of the suspense involves the young D.A. fretting about a romantic conflict of interest. The underlying tone of the film is sweet, fond, and a little sad: These characters believe the disco period was the most wonderful period of their lives, and we realize that it wasn't disco that was so special, but youth. They were young, they danced, they drank, they fell in love, they learned a few lessons, and the music of that time will always reawaken those emotions.

It's human nature to believe that if a club admits people like you, you will find the person you are looking for inside. The problem with that theory is that wherever you go, there you are. At the end of *The Last Days of Disco,* as the club scene fades, people are hired to stand outside and pretend they have been turned away. When they get off work, what clubs do they go to? So it goes.

Lawn Dogs ★ ½

R, 101 m., 1998

Mischa Barton (Devon), Sam Rockwell (Trent), Kathleen Quinlan (Clare), Christopher McDonald (Morton), Bruce McGill (Nash), Eric Mabius (Sean), David Barry Gray (Brett), Miles Meehan (Billy). Directed by John Duigan and produced by Duncan Kenworthy. Screenplay by Naomi Wallace.

John Duigan's *Lawn Dogs* is like a nasty accident at the symbol factory. Pieces are scattered all over the floor, as the wounded help each other to the exits. Some of the pieces look well made and could be recycled. We pick up a few of them, and put them together to see if they'll fit. But they all seem to come from different designs.

The movie isn't clear about what it's trying to say—what it wants us to believe when we leave. It has the form of a message picture, without the message. It takes place in an upscale Kentucky housing development named Camelot Gardens, where the $300,000 homes sit surrounded by big lawns and no trees. It's a gated community; the security guard warns one of the "lawn dogs"—or yard workers—to be out of town by 5:00 P.M.

In one of the new houses lives ten-year-old Devon (Mischa Barton), who has a scar running down her chest after heart surgery. Her insipid parents are Morton (Christopher McDonald) and Clare (Kathleen Quinlan). Morton plans to run for office. Clare has casual sex with local college kids. And Trent (Sam Rockwell) mows their lawn.

Devon is in revolt, although she doesn't articulate it as interestingly as the heroine of *Welcome to the Dollhouse.* She wanders beyond the gates, finds Trent's trailer home in the woods, and becomes his friend. There are unrealized undertones of sexuality in her behavior, which the movie never makes overt, except in the tricky scene where she asks Trent to touch her scar. He has a scar, too; here's a new version of you show me yours and I'll show you mine.

The people inside Camelot Gardens are all stupid pigs. That includes the security guard, the parents, and the college kids, who insult and bully Trent. Meanwhile, Trent and Devon spend idyllic afternoons in the woods, being friends, until there is a tragic misunderstanding that leads to the death of a dog and even more alarming consequences.

Nobody makes it into the movie just as an average person. Trent's dad is a Korean vet whose lungs were destroyed by microbes in the K rations, and who is trying to give away his American flag collection. Trent is the kind of guy who stops traffic on a one-lane bridge while he strips, dives into the river, and walks back to his pickup boldly nude. Devon is the kind of little girl who crawls out onto her roof, throws her nightgown into the sky, and utters wild dog cries at the Moon.

All of these events happen with the precision and vivid detail of a David Lynch movie, but I do not know why. It is easy to make a film about people who are pigs and people who are free spirits, but unless you show how or why they got that way, they're simply characters you've created. It's easy to have Devon say, "I don't like kids—they smell like TV." But what does this mean when a ten-year-old says it? It's easy to show good people living in trailers and awful people living in nice homes, but it can work out either way. It's easy to write about a father who wants his little girl to have plastic surgery so her scar won't turn off boys, and then a boy who thinks it's "cool." But where is it leading? What is it saying? Camelot Gardens is a hideous place to live. So? Get out as fast as you can.

The Leading Man ★ ★ ★

R, 96 m., 1998

Jon Bon Jovi (Robin Grange), Lambert Wilson (Felix Webb), Anna Galiena (Elena Webb), Thandie Newton (Hilary Rule), Barry Humphries (Humphrey Beal), David Warner (Tod), Patricia Hodge (Delvene), Diana Quick (Susan). Directed by John Duigan and produced by Bertil Ohlsson and Paul Raphael. Screenplay by Virginia Duigan.

The Leading Man begins as a backstage story about the London theater world, and then a little Hitchcockian intrigue edges into the frame. The movie's about "Britain's greatest living playwright," a bedeviled middle-aged man with a wife and a mistress, both angry with him. A Hollywood sex symbol, who is starring in his new play, offers to solve all his problems by seducing the wife.

This is a little like Hitchcock's setup in *Strangers on a Train,* where an outsider sees a need and volunteers to meet it—at a price. The neat trick in *The Leading Man* is that we never quite understand the movie star's complete plan. Why is he doing this (apart from getting the husband's license to seduce the wife?). What else does he have in mind?

The movie star, Robin Grange, is played by the rock musician Jon Bon Jovi, who is convincing as a man who is completely confident of his ability to seduce any woman, anywhere, anytime. Like Richard Gere, he has a way of looking at a woman as if they're both thinking the same thing. The playwright, Felix Webb (Lambert Wilson), is one of those men for whom romantic intrigue is hardly worth the trouble: His wife is bitter at his treatment of his family, and his mistress is tired of listening to his promises about how someday, very soon, he will leave his wife. He can't be happy anywhere.

Felix's problems come to a boil during rehearsals for his new play, which stars both Robin and Hilary (Thandie Newton), his mistress. It also stars two dependable British veterans, played by David Warner and Patricia Hodge, who have seen backstage affairs before, and will see them again, and simply turn up to do their jobs. (While the younger actors are doing nervous deep-breathing exercises before the curtain goes up, Warner's character listens to cricket and plays solitaire.)

The playwright could be leading a very happy life. He has a big, old house on the banks of the Thames, down from Hammersmith Bridge, where his happy children play in the garden while his wife, Elena (Anna Galiena), steeps in resentment (one night as he sleeps she takes a scissors and chops off his famous forelock). Elena is younger than Felix, and Hilary is younger still, living with roommates who race out to dance clubs and are amused by the fogey she has taken into her bed. But here's a twist: The young girl is steadfast and sincere in her love for him, and not portrayed as a flirt or a siren.

Robin, the American, quickly sees what Felix thinks is a secret, his affair with his leading lady. Robin makes the great man an offer: He will seduce Elena, clearing the field. "It would be doing a favor for a friend," he explains. "Besides, I've seen her photographs. She's a beautiful woman."

So she is, and a faithful one, up to a point. But Robin studies his quarry carefully, making lists of the books she reads and the music she listens to (these details are not very convincing), and discovering her own secret—she is also a playwright, but her writing is hidden in the shadow of Felix's great reputation. He can help her, but is something sinister concealed in Robin's helpfulness? Robin is also growing closer to his costar, Hilary. Does he plan to take both women away from the playwright? And what about the gun he likes to play with?

The film, directed by John Duigan and written by his sister Virginia, is completely familiar with its showbiz world. Virginia is married to the director Bruce Beresford, and Duigan himself has long been linked romantically with Newton, whom he directed in the wonderful film *Flirting* (1992). Little biographical details—like Newton's degree from Oxford—are lifted from life.

But the climax does not, I'm afraid, do justice to the setup. Hitchcock, having brought the gun and the matching love triangles onstage, would have delivered. Still, Duigan keeps us interested right up to the overwrought final developments, and his portrait of the London theater world is wry and perceptive. The way he uses the actor Barry Humphries as the director of Felix's play, and Warner and Hodge as the seasoned pros, adds a certain ironic perspective to all the heavy breathing in the foreground.

Leave It to Beaver ★ ★ ★

PG, 88 m., 1997

Christopher McDonald (Ward), Janine Turner (June), Cameron Finley (Beaver), Erik von Detten (Wally), Adam Zolotin (Eddie), Barbara Billingsley (Aunt Martha), Ken Osmond (Eddie Sr.), Frank Bank (Frank). Directed by Andy Cadiff and produced by Robert Simonds. Screenplay by Brian Levant and Lon Diamond, based on the TV series created by Bob Moser and Joe Connelly.

Leave It to Beaver is a gentle, good-hearted movie about an eight-year-old who sighs, "I used to want to be a kid the rest of my life, but lately I just want to get it over with." Beaver Cleaver despairs of ever being as smart, as popular, as talented, and (especially) as old as his teenage brother, Wally, and all of his schemes to evolve in that direction seem doomed. Even when he finally gets the bicycle of his dreams, he's allowed to ride it only on the sidewalk: He's a "flat-lander."

The movie is based on the popular TV series. I've never watched a single episode of the series all the way through, but like most Americans I have a working knowledge of the Cleavers: Ward and June and their sons Beaver and Wally, and Wally's friend, the conniving Eddie Haskell. They lead the kinds of lives in which all problems can be solved in 22.5 minutes of program time; faced with an eighty-eight-minute movie, they almost run out of plot.

But the film is disarmingly charming, and, like *Good Burger*, pitched at young audiences. Whether they'll want to see it is a good question; kids these days seem to tilt more toward violent action pictures. I was surprised to find myself seduced by the film's simple, sweet story, and amused by the sly indications that the Cleavers don't live in the 1950s anymore.

In a way, all sitcom families are profoundly mad. They must be, to generate so many shallow emergencies, to talk only in one-liners, and to never leave the room without a punch line. *Leave It to Beaver* suggests a certain dark component to the Cleaver's sunniness, as in a moment when Ward (Christopher McDonald) experiences suppressed apoplexy after learning that the Beaver has "lost" his new bike, or in another moment when we learn that June (Janine Turner), who always wears pearls and heels while vacuuming, may know it's a turn-on for her husband.

They live in a time suspended between 1957 and 1997. The cars look new, but they still use glass milk bottles. As the film opens, Beaver (Cameron Finley) wants a bike as badly as his father wants him to join the school football team. Easy, says Eddie Haskell (Adam Zolotin): Pretend to join the team, and your dad will buy you the bike.

The Beaver is so much smaller than the other team members that giving him a uniform seems like a form of child abuse. But he does join the team, briefly, and he does get the bike—only to have it stolen by a mean kid. Much of the plot involves the Beaver's attempts to get the bike back, and to conceal from his father that he's not playing in any games because of homework difficulties.

When he finally does get in a game (because of a rule that everybody on the bench has to play at least a little), he's on his way to scoring a touchdown when a kid from the other team shouts, "Throw me the ball," and he does. This, of course, causes him bottomless shame and remorse, and stirred ancient memories of my own about falling for such tricks—and practicing them. Meanwhile, there's a parallel plot involving Wally (Erik von Detten) and Eddie—kind of a romantic triangle, in which Wally coaches Eddie on how to win a girl, while the girl secretly has a crush on Wally.

The dialogue, by Brian Levant and Lon Diamond, has some nice moments: "For a second he had the same kind of blubbering look he had when the lights came up at the end of *The Lion King*." Or, when older brother Wally is asked to accompany the Beaver to school on the new bike: "I get it—you don't want some truck turning the Beaver into road kill." Or, when the hostile girl rejects Eddie's advances: "Take another step, and I'll file a restraining order."

It's all sort of low-key, and innocent, and depends on the guileless charm of young Cameron Finley, whose needs are simple: He only wants to be loved, respected, and understood, and doesn't know yet that he'll feel that way for the rest of his life.

Les Miserables ★ ★ ½

PG-13, 129 m., 1998

Liam Neeson (Valjean), Geoffrey Rush (Javert), Uma Thurman (Fantine), Claire Danes (Cosette), Hans Matheson (Marius). Directed by Bille August and produced by Sarah Radclyffe and James Gorman. Screenplay by Rafael Yglesias, based on the novel *Les Miserables* by Victor Hugo.

Les Miserables is like a perfectly respectable Classics Illustrated version of the Victor Hugo novel. It contains the moments of high drama, clearly outlines all the motivations, is easy to follow, and lacks only passion. A story filled with outrage and idealism becomes somehow merely picturesque.

Liam Neeson stars as Jean Valjean, and the movie makes its style clear in an early scene where he stands, homeless and hungry, at the door of a bishop, and says: "I am a convict. My name is Jean Valjean. I spent nineteen years at hard labor. On my passport I am identified as a thief." And so on. "I know who you are," replies the bishop, but not before the audience has been spoon-fed its briefing. Valjean is taken in, fed and sheltered, and tries to steal the bishop's silver. In one of the most famous episodes from Hugo's novel, the bishop tells the police he *gave* the tramp the silver, and later tells Valjean: "I've ransomed you from fear and hatred and now I give you back to God." There was a similar scene in Claude Lelouch's 1995 *Les Miserables,* which intercut passages from the novel with a story set during World War II; it was touching, but this version feels more like a morality play.

Valjean sells the silver, gets a job in a provincial factory, and uses the nest egg to buy the factory. As we rejoin him some years later, he is the local mayor, respectable and beloved, trying to teach himself to read and write. Then fate reenters his life in the person of Inspector Javert (Geoffrey Rush), a police official who recognizes him from his years at hard labor and wants to expose him: In this world, if you once do something wrong, you are banished forever from the sight of those lucky enough not to have been caught.

Consider, in the same light, poor Fantine (Uma Thurman), fired from the factory and forced into prostitution because it is discovered she has a child out of wedlock. Valjean discovers her plight (he was unaware of the firing), nurses her through a fatal illness, and promises to care for the child. Thurman's performance is the best element of the movie.

With the unyielding Javert forever at his back, Valjean takes his money and flees to Paris, taking refuge in a convent he had once (foresightedly) given money to. There he and the child, Cosette, spend ten years. Then Cosette, now a young woman played by Claire Danes, yearns for freedom; Valjean, against his better wisdom, takes a house for them. Cosette falls for the fiery radical Marius (Hans Matheson), who is being tailed by the police, which puts Javert once more onto the trail of poor Valjean.

Javert is the kind of man who can say with his dying breath, "I've tried to lead my life without breaking a single rule." He means it, and will never cease his pursuit of Valjean, even though the other man, as mayor, spared his job: "I order you to forgive yourself." As Javert pursues his vendetta against a man who has become kind and useful, Marius leads the mobs to the barricades, which look a lot here as they do in the stage musical.

That musical, by the way, is a long time coming. This is the second movie made of *Les Mis* during a decade when the "musical version" has been promised annually. There is, I think, an obvious person to direct it: Alan Parker, whose *Evita* and *Pink Floyd the Wall* show he is one of the few modern filmmakers who understands musicals. In the meantime, this dramatic version is by the Danish director Bille August, whose work *(Pelle the Conqueror, The Best Intentions* from the Bergman screenplay, *The House of the Spirits),* while uneven, has shown a juiciness and complexity.

Here we have a dutiful, even respectable, adaptation that lacks the rabble-rousing usually associated with *Les Miserables.* The sets and locations are handled well, the period looks convincing, but the story is lame. When Cosette pleads with her father to leave the convent, she sounds more like a bored modern teenager than a survivor of murderous times. ("Don't leave the cab!" he tells her on their first venture into the world, so of course she immediately does.)

Her father could, of course, settle all her objections with a few words of explanation, but in the great movie tradition of senselessly withholding crucial information, he refuses to; it must have been difficult for Neeson to maintain that expression of fearful regret in scene after scene. Rush, in his first major role since *Shine,* somehow doesn't project the fevered ethical madness that drives Javert; he comes across more as a very stubborn bore.

It's hard to make a period picture come alive, but when it happens *(Restoration, Dangerous Beauty, Amistad)* we feel transported back in time. *Les Miserables* only made me feel transported back to high school history class.

Lethal Weapon 4 ★ ★

R, 128 m., 1998

Mel Gibson (Martin Riggs), Danny Glover (Roger Murtaugh), Joe Pesci (Leo Getz), Rene Russo (Lorna Cole), Chris Rock (Lee Butters), Steve Kahan (Captain Travis). Directed by Richard Donner and produced by Donner and Joel Silver. Screenplay by Channing Gibson, Jonathan Lemkin, Alfred Gough, and Miles Millar.

Lethal Weapon 4 has all the technical skill of the first three movies in the series, but lacks the secret weapon, which was conviction. All four movies take two cop buddies and put them into spectacular and absurd action sequences, but the first three at least went through the motions of taking the plot seriously (and the first one did such a good job it made my "best 10" list). This time, we're watching an exercise.

Mel Gibson and Danny Glover star once again, as Riggs and Murtaugh, two cops who alternate between nonstop banter and dangerous action. Along the way, they've picked up a supporting cast: Leo Getz (Joe Pesci), the obnoxious but lovable accountant who joined them in the second film; Lorna Cole (Rene Russo), the Internal Affairs investigator and karate expert who came aboard in the third; Captain Travis (Steve Kahan), their long-suffering commanding officer; and, new this time, Lee Butters (Chris Rock), the cop who is secretly married to Murtaugh's pregnant daughter.

Most action movies don't stop for dialogue, but the *Lethal Weapon* pictures have always had a soft spot for human comedy, and there's a lot of repartee in this movie, some of it funny, as when Murtaugh and Riggs debate whether to take another deadly chance or not. There's a scene where they all wind up inhaling laughing gas in a dentist's office, and it works, too, but other dialogue scenes are just mechanical exercises: characters talking as if oblivious to danger.

The other trademark of the series is its spectacular special effects and stunt sequences. Here there's a brilliant freeway chase that involves a mobile home and a long sheet of plastic that drags Gibson behind it down the highway. Also one of those obligatory self-contained opening sequences (man in armor sprays city with flame-thrower and automatic rifle fire, is distracted by Murtaugh in underwear while Riggs shoots his fuel tank and he jets into a gas truck, etc.). And a climax in one of those factory spaces that seems to manufacture mostly water and steam.

The plot is so impenetrable that at one point the dialogue simply stops to explain it: A corrupt Chinese general has brought the Four Fathers of organized crime to the United States, and the Triads are trying to buy them back with counterfeit money. Yes. And that also involves a shipload of Chinese slave laborers, which is intercepted by Murtaugh, Riggs, and Getz, and Murtaugh ends up adopting one of the refugee families. Oh, and there's a sequence where all of the good guys are tied up on the floor of a burning house. And an underwater fight and rescue. And so on.

All done very well, you understand. Richard Donner is a master of what might be called elevated action. Martial arts fans will enjoy a newcomer named Jet Li, who has a lot of neat moves. And there are parallel pregnancies to create human interest, and a switch on the obligatory scene where the captain calls the rogue cops on the carpet: to control them, he tries promoting them.

But somehow it's all kind of hollow. By the numbers. I really did care for Murtaugh and Riggs in the first movie—and Leo, the Pesci character, was so much fun in the second one, he deserved an Oscar nomination. There was human interest in all the family scenes (especially involving Murtaugh's concern for his wife and kids), and poignancy in Riggs's lonely widower status. But all that has already happened by the beginning of this movie, and in a funny sense I felt like *Lethal Weapon 4* was outtakes—stuff they didn't use earlier, pieced together into a movie that doesn't really, in its heart, believe it is necessary. ☞

Let's Talk About Sex ★

R, 82 m., 1998

Troy Beyer (Jazz), Paget Brewster (Michelle), Randi Ingerman (Lena), Joseph C. Phillips (Michael), Michaline Babich (Morgan), Tina Nguyen (Drew). Directed by Troy Beyer and produced by Deborah Ridpath. Screenplay by Beyer.

It's hard to feel much sympathy for the heroine of *Let's Talk About Sex*, as she regards the wreckage of her dreams. Jazz (Troy Beyer) is a newspaper advice columnist in Miami who wants her own TV show, and the movie is about a very long weekend during which she interviews lots of women about lots of sex, and then edits together a pilot of a show to be called "Girl Talk."

Alas, the pilot tape is mistakenly destroyed. When Jazz hears the news, she is as distraught as a heroine in Greek tragedy. She doubles up in pain. Her body is wracked by great, cataclysmic sobs. Her two friends weep in sympathy, the three of them wailing and gnashing.

So great is their grief that mere words cannot encompass it, and they sink to the ultimate form of lamentation: They clean house. Bitter salt tears course down their cheeks as they Ajax the bathtub and Bab-O the pots and pans, while the audience collapses in disbelieving laughter.

Jazz's reaction seems a tad extreme, especially in comparison with her other big tearful moment, when she confesses she cannot have children. That merely makes her sob. Losing the tape turns her into Lady Macbeth. She was so distraught I wanted to climb right up there on the screen, squeeze her hand, and comfort her. "Look," I would have said, "first of all, you still have all the raw footage, so you can easily re-create the film in no time. Second, almost everything you had on your pilot tape is too raunchy to be played on a commercial television station anyway, so maybe it's better this way."

Let's Talk About Sex, written and directed by Beyer, plays like two bad films trying to elbow each other out of the frame. Film One consists of the documentary footage gathered by Jazz and her friends as they ask Miami Beach women to talk about sex (a lot of this footage seems to involve real women who think they are in a real documentary). Film Two involves the romantic ordeals of Jazz and her two roommates, Michelle (Paget Brewster) and Lena (Randi Ingerman).

They all have problems. Jazz has just broken off a long-running engagement with her boyfriend. Michelle dates men for sex but not for intimacy. Lena attracts men who treat her the way Michelle treats men. All three women are drop-dead beautiful and live in a Miami Beach penthouse that illustrates the rule that characters in movies always live in more expensive housing than they could afford in real life.

Leaving aside the melodrama about the three friends (and the sub-melodramas of Michelle's lesbian sister and Lena's no-good musician boyfriend), we're left with a lot of footage of very strange women describing their very strange sex lives. The movie shows the women being recruited with fliers, but they talk more like they're involved in a slam at Penthouse Forum. It's enlightening to learn you can practice for deep throat by using antiseptic throat spray and a cucumber, but even in the post-Monica age, the audience for this information must be finite.

Few of the interviews will give male audience members even a shred of hope that they will ever succeed in truly pleasing a female. We learn that men are uncaring, unskilled, and underequipped; worse, we go to sleep after sex, when women know that's the perfect time for deep, meaningful conversation. Remember that old college boy joke about how, after sex, the ideal women turns into a pizza and a six-pack? In this movie, the ideal man turns into a vibrator and Ted Koppel.

Liar Liar ★ ★ ★

PG-13, 86 m., 1997

Jim Carrey (Fletcher Reede), Maura Tierney (Audrey Reede), Justin Cooper (Max Reede), Cary Elwes (Jerry), Jennifer Tilly (Samantha Cole), Amanda Donohoe (Miranda), Swoosie Kurtz (Dana Appleton). Directed by Tom Shadyac and produced by Brian Grazer. Screenplay by Paul Guay and Stephen Mazur.

I am gradually developing a suspicion, or perhaps it is a fear, that Jim Carrey is growing on me. Am I becoming a fan? In *Liar Liar* he works tirelessly, inundating us with manic comedy energy. Like the class clown who'll do anything for a laugh, Carrey at one point actually pounds himself with a toilet seat. And gets a laugh.

The movie is a high-energy comeback from 1996's dismal *The Cable Guy,* which made the mistake of giving Carrey an unpleasant and obnoxious character to play. Here Carrey is likable and sympathetic, in a movie that will play for the whole family, entertaining each member on a different level (he's a master at combining slapstick for the kids with innuendo for the grown-ups).

Carrey plays a yuppie lawyer whose career is on the rise but whose wife (Maura Tierney) has divorced him and whose five-year-old son (Justin Cooper) no longer believes a word he says. "My dad's a liar," the kid says in class. "You mean a *lawyer,*" the teacher says. The kid shrugs. Whatever. Carrey is so wrapped up in cases that he even misses the kid's birthday party. So the kid closes his eyes and blows out the candles on the cake and makes a wish: He hopes that for one day his dad won't tell a lie.

The wish comes true. It is, of course, impossible to be a lawyer (or any other form of adult) if you are not prepared to lie, and so the day goes badly. He's defending the respondent in a big-bucks divorce case; his client (Jennifer Tilly) is a buxom sex bomb who is charged with one count of adultery but insists, somewhat proudly, that the actual count is closer to seven. This is not the sort of information you want to give to an attorney who cannot lie.

The screenplay, by Paul Guay and Stephen Mazur, takes this simple premise and applies it to the lawyer's workday. I can imagine the idea getting old really fast with a lesser actor, but Carrey literally throws himself into the story. Struggling to force himself to tell a lie, he goes mano-a-mano with a blue felt-tip pen. He tries to say it's red. He fails. His rubber face contorts itself in agony, but he *cannot* tell a lie.

There's trouble in the courtroom. "How are you today, counselor?" asks the judge. "I'm a little upset about a bad sexual episode last night," he replies. He can't even plead his client's case, since he knows it's false. As the judge and courtroom look on, Carrey climbs the walls and rolls on the floor, and finally escapes to the men's room, where in an astonishing display of comic energy he mugs himself, hoping to get the case continued until tomorrow.

The movie orchestrates one situation after another in which he has to tell the truth. "Do you know why I pulled you over?" a traffic cop asks. "That depends on how long you were following me," Carrey says. In one of the best sequences, he disrupts a partners' meeting at his law firm by telling the complete truth about everyone present.

The movie has been directed by Tom Shadyac, who also did *Ace Ventura: Pet Detective,* and it's mostly content to plant the camera and watch as Carrey goes bananas. He's a remarkable physical comedian. At one point, during a truth-telling session with his son, the kid twists his mouth out of shape and asks, "If I keep making this face, will it get stuck that way?" Absolutely not, says Carrey: "In fact, some people make a good living that way."

Life ★★★

R, 100 m., 1999

Eddie Murphy (Ray Gibson), Martin Lawrence (Claude Banks), Obba Babatunde (Willie Long), Ned Beatty (Dexter Wilkins), Bernie Mac (Jangle Leg), Rick James (Spanky), Miguel A. Nunez Jr. (Biscuit), Clarence Williams III (Winston Hancock), Bokeem Woodbine (Can't Get Right). Directed by Ted Demme and produced by Brian Grazer and Eddie Murphy. Screenplay by Robert Ramsey and Matthew Stone.

Eddie Murphy and Martin Lawrence age more than fifty years in *Life,* the story of two New Yorkers who spend their adult lives on a Mississippi prison farm because of some very bad luck. It's an odd, strange film—a sentimental comedy with a backdrop of racism—and I kept thinking of *Life Is Beautiful,* another film that skirts the edge of despair. *Life Is Beautiful* avoids it through comic inspiration, and *Life* by never quite admitting how painful its characters' lives must really have been.

The movie is ribald, funny, and sometimes sweet, and very well acted by Murphy, Lawrence, and a strong supporting cast. And yet the more you think about it, the more peculiar it seems. Murphy created the original story line, and Ted Demme *(The Ref)* follows his lead; the result is a film that almost seems nostalgic about what must have been a brutal existence. When was the last time a movie made prison seem almost pleasant?

Life opens in 1932 in a Harlem nightclub, with a chance encounter between a bank teller named Claude (Lawrence) and a pickpocket named Ray (Murphy). They both find themselves in big trouble with Spanky, the club owner (Rick James), who is in the process of drowning Claude when Ray saves both their lives by talking them into a job: They'll drive a truck to Mississippi and pick up a load of moonshine.

The trip takes them into Jim Crow land, where Claude is outspoken and Ray more cautious in a segregated diner that serves "white-only pie." Then they find the moonshiner, load the truck, and allow themselves to get distracted by a local sin city, where Ray loses all his money to a cheat (Clarence Williams

III) and Claude goes upstairs with a good-time girl. The cheat is found dead and Claude and Ray are framed by the sheriff who actually killed him, and given life in prison.

The early scenes move well (although why was it necessary to send all the way to Mississippi for moonshine, when New York was awash in bootleg booze during Prohibition?). The heart of the movie, however, takes place in prison, where after an early scene of hard physical labor, life settles down into baseball games, talent shows, and even, at one point, a barbecue. Bokeem Woodbine plays Can't Get Right, a retarded prisoner who hits a homer every time at the plate, and Ray and Claude become his managers, hoping to get a free ride out of prison when he's recruited by the Negro Leagues.

But it doesn't work that way, and life goes on, decade after decade, while the real world is only hearsay. Demme has two nice touches for showing the passage of time: Prison inmates are shown simply fading from the screen, and in the early 1970s Claude gets to drive the warden (Ned Beatty) into nearby Greenville, where he sees hippie fashions and his first Afro. Meanwhile, Rick Baker's makeup gradually and convincingly ages the two men, who do a skillful job of aging their voices and manners.

All of this time, of course, they dream of escaping. And they maintain the fiction that they don't get along, although in fact they've grown close over the years (comparisons with *The Shawshank Redemption* are inevitable). Ray remains the realist and compromiser, and Claude remains more hotheaded; the warden likes them both, and eventually assigns them to his house staff.

But what are we to make of their long decades together? That without the unjust prison term, they would never have had the opportunity to enjoy such a friendship? That prison life has its consolations? That apart from that unfortunate lifetime sentence, the white South was actually pretty decent to the two friends? *Life* simply declines to deal with questions like that, and the story makes it impossible for them to be answered. It's about friendship, I guess, and not social issues.

Murphy and Lawrence are so persuasive in the movie that maybe audiences will be carried along. Their characters are likable, their performances are touching, they age well, they survive. And their lives consist of episodes and anecdotes that make good stories—as when the white superintendent's daughter has a black baby, and the super holds the kid up next to every convict's face, looking for the father. That's a comic scene in the movie; real life might have been different. But life flows along and we get in the mood, and by the end we're happy to see the two old-timers enjoying their retirement. After all, they've earned it.

Life Is Beautiful ★ ★ ★ ½

PG-13, 114 m., 1998

Roberto Benigni (Guido), Nicoletta Braschi (Dora), Giorgio Cantarini (Giosue), Giustino Durano (Zio), Sergio Bustric (Ferruccio), Marisa Paredes (Dora's Mother), Horst Buchholz (Doctor Lessing), Lydia Alfonsi (Guicciardini). Directed by Roberto Benigni and produced by Elda Ferri and Gianluigi Braschi. Screenplay by Vincenzo Cerami and Benigni.

Some people become clowns; others have clownhood thrust upon them. It is impossible to regard Roberto Benigni without imagining him as a boy in school, already a cut-up, using humor to deflect criticism and confuse his enemies. He looks goofy, and knows how he looks. I saw him once in a line at airport customs, subtly turning a roomful of tired and impatient travelers into an audience for a subtle pantomime in which he was the weariest and most put-upon. We had to smile.

Life Is Beautiful is the role he was born to play. The film falls into two parts. One is pure comedy. The other smiles through tears. Benigni, who also directed and cowrote the movie, stars as Guido, a hotel waiter in Italy in the 1930s. Watching his adventures, we are reminded of Chaplin.

He arrives in town in a runaway car whose brakes have failed, and is mistaken for a visiting dignitary. He falls in love instantly with the beautiful Dora (Nicoletta Braschi, Benigni's wife). He becomes the undeclared rival of her fiancé, the fascist town clerk. He makes friends with the German doctor (Horst Buchholz), who is a regular guest at the hotel and shares his love of riddles. And by the fantastic manipulation of carefully planned coincidences, he makes it appear that he is fated to replace the dour fascist in Dora's life.

All of this early material, the first long act of the movie, is comedy—much of it silent comedy involving the fate of a much-traveled hat. Only well into the movie do we even learn the crucial information that Guido is Jewish. Dora, a gentile, quickly comes to love him, and in one scene even conspires to meet him on the floor under a banquet table; they kiss, and she whispers, "Take me away!" In the town, Guido survives by quick improvisation. Mistaken for a school inspector, he invents a quick lecture on Italian racial superiority, demonstrating the excellence of his big ears and superb navel.

Several years pass, offscreen. Guido and Dora are married, and dote on their five-year-old son, Giosue (Giorgio Cantarini). In 1945, near the end of the war, the Jews in the town are rounded up by the fascists and shipped by rail to a death camp. Guido and Giosue are loaded into a train, and Guido instinctively tries to turn it into a game, to comfort his son; he makes a big show of being terrified that somehow they will miss the train and be left behind. Dora, not Jewish, would be spared by the fascists, but insists on coming along to be with her husband and family.

In the camp, Guido constructs an elaborate fiction to comfort his son and protect his life. It is all an elaborate game, he explains. The first one to get 1,000 points will win a tank—not a toy tank but a real one, which Giosue can drive all over town. Guido acts as the translator for a German who is barking orders at the inmates, freely translating them into Italian designed to quiet his son's fears. And he literally hides the child from the camp guards, with rules of the game that have the boy crouching on a high sleeping platform and remaining absolutely still.

Benigni told me at the Toronto festival that the movie has stirred up venomous opposition from the right wing in Italy. At Cannes, it offended some left-wing critics with its use of humor in connection with the Holocaust. What may be most offensive to both wings is its sidestepping of politics in favor of simple human ingenuity. The film finds the right notes to negotiate its delicate subject matter. And Benigni isn't really making comedy out of the Holocaust, anyway. He is showing how Guido uses the only gift at his command to protect his son. If he had a gun, he would shoot at the fascists. If he had an army, he would destroy them. He is a clown, and comedy is his weapon.

The movie actually softens the Holocaust slightly, to make the humor possible at all. In the real death camps there would be no role for Guido. But *Life Is Beautiful* is not about Nazis and fascists, but about the human spirit. It is about rescuing whatever is good and hopeful from the wreckage of dreams. About hope for the future. About the necessary human conviction, or delusion, that things will be better for our children than they are right now. ☞

A Life Less Ordinary ★ ★

R, 90 m., 1997

Ewan McGregor (Robert), Cameron Diaz (Celine), Ian Holm (Naville), Delroy Lindo (Jackson), Holly Hunter (O'Reilly), Dan Hedaya (Chief Gabriel), Stanley Tucci (Elliot). Directed by Danny Boyle and produced by Andrew Macdonald. Screenplay by John Hodge.

A Life Less Ordinary is from the team that gave us *Shallow Grave* and *Trainspotting*, so maybe it's a penance that their characters this time are angels and lovers, rather than body snatchers and druggies. See, ma? We're good lads at heart.

The film expends enormous energy to tell a story that is tedious and contrived. It begins in heaven's police station, where Chief Gabriel (acting on orders from the top) dispatches two angels to Earth to engineer a romance. It appears that God is displeased by the divorce rate.

We meet the two lovers that heaven plans to unite. Robert (Ewan McGregor) is a janitor. Celine (Cameron Diaz) is a millionaire's daughter who amuses herself by using a handgun to shoot apples off the head of her fiancé (Stanley Tucci). (She misses, and a friend observes, "He'll live, but he'll never practice orthodontics again.")

Robert works for her father's company, and when he's replaced by robots, he seizes one of the squat little machines and tries to smash it against the wall of the chairman's office. The millionaire (Ian Holm) calls security, Robert grabs one of the guards' guns, and at a crucial point Celine kicks the gun back into his grasp—maybe because she hopes he will kidnap her, which he does.

The film then settles into a formula familiar from two other recent films, *Excess Baggage* and *Nothing to Lose.* The kidnapper and his victim grow friendly, and eventually become conspirators. Robert turns out to be inept at making threatening phone calls, and Celine starts with helpful hints and ends up stage-managing the kidnapping herself. ("That's all I am to you," he complains bitterly. "Your latest kidnapper—a fashion accessory!")

All of this is being manipulated, in a sense, by two angels, Jackson (Delroy Lindo) and O'Reilly (Holly Hunter). For reasons unclear to me, they are hired by the millionaire to track down his daughter and the kidnapper, and the movie develops into a long, unhinged chase sequence in which the angels act more like cops than matchmakers. By this point I was well past caring.

After the anarchic glee of *Trainspotting,* this film is a move toward the mainstream by the team of director Danny Boyle, producer Andrew Macdonald, and writer John Hodge. It's a conventional movie that never persuades us it needed to be made. Most films with angels depend more on supernatural intervention than character development, but in this case the film seems completely confused about the nature the intervention should take, and so are we. The plot's a mess, the characters flail about in scenes without points, and the more we see of Cameron Diaz and Ewan McGregor the more we yearn for a nice, simple little love story—say, about the rich girl who falls in love with the Scots janitor and gets along just fine without any angels.

Limbo ★ ★ ★ ½

R, 126 m., 1999

Mary Elizabeth Mastrantonio (Donna De Angelo), David Strathairn (Joe Gastineau), Vanessa Martinez (Noelle De Angelo), Casey Siemaszko (Bobby Gastineau), Kris Kristofferson (Smilin' Jack), Kathryn Grody (Frankie), Rita Taggart (Lou). Directed and edited by John Sayles and produced by Maggie Renzi. Screenplay by Sayles.

Limbo sure isn't heaven and it's too cold to be hell.
—From the diary read by Noelle

Juneau is the only state capital with roads that lead nowhere. Every highway out of town ends in the wilderness. That serves as a metaphor for the characters in John Sayles's *Limbo,* a movie about people whose lives are neither here nor there, but stuck in between. It also helps explain the movie's surprising story structure, which doesn't obediently follow our expectations, but reflects the way a wilderness like Alaska can impose its own abrupt reality.

We meet a local handyman named Joe (David Strathairn), who was a high school All-American until he wrecked his knee, and a fishing boat skipper until he lost two lives and quit the trade. And we meet a singer named Donna (Mary Elizabeth Mastrantonio), whose career on the club circuit has ended her up at the Golden Nugget Lounge, pretty much the end of the line. She's had bad luck with men, and we see her breaking up with her latest guy at a wedding reception. Joe gives her a lift back to town.

The movie seems to be announcing it is about a relationship. We meet Donna's daughter, Noelle (Vanessa Martinez), who is exasperated by her mom's taste in men but begins to like Joe. The backdrop also seems to fall into place. We learn about local campaigns to save the environment, and about ways to get around them ("Quit with the chain saws when you get to where people can see"). We meet some of the local fauna, including the high-spirited lesbian couple, Lou (Rita Taggart) and Frankie (Kathryn Grody), who have taken over a valued commercial fishing license.

Mastrantonio is a splendid presence in her role. She can sing well and talks about how sometimes in a song she'll find a moment of grace. She doesn't know what she's doing in Alaska: "Anything where you need equipment instead of clothing, I don't do." Strathairn's character has lived in Alaska most of his life, and it has taught him not to hope for much, and to expect anything. But just now it's summer, and the living looks easy. A romance seems to be forming.

We assume we're in familiar John Sayles territory; he likes to populate his stories with large, interlocking casts, and then show how the local politics and economy work. That's what he did in *City of Hope* (1991), set in New Jersey, and the great *Lone Star* (1996), set on the Tex-Mex border. But he has a surprise ready for us. (Although the ads and review clips reveal it, you might not want to read beyond this point before seeing the movie.)

The surprise is a complete overthrow of all of our expectations for the story, a sharp turn in the narrative that illustrates how Alaska is domesticated only up to a point—that the wilderness is only a step away, and death only a misstep. I was reminded of the chilling book *Into the Wild*, about the young dropout who went on an Alaskan camping trip where everything went wrong.

Joe has a half-brother named Bobby (Casey Siemaszko), who talks him into crewing his boat on a "business trip." Joe innocently invites Donna and Noelle along. The purpose of the trip is far from innocent. After narrowly surviving a storm, Joe guides the boat into an inlet where few boats ever come. And then there are more unexpected developments, and three of them (Joe, Donna, and Noelle) find themselves castaways on an island far from anyone else.

What I liked so much about this story structure is that it confounded my expectations at every step. I expected the story to stay in Juneau, but it didn't. When it took a turn toward adventure, I thought the threat would come from nature—but it comes from men. After the three characters are stranded, I expected—I don't know what, maybe Swiss Family Robinson–style improvisation.

But Sayles gradually reveals his buried theme, which is that in a place like the Alaskan wilderness you can never be sure what will happen next. And that optimism, bravery, and ingenuity may not be enough. Some of the best dialogue passages in the film involve Joe's quiet realism. He refuses to raise false hopes. And of course even the hope of rescue comes with a hidden barb: Will they be found by friends, or death?

The movie leaves conventional plot structure behind and treks off into the wilderness itself. There's even a story within the story, based on a journal Noelle finds—and it contains a surprise too. Then comes the film's ending. Watching the screen, I felt confident that I knew exactly what would have to happen. What, and how, and why. And I was wrong. The more you think about the way *Limbo* ends, the more you realize that any other ending would betray the purpose of the story. Sayles has started with a domestic comedy, and led us unswervingly into the heart of darkness.

Little Dieter Needs to Fly ★ ★ ★ ½

NO MPAA RATING, 80 m., 1998

Dieter Dengler (Himself). A documentary directed and produced by Werner Herzog.

"Men are often haunted," Werner Herzog tells us at the beginning of *Little Dieter Needs to Fly*. "They seem to be normal, but they are not." His documentary tells the story of such a haunted man, whose memories include being hung upside down with an ant nest over his head, and fighting a snake for a dead rat they both wanted to eat.

The man's name is Dieter Dengler. He was born in the Black Forest of Germany. As a child, he watched his village destroyed by American warplanes, and one flew so close to his attic window that for a split second he made eye contact with the pilot flashing past. At that moment, Dieter Dengler knew that he needed to fly.

Dengler is now in his fifties, a businessman living in northern California. He invites us into his home, carefully opening and closing every door over and over again, to be sure he is not locked in. He shows us the stores of rice, flour, and honey under his floor. He obsesses about being locked in, about having nothing to eat. He tells us his story.

As an eighteen-year-old, he came penniless to America. He enlisted in the navy to learn to fly. He flew missions over Vietnam, but "that there were people down there who suffered, who died—only became clear to me after I was their prisoner." He was shot down, made a prisoner, became one of only seven men to escape from prison camps and survive. He endured tortures by his captors and from nature: dysentery, insect bites, starvation, hallucinations.

Werner Herzog's *Little Dieter Needs to Fly* lets Dieter tell his own story, which he does in rushed but vivid English, as if fearful there will not be time enough if he doesn't speak fast. As he talks, Herzog puts him in locations: his American home, his German village of Wildberg, and then the same Laotian jungles where he was shot down. Here certain memories are reenacted: He is handcuffed by villagers, made to march through the forest, and demonstrates how he was staked down at night. "You can't imagine what I'm thinking," he says.

The thing about storytelling is that it creates pictures in our heads. I can "see" what happened to Dieter Dengler as clearly as if it has all been dramatized, and his poetry adds to the images. "As I followed the river, there was this beautiful bear following me," he remembers. "This bear meant death to me. It's really ironic—the only friend I had at the end was death." At another point, standing in front of a giant tank of jellyfish, he says, "This is basically what Death looks like to me," and Herzog's camera moves in on the dreamy floating shapes as we hear the sad theme from *Tristan and Isolde.*

Now here is an interesting aspect. Dieter Dengler is a real man who really underwent all of those experiences (and won the Medal of Honor, the Distinguished Flying Cross, and the Navy Cross because of them). His story is true. But not all of his words are his own. Herzog freely reveals in conversation that he suggested certain images to Dengler. The image of the jellyfish, for example—"That was my idea," Herzog told me. Likewise the opening and shutting of the doors, although not the image of the bear.

Herzog has had two careers, as the director of some of the strangest and most fascinating features of the last thirty years, and some of the best documentaries. Many of his docs are about obsessed men: the ski-jumper Steiner, for example, who flew so high he overjumped his landing areas. Or Herzog himself, venturing onto a volcanic island to interview the one man who would not leave when he was told the volcano would explode.

Herzog sees his mission as a filmmaker not to turn himself into a recording machine, but to be a collaborator. He does not simply stand and watch, but arranges and adjusts and subtly enhances, so that the film takes the materials of Dengler's adventure and fashions it into a new thing.

You meet a person who has an amazing story to tell, and you rarely have the time to hear it, or the attention to appreciate it. The attendants in nursing homes sit glued to their Stephen King paperbacks; the old people around them have stories a thousand times scarier to tell. A colorful character dies and the obituaries say countless great stories were told about him—but at the end, did anybody still care to listen?

Herzog starts with a balding, middle-aged man driving down a country lane in a convertible, and listens, questions, and shapes until the life experience of Dieter Dengler becomes unforgettable. What an astonishing man! we think. But if we were to sit next to him on a plane, we might tell him we had seen his movie, and make a polite comment about it, and go back to our magazine. It takes art to transform someone else's experience into our own.

Little Men ★ ½

PG, 98 m., 1998

Michael Caloz (Nat Blake), Mariel Hemingway (Jo Bhaer), Ben Cook (Dan), Ricky Mabe (Tommy Bangs), Chris Sarandon (Fritz Bhaer), Kathleen Fee (Narrator). Directed by Rodney Gibbons and produced by Pierre David and Franco Battista. Screenplay by Mark Evan Schwartz, based on the novel by Louisa May Alcott.

In my review of *Little Women* (1994), I wrote, "the very title summons up preconceptions of treacly do-gooders in a smarmy children's story." I was relieved to report, however, that the movie itself was nothing of the sort; it was a spirited and intelligent retelling of the Louisa May Alcott classic. Now, alas, comes *Little Men,* which is indeed about treacly do-gooders in a smarmy children's story.

Although younger children may enjoy the movie on a simple and direct level, there's little depth or texture to make it interesting for viewers over the age of, say, about ten. It's all on one note. The adults are all noble and enlightened, the boys are all basically good, and the story is all basically a sunny, innocent fable.

The year is 1871. The "little women" have all grown up, according to a narrator who tells us far more than she should have to. Jo (Mariel Hemingway) has married Fritz Bhaer (Chris Sarandon), and together they run Plumfield School, a country home for wayward or orphaned boys.

To Plumfield comes the Boston street urchin Nat (Michael Caloz) and, not long after, his best friend Dan (Ben Cook). There they find love, acceptance, and such lessons as, "If a pie has twelve pieces and three-quarters of them are served at dinner, how many pieces are left?" All of the boys scribble industriously on their chalkboards to solve the puzzle, although since several of them are later involved in a game of poker, they would seem to have the necessary skills for mental calculation.

Plumfield has limited funds, and perhaps cannot afford to keep Dan. And then Dan causes some problems, as when he sponsors the secret poker game (complete with beer and cigars) and it almost results in Plumfield being burned down. Apart from such hitches, Plumfield is an ideal haven, with pillow fights scheduled every Saturday night, and the narrator informs us that "the feeling that someone cared for him made that playroom seem like heaven for the homeless child."

There is a certain complexity in Fritz, Jo's husband, who recalls that his grandmother taught him to think before he spoke by cutting the end of his tongue with her scissors. His idea of punishment is to have the boys cane him, a practice that will not withstand a single moment's more thought than the movie gives it. He rumbles suspiciously about Dan, but Dan "has the makings of a fine man," Jo declares, and although another boy is sent away for stealing, Dan survives the poker, beer, and cigar scandal.

There is a horse at Plumfield. Only one, untamed and unruly. In an early scene, we see the hired man trying to tame it. We know with complete certainty that Dan was born to tame that horse, which indeed is waiting (all saddled up) when the lad's rebellious spirit requires such a test.

I have no doubt that Louisa May Alcott wrote something resembling this plot, although nothing in it sends me hurrying to the bookshelf. *Little Men* is an example of the kind of movie that wins approval because of what it doesn't have, not for what it has. It is wholesome, blameless, positive, cheerful, well photographed, and nicely acted (especially by Ben Cook), and it has a PG rating. But, man, is it smarmy.

Little Voice ★ ★ ★

R, 99 m., 1998

Jane Horrocks (Laura [Little Voice]), Brenda Blethyn (Mari), Michael Caine (Ray Say), Jim Broadbent (Mr. Boo), Ewan McGregor (Billy), Philip Jackson (George), Annette Badland (Sadie). Directed by Mark Herman and produced by Elizabeth Karlsen. Screenplay by Herman, based on the stage play by Jim Cartwright.

Little Voice is unthinkable without the special and unexpected talent of its star. She is Jane Horrocks, from TV's *Absolutely Fabulous* and the Mike Leigh movie *Life Is Sweet*, and nothing I've seen her do prepared me in any way for the revelation that she is a singer. And not just a singer, but an impressionist who can perform in the voices of Judy Garland, Shirley Bassey, Marilyn Monroe, and Billie Holiday, among others. And not just an impressionist, but a mimic so skillful that the end credits make it a point to inform us that Horrocks sang all her own songs in the movie. We need to know that, because her mimicry is so exact that we assume it must be lip-synching.

Horrocks first appeared in this story on the stage (it was written for her by Jim Cartwright), and now in the movie she repeats an astonishing performance, which is plopped down into an amusing but uneven story about colorful characters in a northern England seaside resort town. She plays a young woman named Laura, who mopes in her bedroom above the record store that her late, beloved dad used to run. She shares his taste for classic pop records, and plays them again and again, memorizing the great performances.

The rest of the house is ruled by her mother, Mari (Brenda Blethyn, the Oscar nominee from

Secrets and Lies). She's a loud, blowzy tart who picks up lads at pubs and brings them home. Her new squeeze is Ray Say (Michael Caine), a onetime London club promoter now reduced to managing strippers in this northern backwater. Mari's approach to Ray is direct. She brings him home from a pub and suggests, "Let's roll about."

One night a duel develops between Mari playing "It's Not Unusual" downstairs while Laura does "That's Entertainment" upstairs. Ray hears the singing, and realizes at once that he's in the presence of an extraordinary talent. But Laura's voice is not reflected in a big personality; she's a shy recluse who speaks in such a small voice that it has supplied her nickname.

Ray brings home his friend Mr. Boo (Jim Broadbent), owner of a local club, to audition Little Voice. They can't get her to sing, but afterward, while they're standing on the sidewalk, they hear her doing "Over the Rainbow" and Mr. Boo knows a big draw when he hears one. (His club books acts more along the lines of an elderly knife-thrower who aims blades at his wife to the strains of "Rawhide.")

The plot involves Ray's struggle to lure Little Voice onto the stage (he tells her a touching parable about a little bluebird) and his struggle to discourage Mari's amorous intensity. There is also a struggle going on for Little Voice's heart. A telephone lineman (Ewan McGregor) is in love with her, and uses his cherry-picker to levitate himself to her bedroom window. Will he win her love? Will she agree to sing?

Little Voice, written and directed by Mark Herman *(Brassed Off)*, seems to have all the pieces in place for another one of those whimsical, comic British slices of life. But the movie doesn't quite deliver the way we think it will. One problem is that the Michael Caine character, sympathetic and funny in the opening and middle scenes, turns mean at the end for no good reason. Another is that the romance, and a manufactured crisis, distract from the true climax of the movie.

That would be Jane Horrocks's vocal performance. Watching her belt out one great standard after another, I was reminded of old musicals that were handmade as showcases for big stars. The plot was just a clothesline for Astaire's big dance number or Mario Lanza's solo. Here everything leads up to (and wilts after) Horrocks's show-stopper. But she is amazing. Absolutely fabulous. ☞

Live Flesh ★ ★ ★ ½

R, 101 m., 1998

Liberto Rabal (Victor Plaza), Francesca Neri (Elena), Javier Bardem (David), Angela Molina (Clara), Jose Sancho (Sancho). Directed by Pedro Almodovar and produced by Agustin Almodovar. Screenplay by Pedro Almodovar, based on the novel by Ruth Rendell.

Pedro Almodovar's *Live Flesh* is the kind of overwrought melodrama, lurid and passionate, that I have a weakness for. It dives in headfirst, going for broke, using the entire arsenal of coincidence, irony, fire, and surprise. It's about cops, lovers, paralysis, prostitution, adultery, deception, and revenge, and it is also surprisingly tender in its portrait of a man who gets into a lifetime of trouble just because he wants to make a woman happy.

Because it is by Almodovar, that Spanish poet of the perverse, none of these elements are come by easily. Victor, the hero, is born on a bus, the child of a prostitute, with a madam as midwife (the Madrid bus company gives him a lifetime pass). Twenty years pass and we find him ringing the doorbell of Elena, a woman he has met only briefly. He recalls their brief encounter at a disco: "The guy you had sex with in the toilet—remember?" She does, but wants nothing to do with him. She's waiting for her drug dealer and all Victor has brought her is a pizza.

But Victor is stubborn. His encounter with Elena was his first sexual experience, and he is doe-eyed with desire to know her better. She's in no condition to be known. They argue, the cops are called, and a gun discharges, striking a young cop and paralyzing him. Flash forward: Victor, in prison, is surprised to see that the cop is now a wheelchair basketball star, and Elena, cheering from the sidelines, has cleaned up her act and is now his devoted wife. Meanwhile, Victor rots behind bars, an innocent man.

Innocent, yes, because he did not fire the gun. In the struggle, it was the other cop—the alcoholic Sancho (Jose Sancho)—who pulled the trigger and hit his young partner, David (Javier Bardem). Why? Because he suspected David of having an affair with his wife, Clara. Of course, it is only a matter of time until Victor, released from prison, is having an affair with Clara himself.

Don't be concerned if you have not quite followed every twist and turn of this convoluted story. Almodovar makes it clear as it unfolds; his screenplay is based on a novel by Ruth Rendell, the British mistress of plots that fold back upon themselves. Another source for the film's style is Douglas Sirk, the master of 1950s Hollywood melodrama, whose films Almodovar claims to have seen hundreds of times, and who manufactured melodramatic plots with the ingenuity of chess puzzles.

Almodovar's films are often intended as put-ons. This one may be, too, but it's played more or less straight (for him, anyway). The actors understand that in melodrama of this sort, the slightest suggestion of irony is fatal, and they play everything with desperate intensity, while inhabiting screens so filled with bright colors it's a wonder they don't wince.

For Victor (Liberto Rabal), life has not been fair. But his luck changes when, after being released from prison, he goes to visit the grave of his mother. There he meets Clara (Angela Molina), an older woman, and after a strictly routine night of love he pleads inexperience and begs her to teach him everything she knows. She proves to be a gifted teacher. His long-term plan is to spend one night with the cruel Elena, proving himself the world's greatest lover and leaving her sobbing for more. Many men dream of such scenarios, but few have Victor's dedication to the necessary training regimen.

There are many other coincidences in the film, which I will not reveal. Some we can anticipate; others are complete surprises. It's interesting how Almodovar anchors the story so concretely in a real world, with everyday jobs and concerns; in the midst of jealousy and lust, the characters somehow retain a certain depth and plausibility. I especially liked the work of Molina, a frequent actress in Almodovar's films, as an older woman whose experience and wisdom have not been enough to protect her from a brutish husband.

And Javier Bardem takes a refreshing approach to the role of the paralyzed ex-cop: Of all the men in the movie, he has the strongest physical presence and the greatest menace. There's a scene where he goes in his chair to call on the young ex-convict, and the way he enters the room and establishes himself makes him the aggressor, not the handicapped one.

Movies like *Live Flesh* exist for the joy of telling their stories. They recall a time before high romance was smothered by taste. They don't apologize for breathless energy and cheerful implausibility, and every time a character walks into a room we feel like bracing ourselves for a new shock. Almodovar cannot be called "sincere" on the basis of this film—there's still a satirical glint in his eye—but by choosing to stick with the story and downplay his usual asides, nudges, and in-jokes, he's made a *film noir* of great energy.

Living Out Loud ★ ★ ★ ½

R, 102 m., 1998

Holly Hunter (Judith), Danny DeVito (Pat), Queen Latifah (Liz Bailey), Martin Donovan (Dr. Nelson), Elias Koteas (Stranger). Directed by Richard LaGravenese and produced by Danny DeVito, Michael Schamberg, and Stacey Sher. Screenplay by LaGravenese.

He is a short, pudgy elevator operator. She is the newly dumped wife of a doctor. They meet in his elevator, in her co-op building on Fifth Avenue. They seem to have little in common, until they start talking. This is a setup for a love story involving all the usual clichés, but *Living Out Loud* isn't a love story and is not made from standard parts. It's the film you need to see in order to understand why the ending of *As Good As It Gets* was phony.

The movie stars two of the most intensely interesting actors in the movies today, Danny DeVito and Holly Hunter. Not many actors can hold the screen against them. There's a dialogue scene where they talk about whether he should ask her out for dinner, and we're seeing a master class on the craft of acting in the movies. We don't *want* them to live happily ever after, because that would drain all of the interest out of their situation.

The movie has been written and directed by Richard LaGravenese, the gifted screenwriter of *The Horse Whisperer, The Bridges of Madison County,* and *Beloved.* He's more interested in characters and dialogue than in shaping everything into a conventional story. He aims for the kind of bittersweet open ends that life itself so often supplies; he doesn't hammer his square pegs into round holes, as James L. Brooks did by insisting in *As Good As It Gets* that the Jack Nicholson character could, should, or would ever be able to live happily with anyone else.

The movie opens with Judith (Hunter) breaking up with her husband of fifteen years (Martin Donovan). He's been cheating on her—and, worse, insulting her intelligence by thinking he could get away with it. Later we meet Pat (DeVito), an elevator operator whose wife has thrown him out because of his gambling debts and a whole lot more, and whose daughter is dying. Pat's brother, a saloon keeper, offers him a job, but Pat clings to his independence. The elevator job is temporary. He has plans.

To be cut adrift in uncertainty and grief is something to share, and soon they are sharing it. Feeling sorry for him and having drunk too much, which she often does, she hugs him, causing unruly feelings to stir within Pat. He subtly borrows $200 (the loan sharks are after him), and when he repays her he brings along a bottle of wine, and she confesses she saw through his story about why he needed the money, but gave it to him anyway, because . . . because . . .

Well, because it was a point of contact in a life that has become empty. (She has a day job as a caregiver for a singularly uncareworthy old lady.) Will they go on to share their innermost feelings and fall in love, as in a standard plot? Not necessarily. He thinks she's the perfect woman. But when she drinks she fantasizes about hunks, which is maybe how she wound up with a creep for a husband.

Need draws them together. Fantasies keep them apart. And then an extraordinary third character enters their lives. This is Liz Bailey (Queen Latifah), a torch singer in a nightclub where Judith likes to drink too many martinis, smoke too many cigarettes, and display too much grief. Liz is tall, striking, carries herself with placid self-confidence, and wears dresses that display her magnificent bosom—not as an advertisement, but more in a spirit of generosity toward the world.

Liz and Judith become unlikely confidantes one boozy night, after Judith blurts out that she's sure Liz's boyfriend is gay. Well, he is: "I've always had this thing for beautiful, sensitive men." She takes Judith to a lesbian nightclub that looks recycled from German expressionist wet dreams; the scene doesn't seem out of place, but falls into the flow of a long, confusing, drunken night.

Judith and Pat both become friends of Liz, who is a confidante and counselor. But LaGravenese is too smart to involve Liz in an affair with Pat (or Judith). He's intrigued by how people can bounce around town when they're cut loose from their routines and marriages. How they find relief in a flood of confession and autobiography. ("His father was one of the first neurosurgeons in the city," Judith tells Pat about her first husband, and he nods and notes that his wife was an Oldsmobile saleswoman on Staten Island.)

Another man turns up in Judith's life, unexpectedly and accidentally, but I will leave it to you to find out how and why. And there's an appointment with an agreeable masseuse (an encounter that's just about perfectly written and acted). It's always confusing to meet your sexual fantasies in the flesh, because you have to deal with them—they won't obligingly evaporate when you're finished.

Living Out Loud is based on two short stories by Chekhov. It plays like a short story. A novel has beginning, middle, end, theme, conflict, resolution. A short story looks intensely at a shorter period of time during which closely observed characters go through experiences that change them. No doubt Judith, Pat, and Liz will drift apart again. There are more happy endings (and endings of any kind) in the movies than in life, which more closely resembles the beginnings of one unfinished story after another.

What I enjoyed in *Living Out Loud* was the comfort of these lives flowing briefly in the same stream. The sense that the unexpected was free to enter the story, and would not be shouldered aside by the demands of conventional plotting. And delight at the voluptuous complications of Liz Bailey. Queen Latifah shows here (as she did in *Set It Off*) that her screen presence makes a scene stand up and hum. Anyone who can steal a scene from Danny DeVito and Holly Hunter can do just about anything in a movie.

Lock, Stock and Two Smoking Barrels

★★★

R, 106 m., 1999

Jason Flemyng (Tom), Dexter Fletcher (Soap), Nick Moran (Eddy), Jason Statham (Bacon), P. H. Moriarty (Hatchet Harry), Lenny McLean (Barry the Baptist), Steven Mackintosh (Winston), Sting (JD), Nicholas Rowe (J), Vinnie Jones (Big Chris). Directed by Guy Ritchie and produced by Matthew Vaughn. Screenplay by Ritchie.

Lock, Stock and Two Smoking Barrels is like Tarantino crossed with the Marx Brothers, if Groucho had been into chopping off fingers. It's a bewilderingly complex caper film, set among the lowlifes of London's East End, and we don't need to be told that the director used to make TV commercials; we figure that out when a cook throws some veggies into water, and the camera shoots up from the bottom of the pot.

The movie is about a poker player named Eddy (Nick Moran), who is bankrolled by three friends for a high-stakes game with Hatchet Harry (P. H. Moriarty), a gambling and porn kingpin. Harry cheats, Eddy runs up an enormous debt, and Harry's giant enforcer, Barry the Baptist (Lenny McLean), explains that he will start chopping fingers if the friends don't pay up—or hand over a pub belonging to Eddy's father (Sting).

What to do? Eddy and his mates eavesdrop on neighbors in the next flat—criminals who are planning to rob a rich drug dealer. Meanwhile, Barry assigns two dimwits to steal a couple of priceless antique shotguns for Harry. The shotguns end up in the hands of Eddy and friends, who steal the drug money from the other thieves, and then—but you get the idea.

Or maybe you don't. The movie, which is an enormous hit in Britain, had its American premiere at the Sundance Film Festival, where I lost track of the plot and some of the dialogue. Seeing it again recently, I found the dialogue easier to understand, and the labyrinthine plot became a little clearer—although it's designed to fold back upon itself with unexpected connections.

The actors seem a little young for this milieu; they seem to be playing grown-up. Tarantino's *Reservoir Dogs* had characters with mileage on them, played by veterans like Harvey Keitel, Lawrence Tierney, and Michael Madsen.

But the heroes of *Lock* (Jason Flemyng, Dexter Fletcher, Jason Statham, and Moran) seem a little downy-cheeked to be moving in such weathered circles. And as the cast expands to include the next-door neighbors and the drug dealers, there are times when, frankly, we wish everybody would wear name tags ("Hi! I'm the effete ganja grower!").

I was convinced, however, by Harry and Barry—and also by Harry's collector, Big Chris, who is played by a soccer star named Vinnie Jones who became famous for squeezing in his vicelike grip that part of an opponent's anatomy that most quickly gains his full attention. They seemed plausible as East End vice retailers—seamy, cynical, middle-aged professionals in a heartless business.

I also liked the movie's sense of fun. The sound track uses a lot of rock music and narration to flaunt its attitude, it keeps most of the violence offscreen, and it's not above throwaway gags. While Eddy plays poker, for example, his three friends go next door to a pub. A man on fire comes staggering out of the door. They look at him curiously, shrug, and go in. The pub is named Samoa Joe's, which seems like a sideways nod to *Pulp Fiction* (Big Kahuna burgers crossed with Jack Rabbit Slim's restaurant). The guys sip drinks with umbrellas in them.

I sometimes feel, I confess, as if there's a Tarantino reference in every third movie made these days. *Lock, Stock and Two Smoking Barrels* is the kind of movie where you naturally play Spot the Influence: Tarantino, of course, and a dash of Hong Kong action pictures, and the old British crime comedies like *The Lavender Hill Mob.* The director, Guy Ritchie, says his greatest inspiration was *The Long Good Friday* (1980), the Cockney crime movie that made a star out of Bob Hoskins. Lurking beneath all the other sources, I suspect, is *Night and the City* (1950), Jules Dassin's masterful *noir,* also about crime in the East End, also with a crime kingpin who employs a giant bruiser.

By the end of it all, as you're reeling out trying to make sense of the plot, *Lock, Stock, etc.* seems more like an exercise in style than anything else. And so it is. We don't care much about the characters (I felt more actual affection for the phlegmatic bouncer, Barry the Baptist, than for any of the heroes). We realize that the film's style stands outside the material and is lathered on top (there are freeze-frames, jokey subtitles, speed-up, and slo-mo). And that the characters are controlled by the demands of the clockwork plot. But it's fun, in a slapdash way; it has an exuberance, and in a time when movies follow formulas like zombies, it's alive.

The Locusts ★ ★ ½

R, 124 m., 1997

Kate Capshaw (Mrs. Potts), Jeremy Davies (Flyboy), Vince Vaughn (Clay), Ashley Judd (Kitty), Paul Rudd (Earl), Daniel Meyer (Joel), Jessica Capshaw (Patsy), Jessie Robertson (Ellen). Directed by John Patrick Kelley and produced by Brad Krevoy, Steve Stabler, and Bradley Thomas. Screenplay by Kelley.

Watching *The Locusts* was like being whirled back in a time warp to the 1950s—to the steamiest and sultriest new work by William Inge or Tennessee Williams about claustrophobic lust in a twisted family. This is the kind of movie that used to star Paul Newman or William Holden, Kim Novak or Natalie Wood or Elizabeth Taylor, with Sal Mineo as the uncertain kid who's lost in confusion and despair.

Even the big emotional outbursts seem curiously dated. When the alcoholic, resentful, sluttish mother wants to wound her hated and helpless son, for example, what does she do? Staggers out into the rain and castrates his beloved bull, of course. And when it's truth time, the family secret seems almost inevitable.

The movie is not bad so much as it's absurd. I never felt I was in the hands of incompetent or untalented filmmakers, and indeed on the basis of *The Locusts,* I anticipate the next film by John Patrick Kelley, its writer-director. He has a talent for rhythm, for mood, for Gothic weirdness. This is his first film, and perhaps in trying to fill it with as much atmosphere and passion as possible, he allowed it to become overwrought.

He also has a gift for casting, and the highest praise I can give the performers here is to say they measure up to the 1950s icons I can so easily imagine in the roles. Kate Capshaw is wonderful as Mrs. Potts, the sultry widow who runs a Kansas feed lot, circa 1960, and takes one of her ranch hands into her bed every night. Vince Vaughn, from *Swingers,* is far from the fleshpots of Hollywood in this second role, as Clay, a drifter with a secret in his past, who turns up in town and is soon parked on lover's lane with Ashley Judd, as Kitty, the warmhearted local girl who wants to heal his soul. And Jeremy Davies is touching and brave in the role of Flyboy, Mrs. Potts's son, who has the full gamut of 1950s symptoms: He feels guilty about his father's suicide, he has spent eight years in an institution getting shock treatment, and now he shuffles around the house as a cowering, mute servant.

All of these characters are created in bold, confident performances of well-written roles. I liked the way Kitty, the Ashley Judd character, cuts to the chase in her dialogue, telling Clay, "So now we're going to skip the sex and go straight to the brooding?" And Kate Capshaw, her cigarette seen glowing through the porch screens on hot summer nights, brings a certain doomed poignancy to the role of a woman whose consolations are whiskey and hired studs.

Because the movie is in some ways so good, it's a shame it's so utterly, crashingly implausible. It's like an anthology of clichés from the height of Hollywood's love affair with Freud. Of course Clay is running away from a tragedy in his past, and of course Kitty wants to heal him, and of course Mrs. Potts knows a lot more than she's telling about Flyboy, and of course there will eventually be a showdown between the widow and her new hired hand.

But listen carefully when Clay tells Kitty what happened back in Kansas City. Ask yourself if Clay wasn't perhaps a mite careless in allowing that incredible chain of events. And ask yourself about the exact chronology of impregnation in the Potts household, and how its menfolk sorted it out. And remind yourself of the old theatrical rule that if a gun comes onstage in the first act it must be discharged in the third, and ask how that applies to the grisly early scene in which Clay learns how a bull becomes a steer.

There are small, quiet scenes here, however, that are just right. I was moved by Jeremy Davies in a scene where Flyboy pins one of Clay's *Playmate* foldouts to a bathroom mirror, lights an unfamiliar cigarette, and engages in conversation with the pinup (he thinks she will be interested in hearing about his bull). I admired the real pain Capshaw brought to her final scenes. And there is a wonderful moment when Kitty teaches Flyboy to dance, and then says, "Thank you for the date. It was the best one I ever had." And Flyboy has a spastic little gesture of joy.

The Locusts is not successful. Its material is so overwrought and incredible, so curiously dated, that it undermines the whole enterprise. But it was not made carelessly or cynically, it shows artists trying to do their best, and its makers had ambition. You can sense they wanted to make a great film, and that is the indispensable first step to making one—a step most films do not even attempt.

The Loss of Sexual Innocence ★ ★ ★ ½

R, 101 m., 1999

Julian Sands (Adult Nic), Johanna Torrel (His Wife), Saffron Burrows (Twins), Stefano Dionisi (Lucca), Kelly MacDonald (Susan), Jonathan Rhys-Meyers (Nic, Age Sixteen), Hanne Klintoe (Eve), Femi Ogumbanjo (Adam). Directed by Mike Figgis and produced by Figgis and Annie Stewart. Screenplay by Figgis.

Mike Figgis, who pays so much attention to the music in his films, has made one that plays like a musical composition, with themes drifting in and out, and dialogue used more for tone than speech. *The Loss of Sexual Innocence* is built of memory and dreams, following a boy named Nic as he grows from a child into a man, and intercutting his story with the story of Adam and Eve. Not all of it works, but you play along, because it's rare to find a film this ambitious.

Figgis knows how to tell a story with dialogue and characters (*Leaving Las Vegas* is his masterpiece), but here he deals with impressions, secrets, desires. His story is about the way the world breaks our own Gardens of Eden, chopping down the trees and divesting us of our illusions. The process begins early for Nic, a British boy being raised in Kenya in 1953, when through a slit in a window he observes an old white man watching while a young African girl, dressed only in lingerie, reads to him from the Bible.

We move forward ten years or so to England, where Nic, now sixteen or so, is ignored by his girlfriend, Susan, at a family function. Susan gets drunk, and Nic discovers her upstairs, necking with an older man on the bed. Later there is an earlier scene from their courtship, when Nic and Susan are younger and steal into her house at night. She makes him coffee, they kiss by the fire, and then her father enters. He doesn't "catch" them and hardly notices them; he is in pain, and takes pills. Their young love is contrasted with the end that awaits us all.

These episodes are intercut with "Scenes from Nature," as Adam and Eve (Femi Ogumbanjo and Hanne Klintoe) emerge from a pond and explore the world, and their own bodies, with amazement. The nudity here, while explicit, is theologically correct; we didn't need clothing until we sinned. The whole Eden sequence could have been dispatched with, I think (its surprise payoff tries too hard to make a point that the ending of *Walkabout* made years ago). Yet the Eden scenes are so beautifully photographed that you enjoy them even as you question them. (The first shot of Eden is a breathtaking optical illusion.)

Nic's story, as it unfolds, reveals unhappiness. As he becomes an adult, now played by Julian Sands, we see glimpses of a marriage underlined with tension. He is a film director, and there is a trip to Tunisia that ends with a surprise development that is a sudden, crushing loss of innocence. And Figgis also weaves in a strand involving twins (played by Saffron Burrows) who are separated shortly after birth, and come face-to-face with one another in an airport years later. To look at your own face on another person is a fundamental loss of innocence, because it deprives you of the assumption that you are unique.

The film has no particular statement to make

about its material (apart from the symbolism of the Eden sequence). It wants to share feelings, not thoughts. A lot of the dialogue sounds remembered, or overheard from a distance. (I was reminded of the dialogue treatment in *Bonnie and Clyde* when Bonnie goes to a family picnic and talks with her mother). We get the points that are being made, but this movie isn't about people talking to one another.

The film itself moves forward, but there are flashbacks of memory, as Nic, driving, recalls scenes from earlier life. There are two dream sequences—one for him, one for his wife, played by Johanna Torrel. Hers is about his indifference as he plays the piano while she makes love with another man. His is about his own death. We don't know if this material comes from Mike Figgis's life, but we're sure it comes from his feelings.

The Loss of Sexual Innocence is an "art film," which means it tries to do something more advanced than most commercial films (which tell stories simple enough for children, in images shocking enough for adults). It wants us to share in the process of memory, especially sexual memory. It assumes that the moments we remember most clearly are those when we lost our illusions—when we discovered the unforgiving and indifferent nature of the world. It's like drifting for a time in the film's musings, and then being invited to take another look at our own.

Lost & Found ★

PG-13, 98 m., 1999

David Spade (Dylan), Sophie Marceau (Lila), Artie Lange (Wally), Patrick Bruel (Rene), Mitchell Whitfield (Mark), Martin Sheen (Millstone), Jon Lovitz (Uncle Harry). Directed by Jeff Pollack and produced by Wayne Rice, Morrie Eisenman, Andrew A. Kosove, and Broderick Johnson. Screenplay by J. B. Cook, Marc Meeks, and David Spade.

Lost & Found is a movie about characters of limited intelligence who wander through the lonely wastes of ancient and boring formulas. No one involved seems to have had any conviction it could be great. It's the kind of movie where the hero imitates Neil Diamond—and he's not making fun of him, he's serious.

In asking us to believe David Spade as a romantic lead, it miscalculates beyond all reason. Spade is wrong by definition for romantic leads, because his persona is based on ironic narcissism and cool detachment. A girl has to be able to believe it when a guy says he loves her more than anything else in the world. When Spade says it, it means he doesn't love anything else in the world, either.

Spade plays the owner of an Italian restaurant in Los Angeles. Like not very many owners of Italian restaurants, his name is Dylan. I have three hints for Dylan: (1) Unless you know them very well, customers do not like to be caressed on their arms as you pass their tables. (2) Although waiters must touch plates while serving them, it is bad form for the owner to put his thumb on a plate while it is being eaten from. (3) During renovations, do not seat customers directly below drywall with holes ripped in it.

Most L.A. restaurant owners do not live in colorful apartment buildings where all the neighbors know each other and little old ladies play strip poker. But the screenplay throws in the colorful rental units as a way of supplying recycled sitcom characters, and to place Dylan near the apartment of Lila (Sophie Marceau), a French cellist. She has a former boyfriend named Rene (Patrick Bruel), whose function is to look pained and supply straight lines to Dylan. And she has a dog named Jack, who is treated as much like the dog in *There's Something About Mary* as is possible without actually including clips from the other movie.

Dylan and Lila have a Meet Cute. She runs into him and knocks him flat, with her landing on top, which is about the cheapest Meet Cute you can buy at the Movie Cliché Store. He falls in love with Lila, gets nowhere, and steals her dog so that he can claim to have found it and thus win her love. Lila is so unobservant that Dylan often carries the dog past her windows, and even walks it in a nearby park, without Lila ever seeing them together. When the dog needs to poop, Dylan wears one of those tool belts you see on power company linemen, with eight or nine bright plastic pooper-scoopers dangling from it. Supplying a character with too much equipment is a creaky comedy wheeze; in a good movie, they'd give him one pooper-scooper and think of something funny to do with it.

Anyway. Dylan has an employee at the restaurant named Wally (Artie Lange), who is tall, fat, and dumb, sleeps over one night, and ends up in Dylan's bed because he gets scared. As they leap to attention in the morning, they can't even think of a funny payoff (such as Steve Martin in *Planes, Trains & Automobiles,* shouting at John Candy, "That wasn't a pillow!"). Instead, when Lila rings the doorbell, they both answer the door in their underpants and she assumes they're gay. Ho, ho.

Meanwhile, Jack the dog eats junk food and throws up. When Dylan comes home, we get a nauseated-dog's-eye-view of an optically distorted Dylan dressed in 1970s disco gear while dancing to a record on the sound track. Don't ask how a dog could have this hallucination; be thankful instead that the dog's fantasies are more interesting than any other visual in the movie.

Lost & Found ends at a big lawn party for rich people, which in movies about people over twenty-one is the equivalent of the Senior Prom scene in all other movies. There is a role for Martin Sheen, as Mr. Millstone, the tight-fisted banker who wants to fly in Neil Diamond as a surprise for his wife. In 1979, Martin Sheen starred in *Apocalypse Now.* In 1999, he plays Mr. Millstone. I wish he had taken my advice and gone into the priesthood.

As for the Neil Diamond imitation, my best guess is that David Spade secretly thinks he could have a parallel career as a Las Vegas idol, and is showing us how he can do Neil Diamond better than Diamond himself. All that's lacking is for Spade to take that hank of hair that hangs in front of his eyes and part it, so that it hangs over his ears.

Truth in Criticism: The movie has one funny scene, starring Jon Lovitz, as a dog whisperer.

Lost Highway ★ ★

R, 135 m., 1997

Bill Pullman (Fred Madison), Patricia Arquette (Renee/Alice), Balthazar Getty (Pete Dayton), Robert Blake (Mystery Man), Gary Busey (Bill Dayton), Robert Loggia (Mr. Eddy/Dick Laurent), Natasha Gregson Wagner (Sheila), Richard Pryor (Arnie), Michael Massee (Andy), Jack Nance (Phil). Directed by David Lynch and produced by Deepak Nayar, Tom Sternberg, and Mary Sweeney. Screenplay by Lynch and Barry Gifford.

David Lynch's *Lost Highway* is like kissing a mirror: You like what you see, but it's not much fun and kind of cold. It's a shaggy ghost story, an exercise in style, a film made with a certain breezy contempt for audiences. I've seen it twice, hoping to make sense of it. There is no sense to be made of it. To try is to miss the point. What you see is all you get.

That's not to say it's without interest. Some of the images are effective, the sound track is strong and disturbing, and there is a moment Hitchcock would have been proud of (although Hitchcock would not have preceded or followed it with this film). Hope is constantly fanned back to life throughout the story; we keep thinking maybe Lynch will somehow pull it off until the shapeless final scenes, when we realize it really is all an empty, stylistic façade. This movie is about design, not cinema.

It opens with two nervous people living in a cold, threatening house. They hate or fear each other, we sense. "You don't mind if I don't go to the club tonight?" says the wife (Patricia Arquette). She wants to stay home and read. "Read? Read?" he chuckles bitterly. We cut to a scene that feels inspired by a 1950s roadhouse movie (*Detour,* maybe), showing the husband (Bill Pullman) as a crazy hep-cat sax player. Cut back home. Next morning. An envelope is found on their steps. Inside, a videotape of their house (which, architecturally, resembles an old IBM punch card).

More tapes arrive, including one showing the couple asleep in bed. They go to a party and meet a disturbing little man with a white clown face (Robert Blake), who ingratiatingly tells Pullman, "We met at your house. As a matter of fact, I'm there right now. Call me." He does seem to be at both ends of the line. That mirrors another nice touch in the film, which is that Pullman seems able to talk to himself over a doorbell speakerphone.

Can people be in two places at once? Why not? (Warning: Plot point coming up.) Halfway through the film, Pullman is arrested for the murder of his wife and locked in solitary confinement. One morning his guard looks in the cell door, and—good God! It's not the same man inside!

Now it's a teenager (Balthazar Getty). The prison officials can't explain how bodies could be switched in a locked cell, but have no reason to hold the kid. He's released and gets his old job at the garage. A gangster (Robert Loggia) comes in with his mistress, who is played by Patricia Arquette. Is this the same person as the murdered wife? Was the wife really murdered? Hello?

The story now focuses on the relationship between Getty and Loggia, a ruthless but ingratiating man who, in a scene of chilling comic violence, pursues a tailgater and beats him senseless ("Tailgating is one thing I can't tolerate"). Arquette comes to the garage to pick up the kid ("Why don't you take me to dinner?") and tells him a story of sexual brutality involving Loggia, who is connected to a man who makes porno films. This requires a scene where Arquette is forced to disrobe at gunpoint and stand naked in a roomful of strange men; an echo of Isabella Rossellini's humiliation in Lynch's *Blue Velvet.*

Does this scene have a point? Does any scene in the movie have a point? *Lost Highway* plays like a director's idea book in which isolated scenes and notions are jotted down for possible future use. Instead of massaging them into a finished screenplay, Lynch and collaborator Barry Gifford seem to have filmed the notes.

Is the joke on us? Is it our error to try to make sense of the film, to try to figure out why protagonists change in midstream? Let's say it is. Let's say the movie should be taken exactly as is, with no questions asked. Then what do we have? We still have just the notes for isolated scenes. There's no emotional or artistic thread running through the material to make it seem necessary that it's all in the same film together. The giveaway is that the characters have no interest apart from their situation; they exist entirely as creatures of the movie's design and conceits (except for Loggia's gangster, who has a reality, however fragmentary).

Luis Buñuel, the Spanish surrealist, once made a film in which two actresses played the same role interchangeably, in the appropriately titled *That Obscure Object of Desire* (1977). He made absolutely no attempt to explain this oddity. One woman would leave a room, and the other would reenter. And so on.

But when Lynch has Patricia Arquette apparently play two women (and Bill Pullman and Balthazar Getty perhaps play the same man), we don't feel it's a surrealistic joke. We feel—I dunno, I guess I felt jerked around. Lynch is such a talented director. Why does he pull the rug out from under his own films? I have nothing against movies of mystery, deception, and puzzlement. It's just that I'd like to think the director has an idea, a purpose, an overview beyond the arbitrary manipulation of plot elements. He knows how to put effective images on the screen, and how to use a sound track to create mood, but at the end of the film our hand closes on empty air.

Lost in Space ★ ½

PG-13, 130 m., 1998

Matt LeBlanc (Major Don West), Gary Oldman (Dr. Zachary Smith), William Hurt (Professor John Robinson), Mimi Rogers (Maureen Robinson), Heather Graham (Judy Robinson), Lacey Chabert (Penny Robinson), Jack Johnson (Will Robinson). Directed by Stephen Hopkins and produced by Mark W. Koch, Hopkins, and Akiva Goldsman. Screenplay by Goldsman.

Lost in Space is a dim-witted shoot-'em-up based on the old (I hesitate to say "classic") TV series. It's got cheesy special effects, a muddy visual look, and characters who say obvious things in obvious ways.

If it outgrosses the brilliant *Dark City,* the previous science-fiction film from the same studio, then audiences must have lost their will to be entertained.

The TV series was loosely modeled on the novel *The Swiss Family Robinson,* about a family shipwrecked far from home and using wit and ingenuity to live off the land. I loved that book, especially its detailed description of how the family made tools, machines, and a home for themselves, and trained the local animals.

The movie doesn't bother with such details. After a space battle that is the predictable curtain-raiser, and a quick explanation of why and how the Robinson family is setting off for a planet called Alpha Prime, the film takes place mostly on board their saucer-shaped ship, and involves many more space battles, showdowns, struggles, attacks, hyperspace journeys, and exploding planets. In between, the characters plow through creaky dialogue and exhausted relationship problems.

Imagine the film that could be made about a family marooned on a distant planet, using what they could salvage from their ship or forage from the environment. That screenplay would take originality, intelligence, and thought. *Lost in Space* is one of those typing-speed jobs where the screenwriter is like a stenographer, rewriting what he's seen at the movies.

The story: Earth will not survive another two decades. Alpha Prime is the only other habitable planet mankind has discovered. Professor John Robinson (William Hurt) and his family have been chosen to go there and construct a hypergate, to match the gate at the Earth end. Their journey will involve years of suspended animation, but once the other gate is functioning, humans can zip instantaneously to Alpha Prime.

There needs to be a hypergate at both ends, of course, because otherwise there's no telling where a hyperdrive will land you—as the Robinsons soon find out. Also on board are the professor's wife, Maureen (Mimi Rogers), their scientist daughter, Judy (Heather Graham), their younger daughter, Penny (Lacey Chabert), and their son, Will (Jack Johnson), who is the brains of the outfit. The ship is piloted by ace space cadet Don West (Matt LeBlanc), and includes an intelligent robot who will help with the tasks at the other end.

Oh, and lurking below deck is the evil Dr. Zachary Smith (Gary Oldman), who wants to sabotage the mission, but is trapped on board when the ship lifts off. So he awakens the Robinsons, after which the ship is thrown off course and seems doomed to fall into the Sun.

Don West has a brainstorm: They'll use the hyperdrive to zap right *through* the Sun! This strategy of course lands them in a galaxy far, far away, with a sky filled with unfamiliar stars. And then the movie ticks off a series of crises, of which I can enumerate a rebellious robot, an exploding planet, mechanical space spiders, a distracting romance, and family issues of trust and authority.

The movie might at least have been more fun to look at if it had been filmed in brighter colors. Director Stephen Hopkins and his cinematographer, Peter Levy, for some reason choose a murky, muted palate. Everything looks like a drab brown suit or a cheap rotogravure. You want to use some Windex on the screen. And Bruce Broughton's musical score saws away tirelessly with counterfeit excitement. When nothing of interest is happening on the screen, it just makes it worse when the music pretends it cares.

Of the performances, what can be said except that William Hurt, Gary Oldman, and Mimi Rogers deserve medals for remaining standing? The kids are standard-issue juveniles with straight teeth and good postures. And there is a monkeylike little alien pet who looks like he comes from a world where all living beings are clones of Felix the Cat. This is the kind of movie that, if it fell into a black hole, you wouldn't be able to tell the difference.

The Lost World: Jurassic Park ★ ★

PG-13, 134 m., 1997

Jeff Goldblum (Dr. Ian Malcolm), Julianne Moore (Dr. Sarah Harding), Pete Postlethwaite (Roland Tembo), Arliss Howard (Peter Ludlow), Richard Attenborough (John Hammond), Vince Vaughn (Nick Van Owen), Vanessa Lee Chester (Kelly Curtis), Peter Stormare (Dieter Stark), Harvey Jason (Ajay Sidhu), Richard Schiff (Eddie Carr), Thomas F. Duffy (Dr. Robert Burke), Joseph Mazzello (Tim), Ariana Richards (Lex). Directed by Steven Spielberg and produced by Gerald Molen and Colin Wilson. Screenplay by David Koepp, based on the novel by Michael Crichton.

Where is the awe? Where is the sense that if dinosaurs really walked the earth, a film about them would be more than a monster movie? Where are the ooohs and ahhhs? *The Lost World: Jurassic Park* demonstrates even more clearly than *Jurassic Park* (1993) that the underlying material is so promising it deserves a story not written on autopilot. Steven Spielberg, a gifted filmmaker, should have reimagined the material; should have seen it through the eyes of someone looking at dinosaurs, rather than through the eyes of someone looking at a box-office sequel.

The movie is well done from a technical viewpoint, yes. The dinosaurs look amazingly real, and we see them plunge into the midst of

360-degree action; a man on a motorcycle even rides between the legs of a running beast. It can be said that the creatures in this film transcend any visible signs of special effects, and seem to walk the earth. But the same realism isn't brought to the human characters, who are bound by plot conventions and action formulas, and scripted to do stupid things so that they can be chased and sometimes eaten by the dinosaurs.

Maybe it was already too late. Perhaps the time to do the thinking on this project was before the first film, when all the possibilities lay before Spielberg. He should have tossed aside the original Michael Crichton novel, knowing it had given him only one thing of use: an explanation for why dinosaurs might walk among us. Everything else—the scientific mumbo-jumbo, the theme-park scheme—was already just the recycling of other movies. We know the tired old plot lessons already, about man's greed and pride, and how it is punished, and why it does not pay to interfere with Mother Nature.

Why not a pseudodocumentary in which the routine plot elements are simply ignored, and the characters venture into the unknown and are astonished and frightened by what they find? There are moments in the first *Jurassic Park* that capture a genuine sense of wonder, the first time we see the graceful, awesome prehistoric creatures moving in stately calm beyond the trees. But soon they are cut down to size by a plot that has them chasing and scaring the human characters, as in any monster movie.

The Lost World is even more perfunctory. The plot sets up a reason for a scientist (Jeff Goldblum) to return to an island where dinosaurs survive. His girlfriend (Julianne Moore) is already there. He takes along an equipment specialist and a "video documentarian" (who comes equipped with a tiny tourist toy of a video camera and doesn't seem sure how to use it). They land on the island, are soon photographing prehistoric creatures, and so careless is the screenplay that the newcomers to the plot are not even allowed to express their amazement the first time they see their prey.

Much of the film, especially the action scenes, is shot at night in the rain. I assume that's to provide better cover for the special effects; we see relatively few dinosaurs in bright light, and the conceit is taken so far that even the press conference announcing a new dinosaur park in San Diego is held in the middle of the night. The night scenes also allow Spielberg to use his most familiar visual trademark, the visible beams from powerful flashlights, but apart from that touch Spielberg doesn't really seem present in the picture: This feels like the kind of sequel a master hands over to an apprentice, and you sense that although much effort was lavished on the special effects, Spielberg's interest in the story was perfunctory.

Here's the key to the movie's weakness: Many elaborate sequences exist only to be . . . elaborate sequences. In a better movie they would play a role in the story. Consider the drawn-out episode of the dangling research trailer, for example, which hangs over a cliff while the characters dangle above a terrifying drop and a hero tries to save the trailer from falling while a dinosaur attacks. This is only what it seems to be, an action sequence. Nothing more. It doesn't lead into or out of anything, and is not necessary, except to fill screen time. It plays like an admission that the filmmakers couldn't think of something more intriguing involving the real story line.

Consider, too, the character of Goldblum's daughter (Vanessa Lee Chester). Why is she here? To be placed in danger, to inspire contrived domestic disagreements, and to make demands so that the plot can get from A to B. At one point, inside the trailer, she gets frightened and says urgently that she "wants to go someplace real high—right now! Right now!"

So Goldblum and another character put her in a cage that lifts them above the forest, after which Goldblum must descend from the cage, after which I was asking why they had ascended in it in the first place. (Early in the film it is established that the girl is a gymnast; later the film observes the ancient principle that every gymnast in a movie sooner or later encounters a bar.)

There are some moments that work. Pete Postlethwaite, as a big game hunter who flies onto the island with a second wave of dinosaur mercenaries, doesn't step wrong; he plays a convincing, if shallow, character, even if he's called upon to make lengthy speeches in speeding jeeps, and to utter arty lines about "movable feasts" and having "spent enough time in the company of death." He alone among the major characters seems convinced he is on an island with dinosaurs, and not merely in a special-effects movie about them.

The film's structure is weird. I thought it was over, and then it began again, with a San Diego sequence in which Spielberg seemed to be trying to upstage the upcoming *Godzilla* movie. The monster-stepping-on-cars sequences in the Japanese import *Gamera: Guardian of the Universe* are more entertaining. And can we really believe that a ship could ram a pier at full speed and remain seaworthy?

The problem with the movie is that the dinosaurs aren't allowed to be the stars. They're marvelously conceived and executed, but no attempt is made to understand their fearsomeness; much of the plot hinges on mommy and daddy T-Rexes exhibiting parental feelings for their offspring. Must we see everything in human terms? At one point one character tells another, "These creatures haven't walked the earth for tens of millions of years, and now all you want to do is shoot them?" Somebody could have asked Spielberg the same question.

Love Always ½★

R, 90 m., 1997

Marisa Ryan (Julia Bradshaw), Moon Zappa (Mary Ellen), Beverly D'Angelo (Miranda), Michael Reilly Burke (Mark Righetti), James Victor (Sean), Mick Murray (Will Bradshaw), Doug Hutchinson (James), Beth Grant (Stephanie). Directed by Jude Pauline Eberhard and produced by Isaac Artenstein. Screenplay by Eberhard and Sharlene Baker.

"You are like a cluster bomb that explodes in a thousand different ways at once," the heroine is told in *Love Always.* As opposed to a cluster bomb that doesn't? I dunno. This movie is so bad in so many different ways you should see it just to put it behind you. Let's start with the dialogue. Following are verbatim quotes:

—"Someday you'll love somebody with all the intensity of the Southern Hemisphere."

—"There's a Starbuck-free America out there!"

—"To be young and in love! I think I'm gonna head out for some big open spaces."

—"Like sands in an hourglass, these are the days of our lives. That's the way the cookie crumbles."

—"Watch your back."

And my favorite, this advice from the heroine's girlfriend (Moon Zappa) as she sets out on her hitchhike odyssey across America: "Follow your intestines."

Does Jude Pauline Eberhard, the writer and director, intend these lines to be funny? Does this film belong in one of those funky festivals where people understand such things? Alas, I fear not. *Love Always* is sincere in addition to its other mistakes.

The movie tells the story of Julia Bradshaw (Marisa Ryan), an intrepid San Diego woman who finds herself in a series of situations that have no point and no payoff, although that is the screenplay's fault, not hers. Early in the film, for example, she goes to the racetrack and her horse comes in, and she says "Yes!" and rides her bike home along the beach, and we never really find out why she was at the track, but no matter, because before long the film goes to visit an amateur theatrical and we see an *entire* "rooster dance," from beginning to end, apparently because film is expensive and since they exposed it they want to show it.

The rooster dance also has nothing to do with the film, which properly gets under way when Julia gets a postcard from her onetime lover Mark, asking her to come to Spokane so he can marry her. This information is presented by filling the screen with a big close-up of the postcard, which Julia then reads aloud for us. Soon we find her in the desert with a bedroll on her back, posing photogenically on the windowsill of a deserted house so that interesting people can brake to a halt and offer her rides.

Her odyssey from San Diego to Spokane takes her via a wedding in Boston. That's a road movie for you. At one point along the way she shares the driving with a woman who is delivering big ceramic cows to a dairy. After Julia drops a ceramic calf and breaks it, she drives the truck to Vegas to get another calf, but when she gets there the ceramic cow lady's husband tells her the dairy canceled the order, so Julia wanders the Strip in Vegas, no doubt because the Road Movie Rule Book requires at least one montage of casino signs.

Back on the road, Julia meets a band of women in a van. They are the Virgin Sluts. They dress like models for ads for grunge clubs in free weeklies in the larger cities of smaller states. She is thrilled to meet them at last. She also meets a make-out artist, a sensitive photographer, and a guy who is convinced he has the movie's Dennis Hopper role. On and on her odyssey goes, until finally she gets to Spokane, where she finds out that Mark is a louse, as we knew already because he didn't send her bus fare.

Love and Death on Long Island

★★★½

PG-13, 93 m., 1998

John Hurt (Giles De'Ath), Jason Priestley (Ronnie Bostock), Fiona Loewi (Audrey), Sheila Hancock (Mrs. Barker), Maury Chaykin (Irving), Gawn Grainger (Henry), Elizabeth Quinn (Mrs. Reed), Linda Busby (Mrs. Abbott). Directed by Richard Kwietniowski and produced by Steve Clark-Hall and Christopher Zimmer. Screenplay by Kwientniowski, based on the novel by Gilbert Adair.

A creaky British writer, who has lived for decades in a cocoon of his books and his musings, locks himself out of the house one day in the rain. He takes refuge in a nearby movie theater, choosing a film based on a novel by Forster. After a time he murmurs, "This isn't E. M. Forster!" And he begins to collect his coat and hat so that he can leave.

Indeed it is not Forster. The film is *Hotpants College II,* about the hijinks of a crowd of randy undergraduates. But as the writer, named Giles De'Ath, rises to his feet, he sees an image that causes him to pause. The camera slowly zooms in on his face, illuminated by the flickering light reflected from the screen, as he stands transfixed by the sight of a young actor named Ronnie Bostock.

It is this moment of rapture that gives *Love and Death on Long Island* its sly comic enchantment. Giles De'Ath, played by John Hurt as a man long settled in his dry and dusty ways, has fallen in love with a Hollywood teen idol, and his pursuit of this ideal leads him stumbling into the twentieth century. He finds that films can be rented, and goes to a video store to obtain two other Ronnie Bostock titles, *Tex Mex* and *Skidmarks.*

Dressed like an actor playing T. S. Eliot, discussing the titles with the clerk as if he were speaking to a librarian in the British Museum, he rents the tapes and brings them home, only to find that he needs a VCR. He purchases the VCR, and has it delivered to his book-lined study, where the delivery man gently explains why he will also require a television set.

At last, banishing his housekeeper from his study, Giles settles down into a long contemplation of the life and work of Ronnie Bostock. He even obtains teenage fan magazines (the cover of one calls Bostock "snoggable!"), and cuts out Ronnie's photos to paste them in a scrapbook, which in his elaborate cursive script he labels "Bostockiana." He sneaks out to dispose of the magazines as if they were pornography, and daydreams of a TV quiz show on which he would know all the answers to trivia questions about Ronnie (Favorite author: Stephen King. Favorite musician: Axel Rose).

These opening scenes of *Love and Death on Long Island* are funny and touching, and Hurt brings a dignity to Giles De'Ath that transcends any snickering amusement at his infatuation. It's not even perfectly clear that Giles's feelings are homosexual; he has been married, now lives as a widower, and there is no indication that he has (or for that matter had) any sex life at all. At lunch with his bewildered agent, he speaks of "the discovery of beauty where no one ever thought of looking for it." And in a lecture on "The Death of the Future," he spins off into rhapsodies about smiles (he is thinking only about Ronnie's).

There is something here like the obsession of the little man in *Monsieur Hire,* who spies adoringly on the young woman whose window is opposite his own. No physical action is contemplated: Sexual energy has been focused into the eyes and the imagination. The cinema of Ronnie Bostock, Giles believes, "has brought me into contact with all I never have been."

It is always a disappointment when fantasies become real; no mere person can equal our imaginings. Giles actually flies to Long Island, where he knows Bostock has a home, and sets out to find his idol. This journey into the new land is not without hazards for the reclusive London writer, who checks into a hot-sheets motel and soon finds himself hanging out at Chez D'Irv, a diner where the owner (Maury Chaykin) refers to almost everything as "very attractive."

But eventually Giles does find his quarry. First he meets Audrey (Fiona Loewi), Ronnie's girlfriend, and then Ronnie himself, played by Jason Priestley with a sort of distant friendliness that melts a little when Giles starts comparing his films with Shakespeare's bawdy passages. The film doesn't commit the mistake of making Ronnie stupid and shallow, and Audrey is very smart; there's a scene where she looks at Giles long and hard, as his cover story evaporates in her mind.

I almost wish Giles had never gotten to Long Island—had never met the object of his dreams. The film, directed by Richard Kwietniowski and based on a novel by the British film critic Gilbert Adair, steps carefully in the American scenes, and finds a way to end without cheap melodrama or easy emotion. But the heart of the film is in Giles's fascination, his reveries about Ronnie's perfection.

There is a scene in *Hotpants College II* in which Ronnie reclines on the counter of a hamburger joint, and his pose immediately reminds Giles of Henry Wallis's famous painting *The Death of Chatterton,* in which the young poet is found dead on his bed in a garret. Thomas Chatterton was to the eighteenth century as Bostock is to ours, I suppose: sex symbol, star, popular entertainer, golden youth. It's all in how you look at it.

Love and Other Catastrophes ★ ★

R, 79 m., 1997

Alice Garner (Alice), Frances O'Connor (Mia), Matthew Dyktynski (Ari), Matt Day (Michael), Radha Mitchell (Danni), Suzi Dougherty (Savita), Kim Gyngell (Professor Leach). Directed by Emma-Kate Croghan and produced by Stavros Andonis Efthymiou. Screenplay by Yael Bergman, Croghan, and Helen Bandis, based on a story by Efthymiou.

Love and Other Catastrophes is one of those first films that makes you long for the second one. Shot in seventeen days on lunch money, it's a campus comedy about love, roommates, professors, sex, and paying your overdue library fine so you can switch departments. There's a lot of potential charm here, but the director, Emma-Kate Croghan, is so distracted by stylistic quirks that the characters are forever being upstaged by the shots they're in.

The movie has been described as a Generation X film from Australia, although most of the students seem young enough to belong to that unnamed generation that has come along since X. True Xers, I think, are now thirtyish, and if you're twentyish you'd no more want to be described as an Xer than a hippie would want to be called a beatnik. Time flies; the generational nicknames ought to keep up with it.

The film's central characters are two roommates: Mia (Frances O'Connor), a lesbian who's breaking up with her girlfriend, and Alice (Alice Garner), who has a crush on one guy while another guy has a crush on her. The other potential romantic partners: Danni (Radha Mitchell), who in retaliation against Mia is seeing another woman; Ari (Matthew Dyktynski), the sort of playboy that Alice likes; and Michael (Matt Day), shy and inarticulate, who is in love with Alice.

All of these people are, of course, terminally cool about their sexuality. That's too bad, because a little uncertainty and doubt can make a great contribution to a comedy (see Kevin Smith's *Chasing Amy,* in which the hero's discovery that the girl he loves is a lesbian leads to inspired dialogue and deeply heartfelt misunderstandings). To put it another way, the characters in *Love and Other Catastrophes* don't seem *needy* enough to require a movie about them; they're self-contained as they are.

The amusing stuff in the movie has to do with campus bureaucracy. Most campuses, everywhere in the world, are run not by their faculties but by two ubiquitous types of staff members: (1) part-time or dropout students who affect a studied disdain for their jobs, and (2) local clerical employees who follow all of the rules as a form of sadism. Alice's best scenes involve her thesis ("Doris Day: Feminist Warrior"), which is four years past due, and her cinema professor (Kym Gyngell), who eats a doughnut in every single scene. (They must not have Dunkin' Donuts shops in Australia, since no company works harder at placing its products in movie scenes, and yet these doughnuts are merely generic.)

Meanwhile, Mia is trying to change departments, but first must pay a library fine, which requires her to shuttle from one uninterested bureaucrat to another in a frustrating process that reminded me of the similar but better scenes in *Gridlock'd.* These academic crises are the counterpoint to the challenges in their sex lives.

The characters are all bright and edgy, and I expect to see them again in movies that feel more finished. *Love and Other Catastrophes* affects a visual style in the same spirit of the unreadable graphics of many new magazines, where typefaces slam up against each other and yellow print is put on brown backgrounds. The whole movie seems to have been subtly tinted brown, scenes play more like sketches for scenes, and there is a general air of self-congratulation on how clever everyone is.

Movies like this are intensely interesting to the people in them, just as people like this are intensely interesting to one another. Outsiders (moviegoers, say) are justified in asking what larger appeal the characters have. I admit they have some interest: I would like to know more about them, and if the movie had told me more, I might have liked it more. Emma-Kate Croghan has talent or she wouldn't have been able to get this movie made. Now she needs time and money. And a less insistent style. And a better screenplay.

Love Is the Devil ★ ★ ★ ½

NO MPAA RATING, 91 m., 1998

Derek Jacobi (Francis Bacon), Daniel Craig (George Dyer), Tilda Swinton (Muriel Belcher), Anne Lambton (Isabel Rawsthorne), Adrian Scarborough (Daniel Farson), Karl Johnson (John Deakin), Annabel Brooks (Henrietta Moraes). Directed by John Maybury and produced by Chiara Menage. Screenplay by Maybury.

I almost climbed the stairs to the Colony Room once. I wanted to see what it looked like inside. I'd read Daniel Farson's *Soho in the 1950s,* and knew that in a shabby room over Trattoria Otello on Dean Street a woman named Muriel Belcher had long presided over the maintenance and upkeep of a generation of Soho alcoholics. After her death, Ian Board continued the tradition, but did not insult the inmates as much.

I knew that the painters Francis Bacon and Lucian Freud, the writer Jeffrey Bernard, the disgraced *Vogue* photographer John Deakin, and Farson himself had frequented the club, along with such celebrity visitors as Peter O'Toole and Richard Harris. In a time when the London pubs closed in the afternoons and again at 11 P.M., it was a place where you could get a drink pretty much whenever you wanted one.

I didn't climb the stairs. I felt too acutely that I didn't belong. I was not and never would be a member. No matter all the books I'd read, all the things I thought I knew about the Colony Room, I would be seen as a tourist, a foolish grin on my face. That was something I could not abide. I stood on the street and looked upstairs and walked on.

Love Is the Devil, the new film by John Maybury, takes me at last up those stairs and back in time to the decades when Francis Bacon presided over a scruffy roomful of bohemians—some rich, some poor, some gay, some straight, all drunks. The movie is loosely inspired by Farson's *The Gilded Gutter Life of Francis Bacon,* which documents the life of the greatest modern English painter as a dour and bitter ordeal, the bitchiness relieved intermittently by a good vintage and the Dover sole at Wheeler's. (Bacon liked a crowd at lunch, and didn't mind picking up the check.)

To look at a Francis Bacon painting is to get a good idea of the man who painted it. In an era of abstract expressionism, he defiantly painted the figure, because he wanted there to be no mistake: His subject was the human body seen in anguish and ugliness. Flesh clung to the bones of his models like dough slapped on by a careless god. His faces were often distorted into grimaces of pain or despair. His subjects looked like mutations, their flesh melting from radiation or self-loathing. His color sense was uncanny, his draftsmanship was powerful and unmistakable, his art gave an overwhelming sense of the artist.

There are no paintings by Francis Bacon in *Love Is the Devil.* Permission was refused by the estate. What are they waiting for, a film that shows him as a nice guy? It is an advantage to the movie, actually, to do without the actual work: Maybury doesn't have to photograph it devoutly, and the flow of the film is not interrupted by our awareness that we are looking at the real thing. Instead, Maybury and his cinematographer, John Mathieson, make the film itself look like a Bacon. They use filters and lenses to distort faces. They shoot reflections in beer mugs and ashtrays to elongate and stretch images. They use reflections to suggest his diptychs and triptychs. A viewer who has never seen a Bacon would be able to leave this film and identify one instantly in a gallery.

Bacon is played by Derek Jacobi (the king in Branagh's *Hamlet*) as a cold and emotionally careless man, a ginger-haired chipmunk who occupies a studio filled with the debris of his art. (He worked from photographs that fell to the floor and built up into a mulch beneath his feet.) One night while he is sleeping, a burglar breaks in through the skylight. The paintings inside are worth millions, but this burglar, named George Dyer (Daniel Craig), knows nothing of Bacon or his paintings. He's looking for pawnable loot. Bacon awakens and makes him a deal: "Take your clothes off and come to bed. Then you can have whatever you want."

George stays on as Bacon's lover. Bacon is a masochist in private, a sadist in public; at first he is touched by George's naïveté ("You actually make money out of painting?"), but eventually he tires of him. George is neurotic, always obsessively scrubbing his nails, and when he threatens suicide Bacon leaps to the attack, referring to "the beam in the studio screaming to have a rope thrown over it."

Whether *Love Is the Devil* is an accurate portrait of Bacon I have no idea. It faithfully reflects the painter as he is described in Farson's book, which is cited as a source for the movie. No one who has seen a Bacon painting expects a portrait much different than this one. From glimpses of the same Soho haunts in books by the late, celebrated drunk Jeffrey Bernard (whose weekly column in the *Spectator* was described as the world's longest-running suicide note), I recognized Belcher and Board and all the others who used the Colony Room as a refuge from an outer world in which they were always two or three drinks behind.

love jones ★ ★ ★

R, 110 m., 1997

Larenz Tate (Darius), Nia Long (Nina), Bill Bellamy (Hollywood), Isaiah Washington (Savon), Lisa Nicole Carson (Josie), Bernadette Clarke (Sheila), Khalil Kain (Marvin). Directed by Theodore Witcher and produced by Nick Wechsler and Jeremiah Samuels. Screenplay by Witcher.

love jones is a love story set in the world of Chicago's middle-class black artists and professionals—which is to say, it shows a world more unfamiliar to moviegoers than the far side of the Moon. It is also frankly romantic and erotic, and smart; this is the first movie in a while where the guy quotes Mozart and the girl tells him he's really thinking of Shaw.

The movie stars Nia Long as Nina, a professional photographer, and Larenz Tate as Darius, a novelist. After an opening montage of great black and white Chicago scenes (Nina's photographs, we learn), they Meet Cute at the Sanctuary, a club inspired by the various venues around town for poetry slams, cool jazz, and upscale dating. His moves are smooth: He meets her, walks to the mike, and retitles his poem "A Blues for Nina," reading it to her across the smoky room. She likes that. "Maybe next week you'll write something for me," he says. They engage in flirt-talk. "There are other things than sex," she tells him. Like what? he wants to know. She takes a pen and writes "love" on his wrist.

As their relationship develops, we see it in the context of the world they live in, a world of African-American artists, writers, teachers, and intellectuals. The film's writer-director, Theodore Witcher, says he wanted to suggest a modern Chicago version of the Harlem Renaissance, but this is the 1920s filtered through modern eyes, and some of the parties they attend have conversation that sounds like hip campus faculty talk.

The relationship between Darius and Nina proceeds, but not smoothly. Is it just a sex thing? They talk about that. She's on the rebound from her last man, and tells Darius "the timing is bad," but it starts looking pretty good. And their chemistry, as characters and actors, is hot. There's a sensuous scene where they go to her place, and she loads her camera and tells him to strip, and shoots him while he's teasing her. This nicely turns the gender tables on the famous *Blow Up* scene where the photographer made love through his camera.

Witcher's screenplay is not content to move from A to B to love. There are hurt feelings and misunderstandings, and Nina goes to New York at one point to see her former fiancé and find out if there's still life in their relationship. I didn't buy that New York trip; it seemed clear to me that Darius was her love, and if she was merely testing him, why take a chance of losing a good thing? Darius starts seeing another woman, she starts dating his best friend, and a completely avoidable misunderstanding develops.

I felt frustrated, but I was happy to. When movie characters inspire my affection so that I want them to stay together when they don't, that shows the movie's working. And there is a very nice sequence when they both end up at a party with other people, and see each other across the room, and are hurt.

These two characters are charismatic. There's electricity when they go on a date to the weekly Steppin' ball hosted by Herb Kent the Cool Gent, who plays himself. Steppin' is a Chicago dance style that comes out of jitterbug, cooled down, and as we watch this scene we get that interesting feeling when a fiction film edges toward documentary and shows us something we haven't seen before.

Nia Long and Larenz Tate are destined for more starring roles. They embody qualities we associate with Whitney Houston and Denzel Washington: They're fresh, have a sense of humor, and are almost implausibly good-looking. It's hard to believe that Tate—so smooth, literate, and attractive here—played the savage killer O-Dog in *Menace II Society.* Nia Long was Brandi, one of the girlfriends, in *Boyz N the Hood. love jones* extends their range, to put it mildly.

Witcher has a good eye for locations. You can see Loop skyscrapers in the backgrounds of a lot of shots, so you know this is Chicago, but movies haven't shown us these neighborhoods before. Scenes are set in Hyde Park, on the near North Side, and in between. As the characters move from coffee bars to record stores to restaurants to the Sanctuary, we realize how painfully limited the media vision of urban black life is. Why do the movies give us so many homeboys and gangstas and druggies and so few photographers, poets, and teachers?

The title is spelled all lower case. That kind of typography was popular in avant-garde circles from the 1920s through the 1950s, on everything from book covers to record album jackets. I think Witcher is trying to evoke the tone of that period when bohemia was still somewhat secret, when success was not measured only by sales, when fictional characters wrote novels instead of computer programs and futures contracts. There is also a bow to the unconventional in the ending of his film. Many love stories contrive to get their characters together at the end. This one contrives, not to keep them apart, but to bring them to a bittersweet awareness that is above simple love. Some audience members would probably prefer a romantic embrace in the sunset, as the music swells. But *love jones* is too smart for that.

Lovers of the Arctic Circle ★ ★ ★

R, 112 m., 1999

Fele Martinez (Otto), Najwa Nimi (Ana), Nancho Novo (Alvaro), Maru Valdivielso (Olga), Peru Medem (Otto [Child]), Sara Valiente (Ana [Child]), Victor Hugo Oliveira (Otto [Teenager]), Kristel Diaz (Ana [Teen ager]). Directed by Julio Medem and produced by Fernando Bovaira and Enrique Lopez Lavigne. Screenplay by Medem.

palindrome, n. Word, verse, sentence, etc., that reads the same backward as forward (e.g., madam, radar).

There is a certain kind of mind that enjoys difficulties. It is not enough to reach the objective; one must do it in a certain way. We begin by not stepping on the cracks in the sidewalk. Some never stop. Ernest Wright wrote an entire novel without using the letter "e." Hitchcock made a film without a single visible edit. There are paintings made of dots, piano compositions for one hand, and now here is a strange and haunting movie that wants to be a palindrome.

Lovers of the Arctic Circle tells the story of Ana and Otto, whose names are palindromes, and whose lives seem governed by circular patterns. Events at the beginning are related to events at the end. The movie is about love—or, rather, about their grand ideas of romance. It is comforting to think that we can love so powerfully that fate itself wheels and turns at the command of our souls.

Ana and Otto are seen at three periods of their lives. When they are small, they have a chance meeting in the woods, and Otto falls in love with Ana. A message he writes on a paper airplane leads to a meeting between their parents, who fall in love, and there is a marvelous shot of Otto's face when he realizes that the girl he loves is going to become his stepsister. As teenagers, they are lovers. As adults, they are separated—although for one heart-stopping moment they sit back to back in a Spanish café, each unaware of the other. And then fate takes them both to Finland, where the great circles of their lives meet again.

Julio Medem, who wrote and directed *Lovers of the Arctic Circle,* suggests that plot alone is not enough to explain a great love; faith is necessary, and an almost mystical belief that one is destined to share life with a single chosen person. His film more or less begins when Ana and Otto are young, and ends when they are older, but the story line is intercut with scenes and images that move back and forth in time and only gradually reveal their meanings. The shot at the beginning, for example, when one character is reflected in the eyes of another—we find out what that means at the end. And there are moments when a car either does, or does not, crash into a red bus. All becomes clear.

When you have a metaphysical system tiptoeing through a film, it's important that the actors provide a grounding of reality; otherwise, we're down the rabbit hole. There are many stretches in *Lovers of the Arctic Circle* that play just like ordinary drama, as we see the children growing up, we see their parents falling in love, we share the anger of Otto's mother when his father chooses the other woman, and we sense her hurt when Otto announces he wants to move in with the other family (it's not that he doesn't love his mother—but that he loves Ana more). There's even room for Ana's discovery that her mother may not be entirely faithful.

The romance between Ana and Otto (played by three sets of actors) is seen growing over many years, from a moment when young Otto wants to tell Ana he loves her, to a moment when he touches her leg, to a moment in their adolescence when she sends him a note: "Come to me tonight! Jump through the window. Be brave!" The movie doesn't linger on sexual details, but is interested instead in the whole arc of a life. It reminded me of the Kieslowski films in which characters are buffeted by chance, fate, and coincidence. And of Vincent Ward's *A Map of the Human Heart.* Yes, we have free will, such films are saying, and can choose as we want—but what ungoverned forces produce the choices we choose from?

Everything in the film is connected. A German pilot in World War II is linked to another pilot, years later. A story in a newspaper changes its meaning the more we learn. Who steps into the street at the wrong moment, and what happens then? It would be unfair to the film to tell. This is not the sort of movie where you can give away the ending. It is all ending. "In my end is my beginning," T. S. Eliot wrote. By now you are either confused by my description of the film, or intrigued by it. There is a certain kind of mind that enjoys difficulties. Are we not drawn onward to a new era? Give or take an "a"?

Love Serenade ★ ★ ★

R, 101 m., 1997

Miranda Otto (Dimity Hurley), Rebecca Frith (Vicki-Ann Hurley), George Shevtsov (Ken Sherry), John Alansu (Albert Lee), Jessica Napier (Deborah), Jill McWilliam (Curler Victim), Ryan Jackson (Boy on Ride), Sabrina Norris (Beautiful Baby). Directed by Shirley Barrett and produced by Jan Chapman. Screenplay by Barrett.

"I've come to Sunray to escape the hustle and bustle of the big city," Ken Sherry explains. He says that like he says everything else, in a dry, flat voice that defies you to believe him. He is the new disc jockey at the local radio station, a fifty-watt operation in a ramshackle hut where all the songs are still on vinyl. He has been divorced three times.

Dimity and Vicki-Ann Hurley live next door

to the house he's rented. They are unspeakably thrilled to think that a big radio personality like Ken Sherry (George Shevtsov) would come all the way from Brisbane to live in their moribund corner of the Australian outback. Until he arrived, the only way to pass the time was to go fishing. They offer him a fish. He says he doesn't eat fish. Then how about a chicken casserole?

The opening scenes of *Love Serenade* play like a definition of the kind of movie that fascinates me. I like films with a very specific sense of place, with characters who are defiantly individual, with plots it is impossible to anticipate. There is the suggestion that *Love Serenade* will be some kind of a love triangle, with both sisters competing for the disc jockey's attention—but something about Ken Sherry's implacable, insolent, lazy personality suggests that he has secrets we have not even remotely guessed.

Australian films love to create strange characters. Movies like *Sweetie*, *Muriel's Wedding*, and *Strictly Ballroom* were populated by people whose lives seem made out of pop fantasies and sheer desperation. The Hurley girls are like that. Vicki-Ann (Rebecca Frith) works in a hair salon (the Hairport), and Dimity (Miranda Otto) is a waitress at the downtown Chinese restaurant, where the owner, Albert Lee (John Alansu), sings "Wichita Lineman" in a mournful baritone. When Ken Sherry walks into the restaurant, Dimity breathlessly blurts out, "Excuse me for interfering, but my sister Vicki-Ann is looking for a boyfriend and we live right next door to you!" Sherry regards her like a specimen on a microscope slide: "What about you? Are *you* looking for a boyfriend?"

She is. Their seduction scene is the least erotic in the history of movies. They discuss whether fish have souls and if they can go to heaven. He speaks about how lonely he is. She offers to ease his loneliness. He remains so impassive that his seduction technique seems to involve challenging women to make him notice them. (The long-faced George Shevtsov plays the character with such snaky detachment that even while we're watching this film we want to see him in others.)

Vicki-Ann, who believes the theory that the way to a man's heart is through his stomach, has adopted the casserole method of seduction, and is shattered to learn that her kid sister has scored first, using more direct methods. But soon both sisters have enjoyed, or endured, or survived Ken Sherry's charms. And peering out from behind their blinds or peeking over the top of the backyard fence, they remain fascinated by his lifestyle. What does he do in there? What is he like?

The film gives an almost physical sense of the small town of Sunray. The sisters meet for lunch at a picnic table in an exhausted park. The main street is almost always deserted. A creek bed is dried up. The sun beats down. The buildings seem to wince in its heat. The radio station is the local outpost, however attenuated, of the glamorous world of show business. Ken Sherry pulls the microphone closer and dedicates songs to "broken dreams." He plays the kind of 1970s songs favored by lounge acts.

And then there is a secret, gradually revealed, about the deejay. Is it strange? Very strange. Does it provide the film with an ending that could not under any circumstances have been guessed? It does. Is it necessary? I don't know. The flat, ironic, desperate but hopeful lives of the sisters might have supplied all the humor the movie needed, and Ken Sherry was certainly odd enough before the final revelations. Still, I am always grateful when a movie shows me something I have never seen before. And in this case, something I shall undoubtedly never see again.

Love! Valour! Compassion! ★ ★ ★

R, 115 m., 1997

Jason Alexander (Buzz Hauser), Randy Becker (Ramon Fornos), Stephen Bogardus (Gregory Mitchell), John Glover (John and James Jeckyll), John Benjamin Hickey (Arthur Pape), Justin Kirk (Bobby Brahms), Stephen Spinella (Perry Sellars). Directed by Joe Mantello and produced by Doug Chapin and Barry Krost. Screenplay by Terrence McNally, based on his play.

In its structure, Terrence McNally's *Love! Valour! Compassion!* is as old-fashioned as a nineteenth-century three-act play. A group of friends meet for a June weekend in a country house. In midsummer, they meet again. At summer's end, they meet a third time. In the first act the characters are introduced and their problems are established. In the second, there is conflict and crisis. In the third, truth and resolution. When this play won its 1994 Tony Award, it wasn't for technical innovation.

In content, too, the material is not original. All of the friends are gay men, and during the course of the drama some of their relationships will dissolve and some will strengthen, and new ones will form. And the specter of AIDS will hover over the drama, which is one of the ways these characters must be different from, say, the characters in *The Boys in the Band.* In crisis, some of the characters will behave well and others badly, and there will be a bittersweet conclusion in which we discover that some will die and others will live, some will be happy and others will remain sad and lonely.

As a formula, this will do nicely for any set of characters of your choice. The dramatic arc is so traditional it's almost reassuring. Yet *Love! Valour! Compassion!* has power and insight, and perhaps what makes it strong is its disinterest in technical experiments: It is about characters and dialogue, expressed through good acting—the very definition of the "well-made play."

Joe Mantello, who directed the play off-Broadway and makes his film debut here, is more concerned with recording the performances than with visual innovation. He allows himself small flashes of wit (one of the characters, packing his bag, throws in flannel shirts, Winstons, and handcuffs).

But basically he's at the service of the material, which builds firmly and observantly into a touching record of human life—not gay, but universal, since the real issues in the play do not depend on sexuality but on character.

"I hope you appreciate the details," says the narrator, Gregory (Stephen Bogardus), taking us on a tour of his rambling Victorian lakeside home. He's proud of the architecture and the furnishings. He is a successful choreographer, and lives there with his lover, Bobby (Justin Kirk), who is blind. We see some of the guests arriving, including the acerbic, lonely British composer John Jeckyll (John Glover), who observes acidly, "What kind of statement do you think a choreographer is making about his work when he lives with a blind person?"

John has a new boyfriend along, named Ramon (Randy Becker), who is a darkly handsome hunk. Other guests include Buzz (Jason Alexander), who has memorized countless Broadway musicals and quotes them compulsively; and Perry (Stephen Spinella) and Arthur (John Benjamin Hickey), who will celebrate their fourteenth anniversary this summer.

Ramon, of course, is the equivalent of the loaded gun which, brought onstage in the first act, must eventually fire. In an early scene that will not puzzle Freudians, he encounters the blind Bobby feeling a tree, and silently places himself in Bobby's way. Soon the two of them are grappling passionately in the kitchen at night, and when Bobby confesses his infidelity to Gregory, their relationship is shaken. That will not be the last of the mischief provoked by Ramon, although he is not a bad person, simply a young one more concerned with pleasure than commitment.

The relationship between John and Ramon is exclusively a sexual one, we see; John is a bitter misanthrope who likes to stand apart from the others, smoking and brooding. In midsummer he gets a call from his twin, James, an AIDS sufferer who needs help and arrives to join the house party. Both characters are played by Glover, who won a Tony for this dual role on Broadway and contributes the two best performances in the film.

It's almost impossible to play a dual role without falling into the *Parent Trap* syndrome, in which the audience spends most of the movie trying to spot the secrets of the trick photography and camera angles, but Glover does it: Both of the Jeckyll brothers are so well acted that we believe in them as individuals, even when they have scenes together.

James is the sweet twin, the one everyone likes. John has spent a lifetime mired in resentment. "You got the good soul; I got the bad one," John tells James, and in a strong late scene: "What's the secret of unconditional love? I'm not going to let you die with it." But it is Buzz (Alexander) who finds and shares that secret, and the movie's best single scene is a quiet conversation on a shaded porch between Buzz and James.

Love! Valour! Compassion! has, of course,

been compared to *The Boys in the Band* because of their obvious similarities, but there are as many differences, and one of them is crucial: This story is not about homosexuality, but about homosexuals. The 1970 movie was the first frank big-studio treatment of uncloseted gays, and much of the movie was preoccupied with how they "got" to be gay, and how they felt about being gay, and how they "accepted" their homosexuality, etc.—an encounter group with drinks served. In *Love! Valour! Compassion!* the characters' sexuality is the air they breathe, the natures they were given; the point is not how they make love, but simply how they love, or fail to love.

There is still ground to be broken and depths to be discovered in drama about homosexuals. There will eventually be a play like this in which one of the characters need not be an expert on the works of Ethel Merman and Gertrude Lawrence, and none of the characters will perform in tutus. The most successful film explorations of homosexuality so far have been about lesbians *(Lianna, The Incredibly True Adventures of Two Girls in Love)*. Perhaps that's because women, as a gender, prefer to begin with a relationship and move on to sexuality, while men usually approach it the other way around. But *Love! Valour! Compassion!* is a touching and perceptive film, about themes anyone can identify with: loneliness, jealousy, need, generosity.

Love Walked In ★ ★

R, 90 m., 1998

Denis Leary (Jack Hanaway), Terence Stamp (Fred Moore), Aitana Sanchez-Gijon (Vicki Rivas), Danny Nucci (Cousin Matt), Moira Kelly (Vera), Michael Badalucco (Eddie Bianco), Gene Canfield (Joey), Marj Dusay (Judith Moore). Directed by Juan J. Campanella and produced by Ricardo Freixa. Screenplay by Campanella, Lynn Geller, and Larry Golin, based on a novel by Jose Pablo Feinmann.

Love Walked In proves something that nobody ever thought to demonstrate before: You can't make a convincing *film noir* about good people. *Noir* is about weakness and temptation, and if the characters are going to get soppy and let their better natures prevail, what's left? Has there ever been a thriller about resisting temptation?

The movie has two other problems: It requires the female lead to behave in a way that's contrary to everything we know about her. And it intercuts the action with an absurd parallel story, a fantasy the hero is writing. He hopes to become a novelist, but on the basis of this sample he should stick to playing the piano. Oh, and the filmmakers should have guessed that the big ending, where the hero falls out of a tree, would inspire laughs just when the movie doesn't need any.

Yet the elements are here for a decent *film noir.* There is, first of all, good casting. Denis Leary plays Jack, a world-weary pianist in a fleapit lounge named the Blue Cat. Aitana Sanchez-Gijon is Vicki, his wife, a songstress who has a way with the pseudo-Gershwin tunes Jack writes. And Terence Stamp, he of the penetrating blue eyes and saturnine features, is a rich man named Moore who frequents the lounge and whose desire stirs for Vicki. Leary has been in a lot of movies lately *(The Real Blonde, Wag the Dog)*, but this is the one where he really emerges: He began as a comedian learning to act, but now you can see that he has the stuff, that given a good script he could handle an important role.

Aitana Sanchez-Gijon (Keanu Reeves's love in *A Walk in the Clouds*) is also just right; you can see how this situation could have been rewritten into a workable *noir.* But neither she nor any other actress could convincingly handle the scenes where she is required to mislead Moore. Women don't work that way. Oh, a femme fatale might, but the whole point is that Vicki's heart is in the right place.

The setup: Jack and Vicki are desperately poor after ten years of touring crummy clubs. (Strange, since they're talented.) Jack's old buddy Eddie (Michael Badalucco), now a private eye, turns up and reveals he's been hired by Moore's jealous wife to get the dirt on him. Since Moore has the hots for Vicki, Eddie says, why not blackmail him—which would rescue Vicki and Jack from poverty row: "You guys have the real thing. All you need is a little dough to complete the picture."

This is a classic *noir* suggestion. And in a different kind of film we'd believe it when Jack suggests this plan to Vicki. But we never sense that Vicki is that kind of girl. She's wounded when she first hears the plan; Jack says she'd only have to "make out" with Moore long enough for Eddie to take photos, and Vicki shoots back, "Make out? How much? Second base? Third? Home run?" But she goes along with the scheme, even though the movie lacks any scene or motivation to explain her change of heart—or indeed, any way of telling what she's really thinking most of the time. Her character is seen entirely from the outside, as an enigma, and maybe that's exactly what she was to the writer-director, Juan J. Campanella.

As for Jack, his character is confusingly written, and it doesn't help that he constantly interrupts the action with cutaways to a parallel story, which he narrates with Rod Serlingesque solemnity. The plot whips itself into a frenzied payoff, with thunder and lightning on cue, as Jack finds himself out on a limb in a scene that would be plausible, unfortunately, only if played by John Belushi in *Animal House.*

Love Walked In has the right moves for *noir:* the melancholy, the sexiness, the cigarettes, the shadows. But you have to believe in the characters and their capacity for evildoing. These characters act like they saw *Double Indemnity* on TV once and thought they could do that stuff themselves, and were wrong.

M

Maborosi ★ ★ ★ ★

NO MPAA RATING, 110 m., 1997

Makiko Esumi (Yumiko), Takashi Naitoh (Tamio, Second Husband), Tadanobu Asano (Ikuo, First Husband), Gohki Kashiyama (Yuichi, Yumiko's Son), Naomi Watanabe (Tomoko, Tamio's Daughter), Midori Kiuchi (Michiko, Yumiko's Mother), Akira Emoto (Yoshihiro, Tamio's Father), Mutsuko Sakura (Tomeno). Directed by Hirokazu Kore-Edaand produced by Naoe Gozu. Screenplay by Yoshihisa Ogita, based on a story by Teru Miyamoto.

Maborosi is a Japanese film of astonishing beauty and sadness, the story of a woman whose happiness is destroyed in an instant by an event that seems to have no reason. Time passes, she picks up some of the pieces, and she is even distracted sometimes by happiness. But at her center is a void, a great unanswered question.

The woman, named Yumiko, is played by the fashion model Makiko Esumi. Models are not always good actresses, but Esumi is the right choice for this role. Tall, slender, and grave, she brings a great stillness to the screen. Her character speaks little; many shots show her seated in thought, absorbed in herself. She is dressed always in long, dark dresses—no pants or jeans—and she becomes after a while like a figure in an opera that has no song.

She is twenty when we meet her. She is happily, playfully married to Ikuo (Tadanobu Asano). They have a little boy, and there is a sunny scene where she bathes him. Then an inexplicable event takes place, and she is left a widow. Five years pass, and then a matchmaker finds a husband for her: Tamio (Takashi Naitoh), who lives with his young son in an isolated fishing village. At twenty-five, she starts her life again.

This is the first film by Hirokazu Kore-Eda, a young Japanese director whose love for the work of the great Yasujiro Ozu (1903–1963) is evident. Ozu is one of the four or five greatest directors of all time, and some of his visual touches are visible here. The camera, for example, is often placed at the eye level of someone kneeling on a tatami mat. Shots begin or end on empty rooms. Characters speak while seated side by side, not looking at one another. There are many long shots and few close-ups; the camera does not move, but regards.

In more obvious homage, Kore-Eda uses a technique which Ozu himself borrowed from Japanese poetry: the "pillow shot," inspired by "pillow words," which are words that do not lead out of or into the rest of a poem but provide a resting place, a pause or punctuation. Kore-Eda frequently cuts away from the action to simply look for a moment at something: a street, a doorway, a shop front, a view. And there are two small touches in which the young director subtly acknowledges the master: a characteristic tea kettle in the foreground of a shot, and a scene where the engine of a canal boat makes a sound so uncannily similar to the boat at the beginning of Ozu's *Floating Weeds* (1959) that it might have been lifted from the sound track.

But what, you are asking, do these details have to do with the movie at hand? I mention them because they indicate the care with which this beautiful film has been made, and they suggest its tradition. *Maborosi* is not going to insult us with a simpleminded plot. It is not a soap opera. Sometimes life presents us with large, painful, unanswerable questions, and we cannot simply "get over them."

There isn't a shot in the movie that's not graceful and pleasing. We get an almost physical sensation for the streets and rooms. Here are shots to look for:

The first husband walking off cheerfully down the street, swinging an umbrella. Yumiko's joy in bathing the baby. A child playing with a ball on a sloping concrete courtyard. Yumiko and her second husband sitting in front of an electric fan in the hot summertime, too exhausted to make love any longer. Yumiko, wearing a deep blue dress, almost lost in shadow at a bus stop. A funeral procession, framed in a long shot between the earth, the sea, and the sky. And a reconciliation seen at a great distance.

Maborosi is one of those valuable films where you have to actively place yourself in the character's mind. There are times when we do not know what she is thinking, but we are inspired with an active sympathy. We want to understand. Well, so does she. There's real dramatic suspense in the first scenes after she arrives at the little village. Will she like her new husband? Will their children get along? Can she live in such a backwater?

It's lovely how the film reveals the answers to these questions in such small details as a shot where she walks out her back door into the sunshine. Underneath these immediate questions, of course, lurk the bigger ones. "I just don't understand!" she says. "It just goes around and around in my head!" Her second husband offers an answer of sorts to her question. It is based on an experience fishermen sometimes have at sea, when they see a light or mirage that tempts them farther from shore. But what is the reason for the light?

Madadayo ★★★

NO MPAA RATING, 134 m., 1998

Tatsuo Matsumura (Hyakken Uchida), Kyoko Kagawa (Uchida's wife), Hisashi Igawa (Takayama), George Tokoro (Amaki). Directed by Akira Kurosawa and produced by Hisao Kurosawa. Screenplay by Akira Kurosawa.

Made in 1993 when he was eighty-three, *Madadayo* is possibly the last film by the Japanese master Akira Kurosawa, who is the greatest living filmmaker. And yet the very title of the film argues otherwise; it means "not yet!" That is the ritual cry that the film's old professor shouts out at the end of every one of his birthday parties, and it means that although death will come and may be near, life still goes on.

This is the kind of film we would all like to make, if we were very old and very serene. There were times when I felt uncannily as if Kurosawa were filming his own graceful decline into the night. It tells the story of the last two decades in the life of Hyakken Uchida, a writer and teacher who retires in the war years of the early 1940s. He was the kind of teacher who could inspire great respect and affection from his students, who venerate him and, as a group, help support him in his old age.

In Japan they have a tradition of "living national treasures"—people who because of their gifts and knowledge are treated like national monuments. Uchida is such a man, who has taught all his life and now finds that his books are selling well enough that he can move with his wife to a pretty little house, and sit in the entranceway: "That will be my study, and at the same time I will be the gatekeeper."

Kurosawa's career has itself spanned some sixty years, and the titles of his films are spoken with awe by those who love them. Consider that the same man made *Rashomon, Yojimbo, Ikiru, The Seven Samurai, The Hidden Fortress, Red Beard, Throne of Blood, Kagemusha, Ran,* and twenty-five more. His movies have been filled with life and spectacle, but here, in *Madadayo,* he has made a film in the spirit of his near-contemporary Yasujiro Ozu, whose domestic dramas are among the most quietly observant and contemplative of all films.

Very little happens in *Madadayo.* The old man (Tatsuo Matsumura) and his wife (Kyoko Kagawa) are feted by his students on his sixtieth birthday, and go to live in the fine little house. The house is destroyed in an air raid. They move to a little hut, hardly more than a room and a half, and there the professor also sits in the doorway and writes. His students come to see him, and every year on his birthday they have the ritual party at which he downs a big glass of beer and cries out "not yet!"

The students conspire to find the professor a larger house. Then something very important happens. A cat named Nora wanders into their house, and the professor and his wife come to love it. Nora disappears. The professor is grief-stricken. Leaflets are circulated, and his students, now middle-aged businessmen, scour the neighborhood for Nora, without success. Then another cat walks into their house, and the wound is healed.

At the professor's seventy-seventh birthday dinner, we see that things have changed. The early events were held Japanese-style, with men only. Now women are present, too: wives, daughters, even grandchildren, in a Western-style banquet room. And still the cry is "not yet!"

Like Ozu, Kurosawa is content to let his camera rest and observe. We never quite learn what sorts of things the professor writes (the real Uchida was in fact a beloved essayist), but we know he must be a great man because his students love him so. We learn few intimate details about his life (not even, if I recall, his wife's first name). We see him mostly seated in his front door, as a stranger might.

Like his students, we are amused by his signs forbidding visitors and warning away those who would urinate on his wall. We learn about the burglar-proofing strategies in his first, larger, house: He leaves a door open, with a sign saying "Burglar's Entrance." Inside, signs indicate "Burglar's Passage," "Burglar's Recess Area" and "Burglar's Exit." He guesses right that burglars would prefer to operate in a house that grants them more anonymity.

The movie is as much about the students as the professor, as much about gratitude and love as about aging. In an interview at the time of the film's release, Kurosawa said his movie is about "something very precious, which has been all but forgotten: the enviable world of warm hearts." He added, "I hope that all the people who have seen this picture will leave the theater feeling refreshed, with broad smiles on their faces."

Mad City ★ ★ ½

PG-13, 120 m., 1997

John Travolta (Sam), Dustin Hoffman (Brackett), Mia Kirshner (Laurie), Alan Alda (Hollander), Robert Prosky (Lou Potts), Blythe Danner (Mrs. Banks), William Atherton (Dohlen). Directed by Constantin Costa-Gavras and produced by Arnold Kopelson and Anne Kopelson. Screenplay by Tom Matthews.

Mad City arrives with the last thing a movie about journalism needs—last year's news. It's about the media feeding frenzy that erupts when a museum guard takes hostages. A TV newsman is one of them, the news channels carry the story around the clock, the museum is ringed with cops and cameras, and we get lots of scenes showing the vanity and hypocrisy of anchormen. This is not news.

It's time to admit the obvious: The public enjoys sensational journalism, and the media are only giving them what they demand. People who say they deplore paparazzi journalism are approximately as sincere as smokers who lecture you on how bad their habit is.

Mad City might have been more fun if it had added that extra spin—if it had attacked the audience as well as the perpetrators. It's too predictable: A media circus springs up when the museum guard, a likable everyman played by John Travolta, creates a hostage crisis and finds himself bonding with a TV newsman (Dustin Hoffman). The movie is obviously inspired by *Ace in the Hole*, the knife-edged 1951 satire by Billy Wilder, about a man trapped in a cave, and the broken-down newsman (Kirk Douglas) who spins out the crisis to rescue his own career. But while Wilder's movie was smart and ironic, *Mad City* is dumbed down into a roundup of the usual suspects: the old-fashioned news director, the egotistical network star, the young intern on the make, etc. Costa-Gavras, who directed the film, should have remembered that satire depends on exaggeration, not attack.

As the film opens, Hoffman is at the museum to cover a story when Travolta walks in and demands a hearing with his boss (Blythe Danner). He's been fired from his low-wage job and wants it back. The guard is not too bright, and has brought along a duffel bag containing a shotgun and sticks of dynamite—to get her attention, he says. Soon he has inadvertently taken a group of children hostage and accidentally shot his best friend, another guard. He's having the kind of day Jim Carrey might have scripted.

Hoffman was once a network star, but after running afoul of an egomaniacal anchor (Alan Alda), he's been exiled to the sticks. This is the big story that can rebuild his career. He stays inside the museum, broadcasting from a battery-powered lapel mike, and over the course of long hours and nights he becomes friends with the hapless guard, who only wanted his job back, and is terrified that now his wife will be mad at him.

Hoffman's performance is on target, and would have served a better screenplay. Alan Alda has some well-observed moments as the star anchorman. There are nice little digs, as when it's suggested to Travolta that Thursday prime time would be the best time to surrender, ratings-wise. But the movie makes its points early and often, and the Travolta character, too familiar from similar roles in *Phenomenon, Michael,* and *White Man's Burden,* keeps playing the same scene: remorse, confusion, resolve.

What I liked was a lot of screenwriter Tom Matthews's dialogue for the Hoffman character, who in effect turns into the guard's unofficial media adviser: "That's your jury pool out there," he tells him. The movie knows what it wants to do, but lacks the velocity for liftoff. There is no moment where satire and human nature meet in perfect union, as there is in *Ace in the Hole*, when Kirk Douglas advises the wife of the trapped man to get herself photographed while praying in church, and she replies, "I don't pray. Kneeling bags my nylons."

Madeline ★ ★ ★

PG, 89 m., 1998

Frances McDormand (Miss Clavel), Nigel Hawthorne (Lord Covington), Hatty Jones (Madeline), Ben Daniels (Leopold the Tutor), Stephane Audran (Lady Covington), Arturo Venegas (Mr. Spanish Ambassador), Katia Caballero (Mrs. Spanish Ambassador), Chantal Neuwirth (Helene the Cook). Directed by Daisy von Scherler Mayer and produced by Saul Cooper, Pancho Kohner, and Allyn Stewart. Screenplay by Mark Levin and Jennifer Flackett, based on the book *Madeline* by Ludwig Bemelmans.

It is a great sadness that a witty and graceful prose stylist like Ludwig Bemelmans should today be remembered primarily for his children's books about Madeline. His works should be in every bookstore, somewhere near Waugh and Thurber, and studied by anyone who wants to learn how to put a sentence together without any nails.

Still, to have a degree of immortality is a blessing, and today there are little girls (and some boys) all over the world who can recite for you the opening lines of Bemelmans's first book about Madeline:

In an old house in Paris that was covered with vines,
Lived 12 little girls in two straight lines.

Bemelmans illustrated the books himself—made the drawings, indeed, for many of his books, which involved sophisticated but penniless European exiles who found themselves in such unfamiliar places as South American palaces and Manhattan hotels. There is a prejudice against adult books with illustrations; readers generally put them down with a sniff. In the case of Bemelmans, they are missing some of the slyest and most seductive writing of the century. And enchanting drawings.

But the riches of Bemelmans are years in the future for the intended audience for *Madeline,* a family movie that does a surprisingly good job of using real actors and locations and making them look and feel like the books it is based on.

Some of the episodes are by Bemelmans, such as Madeline's appendectomy, or her fall into the Seine and rescue by the brave dog Genevieve. Others are invented. Even though the inventions involve an attempted kidnapping, this is not one of those children's movies that depends on noise and action to keep the attention of the audience. The movie has some of the same decorum and understated humor as the books.

Madeline is, of course, one of the twelve little girls who attends a boarding school in Paris run by Miss Clavel (Frances McDormand). An orphan, she is the smallest of the girls, who line up according to height before marching out in their straw hats for processions past Paris landmarks. Both her school and the house next door, which is purchased for the Spanish embassy, look gratifyingly like the Bemelmans drawings (there's a perfect match in the opening fade from drawing to real life).

The plot also involves Pepito, the show-off son of the Spanish ambassador, who roars around the courtyard on his motor scooter and dresses as a matador for his birthday. The girls peer at him from their windows, endure his bragging, and survive his willingness to demonstrate how to decapitate a white mouse before feeding it to his pet snake. Little does Pepito suspect that he figures in the plans of his tutor and a circus clown, who plot to abduct him.

Meanwhile, kind Lady Covington (Stephane Audran), who provides for the school, dies in the hospital, and her glint-eyed husband, Lord Covington (Nigel Hawthorne, from *The Madness of George V*), starts leading potential purchasers through the house. He wants to sell it for an embassy, and his ruthlessness is such that he even paints over the marks on the wall showing how the girls have grown during the year.

Hatty Jones makes an admirable Madeline, small and intent, and I liked her determination. When it appears the school will be sold, she decides to run away to join the circus, and that's how she discovers the plot against Pepito. Amazing that Miss Clavel didn't sniff it out first; she has a way of stopping stock-still, listening to unheard sounds, and announcing, "Something . . . is not right!"

Madeline is a quietly charming movie for kids not too hyped on action and candy. It's assisted mightily by the presence of McDormand and Hawthorne, who play their roles precisely, not broadly, and come across as people, not caricatures. It's not the noisy kind of movie that steamrollers kids into acceptance, like *Mortal Kombat*—but one, like *Mulan* or *Doctor Dolittle,* that actually expects them to listen, and pick up on some of the character humor. Observe, for example, how the movie handles the impending death of the chicken Fred, and Madeline's conversion to vegetarianism. ☞

Mafia! ★★

PG-13, 86 m., 1998

Jay Mohr (Anthony Cortino), Billy Burke (Joey Cortino), Christina Applegate (Diane), Pamela Gidley (Pepper Gianini), Olympia Dukakis (Sophia), Lloyd Bridges (Vincenzo Cortino), Jason Fuchs (Young Vincenzo), Joe Viterelli (Clamato). Directed by Jim Abrahams and produced by Bill Badalato. Screenplay by Abrahams, Greg Norberg, and Michael McManus.

Yes, I laughed during Jim Abrahams's *Mafia!,* but even in midchortle I was reminded of the gut-busting experience of seeing *There's Something About Mary.* It is the new movie's misfortune to arrive after, instead of before, the funniest comedy of the year. I suppose it's not fair to penalize *Mafia!* for its timing, but on the other hand, how can I ignore it?

The movie, titled *Jane Austen's Mafia!* on the screen but not in the ads, is another in the series of gag-a-minit parodies worked on by Abrahams, like *Airplane!, Top Secret,* and the *Naked Gun* movies. It's a takeoff on Coppola's *The Godfather* and *Godfather, Part II* and Scorsese's *Casino,* with a few touches of *Il Postino.*

The opening shot is the best one, as Anthony Cortino (Jay Mohr), the mob's man in a Las Vegas casino, turns the ignition on his Cadillac and is blown sky-high. In the Scorsese picture Robert De Niro rotated dreamily against a backdrop of flames; here the actor catches a Frisbee in his mouth, scores a basket, and watches the *Twister* cow drift by.

The movie, narrated by this character, tells the story of his father's youth in Sicily *(Godfather II)* and his own rise through the mob. Young Vincenzo Cortino, who is raised in the town of Salmonella ("Home of Warm Mayonnaise"), is played by Jason Fuchs. He immigrates to America (where the Ellis Island guards try to name him "Armani Windbreaker" after his jacket), and by the time he reaches Godfather status he's played by the late Lloyd Bridges, who has fun kidding Brando's famous tomatoes-and-death scene.

The don's older son, Joey (Bully Burke), is a short-tempered hothead, and power in the family devolves to Anthony (Mohr), based on the Al Pacino character. Familiarity with the earlier films is helpful, but then who isn't familiar with the *Godfather* movies—and who won't appreciate it when the Diane Keaton character (played by Christina Applegate) complains, "I'm always gonna just be that Protestant chick who never killed anyone."

In Vegas, Cortino runs a casino that includes such games as Go Fish and Snakes and Ladders. My favorite: Guess the Number. "Two?" says a gambler. "Sorry," says the dealer. "I was thinking of three." When cheats are discovered signaling to one another, a tough enforcer with a cattle prod sidles up to the wrong man, zaps him, and then zaps everyone else in the area. Anthony's life in Vegas gets complicated when he falls for a dancer named Pepper Gianini (Pamela Gidley), based on the Sharon Stone character in *Casino.*

I smiled through a lot of this, including Cortino's tip for the casino doorman ("Keep the car"), but by the time the projectile vomiting came around I was wondering if that was a homage to *Animal House* or only a lift. *Mafia!*

is the kind of movie that can never entirely fail, but can succeed to various degrees. It doesn't rank with Abrahams's earlier efforts. And in a town where *There's Something About Mary* is playing, it's not the one to choose. ☞

Mandela ★★★

NO MPAA RATING, 120 m., 1997

A documentary on the life of Nelson Mandela, directed by Jo Menell and Angus Gibson and produced by Jonathan Demme, Edward Saxon, and Menell.

Nelson Mandela is one of the great men of our century. The leader of South Africa's banned African National Congress, he was condemned in 1964 to life imprisonment on Robben Island, off Cape Town. As he entered the prison, he believed "the way you are treated by prison authorities depends on your demeanor." Such was his demeanor that while imprisoned he became the obvious choice to lead his country, and was eventually released to lead a successful campaign that replaced white rule.

Mandela, a new documentary, charts his life from obscure beginnings to the Nobel Prize, and focuses on his steadfast vision of a multiracial South Africa where all would live together peacefully. When I spent 1965 as a student at the University of Cape Town, most people, black and white, believed the apartheid system would end in a bloody civil war. That there was a peaceful, democratic exchange of power is a tribute above all to Mandela's moral leadership.

But it was also because of the courage and imagination of F. W. de Klerk, the white South African president who freed Mandela from prison, lifted the ban on the ANC, and then ran against Mandela in a general election—and lost, as he knew he would. The two men shared the Nobel Peace Prize in 1993.

I mention de Klerk because this film essentially writes him out of the story; it so simplifies the transfer of power in South Africa that it plays more like a campaign biography than a documentary. Why did de Klerk arrive at his decision? Civil unrest and international economic sanctions forced his hand, we are told, and then we see de Klerk informing the South African Parliament that his government had reached an irreversible decision to free Mandela and hold multiracial elections.

The actual story of the events leading to the election is more complicated and interesting than that. Yes, South Africa suffered from economic sanctions. But it could have survived for many years before caving in; it forged clandestine trading arrangements with countries ranging from China to Israel, and its diamonds still found their way onto the fingers of brides all over the world. Civil unrest was widespread, but South Africa had a fearsome array of police and military forces to counter it. If South Africa had chosen, apartheid might still be its law.

What happened was a political miracle. Mandela's unswerving moral and political strength coincided with the growing conviction within the ruling Nationalist Party (and its secret lodge, the Broderbund, and the quasi-official Dutch Reformed Church) that apartheid was, simply, wrong. While de Klerk's predecessor, F. W. Botha, pledged eternal white defiance, de Klerk and other younger ministers instituted secret contacts with Mandela, and the new future of South Africa was hashed out in meetings over a period of years.

De Klerk, when he became president, wanted to free Mandela immediately. Mandela insisted he be "the last man off" of Robben Island; his colleagues and fellow political prisoners had to be freed first, and the ANC had to be recognized as a legitimate political party, not a terrorist underground. Mandela, essentially running a government in exile, moved into the prison warden's house, and often made secret trips elsewhere in South Africa. One famous story tells of a hot day when Mandela's government driver stopped outside a store to buy cold soda, and the world's most famous political prisoner was left alone in the car. He could have simply walked away. But he realized he was more useful to the cause as a prisoner.

None of those events are told in *Mandela*, which simplifies the transfer of power into a fable of black against white, and all but implies that de Klerk was unwilling to see power change hands. The hope for the new South Africa's future lies in multiracialism, and its foundation story is a good place to start.

Still, what a fascinating portrait this film paints of Mandela! Named "Nelson" by a teacher who did not like his tribal name, Mandela was one of nine children of a polygamist father who had four wives (how did Mandela feel about that? The movie doesn't ask). When his father died, the bright boy was adopted by a chief, and prepared to become counselor to the king. He ran away to Johannesburg in the early 1940s to escape an arranged marriage, and had soon moved into the Soweto Township home of Walter Sisulu, who with Oliver Tambo would join him in leading the ANC.

Mandela worked hard to support himself while studying for the law, became a lawyer, and was soon a key leader of the ANC. His cause was never "black power," but "one man, one vote." That led him to Robben Island, and for thirteen years he did hard physical labor in a limestone quarry while continuing to lead classes and discussion groups among his fellow prisoners.

The film has many revealing personal touches: his childhood fear, during a circumcision ceremony, that he would not be as "forthright and strong" as the other boys. His wry imitation of a teacher repeating, "I am a descendant of the famous Duke of Wellington." His memories of hunting animals on the veld. His passion for his second wife, Winnie Mandela, in hundreds of tender letters written from prison—and his anguished decision to divorce her. There are amusing glimpses of Mandela under the guidance of personal aides, including a maternal Indian woman who advises him on wardrobe (he feels choked when he wears a tie).

Mandela delivers a powerful emotional charge in its closing scenes of the Nobel Prize and Mandela's election victory. Today the new South Africa offers the best hope for a new Africa. Its engine might be able to pull the train of corrupt regimes to the north and lead the way to reform. Mandela's South Africa seems to be working, despite worrisome crime rates. It is one of the most inspiring stories of our time. But there is more to it than *Mandela* chooses to tell.

The Man in the Iron Mask ★ ★ ½

PG-13, 117 m., 1998

Leonardo DiCaprio (King Louis/Phillippe), Jeremy Irons (Aramis), John Malkovich (Athos), Gérard Depardieu (Porthos), Gabriel Byrne (D'Artagnan), Anne Parillaud (Queen Anne), Judith Godreche (Christine), Peter Sarsgaard (Raoul). Directed by Randall Wallace and produced by Wallace and Russell Smith. Screenplay by Wallace, based on the novel by Alexandre Dumas.

On the island of St. Marguerite, offshore from Cannes of all places, still stands the rude stone fortress where the Man in the Iron Mask spent his lonely days. I have sat below his window while the owner of the little Italian trattoria assured me that the man in the mask was no less than the twin brother of Louis XIV, held there because the state could not tolerate another claimant to the throne.

No one knows who the man in the mask was, but his dangerous identity must have been the whole point of the mask, so the twin brother theory is as good as any. *The Man in the Iron Mask* is "loosely based" on the Dumas novel, and includes a return appearance by the Three Musketeers. They come out of retirement in a scheme to rescue France from the cruel fist of the young, spoiled king.

Louis XIV and his brother are played by Leonardo DiCaprio in a dual role, his first film since *Titanic.* He looks well fed as the despotic ruler and not particularly gaunt, for that matter, as the man in the mask. As the film opens, he presides over a court that lives in decadent luxury, while mobs riot for bread in the streets. The beautiful Christine (Judith Godreche) catches his eye, and since she's engaged to the young Raoul (Peter Sarsgaard), the king sends Raoul off to war and makes sure he gets killed there.

The death of Raoul enrages his father, Athos (John Malkovich), one of the original musketeers, who enlists his comrades Aramis (Jeremy Irons) and Porthos (Gérard Depardieu) in a plan for revenge. Also involved, on the other side, is the original fourth musketeer, D'Artagnan (Gabriel Byrne), who remains loyal to Louis XIV and the twins' mother, Queen Anne (Anne Parillaud).

This setup, easy enough to explain, takes director Randall Wallace too long to establish, and there are side plots, such as the king's war against the Jesuits, that will confuse audiences. There was once a time when everyone had heard of the musketeers and the Man in the Iron Mask, but history these days seems to start with the invention of MTV, and those not familiar with the characters will take some time to get oriented.

The screenplay by Wallace (who wrote *Braveheart*) is not well focused, and there are gratuitous scenes, but finally we understand the central thread: The musketeers will spring the Man in the Iron Mask from captivity, and secretly substitute him for his brother. The actual mechanics of their plan left me shaking my head with incredulity. Does anyone think Jeremy Irons is large enough to smuggle Leonardo DiCaprio past suspicious guards under his cloak? Wallace should have dreamed up a better plan.

The substitution of the king and his twin is accomplished at a fancy dress ball, where the conspirators drive Louis XIV wild with fear by convincing him he sees iron masks everywhere. But the movie, alas, limits itself to the action in the plot—escapes, sword fights, the frequent incantation "all for one and one for all"—and ignores the opportunity to have more fun with the notion of a prisoner suddenly finding himself king.

Leonardo DiCaprio is the star of the story without being its hero, although his first emergence from the mask is an effective shot. The three musketeers are cast with big names (Irons, Malkovich, Depardieu), but to my surprise the picture is stolen by Gabriel Byrne, who has the most charisma and is the most convincing. His scenes with Parillaud (from *La Femme Nikita*) are some of the best in the movie. Once all the pieces of the plot were in place, I was at least interested, if not overwhelmed; I could see how, with a rewrite and a better focus, this could have been a film of *Braveheart* quality instead of basically just a costume swashbuckler.

The Man Who Knew Too Little ★

PG, 95 m., 1997

Bill Murray (Wallace Ritchie), Peter Gallagher (James Ritchie), Joanne Whalley (Lori), Alfred Molina (Boris), Richard Wilson (Daggenhurst). Directed by Jon Amiel and produced by Arnon Milchan, Michael Nathanson, and Mark Tarlov. Screenplay by Robert Farrar and Howard Franklin, based on the novel *Watch That Man* by Farrar.

The funniest thing about *The Man Who Knew Too Little* is the title; that melancholy truth develops with deadening finality as the movie marches on. The movie develops endless permutations on an idea that is not funny, until at last, in desperation, we cry, "Bring on some dancing Cossacks!" and it does.

Bill Murray stars, as Wallace, a clueless American tourist, visiting London to see his brother (Peter Gallagher). The brother is a banker throwing a big business dinner, so to get rid of Wallace he buys him a ticket to the "Theater of Life," a troupe that works on the city streets and involves one audience member at a time in a real-life drama.

Wallace, alas, answers a pay phone at the wrong time and finds himself involved in a real spy drama instead of a fake theatrical one. This leads to no end of misunderstandings, and when I say "no end," please assume a tone of despair mixed with exhaustion.

The movie is simply not funny. It is clever, yes. Based on a book by Robert Farrar, it concocts conversations that all have the same thing in common: They can be taken both ways. So Wallace means one thing and the spies think he means another, and on and on and on and on and on.

When he is funny, Bill Murray is very funny. But he needs something to push against. He is a reactor. His best screen characters are passive aggressive: They insinuate themselves unwanted into ongoing scenarios. Here he's the center of the show, and all of the other characters are carefully tailored to fit precisely into the requirements of his misunderstanding, like pieces of a jigsaw.

There are sequences here dripping with desperation, like the whole business involving the window ledge. The dancing Cossack scene involves many Chinese dolls, one containing a bomb with a red digital readout (RDR). Here is a movie gasping for diversions, and does it think of any gags involving the RDR? It does not. It never even clearly establishes how we can *see* the RDR, since it is inside the doll. Or maybe (sound of critic's palm smacking against forehead) that's the joke.

Margaret's Museum ★ ★ ★ ½

R, 118 m., 1997

Helena Bonham Carter (Margaret MacNeil), Clive Russell (Neil Currie), Craig Olejnik (Jimmy), Kate Nelligan (Catherine), Kenneth Welsh (Angus), Andrea Morris (Marilyn). Directed by Mort Ransen and produced by Ransen, Christopher Zimmer, Claudio Luca, and Steve Clark-Hall. Screenplay by Gerald Wexler and Ransen, based on stories by Sheldon Currie.

The opening shot of *Margaret's Museum* looks like a painting by Andrew Wyeth of a little clapboard cottage in a sea of grass on a cliffside. Two visitors drive up to visit the "museum," and a moment later one runs from the house, screaming. Then a title card takes us back "three years earlier."

As openings go, this one plays like it belongs on another film. That it doesn't gradually becomes clear. We are in the mining town of Glace Bay on Cape Breton Island in Nova Scotia, in the late 1940s, where the coal pits take a terrible toll in life and limb—and where Margaret (Helena Bonham Carter) and her family live in half a house because the earth subsided into a mine shaft beneath the other half.

Margaret scrubs floors at the hospital. One day a strapping tall fellow named Neil (Clive Russell) walks into a restaurant, half-drunk, and begins to serenade her with big bagpipes. She scorns men but likes this one, and brings him home to meet her bitter mother (Kate Nelligan), who has buried a husband and a son after pit disasters, and cares for a father whose lungs are so filled with dust that he needs to be regularly slammed on the back ("Don't forget to thump your grandfather!").

Margaret's Museum is the story of the people who must make their living from the cold-hearted, cost-conscious mining company, but it isn't like other films with similar themes (*Sons and Lovers*, *The Molly Maguires*, or *Matewan*). It's quirkier and more eccentric, and has a thread of wry humor running through it. The dialogue, inspired by the short stories of Sheldon Currie, shows that Celtic wit has traveled well to the new land. (When Margaret encourages her younger brother to ask his girl to the Sunday dance, he replies, "They're not supposed to dance on Sunday." She tells him, "They're not supposed to work. Dancing's not work." And he replies, "They're Protestant, aren't they? For them, it's work.")

Most of the movie is the love story of Margaret and Neil. He towers above her slight frame and threatens to force them all out of the house with his drinking, his buddies, and his songs. But he listens when she protests, and mends his ways. Soon he has built her the curious house near the sea, using parts scrounged around town. (The bedroom, with walls and a ceiling made from old windows, is going to be bloody cold in a Nova Scotia winter.)

As Margaret's mother, Nelligan is hard and dour, and can see no point in a life that snatches all of your loved ones away from you. "I'll have five sons and three daughters," Margaret tells her. "I can hear them in the bagpipe, screaming to be born." Her mother's predictions about the fates of these unborn infants are blood-chilling.

The margins of the movie are filled with colorful characters. With old grandfather, who coughs and writes his song requests on a notepad. With Uncle Angus (Kenneth Welsh), who dreams of sparing his nephew a life in the mines, and works double shifts in hopes that if he just once sees Toronto, he'll see there is a different life waiting for him. With the pit manager, who orders his red-haired daughter (Andrea Morris) not to see Margaret's brother (Craig Olejnik). The daughter and the brother perform their own marriage ceremony, solemnly, before two candles in a root cellar.

The destination of the film may be guessed by some, but I will not reveal it, nor how it contributes to Margaret's museum and its sign, THE COST OF COAL. What is surprising about the film is not its ending, but how it gets there. Helena Bonham Carter might seem an unlikely candidate for this role (she took it in preference to the lead in *Breaking the Waves*), but she is just right—plucky, sexy, bemused, glorious in a scene where Neil sneaks her into the miner's cleaning area and she takes the first hot shower of her life. Russell, as Neil, is sort of a rougher-hewn Liam Neeson, strong, gentle, and poetic. And Nelligan is astounding in the way she allows her humanity to peek out from behind the mother's harsh defenses.

Margaret's Museum is one of those small, nearly perfect movies that you know, seeing it, is absolutely one of a kind.

Marie Baie des Anges ★

R, 90 m., 1998

Vahina Giocante (Marie), Frederic Malgras (Orso), Amira Casar (Young Woman), David Kilner (Larry), Jamie Harris (Jim), Frederic Westerman (Ardito), Nicolas Welbers (Goran), Swan Carpio (Jurec). Directed by Manuel Pradal and produced by Philippe Rousselet. Screenplay by Pradal.

At the height of the storm over *Last Tango in Paris,* Art Buchwald, who had lived in Paris for years, weighed in with some common sense: The movie, he explained, is really about real estate. Both characters want the same apartment and are willing to do anything to get it.

Marie Baie des Anges is not really about real estate. It is about sex. But I thought a lot about real estate while I was watching it. It takes place on the French Riviera, which is pictured here as an unspoilt Eden in which the film's adolescent lovers gambol and pose, nude much of the time, surfacing only occasionally for the dangers of the town.

Anyone who has visited the French Riviera knows that it has more in common with Miami than with Eden. It is a crowded, expensive perch for ugly condos and desperate beachgoers, and the only place where teenage lovers can safely gambol is in their bathtubs. *Marie Baie des Anges* is as realistic as *Blue Lagoon,* although without any copulating turtles.

The movie stars Vahina Giocante as Marie, a fifteen-year-old who spends her vacations on the Riviera picking up American sailors and sleeping under the stars. No mention of her parents, home, income, past, experience, etc. She is the pornographer's dream: an uncomplicated, nubile teenager who exists only as she is. Giocante has been billed as "the new Bardot," and she's off to a good start: Bardot didn't make many good films either.

On the beach, she meets Orso (Frederic Malgras), a sullen lout who lurks about looking like a charade, with the answer "Leonardo DiCaprio." Together they run, play, boat, swim, eat strawberries, and flirt with danger, and inevitably a handgun surfaces, so we will not be in suspense about the method used to bring the film to its unsatisfactory conclusion. "Get me the best-looking gun you can find," Orso tells Marie, who steals it from a one-night stand.

The movie is yet one more evocation of doomed youth, destined for a brief flash of happiness and a taste of eroticism before they collide with the preordained ending. All of these movies end the same way, with one form of death or another, which casts a cold light on the events that went before, showing you how unlucky these young people were to be in a story written by a director who lacked the wit to think of anything else that might happen.

The filmmaker is Manuel Pradal, who in addition to recycling exhausted clichés also fancies himself at the cutting edge of narrative. He tells his story out of sequence, leaving us to collect explanations and context along the way; one advantage of this style is that only at the end is it revealed that the story was not about anything. We get glimpses and fragments of actions; flashforwards and flashbacks; exhausting, self-conscious artiness.

Yes, there is beautiful scenery. And nice compositions. Lots of pretty pictures. Giocante and Malgras are superficially attractive, although because their characters are empty vessels there's no reason to like them much or care about them. The movie is cast as a tragedy, and it's tragic, all right: Tragic that these kids never developed intelligence and personalities.

Marius and Jeannette ★ ★

NO MPAA RATING, 1998

Ariane Ascaride (Jeannette), Gerard Meylan (Marius), Pascale Roberts (Caroline), Jacques Boudet (Justin), Frederique Bonnal (Monique), Jean-Pierre Darroussin (Dede), Laetitia Pesenti (Magali), Miloud Nacer (Malek). Directed by Robert Guediguian and produced by Gilles Sandoz. Screenplay by Guediguian and Jean-Louis Milesi. In French with English subtitles.

Marius and Jeannette is a sentimental fantasy of French left-wing working-class life, so cheerful and idealized that I expected the characters to break into song; they do all dance together, in the forecourt of a shuttered cement factory.

Set in a blue-collar district of Marseilles, it plays like a sitcom spin-off of *Carmen,* with everyone popping in and out of each other's houses and lives, while all personal emergencies are handled in public, collectively.

The director, Robert Guediguian, has visited this territory before; his 1980 film *Last Summer* dealt with workers in the same factory when it was still in operation. Now the jobs have fled to Malaysia, the workers tell each other, although they are none too sure where that is, and they sit outside their doors in beach chairs, unemployed but unbowed.

The movie's heroine is Jeannette (Ariane Ascaride, the director's wife). She's raised two kids by different fathers, and as the movie opens she tries to steal cans of paint from the factory. She's stopped by a security guard, Marius (Gerard Meylan), who limps around in an orange one-piece suit, patrolling the ruins. "My house will collapse without a paint job!" Jeannette shouts, calling him a fascist. The next day, he delivers the cans to her door, and that's the beginning of a romance.

Well, we like these two people, and that's the argument for liking the movie. Jeannette is irredeemably cheerful and upbeat, a pal to her children, a no-nonsense figure in jeans and a Levi's jacket. Sample dialogue: "You're beautiful," she tells her teenage daughter Magali, who tries on a lacy minidress. "But I look cheap," the daughter says. "Yes, but it suits you." "If I wear this I'll be pregnant before I get to the end of the street," Magali says. Jeannette smiles: "I'd like to be a grandma."

Not your typical mother, eh? Jeannette combines elements of old-time leftist idealism with the hippie commune spirit. She and her neighbors live in each other's pockets; they occupy a little courtyard with windows that open onto a common space, and even the most intimate matters are freely discussed. They also laugh a lot—too much, I thought. At one point the neighbor's husband lands in the hospital after getting drunk and throwing rocks at right-wing political posters. The rocks bounce back and hit him in the head. At this news everyone laughs so uproariously that they have to wipe away the tears. I didn't believe I was looking at laughter: It looked more like overacting in response to the screenplay instruction, "They laugh uncontrollably."

There must be an arc in all romances, a darkness before the dawn. Marius and Jeannette fall in love, but then he unexpectedly disappears, and the movie falls back on that most ancient of clichés, that in wine there is truth. The neighborhood guys get him drunk, and he confesses his innermost fears and insecurities. There is also an unnecessary and unmotivated bar brawl. Then, in a tactic that takes communal living too far, they haul him unconscious back to Jeannette's bed.

Meanwhile, Jeannette conducts her private war against the bosses. She's a checkout clerk at a supermarket, where the chair hurts her back (she should try standing up like an American grocery clerk). She shouts at the manager, "The Gestapo could have used these chairs for torture!" Since the movie is set much too late for Jeannette to have had any experience of World War II, this seems more like a dated, ritualized left-wing attribution of fascism to all the enemies of the workers.

By the end of the film, I was fed up. Yes, I liked Jeannette and Marius as individuals; they're a warm, attractive, funky couple on the shores of middle age who find happiness. But the movie forces its politics until it feels like a Pete Seeger benefit. And, hey, I like Pete Seeger. It's just that the love story of *Marius and Jeannette* is at an awkward angle to the politics, and the lives and dialogue of these characters seem impossibly contorted to reflect the director's politics.

Marvin's Room ★ ★ ★ ½

PG-13, 98 m., 1997

Meryl Streep (Lee), Leonardo DiCaprio (Hank), Diane Keaton (Bessie), Robert De Niro (Dr. Wally), Hume Cronyn (Marvin), Gwen Verdon (Ruth), Hal Scardino (Charlie), Dan Hedaya (Bob), Margo Martindale (Dr. Charlotte), Cynthia Nixon (Home Director). Directed by Jerry Zaks and produced by Scott Rudin, Jane Rosenthal, and Robert De Niro. Screenplay by Scott McPherson, based on his stage play.

There is a line of dialogue that occurs late in *Marvin's Room* and contains the key to the whole film. It is spoken by a woman who has put her life on hold for years to care for a father who "has been dying for twenty years—

slowly, so that I won't miss anything." Has her life been wasted? She doesn't believe so. She says: "I've been so lucky to have been able to love someone so much."

The woman's name is Bessie (Diane Keaton). She lives in Florida with her still-dying father, Marvin (Hume Cronyn), and a dotty aunt (Gwen Verdon), who wears some kind of medical device that is always opening the garage door. Bessie has discovered that she has cancer, but that her life might be saved by a bone marrow transplant. The only candidates for donors are Lee (Meryl Streep), a sister she has not seen in years, and Lee's two children. If they are to be of any help, some old wounds will have to be reopened.

Lee lives in Ohio, where her precarious life has recently taken an upturn; she's received her degree in cosmetology. It has also taken a downturn; her older son, Hank (Leonardo DiCaprio), has just burned down the house. Her younger son, Charlie (Hal Scardino), has reacted to this development as he reacts to most, by burying his nose in a book. Lee visits Hank in an institution, where he proudly reports, "They're not strapping me down anymore!" "Don't abuse that privilege," she tells him. The two sisters have not so much as exchanged Christmas cards in years, for reasons which they would certainly not agree on.

In broad outlines, this story goes on the same shelf with *What's Eating Gilbert Grape?*, another drama about a malfunctioning family (also starring DiCaprio). Both have children who are the captives of chronically housebound parents; both have a child whose behavior is unpredictable and perhaps dangerous; both have a rich vein of bleak humor; both are about the healing power of sacrifice.

One of the big differences between the films, for a viewer, is that *Marvin's Room* has so much star power: not only Streep and Keaton, but also Robert De Niro, as a detached, apologetic doctor whose attempts to sound reassuring are always alarming. (How many spins can a doctor put on the words "test results"?) The famous faces make it difficult at first to sink into the story, but eventually we do; the characters become so convincing that even if we're aware of Keaton and Streep, it's as if these events are happening to them. (De Niro never becomes that real, and neither does Dan Hedaya, who is brilliant as his problematic brother, but that doesn't matter because they function like the fools in a tragedy.)

Lee piles Hank and Charlie into the car for the drive down south, during which she keeps Hank (on release from a juvenile home) on a very short chain. (Having burned down the house, he naturally is not allowed matches, so when he wants to smoke she has Charlie, the ten-year-old, light his cigarette.) When she first sees Bessie, there is bluntness and disbelief: Both have aged by twenty years, except in each other's minds—and in their own.

Once the sisters are reunited, the material boils down into a series of probing conversations, and we sense the story's origin as a play. (It was written by Scott McPherson, and first produced at the Goodman Theater in Chicago in 1990; McPherson wrote a version of the screenplay before he died in 1992.) The stage origins, although we sense them, are not a problem because these two women *need* to talk to one another. There is a lot to say, and director Jerry Zaks lets them say it.

How do families fall apart? Why do many have one sibling who takes on the responsibilities of maintaining the "family home" and being the caregiver, while others get away as far and fast as they can? Is one the martyr and are the others taking advantage? Or does everyone get the role they really desire?

What *Marvin's Room* argues is that Lee, by fleeing the sick people at home, may have shortchanged herself, and that Bessie, "chained" to the bed of her slowly dying father, might have benefited. Or perhaps not; perhaps Lee was constitutionally incapable of caring for her father and was better off keeping out of the way. There is a point in *Marvin's Room* where such questions inspired parallel questions in my own mind; all families have illness and death, and therefore all families generate such questions.

Is one of the three visitors from Ohio a match for the transplant operation? Will Bessie live? Will her father die? The true depth of *Marvin's Room* is revealed in the fact that the story is not about these questions. They are incidental. The film focuses instead with the ways the two sisters deal with their relationship—which they both desperately need to do—and the way the sons learn something, however haphazardly, about the difference between true unhappiness and the complaints of childhood.

Streep and Keaton, in their different styles, find ways to make Lee and Bessie into much more than the expression of their problems. Hal Scardino has some wonderful moments as the "good" boy of a mother who is a borderline control freak (watch how he meticulously eats a potato chip just as she instructs). DiCaprio on his good days is one of the best young actors we have. Here he supplies the nudge the story needs to keep from reducing itself to a two-sided conversation; he is the distraction, the outside force, the reminder that life goes on and no problem, not even a long dying, is forever.

The Mask of Zorro ★ ★ ★

PG-13, 136 m., 1998

Antonio Banderas (Alejandro/Zorro), Anthony Hopkins (Don Diego/Zorro), Catherine Zeta-Jones (Elena Montero), Stuart Wilson (Don Rafael Montero). Directed by Martin Campbell and produced by Doug Claybourne and David Foster. Screenplay by John Eskow, Ted Elliott, and Terry Rossio.

The Mask of Zorro has something you don't often see in modern action pictures, a sense of honor. The character takes sides, good versus evil, and blood debts are nursed down through the generations. It also has a lot of zest, humor, energy, and swordplay; it's fun, and not an insult to the intelligence.

The movie resurrects a character first played in silent films by Douglas Fairbanks Sr., and again on TV in the 1950s by Guy Williams, and launches him in what the producers no doubt hope will be a series. The director, Martin Campbell, did the Bond picture *GoldenEye*, and in a sense, *The Mask of Zorro* is a Bond picture on horseback: There's the megalomaniac villain, the plan to take over the world (or, in this case, California), the training of the hero, the bold entry into the enemy's social world, the romance with the bad guy's stepdaughter, and the sensational stunts. There's even the always-popular situation where the hero and the girl start out in a deadly struggle and end up in each other's arms.

All of this action is set in Mexico and California as they were in the first half of the nineteenth century, when the evil Don Rafael Montero (Stuart Wilson) rules the land, chooses peasants at random to be shot by a firing squad, and earns the enmity of the mysterious masked man Zorro.

In an opening setup, Zorro interrupts a public killing, inspires the population, and escapes back into domestic bliss. He's played by Anthony Hopkins, who in his daytime identity as Don Diego de la Vega has a beautiful wife and child. But Don Rafael invades his home, his men shoot the wife, Don Diego is imprisoned, and Don Rafael raises the daughter as his own.

Twenty years pass, and the movie's central story begins. It involves a street urchin named Alejandro, once befriended by Zorro, now grown into a bandit played by Antonio Banderas. Alejandro and Don Diego, now older and gray, meet and join forces, and Don Diego trains the youth to inherit the legend of Zorro. "You know how to use that?" the old man asks, pointing to the younger one's sword. "Yes," he says, "the point goes into the other man." Ah, but it's not as simple as that, and after lessons in fencing, horsemanship, hand-to-hand combat, and the arts of swinging from ropes and somersaulting out of danger, the older man thinks the younger one might be ready to foil old Don Rafael's plans. There's just one final lesson: "I must teach you something that is completely beyond your reach—charm."

Don Rafael's plans have now matured: He's amassed a fortune in gold from secret mines on Mexican land, and now wants to use the gold to buy California from General Santa Anna, who needs cash to fund his war against the United States. Since it's Santa Anna's gold, this is a brilliant plan—if Don Rafael can pull it off. As the rich plot unfolds, the new young Zorro, disguised as a Spanish nobleman, infiltrates Don Rafael's social circle, and romance blossoms between the newcomer and the beautiful daughter, Elena (Catherine Zeta-Jones).

The best scenes in the movie are between Banderas and Zeta-Jones, who share chemistry and, it turns out, a sense of justice. There is a dance at Don Rafael's house at which the daughter and the visitor take over the dance floor in a passionate pas de deux, and another scene where the outlaw hides in a confessional and listens with great interest as the young woman confesses her feelings of lust for a mysterious masked man. All of these threads come together in what starts as a duel to the death between the man and the woman, and ends in a surprised embrace.

The movie celebrates the kind of Western location shooting that's rarely seen these days: horses and haciendas, gold mines and dungeons, and a virtuoso display of horsemanship. The back story, involving the first Zorro's abiding love for the daughter who was stolen from him, is pure melodrama, but Anthony Hopkins brings it as much dignity and pathos as possible, and Zeta-Jones does a good job of handling the wide-eyed, heaving bosom, tears-in-eyes kind of stuff.

The movie is a display of traditional movie craftsmanship, especially at the level of the screenplay, which respects the characters and story and doesn't simply use them for dialogue breaks between action sequences. It's a reminder of the time when stunts and special effects were integrated into stories, rather than the other way around. And in giving full weight to the supporting characters and casting them with strong actors, *The Mask of Zorro* is involving as well as entertaining. I was surprised how much I enjoyed it. ☞

Masterminds ½★

PG-13, 106 m., 1997

Patrick Stewart (Raif Bentley), Vincent Kartheiser (Ozzie), Brenda Fricker (Principal Maloney), Brad Whitford (Miles Lawrence), Matt Craven (Jake), Annabelle Gurwitch (Helen), Jon Abrahams (K-Dog), Katie Stuart (Melissa). Directed by Roger Christian and produced by Robert Dudelson and Floyd Byars. Screenplay by Byars, based on a story by Byars, Alex Siskin, and Chris Black.

Patrick Stewart, best known for his work on *Star Trek*, is an actor of effortless class and presence, and *Masterminds* is like an obstacle course he has to run. Can he make it from beginning to end of this dreadful movie without lowering himself to its level of idiocy? Or will he go down with the material? The answer to that question provides the only suspense and nearly the only interest in one of the worst films of the year.

The premise: Young Ozzie (Vincent Kartheiser) is a computer hacker who has been exiled for life from the exclusive Shady Glen School. His father threatens to send him to a military academy. He has his bedroom rigged with motion detectors and spends his days downloading pirated software.

He takes his little sister, Melissa (Katie Stuart), to the school, which is walled and guarded like the CIA, and talks his way past the security guard. Inside, he confronts the bossy principal (Brenda Fricker) and the ominous Raif Bentley (Patrick Stewart), the school's newly-hired chief of security, who has been brought on staff mostly because of the recent depredations of Ozzie.

To make a long but shallow story into a short but no less shallow one, it turns out that Bentley plans to kidnap ten of the kids, whose parents are among the richest people in America. And Ozzie, locked inside the school during a hostage crisis, uses his skills as a hacker and troublemaker to battle the evil scheme.

More than that you do not need to know, since already in your mind you are conjuring up images of air shafts, abandoned boiler rooms, hacked computers, obscure electrical connections, and ways to commandeer the school's public address system. The details run together in my mind. I lost all interest. I stopped taking notes on my Palm Pilot and started playing the little chess game.

Since we have all seen this movie several times (all of the pieces have been assembled from better films, but then there are few worse films to borrow from), the sole remaining interest comes from the presence of Patrick Stewart. He is clipped, trim, precise, wise. He narrows his eyes impressively. He is a good actor, and no doubt signed up for this movie for the same reason as everyone else involved: A case of mass hallucination in which the screenplay appeared to be for another film.

Does Stewart emerge unsullied? Very nearly. I give him credit for that. Right up until almost the very end of the film, he retains a certain poise and dignity. But then (do not read further if you intend to see this film) he is placed in a situation that, I submit, no actor could survive. Not De Niro. Not Olivier. He is made to take little Melissa hostage and then engage in a high-speed chase with Ozzie through a sewer system, using souped-up dune buggies.

If you go to see *Masterminds*, do not by any means walk out early. You must stay, simply to appreciate Stewart's expression as he struggles with the little hostage who is trying to jump off his dune buggy. I cannot read lips or minds, but I intuit that what he is saying, if only as an interior monologue, runs along the lines of, "Beam me the hell up outta here!"

The Matchmaker ★ ★ ★

R, 96 m., 1997

Janeane Garofalo (Marcy), David O'Hara (Sean), Jay O. Sanders (McGlory), Denis Leary (Nick), Milo O'Shea (Dermot). Directed by Mark Joffe and produced by Tim Bevan, Eric Fellner, and Luc Roeg. Screenplay by Karen Janszen, Louis Nowra, and Graham Linehan, based on a screenplay by Greg Dinner.

I attempted once in a review to write that the Irish "have the gift of gab," and was reprimanded by an editor who told me this was an unwarranted and possibly offensive generalization about an ethnic group.

That editor has moved on and a new regime rules, which allows me to risk offending readers of Irish descent by stating that, yes, the Irish do indeed often express themselves with freedom and an innate poetry.

Some Americans, especially northerners and those involved in political campaigns, also have a certain vocal style, which might be described as "cutting out the crap and getting to the bottom line." And one of the pleasures of *The Matchmaker* is to hear these two styles in conflict. Milo O'Shea, that twinkly professional Irishman, has enormous fun expounding on his theories of romance, and Janeane Garofalo, who has a built-in blarney detector, cuts to the chase.

The movie stars Garofalo as Marcy, an aide to the fatuous Senator McGlory from Massachusetts (Jay O. Sanders), who is behind in his campaign for reelection and dispatches her to Ireland to round up some ancestors so he can visit them.

This is not her idea of a good time. In Ireland, on a bus to McGlory's ancestral village of Ballinagra, she finds herself surrounded by ebullient women who seem on the brink of song. "Do men and women have to travel separately in Ireland?" she asks grumpily, only to discover she is en route to the village's annual matchmaking festival, at which unattached men and women size up the opposition.

In Ballinagra, the hotel facilities are primitive ("a little bijou," is how the clerk puts it), the locals seem to be speaking in code, the customs are incomprehensible, and the local color is seductive.

There have been a lot of good-hearted comedies from Ireland in recent years, and many of them argue more or less the same thing: Instead of watching the telly and cowering behind locked doors, we'd be better off among people who know each other and enjoy singsongs in pubs. I am always persuaded by this argument.

In Ballinagra, Marcy meets Sean (David O'Hara), a former journalist who has retreated to this rural backwater in order to work on a book. He is not her idea of sophistication, especially when he has a Kleenex stuck up his nostril because of a nosebleed. They strike uneasy sparks.

Meanwhile, the professional matchmaker Dermot (Milo O'Shea) drums up customers for his other business, Turbo Tans, and keeps an eye on Marcy and Sean. He senses a certain chemistry there, and when a competitor bets him £100 he can't match them up, he takes the bet and contrives to send them to one of the isolated Aran Islands, where, he says, lives the only genealogist in Ireland capable of tracing the senator's ancestors.

The scenes on the island are magnificent. The scenery is wild and forbidding, the sea is awesome, the people are suspicious at first and then quickly friendly, and in no time Marcy finds herself judging the song contest at the local pub. (Sample lyrics: "In eighteen hundred and forty-one, my corduroy britches I put on.")

Whether Marcy and Sean will find love, I leave you to discover. Whether the senator will personally arrive on the scene, I leave you to predict. Whether the action returns to America, I reluctantly confirm, since the Irish center of the film is so charming we feel distracted by the bookends.

Matchmaker might have been better if it hadn't shoehorned in the Massachusetts scenes, but it could hardly be more entertaining in its Irish material. Garofalo, fresh from the magical *Truth About Cats and Dogs,* is one of the most engaging actresses around. We relate with her cynical intelligence and the warmth of her smile as she makes observations such as, "The basis of any friendship is that the two people not hate each other." Somehow we are not surprised that this is the only romantic comedy in which a downhearted lover attempts suicide by tanning.

The Matrix ★ ★ ★

R, 135 m., 1999

Keanu Reeves (Neo), Laurence Fishburne (Morpheus), Carrie-Anne Moss (Trinity), Hugo Weaving (Agent Smith), Joe Pantoliano (Cypher), Gloria Foster (Oracle). Directed by Larry and Andy Wachowski and produced by Joel Silver and Dan Cracchiolo. Screenplay by Larry and Andy Wachowski.

The Matrix is a visually dazzling cyberadventure, full of kinetic excitement, but it retreats to formula just when it's getting interesting. It's kind of a letdown when a movie begins by redefining the nature of reality and ends with a shoot-out. We want a leap of the imagination, not one of those obligatory climaxes with automatic weapons fire.

I've seen dozens if not hundreds of these exercises in violence, which recycle the same tired ideas: Bad guys fire thousands of rounds, but are unable to hit the good guy. Then it's down to the final showdown between good and evil—a martial arts battle in which the good guy gets pounded until he's almost dead, before he finds the inner will to fight back. Been there, seen that (although rarely done this well).

Too bad, because the setup is intriguing. *The Matrix* recycles the premises of *Dark City* and *Strange Days,* turns up the heat and the volume, and borrows the gravity-defying choreography of Hong Kong action movies. It's fun, but it could have been more. The directors are Larry and Andy Wachowski, who know how to make movies (their first film, *Bound,* made my ten best list in 1996). Here, with a big budget and veteran action producer Joel Silver, they've played it safer; there's nothing wrong with going for the Friday night action market, but you can aim higher and still do business.

Warning; spoilers ahead. The plot involves Neo (Keanu Reeves), a mild-mannered software author by day, a feared hacker by night. He's recruited by a cell of cyber-rebels, led by the profound Morpheus (Laurence Fishburne) and the leather-clad warrior Trinity (Carrie-Anne Moss). They've made a fundamental discovery about the world: It doesn't exist. It's actually a form of Virtual Reality, designed to lull us into lives of blind obedience to the "system." We obediently go to our crummy jobs every day, little realizing, as Morpheus tells Neo, that "Matrix is the wool that has been pulled over your eyes—that you are a slave."

The rebels want to crack the framework that holds the Matrix in place and free mankind. Morpheus believes Neo is the Messianic "One" who can lead this rebellion, which requires mind power as much as physical strength. Arrayed against them are the Agents, who look like Blues Brothers. The movie's battles take place in Virtual Reality; the heroes' minds are plugged into the combat. (You can still get killed, though: "The body cannot live without the mind.")

"Jacking in" like this was a concept in *Strange Days* and has also been suggested in novels by William Gibson *(Idoru)* and others. The notion that the world is an artificial construction, designed by outsiders to deceive and use humans, is straight out of *Dark City.* Both of those movies, however, explored their implications as the best science fiction often does. *Dark City* was fascinated by the Strangers who had a poignant dilemma: They were dying aliens who hoped to learn from human methods of adaptation and survival.

In *Matrix,* on the other hand, there aren't flesh-and-blood creatures behind the illusion—only a computer program that can think and learn. The Agents function primarily as opponents in a high-stakes computer game. The movie offers no clear explanation of why the Matrix-making program went to all that trouble. Of course, for a program, running is its own reward—but an intelligent program might bring terrifying logic to its decisions.

Both *Dark City* and *Strange Days* offered

intriguing motivations for villainy. *Matrix* is more like a superhero comic book in which the fate of the world comes down to a titanic fistfight between the designated representatives of good and evil. It's cruel, really, to put tantalizing ideas on the table and then ask the audience to be satisfied with a shoot-out and a martial arts duel.

Let's assume Neo wins. What happens then to the billions who have just been "unplugged" from the Matrix? Do they still have jobs? Homes? Identities? All we get is an enigmatic voice-over exhortation at the movie's end. The paradox is that the Matrix world apparently resembles in every respect the pre-Matrix world. (I am reminded of the animated kid's film *Doug's 1st Movie,* which has a VR experience in which everything is exactly like in real life, except more expensive.)

Still, I must not ignore the movie's virtues. It's great-looking, both in its design and in the kinetic energy that powers it. It uses flawlessly integrated special effects and animation to visualize regions of cyberspace. It creates fearsome creatures, including mechanical octopi. It morphs bodies with the abandon of *Terminator II.* It uses f/x to allow Neo and Trinity to run horizontally on walls, and hang in the air long enough to deliver karate kicks. It has leaps through space, thrilling sequences involving fights on rooftops, helicopter rescues, and battles over mind control.

And it has performances that find the right notes. Keanu Reeves goes for the impassive Harrison Ford approach, "acting" as little as possible. I suppose that's the right idea. Laurence Fishburne finds a balance between action hero and Zen master. Carrie-Anne Moss, as Trinity, has a sensational title sequence, before the movie recalls that she's a woman and shuttles her into support mode. Hugo Weaving, as the chief Agent, uses a flat, menacing tone that reminded me of Tommy Lee Jones in passive-aggressive overdrive. There's a well-acted scene involving Gloria Foster as the Oracle, who like all oracles is maddeningly enigmatic.

The Matrix did not bore me. It interested me so much, indeed, that I wanted to be challenged even more. I wanted it to follow its material to audacious conclusions, to arrive not simply at victory, but at revelation. I wanted an ending that was transformational, like *Dark City*'s, and not one that simply throws us a sensational action sequence. I wanted, in short, a third act. ☞

Ma Vie en Rose ★ ★ ★

R, 88 m., 1998

Georges Du Fresne (Ludovic), Michele Laroque (Hanna), Jean-Philippe Ecoffey (Pierre), Helene Vincent (Elisabeth), Julien Riviere (Jerome), Cristina Barget (Zoe), Gregory Diallo (Thom), Erik Cazals De Fabel (Jean). Directed by Alain Berliner and produced by Carole Scotta. Screenplay by Chris vander Stappen and Berliner.

Ludovic is a seven-year-old boy who likes to dress in girl's clothes, not so much because he likes the clothes as because he is convinced he is a girl. It all seems very clear. After he learns about chromosomes, he explains to his parents that instead of the female XX chromosomes he was intended to get, he received the male XY after "my other X fell in the garbage."

Ludovic's parents have just moved to a suburb of Paris that looks for all the world like a set for *Ozzie and Harriet.* Ominously, they live next door to his father's boss. A barbecue is planned to welcome the newcomers, and it's at this party that Ludovic makes his dramatic entrance, dressed in pink. The adults, who would not have looked twice at a little girl wearing jeans and sneakers, are stunned. "It's normal until seven," Ludovic's mother explains bravely. "I read it in *Marie-Claire.*"

Ma Vie en Rose offers gentle fantasy, and a little hard reality, about Ludovic's predicament. He is convinced he is a girl, knows some sort of mistake was made, and is serenely intent on correcting it. Soon he's making the arrangements for a play "marriage" with Jerome, his best friend, who lives next door and is therefore, unluckily, the boss's son. Since the boss is a blustering bigot, this is not a good idea. Indeed, most of the adults in the movie seem like members of the Gender Role Enforcement Police.

The film is careful to keep its focus within childhood. It's not a story about homosexuality or transvestism, but about a little boy who thinks he's a little girl. Maybe Ludovic, played by a calmly self-possessed eleven-year-old named Georges Du Fresne, will grow up to be gay. Maybe not. That's not what the movie is about. And the performance reflects Ludovic's innocence and naïveté; there is no sexual awareness in his dressing up, but simply a determination to set things right.

The movie is about two ways of seeing things: the child's and the adult's. It shows how children construct elaborate play worlds out of dreams and fantasies, and then plug their real worlds right into them. Ludovic's alternate universe is ruled by his favorite TV personality, named Pam, who dresses like a princess and has a boyfriend named Ken and flies about the house with her sparkling magic wand. It also contains his beloved grandmother. In this world Ludovic is sort of an assistant princess, and we can see how his worship of Pam has made him want to be just like her.

Adults, on the other hand, see things in more literal terms and are less open to fantasy. No one is threatened by a girl who dresses like a boy, but the father's boss is just one of the people who sees red whenever Ludovic turns up in drag. This innocent little boy is made to pay for all the gay phobias, fears, and prejudices of the adult world.

Because *Ma Vie en Rose (My Life in Pink)* is a comedy, however, the going never gets too heavy. Ludovic is taken to a psychiatrist, he is shouted at by his (mostly sympathetic) parents, he is a figure of mystery to his three well-adjusted siblings, and he is a threat to the stability of his neighborhood. Since it's one of those sitcom neighborhoods where everyone spends a lot of time out on the lawn or gossiping over the driveways, what happens to one family is the concern of all.

Ma Vie en Rose is the first film by Alain Berliner, a Belgian, who worked from the original screenplay of Chris vander Stappen, herself a tomboy who got a lot of heat as a child. There are clearly important personal issues at work beneath the surface, especially for Ms. vander Stappen, who identifies herself as a lesbian, but they skate above them. And there is a certain suspense: Surely Ludovic cannot simply be humored? Simply allowed to dress as a girl? Or can he?

Meet Joe Black ★ ★ ★

PG-13, 174 m., 1998

Brad Pitt (Joe Black), Anthony Hopkins (William Parrish), Claire Forlani (Susan Parrish), Jake Weber (Drew), Marcia Gay Harden (Allison), Jeffrey Tambor (Quince), David S. Howard (Eddie Sloane), Lois Kelly-Miller (Jamaican Woman). Directed and produced by Martin Brest. Screenplay by Ron Osborn, Jeff Reno, Kevin Wade, and Bo Goldman.

Meet Joe Black is a movie about a rich man trying to negotiate the terms of his own death. It is a movie about a woman who falls in love with a concept. And it is a meditation on the screen presence of Brad Pitt. That there is also time for scenes about sibling rivalry and a corporate takeover is not necessarily a good thing. The movie contains elements that make it very good, and then a lot of other elements besides. Less is more.

As the movie opens, a millionaire named William Parrish (Anthony Hopkins) is pounded by a heart attack, the sound track using low bass chords to assault the audience. He hears a voice—his own—in his head. On the brink of his sixty-fifth birthday, he senses that death is near. He tells his beloved younger daughter, Susan (Claire Forlani), that he likes her fiancé, but doesn't sense that she truly loves him: "Stay open. Lightning could strike."

It does. A few hours later in a coffee shop, she meets a stranger (Brad Pitt). They talk and flirt. He says all the right things. Lightning makes, at the very least, a near miss. They confess they really like one another. They part. He is killed. That night at dinner, she is startled to find him among her father's guests. The body of the young man is now occupied by Death, who has come to inform Parrish that his end is near.

He does not recognize Susan. That's odd. Isn't Death an emissary from God? Shouldn't he know these things? He's been around a long time (one imagines him breaking the bad news to amoebas). This Death doesn't even know what peanut butter tastes like, or how to kiss. A job like that, you want a more experienced man.

No matter. We accept the premise. We're distracted, anyway, by the way Brad Pitt plays the role. As both the young man in the coffee shop and as "Joe Black" (the name given him by Parrish), he is intensely aware of himself—too aware. Pitt is a fine actor, but this performance is a miscalculation. Meryl Streep once said that an experienced actor knows that the words "I love you" are really a question. Pitt plays them as a compliment to himself. There is no chemistry between Joe Black and Susan because both parties are focused on him.

That at least leads to the novelty of a rare movie love scene where the camera is focused on the man's face, not the woman's. Actresses have become skilled over the years at faking orgasms on camera, usually with copious cries of delight and sobs of passion. (As they're buffeted by their competent male lovers, I am sometimes reminded of a teenager making the cheerleader team, crossed with a new war widow.) A male actor would have to be very brave to reveal such loss of control, and Pitt's does not cry out. His orgasm plays in slow motion across his face like a person who is thinking, "This is way better than peanut butter."

I was not, in short, sold on the relationship between Susan and Joe. She spends most of the movie puzzling about a very odd man who briefly made her heart feel gooey. There is no person there for her, just the idea of perfect love. Joe Black is presented as a being who is not familiar with occupying a human body or doing human things. One wonders—is this the first time Death has tried this approach? Parrish strikes a deal with him (he won't die as long as he can keep Joe interested and teach him new things) and he takes him everywhere with him, including board meetings, where Joe's response to most situations is total silence, while looking like the cat that ate the mouse.

The Parrish character, and Anthony Hopkins's performance, are entirely different matters. Hopkins invests the dying millionaire with intelligence and acceptance, and he talks wonderfully well. *Meet Joe Black* consists largely of conversations, which are well written and do not seem false or forced as long as Parrish is involved in them. His key business relationships are with the snaky Drew (Jake Weber), whom Susan dumps for Joe, and with the avuncular Quince (Jeffrey Tambor), his loyal but bumbling son-in-law. Quince is married to Allison (Marcia Gay Harden), who knows Susan is her father's favorite but can live with that because Parrish is such a swell guy. (He's ethical, sensitive, and beloved—the first movie rich man who could at least squeeze his head and shoulders through the eye of the needle.)

What's fascinating about Parrish is that he handles death as he has handled everything else. He makes a realistic assessment of his chances, sees what advantages he can extract, negotiates for the best possible terms, and gracefully accepts the inevitable. There are times when he handles his talks with Death so surely that you wish heaven had sent a more articulate negotiator.

The movie's ending takes too long. There are farewells, reflections, confessions, reassurances, reconciliations, partings, and surprises. Joe Black begins to get on our nerves with his knack of saying things that are technically true, but incomplete and misleading. The film would play better if he didn't always have to talk in epigrams. Even at the very end, when a line or two of direct dialogue would have cleared the air, he's still talking in acrostic clues.

Still, there's so much that's fine in this movie, directed by Martin Brest *(Scent of a Woman)*. Claire Forlani has a touching vulnerability as she negotiates the strange terms of her love. Marcia Gay Harden plays a wise, grown-up scene with Hopkins, as a loving daughter who knows she isn't the favorite. Jeffrey Tambor's performance is crucial; through his eyes, we understand what a good man Parrish is. And Anthony Hopkins inhabits a story that tends toward quicksand and finds dry land. You sense a little of his *Nixon* here: A man who can use anger like a scalpel, while still standing back to monitor the result.

Meet the Deedles ★ ½

PG, 90 m., 1998

Steve Van Wormer (Stew Deedle), Paul Walker (Phil Deedle), A. J. Langer (Jesse Ryan), John Ashton (Captain Douglas Pine), Dennis Hopper (Frank Slater), Eric Braeden (Elton Deedle), Richard Lineback (Crabbe), Robert Englund (Nemo). Directed by Steve Boyum and produced by Dale Pollock and Aaron Meyerson. Screenplay by Jim Herzfeld.

The cult of stupidity is irresistible to teenagers in a certain mood. It's a form of rebellion, maybe: If the real world is going to reject them, then they'll simply refuse to get it. Using jargon and incomprehension as weapons, they'll create their own alternate universe.

All of which is a tortuous way to explain *Meet the Deedles*, a movie with no other ambition than to create mindless slapstick and generate a series in the tradition of the *Bill and Ted* movies. The story involves twin brothers Stew and Phil Deedle (Steve Van Wormer and Paul Walker), slackers from Hawaii who find themselves in the middle of a fiendish plot to sabotage Old Faithful in Yellowstone National Park.

As the movie opens, Stew and Phil are hanging beneath a balloon being towed above the Hawaiian surf, while being pursued by a truant officer on a Jet Ski. Soon they're called on the carpet before their millionaire father (Eric Braeden), who snorts, "You will one day take over the entire Deedles empire—and you are surf bums!" His plan: Send them to Camp Broken Spirit, a monthlong experience in outdoor living that will turn them into men.

Through plot developments unnecessary to relate, the Deedles escape the camp experience, are mistaken for Park Ranger recruits, come under the command of Ranger Pine (John Ashton), and stumble onto the solution to a mysterious infestation of prairie dogs.

Now prairie dogs can be cute, as anyone who has seen Disney's *The Living Prairie* nature documentary can testify. But in large numbers they look alarmingly like herds of rats, and the earth trembles (slightly) as they scurry across the park. Why so many prairie dogs? Because an evil ex-ranger named Slater (Dennis Hopper) has trained them to burrow out a cavern around Old Faithful, allowing him to redirect the geyser's boiling waters in the direction of New Faithful, to which he plans to sell tickets.

Hopper lives in the cavern, relaxing in his E-Z-Boy recliner and watching the surface on TV monitors. His sidekicks include Nemo, played by Robert Englund, Freddy of the *Nightmare on Elm Street* pictures. At one point he explains how he trained the prairie dogs, and I will add to my permanent memory bank the sound of Dennis Hopper saying, "Inject kibble into the dirt, and a-tunneling they would go." Study his chagrin when the Deedles employ Mentholatum Deep Heat Rub as a weapon in this war.

While he schemes, the Deedles fumble and blunder their way through ranger training, and Phil falls for Jesse (A. J. Langer), the pretty stepdaughter of Ranger Pine. There are a lot of stunts, involving mountains, truck crashes, and river rapids, and then the big showdown over Old Faithful. The Deedles relate to everything in surfer terms (plowing into a snowbank, they cry, "We've landed in a Slurpy!").

I am prepared to imagine a theater full of eleven-year-old boys who might enjoy this movie, but I can't recommend it for anyone who might have climbed a little higher on the evolutionary ladder. The *Bill and Ted* movies had a certain sly self-awareness that this one lacks. Maybe that's a virtue. Maybe it isn't.

Men in Black ★ ★ ★

PG-13, 98 m., 1997

Tommy Lee Jones (K), Will Smith (J), Linda Fiorentino (Laurel), Vincent D'Onofrio (Edgar), Rip Torn (Zed), Tony Shalhoub (Jeebs), Siobhan Fallon (Beatrice). Directed by Barry Sonnenfeld and produced by Walter F. Parkes and Laurie MacDonald. Screenplay by Ed Solomon.

There is a moment in *Men in Black* when a grim government official shows a wall chart of "every alien on Earth." We're not too surprised to see some of the faces on display: Sylvester Stallone, Al Roker, Newt Gingrich, Dionne Warwick. (When the movie comes out on video, I'll use freeze frames to capture the rest.) Wicked little side jokes like that are the heart and soul of *Men in Black* (or *MiB*, as it is already being called, no doubt in the movie title-as-software tradition of *ID4*).

A lot of big-budget special-effects films are a hair this side of self-parody and don't know it. *Men in Black* knows it and glories in it; it's a refreshing Bronx cheer aimed at movies that think $100 million budgets equal solemnity. This is not a film about superheroes, but the adventures of a couple of hardworking functionaries whose assignment is to keep tabs on the sizable alien population of the United States.

Tommy Lee Jones, never more serious, unsmiling, and businesslike, stars as K, the veteran agent of Division 6, whose members dress, as William Morris agents used to, in black suits and black ties. The agency is headed by Zed (Rip Torn), who grows alarmed at the latest threat to Earth's sovereignty, and assigns K a young assistant code-named J (Will Smith).

Their biggest problem materializes when a flying saucer strikes the truck of a hillbilly named Edgar (Vincent D'Onofrio), and the alien inside occupies his body, none too comfortably. Imagine Orson Welles in a suit of armor and you will have a rough approximation of how easily the Edgar-alien inhabits his skin.

The running gag in the movie is that almost anyone could be an alien; the film begins on the Mexican border, where Jones takes charge of a group of lawmen who have nabbed some illegal aliens, and picks out the one who is *really* an alien: a fantastical, blobby, bug-eyed monster with a realistic human face mask.

The special effects are by Industrial Light and Magic, and the aliens are by Rick Baker, perhaps Hollywood's greatest creator of monsters. Here he goes hog-wild. Instead of being asked to create one alien race, he's been assigned to create a galaxy-full, and every one is a new surprise. There were times I thought we were seeing the new seven dwarfs: Slimy, Gooey, Icky, Creepy, Sticky, Barfy, and Pox.

The plot (if there can be said to be one, and if I understood it) involves Edgar's scheme to somehow use a captured galaxy to conquer Earth. Although aliens would presumably be more advanced than we laggards on Earth, many of these aliens seem to have advanced only to the approximate level of the Three Stooges, and are vanquished by a series of bizarre weapons employed by J and K (you may have seen the previews: "Any idea how to use this?" "None whatsoever").

Linda Fiorentino, still looking for the right role to follow her triumph in *The Last Seduction*, hasn't found it here—but her hard-bitten coroner will do nicely as an intermediate step. Performing autopsies on some of these creatures is a process much like dissecting very old spinach lasagna.

The movie makes good use of a lot of New York landmarks (there's a chase through the Guggenheim, a flying saucer lands in Shea Stadium, and another one has been disguised as an exhibit at the 1964 World's Fair). Director Barry Sonnenfeld (*The Addams Family* and its sequel) shows a cheerful willingness in the movie's first hour or so to completely cut loose from all conventions of dreary storytelling and simply let the story follow the laughs and absurdities. Writer Ed Solomon, who on the basis of this irreverent screenplay could probably play all three of the critics on MST3K, deflates one sci-fi pomposity after another.

When the plot finally does click in, it slows down the trajectory a little, but not fatally. *Men in Black* expands on the tradition of big-budget action pictures that at least have the wit to know how silly they are.

Men With Guns ★ ★ ★ ★

R, 128 m., 1998

Federico Luppi (Dr. Fuentes), Damian Delgado (Domingo, the Soldier), Dan Rivera Gonzalez (Conejo, the Boy), Tania Cruz (Graciela, the Mute Girl), Damian Alcazar (Padre Portillo, the Priest), Mandy Patinkin (Andrew), Kathryn Grody (Harriet). Directed by John Sayles and produced by R. Paul Miller and Maggie Renzi. Screenplay by Sayles.

Men With Guns tells the story of a doctor in an unnamed Central American country who makes a trip into the rain forest to visit the young medical students he trained some years earlier. They were supposed to fan out among the Indian villages, fighting tapeworm and other scourges. The doctor has reason to believe many of them have been killed.

The doctor's journey is enlarged by John Sayles into an allegory about all countries where men with guns control the daily lives of the people. Some of the men are with the government, some are guerrillas, some are thieves, some are armed to protect themselves, and to the ordinary people it hardly matters: The man with the gun does what he wants, and his reasons are irrelevant—unknown perhaps even to himself.

The film takes the form of a journey, sometimes harrowing, sometimes poetic. It has a backbone of symbolism, as many great stories do. As the doctor moves from the city to the country, from the shore to the mountains, he also moves through history. We see the ruins of older civilizations that lived in this land, and we see powerless villagers moved here and there according to arbitrary whims. They are killed by the military for helping the guerrillas, and killed by the guerrillas for helping the military, and their men are killed simply because they are men without guns. There is no suggestion that either military or guerrillas have any larger program than to live well off the spoils of power.

The doctor (Federico Luppi), tall and white-haired, has a grave dignity. He is not an action hero, but a man who has been given a pass in life; while he has lived comfortably in the capital with a nice practice, his country's reality has passed him by. As he ventures into the countryside, he gathers four traveling companions. There is an army deserter, now a thief, who first steals from him, then joins him. A former priest ("his church calls it liberation theology, but he preferred to liberate himself"). A young boy who knows the area better than any of them and has an uncanny ability to judge the essence of a situation. And a woman who has not spoken since she was raped.

The critic Tom Keogh suggests that there is an element of *The Wizard of Oz* in the doctor and his companions, who need a heart, a voice, and courage. There are also suggestions of *Treasure of the Sierra Madre* and other stories in which a legendary goal—Oz, gold, El Dorado—is said to be hidden further on. In this case the travelers begin to hear about a village named "The Circle of Heaven," which is so high on a mountain and so deep in the trees that the helicopters cannot find it, and people live free. Sayles tells his story in a series of vignettes—encounters on the road, stories told, flashbacks of earlier experiences, a touch of magic realism.

From time to time, the travelers and their journey are interrupted by two other characters, chatty American tourists (Mandy Patinkin and Kathryn Grody) who are looking for "antiques" and haven't a clue about the reality of the land and people behind them.

The tourists serve a satirical purpose, but I found myself seeing them in a different light. From time to time, reviewing a movie, I'll say the leading characters were shallow but the people in the background seemed interesting. In that sense, *Men With Guns* is about the background. Sayles finances his own films. If he had taken this script to a studio executive, he no doubt would have been told to beef up the American tourist roles and cast the roles with stars. The film would have become an action sitcom with Indians, doctors, priests, and orphans in the background as local color.

If you doubt me, look again at *Medicine Man* (1992), with Sean Connery in the rain forest, or *Anaconda* (1997), with snake-hunters up the Amazon. In my bemusement, every time the American tourists turned up, I thought of them as visitors from the phantom Hollywood revision of this material: magic realism of a different sort. It's as if Sayles is saying, "Here's what the studios would have made this movie into."

When the history of the century's films is written, John Sayles will stand tall as a director who went his own way, made his own films, directed and edited them himself, and operated completely outside the traditional channels of distribution and finance. When we hear Francis Coppola's lament that he has to make a John Grisham film in order to make one of his "own" films, we can only reflect that Sayles has demonstrated that a director can be completely independent if he chooses.

Men With Guns is immensely moving and sad, and yet because it dares so much, it is an exhilarating film. It frees itself from specific stories about *this* villain or *that* strategy to stand back and look at the big picture: at societies in collapse because power has been concentrated in the hands of small men made big with guns. I understand guns in war, in hunting, in sport. But when a man feels he needs a gun to leave his house in the morning, I fear that man. I fear his fear. He believes that the only man more powerless than himself is a dead man.

Mercury Rising ★★

R, 108 m., 1998

Bruce Willis (Art Jeffries), Alec Baldwin (Kudrow), Miko Hughes (Simon), Chi McBride (Bizzi Jordan), Kim Dickens (Stacey), Robert Stanton (Dean), Bodhi Pine Elfman (Leo).

Directed by Harold Becker and produced by Brian Grazer and Karen Kehela. Screenplay by Lawrence Konner, Ryne Douglas Pearson, and Mark Rosenthal, based on the novel by Pearson.

Mercury Rising is about the most sophisticated cryptographic system known to man, and about characters considerably denser than anyone in the audience. Sitting in the dark, our minds idly playing with the plot, we figure out what they should do, how they should do it, and why they should do it, while the characters on the screen strain helplessly against the requirements of the formula.

The movie begins with the two obligatory scenes of most rogue lawman scenarios: (1) Opening hostage situation, in which the hero (Bruce Willis) could have saved the situation if not for his trigger-happy superiors; (2) The calling on the carpet, in which his boss tells the lawman he's being pulled off the job and assigned to grunt duty. "You had it—but the magic's gone," the boss recites. Willis's only friend is a sidekick named Bizzi Jordan (Chi McBride), who has, as is the nature of sidekicks, a wife and child, so that the hero can gaze upon them and ponder his solitude.

Experienced moviegoers will know that in the course of his diminished duties, Willis (playing an FBI man named Jeffries) will stumble across a bigger case. And will try to solve it single-handedly, while he is the object of a police manhunt. And will eventually engage in a hand-to-hand struggle with the sinister man behind the scheme. This struggle will preferably occur in a high place (see "Climbing Killer," from *Ebert's Little Movie Glossary*). Plus, there's a good bet the hero will enlist a good-looking woman who will drop everything for a chance to get shot at while by his side.

The new twist this time is explained by the evil bureaucrat (Alec Baldwin) in one of several lines of dialogue he should have insisted on rewriting: "A nine-year-old has deciphered the most sophisticated cipher system ever known—and he's autistic!?!" Yes, little Simon (Miko Hughes) looks at a word game in a puzzle magazine, and while the sound track emits quasi-computeristic beeping noises, he figures out the code concealed there, and calls the secret phone number, causing two geeks in a safe room to leap about in dismay.

Agents are dispatched to try to kill the kid and his parents, who live in Chicago. FBI agent Jeffries comes late to the scene, eyeballs the dead parents, immediately intuits it wasn't really a murder-suicide ("How's a guy that's so broke afford a $1,500 handgun?"), and then finds Simon hiding in a crawl space. Putting two and two together (without beeping noises), he deduces that Simon knows a secret, and powerful people want to destroy him.

The movie then descends into formula again, with obligatory scenes in which the police guard is mysteriously pulled off duty in a hospital corridor (see *The Godfather*), and Jeffries runs down corridors with the kid under his arm while evil agents demonstrate that no marksman, however well trained, can hit anyone important while there's still an hour to go. (The David Mamet movie *The Spanish Prisoner,* which is as smart as *Mercury Rising* is dumb, has the hero ask a markswoman: "What if you had missed?" and supplies her with the perfect answer: "It would be back to the range for me!")

The movie's greatest test of credibility comes when Jeffries, object of a citywide manhunt, walks into a restaurant in the Wrigley Building, meets a complete stranger named Stacey (Kim Dickens), and asks her to watch the kid for him while he goes on a quick mission. Of course Stacey agrees, and cooperates again when the agent and the kid turn up at her house in the middle of the night and ask for a safe place to stay. Before long, indeed, she's blowing off a business trip to Des Moines because, well, what woman wouldn't instinctively trust an unshaven man in a sweaty T-shirt, with an autistic kid under his arm and a gun in his belt—especially if the cops were after him?

What is sad is that the performances by Willis, Dickens, and young Miko Hughes are really pretty good—better than the material deserves. Willis doesn't overplay or overspeak, which redeems some of the silly material, and Dickens somehow finds a way through the requirements of her role that allows her to sidestep her character's wildly implausible decisions.

But what happened to Alec Baldwin's BS detector? Better replace those batteries! His character utters speeches that are laughable in any context, especially this one: "You know," he says, "my wife says my people skills are like my cooking skills—quick and tasteless." And listen to his silky speech in the rain as he defends his actions.

Here are the two most obvious problems that sentient audiences will have with the plot. (1) Modern encryption cannot be intuitively deciphered, by rainmen or anyone else, without a key. And (2) if a nine-year-old kid can break your code, don't kill the kid; kill the programmers.

A Merry War ★ ★ ★

NO MPAA RATING, 100 m., 1998

Richard E. Grant (Gordon Comstock), Helena Bonham Carter (Rosemary), Julian Wadham (Ravelston), Jim Carter (Erskine), Harriet Walter (Julia Comstock), Lesley Vickerage (Hermione), Liz Smith (Mrs. Meakin), Barbara Leigh Hunt (Mrs. Wisbeach). Directed by Robert Bierman and produced by Peter Shaw. Screenplay by Alan Plater, based on the novel by George Orwell.

A Merry War is the insipid and enigmatic new title for a film released in England as *Keep the Aspidistra Flying.* That may not be an inspired title either, but at least it is the title of the famous 1936 novel by George Orwell, and a play on the communist slogan "Keep the Red Flag Flying." In Orwell's England, the aspidistra, a house plant almost impossible to kill through neglect, was a symbol of suburban living rooms. And his hero, Gordon Comstock, seems determined to find out how much neglect he can endure.

Comstock is a version of Orwell with many autobiographical parallels, I suspect, and as played by Richard E. Grant, has the same long face, deep eyes, towering brow, and morose demeanor. The film begins with Comstock quitting his job at an advertising agency in order to write poetry, only to find that poets, like everyone else, need money.

He gets a job in a ratty used bookstore in the slums of Lambeth but is reminded by the dusty shelves and sparse business that his boss at the ad agency was probably right when he asked, "Isn't there enough poetry in the world already?" The final straw comes when Gordon finds his own slim volume of verse marked down to three pence.

In Gordon's life there is one sparkle of sunshine, and it is provided by Rosemary (Helena Bonham Carter), an artist at the agency, who rather improbably loves him and even believes in him. But Gordon has no money to take her out, no money for a clean shirt or laundry, no money for smokes or even for tea (he cadges off his sister, who works in a tea shop). The movie, and the novel, capture the desperation of the Great Depression, when people like Gordon, whose family had just barely slipped into the middle class, were in danger of slipping out again.

Orwell himself was a connoisseur of poverty. His book *Down and Out in Paris and London* chronicles time spent living among the poor; he supported himself as a dishwasher in Paris, inhabiting another universe from the diners who dirtied the dishes. And he worked for a time in a London used bookstore; you can see his face gazing down from the wall of a pizza parlor at 1 South End Street in Hampstead, where the bookstore once operated.

The novel is billed as "Orwell's only comedy," although a better case can be made for *Animal Farm,* and the humor in *Keep the Aspidistra Flying* is of a sardonic turn: "The public are swine; advertising is the rattling of a stick inside a swill-bucket." The movie plays more as a morality tale, in which Gordon thinks he can escape advertising and is proven wrong. "I was called 'promising' by the *Times Literary Supplement,*" he tells his long-suffering publisher. "I know," says the publisher. "I wrote it."

Gordon hardly deserves Rosemary's sweetness and trust, but she is his savior. As played by Helena Bonham Carter, she is a small, intense, focused, and serious young woman who has her standards. They are in love but have never made love, mostly because Gordon has a sharp-eyed landlady and no money to rent a room, and Rosemary sharply lays down the law: "I will not make love where dogs have peed." When they do finally achieve union, of course she gets pregnant, but even then offers him his freedom: "Remember—you're a poet. And a free man."

Babies. What does Gordon know of them? He goes to the public library and has a classic exchange with the librarian (Alan Plater's screenplay concisely punches up Orwell's dialogue). "Do you have any books on pregnancy?" he asks. "Not for the general public!" she snaps. "I'm not the general public," he corrects her condescendingly. "I'm the father of an unborn child." And as he regards the engraving of a fetus, he knows what his duty is. After all, as his boss also observed, "Poetry and advertising all use the same words—just in a different order."

A Merry War is the kind of movie that doesn't reach large audiences, but some will find it appealing. For me it works not only as a reasonable adaptation of an Orwell novel I like, but also as a form of escapism since, if the truth be known, I would be happy as a clerk in a London used bookstore. For a time.

Message in a Bottle ★★

PG-13, 126 m., 1999

Kevin Costner (Garret Blake), Robin Wright Penn (Theresa Osborne), John Savage (Johnny Land), Illeana Douglas (Lina Paul), Robbie Coltrane (Charlie Toschi), Jesse James (Jason Osborne), Paul Newman (Dodge Blake). Directed by Luis Mandoki and produced by Denise Di Novi, Jim Wilson, and Kevin Costner. Screenplay by Gerald DiPego, based on the novel *The Notebook* by Nicholas Sparks.

Message in a Bottle is a tearjerker that strolls from crisis to crisis. It's curiously muted, as if it fears that passion would tear its delicate fabric; even the fights are more in sorrow than in anger, and when there's a fistfight, it doesn't feel like a real fistfight—it feels more like someone thought the movie needed a fistfight 'round about then.

The film is about a man and a woman who believe in great true love. The man believes it's behind him; the woman hopes it's ahead of her. One of their ideals in life is "to be somebody's true north." Right away we know they're in trouble. You don't just find true love. You team up with somebody, and build it from the ground up. But *Message in a Bottle* believes in the kind of love where the romantic music comes first, trembling and sweeping under every scene, and the dialogue is treated like the lyrics.

Yet it is about two likable characters—three, really, since Paul Newman not only steals every scene he's in, but puts it in the bank and draws interest on it. Robin Wright Penn plays Theresa, a researcher for the *Chicago Tribune*, who finds a letter in a bottle. It is a heartbreaking love note to "Catherine," by a man who wants to make amends to his true north.

Theresa, a divorced mother of one, is deeply touched by the message, and shares it with a columnist named Charlie (Robbie Coltrane), who of course lifts it for a column. Theresa feels betrayed. (If she thinks she can show a letter like that to a guy with a deadline and not read about it in tomorrow's paper, no wonder she's still a researcher.) The column leads to the discovery of two other letters on the same stationery. Charlie has the bottle, the cork, the stationery, and the handwriting analyzed, and figures the messages came from the Carolinas. A few calls to gift shops, and they know who bought the stationery.

It's Garret Blake (Kevin Costner). Theresa is sent out on a mission to do research about him. She meets his father (Newman), and then the man himself, a shipwright who handcrafts beautiful vessels. He takes her for a test sail. The wind is bracing and the chemistry is right. "You eat meat?" he asks her. "Red meat? I make a perfect steak. It's the best thing I do." With this kind of buildup, Linda McCartney would have tucked into a T-bone.

Soon it's time for Theresa to return home (where after she writes one column, the paper promotes her and gives her an office with a window view; at that rate, in six weeks she'll be using Colonel McCormick's ancestral commode). Of course she wants him to come and see her—to see how she lives. "Will you come and visit me?" she asks. His reply does not represent the proudest moment of the screenwriter: "You mean, inland?"

Sooner or later he's going to find out that she found his letter in a bottle and is not simply a beautiful woman who wandered onto his boat. That his secrets are known in those few places where the *Tribune* is still read. Yes, but it takes a long time, and when his discovery finally comes, the film handles it with a certain tact. It's not just an explosion about betrayal, but more complicated—partly because of the nature of the third letter.

As morose and contrived as the movie is, it has a certain winsome charm because of the personal warmth of the actors. This is Robin Wright Penn's breakthrough to a different kind of acting, and she has a personal triumph; she's been identified with desperate, hard-as-nails characters, but no more. Costner finds the right note of inarticulate pain; he loves, but doesn't feel he has the right to. Paul Newman handles his role, as Costner's ex-drunk father, with the relaxed confidence of Michael Jordan shooting free throws in your driveway. It is good to see all three of them on the screen, in whatever combination, and the movie is right to play down the sex scenes and underline the cuddling and the whispers.

But where, oh where, did they get the movie's ending? Is it in the original novel by Nicholas Sparks? Don't know. Haven't read it. The climactic events are shameless, contrived, and wildly out of tune with the rest of the story. To saddle Costner, Penn, and Newman with such goofy melodrama is like hiring Fred Astaire and strapping a tractor on his back. ☞

Metro ★ ★ ★

R, 117 m., 1997

Eddie Murphy (Scott Roper), Michael Rapaport (Kevin McCall), Carmen Ejogo (Ronnie Tate), Michael Wincott (Michael Korda), Denis Arndt (Captain Frank Solis), Art Evans (Lieutenant Sam Baffert), Donal Logue (Earl), Paul Ben-Victor (Clarence Teal). Directed by Thomas Carter and produced by Roger Birnbaum. Screenplay by Randy Feldman.

In formula action pictures, there are always setup scenes early in the movie that trigger payoff scenes later on. *Metro* is a movie so preoccupied with its chases, stunts, and special effects that it never gets around to the payoffs. That's not a criticism, just an observation. Leave out the setups *and* the payoffs, and you'd have wall-to-wall action, which is the direction I suspect we're heading in.

Metro stars Eddie Murphy in a muscular, energetic performance as Roper, a star hostage negotiator for the San Francisco Police Department. He's the guy who walks unarmed into the bank where the robber is holding a gun to a hostage's head, and gets the guy talking. Murphy has always been a good talker, and he has fun with some of this dialogue. Taking a bag of doughnuts in to a manic madman, Roper explains, "I'm duty-bound under my oath as a negotiator to take out this wounded man." And does.

This opening scene of course has nothing to do with the rest of the movie. Action movies always start in the middle of a crisis, establish the hero, and then move into the story. Usually the early crisis is followed by a quiet domestic scene (Roper meets his former girlfriend) and the introduction of the police chief, etc., before another crisis develops. Oh, and the cop has to meet his New Partner.

Metro makes all the early stops, which makes it interesting that it never doubles back to refer to them again. For example:

1. Roper gets a new partner named McCall (Michael Rapaport) who is a marathon runner, can lip-read, is a sharpshooter, etc., but has never done hostage negotiations before. The formula calls for the veteran to resent the kid and make it hard for him. Not here. Roper asks his chief for a raise, gets it, and takes the kid to the racetrack.

2. After a friend of Roper's is killed by Korda (Michael Wincott), the movie's homicidal diamond thief, Roper vows revenge. Then, of course, the chief Takes Him Off the Case. Roper continues to chase the guy anyway—no one says a word to reprimand him, and his badge and gun are never taken away.

3. In a mock-up of a grocery store, Roper uses department store mannequins to represent stickup guys, and rehearses his new partner in the methods of handling such a situation. This will inevitably pay off when the kid has to handle such a situation, right? Wrong.

4. Roper is seen as a compulsive gambler. This will have something to do with the plot, right? Wrong again. It's a meaningless character detail.

5. Roper's girlfriend, Ronnie (Carmen Ejogo), has left him for a baseball star. The two men meet briefly, and coldly, at her apartment. Then she gets back with Roper. The baseball player will turn up later, angry and possibly dangerous, right? Nope; he's never seen again.

These aren't loose threads, because the plot doesn't matter anyway. They're simply punctuation marks between the extravagant stunt scenes. The reason to see *Metro* is because it has two ingenious action sequences. One occurs when Korda, fleeing Roper, leaps aboard a San Francisco streetcar and kills the driver. The streetcar speeds downhill out of control, crashing into dozens of cars, and Roper and McCall chase it in a vintage Cadillac before Roper jumps onto the streetcar and McCall steers the Caddy broadside in front of it, slowing it before it plows into dozens of victims at the bottom of the slope.

This is, of course, impossible (the Caddy's tires don't even blow after scraping sideways for a couple of thousand yards), but so what? It's fun, and skillfully directed by Thomas Carter. And there's an ingenious scene later in the film where Ronnie, the hapless girlfriend, is strapped to a piece of machinery that functions in exactly the same way that sawmills did in old silent movies: If Roper takes his hand off the red button, the girl will be cut in two. If he doesn't, he'll be killed. Neat.

The movie also has fun with horror movie clichés. Ronnie keeps closing her bathroom mirror so we can see the killer behind her—and the movie's music swells ominously, but there's no killer. She calls for her dog, and the dog doesn't come. More swelling music. But the dog isn't dead. And *Metro* should get a gold star for being the first movie in the history of San Francisco to stage a chase through Chinatown without having the cars get stuck in the middle of a parade. On the debit side, after Roper knows the villain has escaped jail and vowed revenge, he lets Ronnie go back into her apartment alone. "I'll be right back," she says, when, as the characters in *Scream* observe, hardly anyone who says that ever is.

The movie works well on its chosen level. The big action scenes are cleverly staged and Eddie Murphy is back on his game again, with a high-energy performance and crisp dialogue. Rapaport makes a good foil—stalwart, with good reaction shots—and Wincott is a smart, creepy killer. There are some nice twists. Perhaps it is even a good thing that this is the first cop buddy movie that uses all the clichés from the first half of the formula and none from the second. It's not like I missed them.

Metroland ★ ★ ★

NO MPAA RATING, 101 m., 1999

Christian Bale (Chris), Emily Watson (Marion), Lee Ross (Toni), Elsa Zylberstein (Annick), Rufus (Henri), Jonathan Aris (Dave), Ifan Meredith (Mickey), Amanda Ryan (Joanna). Directed by Philip Saville and produced by Andrew Bendel. Screenplay by Adrian Hodges, based on the novel by Julian Barnes.

There are a lot of movies about escaping from the middle class, but *Metroland* is one of the few about escaping into it. In 1968, Chris is a footloose British photographer in Paris, who has an affair with a French woman and drifts through streets alive with drugs and revolution. In 1977, Chris has become a married man with a child, living in a London suburb at the end of the Metropolitan line of the Underground. Is he happier now?

Not according to his friend Toni, who joined Chris in sixties hedonism and never looked back. Toni (Lee Ross) has just returned from America, after dropping out in Africa and Asia. He's returned to the United Kingdom for one reason only: to convince Chris (Christian Bale) to leave his family behind and join him on the road. *Metroland*, based on a 1980 novel by Julian Barnes, who became famous after *Flaubert's Parrot*, watches Chris as he is enticed by temptation and memory.

The memories are often about the two women he met in Paris that year—the one he married and the one he didn't. Annick (Elsa Zylberstein) is one of those young Parisians who live on air and use the cafés as living rooms. They meet, they flirt, they become a couple. The sound track of their romance is sixties rock, mixed with Django Reinhardt, and with Annick he learns about sex ("Is it the first time?" she asks, with reason). Then into his world drifts a visiting English girl, Marion (Emily Watson), who is sensible, cheerful, supportive, reassuring, and wholesome. She sizes him up and informs him that he will get married, probably to her, because "you're not original enough not to."

He does, and life in Metroland continues happily until Toni calls at 6 A.M. one morning. Toni tempts Chris with tastes of the life he left behind, and at a party they attend, an available girl makes him an offer so frank and inviting he very nearly cannot refuse. Yet the movie is not about whether Chris will remain faithful to Marion; it's about whether he chose the right life in the first place.

Philip Saville, who directs from a screenplay by Adrian Hodges, starts with a straightforward story of life choices (the plot could as easily be from Joanna Trollope as Julian Barnes), and slips in teasing asides, as in a scene where Toni almost has Chris and Marion believing he has "always been in love with Chris." Or when Chris daydreams about Marion telling him, "of course, I expect you to have affairs." What Saville doesn't do, mercifully, is depend on sentiment: Chris is not asked to make his decision based on loyalty to wife and daughter, but on the actual issue of his choice to live in the London outskirts and raise a family. There is a cold-blooded sense in which he could decide, objectively, dispassionately, that he took the wrong turn—that it is his right to join Toni in a life of wandering, sex, and mind-altering.

What's curious, given how everything depends on Chris, is the way the movie is really centered on the two women. Annick almost deliberately plays the role of a cliché—the brainy, liberated French woman showing the Englishman the sensual ropes. Elsa Zylberstein finds the right note: The woman proud to have "a beautiful British boyfriend," and hurt when she's dumped, but not blinded by dreams of eternal love. And then there's Marion, played by Emily Watson in a radical departure from her tormented characters in *Breaking the Waves* and *Hilary and Jackie*. Here she is cheerfully normal—an ideal wife, if that's what Chris is looking for. "No wonder you're bored," says Toni. But why did Toni come back, if he wasn't bored too?

Microcosmos ★ ★ ★ ★

G, 77 m., 1997

A documentary directed by Claude Nuridsany and Marie Perennou and produced by Galatee Films, Jacques Perrin, Christophe Barratier, and Yvette Mallet. Screenplay by Nuridsany and Perrenou.

There are so many different insect species that there's a famous biologists' quip: Essentially *all* species are insects. Their biomass—the combined weight of the creepy-crawly things—is many times greater than the combined weight of everything else that swims, flies, walks, and makes movies. Insects are the great success story on planet Earth; they were here before we arrived and will remain long after we've gone, inhabiting their worlds of mindless and intricate beauty.

Children, being built nearer to the ground and having more time on their hands, are close observers of ants and spiders, caterpillars and butterflies. Adults tune them out; bugs are things you slap, swat, step on, or spray. *Microcosmos* is an amazing film that allows us to peer deeply into the insect world, and marvel at creatures we casually condemn to squishing. The makers of this film took three years to design their close-up cameras and magnifying lenses, and to photograph insects in such brilliant detail that if they were cars we could read their city stickers.

The movie is a work of art and whimsy as much as one of science. It uses only a handful of words, but is generous with music and amplified sound effects, dramatizing the unremitting struggle of survival that goes on in a meadow in France. If a camera could somehow be transported to another planet, there to photograph alien life forms, would the result be any more astonishing than these invasions into the private lives of snails and bees, mantises and beetles, spiders and flies?

Where did these forms come from? These legs—two, four, six, a thousand? Eyes like bombardiers' turrets? Giant pincers? Honeyed secretions? Metamorphosis from a wormy crawling thing into a glorious flying thing? Grasshoppers that look like plants, and beetles that look like ants? Every one of these amazing creatures represents a successful Darwinian solution to the problem of how to reproduce and make a living. And so do we.

One beautiful creature after another takes the screen. There is a parade of caterpillars. A dung beetle, tirelessly moving his treasure. Two snails engaging in a long and very loving wet kiss. Spiders methodically capturing and immobilizing their prey (what a horrible fate;

does the victim understand what has happened to it?). Ants construct lives of meticulous order and then a hungry bird comes along and gobbles up thousands of them. More ants construct more anthills, flawless in design and function, and then the hills are bombed by raindrops that look to them as big as beach balls.

There is a fight to the death between two beetles, and their struggle looks as gargantuan as the battling dinosaurs in *Jurassic Park.* There are tiny insects who live in, on, and for the nectar supplied by plants that are perfectly designed for them. Ladybugs seem so ill-designed to fly that every takeoff looks like a clumsy miracle; do they get sweaty palms? Overhead there is a towering canopy of jungle foliage, consisting of the grasses and flowers of the meadow.

Microcosmos is in a category of its own. There is no other film like it. If the movies allow us to see places we have not been and people we do not know, then *Microcosmos* dramatically extends the range of our vision, allowing us to see the world of the creatures who most completely and enduringly inhabit Earth.

Sometimes the close-up cameras are almost embarrassingly intimate; should we blush to see these beings engaged in their crucial daily acts of dining, loving, fighting, being born, and dying? You may leave this movie feeling a little like a god. Or like a big, inelegant and energy-inefficient hunk of clunky design. Of course, we're smart and they're not. We know the insects exist, and they don't know we exist. Or need to.

Midnight in the Garden of Good and Evil ★ ★ ½

R, 154 m., 1997

Kevin Spacey (Jim Williams), John Cusack (John Kelso), Jack Thompson (Sonny Seiler), The Lady Chablis (Herself), Alison Eastwood (Mandy Nichols), Irma P. Hall (Minerva), Paul Hipp (Joe Odom), Jude Law (Billy Hanson). Directed by Clint Eastwood and produced by Eastwood and Arnold Stiefel. Screenplay by John Lee Hancock, based on the book by John Berendt.

Midnight in the Garden of Good and Evil is a book that exists as a conspiracy between the author and the reader: John Berendt paints a portrait of a city so eccentric, so dripping with Southern Gothic weirdness, that it can't survive for long when it's removed from the life-support system of our imagination. Clint Eastwood's film is a determined attempt to be faithful to the book's spirit, but something ineffable is lost just by turning on the camera: Nothing we see can be as amazing as what we've imagined.

The book tells the story of a New York author who visits Savannah, Georgia, is bewitched, and takes an apartment there. Gradually he meets the local fauna, including a gay antiques dealer, a piano bar owner of no fixed abode, a drag queen, a voodoo sorceress, a man who keeps flies on leashes, a man who walks an invisible dog, and the members of the Married Women's Card Club. The plot grows labyrinthine after the antiques dealer is charged with the murder of a young hustler.

Berendt introduces these people and tells their stories in a bemused, gossipy fashion; he's a natural storyteller who knows he has great stories to tell and relishes the telling. He is not, however, really a major player in the book, and the movie makes a mistake by assigning its central role to a New York writer, now named John Kelso, through whose hands all of the action must pass.

There is nothing wrong with the performance by John Cusack except that it is unnecessary; if John Lee Hancock's screenplay had abandoned the Kelso character and just jumped into the midst of Savannah's menagerie with both feet, the movie might have had more energy and color. Or if Kelso had been a weird character, too, that might have helped; he's written and played as a flat, bland witness, whose tentative love affair with a local temptress (Alison Eastwood) is so abashed we almost wonder if he's ever dated before.

Berendt's nonfiction book (the credits inexplicably call it a novel) circulates with amusement and incredulity among unforgettable characters. But the screenplay whacks the anecdotal material into shape to fit the crime-and-courtroom genre. A doped-up young bisexual hothead (Jude Law) is introduced in two overplayed scenes, and then found dead on the floor of the antiques dealer's office. His death inspired an unprecedented four trials in real life, which the movie can be excused for reducing to one—but as the conventions of courtroom melodrama take over, what makes Savannah unique is gradually lost sight of. Jack Thompson gives a solid performance as Sonny Seiler, the defense attorney, but he's from Grisham territory, not Savannah.

The characters in the book live with such vivid energy that it's a shame we see them only in their relations with Kelso, the quiet outsider (there's hardly a scene in the movie of the locals talking to each other without the Yankee witness). Kevin Spacey plays Jim Williams, the antiques dealer, who holds two Christmas parties—one so famous that *Town & Country* magazine has assigned Kelso to cover it, and another, the night before, "for bachelors only." Spacey's performance is built on a comfortable drawl, perfect timing, a cigar as a prop, and the actor's own twinkling warmth: We like Jim Williams so much we're surprised we don't see more of him. "What money I have," he explains, "is about eleven years old. Yes, I am 'nouveau riche'—but it's the 'riche' that counts."

Kelso also encounters The Lady Chablis, a drag queen played by the real Lady Chablis, who specializes in shocking the bourgeoisie. She has some one-liners that are real zingers, but her big scene—crashing the black debutante ball to embarrass Kelso—is a scene so lacking in focus and structure that it brings the movie to a halt. My guess is that The Lady Chablis would be well known to the black middle class of Savannah (where everybody knows everybody), and the blank stares she gathers make you realize the scene lacks setup, purpose, and payoff.

Another colorful character in the book is Joe Odom, who makes himself at home as an unpaid (and unauthorized) "house-sitter" in historic mansions, supporting himself as the host of the longest-running house party in Georgia. He's a charmer who has the misfortune to be dating Mandy Nichols (Alison Eastwood), and so the movie has to hustle him out of sight to free Mandy for her frictionless dalliance with Kelso—who mutters vaguely about his "track record" in romance, and has to be instructed to kiss her after their first date. What's the point?

Much is made of Minerva (Irma P. Hall), the voodoo priestess, who casts hexes against the prosecuting attorneys and leads midnight forays into local cemeteries. In the book some local residents, Jim Williams included, halfway believe in her magic; in the movie, she comes across more as a local eccentric.

In a way, the filmmakers faced the same hopeless task as the adapters of Tom Wolfe's *The Bonfire of the Vanities.* The Berendt book, on best-seller lists for three years, has made such a vivid impression that any mere mortal version of it is doomed to pale. Perhaps only the documentarian Errol Morris, who specializes in the incredible variety of the human zoo, could have done justice to the material.

Still, I enjoyed the movie at a certain level simply as illustration: I was curious to see The Lady Chablis, and the famous old Mercer House where the murders took place, and the Spanish moss. But the movie never reached takeoff speed; its energy was dissipated by being filtered through the deadpan character of Kelso. They say people who hadn't read *The Bonfire of the Vanities* liked the movie more than those who knew the book. Maybe the same thing will happen with *Midnight.*

The Mighty ★★★

PG-13, 100 m., 1998

Elden Henson (Max), Kieran Culkin (Kevin), Sharon Stone (Kevin's Mother), Gena Rowlands (Max's Grandmother), Harry Dean Stanton (Max's Grandfather), Gillian Anderson (Loretta Lee), James Gandolfini (Max's Father), Meat Loaf (Iggy). Directed by Peter Chelsom and produced by Jane Startz and Simon Fields. Screenplay by Charles Leavitt, based on the novel *Freak, the Mighty* by Rodman Philbrick.

"You need a brain, I need legs—and the Wizard of Oz doesn't live in South Cincinnati."

So speaks a twisted little boy named Kevin to a hulking giant named Max, in the new movie *The Mighty.* They're both in the seventh grade in Cincinnati—Max for the third time—and they're both misfits.

Max, known to his cruel classmates as the Missing Link, feels like Godzilla as he lumbers down the school corridors, and says, ". . . sometimes seems like the whole world has just seen me on *America's Most Wanted.*" Kevin has Morquio's Syndrome, which causes his bones to stop growing even though his organs continue to expand, until finally, in the movie's words "his heart will get too big for his body."

Kevin and Max are the heroes of *Freak, the Mighty,* a best-selling children's book by Rodman Philbrick that has been embraced by kids who feel they stand out like sore thumbs (and what kid doesn't?). It's a fable about how two friends can work together to take on the world, and it's about how Kevin's example helps Max repair a life that began with his father killing his mother.

At first, it's not a friendship made in heaven. Kevin moves in next door to Max, who spies across the back fence as the little kid, who wears braces and glasses, test-flies a birdlike model flying machine he calls an "Ornothopter." ("I gave birth to a seven-and-a-half-pound dictionary," sighs his mother.) In gym class, a cruel kid throws a basketball to knock Kevin off his crutches, and Max is blamed for the stunt. It's ironic when Max goes for remedial reading lessons and finds out that Kevin is his tutor. "I didn't throw the basketball," he tells the little kid, who says he was a chump to take the rap for someone else.

The book they read is *King Arthur and the Knights of the Round Table,* and it is Arthurian chivalry that Kevin believes should guide their lives. Soon they arrive at a working arrangement that takes advantage of both their needs: Kevin rides around on Max's shoulders, and they even play basketball that way. The extra height is great for layups. (Did the book's author see *Mad Max Beyond Thunderdome,* where another giant and another dwarf teamed up to create the character Master-Blaster?)

We meet the people in their lives. Kevin's mother (Sharon Stone) struggles to keep him out of "special schools" and help him lead the fullest possible life. Max's grandparents, Gram and Grim (Gena Rowlands and Harry Dean Stanton), are raising him, not without love, after the death of his mother and the imprisonment of his father (James Gandolfini).

The last third of the movie involves derring-do that's highly improbable, especially a makeshift toboggan ride. But for the younger audiences the movie is aimed at, these adventures will be thrilling and not too violent, and they do give both boys a chance to put the code of the Round Table into practice.

The Mighty is an emotionally affecting movie (much like the somewhat similar *Simon Birch,* which is about a friendship between a fatherless boy and a dwarf). It is a little stronger in its central theme, which is that we all have weaknesses, we are not perfect, but together we can be more than the sum of our parts.

Much of the film's appeal comes from the performances. Elden Henson, with his big, round, Scandinavian face and football lineman's body, brings a shyness and vulnerability to Max. He's stronger than the bullies who pick on him, but he has retreated into himself. Kieran Culkin, as Max, looks like his older brother Macaulay, but doesn't play the cute card as much, and has a nice unsentimental streak when he levels with Max. And the adults tactfully do what their roles require without trying to steal the movie from its heroes. (There's also a nice supporting role for Gillian Anderson as a woman whose stolen purse sets up the movie's climax.)

What I liked most about the movie is the way it shows that imagination can be a weapon in life. At their first reading lesson, Kevin tells Max that every word is part of a picture, and every sentence is a picture, and you put them all together in your head. That has never occurred to Max, who in reading about the Round Table is taken to a place outside his lonely bedroom and solitary school existence, and learns of nobility and romance. No child is completely a captive of a sad childhood if he can read and has books; they are the window to what can be, and that is the underlying message of *The Mighty.*

Mighty Joe Young ★ ★ ★

PG, 114 m., 1998

Charlize Theron (Jill Young), Bill Paxton (Gregg O'Hara), Rade Serbedzija (Strasser), Peter Firth (Garth), David Paymer (Harry Ruben), Regina King (Cecily Banks), Robert Wisdom (Kweli), Naveen Andrews (Pindi). Directed by Ron Underwood and produced by Ted Hartley and Tom Jacobson. Screenplay by Mark Rosenthal and Lawrence Konner, based on a screenplay by Ruth Rose.

Mighty Joe Young is an energetic, robust adventure tale: not too cynical, violent, or fragmented for kids, not too tame for adults. After all the calculation behind *Godzilla* or *Armageddon,* it has a kind of innocence to it. It's not about a monster but about a very big, well-meaning gorilla that just wants to be left in peace. And about a woman who treasures the gorilla. And about a zoologist who loves the woman. All that stuff.

Charlize Theron stars as Jill Young, a woman whose mother is a famed gorilla expert of the *Gorillas in the Mist* variety. Jill is raised with Joe, who even as a baby is big for his size. They grow up together, and Joe just keeps on growing, until you can tell he's approaching because the treetops shake.

Bill Paxton, from *Twister,* stars as Gregg O'Hara, a zoologist who wants samples of Joe's blood. Alas, the snaky types he hires as assistants are crooked, and try to sell information about the gorilla to a sleazy Los Angeles promoter named Strasser (Rade Serbedzija). This same Strasser is a poacher with a history with Joe, who once bit off his thumb and forefinger.

The African scenes are remarkable in the way they create a convincing giant gorilla and place him in the wild. The majority of the shots of Joe in this movie are special effects; we are rarely looking at a real gorilla. You can't tell that by anything on the screen—apart from Joe's size, of course. Joe isn't simply seen as he lumbers past. The camera is free to circle and approach him. In a sequence where he's being pursued by men in Land Rovers, the camera parallels him, then swings in front of him, then moves in for a close-up. It's a remarkable demonstration of technical skill.

Close-ups of Joe's face and upper body use superb animatronics. The only thing dubious about Joe is his attitude; when Jill cuddles and comforts him, he's more like a gentle little chimp than a fearsome beast. His eyes, lips, and facial movements are expressive even in the close shots. Theron treats him like a pet, whistling to make him approach her, sure of her authority.

The romance between Theron and Paxton is inevitable, but not intrusive. It's more of an obligatory subplot than a big deal. More interesting is the devious scheming of Strasser and his henchmen after Joe is brought to California. There's a scene where Mighty Joe freaks out at a charity benefit, and then the payoff as he scales Graumann's Chinese Theater, visits the Hollywood sign, and ends up in that dependable refuge of all thrillers, a carnival midway, where a child is in danger on top of a Ferris wheel.

The payoff of that scene owes more than a little to a certain scene in *E.T.*, and indeed the director, Ron Underwood, shows he's studied *E.T.* carefully. An early scene of poachers in the jungle is framed much like the early hunt for *E.T.* The camera is at boot level, there are loud jangles of keys and weapons on the sound track, and powerful flashlight beams cut Spielbergian laser-tracks through the mist.

One positive aspect is the film's relative civility. So many special-effects movies seem angry and aggressive; smaller kids are blown out of the theater by the force of the noise and special effects. *Mighty Joe Young* is not meek and harmless; it's a full-blooded action picture, all right, but with a certain warmth and humor instead of a scorched-earth approach. You feel good at the end, instead of merely relieved.

Mighty Peking Man ★★★

NO MPAA RATING, 100 m., 1977 (rereleased 1999)

Danny Lee (Li Hsiu-Hsien) (Johnny Feng), Evelyne Kraft (Samantha [Ah Wei]), Hsiao Yao (Huang Tsui-Hua), Ku Feng (Lu Tien), Lin Wei-Tu (Chen Shi-Yu), Hsu Shao-Chiang (Ah Lung), Wu Hang-Sheng (Ah Pi), Cheng Ping (Lucy). Directed by Ho Meng-Hua and produced by Runme Shaw. Screenplay by I. Kuang.

There is an earthquake near the beginning of *Mighty Peking Man,* but unlike the earthquake in the fondly remembered *Infra-Man,* it does not unleash the Slinky-necked robots and hairy mutant footstools controlled by Princess Dragon Mom. Still, it offers attractions of its own. It disturbs a giant ape, for example, which lumbers down from its mountain home and heads for the jungles of India. And it is no ordinary tremor; it unfolds progressively.

First, a character shouts that there's an earthquake. Then we hear it, although we do not see anything alarming. Then the back-projected landscape begins to shake violently, although the foreground does not shake. Then the camera begins to shake, while the foreground still holds steady. Later, finally, Earth moves. This may be the first special effects–generated earthquake in which the back projection shakes so hard it moves Earth.

The earthquake doesn't really have an impact on the plot. It's simply an earthquake scene, just as later there is a quicksand scene, a scene where a python fights a tiger, etc. *Mighty Peking Man,* made in 1977, is being rereleased by Quentin Tarantino's Rolling Thunder Pictures, and we can only imagine young QT behind the counter of that legendary video store of his youth, watching this on the monitor and realizing he'd struck gold.

The plot involves an expedition to discover the giant apelike Peking Man, who is said at one point to be ten feet tall—although a grown man is able to stand inside one of its footprints. Later in the film, however, the creature has grown enough to knock down tall buildings, although later still it has shrunk enough to climb one.

The dialogue is to the point. After the expedition is suggested, a character says: "I know an explorer here in Hong Kong! He just lost his girl! He wants to get away!" The explorer, whose name is Johnny Feng (Danny Lee), is drunk when we first meet him; a flashback reveals that his girlfriend is having an affair with his brother. That doesn't dissuade Lu Tien, the hunt financer: "You're going to lead our expedition into the Himalyan jungle! You're the only one I trust!"

Soon the expedition sets off, not in Land Rovers as we might expect, but in tall two-wheeled ox carts. There are hazards along the way. My favorite is when a Sherpa gets his leg bitten off above the knee. Johnny wants to summon medical help, but Lu Tien simply shoots the man in the head. The expedition soon encounters a blond woman named Samantha (Evelyne Kraft) who has lived in the jungle since the crash long ago of a plane carrying her family (in a flashback, we see the tot crying out, "Mama! Papa!"). Mighty Peking Man and Samantha hang out together, but are just friends.

Samantha doesn't speak English at first, but quickly learns, no doubt in the same way the other actors have learned: by speaking their usual language and having it dubbed. What is amazing is that Mighty Peking Man, when encountered, also speaks English. Samantha's savage existence has given her time to design an off-the-shoulder leopard-skin brassiere, and to find a supply of lip gloss and eyeliner. Soon Samantha and Johnny are an item.

Lu Tien sees a fortune in Mighty Peking Man, and brings him to Hong Kong, where he is displayed in a stadium before thousands of people, while chained to big trucks. Samantha meanwhile has found Johnny in bed with his original girlfriend, and races distraught to the stadium when she sees Mighty Peking Man on TV, tossing the trucks around like large toys (which they are). She desperately pleads with the implacable security forces to spare the beast because he has been misunderstood. But too late: MPM goes on a rampage through downtown Hong Kong, knocking over buildings and batting helicopters out of the sky in a sequence that was surely not an attempt to rip off Dino De Laurentiis's *King Kong,* made a year earlier.

Mighty Peking Man is very funny, although a shade off the high mark of *Infra-Man,* which was made a year earlier and is my favorite Hong Kong monster film. Both were produced by the legendary Runme Shaw, who, having tasted greatness, obviously hoped to repeat. I find to my astonishment that I gave *Infra-Man* only two and a half stars when I reviewed it. That was twenty-two years ago, but a fellow will remember a lot of things you wouldn't think he'd remember. I'll bet a month hasn't gone by since that I haven't thought of that film. I am awarding *Mighty Peking Man* three stars, for general goofiness and a certain level of insane genius, but I cannot in good conscience rate it higher than *Infra-Man.* So, in answer to those correspondents who ask if I have ever changed a rating on a movie: Yes, *Infra-Man* moves up to three stars.

Mimic ★ ★ ★ ½

R, 104 m., 1997

Mira Sorvino (Susan Tyler), Jeremy Northam (Peter Mann), Alexander Goodwin (Chuy), Giancarlo Giannini (Manny), Charles S. Dutton (Leonard), Josh Brolin (Josh), Alix Koromzay (Remy), F. Murray Abraham (Dr. Gates). Directed by Guillermo Del Toro and produced by Bob Weinstein, B. J. Rack, and Ole

Bornedal. Screenplay by Matthew Robbins and Del Toro, based on the short story "Mimic" by Donald A. Wolheim.

There is a sense in which *Mimic* is exactly the same movie as *Event Horizon,* which is exactly the same movie as *The Relic,* which like many other movies was descended from *Alien,* which itself was the child of a well-established horror tradition.

All of these movies, and there are hundreds more, follow a formula in which a pseudoscientific setup in the opening act leads to a series of scenes in which the heroes are trapped (in a subway system, spaceship, tunnel, etc.) with a new and terrifying monster in a form not previously known to man, and the monster leaps out of hiding at them in ways long known to special-effects technicians.

One does not attend *Mimic* hoping for more than a few new twists on the durable old idea; such movies, like thrill rides at parks, work every single time if they have been well planned and constructed. But *Mimic* is superior to most of its cousins, and has been stylishly directed by Guillermo Del Toro, whose visual sense adds a certain texture that makes everything scarier and more effective. It's not often that a movie like this can frighten me, but I was surprised how effective *Mimic* was.

The film begins with ominous reports of a plague that has devastated Manhattan, claiming mostly young children. It is spread by cockroaches, and Mira Sorvino plays a scientist named Susan Tyler who, with her colleagues, is able to use genetic engineering to create the "Judas Breed," a designer bug (half-mantis, half-termite) that can mimic cockroaches, infiltrate their strongholds, and kill them. Soon the plague has ended, three years have passed, and apparently those new little bugs (which were supposed to be sterile) have kept right on evolving.

This is all pretty standard stuff. Originality is in the details. Del Toro, whose movie *Cronos* (1992) was about a nasty little antique metal vampire bug, creates thrills by manipulating human nature. We're all squeamish about sticking our hands into unseen dark places where something might bite us. We're all concerned when we see children who don't know they're in danger. We're instinctively frightened when an entity looks like one thing and suddenly reveals itself as something else.

Del Toro touches all of those bases. The hand reaching into darkness had me sliding down in my seat. I liked the two little kids who are bug collectors and know their way around the subway system. And there's a shoeshine man's kid who clicks spoons together in such a way that he mimics the clicking sounds of the Judas Breed. That sets up an expectation that sooner or later the kid will send the wrong (or right) message by accident. Tactical suspense like that is hard to create, but effective: As Hitchcock pointed out, it's more fun to wait for a payoff than to see one.

As for the insect predators, what they have learned to mimic, and how they do it, provides one of the best payoff shots in the movie. There is also a visual intrigue in the locations. Instead of locking us forever into dark, claustrophobic tunnels, Del Toro creates an abandoned subway station with a vaulted ceiling and overhead windows; we could be somewhere on the Paris Metro. There's a shot where a character, trapped below, can look up and see people walking in the daylight above—so close, and so far away. And an old subway car provides a useful prop.

Mira Sorvino's casting in the role of the scientist has been questioned in some quarters, perhaps because she is remembered as the ditzy hooker in Woody Allen's *Mighty Aphrodite.* But here she comes across as the smart but unfocused graduate student who knows everything and hopes she got it right. (I liked the scene where she grabs insect goo and tells her friends, "Here! Rub it all over yourself!") Jeremy Northam plays her husband, also a scientist; Charles S. Dutton is a subway guard with a lot of information about the underground system, and Giancarlo Giannini is the shoeshine man.

There are expected payoffs, yes, and the usual scenes where a false shock is followed by a real one. *Mimic* is a loyal occupant of its genre. But Del Toro is a director with a genuine visual sense, with a way of drawing us into his story and evoking the mood with the very look and texture of his shots. He takes the standard ingredients and presents them so effectively that *Mimic* makes the old seem new, fresh, and scary.

The Mod Squad ★ ★

R, 94 m., 1999

Claire Danes (Julie), Giovanni Ribisi (Pete), Omar Epps (Linc), Dennis Farina (Greer), Josh Brolin (Billy), Michael Lerner (Wiseman), Steve Harris (Briggs), Richard Jenkins (Mothershed), Larry Brandenburg (Eckford). Directed by Scott Silver and produced by Ben Myron, Alan Riche, and Tony Ludwig. Screenplay by Stephen Kay, Silver, and Kate Lanier.

The Mod Squad has an intriguing cast, a director who knows how to use his camera, and a lot of sly humor. Shame about the story. When you see this many of the right elements in a lame movie, you wonder how close they came to making a better one. The director, Scott Silver, cowrote the script himself, and has to take some of the blame: This is a classy production and deserves better.

The premise is from the old TV series. Three young screw-ups are interrupted at the beginning of criminal careers and recruited by a police captain to form an undercover squad. Their assignment: Infiltrate a club where prostitution and drug dealing seem to be happening. The mod squad doesn't carry guns (officially, anyway), doesn't have badges, and I'm not sure if they can make arrests; maybe they're more like high-level snitches.

The members are described by a Rod Serling–type voice over the opening credits. Julie (Claire Danes) was "a runaway—an addict at eighteen." Pete (Giovanni Ribisi) "went straight from Beverly Hills to county jail." Linc (Omar Epps) "doesn't blame his crimes on anything." (He's black, and so the implication, I guess, is that this is worthy of comment.) In the good-looking opening sequence, filmed by Ellen Kuras, they're intercut with dancers at a club, get into a fight, and then find themselves being debriefed and lectured by Captain Greer (Dennis Farina), who orders them to stand up when they talk to him, quit sitting on his desk, etc. Of course, their bad manners are a curtain-raiser to bravery, heroism, and astonishing crime-fighting skills.

The skills, alas, are astonishing because they're so bush-league. The main investigative technique in this movie consists of sneaking up on people and eavesdropping while they explain the entire plot and give away all the secrets. Julie falls for a former lover, follows him to a rendezvous with a drug kingpin (Michael Lerner), and overhears choice nuggets of conversation ("None of them have any idea I know they're cops!"). Then she follows him home and hides in his closet while the faithless louse does the rumpy-pumpy with another woman.

Petey, meanwhile, is even more clever. He creeps up on a hideout and hides behind a wall while tape-recording a full confession. It goes without saying his tape will later be played over a loudspeaker in order to incriminate the bad guys. He uses one of those little $29 microcassette recorders—you know, the kind that can record with perfect fidelity at twenty yards outdoors on a windy day.

As the mod squaders were creeping around, eavesdropping and peeping through windows, I grew restless: This is the kind of stuff they rewrote the Nancy Drew books to get rid of. Too bad, because I liked the pure acting touches that the cast brought to their roles. Ribisi (from *Friends, Saving Private Ryan,* and *The Other Sister*) has a kind of poker-faced put-upon look that's appealing, especially when he gets beat up and goes back to Beverly Hills and his dad chortles heartily at the claim that his kid is now a cop. Danes *(Romeo and Juliet)* has a quick intelligence that almost but not quite sells the dumb stuff they make her do. Epps *(Scream 2, Higher Learning)* is the dominant member of the squad, who tries to protect the others from their insane risk-taking.

And there's a small but indispensable supporting role by Michael Lerner as the crewcut evil kingpin, who intimidates his enemies by dancing with them ("I'm not a fairy—I just like to dance"). He delivers his dialogue indirectly, as an ironic commentary on the horrible things he always seems about to do.

So all of this is a good start, but the screenplay just doesn't provide the foundation. Consider Billy, the Josh Brolin character, who is Julie's once and future boyfriend. We know from the first moment we see him that he's no good. We're tipped off by how suddenly Julie goes for him; if the point were romance, the movie would let them take longer, but since the point is for her to be deceived, she has to rush in heedlessly. No girl meets a guy who dumped her and broke her heart, and immediately drags him into a toilet stall for sex. Especially not now that she's clean and sober, as Julie is (although the movie repeats the tiresome cliché that all recovering alcoholics immediately turn to drink after a setback—preferably swigging from a fifth).

What I'd love to know is how the screenplay got green-lighted. This is a top-drawer film with a decent budget and lots of care about the production values. The cast is talented and well chosen. The movie is even aware of potential clichés (before the last shoot-out, Julie says, "At least it's not going down in an abandoned warehouse"). And then what do they end up with? The most expensive Nancy Drew mystery ever filmed.

Money Talks ★ ★ ★

R, 92 m., 1997

Charlie Sheen (James Russell), Chris Tucker (Franklin Hatchett), Paul Sorvino (Guy Cipriani), Heather Locklear (Grace Cipriani), David Warner (Barclay), Gerard Ismael (Villard), Paul Gleason (Pickett), Elise Neal (Paula). Directed by Brett Ratner and produced by Walter Coblenz and Tracy Kramer. Screenplay by Joel Cohen and Alec Sokolow.

How does a guy like Jim Carrey get his first chance to perform anarchic comedy in a movie? Now that he's a star, directors are of course happy to let him run wild. But how did he get his foot in the door in the first place? How did they know they should hand him the scenery and a knife and a fork? I wonder because in *Money Talks*, a comedian named Chris Tucker has his own foot jammed in the same door, and you can see his talent blossom right there before your eyes.

The movie is not distinguished. It's a clone of the black-and-white buddy pictures, with a little of *48 HRS* and *Lethal Weapon* and *Nothing to Lose*. The plot is so dumb that at one point terrorists blow up a prison bus so that their leader can escape, and no one even considers the possibility that, gee, maybe the leader could get blown up along with everyone else on the bus. He isn't, and that's just as well, because he's handcuffed to Franklin Hatchett, the Chris Tucker character, and we're going to need him for the rest of the movie.

You may remember Tucker from *The Fifth Element*, where his character went on endlessly, as an emcee in a nightclub on a space station. Watching that movie, I felt the Tucker role derailed the ending by continuing too long on the wrong note, as a distraction. But in *Money Talks*, where he has more of a chance to develop a character and experiment with his voice and style, Tucker has a personal triumph. He's funny in that cocky, free-fall way that Carrey and Jerry Lewis get away with: He's floating on inspiration and improvisation, like a musician.

Consider the scene where he is presented at a black-tie wedding party for a rich Italian-American, played by Paul Sorvino. Sorvino is dubious about this black man he's never seen before. But Tucker, who earlier in the day happened to watch a TV ad for the greatest hits of Vic Damone, has a brainstorm: He introduces himself as Vic Damone Jr., the son of the singer and Diahann Carroll. Sorvino embraces the Italian connection, ignores the African-American component, and is blissful as Tucker recalls a childhood spent among other juniors: "Junior Walker Junior, Sammy Davis Junior Junior . . ."

I'm not giving Tucker credit for this hilarious scene, which was written by Joel Cohen and Alec Sokolow. But I'm crediting him with how he sells it: The lines are funny, but Tucker runs with them, and there's a kind of wink to the audience as he relaunches himself as Vic Damone's son: We know he knows exactly what he's doing.

He was invited to the prewedding party by a TV newsman named James Russell (Charlie Sheen), who plays his sidekick through most of the movie. Russell is not a great newsman (and it doesn't help that nobody connected with the movie knows anything about how real TV news reporters talk or behave). In fact, he's just been fired by his weary, cynical boss (David Warner, very funny in an engaging, attention-getting role). But when there's a manhunt for the escaped terrorist, and the Tucker character is fingered as the mastermind behind the prison break, Tucker turns to Sheen for protection—and Sheen agrees to hide him for a weekend (under cover of his own wedding) in order to produce him in time for a sweeps ratings period.

Sheen has the most thankless role in the

movie, as the straight man, and there are scenes where he seems to realize that Tucker, Sorvino, and Warner have all the best lines. He stands there while Tucker goes on wild verbal riffs and has the thankless task of appearing to take him seriously. Some critics have disliked Sheen's performance, but I think it's more or less what's called for: He provides the solid backdrop for the anarchy, and probably feels like Margaret Dumont to Tucker's Groucho Marx.

The movie is the directing debut of Brett Ratner, who has not made a flawless film but at least has made an interesting one, and who understands what Tucker is able to do, and helps him do it. And Tucker, like Carrey, comes on obnoxious and irritating at first, and then you see the smile and the intelligence underneath, and he begins to grow on you.

Mon Homme ★ ★

NO MPAA RATING, 95 m., 1998

Anouk Grinberg (Marie), Gérard Lanvin (Jeannot), Valeria Bruni-Tedeschi (Sanguine), Olivier Martinez (Jean-Francois), Sabine Azema (Berangere), Dominique Valadie (Gilberte), Mathieu Kassovitz (First Client), Jacques Francois (Second Client). Directed by Bertrand Blier and produced by Alain Sarde. Screenplay by Blier. In French with English subtitles.

"What I sell is true love," says the heroine of Bertrand Blier's *Mon Homme.* "With me they hear the music." She says her name is Marie (Anouk Grinberg) and she is the hooker of a john's dreams: "I should pay you," she tells one client. As the film opens, we find her sitting outside a hotel ("This is where I spin my web"), explaining how much she enjoys prostitution. "Ever thought of being paid for it?" she asks a matron who is passing by. The matron has. In no time at all, Marie has talked her into turning her first trick.

Blier's films are often about men in the service of their sexual needs. *Too Beautiful for You* (1988) starred Gérard Depardieu as a man who leaves his elegant wife for the dowdy secretary who obsesses him. The Oscar winner *Get Out Your Handkerchief* (1977) starred Depardieu as a man who despairs of satisfying his wife. In *Mon Homme,* Blier in a sense has cast the male role with a woman: Marie calls the shots, satisfies herself, sleeps with whom she wants, and gets paid for it.

But her life is not perfect until one day she discovers a derelict sleeping near a garbage heap. She brings him home, feeds him (leftover veal stew; French refrigerators never contain old pizzas and doggie bags from the Chinese restaurant). Then they make love. Grinberg is awesome in suggesting her passion; the earth shakes because she's shaking it. There is a small detail that's just right: the way she bites his chin through his beard. Jeannot (Gérard Lanvin) is expert and enduring. She bathes him, shaves him, and asks him to be her pimp and take all her money.

He: What if you want money?

She: I'll ask you for it.

He: And if I refuse?

She: Then you'll be a real pimp.

I wouldn't go so far as to say there are *no* hookers like this in Paris, but Blier may have found the only one.

I was distracted, during their lovemaking, by the thought that a homeless man, found on a garbage heap, would be aromatic. Shouldn't she have bathed him before sex? But a moment's thought reveals that Marie is not being entirely truthful about her needs: It is not so much that she loves sex and prostitution as that she's a masochist, as Jeannot intuits when he slaps her after she has given him stew, sex, and what he concedes is a rather nice red wine. ("Like the smack?" She nods. Later, good fellow that he is, he instructs her on how to duck when she senses a slap on its way.)

If Blier had been true to the logic of the story, he would have followed Marie's compulsions to their bitter end. Instead, he spins off into Jeannot's story, as the new pimp (who cleans up nicely) who seduces a manicurist, names her Tangerine, and tries to set her up in business. Tangerine, who thinks with her mouth open, does not have enough wit for the game, and soon Jeannot is being slapped around by the cops; in France, it is legal to be a prostitute but not to be a pimp.

The film drifts away into developments, fantasies, whimsy, and conceit. Its energy is lost. Blier has a strong central character and abandons her rather than accept the inescapable implications of her behavior. I do not argue that prostitutes cannot be happy (indeed, I have here a letter from a prostitute taking me to task for calling all the characters in *Boogie Nights* sad). But I argue that Marie is not happy, and that Blier's view of women and their sexuality is so narrow that he simply cannot accommodate that inconvenience.

Monument Ave. ★★★

NO MPAA RATING, 90 m., 1998

Denis Leary (Bobby), Colm Meaney (Jackie), Billy Crudup (Teddy), Jason Barry (Seamus), Ian Hart (Mouse), Famke Janssen (Katy), Martin Sheen (Hanlon), John Diehl (Digger), Greg Dulli (Shang), Jeanne Tripplehorn (Annie). Directed Ted Demme and produced by Joel Stillerman, Demme, Jim Serpico, Nicolas Clermont, and Elie Samaha. Screenplay by Mike Armstrong.

Watching *Monument Ave.*, I was reminded of the recent tragedy in Chicago when a young black man, bicycling through Bridgeport, was beaten almost to death. There is a chillingly similar scene in this movie, with a revealing twist on the sickness of racism.

The film takes place in an Irish-American section of Boston, where a gang of childhood friends, now in their thirties, support their booze and coke habits with a loosely organized car theft ring. Their leader is Jackie (Colm Meaney), who is capable of ordering an informer to be shot dead in a saloon, and then attending the wake to pass out $100 bills to the dead boy's relatives. Second in command is Bobby (Denis Leary), who is drifting out of control, and is usually in debt to Jackie because of gambling bets made during blackouts.

One night Bobby and his friends are cruising their neighborhood in a friend's cab, when they see a young black man walking alone on the street. One of the gang says they ought to beat him up "to teach him a lesson." The others are not so enthusiastic, but the guy keeps talking, until finally Bobby, fueled by cocaine and booze, orders the driver to turn the cab around. "Give me the gun," Bobby says.

With Bobby as the instigator, they pile out of the taxi and force the black man inside. They drive around, as Bobby makes violent threats. There is a fake execution before Bobby sets his victim free. "There's a subway stop a block from here," he says. "Ask around at school to see where it's safe to go."

Then he turns on his racist friend and berates him for talking big but being gutless. And we get the point: Bobby never intended to harm the black man, but staged the whole charade to teach his friend a lesson—to show him up as a phony. Bobby is the good guy here. And as that sinks in, we realize the depth of the sickness in Bobby's society. He was concerned only with making a point to his friend. He felt not a shred of empathy for the victim. He was incapable of sharing or perhaps even seeing the man's terror. Bobby, like the others, is trapped inside a watertight, airtight, thought-proof cocoon of blind tribalism.

Gangs of every color are like that. Their values are entirely within the gang structure; outsiders are irrelevant. In *Monument Ave.*, the characters drink together, snort together, play stick hockey together. The movie, directed by Ted Demme and written by Mike Armstrong, has a good ear for their dialogue, and it's not the funny, colorful dialogue of other lowlife movies; a kind of exhausted desperation creeps even into their humor.

There's a minimal plot; the movie is mostly concerned with showing the lifestyle. In a key early scene, Bobby goes to the local bar and sees that his friend Teddy (Billy Crudup) is home from prison. Teddy is obviously high in a dangerous way. Bobby tries to give him money and send him home. No luck. Teddy settles in, and when Jackie the ringleader turns up, he unwisely goes into a disorganized ramble about what he did, and didn't, tell the cops who quizzed him. Everybody at the table knows that Teddy has made a big mistake. Bobby tells a funny story. Jackie's men shoot Teddy dead. The beat detective (Martin Sheen) arrives and makes cynical noises about how he supposes all the witnesses were in the men's room at the time.

As the central character, Denis Leary gives a thoughtful and effective performance. He is tired of his life of crime, tired of drugs and drinking, tired of always playing catch-up. Teddy's friends huddle in a corner at the funeral home and watch disbelievingly as Jackie, the big man, hands out the bills and sympathy. His mother, after still another wake, tells him,

"Somebody ought to say something this time." But nobody ever does.

The characters talk about family, neighborhood, loyalty, tradition, as if their gang represents the neighborhood (which is terrified of them). Certainly there are a lot of good people in the neighborhood, and we glimpse them in the background, but in Bobby's crowd, all of the good has been drained out, and they are demoralized by the half-realized fact that they are bad and worthless, their code a hollow shell.

The film is populated with many other sharply seen characters. Katy (Famke Janssen) is officially Jackie's girlfriend, but gets drunk and comes over to Bobby's house. All life centers in the tavern, which is a stage for nightly dramas, as when Bobby sees Katy with Jackie, and deliberately picks up a yuppie girl (Jeanne Tripplehorn) just to make her mad at him. It's the kind of bar where two men put their bare arms side by side, and the bartender puts a lighted cigarette on them, and they bet on who'll be the first to pull his arm away. You see somebody playing that game, you know all you need to know about them.

There is a whole genre of films about childhood friends still living in the old neighborhood, and going down the drain of crime and drugs. Few of them capture the fatigue and depression, the futility, as well as this one, in which the characters hold on to their self-respect by obeying the very rules that are grinding them down.

Mother ★ ★ ★ ½

PG-13, 104 m., 1997

Albert Brooks (John Henderson), Debbie Reynolds (Beatrice), Rob Morrow (Jeff), Lisa Kudrow (Linda), Isabel Glasser (Cheryl, Jeff's wife), Peter White (Charles). Directed by Albert Brooks and produced by Scott Rudin and Herb Nanas. Screenplay by Brooks and Monica Johnson.

The mother in Albert Brooks's *Mother* knows how to push the secret buttons to drive her son up the wall. All it takes is a slight intonation, a little pause, a wicked word choice no outsider would notice. And she's so sweet while making her subtle criticisms; why, you'd almost think she didn't know what she was doing.

Mother opens with John Henderson (Brooks) in despair because his second marriage has ended in divorce. In the lawyer's office, his ex-wife holds herself apart from him like the survivor of a long and exquisitely unpleasant experience. "She brought a lot of great furniture to the marriage," Henderson reflects, returning to a house now furnished with one chair, which he spends the afternoon rearranging. Then he telephones his mother, tells her his problems with women all started with her, and says he wants to move back home and get it right this time.

Beatrice Henderson (Debbie Reynolds) is not pleased. She's paid her dues, raised her children, and embraced the solitude of widowhood. She doesn't really seem to be focusing on his anguish; she constantly interrupts his emergency telephone call with call waiting, even though she doesn't know how it works. We see the nature of the difficulty: A mother who insists on her right to do things wrong is a torture to a perfectionist son.

Brooks is working with materials which look like the stuff of a sitcom; there is an *Odd Couple* spin-off here, waiting to happen. But Brooks, who cowrote (with Monica Johnson) and directed as well as starred, is much too smart to settle for the obvious gags and payoffs. All of his films depend on closely observed behavior and language, on the ways language can refuse to let us communicate no matter how obsessively we try to nail things down. In his scenes with Reynolds, they talk quietly, conversationally; they're not pounding out punch lines, and that's why the dialogue is so funny.

The experiment begins. John moves in with Beatrice and their first battles are joined over the issue of food. Beatrice puts salads in the freezer along with ancient blocks of Swiss cheese large enough to feed a day-care center. She buys the cheapest brands of everything, including "Sweet Tooth" orange sherbet, which has been hibernating in the freezer for years, growing what she happily describes as a "protective ice coating." ("This tastes," he tells her, "like an orange foot.") When he says he's a vegetarian, she offers to "scrape the top off the meat loaf."

Reynolds, who has not had a leading role in twenty-seven years, has two scenes with Brooks which are triumphs of perfect tone and timing. One is the scene just mentioned, where she tries to feed him dinner. Another is when they go shopping and get into arguments about everything that goes into the shopping cart; when she selects a generic brand of peanut butter, he cries out, "Just once, I want an experience where we throw away ninety-one cents together."

These tussles over superficial issues reveal underlying problems. Yes, Beatrice is maddening. But if John wants to improve his track record with women, he's going to have to learn not to be maddened. And the screenplay has some sly tricks up its sleeve: Perhaps, for example, it is absolutely true that Beatrice favors her other son (Rob Morrow) over John. The Morrow character is handled with a sharper edge than Beatrice and John. We see him at home with his wife (Isabel Glasser) in a scene that is deadly serious, as they argue over his possessiveness and insecurity about his mother.

The dialogue in *Mother* is written so carefully that some lines carry two or three nuances. That's especially so when John discovers that his mother has a gentleman friend (Peter White) who comes to visit once a month or so for dinner and sex. John has by now moved back into the room he had in high school (and decorated it with all the same old posters and sports pennants). His mother tiptoes down the corridor to be sure he's asleep, while the friend waits eagerly in the foyer.

I've seen *Mother* twice, once at the Toronto film festival and again with a capacity audience in Santa Monica. There was a lot of laughter both times, and the second time, listening closely, I recognized a certain quality in it. It wasn't the automatic laughter produced by slam-dunk punch lines, but the laughter of recognition, of insight, even sometimes of squirmy discomfort, as the truths hit close to home.

The audiences appreciated the film; they seemed grateful for its invention and intelligence, which didn't insult them, and on the way out they were repeating some of the best lines. I don't know if you can improve your romantic life by moving back in with your mother, but it might be a help to see this movie. Maybe with your mother. Maybe not.

The Mother and the Whore ★★★★

NO MPAA RATING, 215 m., 1973 (rereleased 1999)

Jean-Pierre Leaud (Alexandre), Bernadette Lafont (Marie), Francoise Lebrun (Veronika), Isabelle Weingarten (Gilberte), Jean Douchet (Man at Café Flore), Jean-Noel Picq (Offenbach Lover). Directed by Jean Eustache and produced by Pierre Cottrell. Screenplay by Eustache.

When Jean Eustache's *The Mother and the Whore* was released in 1973, young audiences all over the world embraced its layabout hero and his endless conversations with the woman he lived with, the woman he was dating, the woman who rejected him, and various other women encountered in the cafés of Paris. The character was played by Jean-Pierre Leaud, star of *The 400 Blows* and two other autobiographical films by François Truffaut. In 1977, Truffaut made *The Man Who Loved Women.* This one could have been titled *The Man Who Loved to Hear Himself Talk.*

At three and a half hours, the film is long, but its essence is to be long: Make it any shorter, and it would have a plot and an outcome, when in fact Eustache simply wants to record an existence. Alexandre (Leaud), his hero, lives with Marie (Bernadette Lafont), a boutique owner who apparently supports him; one would say he was between jobs if there were any sense that he'd ever had one. He meets a blind date named Veronika (Francoise Lebrun) in a café, and subjects her to a great many of his thoughts and would-be thoughts. (Much of Lebrun's screen time consists of close-ups of her listening.) In the middle of his monologues, Alexandre has a way of letting his eyes follow the progress of other women through his field of view.

Alexandre is smart enough, but not a great intellect. His favorite area of study is himself, but there he hasn't made much headway. He chatters about the cinema and about life, sometimes confusing them ("films tell you how to live, how to make a kid"). He wears a dark coat and a very long scarf, knotted around his neck and sweeping to his knees; his best friend dresses the same way. He spends his days in cafés, holding (but not reading) Proust. "Look there's Sartre—the drunk," he says one day in Café Flore, and Eustache supplies a quick shot of several people at a table, one of whom may or may not be Sartre. Alexandre talks about Sartre staggering out after his long intellectual chats in the café, and speculates that the great man's philosophy may be alcoholic musings.

The first time I saw *The Mother and the Whore*, I thought it was about Alexandre. After a viewing of the newly restored 35mm print being released for the movie's twenty-fifth anniversary, I think it is just as much about the women, and about the way that women can let a man talk endlessly about himself while they regard him like a specimen of aberrant behavior. Women keep a man like Alexandre around, I suspect, out of curiosity about what new idiocy he will next exhibit.

Of course, Alexandre is cheating—on Marie, whom he lives with, and on Veronika, whom he says he loves. Part of his style is to play with relationships, just to see what happens. The two women find out about each other, and eventually meet. There are some fireworks, but not as many as you might expect, maybe because neither one would be that devastated at losing Alexandre. Veronika, a nurse from Poland, is at least frank about herself: She sleeps around because she likes sex. She has a passionate monologue about her sexual needs and her resentment that women aren't supposed to admit their feelings. Whether Alexandre has sex with Marie is a good question; I suppose the answer is yes, but you can't be sure. She represents, of course, the mother, and Veronika thinks of herself as a whore; Alexandre has positioned himself in the crosshairs of the classic Freudian dilemma.

Jean-Pierre Leaud's best performance was his first, as the fierce young thirteen-year-old who roamed Paris in *The 400 Blows*, idolizing Balzac and escaping into books and trouble as a way of dealing with his parents' unhappy marriage. In a way, most of his adult performances are simply that boy, grown up. Here he smokes and talks incessantly, and wanders Paris like a puppet controlled by his libido. It's amusing the way he performs for the women; there's one shot in particular, where he takes a drink so theatrically it could be posing for a photo titled, "I Take a Drink."

The genuine drama in the movie centers on Veronika, who more or less knows they are only playing at love while out of the sight of Marie. We learn a lot about her life—her room in the hospital, her schedule, her low self-esteem. When she does talk, it is from brave, unadulterated self-knowledge.

The Mother and the Whore made an enormous impact when it was released. It still works a quarter-century later, because it was so focused on its subjects and lacking in pretension. It is rigorously observant, the portrait of an immature man and two women who humor him for a while, paying the price that entails. Eustache committed suicide at forty-three, in 1981, after making about a dozen films, of which this is by far the best-known. He said his film was intended as "the description of a normal course of events without the shortcuts of dramatization," and described Alexandre as a collector of "rare moments" that occupy his otherwise idle time. As a record of a kind of everyday Parisian life, the film is superb. We think of the cafés of Paris as hotbeds of fiery philosophical debate, but more often, I imagine, they are just like this: people talking, flirting, posing, drinking, smoking, telling the truth, and lying, while waiting to see if real life will ever begin.

Mouse Hunt ★ ★

PG, 97 m., 1997

Nathan Lane (Ernie Smuntz), Lee Evans (Lars Smuntz), Christopher Walken (Caesar), Vicky Lewis (April Smuntz), Eric Christmas (Lawyer), Maury Chaykin (Alexander Falko), Michael Jeter (Quincy Thorpe), William Hickey (Rudolph Smuntz). Directed by Gore Verbinski and produced by Alan Riche, Tony Ludwig, and Bruce Cohen. Screenplay by Adam Rifkin.

Mouse Hunt is not very funny, and maybe couldn't have been very funny no matter what, because the pieces for comedy are not in place. It's the story of two luckless brothers who inherit a priceless architectural treasure and hope to auction it for a big bundle, but are frustrated at every turn by the house's only inhabitant, a very clever mouse. Quick: Whom do we sympathize with? The brothers or the mouse?

The movie doesn't know, and as a result the

payoffs are lost in a comic vacuum. Pratfalls, slapstick, and special effects are not funny in themselves (something Hollywood keeps forgetting). They're only funny when they apply to someone we have an attitude about, so that we want them to succeed or fail. A comedy that hasn't assigned sympathy to some characters and made others hateful cannot expect to get many laughs because the audience doesn't know who to laugh at, or with.

Consider the rodent itself. In appearance, it is a common field mouse. Sort of cute. It has been cinematically assembled from many sources (real trained mice, animated mice, an animatronic mouse for the close-ups), but it has never been given a goal in life, other than to function as a plot device. Is the mouse intelligent? Does it know and care what is happening? Or is it simply a movie prop to be employed on cue? We aren't told, and we don't know. Because the mouse has no personality or personal history, because it has no particular goals other than to continue being a mouse, it isn't a sympathetic character, but simply an ingenious prop.

Now what about the brothers Smuntz? Ernie (Nathan Lane) and Lars (Lee Evans) have inherited the string factory of their father (William Hickey), and also a run-down old Victorian mansion that turns out to be a lost masterpiece of a great architect. They can get rich by selling it, but first they have to make some repairs—and get rid of the mouse. To help themselves, they bring in an exterminator named Caesar (Christopher Walken).

At some point in the production, someone undoubtedly said, "Wouldn't it be great to get Christopher Walken as the exterminator!" But why? Yes, Walken is an actor who inspires strong audience reactions, and, yes, his baggage from previous roles makes him a plausible exterminator. But what is funny about the character *other* than that it's played by Walken? Are we supposed to laugh when he's humiliated by the mouse? Not unless we care about him—and we don't, since he's obviously as much a prop as the mouse.

What about the brothers? Are they funny? No. But it is supposed to be funny that they can't get rid of the mouse, which is able to set off all their traps, figure out all their plans, and anticipate all their schemes. Since we never believe the mouse is doing that (we believe the screenplay is doing it), we don't much care that it's done.

Mouse Hunt is an excellent example of the way modern advances in special effects can sabotage a picture (*Titanic* is an example of effects being used wisely). Because it is possible to make a movie in which the mouse can do all sorts of clever things, the filmmakers have assumed incorrectly that it would be funny to see the mouse doing them.

Years ago, a comedy with a similar theme would have established the mouse, but would have been about the people. The characters would have reacted to the simple presence of a mouse, not to the incredibly elaborate stunts the mouse performs. The brothers and their auctioneer could have been developed as desperate for money, as eager to deceive, as pathetic liars, as hapless victims. The mouse would have been there, but wouldn't have had more screen time than most of the characters.

Mouse Hunt is a film that has gone to incredible effort and expense in order to sidetrack itself from comic payoffs. Less mouse, better dialogue, and more strongly drawn characters might have made a funnier movie. I believe a mouse can be trained to pick up an olive and run with it, but I don't believe it's funny. Not unless I know the mouse.

Mr. Jealousy ★ ★ ½

R, 103 m., 1998

Eric Stoltz (Lester Grimm), Annabella Sciorra (Ramona Ray), Chris Eigeman (Dashiell Frank), Carlos Jacott (Vince), Marianne Jean-Baptiste (Lucretia), Brian Kerwin (Stephen), Peter Bogdanovich (Dr. Poke), Bridget Fonda (Irene). Directed by Noah Baumbach and produced by Joel Castleberg. Screenplay by Baumbach.

Lester Grimm, the hero of *Mr. Jealousy,* is the kind of guy who can grow so obsessed with a girl that he shadows her all the time, hiding in shrubbery to see where she goes and what she does—until she drops him because he never seems to be around. His insecurity started early. At fifteen, he took a girl to a movie and an Italian restaurant on what he thought was a perfectly acceptable date, only to spot her later at a party, making out with a twenty-four-year-old club promoter.

Ever since, Lester (Eric Stoltz) has been tormented by images of his dates in the arms of other guys. Who did they date before they met him? How did they feel about their former lovers? How do they still feel? At thirty-one, Lester is still single, and working as a substitute teacher of Spanish, a language he does not speak. He is dating Ramona (Annabella Sciorra), who conducts museum tours and is getting her doctoriate in abstract expressionism. Can he trust her? Did she have a life before he met her?

She sure did. She used to date Dashiell Frank (Chris Eigeman), "the generation-defining writer" whose novels speak powerfully to Generation Xers. When Ramona and Dashiell accidentally encounter one another, Lester's jealousy is inflamed by their air of easy affection, and he starts following Dashiell. Discovering that the writer is a member of a therapy group, Lester signs up for the same group—not under his own name, but as "Vince," the name of his best friend (Carlos Jacott).

That's the setup for Noah Baumbach's film, which, like his observant *Kicking and Screaming* (1995), is about characters who are too old for college but unready for real life. Baumbach has a good ear for how these characters talk, but the unforced originality of his earlier film is joined here by homages to other directors; he gets the iris shots and narration from Francois Truffaut, the nebbishy insecurity from Woody Allen and Henry Jaglom, and the self-analytical dialogue from Whit Stillman. I'm not bothered by his homage to them so much as I miss his confidence in himself.

That earlier film nailed the characters and the dialogue so accurately that you remembered people exactly like that; indeed, you recalled *being* like that. *Mr. Jealousy* pumps in more plot, and I'm not sure that's the right decision. Mistaken identities and mutual misunderstandings can only be taken so far before the plot seems to be leading the characters. That's okay in farce, but in more thoughtful comedies the characters should appear to be making their decisions entirely unprompted by the requirements of the genre.

Baumbach is a gifted filmmaker, however, and many of his scenes are just right, including a sequence where Dashiell, the writer, reads a story to the group and Lester thinks it must be based on Dashiell's relationship with Ramona. He challenges the writer to "reveal more about his characters," and learns what he didn't want to know, that the original of the woman in the story "was a bit of a tart."

Well, was she? Ramona strikes us as sensible and restrained, and discriminating enough in her relationships that she probably shouldn't even be dating Lester. But we begin to sense uneasily that a story arc is being shaped here, and that the movie will require Lester to almost lose Ramona, and for secrets to be revealed and emotional showdowns to be arrived at, and for events to replace insights.

Eric Stoltz, who also starred in *Kicking and Screaming,* is well cast as Lester; he has a quiet intelligence matched with a kind of laconic earnestness about himself. Chris Eigeman, a veteran of Stillman's films, finds and holds a difficult note as a writer who is young and famous without being any more insufferable as a result than is absolutely necessary. Annabella Sciorra does a good job of creating the kind of woman who puts up with a lot from a guy if she likes him; she has her own life, doesn't need to live through his, and only gradually realizes that in a quiet, elusive way he is stark staring mad.

Mr. Jealousy isn't quite successful, but it does provide more evidence of Baumbach's talent. So many young filmmakers aim merely for success, and throw anything at us that they think we'll buy. Only a few are trying to chronicle their generation, listening to how it talks and watching how it behaves. That number includes the Whit Stillman of *The Last Days of Disco,* the Richard Linklater of *subUrbia,* the Kevin Smith of *Chasing Amy,* and the Nicole Holofcener of *Walking and Talking. Mr. Jealousy* shows that Baumbach is the real thing, but he needs to focus.

Mr. Magoo ½★

PG, 97 m., 1997

Leslie Nielsen (Mr. Magoo), Kelly Lynch (Luanne), Matt Keeslar (Waldo), Nick Chinlund (Bob Morgan), Stephen Tobolowsky (Agent Chuck Stupak), Ernie Hudson (Agent Gus Anders), Jennifer Garner (Stacey

Sampanahoditra), Malcolm McDowell (Austin Cloquet). Directed by Stanley Tong and produced by Ben Myron. Screenplay by Pat Proft and Tom Sherohman.

Magoo drives a red Studebaker convertible in *Mr. Magoo,* a fact I report because I love Studebakers and his was the only thing I liked in the film. It has a prescription windshield. He also drives an eggplantmobile, which looks like a failed wienermobile. The concept of a failed wienermobile is itself funnier than anything in the movie.

Mr. Magoo is transcendentally bad. It soars above ordinary badness as the eagle outreaches the fly. There is not a laugh in it. Not one. I counted. I wonder if there *could* have been any laughs in it. Perhaps this project was simply a bad idea from the beginning, and no script, no director, no actor, could have saved it.

I wasn't much of a fan of the old cartoons. They were versions of one joke, imposed on us by the cantankerous but sometimes lovable nearsighted Magoo, whose shtick was to mistake something for something else. He always survived, but since it wasn't through his own doing, his adventures were more like exercises in design: Let's see how Magoo can walk down several girders suspended in midair, while thinking they're a staircase.

The plot involves Magoo as an innocent bystander at the theft of a jewel. Mistaken as the thief, he is pursued by the usual standard-issue CIA and FBI buffoons, while never quite understanding the trouble he's in. He's accompanied on most of his wanderings by his bulldog and his nephew, Waldo, of which the bulldog has the more winning personality.

Magoo is played by Leslie Nielsen, who could at the very least have shaved his head bald for the role. He does an imitation of the Magoo squint and the Magoo voice, but is unable to overcome the fact that a little Magoo at six minutes in a cartoon is a far different matter than a lot of Magoo at ninety minutes in a feature. This is a one-joke movie without the joke. Even the outtakes at the end aren't funny, and I'm not sure I understood one of them, unless it was meant to show stunt people hilariously almost being drowned.

I have taken another look at my notes, and must correct myself. There is one laugh in the movie. It comes after the action is over, in the form of a foolish, politically correct disclaimer stating that the film "is not intended as an accurate portrayal of blindness or poor eyesight." I think we should stage an international search to find one single person who thinks the film is intended as such a portrayal, and introduce that person to the author of the disclaimer, as they will have a lot in common, including complete detachment from reality.

Mr. Nice Guy ★ ★ ★

PG-13, 90 m., 1998

Jackie Chan (Jackie), Richard Norton (Giancarlo), Gabrielle Fitzpatrick (Diana), Miki Lee (Miki), Karen McLymont (Lakeisha), Vince Poletto (Romeo), Barry Otto (Baggio), Sammo Hung (Cyclist). Directed by Sammo Hung and produced by Chua Lam. Screenplay by Edward Tang and Fibe Ma.

Jackie Chan's *Mr. Nice Guy* was originally titled *No More Mr. Nice Guy,* which would also have worked; as the film opens he's a smiling chef on a TV show, and as it closes he's single-handedly destroying a house with a giant piece of earthmoving equipment. Still, I like the new title, because Chan *is* a nice guy, with his infectious grin, potato nose, and astonishing physical comedy.

In a seminar last year at the Hawaii Film Festival, I compared some of Chan's action sequences to work by Buster Keaton. That may seem like a stretch, but look at his films and it's obvious Chan is more in the tradition of silent comedy than of the chop-socky genre. He kids himself, he pretends to be in over his head, and he survives by luck and skill instead of brute force.

In *Mr. Nice Guy,* he's the innocuous bystander who gets involved only to save a pretty girl, and wanders into a drug war by accident. The plot is a clothesline for the action sequences. A TV reporter (Gabrielle Fitzpatrick) has a videotape incriminating some drug lords. The bad guys want it back. They chase her. Jackie helps her. The bad guys become convinced Jackie has the tape. They chase both of them. Jackie's TV show assistant (Karen McLymont) turns up and gets chased too. Jackie's girlfriend from Hong Kong (Miki Lee) flies into town. Then the bad guys chase Jackie and all three women.

Sample dialogue. Goon tells boss: "I'm sorry, boss. We didn't get the tape, and four of our guys got blown up!" Boss tells goon: "Get the tape or you'll never be seen again." So far, so good, but then the boss grabs the goon's tie and starts slapping him on his face with the end of it, and this is so unexpected and weirdly goofy that it gets a laugh.

The plot is an excuse for sight gags, physical humor, stunts, and exquisite timing. There are big action ballets, but one of my favorite moments is a quieter one that happens so fast you'll miss it if you blink. Jackie is holding a gun he knows is not loaded. He comes around a corner and is face-to-face with a bad guy, also with a gun. The guy points the gun at Jackie. Jackie hands his own gun to the guy. The guy looks at the gun he's been given, and Jackie simply takes the other gun, as if in trade. Then the guy shoots Jackie—but with the unloaded gun. It's like a three-card monte trick. I think I've left out a couple of steps, but you get the idea: The logic of the physical movements drives the drama.

Another neat sequence: Jackie is demonstrating cooking skills in a shopping center by flipping bite-sized pieces of crepes twenty yards into the mouths of his fans. A bad guy steps in front of a fan, and intercepts one of the bites. Jackie grins and flips him another bite. This time it's a fiery pepper. Okay, so this isn't Antonioni.

The big action sequences involve runaway horses, a chase through a shopping center, the use of a crane, and an escape across a steel beam high in the air. Some of the stunts are amazing. That giant earthmoving vehicle, for example, has wheels that look twelve feet high. In one shot, as a wheel approaches Jackie to crush him, he keeps himself away from it—by pushing off with his feet against the moving wheel to scoot himself along on his back. Get that one wrong, and you have tire treads where your face used to be.

There's a stunt, too, where Jackie is hanging out the side of a moving carriage, about to fall, and braces himself by running sideways, as it were, down the side of a passing trolley car. Hard to describe, and almost impossible to do, but for Chan it's a throwaway, a few seconds in length.

The movie ends, as always, with credit cookies showing outtakes of Jackie landing wrong and nearly getting creamed. They prove what we know, that he does his own stunts. You watch how good he is and how hard he works, and you're glad his plots are an afterthought, because you don't want anything distracting from his sheer physical exuberance.

Mrs. Brown ★ ★ ★ ½

PG, 103 m., 1997

Judi Dench (Queen Victoria), Billy Connolly (John Brown), Geoffrey Palmer (Henry Ponsonby), Antony Sher (Disraeli), Gerald Butler (Archie Brown), Richard Pasco (Doctor Jenner), David Westhead (Prince of Wales). Directed by John Madden and produced by Sarah Curtis. Screenplay by Jeremy Brock.

"Honest to God," the man tells the woman, "I never thought to see you in such a state. You must miss him dreadfully." Between ordinary people, ordinary words. Between a commoner and a queen, sheer effrontery. How can this bearded man, a Scotsman who oversees Queen Victoria's palace at Balmoral, have the gall to look her in the eye and address her with such familiarity?

The atmosphere in court is instantly tense and chilling. But the man, John Brown, has caught the queen's attention and cut through the miasma of two years' mourning for her beloved consort, Prince Albert. The little woman—a plump pudding dressed all in black—looks up sharply, and a certain light glints in her eyes. Before long she is taking Brown's advice that she must ride out daily for the exercise and the fresh air.

Mrs. Brown is a love story about two strong-willed people who find exhilaration in testing one another. It is not about sexual love, or even romantic love, really, but about that kind of love based on challenge and fascination. The film opens in 1864, when Queen Victoria (Judi Dench), consumed by mourning, has already been all but invisible to her subjects for two years. Her court coddles and curtseys to her, and that's what she expects: A nod or a glance from her can subdue an adviser.

Her household thinks perhaps riding might help her break out of her deep gloom, and import John Brown (Billy Connolly), a Scotsman in a kilt, who arrives with one of the queen's horses and is promptly ignored. Not to be trifled with, he stands at attention in her courtyard next to the horse. The next day he is there again. Proper behavior would have him waiting, docile and invisible, in the stables. "The queen will ride out if and when she chooses," Victoria informs him.

"And I intend to be there when she is ready," Brown informs Victoria.

Nobody in her life had spoken to her in this way, except perhaps for the beloved Albert. A charge forms in the air between them. Victoria is a complex and observant woman, who knows exactly what he is doing, and is thrilled by it: Queens perhaps grow tired of being fawned upon. Soon Brown and the queen are out riding, and soon the color has returned to her cheeks, and soon Brown is offering advice on how she should manage her affairs, and soon the household and the nation are whispering that this beastly man Brown is the power behind the throne.

"Mrs. Brown," they called her behind her back. Her son the Prince of Wales (David Westhead) is enraged to find that at Brown's order the smoking room is to be closed at midnight ("Mr. Brown needs his rest," the queen serenely explains). Brown takes her riding in the country and they call at a humble cottage, and the queen is offered Scotch whisky. The national newspapers raise their eyebrows. Finally the prime minister, Benjamin Disraeli (Antony Sher), pays a visit to see for himself what is happening in the royal household.

Judi Dench has long been one of the reigning stars of the London stage. She often plays strong-willed, intelligent women. She has never been much interested in the movies, although she did play "M" in a Bond film. This is her first starring role. She is wonderful in it, building the entire character on the rock of utter self-possession, and then showing that character possessed by another. Entrenched behind her desk, dressed in mourning, coils of braids framing her implacable face, she presents such a formidable facade that it is curiously erotic when Brown melts through it.

Billy Connolly is also little known in films; he is a stand-up comic, I learn, although here he has the reserve and self-confidence that most stand-up comics lack almost by definition. There is a manliness to him, a robust defiance of the rules. He also drinks too much, and although he seems for a long time able to hold it, one of the movie's subtle themes is that the better he gets to know the queen the less sure he is of how be should proceed.

Would there be, could there be, physical sex between them? Almost certainly not. But they both tacitly recognize that they might enjoy it. The queen is not an attractive woman, but she is powerful, and power is thrilling; in one key scene Brown swims naked in the highlands, intoxicated by his closeness to the throne. Victoria is like a movie nun-like Deborah Kerr in *Black Narcissus*—in being all the more intriguing because forbidden.

Mrs. Brown was written by Jeremy Brock and directed by John Madden, whose first film, the torturous *Ethan Frome*, gave little promise of his confidence here. The movie is insidious in its methods, asking us to see what is happening beneath the guarded surfaces. The behavior of a queen and her servant is so minutely dictated by rules and customs that they may look much the same when breaking them as when following them. So much depends on the eyes.

Mrs. Dalloway ★ ★ ★ ½

PG-13, 97 m., 1998

Vanessa Redgrave (Mrs. Dalloway), Natascha McElhone (Young Clarissa), Rupert Graves (Septimus Smith), Michael Kitchen (Peter Walsh), Alan Cox (Young Peter), Sarah Badel (Lady Rosseter [Sally]), Lena Headey (Young Sally), John Standing (Richard Dalloway), Robert Portal (Young Richard), Amelia Bullmore (Rezia Smith). Directed by Marleen Gorris and produced by Stephen Bayly and Lisa Katselas Pare. Screenplay by Eileen Atkins, based on a novel by Virginia Woolf.

In many lives there is a crossroads. We make our choice and follow it down to the present moment. Still inside of us is that other person, who stands forever poised at the head of the path not chosen. *Mrs. Dalloway* is about a day's communion between the woman who exists and the other woman who might have existed instead.

The film's heroine muses that she is thought of as "Mrs. Dalloway" by almost everybody: "You're not even Clarissa any more." Once she was young and fair, and tempted by two daring choices. Young Peter would have been a risk, but he was dangerous and alive. Even more dangerous was Sally, with whom flirtation threatened to develop into something she was unwilling to name. Clarissa took neither choice, deciding instead to marry the safe and sound Richard Dalloway, of whom young Peter sniffed, "He's a fool, an unimaginative, dull fool."

Now many years have passed. Mrs. Dalloway is giving a party. The caterer has been busy since dawn, the day is beautiful, and she walks through Hyde Park to buy the flowers herself. So opens Virginia Woolf's famous 1923 novel, which follows Clarissa Dalloway for a day, using the new stream-of-consciousness technique James Joyce was experimenting with. We will follow her through until the end of her party, during a day in which no one she meets will know what she's really thinking: All they will see is her reserved, charming exterior.

The novel stays mostly within the mind of Clarissa, with darts into other minds. Film cannot do that, but *Mrs. Dalloway* uses a voice-over narration to let us hear Clarissa's thoughts, which she never, ever, shares with anybody else. To the world she is a respectable, sixtyish London woman, the wife of a Cabinet official. To us, she is a woman who will always wonder what might have been.

Vanessa Redgrave so loved the novel that she commissioned this screenplay by Eileen Atkins, an actress who has been involved in a lot of Woolf-oriented stage work. Redgrave, of course, seems the opposite of a woman like Clarissa Dalloway, and we assume she has few regrets. But we all wonder about choices not made, because in our memories they still glow with their original promise, while reality is tied to the mundane.

As the film makes its way through Clarissa's day, there are flashbacks to long-ago summers when young Peter (Alan Cox) was courting young Clarissa (Natascha McElhone), and young Sally (Lena Headey) was perhaps courting her, too, although the movie is cagier about that than the novel. But Woolf is too wise to let Peter and Sally remain in the sunny past of memory. They both turn up on this day.

In middle age, Peter (Michael Kitchen) is rather pathetic, just returned from what seems to have been an unsuccessful romance and career in India. And Sally (Sarah Badel) is now the distinguished Lady Rosseter. There is a wonderful scene where Peter and Sally find a quiet corner of the party, and he tells her of Clarissa, "I loved her once, and it stayed with me all my life, and colored every day." Sally nods, keeping her own thoughts to herself. We gather that Sally, in middle age, may be practicing the same sort of two-track thinking that Clarissa uses: Both women see more sharply, and critically, than anyone imagines, although with Sally we must guess this from the outside.

There is another crucial character in the film. Unless you've read the novel you may have trouble understanding his function. This is Septimus Warren Smith (Rupert Graves), who in an early scene watches as a friend is blown up in the no-man's-land of the trenches in France. Now five years or more have passed, but he suffers from shell shock, and has a panic attack outside a shop where Clarissa pauses. She sees him, and although they never meet, there is a link between them: Both have seen beneath the surface of life's reassurance, to the possibility that nothing, or worse than nothing, lurks below. Woolf is suggesting that World War I unleashed horrors that poisoned every level of society.

The subtext of the story is suicide. Woolf is asking what purpose is served by the decisions of Clarissa and Septimus to go on living lives that they have seen through. A subtle motif throughout the film is the omnipresence of sharp fence railings—spikes, like life, upon which one could be impaled.

The director, Marleen Gorris, previously made the Oscar-winning Dutch film *Antonia's Line,* about a woman who makes free choices, survives, and prevails. Here is the other side. It's surprising that Gorris, who was so open about Antonia's sexuality, is so subtle about the unspoken lesbianism in Woolf's story, but it's there for those who can see it.

More important is the way she struggles with form, to try to get an almost unfilmable novel on the screen. She isn't always successful; the first act will be perplexing for those unfamiliar with the novel, but Redgrave's performance steers us through, and by the end we understand with complete, final clarity what the story was about. Stream-of-consciousness stays entirely within the mind. Movies photograph only the outsides of things. The narration is a useful device, but so are Redgrave's eyes, as she looks at the guests at her party. Once we have the clue, she doesn't really look at all like a safe, respectable, middle-aged hostess. More like a caged animal—trained, but not tamed.

Mulan ★ ★ ★ ½

G, 98 m., 1998

With the voices of: Ming-Na Wen (Mulan), Lea Salonga (Mulan, Singing), Eddie Murphy (Mushu), B. D. Wong (Shang), Donny Osmond (Shang, Singing), Harvey Fierstein (Yao), Jerry Tondo (Chien-Po), Gedde Watanabe (Ling). Directed by Barry Cook and Tony Bancroft and produced by Pam Coats. Screenplay by Rita Hsiao, Christopher Sanders, Philip LaZebnik, Raymond Singer, and Eugenia Bostwick-Singer, based on a story by Robert D. San Souci.

Mulan charts a new direction for Disney's animation studio, combining the traditional elements (brave heroine, cute animal sidekicks) with material that seems more adventuresome and grown-up. Like Fox's *Anastasia,* this is a film that adults can enjoy on their own, without feeling an obligation to take along kids as a cover.

The story this time isn't a retread of a familiar children's classic, but original material, about a plucky Chinese teenage girl who disguises herself as a boy to fight the invading Huns. When the invaders and their implacable leader Shan-Yu (who looks alarmingly like Karl Malone) sweep down on the Great Wall, the emperor calls up all able men to defend the kingdom. Mulan's father is old and feeble, but throws away his crutch to volunteer. To spare him, Mulan steals the family sword, summons the family ancestors for aid, and secretly goes in his place.

Ah, but it isn't as simple as that. Mulan is defying not simply convention, but her family's desire that she abide by the plans of a matchmaker and marry whomever she selects for her. Opening scenes in the film show her botching the interview with the matchmaker (she sets her pants on fire, a nice Freudian touch), and asking, "When will my reflection show who I am inside?"

The message here is standard feminist empowerment: Defy the matchmaker, dress as a boy, and choose your own career. But *Mulan* has it both ways, since inevitably Mulan's heart goes pitty-pat over Shang, the handsome young captain she's assigned to serve under. The movie breaks with the tradition in which the male hero rescues the heroine, but is still totally sold on the Western idea of romantic love. (In an Eastern culture, the ending might have involved an arranged match between Mulan and Shang, which she has earned by her exploits.)

Disney movies since time immemorial have provided their leads with low-comedy sidekicks, usually in the form of animals, although teacups and chandeliers are not unheard-of. Mulan is accompanied on her journey by a scrawny dragon named Mushu, whose voice is performed by Eddie Murphy. It's a little disconcerting the first time we hear his street-smart lingo (a black dude in medieval China?), but Mushu quickly grows on us. Murphy, working in the tradition of Robin Williams's genie in *Aladdin,* is quick, glib, and funny. He is also offended when people doubt he is a real dragon and refer to him as a lizard.

The action plot involves Mulan training for battle (the song promises, "I'll make a man out of you"), and using quick thinking to save Shang's troops from certain defeat. There are a couple of scenes where she narrowly escapes detection, including one at a swimming hole, and then, when she's unmasked, Shang's snaky adviser whispers that to impersonate a man is "treason." The outcome manages somehow to be true simultaneously to feminist dogma and romantic convention.

The visual style breaks slightly with the look of modern Disney animation to draw from Chinese and Japanese classical cartoon art; in the depiction of nature, there's an echo of the master artist Hiroshige. In a scene where the Hun troops sweep down the side of a snowy mountain, I was reminded of the great battle sequence in Eisenstein's *Alexander*

Nevsky. There are scenes here, indeed, where the Disney artists seem aware of the important new work being done in Japanese anime; if American animation is ever going to win an audience beyond the family market, it will have to move in this direction, becoming more experimental in both stories and visual style.

Animation often finds a direct line to my imagination: It's pure story, character, movement, and form, without the distractions of reality or the biographical baggage of the actors. I found myself really enjoying *Mulan,* as a story and as animated art. If the songs were only more memorable, I'd give it four stars, but they seemed pleasant rather than rousing, and I wasn't humming anything on the way out. Still, *Mulan* is an impressive achievement, with a story and treatment ranking with *Beauty and the Beast* and *The Lion King.* ☞

The Mummy ★★★

PG-13, 124 m., 1999

Brendan Fraser (Rick O'Connell), Rachel Weisz (Evelyn), John Hannah (Jonathan), Kevin J. O'Connor (Beni), Arnold Vosloo (Imhotep), Jonathan Hyde (Egyptologist), Oded Fehr (Ardeth Bay), Omid Djalili (Warden). Directed by Stephen Sommers and produced by James Jacks and Sean Daniel. Screenplay by Sommers.

There is within me an unslaked hunger for preposterous adventure movies. I resist the bad ones, but when a *Congo* or an *Anaconda* comes along, my heart leaps up and I cave in. *The Mummy* is a movie like that. There is hardly a thing I can say in its favor, except that I was cheered by nearly every minute of it. I cannot argue for the script, the direction, the acting, or even the mummy, but I can say that I was not bored and sometimes I was unreasonably pleased. There is a little immaturity stuck away in the crannies of even the most judicious of us, and we should treasure it.

This is a movie about a man who fooled around with the pharaoh's mistress and lived (and died, and lived again) to regret it. As his punishment he is "mummified alive," sealed inside a sarcophagus with thousands of flesh-eating beetles (which eat flesh "very slowly," we learn). Millennia pass. In the 1920s, a French foreign legionnaire named Rick meets a librarian named Evelyn, and joins with her and her brother in an unwise quest to find Hamunaptra, the City of the Dead. (Sample dialogue: "Are we talking about *the* Hamunaptra?") They get into a race with other fortune-hunters, who have heard of untold treasure buried beneath the sands, and meanwhile the descendants of the high priests, who have guarded the city for 3,000 years, move against them.

There is good reason not to disturb the mummy, named Imhotep. If he is brought back to life, he will "arise a walking disease," we learn, and unleash the ten proverbial plagues upon Egypt, of which in the course of the movie I counted locusts, fireballs from the sky, rivers running with blood, earthquakes, and flies. Also, of course, the flesh-eating beetles, although I was not certain whether they were a plague or came with the territory.

Brendan Fraser plays Rick, a low-rent Indiana Jones who single-handedly fights his way through a bewildering series of battles. Evie (Rachel Weisz) is too clumsy to be much help (in a delightful early scene, she knocks over one bookcase and the domino effect knocks over every single bookcase in the Museum of Antiquities). Her brother Jonathan (John Hannah) is a spoiled rich kid who specializes in the sorts of asides that butlers used to make. Arnold Vosloo plays Imhotep the mummy in the later scenes, after Imhotep has absorbed the inner organs of enough victims to reconstitute himself. In the earlier scenes, Imhotep is a ghastly special-effects creature who seems made of decomposed cardboard, and lets out a cloud of dust every time Rick slices him.

None of this has anything to do with the great horror classic *The Mummy* (1932), which starred Boris Karloff in a strangely poignant performance as a long-dead priest who returns to life and falls in love with the modern reincarnation of the woman he died for. The 1932 movie contains no violence to speak of; there's hardly any action, indeed, and the chills come through slow realizations (hey, did that mummy move?). This 1999 mummy does indeed mumble something about his feelings for Evie, who may be descended from the pharaoh's mistress on her mother's side. But the bass on his voice synthesizer was set to Rumble, and so I was not quite sure what he said. It sounded vaguely affectionate, in the way that a pit bull growling over a T-bone sounds affectionate, but how can Imhotep focus on rekindling a 3,000-year-old romance when he has ten plagues to unleash?

There's a lot of funny dialogue in the movie, of which my favorite is a line of Evie's after she hears a suspicious noise in the museum library: "Abdul? Mohammed? Bob?" I liked the Goldfinger paint job on the priests in ancient Thebes. And the way a beetle burrowed in through a guy's shoe and traveled through his body, a lump under his flesh, until it could dine on his brain. And the way characters were always reading the wrong pages of ancient books, and raising the dead by accident.

Look, art this isn't. Great trash, it isn't. Good trash, it is. It's not quite up there with *Anaconda,* but it's as much fun as *Congo* and *The Relic,* and it's better than *Species.* If those four titles are not intimately familiar to you, *The Mummy* might not be the place to start.

Murder at 1600 ★ ★ ½

R, 106 m., 1997

Wesley Snipes (Harlan Regis), Diane Lane (Nina Chance), Alan Alda (Alvin Jordan), Daniel Benzali (Nick Spikings), Dennis Miller (Detective Stengel), Ronny Cox (President Jack Neil). Directed by Dwight Little and produced by Arnold Kopelson and Arnon Milchan. Screenplay by Wayne Beach and David Hodgin.

There is an opening sequence that's familiar from a lot of cop movies. A madman is waving a gun and threatening bystanders. He is surrounded by cops. Then the department's hot shot drives up, sizes up the situation, intuits how to push the madman's buttons, walks up to him unarmed, distracts him, disarms him, and the crisis is over.

That's how Eddie Murphy's *Metro* opened, and that's Wesley Snipes's big opening scene in *Murder at 1600.* This cliché serves useful purposes: (1) it opens the movie with an action scene, (2) it establishes the hero's credentials as a guy who doesn't play by the rules, and (3) it's the setup for a payoff later in the movie—usually in a minor comic key.

That's what happens this time. Turns out the guy waving the gun is a depressed government commissioner. Turns out Snipes has had problems with the same agency: It wants to tear down his apartment building and put up a parking lot. In a movie involving a White House murder, the odds are excellent that sooner or later the cop and the president are going to be chatting about that parking lot.

Snipes plays Harlan Regis, a Washington police detective who is assigned when a woman is found murdered in the White House. He gets into a territorial struggle with Spikings (Daniel Benzali), the head of the Secret Service detail, who gives him absolutely no cooperation.

"She was killed in my city," Regis barks.

"She was killed in my house," Spikings growls.

Why was a city cop assigned in the first place? "They got you in to make it look real," Regis is told, and indeed there seems to be a cover-up under way. Among the suspects: the president's son, who was a lover of the dead woman, and perhaps the president himself (Ronny Cox). A voice of reason seems to be the national security adviser (Alan Alda), who's a contrast to the demented Mr. Clean image of Spikings.

Because this is a cop movie, Regis is supplied with a partner (Dennis Miller). Miller serves no function except to take phone calls, but soon we understand: He's a seat-warmer, brought in to provide a virtual partner until the movie can supply a real one. Regis quickly meets Nina Chance (Diane Lane), a member of the Secret Service detail and an Olympic Gold Medal sharpshooter. Even though they're on opposite sides of the jurisdictional divide, they share the conviction that an innocent man is being framed.

A lot of *Murder at 1600* is well done. Characters are introduced vividly, there's a sense of realism in the White House scenes, and some of the dialogue by Wayne Beach and David Hodgin hits a nice ironic note. (In a briefing, White House spokesmen are told: "We would like you to avoid two words when talking to the media. The words are 'woman' and 'murder.'") The cop and the sharpshooter achieve an easy rapport; she likes it that his apartment is filled with incredibly elaborate reconstructions of Civil War battles.

But then the movie kicks into autopilot. The last third of the film is a ready-made action movie plug-in. Without giving away a single secret, I can tell you that Regis and Chance find it necessary to break into the White House. And to do this, they must traverse a forgotten series of tunnels that lead by labyrinthine twists into the White House basement. The movie does what too many thrillers do: It establishes an interesting premise, and then instead of following it, substitutes standard action clichés. Will there be water, rats, electricity, dangerous secrets, hazards, security traps, flames, explosions, and gunshots in the tunnel? If you think not, you haven't seen *The Rock* or all the other movies that inspire this sequence.

While our heroes are wading through the dangerous subterranean waters, let's step back and think. They need to tell the president something. He is walled off by a conspiracy. How can they get the information to him? I can think of two answers: (1) the president's son has a personal motive for wanting his father to get the information, and has complete access to him; and (2) the cop is surrounded by TV cameras every time he steps outside. He could simply blurt out the truth, since there is no need to keep it secret. Neither of these alternatives would be as much fun as breaking into the White House, but they would have a better chance of success.

The fact is, the entire movie is fiction, and so if it's entertaining me, then I'm grateful. It's only when a movie stops working that I ask questions. For example, in a later scene, Regis masquerades as a janitor and pushes a cart through the White House while holding his head down and whistling tunelessly. Doesn't he know that holding your head down and whistling tunelessly is what *all* suspicious characters do when they disguise themselves as janitors? Isn't that like wearing a neon sign saying IMPOSTOR?

I'd love to see a taut, competent police procedural based on a murder in the White House—one that followed standard procedures to see how they were warped by presidential power. *Murder at 1600* seems to have started in that direction, before the fatal decision was made to cut out large chunks of the story in order to import weary thriller clichés. If I want to see a movie about slogging through flooded tunnels, I'll watch *The Third Man.*

My Best Friend's Wedding ★ ★ ★

PG-13, 105 m., 1997

Julia Roberts (Julianne Potter), Dermot Mulroney (Michael O'Neal), Cameron Diaz (Kimmy Wallace), Rupert Everett (George Downes), Philip Bosco (Walter Wallace), M. Emmet Walsh (Joe O'Neal), Rachel Griffiths (Samantha Newhouse), Carrie Preston (Amanda Newhouse). Directed by P. J. Hogan and produced by Jerry Zucker and Ronald Bass. Screenplay by Bass.

When she dumped Michael as a boyfriend in college, Julianne made him her new best friend. And they made a pact: If they were still single at twenty-eight, they'd marry each other. Now they're almost twenty-eight. And Michael is in Chicago. And wants Julianne to call him. She's touched. She's always really loved the guy. But he's not calling to propose. He's calling to explain he's engaged to be married in three days—to a junior at the University of Chicago, whose father owns the White Sox and a cable TV empire.

This is not good news for Julianne. P. J. Hogan's *My Best Friend's Wedding* tells the story of how she tries to sabotage the wedding and win the man she should have married all along. And since Julianne, a famous food critic, is played by the luminous Julia Roberts, we know how the movie will end, right? Not necessarily.

One of the pleasures of Ronald Bass's screenplay is the way it subverts the usual comic formulas that would fuel a plot like this. It makes the Julia Roberts character sympathetic at first, but eventually her behavior shades into cruel meddling. It gives Kimmy Wallace (Cameron Diaz), the fiancée, goodness and warmth instead of a ditzy facade. It makes Michael (Dermot Mulroney) an intelligent player in the drama, rather than the easily manipulated male we might expect. And out of left field it brings in another character, George (Rupert Everett), who is Julianne's editor, gay, and playfully wise.

The movie takes place over a few days in summer in Chicago. Julianne is devastated to learn that Michael is marrying this rich young beauty, and her strategy is simple: Put on a happy face, pretend to go along, and destroy from within. Kimmy knows she's got a formidable opponent, and her strategy is niceness: "You win. He's got you on a pedestal and me in his arms." She asks Julianne to be maid of honor.

How does Michael feel? He's a sportswriter who's always working, whose idea of a honeymoon is taking his bride on a baseball road trip, whose occupation, as Julianne observes, involves spending a great deal of time in places like College Station, Texas. He loves Kimmy. Truly loves her. The fact that her dad is a zillionaire sports owner isn't relevant because Michael, of course, would never accept a job from him. And Kimmy's dad (Philip Bosco), of course, would never offer him a job—not until the scheming Julianne convinces Kimmy to ask her dad to do that.

The fight over the job offer is a disaster, because it ends in reconciliation and forgiveness. It is also a bad idea when Julianne forces Kimmy to sing in a karaoke bar. Will Michael see his fiancée in a different light when he discovers what a lousy singing voice she has? Not at all, because she has moxie, and saves her bad performance with showmanship. That's when Julianne gets the idea of forging an e-mail from Kimmy's rich dad to the editor of Michael's sports magazine.

The e-mail is the movie's turning point. Until then, we've been more or less on familiar ground, in a tables-turned romantic comedy. But the e-mail is really sneaky, and really mean, and we realize with a little start that Julia Roberts is not the heroine of this movie. We were identifying with the wrong person. We hope, guiltily, that Michael and Kim will get married.

That makes the movie's third act surprisingly interesting: We don't have any idea what will happen. The screenplay has never been on autopilot; it just fooled us into thinking it was, in order to sneak up on the unpredictability. Ronald Bass, who wrote this as an original, has credits including some of the best recent women's roles: *Sleeping with the Enemy, The Joy Luck Club, When a Man Loves a Woman, Dangerous Minds, Waiting to Exhale.* Here he takes a romantic formula, turns it inside out, and adds a wild card in the character of George, who is played by Rupert Everett as a man comfortable with himself and insightful about others (he gives Julianne the only advice that could ever work—"tell him you love him!"—even though it may come too late).

Stories like this are tricky for the actors. They have to be light enough for the comedy, and then subtle in revealing the deeper tones. Roberts, Diaz, and Mulroney are in good synch, and Roberts does a skillful job of negotiating the plot's twists: We have to care for her even after we stop sharing her goals. I was wondering, toward the end, how the story could possibly stay true to itself and still contrive a happy ending. It does, but not at all the one we're expecting. This is subtle writing, to end a movie not with a clear-cut plot resolution, but with the right note, struck and then held.

My Favorite Martian ★★

PG, 93 m., 1999

Christopher Lloyd (Uncle Martin), Jeff Daniels (Tim O'Hara), Elizabeth Hurley (Brace Channing), Daryl Hannah (Lizzie), Wallace Shawn (Coleye), Christine Ebersole (Mrs. Brown), Michael Lerner (Mr. Channing), Ray Walston (Armitan). Directed by Donald Petrie and produced by Robert Shapiro, Jerry Leider, and Mark Toberoff. Screenplay by Sherri Stoner and Deanna Oliver.

My Favorite Martian is slapstick and silliness, wild sight gags and a hyped-up acting style. The Marx Brothers would have been at home here. The movie is clever in its visuals, labored in its audios, and noisy enough to entertain kids up to a certain age. What age? Low double digits, I'd say.

It stars Jeff Daniels, a seasoned straight man *(Dumb and Dumber)*, as a TV producer named Tim. He sees a flying saucer crash and is soon adopted by its occupant, a Martian named, for purposes of the human appearance he assumes, Uncle Martin. The Martian is played by Christopher Lloyd with zestful looniness, and the Martian's space suit, named Zoot, becomes a character in its own right. Both Uncle Martin and Zoot are capable of instant shape-shifting, and depending on what color of extraterrestrial gumball they're chewing, Martin (and the humans) can turn into a variety of monsters.

There's a love story in the frenzy. As the film

opens, Tim is in love with his on-air talent, a reporter named Brace (Elizabeth Hurley). By the end, he has come to realize that Lizzie (Daryl Hannah), his technician, is a better choice in every way. All of this is decided at breakneck speed, and at one point Lizzie even turns into a bug-eyed monster and entirely devours a bad guy. (Soon after, defying one of Newton's laws, I'm not sure which one, she turns back into a lithesome young woman who has not put on any weight.)

The villains are all government scientists, led by Coleye (pronounced "coli," as in "e coli"), a bureaucrat obsessed with aliens. Played by Wallace Shawn, who often looks as if he is about to do something immoral with a clipboard, he desperately chases Tim and Uncle Martin because he wants to prove there is intelligent life on other planets. Uncle Martin, on the other hand, only wants to lie low, be friends with Tim and Lizzie, repair his spaceship, and go home. Then he discovers ice cream, and all he wants to do is eat ice cream.

There are some good moments in *My Favorite Martian,* and the best comes right at the top, where we see one of NASA's Martian exploratory vehicles roll up to a rock, stop, and run out of juice just before it would have stumbled upon an amazing sight. I also liked the gyrations of Zoot the suit, which develops an addiction to washing machines. And the scene where Martin chug-a-lugs a lava lamp. I also appreciated the information that a space probe contained the ashes of Jerry Garcia.

It looks as if everyone who made this film had a lot of fun. Spirits and energy are high, mugging is permitted, dialogue is rapid-fire, nobody walks if they can run. As kids' entertainment, it's like a live-action cartoon, and I can recommend it on that level, although not on a more ambitious plane. I came upon the movie just a few days after seeing *Children of Heaven,* a children's film from Iran that has the power to absorb and teach any child, and I found *My Favorite Martian* noisy and superficial by comparison. (But of *course* it's noisy and superficial. That's its mission. I keep forgetting.)

My Giant ★ ★

PG, 107 m., 1998

Billy Crystal (Sammy), Kathleen Quinlan (Serena), Gheorghe Muresan (Max), Joanna Pacula (Lilianna), Zane Carney (Nick), Jere Burns (Weller), Steven Seagal (Himself). Directed by Michael Lehmann and produced by Billy Crystal. Screenplay by David Seltzer, based on a story by Crystal and Seltzer.

The posters for *My Giant* show the seven-foot, seven-inch basketball star Gheorghe Muresan holding Billy Crystal (who is at least two feet shorter) under his arm. That looks funny. Who could guess it's a heartfelt friendship?

We go into the movie and meet Crystal, who plays Sammy, a Hollywood agent visiting the set of his single remaining client, in Romania. He's not having a good day. His wife announces she's leaving him, his client fires him, and then his car swerves into a creek. It looks like he'll drown, until he is saved by two enormous hands.

Regaining consciousness later in a monastery, he discovers that the hands belong to Max (Muresan), a local giant who is the ward of the monks. In the monastery he reads Shakespeare and pines for his lost love, who jilted him and moved to New Mexico. He is a big, sweet guy. Very big. Muresan may not have heard of Rossellini's belief that everyone has at least one movie performance in him (playing himself), but he illustrates that principle nicely.

Sammy, a desperate hustler, sees Max as his meal ticket out of Romania and back into the business. Promising him an eventual reunion with his lost beloved, he flies the two of them back to America, where the plot grows mired in sentimentality and we gradually realize this is not a comedy after all, but a greeting card crossed with a guide to improved self-esteem. The movie, which could have been a funny send-up of Hollywood talent requirements, gets distracted by subplots: Can Sammy's marriage be saved? Will his son learn to trust him again? Will that heartless girl in New Mexico give a break to the big lug whose heart she shattered?

Why is it that comics are always the biggest pushovers when it comes to sentiment? Do people who are funny have a greater than ordinary need to be loved? Is that why they want to make us laugh in the first place? After its promising start, *My Giant* isn't a comedy about an agent and a giant, so much as the heartwarming tale of a guy who learns to be a better family man.

It's interesting, the way Muresan establishes himself on screen as a stable area of calm, while the plot scurries around him. His English is not the best, but we believe he is who he's playing, and that's a test not every actor can pass. There are a few attempts to insert him into the world of showbiz, and they provide the movie's biggest laughs. There's a talk show sequence, a wrestling gig, and a funny send-up of Steven Seagal, in which Seagal does a good job of cheerfully skewering himself. That comes as Sammy tries to get Max a job on the new Seagal thriller, being shot in Las Vegas, and suggests how the whole movie could have worked, if it hadn't headed straight for the heart-tug department.

But most of the movie is lugubrious. Way too much dialogue is about whether Sammy forgot his son's birthday, and whether his wife (Kathleen Quinlan) can trust him to ever remember it again, and whether Max's lifelong happiness really does depend on the cold-hearted woman in New Mexico. Do you know anyone who wanted to see a heartwarming story about Gheorghe Muresan helping Billy Crystal get in touch with his better nature? I don't think I do.

My Name Is Joe ★ ★ ★ ½

R, 108 m., 1999

Peter Mullan (Joe), Louise Goodall (Sarah), Gary Lewis (Shanks), Lorraine McIntosh (Maggie), David McKay (Liam), Anne-Marie Kennedy (Sabine), David Hayman (McGowan), Scott Hannah (Scott), David Peacock (Hooligan). Directed by Ken Loach and produced by Rebecca O'Brien. Screenplay by Paul Laverty.

His name is Joe, and he's an alcoholic. He's been sober for only ten months, and although AA advises against romance in the first year of recovery, Joe falls in love with a nurse named Sarah. She's a social worker who has seen a lot of guys like Joe, but there's something about him—a tenderness, a caring—that touches her.

They're both wounded and cautious, but a romance slowly grows at moments like the one where he invites her in for tea and plays some classical music. He explains: In his drinking days he stole some cassettes and sold them, but the classical tape didn't sell. One night he got drunk and played it, and "it was just lovely."

Joe is played by Peter Mullan, who won the 1998 Best Actor Award at Cannes. He's a compact, ginger-haired man around forty, who moves with a physical efficiency that suggests he's focused and impatient. He looks a little like Paul Newman, with the same slender energy. He keeps busy. He doesn't have work, but he manages a soccer team and picks up the members in a city van, fussing over them like a brood hen. He wears a windbreaker and sneakers, and is always in a hurry. And he takes his newfound sobriety seriously (the opening scene shows him telling his story at an AA meeting).

Joe lives in a rough neighborhood of Glasgow, where drugs and crime are a way of life. One of his friends is Liam (David McKay), a kid who did time for drugs. Liam's wife, Sabine (Anne-Marie Kennedy), dealt while Liam was inside, but now he's out and, Joe thinks, clean and sober. But it's not that simple. Sabine is using, and they're into the local druglord, McGowan, for a total of 2,000 pounds. McGowan's thugs have offered to break Liam's legs, and nobody thinks they're kidding.

My Name Is Joe takes these elements and puts them together into a story that forces Joe to choose between the twelve steps of AA and the harder, more painful steps he learned on the street. In theory, a recovering alcoholic doesn't allow himself anywhere near drink or drugs. But McGowan offers Joe a deal: If he makes two trips up north and drives back cars containing drugs, Liam's debt will be forgotten. Why doesn't McGowan simply have Liam do this? Because McGowan isn't dumb. He knows Liam can't be trusted—and he also enjoys, perhaps, compromising a community leader who no longer adorns McGowan's pub.

The film is another one of Ken Loach's tales of working-class life; like *Riff-Raff*, it is told in a regional British accent that's so thick it has been subtitled. (I understood most of it when I saw it without subtitles in Cannes, but I have to say they help.) His screenplay is ingenious in bringing together the romance, the crime elements, and the challenge of being sober in a community where drink and drugs provide the primary pastime (and employment).

The romance is all the more absorbing because it's between two streetwise people in early middle age who have no illusions. The nurse, Sarah, is played by Louise Goodall with a careworn face but a quick smile; she's had to harden herself against the sad cases she encounters as a community health worker, but she's able to be moved by Joe's spirit and sincerity.

I have made the film sound too depressing, perhaps. It is about depressing events, but its spirit is lively, and there's a lot of humor wedged here and there, including a walk-on for a bagpiper who knows three songs, plays them, and then peddles shortbread to tourists. And there's humor involving the soccer team, their bad luck and their uniforms.

Often with a film like this you think you know how it has to end. The ending of *My Name Is Joe* left me stunned. I've rarely seen a film where the conclusion is so unexpected, and yet, in its own way, so logical, and so inevitable.

The Myth of Fingerprints ★ ½

R, 90 m., 1997

Blythe Danner (Lena), Hope Davis (Margaret), Laurel Holloman (Leigh), Brlan Kerwin (Elliot), James LeGros (Cézanne), Julianne Moore (Mia), Roy Scheider (Hal), Noah Wyle (Warren), Arija Bareikis (Daphne), Michael Vartan (Jake). Directed by Bart Freundlich and produced by Mary Jane Skalski, Tim Perell, and Freundlich. Screenplay by Freundlich.

Some families cannot be saved. The family in *The Myth of Fingerprints* is one of them. There have been a lot of movies where dysfunctional families return home for uneasy Thanksgiving weekends (*Home for the Holidays* and *The Ice Storm* come to mind), but few in which the turkey has less to complain about than anyone else at the table.

The film takes place in chilly light at a farmhouse somewhere in New England, where angry and sullen grown children return for Thanksgiving, bringing along apprehensive lovers and angry memories. Waiting to welcome them is their mother, Lena (Blythe Danner), whose relative cheer under these circumstances is inexplicable but welcome, and their father, Hal (Roy Scheider), who, like so many WASP fathers in recent films, is by definition a monster (aware of his pariah status, he walks and talks like a medieval flagellant).

The family drags itself together like torture victims returning to their dungeons. The dialogue, wary and elliptical, skirts around remembered wounds. Angriest of all is Mia (Julianne Moore), who glowers through the entire film, nursing old grudges, and lashes out at her hapless fiancé, Elliot (Brian Kerwin), a psychotherapist who, if he were any good at all, would prescribe immediate flight for himself. Mia's younger sister, Leigh (Laurel Holloman), seems relatively unscathed by the family experience, maybe because her siblings exhausted the family's potential for damage before she grew into range.

Also in the family are two sons. Warren (Noah Wyle) is interested to learn that the great love of his life, Daphne, is back in town. Jake (Michael Vartan) has brought along his fiancée, Margaret (Hope Davis), who has an alarming taste for immediate sexual gratification ("anywhere, anytime," as Travis Bickle once said).

During the weekend, two of these characters will meet people from their pasts. For Warren, the reunion with Daphne (Arija Bareikis) will be a chance to explain why he broke off their warm relationship so suddenly and seemed to flee. Mia meets an old schoolmate who now calls himself Cézanne (James LeGros), and who represents, I think, a life principle the family would be wise to study.

Frequently in the movies, when an alienated, inarticulate, and depressed father starts cleaning his rifle, we can anticipate a murder or a suicide by the end of the film. Here we're thrown off course when Hal, the dad, buys a turkey at the grocery store and then shoots it with his rifle, so his family will think he hunted it down himself. (I would have appreciated a scene where he explained the plastic bag with the gizzards.)

The movie is not unskillful. The acting is much better than the material deserves, and individual scenes achieve takeoff velocity, but the movie ends without resolution, as if its purpose was to strike a note and slink away. *The Myth of Fingerprints* makes one quite willing to see the same actors led by the same director—but in another screenplay. This one is all behavior, nuance and angst, seasoned with unrelieved gloom. Some families need healing. This one needs triage.

N

The Negotiator ★★★½

R, 141 m., 1998

Samuel L. Jackson (Danny Roman), Kevin Spacey (Chris Sabian), David Morse (Commander Adam Beck), Ron Rifkin (Commander Frost), John Spencer (Chief Al Travis), J. T. Walsh (Inspector Niebaum), Regina Taylor (Karen Roman). Directed by F. Gary Gray and produced by Arnon Milchan and David Hoberman. Screenplay by James DeMonaco and Kevin Fox.

The Negotiator is a triumph of style over story, and of acting over characters. The movie's a thriller that really hums along, and I was intensely involved almost all the way. Only now, typing up my notes, do I fully realize how many formula elements it contains.

Consider. In the opening scene, a Chicago police negotiator named Danny Roman (Samuel L. Jackson) calmly talks with a madman who has taken his own daughter hostage. The siege ends in victory, just as it does in every other cop movie. Next scene, of course, is the cops celebrating in a bar and watching coverage of themselves on TV. There's always one sorehead who makes a point of *not* celebrating the hero's triumph. Pay close attention to this character, who is the False Villain and is there to throw you off the track.

Next major sequence: Hero cop faces sudden disgrace. Is accused of embezzling funds from police pension fund. Is framed to look like bad guy. Has no friends anymore. I don't have to tell you this always leads to the Gun and Badge scene, in which the hero drops the tools of his trade on the chief's desk.

The film now moves quickly toward its central notion, which is that one trained negotiator faces another one—meaning that these men understand each other's strategies. Roman, facing jail as the victim of a frame-up, takes hostages, including Niebaum (J. T. Walsh), an investigator looking into the missing pension funds. Roman says there is only one negotiator he will deal with—Chris Sabian (Kevin Spacey), a man who is not part of the department and unlikely to be in on the frame-up.

Until Sabian's arrival on the scene, *The Negotiator* has been assembled from off-the-shelf parts. But then the movie comes alive. There's a chemistry between the negotiators played by Jackson and Spacey; sometimes they seem to be communicating in code, or by the looks in their eyes. The screenplay, by James DeMonaco and Kevin Fox, shows evidence of much research into the methods of negotiators, but it uses its knowledge only when it's needed. (I liked the little lecture on eye language.) And the direction by F. Gary Gray is disciplined, taut, and smart: When he touches a base, he's confident enough to keep on running, instead of jumping up and down on it like a lot of directors would.

I don't know a lot about Gray, but I know he has a greater curiosity about the human element than a lot of men who make thrillers. His first film was *Friday* (1995), written by and starring Ice Cube in a character study of two homeboys hanging out in the neighborhood, engaged in intense people-watching and dope-smoking. His second film, *Set It Off* (1996), was about four black women who get involved in a bank robbery, and who emerge as touching and convincing characters, vividly seen.

Now comes *The Negotiator*, which essentially consists of two men talking to one another, intercut with action. It could have dragged. It could have locked into sets. It doesn't. Gray makes us care about the characters, to share some of Roman's frustration and rage, to get involved in the delicate process of negotiations. The plot makes good use of the fact that the Chicago policemen surrounding Danny Roman (who has taken his hostages in a West Wacker Drive high-rise) may also be in on the embezzlement. They want him dead. Spacey, as Sabian, is fighting for time before the hotheads send in the SWAT teams.

There are also quiet passages, in which some of the hostages begin to feel sympathy for Danny Roman. J. T. Walsh, in one of his last performances before his untimely death, is effective at concealing how much he might really know, and what his involvement is. But Roman is right in suspecting that his loyal secretary might know where all the secrets are hidden and want to go home to her family in one piece.

Yes, there are clichés all through the movie, including the obligatory role of Roman's new wife (Regina Taylor), who wants him to stop taking the dangerous assignments. Yes, the TV news crews supply the usual breathless bulletins and obnoxious questions. Yes, the action scenes are unlikely (Roman uses the SWAT teams' own percussion bombs against them—but in a confined space wouldn't the percussion affect him as much as them?).

But *The Negotiator* works because it takes its conventional story and jacks it up several levels with Gray's craft and style. And because Jackson and Spacey are very good. Much of the movie simply consists of close-ups of the two of them talking, but it's not simply dialogue because the actors make it more than dialogue—investing it with conviction and urgency. Here is one of the year's most skillful thrillers.

Nenette et Boni ★ ★ ★

NO MPAA RATING, 103 m., 1997

Gregoire Colin (Boni), Alice Houri (Nenette), Valeria Bruni-Tedeschi (Baker-Woman), Vincent Gallo (Baker), Jacques Nolot (Mr. Luminaire), Gerard Meylan (Uncle), Alex Descas (Gynecologist), Jamila Farah (Wise Woman). Directed by Claire Denis and produced by Georges Benayoun. Screenplay by Jean-Pol Fargeau and Denis.

There's an offhand cockiness to the characters in *Nenette et Boni* that reminded me of *Jules and Jim* and the other early Truffaut films where characters acted tough but were really emotional pushovers. Boni, a dreamy nineteen-year-old kid in Marseilles, shoots his pellet gun at a neighbor's cat, but has untapped reserves of romanticism and tenderness. It's Nenette, his fifteen-year-old sister, who's been tempered by life.

Claire Denis, the gifted French director, tells their story as if we already knew it. There are throwaway details, casual asides, events that are implied rather than shown. This creates a paradoxical feeling: We don't know as much, for sure, as we would in a conventional film, but we somehow feel more familiar with the characters because of her approach.

Nenette and Boni are the survivors of an apparently ugly divorce. After the breakup, Nenette (Alice Houri) lived with her father, and Boni (Gregoire Colin) with his mother. Now Boni lives alone, and one day Nenette turns up, seven months pregnant. She doesn't want the baby, but it's too late for an abortion, and so she accepts approaching motherhood with a grim indifference. Boni, on the other hand, is thrilled; he cares tenderly for the young mother-to-be, and dotes on every detail of the pregnancy.

They form, if you will, a couple. Not one based on incestuous feelings, but on mutual need and weakness: Boni provides what emotional hope Nenette lacks, and her pregnancy adds a focus and purpose to his own life. It is something real. And reality is what he's been lacking in a love life based largely on his inflamed fantasies about the plump wife (Valeria Bruni-Tedeschi) of the local baker (Vincent Gallo, playing an American in France).

Nenette et Boni is one of those movies that is saturated with sensuality but not with explicit detail. One of the most extended sex scenes involves Boni kneading pizza dough; what he does to the dough he does, in his imagination, to the baker's wife, and that is going to be one happy pizza.

Boni is sort of a moony kid, who keeps a pet rabbit and is apt to fall thunderstruck into long reveries of speculation or desire. The approaching childbirth is a reality check for him; we sense it will be one of the positive, defining moments of his life. About Nenette we aren't so optimistic. There are vague, alarming possibilities about the father of her child—the film acts like a family member that knows more than it says—and it may be years before Nenette recovers her emotional health.

Claire Denis, born in French Africa, is a director who seems drawn to stories about characters who want to build families out of unconventional elements. I have never forgotten the haunting emotional need in her first film, *Chocolat* (1988), about a mother and daughter living in an isolated African outpost, the father absent, and finding themselves drawn to an African foreman whose ability and stability offered reassurance.

With *Nenette et Boni,* she makes a more delicate film. She feels affection for the characters, especially Boni, and is very familiar with them. Maybe that's why she feels free to tell the story so indirectly. This isn't a chronicle of events in two lives told one after another. It's more like an affectionate, fond chat. "And Boni? How is he?" you imagine the audience asking her just before the movie begins. And Denis replying, "Oh, you know that Boni . . ."

Never Been Kissed ★ ★ ★

PG-13, 107 m., 1999

Drew Barrymore (Josie Geller), David Arquette (Rob Geller), Michael Vartan (Sam Coulson), Molly Shannon (Anita), Leelee Sobieski (Aldys), John C. Reilly (Gus), Garry Marshall (Rigfort), Sean Whalen (Merkin). Directed by Raja Gosnell and produced by Sandy Isaac and Nancy Juvonen. Screenplay by Abby Kohn and Marc Silverstein.

Never Been Kissed stars Drew Barrymore as a copy editor for that excellent newspaper the *Chicago Sun-Times.* I recommend its use as a recruiting film—not because it offers a realistic view of journalistic life, but because who wouldn't want to meet a copy editor like Barrymore? Even when she's explaining the difference between "interoffice" and "intraoffice," she's a charmer. The movie's screenplay is contrived and not blindingly original, but Barrymore illuminates it with sunniness and creates a lovable character. I think this is what's known as star power.

She plays a twenty-five-year-old named Josie Geller who, despite a few unhappy early experiences with spit-swapping, has indeed never *really* been kissed. At the paper, she issues copyediting edicts while hiding behind a mousy brown hairdo and a wardrobe inspired by mudslides. Her editor, played as subtly as one of the Three Stooges by Garry Marshall, likes to pound the conference table with a bat while conducting editorial meetings; he wants an undercover series on life in high school and assigns Josie because she looks young enough.

That sets up Josie's chance to return to high school and get it right. The first time around, she was known as "Josie Grossie," an ugly duckling with braces on her teeth, hair in her eyes, baby fat, and pimples. Barrymore does a surprisingly convincing job of conveying this insecure lump of unpopularity; it's one of the reasons we develop such sympathy for Josie.

Josie borrows a car from her brother Rob (David Arquette), a once-promising baseball player who now works in a store that's a cross between Kinko's and Trader Vic's. She adopts a new blond hairstyle and gets rid of the glasses. But her first day on her secret assignment gets off to the wrong start, thanks to a wardrobe (white jeans and a gigantic feather boa) that might have been Cruella DeVil's teenage costume. The popular girls mock her, but she's befriended by Aldys (Leelee Sobieski), leader of the smart kids: "How are you at calculus? How would you like to join the Denominators?" That's the math club, with matching sweatshirts.

Josie's unpopularity reaches such a height that her car is deposited by pranksters in the middle of the football field. Rob analyzes the situation and says she needs to be certified as acceptable by a popular kid. What kid? Rob himself. He enrolls in high school and is popular by lunchtime, after winning a coleslaw-eating contest. Following his example, the students accept Josie, while Rob reawakens his fantasy of playing for a state championship baseball team.

The title *Never Been Kissed* gives us reason to hope that Josie will, sooner or later, be kissed. Soon we have reason to believe that the kisser may be Mr. Coulson (Michael Vartan), the English teacher, and of course the taboo against student-teacher relationships adds spice to this possibility. Meanwhile, Josie's adventures in high school are monitored at the *Sun-Times* through a remarkable invention, a brooch pin that contains a miniature TV camera and transmits everything she sees back to the office. We do not actually have such technology at the *Sun-Times*, and thank heavens, or my editors would have had to suffer through *Baby Geniuses.*

The story develops along a familiar arc. Josie has flashbacks to her horrible high school memories, but this time around, she flowers. Unspoken romance blooms with Mr. Coulson. Comic relief comes from Josie's friend Anita (Molly Shannon), who is mistaken for a high school sex counselor and offers advice startling in its fervor. Alas, Josie gets scooped on a story about the local teenage hangout, and her editor bangs the conference table some more. We are left to marvel at the portrait of Chicago journalism in both this movie and *Message in a Bottle*, which had Robin Wright Penn as a researcher at the *Tribune*. Apparently at both papers the way to get a big salary and your own office is to devote thousands of dollars and weeks of time to an assignment where you hardly ever write anything.

Never Been Kissed is not deep or sophisticated, but it's funny and bighearted and it wins us over. The credit goes to Barrymore. In this movie and *Ever After* (and in *The Wedding Singer*, where I liked her a lot more than the movie), she emerges as a real star—an actor whose personality and charisma are the real subject of the story. *Never Been Kissed* ends in a scene that, in any other movie, I would have hooted at. Without revealing it, I'll identify it as the five-minute wait. This scene is so contrived and artificial it could be subtitled "Shameless Audience Manipulation." But you know what? Because the wait involved Barrymore, I actually cared. Yes, I did.

The Newton Boys ★ ★

PG-13, 122 m., 1998

Matthew McConaughey (Willis Newton), Skeet Ulrich (Joe Newton), Ethan Hawke (Jess Newton), Julianna Margulies (Louise Brown), Dwight Yoakam (Brentwood Glasscock), Vincent D'Onofrio (Dock Newton), Gail Cronauer (Jess Newton), Chloe Webb (Avis Glasscock). Directed by Richard Linklater and produced by Anne Walker-McBay. Screenplay by Linklater, Claude Stanush, and Clark Lee Walker, based on the book by Stanush.

The Newton boys were the most successful bank robbers in American history, up until the savings and loan bandits of the 1980s. Operating in the Roaring Twenties, they hit as many as two hundred banks, and then pulled off the nation's biggest train robbery, a mail train heist in northern Illinois. Despite their remarkable record, they never became as famous as John Dillinger or Bonnie and Clyde. On the basis of this movie I suspect it was because they were too respectable.

The Newton Boys tells the story of the four brothers and a friend who knew how to handle nitroglycerine. Operating mostly at night, blowing up safes that were no match for their skill, they worked under a simple code: no killing, no stealing from women and children, and no snitching. According to the film, they actually managed to complete their criminal careers without shooting anybody except for one of their own brothers, by accident.

The brothers are played by a roll call of gifted young actors: Matthew McConaughey (Willis, the oldest), Skeet Ulrich (Joe), Ethan Hawke (Jess), and Vincent D'Onofrio (Dock). Dwight Yoakam is Brentwood Glasscock, their explosives expert, who pours nitro as if intensely curious about what it would feel like to be vaporized in the next nanosecond. Julianna Margulies plays Louise, the cigar-store girl who hitches up with Willis without knowing his real name or occupation, and Chloe Webb is Glasscock's approving wife. It's not an enormous cast, and yet somehow the Newtons are hard to tell apart—not in appearance, but in personality. Their dialogue mostly strikes the same musing, loquacious note.

The film chronicles their criminal career in a low-key, meandering way; we're hanging out with them more than we're being told a story. There are a lot of conversations about the profession of bank robbery—which, as a topic for conversation, is not a whole lot more interesting than double-entry bookkeeping. And when there is action (as in a scene where they're unexpectedly chased by bank guards), it plays like a pale shadow of this film's master, *Bonnie and Clyde*.

The *B&C* influences are everywhere: in the period, the clothes, the cars, the banjo music on the sound track, the reunions between brothers, the suspicions of girlfriends, and even in the character of Texas Ranger Frank Hamer, who arrests the Newtons. Hamer was the ranger forced to pose for photos with Bonnie and Clyde; to be fair, his inclusion is probably a deliberate in-joke by Richard Linklater, the director and cowriter, but the film as a whole seems drained of thrust and energy—especially compared to his earlier films.

Linklater is the talented maker of *Slacker*, *Dazed and Confused*, *Before Sunrise*, and the underrated *subUrbia*. Those have all been pigeonholed as Gen-X movies, although there's a wide range of material. What none of them lack is energy: He's intensely involved in the lives of his characters, whether the preppies of *Before Sunrise* or the losers hanging out in a strip-mall parking lot in *subUrbia.*

He just doesn't seem as interested in the Newton Boys. Sure, they were great bank robbers—but their very success may help explain why their legend hasn't placed as high in the charts as Dillinger, Baby Face Nelson, or Pretty Boy Floyd. They were efficient professionals. And the movie sits there on the screen like a biopic of traveling salesmen who crack safes instead of prospects.

The most entertaining footage in the film comes at the end, during the credits, when we see the real Willis Newton, in his eighties, being interviewed by Johnny Carson, and see scenes from a home movie interview with the real Joe Newton. Willis makes a spirited defense of their trade to Carson. Since the insurance companies were crooks, too, and since the banks always exaggerated the amount of their losses, he says, it was "just one thief a-stealing from another."

Niagara, Niagara ★ ★ ★

R, 93 m., 1998

Robin Tunney (Marcy), Henry Thomas (Seth), Michael Parks (Walter), Stephen Lang (Claude), John MacKay (Seth's Father), Alan Pottinger (Lot Cop), Sol Frieder (Pawn Broker), Candy Clark (Sally). Directed by Bob Gosse and produced by David L. Bushell. Screenplay by Matthew Weiss.

Niagara, Niagara is about two misfits who become lovers and hit the road, where the cruel world boots them toward a tragic conclusion. This is not a new idea, as the current revival of *Badlands* (1973) reminds us. But the movie contains three strong performances and a subject I haven't seen before: the affliction of Tourette's syndrome.

Marcy (Robin Tunney) and Seth (Henry Thomas) meet while shoplifting. In the parking lot outside the store, they share a broken conversation, until Marcy finally admits that she can't look at people while talking to them and notices that Seth can't either: "I like that." Outsiders and loners, they fall into one another's arms by default, and Seth is too shy or uncertain to show that he notices her sometimes strange behavior.

She levels with him: She has Tourette's syndrome, which in her case takes the form of sudden tics, contortions, arm-flailing, bursts of aggressive behavior, and acting out. There's medication to control it. And she constantly takes little drinks out of a flask because booze seems to help. "And sex helps. For some reason, sex helps."

We get a glimpse of their home lives. Seth lives with a violent, abusive father. Marcy lives in a cluttered school bus behind a mansion that I assume belongs to her parents. She has always wanted a "black Barbie head," but cannot find one on local shelves, so they decide to run away together. Maybe she can find one in Toronto.

The parabola of a road movie is as reassuring as a nursery rhyme. It is required that the heroes drive a full-sized American car, preferably an older model. That there be long shots showing them on the open road. That there be a montage of the roadside sights and signs. And eventually that there be a collision with the unbending requirements of society.

Marcy needs pills. They try to get them from a drugstore. They don't have a prescription. Since the medication she needs isn't a controlled substance, it's likely she could find someone to prescribe it for her, maybe in a free clinic, but no: They stick up the store that night, Seth is wounded, their car overturns in the getaway, and then the movie's strange, enchanted centerpiece begins.

They're found by an old geezer named Walter (Michael Parks) in a tow truck. He takes them to his ramshackle spread, tends the wound, and tells them of his late wife, whom he loved, and his favorite chicken, which he still loves. Seth is afraid of fish, but somehow finds the courage to go fishing with Walter. The writing and acting here blossom, and we get a glimpse of how the movie might have developed without the road formula to contain it.

What happens later in their journey I shall not reveal. We do indeed see Niagara Falls, which inspires some easy symbolism, and we do eventually see the rare Barbie head. But what disappointed me was the film's need to hold itself within the narrow requirements of the genre.

How many times have we seen Tourette's syndrome on the screen? Hardly ever. So why not devise a story that would be about these two characters and their problems, rather than plugging them into a road movie? They're packaged much as Barbie comes boxed in different roles. The movie is good, but could have been better if it has been set free to explore.

Robin Tunney is sometimes scary, she's so good at conveying her character's torment (she won the Best Actress Award at Venice). And Henry Thomas, who fifteen years ago was the little boy in *E.T.*, has developed into a fine actor, able to be quiet and absorbed. The materials were here for a different kind of film, in which the souls of the characters had an effect on the outcome. In *Niagara, Niagara,* we want to warn them there's no hope. They're in the wrong genre for that.

Nick and Jane ½★

R, 96 m., 1997

Dana Wheeler-Nicholson (Jane Whitmore), James McCaffrey (Nick Miller), Gedde Watanabe (Enzo), David Johansen (Carter), Clinton Leupp (Miss Coco Peru), John Dossett (John Price). Directed by Richard Mauro and produced by Bill McCutchen III. Screenplay by Mauro, Neil William Alumkal, and Peter Quigley.

You don't want to watch *Nick and Jane;* you want to grade it. It's like work by a student inhabiting the mossy lower slopes of the bell curve. Would-be filmmakers should see it and make a list of things they resolve never to do in their own work.

The story involves Jane (Dana Wheeler-Nicholson), a business executive, and Nick (James McCaffrey), a taxi driver. She is unaware of the movie rule that requires that whenever a character arrives unannounced at a lover's apartment for a "surprise," the lover will be in bed with someone else. She finds the faithless John (John Dossett) in another's arms, bolts out of the building, and into Nick's cab. Then follow the usual scenes in which they fall in love even though two different worlds, they live in.

I call that the story, but it's more like the beard. Inside *Nick and Jane*'s heterosexual cover story is a kinky sex comedy, signaling frantically to be released. Consider. Nick's neighbor in his boardinghouse is Miss Coco Peru (Clinton Leupp), a drag queen. Nick's roommate is Enzo (Gedde Watanabe), whose passion for feet is such that he drops to his knees to sniff the insteps of complete strangers. The friendly black woman at the office is into bondage and discipline with the naughty boss. Carter (David Johansen), the boss's special assistant, is Miss Coco's special friend. Key scenes take place at a drag club where Miss Coco is the entertainer (her act consists of singing "The Lord's Prayer"—in all seriousness, and right down to the "forever and ever, Amen," I fear).

These elements could possibly be assembled into quite another movie (for all I know, they were disassembled from quite another movie). But they don't build into anything. They function simply to show that the filmmakers' minds are really elsewhere—that the romance of Nick and Jane is the bone they're throwing to the dogs of convention. I kept getting the strange feeling that if they had their druthers, director Richard Mauro and writers Neil William Alumkal and Peter Quigley would have gladly ditched Nick and Jane and gone with Miss Coco as the lead.

As for Nick and Jane, they have alarming hair problems. Dana Wheeler-Nicholson goes through the movie wearing her mother's hairstyle, or maybe it's Betty Crocker's. James McCaffrey starts out with the aging hippie look, but after an expensive makeover paid for by Jane, he turns up with his hair slicked back in the Michael Douglas Means Business mode. I think the idea was to show him ever so slightly streaked with blond, but they seem to have dismissed the stylist and done the job themselves, maybe over Miss Coco's sink with a bottle of something from Walgreen's, and Nick looks like he was interrupted in the process of combing yolks through his hair.

The camera work is sometimes quietly inept, sometimes spectacularly so. Consider the scene involving a heated conversation, during which the camera needlessly and distractingly circles the characters as if to say—look, we can needlessly circle these characters! The dialogue is written with the theory that whatever people would say in life, they should say in a movie ("This is a wonderful view!" "I've never been in the front seat of a cab before!").

There is one scene where Nick bashfully confesses to having studied art, and reluctantly lets Jane see some sketches he has done of her. The usual payoff for such scenes is a drawing worthy of Rembrandt, but what Nick shows her is one of those Famous Artist's School approaches where he drew an egg shape and then some crosshairs to mark where the ears and eyes should line up.

Nick's artistry knows no bounds. While masquerading as a business executive, he effortlessly absorbs the firm's current challenge, which apparently involves saving 25 percent on the importation of scrap metal from Surinam. He dispatches Enzo (wearing those L.A. Gear shoes with heels that light up) to collect lots of scrap metal from a junkyard, after which Nick dons a handy welder's helmet to fashion a sculpture, which he hauls into the CEO's office, explaining it is intended "to punctuate the enormity of the idea I'm about to present." Yes. That's what he says.

A Night at the Roxbury ★

PG-13, 84 m., 1998

Will Ferrell (Steve Butabi), Chris Kattan (Doug Butabi), Molly Shannon (Emily Sanderson), Richard Grieco (Himself), Loni Anderson (Barbara Butabi), Dan Hedaya (Kamehl Butabi), Chazz Palminteri (Club Owner), Elisa Donovan (Cambi), Gigi Rice (Vivica), Lochlyn Munro (Craig). Directed by John Fortenberry and produced by Lorne Michaels and Amy Heckerling. Screenplay by Steve Koren, Will Ferrell, and Chris Kattan.

D. Kepesh of Chicago writes: "Do you ever find yourself distracted during a screening by thoughts of the review you will later write? Distracted to the point of missing part of the film?" Sometimes it gets much worse than that, D. Sometimes a movie is so witless that I abandon any attempt to think up clever lines for my review, and return in defeat to actually watching the film itself. I approach it as an opportunity for meditation. My mantra is "aargh . . . aargh. . . ."

A Night at the Roxbury is such a movie. It's based on the *Saturday Night Live* skits about the Butabi brothers, Steve and Doug (Will Ferrell and Chris Kattan), who snap their heads in unison with the music and each other, while trying out pickup lines in spectacularly unlikely situations. I liked the first sixty seconds of the first Butabi brothers sketch I saw because I found the head-snapping funny. Apart from that, I relate to the sketches basically as a waste of the talent of Kattan, who as Mr. Peepers, the Missing Link, is very funny.

No doubt we will get a Mr. Peepers movie one of these days. Lorne Michaels seems determined to spin out every one of the *SNL* characters into a feature-length movie—even if this one barely makes it to that length (the studio pegs it at eighty-four minutes but I didn't stay for the closing credits and was out in closer to seventy-five).

The sad thing about *A Night at the Roxbury* is that the characters are in a one-joke movie, and they're the joke. The premise: The Butabi brothers work for their dad (Dan Hedaya) in his artificial flower store. They still live at home with Dad and Mom (Loni Anderson), but dream of meeting great chicks in Los Angeles night clubs, where the bouncers treat them like target practice. Finally they get inside on the coattails of TV star Richard Grieco (playing himself, none too well), find a wonderland of improbably buxom babes (Elisa Donovan and Gigi Rice), and get picked up under the mistaken impression that they're part of Grieco's entourage. One suspects that the movie is poking fun at Grieco, but the cues are so muddled that on the other hand, maybe not. The whole party moves on to the home of the club's owner (Chazz Palminteri in an unbilled role), where the brothers demonstrate that, for them, getting lucky and falling in love are synonymous.

Meanwhile, Emily (Molly Shannon), daughter of the man who owns the store next door, dreams of marrying Steve so her dad can merge their retail empires. She's up-front about sex (especially as a means of fulfilling her business ambitions), and although the boys would rather throw themselves away on mindless bimbos, they're no match for her strategy, perhaps because the boys *are* mindless bimbos.

Steve and Doug, who took seven years to graduate from high school, still share the same bedroom, which seems to have been decorated when they were in junior high. They have a falling out and Doug moves into the pool house. And then there's an engagement, and a wedding, and . . . the script fairly wheezes with exhaustion. *A Night at the Roxbury* probably never had a shot at being funny anyway, but I don't think it planned to be pathetic. It's the first comedy I've attended where you feel that to laugh would be cruel to the characters.

Night Falls on Manhattan ★ ★ ★ ½

R, 114 m., 1997

Andy Garcia (Sean Casey), Lena Olin (Peggy Lindstrom), Richard Dreyfuss (Sam Vigoda), Ian Holm (Liam Casey), Ron Leibman (Morgenstern), James Gandolfini (Joey Allegretto), Shiek Mahmud-Bey (Jordan Washington), Colm Feore (Elihu Harrison), Paul Guilfoyle (McGovern). Directed by Sidney Lumet and produced by Thom Mount and Josh Kramer. Screenplay by Lumet, based on the novel *Tainted Evidence* by Robert Daley.

I see a slick, bemused man sitting behind a big desk in a dark room, flanked by his lieutenants. An evil man. I see a movie in which this sadistic puppet master devises diabolical schemes to destroy lives—until he is at last destroyed himself by the hero in a series of chase scenes and shoot-outs.

This man I see has absolutely nothing to do with Sidney Lumet's *Night Falls on Manhattan.* Why do I begin with him? Because he is not in the movie. Because a clone of him is at the center of so many films about police and criminals, law and order. Because he is an example of creative bankruptcy—the stereotyped villain who toys with a paperweight or a kitten, representing the inability of the filmmakers to find a good story in the world around them.

Night Falls on Manhattan is based on a book by Robert Daley, a New York writer who specializes in the shadowlands between right and wrong. It is about characters who have held onto what values they could while dealing in a flawed world. It has characters who do wrong and are therefore bad, but it doesn't really have "villains" in the usual movie sense of the word. It's too smart and grown-up for such lazy categories.

As the film opens, a lawyer named Sean Casey (Andy Garcia) is being trained as an assistant district attorney. Those scenes are intercut with some cops on a stakeout: Casey's father, Liam (Ian Holm), and the father's partner, Joey (James Gandolfini). They're after the biggest drug dealer in Harlem. But when they try to burst through his door, a barrage of gunfire answers them, and Liam is critically wounded. The call for help is answered by three precincts and ends in a fiasco: One cop is shot by another when a tire blowout is mistaken for gunfire, and the drug dealer ends up escaping in a squad car, while three cops are dead.

This creates a political hot potato for Morgenstern (Ron Liebman), the district attorney. His chief assistant, Harrison (Colm Feore), expects to be assigned the case, but instead, for publicity reasons, Morgenstern gives it to young Sean Casey, the hero cop's son. Leading the defense is hotshot Sam Vigoda (Richard Dreyfuss), who resembles Alan Dershowitz. One of the things Vigoda would like to reveal in court is why three precincts responded to the call when only one was supposed to: Were they turning up because they were all on the dealer's payroll?

Vigoda has a brilliant opening ploy: He produces his client (Shiek Mahmud-Bey) at a press conference and has him strip, so the reporters can be witnesses: "I am delivering my client in perfect condition. I want to be sure he turns up for trial in the same condition."

You see here how the complexities coil in upon themselves. The drug dealer is bad, yes, but are the cops heroes? Was the bust clean? Is there anything the young assistant D.A. doesn't know about his father, or his father's partner? There is a scene in a steam bath (where no one can wear a wire) between Casey and Vi-goda, in which real motives and possibilities are gingerly explored. And as a result of the case, Casey finds himself sleeping with Peggy Lindstrom (Lena Olin), a lawyer in Vigoda's office, who frankly tells him, "I knew I was seeing the start of a great career and I knew I couldn't wait until I got you into bed."

Sidney Lumet is a director who is bored by routine genre filmmaking in which everything is settled with a shoot-out. In movies like *Dog Day Afternoon* (1975), *Prince of the City* (1981, also based on a Daley book), *The Verdict* (1982), *Running on Empty* (1988), and *Q & A* (1990), he shows how well he knows his way through moral mazes, where what is right and what is good may not coincide.

In this film he finds performances that suggest how tangled his characters are. Consider Liebman's scene-stealing work as the district attorney: The character (not the actor) is sort of a ham, who enjoys pushing his personal style as far as it will go, this side of parody. The way he speaks and moves fills all the volume of space around him. Is he a completely political animal? Not wholly. He has a very quiet, introspective late scene in which he reveals a deep, sad understanding of his own world. It is a fine performance.

Consider, too, James Gandolfini as Allegretto, one of the cops on the original bust. What does he know that he isn't telling? Young Sean has known his father's partner for a long time. Can he trust him? "I swear to God, Sean," the partner says, looking him straight in the eye, "your father is clean." But can he even trust his father? When asked why only two cops were on such an important bust, the old man testifies significantly, "In narcotics you gotta be careful. On a good lead you don't want too much word out."

Night Falls on Manhattan is absorbing precisely because we cannot guess who is telling the truth, or what morality some of the characters possess. In a lesser movie, we'd be cheering for the young assistant D.A. and against the slickster defense attorney. When the Lena Olin character climbed into bed with the hero, we'd suspect treachery or emotional blackmail. We'd assume the original cops were either heroes or louses. We'd assume that Harrison, the D.A.'s second-in-command, would be a schemer out to further his own career at any cost.

Here we don't know. Here intelligence is required from the characters: They're feeling their way. They've been around. They know movie courtrooms aren't like real ones, and that movies simplify life. They know that sometimes good people make mistakes, and that even those who break the law may be fundamentally committed to upholding it. That in a society where people find a choice between abject poverty and selling drugs, not everyone has the luxury of deciding in the abstract.

This movie is knowledgeable about the city and the people who make accommodations with it. It shows us how boring that obligatory evil kingpin is in so many other crime movies—sitting in his room, flanked by his henchmen, a signal that his film is on autopilot and we will not need to think.

Nightwatch ★★

R, 105 m., 1998

Ewan McGregor (Martin Bells), Nick Nolte (Inspector Gray), Josh Brolin (James), Patricia Arquette (Katherine), Alix Koromzay (Joyce), Lauren Graham (Marie), Erich Anderson (Newscaster), Lonny Chapman (Old Watchman), Scott Burkholder (College Professor), Brad Dourif (Duty Doctor). Directed by Ole Bornedal and produced by Michael Obel. Screenplay by Bornedal and Steven Soderbergh, based on the film *Nattevagten* by Bornedal.

Horror films often bring out the best in a director's style but not in his intelligence. *Nightwatch* is an example. It's a visually effective and often scary film to watch, but the story is so leaky that we finally just give up: Scene after scene exists only to toy with us and prop up the impossible plot.

Ewan McGregor, from *Trainspotting,* stars as Martin Bells, a law student who takes a night watchman's job in the local morgue. It's a creepy building, not improved by two giant pine trees that flank the doors and have been wrapped in plastic, so that they look like swaying bodies in huge garbage bags.

Inside, we find the usual lighting problem: Corridors have small bulbs and are spooky, but the cold room for the corpses is brightly lit so we can see what we don't much want to see. The building itself has a certain eerie charm, with its large empty spaces and its institutional chill.

There's a nice sequence with Lonny Chapman as the retiring watchman, who shows the kid the ropes, filling him in on creepy old stories, and entreating, "Get a radio!" Much is made of the alarm that will go off if one of the corpses should suddenly come to life ("It's not going to happen," the old man assures Martin). The story is repeated about a watchman from "several years ago," who was dismissed in a messy scandal. There are murky shots of vats of chemicals, one of which, Martin is disturbed to discover, contains "feet—nothing but feet!"

Of course, the watchman's rounds include a time clock on the far wall of the cold room, which must be punched once an hour. (The morgue door has no handle on the inside, which if you really think about it makes sense, from the point of view of the corpses.) Each marble palette has a cord above it, within reach of a body that returns to life, although in the absolute dark of the storage room it would be a clever resurrectionist who thought to wave his hand in search of it.

The other characters: Martin's best friend, James (Josh Brolin), who gets in bar fights because he likes the rush ("my tolerance level has increased"). Martin's girlfriend, Katherine (Patricia Arquette), who puts up with his bad breath, a by-product of working around formaldehyde. The creepy doctor (Brad Dourif) who works in the morgue. The frightened hooker (Alix Koromzay), who has a client who wants her to play dead. And the cop, Inspector Gray (Nick Nolte), who is sad, rumpled, and wise, and warns Martin that he is being framed for murder: "There's someone really dangerous standing right behind you."

One of these people is responsible for a series of murders of local prostitutes. I was able to guess which one in the opening credits, although I wasn't sure I was right for a while—and the movie gives him (or her) away in such a sneaky way that for a moment there even seems to be another explanation for his (or her) presence at the murder scene.

The movie is a remake of *Nattevagten,* a Danish film by Ole Bornedal, who also directed this English-language version. Dimension Films bought the original film, a hit in Europe, and kept it off the market here while producing the retread, no doubt to forestall the kinds of unfavorable comparisons that came up when the Dutch director George Sluizer remade his brilliant *The Vanishing* (1988) into a sloppy, spineless 1993 American film.

I haven't seen *Nattevagten,* and don't know how it compares with *Nightwatch,* but this film depends so heavily on horror effects, blind alleys, false leads, and red herrings that eventually watching it stops being an experience and becomes an exercise.

Nil by Mouth ★ ★ ★ ½

R, 128 m., 1998

Ray Winstone (Raymond), Kathy Burke (Valerie), Charlie Creed-Miles (Billy), Laila Morse (Janet), Edna Dore (Kath), Chrissie Coterill (Paula), Jon Morrison (Angus), Jamie Forman (Mark), Steve Sweeney (Danny). Directed by Gary Oldman and produced by Luc Besson, Douglas Urbanski, and Oldman. Screenplay by Oldman.

Gary Oldman's *Nil by Mouth* descends into a domestic hell of violence, drugs, and booze, where a man can kick his pregnant wife and then, drunk, scrape out the words "My Baby" on the wallpaper with his bloody fingernails. It takes place in the pubs and streets of South London, where the actor grew up, and is dedicated enigmatically, "In memory of my father." We want to stand back out of the way; something primal, needful, and anguished is going on here.

Using a handheld camera and close-up style, Oldman plunges into the middle of this family as they spend a night at their local pub. At first we don't understand all the relationships, but Oldman uses the right approach: These people know each other so intimately and in such fearsome ways that any "establishing" scenes would dilute the impact.

The center of authority in the film is Janet (Laila Morse), the worn blond mother whose factory job is one of the family's few steady sources of income. Her own aged, feisty mother, Kath (Edna Dore), is still around. Janet's daughter is Valerie (Kathy Burke, who won the Best Actress award at Cannes). Val's husband, Ray (Ray Winstone), is a violent drunk whose rage alternates with self-pity. Val's brother, Janet's son, is Billy (Charlie Creed-Miles). He has a drug habit. Ray's best friend Mark (Jamie Forman) is emotionally dependent on him—maybe he's an excitement junkie, who feeds on the moments when Ray explodes.

This family weeps, bleeds, and endures. Billy, who lives with Val and Ray, is thrown out of the house after some money is missing; Ray beats him and bites his nose, and Billy staggers into a bleak dawn—homeless, although he still lives on the outskirts of the family, like a wounded wolf following the pack.

A day or so later, Ray walks into a pub and finds his wife, Val, playing pool with a casual friend. Ray seems cheerful at first, but he has the personality changes of the alcoholic, and orders her home, where he weeps and explodes in a jealous rage, sure Val (who is large with child) was having an affair with the man. She miscarries after his beating.

One of the film's key scenes comes after Val returns home and is seen, black, blue, and bandaged, by her mother. She tells Janet she was struck by a hit-and-run driver. Janet clearly knows Ray beat her daughter, but accepts the story. The dialogue here is precise in its observation; Val's details all have to do with the location ("You know, down by the shops"), as if the story is proven by the fact that the shops exist. Her mother vows revenge on the bastard driver who committed the hit and run; both women understand this is code for Ray. ("You know what it's like going to hospitals late at night," Janet says at one point. In most healthy families this is not something everyone knows.)

The film's portrait of street life in South London is unflinching and observant. Billy, drifting, looking for a fix, gets involved in a strange fight over a tattooed street person and his little pet dog. He goes to his mother's factory to borrow money for a fix, and then asks her to drive him to a dealer. Back in her van, he starts to shoot up, and she snaps, "Get in the back of the van where no one can see you." Just like a mother. The cost of Billy's habit is something Janet knows, just as in another family the mother would know the size of her son's paycheck.

Gary Oldman is clearly dealing here with autobiographical wounds. I saw him after the film played at Cannes, and he volunteered the information that a chair in the film is the same one his father sat in while drinking at home. He spoke in a flat voice, giving information, but I sensed that the chair was still occupied by the stabbing ghosts of days and words.

Yet *Nil by Mouth* is not an unrelieved shriek of pain. There is humor in it, and tender insight. After he almost kills himself on a bender, Ray is hospitalized, and Mark visits him. In a monologue brilliantly delivered by Winstone, Ray complains about the lack of love from his own father: "Not one kiss. Not one cuddle." In Ray's mind, he is the abused child. We sense Oldman's ability to understand, if not forgive.

At the beginning of *Nil by Mouth* we cannot understand the South London dialect very easily, and aren't sure who all the characters are. By the end, we know this family and we understand everything they say, and many things they do not say. And we remember another very minor character in the film, the small child of Ray and Val, who sits at the top of the stairs during a bloody fight and sees everything.

Footnote: Dedicated to Oldman's father, the film is filled with personal touches. The actress who plays Janet, billed as "Laila Morse," is the author's sister; her stage name is an anagram of "my sister" in Italian. When Kath sings "Can't Help Lovin' That Man" over the closing credits, the voice dubbed onto the track belongs to Oldman's seventy-five-year-old mother. And that is his father's chair.

No Looking Back ★ ★

R, 96 m., 1998

Jon Bon Jovi (Michael), Edward Burns (Charlie), Lauren Holly (Claudia), Connie Britton (Kelly), Blythe Danner (Claudia's Mom), Jennifer Esposito (Teresa), Shari Albert (Shari), Kathleen Doyle (Mrs. Ryan). Directed by Edward Burns and produced by Ted Hope, Michael Nozik, and Burns. Screenplay by Burns.

Hobbies. That's what the characters in *No Looking Back* need. Bowling or yard sales or watching the Knicks on television. Anything. Although the movie wants us to feel sympathy for them, trapped in meager lives and empty dreams, I saw them as boring slugs. There is more to existence than moping about at bars and kitchen tables, whining about unhappiness while endlessly sipping from long-neck Budweiser bottles. Get a life.

The movie is the latest from Ed Burns, who won the Sundance Film Festival in 1995 with his rich and moving *The Brothers McMullen*, but has since made two thin and unconvincing films: *She's the One* (1996) and now this one, in which self-absorbed characters fret over their lives. I have no brief against that subject matter; I simply wish the characters and their fretting were more interesting, or their unhappiness less avoidable.

The film is set in the bleak, wintry landscape of Rockaway Beach, New York, where Claudia (Lauren Holly) works in a diner and lives with Michael (Jon Bon Jovi), a mechanic. They are engaged, in a sense, but with no plans for marriage; Michael wants to marry her, but she's "afraid to wake up ten years from now" still working in the diner.

As the film opens, Charlie (Edward Burns) returns to town on the bus after an absence of three years. He was once Claudia's lover, but ditched her without a farewell. Now he apparently hopes to pick up where they left off. He moves into his mother's house; she has his number and tells him to get a job. And then Michael, who was his best friend, comes over for more beer and conversation, and explains that he and Claudia are "together" now.

Will Claudia accept the dependable Michael? Or will she be swept off her feet once again by the flashier, more charismatic Charlie? "It's different this time," he tells her. "This time I need you. I love you." He's not the soul of eloquence, but she is willing to be persuaded.

The problem is, Charlie is an enigma. Where was he for three years? Why is he back? What are his skills, his plans, his strategies? His vision for the two of them is not inspiring: They'll leave town and go to Florida, where he has no prospects, and "start over." Still, Charlie paints a seductive picture.

Or does he? The film wants us to see Michael, the Bon Jovi character, as a boring, safe, faithful, but unexciting choice. But I sort of liked him; Bon Jovi plays the role for its strengths, which involve sincerity and a certain bottom line of integrity. Charlie, on the other hand, is one of those men who believe that true happiness, for a woman, consists of doing what he wants. He offers Claudia not freedom, but the choice of living in his shadow instead of her own.

The story plays out during overcast days and chilly nights, in lonely barrooms and rented houses. Some small life is provided by Claudia's family, which includes her mother (Blythe Danner) and her sister. The mother is convinced her husband, who has deserted her, will return someday. The sister is dating the local fishmonger. As the three women discuss the comings and goings of the men in their lives, they scheme like some of Jane Austen's dimmer characters, for whom the advent of the right man is about the most a girl can hope for.

It is extremely important to some men that the woman of their choice sleep with them. This is a topic not of much interest to outside observers, and often not even to the woman of their choice. *No Looking Back* is really only about whether Claudia will sleep with Charlie, stay with Michael, or leave town. As the characters unhappily circled those possibilities, I felt like asking Claudia to call me back when she made up her mind.

Nothing to Lose ★★

R, 97 m., 1997

Martin Lawrence (T. Paul), Tim Robbins (Nick Beam), John C. McGinley (Davis "Rig" Lanlow), Giancarlo Esposito (Charlie Dunt), Kelly Preston (Ann), Irma P. Hall (Bertha), Michael McKean (Philip Barrow), Rebecca Gayheart (Danielle), Susan Barnes (Delores). Directed by Steve Oedekerk and produced by Martin Bregman, Dan Jinks, and Michael Bregman. Screenplay by Oedekerk.

Nothing to Lose is a five-peat: Buddy Movie, Fish-Out-of-Water Movie, Road Movie, Mistaken Identity Movie, and Corporate Espionage Movie.

Okay, so maybe the fifth one isn't a genre of its own yet, but it sure seemed familiar when the heroes were creeping around the halls of power, eluding security guards.

The writer-director, Steve Oedekerk, is at least an attentive student of what's been done before. Notice how subtly he sets up the plot as a Strange Bedfellows Movie and then slips into Buddy Movie mode. You can hardly hear the gears meshing as *Nothing to Lose* shifts between one set of obligatory scenes and another.

The film stars Tim Robbins as Nick Beam, a corporate executive who comes home one afternoon to find his wife (Kelly Preston) in bed with another man. Cufflinks in the living room provide a fatal clue: It's his boss. Angered and distraught, Nick drives out into the night, where before he can do something reckless he is carjacked by T. Paul (Martin Lawrence), an unemployed man who looks more dangerous than he is.

"You sure picked the wrong guy," Nick tells him, flooring the accelerator and taking T. Paul on a hair-raising wild ride. Through a series of plot devices, Nick is soon deprived of his wallet and credit cards, and the two men find themselves in the middle of the Arizona desert, living by their wits and an occasional stickup while having heartfelt conversations about life in America today.

Oedekerk's previous movie was *Ace Ventura: When Nature Calls*. This time he offers some of the same comic spirit, interlarded with messages about how T. Paul can't get a job, corporate America is racist, and Nick's life is built on a shaky foundation of unexamined assumptions.

The movie wants to be two or three things at once, and while I applaud the ambition, the result is kind of shapeless.

There are good moments. The biggest laugh in the entire film belongs to that splendid character actress Irma P. Hall, who plays T. Paul's mother and leaves no doubt about who is boss. Another wonderful scene features Patrick Cranshaw as a convenience-store clerk who, in the process of being stuck up, is asked to judge which of two approaches is the scarier, and offers some helpful suggestions. A third good scene belongs to a security guard in corporate headquarters who, in the middle of the night in what he thinks is an empty office, unleashes his disco spirit.

In a way, this is not as it should be. The biggest laughs shouldn't come from walk-on characters. But Robbins and Lawrence have been supplied with so much quasi-serious motivation that it's hard for them to free themselves from the requirements of the plot and seize the moment; there should be more scenes like the one where Robbins's shoes catch on fire.

Two other dependable character actors, Giancarlo Esposito and long-faced John C. McGinley, play a couple of stickup artists who trail Nick and T. Paul, trying to rob them—but their characters and scenes seem manufactured only for the convenience of the plot. (It's nice to have two antagonists who follow you around in a Road Movie, popping up when needed.)

Oedekerk's screenplay has serious ambitions, which it should have suppressed. A scene with T. Paul's family is sweet, but belongs in a different movie. And Nick's scenes with the good-hearted woman who runs the flower shop in his building don't seem consistent with how the movie turns out.

At the end, *Nothing to Lose* turns out to be a textbook example of our old friend the Idiot Plot, in which everything depends on a crucial but unconvincing misunderstanding that needs to be laboriously contrived. Sometimes you can watch movies in the spirit in which you solve Acrostics; the trick is in interpreting the clues. Advanced students of the genre will find their ears pricking up the moment Nick's wife mentions her sister. Catch that clue, and everything falls into place.

Notting Hill ★ ★ ★

PG-13, 125 m., 1999

Julia Roberts (Anna Scott), Hugh Grant (William Thacker), Richard McCabe (Tony), Rhys Ifans (Spike), Emma Chambers (Honey), Tim McInnerny (Max), Gina McKee (Bella), Hugh Bonneville (Bernie), James Dreyfus (Martin). Directed by Roger Michell and produced by Duncan Kenworthy. Screenplay by Richard Curtis.

Well of course the moment we see Julia Roberts and Hugh Grant together on the screen, we want to see them snoggling, but a romantic comedy like *Notting Hill* is about delaying the inevitable. After all, two different worlds they live in. Her character, Anna, is one of the most famous movie stars in the world. His character, William, runs a modest little travel bookshop in London. We know they're destined for one another, but we're always quicker to see these things than the characters are.

Notting Hill reassembles three of the key players from *Four Weddings and a Funeral* (1994), which made Hugh Grant a star: Grant, screenwriter Richard Curtis, and producer Duncan Kenworthy. In the earlier film Grant fell for a beautiful American (Andie MacDowell), and that's what happens this time too. And both films surround the romantic couple with a large, cheerful assortment of weird but lovable friends.

The film, of course, begins with a Meet Cute; she wanders into his bookstore, enjoys the way he handles a would-be shoplifter, and their eyes, as they say, meet. He tries to keep his cool, although he's as agog as if she were, well, Julia Roberts. She acknowledges his unspoken adoration, and is grateful that it remains unspoken, and although there's enough electricity between them to make their hair stand on end, she leaves. They will have to meet again. If there's one thing this movie has, luckily, it's an endless supply of Meet Cutes. The next time they meet, it's by accident, and he spills orange juice all over her. That leads to an invitation to clean up at his nearby flat, which leads to some flirtatious dialogue and a kiss, but then they separate again.

Will Anna and William never find the happiness they deserve? We slap our foreheads in frustration for them. Eventually they meet again during her press junket at the Ritz Hotel, where he is mistaken for a journalist, identifies himself as the film critic for *Horse & Hound* magazine, and quizzes her about her horses—and hounds, I think. The absurdities of a press junket are actually pretty clearly seen, allowing for some comic exaggeration, and the movie is more realistic about the world of a movie star than I expected it to be.

Anna Scott, the Julia Roberts character, is seen not simply as a desirable woman, but as a complicated one, whose life doesn't make it easy for her to be happy. There are moments of insight in the middle of this comedy that bring the audience to that kind of hushed silence you get when truths are told. One comes when Roberts looks into the camera and predicts Anna's future: "One day my looks will go, and I'll be a sad middle-aged woman who looks like someone who was famous for a while." Another comes when she kids with the bookseller that the price of her beauty was two painful operations. She points silently to her nose and her chin. Is Roberts talking about herself? Doesn't matter. The scene is based on a fact of life: Anyone who gets paid $15 million a picture is going to perform the necessary maintenance and upkeep.

To be beautiful and famous is, the movie argues, to risk losing ordinary human happiness. The first "date" between Anna and William is at his sister's birthday party, where a mixed bag of friends take her more or less at face value, and allow her to enjoy what is arguably the first normal evening she's had in years. There are other moments when they are basically just a boy and a girl, hand in hand, wandering at night through London. And then her "real life" kicks in, complete with a movie star boyfriend (Alec Baldwin) who thinks William is from room service.

From *Four Weddings*, we remember the extended family and friends such as Simon Callow, so good as the gay friend who has the heart attack. In *Notting Hill* William's circle includes his airhead sister Honey (Emma Chambers); his best friend Max (Tim McInnerny); Max's beloved wife, Bella (Gina McKee), who is in a wheelchair; and his stockbroker pal Bernie (Hugh Bonneville), who is like one of those friends we all accumulate—boring, but reassuring to have around. William also has a Welsh roommate named Spike (Rhys Ifans), who seems to regard his bodily functions as performance art. These friends and others, like a restaurant owner, represent a salt-of-the-earth alternative to Anna's showbiz satellites.

The movie is bright, the dialogue has wit and intelligence, and Roberts and Grant are very easy to like. By the end, as much as we're aware of the ancient story machinery groaning away below deck, we're smiling. I have, however, two quibbles. The first involves the personality of Grant's character. Nobody is better at being diffident, abashed, and self-effacing than Hugh Grant, but there comes a point here where the diffidence becomes less a manner, more of a mannerism. Hint: Once a woman spends the night with you, you can stop apologizing for breathing in her presence.

My other problem is with the sound track, which insists on providing a running commentary in the form of song lyrics that explain everything. There is a moment, for example, when Anna disappears from William's life, and he is sad and lonely and mopes about the city. A few violins and maybe some wind in the trees would have been fine. Instead, the sound track assaults us with "Ain't No Sunshine When She's Gone," which is absolutely the last thing we need to be told.

O

The Object of My Affection ★ ★

R, 111 m., 1998

Jennifer Aniston (Nina Borowski), Paul Rudd (George Hanson), John Pankow (Vince McBride), Alan Alda (Sidney Miller), Tim Daly (Dr. Robert Joley), Nigel Hawthorne (Rodney Fraser), Allison Janney (Constance Miller), Amo Gulinello (Paul James). Directed by Nicholas Hytner and produced by Laurence Mark. Screenplay by Wendy Wasserstein, based on the novel by Stephen McCauley.

There is a movie fighting to get out of *The Object of My Affection,* and I like it better than the movie it's trapped in. It involves a wise old man who has arrived at some useful insights about life. If they did spin-offs of movie characters the way they do on TV, he'd be in a movie of his own.

Alas, this touching and fascinating character is mired in the worst kind of sitcom—a serious one (seriocom?). *The Object of My Affection* deals with some real issues and has scenes that work, but you can see the wheels of the plot turning so clearly that you doubt the characters have much freedom to act on their own.

The story involves a social worker named Nina (Jennifer Aniston) and a first-grade teacher named George (Paul Rudd). Nina is engaged to a creep named Vince (John Pankow), and George is living with a literary critic named Robert (Tim Daly), who, like all Bernard Shaw experts, can afford a BMW convertible and a luxurious apartment in Manhattan. At a dinner party, Nina finds out that Robert is leaving George, and tells George—alas, before Robert has. George is crushed, but soon has moved into Nina's Brooklyn apartment, where they will live as good friends.

Then Nina gets pregnant. Vince, the father, keeps talking about "our" baby until Nina announces it is her baby and she has no plans to marry Vince, and Vince stalks out after declaring, "I never want to see you again," a line that sounds for all the world like a screenwriter's convenience to get him out of the cluttered plot for a scene or two. Nina, who really likes George, asks him to share the fathering: They could be a couple in everything but sex. George agrees, but then he falls for Paul (Amo Gulinello), and Nina feels hurt and jealous.

All of this material, which is promising, is dealt with on that level where characters are not quite allowed to be as perceptive and intelligent as real people might be in the same circumstances. That's because they're shuttled hither and yon by the plot structure, which requires, of course, a false crisis and false dawn (Nina and George dance to "You Were Meant for Me") before the real crisis and real dawn. At least we're spared a live childbirth scene, although to be sure, we do get the listening-to-the-embryo's-heartbeat scene.

Aniston and Rudd are appealing together; however, Pankow's crudely written role puts him through bewildering personality shifts. But then, suddenly, a character walks in from nowhere and becomes the movie's center of interest. This is the aging drama critic Rodney, played by Oscar nominee Nigel Hawthorne of *The Madness of King George.* He is gay, and Paul is his young protégé. They do not have sex, Paul makes clear to George. But Rodney clearly loves the young man, and there are a couple of scenes in which he says and does nothing, and achieves a greater emotional effect than is reached by any dialogue in the movie.

He also offers Nina hard-won advice: In the long run, her arrangement with George will not work. "Don't fix your life so that you're left alone just at the middle of it," he says, and we sense that the movie has quieted down and found its focus and purpose. You ask yourself, what would the whole film have been like if it had been written and acted at this level? The answer, sadly, is—not much like *The Object of My Affection.*

October Sky ★ ★ ★ ½

PG, 108 m., 1999

Jake Gyllenhaal (Homer Hickam), Chris Cooper (John Hickam), Laura Dern (Miss Riley), Chris Owen (Quentin), William Lee Scott (Roy Lee), Chad Lindberg (Odell), Natalie Canerday (Elsie Hickam), Scott Thomas (Jim Hickam), Chris Ellis

(Principal). Directed by Joe Johnston and produced by Charles Gordon and Larry Franco. Screenplay by Lewis Colick, based on the book *Rocket Boys* by Homer H. Hickam Jr.

Like the hero of *October Sky,* I remember the shock that ran through America when the Russians launched *Sputnik* on October 4, 1957. Like the residents of Coalwood, West Virgina, in the movie, I joined the neighbors out on the lawn, peering into the sky with binoculars at a speck of moving light that was fairly easy to see. Unlike Homer Hickam, I didn't go on to become a NASA scientist or train astronauts. But I did read Willy Ley's *Rockets, Missiles and Space Travel* three or four times, and Arthur Clarke's *The Making of a Moon.* I got their autographs, too, just as Homer sends away for a signed photo of Werner von Braun.

That first shabby piece of orbiting hardware now seems like a toy compared to the space station, the shuttle, and the missions to the moon and beyond. But it had an impact that's hard to describe to anyone who takes satellite TV for granted. For the first time in history, man had built something that went up, but did not come down—not for a long time, anyway. *Sputnik* was a tiny but audacious defiance of the universe.

October Sky tells the story of four boys in a poverty-stricken corner of Appalachia who determine to build their own rocket and help get America back in the "space race." It's seen through the eyes of their leader, young Homer Hickham (Jake Gyllenhaal), who sees the speck of light in the sky and starts reading the science fiction of Jules Verne. Homer is a good student, but math and science are his weak points. He knows he needs help, and breaks all of the rules in the school lunchroom by approaching the class brain, an outcast named Quentin (Chris Owen).

They talk about rocket fuel, nozzles, velocity. Two other boys get involved: Roy Lee (William Lee Scott) and Odell (Chad Lindberg). Their first rocket blows a hole in the picket fence in front of Homer's house. The second one narrowly misses some miners at the coal mine, and Homer's dad, John (Chris Cooper), the mine supervisor, forbids further experimentation and confiscates all of the "rocket stuff" from the basement. But the kids labor on in an isolated patch of woods, building a shelter to protect themselves from exploding rockets. They talk a machinist at the mine into building them a rocket casing of stronger steel, and they use alcohol from a moonshiner as an ingredient in the fuel.

The tension in the movie is not between the boys and their rockets, but between the boys and those who think that miners' sons belong down in the mines and not up in the sky. Homer's father is not a bad man; he fights for the jobs of his men, he rescues several in a near-disaster, he injures his eye in another emergency. He wants Homer to follow in his footsteps. The mine may seem an unhealthy and hateful place to some, but when John takes Homer down for his son's first day on the job, his voice glows with poetry: "I know the mine like I know a man. I was born for this."

The high school principal (Chris Ellis) believes the job of the school to is send miners' sons down to the coal face. But a young teacher (Laura Dern) tells Homer she feels her life will have failed if some of the kids don't get out and realize their dreams. Then there's a crisis (did a rocket set a forest fire?), and a scene in which Homer and his friends use trigonometry to argue their innocence.

There have been a lot of recent movies set in high school: *She's All That, Varsity Blues, Jawbreaker.* In those movies, even the better ones, "teenagers" who look like soap stars in their twenties have lives that revolve around sex and popularity. The kids in *October Sky* look like they're in their mid-teens, and act that way too. Watching Homer get out the trig book, I was reminded how rarely high school movies have anything to do with school—with how an education is a ticket to freedom.

Perhaps because *October Sky* is based on a real memoir, Homer Hickam's *Rocket Boys,* it doesn't simplify the father into a bad guy or a tyrant. He understandably wants his son to follow in his footsteps, and one of the best elements of the movie is when the son tries to explain that in breaking free, he is respecting his father. This movie has deep values. ☞

The Odd Couple II ★ ½

PG-13, 107 m., 1998

Jack Lemmon (Felix Ungar), Walter Matthau (Oscar Madison), Christine Baranski (Thelma), Barnard Hughes (Beaumont), Jonathan Silverman (Brucey Madison), Jean Smart (Holly), Lisa Waltz (Hannah Ungar), Mary Beth Peil (Felice). Directed by Howard Deutch and produced by Neil Simon, Robert W. Cort, and David Madden. Screenplay by Simon.

Watching Walter Matthau and Jack Lemmon make the talk show circuit, trading one-liners and barbs like a vaudeville team, I imagined a documentary simply showing them promoting this film. They're funny, familiar, edgy, and smart. *The Odd Couple II* is none of those things, and a much longer list could be made of other things it is not.

Lemmon and Matthau are perfectly suited for working together. In life as in fiction, they *are* a little like the original odd couple, Felix and Oscar: Lemmon concise and tidy, Matthau rambling, shambling, and gambling. When they're given a decent screenplay, as in the original *Odd Couple* (1968) or last year's engaging *Out to Sea*, they're fun to watch; their timing is impeccable, and you can sense their joy of work.

Odd Couple II is not, alas, such a screenplay. It has been written by the master, Neil Simon, who in this case is an emperor without any clothes. Did no one have the nerve to suggest a rewrite? To tell him that his story was slight, contrived and flat? Perhaps it seemed to the film's producers that the combination of Simon, Lemmon, Matthau, and the words "odd couple" were a sufficient guarantee of success. The difference between a creative executive and a contract signer lies precisely in the ability to see, in a case like this, that they were not. (Of course, Simon himself is one of the producers on this film, so in a way he was working without a net.)

The story opens seventeen years after Oscar and Felix last saw one another. (It's thirty years since the movie, but that would make their children middle-aged, so never mind.) Both now live in Florida, where Felix plays cards with old cronies and fusses over the snacks, while Oscar practices trying to hit his garbage can with a Hefty bag from an upper floor. They get calls: Oscar's son is engaged to marry Felix's daughter.

This inevitably requires them to fly to Los Angeles, where they plan to rent a car and drive to the town where the wedding is being held (it's "San something," but they can't remember what). Felix injures his foot while crashing into Oscar at the airport, they rent a car, the car rolls over a cliff and explodes, etc., and they find themselves in a road movie, complete with seamy motels and colorful characters along the way.

Simon's borscht-belt humor still prevails in the dialogue. ("My sister lost three pairs of dentures in the earthquake." "What did she do to eat?" "She sent out.") There are jokes about age, sex, and death, and a nice sight gag after they get a lift in a Rolls-Royce driven so slowly by a millionaire that they are passed up first by runners, and then by walkers.

But the movie has no purpose for being. That's revealed by the road movie premise: The genre is ideal for throwing characters and dialogue at situations without the bother of contriving any kind of a dramatic or comedic reason for them to be together. More honest, and maybe even funnier, would have been the story of the two old adversaries forced to be roommates in a retirement village. The movie slogs on and on, Matthau and Lemmon gamely delivering lines that may contain mechanical wit, but no impulse or dramatic purpose.

Office Space ★ ★ ★

R, 90 m., 1999

Ron Livingston (Peter), Jennifer Aniston (Joanna), Stephen Root (Milton), Gary Cole (Bill Lumbergh), David Herman (Michael Bolton), Ajay Naidu (Samir), Richard Riehle (Tom Smykowski), Diedrich Bader (Lawrence), Alexandra Wentworth (Anne). Directed by Mike Judge and produced by Michael Rotenberg and Daniel Rappaport. Screenplay by Judge, based on his *Milton* animated shorts.

Mike Judge's *Office Space* is a comic cry of rage against the nightmare of modern office life. It has many of the same complaints as *Dilbert* and the movie *Clockwatchers*—and, for that matter, the works of Kafka and the Book of Job. It is about work that crushes the spirit. Office cubicles are cells, supervisors are the wardens, and modern management theory is skewed to employ as many managers and as few workers as possible.

As the movie opens, a cubicle slave named Peter (Ron Livingston) is being reminded by his smarmy supervisor (Gary Cole) that all reports now carry a cover sheet. "Yes, I know," he says. "I forgot. It was a silly mistake. It won't happen again." Before long another manager reminds him about the cover sheets. "Yes, I know," he says. Then another manager. And another. Logic suggests that when more than one supervisor conveys the same trivial information, their jobs overlap, and all supervisors after the first one should be shredded.

Peter hates his job. So do all of his coworkers, although one of them, Milton (Stephen Root), has found refuge through an obsessive defense of his cubicle, his radio, and his stapler. Milton's cubicle is relocated so many times that eventually it appears to have no entrance or exit; he's walled in on every side. You may recognize him as the hero of cartoons that played on *Saturday Night Live*, where strangers were always arriving to use his cubicle as storage space for cardboard boxes.

Mike Judge, who gained fame through TV's *Beavis and Butt-head*, and made the droll animated film *Beavis and Butt-head Do America* (1996), has taken his *SNL Milton* cartoons as an inspiration for this live-action comedy, which uses Orwellian satirical techniques to fight the cubicle police: No individual detail of office routine is too absurd to be believed, but together they add up into stark, staring insanity.

Peter has two friends at work: Michael Bolton (David Herman) and Samir (Ajay Naidu). No, not that Michael Bolton, Michael patiently explains. They flee the office for coffee breaks (demonstrating that Starbucks doesn't really sell coffee—it sells escape from the office). Peter is in love with the waitress at the chain restaurant across the parking lot. Her name is Joanna (Jennifer Aniston), and she has problems with management too. She's required to wear a minimum of fifteen funny buttons on the suspenders of her uniform; the buttons are called "flair" in company lingo, and her manager suggests that wearing only the minimum flair suggests the wrong spirit (another waiter has "forty-five flairs" and looks like an exhibit at a trivia convention).

The movie's dialogue is smart. It doesn't just chug along making plot points. Consider, for example, Michael Bolton's plan for revenge against the company. He has a software program that would round off payments to the next-lowest penny and deposit the proceeds in his checking account. Hey, you're thinking—that's not original! A dumb movie would pretend it was. Not *Office Space*, where Peter says he thinks he's heard of that before, and Michael says, "Yeah, they did it in *Superman 3*. Also, a bunch of hackers tried it in the seventies. One got arrested."

The movie's turning point comes when Peter seeks help from an "occupational hypnotherapist." He's put in a trance with long-lasting results; he cuts work, goes fishing, guts fish at his desk, and tells efficiency experts he actually works only fifteen minutes a week. The experts like his attitude and suggest he be promoted. Meanwhile, the Milton problem is ticking like a time bomb, especially after Milton's cubicle is relocated into a basement storage area.

Office Space is like the evil twin of *Clockwatchers*. Both movies are about the ways corporations standardize office routines so that workers are interchangeable and can be paid as little as possible. *Clockwatchers* was about the lowest rung on the employment ladder—daily temps—but *Office Space* suggests that regular employment is even worse, because it's a life sentence. Asked to describe his state of mind to the therapist, Peter says, "Since I started working, every single day has been worse than the day before, so that every day you see me is the worst day of my life."

Judge, an animator until now, treats his characters a little like cartoon creatures. That works. Nuances of behavior are not necessary, because in the cubicle world every personality trait is magnified, and the captives stagger forth like grotesques. There is a moment in the movie when the heroes take a baseball bat to a malfunctioning copier. Reader, who has not felt the same?

187 ★★

R, 121 m., 1997

Samuel L. Jackson (Trevor Garfield), John Heard (Dave Childress), Kelly Rowan (Ellen Henry), Clifton Gonzalez Gonzalez (Cesar), Karina Arroyave (Rita), Jonah Rooney (Stevie Middleton), Lobo Sebastian (Benny Chacon). Directed by Kevin Reynolds and produced by Bruce Davey and Steve McEveety. Screenplay by Scott Yagemann.

187 tells the story of a high school teacher who is driven mad by the system. We can well believe it, especially given the schools portrayed in the movie, where violent bullies control the classrooms, and the spineless administration—terrified of lawsuits—refuses to back up the teachers. But the movie ends in a way that will disturb its more thoughtful viewers.

Samuel L. Jackson stars as Trevor, a dedicated and gifted teacher who does a demonstration of centrifugal force that I, for one, wanted to try for myself. He finds the pages of his textbook defaced with the scrawl "187," which is police code for "homicide." It's a warning, he thinks, from a dangerous student. He gets no sympathy or support from his principal, who says: "You know what your problem is? On the one hand, you think someone is going to kill you, and on the other hand, you actually think kids are paying attention in your class."

The warning is real; Trevor is attacked and seriously wounded, and then the main story begins fifteen months later, after the teacher has switched coasts and is trying to make a fresh start as a substitute science teacher in the San Fernando Valley. Trevor is no longer quite the man he was. He confides in Ellen, a friendly fellow teacher, that the assault meant "the robbery of my passion, my spark, my unguarded self. I miss them."

This California school is no better than the one he left in New York. Thugs and gangbangers challenge the teachers for control of the classroom and threaten lawsuits if teachers try to take firm measures. The administration gives no support. It's as if the whole system is engaged in a charade. The students pretend to study, the teachers pretend to teach, and nobody rocks the boat.

But Trevor is different. He really wants to teach. He draws closer to Ellen (Kelly Rowan), but she senses a wall that will always be there, and he quotes Thomas Wolfe's despairing cry that loneliness is the human condition. He does what he can. He offers to tutor a student named Rita, but she misinterprets his attention and offers him sex. He visits the home of a violent student named Benny, and wishes he hadn't. He is counseled by a disillusioned teacher named Childress (John Heard), who then finds out he's the famous teacher who was attacked out east, and says, "I'm giving advice to a guy with a purple heart."

And then all of the plot threads come together in a way I will not reveal, but which raised serious questions in my mind about motivation, about plausibility, and even about whether a climactic final scene should have been in the movie at all. The movie, written by Scott Yagemann and directed by Kevin Reynolds *(Waterworld),* has elements that are thoughtful and tough about inner-city schools, and other elements that belong in a crime thriller or a war movie.

At the end, I know, Trevor has come unhinged. I accept that and believe it. But it feels like the movie lost the nerve of its original story impulse and sought safety in elements borrowed from thrillers. Its destination doesn't have much to do with how it got there.

Too bad, because this is a strong and sympathetic performance by Samuel L. Jackson, who has so many different notes in his work and here is able to make the teacher come completely alive—right until the end, when the plot manipulations bury him. I also liked the tentative sweetness of Kelly Rowan as the friendly teacher, although the relationship isn't resolved very neatly. The young actors playing the dangerous students are focused and effective; they include Lobo Sebastian as Benny and Clifton Gonzalez Gonzalez as Cesar.

But . . . I dunno. If you see the movie, ask yourself if the last third is really satisfying. Was there another way to present the same kind of frustration and despair? Are they really proving anything in the final confrontation? What do they think they're proving? The motivation seems cloudy on both sides.

One Night Stand ★ ★ ★

R, 105 m., 1997

Wesley Snipes (Max Carlyle), Nastassja Kinski (Karen), Ming-Na Wen (Mimi), Robert Downey Jr. (Charlie), Kyle MacLachlan (Vernon). Directed by Mike Figgis and produced by Figgis, Annie Stewart, and Ben Myron. Screenplay by Figgis.

One Night Stand is work in a minor key from Mike Figgis, whose previous film was the symphonic *Leaving Las Vegas.* The romance this time is lighter and more cheerful, but the result is peculiar: I liked almost everything about the film except for the central relationship, which struck me as just an excuse for everything else.

The story opens with a Meet Cute. Max (Wesley Snipes), a director of TV commercials, misses his flight out of New York. There are no rooms left when he returns to his hotel. Sitting in the lobby, he's told by a pretty blonde (Nastassja Kinski) that his fountain pen is leaking. They attend a chamber music concert, she touches his shoulder as the music weaves a romantic mood, she lets him use the extra bed in her room, and soon the extra bed is not required.

Max was in New York to visit his best friend, Charlie (Robert Downey Jr.), who is HIV-positive. He returns to Los Angeles and his wife, Mimi (Ming-Na Wen), his children, and the family dog, who growls softly while sniffing his crotch. You can't fool a dog. One year passes. Read no further unless you want to know that Charlie is in the hospital with weeks to live. Max flies back to New York, meets Charlie's brother Vernon (Kyle MacLachlan) and his wife, Karen—who is, of course, Kinski.

That's the setup. The central question would seem to be, how do Max and Karen handle this embarrassing development? The two adulterers go through the motions required by movie convention ("As far as I'm concerned," Karen says, "nothing happened"). And eventually all of the romantic problems are sorted out. But I didn't much care, because the real interest in the film is not the relationship between Max and Karen, and the Karen character is so underwritten that Kinski has to create it mostly out of surfaces and body language.

I did find myself caring about Charlie, the best friend with AIDS, who is played by Downey as a man determined not to go solemnly into that good night. He has a sense of humor even on his deathbed, and gets one of the movie's best laughs just by raising his eyebrows. I liked him, and I also liked the character of Max's wife, Mimi, who is written with much more detail than the Kinski character, and played by Ming-Na Wen as smart, observant, fiery and extremely clear about what she likes in bed.

The writing credit for *One Night Stand* goes to Figgis. The original screenplay was by Joe Eszterhas, who removed his name after reading Figgis's rewrite. (Figgis observed at the Toronto Film Festival that Eszterhas's partner Ben Myron still has a producer's credit—"although I never met him.") What Figgis liked, he said, was the three-act structure of the original script, by which I think he means the way that the lovers Meet Cute, part, and Meet Cuter. I wonder if the Eszterhas version paid more attention to Karen. This version adds several scenes that play well, but seem to belong in a movie about Max, not Max and Karen. For example, a discussion of an ad campaign for a pickle manufacturer, and a fight between Max and his wife.

In the last act of the movie, the romance essentially becomes a backdrop for the real drama, which involves Charlie's illness. There's a party in his hospital room and a celebration held by his friends, both recalling the tenderness of the 1996 movie *It's My Party,* where Eric Roberts was the dying man. Compared to the power of these scenes, the movie's ending plays as a Meet Cutest, with some sly exploitation of what we assume about a series of two-shots.

Strange, that these observations did not get in the way of my enjoyment of the movie as a whole. It is so well acted and written that it convincingly shoulders aside its central premise and works because of the subplots and the supporting characters. Even the Wesley Snipes character, presumably at the center of the action, acts more as a master of ceremonies, leading us from one diversion to another. And Kinski, although underused, is warm and fetching, and gets maybe the movie's best line. "What do you do, Karen?" asks Mimi. And she replies: "I'm a rocket scientist."

One Tough Cop ★

R, 92 m., 1998

Stephen Baldwin (Bo Dietl), Chris Penn (Duke), Mike McGlone (Richie La Cassa), Gina Gershon (Josephine "Joey" O'Hara), Paul Guilfoyle (Frankie "Hot" Salvano), Amy Irving (Jane Devlin), Victor Slezak (Bruce Payne). Directed by Bruno Barreto and produced by Michael Bregman and Martin Bregman. Screenplay by Jeremy Iacone, inspired by the novel by Bo Dietl.

As the opening credits on *One Tough Cop* rolled, I made a bet with myself that the opening sequence would involve a hostage crisis. I lost. There was another short scene first, and *then* the hostage crisis. A tough cop named Bo Dietl (Stephen Baldwin) walks past the uniformed officers and confronts the madman who has taken his daughter hostage. Just like in dozens of other cop movies. Of course, the hostage sequence must stand alone, and not have any attachment to the rest of the movie.

Okay, I'm thinking. What scene *always* follows a hostage scene in a cop movie? A bar scene. Cops drinking. I am correct. Dietl and his partner Duke (Chris Penn) are in a bar, while the movie establishes that Duke has drinking and gambling problems. (It's always a danger signal when your partner advises you to "put something on your stomach.") Then Dietl ends up at a birthday party for Richie La Cassa (Mike McGlone), his friend since kindergarten. Is Richie in the mob? (It's always a danger signal when your best friend has an uncle named Sal who travels with bodyguards.)

I'm checking my Timex Indiglo, waiting to see how long it will take for the rogue cop to be called on the carpet by his superior. Answer: Four minutes. "Bo," says the chief, "you're the best cop I have working for me, but, swear to God, you're your own worst enemy!"

Bo is confronted by two feds (Amy Irving and Victor Slezak), who show him photos of himself hugging his childhood buddy Richie at last night's party. In a dialogue scene so talky it brings the movie to a halt, they want him to turn rat and plant a bug on Richie. But Bo won't. The movie is filled with speeches in which he explains that these Mafia guys are his childhood friends from the old neighborhood, who he saw on Sundays at church and never asked what they did for a living.

Meanwhile, Duke continues to drink and gamble, and then the two cops happen upon a crime scene in which a nun has been raped and tortured. I'm counting down, five, four, three . . . and sure enough, on two we hear the obligatory line, "What kind of an animal would do this?"

This Bo Dietl is apparently a real person, an ex-cop who reviews movies on the Don Imus radio program. *One Tough Cop* is based on a book that is somewhere between memoir and fiction. The movie ends with its only laugh, a title card which informs us: "Except for the character of Bo Dietl, all characters and events in this movie are fictional." How real can a character be, you ask, in a totally fictional story? Think Michael Jordan in *Space Jam.*

To the degree that Dietl's book does reflect events in his life, his life has been remarkable in incorporating all the clichés of cop movies. There's even a *noir* heroine, Joey (Gina Gershon), whose purpose is to be backlit in slinky poses while making me wonder why this movie got released when her infinitely better work in the incomparably better murder-'n'-incest film *This World, Then the Fireworks* (1997) never got a theatrical run.

The movie misses sure bets in scene after scene. Consider a confrontation in a bawdy house between Duke and Frankie "Hot" Salvano (Paul Guilfoyle), a mob gambling collector. "Hot" insultingly throws crumpled $100 bills at Duke, who boils over, smashes "Hot" against a table, and stalks out. My best guess is that the hookers would immediately dive for the floor, butting heads in the scramble for the C-notes, but no. They just sit there, forgotten by the screenplay.

The movie forgets lots of things. If you were Bo Dietl, for example, and had already been shown eight-by-ten glossies of yourself at a private birthday party with your mob friend Richie, would you select a table in the front window of a coffee shop as the ideal place to openly hand $5,000 in gambling debts to "Hot"? That's professional suicide. Maybe Dietl is thinking, one tough cop is one tough cop too many.

One True Thing ★ ★ ★

R, 121 m., 1998

Meryl Streep (Kate Gulden), Renee Zellweger (Ellen Gulden), William Hurt (George Gulden), Tom Everett Scott (Brian Gulden), Lauren Graham (Jules), Nicky Katt (Jordan Belzer), James Eckhouse (District Attorney), Patrick Breen (Mr. Tweedy). Directed by Carl Franklin and produced by Harry Ufland and Jesse Beaton. Screenplay by Karen Croner, based on the novel by Anna Quindlen.

No matter how well we eventually come to understand our parents, our deepest feelings about them are formed at a time when we are young and have incomplete information. *One True Thing* is about a daughter who grows up admiring her father and harboring doubts about her mother, and finds out she doesn't know as much about either one as she thinks she does.

The movie is based on the 1995 novel by Anna Quindlen, about a New York magazine writer whose father is "Mr. American Literature" and whose mother seems to have been shaped by the same forces that generated Martha Stewart's hallucinations. Ellen (Renee Zellweger) is bright and pretty, but with a subtle wounded look: She has that way of signaling that she's been hurt and expects to be hurt again.

She comes home to upstate New York for a surprise birthday party for her father, a professor named George (William Hurt), and is not surprised to see her mother, Kate (Meryl Streep), prancing around the house dressed like Dorothy in *The Wizard of Oz.* Yes, it's a costume party, but Kate is the kind of woman who can find costumes like that right in her own closet. Eventually Ellen gets a chance to ask her dad about her latest magazine article, which he has read, and, "writer to writer," thinks should be "more muscular."

Later he muses, "When I was twenty and working at *The New Yorker* I would spend a whole day working on a single sentence." That's the kind of statement that deserves pity rather than respect; if it is true, then to meet his deadlines he must have had to dash off his other sentences in heedless haste. Ellen should be able to feel a certain contempt for her father for even using such a ploy, but she is blinded by his tweeds, his National Book Award, his seminars, his whole edifice of importance. He thinks he's a big shot, and she buys it.

Ellen's hurt, we see, comes because her father, who she admires, does not sufficiently show his love for her—while her mother, of whom she disapproves, has a love that is therefore unwelcome. All of this begins to matter in the next months, as it develops that Kate has cancer, and George wants his daughter to move back home and take care of her.

But, I have a career, Ellen argues. "You can work as a freelancer from home," the professor says, clearly not convinced that whatever his daughter has can be described as a career. He, of course, is too busy with midterms to take care of Kate. The family's younger brother, Brian (Tom Everett Scott), must stay in school. Yes, a nurse could be hired, but the professor doesn't want a nurse poking around the house and disturbing his routine. Kate herself doesn't want Ellen to stay but wasn't consulted (by her husband or her daughter) about the decision.

As autumn winds down into winter, Ellen coexists in the house with a mother who is clearly demented in the area of domestic activities. She belongs to a local group named the Minnies, who decorate Christmas trees with the fury of beavers rebuilding a dam. The luncheon meetings of the Minnies could be photographed for layouts in food magazines, and of course the Minnies cook everything themselves. When Ellen breaks a piece of Kate's china, Kate asks her to save the pieces because she can use them in her mosaic table. Ellen finally tells Kate she thinks the Minnies are like a cult group.

George, on the other hand, throws his daughter a bone; he asks her to write an introduction to his collected essays. She is flattered, although a little wounded that he immediately afterward asks her, in more or less the same spirit, to launder some shirts. As winter unfolds and Kate's illness grows more severe, Ellen begins to suspect things about her father, and her mother observes this and finally tells her: "There's nothing that you know about your father that I don't know—and better." And we see that the buried story of the movie is the hurt that Kate has borne, all these years, over the way her daughter's love was quietly directed away from her.

It is the craftsmanship that elevates *One True Thing* above the level of a soaper. The director, Carl Franklin *(One False Move)*, goes not for big melodramatic revelations but for the accumulation of emotional investments. Hurt and Streep are so well cast they're able to overcome the generic natures of their roles and make them particular people. And Renee Zellweger, as Streep observed at the Telluride Film Festival, is able to create a place for herself and work inside of it, not acting so much as fiercely possessing her character. The movie's lesson is that we go through life telling ourselves a story about our childhood and our parents, but we are the authors of that story, and it is less fact than fiction. ☞

Operation Condor ★★★

PG-13, 92 m., 1997

Jackie Chan (Jackie), Carol Cheng (Ada), Eva Cobo De Garcia (Elsa), Shoko Ikeda (Momoko), Alfred Brel Sanchez (Adolf), Ken Goodman (Adolf's Guard). Directed by Jackie Chan and produced by Leonard Ho. Screenplay by Chan and Edward Tang.

The knowledge that Jackie Chan performs all of his own stunts brings a certain intensity to the act of watching his movies: A real person in real time is really doing something dangerous. There's an element of Evel Knievel to it. And also an element of Buster Keaton, because Chan is above all a silent comedian who depends on broad humor and timing to make action comedies in which the violence is secondary ("No guns!" he likes to shout).

Although Chan does his own stunts, they are, of course, stunts—safety precautions are taken, and camera angles are chosen to make things look more difficult than they are. Sometimes there is a certain clumsiness that makes the realism even more effective.

Early in *Operation Condor,* for example, Jackie straps on a hang-gliding outfit powered by an airplane engine, fires it up, and runs with mounting desperation across a meadow, trying to get airborne. Eventually, he does. In a slicker action picture, the flight would have been effortless. It's more fun to watch Chan sweating a little. And that's really him in the air.

There are a couple of other stunts in the film that had me seriously impressed. In one of them, Chan is hanging from a beam near the roof of a warehouse. A car catapults through the air, straight at him. He swings up out of the way and the car misses him. It looked to me as if trick photography wasn't involved; there was a real car and perfect timing. In another stunt, he leaps from a motorcycle speeding off of a pier and grabs a safe hold on a fisherman's net. And there's a wonderfully choreographed fight above odd, flat, moving steel platforms high above a hangar floor.

Even the little moments are a kind of perfection. Chan jumps against a wall, pushes off to the parallel wall, and leaps over a gate in the wall. The stunt combines an acrobat's skill with a dancer's grace. And there are scenes where he kids himself, as when he rescues a baby carriage in the middle of a breakneck chase, or when he makes a quick getaway by bouncing down a hill inside what looks like a large inflated volleyball.

Operation Condor was originally released in Asia in 1991 with the prefix *The Armor of God II.* Chan is the writer, director, and star. The plot is about as silly as most of his movies. A European count hires him on behalf of the United Nations to find Nazi loot—a fortune in gold buried in the North African desert near the end of World War II. Chan is supplied with a sidekick, an agent named Ada (Carol Cheng), and eventually collects two more bodacious babes: Elsa (Eva Cobo De Garcia), who is the granddaughter of the Nazi who hid the gold, and Momoko (Shoko Ikeda), an innocent soul they encounter in the desert, who is searching for the meaning of life and death, and keeps a pet scorpion.

It's a little dizzying, the way the movie switches locations from the desert to Arab bazaars to fleabag hotels to a really elaborate set representing some kind of long-lost Nazi headquarters with a built-in wind tunnel that stars in the final action scene. (There is a bomb in the buried headquarters, and in a nod to period detail, it has a countdown timer that uses analogue hands instead of a digital readout.) The screenplay pauses for as little dialogue as possible ("Look out behind you!" "Take this!"), and provides a couple of teams of bad guys whose motivations are barely described—but then, what do we really need to know, except that they want the gold and are enemies of Jackie?

Most action pictures are, at some level, a little mean-spirited: They depend upon macho brutes getting their way. Jackie Chan is self-effacing, a guy who grimaces when he's hurt, who dusts himself off after close calls, who goes for a gag instead of a gun. It adds to the amusement that he bears an uncanny resemblance to Tom Hayden. He brings that lighthearted persona to the fact that he is also a superb athlete and does amazing things in every film. There's a kind of innocence to it all, and a joy of performance. Half of the time, you find yourself wearing a silly grin.

The Opposite of Sex ★ ★ ★

R, 105 m., 1998

Christina Ricci (Dedee Truitt), Martin Donovan (Bill Truitt), Lisa Kudrow (Lucia), Lyle Lovett (Carl Tippett), Johnny Galecki (Jason), Ivan Sergei (Matt Mateo), William Lee Scott (Randy). Directed by Don Roos and produced by David Kirkpatrick and Michael Besman. Screenplay by Roos.

The Opposite of Sex is like a movie with the *Mystery Science Theater 3000* commentary built right in. It comments on itself, with the heroine as narrator. Dedee Truitt, a trash-talking teenager from Louisiana, chats on the sound track during and between many of the scenes, pointing out the clichés, warning us about approaching plot conventions, and debunking our desire to see the story unfold in traditional ways.

Watching the movie is like sitting through a film in front of a row of wisecracking cult movie fans. It's also sometimes very funny. Dedee (the name may relate to her bra size) is played by Christina Ricci, who is having a very good year, and has left all memories of *The Addams Family* far behind with roles in movies such as *The Ice Storm* and *Fear and Loathing in Las Vegas.* Here she shows a cocky, smart-aleck side. She's the kind of actress who makes an audience sit up and take notice, because she lets us know she's capable of breaking a movie wide open.

In *The Opposite of Sex,* her sixteen-year-old character Dedee bails out from an unhappy home life in Louisiana and makes her way to Indiana, where an older half-brother named Bill (Martin Donovan) teaches high school. Bill is gay, and until recently lived with a stockbroker named Tom, who died of AIDS and left him all his money. Now he lives with a younger man named Matt (Ivan Sergei) and gets frequent visits from Lucia (Lisa Kudrow), who was Tom's sister.

It's a good thing we have Dedee to explain all of this to us, usually in cynical terms. Dedee is advanced sexually, if not intellectually, and soon sets about trying to convince Matt that he is not really gay at all, but has just been killing time while waiting for Dedee to come along. She has a good reason for snaring Matt: She got pregnant in Louisiana and is recruiting a partner.

Dedee and her brother Bill have obviously had quite different childhoods. Bill is quiet, civilized, accepting. When he finds a student writing a crude graffiti about him on the wall of the high school men's room, he suggests grammatical improvements. Dedee is loud, brash, and in your face—a hellion whose master plan includes seducing Matt and stealing $10,000 from Bill so she and Matt can flee to Los Angeles for the good of "their" baby.

Meanwhile, an obnoxious dropout named Jason (Johnny Galecki from *Roseanne*) claims Bill has molested him. It's a blackmail scheme, but the sheriff (Lyle Lovett) has to investigate anyway, even though he more or less sees through Jason. Working behind the scenes, Lucia, the Kudrow character, wonders if maybe Bill would like to live with her in whatever arrangement might seem to work. The sheriff likes Lucia in his earnest and plodding way, but she can't really focus on him.

In its plot outlines, *The Opposite of Sex* is an R-rated sitcom. But first-time director Don Roos (who wrote *Single White Female* and *Boys on the Side*) redeems it with Dedee's narration. When a gun turns up on the screen, Dedee tells us: "This is foreshadowing. Duh!" She likes to tell us she knows what we're thinking, and we're wrong.

The approach is refreshing. Most movies are profoundly conservative at the level of plot construction, no matter how offbeat their material may be. They believe that all audiences demand happy endings, and want to be led lockstep through traditional plot construction. When you've seen enough movies, alas, you can sense the gears laboriously turning, and you know with a sinking heart that there will be no surprises. The Dedee character subverts those expectations; she shoots the legs out from under the movie with perfectly timed zingers. I hate people who talk during movies, but if she were sitting behind me in the theater, saying all of this stuff, I'd want her to keep right on talking. ☞

Orgazmo ½★

NC-17, 94 m., 1998

Trey Parker (Elder Joe Young), Matt Stone (His Friend), Dian Bachar (Ben [Choda-Boy]), Michael Dean Jacobs (Maxxx Orbison), Robyn Lynne (Joe's Fiancée), Masad "Maki" San (G-Fresh), Ron Jeremy (Clark), Chasey Lain (Candi). Directed by Trey Parker and produced by Fran Rubel Kuzui, Jason McHugh, and Matt Stone. Screenplay by Parker.

When a critic uses the word "sophomoric," it's a good sign you're dealing with an amateur. Once you get to be a junior, you should more or less retire "sophomoric" from your vocabulary, unless no other word will do.

A database search through my old reviews reveals that I have used it only twice in the 1990s (once to refer to the plot of *Wild at Heart*, and again to describe Jim Morrison's lyrics) and in only eleven reviews in total. (They included *National Lampoon's Animal House, Airplane!* and the surfing documentary *Endless Summer;* in all three cases I'm sure the directors themselves would agree it was appropriate.)

Now I must use the word again. *Orgazmo,* a comedy by *South Park* cocreator Trey Parker, is the very soul of sophomorism. It is callow, gauche, obvious, and awkward, and designed to appeal to those with similar qualities. It stars Parker himself as Elder Joe Young, a Mormon missionary who agrees to appear in a porn film in order to raise $20,000 so that he can be married in the temple in Salt Lake City. True to the film's sophomorism, it is not a satire of Mormonism, but simply uses Mormons in the conviction that their seriousness will be funny to gapejaws in the audience—to whom all sincerity is threatening, and therefore funny.

Sophomorism uses a sledgehammer; wit uses a scalpel. Sophomorism cries out for your attention; wit assumes it has it. Sophomorism shocks by presenting sexuality; wit shocks by using it. A sophomoric film will think it is funny when hairy buttocks block the camera's view. A witty film will ask, whose buttocks? Why now? What next?

I will provide an example. Early in the film, Elder Young (whose name would have been funnier if it had been Elder Younger) and another missionary are knocking on doors in Los Angeles, seeking converts. One door is opened by a sweet little old lady. The instant I saw her, I knew, with the same certainty that a Mormon missionary knows he will go to heaven, that the sweet little old lady would shout a stream of vile obscenities. She did.

That is sophomorism. What would wit have done? The missionaries would have knocked on the door, the sweet little old lady would have opened it, and wit would have known that the audience anticipated obscenities, so wit would have had the little old lady say: "I know that in the movies we sweet little old ladies are always getting a cheap laugh by using the f-word to missionaries, but that lacks imagination, don't you think? That's what my son, Quentin Tarantino, always says. Here, have some cookies."

The plot thickens when Elder Young knocks on the door of Maxxx Orbison (Michael Dean Jacobs), a porno filmmaker. After Young beats up the pornographer's bodyguards, the director offers him $20,000 for two days' work, and even agrees that a body-part double will be used. That he will pay extra for star quality is proven by the presence of Ron Jeremy as the costar of the movie he is making. Ron Jeremy, for those not willing to admit they know who he is, has been in more porn films than anyone else. His popularity is easily explained: Every man alive believes that any woman would prefer him to Ron Jeremy.

Elder Young is given the role of Orgazmo, a porno superhero with a sidekick named Choda-Boy (Dian Bachar). They crash through cardboard walls to rescue damsels in distress (or damsels being ravished by Ron Jeremy, which amounts to the same thing). His weapon (Orgazmo's) is an Orgazmorator, which immobilizes his enemies with multiple orgasms. In a movie with wit, people would be lining up to become Orgazmo's enemies.

Elder Young calls his fiancée, Lisa (Robyn Lynne), in Utah and explains that he has been cast in a movie. She wants to know the title. *Death of a Salesman,* he says, and Lisa intuits that he has bagged the plum role of Biff. She flies to L.A. and is soon tied to the bed in Maxxx Orbison's house. I was by now so desperately longing for a reason to laugh that, yes, I did laugh at a scene where all of the characters leave the frame and fight offscreen, and debris is thrown on-screen from beyond the edges to indicate what a battle it is.

Orgazmo was made before Trey Parker and Matt Stone became famous for the *South Park* cable cartoon program. (There is an even earlier film, *Cannibal: The Musical,* which is unseen by me and has an excellent chance of remaining so.) *South Park* is elegant, in its way: a self-contained animated universe that functions as a laboratory to conduct experiments in affronting the values of viewers, who, if they held them, would not be watching. I like *South Park.* It has wit. I guess *Orgazmo* was a stage the boys had to go through. They're juniors now.

Oscar and Lucinda ★ ★ ★ ★

R, 133 m., 1998

Ralph Fiennes (Oscar Hopkins), Cate Blanchett (Lucinda Leplastrier), Ciaran Hinds (Reverend Dennis Hasset), Tom Wilkinson (Hugh Stratton), Richard Roxburgh (Mr. Jeffris), Clive Russell (Theophilus), Bille Brown (Percy Smith), Josephine Byrnes (Miriam Chadwick), Geoffrey Rush (Narrator). Directed by Gillian Armstrong and produced by Robin Dalton and Timothy White. Screenplay by Laura Jones from the original novel by Peter Carey.

"In order that I exist," the narrator of *Oscar and Lucinda* tells us, "two gamblers, one obsessive, one compulsive, must declare themselves." The gamblers are his grandparents, two oddball nineteenth-century eccentrics, driven by faith and temptation, who find they are freed to practice the first by indulging in the second. Their lives form a love story of enchantment and wicked wit.

When we say two people were born for each other, that sometimes means their lives would have been impossible with anyone else. That appears to be the case with Oscar and Lucinda. Their story, told as a long flashback, begins with Oscar as the shy son of a stern English minister, and Lucinda as the strong-willed girl raised on a ranch in the Australian outback. We see them formed by their early lives; he studies for the ministry, she inherits a glassworks and becomes obsessed with glass, and they meet during an ocean voyage from England to Australia.

They meet, indeed, because they gamble. Oscar (Ralph Fiennes) has been introduced to horse racing while studying to be a clergyman, and is transformed by the notion that someone will actually pay him money for predicting which horse will cross the line first. Lucinda (Cate Blanchett) loves cards. Soon they're playing clandestine card games on board ship, and Oscar is as thrilled by her descriptions of gambling as another man might be by tales of sexual adventures.

Oscar and Lucinda is based on a novel by Peter Carey, a chronicler of Australian eccentricity; it won the 1988 Booker Prize, Britain's highest literary award. Reading it, I was swept up by the humor of the situation and by the passion of the two gamblers. For Oscar, gambling is not a sin but an embrace of the rules of chance that govern the entire universe: "We bet that there is a God—we bet our life on it!"

There is also the thrill of the forbidden. Once ashore in Sydney, where Oscar finds rooms with a pious church couple, they continue to meet to play cards, and when they are discovered, they're defiant. Oscar decides he doesn't fit into ordinary society. Lucinda says it is no matter. Even now they are not in love; it is gambling that holds them together, and Oscar believes Lucinda fancies another minister who has gone off to convert the outback. That gives him his great idea: Lucinda's glassworks will fabricate a glass cathedral, and Oscar will superintend the process of floating it upriver to the remote settlement.

For madness, this matches the obsession in Herzog's *Fitzcarraldo* to move a steamship across a strip of dry land. For inspiration, it seems divine—especially since they make a bet on it. Reading the novel, I pictured the glass cathedral as tall and vast, but of course it is a smaller church, one suitable for a growing congregation, and the photography showing its stately river progress is somehow funny and touching at the same time.

Oscar and Lucinda has been directed by Gillian Armstrong, whose films often deal with people who are right for each other and wrong for everyone else (see her neglected 1993 film *The Last Days of Chez Nous,* about a troubled marriage between an Australian and a Frenchman, or recall her 1979 film *My Brilliant Career,* in which Judy Davis played a character not unlike Lucinda in spirit). Here there is a dry wit, generated between the well-balanced performances of Fiennes and Blanchett, who seem quietly delighted to be playing two such rich characters.

The film's photography, by Geoffrey Simpson, begins with standard, lush nineteenth-century period evocations of landscape and sky, but then subtly grows more insistent on the quirky character of early Sydney, and then cuts loose altogether from the everyday in the final sequences involving the glass church. In many period films, we are always aware that we're watching the past: Here Oscar and Lucinda seem ahead of us, filled with freshness and invention, and only the narration (by Geoffrey Rush of *Shine*) reminds us that they were, incredibly, someone's grandparents.

Oscar and Lucinda begins with the look of a period literary adaptation, but this is not Dickens, Austen, Forster, or James; Carey's novel is playful and manipulative, and so is the film. Oscar is shy and painfully sincere, Lucinda has evaded her century's strictures on women by finding a private passion, and they would both agree, I believe, that people who worship in glass churches should not throw stones.

The Other Sister ★

PG-13, 130 m., 1999

Juliette Lewis (Carla), Diane Keaton (Elizabeth), Tom Skerritt (Radley), Giovanni Ribisi (Danny), Poppy Montgomery (Caroline), Sarah Paulson (Heather), Linda Thorson (Drew), Joe Flanigan (Jeff). Directed by Garry Marshall and produced by Mario Iscovich and Alexandra Rose. Screenplay by Marshall and Bob Brunner.

The Other Sister is shameless in its use of mental retardation as a gimmick, a prop, and a plot device. Anyone with any knowledge of retardation is likely to find the film offensive. It treats the characters like cute little performing seals—who always deliver their "retarded" dialogue with perfect timing and an edge of irony and drama. Their zingers slide out with the precision of sitcom punch lines.

The film stars Juliette Lewis as Carla, a rich San Francisco girl of seventeen or eighteen who has just returned home after several years in an institution. Her ambition is to train as a veterinarian's assistant. Her father (Tom Skerritt) thinks she should go for it, but her mother (Diane Keaton) is opposed. If there is a convincingly retarded character in the movie, it's the mother. She's borderline hysterical in insisting her daughter is not ready for junior college, dating, dancing, sex, living in her own apartment, or anything else.

In flashbacks to the girl's childhood, we see the mother crying out, "I don't want her to be retarded!" Now she doesn't want her to be anything else. Her opposition to any sign of Carla's independence is handled oddly, however. Every once in a while, she has a brief moment of humanity, in which she softens and says sensible things like, "I'll try to see it your way." These interludes play suspiciously as if they were inserted into the script to lighten the character and make her less of a harridan. Then it's back to bullheaded denial again.

Carla does eventually get into the local polytechnic, where she makes a friend of Danny (Giovanni Ribisi). The two of them are the butts of some cruel treatment, but Danny has found a haven in the music department, where, he proudly tells Carla, he has a real job: "cleaning the marshmallows out of the tubas."

That's because at football games students throw marshmallows at the tubas in the marching bands. I am prepared to believe they do that, but not so prepared to believe that something equally cute comes up at every juncture, as when Carla and her mother attend a benefit at a dog shelter and Carla starts barking at the strays and releases them, disrupting a reception. Or when she gets a free beauty makeover at the mall and is surprised to find it covers only half her face. Or when she's garbed in an absurd swan costume for a social event. Or when she and Daniel, alone at last, study positions in *The Joy of Sex.*

The movie's dialogue knows it's funny—a fatal error. "I wonder who thought up sex in the first place?" one of them muses, studying the sex books. The answer: "I think it was Madonna." Sure, that's exactly what would be said. And how about when Daniel tells Carla, "I love you more than band music and cookie making." All of their words are pronounced as if the characters have marbles in their mouths, and when they walk, it's a funny little modified duck walk. It's like they learned how to act retarded by studying under Jerry Lewis.

Moment after moment is utterly false. Take the climax at the country club, where a bartender keeps pouring triple shots of green Chartreuse for Danny. Not likely, because: (1) Danny is obviously a novice drinker. (2) He is obviously underage. (3) Green Chartreuse is one of the strongest liquors in the world, so that several full snifters would paralyze an inexperienced drinker. And (4) country club bartenders like their jobs and know they can get fired for getting underage drinkers blind drunk.

Of course, Danny doesn't get *really* drunk—only drunk enough to make a speech that is cunningly calculated to offend those who need to be offended, please those who need to be pleased, and move the wheels of the plot. All in "retarded" language that is perfectly chosen and timed, of course.

Am I getting too technical here? I don't think so. The truth is in the details. The details of *The Other Sister* show a movie with no serious knowledge of retardation and no interest in learning or teaching. I never tire of quoting Godard, who tells us that the way to criticize a movie is to make another movie. The movie that shames *The Other Sister* was made in 1988 by Robert M. Young. It is called *Dominick and Eugene,* and it stars Tom Hulce and Ray Liotta in the story of a retarded man and his brother. See that, and you will cringe when you compare it to *The Other Sister.*

Out of Sight ★ ★ ★ ½

R, 123 m., 1998

George Clooney (Jack Foley), Jennifer Lopez (Karen Sisco), Ving Rhames (Buddy Bragg), Isaiah Washington (Kenneth), Don Cheadle (Maurice Miller), Steve Zahn (Glenn Michaels), Keith Loneker (White Boy Bob), Dennis Farina (Marshall Sisco), Albert Brooks (Ripley). Directed by Steven Soderbergh and produced by Danny DeVito, Michael Shamberg, and Stacey Sher. Screenplay by Scott Frank, based on the novel by Elmore Leonard.

Steven Soderbergh's *Out of Sight* is a crime movie less interested in crime than in how people talk, flirt, lie, and get themselves into trouble. Based on an Elmore Leonard novel, it relishes Leonard's deep comic ease; the characters mosey through scenes, existing primarily to savor the dialogue.

The story involves a bank robber named Foley (George Clooney) and a federal marshal named Sisco (Jennifer Lopez), who grow attracted to one another while they're locked in a car trunk. Life goes on, and in the nature of things, it's her job to arrest him. But several things might happen first.

This is the fourth recent adaptation of a Leonard novel, after *Get Shorty, Touch,* and *Jackie Brown,* and the most faithful to Leonard's style. What all four movies demonstrate is how useful crime is as a setting for human comedy. For example: All caper movies begin with a self-contained introductory caper that has nothing at all to do with the rest of the plot. A cop will disarm a hostage, or a terrorist will plant a preliminary bomb. *Out of Sight* begins with as laid-back a bank robbery as you'd want to see, as Clooney saunters up to a teller's window and politely asks, "This your first time being held up?" How he cons the teller is one of the movie's first pleasures. The point of the scene is behavior, not robbery.

It turns out that this robbery is not, in fact, self-contained—it leads out of and into something—and it's not even really the first scene in the story. *Out of Sight* has a time line as complex as *Pulp Fiction,* even though at first we don't realize that. The movie's constructed like hypertext, so that, in a way, we can start watching at any point. It's like the old days when you walked in to the middle of a film and sat there until somebody said, "This is where we came in."

Elmore Leonard is above all the creator of colorful characters. Here we get the charming, intelligent Foley, who is constitutionally incapable of doing anything but robbing banks, and Sisco, the marshal, who has already had a previous liaison with a bank robber (admittedly, she eventually shot him). They are surrounded by a rich gallery of other characters, and this movie, like *Jackie Brown,* takes the time to give every character at least one well-written scene showing them as peculiar and unique.

Among Foley's criminal accomplices is his criminal partner, Buddy Bragg (Ving Rhames, who played Marcellus Wallace in *Pulp Fiction*). He's waiting on the outside after the prison break. In prison, Foley met a small-time hood named Glenn (Steve Zahn), who "has a vacant lot for a head." They're highly motivated by one of their fellow prisoners, a former Wall Street leverage expert named Ripley, who unwisely spoke of a fortune in uncut diamonds that he keeps in his house. (Ripley is played by Albert Brooks with a Michael Milkin hairstyle that is not a coincidence.)

Then there's the threesome that join Foley and his friends in a raid on Ripley's house. Snoopy Miller (Don Cheadle) is a nasty piece of work, a hard-nosed and violent former boxer; Isaiah Washington plays his partner; and Keith Loneker is White Boy Bob, his clumsy but very earnest bodyguard. It's ingenious how the raid involves shifting loyalties, with Foley and Sisco simultaneously dueling and cooperating.

All of these characters have lives of their own and don't exist simply at the convenience of the plot. Consider a tender father-daughter birthday luncheon between Karen Sisco and her father (Dennis Farina), a former lawman who tenderly gives her a gun.

At the center of the film is the repartee between Jennifer Lopez and George Clooney, and these two have the kind of unforced fun in their scenes together that reminds you of Bogart and Bacall. There's a seduction scene in which the dialogue is intercut with the very gradual progress of the physical action, and it's the dialogue that we want to linger on. Soderbergh edits this scene with quiet little freeze-frames; nothing quite matches up, and yet everything fits, so that the scene is like a demonstration of the whole movie's visual and time style.

Lopez had star quality in her first role in *My Family,* and in *Anaconda, Selena,* and the underrated *Blood and Wine* she has only grown; here she plays a role that could be complex or maybe just plain dumb, and brings a rich comic understanding to it. She wants to arrest the guy, but she'd like to have an affair with him first, and that leads to a delicate, well-written scene in a hotel bar where the cat and mouse hold negotiations. (It parallels, in a way, the "time out" between De Niro and Pacino in *Heat.*)

Clooney has never been better. A lot of actors who are handsome when young need to put on some miles before the full flavor emerges; observe how Nick Nolte, Mickey Rourke, Harrison Ford, and Clint Eastwood moved from stereotypes to individuals. Here Clooney at last looks like a big-screen star; the good-looking leading man from television is over with.

For Steven Soderbergh, *Out of Sight* is a paradox. It's his best film since *sex, lies, and videotape* a decade ago, and yet at the same time it's not what we think of as a Soderbergh film—detached, cold, analytical. It is instead the first film to build on the enormously influential *Pulp Fiction* instead of simply mimicking it. It has the games with time, the low-life dialogue, the absurd violent situations, but it also has its own texture. It plays like a string quartet written with words instead of music, performed by sleazeballs instead of musicians. ☞

The Out-of-Towners ★ ½

PG-13, 91 m., 1999

Steve Martin (Henry Clark), Goldie Hawn (Nancy Clark), John Cleese (Hotel Manager), Tom Riis Farrell (Mugger). Directed by Sam Weisman and produced by Robert W. Cort, Robert Evans, and Christine Forsyth-Peters. Screenplay by Marc Lawrence, based on the screenplay by Neil Simon.

The Out-of-Towners jogs doggedly on the treadmill of comedy, working up a sweat but not getting much of anywhere. It's a remake of the 1970 Neil Simon screenplay, with Steve Martin and Goldie Hawn now taking the roles played by Jack Lemmon and Sandy Dennis. The most valuable addition to the cast is John Cleese, as the hotel manager; he's doing his character from *Fawlty Towers*, but at least it's a role worth repeating.

Martin and Hawn play the Clarks, Henry and Nancy, who are empty nesters in Ohio now that their daughter has moved to New York and their son is studying abroad. Henry has a secret: He's been fired at his ad agency. He flies to New York for a job interview, Nancy tags along, and we sense the movie's desperation in a scene on the plane. She's seated several rows behind him, and asks the passengers in between to pass up his Foot Chums and rash ointment. A woman like that deserves to be in an empty nest all by herself.

But the thing is, Nancy isn't really that lamebrained. She can be smart, or tender, or goofy, or stubborn—or whatever the screenplay requires from moment to moment. That's because she isn't really anybody at all, and neither is Henry. They're devices to be manipulated by the film—figures on a chessboard.

Lots of things go wrong on the trip, which is taken by plane, train, and automobile, providing a melancholy reminder of Martin's much better 1987 movie—and also of *Forces of Nature*, in which Ben Affleck and Sandra Bullock go through a similar ordeal. The trick in a film like this is to keep the characters consistent as the situations change. If both the characters and the situations are slippery, there's no place to stand. And if you're determined to have a sweet, uplifting ending, all is lost.

It helps to observe situations closely, to find humor in the details rather than trusting the general scene. Consider, for example, a sequence where Henry and Nancy blunder into a meeting of Sex Addicts Anonymous because they're starving and spot the free sweet rolls. They don't realize what kind of a meeting it is, and the movie thinks that's joke enough, so it doesn't really "see" the other people at the meeting. I'm reminded of a scene in John Waters's *Polyester*, where Tab Hunter blunders into an AA meeting and is asked to introduce himself. He gives his name. "And?" ask the assembled members. "AND? AAANNNDDD???" They're shot with a fish-eye lens as they peer at him, waiting for the magic words, "and I'm an alcoholic."

In *The Out-of-Towners*, the filmmakers think it's funny enough that the sex addicts are creepy, and Henry and Nancy are grossed out by their stories. That misses the point. In comedy, you figure out what the objective is, and go for it single-mindedly. Why are Henry and Nancy at the meeting? Because they want those sweet rolls! So what should they do? Win the sweet rolls by any means necessary, telling the members whatever they want to hear. I can imagine Martin and Hawn improvising sexual addictions all night long. But not in this movie, which skims the surface.

There are a couple of sequences that work. I liked the absurdity of the scene where they're approached on the street by a well-dressed, well-spoken man (Tom Riis Farrell) who asks for $5 to get to a business meeting. He doesn't look like a panhandler, and his British accent is curious. Nancy finally asks, "Aren't you . . . Andrew Lloyd Webber?" Well, yes, he confesses, it's embarrassing to be caught short of funds, but yes, he is. The scene develops nicely.

And then there is John Cleese, who perhaps had a hand in the precise wording of some of his own dialogue, which spins easily between ingratiating toadiness and loathsome sneering. There are few things funnier than Cleese playing a snob who is pretending to be a democrat.

But even some of the movie's surefire ideas don't seem to work. There's a moment, for example, when the Clarks are embracing on the grass in Central Park, and are suddenly hit with spotlights and seen by dozens of people inside the Tavern on the Green, including Mayor Rudy Giuliani, playing himself. Incredible as it may seem, this is not funny.

We observe that, yes, it's the mayor. We understand that the Clarks are embarrassed. But the movie stands flat-footed and smugly regards the situation, instead of doing something with it. If you're going to have a celebrity in your movie, make him work for his cameo. Why not have Giuliani personally take charge of the police investigation? Or claim the spectacle as an example of how people-friendly the park is? Or get turned on?

As it became increasingly clear that *The Out-of-Towners* was not a proud moment in the often inspired careers of Martin and Hawn, I started looking for evidence of little moments of genius that the stars may have slipped into the crevices of the movie on their own. Surely it was Martin's idea to suggest renting advertising space on the tongues of dogs to tattoo the word "Alpo."

Outside Ozona ★★

R, 98 m., 1998

Robert Forster (Odell Parks), Kevin Pollak (Wit Roy), Sherilyn Fenn (Marcy Duggan), David Paymer (Alan Defaux), Penelope Ann Miller (Earlene Demers), Swoosie Kurtz (Rosalee), Taj Mahal (DJ), Meat Loaf (Floyd Bibbs), Lois Red Elk (Effie Twosalt), Kateri Walker (Reba Twosalt), Lucy Webb (Agent Deene). Directed by J. S. Cardone and produced by Avi Lerner. Screenplay by Cardone.

When I say that all the plot threads in *Outside Ozona* come together in one closing scene, you can't imagine how literally I mean that. The movie builds up an incredible series of coincidences, in which the good are rewarded, the evil are punished, the lovelorn are thrown into one another's arms, all mysteries are solved, and a homeless dog named Girl lives to bark another day. There was feverish scribbling in the dark as my colleagues and I tried to keep up with the cascade of developments.

An ending like this is either naive or deeply profound. After all the slick formula movies, it's refreshing sometimes to see a film that isn't working from the rule book. J. S. Cardone, who wrote and directed, provides clumsy parallels and too many speeches that sound written, but his heart is sound: He's going for something touching and sincere, and some of his scenes get there.

The movie takes place during a long night on the lonely highways outside Ozona, Oklahoma. The local radio DJ (Taj Mahal) calls this area the "badlands," and indeed it's so far from anywhere else that everyone has to listen to the same radio station. In movie theory, much is made of "offscreen space," which is the implied environment outside the frame. Cardone creates an almost palpable sense that the offscreen space is dark, hostile, and abandoned to the wolves.

We meet a lot of characters. The movie will cut between their stories. Many of the scenes are conversations in the front seats of cars that are allegedly traversing the lonely badlands highways, but are obviously on darkened sound stages. This is a stylistic decision, not a weakness; it increases focus as the film breaks out into dialogues between the people whose lives we glimpse.

Among them are a circus clown (Kevin Pollak) who has just been fired and his girlfriend, an ex–lap dancer (Penelope Ann Miller). They have a clever scene in which she interrupts his robbery attempt and makes him apologize, but we could have been spared his monologue about the fate of Jumbo the famous elephant.

Then there's a lonely trucker (Robert Forster, who stepped into the role after J. T. Walsh died) and a Navaho woman (Lois Red Elk). He gives her a ride, and there is mutual attraction. Later, in a car with her grandmother (Kateri Walker), she learns the old woman's lessons about love.

Sherilyn Fenn plays one of two sisters who pick up a hitchhiker (David Paymer) who may or may not be the serial killer haunting these highways. And we meet a truck stop waitress (Swoosie Kurtz), a radio station manager (Meat Loaf), and the FBI. For lost highways in the badlands, these are well-traveled roads.

The dialogue exchanged by these people doesn't further the plot, because there is no central plot; the strategy of the movie is simply to watch and listen as its characters speed toward their rendezvous with destiny. There are some grisly interludes (the killer's victims are left holding their own hearts), some heavy-handed preaching (the DJ uses the killer's calls as his cue for a political rant), and some oddly low-key FBI work.

I'm not sure what the movie thinks its purpose is; at the end, we are pleased with the outcome but not enlightened. But there are moments I will remember, and Cardone evokes a real sense for the deserted night highways.

Out to Sea ★★★

PG-13, 106 m., 1997

Jack Lemmon (Herb), Walter Matthau (Charlie), Dyan Cannon (Liz), Gloria De Haven (Vivian), Brent Spiner (Godwyn), Elaine Stritch

(Mavis), Hal Linden (Mac), Donald O'Connor (Jonathan). Directed by Martha Coolidge and produced by John Davis and David T. Friendly. Screenplay by Robert Nelson Jacobs.

The grumpys have never been funnier than they are in *Out to Sea*, which continues the comic relationship of Jack Lemmon and Walter Matthau on board a cruise ship. They are not, strictly speaking, the original grumpy old men—they're Herb and Charlie instead of John and Max—but they might as well be, since this movie uses a lot of the same elements, including romance in the sunset years.

The setup: Matthau is a gambler who is deeply in debt to various bookies and other shady associates. Lemmon is his brother-in-law. Lemmon's wife is dead, his life is empty, and Matthau thinks it's time for them to have a change of scenery. So he arranges free tickets for them on the cruise ship *Westerdam*. The only catch is, they have to work for their passage: They'll be professional dance partners for the widows on board.

Matthau and Lemmon have long since settled into comfortably comic persona: Matthau rumpled and raffish, Lemmon uncertain and fretting. That's how it goes on board the ship, where Lemmon tries to please the militaristic cruise director, while Matthau sneaks off to the high-stakes poker games.

Their fellow passengers include a sweet-faced widow (Gloria De Haven) and a brassy blonde (Dyan Cannon), whose mother (Elaine Stritch) is engineering her attempts to snag a Daddy Warbucks. It goes without saying that Lemmon falls at once into love with the widow, while Matthau lays siege to the gold digger.

It's hard to describe just why *Out to Sea* is so funny and charming. Part of it may be due to the tender touch of Martha Coolidge, the director, whose films *(Rambling Rose, Lost in Yonkers, Real Genius)* always find humor in the human aspects of her stories. There is sheer slapstick here, including an inevitable scene in a lifeboat, but the human comedy is funnier—especially when it involves Brent Spiner, as the cruise director who introduces himself in glowing terms, and tells his dance partners: "I'm your worst nightmare: a song-and-dance man raised on a military base."

Matthau, who can't dance, fakes injuries and tries to hide from his martinet boss. Lemmon, who can dance, finds himself in the arms of De Haven and starts feeling guilty about his own departed wife, to whom he pledged eternal love. De Haven's role would seem to be thankless, but this movie veteran (whose first role was in Charlie Chaplin's *Modern Times*) looks warm and dazzling and finds just the right note in several tricky scenes.

Matthau and Lemmon are easy together, and no wonder; this is their seventh major film together, not counting a few footnotes. "Years of insanity have made you crazy," Lemmon tells Matthau, but when Lemmon is afraid it's too late for him to find love again, Matthau offers sound advice: "There's no such thing as too late. That's why they invented death."

Is the movie's ending, involving not only a lifeboat but also a seaplane, preposterous? Of course. Do we care? Not at all. In an industry overwhelmed with $100 million special-effects pictures, here's an alternative: a classic romantic comedy with big laughs and a sweet story.

P

Palmetto ★★

R, 113 m., 1998

Woody Harrelson (Harry Barber), Elisabeth Shue (Rhea), Gina Gershon (Nina), Rolf Hoppe (Felix Malroux), Michael Rapaport (Donnelly), Chloe Sevigny (Odette), Tom Wright (John Renick), Marc Macaulay (Miles Meadows). Directed by Volker Schlondorff and produced by Matthias Wendlandt. Screenplay by E. Max Frye, based on the novel *Just Another Sucker* by James Hadley Chase.

Florida is the ideal state for *film noir.* Not the Florida of retirement villas and golf condos, but the Florida of the movies, filled with Spanish moss and decaying mansions, sweaty trophy wives and dog-race gamblers, chain-smoking assistant DAs and alcoholic newspaper reporters. John D. Macdonald is its Raymond Chandler and Carl Hiaasen would be its Elmore Leonard, if Leonard hadn't gotten there first.

Noir is founded on atmosphere, and Florida has it: tacky theme bars on the beach, humid nights, ceiling fans, losers dazed by greed, the sense of dead bodies rotting out back in the Everglades. (Louisiana has even more atmosphere, but in *noir* you need a society where people are surprised by depravity, and Louisiana takes it for granted.)

Palmetto is the latest exercise in Florida *noir,* joining *Key Largo, Body Heat, A Flash of Green, Cape Fear, Striptease,* and *Blood & Wine.* The movie has all the elements of the genre, and lacks only pacing and plausibility. You wait through scenes that unfold with maddening deliberation, hoping for a payoff—and when it comes, you feel cheated. Watching it, I was more than ever convinced that Bob Rafelson's *Blood & Wine* was the movie that got away in 1997—a vastly superior Florida *noir* (with a Jack Nicholson performance that humbles his work in *As Good As It Gets*).

Both films depend on our sense of rich, eccentric people living in big houses that draw the attention of poor people. Both involve deception and hidden identities. Both heroes are once-respectable outsiders, driven to amateurish crime by desperation. Both involve older men blinded to danger by younger women with beckoning cleavage. *Blood & Wine* is the film that works. *Palmetto* is more like a first draft.

Woody Harrelson stars as Harry Barber, a newspaper reporter who tried to expose corruption in the town of Palmetto and was framed and sent to prison. After two years his conviction is overturned and he's released—by a judge who renders the verdict over closed-circuit TV. When Harry starts screaming that he wants his two years back, the judge dismisses him by clicking the channel-changer.

Harry wants to start over, anywhere but in Palmetto. But he's drawn back by his ex-girlfriend, Nina, an artist played by Gina Gershon. He looks for work, can't find it, and amuses himself by hanging around daytimes in bars, ordering bourbon and not drinking it (this is not recommended for ex-drinkers). One day a blonde named Rhea (Elisabeth Shue) undulates into the bar, makes a call, and outdulates without her handbag. Harry finds it in the phone booth, she reundulates for it, and they fall into a conversation during which Harry does not drink bourbon and Rhea holds, but does not light, a cigarette ("I don't smoke").

The sense that Harry and Rhea are holding their addictions at bay does not extend to sex, which Rhea uses to enlist Harry in a mad scheme. She's married to a rich old coot named Felix who is dying of cancer but may linger inconveniently; meanwhile, her stepdaughter, Odette (Chloe Sevigny, from *Kids*), is threatening to run away rather than be parked in a Swiss boarding school. Rhea's proposal: Harry fakes Odette's kidnapping, Felix pays $500,000 in ransom, Harry keeps 10 percent for his troubles, Odette has her freedom with the rest. Lurking in the background: Michael Rapaport, as Felix's stern houseboy.

Well, what mother wouldn't do as much for a child? Harry's misgivings about this plot are silenced by Rhea's seductive charms, while Nina observes in concern (her role here reminded me of Barbara Bel Geddes in *Vertigo*—the good girl with the paint brush, looking up from her easel each time the bad boy slinks in after indulging his twisted libido).

Harry is, of course, spectacularly bad as a kidnapper (I liked the scene where he types a ransom note on his typewriter and flings the machine from a bridge, only to see that he has misjudged the water depth and it has landed in plain sight on the mud). While he busies himself leaving about fingerprints and cigarette butts ("DNA? They can test for that?"), there's a neat twist: The assistant DA in charge of the kidnapping case (Tom Wright) hires Harry as a press liaison. So the kidnapper becomes the official police spokesman.

All of the pieces are here for a twisty *film noir*, and Harry's dual role—as criminal and police mouthpiece—is Hitchcockian in the way it hides the perp in plain sight. But it doesn't crackle. The director, Volker Schlondorff *(The Tin Drum)*, doesn't dance stylishly through the genre, but plods in almost docudrama style. And screenwriter E. Max Frye, working from James Hadley Chase's novel *Just Another Sucker*, hasn't found the right tone for an ending where victims dangle above acid baths. The ending could be handled in many ways, from the satirical to the gruesome, but the movie adopts a curiously flat tone. Sure, we have questions about the plot twists, but a better movie would sweep them aside with its energy; this one has us squinting at the screen in disbelief and resentment.

The casting is another problem. Gina Gershon and Elisabeth Shue are the wrong way around. Gershon is superb as a lustful, calculating femme fatale (she shimmers with temptation in *Bound* and *This World, Then the Fireworks*). Shue is best at heartfelt roles. Imagine Barbara Stanwyck waiting faithfully behind the easel while Doris Day seduces the hero and you'll see the problem. Woody Harrelson does his best, but the role serves the plot, not his character, and so he sometimes does things only because the screenwriter needs for him to. *Palmetto* knows the words, but not the music.

Paperback Romance ★ ★ ★

R, 89 m., 1997

Gia Carides (Sophie), Anthony LaPaglia (Eddie), Rebecca Gibney (Gloria), Jacek Koman (Yuri), Sioban Tuke (Kate), Lewis Fiander (Bruce Wrightman), Robyn Nevin (Anne-Marie LePine), Marshall Napier (George LePine). Directed by Ben Lewin and produced by Bob Weis. Screenplay by Lewin.

The voice describes images of passion in the words of lurid melodrama; we think this must be a dream sequence, and in a way we're right. *Paperback Romance* cuts to reveal that the words are being read aloud by a pretty woman writer in a large and almost empty library, and overheard by a man who asks her out because "conversation with you would be the most exquisite imaginable form of foreplay."

She turns him down. We might ask why, since a writer who reads soft-core pornography aloud in a public place usually does not wish to avoid attention. Then we find out why: After the man leaves, we see that the woman wears a leg brace and uses crutches. Later, we discover she had polio as a child.

My guess is that in the real world this woman would not feel the need to conceal her disability. But in the world of *Paperback Romance* she conceals it for an excellent reason: The entire plot depends on the misunderstandings that result.

The woman's name is Sophie, and she's played by Gia Carides, whom you may remember as the nasty rival in *Strictly Ballroom*. The man, Eddie (Anthony LaPaglia), runs a jewelry store in a mall, and Sophie, who is intrigued, tracks him down there. She wants to remain hidden, especially after she sees him with the attractive Gloria (Rebecca Gibney), but in trying to hurry out of view she stumbles on her crutches, falls into a baby carriage, and is hurtled over the edge of the balcony and into the arms of a rotund opera singer below.

She breaks her leg in the accident. It's the same leg that is crippled, so now she wears a crutch and has an alibi (it was a "skiing accident") as her relationship with Eddie proceeds uncertainly—very uncertainly, since he is scheduled to marry Gloria. Eddie finds himself in the grip of a mad passion involving Sophie, however, and during a sex scene, blind as a bat, he injures his lip on her cast and is unable to speak for several scenes. Sophie can understand his tortured mumblings, and helpfully translates for him with Gloria, adding her own spin to most of what he says.

The pratfall over the edge of the balcony caught me by surprise, since I thought the movie had started on a different kind of note. But the director, Ben Lewin, permits himself screwball comedy at the same time he develops his darker material, and the scenes involving the lip injury are truly funny. So are aspects of a subplot involving a Russian and a stolen necklace, although the setup is pretty conventional.

Paperback Romance comes from Australia, and I was more than mildly surprised to find out that LaPaglia does, too (he's married to Carides). On a quiz, I would have penciled in New Jersey, or maybe Manhattan. The movie's country of origin helps explain its screwy charm. For a long time I've been talking about "offbeat Australian comedies," but on reflection I realize there are no Australian comedies that are on beat. With *Love Serenade*, we had a very strange romance between two sisters and a fishy disk jockey, and of course there have been *Strictly Ballroom, Muriel's Wedding, Priscilla, Queen of the Desert,* and a lot of other films to suggest that perhaps this is more than a trend: Perhaps everyone in Australia *is* goofy.

Paradise Road ★★

R, 130 m., 1997

Glenn Close (Adrienne Pargiter), Pauline Collins (Margaret Drummond), Cate Blanchett (Susan Macarthy), Frances McDormand (Dr. Verstak), Julianna Margulies (Topsy Merritt), Sab Shimono (Colonel Hiroyo), Jennifer Ehle (Rosemary Leighton-Jones), Elizabeth Spriggs (Mrs. Roberts), Joanna Ter Steege (Sister Wilhelminia). Directed by Bruce Beresford and produced by Sue Milliken and Greg Coote. Screenplay by Beresford.

Bruce Beresford's *Paradise Road* tells the story of a group of women who were held prisoner in a Japanese internment camp for most of World War II. If you were told this story by one of the survivors, you would shake your head in amazement and marvel at her courage. You would probably think it would make a good movie; after all, it's even true.

The film begins at Raffles Hotel in Singapore in 1942, at an elegant dinner dance. An alert arrives that Japanese forces are about to take the city. Women and some children are hurried aboard a transport ship, which is attacked a few days later by Japanese aircraft. Life rafts float ashore at Sumatra, where the survivors are taken to a POW camp, there to spend the rest of the war.

The movie now has a delicate balance to find. It is no longer acceptable to portray the Japanese as the embodiment of evil; the monsters of *The Bridge on the River Kwai* now have to be seen in a slightly better light, as harsh and cruel, perhaps, but not inhuman—and capable of sentiment when the prisoners form a choir and begin to perform classical choral works. (Earlier, the screenplay provides racist anti-Japanese slurs at the Singapore party, to show that the British, too, had their flaws; the film is set in 1942, but its attitudes are circa 1997.)

We meet the prisoners. They include a remarkable group of women: the British musician Adrienne Pargiter (Glenn Close); the Australian missionary Margaret Drummond, nicknamed Daisy (Pauline Collins); the nurse Susan Macarthy (Cate Blanchett); the German-accented Dr. Verstak (Frances McDormand); and an American painted in broad strokes, Topsy Merritt (Julianna Margulies).

Conditions are brutal in the tropical climate, food is scarce, living quarters are filthy, and the camp commandant (Sab Shimono) supervises cruel punishments, including one where a woman must kneel for hours in the hot sun, or fall over onto sharp spikes. Yet their music somehow redeems the conditions and elevates their spirits; the choir even soothes the Japanese to such an extent that guards sent to silence them cannot bring themselves to halt such a glorious sound (they, too, hate the war and are moved by beauty).

Told this story, and that it was true, you would think it would be enough for a screenplay. But would you be correct? I didn't want *Paradise Road* to be a melodrama—a *Great Escape,* say, or *Stalag 17* in which the sound of the music distracts from the digging of tunnels. There is not even the possibility of escape, because they are on an island in the middle of a sea controlled by Japan. We realize fairly early on that prison life, within boundaries, will remain much the same until the film's end. But what the movie lacks is a story arc to pull us through.

The performances are moving, especially Glenn Close's work as the strongest of the women, who conducts the choir. It was difficult for me to accept Frances McDormand with a German accent (*Fargo* was too fresh in my mind), but I admired Pauline Collins (of *Shirley Valentine*), whose character's remarkable memory allows her to write down classical music so that they can rehearse it.

There is a possibility in this material for a story that contains more drama. The women are offered an alternative to the prison camp: If they volunteer to be prostitutes and please Japanese officers, they can live in a hotel with clean sheets, hot meals, and nightly dances. (A lapse in the dialogue: When one woman seems tempted, another asks, "But what about the choir?") Some women in such a position did choose to become prostitutes (some women in Raffles in 1942 no doubt had made that career choice even earlier). If the film had intercut the camp scenes with the experiences of a woman who accepted the Japanese offer, it would have brought contrast into the story—and provided an ironic ending for her, no doubt.

Am I being a vulgarian? Given these brave, muddy women singing Dvorak, why am I not content? Why do I want to see one of them sell her body and soul to the Japanese? I think the film cries out for contrast, for tension, for choice. It is too linear. The women are captured, they go to the camp, they suffer and endure, they perform their music, and then the war is over. The movie is an anecdote, not a story.

The Parent Trap ★ ★ ★

PG, 123 m., 1998

Lindsay Lohan (Hallie Parker/Annie James), Dennis Quaid (Nick Parker), Natasha Richardson (Elizabeth James), Elaine Hendrix (Meredith Blake), Lisa Ann Walter (Chessy), Simon Kunz (Martin). Directed by Nancy Meyers and produced by Charles Shyer. Screenplay by David Swift, Meyers, and Shyer.

The Parent Trap is based on story elements so ancient and foolproof they must have their roots in Shakespeare's day: The twins changing places, their divorced parents falling in love again, and, for low comedy, their servants falling in love too. And of course there's a wicked would-be stepmother lurking about. It's the stuff of Elizabethan comedy, resurrected in modern times as the British film *Twice Upon a Time* in 1953, and in the classic 1961 film *The Parent Trap*.

The story is ageless and so is the gimmick: The twins are played by the same actress, using trick photography. Hayley Mills did it in 1961 and Lindsay Lohan does it this time, seamlessly. Although I was aware that special effects and over-the-shoulder doubles were being used, I simply stopped thinking about it, because the illusion was so convincing. One twin is American, one is British, but even their accents don't help us tell them apart, since half of the time they're pretending to be each other.

"I'll teach you to be me, and you teach me to be you," one twin says after they meet by chance at summer camp and realize that they've been raised separately by divorced parents. It's a splendid story premise, but in a way the switch is just the setup, and the real story involves the parents. They're played by Dennis Quaid and Natasha Richardson, who bring such humor and warmth to the movie that I was amazed to find myself actually caring about their romance.

The three important supporting roles are also well filled. Plump, spunky Lisa Ann Walter plays the nanny and housekeeper on Quaid's spread (he runs a vineyard in Napa Valley), and bald, droll Simon Kunz is Richardson's butler (she's a trendy London fashion designer). Elaine Hendrix, coming across a little like Sharon Stone, is the snotty publicist who plans to marry Quaid—until the parent trap springs. She has a thankless role—the only person in the movie we're not supposed to like—but at least they don't make her just stand there and be obnoxious. She gets to earn her stripes in a camping trip during which she demonstrates, for once and all, that she is not the ideal wife for Quaid.

A movie like this has to cover a lot of ground in several different locations. That's why good casting is so important. There's not time to establish the characters carefully, so they have to bring their personalities along with them almost from the first shot. Quaid is instantly likable, with that goofy smile. Richardson, who almost always plays tougher roles and harder women, this time is astonishing, she's so warm and attractive. The two of them have a conversation over an old bottle of wine, and, yes, it's cornball—but quality cornball, earning its sentiment.

Movies like this remember how much fun escapism can be. The film opens with Quaid and Richardson falling in love on the *QE2* and being married in mid-Atlantic. It includes the kind of summer camp where when the kids play pranks, it looks like they had the help of a platoon of art directors and special-effects coordinators. And, of course, both parents live in great houses: Richardson in a London town house with sweeping staircases and *Architectural Digest* interiors, Quaid in a Napa ranch home with a shaded veranda.

The key task in the movie is to make the double photography of the "twins" work. All kinds of tricks are used, and of course the techniques are more advanced than they were in 1961, but since you can't see them anyway, you forget about them. Lindsay Lohan has command of flawless British and American accents, and also uses slightly flawed ones for when the girls are playing each other. What she has all the time is the same kind of sunny charm Hayley Mills projected, and a sense of mischief that makes us halfway believe in the twins' scheme.

The movie was directed by Nancy Meyers and produced by Charles Shyer; they wrote the script with David Swift. Meyers and Shyer have specialized in light domestic comedies *(Baby Boom, Father of the Bride)* and they make this into a good one—a family picture that's not too soppy for adults. My only reservation involves the ear-piercing scene, which I suspect will lead to an epidemic of do-it-yourself home surgery. ☞

Passion in the Desert ★ ★

PG-13, 93 m., 1998

Ben Daniels (Augustin), Michel Piccoli (Venture), Paul Meston (Grognard), Kenneth Collard (Officer), Nadi Odeh (Bedouin Bride), Auda Mohammed Badoul (Shepherd Boy), Mohammed Ali (Medicine Man). Directed and produced by Lavinia Currier. Screenplay by Currier, adapted from the novella *A Passion in the Desert* by Honoré de Balzac.

Passion in the Desert is a brave folly of a film, easy to laugh at but deserving a certain respect, if only because it involves such a foolish and difficult story. For most of its length, it is about a man and a leopard who seem to fall in love with one another (if leopards can be said to fall in love). As they gaze happily into each other's eyes, we agree they make a handsome couple, but what exactly is the filmmaker trying to say?

The film, acted in English despite its French origins, opens in 1798, during Napoleon's North African campaign. The soldier Augustin (Ben Daniels) has been attached as a guide to an artist named Venture (Michel Piccoli), assigned to the campaign. After a bloody attack, Augustin observes, "We seem to have misplaced the French army." No matter: "How can you get lost in Egypt? You have the Nile and the sea."

Yes, but that isn't much help if neither is in walking distance. The two men struggle under the blazing sun until death seems near. Venture drinks his paints and dies. Augustin stumbles across a tent, water, a woman in jewels, but after his depredations are discovered he is chased toward an ancient gathering of monuments, which is guarded by a female leopard.

The beast has already killed a man, but now soldier and leopard make a wary peace, which gradually grows into acceptance and fondness; the soldier even grooms the leopard's coat by licking it. When a male leopard appears and a courtship seems on the horizon, the jealous soldier uses mud to cover himself with spots, so he can seem to be a male leopard too.

The actor worked with three trained leopards in filming these scenes, which win our admiration for their beauty and difficulty even as we're trying to puzzle them out on some plane above the *Wild Kingdom* level. And the film is beautifully photographed. But the longer the courtship continues, the more it seemed like a weird exercise in surrealism; I didn't believe it on a literal level and couldn't get it to work on any other.

Where did the writer-director, Lavinia Currier, get the idea for this story? Not in a million years would I have guessed the answer: from Balzac. Yes, from Honoré de Balzac, the nineteenth-century French saint of social realism. The critic Michael Atkinson has pointed out that Balzac's story, however, is titled *A Passion in the Desert*, and that little "A" makes all the difference—suggesting the suffering of Christ rather than, as Atkinson puts it, "a soft porn Bo Derek film from the '80s."

I am informed by a reader that the Vancouver movie ratings board has, in addition to everything our own MPAA warns us about, a warning about "animal husbandry" scenes in which animals engage in reproductive frolic. Mercifully, Augustin and the leopard hold the line at goo-goo eyes.

Patch Adams ★ ½

PG-13, 110 m., 1998

Robin Williams (Patch Adams), Daniel London (Truman), Monica Potter (Carin), Philip Seymour Hoffman (Mitch), Bob Gunton (Dean Walcott), Josef Sommer (Dr. Eaton), Irma P. Hall (Joletta), Frances Lee McCain (Judy). Directed by Tom Shadyac and produced by Barry Kemp, Mike Farrell, Marvin Minoff, and Charles Newirth. Screenplay by Steve Oedekerk, based on the book *Gesundheit: Good Health Is a Laughing Matter* by Hunter Doherty Adams with Maureen Mylander.

Patch Adams made me want to spray the screen with Lysol. This movie is shameless. It's not merely a tearjerker. It extracts tears individually by liposuction, without anesthesia. It is allegedly based on the life of a real man named Patch Adams, whom I have seen on television, where he looks like Salvador Dali's seedy kid brother. If all of these things really happened to him, they should have abandoned Robin Williams and brought in Jerry Lewis for the telethon.

As the movie opens, a suicidal Patch has checked into a mental hospital. There he finds that the doctors don't help him, but the patients do. On the outside, he determines to become a doctor in order to help people, and enrolls in a medical school. Soon he finds, not to our amazement, that medicine is an impersonal business. When a patient is referred to by bed number or disease, Patch reasonably asks, "What's her name?"

Patch is a character. To himself, he's an irrepressible bundle of joy, a zany live wire who brings laughter into the lives of the sick and dying. To me, he's a pain in the wazoo. If this guy broke into my hospital room and started tap-dancing with bedpans on his feet, I'd call the cops.

The lesson of *Patch Adams* is that laughter is the best medicine. I know Norman Cousins cured himself by watching Marx Brothers movies, but to paraphrase Groucho, I enjoy a good cigar, but not when it explodes. I've been lucky enough to discover doctors who never once found it necessary to treat me while wearing a red rubber nose.

In the movie, Patch plays the clown to cheer up little tykes whose hair has fallen out from chemotherapy. Put in charge of the school welcoming committee for a gynecologist's convention, he builds a papier-mâché prop: enormous spread legs reaching an apex at the entrance to the lecture hall. What a card. He's the nonconformist, humanist, warmhearted rebel who defies the cold and materialist establishment and stands up for clowns and free spirits everywhere. This is a role Robin Williams was born to play. In fact, he was born playing it.

We can see at the beginning where the movie is headed, but we think maybe we can jump free before the crash. No luck. (Spoiler warning!) Consider, for example, the character named Carin (Monica Potter), who is one of Patch's fellow students. She appears too late in the movie to be a major love interest. Yet Patch does love her. Therefore, she's obviously in the movie for one purpose only: to die. The only suspense involves her function in the movie's structure, which is inspired by those outlines that Hollywood writing coaches flog to their students: Will her death provide the False Crisis, or the Real Crisis?

She's only good for the False Crisis, which I will not reveal, except to say that it is cruel and arbitrary, stuck in merely to get a cheap effect. It inspires broodings of worthlessness in Patch, who ponders suicide, but sees a butterfly and pulls himself together for the False Dawn. Life must go on, and he must continue his mission to save sad patients from their depression. They may die, but they'll die laughing.

The False Dawn (the upbeat before the final downbeat) is a lulu. A dying woman refuses to eat. Patch convinces her to take nourishment by filling a plastic wading pool with spaghetti and jumping around in it. This is the perfect approach, and soon the wretched woman is gobbling her pasta. I would have asked for some from the part he hadn't stepped in.

Next comes the Real Crisis. Patch is threatened with expulsion from medical school. I rubbed my eyes with incredulity: *There is a courtroom scene!* Courtrooms are expected in legal movies. But in medical tearjerkers, they're the treatment of last resort. Any screenwriter who uses a courtroom scene in a nonlegal movie is not only desperate for a third act, but didn't have a second act that led anywhere.

What a courtroom. It's like a John Grisham wet dream. This could be the set for *Inherit the Wind.* The main floor and balcony are jammed with Patch's supporters, with a few seats up front for the villains. There's no legalistic mumbo-jumbo; these people function simply as an audience for Patch's narcissistic grandstanding. (Spoiler warning No. 2.) After his big speech, the courtroom doors open up and who walks in? All those bald little chemotherapy kids that Patch cheered up earlier. And yes, dear reader, each and every one is wearing a red rubber nose. Should these kids be out of bed? Their immune systems are shot to hell. If one catches cold and dies, there won't be any laughing during the malpractice suit.

I have nothing against sentiment, but it must be earned. Cynics scoffed at Robin Williams's previous film, *What Dreams May Come,* in which he went to heaven and then descended into hell to save the woman he loved. Corny? You bet—but with the courage of its convictions. It made no apologies and exploited no formulas. It was the real thing. *Patch Adams* is quackery. ☞

Paulie ★ ★

PG, 92 m., 1998

Gena Rowlands (Ivy), Tony Shalhoub (Misha), Cheech Marin (Ignacio), Bruce Davison (Dr. Reingold), Jay Mohr (Paulie/Benny), Trini Alvarado (Adult Marie), Buddy Hackett (Artie), Hallie Kate Eisenberg (Marie). Directed by John Roberts and produced by Mark Gordon, Gary Levinsohn, and Allison Lyon Segan. Screenplay by Laurie Craig.

Paulie tells the story of a parrot who can think like a human and talk like a stand-up comic, but a parrot who really had those gifts wouldn't have the problems this one does. He doesn't come across as a bird at all, but as a small, wisecracking person wearing feathers. He's just a little more interesting than the other guy with the same first name who also stars in—but no, that sentence was headed in an unkind direction.

The film is aimed at children, I suppose, although I don't think they'll like Paulie all that much. I didn't. I know there are people who love parrots, but they love them for being parrots. Would you want to live with a parrot who talked and thought like Buddy Hackett? You would? As long as he cleaned his own cage?

As the movie opens, Paulie is in "purgatory" in the basement of a research lab, where he's been banished for refusing to cooperate with an ambitious scientist (Bruce Davison). How did Paulie get there? After he's befriended by a Russian-American janitor (Tony Shalhoub), he offers to tell his story, and we see it in flashback as an odyssey across the country.

Paulie started, we learn, as the friend of a little girl named Marie. After he's blamed for her fall from a roof, he's dispatched to Buddy Hackett's pawnshop, where he picks up some of his vocal style before he's purchased by a lovable woman named Ivy (Gena Rowlands) who (kids! hide your eyes!) goes blind and dies. Then he travels cross-country to Los Angeles, where he has an unconsummated romance with a girl parrot, and no wonder: If you were as smart as Buddy Hackett, how long would you be able to sustain a relationship with a parrot? Cheech Marin makes a brief appearance as another of Paulie's owners, and the bird even becomes expert at stealing from ATM machines before he ends up in the hands of the scientist.

The movie's slant is that it's wrong to keep animals in cages and do experiments on them, and Paulie makes some dramatic gestures toward this end, but by then my attention was drifting. Dogs and cats, horses and monkeys, and even bears make charismatic movie stars, but *Paulie,* I think, suggests that birds are more decorative than dramatic.

On the other hand, just to be fair, I should mention that parrots make great subjects for jokes. I know about a dozen, including the ones about the parrot in the deep freeze, the insulting parrot, the 300-pound parakeet, and the parrot whose last words were, "Who moved the ladder?"

I even made up a brand-new parrot joke while watching this movie. A parrot has a memory that will hold only the last two things it has heard. A guy buys him, puts him by the front door and tests him. "One, two," the man says. "One, two," the parrot says. "Three," says the man. "Two, three," says the parrot. "Four," says the man. "Three, four," says the parrot. Then the guy shouts to his wife: "So long, honey, I'm going to the office!" When the guy comes home, what does the parrot say?

I'd tell you, but this is a family movie.

Payback ★ ★ ★

R, 102 m., 1999

Mel Gibson (Porter), Gregg Henry (Val), Maria Bello (Rosie), David Paymer (Stegman), Deborah Kara Unger (Lynn), William Devane (Carter), Bill Duke (Detective Hicks), Kris Kristofferson (Bronson), James Coburn (Mr. Fairfax), Lucy Liu (Pearl). Directed by Brian Helgeland and produced by Bruce Davey. Screenplay by Helgeland and Terry Hayes, based on the novel *The Hunter* by Richard Stark.

"Not many people know what their life's worth," the hero of *Payback* tells us right at the beginning. "I do. Seventy grand. That's what they took from me. And that's what I'm gonna get back." If you absorb that statement and take a close look at the title, you'll have a good idea of what the movie's about. The only remaining question: Is it about it entertainingly? Yes.

The movie's publicity makes much of the fact that the hero, named Porter, is a bad guy. It quotes the director, Brian Helgeland: "I wanted to see a bad guy as the hero, but I didn't want to make excuses for him." Of course, if the bad guy is played by Mel Gibson, you don't have to make the same kinds of excuses as if he's played by, say, James Woods. Gibson has a whimsical charm, a way of standing outside material like this and grinning at it. Oh, he's earnest and angry, blood-soaked and beaten nearly to death. But inside, there's a grin. His fundamental personality is comic—he's a joker and a satirist—and he only rarely makes an effort to hide that side (as he did, say, in *The Year of Living Dangerously*).

Brian Helgeland has a sense of style, too (he wrote *L.A. Confidential*), and we get the sense that *Payback* is more interested in style than story; it wants to take a criminal's revenge and make it the story of a guy whose mission edges into monomania. He wants exactly $70,000, no more, no less. More than once in the movie, Porter's enemies try to pay him more than $70,000. They're missing the point. (Porter could save himself a lot of wear and tear by taking $130,000 and mailing the rest back, but you know how it is.)

The setup contains a fundamental double-cross that I dare not reveal, and that will make it a little hard to discuss certain other aspects of the story. Perhaps selected details will give you the flavor. As when Porter's friend Val (Gregg Henry) shows him the weekly routine of some Chinese mobsters picking up cash. "They're not wearing their seat belts," Porter observes, and of course that leads to the logical conclusion that the way to get their money is to crash head-on into their car.

There are also action gags involving severed gas lines on a car, a trick telephone, blackmail by cell phone, kidnapping, and a scene in which Porter comes closer than anyone since James Bond to being killed crotch-first. The film also contains a hooker with a heart of gold (Maria Bello), a two-timing dame (Deborah Kara Unger), a laconic cop (Bill Duke), a big mobster (Kris Kristofferson), and an even bigger one (James Coburn).

Writing a screenplay like this essentially involves finding new bottles for old wine. Tricking the enemy is routine, but doing it in a new way is fun. Turning the tables is standard, but not when you don't expect when, and how, they'll be turned. And cinematographer Ericson Core finds a nice blue-green grittiness in the streets of Chicago, where the exterior scenes are punctuated by elevated trains rumbling past on such a frequent schedule that actual el riders will be chuckling to themselves.

There is much cleverness and ingenuity in *Payback*, but Mel Gibson is the key. The movie wouldn't work with an actor who was heavy on his feet, or was too sincere about the material. Gibson is essentially an action comedian, who enters into violence with a bemused detachment *(Mad Max Beyond Thunderdome).* Here he has fun as the movie goes over the top, as when a doctor operates on him for gunshot wounds, using whiskey as a painkiller (for the doctor, not Gibson). Or when he helps himself to the dollars from a beggar's hat. Or when, and how, he recites "This little piggy." ☞

The Peacemaker ★ ★ ½

R, 122 m., 1997

George Clooney (Thomas Devoe), Nicole Kidman (Julia Kelly), Marcel Iures (Dusan Gavrich), Alexander Baluev (Alexsander Kodoroff), Rene Medvesek (Vlado Mirich), Gary Werntz (Hamilton), Randall Batinkoff (Ken), Jim Haynie (General Garnett). Directed by Mimi Leder and produced by Walter Parkes and Branko Lustig. Screenplay by Michael Schiffer.

At first I wasn't going to mention the red digital readout. I've talked about them so often in the past I was afraid of boring you. Then I thought, hey, I was amazed when I saw it in this movie—so why shouldn't I share? I refer to the wheezy movie device requiring the hero to defuse a bomb or other dangerous device before it explodes. Such devices invariably have red digital readouts, so we can see the seconds ticking away with deadly precision.

RDRs have become a jarring cliché, but they survive because they're a quick, cheap device for manufacturing phony suspense. Already this year we've seen RDRs on a doomed ocean liner *(Speed II)* and onboard *Air Force One,* and now, in *The Peacemaker,* the whole climax comes down to whether Nicole Kidman and George Clooney can disarm a ticking nuclear bomb before it vaporizes Manhattan.

This is the first big release from the new DreamWorks studio, and it looks great. The technical credits are impeccable, and Clooney and Kidman negotiate assorted dangers skillfully. But it's mostly spare parts from other thrillers. There's one flash of originality (the villain is protesting that the world has ignored the killing in Bosnia). Much of the rest is retreaded, including the standard idea of teaming a macho military hero (Clooney) with a bright female government official (Kidman). "Give me a man who knows how to take orders from a woman," she barks, just before the scene where he marches into her briefing, interrupts her, corrects her, and then spends the rest of the film giving her orders.

Kidman plays the "acting head of the White House Nuclear Smuggling Group," and Clooney is an intelligence officer with Army Special Forces. The terrorist (Marcel Iures) is haunted by images of his loved ones slaughtered in the former Yugoslavia.

The film opens with a convincing sequence in which nuclear bombs are stolen from a Russian train carrying them to be defused. ("I didn't join the Russian Army to dismantle it for the Americans," one soldier grumbles.) The train is destroyed in a nuclear blast to make it look like all the bombs were destroyed by accident, but Clooney saves us ten minutes of screen time by seeing through the scheme at once.

The film then assembles off-the-shelf parts. These include such standbys as (1) beetle-browed enemy officials sitting in ornate offices and issuing imprecations; (2) preparations for an emergency mission by the good guys; (3) canned personality conflicts, quickly resolved; (4) exterior shots of ominous-looking places, with captions telling us what they are; (5) rat-a-tat military music over convoys to Iran, etc.; (6) high-tech displays of satellite surveillance; and (7) after a few subtitles, a Russian barking "speak English!" at a subordinate, after which they continue in English for no other reason than that they must realize they're in an American movie.

Everything comes down to a cat-and-mouse chase in Manhattan, where the terrorist hopes to explode his bomb. He's made a videotape arguing that he is not a bad man, but he remains such a cipher we don't know if he's sincerely misguided, or simply mad. No matter; the film goes on autopilot for its last act, with the usual canned chase scenes down Manhattan streets, heroes climbing over automobiles, sirens blaring, cars crashing, etc. This used to be known as "second unit" stuff. Now it's the centerpiece.

Finally we get the red digital readout scene, and I'm thinking—what? A movie this expensive was actually based on the bankrupt climax of the heroes dismantling a bomb while an RDR ticks down? Wasn't it possible to think up an original third act? Three other not dissimilar thrillers released at about the same time *(The Assignment, The Edge,* and *Kiss the Girls)* all featured real endings involving character developments and new surprises. DreamWorks shouldn't have settled for less.

At one point, trying to dismantle the bomb, the Kidman character tells a children's choir director, "Get those kids as far away from here as possible," and the kids scurry out the church door. A nuclear bomb is set to explode in under two minutes. If it does, it won't help that the kids are four blocks down the street. If it doesn't, the kids are safe where they are. A wittier screenplay might have had her say, "Let the kids watch this. They might learn something." And then a cherubic little choir boy hurrying over and saying, "Wow! A red digital readout! Just like in the movies!"

Pecker ★ ★

R, 87 m., 1998

Edward Furlong (Pecker), Christina Ricci (Shelley), Mark Joy (Jimmy), Mary Kay Place (Joyce), Martha Plimpton (Tina), Brendan Sexton III (Matt), Lili Taylor (Rorey Wheeler), Jean Schertler (Memama), Lauren Hulsey (Little Crissy). Directed by John Waters and produced by John Fiedler and Mark Tarlov. Screenplay by Waters.

The hero of John Waters's *Pecker* got his nickname as a kid, we are told, by pecking at his food. Uh, huh. And guys named Studs had fathers in the tuxedo business. Pecker (Edward Furlong) works in a Baltimore sandwich shop and takes photos of the seamy side of life. He has an exhibit in the restaurant, a famous New York art dealer (Lili Taylor) happens to see it, and she mounts a show of his work in her gallery.

Of course all Manhattan is soon agog at the young genius, providing Waters with easy targets in the world of modern art. "Pecker's like a humane Diane Arbus," one critic gushes, when in fact he's more like just plain Diane Arbus. But *Pecker* isn't really about art so much as about the way that fame and fortune upset Pecker's little world.

There is a strong streak of domesticity in Waters's plots (even the characters in *Pink Flamingos* have home lives, although you might need to leave the room if I described them). Pecker's dad (Mark Joy) operates a failing bar. His mom (Mary Kay Place) runs a thrift shop and sells the homeless "a complete Easter outfit" for twenty-five cents. (Pecker assures one of her potential customers that a winter coat is "flameproof—in case someone tries to set you on fire.")

His sister Tina (Martha Plimpton) is the emcee in a male go-go bar, issuing dire warnings against such misbehavior as "tea-bagging." His grandmother (Jean Schertler) has a stand in front of the house to sell something called "pit beef," and has a Virgin Mary statue that talks uncannily like one of Conan O'Brien's speaking TV pictures. And there is a kid sister named Little Crissy (Lauren Hulsey) who stuffs candy into her mouth as if she only feeds on payday; she continues the Waters tradition of at least one addictive character in every movie.

Pecker is the most normal member of the family, I'd say. His girlfriend Shelley (Christina Ricci) runs a Laundromat, is an expert on stains, and sometimes slightly unzips the top of her jumper so Pecker can snap off a few quick shots. His best friend, Matt (Brendan Sexton III), is a compulsive shoplifter who poses while committing crimes and suffers the most from Pecker's fame; he complains, "If I can't shoplift, I don't want to be an artist!"

Waters follows these characters through their fifteen minutes of fame without ever churning up very much interest in them. One problem is that Furlong's performance doesn't project much heat or charisma, while the girlfriend played by Ricci seems constantly to be dampening her own. A simple casting switch, making Ricci the photographer and Furlong the boyfriend, might have improved the movie considerably.

There's also a certain tension between the gentler new Waters and his anarchic past. In the scenes in the male strip bar, for example, we keep waiting for Waters to break loose and shock us, and he never does, except with a few awkward language choices. The miraculous statue of Mary could have provided comic possibilities, but doesn't. In the early scenes it's clear that the grandmother is a ventriloquist, but in the later scenes, when the statue actually does talk, the best it can come up with are some disconnected phrases; one is reminded of HAL 9000 as the memory is being disconnected. Better if Mary had become an art critic.

Some scenes are so flat we squint a little at the screen, trying to see why anyone thought they might be funny. After Shelley the girlfriend thinks she sees Pecker kissing the art dealer, for example, she flees brokenhearted into a voting booth, and Pecker follows her into the booth, where they have loud and active sex. This is supposed to shock the bourgeoisie, but it plays like a bad idea.

The movie is filled with cameos, of which the most suggestive is the artist/photographer Cindy Sherman. She eyes the pit-beef grandma as a possible subject, and started me thinking maybe *that* would have been a better approach: Every member of the family is taken up by a different artist, and the Virgin Mary examines the results and says she doesn't know much about art, but she knows what she likes. After all, she's been in a lot of good paintings herself.

A Perfect Murder ★ ★ ★

R, 107 m., 1998

Michael Douglas (Steven Taylor), Gwyneth Paltrow (Emily Bradford Taylor), Viggo Mortensen (David Shaw), David Suchet (Detective Karaman), Constance Towers (Sandra Bradford), Sarita Choudhury (Raquel Martinez). Directed by Andrew Davis and produced by Arnold Kopelson, Anne Kopelson, Christopher Mankiewicz, and Peter MacGregor-Scott. Screenplay by Patrick Smith Kelly, based on the play *Dial M for Murder* by Frederick Knott.

Michael Douglas is about as good as anyone can be at playing greedy, coldhearted SOBs. He's also good at playing nice guys and victims—he's a versatile pro—but when he goes into his Gordon Gekko mode there's an extra charge on the screen, because we know everything his character says and does will be deceitful and self-interested.

Consider an early scene in Andrew Davis's *A Perfect Murder*. Douglas plays Steven Taylor, a wealthy currency trader. Gwyneth Paltrow plays Emily, his wife. She comes home to their designer apartment to find him dressed for a museum opening. They kiss. She says how nice he looks: "I'll hurry and get dressed so I can catch up." Throughout this entire scene, dislike hangs in the air. There's nothing overt. It's simply a way Douglas has of pronouncing his words, as if he wants to say all the proper things even though he doesn't mean them.

The Paltrow character is an heiress who is having an affair with an artist named David Shaw (Viggo Mortensen). We learn that in the first scene. *A Perfect Murder* doesn't fool around with a misleading opening charade to deceive us. This is not a happy marriage and the movie never pretends otherwise, and when the husband confronts the artist in his studio, there is a kind of blunt savagery to the way he cuts to the bottom line. ("You steal the crown jewel of a man's life, and all you can come up with is some candy-ass Hallmark sentiment?")

A murder is arranged in the movie, but for once the TV ads leave you with a certain doubt about who is doing what and with which and to whom, so I won't reveal the secret. I will say that Paltrow does a convincing job of playing a chic wife who considers love to be a choice more than a destiny. Viggo Mortensen undergoes an interesting transformation in his key scene with Douglas; we believe him when he's a nice guy, and we believe him even more when he's not; he doesn't do a big style shift, he simply turns off his people-pleasing face.

The screenplay, by Patrick Smith Kelly, is based on the play *Dial M for Murder* and the Hitchcock film of the same title. It has little in common with its predecessors. It's about negotiation more than deception, money more than love. Everybody's motives are pretty much clear from the beginning, and when the body is found on the kitchen floor the only mystery is how long it will take the survivor to find the key to the scheme.

Surprisingly, the movie got some negative early reviews. I think it works like a nasty little machine to keep us involved and disturbed; my attention never strayed, and one of the elements I liked was the way Paltrow's character isn't sentimentalized. She says she's in love with the artist, yes, but she gets over it in a hurry; it takes her about one line of dialogue. And there is a moment when it appears that husband and wife will put adultery and violence behind them, and continue their pragmatic liaison as a rich guy and his multilingual trophy wife. Who wouldn't want to keep living in that great apartment?

But there's another problem: Steven is having a portfolio meltdown (his adviser tells him, "Think Chernobyl"). Steven is driven not only by jealousy but by need and greed. Emily has a $100 million trust fund that would help Steven cover those margins (although the markets move a lot faster than probate, and the inheritance is unlikely to arrive in time to do much good).

The movie is a skilled example of what I call the Fatal Basic Genre. Like *Fatal Attraction, Basic Instinct,* and all of their lesser imitators, it's about sex between bad people who live in good houses. Nobody is better at Fatal Basic than Michael Douglas, who doesn't need to read *GQ* because he instinctively knows what clothes to wear and which cigars to smoke.

My only real disappointment with the movie comes at the end, when various differences are resolved with gunshots. This is such a tired story solution. I realize that the Hollywood bylaws require all action movies to end in shoot-outs, but is a gun really necessary in a Fatal Basic movie? I'd prefer the chessmaster approach to the problem, in which a single line of logical dialogue seals a character's fate, and then we get a big close-up of him realizing he's screwed. Gunshots release tension, but they don't provide audience pleasure, because the victim is dead and therefore cannot feel as bad as he deserves to.

Permanent Midnight ★ ★ ★

R, 95 m., 1998

Ben Stiller (Jerry Stahl), Elizabeth Hurley (Sandra), Janeane Garofalo (Jana), Maria Bello (Kitty), Owen C. Wilson (Nicky), Lourdes Benedicto (Volo), Fred Willard (Craig Ziffer), Cheryl Ladd (Pamel Verlaine), Peter Greene (Dealer). Directed by David Veloz and produced by Jane Hamsher and Don Murphy. Screenplay by Veloz, based on the book by Jerry Stahl.

"You're too darn sad-looking to just be another retard in a pink visor," the customer tells the fast-food clerk. That leads into a conversation, and in no time at all they're in bed together, and he's telling her the story of his life—which, in recent years, played more like his slow and agonizing death.

The guy with the drive-thru job is Jerry Stahl (Ben Stiller), who at one point was making $5,000 a week as a TV writer in Hollywood. Nice work, unless your drug habit is running you $6,000 a week. It's a true story. The movie *Permanent Midnight,* based on the autobiography of Stahl, tells how his life spiraled into increasing desperation, even while his TV bosses let him get away with almost everything—as long as he produced.

Stahl, a smart guy with good ideas, gets his TV job through Sandra (Elizabeth Hurley), a British woman he marries for money, so she can get a green card. His first job interview goes strangely. "I'm wondering if your mind can function down at our level," muses his prospective boss (Fred Willard). Asked what he thinks about the show (a puppetcast named Mr. Chompers), he insults the show and is hired. Soon he's turning his own life into fodder for comedy; his father's suicide is recycled into an episode.

The story of every drunk or addict is different in the details but similar in the outlines: Their days center around locating and using a sufficient supply of their substance of choice to avoid acute mental and physical discomfort. Eventually it gets to the point where everything else—job, family, self-image—is secondary. Stahl steals drugs from the medicine cabinet of his friends ("If I was Percodan, where would I be?") and buys drugs from very dangerous people (he's safe only because there's more money in customers who are not dead). He shoots up in risky places, is sometimes caught or almost caught, and finds his anger mounting because it is so very hard and exhausting to get high all the time.

There are bizarre episodes at work and in his private life, where the green-card girl inexplicably begins to take a liking to him, gets pregnant, and finds out too late that he is the wrong pony to bet on. One day, in desperation, she begs him to baby-sit. He sticks the kid in the car and goes looking for drugs; he's eventually stopped by the cops, who arrest him and call family services for the child Does he learn his lesson? Does it help that when he gets out of rehab a friendly dealer

(Peter Greene) is waiting to sell him drugs in the parking lot?

The story in *Permanent Midnight* has been told many times in many forms. Someday I'd like to see a movie based on Julia Phillips's harrowing memoir, *You'll Never Have Lunch in This Town Again.* What Ben Stiller brings to the role is a kind of savage impatience; his character stabs his body anywhere with the needle—even in the neck—because the niceties are no longer of interest to a man who simply needs to get the stuff into his veins, right away.

The movie gets credit for not making the highlife seem colorful or funny. It is not. It is boring, really, because when the drugs are there they simply clear the pain and allow the mind to focus on getting more drugs. Stahl doesn't seek drugs because he wants to feel good but because he wants to stop feeling bad. It isn't the high that makes people into addicts; it's the withdrawal.

Last month I saw a revival of Otto Preminger's *The Man With the Golden Arm,* the first of the Hollywood drug movies, with Frank Sinatra in the title role. Sinatra got an Oscar nomination for the role, in which he portrayed the pain of withdrawal. Stiller, playing Stahl, makes it look incomparably worse. Either the drugs are getting stronger, or the actors are.

Phantoms ★

R, 91 m., 1998

Peter O'Toole (Timothy Flyte), Rose McGowan (Lisa Pailey), Joanna Going (Jenny Pailey), Liev Schreiber (Deputy Stu Wargle), Ben Affleck (Sheriff Bryce Hammond), Nicky Katt (Deputy Steve Shanning). Directed by Joe Chappelle and produced by Joel Soisson, Michael Leahy, Robert Pringle, and Steve Lane. Screenplay by Dean Koontz, based on his book.

Did you know that if a certain kind of worm learns how to solve a maze, and then you grind it up and feed it to other worms, the other worms will then be able to negotiate the maze on their first try? That's one of the scientific nuggets supplied in *Phantoms,* a movie that seems to have been made by grinding up other films and feeding them to this one

As the movie opens, two sisters arrive by Jeep in a quaint mountain town that seems suspiciously quiet, and no wonder: Everybody in town seems to be dead. Some of them have died rather suddenly. The baker's wife, for example. Her hands still grip the rolling pin. Just her hands. The rest of her is elsewhere.

The sisters (Rose McGowan and Joanna Going) find more ominous signs. A dead deputy sheriff, for example. And phones that don't work—but then one does. The older sister picks it up. "Who are you? What do you want?" she asks. It is a test of great acting to be able to say those ancient lines as if you mean them. A test like many others that this movie fails.

The sheriff turns up. He is played by Ben Affleck, wearing an absurd cowboy hat that looks like the kind of unsold stock they unload on city slickers at the end of the season. He is accompanied by another deputy (Nicky Katt), who wears an identical hat. Don't they know it's a rule in the movies: Hero wears neat hat, sidekick wears funny hat?

Joining the two young women, they search the town and find a desperate message written in lipstick on a mirror, which (I'm jumping ahead now) leads them to Dr. Timothy Flyte (Peter O'Toole), an editor of the kind of supermarket rag that features babies with nine-pound ears. Dr. Flyte and U.S. Army troops soon arrive in the small town, dressed like ghostbusters, to get to the bottom of the mystery. "What kind of threat are we dealing with here—biological, chemical, or other?" he's asked. "I'm leaning toward 'other,'" he replies, with all the wisdom and poignancy of a man who once played Lawrence of Arabia and is now playing Dr. Timothy Flyte.

The movie quickly degenerates into another one of those Gotcha! thrillers in which loathsome, slimy creatures leap out of drain pipes and sewers and ingest supporting actors, while the stars pump bullets into it. There are a few neat touches. In front of an altar at the local church, the heroes discover a curious pile of stuff: watches, glasses, ballpoints, pacemakers. At first they think it's an offering to the Virgin Mary. But no: "That's not an offering. Those are undigested remains."

How common are these films getting to be? Two out of the three films I saw today used the formula. With a deep bow (almost a salaam) to *Tremors,* they locate their creatures beneath the surface of the land or sea, so that most of the time, although not enough of the time, you can't see them.

Peter O'Toole is a professional and plays his character well. It takes years of training and practice to be able to utter lines like, "It comes from the deep and secret realms of our Earth" without giggling. It is O'Toole who gets to float the educated tapeworm theory. When these creatures eat a human, they learn everything it knows—and even everything it thinks it knows, so that since many humans think they are being eaten by the devil, the creatures think they are the devil too. If only we could learn to think more kindly of those who digest us, this movie could have ended happily.

π ★★★½

R, 85 m., 1998

Sean Gullette (Maximillian Cohen), Mark Margolis (Sol Robeson), Ben Shenkman (Lenny Meyer), Pamela Hart (Marcy Dawson), Stephen Pearlman (Rabbi Cohen), Samia Shoaib (Devi), Ajay Naidu (Farrouhk). Directed by Darren Aronofsky and produced by Eric Watson. Screenplay by Aronofsky.

π is a study in madness and its partner, genius. A tortured, driven man believes (1) that mathematics is the language of the universe, (2) nature can be expressed in numbers, and (3) there are patterns everywhere in nature. If he can find the patterns, if he can find the key to the chaos, then he can predict anything—the stock market, for example. If the man is right, the mystery of existence is unlocked. If he is wrong, the inside of his brain begins to resemble a jammed stock ticker.

The movie, written and directed by Darren Aronofsky, is a study in mental obsession. His hero, named Maximillian Cohen, lives barricaded behind a triple-locked door, in a room filled with high-powered, customized computer equipment. He wants nothing to do with anybody. He writes programs, tests them, looks for the pattern, gets a 216-digit bug, stomps on his chips in a rage, and then begins to wonder about that bug. Exactly 216 digits. There is a theory among some Jewish scholars, he learns, that the name of God has 216 letters.

The movie is shot in rough, high-contrast black and white. Max, played by Sean Gullette, is balding, restless, paranoid, and brilliant. He has debilitating headaches and nosebleeds, symptoms of high blood pressure—or of the mental torment he's putting himself through. He's suspicious of everyone. The friendly Indian woman next door puts food by his door. He avoids her. He trusts only his old teacher, Sol (Mark Margolis). They play Go, a game deeper than chess, and Sol tells him to stop with the key-to-the-universe business already. He warns that Max's spinning away from science and toward numerology.

Not everybody thinks so. Max's phone rings with the entreaties of Marcy (Pamela Hart), who works for a high-powered Wall Street analysis firm. They want to hire him as a consultant. They think he's onto something. He has predicted some prices correctly. At the deli, he runs into a Hasidic Jew named Lenny (Ben Shenkman), who seems casual and friendly but has a hidden mission: His group believes the Torah may be a code sent from God, and may contain God's name.

Of course, if one finds the mathematical key to everything, that would include God, stock prices, the weather, past and future history, baseball scores, and the response to all moves in Go. That assumes there is a key. When you're looking for something that doesn't exist, it makes you crazier the closer you get to it.

The seductive thing about Aronofsky's film is that it is halfway plausible in terms of modern physics and math. What was numerology a century ago has now been simplified into a very, very vast problem. Chaos theory looks for patterns where common sense says there are none. A computer might be able to give you the answer to anything, if (1) it is powerful enough, and (2) it has all the data. Of course, you might need a computer the size of the universe and containing everything in it, but we're talking theory here.

π is a thriller. I am not very thrilled these days by whether the bad guys will get shot or the chase scene will end one way instead of another. You have to make a movie like that pretty skillfully before I care. But I am thrilled when a man risks his mind in the pursuit of a dangerous obsession. Max is out on a limb There are hungry people circling him. He may be onto something. They want it too. For both the stock market people and the Hasidic cabal, Max's formula represents all they believe in and everything they care about.

And then there is a level, of course, at which Max may simply be insane or physically ill. There are people who work out complicated theories involving long, impenetrable columns of numbers. Newspapers get envelopes filled with their proofs every day. And other people who sit in their rooms, wrapping themselves in the webs of chess or numbers theory, addicted to their fixes. And game players, gamblers, horse players—people bewitched by the mirage of a system.

The beautiful thing about mathematics is that you can't prove it except by its own terms. There's no way to put some math in a test tube and see if it turns purple or heats up. It sits there smugly in its own perfect cocoon, letting people like Max find anything he wants in it—or to think that he has.

Note: Sean Gullette, the star of π, has authored the movie's fascinating Web page at www. pithemovie.com/.

Picture Perfect ★ ★

PG-13, 101 m., 1997

Jennifer Aniston (Kate), Jay Mohr (Nick), Kevin Bacon (Sam), Olympia Dukakis (Rita), Illeana Douglas (Darcy), Kevin Dunn (Mr. Mercer), Anne Twomey (Sela), Faith Prince (Mrs. Mercer). Directed by Glenn Gordon Caron and produced by Erwin Stoff. Screenplay by Arleen Sorkin, Paul Slansky, and Caron.

Sometimes a movie will include a subversive line of dialogue that shows somebody was paying attention. In *Picture Perfect,* that line comes when the devious woman tells the good guy: "This sounds like something out of *The Patty Duke Show.*" That hits the nail on the head. And it's a shame the plot is so contrived, because parts of this movie are really pretty good.

The film has Jennifer Aniston of TV's *Friends* in her first leading movie role, as Kate, an ad executive who has good ideas but projects the wrong image. She dreams up a campaign for Gulden's mustard, but when the client buys it, she's not included on the account team. Why not? Mercer (Kevin Dunn), the agency head, says it's because she's not engaged and not in debt, so there's nothing to stop her from leaving the agency. So her best friend, Darcy (Illeana Douglas), dreams up a scheme: She should claim to be engaged to a guy from Boston.

She has met this guy from Boston just once. His name is Nick (Jay Mohr), he videotapes weddings for a living, and he's in love with her. In a nice, subtle touch, we can sense the moment he first notices her, because we're looking through the POV of his viewfinder at a wedding when his camera focuses on her and freezes. Kate contacts him and offers him $1,000 to come to New York for a weekend, pose as her boyfriend, and break up with her publicly. That way she'll get the job and be able to explain her freedom. It's at this point that she uses the Patty Duke line and he turns down the money.

I'm not sure *Picture Perfect* paints a very accurate portrait of the requirements that modern ad agencies have for their employees; it sounds more as if Kate is being considered for a job as a deaconess. But never mind. The plot thickens when she immediately has an affair with the office bad boy (Kevin Bacon), who thought she was "too nice" until she got "engaged," but is now attracted by the thought that he's stealing her away from her fiancé.

The movie has some nice dialogue touches in it. I like how Darcy justifies her bright idea about the Boston boyfriend to Kate: "We're in advertising, Kate. I didn't lie—I sold." I liked the way Kate prepared a "study guide" so that Nick would know all about her if anybody asked specific questions. And I liked Nick's sweet little speech about why he feels so privileged to videotape the most important moments in his clients' lives.

But against those moments are some huge distractions. One is the plot, which has Kate being so incredibly crass and rude toward Nick that we almost fall out of sympathy with her—and lose respect for Nick for putting up with it. Another is the character of Kate's mother (Olympia Dukakis), who pops up regularly to do things that, frankly, she seems too bright to do.

And the third, which becomes a distraction during at least the last third of the movie, is

Jennifer Aniston's neckline. After the agency boss advises her to buy a new dress, she appears in a series of plunging frocks that seem designed to advertise the powers of the WonderBra. Aniston is pretty and she has a swell body, but these dresses get to be a joke after a while; is she auditioning for *Playboy*'s Girls of Summer? It was W. C. Fields who hated to appear in the same scene with a child, a dog, or a plunging neckline—because nobody in the audience would be looking at him. Jennifer Aniston has the same problem in this movie, even when she's in scenes all by herself.

The Pillow Book ★ ★ ★ ½

NO MPAA RATING, 126 m., 1997

Vivian Wu (Nagiko), Yoshi Oida (The Publisher), Ken Ogata (The Father), Hideko Yoshida (The Aunt/The Maid), Ewan McGregor (Jerome), Judy Ongg (The Mother), Ken Mitsuishi (The Husband), Yutaka Honda (Hoki). Directed by Peter Greenaway and produced by Kees Kasander. Screenplay by Greenaway.

Nagiko's father was a calligrapher, and when she was a little girl he would write his birthday greetings on her face. Her mother would read aloud from a 1,000-year-old manuscript, *The Pillow Book of Sei Shonagon,* which dealt among other things with the arts of love. Because children invest their birthdays with enormous importance, it's no wonder that when Nagiko grows up she finds a powerful link between calligraphy, human flesh, poetry, and sexuality.

Peter Greenaway, born in Australia, long working in England, is not so far from Nagiko himself. His films also work by combining images, words, quotations, and sexual situations. He uses the screen as Nagiko uses flesh, finding an erotic charge not just in the words, but in the surface they are written on. His new film *The Pillow Book,* starring Vivian Wu (from *The Last Emperor*), is a seductive and elegant story that combines a millennium of Japanese art and fetishes with the story of a neurotic modern woman who tells a lover: "Treat me like the pages of a book."

Early in Nagiko's life, she sees something she was not intended to see: her father's publisher (Yoshi Oida), forcing her father (Ken Ogata) to have sex as the price of getting a book published. On another occasion, when she is six or seven, she is introduced to the publisher's ten-year-old nephew and told this will be her future husband. These events set up fundamental tensions in her life, and as an adult, unhappily married to the publisher's nephew, she begins keeping her own pillow book. The nephew (Ken Mitsuishi) is a shallow dolt, who finds her book and in a jealous rage burns her papers and then their house.

Nagiko flees from Kyoto to Hong Kong, where eventually she finds work as a fashion model and begins to seek lovers who will fulfill her dreams. For her the appearance of a person's handwriting is more important than the surfaces of his face; she wants to be used as a book, to be written on, to be read.

Her fetish ties in with two ancient Japanese artistic practices. One is the art of tattooing, which can be much more elegant and artistic than in the West, and is used by the Yakuza as a way of bonding with their criminal brothers. It can be seen as a form of submission—to the will of the tattoo artist, to the will of the group dictating the tattoos, or simply in the willingness of a person to be used as an object.

The other practice is the long-standing Japanese tradition in art of deliberately exposing the artificiality of a work of art. Realism is less prized than style. Landscapes may use great realistic detail, and then have captions written on them, or the bright red artist's mark. Kabuki and Noh theater overlay their stories with ancient layers of style and tradition. To write a poem on a body is much the same as writing it on a landscape: The word and the image create a tension.

Greenaway, whose work includes *The Draughtsman's Contract; The Cook, The Thief, His Wife and Her Lover;* and *Prospero's Books,* uses an essentially Japanese technique. He likes to build up his images in layers, combining film and video, live action and paintings, spoken narration and visual texts. He shoots in color, black and white, and subtle tints. Here he tells a lurid story of sexuality, fetishism, and betrayal, in an elegant and many-faceted way.

The story itself is simple. In Hong Kong, Nagiko takes a British lover, Jerome (Ewan McGregor). He is a good lover and a bad calligrapher; certainly his handwriting is not good enough to decorate her body. Meanwhile, Nagiko's book has been rejected by the publisher (the very same publisher who has caused her so much unhappiness). Jerome hits on an inspiration: Why not use his body as her book, which he will then take to the publisher? She decorates his body, he goes to the publisher, and the publisher and Jerome end by making love—which for Nagiko is a betrayal that spirals back through all her memories.

One of the most elegant parts of the film comes toward the end, as Greenaway illustrates the pages of Nagiko's pillow book. She has used each part of the body for the appropriate texts, even writing on ears and tongues, and here the words (Japanese, English, printed, spoken, Kanji) take on a sort of mystical, abstract quality. The talkies chained pictures to words; Greenaway finds a way out by using words as pictures.

Greenaway once said something that perfectly describes his work: "I don't make pictures that have a sell-by date." Most new American movies have a limited shelf life. They're put in the theaters to sink or swim. If they haven't sold in a week or two, they're yanked like stale bread. Greenaway's notion is that his movies stand outside the ordinary distribution channels. You may see them today or in ten years, as you choose. And when you are ready.

Pink Flamingos

STAR RATING: NOT RELEVANT
NC-17, 92 m., 1972 (rereleased 1997)

Divine (Divine/Babs Johnson), David Lochary (Raymond Marble), Mary Vivian Pearce (Cotton), Mink Stole (Connie Marble), Danny Mills (Crackers), Edith Massey (Mama Edie), Channing Wilroy (Channing), Cookie Mueller (Cookie). Written, produced, and directed by John Waters.

John Waters's *Pink Flamingos* has been restored for its twenty-fifth anniversary revival, and with any luck at all that means I won't have to see it again for another twenty-five years. If I haven't retired by then, I will.

How do you review a movie like this? I am reminded of an interview I once did with a man who ran a carnival sideshow. His star was a geek who bit off the heads of live chickens and drank their blood.

"He's the best geek in the business," this man assured me.

"What is the difference between a good geek and a bad geek?" I asked.

"You wanna examine the chickens?"

Pink Flamingos was filmed with genuine geeks, and that is the appeal of the film to those who find it appealing: What seems to happen in the movie really does happen. That is its redeeming quality, you might say. If the events in this film were only simulated, it would merely be depraved and disgusting. But since they are actually performed by real people, the film gains a weird kind of documentary stature. There is a temptation to praise the film, however grudgingly, just to show you have a strong enough stomach to take it. It is a temptation I can resist.

The plot involves a rivalry between two competing factions for the title of Filthiest People Alive. In one corner: a transvestite named Divine (who dresses like a combination of a showgirl, a dominatrix, and Bozo); her mentally ill mother (sits in a crib eating eggs and making messes); her son (likes to involve chickens in his sex life with strange women); and her lover (likes to watch son with strange women and chickens). In the other corner: Mr. and Mrs. Marble, who kidnap hippies, chain them in a dungeon, and force their butler to impregnate them so that after they die in childbirth their babies can be sold to lesbian couples.

All of the details of these events are shown in the film—oh, and more, including the notorious scene in which Divine actually ingests that least appetizing residue of the canine. And not only do we see genitalia in this movie—they do exercises.

Pink Flamingos appeals to that part of our psyche in which we are horny teenagers at the county fair with fresh dollar bills in our pockets and a desire to see the geek show with a bunch of buddies, so that we can brag about it at school on Monday. (And also because of an intriguing rumor that the Bearded Lady proves she is bearded all over.)

After the restored version of the film has played, director John Waters hosts and narrates a series of outtakes, which (not surprisingly) are not as disgusting as what stayed in the film. We see long-lost scenes in which Divine cooks the chicken that starred in an earlier scene; Divine receives the ears of Cookie, the character who costarred in the scene with her son and the chicken; and Divine, Cookie, and her son sing "We Are the Filthiest People Alive" in Pig Latin.

John Waters is a charming man, whose later films (like *Polyester* and *Hairspray*) take advantage of his bemused take on pop culture. His early films, made on infinitesimal budgets and starring his friends, used shock as a way to attract audiences, and that is understandable. He jump-started his career, and in the movie business, you do what you gotta do. Waters's talent has grown; in this film, which he photographed, the visual style resembles a home movie, right down to the overuse of the zoom lens. (Amusingly, his zooms reveal he knows how long the characters will speak; he zooms in, stays, and then starts zooming out before the speech ends, so he can pan to another character and zoom in again.)

After the outtakes, Waters shows the original trailer for the film, in which, not amazingly, not a single scene from the movie is shown. Instead, the trailer features interviews with people who have just seen *Pink Flamingos,* and are a little dazed by the experience. The trailer cleverly positions the film as an event: Hey, you may like the movie or hate it, but at least you'll be able to say you saw it! Then blurbs flash on the screen, including one comparing *Pink Flamingos* to Luis Buñuel's *An Andalusian Dog,* in which a pig's eyeball was sliced. Yes, but the pig was dead, while the audience for this movie is still alive.

Note: I am not giving a star rating to Pink Flamingos, *because stars simply seem not to apply. It should be considered not as a film but as a fact, or perhaps as an object.*

Player's Club ★ ★ ★

R, 103 m., 1998

Lisa Raye (Diana Armstrong), Bernie Mac (Dollar Bill), Chrystale Wilson (Ronnie), Adele Givens (Tricks), A. J. Johnson (Li'l Man), Larry McCoy (St. Louis), Jamie Foxx (Blue [DJ]), Monica Calhoun (Ebony). Directed by Ice Cube and produced by Patricia Charbonnet and Carl Craig. Screenplay by Ice Cube.

Player's Club, written and directed by the rapper Ice Cube, is a gritty black version of *Showgirls,* set in a "gentlemen's club" where a young college student hopes to earn her tuition. Rich with colorful dialogue and characters, it's sometimes ungainly but never boring, and there's a core of truth in its portrait of sex workers.

Thirty years ago this material would have been forced into the blaxploitation genre—dumbed down and predictable. But *Player's Club* is observant and insightful, and beneath its melodrama lurks unsentimental information about why young women do lap dances for a living, and what they think about themselves and their customers.

The movie stars a convincing newcomer named Lisa Raye as Diana, who has a fight with her father over what college to attend. Pregnant and jobless, she moves away from home, gets a job in a shoe store, and is fairly happy until her child's father wants "more space" and abandons her.

That's when she meets Tricks and Ronnie, two dancers at the Player's Club, who tell her there are ways to make a lot more money. They are correct, but the money comes at a price. The film is knowledgeable about details of the clubs: the camaraderie of the dancers, the flamboyance of the owner and grandiloquence of the doorman, the way the bartenders and the disk jockey keep an eye on the action, and the needy absorption of the customers. "The first dance is degrading," Ronnie (Chrystale Wilson) tells her, "but you get used to it." Her advice to the newcomer: Don't look at the customers, look at yourself in the mirror.

Onto this semidocumentary material, Ice Cube grafts a crime story involving the mysterious St. Louis, a gangster who is owed a lot of money by Dollar Bill (Bernie Mac), the club's fast-talking owner. St. Louis wants his money, Dollar Bill doesn't have it, and at one point Bill is actually inside a car trunk and we think we know what has to happen next, but the action tilts toward farce rather than tragedy. (A lot of people get shot at in the movie, but I don't think anyone ever quite gets killed.)

Problems for Diana begin when Ebony

(Monica Calhoun), her eighteen-year-old cousin, comes to stay with her. She wants to keep Ebony away from the club, but "Ebony jumped headfirst into the lifestyle," and soon Diana, who has drawn the line at prostitution, finds that Ebony treats it more like a career goal. Ice Cube uses strong dramatic intercutting to build suspense in a scene where Ebony, hired as a dancer at a bachelor party, is uneasy to find there aren't any other girls there.

What's interesting about *Player's Club* is the way it moves through various tones and kinds of material. There's the documentary stuff, the crime story, Diana's shaky romance with a new boyfriend, Ebony's problems, and comic relief from the stylized dialogue of Dollar Bill and his doorman, L'il Man (A. J. Johnson). And then a strong underpinning of economic reality, as Diana works hard to pay her bills, and is encouraged by a professor after she finds herself falling asleep in class.

The movie has strong scenes for all its major characters, including a boozy after-hours party being held by some ATF agents who hire Ronnie and some of the other girls as strippers. Ronnie knows these guys from earlier parties and plays the role of dominatrix. (Slapping one officer on the behind with a paddle, she says, "That's one more for Rodney King.") The scene develops interestingly: At first we think Ronnie may be in danger, and when we see she knows what she's doing, Ice Cube resists the temptation to go for a comic put-down of the agents, and stays instead with the real tension of the tables being turned. The scene's effect depends on the way Wilson plays it; a less convincing performance, and we wouldn't buy it.

The movie doesn't preach, but it has values. It sees the Player's Club as a job, and the women there as workers, not sex objects. It's work that pays well, but at a price, and although Diana has rules about drugs and sex, Ebony seems like an excellent candidate to crash and burn. I liked Ice Cube's ambition in writing so many colorful characters and juggling them all at the same time. The movie isn't deep, but it's sophisticated about its people and places, and Diana and Ebony have the clarity of characters who seem drawn from life. It would be easy to dismiss *Player's Club* by looking only at its subject matter, but look a little harder and you see an ambitious filmmaker at work.

Playing by Heart ★ ★ ½

R, 120 m., 1999

Gillian Anderson (Meredith), Ellen Burstyn (Mildred), Sean Connery (Paul), Gena Rowlands (Hannah), Anthony Edwards (Roger), Angelina Jolie (Joan), Jay Mohr (Mark), Ryan Philippe (Keenan), Dennis Quaid (Hugh), Madeleine Stowe (Gracie), Jon Stewart (Trent), Patricia Clarkson (Allison), Nastassja Kinski (Melanie), Alec Mapa (Lana). Directed by Willard Carroll and produced by Meg Liberman, Carroll, and Tom Wilhite. Screenplay by Carroll.

Playing by Heart interweaves the stories of maybe a dozen characters, couples of one sort or another, who try to express how they feel and sometimes succeed. It's like one of those Alan Rudolph films *(Choose Me* or *Welcome to L.A.)* where lonely seekers cruise the city seeking solace. The difference is that Rudolph's characters have tough, wounded personalities, and the characters created here by Willard Carroll are mostly softies—they're in tune with the current trend toward movies that coddle the audience with reassuring sentiments.

Of course, there is some pain along the way. One of the most touching couples consists of a mother (Ellen Burstyn) whose son (Jay Mohr) is dying of AIDS. Their long sickroom conversations contain the stuff of truth. And there is a different kind of truth in the peppy wisecracks of Joan (Angelina Jolie), a club-crawler who meets Keenan (Ryan Philippe), a guy she likes, and can't understand why he goes hot and cold with her. Jolie steals the movie as a woman whose personal style has become so entertaining she can hide behind it.

Other couples include Paul and Hannah (Sean Connery and Gena Rowlands), who are approaching their fortieth wedding anniversary under an unexpected cloud. And Meredith (Gillian Anderson), a theater director who tries dating Trent (Jon Stewart), an architect. And Gracie (Madeleine Stowe), who meets her lover (Anthony Edwards) in hotel rooms, and then comes home to her cold husband, Hugh (Dennis Quaid). And we see Hugh in a different light in a series of deep and deceptive barroom conversations with Patricia Clarkson,

Nastassja Kinski, and a drag queen played by Alec Mapa.

All of these people are articulate, and some of them are glib, and although the dialogue sometimes sounds exactly like dialogue, it's often entertaining. I liked the way the drag queen says he's twenty-nine, "and those are real years, not Heather Locklear years." And the way Keenan tells Joan, "What did I do to deserve this?" and means it gratefully, and she observes that's the kind of line that's usually hurled at her by someone on his way out the door.

In a movie with so many characters, there's no time to deeply develop any of them. Some don't really register. Others we enjoy because of their star power. It's a little unlikely that the couple played by Connery and Rowlands would have quite the conversation they have about an affair Connery almost had twenty-five years ago. That's especially true given more urgent circumstances facing them now. But the affection between the two feels real, and there is an invaluable moment when Connery imitates a puppy dog.

As the movie circled from one story to another, I found myself waiting for Angelina Jolie to come round again. With her pouty lips and punk chic look, she's an original; I like the way she's talking to her sister on the phone and when Keenan turns up unexpectedly, she says, "Let me take care of this call" and takes care of it by hanging up. Their relationship is the one that develops the most during the film—the one we care about.

Where it all ends up, the filmmakers have entreated critics not to say. I will obey. There is not a ban on deciding what it all adds up to, however, and I think it amounts to a near miss. It's easy to like the movie because we like the actors in it, and because the movie makes it easy on us and has charming moments. But it feels too much like an exercise. It's yuppie lite—affluent, articulate people who, except for those who are ill, have problems that are almost pleasant. It has been observed that a lot of recent movies about death have gone all soft and gooey at the center. Here's a movie about life that does the same thing.

Playing God ★ ★ ★

R, 93 m., 1997

David Duchovny (Eugene Sands), Timothy Hutton (Raymond Blossom), Angelina Jolie (Claire), Michael Massee (Gage), Peter Stormare (Vladmir), Andrew Tiernan (Cyril), Gary Dourdan (Yates). Directed by Andy Wilson and produced by Marc Abraham and Laura Bickford. Screenplay by Mark Haskell Smith.

Playing God opens with the hero deep in trouble. Eugene Sands (David Duchovny) is a former surgeon, now a druggie, who's in a scuzzy bar looking to score synthetic heroin. Shabby as he looks, he attracts the eye of a dazzling woman across the room—but then shots ring out and a man is gravely wounded.

Sands argues, not unreasonably, that someone should call 911. But there are reasons why the police should not be involved in this shooting, and soon the defrocked doc is reenacting one of those classic movie situations where he barks orders and prepares for instant surgery. A master of improvisation (few battlefield surgeons must be this creative), he fashions a breathing apparatus out of a plastic pop bottle and some tubing from the club soda siphon, cuts a hole in the guy's chest, plugs the tube into his lung, and restores vital signs. Of course, the beautiful woman, named Claire (Angelina Jolie), has the right stuff and could become an expert ER nurse.

It is a tribute of some sort to Duchovny, the *X-Files* star, that I was almost able to believe this was possible. He's a convincing actor. Among those his character convinces in the movie is Raymond Blossom (Timothy Hutton), a shady millionaire, who invites Sands to his home and gives him $10,000 for saving his colleague's life. Also at Blossom's home is, inevitably, Claire, a not-uncommon type in the movies: Living with a rich and dangerous man, she makes eyes at every poor schmuck who drifts into range.

In a flashback, we learn the sad story of ex–Dr. Sands. Up for twenty-eight hours straight and exhausted, he once tried balancing uppers and downers and did it so well that he came to a complete halt, losing a patient in the process. His license was lifted, and now he's a man without a career or future, until Blossom offers him one. The older man has a lot of pals who get shot, it appears. And none of them much want to go to the hospital. Blossom offers Sands a retainer to come on staff as the house specialist in gunshot wounds.

Playing God, directed by Andy Wilson, a former cameraman, tells a preposterous story in a way that almost makes it credible. It's based on three sound performances. Duchovny finds a delicate balance between action hero and moping antihero. Angelina Jolie (Jon Voight's daughter) finds a certain warmth in a kind of role that is usually hard and aggressive; she seems too nice to be Blossom's girlfriend, and maybe she is.

And the surprise in the movie is Timothy Hutton, as the villain. I sense the curtain rising on the next act of his career. Having outgrown the sensitive-boy roles that established him *(Ordinary People, Made in Heaven),* he returns to his dark side, to notes he struck in such films as *The Falcon and the Snowman* and *Q & A.* He shows here what sets the interesting villains apart from the ordinary ones.

Too many movie villains are simply evil. They sneer, they threaten, they hurt, but they do not much involve us, except as plot devices. The best villains are intriguing. They have a seductive quality, as when Blossom tells the doctor, "Eugene, you should embrace your criminal self." We can believe that beautiful women would be attracted to them. Thin, chain-smoking, with a fashionable two-day beard, Hutton creates a character instead of simply filling a space.

Playing God is David Duchovny's first starring role, unless you count the *Red Shoe Diaries* episodes on cable. It seems crafted to match his new stardom on *The X-Files,* and it does: He has the psychic weight to be a leading man and an action hero, even though his earlier TV and film roles might not have revealed it. And he also has a certain detachment, a way of standing above the action, that stars like Eastwood and Mitchum have. This may not be a great movie, but for both Duchovny and Hutton, it's a turning point.

Pleasantville ★ ★ ★ ★

PG-13, 116 m., 1998

Tobey Maguire (David/Bud), Reese Witherspoon (Jennifer/Mary Sue), Jeff Daniels (Mr. Johnson), Joan Allen (Betty Parker), William H. Macy (George Parker), J. T. Walsh (Big Bob), Don Knotts (TV Repairman), Paul Walker (Skip), Marley Shelton (Margaret), Jane Kaczmarek (David and Jennifer's Mom). Directed by Gary Ross and produced by Steven Soderbergh, Jon Kilik, and Bob Degus. Screenplay by Ross.

In the twilight of the twentieth century, here is a comedy to reassure us that there is hope—that the world we see around us represents progress, not decay. *Pleasantville,* which is one of the year's best and most original films, sneaks up on us. It begins by kidding those old black-and-white sitcoms like *Father Knows Best,* it continues by pretending to be a sitcom itself, and it ends as a social commentary of surprising power.

The movie opens in today's America, which we have been taught to think of as rude, decadent, and dangerous. A teenager named David languishes in front of the tube, watching a rerun of a 1950s sitcom named *Pleasantville,* in which everybody is always wholesome and happy. Meanwhile, his mother squabbles with her ex-husband and his sister Jennifer prepares for a hot date.

Having heard a whisper or two about the plot, we know that the brother and sister will be magically transported into that 1950s sitcom world. And we're expecting maybe something like *The Brady Bunch Movie,* in reverse. We are correct: While David and Jennifer are fighting over the remote control, there's a knock at the door, and a friendly TV repairman (Don Knotts) offers them a device "with more oomphs." They click it, and they're both in Pleasantville.

The movie has been written and directed by Gary Ross, who wrote *Big,* the 1988 movie where Tom Hanks was a kid trapped in an adult body. Here the characters are trapped in a whole world. He evokes the black-and-white 1950s sitcom world of picket fences and bobby sox, where everybody is white and middle class, has a job, sleeps in twin beds, never uses the toilet, and follows the same cheerful script.

Luckily, this is a world that David (Tobey Maguire) knows well; he's a TV trivia expert. It's a mystery to his sister Jennifer (Reese Witherspoon), so he briefs her: Their names are now Bud and Mary Sue, and their parents are Betty and George Parker (Joan Allen and William H. Macy). "We're, like, stuck in Nerdville!" Jennifer complains.

They are. Geography lessons at the local high school are limited to subjects like "Main Street" and "Elm Street" because the world literally ends at the city limits. Space twists back upon itself in Pleasantville, and "the end of Main Street is just the beginning again." Life always goes according to plan, and during basketball practice every shot goes in. (But things change. After one player experiences sex, he is capable of actually missing a shot; a dead silence falls as it rolls away. "Stand back, boys!" warns the coach. "Don't touch it!")

Pleasantville has fun during these middle sequences, as "Bud and Mary Sue" hang out at the malt shop run by Mr. Johnson (Jeff Daniels) and park on Lover's Lane (just to hold hands). Then sparks from the emerging future begin to land here and there in the blandness. Mary Sue shares information about masturbation with her mother, who of course has never dreamed of such a pastime (as a perfect housewife, she has never done anything just for herself). As her mother relaxes in her bath, a tree outside their house breaks into flames—in full color!

Ross and his cinematographer, John Lindley, work with special effects to show a black-and-white world in which some things and a few people begin switching to color. Is there a system? "Why aren't I in color?" Mary Sue asks Bud. "I dunno," he says. "Maybe it's not just the sex." It isn't. It's the change.

The kids at school are the first to start appearing in colors. They're curious and ready to change. They pepper Bud with questions. "What's outside of Pleasantville?" they ask. "There are places," he says, "where the roads don't go in a circle. They just keep going." Dave Brubeck's "Take Five" subtly appears on the sound track.

Bud shows Mr. Johnson a book of color art reproductions, and the soda jerk is thunderstruck by the beauty of Turner and van Gogh. He starts painting. Soon he and Betty Parker have discovered they're kindred spirits. (After Betty turns up in color, she's afraid to show herself, and in a scene of surprising tenderness her son helps her put on gray makeup.) George Parker, meanwhile, waits disconsolately at home for his routine to continue, and the chairman of the chamber of commerce (J. T. Walsh, in his last performance) notes ominously, "Something is happening in our town."

Yes, something, in a town where nothing ever did. The film observes that sometimes pleasant people are pleasant simply because they have never, ever been challenged. That it's scary and dangerous to learn new ways. The movie is like the defeat of the body snatchers: The people in color are like former pod people now freed to move on into the future. We observe that nothing creates fascists like the threat of freedom.

Pleasantville is the kind of parable that encourages us to reevaluate the good old days, and take a fresh look at the new world we so easily dismiss as decadent. Yes, we have more problems. But also more solutions, more opportunities, and more freedom. I grew up in the 1950s. It was a lot more like the world of *Pleasantville* than you might imagine. Yes, my house had a picket fence, and dinner was always on the table at a quarter to six, but things were wrong that I didn't even know the words for. There is a scene in this movie where it rains for the first time. Of course it never rained in 1950s sitcoms. Pleasantville's people in color go outside and just stand in it. ☞

* * *

Note: *Pleasantville* contains the last major role by the much-admired character actor J. T. Walsh. He plays the head of the 1950s sitcom chamber of commerce, a man much threatened by change, who warns, "There is something happening in our town"—a town, we know, where nothing has ever happened.

Walsh, who played roles in nearly sixty movies in a busy acting career that began only in 1983, was also seen recently as an internal affairs investigator in *The Negotiator* and a murdering truck driver in *Breakdown.* He died unexpectedly on February 27, 1998, of a heart attack, at age fifty-three.

"He was so hard on himself," remembers Gary Ross, who directed him in *Pleasantville.*

"I met J. T. at seven in the morning and he was having a big whipped cream cheese, smoking a cigarette while he was eating. He smoked all the time. Tough on himself. And he was so hard on himself as an actor.

"As a director, you try to sort of find what it is they need, a little bit of reassurance, and with J. T. it was—boy, how do I get him to forgive himself and relax a little bit here? He was so brilliant, and I would go, 'This is great, this is great.' But he never believed it."

Walsh came late to acting, Ross said. "He was an encyclopedia salesman. He was so good right from the start. Remember him in *Good Morning, Vietnam*?"

He was also in *Sling Blade, Nixon* (as John Erlichman), *Contact, Red Rock West, Backdraft, Hoffa* (as union leader Frank Fitzsimmons), and many TV programs (he had a continuing role on *L.A. Law* in 1986).

In *Pleasantville,* he leads the forces of the status quo against the threat of change. "J. T. had the best way of describing the movie," Ross remembered. "He said the kids from the future (who stir up the 1950s sitcom universe) are like the sand that gets in the oyster. It was such a perfect metaphor—the irritation that produces something beautiful."

As for Walsh's death so soon after filming was completed: "It's just an insane loss."

Polish Wedding ★ ★

PG-13, 101 m., 1998

Lena Olin (Jadzia Pzoniak), Gabriel Byrne (Bolek Pzoniak), Claire Danes (Hala Pzoniak), Adam Trese (Russell Schuster), Mili Avital (Sofie Pzoniak), Daniel LaPaine (Ziggy Pzoniak), Rade Serbedzija (Roman Kroll). Directed by Theresa Connelly and produced by Tom Rosenberg, Julia Chasman, and Geoff Stier. Screenplay by Connelly.

A movie can get away with anything if it can convince you it believes in itself. Theresa Connelly's *Polish Wedding* doesn't succeed. Too many scenes float above reality, going for cuteness and colorful dialogue and zany quirks, until we begin to question the very possibility that these wonderful, full-hearted characters could actually exist in a suburb of Detroit—or anywhere.

The movie tells the story of a Polish-American family awash with secret romance, buried passion, and fierce pride. Jadzia Pzoniak (Lena Olin), the mother, is a cleaning woman. Bolek (Gabriel Byrne), the father, works nights as a baker. The family lives in one of those houses you see only in the movies—where everyone's always looking out the window and lots of things happen in the yard. There are four sons and a daughter, and the boys all seem to sleep in one bedroom, which is strictly speaking not impossible—but a thrifty Polish-American family that has had two working parents for more than twenty years is more likely, I think, to be living in a larger house by now, instead of one that seems artificially cramped for movie purposes.

Jadzia and Bolek are not happily married. Jadzia says she married her husband for a good reason, but just at the moment she can't remember what it was. She dresses in some kind of women's auxiliary outfit once a week and goes out to her "meeting," which consists of a liaison with her lover, Roman (Rade Serbedzija). He's her boss at work. You might therefore wonder why she's still a cleaning lady, instead of being promoted to receptionist or something, but there's a scene where he enters the restroom she's cleaning and she hurls him to the floor and pounces on him for some inappropriate behavior in the workplace; maybe he'd miss that.

Jadzia's daughter, Hala (Claire Danes), a teenager young enough to be cast as the virgin in the church procession, is sneaking out nights, too, to see a young cop named Russell (Adam Trese). She gets pregnant and tells her dad, "My clock stopped." What clock? "Every woman has that kind of clock that she tells her time by." That leads to the double climax, in which the serenity of the procession is much tested, and the entire Pzoniak family marches on Russell's house for a singularly unconvincing confrontation.

Polish Wedding is the kind of movie that cries out to be set in a country I know little or nothing about. Maybe I would believe this colorful behavior in Albania, or in one of those Italian comedies where Sophia Loren knew everybody in town, biblically and otherwise.

In a Detroit suburb, I don't imagine carefree people gambol in the fields and gather around the breakfast table for family conversations apparently inspired by sitcom dialogue. Oh, I believe all the things happen in Detroit that happen in this movie; I simply don't believe people rant and rave and posture and emote so wildly while they're happening. A lot of the time I'll bet they're monosyllabic, and even during their emotional peaks still spend a lot of time watching TV.

Lena Olin is an actress who could have gotten away with this role, in another movie in another country. She brings it great life and conviction, but since the movie never connects with the world around it she seems, alas, more crazy than colorful. Gabriel Byrne's character is written as an enigma and he plays it as if it's certainly an enigma to him. Claire Danes seems too old for some scenes and too young for others; her character is a utility infielder, playing all positions and trying to field whatever the screenplay hits at her.

The movie's mixture of sex, religion, and family craziness reminded me of *Household Saints,* the Nancy Savocca film in which Lili Taylor's grandmother believes in saints, her parents believe in the American dream, and Lily, by seriously desiring to become a saint, does what would make her grandmother happy and her parents miserable. All the generational values are squished together in *Polish Wedding.* We're not looking at behavior, but at a lot of dubious anecdotes.

Ponette ★ ★ ★ ½

NO MPAA RATING, 92 m., 1997

Victoire Thivisol (Ponette), Matiaz Bureau (Ponette's Cousin), Delphine Schiltz (Ponette's Cousin), Marie Trintignant (The Mother), Xavier Beauvois (The Father), Claire Nebout (The Aunt), Aurelie Verillon (Aurelie), Leopoldine Serre (Ada). Directed by Jacques Doillon and produced by Alain Sarde. Screenplay by Doillon.

Ponette enters the mystery of a little girl's mind at the age of four, when she has all of her intelligence but little experience and information. Ponette has been in a car crash. Her arm was broken. "Mommy may die," her father tells her. How does she deal with that information? What does death mean to a four-year-old? How can it be dealt with?

The most extraordinary thing about *Ponette* is the way it faces these questions while staying resolutely within the focus of the child's mind. It follows the little girl out of the hospital and to her aunt's house, where with two cousins about her own age she tries to puzzle out what is happening to her.

She doesn't get a lot of help from her father. "Mommy's dead," he tells her after a few days. "She was all broken. They couldn't fix her." He is preoccupied with his own grief. He makes her promise not to die. And he talks about how stupid his wife was to get in the car crash. "She's not stupid!" Ponette cries. "It wasn't her fault!"

Played by Victoire Thivisol, she is a small, blond, round-faced little girl, very solemn much of the time, and the film follows her with an intensity that requires her to give a real performance—not as a "child actor," but as a real actor who has to negotiate tricky dialogue and situations. She does. "In the matter of child acting," writes Stanley Kauffmann, "this is the most extraordinary picture I know." (Thivisol's performance won the Best Actress Award at the 1996 Venice Film Festival.)

In preparing the dialogue for Ponette and her young friends, Jacques Doillon, the writer-director, interviewed hundreds of young children, I understand. What he captures is the logical way that kids proceed from what little they know to what, therefore, must be the case. As Ponette copes with the fact that her mother is in a coffin and will soon be under the ground, her little friend explains about crucifixes and pillows under the head and what happens to bodies after a long time, and adds helpfully: "I like living above ground. I really hate skulls."

Whether Ponette understands the finality of death in an adult way is a good question. Certainly she misses her mother, and is not consoled by her aunt's stories about Jesus and resurrection. If Jesus gets to rise from the dead, she asks not unreasonably, why can't her mother? And if it's true, as she's told, that the dead sometimes like to have little gifts or keepsakes left in their coffin to remember things by, then why not offer her mother even larger gifts? There is a scene where Ponette stands fiercely under the empty sky, holding up the offerings she has selected, hoping her mother will come down for them.

The film is not entirely about the aftermath of death. Its real subject, actually, is the development of intelligence in childhood. How do kids interact with their environment and learn from their friends, and fashion theories and test them out? There is a sequence where the children play a game involving an empty dumpster. Is it dangerous? Perhaps. Do they benefit from the game? Yes. Because city streets are no longer considered safe for children, they're kept inside more than earlier generations. Street games are no longer played. In *Ponette* we see how through trial and error these children learn from the lessons and adventures of the neighborhood.

The theology in *Ponette* is direct and challenging. Given the consolations of the Christian faith, Ponette responds with reasonable questions a child might ask and a philosopher might not be able to answer. She also has to deal with the casual cruelties of childhood, as when a friend tells her: "You killed your mother." Applying logic, Ponette determines that if her mother died and went to heaven, then the best way to visit her would be to die and go to the same place. "I want you to make me die," she tells a friend.

The movie's one wrong step is a closing sequence reuniting Ponette with her mother. Is this a fantasy or a miracle? A miracle, I fear—and Ponette deserves better. In the real world, when mothers die they don't come back. Ponette has just about dealt with that when the movie sneaks in a happy ending. She'll never learn that way.

But the ending is an imperfection in a film of great imagination and close observation. I can't even begin to imagine how Doillon obtained these performances from Thivisol and her friends (Matiaz Bureau and Delphine Schiltz). Watching this film is like eavesdropping on bright children and observing the process by which their intelligence builds their personalities, their beliefs, their strategies, and their minds.

The Portrait of a Lady ★ ★ ★

PG-13, 144 m., 1997

Nicole Kidman (Isabel Archer), John Malkovich (Gilbert Osmond), Barbara Hershey (Madame Serena Merle), Mary-Louise Parker (Henrietta Stackpole), Martin Donovan (Ralph Touchett), Shelley Winters (Mrs. Touchett), John Gielgud (Mr. Touchett), Richard E. Grant (Lord Warburton), Shelley Duvall (Countess Gemini), Valentina Cervi (Pansy), Christian Bale (Edward Rosier), Viggo Mortensen (Caspar Goodwood). Directed by Jane Campion and produced by Monty Montgomery and Steve Golin. Screenplay by Laura Jones, based on the novel by Henry James.

For Henry James, who spent most of his life there, Europe was a snake pit for naive Americans, who were prey to the intrigues of more devious races. His Yankees disembark fresh-scrubbed from the land of Lincoln, only to tumble into the coils of greed. Isabel Archer, the heroine of *The Portrait of a Lady*, is one of his most loved and tragic characters; everything she does is inspired by idealism, and leads to heartbreak and ruin.

In Jane Campion's film of the James novel, we meet Isabel (Nicole Kidman) at what could have been the defining moment of her life. Orphaned in America, she visits rich English relatives and receives a proposal of marriage from Lord Warburton (Richard E. Grant). He is rich and titled, and even lives in a house with a moat. She rejects his proposal, although reassuring him that she does love moats.

Why does she turn down Warburton? Because he is too right, too safe and sure, and she seeks a spark of inspiration in her man. One of those astounded by her decision is her cousin Ralph (Martin Donovan), who also loves Isabel, but keeps that a secret because he is dying of consumption. "I shall have the pleasure," he muses, "of seeing what a young lady does who rejects Lord Warburton." It will be no pleasure.

Ralph lives with his parents, the rich Touchetts (John Gielgud and Shelley Winters). Knowing Isabel has rejected Warburton, aware of her poverty, he fears her spirit will be crushed by the hard realities of Europe. He wants her to have a chance to bloom. As his father lays dying, Ralph asks him to leave a large portion of his inheritance to the young woman. Ralph explains, "I call people rich when they are able to meet the requirements of their imagination."

Isabel, surprised by the bequest and never suspecting its reason, embarks on the grand tour. In Rome she swims into the net of Madame Merle (Barbara Hershey), an independent woman who knows everyone and is frank about her purpose: "I don't pretend to know what people are meant for. I only know what I can do with them."

Merle, knowing what she can do with Isabel, delivers her to the indolent expatriate artist Gilbert Osmond (John Malkovich). Osmond is a fake—a lazy fraud with more manner than means. But Isabel, who could see Lord Warburton's flaws, cannot see Gilbert's, and soon she is married. He has a daughter named Pansy; he explains vaguely that his first wife is deceased. Isabel comes to love Pansy, and soon she loves her a great deal more than Osmond.

The story leaps forward three years, to a time when Isabel and Gilbert coexist in a hateful truce. Her cousin Ralph, visiting Rome, sees through their marriage: "Weren't you meant for something better than to keep guard over the sensibilities of a sterile dilettante?" Then the noose tightens, as Isabel discovers the exact nature of her situation.

I will not reveal more. Yet I assume that most of the people going to see this movie will have read the book, and, frankly, you can't easily understand this film if you haven't. Too much is left out, glossed over, or implied.

Why, for example, does Isabel marry Osmond? In the novel there is no mystery. He is an "artist"—able to pose, at least during their courtship, as a man who lives on a higher plane. In Campion's film, Osmond is never allowed the slightest plausibility. Malkovich plays him as a snaky, sinister poseur, tobacco smoke coiling past his hooded eyes. The crucial distinction is: In the novel, Isabel marries him because she is an idealist, but in the movie because she is a masochist.

This difference is fatal to the development of the story. To Ralph, she must seem more stupid than brave. Madame Merle's manipulation becomes cynical, not simply opportunist. Even Osmond seems more a villain here (where he is not deceived by his intentions) than in the novel (where he half-believes his lies).

The Portrait of a Lady ends with a series of hammer blows. Anyone who believes Henry James is bloodless has never really read him. Beneath his meticulous prose are lusts and fears that his characters struggle to contain within the strictures of proper society. His conclusion of this novel is one of incredible power; Isabel is a good woman who has tried to do right, and who has done wrong, wrong, wrong—wrong to Ralph's faith, wrong to Warburton's love, wrong to herself.

In the movie, it just doesn't play that way. Isabel turns too hard in the years the film leaps over. By the time of the final revelations, she is no longer as deserving of Ralph's pity as she should be. By tilting the story at this angle, Campion and her writer, Laura Jones, are said to have brought a "feminist sensibility" to the film. I think the James version was more truly feminist and that this version sees Isabel more as a victim and less as a heroine gone astray.

Yet I think if you care for James, you must see it. It is not an adaptation but an interpretation. It gives us Isabel from a new angle. And it is well acted. Kidman has the bearing and quality of the intelligent young American. Barbara Hershey is magnificent as Madame Merle (who has her own heartbreak, and has worked with the means at her disposal). Martin Donovan is touching as Ralph, whose own love is bravely concealed. Only Malkovich seems wrong; we need an Osmond who seems worthier at first.

The value of Henry James is that he teaches us to consider our motives. Today we rush heedless into life. We believe in "love at first sight." We get our values from TV and film, where the plot exists only to hurry the characters into sex. All modern emotions can be expressed in a sound bite. James's people think before they commit. When they choose wrong, they eventually learn how, and why. Today's Isabel Archer would dump Osmond, sue for her money back, and head for a spa to recuperate. I imagine James's Isabel captured forever in the loveless tomb of her own choosing.

Post Coitum, Animal Triste ★ ★ ★

NO MPAA RATING, 95 m., 1998

Brigitte Rouan (Diane), Boris Terral (Emilio), Patrick Chesnais (Philippe), Nils Tavernier (Francois), Jean-Louis Richard (Weyman-Lebeau). Directed by Brigitte Rouan and produced by Humbert Balsan. Screenplay by Santiago Amigorena, Jean-Louis Richard, Rouan, and Guy Zylberstein.

The first shot is of a cat writhing in lust. The second shot is of a woman writhing in emotional agony. Both feel the same animal need, according to Brigitte Rouan, who directed, stars in, and cowrote the astonishing psychodrama *Post Coitum, Animal Triste,* which is about a woman's transition from wild sexual excitement to love to fury at rejection.

Rouan plays Diane, a Parisian book editor in her forties, who is trying to guide a young author named Francois (Nils Tavernier) through the ordeal of his second novel. At his apartment, she meets Emilio (Boris Terral), Francois's roommate. Their eyes lock. They seem almost immediately to fall into a mutual sexual trance and are making love before they know each other. He is young, wild, reckless. She is a bourgeoisie intellectual with a husband and two children. "I'm a lifetime ahead of you," she complains. "Want to help me buy some socks?" he asks.

The first stage of their relationship is one of urgent risk taking, as they meet whenever and wherever they can. She races across streets, crying out his name. Kissing, they fall onto the hood of a car in the middle of traffic, oblivious. Once they become so reckless that they are requested to leave a restaurant. Diane is amazed to feel so strongly and deeply; at one point, she is literally seen floating on air. The bewitched Emilio seems in a tumescent daze.

Her husband, Philippe (Patrick Chesnais), of course, soon suspects an affair. He is a lawyer, not stupid, whose current client plunged a carving fork into the jugular of her husband; the older woman had put up with years of infidelity and abuse, but could not deal with her husband's threat to leave her. As Philippe quizzes his client about her crime, he senses a certain serenity in her manner; by murdering her husband, she has at last ended her lifetime of suffering. The film teases us with the possibility that Philippe may take the hint.

Then, gradually, in steps as small as a few words murmured to his grandfather, Emilio begins to lose his passion. He is a "hydraulic engineer in the Third World," on leave after mending dikes in Bangladesh, and now he informs Diane he is going to Africa for six months. She interprets this, correctly, as an attempt to get away, and has a breakdown that escalates for most of the rest of the movie.

It is not a pretty sight, seeing a dignified and attractive woman of a certain age as she goes completely to pieces. "I hurt all over and you feel nothing," she tells Emilio. He might have been willing to extend their relationship in a reasonable way, but is frightened by her frenzy. She drinks to oblivion. She starts a fire in her office. She loses her job. She lives on the sofa. She forgets to eat. She cries for hours. Her family moves out. She doesn't kill herself only because, perhaps, she masochistically enjoys her agony.

This breakdown went on too long, I thought; a little forlorn hysteria goes a long way. But by the end of the film, we have come to admire Rouan's courage as a performer and a filmmaker in following Diane's mania as far as it will go. And I liked the way the central drama is surrounded by small, observant moments involving the husband, the children, and even the accused murderer (at one point, Philippe plays tapes of his wife's secret phone calls to his client—to get the benefit of her more direct experience with adultery).

The title translates loosely as "After sex, animal grief." Is it autobiographical? I don't know. My guess is, either these events are inspired by an affair that Rouan once had, or they are a memorandum to herself: Never have one.

The Postman ★ ½

R, 177 m., 1997

Kevin Costner (The Postman), Will Patton (Bethlehem), Larenz Tate (Ford Lincoln Mercury), Olivia Williams (Abby), James Russo (Idaho), Tom Petty (Mayor). Directed by Kevin Costner and produced by Costner and Steve Tisch. Screenplay by Erich Roth and Brian Helgeland.

There are those who will no doubt call *The Postman* the worst film of the year, but it's too good-hearted for that. It's goofy, yes, and pretentious, and Kevin Costner puts himself in situations that get snickers. And it's way too long. But parables like this require their makers to burn their bridges and leave common sense behind: Either they work (as *Forrest Gump* did), in which case everyone involved is a genius, or they don't—in which case you shouldn't blame them for trying.

In choosing *The Postman* as his new project, however, Kevin Costner should perhaps have reflected that audiences were getting to be overfamiliar with him as the eccentric loner in the wilderness, coming across an isolated community and then joining their war against evil marauders. He told that story magnificently in *Dances With Wolves* (1990) and then did another version in the futuristic fantasy *Waterworld* (1995).

Now he sort of combines them, in a film that takes place in the post-Apocalyptic future like *Waterworld*, but looks and feels like it takes place in a Western.

The movie, based on an award-winning science-fiction novel by David Brin, takes place in 2013. The dust clouds have settled after nuclear war, and scattered communities pick up the reins of civilization. There is no central government. Costner is a lone figure in the wilderness, friendly only with his mule, named Bill. They support themselves by doing Shakespeare for bands of settlers. Bill can hold a sword in his mouth, and in *Macbeth* he plays Birnam Wood. His master recites lines like, "Life is a tale told by a moron," not the sort of mistake he'd be likely to make, especially with a woman helpfully prompting him by whispering, "Idiot! Idiot!" Or maybe she's a critic.

Costner is conscripted into a neofascist army run by General Bethlehem (Will Patton). He escapes, stumbles over an abandoned U.S. Mail van, and steals the uniform, cap, and letter bag of the skeleton inside. At the gates of a settlement called Pineview, he claims he's come to deliver the mail. Building on his fiction, he tells the residents of a restored U.S. government in Minneapolis. The sheriff spots him for a fraud, but the people want to believe, and the next morning, he finds letters pushed under his door. Walking outside, he discovers that all the people of the town have gathered in hushed silence in a semicircle around his lodging, to await his awakening and appearance—the sort of thing townspeople do in movies, but never in real life, where some helpful townsman invariably suggests, "Let's just wake the sonuvabitch up."

In a movie that proceeds with glacial deliberation, the Postman becomes a symbol for the survivors in their struggling communities. "You give out hope like it was candy in your pocket," a young woman tells him. It's the sort of line an actor-director ought to be wary of applying to his own character, but Costner frankly sees the Postman as a messiah, and there is a shot late in the film where he zooms high above a river gorge in a cable car that serves absolutely no purpose except to allow him to pose as the masthead on the ship of state.

That young woman (Olivia Williams), by the way, wants the Postman's semen. Her husband is infertile after the "bad mumps," and the couple desires a child. The Postman eventually obliges, and she makes love with him in a scene reminiscent of those good Victorian wives who closed their eyes and thought of the empire. Her husband is murdered, and she's kidnapped by General Bethlehem, who has seen *Braveheart* and knows about the feudal system where the lord gets first dibbies on the wedding nights of his vassals. She and the Postman eventually escape into the wilderness and spend the winter together while she comes full term. This is some frontier woman; in the spring, she burns down their cottage so they'll be forced to move on, and "we can find someplace nice for the baby."

In his absence, the Postman's legendary status has been magnified by young Ford Lincoln Mercury (Larenz Tate), who has named himself after an auto dealership and in the absence of the Postman has organized a postal service in exile. It is clear that the Postman and Bethlehem will sooner or later have to face each other in battle. When they do, the general produces a hostage he has captured—Ford L. Mercury—and the Postman pales and pauses at the prospect of F. L. Mercury's death, even though the Postman's army consists mostly of hundreds of women and children he is cheerfully contemplating leading to their slaughter.

The movie has a lot of unwise shots resulting in bad laughs, none more ill-advised than one where the Postman, galloping down a country lane, passes a gate where a tow-headed little tyke holds on to a letter. Some sixth sense causes the Postman to look back, see the kid, turn around, then gallop back to him, snatching up the letter at full tilt. This touching scene, shot with a zoom lens in slow motion to make it even more fatuous than it needed to be, is later immortalized in a bronze statue, unveiled at the end of the movie. As a civic figure makes a speech in front of the statue, which is still covered by a tarpaulin, a member of the audience whispered, "They've bronzed the Postman!" Dear reader, that member was me, and I guess I shouldn't have been surprised that I was right.

Practical Magic ★ ★

PG-13, 105 m., 1998

Sandra Bullock (Sally Owens), Nicole Kidman (Gillian Owens), Aidan Quinn (Gary Hallett), Dianne Wiest (Aunt Jet), Stockard Channing (Aunt Frances), Goran Visnjic (Jimmy), Evan Rachel Wood (Kylie), Alexandra Artrip (Antonia). Directed by Griffin Dunne and produced by Denise Di Novi. Screenplay by Robin Swicord, Akiva Goldsman, and Adam Brooks, based on the novel by Alice Hoffman.

Practical Magic is too scary for children and too childish for adults. Who was it made for? On the one hand, you have cute witches making jokes about magic potions and herbal shampoos, and on the other hand you have a kidnapping by an abusive boyfriend who dies of an overdose—but not for long. Moldy evil spirits rise up out of other people's bodies, and teaspoons stir on their own.

The movie doesn't seem sure what tone to adopt, veering uncertainly from horror to laughs to romance. To cue us, it puts lots of songs on the sound track. A movie lacks confidence when it uses music to tell us how to feel; here the music intrudes, insists, explains, and tries to force segues between events that are not segueable. Example: Early in the film, an impending kiss is accompanied by "This Kiss," by Faith Hill.

The story involves a family that has had witches for 300 years. Because of an ancient curse, all of their husbands die. The chirp of a deathwatch beetle provides advance warning. So it is best for the womenfolk (and in the long run this family has nothing but womenfolk) to avoid heartbreak by not falling in love. Two sisters named Sally and Gillian (Sandra Bullock and Nicole Kidman) grow up with the curse, and Sally protects against it by casting a spell for a man she trusts will be impossible to find. He has to have one blue eye and one green eye, be able to flip pancakes in the air, and have other attributes that are not nearly as rare as Sally thinks.

Flash-forward. Sally marries. She is happy. She and her husband have two lovely daughters. One day she hears the deathwatch beetle beneath the floorboards. Desperate, she tears up one floorboard, then another. How does this work? Your husband lives if you squish the beetle in time? Soon she has torn up the entire floor—a job that would take union carpenters hours if not days, and is not necessary because anguish can actually be demonstrated by the manner in which you tear up floorboards, not by how many you are able to get through. The extra floorboards, like the extra songs, are overkill.

Later, Gillian sends Sally a psychic distress call, and Sally speeds to the rescue, finding Gillian shacked up in a motel with Jimmy (Goran Visnjic), a "Transylvanian cowboy" who beats her up. (She can't marry him and trigger the beetle scenario because she doesn't love him.) He kidnaps the two women, and eventually supplies the evil spirit that fuels the rest of the plot. Aidan Quinn plays Gary Hallett, a cop who comes to investigate the missing Transylvanian. "Is he cute?" asks Gillian about the cop. "Yeah," says Sally, "in a penal code sort of way." No prizes for guessing his eye color.

Comic relief is provided by the sisters' two maiden aunts, Jet (Dianne Wiest) and Frances (Stockard Channing). The whole movie would have been funnier if they, and not the younger women, had been involved with the Transylvanian cowboy and the cop, but that would have required wit and imagination beyond the compass of this material. Still pending at the outcome is whether pancake flipping somehow immunizes Gary from the knell of the deathwatch beetle.

Prefontaine ★ ★ ★

PG-13, 106 m., 1997

Jared Leto (Steve Prefontaine), R. Lee Ermey (Bill Bowerman), Ed O'Neill (Bill Dellinger), Breckin Meyer (Pat Tyson), Lindsay Crouse (Elfriede Prefontaine), Amy Locane (Nancy Alleman), Laurel Holloman (Elaine Finley), Brian McGovern (Mac Wilkins). Directed by Steve James and produced by Irby Smith, Jon Lutz, Mark Doonan, and Peter Gilbert. Screenplay by James and Eugene Corr.

Steve Prefontaine was one of the greatest runners produced in the United States, and one of the most abrasive. This film based on his life makes him seem fairly unlikable, and that's one of its best qualities: Here is a sports movie in the tradition of the best sportswriting, where athletes are portrayed warts and all. You do not have to be nice to win races, but you have to be good.

Prefontaine opens in the 1960s, with Steve (Jared Leto) as a kid whose short stature and "bad hand-eye coordination" make him the most hapless player on the football team. Determined to be good at something—to get even with those who dismissed him—he turns to track, and even though he's not built like a runner and one leg is shorter than the other, he uses sheer determination to win. Soon he's being scouted by the legendary Oregon coach Bill Bowerman (R. Lee Ermey), who manufactures track shoes in his garage, using his wife's waffle iron to mold the rubber treads. Bowerman goes on to cofound Nike, and Pre goes on to hold almost every American record at the longer distances.

Sports movies have traditionally tried to turn their heroes into demigods. Not *Prefontaine*, which sees Pre as a single-minded, self-centered, ruthless competitor. At one point, goofing around on the track with kids, he refuses to even pretend to let a nine-year-old beat him. He has to win even that race. When his girlfriend Nancy (Amy Locane) wonders if that's carrying things too far, he spits out: "All my life people have said to me, 'You're too small, Pre. You're not fast enough, Pre. Give up your foolish dreams, Steve!' They forgot something: I have to win. No fallback here, no great stride, no long legs—nothing!"

The movie follows Prefontaine to an NCAA championship he wins with twelve stitches in his foot (he runs an extra victory lap in his bloody shoe). It shows him arguing with Bowerman about distance (he wants the higher visibility of the mile); Bowerman correctly sees him at the longer distances, where stamina and guts count for more. He qualifies for the 1972 Olympics—and then the massacre of the Israeli athletes takes place the night before his big race. The race is eventually held, even though Pre tells his assistant coach (Ed O'Neill) he "can't run over the bodies of those dead athletes."

Does he win? You will have to see for yourself. What sets *Prefontaine* aside from most sports movies is that it's not about winning the big race. It's about the life of a runner. After he returns from Munich, Prefontaine supports himself by bartending and lives in a mobile home. Other nations support their athletes in style, but the rules of American amateur sports at that time essentially required a life spent in training and poverty. (Much is made of the shabby quarters supplied to U.S. athletes in Munich while 100 adult "officials" lived in splendor at a luxury hotel.)

After Munich, Bowerman retires to start his track shoe empire (Pre says the Nike trademark "looks like needless air resistance to me"). What Prefontaine eventually does is break the nerve of the American amateur athletic establishment by getting his teammates (including discus champion Mac Wilkins) to join him in an unsanctioned invitation for the Finnish national team to visit Oregon. Accused of betraying the U.S. national team, he tells a press conference, typically: "To hell with love of country; I'm looking out for me."

Prefontaine, which is smart, quirky, and involving, is the first fiction film by Steve James, who directed the great sports documentary *Hoop Dreams*. In a sense, this is a continuation of the same story, about how the sports establishment uses and then discards gifted young athletes with little regard for their personal welfare.

If the two young subjects of *Hoop Dreams* won a victory of sorts (they got college educations and were able to use basketball to better their prospects in life), Steve Prefontaine won one too. In the process he may have dismantled the idea of pure amateur athletics in this country, but the movie shows how much hypocrisy was masked by that ideal. By the end of the film we may not like Pre, but we understand and respect him. The movie shows an athlete for whom winning wasn't everything—but *having* to win was.

A Price Above Rubies ★★★

R, 116 m., 1998

Renee Zellweger (Sonia), Christopher Eccleston (Sender), Julianna Margulies (Rachel), Allen Payne (Ramon), Glenn Fitzgerald (Mendel), Kim Hunter (Rebbitzn), John Randolph (Rebbe), Phyllis Newman (Mrs. Gelbart). Directed by Boaz Yakin and produced by Lawrence Bender and John Penotti. Screenplay by Yakin.

A Price Above Rubies tells the story of a woman who burns for release from the strictures of a closed society. We learn much about her during the film, but not much about her society—a community of Orthodox Hasidic Jews, living in Brooklyn. Perhaps that's in the nature of commercial filmmaking; there is a larger audience for a story about the liberation of proud, stubborn Renee Zellweger (from *Jerry Maguire*) than there is for a story about why a woman's place is in the home.

During the film, however, questions about the message were not foremost in my mind. I was won over by Zellweger's ferociously strong performance, and by characters and scenes I hadn't seen before: the world, for example, of Manhattan diamond merchants, and the parallel world of secret (untaxed) jewel shops in Brooklyn apartments, and the life of a young Puerto Rican who is a talented jewelry designer. The film also adds a level of magic realism in the character of an old homeless woman who may be "as old as God himself."

Zellweger plays Sonia, the daughter of gemologists who steer her away from the family business and into marriage with a young scholar named Mendel (Glenn Fitzgerald), who prefers prayer and study to the company of his wife. (During sex, he turns off the light and thinks of Abraham and Isaac.) Sonia's unhappiness makes her an emotional time bomb, and it is Mendel's older brother Sender (Christopher Eccleston) who sets her off. First he tests her knowledge of jewelry. Then he offers her a job in his business. Then he has sex with her. It's rape, but she seems to accept it as the price of freedom.

A Price Above Rubies is the second film by writer-director Boaz Yakin, whose *Fresh* (1994) was able to see clearly inside a black community; here, although he is Jewish, he is not able to bring the Hasidim into the same focus. All I learned for sure about them is that the men wear beards and black hats and suits, and govern every detail of daily life according to the teachings of rabbis and scholars. The women obey their fathers and husbands, and the group as a whole shuns the customs of the greater world and lives within walls of rules and traditions. There is not a lot of room for compromise or accommodation in their teachings, which is a point of tension in modern Israel between Orthodox and other Jews.

Sonia does not find this a world she can live in. She is rebellious when her husband insists their newborn son be named after the rabbi rather than after Sonia's beloved brother, who drowned when he was young. She is opposed to the boy's circumcision ("He's like a sacrifice!")—but, to be sure, her husband also faints at the sight of blood. She is as resentful at Mendel's long hours at study and prayer as another wife might be at a husband who spent all of his time in a bar or at the track. And there is that unquenched passion burning inside of her. (In equating her sexual feelings with heat, Yakin unwittingly mirrors the convention in porno films, where women complain of feeling "hot . . . so hot" and sex works like air-conditioning.)

After her brother-in-law sets her up in the jewelry business, she glories in her freedom. She wheels and deals with the jewelry merchants of the city, and runs his illicit store from a garden apartment. On a park bench one day, she sees a black woman with beautiful earrings, and this sends her on a search for their maker, Ramon (Allen Payne), a Puerto Rican who sells schlock in Manhattan to make money, and then does his own work for love.

This man is unlike any Sonia has ever met, but at first her love is confined to his jewelry. She encourages him, commissions him, reassures him that his work is special. But then

Sender discovers their connection and tells Sonia's husband and family, and Sonia is locked out of her house, cut off from her child, and divorced.

It is hard to see why Sender would take that risk, considering what a powerful weapon Sonia has: She could accuse him of rape. But perhaps he knows she wouldn't be believed. His values are hardly those of his prayerful brother's; he believes we sin in order to gain God's forgiveness (or perhaps even his attention), and that "the quality of our sins sets us apart."

I was always completely absorbed in Sonia's quest. Zellweger avoids all the cute mannerisms that made her so lovable in *Jerry Maguire*, and plays this young woman as quiet, inward, even a little stooped. She knows she must find a different kind of life for herself, and does.

The film has been protested by some Hasidic Jews, who especially disliked the circumcision scene. Yakin did little for his defense by claiming it was "comedic"—which it is not remotely. Like the Amish of *Kingpin* and the Catholics of the early scenes in *Household Saints*, these Jews come across as exotic outsiders and holdouts in the great secularized American melting pot. What may offend them as much as anything is that their community is reduced to a backdrop and props for Sonia's story. It would be an interesting challenge for a filmmaker to tell a story from inside such a community. *Witness* came close to suggesting the values of the Amish, I think, but then how would I really know?

Primary Colors ★ ★ ★ ★

R, 135 m., 1998

John Travolta (Governor Jack Stanton), Emma Thompson (Susan Stanton), Billy Bob Thornton (Richard Jemmons), Kathy Bates (Libby Holden), Adrian Lester (Henry Burton), Maura Tierney (Daisy), Larry Hagman (Governor Fred Picker), Diane Ladd (Mamma Stanton). Directed and produced by Mike Nichols. Screenplay by Elaine May, based on the novel by "Anonymous."

Here's the surprising thing: *Primary Colors* would seem just about as good, as tough, and as smart if there had never been a president named Bill Clinton. Of course the movie resonates with its parallels to the lives of Bill and Hillary Clinton, but it's a lot more than a disguised exposé. It's a superb film—funny, insightful, and very wise about the realities of political life.

The director, Mike Nichols, and the writer, his longtime collaborator Elaine May, have put an astonishing amount of information on the screen, yes, but that wasn't the hard part. Their real accomplishment is to blend so many stories and details into an observant picture that holds together. We see that Jack Stanton, the presidential candidate in the film, is a flawed charmer with a weakness for bimbos, but we also see what makes him attractive even to those who know the worst: He listens and cares, and knows how to be an effective politician.

John Travolta and Emma Thompson play Stanton and his wife, Susan, as a couple who, we feel, have spent many long hours and nights in mind-to-mind combat. Her true feelings about his infidelity remain unexpressed, but she is loyal to a larger idea of the man, and not as hurt that he fools around as that she's lied to about it. Much will be written about how much Travolta and Thompson do or do not resemble the Clintons, but their wisest choice as actors is to preserve their mystery.

By *not* going behind their bedroom door, by not eavesdropping on their private moments, the movie avoids having to explain what perhaps can never be understood: why a man is driven to self-destructive behavior, and how his wife might somehow remain at his side anyway. The movie wisely stays a certain distance from the Stantons. There are no important scenes in which they are alone together in a room.

Instead, *Primary Colors* centers its point of view in a character named Henry Burton (Adrian Lester), grandson of a civil rights leader, who doesn't join the campaign so much as get sucked into its wake. Before he has even agreed to join Stanton's team, he finds himself on a chartered plane to New Hampshire with the candidate asleep on his shoulder. Earlier, he saw Stanton at work. At an illiteracy class, a black man (Mykelti Williamson in a powerful cameo) tells of the pain of not being able to read. Stanton empathizes with him, telling the story of his Uncle Charlie, who was a Medal of Honor winner but passed up college scholarships because he was ashamed to admit his illiteracy, and instead "just laid down on his couch and smoked his Luckies."

Of course, the Uncle Charlie story may not be entirely true, and later that day Henry sees Stanton emerging from a hotel bedroom with the flustered woman who runs the illiteracy program, but for Henry and the other campaign workers it eventually comes down to this: All the candidates are flawed in one way or another, but some have good ideas, and of those only a few might be able to win.

John Travolta dominates the movie, in part, by his absence. Nichols and May must have decided it would be a mistake to put him into every scene: A man like Jack Stanton is important because of the way people talk, speculate, and obsess about him in his absence.

Through Henry, we meet the campaign's inner circle. Richard Jemmons (Billy Bob Thornton), obviously based on Clinton's strategist James Carville, is a cynical realist who provides running commentary on the stages of the campaign. Libby Holden (Kathy Bates), the "dust-buster," is a longtime Stanton confidant and recent mental patient who comes out of retirement, foul-mouthed and lusty, to dig up the dirt before the other side can. And Daisy (Maura Tierney), quiet and observant, is a scheduler who eventually finds herself in Henry's bed, not so much out of choice as default. Of the crowd, Bates is the dynamo, playing a hard-living lesbian with a secret center of idealism; it's an Oscar-caliber performance.

The movie ticks off episodes based on real life. There's a woman from the candidate's home state who claims to have had an affair with him and to have tapes to prove it. And a dramatic appearance on national TV, where Susan Stanton holds her husband's hand and defends him (her hand snaps away from his as the show goes off the air). It intercuts these with fiction, created in the novel by "Anonymous," now revealed as ex-*Newsweek* writer Joe Klein. There's the pregnancy of the teenage daughter of Stanton's favorite barbecue chef. And the populist Florida governor (Larry Hagman), who looks good against Stanton until his past returns to haunt him.

Much of the movie's ethical content revolves not around sex, but around how a primary campaign should handle damaging information it turns up about its opponent. Libby argues that they shouldn't use it. Jack says that if they don't, the other side will. Better to get it out before it does more harm.

In the way *Primary Colors* handles this issue, it shows more insight and maturity than all but a handful of recent mainstream movies: This is a grown-up film about real issues in the real world. Among its pleasures is the way it lets us examine the full frame, and observe how characters at the side or in the background react; whole characters are developed in asides.

It is also very funny at times, as when Stanton, Jemmons, and others get in a "mommathon," praising their mothers into the night. Or when Susan snatches Jack's ever-present chicken drumstick out of his hand. Or when the candidate, his wife, and his aides search a roadside for a cell phone thrown from a car in anger. The movie is endlessly inventive and involving: You get swept up in the political and personal suspense, and begin to understand why people are engulfed in political campaigns.

Will *Primary Colors* hurt or help the Clinton presidency? To some degree, neither; it's a treatment of matters the electorate has already made up its mind about. The film has certainly not in any sense "softened" its portrayal of its Clintonesque hero—those rumors are exposed by its almost brutal candor. But in a strange way *Primary Colors* may actually work to help Clinton. While a lesser film would have felt compelled to supply an "answer," this one knows that the fascination is in the complexity, in the strong and weak qualities at war with one another. The secret of what makes Jack Stanton tick is as unanswerable as the meaning of Citizen Kane's "Rosebud." And the resemblance doesn't stop there.

The Prince of Egypt ★ ★ ★ ½

PG, 99 m., 1998

With the voices of: Val Kilmer (Moses), Sandra Bullock (Miriam), Ralph Fiennes (Rameses), Danny Glover (Jethro), Jeff Goldblum (Aaron), Steve Martin (Hotep), Helen Mirren (Queen), Michelle Pfeiffer (Tzipporah), Patrick Stewart (Seti). Directed by Brenda Chapman, Steve

Hickner, and Simon Wells and produced by Penney Finkelman Cox and Sandra Rabins. Screenplay by Philip LaZebnik.

Not long ago I saw the first of the great screen epics about Moses and his people, the 1923 silent version of Cecil B. DeMille's *The Ten Commandments.* Everyone must be familiar with DeMille's 1956 sound version, which plays regularly on television. Now here is *The Prince of Egypt,* an animated version based on the same legends. What it proves above all is that animation frees the imagination from the shackles of gravity and reality, and allows a story to soar as it will. If DeMille had seen this film, he would have gone back to the drawing board.

The story of Exodus has its parallels in many religions, always with the same result: God chooses one of his peoples over the others. We like these stories because in the one we subscribe to, we are the chosen people. I have always rather thought God could have spared Man a lot of trouble by casting his net more widely, emphasizing universality rather than tribalism, but there you have it. Moses gives Ramses his chance (free our people and accept our god) and Ramses blows it, with dire results for the Egyptian side.

Prince of Egypt is one of the best-looking animated films ever made. It employs computer-generated animation as an aid to traditional techniques, rather than as a substitute for them, and we sense the touch of human artists in the vision behind the Egyptian monuments, the lonely desert vistas, the thrill of the chariot race, the personalities of the characters. This is a film that shows animation growing up and embracing more complex themes instead of chaining itself in the category of children's entertainment.

That's established dramatically in the wonderful prologue scenes, which show the kingdom and Hebrew slaves building pyramids under the whips of the pharaoh's taskmasters. The "sets" here are inspired by some of the great movie sets of the past, including those in DeMille's original film and Griffith's *Intolerance.* A vast sphinx gazes out over the desert, and slaves bend to the weight of mighty blocks of stone. In crowd scenes, both here and when the Hebrews pass through the Red Sea, the movie uses new computer techniques to give the illusion that each of the countless tiny figures is moving separately; that makes the "extras" uncannily convincing.

The film follows Moses (voice by Val Kilmer) from the day when he is plucked from the Nile by the queen (Helen Mirren) to the day when he returns from the mountain with the Ten Commandments. What it emphasizes more than earlier versions is how completely the orphan child is taken into the family of the pharaoh (Patrick Stewart); he is a well-loved adopted son who becomes the playmate and best friend of Ramses (Ralph Fiennes), the pharaoh's son. As boys, they get in trouble together (one drag race in chariots, which speed excitingly down collapsing scaffolds, results in the destruction of a temple). And when Ramses is named regent, his first act is to name Moses as royal chief architect.

But something in Moses knows that the Egyptians are not his people. After he happens to meet his real brother and sister, Aaron (Jeff Goldblum) and Miriam (Sandra Bullock), and learns the truth about his heritage, he runs away into the desert. At an oasis, he encounters the former slave girl Tzipporah (Michelle Pfeiffer), whom he earlier helped escape from the pharoah's kingdom, and her father, Jethro (Danny Glover), the Hebrew high priest. While staying with them, Moses hears the voice from the burning bush: "I am that I am, the god of your fathers."

For Moses, accepting this god means renouncing untold power and riches, and Ramses (now the pharaoh) is first incredulous, then angered. "I am a Hebrew," Moses sternly informs him, "and the god of the Hebrews came to me and commands that you let my people go." When Ramses disagrees (and doubles the slaves' workload), God unleashes a series of punishments. Fire rains from the sky, locusts descend in clouds, and all the firstborn are killed. All leads up to the spectacular parting of the Red Sea, an event made for animation; unlike DeMille's oddly unconvincing vertical walls of water, the parting here has an almost physical plausibility; we can see how the water parts and where it goes.

The movie is not shy about being entertaining, but it maintains a certain seriousness. In place of the usual twosomes and threesomes of little characters doing comic relief, we get two temple magicians (voices by Steve Martin and Martin Short), and a duet ("You're Playing With the Big Boys Now") after Moses turns his staff into a snake to impress Ramses, and magicians show how the trick has been done. It's not that easy to explain the fire and the locusts.

The more movies I see, the more grateful I am for new films that go to the trouble of creating astonishing new images. One of the reasons I was so enthusiastic about *Dark City, What Dreams May Come,* and *Babe: Pig in the City* is that they showed me sights I had never imagined before, while most movies were showing me actors talking to one another. (Those who found *Dreams* cornball were correct, but they missed the point.)

Prince of Egypt is the same kind of film (as were, on quite a different scale, *A Bug's Life, Antz,* and *Kiki's Delivery Service*). It addresses a different place in the moviegoer's mind, one where vision, imagination, and dream are just barely held in rein by the story. One imagines that DeMille had a film like this in his mind before he had to plod out and translate it to reality.

Prisoner of the Mountains ★ ★ ★ ½

R, 99 m., 1997

Oleg Menshikov (Sacha), Sergei Bodrov Jr. (Vania), Jemal Sikharulidze (Abdoul-Mourat), Susanna Mekhralieva (Dina), Alexei Jharkov (The captain), Valentina Fedotova (The mother). Directed by Sergei Bodrov and produced by Boris Giller and Bodrov. Screenplay by Arif Aliev, Bodrov, and Giller.

An old man, the Muslim patriarch of a mountain village, takes two Russian soldiers prisoner because he wants to trade them for his own son. The mother of one of his prisoners comes to see him, to make a trade to save her son. "I know your son is a teacher," she tells him. "I am a teacher too." The old man shakes his head: "It doesn't matter. We are enemies."

Sergei Bodrov's *Prisoner of the Mountains,* a thoughtful and moving film about war, exists on the line between the individual and "the enemy." Because we have seen similar stories before, we expect that eventually the two Russian soldiers will become the friends of their captors, who will begin to see them as human beings. It is not going to be that simple. The war that brings them together—a war between the Russian central government and Muslim rebels in the Caucasus mountains—is based on a hatred so old and durable that this movie, set in the present day, is based on a short story written by Leo Tolstoy more than 150 years ago.

The soldiers are Sacha (Oleg Menshikov) and Vania (Sergei Bodrov Jr.). Sacha is older, more confident, dashing. Vania is an uncertain kid. They meet in training, go on a tank patrol, and are almost immediately captured by a freelance rebel ambush headed by old Abdoul-Mourat (Jemal Sikharulidze), the tall, intimidating leader of a mountain village. Placed in shackles, they are kept prisoner and put to hard labor. Abdoul's sweet, dark-eyed daughter (Susanna Mekhralieva), who is about twelve, soon begins to like them, although she never questions their captivity. "My dowry," she boasts complacently, "will include two Russian slaves."

This war zone seems so small that some of the participants know each other (in fact, Bodrov shot the whole movie within twenty miles of actual fighting). Abdoul sends off his ransom letter (learning that the mail delivery will take about ten days). But Vania's mother simply goes to the front, confronts her son's former commander, and says she wants to deal directly with the rebels. The commander discourages her ("You can't trust anyone here. Soldiers traded grenades for hash, and kids threw the grenades back at them."). The mother swings her purse at his head, and he ducks, apologizing, "Mother, you don't understand. We have casualties every day."

She sets off alone for a rendezvous with Abdoul in a café. They are two parents negotiating for the lives of their sons. The difference is that the Russian woman places her son above ideology, and the patriarch believes in the value of a glorious death. Meanwhile, the two soldiers, chained together, sing songs, drink smuggled booze, and one night are taken out on a patrol by regular troops, who force them to look for land mines.

When they are not blown up as expected, we get a scene which shows the greater maturity of this film, as opposed to standard Hollywood war movies. The Muslim troops have gathered on a bleak hillside for a little entertainment: all-in fighting, starring their defending champion, who leaves his opponents broken and bloody. We watch while the fighter wins his latest bout, and then one of the prisoners is ordered to fight him. Frightened, trembling, he approaches the champion. In most Hollywood films, this scene would end with the good guy being beaten to a pulp, yes, but then staging a comeback and hammering the champion. *Prisoner of the Mountains* is wiser about human nature: The champion, who is a fighter but not a murderer, takes one look at his puny challenger and dismisses him with a laugh. It is a special moment.

The movie has an acute sense of place and the passage of time. The mountain village seems unchanged over the centuries ("The wind frightens the hearts of strangers here," the children say). When we hear Louis Armstrong on a radio, it is like a signal from space. Modern methods of warfare are meaningless here; the rebels know the mountain passes, and fight with greater zeal. The little girl, who in a conventional film would befriend the soldiers, does befriend them, but after the style of her people: She promises them a proper burial. Because the film is about these specific characters and not about a formula with a happy ending, we are wrapped in the story: We have no way of knowing how it will turn out.

Movies can have a way of putting faces to headlines. I have been reading for years about the various obscure (to me) rebellions in the old Soviet Union, and now I can put faces to them and see what they come down to: bureaucracy against zealotry, weary regular troops against fierce men who burn with conviction. When your enemy considers his death a victory, it is impossible to defeat him. In a way, this movie is about how the two prisoners come to terms with that realization.

Private Parts ★ ★ ★

R, 111 m., 1997

Howard Stern (Himself), Robin Quivers (Herself), Mary McCormack (Alison Stern), Paul Giamatti (Pig Vomit), Fred Norris (Himself), Jackie Martling (Himself), Gary Dell'Abate (Himself), Richard Portnow (Ben Stern), Kelly Bishop (Ray Stern). Directed by Betty Thomas and produced by Ivan Reitman. Screenplay by Len Blum.

Howard Stern has been accused of a lot of things, but he has never been accused of being dumb. With *Private Parts*, his surprisingly sweet new movie, he makes a canny career move: Here is radio's bad boy walking the finest of lines between enough and too much. His fans will find enough of the Howard whose maxims include "lesbians equal ratings." General audiences will be seduced by the film's story line, which exploits three time-honored Hollywood formulas: (1) rags to riches, (2) I gotta be me, and (3) hey, underneath it all I'm really just a cuddly teddy bear.

The movie shows the coronation of a geek. In grade school, we learn, Howard's father made a more or less daily practice of calling him a moron. Howard was the only white kid in an all-black high school. He didn't date until college (even a blind girl turns him down, after feeling his nose), and he married almost the first woman who was nice to him. Played by Mary McCormack, his wife, Alison, plays a key role in the film, which asks as its underlying subplot, "How much will this woman put up with before she dumps him?" The answer, as Stern listeners know, is "a lot."

Private Parts is a biopic about an awkward kid with a bad radio voice and such shaky breath control that he was always running out of steam in the middle of the call letters. Working at a 40-watt station, he's promoted to program manager because he's such a lousy DJ, and told by the station owner: "Disc jockeys are dogs. Your job is to make them fetch." Fired from a country station he hates, Howard tells Alison: "I have to be myself on the radio, and tell the truth. I have to go all the way." He does. He reveals things about their marriage on the radio that would be grounds for divorce in any civilized land.

In 1981, Howard arrives at a Washington station and is paired for the first time with Robin Quivers, who plays herself in the movie and functions as ballast, steadying Howard in his manic phases and speaking for many members of the audience when she tells him, over and over, that this time he's gone too far. Stern and Quivers are both making their screen acting debuts here, and they do what seasoned actors claim is very difficult: They play convincing, engaging versions of themselves.

The final third of the movie shows Howard in his modern incarnation, as the shock jock who will say almost anything on the radio. He crowns himself King of All Media (tough to do, since by his account he rarely has both hands free at the same time). And he gets into trouble after WNBC, the network's New York flagship, hires him apparently without having listened to his show. His new boss is a program director quickly nicknamed Pig Vomit (well played by Paul Giamatti), who promises his superior, "Either I tame him or I make him so crazy he quits." The process includes lessons in the proper sing-song pronunciation of the call letters.

When one bit goes over the top, Howard makes Robin the fall guy and she's fired and feels betrayed. This episode, based on life, is played honestly; Howard acts like a creep and doesn't resign on principal, although perhaps he is right, strategically, to see the firing as a ploy to get him to resign.

The film has been directed by Betty Thomas (*The Brady Bunch, The Late Shift*), whose steadying hand makes it play like a movie and not a series of filmed radio shows. Many sequences are very funny, including one where Howard uses a listener's subwoofer to create effects for which it was not designed. Stern on-air regulars like Fred Norris, Jackie (the Joke Man) Martling, and Stuttering John play themselves, and producer Gary Dell'Abate hosts inserts that feel unrehearsed, including one where a donkey makes a surprise appearance.

Stern reportedly rejected some two dozen scripts before settling on this one, written by Len Blum. He made the prudent choice. The material is just outrageous enough to be convincingly Stern, but not so far out it will offend those likely to see this movie (*Booty Call*, by contrast, is more uninhibited). The movie successfully launches Stern's screen career, and it will be interesting to see how its inevitable sequel, *Miss America*, will develop. What is certain about Stern is that he will find a way to stretch the envelope without tearing it; he may have paid $1 million in fines to the FCC, as his publicity boasts, but he is still, after all, on the air.

Psycho ★ ½

R, 106 m., 1998

Vince Vaughn (Norman Bates), Anne Heche (Marion Crane), Julianne Moore (Lila Crane), Viggo Mortensen (Sam Loomis), William H. Macy (Milton Arbogast), Robert Forster (Dr. Simon), Philip Baker Hall (Sheriff Chambers), Anne Haney (Mrs. Chambers). Directed by Gus Van Sant, and produced by Brian Grazer and Van Sant. Screenplay by Joseph Stefano, based on the novel by Robert Bloch.

The most dramatic difference between Alfred Hitchcock's *Psycho* (1960) and Gus Van Sant's "shot-by-shot" remake is the addition of a masturbation scene. That's appropriate, since this new *Psycho* evokes the real thing in an attempt to re-create remembered passion.

Curious, how similar the new version is, and how different. If you have seen Hitchcock's version, you already know the characters, the dialogue, the camera angles, the surprises. All that is missing is the tension—the conviction that something urgent is happening on the screen at this very moment. The movie is an invaluable experiment in the theory of cinema, because it demonstrates that a shot-by-shot remake is pointless; genius apparently resides between or beneath the shots, or in chemistry that cannot be timed or counted.

Students of trivia will note the differences. The opening shot is now an unbroken camera move from the Phoenix skyline into the hotel room where Marion Crane (Anne Heche) is meeting with her lover, Sam Loomis (Viggo Mortensen). There is a shot of Loomis's buttocks, and when he turns toward her, a quick downward glance of appreciation by Marion. In the scene where Marion packs while deciding to steal the money, Heche does more facial acting than Janet Leigh did in the original—trying to signal what she's thinking with twitches and murmurs. Not necessary.

The highway patrolman who wakes her from her roadside nap looks much the same as in the original, but has a speaking voice which, I think, has been electronically tweaked to make it deeper—and distracting*. We never get the chilling closer shot of him waiting across the street from the car lot, arms folded on his chest. When Marion goes into the "parlor" of Norman Bates (Vince Vaughn), the stuffed birds above and behind them are in indistinct soft focus, so we miss the feeling that they're poised to swoop. There is a clearer shot of "Mrs. Bates" during the knife attack in the shower. And more blood.

As for the masturbation scene, as Norman spies on Marion through the peephole between the parlor and Room No. 1: Even if Hitchcock was hinting at sexual voyeurism in his 1960 version, it is better not to represent it literally, since the jiggling of Norman's head and the damp offscreen sound effects inspire a laugh at the precise moment when one is not wanted.

All of these details would be insignificant if the film worked as a thriller, but it doesn't. One problem is the casting of Vaughn in the Norman Bates role. He isn't odd enough. Norman's early dialogue often ends in a nervous laugh. Anthony Perkins, in the original, made it seem compulsive, welling up out of some secret pool of madness. Vaughn's laugh doesn't seem involuntary. It sounds as if he intends to laugh. Possibly no actor could have matched the Perkins performance, which is one of the unique creations in the cinema, but Vaughn is not the actor to try. Among actors in the correct age range, my suggestion would be Jeremy Davies, who was the frightened Corporal Upham in *Saving Private Ryan.*

Anne Heche, as Marion Crane, lacks the carnal quality and the calculating detachment that Janet Leigh brought to the original film. She is less substantial. Van Sant's decision to shoot in color instead of black and white completes the process of de-eroticizing her; she wears an orange dress that looks like the upholstery from my grandmother's wingback chair. Viggo Mortensen is also wrong for Sam Loomis, the lover. Instead of suggesting a straight arrow like John Gavin in the original film, he brings an undertow of elusive weirdness. The only new cast members who more or less get the job done are William H. Macy, as the private eye Arbogast, and Philip Baker Hall, as Sheriff Chambers. By having a psychiatrist (Robert Forster) reproduce a five-minute speech of clinical diagnosis at the end of the film, Van Sant demonstrates that a completely unnecessary scene in the original, if reproduced, will be completely unnecessary in the remake as well.

I viewed Hitchcock's *Psycho* a week ago. Attending this new version, I felt oddly as if I were watching a provincial stock company doing the best it could without the Broadway cast. I was reminded of the child prodigy who was summoned to perform for a famous pianist. The child climbed into the piano stool and played something by Chopin with great speed and accuracy. When the child had finished, the great musician patted it on the head and said, "You can play the notes. Someday, you may be able to play the music." ☞

**I was wrong. That's the real voice of James Remar.*

Public Housing ★★★

NO MPAA RATING, 210 m., 1997

A documentary by Frederick Wiseman.

If I told you I've seen a documentary about public housing in Chicago, you might immediately assume it shows poverty, illiteracy, welfare, drugs, and crime. If I told you that the documentary had moved me almost to tears with the kindness, courage, tenacity, and hope that it displayed, you might wonder what miracle the filmmaker had witnessed—or evoked. But all Frederick Wiseman has done is point his camera, and look and listen.

His new film *Public Housing,* is the record of a lot of time spent among the residents of the Ida B. Wells homes on the South Side. These are poor people, mostly unemployed, one step from homelessness, preparing for the coming changes in the welfare system.

Watching the film, I came to the uneasy conclusion that the Chicago Housing Authority bureaucracy is a pyramid of jobholders balanced precariously on the backs of the poor. Residents speak helplessly of the steps necessary to get anything done. There's a woman who needs an ink cartridge for a copying machine: Her request has to go through four levels of authorization to be approved. Then it has to be put out for three bids. Then the lowest bid has to go through an approval process. "I finally went out and just bought the thing myself," she says.

Yet many of the people involved at ground level in the system, including maintenance men, residents, volunteers, social workers, and police officers, are so generous and patient in their efforts that their everyday lives take on a sort of quiet heroism.

Yes, heroism. The news is filled with stories about bad cops. But look at the cops in *Public Housing.* Two stand for fifteen minutes on a street corner with a young woman who is apparently involved in the drug business. They find no drugs, but they, and eventually we, can see what's up. Finally one cop tells her: "Six months from now you're gonna have all your teeth broken out, and your eyeball hanging down on your cheek. You still got a life ahead of you. You can beat these drugs. I'm gonna remember you. You're gonna be my special project. Every time I see you I'm gonna pull over."

Then there are two other cops, evicting an old man who is being sent to a nursing home. Look at their tenderness. The old man is surrounded by the scant remains of a lifetime. One cop sighs and shakes open a brown paper bag, and begins to fill it with canned goods.

There's an exterminator, patiently giving a woman tips on how to catch bugs off guard. A plumber, fixing a leaking drain and obviously concerned about a young man who seems to wander through an old woman's apartment at will. A police captain, talking quietly with a man who owes $80 to drug dealers; they both know the man will be beaten later that night. "Have you got any relatives you could go to?" the cop asks. And, "Well, your wife hung in there for a while, huh?"

There is a woman named Helen Finner, who has been president of the Ida B. Wells Resident's Association for twenty years, and who works the phone in her office while a sad young girl sits huddled in a blanket. "You have 200 vacancies waiting for somebody to move into them, and you have mothers with children, homeless, sitting around in the lobby of the hospital, who can't find a place to spend the night," she says into the phone. "If I haven't heard from (you) by one o'clock Monday, then I'm gonna call down there and act crazy."

There are meetings. The Men of Wells sit behind folding tables and discuss commitments for volunteer work. A teacher from a junior college explains ways residents can qualify for funds to start small businesses. There's a meeting about the Child Family Preservation Center, and the speaker tells a story I will not forget. She has just seen a young mother's children taken away from her in court. When her own mother tries to comfort her, the younger woman tells her frankly, "If they had taken me away from you, I wouldn't be here today."

And on and on. Frederick Wiseman has spent his lifetime filming the institutions of society: hospitals, high schools, mental homes, even a monastery. He doesn't bring an attitude to his work. He visits, looks, and listens. To watch his films is to spend some time in the lives of other people.

Those who do not live in public housing have a lot of ideas about those who do. Most of them are formed by crime reports in the news. What you see in *Public Housing* is a neighborhood with many people, some bad, some devastated by drugs, yes—but most just sincerely trying to get by, live right, improve themselves, and stick together. If you were in big trouble, these might be neighbors you would be happy to have.

Pushing Tin ★ ★ ★

R, 124 m., 1999

John Cusack (Nick Falzone), Billy Bob Thornton (Russell Bell), Angelina Jolie (Mary Bell), Cate Blanchett (Connie Falzone), Jake Weber (Barry Plotkin), Vicki Lewis (Tina). Directed by Mike Newell and produced by Art Linson. Screenplay by Glen and Les Charles, based on an article by Darcy Frey.

Like an overloaded airplane struggling to lift off, the characters in *Pushing Tin* leap free of the runway only to be pulled back down by the plot. John Cusack and Billy Bob Thornton play two air-traffic controllers who are prickly and complex, who take hold of a scene and shake it awake and make it live, only to be brought down by a simpering series of happy endings.

For at least an hour, there is hope that the movie will amount to something singular. It takes us into a world we haven't seen much of—an air-traffic control center. Controllers peer into their computer screens like kids playing a video game, barking instructions with such alarming quickness that we wonder how pilots can understand them. They use cynicism to protect themselves from the terrors of the job. One guy "has an aluminum shower in his future." The movie opens with the laconic observation, "You land a million planes safely, then you have one little midair, and you never hear the end of it." This movie is not going to be shown on airplanes.

Cusack plays Nick Falzone, hotshot controller, on top of his job, happily married to his sweet wife, Connie (Cate Blanchett, astonishingly transformed from Elizabeth I into a New Jersey housewife). He works a night shift, ingests a plateful of grease at the local diner, is tired but content. Then into his life comes Russell Bell (Billy Bob Thornton), a cowboy controller from out west, who gets under people's skins. He rides a hog, needs a shave, schedules planes so close together that the other controllers hold their breaths. He's married to a twenty-year-old sex bomb named Mary (Angelina Jolie), who dresses like a lap dancer.

These four characters are genuinely interesting. Russell is an enigma and likes it that way. He speaks seldom, has tunnel vision when concentrating on a task, and once stood on a runway to see what the backwash from a 747 felt like. (The controllers watch him doing this, in a video that shows him blown away like a rag doll; in real life, paralysis or death would probably result.) Thornton, who is emerging as the best specialist in scene-stealing supporting roles since Robert Duvall, is able to maintain the fascination as long as the screenplay maintains Russell's mystery.

Alas, Hollywood grows restless and unhappy with characters who don't talk much; that's why the typical American screenplay is said to be a third longer than most French screenplays. It's hard to be chatty and still maintain an air of mystery; the key to Bogart's appeal is in enigmatic understatement. When Russell does start speaking (or "sharing") with Nick, he turns out, alas, to have the mellow insights of a self-help tape, and at one point actually advises the younger man to learn to "let go." This is not what we want to hear from the same man who, earlier in the movie, when asked if he has any hobbies, growls, "I used to bowl, when I was an alcoholic."

The Cusack character is also given a rocky road by the screenwriters (Glen and Les Charles). He's a happily married man, but when he sees the Angelina Jolie character, he melts. She's weeping in the supermarket over a cart full of vodka, and he helpfully invites her to a nearby restaurant. After predictable consequences, she has a line that would have made her husband proud ("Mr. Falzone, what's the fewest number of words you can use to get out that door?"), but instead of following the emotional and sexual consequences to some kind of bitter end, the movie goes all soft and sentimental.

Cusack does what he does best: incisive intelligence, combined with sincere but sensible emotion. Blanchett, eccentric in *Oscar and Lucinda* and regal in *Elizabeth,* is cheery and normal here, chatting about taking art classes. Jolie's sexuality is like a bronco that keeps throwing her; she's too young and vulnerable to control it. One can imagine a movie that linked these characters in unforgettable ways, and this one seems headed for a showdown before it veers off into platitudes.

At least it spares us an airplane crash. And it gives us a good scene where Nick, aboard a plane, becomes convinced that Russell is steering them through a thunderstorm. (His behavior here should get him handcuffed by the flight crew and arrested by the FBI, but never mind.) The movie also does an observant job of showing us the atmosphere inside an air-traffic control center, where the job description includes "depression, nervous breakdowns, heart attacks, and hypertension."

The movie is worth seeing for the good stuff. I'm recommending it because of the performances and the details in the air-traffic control center. The director is Mike Newell *(Donnie Brasco, Four Weddings and a Funeral).* His gift in making his characters come alive is so real that it actually underlines the weakness of the ending. We believe we know Russell and Nick—know them so well we can tell, in the last half-hour, when they stop being themselves and start being the puppets of a boring studio ending.

Q

Quest for Camelot ★ ★

G, 83 m., 1998

With the voices of: Jessalyn Gilsig (Kayley), Andrea Corr (Kayley Singing), Cary Elwes (Garrett), Bryan White (Garrett Singing), Gary Oldman (Ruber), Eric Idle (Devon), Don Rickles (Cornwall), Jane Seymour (Juliana), Celine Dion (Juliana Singing). Directed by Frederik Du Chau and produced by Dalisa Cooper Cohen. Screenplay by Kirk De Micco, William Schifrin, Jacqueline Feather, and David Seidler, based on the novel *The King's Damosel* by Vera Chapman.

Quest for Camelot is still another big-studio attempt to wrest the crown of family animation away from Disney. It's from Warner Bros., which scored with the bright and amusing *Space Jam*, but now seems to fall back into the pack of Disney wanna-bes. The animation isn't vivid, the characters aren't very interesting, and the songs are routine.

Space Jam and Fox's *Anastasia* are the only recent non-Disney features to steal some of the magic from Walt's heirs. Since *Quest for Camelot* cost a rumored $100 million and yet lacks the sparkle of a *Beauty and the Beast*, perhaps it's time for Warners to explore a different approach—perhaps animation aimed at the teenage and adult market, which does so well in Japan.

Quest for Camelot, like so many animated features, is a template into which superficially new characters are plugged. We need a young hero, and get one in Kayley, the brave teenage daughter of Lionel, one of Arthur's knights. Lionel, of course, is killed in an early scene while defending Arthur, because the heroes of animated films must always lack at least one parent (later, Kayley's mother is conveniently kidnapped).

We also need—let's see, a villain (Ruber, the evil and jealous knight), a villain's cruel sidekick (the wicked griffin), and a villain's good-hearted sidekick (Bladebeak the chicken). We need a young man to help the heroine on her quest (Garrett, the blind forest dweller), a hero's noble friend (a silver-winged falcon), and the hero's low comedy team (Devon and Cornwall, the two-headed dragon). Then have Ruber steal the magic sword Excalibur, and have Kayley and Garrett try to recapture it, throw in some songs and a lot of animated action, and you have your movie.

I'm not putting the formula down. Done well, it can work, and some version of these ingredients now seems to be required in all feature-length animated films. But *Quest for Camelot* does a fuzzy job of clearly introducing and establishing its characters, and makes them types, not individuals. Their personalities aren't helped by the awkward handling of dialogue; in some of the long shots, we can't tell who's supposed to be speaking, and the animated lip synch is unconvincing. Another problem is the way the songs begin and end abruptly; we miss the wind-up before a song and the segue back into spoken dialogue. The movie just doesn't seem sure of itself.

Will kids like it? I dunno. I saw it with a theater filled with kids, and didn't hear or sense the kind of enthusiasm that good animation can inspire. The two-headed dragon gets some laughs with an Elvis imitation. But there's a running joke in which one head is always trying to smooch the other one, and the kids didn't seem sure why they were supposed to laugh. There's also the problem that Ruber is simply a one-dimensional bad guy, with no intriguing personality quirks or weaknesses; he pales beside Rasputin in *Anastasia* or Scar in *The Lion King*.

Of the supporting animals, the falcon has no particular personality, and Bladebeak is a character in search of a purpose. Even the vast, monstrous dragon that ends up with Excalibur (as a toothpick) is a disappointment. When the heroes find him in a cave, he doesn't exude much menace or personality; he's just a big prop.

The most interesting character is Garrett, who (we learn) was rejected from Camelot because he was blind, and now lives in the forest with the falcon. "I stand alone," he sings, but his friendship with Kayley is the only meaningful one in the movie. It's also curious that the plants in his forest are more interesting than most of the animals. There are eyeball plants that snap at people, and helicopter plants that give free rides (more could have been made of these), and plants that snap at ankles and elbows.

Really good animation can be exhilarating; I remember the "Under the Sea" sequence from *The Little Mermaid*, and "Be Our Guest" from *Beauty and the Beast.* In *Quest for Camelot* there are no sequences that take off and soar, and no rules to give shape to the action scenes (if Excalibur is really all-powerful, how is its power exercised, and why can its bearer be defeated?). The movie's underlying formula is so familiar that there's no use bothering with a retread unless you have compelling characters and good songs. Enormous resources went into the making of this film, but why wasn't there more stretching and creativity at the screenplay level? Why work so hard on the animation and run the plot on autopilot?

R

The Rage: Carrie 2 ★ ★

R, 104 m., 1999

Emily Bergl (Rachel Lang), Jason London (Jesse Ryan), Dylan Bruno (Mark), J. Smith-Cameron (Barbara Lang), Amy Irving (Sue Snell), Zachery Ty Bryan (Eric), John Doe (Boyd), Gordon Clapp (Mr. Stark). Directed by Katt Shea and produced by Paul Monash. Screenplay by Rafael Moreu.

The Rage: Carrie 2 opens with a woman painting a red stripe at eye-level completely around her living room, while screaming, "You can't have my daughter!" Soon the woman is being carried out of the house in restraints, and her daughter, little Rachel, is being reassured by a cop, who for some reason thinks they should stand outside in the pouring rain instead of inside where it's dry.

Why the rain? For the same reason the movie has all the other props of macabre thrillers, such as blinding flash-frames accompanied by loud whooshes on the sound track. And the snicker-snack noise of two blades clashing, even when there are no blades anywhere around. And, of course, a room filled with hundreds of burning candles. And flashbacks to blood-soaked horrors in the past.

After her mother is shipped off to the asylum, Rachel grows up to become an unpopular teenager (played pretty well, under the circumstances, by Emily Bergl). She's a loner, works at a Fotomat booth, lives with a cruel foster family (even its dog is always trying to run away). One day her best friend Lisa is distraught after a boy seduces and betrays her, and throws herself off the high school roof. Rachel is distraught, and all of the lockers in the high school spring open and start banging.

The wise teacher Mrs. Snell (Amy Irving) has seen this before. Twenty years earlier, she was the friend of Carrie, the jilted girl whose psychic meltdown at a prom killed seventy-three people and burned the high school to the ground. Mrs. Snell tries to counsel Rachel, who gets upset and causes the teacher's paperweight to explode. Soon Mrs. Snell tracks down the secret of Rachel's uncontrollable powers and offers her help.

Rachel is telekinetic, we learn. Well, we knew that. What we didn't know, what indeed has escaped the attention of the ESP industry, is that telekinesis is a genetic trait. Yes, Mrs. Snell tells Rachel: "There's a lab at Princeton working on this. The male is the carrier. It's an inherited recessive trait." Why recessive? If Darwin was right, since telekinesis is so useful, it should be a dominant trait, so that Mayflower guys could move the piano upstairs while relaxing in lawn chairs.

The Rage: Carrie 2 faithfully follows the story arc of Brian De Palma's 1976 thriller. Rachel, like Carrie, is a plain and unpopular girl who is unexpectedly asked out by a popular guy (Jason London). Instead of a prom, the movie leads up to a party after the opening game of the football season. The guy, named Jesse, really does like Rachel, but nevertheless she's set up for heartbreak by cruel girls and heartless football jocks, and responds in a terrifically unrecessive way.

All of this happens like dreamwalking, as if the characters in this movie knew they were doomed to follow the scenario laid down in the first one. Some scenes exist only for contrived distraction, like the utterly pointless one where Rachel's family dog runs into traffic. (Okay, to be fair, it doubles as a Meet Cute, when Jesse takes them to the all-night animal clinic.) There is a scene where Mrs. Snell takes Rachel on a tour of the ruins of the high school that Carrie burnt down, and even she thinks it's curious that the ruins (which are practically still smoldering) haven't been cleared after two decades. Amy Irving intones her dialogue in this scene as if evoking ancient disappointments.

The original *Carrie* worked because it was a skillful teenage drama grafted onto a horror ending. Also, of course, because De Palma and his star, Sissy Spacek, made the story convincing. *The Rage: Carrie 2* is more like a shadow. I can imagine the story conference: "Let's think up some reason why the heroine has exactly the same ability Carrie had, and then let's put her in a story where exactly the same things happen to her, with the same result." People actually get paid for thinking up things like that. Too much, if you ask me.

The Rainmaker ★★★

PG-13, 137 m., 1997

Matt Damon (Rudy Baylor), Danny DeVito (Deck Shifflet), Claire Danes (Kelly Riker), Jon Voight (Leo F. Drummond), Mary Kay Place (Dot Black), Teresa Wright (Miss Birdie), Mickey Rourke (Bruiser Stone), Danny Glover (Judge Tyrone Kipler), Virginia Madsen (Jackie Lemanczyk), Red West (Buddy Black), Johnny Whitworth (Donny Ray), Dean Stockwell (Judge Hale). Directed by Francis Ford Coppola and produced by Michael Douglas, Steven Reuther, and Fred Fuchs. Screenplay by Coppola and Michael Herr, based on the novel by John Grisham.

Rudy Baylor, the hero of *The Rainmaker,* works the other end of the scale from the legal superpowers in most of John Grisham's stories. He's a poor kid who has scraped through law school by the skin of his teeth, is living in his car as the film begins, and signs on with a firm where most of the work is done by a paralegal, and the boss wears the kinds of cufflinks you can get rid of in a hurry at a pawn shop.

Francis Ford Coppola, who wrote and directed the film, has made the most of Grisham's ground-level realism. This is not a film that loves the legal profession, and yet it loves some of those who labor in it—not only Baylor, played by Matt Damon with the earnestness of an Eagle Scout, but also Deck Shifflet (Danny DeVito), the kind of courthouse handyman who has never passed the bar exam, perhaps because a license would slow him down. Their give-and-take is the soul of the film; they form a desperate democracy made possible because *The Rainmaker,* unlike most Grisham films, doesn't have to drag a high-paid superstar around and give him all the best lines. DeVito's role is in the fading tradition of the star character actor.

The movie takes place in Tennessee, where Baylor has just graduated from a second-rate law school, and goes to work for Bruiser Stone (Mickey Rourke), a flashy fraud with charm where his morals should be. The law is closing in on Bruiser. Deck Shifflet sees the end coming and convinces Rudy to open a storefront office, with Deck as the legman who knows all the ropes. (Deck's credo: "A lawyer should fight for his client, refrain from stealing money, and try to tell the truth.") One of Baylor's first clients is Miss Birdie (Teresa Wright), a sweet old lady who plans to leave her money to a TV preacher ("he needs it for his airplane"), and who rents Rudy a cheap apartment. She doesn't actually have much money, but Rudy observes that her son treats her better after being told she does.

Soon Baylor and Shifflet are involved in trickier cases. One involves Kelly Riker (Claire Danes), whose husband plays softball and likes to practice his swing on her. The other involves Dot and Buddy Black (Mary Kay Place and Red West), whose son Donny Ray (Johnny Whitworth) is dying of cancer and has been refused treatment by his insurance company.

Coppola juggles these three cases with side stories involving the insurance company's amoral, high-paid lawyer (Jon Voight) and the continuing threat to Kelly from her husband. Along the way, Rudy finds it necessary to violate what he understands of legal ethics, particularly when he gets personally involved with Kelly and she convinces him there is only one right thing to do in a desperate situation.

Kelly and Rudy don't have a romance, exactly; Coppola's screenplay is too smart to stop the action for obligatory love scenes, and Rudy's legal life has become so complex that there's no time for personal matters. Hey, he hasn't even had time to be sworn in—a service the judge (Dean Stockwell) obligingly performs before his first case. The DeVito character is like a wise, profane little shadow, stage-managing his court appearances and finding the crucial evidence.

Coppola assigns Michael Herr, one of his screenwriters on *Apocalypse Now* (1979), to write a narration that casts all of these events in a jaundiced light; Rudy Baylor's tone throughout is that of a man who has drifted into a profession that makes his skin crawl. Much is made of the hourly billing rates of the insurance company's lawyers, and Voight does a quietly masterful job of being elegantly sleazy. One strong scene is blindsided by a woman (Virginia Madsen) who knows more about the inner workings of the insurance company than perhaps she should.

I have enjoyed several of the movies based on Grisham novels *(A Time to Kill, The Pelican*

Brief, The Firm), but I've usually seen the storyteller's craft rather than the novelist's art being reflected. Coppola says he picked up *The Rainmaker* in an airport, was intrigued by the story, and asked to direct it. What attracted him, I imagine, was the richness of the supporting characters: Miss Birdie, Deck, Bruiser, Kelly, and the scorned woman from the insurance company. The gallery is so colorful this could almost be a movie based on a Carl Hiassen story. By keeping all of the little people in focus, Coppola shows the variety of a young lawyer's life, where every client is necessary and most of them need a lot more than a lawyer.

Ravenous ★ ★ ★

R, 101 m., 1999

Guy Pearce (Boyd), Robert Carlyle (Colqhoun/Ives), David Arquette (Cleaves), Jeremy Davies (Toffler), Jeffrey Jones (Hart), John Spencer (General Slauson), Stephen Spinella (Knox), Neal McDonough (Reich). Directed by Antonia Bird and produced by Adam Fields and David Heyman. Screenplay by Ted Griffin.

I said no food. I didn't say nothing to eat.
—dialogue from *Ravenous*

Of course a vampire is simply a cannibal with good table manners, and *Ravenous* is a darkly atmospheric film about an epidemic of flesh-eating and the fearsome power that it brings. It takes place during the Mexican-American War in an isolated U.S. Army outpost in the Sierra Nevadas, when a half-dead man (Robert Carlyle) staggers into the fort with the story of snowbound travelers, starvation, and worse: "We ate the oxen, then the horses, then a dog, then our belts and shoes . . ."

Eventually one of the party died of starvation, and they ate him. Then they ate others . . . and by now the commander of the fort has heard enough, and determines to send out a party to investigate. All of this is shown in wet, dark colors, with a sound track of chimes and mournful cries, low, ominous, burbling percussion, and far-off female laments. *Ravenous* is the kind of movie where you savor the texture of the filmmaking, even when the story strays into shapeless gore.

The movie stars Guy Pearce, the honest cop from *L.A. Confidential*, as a man named Boyd who becomes an accidental hero during a battle. Mistaken for dead, he's piled under corpses; blood trickles into his mouth and gives him the strength to capture an enemy outpost. He's decorated, but his commanding officer sees the cowardice beneath his luck, and sends him to a godforsaken outpost where the story takes place.

Fort Spencer is a caretaking operation in a vast wilderness, presided over by Hart (Jeffrey Jones), a genial commanding officer who acts more like a host. The soldiers are all cracking up in one way or another, except for Reich (Neal McDonough), a gung ho warrior. The others include the second in command, Knox (Stephen Spinella), the religious Toffler (Jeremy Davies), Cleaves the cook (David Arquette), and some Indians. From the Indians comes the legend that when you eat another man's flesh, you possess his past and assume his strength, and your hunger becomes insatiable.

The movie has established its cold, ominous tone long before the real story reveals itself. That happens when the characters return to the cave where the travelers are said to have taken shelter. There's a creepy sequence in which Reich and Toffler enter the cave, and then traverse into an inner cave where what they find is not a pretty sight. Then there are surprises and revelations, and unspeakable things happen to some of the characters, or at least we think they do.

The director is a British woman named Antonia Bird; I didn't admire her *Priest*, but she shows she's a real filmmaker. She is wisely more interested in atmosphere than plot, and has an instinct for scenes like the one where a visiting general savors the broth of a bubbling stew. Her shots of meat are all cheerfully off-putting; she revealed at the Sundance premiere that she is a vegetarian, which came as no surprise. She does what is very hard to do: She makes the weather feel genuinely cold, damp, and miserable. So much snow in the movies looks too pretty or too fake, but her locations (in Slovakia) are chilly and ominous.

The film's setup is more fun than its payoff because in a story of this nature we would rather dread what is going to happen than see it. The movie makes much of the strength to be gained by eating human flesh, and there is a final confrontation between two men, both much fortified by their fellows, that feels like one of those superhero battles in a comic book, where neither side can lose.

The screenplay, by Ted Griffin, provides nice small moments of color for the characters (I liked the way Jeffrey Jones's C.O. seemed reasonable in the most appalling ways), and short, spare lines of dialogue that do their work ("He was licking me!"). I also liked the way characters unexpectedly reappeared, and how the movie savors Boyd's inability to get anyone to believe him. And I admired the visceral music, by Michael Nyman and Damon Albarn, which calls attention to itself (common) but deserves to (rare). *Ravenous* is clever in the way it avoids most of the clichés of the vampire movie by using cannibalism, and most of the clichés of the cannibal movie by using vampirism. It serves both dishes with new sauces.

Reach the Rock ★

R, 100 m., 1998

Alessandro Nivola (Robin), William Sadler (Phil Quinn), Bruce Norris (Ernie), Brooke Langton (Lise), Karen Sillas (Donna). Directed by William Ryan and produced by John Hughes. Screenplay by Hughes.

Reach the Rock plays like an experiment to see how much a movie can be slowed down before it stops. It was produced and written by John Hughes, who should have donated his screenplay to a nearby day-care center for use by preschoolers in constructing paper chains. How can the man who made *Plains, Trains and Automobiles* have thought this material was filmable?

The story involves an unhappy young man named Robin (Alessandro Nivola), who in the opening scene uses a flagpole to break the window of a hardware store. When Ernie the small-town cop (Bruce Norris) arrives, he finds Robin seated in a beach chair before the window, cooling himself with an electric fan. Robin is returned to the station, where the only other cop on the overnight shift is Sergeant Phil Quinn (William Sadler).

Robin is well known to the officers. His arrest sheet lists such offenses as loitering, disturbing the peace, vandalism, etc. The sergeant and the kid dislike each other, and the actors demonstrate this with various reliable techniques, including the always dependable flaring of the nostrils.

The cops lock Robin in a cell. He steals the keys to the cell, lets himself out, steals a squad car, drives downtown, fires a shotgun through a coffee shop window, returns, and locks himself back in. This is a pattern that will repeat itself many times during the long night. "How are you gettin' out of here?" asks Sergeant Quinn, convinced that Robin is the culprit. It never occurs to him to search the prisoner for the keys. I can't say much for his police work. (That line is borrowed from *Fargo*, a movie I thought of during this one as a drowning man will think of an inflatable whale.)

Robin's sneaky activities unfold with the velocity of sleepwalking. There are two cells in the jail, and at various times Robin is locked in both, Ernie is locked in one, Quinn is locked in the other, a bunk catches fire, Robin's old girlfriend is locked in with him, and Quinn is locked out of the building. Sounds like a maelstrom of activity with all those cell doors banging open and shut, but imagine the stateroom scene in *A Night at the Opera*, enacted in slow motion, and with sadness.

Yes, *Reach the Rock* is very sad. Halfway through the film we learn that Sergeant Quinn blames Robin for the drowning death of his nephew. Even later, we learn that Robin has been moping and pining for four years because a rich local girl (Brooke Langton) dated him in high school but dropped him when she went to college—except, of course, for summers, when she comes home and resumes their sexual relationship, which seems sporting of her. "Time stopped for you about four years ago," somebody tells Robin, or maybe it is everybody who tells Robin that.

There is a subplot. When we first see Ernie the dim-witted deputy, he is drinking in a parked squad car with a local woman named Donna (Karen Sillas). He's about to make a move when he gets the call to check out the alarm at the hardware store. Throughout the entire movie, Ernie and Donna try to get horizontal and are repeatedly interrupted. This is a running gag, or, in this movie, a walking gag. Donna grows frustrated and wanders the deserted night streets in her nightgown—forlorn, neglected, and in heat. At one point, when Ernie arrives for yet another rendezvous, she warns him, "This is your last chance," but one senses that with Donna there are as many last chances as with Publishers Clearing House.

All of the elements of the plot at long last fall into place, including an old tattoo that explains an earlier parable. Comes the dawn, and we are left with questions only a policeman could answer. (Spoiler Warning—read no further if you intend to see the film.)

Attention, officers! If a perpetrator has a three-page arrest record and during one night, angry at being dumped by an old girlfriend, he breaks a store window, breaks out of a jail cell, steals a police car, uses a police shotgun to shoot out another window, locks an officer out of the police station, locks two officers into cells, starts a fire, and tries to frame an officer for the crimes, would you, in the morning, release the kid and tell him to go home because "her old man has insurance"? Just wondering.

The Real Blonde ★★★

R, 107 m., 1998

Matthew Modine (Joe), Catherine Keener (Mary), Daryl Hannah (Kelly), Maxwell Caulfield (Bob), Elizabeth Berkley (Tina), Marlo Thomas (Blair), Bridgette Wilson (Sahara), Buck Henry (Dr. Leuter), Christopher Lloyd (Ernst), Denis Leary (Doug), Kathleen Turner (Dee Dee). Directed by Tom DiCillo and produced by Marcus Viscidi and Tom Rosenberg. Screenplay by DiCillo.

Tom DiCillo's *The Real Blonde* is a meandering movie that usually meanders in entertaining directions. It has too many characters and not much of a plot, but that didn't bother me while I was watching it. It's a sketchbook in which the director observes certain types he seems familiar with. A lot of them are actors and models, who are understandably confused because they don't know if they're being paid to be someone else, or just because of who they are.

The central couple are Joe (Matthew Modine) and Mary (Catherine Keener), who have been together so long they feel they should either break up or get married. Not that it isn't working the way it is, but they feel embarrassed, somehow, by not having chosen one path or the other. Joe is an actor with such high standards that he never works. Mary is a makeup artist in the fashion industry, skilled at calming restless models before they go in front of the camera.

The movie proceeds as a sort of tag game, as each new character introduces other ones. Through Mary we meet a famous photographer (Marlo Thomas) and an insecure model named Sahara (Bridgette Wilson). Through Joe we meet the punctilious caterer (Christopher Lloyd) he works for, and Joe's best friend Bob (Maxwell Caulfield), a soap opera actor obsessed with dating a real blonde. And then through Bob we meet a real blonde named Kelly (Daryl Hannah) and, full circle, Bob also meets Sahara.

Meanwhile, Mary's therapist (Buck Henry) leads her to discover a self-defense instructor (Denis Leary), while Joe's agent (Kathleen Turner) gets him a job in a Madonna video directed by Steve Buscemi, where he meets Madonna's body double (Elizabeth Berkley) and almost has an affair with her, while Mary is almost having an affair with the karate teacher.

You see what I mean. There are so many characters that none of them is really developed, except to a certain degree Joe and Mary. But the film isn't about psychological insight. It has about the same depth as many real relationships in the same circles, where ego and job demands fit right into the lifestyle: People meet and feel like they know one another because they share the same jargon and reference points. They flirt, talk, and dart away like mayflies who must mate before the end of the day—or the current shoot, whichever comes first.

DiCillo is a quixotic director, who began as a cinematographer for directors like Jim Jarmusch, and whose take is always a little skewed. His credits include the ambitious, oddball but not compelling *Johnny Suede* (an early Brad Pitt film); the satirical *Living in Oblivion*, about a cheap horror movie production; and *Box of Moonlight*, about a man who goes in search of . . . well, in search of something to go in search of.

Here he devises brief, sharply observed scenes. He notices, for example, the way a makeup artist makes up not only a model's face but also her attitude. The way the karate instructor, playing an aggressor, takes a sly pleasure in using sexist insults. The way people talk knowledgeably about movies they haven't seen. The way a guy who's embarrassed to be in a porno store will brazen it out. All of the actors are right for their roles, because a degree of typecasting has been done, but Daryl Hannah brings a particularly focused energy to the role of a soap opera actress who is not impressed that a guy is impressed by her. And Catherine Keener brings a kind of wry wit to her character; she sees models in billboards on Times Square and knows what it took to get them there.

The film's opening titles are a visual tease: We see parts of two torsos, gradually revealed, like shards of a giant sculpture, until finally they resolve themselves into a blonde with a man who kneels to embrace her. Later in the film, we see the Marlo Thomas photographer taking that shot, and we learn the real story: The model, a European Fabio clone, is embarrassed because he "released the gas," as he puts it, and the model consoles him. Thus are legends born.

As for Joe and Mary, their threatened relationship and their temptations to stray: *The Real Blonde* is so much more adult in its attitudes than a shallow film like, say, *Kissing a Fool.* The characters are articulate enough to talk about what really moves them; they don't play sitcom games. DiCillo never puts two and two together, but somehow it all adds up.

Red Corner ★★

R, 119 m., 1997

Richard Gere (Jack Moore), Bai Ling (Shen Yuelin), Bradley Whitford (Bob Ghery), Byron Mann (Lin Dan), Peter Donat (David McAndrews), Robert Stanton (Ed Pratt), Tsai Chin (Chairman Xu), James Hong (Lin Shou). Directed by Jon Avnet and produced by Avnet, Jordan Kerner, Charles B. Mulvehill, and Rosalie Swedlin. Screenplay by Robert King.

Red Corner is a contrived and cumbersome thriller designed to showcase Richard Gere's unhappiness with Red China, which it does with such thoroughness that story and characters are enveloped in the gloom. The Chinese do this better to themselves. Unlike such Chinese-made films as *The Blue Kite, To Live,* and *The Story of Qui Ju,* which criticize China with an insider's knowledge and detail, *Red Corner* plays like a xenophobic travelogue crossed with *Perry Mason.*

Gere plays an American TV executive with a bathetic life story, who has been reduced to wandering the globe, living in anonymous hotel rooms and selling syndicated TV programming that one character describes, probably overoptimistically, as "pornographic, violent, and superstitious" (sounds like *Xena* reruns to me). He meets a pretty girl in a bar, they go back to his hotel, and the next morning he's awakened by the police, who point out disapprovingly that the girl is dead and Gere is covered with her blood. Still worse, the dead girl is the daughter of an important general.

Gere protests his innocence, and, of course, we believe him, but if it's all a setup (a) did the girl volunteer to be killed, or (b) were the conspirators not clever enough to find a victim with less clout? No matter; Gere is soon inside the Chinese legal system, which is portrayed as biased, brutish, and slanted in favor of the prosecution.

He is assigned a lawyer (another pretty young woman, well played by Bai Ling), who advises him to plead guilty because, "It can be more easy if you confess your crime." Given the dead body and the blood, he might get similar advice in the United States, especially since his attorney sincerely believes he's guilty.

I have no doubt that the Chinese court system could use reform. It does, however, have the advantage of allowing the hero of a movie considerable latitude to cross-examine witnesses, spring surprise developments, and generally run the show from the defendant's box—even being able to return to the courtroom and pick up the reins after an escape attempt. Chinese courts also add the interesting touch of "people's assessors"—two ordinary citizens who flank the judge and can express their own opinions, speaking for the People. Amazing that so fiendish a conspiracy was not able to control them along with everyone else. Haven't they ever heard of jury-tampering in China?

There are billions to be made for whoever gets the license to sell pornography, violence, and superstition (not to mention ESPN) to the Chinese via satellite TV, and so perhaps Gere has been framed by his business competitors. Before the movie explores this possibility, we get scenes of Gere in solitary confinement, Gere having his glasses stepped on, Gere having his law books taken away, and a ludicrous scene in which he escapes from his guards in a chase down crowded alleyways and across rooftops. He was, as I recall, handcuffed during this chase. It must not be easy to outrun dozens of cops across rooftops while handcuffed.

He gains the safety of the U.S. Embassy, only to discover that his attorney gave her personal guarantee of his return, and will lose her license as a result. Rather than have this happen to her, he voluntarily returns to what looks like certain and quick execution. What a great guy. Then what happens is worthy of a *Perry Mason* showdown, involving secret photos inside lockets, surprise last-minute confessions, and suspicions about the odor of chloroform. Only the portentous music keeps this silliness earthbound.

Red China has indeed been guilty of human rights violations, the criminal mistreatment of Tibet, persecution of minority religions, and general surliness. What is interesting, as I mentioned, is that Red Chinese films have done a good job of portraying some of those evils (particularly the nightmare of the Cultural Revolution). To some degree, Richard Gere set himself up by appearing in this film; as an outspoken critic of China and follower of the Dalai Lama, he has a case to plead. It's surprising, then, that he chooses to do it so lamely in such a lugubrious movie.

The Red Violin ★ ★ ★ ½

NO MPAA RATING, 126 m., 1999

Carlo Cecchi (Nicolo Bussotti), Irene Grazioli (His Wife, Anna), Samuel L. Jackson (Charles Morritz), Sylvia Chang (Xiang Pei), Colm Feore (Auctioneer), Don McKellar (Evan Williams), Greta Scacchi (Victoria Byrd), Jason Flemyng (Frederick Pope), Jean-Luc Bideau (Georges Poussin), Christoph Koncz (Kasper Weiss). Directed by Francois Girard and produced by Niv Fichman. Screenplay by Don McKellar with Girard.

There is a kind of ideal beauty that reduces us all to yearning for perfection. *The Red Violin* is about that yearning. It traces the story of a violin ("the single most perfect acoustical machine I've ever seen," says a restorer) from its maker in seventeenth-century Italy to an auction room in modern Montreal. The violin passes from the rich to the poor, from Italy to Poland to England to China to Canada. It is shot, buried, almost burned, and stolen more than once. It produces music so beautiful that it makes you want to cry.

The film is heedlessly ambitious. In a time of timid projects and easy formulas, it has the kind of sweep and vision we identify with elegant features from decades ago—films that followed a story thread from one character to another, like *Tales of Manhattan* or *La Ronde.* There really is a little something here for everyone: music and culture, politics and passion, crime and intrigue, history and even the backstage intrigue of the auction business. Not many films can encompass a British aristocrat who likes to play the violin while he is having sex, and a Chinese woman who risks her life to protect a violin from the martinets of the Cultural Revolution.

The violin is crafted in Cremona, Italy, in 1681—made by the craftsman Nicolo Bussotti (Carlo Cecchi) for his unborn son. But his wife, Anna (Irene Grazioli), dies in childbirth after hearing a series of prophecies from a village crone who reads the Tarot deck. The cards provide a structure for flash-forwards to the future adventures of the violin, and at the same time there is a flashback structure, as bidders arrive at the auction house in Montreal and we learn why they desire the instrument.

The film is easy to follow, and yet reveals its secrets slyly. The tale of the violin is a series of stories involving the people who own it over a period of 300 years. Then there is another story, hinted at, slowly revealing itself, involving an expert evaluator of instruments (Samuel L. Jackson). He is the person who proves that this is indeed Bussotti's famous red violin, and solves the mystery of its color. He is also perhaps the person best equipped to appreciate how rare and wonderful the instrument is—

but, like many passionate connoisseurs, he lacks the wealth to match his tastes. His plans for the instrument supply a suspenseful ending to a movie that has already given us just about everything else.

The film was directed by the Canadian Francois Girard, and written by him and the actor-director Don McKellar. They also cowrote Girard's brilliant first film, *Thirty-two Short Films About Glenn Gould* (1994), which considered the life and work of the great Canadian pianist in thirty-two separate episodes. *The Red Violin* uses a similar approach, spinning stories and tones out of the central thread.

After the opening sequence involving Bussotti, the violin drifts into the hands of an order of monks, and we rejoin it 100 years later at their orphanage. They dote on a young prodigy named Kasper (Christoph Koncz), who plays with the purity of an angel. The musician Poussin (Jean-Luc Bideau), expert but poor, hears the boy play and adopts him on the spot, despite the doubts of his wife. This sequence develops tenderly, as the old couple grow to love the boy—who sleeps with his violin.

Flash-forward. The violin is in the possession of gypsies (I am not revealing the details of the transfers). It is played by many hands and travels from Poland to England where, in the nineteenth century, it is heard by a rich virtuoso named Frederick Pope (Jason Flemyng), who incorporates it into his concerts and into his lovemaking with his mistress, Victoria (Greta Scacchi). It is she who fires a bullet at it. The violin next surfaces in a pawn shop in Shanghai where, during the Cultural Revolution, it stands as a symbol of Western decadence. It's defended by a brave musician who points out that Beethoven and Prokofiev were revolutionaries, but is saved only when a music lover (Sylvia Chang) risks her life. Eventually the now-capitalist Chinese government sends it off to Montreal, where it attracts the attention of the Samuel Jackson character.

A brief outline doesn't begin to suggest the intelligence and appeal of the film. The story hook has been used before. *Tales of Manhattan* followed an evening coat from person to person, and *The Yellow Rolls-Royce* followed a car. Max Ophuls's *La Ronde* (1950), Luis Buñuel's *The Phantom of Liberty,* (1974) and Richard Linklater's *Slacker* (1991) all follow chains of characters, entering a scene with one person and exiting it with another. Such structures take advantage of two contradictory qualities of film: It is literal, so that we tend to believe what we see; and it is fluid, not tied down to times and places. All of those titles more or less observe time and place, however; *The Red Violin* follows not a person or a coat, but an idea: the idea that humans in all times and places are powerfully moved, or threatened, by the possibility that with our hands and minds we can create something that is perfect. ☞

The Relic ★ ★ ★

R, 110 m., 1997

Penelope Ann Miller (Margo Green), Tom Sizemore (Lieutenant Vincent D'Agosta), Clayton Rohner (Hollingsworth), Linda Hunt (Ann Cuthbert), Chi-Muoi Lo (Greg Lee), James Whitmore (Dr. Frock), Audra Lindley (Coroner), Robert Lesser (Mayor Owen). Directed by Peter Hyams and produced by Gale Anne Hurd and Sam Mercer. Screenplay by Rick Jaffa, Amy Holden Jones, John Raffo, and Amanda Silver, based on the novel by Lincoln Child and Douglas Preston.

The Relic begins with a boiling cauldron deep in the Amazonian jungle, and includes not only a cat that leaps out and frightens someone but such other horror film standbys as kids locked into a museum after hours, a lucky bullet, a hard-boiled coroner who thinks she has seen everything (but is wrong), and the mayor of Chicago fleeing with socialites through waist-deep water in a tunnel linking the Field Museum of Natural History to Lake Michigan.

He is not simply fleeing, but being chased by a monster that decapitates its victims and chews a hole in their skulls to suck out their thalamus and pituitary glands. A monster, mind you, that has genes combining human, insect, and reptile DNA, and might be the product of an "evolutionary leap that causes grotesque and short-lived aberrant species." The species looks plenty aberrant to me: It's twice the size of a raptor, looks like a cross between a kangaroo and Godzilla, has teeth the size of fence pickets, and a long, red, forked tongue it uses to lick the face of the pretty young anthropologist.

Her name is Dr. Margo Green (Penelope Ann Miller). She works at the museum, where two large crates have arrived from a colleague in South America. Not long after, a security guard is found dead (decapitated, hole in skull, pituitary missing, etc.). The cop assigned to the case is Lieutenant D'Agosta (Tom Sizemore), who makes a quick link between this death and the mysterious case of a South American freighter found floating in Lake Michigan with a bilge full of corpses (all missing their pituitaries, etc.). When he discovers there is a tunnel from the lake to the museum, he asks ominously if it would be possible to enter the museum from the lake that way.

Why would a monster from a ship want to go to all that trouble? Maybe because one of the crates in the museum contains the leaves he likes to eat. Or maybe because the beast was in the crate with the leaves, escaped, and nailed the crate shut again, so people would think it was merely a crate of leaves. This is a clever monster. At one point, even though steel security doors have slammed down and isolated all parts of the museum from each other, the monster seems capable of simultaneously chasing the mayor and his friends down the tunnel, terrorizing scientists in the museum basement, and chewing up cops who are trying to attack it from the skylights. It gets around.

All of this is actually a lot of fun, if you like special effects and gore. To see this movie in the same week as the hapless and witless *Turbulence* is to understand how craft and professionalism can let us identify with one thriller heroine and laugh at another. Peter Hyams is a skillful action director, working here with the veteran "creature-effects" specialist Stan Winston and so many special-effects technicians that they could have played the entire sound track album under the end credits.

It's clever the way the movie combines the conventions of the horror and disaster genres. Although this is technically a science-fiction movie about a mutant monster, Hyams adds another level by having the mayor insist that a black-tie charity benefit proceed inside the museum as planned, even though the cops are convinced that it's not safe. After the steel doors slam shut, the sprinkler system drenches everyone, and decapitated bodies start dropping from above, the guests are in roughly the same predicament as in a disaster movie: trapped, in danger, and helpless to escape.

The level of horror and violence in *The Relic* is a notch or two above the industry average. There's a scary scene where a flaming monster pursues Dr. Green down a corridor of exploding specimen bottles. And a gory scene involving an autopsy, with Audra Lindley chillingly effective as the coroner. And scenes where cops get half their bodies chewed off, and a lot of scenes involving heads and brains, and lots of scientific double-talk to go with it. *The Relic* is not for younger viewers.

There are a few loose ends. Early in the film, Dr. Green tells Lieutenant D'Agosta about the tanks of chemicals they use to strip the flesh from rhino bones. Later in the film, she hides in such a tank herself, yet emerges with all her flesh. I am not sure what connection the monster has with the little red fungus pellets on the imported leaves. And there is the matter of the relic itself—a stone devil that was damaged in shipment. For most of the movie, a restoration expert is ominously piecing it back together, but I don't think the relic actually has anything to do with the man-lizard-insect creature.

I know Chicago mayor Richard M. Daley is a movie fan, and I imagine he will check out this one. He'll be disappointed by Robert Lesser as the mayor (instead of using a Chicago accent, he talks much like Al Pacino). But Daley might enjoy some of the other stuff, including city cops using acetylene torches to burn through the steel doors of the museum and rescue the terrified millionaires inside—proving Chicago is "the city that works." And he will reflect that in the real world, no Chicago mayor would ever be so reckless as to order a society benefit to proceed in a museum still being scoured for vicious decapitating pituitary-suckers. A guy gets his pituitary sucked out, he's not going to contribute to your next campaign.

The Replacement Killers ★ ★ ★

R, 88 m., 1998

Chow Yun-Fat (John Lee), Mira Sorvino (Meg Coburn), Michael Rooker (Stan "Zeedo" Zedkov), Kenneth Tsang (Terence Wei), Jurgen Prochnow (Michael Kogan), Til Schweiger (Ryker), Danny Trejo (Collins), Clifton Gonzalez

Gonzalez (Loco). Directed by Antoine Fuqua and produced by Brad Grey and Bernie Brillstein. Screenplay by Ken Sanzel.

The Replacement Killers is all style. It's a high-gloss version of a Hong Kong action picture, made in America but observing the exuberance of a genre where surfaces are everything. The characters are as flat as figures on a billboard, but look at the way everything is filmed in saturated color, and anything that moves makes a metallic whooshing sound that ends in a musical chord, and how when the hero walks down a corridor at a car wash, it's done with a tilt and a zoom. In a movie like this, the story is simply a device to help us tell the beginning from the end.

The film is the American debut for Chow Yun-Fat, a popular star in Asia for twenty years and for the last ten a frequent collaborator with John Woo, the Hong Kong action wizard also now working in Hollywood (he produced this film). Chow is good-looking, open-faced, with a hint of sadness that reminded me of Charles Bronson in repose. Here he plays a Chinese immigrant to America, who owes a favor to the drug lord Terence Wei (Kenneth Tsang), whose son has been killed by a cop (Michael Rooker).

Chow's assignment: Kill someone important to the cop. But with the target framed in his telescopic sights, Chow just can't do it. "I went against Mr. Wei," he tells a wise Buddhist monk. "There will be consequences." He knows Wei will go after his mother and sister in Shanghai, and he needs a forged passport to fly home and protect them. That leads him to the lair of Meg Coburn (Mira Sorvino), a master forger whose first appearance is a good example of the movie's visual lushness: Leaning over her computer, she's in red lipstick and a low-cut dress in a hideaway that looks like a cross between Skid Row and a cosmetics ad.

Meg is a tough girl, played by Sorvino with a nice flat edge (while Chow's posing for his passport picture, she says "Smile, and say, 'Flight from prosecution.'"). She wants no part of his troubles, but soon they've teamed up as Wei throws squadrons of killers at them, including two "replacements" flown in to kill the cop's son.

In movies like this, everyone knows everyone. Chow and Sorvino go into an amusement arcade, and she's hit on by a gold-toothed creep. Her reaction: "I try to stick to my own species." The creep of course is in the hire of Wei, and soon a gun battle rages through the arcade. Other elaborately choreographed shootouts take place in a car wash, and in a theater where the cop has taken his son for a cartoon festival (the gunfire is intercut with Mr. Magoo).

There's a moment in the recent *Desperate Measures* where violence erupts as a father tries to save the life of his son, and a cop asks, "How many people are gonna have to die here tonight so that kid of yours can live?" I had the same thought in *The Replacement Killers.* Because Chow spares Wei's target, approximately two dozen people die, or maybe more (in the dark it's hard to see what happens to all the Magoo fans).

What I liked about the film was its simplicity of form and its richness of visuals. There's a certain impersonality about the story; Chow and Sorvino don't have long chats between the gunfire. They're in a ballet of Hong Kong action imagery: bodies rolling out of gunshot range, faces frozen in fear, guys toppling off fire escapes, grim lips, the fetishism of firearms, cars shot to pieces, cops that make *Dragnet* sound talky. The first-time director, Antoine Fuqua, is a veteran of commercials and music videos; with cinematographer Peter Lyons Collister he gets a sensuous texture onto the screen that makes you feel the roughness of walls, the clamminess of skin, the coldness of guns. *The Replacement Killers* is as abstract as a jazz instrumental, and as cool and self-assured.

Return of the Jedi (Special Edition) ★ ★ ★ ★

PG, 133 m., 1983 (rereleased 1997)

Mark Hamill (Luke Skywalker), Harrison Ford (Han Solo), Carrie Fisher (Princess Leia), Billy Dee Williams (Lando Calrissian), Anthony Daniels (C-3PO), Peter Mayhew (Chewbacca), Sebastian Shaw (Anakin Skywalker), Ian McDiarmid (Emperor). Directed by Richard Marquand and produced by Howard Kazanjian. Screenplay by Lawrence Kasdan and George Lucas, based on a story by Lucas.

Return of the Jedi completes the epic Star Wars cycle with the final destruction of the Empire and the inevitable face-off between Luke Skywalker and the evil Darth Vader, now revealed, as we surmised, to be his father. The film has a tone of its own. If *Star Wars* was a brash space opera and *The Empire Strikes Back* was a visual feast, *Return of the Jedi* is a riot of character invention. We get a good look at Jabba the Hutt and his court, we meet the fuzzy-wuzzy Ewoks, and we are confronted by two wonderfully loathsome creatures—the beast in the dungeon beneath Jabba's throne room, and the desert monster made of teeth and gullet.

If I had to choose, I would say this is the least of the Star Wars films. It lacks the startling originality of the first two: It's more concerned with loose ends and final resolutions. It was the correct decision for George Lucas to end with a trilogy and then move to another point in time for the continuation of the saga; to return to these characters a fourth time would destroy the mythic structure of the story and turn it simply into a series.

Still, there are inspired things here. The early scenes are dominated by Jabba the Hutt, whose cavern is populated with lots of small, obnoxious creatures in the corners, and with a grotesque intergalactic jazz band that seems to have been improvised along with its music. Secure in his lair, Jabba has Han Solo frozen in a sculpture on the wall, and eventually takes all of our heroes captive. His gurgling voice is wonderfully reprehensible, and he squats beneath his cavern ceiling like a stalagmite of slime. (It has been observed that Jabba seems much larger here than in *Star Wars.* Some say it is because he is on a platform, some say it is an optical illusion; I suggest that a hutt is a slug, and slugs continue to grow all of their lives.)

The monster in the dungeon, made of teeth and scales, is the embodiment of disgusting aggression, and yet its death provides one of the movie's finest moments. The creature is crushed beneath a heavy door, and then we see its keeper come forward, weeping to have lost his pet. It's a throwaway moment, but typical of the film's richness.

An extended sequence takes place in the desert, where Jabba's hovercraft positions itself over the creature in the sand, which seems to consist primarily of a large digestive system. He intends to force his captives to walk the plank, but the tables are nicely turned. I have always felt Lucas lost an opportunity here; since Jabba obviously must die at some point, why not feed him to the sand thing? I can envision the hutt's globular body slithering along the plank and plopping down into the big open mouth—and then being spit up again, as too unsavory even for this eating machine. Final shot: Green gooey Jabba-stuff dissolving in the monster's digestive juices under a pitiless sun.

The Ewoks (never referred to by name in the film) are as cute as stuffed animals, and bring a kind of innocence to the Forest Moon, where the power station for the orbiting Death Star is located. Their forest provides the location for the movie's most inexplicable sequences, in which characters chase each other on high-speed hover-scooters. As you know if you have seen the film (and *USA Today* assures us the average American has seen it several times), bad guys regularly get wiped out by running their scooters into trees. Question: Isn't a thickly forested area the wrong venue for these vehicles? How about flying above the treetops, where there's nothing to run into?

This third movie lacks the resonance that Obi-Wan and Yoda brought to the second one (they make cameo appearances, but are not major players). We see a great deal more, however, of Darth and the Emperor, who looks uncannily like Death in *The Seventh Seal.* There is, of course, the climactic moment when Vader reveals his real face, allowing the character to become the first in movie history to be played by three actors (body by David Prowse, voice by James Earl Jones, face by Sebastian Shaw). By this third installment, I think, we've seen quite enough of the swordplay with laser beams, and those scenes could be shortened. The Sharper Image catalog, I see, is offering replicas of the lightsabers for $350 to $450—pricey, when you consider the original prop was a photoflash grip.

At the end of it all, after the three movies, we've taken an epic fantasy journey. George Lucas has in common with all great storytellers the ability to create a complete world; these films may spring from space opera, science fiction, and Saturday serials, but they are done so superbly that they transcend all genres, and become a reverberating place in our imaginations.

Thinking back over the three, I find that the most compelling characters are Darth Vader, Yoda, and Obi-Wan Kenobi. That is because their lives and thoughts are entirely focused on the Force. To the degree that characters have distance from the Force, they resonate less: Skywalker is important although boyishly shallow, and Princess Leia harbors treasured secrets, but Han Solo, for all his importance to the plot, is not very interesting as a person, and a little of Chewbacca, as observed earlier, goes a long way.

The droids, R2-D2 and C-3PO, play much the same role here as their originals did in the movie that inspired them, Kurosawa's *The Hidden Fortress.* They're a team, Laurel and Hardy or Vladimir and Estragon, linked together by fate and personality. The other characters—Lando, Jabba, the Grand Moff Tarkin, and the many walk-ons and bit players—function, in Eliot's words, to swell the progress of a scene or two.

At the end, what are we left with? Marvelous sights: the two Death Stars, the lumbering war machines on the snow planet, space warfare, the desert monster, buccaneering action. Marvelous sounds: the voices of Darth Vader, Jabba, and the chirpy little R2-D2. And an idea—the Force—that in encompassing everything may, perhaps, encompass nothing, and conceal another level above, or beneath. I'm guessing that will be the subject of the next trilogy.

Return to Paradise ★ ★ ★ ½

R, 109 m., 1998

Vince Vaughn (Sheriff), Anne Heche (Beth), Joaquin Phoenix (Lewis), David Conrad (Tony), Vera Farmiga (Kerrie), Nick Sandow (Ravitch), Jada Pinkett Smith (M. J. Major). Directed by Joseph Ruben and produced by Alain Bernheim, Steve Golin, and Ezra Swerdlow. Screenplay by Bruce Robinson and Wesley Strick.

Joseph Ruben's *Return to Paradise* is a thriller that traps its characters in an exquisite dilemma involving life and death. Lewis, Sheriff, and Tony are three Americans who meet in Malaysia and fool around in cheap huts on the beach, "God's own bathtub," enjoying the rum, the girls, and the hashish. Sheriff and Tony return to New York. Lewis plans to go on to Borneo for a Greenpeace project to protect the orangutan. Instead, he's arrested with the leftover hash and sentenced to death.

Two years pass before Sheriff (Vince Vaughn) and Tony (David Conrad) are contacted in Manhattan and told all of this by Lewis's advocate, Beth (Anne Heche). The problem, she explains, is that Lewis (Joaquin Phoenix) was over the legal limit for possession by one person, making him a trafficker, not a user. However, she's cut a deal with the authorities. If Sheriff and Tony will return to Malaysia and testify that they all owned the hashish together, Lewis will be allowed to live, and Sheriff and Tony will each have to spend three years apiece in prison. If only one of them returns, it'll be six years.

Students of logic will recognize this choice immediately. It's a variation of the Prisoner's Dilemma, one of the oldest puzzles in mathematics and philosophy. Obviously, neither Tony nor Sheriff want Lewis to die. But they didn't know him *that* well, and they hardly want to spend three years of their lives in a Third World prison—let alone six years. The ideal solution for either Tony and Sheriff would be for the other guy to do six years while one gets off free. But if both guys try this tactic, Lewis dies.

Hemingway, defining morality, once said that something is good if you feel good after doing it, and evil if you feel bad after doing it. How would you feel if you let Lewis hang? Good, because you were not spending three or six years in prison in Malaysia? Or bad, because you know it was your hashish too? *Return to Paradise* watches Sheriff and Tony as they decide. And they do decide; this is not going to be one of those teasers that sets you up for a moral dilemma and then pulls a switcheroo and solves everything with an action climax.

All of the performances are convincing, but Anne Heche's is especially effective. She walks a fine line between inviting Tony and Sheriff to save Lewis's life, and pummeling them with moral blackmail. It is not an easy decision to walk out of freedom in Manhattan and into three years in a jail where disease, brutality, malnutrition, and dysentery have been reported. Heche looks very concentrated in her scenes: intense, focused, trying to read all of the signs.

Sheriff (Vince Vaughn) is now working as a limo driver. He doesn't have much of a life, but at least it's his. Tony is engaged to be married. As for Beth, we only gradually learn her full story, which catches Sheriff in a tricky emotional vise. Joaquin Phoenix, as the prisoner, is not stoic or philosophical, but feels the way most people would when a death sentence appears out of the blue.

The director, Joseph Ruben *(The Stepfather, Sleeping With the Enemy)*, uses a kind of flat, logical storytelling that leads us inexorably toward his conclusions. The suspense is not so much over what happens as about how it will happen to us—how the movie will make us experience what clearly must happen. His screenplay, by Bruce Robinson and Wesley Strick, doesn't make things easy by portraying the Malaysians as particularly villainous; the judge, indeed, makes sense when he expresses puzzlement that America would permit its streets to be endangered by drugs: Better that the drug dealers should suffer instead of the general population.

The only real villain in the movie, indeed, is a journalist played by Jada Pinkett Smith, whose eagerness to get Lewis's story may endanger the efforts to free him. She's seen as a little too eager and careless, but there is an element of truth in her behavior: Many journalists would and do get stories at a human cost that the story cannot possibly justify.

Return to Paradise has been compared to *Midnight Express*, another film about a thoughtless American facing the forfeit of his life in prison far from home. That was more of a visceral film. This one is more cerebral. Like Sheriff and Tony, we're pulled both ways by the story: We want them to go back and save Lewis, but we're not exactly sure we'd do the same. That's the Prisoner's Dilemma in a nutshell. ☞

Ringmaster ★ ★

R, 95 m., 1998

Jerry Springer (Jerry Farrelly), Jaime Pressly (Angel Zorzak), Molly Hagan (Connie Zorzak), Michael Dudikoff (Rusty), Ashley Holbrook (Willie), Michael Jai White (Demond), Wendy Raquel Robinson (Starletta), Tangie Ambrose (Vonda), Nicki Micheaux (Leshawnette). Directed by Neil Abramson and produced by Jerry Springer, Gina Rugolo-Judd, Brad Jenkel, Steve Stabler, and Gary W. Goldstein. Screenplay by Jon Bernstein.

Jerry Springer's *Ringmaster* creates an understandable anticipation in the audience that the film will be largely about Springer. But Springer appears more as a by-product. He stands to one side looking morose and regretful, while human flotsam occupies his stage. He's like a sorrowful deer caught in the headlights, except for a big speech where he lectures sternly that the poor have just as much right as the rich to be humiliated in public.

The difference, of course, is that the rich have public humiliation thrust upon them, while the poor have to angle for it. The movie's plot is mostly about two sets of would-be guests who apply to the show, hoping for free airline tickets. The movie wisely focuses on them, and that's the key to its occasional charm: It doesn't make the mistake of thinking we're much interested in Springer himself. What we want to know is, what kind of people would want to be guests on that show?

Was ever the word "guest" more cruelly misused than as a description of the victims of the Springer program? And yet that's how they see themselves. "This is the first family vacation we've ever had," says Connie Zorzak (Molly Hagan), the heroine of the film, who volunteers her daughter, Angel (Jaime Pressly), and husband (Angel's stepfather), Rusty (Michael Dudikoff), for the Springer show after catching them in bed with one another. As a fillip, she throws in Angel's boyfriend, Willie (Ashley Holbrook), who she (Connie) has been having sex with—as revenge against Angel, of course.

They all live in a trailer park near Miami. Connie and Angel are employed, Connie as the proprietor of a snack wagon that never seems to have any customers, Angel as a maid in a motel where the male customers all seem to know that, for a good time, they should see Angel. Rusty sits at home drinking beer and watching the dog races on TV. Occasionally he has to deal with Connie calling him up and telling him about openings for fork lift operators. All three actors are effective at finding the note that passes caricature but stops short of parody; I was reminded of scenes from *The Positively True Adventures of the Alleged Texas Cheerleader-Murdering Mom.*

They're accepted for the TV segment "You Did WHAT With Your Stepdaddy?" Meanwhile, we meet other guests. Starletta (Wendy Raquel Robinson) has a straying boyfriend named Demond (Michael Jai White), who has cheated on her with two other women: Vonda (Tangie Ambrose) and Leshawnette (Nicki Micheaux). They all qualify for the Jerry show "My Traitor Girlfriends," where almost inevitably some of these cheerful cheaters find new possibilities backstage.

You'd expect this material to be dealt with in a careless and seamy way, but *Ringmaster* is a better movie than I expected. The guests come across as pathetic but spirited, and are acted with some sympathy. And the show tapings look like outtakes from TV, including tongue-kissing lesbians and black-shirted security guards to pull apart hair-pulling guests. (The preshow announcements have a charm of their own: "The No. 1 rule is: No weapons whatsoever. Can you be arrested for a crime you commit on the Jerry show? The answer is, yes.")

Molly Hagan brings poignancy to Connie, the trailer park mom. She was pregnant at fifteen, we learn, and blames herself for the shabby life she has created for her daughter. When she finds Angel in bed with her husband, she sees it less as a betrayal than as an opportunity for free airfare. Like Robert De Niro in *Taxi Driver,* she practices her lines in the mirror: "You did WHAT with my husband?" Jaime Pressly has a good scene as she tries to cash her paycheck and is told she has the wrong ID; her lifestyle includes weekly challenges to accepted banking practices.

Jon Bernstein's screenplay has some nice lines ("I like to think of us as the Judds without the talent"). Jerry Springer probably supplied most of his own dialogue ("This is a slice of American life, and if you don't like it, bite something else"). At times he looks like he's trying to send us a telepathic appeal for forgiveness. True story: One day Springer encountered a Chicago news anchor. Out of a blue sky, he volunteered, "I know I'm going to go to hell for doing this show." He should learn to forgive himself (a current Oprah topic). Somebody must be watching. I watch sometimes. And so do you.

Rocket Man ★ ★ ★

PG, 93 m., 1997

Harland Williams (Fred Z. Randall), Jessica Lundy (Julie Ford), William Sadler ("Wild Bill" Overbeck), Jeffrey DeMunn (Paul Wick), James Pickens Jr. (Ben Stevens), Beau Bridges (Bud Nesbitt), Peter Onorati (Gary Hackman). Directed by Stuart Gillard and produced by Roger Birnbaum. Screenplay by Craig Mazin and Greg Erb.

The thought never occurred to me that Jim Carrey made grown-up films—until halfway through *Rocket Man,* when I realized that Harland Williams was basically a Jim Carrey for the six-to-fourteen set. Filling the void in our national life left by the retirement of Peewee Herman, he plays the kind of guy who lands on Mars and tells Mission Control: "Look! I'm the first man to walk backward on Mars!"

Williams (from TV's *Simon*) plays Fred Z. Randall, computer nerd, whose dream since childhood has been to be an astronaut. We see him first inside a washing machine, pretending the window is a spaceship porthole. (He sets the machine to spin, which may give kids dangerous ideas, but pays off with a big laugh when his mother liberates him and he tumbles onto the floor explaining, "I come in peace!")

As an adult, Randall is responsible for a computer guidance program for the manned mission to Mars. The ace pilot, however, keeps crash-landing in training simulations, and Fred is able to prove it's because the pilot's feeding in the wrong figures. Fred's helpful demonstration lands the pilot in a cast, and there's only one other person qualified to join the three-man crew: Fred himself.

Rocket Man is cheerfully oblivious to any scientific discoveries about Mars more advanced than that the planet is red. (It assumes, for example, that instantaneous two-way communication could take place with a lander on the Martian surface.) But this is not a science movie, to put it mildly. It's a wacky comedy in the Jerry Lewis–Jim Carrey mold, with lots of jokes about two astronauts who share the same air hose while one of them passes enormous volumes of gas. Guess which one.

Harland Williams comes across uncannily like a man born to annoy you with everything he says. The movie exploits this. After the mission lands on Mars and he gets into an explorer vehicle with the mission commander (William Sadler), he badgers the commander with little-kid questions: "Are we almost there? Can I drive?" He bungles the dramatic moment when they plan to raise the American flag on Mars by dropping it over a cliff—but he saves the day with his own substitute flag, which waves proudly on TV for the folks at home: his pair of stars-and-stripes boxer shorts.

Jessica Lundy and Sadler, who play his fellow crew members, are deployed mostly as foils. And the movie has fun with the obligatory shots of Mission Control, with rows of men in white shirts and ties, stationed solemnly at computers but jumping up on cue to cheer successful developments. (There's a bald-headed actor playing a Mission Control guy here who has had similar roles, I'll bet, in half the space pictures made; no, not Clint Howard, but you get the idea.) Most of the technical dialogue is right out of other space movies, but there's the occasional zinger, such as "Your promises are worth about as much as dental floss at a Willie Nelson concert."

Rocket Man is not inspired or brilliant or original, but it's the kind of movie that gives you a goofy grin half of the time. A lot of the credit goes to Williams, who has the knack of almost making you think he doesn't know how obnoxious his character is. "It wasn't me!" he shouts, every time he screws up. For example, when he falls out of the lander door and inadvertently becomes the first man on Mars. And when his air hose is linked to Sadler's, and Sadler realizes someone has cut the cheese.

Romy and Michele's High School Reunion ★ ★ ★

R, 91 m., 1997

Mira Sorvino (Romy), Lisa Kudrow (Michele), Janeane Garofalo (Heather), Alan Cumming (Sandy Frink), Camryn Manheim (Toby), Justin Theroux (Cowboy). Directed by David Mirkin and produced by Laurence Mark. Screenplay by Robin Schiff.

"I just get really happy when they let her shop," Michele tells Romy, tears in her voice, as they watch the video of *Pretty Woman* for the umpteenth time. Romy agrees. The two women, curled up on their beds, have been pals since high school, and now, in Los Angeles and pushing thirty, they're still single but still making the dance club scene and still looking for Mr. Okay. Here they are in front of the mirror: "I can't believe how cute I look."

"Don't you love how we can say that to each other and we know we're not being conceited?"

"No, we're just being honest."

The two women have been friends so long they talk the same way, sounding a little like the *Saturday Night Live* version of Tori Spelling. Romy (Mira Sorvino) is a cashier at a Jaguar dealership, and Michele (Lisa Kudrow) is unemployed at the moment, but, honestly, they think their lives are pretty darn exciting.

Memories of their painful and dreadful days in high school are all but obliterated until one day an old classmate named Heather (Janeane Garofalo) walks into the Jaguar shop, is recognized by Romy, and tells her their tenth reunion is coming up at Sagebrush High in Tucson. Will she be there?

Romy and Michele at first decide not to go. They recall nothing but agony. They were labeled as "kooks" and persecuted by the popular girls. But then . . . then . . . they start thinking maybe they could go and make a different impression. Romy can borrow a used Jag from the dealership. And they can pose as business executives. What business? They decide to tell everyone they invented Post-It Notes. "Well, I invented them," Romy tells Michele, "but you were instrumental in the development and marketing."

There have been a lot of high school reunion movies, and they all hinge on long-lasting insecurity. Apparently *everyone* was miserable during high school, and even the popular kids didn't seem successful to themselves. (I recently got a note from a high school classmate who described herself as painfully shy and dyslexic. Looking at the signature, I recognized the name of a woman I'd always thought of as the epicenter of popularity.)

Romy and Michele's High School Reunion, written by Robin Schiff (based on her play) and directed by David Mirkin, is one of the brightest and goofiest comedies in a while, a film that has a share of truth, but isn't afraid to cut loose with the weirdest choreography I have seen outside of a 1960s revival.

It alternates scenes from the reunion with flashbacks to real memories of high school and fantasy scenes (the funniest is when Michele is challenged to explain how she invented Post-It Notes, and responds with a detailed and technical explanation that sounds pretty good to me).

In high school, Romy and Michele were scorned by a trio of the most popular girls. Romy had a crush on cute Billy Christiansen, who wouldn't give her the time of day. Michele had scoliosis and had to wear an unsightly neck brace that squeaked every time she moved. Times were not good, especially when the popular girls stuck refrigerator magnets to her brace.

For everyone who is unpopular, there is someone more unpopular still. Sandy Frink (Alan Cumming), the class nerd, had such a hopeless crush on Michele that he carried a giant notebook with him everywhere, for camouflage in case of unwanted physical responses to her mere presence. And there was plump, plain Toby (Camryn Manheim), who exuded school spirit but was always ignored.

Now Sandy has become incredibly wealthy (he's a Bill Gates clone) and arrives by helicopter. He even looks better: "When I made my first million, my present to myself was a new face," he tells Michele during a dream sequence. He still carries a torch for her, which helps set up the funny closing sequences at the reunion dance, where old wrongs are righted and old enemies are slighted.

Mira Sorvino and Lisa Kudrow work easily and wickedly together, playing conspirators who are maybe just a little too dense to realize how desperate they are, or maybe just a little too bright to admit it. Janeane Garofolo, looking fearsomely hard-boiled, is the *really* successful businesswoman from the class, chain-smoking and blurting out the truth, and at the reunion she, too, runs into an old nemesis: Cowboy (Justin Theroux), who she used to meet when she slipped behind the building to sneak a cigarette. He has a secret too.

Comedies are hard to make well. The proof is in how many are made badly. *Romy and Michele's High School Reunion* is light as a feather and cheerfully inconsequential, and most of the developments are predictable, but it has charm, a sly intelligence, and the courage to go for special-effects sequences like a weird run-in with a limo. And then there's that three-way dance number at the reunion. I can't believe how cute they look. Honest.

Ronin ★ ★ ★

R, 121 m., 1998

Robert De Niro (Sam), Jean Reno (Vincent), Stellan Skarsgard (Gregor), Skipp Sudduth (Larry), Jan Triska (Dapper Gent), Natascha McElhone (Deidre), Sean Bean (Spence), Michael Lonsdale (Jean-Pierre). Directed by John Frankenheimer and produced by Frank Mancuso Jr. Screenplay by J. D. Zeik and Richard Weisz.

The "ronin" of Japanese legend were samurai whose lords were killed. Left with no leader to dedicate their lives to, they roamed the countryside, freelancers for hire. The same definition would apply to the rough band of killers who assemble in a Paris bistro at the beginning of John Frankenheimer's *Ronin.*

They're an international crew. From America comes Sam (Robert De Niro), who the others think is ex-CIA. From France, Vincent (Jean Reno). From Russia, Gregor (Stellan Skarsgard), who may be ex-KGB and is a computer expert. From England, Spence (Sean Bean), a munitions and bomb man. And there's another American, Larry (Skipp Sudduth)—who is supposed to be a great driver but is too much of a showboat, choosing as he does to replicate the Diana death chase (actually, that's just the movie's in-joke, if it's a joke at all).

The movie is essentially bereft of a plot. There's an explanation at the end, but it's arbitrary and unnecessary. *Ronin* is really about characters, locations, and behavior. Consider the elaborate opening setup in which Sam, the De Niro character, reconnoiters the bistro before going in. We assume he's going to attack those inside, but actually he's only attending a meeting of all the men that has been called by an IRA paymistress named Deidre (Natascha McElhone). "Why did you go around to the back?" she asks him. "I never walk into a place I don't know how to walk out of," says De Niro, who spends most of the rest of the movie walking into places he doesn't know how to walk out of.

Frankenheimer milks that opening for ten minutes of pure cinema. Once De Niro gets inside, the opening is revealed as just an exercise, but in a film like this you stay in the present and don't ask questions (like, why hold the meeting in a public place?).

The IRA has assembled these five men to get a briefcase. We never learn what is in the briefcase. It's the perfect McGuffin, as defined by Hitchcock (something everyone cares about, although it doesn't matter what it is). My guess: Inside this briefcase is the briefcase from *Pulp Fiction.* The briefcase is in the possession of "five to eight men," Deidre tells them, and the ronin set out to track them to Cannes, Nice, and other attractive locations (an obligatory encounter in an ancient Roman arena is not overlooked). Every encounter leads to a violent bloodbath and a high-speed chase, so that in the real world the headlines would be screaming about streets in flames and dozens dead—but in a thriller, of course, to be dead is to be forgotten.

I enjoyed the film on two levels: for its skill and its silliness. The actors are without exception convincing in their roles, and the action makes little sense. Consider the Stellan Skarsgard character, who is always popping out his laptop computer and following the progress of chase scenes with maps and what I guess are satellite photos. Why does he do this? To affirm to himself that elsewhere something is indeed happening, I think.

The best scene is one of the quieter ones, as De Niro's character gives instructions on how a bullet is to be removed from his side. "I once removed a guy's appendix with a grapefruit spoon," he explains, and more urgently: "Don't take it out unless you really got it." The scene ends with a line that De Niro, against all odds, is able to deliver so that it is funny and touching at the same time: "You think you can stitch me up on your own? If you don't mind, I'm gonna pass out."

John Frankenheimer is known as a master of intelligent thrillers *(Manchurian Candidate, 52 Pick-Up)*, and his films almost always have a great look: There is a quality in the visuals that's hard to put your finger on, but that brings a presence to the locations, making them feel like more than backdrops.

Here, with a fine cast, he does what is essentially an entertaining exercise. The movie is not really about anything; if it were, it might have really amounted to something, since it comes pretty close anyway. The screenplay credits conceal the presence of hired hand David Mamet, who reportedly wrote most of the final draft, and who gives the dialogue a deadpan, professional sound. For a little more maybe he would have thrown in a plot.

Rosewood ★ ★ ★ ½

R, 142 m., 1997

Jon Voight (John Wright), Ving Rhames (Mann), Don Cheadle (Sylvester Carrier), Bruce McGill (Duke), Loren Dean (James Taylor), Esther Rolle (Sarah Carrier), Elise Neal (Scrappie), Catherine Kellner (Fannie Taylor), Michael Rooker (Sheriff Walker). Directed by John Singleton and produced by Jon Peters. Screenplay by Gregory Poirier.

John Singleton's *Rosewood* re-creates the story of a shameful event in American history, the race riot by whites against blacks in 1922 in the small Florida town of Rosewood, that left the town a smoking ruin while dozens of its residents were shot, burned to death, or lynched. But if the movie were simply the story of this event, it would be no more than a sad record. What makes it more is the way it shows how racism breeds and feeds, and is taught by father to son.

Early in the film we see a young white boy named Everett whose best playmate is a black boy about the same age. His father forbids him to "pal around with that little nigger boy." During the course of the film, this father will show his son how to tie a hangman's noose, and he will shove others aside, crying out "make way for a boy to look!" so his son can peer down into a mass grave filled with the bodies of African-Americans—some of them babies.

We do not need to be told that many of the white men in the mob had similar childhood experiences, and that their own guilt was mixed with fear, envy, and the intoxicating frenzy of the mob to create the bloodbath of Rosewood. "Between 70 and 250 African-Americans" were killed during the violence, according to recent reconstructions (state authorities at the time estimated "2 to 6"). But Rosewood remained a secret until newspaper reports in the *St. Petersburg Times* and a recent ABC news documentary on the Discovery channel—perhaps because there were few survivors, or they were too frightened to talk.

As the film opens in 1922, we see a prosperous town owned by its African-American residents, who have only a few white families living among them—the grocer, Mr. Wright (Jon Voight), whose affection for his neighbors extends to sexual relations with his pretty seventeen-year-old clerk. The black families own their own land and run their own businesses, and are resented by poorer whites living in a neighboring town. ("Why does that nigger have a piano when I don't?" one man asks; he is offended on principle, since he can't play the piano.)

Early in the film, Singleton and his screenwriter, Gregory Poirier, introduce a key story element not based on fact: the character of Mann (Ving Rhames), who rides into town on a handsome horse, has money, and bids at auction for five acres of land coveted by the white grocer. A black convict has just escaped from a chain gang in the area: Is Mann the escapee? Almost certainly not, although rumors feed the fires of suspicion when a local white woman claims she was beaten (but not raped, she is careful to add) by a black man who invaded her home.

We saw the event and know what happened. She was beaten by her own white lover, and has made up the story to explain her bruises to a jealous husband. Two local black women also know the story, but remain silent until it is too late because they fear retribution. The white woman's report inspires white mob violence.

One of the crucial figures in these events is the white sheriff (Michael Rooker), who has a good idea of what really happened and tries ineffectually at times to cool the mob, but is powerless because he is the creature of its collective will. He makes attempts to warn blacks—especially the stubborn, courageous Sylvester Carrier (Don Cheadle)—to get out of town and save their lives, but their understandable desire to protect their property causes them to delay until it is too late. (The older woman who witnessed the original attack, played by Esther Rolle, was midwife to half the local whites, and perhaps has a misplaced belief that people who were so lovable as babies could hardly grow up to attack her family.)

The character named Mann is also aware of the dangers ("If I stay I'm sure to be hung"), but he becomes the leader of the defense, especially in a sequence where he leads women and children to a train—operated by friendly whites—that will help them escape. Although the train escape is based on historical events, this sequence plays a little too much like an action movie to fit convincingly with the rest of the story.

Singleton is the young director who burst onto the scene with *Boyz N the Hood* (1991). *Rosewood* represents an important step in his growth; it's a period picture painted on a large canvas, and he handles his large cast effortlessly, establishing a good sense of the community's life.

The *Rosewood* project began with the screenplay by Poirier; Singleton was brought in at a time when a more "positive" black lead than Ving Rhames was being sought (that's Rhames's own word). But his performance here finds the right note, and is essential to the film. Rhames became famous as the mob boss in *Pulp Fiction* and played a South African drug lord in *Dangerous Ground*. He is a powerful, direct actor, who takes up considerable psychic space. Here, in a partly symbolic role, as the strong independent counterpoint to the local blacks who are reluctant to fear the worst, he convinces at first sight and keeps on convincing. Rhames at this point has an element of mystery and unfamiliarity that's effective.

Rosewood was expensive, and a box office disappointment. It didn't obviously appeal to either blacks (since it documents such a depressing chapter) or whites (depicted as murderous or ineffectual). Perhaps on video it will appeal to people looking for a well-made film that tells a gripping, important story. Now there's a notion.

Rough Magic ★★

PG-13, 104 m., 1997

Bridget Fonda (Myra Shumway), Russell Crowe (Alex Ross), Jim Broadbent (Doc Ansell), D. W. Moffett (Cliff Wyatt), Kenneth Mars (Magician), Paul Rodriguez (Diego), Andy Romano (Clayton), Richard Schiff (Wiggins), Euva Anderson (Diego's Wife/Tojola). Directed by Clare Peploe and produced by Laurie Parker and Declan Baldwin. Screenplay by Robert Mundy, William Brookfield, and Peploe, based on the novel *Miss Shumway Waves a Wand* by James Hadley Chase.

If ever there were two genres that don't seem to fit together, they're *film noir* and magic realism. The one grovels in gritty reality, the other dissolves into clouds of butterflies. Clare Peploe deserves credit for the uncompromising way in which she stage-manages a head-on collision between them in *Rough Magic*, an oddly enchanting fantasy that almost works.

The story, set in 1952, follows a magician's assistant named Myra (Bridget Fonda) as she flees from a Los Angeles murder scene and the arms of an arranged marriage. Her fiancé, a Howard Hughes type named Wyatt (D. W. Moffett), sends a private eye named Alex (Russell Crowe) after her, and then flies down himself, piloting his private DC-3. But by then she's fallen in love with Alex, and fallen into the clutches of a quack named Doc Ansell (Jim Broadbent), who sells a constipation cure (not that it doesn't work). The doc realizes she's the real thing. So he arranges for her to go on a solo mission: She crosses a lake and engages in rituals with ancient shaman women, drinks a secret potion, and finds that she possesses real magic (she also lays a blue egg).

It can be dangerous, being a genuine magician. At one point she unintentionally turns an ominous Mexican bandit into a sausage, which is gobbled up by Doc Ansell's beloved terrier. At another point, she makes love with Alex so enthusiastically that they levitate. She kills someone without meaning to, but not to worry: Hardly anyone is dead for long in this movie.

My favorite dialogue exchange comes after she turns the guy into a sausage: "Those guys would have made a hamburger out of me," Alex says. She frowns and says thoughtfully, "Don't say things like that."

Rough Magic is based on a novel by the *noir* novelist James Hadley Chase, best known for *No Orchids for Miss Blandish*. I haven't read it, but I'll bet nobody lays a blue egg in it. The screenplay, written by Peploe with Robert Mundy and William Brookfield, is curiously serious even in its most absurd moments; Bridget Fonda looks at times as if she thinks she may be in a comedy, but can't be sure. Neither can we. A whimsical fantasy may be the correct description.

Peploe, who is married to Bernardo Bertolucci, cowrote his *Luna* (1979) and Antonioni's *Zabriskie Point* (1970), and has directed one previous feature, *High Season* (1987), an engagingly goofy comedy set on a Greek island and involving tourists and spies. Nothing she has done before is anything like *Rough Magic*, which seems to be a visitor from a parallel time line: If *film noir* had developed in South America instead of California, maybe we would have seen more films like this.

Apart from anything else, the movie is wonderful to look at. It's a cliché to talk about great visuals, since if you point a camera in the right direction you can make almost anything look good. But John J. Campbell and Peploe create painterly compositions with rich Mexican colors, and there are landscape shots and atmospheric effects here that are astonishing.

The acting is quirky in an engaging way. Moffett is dry and opaque as the ambiguous Hughes clone, Broadbent is a likable scoundrel as the snake oil salesman, and Russell Crowe is steady in the Mitchum role, as a guy hired to do a job who falls in love with the dame. At one point in the movie he starts calling Bridget Fonda "Slim," and indeed her hairstyle and costumes are intended to evoke Lauren Bacall, but it's hard for her to maintain an air of mystery while laying eggs.

In casting the lead, Peploe obviously leaned toward the *noir* side of her material, and went for an actress who could project 1950s allure. Maybe she should have tilted toward the Latin elements of magic realism, and picked somebody like Maria Conchita Alonso or Jennifer Lopez—somebody who, when presented with a mysterious green goblet of liquid prepared by an ancient priestess on the slopes of a volcano, would be able to look eager to taste it. Or maybe the project was so weird it was doomed from the start. Give *Rough Magic* credit, however, for possessing all the pieces necessary to make two other movies that both might have worked.

Rounders ★★★

R, 115 m., 1998

Matt Damon (Mike McDermott), Edward Norton (Worm), John Malkovich (Teddy KGB), Gretchen Mol (Jo), John Turturro (Joey Knish), Martin Landau (Petrovsky), Famke Janssen (Petra). Directed by John Dahl and produced by Joel Stillerman and Ted Demme. Screenplay by David Levien and Brian Koppelman.

Rounders cheerfully buys into compulsive gambling. The hero gambles away his tuition money, his girlfriend, his law degree, and nearly his life, and at the end he's still a happy gambler. If this movie were about alcoholism, the hero would regain consciousness after the DTs and order another double. Most gambling movies are dire warnings; this one is a recruiting poster.

I think that's because the movie would rather recycle the *Rocky* genre than end on a sour note. It stars Matt Damon as a New York law student who is a truly gifted poker player, and since the movie ends with a big game you somehow kinda know he's not going to lose it. Since the genre insists on a victory at the end, the movie has to be in favor of poker; you don't see Rocky deciding to retire because of brain damage.

As a poker movie, it's knowledgeable and entertaining. And as a mediocre player who hits the poker room at the Mirage a couple of times a year and has read a fair share of books about the World Series of Poker, I enjoyed it. It takes place within the pro poker underground of New York and Atlantic City, where everybody knows the big games and the key players. And it shows brash, clean-cut, young Mike McDermott (Damon) venturing into the world of cutthroats like Teddy KGB (John Malkovich), the poker genius of the Russian-American Mafia.

Mike is a law student, living with fellow student Jo (Gretchen Mol). As the movie opens, he gathers his entire stake of $30,000 and loses it all to Teddy KGB. Jo has been trying to talk him into quitting poker, and he promises to reform. But the next day his best friend, Worm (Edward Norton), gets out of prison, and of course he has to meet him at the prison gates, and of course that leads to a poker game that night, and to an escalating and dangerous series of problems.

Worm owes a lot of money to bad people. Mike unwisely becomes his coguarantor. It becomes necessary for them to win a lot of money in a short period of time or be hurt very badly, and the movie is about the places they go and the weird people they encounter in the process. Although it's not necessary to play poker to understand the movie, the screenwriters (David Levien and Brian Koppelman) have done their homework, and approvingly quote such truisms as, "If you can't spot the sucker in your first half-hour at the table, you are the sucker."

The movie buys into the seedy glamour of poker, romanticizing a game that essentially consists of exhausted technicians living off brief bursts of adrenaline generated by risking everything they own or can borrow. All gambling comes down to that—the queasy combination of thrill and fear as you win or lose—and real gambling ideally involves more of your money than it reasonably should.

Mike is established as a brilliant poker player in a scene where he walks into a game between some judges and tells every player what's in his hand. The movie doesn't have him in the room long enough to be able to do that, but never mind: The point is made, and one of the players is his mentor, Professor Petrovsky (Martin Landau), who tells him, "Our destiny chooses us." Sounds like Mike's destiny is not the law but poker, although I am not sure I follow the professor's reasoning when he lends his student $10,000 and calls it a mitzvah. (The professor remembers someone who helped him when he decided to become a lawyer instead of a rabbi, but that's not quite the same thing as deciding to become a gambler instead of a lawyer.)

The movie's best scenes contrast the personalities of Mike and Worm. Mike wants to win by playing well. Worm wants to hustle. He's a card mechanic who takes outrageous chances, and his intoxication with danger leads them both into trouble—not least when they find themselves in a high-stakes game in a roomful of state troopers. Not for Worm is the cautious lifestyle of Joey Knish (John Turturro), who has ground out a living for fifteen years by folding, folding, folding, until he draws a good hand.

There's humor in the film, especially when a lot of professional players find themselves at the same table in Atlantic City, and Mike's droll voice-over narration describes the unsuspecting suckers who sit down at the table. ("We weren't working with one another, but we weren't working against one another, either. It's like the Nature Channel; you don't see piranhas eating each other.")

The movie was directed by John Dahl, whose *Red Rock West* and *The Last Seduction* are inspired neo-*noirs. Rounders* sometimes has a *noir* look but it never has a *noir* feel, because it's not about losers (or at least it doesn't admit it is). It's essentially a sports picture, in which the talented hero wins, loses, faces disaster, and then is paired off one last time against the champ. For a grimmer and more realistic look at this world, no modern movie has surpassed Karel Reisz's *The Gambler* (1974), starring James Caan in a screenplay by self-described degenerate gambler James Toback. Compared to that, *Rounders* sees compulsive gambling as a lark—as long as it's not your money. ☞

Rudyard Kipling's Second Jungle Book: Mowgli and Baloo ★ ½

PG, 88 m., 1997

Jamie Williams (Mowgli), David Paul Francis (Chuchandra), Bill Campbell (Harrison), Dyrk Ashton (Karait), Roddy McDowell (King Murphy), Gulshan Grover (Buldeo). Directed by Duncan McLachlan and produced by Raja Patel. Screenplay by Bayard Johnson and Matthew Horton, inspired by the book by Kipling.

One of the reasons to make a movie is to tell a good story, which makes it all the more mysterious that so many storytelling opportunities are lost in *Rudyard Kipling's Second Jungle Book: Mowgli and Baloo.* The move is in no sense authored by Kipling, who knew how to tell a story; its primary connection to the *Jungle Books* is the name of the hero and the name of the bear. But it has a promising premise: Boy is raised in the jungle by animals, lives with them as an equal, then falls afoul of evil civilized men who want to exploit him.

Can you imagine a film involving a boy, animals, and the jungle? I can. It would involve a lot of storytelling imagination, since there would presumably be no dialogue. And it would be hard to photograph the animals convincingly. But a film could be made—maybe a good one.

Rudyard Kipling's Second Jungle Book: Mowgli and Baloo (which has the longest movie title since *Swept Away by an Unusual Destiny in the Blue Sea of August*) is not the one. It gives us a child actor whose acting is limited largely to looking agog in close-ups, while the editor cuts to shots of animals. Adult characters are thrown in for broad comedy and manufactured thrills. Great effort was obviously expended on the film—some of these sequences could not have been easy to shoot, and they look good—but the filmmakers were content with a limp story, one of those ready-made combinations of chases that aren't exciting and pratfalls that aren't funny.

Consider Chuchandra (David Paul Francis), the major Indian character. He's a caricature, a collection of Indian stereotypes. When we first see him, he's aghast because his pet monkey has escaped and is frolicking with Mowgli (Jamie Williams) on a train. The monkey is referred to as dirty. "He is not filthy!" the Indian cries. "I am picking off his fleas every day!" Ho, ho. Later Chuchandra exhibits exaggerated fright at sounds he must have been long familiar with (thunder, and animal roars) and races about waving his hands like a silent comedian.

The film opened with Mowgli swinging through the treetops like a junior Tarzan. He comes upon a railway track and tries to stop the train, only to be chased through the car (he may be small, but he's strong enough to drag a grown man the length of a carriage). Among those coveting him: Harrison (Bill Campbell), who works for P. T. Barnum and intends to exhibit the boy in the circus. Harrison teams up with Buldeo (Gulshan Grover), a local with a secret: Mowgli is probably his lost nephew, and Buldeo has stolen his hereditary fortune.

An even more villainous character is Karait (Dyrk Ashton), who has trained a snake to hunt; the snake can wrap itself around the sleeping Mowgli—who, after years in the jungle, doesn't have instincts that awaken him. The snake then helpfully drops Mowgli into a net. After Mowgli escapes and stumbles upon a lost city, there is the character of King Murphy (Roddy McDowell), who lives half-mad in a jungle ruin, expecting visits from royalty.

All of these adult characters are arbitrary. They have little to do with Mowgli or with one another, they are invented out of whole cloth and put into a series of lame chases, double takes, frights, surprises, sinister developments, and contrived escapes.

It is not easy to get a movie made, and even harder to make one for young audiences. If you're going to the effort, why not make a smart one? Young moviegoers, in my experience, are sharp and observant: Bored by countless hours of brainless television, they don't want the same old stuff on a movie screen. At a time when a film like *Shiloh* is playing in theaters, there is no reason to see *Rudyard Kipling's etc., etc.*

Rugrats ★ ★

G, 84 m., 1998

Voices of: E. G. Daily (Tommy Pickles), Christine Cavanaugh (Chuckie Finster), Kath Soucie (Phil and Lil DeVille), Cheryl Chase (Angelica Pickles), Tara Charendoff (Dil Pickles), Melanie Chartoff (Didi Pickles), Jack Riley (Stu Pickles), Joe Alaskey (Grandpa Pickles). Directed by Norton Virgien and Igor Kovalyov and produced by Arlene Klasky and Gabor Csupo. Screenplay by David N. Weiss and J. David Stem.

Rugrats is kind of an animated *Kids Say the Darndest Things* for kids. They also do the darndest things, many of them involving poo and pee. I don't know if I can use those words in the paper, but they use them all the time in this G-rated movie, which is pitched at kids so young that poo and pee are substances over which they are still celebrating recent victories.

Consider an opening musical number set in a maternity ward, where Tommy Pickles and his friends Chuckie Finster and Phil and Lil DeVille are hoping for a look at Tommy's new kid brother, Dilbert. (Dil Pickles—get it? For *Rugrats* fans, this is humor of the highest order.) They wake up the babies, who do a musical number that seems inspired by Busby Berkeley, except that the Berkeley girls never had to supply their own dancing waters, if you get my drift. The song is "This World Is Something New to Me," and like most of the movie, it's scored by pop performers—Busta Rhymes, Lou Rawls, and the B-52s among them. The sound track would be fun.

The movie, based on the popular Nickelodeon series, doesn't have a plot so much as a series of cliff-hanging adventures, many of them containing satirical movie references (I noticed *Raiders of the Lost Ark, The Fugitive,* and *2001*). Led by Tommy, who has a gift for finding danger, the Rugrats commandeer the new Reptorwagon designed by his dad, Stu. This vehicle, which may have some connection to the SUVs in *Jurassic Park: The Lost World,* or then again may not, takes them on a harrowing ride that ends shuddering at the edge of a precipitous drop.

Adventures in the woods include a run-in with a wolf. ("He ate that Little Red Riding Girl!" "The wolf ate a girl?" "They got her out.") And adventures with monkeys from a circus train. And adventures inside a mattress truck. And mud, a lot of mud. Much of the humor comes from the way the Rugrats talk, in a kind of marble-mouthed free association that leads to lines like, "I want those fugitives back in custard-y!"

I saw *Rugrats* the same day I saw *A Bug's Life,* and not long after seeing *Antz.* Both of the insect pictures were more to my taste. But when Adam Sandler's *The Waterboy* grossed $76 million in its first two weeks in release, all sorts of articles appeared that said that although critics hated it, they were "out of touch with the target audience." (At today's press screening, we took a twenty-two-year-old colleague severely to task for disliking the movie, since he was a member of the target audience and thus guilty of betraying his age group by a display of advanced taste.)

The target audience for *Rugrats* is, I think, kids under ten. Unlike both insect cartoons, the movie makes little effort to appeal to anyone over that age. There is something admirable about that. Trying to liberate myself from my box of space and time, I traveled in my memory back to my tenth year to ask if I would have liked *Rugrats*. The answer was, no—but when I was eight I might have. Is it bright, cheerful, colorful, and fast-moving? Yes. Is it for me? No. Would I recommend it to kids? Yeah, my guess is they would like it. I would also recommend it to those who liked *The Waterboy*, because *Rugrats* is the next step up the ladder of cinematic evolution.

Rush Hour ★ ★ ★

PG-13, 94 m., 1998

Jackie Chan (Detective Lee), Chris Tucker (James Carter), Tom Wilkinson (Thomas Griffin), Elizabeth Pena (Tania Johnson), Tzi Ma (Consul Han), Julia Hsu (Soo Yung), Philip Baker Hall (Chief). Directed by Brett Ratner and produced by Roger Birnbaum, Arthur Sarkissian, and Jonathan Glickman. Screenplay by Jim Kouf and Ross Lamanna.

Rush Hour is our reliable friend, the Wunza Movie, pairing two opposites: Wunza legendary detective from Hong Kong, and wunza Los Angeles cop. And wunza Chinese guy, and wunza black guy. And wunza martial arts expert and wunza wisecracking showboat. Neither wunza original casting idea, but together, they make an entertaining team.

The movie teams up Jackie Chan, king of lighthearted action comedy, and Chris Tucker, who crosses Eddie Murphy with Chris Rock and comes up with a guy that, if you saw him a block away, you'd immediately start wondering how he was going to con you. There are comic possibilities even in their personal patterns. Chan is not known for his effortless command of English, and Tucker is a motormouth. Chan's persona is modest and self-effacing, and Tucker plays a shameless self-promoter.

The story: During the last days of Hong Kong's status as a British colony, supercop Chan busts up a smuggling ring, but the masterminds escape to the United States. There they kidnap the daughter of the Chinese consul, who tells the FBI he wants Chan, a family friend, flown in to help with the investigation. The feds want nothing to do with a cop from overseas, and they also don't want the LAPD involved. So they get the idea of pairing up the Chinese guy and the L.A. cop, so they can keep each other out of the way.

At L.A. police headquarters, this idea is well received after the chief (the redoubtable Philip Baker Hall) realizes it's a way to get his most troublesome detective out of his hair. That would be Carter, played by Chris Tucker as the kind of loose cannon who roars around the streets in a vintage Corvette and works undercover in dangerous situations.

Neither cop likes teamwork. Both work best alone. But Chan doesn't know his way around L.A., and Tucker needs to earn points with his chief. That's enough to fuel the lightweight screenplay by Jim Kouf and Ross Lamanna, which contains a lot of genuinely funny lines and even a reference to Roscoe's Chicken and Waffles, of *Jackie Brown* fame.

Chan is, of course, noted for his stunts, which he performs himself, without doubles. *Rush Hour* has a neat little example of his wall-climbing ability, and a breathtaking sequence in which he leaps from a double-decker bus to an overhead traffic sign to a truck. And there's a scene in a high atrium where he falls from a beam and slides to safety down a silk streamer. (It's useful to point out, I suppose, that although Chan does his own stunts, they are indeed stunts and not death-defying risks; he does what a stunt man would do, but with the same safeguards and deceptive camera angles. He is brave, agile, and inventive, but not foolish.)

I like the way the plot handles Soo Yung (Julia Hsu), the consul's young daughter. Instead of being treated like a helpless pawn, she's portrayed as one of Jackie's little martial arts students in Hong Kong ("Have you been practicing your eye gouges?"), and when the kidnappers try to carry her off, she causes them no end of trouble. I also liked the way Chris Tucker (who was funny in *Money Talks*) talks his way into and out of situations, using a distracting stream of dialogue while he figures out what to do next. *Rush Hour* is lightweight and made out of familiar elements, but they're handled with humor and invention, and the Wunza formula can seem fresh if the characters are Botha couple of engaging performers. ☞

Footnote: All Jackie Chan movies end with outtakes, which usually show him missing on stunts and breaking bones, etc. This time the emphasis is mostly on bloopers, where he and Tucker blow their lines. I like the missed stunts better. It's not that I enjoy *seeing Jackie waving bravely from the stretcher as they wheel him into the ambulance, but that there's a tradition involved. To be sure, with the two major stunts in this movie, any mistakes could have been his last.*

Rushmore ★ ★ ½

R, 93 m., 1999

Jason Schwartzman (Max Fischer), Bill Murray (Mr. Blume), Olivia Williams (Miss Cross), Brian Cox (Dr. Guggenheim), Seymour Cassel (Bert Fischer), Mason Gamble (Dirk Calloway), Sara Tanaka (Margaret Yang), Stephen McCole (Magnus Buchan). Directed by Wes Anderson and produced by Barry Mendel and Paul Schiff. Screenplay by Anderson and Owen Wilson.

Max Fischer, the hero of *Rushmore,* is an activity jock, one of those kids too bright and restless to color inside the lines. Although he's a lousy student, that doesn't stop him from organizing a movement to keep Latin on the curriculum of his exclusive prep school. His grades are so bad he's on "sudden death probation," but in his spare time he edits the school magazine and runs the fencing club, the bee-keeping club, the karate team, the French club, and the Max Fischer Players. With his bushy eyebrows and black horn-rims, he looks a little like a young Benjamin Braddock from *The Graduate.*

Max, played by Jason Schwartzman, has a secret. He's in the exclusive Rushmore Academy on a scholarship; his dad is a barber. Always dressed in a tie and snappy blazer (unless in costume for one of his activities), he speaks with an unnerving maturity, and is barely able to conceal his feelings of superiority for the headmaster (Brian Cox) and other adults, who enforce their stuffy rules because they are not, and never were, able to play without a net the way Max can.

Then Max encounters a problem even he cannot outflank. Reading a book in the school library, he finds a quote by Jacques Cousteau written in the margin. The book was recently checked out, he discovers, by Miss Cross (Olivia Williams), a first-grade teacher at Rushmore. She is, he finds, incredibly beautiful, and he falls instantly in love, devising a scheme to attract her attention by running a campaign for a school aquarium. Among the potential donors is a steel tycoon named Blume (Bill Murray). Murray has kids in Rushmore, but hates them. Soon he, too, is in love with Miss Cross.

Up until this point, even a little further, *Rushmore* has a kind of effortless grace. Max Fischer emerges as not just a brainy comic character, but as a kid who could do anything if he weren't always trying to do everything. It's ingenious the way he uses his political and organizing abilities to get his way with people, how he enlists a younger student (Mason Gamble) as his gofer, how he reasons patiently with the headmaster and thinks he can talk Miss Cross into being his girlfriend ("Max, has it ever occurred to you that you're far too young for me?").

Blume is played by Bill Murray with the right note to counter Max's strategies. He is, essentially, a kid himself—immature, vindictive, love-struck, self-centered, physically awkward, but with years more experience in getting his way. (Still, he winds up hiding from life at the bottom of a swimming pool, just like Benjamin.) The movie turns into a strategic duel between Max and Blume, and that could be funny, too, except that it gets a little mean when Max spills the beans to Blume's wife, and it feels too contrived. When plotting replaces stage-setting and character development, the air goes out of the movie.

Rushmore was directed by Wes Anderson and written by Anderson and his college friend, Owen Wilson. It's their second film, after the slight but engaging *Bottle Rocket* (1996). The legend of that film is well known, and suggests that Anderson and Wilson may have a little of Max Fischer in their own personalities—the film may have elements of self-portraiture.

They were friends at the University of Texas

who made a short film, pitched it to screenwriter L. M. (Kit) Carson, got his encouragement, took it to the Sundance Film Festival, and cornered famous director James L. Brooks *(As Good As It Gets)*, who liked it enough to help them get financing for a feature from Columbia. I am writing this review during the Sundance festival, where I have met a lot of kids trying to pitch their short films and get production deals, and having a good film is not enough: You also need the relentless chutzpah of a Max Fischer.

Bill Murray has a way of turning up in perfect smaller roles; he stars in his own films, but since *Tootsie*, he has made supporting roles into a sort of parallel career. His Blume admires and hates Max for the same reason: Because he is reminded of himself. There are times when Blume is frustrated in his desire to win Miss Cross for himself, but from an objective viewpoint he can't resist admiring Max's strategy.

Anderson and Wilson are good offbeat filmmakers. They fill the corners of their story with nice touches, like the details of Max's wildly overambitious stage production of *Serpico*. But their film seems torn between conflicting possibilities: It's structured like a comedy, but there are undertows of darker themes, and I almost wish they'd allowed the plot to lead them into those shadows. The Max Fischer they give us is going to grow up into Benjamin Braddock. But there is an unrealized Max who would have become Charles Foster Kane.

S

Safe Men ★

R, 89 m., 1998

Sam Rockwell (Sam), Steve Zahn (Eddie), Paul Giamatti (Veal Chop), Michael Schmidt (Bernie Jr.), Michael Lerner (Big Fat Bernie Gayle), Harvey Fierstein (Goodstuff Leo), Mark Ruffalo (Frank), Christina Kirk (Hannah). Directed by John Hamburg and produced by Andrew Hauptman, Ellen Bronfman, Jeffrey Clifford, and Jonathan Cohen. Screenplay by Hamburg.

Safe Men whirls wildly from one bright idea to the next, trying to find a combo that will hold the movie together. No luck. This is one of those movies where you picture the author at his keyboard, chortling so loudly that he drowns out his own thoughts.

The movie takes place in Providence, Rhode Island, where Sam (Sam Rockwell) and Eddie (Steve Zahn) are the two dismally untalented members of a pathetic lounge act. (They're dismal; the lounge is pathetic—the scene looks like it was shot in somebody's rec room.) After their gig, they go to a bar where they're approached by a stranger with a weird story about a rich old man who has forgotten all about the oodles of cash in his safe.

The safe is ripe for cracking, the stranger says, but the guy can't do it himself; he's a male nurse with "Lawrence Nightingale Syndrome." Florence, Lawrence—they sound alike, but it's the kind of gag that only works in print, and that's the problem with a lot of the movie's dialogue.

Anyway, the whole con is a setup by a local Mafia boss who is convinced that Sam and Eddie are actually a couple of famous safecrackers. They're not, but they find themselves just as involved as if they were, as a bitter competition breaks out between the two powerful Jewish gangsters: Big Fat Bernie Gayle (Michael Lerner) and Goodstuff Leo (Harvey Fierstein). At stake is a valuable cup that one of them has in his safe and the other wants to present at his son's bar mitzvah. To name the cup would reveal the joke, although it's not much of a joke.

Sam and Eddie find themselves actually cracking safes, sometimes simultaneously with the two *real* safecrackers, leading to a series of coincidences in which it seems like they know what they're doing even though they don't. There is also some weak humor depending on the possibility that the tough mobsters (also including Paul Giamatti as a henchman) will hurt them badly if they don't go along.

There are isolated flashes of wit, especially in the satirically exaggerated bar mitzvah scene. And there's a certain amount of pleasure to be had from watching Lerner and Fierstein try to out-Mafia one another. And a small subplot when Sam gets a crush on Leo's daughter (Christina Kirk). But this is basically the kind of freshman project that should go straight to cable or video, clearing the way for its young writer-director, John Hamburg, to get on with his career.

The Saint ★ ★

PG-13, 117 m., 1997

Val Kilmer (Simon Templar), Elisabeth Shue (Dr. Emma Russell), Rade Serbedzija (Ivan Tretiak), Valery Nikolaev (Ilya). Directed by Phillip Noyce and produced by David Brown, Robert Evans, and Mace Neufeld. Screenplay by Jonathan Hensleigh and Wesley Strick.

The Saint is a James Bond wanna-be, which is an irony, since James Bond in a way is a Saint clone. Leslie Charteris created his gentleman crook in 1926 and wrote about him in dozens of novels before his death in 1993. The Saint also inspired fourteen movies and a 1960s TV series starring Roger Moore, a future Bond. When Ian Fleming began writing his Bond stories, he must have had the Saint in mind: The two characters share a debonair sophistication, a gift for disguise, a taste for beautiful women, a fetish for expensive toys, and a thorough working knowledge of fine wines and fast cars.

If the Saint inspired Bond, the Bond films have obviously inspired *The Saint*, which stars Val Kilmer as Simon Templar, a man of constantly shifting appearances and identities. "Who *are* you?" asks the woman who loves him. "No one has a clue," he says. "Least of all me."

The movie opens with the Saint's origination story, although the time line seems a bit askew. The man who was to name himself after the Knights Templar spent his boyhood, we learn, in a Dickensian orphanage somewhere in the Far East. When the cruel headmaster locks all the food in a storage cart as a punishment, young Simon picks the lock, and is launched on his life of adventure.

What does he do? Steals things for people, sometimes with legal sanction, more often not. This Saint is more high-tech than his pulp predecessors, and uses a Mac Powerbook and a palmtop to dial the Internet and check on his Swiss bank account, which is creeping toward $50 million. His latest assignment is to steal the secret of cold fusion from an unsuspecting Oxford scientist named Emma Russell (Elisabeth Shue).

Cold fusion, of course, would provide unlimited free power, and that is of great interest to the man who has hired the Saint, Ivan Tretiak (Rade Serbedzija). He was once a communist boss, is now an oil billionaire, and is secretly withholding vast stores of heating oil in an attempt to freeze Russian citizens into an uprising that would sweep him into office. The Saint's assignment involves a trip to Moscow in midwinter, some impressive location shots of Red Square, and a scene where he sneaks into what I guess is the Kremlin, wearing goggles and a black ski mask so that anyone who sees him will instantly know he's up to no good.

Most of his costumes are more wisely chosen. When he goes to Oxford, he poses as an Austin Pendleton lookalike—a chatty egghead who attends Shue's lectures and learns that she is on the verge of providing Earth with free energy. Then he poses as an artist to win her trust, gets her drunk, inveigles his way into her arms, and is on the brink of learning the secret of cold fusion when an inconvenient thing happens: He falls in love with her.

All of this involves some of the same ingredients that have been road tested in Bond movies, and indeed there's speculation that *The Saint* is also the first of a series. If so, they'll have to wind the plot a little tighter. Compared to the sensational stunts and special effects in the Bond series, *The Saint* seems positively leisurely. The fight scenes go on too long and are not interesting, the villains aren't single-minded enough, and the Saint seems more like a disguise fetishist than a formidable international operative. What does work is the chemistry between Kilmer and Shue, whose scenes have a certain charm, especially the one where she says she'll give away the secret of cold fusion to avoid anyone getting rich with it.

I've been trying to put my finger on the movie's key problem, and I think it may be that Kilmer plays the Saint too realistically. If you take a step back and really think about James Bond, you will realize that he is mad. So is Batman. So is the Phantom (the most unfairly overlooked recent movie superhero). They live in fantasy worlds of their own creation, and bring a certain style to their delusions. The Saint still harbors ordinary human emotions, and that will not do.

Saving Private Ryan ★ ★ ★ ★

R, 170 m., 1998

Tom Hanks (Captain Miller), Tom Sizemore (Sergeant Horvath), Edward Burns (Private Reiben), Barry Pepper (Private Jackson), Adam Goldberg (Private Mellish), Vin Diesel (Private Caparzo), Giovanni Ribisi (T/4 Medic Wade), Jeremy Davies (Corporal Upham), Harve Presnell (General George Marshall), Matt Damon (Private Ryan). Directed by Steven Spielberg and produced by Spielberg, Ian Bryce, Mark Gordon, and Gary Levinsohn. Screenplay by Robert Rodat.

The soldiers assigned to find Private Ryan and bring him home can do the math for themselves. The army chief of staff has ordered them on the mission for propaganda purposes: Ryan's return will boost morale on the home front and put a human face on the carnage at Omaha Beach. His mother, who has already lost three sons in the war, will not have to add another telegram to the collection. But the eight men on the mission also have parents—and besides, they've been trained to kill Germans, not to risk their lives for publicity stunts. "This Ryan better be worth it," one of the men grumbles.

In Hollywood mythology, great battles wheel and turn on the actions of individual heroes. In Steven Spielberg's *Saving Private Ryan*, thousands of terrified and seasick men, most of them new to combat, are thrown into the face of withering German fire. The landing on Omaha Beach was not about saving Private Ryan. It was about saving your ass.

The movie's opening sequence is as graphic as any war footage I've ever seen. In fierce dread and energy it's on a par with Oliver Stone's *Platoon,* and in scope surpasses it—because in the bloody early stages the landing forces and the enemy never meet eye to eye, but are simply faceless masses of men who have been ordered to shoot at one another until one side is destroyed.

Spielberg's camera makes no sense of the action. That is the purpose of his style. For the individual soldier on the beach, the landing was a chaos of noise, mud, blood, vomit, and death. The scene is filled with countless unrelated pieces of time, as when a soldier has his arm blown off. He staggers, confused, standing exposed to further fire, not sure what to do next, and then he bends over and picks up his arm, as if he will need it later.

This landing sequence is necessary in order to establish the distance between those who give the order that Private Ryan be saved, and those who are ordered to do the saving. For Captain Miller (Tom Hanks) and his men, the landing at Omaha has been a crucible of fire. For Army Chief George C. Marshall (Harve Presnell), in his Washington office, war seems more remote and statesmanlike; he treasures a letter Abraham Lincoln wrote consoling Mrs. Bixby of Boston about her sons who died in the Civil War. His advisers question the wisdom and indeed the possibility of a mission to save Ryan, but he barks, "If the boy's alive we are gonna send somebody to find him—and we are gonna get him the hell out of there."

That sets up the second act of the film, in which Miller and his men penetrate into French terrain still actively disputed by the Germans, while harboring mutinous thoughts about the wisdom of the mission. All of Miller's men have served with him before—except for Corporal Upham (Jeremy Davies), the translator, who speaks excellent German and French but has never fired a rifle in anger and is terrified almost to the point of incontinence. (I identified with Upham, and I suspect many honest viewers will agree with me: The war was fought by civilians just like him, whose lives had not prepared them for the reality of battle.)

The turning point in the film comes, I think, when the squadron happens upon a German machine-gun nest protecting a radar installation. It would be possible to go around it and avoid a confrontation. Indeed, that would be following orders. But they decide to attack the emplacement, and that is a form of protest: At risk to their lives, they are doing what they came to France to do, instead of what the top brass wants them to do.

Everything points to the third act, when Private Ryan is found and the soldiers decide what to do next. Spielberg and his screenwriter, Robert Rodat, have done a subtle and rather beautiful thing: They have made a philosophical film about war almost entirely in terms of action. *Saving Private Ryan* says things about war that are as complex and difficult as any essayist could possibly express, and does it with broad, strong images, with violence, with profanity, with action, with camaraderie. It is possible to express even the most thoughtful ideas in the simplest words and actions, and that's what Spielberg does. The film is doubly effective because he communicates his ideas in feelings, not words. I was reminded of *All Quiet on the Western Front.*

Steven Spielberg is as technically proficient as any filmmaker alive, and because of his great success he has access to every resource he requires. Both of those facts are important to the impact of *Saving Private Ryan.* He knows how to convey his feelings about men in combat, and he has the tools, the money, and the collaborators to make it possible.

His cinematographer, Janusz Kaminski, who also shot *Schindler's List,* brings a newsreel feel to a lot of the footage, but that's relatively easy compared to his most important achievement, which is to make everything visually intelligible. After the deliberate chaos of the landing scenes, Kaminski handles the attack on the machine-gun nest, and a prolonged sequence involving the defense of a bridge, in a way that keeps us oriented. It's not just men shooting at one another. We understand the plan of the action, the ebb and flow, the improvisation, the relative positions of the soldiers.

Then there is the human element. Hanks is a good choice as Captain Miller, an English teacher who has survived experiences so unspeakable that he wonders if his wife will even recognize him. His hands tremble, he is on the brink of breakdown, but he does his best because that is his duty. All of the actors playing the men under him are effective, partly because Spielberg resists the temptation to make them zany "characters" in the tradition of World War II movies, and makes them deliberately ordinary. Matt Damon, as Private Ryan, exudes a different energy because he has not been through the landing at Omaha Beach; as a paratrooper, he landed inland, and although he has seen action, he has not gazed into the inferno.

They are all strong presences, but for me the key performance in the movie is by Jeremy Davies, as the frightened little interpreter. He is our entry into the reality because he sees the war clearly as a vast system designed to humiliate and destroy him. And so it is. His survival depends on his doing the very best he can, yes, but even more on chance. Eventually he arrives at his personal turning point, and his action writes the closing words of Spielberg's unspoken philosophical argument.

Saving Private Ryan is a powerful experience. I'm sure a lot of people will weep during it. Spielberg knows how to make audiences weep better than any director since Chaplin in *City Lights*. But weeping is an incomplete response, letting the audience off the hook. This film embodies ideas. After the immediate experience begins to fade, the implications remain, and grow. ☞

Savior ★ ★ ★ ½

R, 103 m., 1998

Dennis Quaid (Guy), Natasa Ninkovic (Vera), Nastassja Kinski (Maria), Stellan Skarsgard (Dominic), Sergej Trifunovic (Goran), Neboisa Glogovac (Vera's Brother), Vesna Trivalic (Woman on Bus). Directed by Peter Antonijevic and produced by Oliver Stone and Janet Yang. Screenplay by Robert Orr.

Savior is a brutally honest war film that looks unblinkingly at how hate and prejudice can pose as patriotism. It stars Dennis Quaid as an American named Guy, whose wife and child are killed by a Muslim terrorist bomb in Paris. He walks into the nearest mosque, murders men at prayer, and then disappears into the French Foreign Legion. Six years later he is in Bosnia as a mercenary fighting for the Serbs against the Bosnians.

"We fight for no country, no faith, no political cause," he is told on the day he's sworn into the legion. "We fight for honor." One would like to think that honor might involve country, faith, or politics, but only the legion deserves the loyalty of a legionnaire, and it's this kind of macho, death-intoxicated craziness that Guy encounters in Bosnia. The Bosnians and Serbs have religious differences, but the film argues that much of the blood-hate on both sides involves psychotic male societies in which women are chattel—to be raped if they're not yours, and killed if they're yours and have been raped.

Guy buys into this ethic in the early scenes of the movie, blaming all Muslims for his family's murder by a lunatic fringe. Later, he is forced to focus on individual people, and finds it is not so easy to hate when you know someone. Empathy is the enemy of tribalism.

In Bosnia, he and his best friend Dominic (Stellan Skarsgard) kill for hire, and sometimes discuss what they do. Guy: "You've done nothing wrong here." Dominic: "It feels like I did." We see Guy use a sniperscope to take aim on an innocent young boy looking for his goat. Guy kills him. A flashback shows how Guy's friend was killed by a young girl concealing a grenade. An eye for an eye.

A truce is declared. Guy and his Serbian comrade Goran (Sergej Trifunovic) take custody of a very pregnant Serbian woman. Goran knows the woman's family. In a tunnel, he drags the woman out of the car and starts kicking her in the stomach. Her crime: being pregnant with a Muslim child. "She was raped," Guy protests. This is a meaningless concept to Goran. She has been defiled, and if she were a decent woman, then of course she would already have killed herself. No blame attaches to her rapists, and we assume Goran himself has enthusiastically raped as many Bosnian women as convenient, trusting them to kill themselves or be killed by their fathers, brothers, or helpful male neighbors.

Guy, who has spent years killing for hire, who himself has killed in revenge, now finds he can stomach no more. He kills Goran and finds himself in possession of the woman, named Vera (Natasa Ninkovic), and her child. All of this is prologue to the film's central sections, in which Guy undergoes a change of heart because circumstances force him to empathize with these people instead of objectifying them as targets. His situation is complicated because Vera buys into the poisoned macho logic, and refuses to nurse or care for the baby. The story arrives at a point where her own father hands her a gun and expects her to shoot herself.

Truffaut once wondered if it was really possible to make an antiwar movie, since war films were inherently exciting and we tend to identify with one side or the other. Here is an antiwar film. It helps, I suppose, that we see it from outside: Most American audiences view the civil wars in Yugoslavia as insane. While one side or the other might seem to make a better ideological case, the fighting is based on ancient blood hatred, and the hatred is founded not on religion but on tribalism: If you are not like me, then I hate you. The primitive attitudes toward women make it easier to see how many fighters on both sides are killing for reasons more pathological than patriotic.

Quaid is an actor who is innately likable. Here we don't ever see the famous grin, the easy charm. He plays Guy as a man who essentially shares the values of the men on both sides of the war he finds himself in, until responsibility for an infant forces him back in touch with more civilized values.

Savior is not subtle. Directed by Peter Antonijevic, a Serbian who is evenhanded in his treatment of both sides, it was produced by Oliver Stone and his longtime colleague Janet Yang from a screenplay they purchased from Robert Orr, who was inspired by a true story. The symbolism is heavy-handed and the movie pounds its insights home with big, bold strokes. But Quaid and Ninkovic find the right tone for their relationship; it doesn't get soppy or turn into phony romance, but remains hardened by war. And the end of the story is cathartic but not "happy" in a contrived way. Too bad the music is allowed to swell into an inappropriate chorus, when the single woman's voice that began the song would have been a more effective closing note

A movie like *Savior* is a reminder that human nature does not inevitably take us upward to higher moral ground, but sometimes drags us down to our dog-eat-dog beginnings. It is so easy to blame a group for the actions of a few of its members—to make them seem less than human, to justify our hatred for them. Of course, movies that demonstrate that are not as much fun as the other kind, in which those bastards get what they have coming to them.

The School of Flesh ★ ★ ★

R, 102 m., 1999

Isabelle Huppert (Dominique), Vincent Martinez (Quentin), Vincent Lindon (Chris), Marthe Keller (Madame Thorpe), Francois Berleand (Soukaz), Daniele Dubroux (Dominique's Friend), Bernard Le Coq (Cordier), Roxane Mesquida (Marine). Directed by Benoit Jacquot and produced by Fabienne Vonier. Screenplay by Jacques Fieschi, based on the novel by Yukio Mishima.

We look at French films about love like schoolchildren with our noses pressed against a window. We are so direct about love in North America. We date, we have relationships, we fall in love—as if a natural, unconscious process is taking place. In France, love is more like a discussion, a debate. One has to be right or wrong about it. Not about the other person—about the idea of love itself.

"I don't think you'll go the distance," the older woman says to the younger man in Benoit Jacquot's *The School of Flesh.* Later in the film, he tells her, "One day I decided to live without feelings." The first time she takes him out to dinner, he uses his fingers to pick up the fish on his plate. "Put it down," she says. "Why?" Her face betrays absolutely no expression: "You're with me."

One guesses that in another restaurant, with another woman, he would have used his fork for the fish. He is not without some sophistication; she found him as a bartender in a gay club. Using his fingers was a way of testing her; her response was the answer to an exam question. The exam involved the matter of class differences. They are not concerned that he is working class and she is a professional; what matters is the tug-of-war and who will win as their styles clash.

It's a good question whether romance is involved at all in *The School of Flesh,* which is based on a Japanese novel by Yukio Mishima, who also wrote of class and power. Love is mentioned at various times, but is it a fact or a concept? How much is sex involved, for that matter? The man and woman have sex together, yes, but it doesn't seem as important to them as the battle of wills they engage in. The first time they see each other, they issue a mutual challenge with their eyes. The look they exchange isn't about lust, but power.

That first meeting is in a bar with a primarily gay clientele. Dominique (Isabelle Huppert), who works in the fashion business, sees Quentin (Vincent Martinez) behind the bar. He's a boxer, is twenty years younger, looks tough, has cold eyes—but not colder than Dominique's. Huppert, who is famous for impassivity in her movie roles, has rarely revealed less than here (Stephen Holden wrote that her tears appear "to emanate from a realm somewhere beyond feeling"). Their eyes lock, they size each other up, she leaves and she is back the next night.

She knows from a transvestite in the bar that Quentin is bisexual. Doesn't matter. She is in the grip of the kind of erotomania that must have what it must have. He realizes this and plays with it; there's a scene where he plays a video game in an arcade while she shifts impatiently on her feet, asks that they leave, leaves alone, turns around, comes back—and only then does he acknowledge her. The twist in the movie comes when he starts to become as obsessed with her as she is with him. And when she finds out his secrets—not the ones she thought she knew, but others.

I cannot imagine a Hollywood movie like this. Audiences would be baffled. Imagine two fairly tough stars—a younger guy like Vincent Gallo, say, and an alluring older woman like Susan Sarandon. I can imagine their sex scenes (indeed, I've seen them, between Sarandon and James Spader in *White Palace*). I can imagine conversations in cafés and arguments in bedrooms. What I cannot imagine is the holding back, the restraint, the intellectual side, as the two characters engage in a debate about the proper form of an affair. Ever hear the one about the three guys who see a couple through a window? "What are they doing?" asks the Englishman. "Making love," says the American. "Very badly," says the Frenchman.

Scream 2 ★★★

R, 122 m., 1997

Neve Campbell (Sidney Prescott), David Arquette (Dewey Riley), Courteney Cox (Gale Weathers), Liev Schreiber (Cotton Weary), Sarah Michelle Gellar (Cici), Jamie Kennedy (Randy Meeks), Elise Neal (Hallie), Jerry O'Connell (Derek), Jada Pinkett (Maureen), Omar Epps (Phil). Directed by Wes Craven and produced by Cathy Konrad and Marianne Maddalena. Screenplay by Kevin Williamson.

Wes Craven's *Scream* (1996) was a revolutionary film, the first horror movie in which the characters had seen other horror movies, knew all the clichés, and tried not to make the obvious mistakes. Now comes *Scream 2,* in which the characters have seen a movie based on the first killings, and are trapped once again in a slasher nightmare.

Like all sequels, this one is a transparent attempt to cash in on the original—but, of course, it *knows* it is, and contains its own learned discussion of sequels. The verdict is that only a few sequels have been as good as the originals; the characters especially like *Aliens* and *Godfather, Part Two.* As for *Scream 2,* it's . . . well, it's *about* as good as the original.

Both movies use a Boo Machine, a plot device for making the audience jump and scream and clutch each other's forearms. The scares this time come from a mad slasher in a curiously unsettling Halloween ghost mask, who stalks a bunch of college freshmen who survived the original slashings. The killer is also interested in such groupies as a TV newsman and a crippled former deputy sheriff.

I have witnessed a lot of slashers jump out of a lot of shadows. When Alan Arkin pounced on Audrey Hepburn in *Wait Until Dark,* that pretty much defined, for me, how scary such an event could be. I was not frightened by the Boo Moments in *Scream 2,* and I found the violence kind of inappropriate; this movie is gorier than the original, and that distracts from the witty screenplay by Kevin Williamson

His premise this time is that violence is quickly translated into marketable form by the media; since he is doing that very thing in *Scream 2*, there are ironies within ironies here. The movie is so articulate about what it's doing, indeed, that you can't criticize it on those grounds—it gets there first.

The film opens with a showing of *Stab*, a movie based on the killing in the first film, and at the screening two audience members (Jada Pinkett and Omar Epps) are . . . well, see for yourself. Soon the slasher has moved to a nearby campus, where survivors, including Sidney Prescott (Neve Campbell), are students, and the wounded Deputy Riley (David Arquette) has found a job as a security guard. Also hanging around is TV newswoman Gale Weathers (Courteney Cox), who covered the first murders and wrote a best-seller about them, which became *Stab* and has now inspired the new murders. Also moping about is Cotton (Liev Schreiber), accused by Sidney in the first film but found innocent, and now demanding a second helping of his fifteen minutes of fame.

Who gets killed, and why, and how, I will not reveal, except to register a useless complaint that there is no way to guess who's doing the killing, and everyone who seems suspicious is (almost) sure to be innocent. Idea: In *Scream 3*, the man behind the mask is a movie critic, trying to discredit horror movies so he won't have to sit through any more.

The Williamson screenplay uses the horror platform as a launching pad for a lot of zingers; I'd like to see his work in a more mainstream film. When the TV newswoman is asked about her nude photos on the Internet, for example, she replies, "It was just my head. It was Jennifer Aniston's body." And a killer says he *wants* to be caught because he's already mapped out his strategy: "The movies made me do it," he'll argue, and he plans to have Bob Dole testify for the defense. ("I'll get Dershowitz! Cochran! The Christian Coalition will pay for my defense!")

Wes Craven was born to direct this material. One of the most successful of horror filmmakers, he made *The Hills Have Eyes* and the *Nightmare on Elm Street* movies, and was already headed in the same direction as the Williamson screenplay when he wrote and directed *Wes Craven's New Nightmare* in 1994. That was a movie (better than either *Scream* picture, I think) in which the cast and crew of a horror film found deadly parallels between the plot and their lives.

Do movies cause people to act violently? *Scream 2* seems to think so—or is that an ironic stance, to make the movie scarier? Will a movie like this, by educating its audience to the conventions and silly clichés of horror films, defuse the violence and make them less likely to be influenced? Now there's an intriguing notion.

See the Sea and A Summer Dress

★★★

NO MPAA RATING, 52 m. and 15 m., 1999

Sasha Hails (Sasha), Marina de Van (Tatiana). Directed by Francois Ozon and produced by Oliver Delbosc and Marc Missonnier. Screenplay by Ozon.

Hitchcock believed that suspense came not in action, but in anticipation: not the bomb exploding, but the bomb under the table, waiting to explode. From the first shots of Francois Ozon's *See the Sea*, we sense impending disaster, but we're not sure what form it will take. There is a simple situation, involving two women and a baby at an isolated beach cottage, and yet the possibilities are many, and we speculate about first one outcome, then another.

Sasha (Sasha Hails), an Englishwoman, is living in a cottage in France with her ten-month-old daughter. Her husband is expected to join them, but seems distant and unreachable. A backpacker knocks at the door. This is Tatiana (Marina de Van), a sullen, expressionless young woman who wants to pitch her tent in the yard. She doesn't ask so much as demand. Sasha's reply is curious: "It's my husband's property. I'd have to ask him." Eventually, maybe because she is lonely or intrigued, Sasha lets Tatiana stay.

What will the outcome be? Ozon creates the atmosphere of hot, drowsy summer moral laxity; we are reminded a little of Laura Dern's erotic boredom in *Smooth Talk*. There is the possibility of sex between the women, reinforced by scenes of casual nudity, but we somehow know that's not the point: Something sinister will happen. And then we're worried about that baby.

Sasha is a loving mother, billing and cooing, but a shockingly irresponsible one. She leaves the infant alone in the bath. Later, she leaves it on the beach while she wanders into a nearby wood, a gay cruising area where one of the anonymous men among the trees supplies what she abruptly indicates she desires. One day Sasha goes into town, and asks Tatiana to baby-sit.

This is not a woman you would choose for a baby-sitter. She is dirty and deliberately ill-mannered, bolting her food and then lifting up her plate to lick it clean. She asks questions in a challenging manner, and her face conceals what she thinks of the answers. We have seen her play a particularly nasty little secret trick on Sasha. In her aimlessness she resembles the heroine of Agnes Varda's *Vagabond,* but that woman was a victim, and Tatiana is not a victim.

The outcome is a surprise, and yet in a way we were waiting for it. The movie is about the waiting. It is fifty-two minutes long, and that's about the right length. Longer, and the plot would have had to add unnecessary details to the spare, clean, ominous style.

On the same program is a fifteen-minute short subject, also by Ozon, named *A Summer Dress,* which is lighter in tone. Apparently filmed on the same beach, it also uses the forest area where men cruise for sex, and also places a heterosexual encounter there, with watching eyes. The film follows a young man, who is perhaps gay, as he goes to the beach for a swim and is boldly invited into the woods by a woman who says she is his age (she looks older). He accompanies her, and what he discovers provides the film's payoff.

Both films are notable for the way they quietly slip into the hidden sexual spaces of their characters. Hollywood movies seem determined these days to present sex as an activity not unrelated to calisthenics. What Ozon knows about sex is like what Hitchcock knows about suspense: not the explosion, but the waiting for the bomb to go off.

Selena ★★★½

PG, 130 m., 1997

Jennifer Lopez (Selena), Edward James Olmos (Abraham Quintanilla), Jon Seda (Chris Perez), Constance Marie (Marcela Quintanilla), Jacob Vargas (Abie Quintanilla), Lupe Ontiveros (Yolanda Saldivar), Jackie Guerra (Suzette Quintanilla), Becky Lee Meza (Young Selena). Directed by Gregory Nava and produced by Moctesuma Esparza and Robert Katz. Screenplay by Nava.

Selena brings freshness and heart to the life story of a little girl from Corpus Christi, Texas, who had big dreams and was lucky enough to realize almost all of them before her life was cut short. Selena Quintanilla was poised to become the first female singer to cross over from Spanish to English markets when she was shot dead on March 31, 1995.

By the time she died, the English-speaking Selena (Jennifer Lopez) had conquered the Spanish charts, dominated Mexican-American pop music, and even won acceptance in Mexico, despite her shaky Spanish and an American accent. She'd had No. 1 hits, won a Grammy award, and was about to go on tour to promote her first English album. "Everybody's gonna wonder how I learned English so fast," she joked. Then it all ended when an employee shot her in an argument over theft.

Selena, written and directed by Gregory Nava *(El Norte, My Family),* places her firmly inside a close, loving family. From the very beginning, "Selena y Los Dinos" was a family act, guided by her father, Abraham (Edward James Olmos), and including sister Susie (Jackie Guerra) on drums and brother Abie (Jacob Vargas) on guitar. They toured county fairs and played school dances, and Abraham even opened a restaurant just so he could book his kids as the entertainment (Selena's big crowd-pleaser was "Over the Rainbow"). It was slow going at first, and when Abraham insisted Selena start singing in Spanish, the young teenager rebelled: "I don't want to learn to sing in Spanish! I don't even *like* Spanish music. I like Donna Summer."

Abraham tells her she has to sing from the inside, from what she is, and she is Mexican-American, between two worlds, and that's tough: "The Americans jump all over us because we don't speak perfect English, and then the Mexicans jump all over us because we don't speak perfect Spanish." So Selena learns from her father to sing Spanish and eventually to speak it, and becomes a regional star of Tejano music—the unique South Texas blend that formed in the early 1900s when Mexican bands mixed in the accordion music of their Czech and Polish neighbors.

The movie opens with Selena singing "I Will Survive" to a packed house in the Houston Astrodome, and then flashes back to the early life of her father, who formed a rock 'n' roll group named "The Dinos." Like his daughter many years later, he found himself caught between two worlds: Anglo clubs didn't want Chicano bands, and Mexican clubs wanted Spanish dance music. After one appearance ends in a fight, a cop asks Abraham, "What'd y'all do?" He answers, "We sang 'We Belong Together.'"

Abraham's band fails, but he starts again, bringing home secondhand instruments to begin a family group, despite the doubts of his wife, Marcela (Constance Marie). In one of the movie's most charming scenes, the family has hit bottom. Abraham promises Selena someday she'll be a big star "and go to Disneyland." Then Marcela hears a familiar song on the radio, and teaches her daughter to dance to it, giving her the trademark of perpetual motion onstage.

Young Selena is played by Becky Lee Meza, who has a big smile and a lot of energy. The teenage and adult Selena is played by Lopez in a star-making performance. After her strong work as the passionate lover of Jack Nicholson in *Blood and Wine,* here she creates a completely different performance, as a loyal Quintanilla who does most of her growing up on a tour bus with her dad at the wheel.

She's very close to Susie and Abie, and finds a trusted confidante in her mother, but when a talented young guitarist named Chris Perez (Jon Seda) joins the band and she falls in love with him, there's trouble. "This stops right now!" Abraham thunders, firing the kid. But it's true love, well written and acted here, and after Selena and Chris elope, the family accepts him. Olmos's scene with his daughter, when she brings her new husband home, is one of the movie's most touching.

The biographical scenes are intercut with a lot of music; Selena's original recordings are used, with Lopez lip-synching and doing a convincing job of being Selena onstage; she has the star presence to look believable in front of 100,000 fans in Monterrey, Mexico. Some of the songs build real power, but others are undercut, I think, by unnecessary visual gimmicks like Woodstock-style double- and triple-split screens, and cutaways to the Moon, roses, and other symbols. In one montage late in the movie, the same song is shown being performed at several concerts, to showcase the many different costumes Selena designed for herself; the costumes come across, but the performance is lost in the cutting. When Lopez (and Selena) are left alone to simply sing, the results are electrifying.

Selena is smart in not letting the singer's death dominate the story of her life. We meet her killer, Yolanda Salvidar (Lupe Ontiveros), almost obliquely, when she's introduced as the manager of Selena's new boutique and the former president of her fan club. Soon there's a discrepancy over missing money, and then the shooting, which the movie wisely deals with only through its aftermath.

Selena succeeds, through Lopez's performance, in evoking the magic of a sweet and talented young woman. And, like Nava's *My Family,* it's insightful in portraying Mexican-American culture as a rich resource with its own flavor and character. It's ironic that the most successful modern Latina female singer could once have had a talk with her dad where he sighed, "You like Donna Summer; I like doo-wop." But he also said, "You gotta be who you are." She was.

A Self-Made Hero ★ ★ ★

NO MPAA RATING, 105 m., 1998

Mathieu Kassovitz (Albert Dehousse), Anouk Grinberg (Servane), Sandrine Kiberlain (Yvette), Albert Dupontel (Dionnet), Nadia Barentin (Mme Louvier/Mme Revuz/General's Wife). Directed by Jacques Audiard and produced by Patrick Godeau. Screenplay by Alain Le Henry and Jacques Audiard, based on the novel by Jean-Francois Deniau.

"The past only drags you down," the Captain advises Albert, who is a beggar at the time. Albert takes him at his word and reinvents himself as a hero of the French Resistance—so successfully that men who really were heroes have tears in their eyes when they think of his bravery. *A Self-Made Hero* is inspired by the way that some French belatedly recalled that they were always against the Nazis in World War II, but it is not simply an attack on hypocrisy. In a larger sense, it's about our human weakness for inventing stories about ourselves and telling them so often that we believe them.

Albert Dehousse (Mathieu Kassovitz) is schooled in deception at his mother's breast. From her he learns that his father was a hero in the first war: Doesn't she have his veteran's pension to prove it? From nasty local urchins Albert learns the more likely story, that his father was a drunk who died of liver failure, and his mother made the whole thing up.

Albert himself is an idle daydreamer, a blank slate on which various versions of a life story can be sketched. He reads romantic novels, and then tells a girl he is a novelist. She believes him and marries him, but her family so mistrusts him that it is only after the war he discovers they were in the Resistance, and sheltered Allied pilots who were shot down.

Albert spends the war as a salesman, having evaded the draft. From his father-in-law he learns that to make a sale, you must determine what a customer wants to believe, and confirm it. Fleeing his first marriage after the liberation, he is penniless in Paris when he meets the Captain (Albert Dupontel), a heroic Resistance parachutist who assumed so many fake identities during the war that he perhaps lost touch with himself and identified only with his deceptions. He bluntly counsels Albert to invent a new past.

This process comes easily to Albert because he has no present. Like Chance, the hero of *Being There,* he is such a cipher that other people see what they want. Albert studies papers on the Resistance, memorizes lists, even inserts himself into old newsreel footage. Some of his skills he learns during a period as private secretary to the enigmatic Mr. Jo, who survived the war by supplying both the Nazis and the Resistance with what they wanted. Albert, indeed, has a gift for finding those who can tutor him in deception: He even learns about the artifices of love from a prostitute.

A Self-Made Hero is not an angry exposé, but a bemused, cynical examination of human weakness. Not a week goes past without another story of an ambassador who invents wartime heroism, an executive who awards himself fictitious degrees, a government official who borrows someone else's childhood trauma and calls it his own. I myself have told stories so often they seem real to me, and can no longer be sure whether my friend McHugh really slapped King Constantine on the back in that hotel bar in Rome. All children tell you with great solemnity about adventures that never happened. Some children don't stop when they grow up.

As it must to all men, some degree of maturity eventually comes to Albert, and with it an uneasiness about what he has done. Even deception has its responsibilities, as when fate requires Albert to decide the fates of six Frenchmen who served in the German army. And then there is a woman he begins to love; he is seized by a great need to tell her the truth.

Albert is played by Mathieu Kassovitz, whose own films as a director *(Cafe au Lait, Hate)* skate along the cutting edge of France's racial tension. In those films he can seem brash, quick, violent. Here he's more of a wraith, and the parallel with Chance is appropriate. Resistance heroes embrace him because his experience enhances their own; the real reason anyone listens to your story is so that you will have to listen to theirs.

Jacques Audiard, who directed the film and cowrote it (the screenplay won an award at Cannes), is of course aware of the way many French collaborationists suddenly discovered Resistance pasts after the war. But that process is too well known to need repeating. His film is more subtle and wide reaching, the story of a man for whom everything is equally unreal, who distrusts his own substance so deeply that he must be somebody else to be anybody at all.

Senseless ★ ★ ½

R, 88 m., 1998

Marlon Wayans (Darryl Witherspoon), David Spade (Scott Thorpe), Matthew Lillard (Tim LaFlour), Rip Torn (Randall Tyson), Tamara Taylor (Janice), Brad Dourif (Dr. Wheedon),

Kenya Moore (Lorraine). Directed by Penelope Spheeris and produced by David Hoberman. Screenplay by Greg Erb and Craig Mazin.

Senseless is a Jim Carrey movie fighting to be a Penelope Spheeris movie, and losing. In this corner is Marlon Wayans, another of the large and talented Wayans family, playing a college student who becomes the pawn of a mad scientific experiment. And in the other corner, Spheeris *(The Decline of Western Civilization, Wayne's World, Black Sheep)*.

Wayans does Jim Carrey–style berserk physical comedy, and does it pretty well. Spheeris fills the crannies of the film with Gen-X counterculture stuff, including Wayans's college roommate, who is so deeply into body piercing that he not only wears studs in his eyebrows, tongue, and lower lip, but wears a gold chain linking those two parts of the anatomy which any prudent man would most hope to keep unbound.

Wayans plays Darryl Witherspoon, who is being dunned for past-due tuition, and in desperation seeks out Dr. Wheedon (Brad Dourif), an owlish scientist whose experimental potion enhances the five senses beyond belief. Darryl hires on as a guinea pig, and the movie's gags involve what he does with his supersenses.

This is a promising idea, and *Senseless* has some fun with it. The slightest sound drives Darryl mad, and side effects make him too itchy to sit through an exam. But soon he's able to see, hear, taste, smell, and feel better than anyone else. That makes him a star on the hockey team, and a virtuoso in other areas too. (He's been raising money by donating blood and sperm, and now asks the sperm bank for a quote on two gallons.)

The film's villain is the supercilious Scott (David Spade), who maneuvers to keep Darryl out of his fraternity. That's important because an important alum of the fraternity (Rip Torn) might help a bright economics major get a job with a Wall Street firm. Darryl and Scott are finalists when tragedy strikes: Darryl incautiously takes a double dose of the magic potion and finds that his senses are cycling out of control. He can count on only four of the five at any given moment, and when Torn takes him to a Knicks game, his hearing cuts out during the national anthem and his eyesight fails as he sits next to an unamused Patrick Ewing.

This is not great comedy, and Wayans doesn't find ways to build and improvise, as Carrey does. But he's talented and has unbounded energy, a plastic face, and a rubber body. I liked him. And I liked his flirtation with Janice (Tamara Taylor), a co-ed who accepts his bizarre misadventures. I was not so fond of a subplot involving Lorraine (Kenya Moore), Janice's buxom sorority sister, who seems written in to supply an awkward and pointless seduction scene.

Penelope Spheeris, whose *Wayne's World* remains one of the funniest of recent movies, never finds a consistent tone here. The broad physical humor of the main plot contrasts weirdly with the character of the roommate (Matthew Lillard), who doesn't seem to vibrate in the same universe. His character could be funny in a different movie, but he seems at right angles to this one.

Seven Years in Tibet ★ ★ ½

PG-13, 131 m., 1997

Brad Pitt (Heinrich Harrer), David Thewlis (Peter Aufschnaiter), B. D. Wong (Ngawang Jigme), Lhakpa Tsamchoe (Pema Lhaki), Mako (Kungo Tsarong), Danny Denzongpa (Regent), Victor Wong (Chinese "Amban"), Ingeborga Dapkunaite (Ingrid Harrer), Jamyang Jamtsho Wangchuck (Dalai Lama [fourteen years]). Directed by Jean-Jacques Annaud and produced by Annaud, John H. Williams, and Iain Smith. Screenplay by Becky Johnston, based on the book by Heinrich Harrer.

Jean-Jacques Annaud's *Seven Years in Tibet* takes the true story of a bright and powerful young boy who meets a stranger from a different land, and buries it inside the equally true but less interesting story of the stranger. The movie is about two characters, and is told from the point of view of the wrong one.

As it opens, we already understand or guess much of what there is to know about Heinrich Harrer (Brad Pitt), an Austrian obsessed by mountain climbing. We know next to nothing about the early life of the Dalai Lama. We know all about the kind of events that occupy the first half of the movie (mountain climbing, POW camps, wilderness treks). We know much less about the world inside the Forbidden City, where lives a fourteen-year-old boy who is both ruler and god.

Seven Years in Tibet is an ambitious and beautiful movie with much to interest the patient viewer, but it makes the common mistake of many films about travelers and explorers: It is more concerned with their adventures than with what they discovered. Consider Livingstone and Stanley, the first Europeans to see vast reaches of Africa, who are remembered mostly because they succeeded in finding each other there.

Vienna, 1939. Harrer is preparing an assault on the difficult Himalayan peak of Nanga Parbat. War is about to break out, but he is indifferent to it, and cold to his pregnant wife ("Go—leave! I'll see you in four months!"). He and a guide named Peter Aufschnaiter (David Thewlis) are soon on the peaks. The mountain-climbing scenes (shot in the Andes) are splendid but not very original; Heinrich saves Peter despite a broken ankle, they are nearly killed by an avalanche, the war begins, and they're interred in a British POW camp, from which they finally escape.

This material occupies the first half of the movie, and yet strictly speaking, it has nothing to do with it. The story proper (the seven years mentioned in the title) begins after they stumble into Tibet and are welcomed uncertainly by the peaceful and isolated civilization they find there.

From the moment of the first appearance of the Dalai Lama (Jamyang Jamtsho Wangchuck), the film takes on greater interest. He stands on the parapet of his palace in Lhasa and surveys his domain through a telescope. He is fascinated by the strangers who have arrived in his kingdom, and soon sends his mother to invite Harrer to visit.

"Yellow Head," he calls him, touching the European's blond hair with fascination, and soon protocol falls aside as he asks Harrer to build him a movie theater and teach him about the world outside. This makes an absorbing story, although I suspect the relationship between pupil and teacher did not feel as relaxed and modern as it does in the film.

Aufschnaiter, the guide, meets a local woman tailor (Lhakpa Tsamchoe) and marries her, and we gather from soulful looks that Harrer would have liked to marry her himself, but the Harrer character is not forthcoming. Brad Pitt plays him at two speeds: cold and forbidding at first, and then charming and boyish. He might have been more convincing if he'd been played by, for example, Thewlis. But *Seven Years in Tibet* is a star vehicle: Pitt is required to justify its $70 million budget, and it would be churlish to blame him for his own miscasting since the movie would not have been made without him.

The film shows the behavior of the Red Chinese toward Tibet as cruel and gratuitous. Why the Chinese so valued this remote, sealed-off kingdom is a mystery; maybe it was a threat to self-righteous, lockstep Marxism. The film shows how Tibet was betrayed from without and within, and then the Dalai Lama, now twenty-one, flees into long years of exile.

He has a more complex face for me, now that I have seen the tortuous journey from his childhood. I wish I had learned more about Tibet: What were the ethnic ramifications, for example, of the marriage between the tailor and the mountain climber? How easily was the language barrier overcome? Why were the Dalai Lama's advisers willing to allow him to come under the influence of a foreigner? How did the boy overcome his godlike upbringing to become open and curious to the outside?

These questions are not exactly answered. But the film does deal with one issue that has been publicized recently: the fact, unknown to the filmmakers when they began, that Harrer had been a Nazi Party member since 1933. Voice-over dialogue establishes him as a Nazi early in the film, and another line later says he "shuddered to recall" his early errors. The information about Harrer should have come as no surprise; would the Nazis have risked letting a nonparty member win the glory of conquering Nanga Parbat?

Shadow Conspiracy ★

R, 103 m., 1997

Charlie Sheen (Bobby Bishop), Linda Hamilton (Amanda Givens), Donald Sutherland (Conrad), Stephen Lang (The Agent), Sam Waterston (President), Ben Gazzara (Vice President Saxon), Henry Strozier (Treasury Secretary

Murphy). Directed by George P. Cosmatos and produced by Terry Collis. Screenplay by Adi Hasak and Ric Gibbs.

Shadow Conspiracy is a simpleminded thriller that seems destined for mercy killing in the video stores after a short run before appalled audiences. There isn't a brain in its empty little head, or in its assembly-line story, which is about how Charlie Sheen pauses occasionally between ludicrous action scenes, some of them ripped off from better films.

Sheen plays a special assistant to the president of the United States. After a dozen people are shot dead in Washington (five victims at a conspiracy center, several reporters at the local paper, etc.), he catches on that something is not right. "Remember that article you wrote about a shadow government?" he askes his former lover, a reporter played by Linda Hamilton. "A conspiracy in the highest levels of government?" She does.

The president (Sam Waterston) threatens to call a halt to all federal spending. His chief of staff (the ominous Donald Sutherland) can't have that. An expert killer (Stephen Lang) is dispatched to kill those who would expose Sutherland's conspiracy. Lang is expert, but not subtle; he pulls women's hair, knocks over laundry carts, runs through public places firing his gun, and tries to assassinate the president with a toy helicopter that fires real machine guns. (If any students of Newton's second law are reading this, I hope they will explain why a toy weighing five pounds would not be disabled by the recoil from these weapons.)

The movie starts with the assault on the center for conspiracy studies, where all of the researchers are apparently deaf, since none of them hear a thing when Lang shoots his first victim through a plate glass window. Later Sheen twigs to the conspiracy and is chased through Washington by Lang; the chase leads into one of my favorite cliché locations, a Steam and Sparks Factory—so named because all it apparently produces are steam and sparks. From the factory Sheen dives into a river, escapes over a waterfall, and dries off with the hot-air blower in a men's room (I will not soon forget him directing the jet of air down the front of his pants). Oh, I almost forgot that the sequence began with Sheen surviving a fall from a high-rise window-washer's platform. ("It's funny how twenty-four hours in this town can put you on the other side of the fence," he philosophizes.)

I especially doubted some of the technical details. Sheen hacks into a top secret National Security database to discover the fate of a colleague, and reads on the screen: "Terminated With Extreme Prejudice. Authorized by Jacob Conrad." Conrad is the Sutherland character. I'm sure secret government agencies carefully enter all of their murders into their databases.

Then there's the matter of the surveillance satellites used by the White House conspirators to track down Sheen and Hamilton in her Jeep. Starting with a view of the hemisphere, the spy cameras can apparently scan every license plate in Washington, and find hers—not once but several times. I'm thinking (a) how come the car is never parked in a garage, or pointing the wrong way, or under a tree? and (b) is this tracking method really the easiest way of spotting two famous people driving around central Washington in an open Jeep?

Such quibbles do not easily slow the director, George P. Cosmatos, whose credits include *Rambo II*, *Cobra*, and *Leviathan*. His movie contains a scene with Lang riding a motorcycle that chases Sheen into the subway system and onto the tracks. Moviegoers with long memories will recall this sequence in its original, much superior incarnation, in *Diva* (1982). Only moviegoers with very, very short memories, however, should attempt to see *Shadow Conspiracy*.

Shadrach ★ ★

PG-13, 88 m., 1998

Harvey Keitel (Vernon Dabney), Andie MacDowell (Trixie Dabney), Scott Terra (Paul Whitehurst), Monica Bugajeski (Ebonia Dabney), John Franklin Sawyer (Shadrach), Daniel Treat (Little Mole Dabney), Darrell Larson (Mr. Whitehurst), Deborah Hedwall (Mrs. Whitehurst). Directed by Susanna Styron and produced by Boaz Davidson, Bridget Terry, and John Thompson. Screenplay by Susanna Styron and Terry, based on a story by William Styron.

It is a strange coincidence that leads me to review *Shadrach,* based on a story by William Styron, on the same day as *Beloved,* based on a story by Toni Morrison. Both are about the aftermath of slavery. In *Shadrach,* a 101-year-old former slave completes a long trek in order to return to the plantation where he was born and wants to be buried. In *Beloved,* a mother kills her children rather than have them returned to the plantation she has escaped from.

It might seem like there are easy points to be scored here against Styron, a white southern novelist, but they wouldn't be fair. He has amply demonstrated, in *The Confessions of Nat Turner,* his own understanding of the horror of slavery.

And he is not arguing that the ancient Shadrach wants to be buried on "Dabney land" out of nostalgia for plantation days under the slave-owning Dabneys. The old man never really explains his motivation, but we sense it is made of nostalgia for his childhood on the plantation, and a feeling that since he worked this land it is more his own than any other land anywhere else.

Still, *Shadrach* is another one of those well-meaning films, like *Amistad,* in which slaves are the supporting characters in their own stories. *Beloved* brings its characters front and center and focuses on how slavery impacted their lives. It doesn't have much screen time for white people, good or bad. It is inescapable that none of the white characters in *Shadrach* have the slightest inkling of the reality of the experience that Shadrach and the characters in *Beloved* endured.

The movie takes place in 1935, in a Virginia deep in the Depression. We meet Paul Whitehurst (Scott Terra), a young boy whose affluent parents are setting out for a funeral. It is a long trip—maybe too long for a young boy. Paul is friendly with some of the children of the Dabney family, poor whites who no longer live in the mansion on the family plantation, but in a sharecropper's cabin. The Dabneys ask Paul to stay with them, and he's delighted at the chance to play with his best friend, Little Mole Dabney (Daniel Treat), and his cheerful sister Ebonia (Monica Bugajeski).

The Dabney parents, who are the best-drawn characters in the story, are Trixie (Andie MacDowell) and Vernon (Harvey Keitel). Vernon is a moonshiner, Trixie has a good heart but swigs too much beer, and the Dabney children are raising themselves to be strangers to soap.

Old Shadrach (John Franklin Sawyer) materializes one day. He is so ancient and feeble it hardly seems possible he walked to "Dabney land," but he did, and now he sits down and tells the Dabneys he wants to be buried there. When he dies, that sets in motion a subplot about the laws against human burial on private ground, and complications involving the segregated cemeteries in Virginia. The Dabneys solve these problems with a subterfuge that edges perilously close to slapstick, considering the issues being considered here.

Shadrach is a well-meaning film, directed by Susanna Styron from her father's autobiographical story. But without diminishing Shadrach's own determination and dignity (evoked in a minimalist, whispering performance by first-time actor Sawyer), it indulges in a certain sentimentality that is hard to accept in the dark weather stirred up by *Beloved.*

The movie even has Vernon Dabney wonder if the slaves weren't better off back when they had an assured place in the social order, and got their meals on time; the movie does not adopt this view as its own, and quietly corrects him, but I was left with a vision of Vernon trying to expound his theories to Sethe, the heroine of *Beloved,* who would rather have a child dead in freedom than alive in slavery.

Shakespeare in Love ★ ★ ★ ★

R, 120 m., 1998

Gwyneth Paltrow (Viola De Lesseps), Joseph Fiennes (Will Shakespeare), Geoffrey Rush (Philip Henslowe), Colin Firth (Lord Wessex), Ben Affleck (Ned Alleyn), Judi Dench (Queen Elizabeth), Simon Callow (Tilney, Master of the Revels), Rupert Everett (Christopher Marlowe), Martin Clunes (Richard Burbage), Tom Wilkinson (Fennyman), Imelda Staunton (Nurse), Anthony Sher (Dr. Moth). Directed by John Madden and produced by David Parfitt, Donna Gigliotti, Harvey Weinstein, Edward Zwick, and Marc Norman. Screenplay by Norman and Tom Stoppard.

There is a boatman in *Shakespeare in Love* who ferries Shakespeare across the Thames while bragging, "I had Christopher Marlowe in my boat once." As Shakespeare steps ashore, the boatman tries to give him a script to read. The contemporary feel of the humor (like Shakespeare's coffee mug, inscribed "Souvenir of Stratford-upon-Avon") makes the movie play like a contest between *Masterpiece Theater* and Mel Brooks. Then the movie stirs in a sweet love story, juicy court intrigue, backstage politics, and some lovely moments from *Romeo and Juliet* (Shakespeare's working title: *Romeo and Ethel, the Pirate's Daughter*).

Is this a movie or an anthology? I didn't care. I was carried along by the wit, the energy, and a surprising sweetness. The movie serves as a reminder that Will Shakespeare was once a young playwright on the make, that theater in all times is as much business as show, and that *Romeo and Juliet* must have been written by a man in intimate communication with his libido. The screenplay is by Marc Norman and Tom Stoppard, whose play *Rosencrantz and Guildenstern are Dead* approached *Hamlet* from the points of view of two minor characters.

Shakespeare in Love is set in late Elizabethan England (the queen, played as a young woman by Cate Blanchett in *Elizabeth,* is played as an old one here by Judi Dench). Theater in London is booming—when the theaters aren't closed, that is, by plague warnings or bad debts. Shakespeare (Joseph Fiennes) is not as successful as the popular Marlowe (Rupert Everett), but he's a rising star, in demand by the impecunious impresario Henslowe (Geoffrey Rush), whose Rose Theater is in hock to a money lender, and Richard Burbage (Martin Clunes), whose Curtain Theater has Marlowe and would like to sign Shakespeare.

The film's opening scenes provide a cheerful survey of the business of theater—the buildings, the budgets, the script deadlines, the casting process. Shakespeare meanwhile struggles against deadlines and complains in therapy that his quill has broken (his therapist raises a Freudian eyebrow). What does it take to renew his energy? A sight of the beautiful Viola De Lesseps (Gwyneth Paltrow), a rich man's daughter with the taste to prefer Shakespeare to Marlowe, and the daring to put on men's clothes and audition for a role in Will's new play.

Players in drag were, of course, standard on the Elizabethan stage ("Stage love will never be true love," the dialogue complains, "while the law of the land has our beauties played by pip-squeak boys"). It was conventional not to notice the gender disguises, and *Shakespeare in Love* asks us to grant the same leeway as Viola first plays a woman auditioning to play a man, and later plays a man playing a woman. As the young man auditioning to play Romeo, Viola wears a mustache and trousers, and yet somehow inspires stirrings in Will's breeches; later, at a dance, he sees her as a woman and falls instantly in love.

Alas, Viola is to be married in two weeks to the odious Lord Wessex (Colin Firth), who will trade his title for her father's cash. Shakespeare nevertheless presses his case, in what turns out to be a real-life rehearsal for Romeo and Juliet's balcony scene, and when it is discovered that he violated Viola's bedchamber, he thinks fast and identifies himself as Marlowe. (This suggests an explanation for Marlowe's mysterious stabbing death at Deptford.) The threads of the story come together nicely on Viola's wedding day, which ends with her stepping into a role she could not possibly have foreseen.

The film has been directed by John Madden, who made *Mrs. Brown* (1997), about the affection between Queen Victoria and her horse trainer. Here again he finds a romance that leaps across barriers of wealth, titles, and class. The story is ingeniously Shakespearean in its dimensions, including high and low comedy, coincidences, masquerades, jokes about itself, topical references, and entrances with screwball timing. At the same time we get a good sense of how the audience was deployed in the theaters, where they stood or sat, and what their view was like—and also information about costuming, props, and stagecraft.

But all of that is handled lightly, as background, while intrigues fill the foreground, and the love story between Shakespeare and Viola slyly takes form. By the closing scene, where Viola breaks the law against women on the stage, we're surprised how much of Shakespeare's original power still resides in lines that now have two or even three additional meanings. There's a quiet realism in the development of the romance, which grows in the shadow of Viola's approaching nuptials: "This is not life, Will," she tells him. "It is a stolen season." And Judi Dench has a wicked scene as Elizabeth, informing Wessex of his bride-to-be, "You're a lordly fool; she's been plucked since I saw her last, and not by you. It takes a woman to know it."

Fiennes and Paltrow make a fine romantic couple, high-spirited and fine-featured, and Ben Affleck prances through the center of the film as Ned Alleyn, the cocky actor. I also enjoyed the seasoned Shakespeareans who swelled the progress of a scene or two: Simon Callow as the Master of the Revels; Tom Wilkinson as Fennyman, the usurer; Imelda Staunton as Viola's nurse; Anthony Sher as Dr. Moth, the therapist.

A movie like this is a reminder of the long thread that connects Shakespeare to the kids opening tonight in a storefront on Lincoln Avenue: You get a theater, you learn the lines, you strut your stuff, you hope there's an audience, you fall in love with another member of the cast, and if sooner or later your revels must be ended, well, at least you reveled. ☞

Shall We Dance? ★ ★ ★ ½

PG, 118 m., 1997

Koji Yakusyo (Shohei Sugiyama), Tamiyo Kusakari (Mai Kishikawa), Naoto Takenaka (Tomio Aoki), Eriko Watanabe (Toyoko Takahashi), Akira Emoto (Toru Miwa), Yu Tokui (Tokichi Hattori), Hiromasa Taguchi (Masahiro Tanaka), Reiko Kusamura (Tamako Tamura). Directed by Masayuki Suo and produced by Yasuyoshi Tokuma, Shoji Masui, and Yuji Ogata. Screenplay by Suo.

One night as he is taking the train home after work, a man sees a beautiful woman standing alone at a second-floor window, lost in thought.

The second night, she is there again. The sign on the window advertises ballroom dancing lessons. The third night, the man gets off the train at an unaccustomed stop and climbs the stairs to the dance studio.

With these simple and direct shots, Masayuki Suo establishes loneliness, mystery, and allure. Later, all will become clear, but it is more intriguing this way: A man seeking not so much a woman as an answer to his question. Why is she sad? What is she thinking?

In Japan the opening scenes would play with an even greater charge. Opening titles, probably added by the distributor, tell us, "Ballroom dancing is regarded with great suspicion, in a country where couples don't go out hand in hand, or say 'I love you.'" The hero of *Shall We Dance?* named Shohei Sugiyama (Koji Yakusyo), is married, a salaryman who works late at night in an office. For him to take dance lessons is as shocking as taking a mistress.

Japan is in some ways still a Victorian society, which makes its eroticism more intriguing. Repression, guilt, and secrecy are splendid aphrodisiacs. Sugiyama creeps up the staircase like a man sneaking into a brothel, and enters a brightly lighted room where other students are already taking their lessons. He is disappointed to learn that his instructor will not be the mysterious stranger at the window (Tamiyo Kusakari), but a friendly, plump, middle-aged woman who teaches him the fundamentals of the fox-trot, and warns him: "She's all the sweeter when viewed from afar."

Shall We Dance? is not about love with a tantalizing mirage, then, but about a man losing his inhibitions and breaking out of the rut of his life. Even Sugiyama's wife thinks he should get out more. "He's working too hard," she tells her daughter; we get a glimpse of the Japanese salaryman's home, where the wage earner often arrives late at night and leaves early in the morning, and may have more important relationships at work than with his own family.

The little crowd at the dance studio has its regulars, including a chubby man who will forever be uncoordinated, and a "wild and crazy" little guy with a mop of hair whose identity provides one of the movie's best moments. Eventually Sugiyama learns that the beautiful woman is embittered because of a breakup with her dance partner, and slowly he is introduced to the world of ballroom dancing competitions, which seem to be the same the world over (the scenes have some of the same feel as the contests in the Australian *Strictly Ballroom*).

There are puzzles at Sugiyama's home. His wife smells unfamiliar perfume on his shirt. His daughter catches him rehearsing alone, late at night. Is he having an affair? Not with the mysterious woman he's not: When he asks her out for dinner, she explains sternly that dancing is her life, and that she certainly hopes he didn't take lessons just in the hopes of meeting her.

The last third of *Shall We Dance?* provides audience-pleasing payoffs that could make this the most successful Japanese film at the Western box office since *Tampopo* ten years ago. But it is the opening material that fascinates. To seek out the secret of a beautiful woman in a window is much more interesting than to discover the secret. Familiarity dissipates eroticism. But of course I realize I am asking the impossible, because of course Sugiyama will mount the stairs, and so of course there must be a story.

Masayuki Suo's direction combines the psychological and intriguing with comedy bits that might be found in a lesser movie. This is often a characteristic of Japanese art; between the moments of drama and truth, lowbrow characters hustle onstage to provide counterpoint. The result is one of the more completely entertaining movies I've seen in a while—a well-crafted character study that, like a Hollywood movie with a skillful script, manipulates us but makes us like it.

As for the happy ending: Well, of course there is one. And it is happy not just for the characters in the movie, but for me, as well, because I imagine the mysterious woman will again appear at her place in the window, gazing out, lost in thought, an inspiration to us all.

Shattered Image ★ ½

NO MPAA RATING, 103 m., 1999

William Baldwin (Brian), Anne Parillaud (Jessie), Graham Greene (Detective), Billy Wilmott (Lamond), Lisanne Falk (Paula/Laura), Bulle Ogier (Mrs. Ford). Directed by Raul Ruiz and produced by Barbet Schroeder, Lloyd Silverman, and Abby Stone. Screenplay by Duane Poole.

Shattered Image is a film so confoundedly and deliberately difficult to view, I felt like the laboratory mouse that fought its way through the maze and was rewarded with nothing more than a chlorophyll gumball. I sat in the dark, earnestly scribbling notes and trying to make mental connections, until it occurred to me that I was being toyed with. Without giving away the ending, I can say that the plot exists at the level of a child's story that ends, "and then I woke up, and it was all a dream!"

Ah, if that only *did* give away the ending! Raul Ruiz, the director, is fond of stories in which the viewer is kept in the dark about the true nature of the characters' reality. In *Shattered Image* he outdoes himself, with the story of a woman named Jessie (Anne Parillaud, of *La Femme Nikita*) who is either a hit woman who dreams she is a rape victim, or a newlywed who dreams she is a hit woman. Each character wakes up from dreams of the other, and as for Brian (William Baldwin)—who is he, really? Her new husband, or what?

Raul Ruiz is a Chilean-born director who has been involved in nearly eighty films since 1970, has shot in several European languages, and moves into English with *Shattered Image.* His interest in narrative game-playing can be seen to better effect in *Three Lives and Only One Death* (1997), the last film starring Marcello Mastroianni, who plays three roles—or maybe only one—in stories that occupy interlocking time lines.

In that film we quickly understand the underlying principle, and it's absorbing to see the time- and space-shifting that goes on. There are rules, even if they are only dimly understood principles of (take your choice) psychology, hallucination, imagination, or magic. In *Shattered Image* all is arbitrary until the end, and then it gets *really* arbitrary.

Faithful readers will know that I am not hostile to stories that conceal their reality. That was the strategy underlying *Dark City,* my choice as the best film of 1998. But in that film (and in *Three Lives*), the director is the audience's coconspirator, allowing glimpses or guesses of the solution.

Shattered Image, which is set alternately in the Caribbean and the Pacific Northwest, keeps the book of its secrets slammed shut. All is mystery until the "answer," which is singularly unsatisfying. And then there is another problem too. In *Three Lives,* we could always be interested in the actual events as they unfolded. In *Shattered Image,* the events seem more like arbitrary behavior designed to give Jessie something to do when loud noises and other triggers jerk her back and forth between dreams and reality (or reality and dreams, or dreams and dreams).

Apart from the narrative gimmick, the story is not intrinsically interesting. So we're like the mouse, negotiating the maze. There's not much of interest along the way, and when we get to the end and the titles roll up the screen, we have a good idea for a song they could play over the credits: Peggy Lee singing "Is That All There Is?"

She's All That ★ ★ ½

PG-13, 97 m., 1999

Freddie Prinze Jr. (Zack Siler), Rachael Leigh Cook (Laney Boggs), Matthew Lillard (Brock Hudson), Paul Walker (Dean Sampson), Jodi Lyn O'Keefe (Taylor Vaughan), Kevin Pollak (Wayne Boggs), Anna Paquin (Mackenzie Siler), Kieran Culkin (Simon Boggs). Directed by Robert Iscove and produced by Peter Abrams, Robert L. Levy, and Richard Gladstein. Screenplay by R. Lee Fleming Jr.

Sometimes while you're watching a movie, you can sense the presence of a wicked intelligence slipping zingers into a formula plot. I had that feeling all during *She's All That,* which is not based on a blindingly original idea (*Pygmalion* and *My Fair Lady* got there first). It's about how the most popular guy in the senior class makes a bet that he can take a dorky girl and turn her into a prom queen.

There's fun in the plot, but there's more fun around the edges. The movie stars Freddie Prinze Jr. as Zack, who has the third best grade point average in his class, and is also the captain of the soccer team and dates the beautiful class sexpot Taylor (Jodi Lyn O'Keefe). But Taylor breaks up with him after going to Daytona Beach and meeting Brock Hudson, star of a cable show in which real kids are cast more or less as themselves (MTV's *The Real World* is the model). I only got a quick glimpse, but I think Brock has a tattoo of himself on his right arm.

Taylor is sure she'll be prom queen. Zack's buddies bet him he can't take another girl and make her the queen. He accepts, and chooses Laney (Rachael Leigh Cook), a mousy wallflower who paints down in her basement. In this affluent southern California community, it doesn't help that her dad is "Dr. Pool" (Kevin Pollak), owner of a pool-cleaning service.

Will Laney undergo a startling transformation? What do you think? I wanted to applaud when Zack unleashed the classic line, "Do you always wear those glasses?" Of course, it is an unbreakable rule of this formula that the ugly duckling is a swan in disguise: Rachael Leigh Cook is in fact quite beautiful, as was Audrey Hepburn, you will recall, in *My Fair Lady.* Just once I'd like to see the *Pygmalion* formula applied to a woman who was truly unattractive.

To give the movie credit, it's as bored with the underlying plot as we are. Even the prom queen election is only a backdrop for more interesting material, as *She's All That* explores differences in class and style, and peppers its screenplay with very funny little moments.

Consider, for example, the scene where Zack seeks Laney in the fast-food joint where she works. McDonald's would be too much of a cliché. This is a Middle Eastern franchise: "Would you like to supersize those falafel balls?" Consider a scene that plays in the foreground while Laney's dad is watching *Jeopardy!* in the background and shouting out the answers. (To a question about the printer of the most famous Bible in history, he shouts out "Hewlett-Packard." I couldn't quite catch the question for which his answer is "Lou Rawls" and the correct answer is "the pope.")

Moments like that are almost better than the movie deserves. So is the way the movie treats Taylor, the villainess, who tries to seduce the vain Brock while he's watching himself on TV, and is told to stop getting spit on his chest. And although it's obligatory to have a party scene at which the bad girl humiliates the good girl by pouring something down her dress, I liked the way Taylor told Laney she was "a waste of perfectly good yearbook space."

High school movies never seem that convincing to me, maybe because all the students seem to be in their twenties and don't have zits. Freddie Prinze Jr., I learn, is twenty-three, and Rachael Leigh Cook is twenty. Still, they have a charm in their roles, muted somewhat in Cook's case because the plot requires her to be sullen much of the time. She lurks in the basement painting large dark canvases, and at first Zack doesn't realize he's really falling in love with her.

But of course he is. And although she resists his advances ("What is this, some kind of a dork outreach program?"), nothing can stand in the way of the happy ending. Watching the movie, I was grateful to the director, Robert Iscove, and the writer, Lee Fleming, for taking this weary material and doing what they could with it. There's so little wit in the movies today. Too many characters speak in big, clunky declarative sentences that serve only to push the plot ahead of them, like people trying to shove their cars out of the snow. *She's All That* is not a great movie, but it has its moments.

She's So Lovely ★★★

R, 112 m., 1997

Sean Penn (Eddie), Robin Wright Penn (Maureen), John Travolta (Joey), Harry Dean Stanton (Shorty), Debi Mazar (Georgie), Gena Rowlands (Miss Green), James Gandolfini (Kiefer), Kelsey Mulrooney (Jeanie). Directed by Nick Cassavetes and produced by Rene Cleitman. Screenplay by John Cassavetes.

At first I didn't understand some of the behavior in the second half of *She's So Lovely,* but then I found the explanation, which is that two of the characters are mad. They often are in the films of John Cassavetes, and this is the last that will bear his credit: Cassavetes, who died in 1989, wrote the screenplay, which has been directed by his son, Nick.

The presence in a small role of Cassavetes's widow, Gena Rowlands, is a reminder of all the characters she played in her husband's movies. Most of them were also mad-deranged, alcoholic, obsessive wives, lovers, or eccentric dames, driven crazy by love and need. Narrow your eyes a little, imagine Rowlands, Cassavetes, and Peter Falk in the roles played here by Robin Wright Penn, Sean Penn, and John Travolta, and you have the key that unlocks the film. Otherwise, you're likely to leave the theater frustrated and confused, asking yourself how any mother could make the choice that the woman in this film makes.

As the story opens, the woman, named Maureen (Wright Penn), lives in a transient hotel with her lover, Eddie (Sean Penn). He has been missing for three days. She seeks him out (and also free drinks and smokes) in a Skid Row bar, and ends up in the room of Kiefer (James Gandolfini), a neighbor across the hall. Through a very large, alcoholic misunderstanding, he assaults her, and Maureen is afraid that when Eddie finds out, he'll kill the guy.

She is nearly right. Eddie, also drunk, succeeds in accidentally shooting a member of an emergency response team, and is sent to prison. At this point, halfway through the movie, everything has advanced according to a certain logic, and we understand that Maureen and Eddie are alcoholics who are obsessively in love, and whose lives, as they say, have become unmanageable.

Ten years pass, handled and explained only with a title on the screen. Maureen is now serenely married to Joey (John Travolta), and lives in a suburban home with her three children, the oldest by Eddie. Then Eddie is released from prison, and the madness begins all over again. Eddie still loves her and wants to see her. In a sequence that has a scary fascination, Joey takes Eddie's daughter, Jeanie, to meet Eddie at a downtown hotel. Would a stepfather do such a thing? Yes, but in such a place? "Shut up and drink your beer," Eddie tells Jeanie at one point, not unkindly.

I was reminded of the Cassavetes film about an obsessive gambler who took his child with him to Vegas and left him in a room at a casino while he disappeared for hours to gamble. Or another where kids are yanked out of school for a weird day at the beach. The families in Cassavetes films are always dysfunctional, the children confronted with irresponsible, deranged adults and trying to make sense of them. Cassavetes's films spun at such a pitch of emotional chaos that no behavior seemed unbelievable, although a lot of it seemed unwise.

The crucial late scene in *She's So Lovely* involves Eddie's visit to the suburban home of Joey and Maureen. This scene will raise questions among logical viewers, but it works as drama, and we cannot look away. Eddie and Maureen are not given a lot of choices (they're locked into a compulsive replay of old tapes), but Travolta finds ways to introduce dark humor into the scene, and we smile sometimes, as we did with so many Cassavetes films, because the characters are mad in such a verbal, screwy, almost pathetic way.

Watching *She's So Lovely,* it's helpful to remember that movies can show behavior without recommending it—that the highest purpose of a movie is not to reflect life realistically, but to filter it through the mind of the artist. *She's So Lovely* does not depict choices most audiences will condone, or even understand, but the film is not boring, and has the dread hypnotic appeal of a slowly developing traffic accident (in which we think there will probably be no fatalities).

Robin Wright Penn and Sean Penn are locked into Maureen and Eddie with a savage zeal; the characters play less implausibly than they sound, because the actors believe in them. Penn is one of our best actors, and his wife (who was so solid as Jenny in *Forrest Gump*) is able to stay with him in these harrowing situations. Travolta finds a way to somehow be outside firing range—his Joey is a man with his own goofiness, who only seems to be ordinary. And there are nice side roles, including one for Harry Dean Stanton, as a drinking buddy who has the classic line, "Nobody brought a piece—it's not that kind of an evening."

Nick Cassavetes, now in his thirties, has been an actor (as indeed anyone with his parents would almost have to be) and is now a director. In *Unhook the Stars* (1996) he directed his mother, Gena Rowlands, as a sensible woman trying to deal with the dysfunctional young mother (Marisa Tomei) across the street, and now here he directs his father's last script.

As a filmmaker, he lacks his father's untidy emotional wildness; he makes films that are more carefully crafted and lack the anarchic spirit. But he understands the territory, and in *She's So Lovely* what he especially understands is that if you want to see true weirdness, you don't look along Skid Row, where the motives are pretty easy to understand, but out in suburbia, where those green lawns can surround human time bombs.

Shiloh ★★★½

PG, 93 m., 1997

Michael Moriarty (Ray Preston), Rod Steiger (Doc Wallace), Blake Heron (Marty Preston), Scott Wilson (Judd Travers), Bonnie Bartlett (Mrs. Wallace), Ann Dowd (Louise Preston), J. Madison Wright (Samantha), Tori Wright (Becky Preston), Shira Roth (Dara Lynn Preston). Directed by Dale Rosenbloom and produced by Zane W. Levitt and Rosenbloom. Screenplay by Rosenbloom, based on the novel by Phyllis Reynolds Naylor.

If I were to say *Shiloh* is the story of a boy and his dog, that would give you a quick idea of the movie, but it would be the wrong idea. The movie is about growing up and taking responsibility, and it is also about the fierce emotions that children have about pets. It is such an awesome duty when you are eleven years old to have a living thing that is your responsibility—that you care for, and that loves you.

When I was ten, I was given a dog named Blackie. He was half Beagle, half mutt. My parents would not allow him in the house; we had just had wall-to-wall carpeting installed. Blackie lived in a doghouse in the backyard. All summer long he was my friend and playmate, and went everywhere with me, and I fed and combed him. That winter, however, it was cold for a dog. Too cold, and Blackie would howl mournfully all night long, and the neighbors complained, and I lay in my bed listening, with a knot in my stomach.

One weekend I was sent on my first plane journey to visit relatives. When I returned, I was told that Blackie had been hit by a car and killed. I didn't believe it then and I don't believe it now, and inside of me, all of these years later, is fury that has not gone away. Adults may have the power to take away a kid's dog and tell him a story about it, but they do not have the right.

Some of those feelings came into play when I saw *Shiloh,* which is a remarkably mature and complex story about a boy who loves a dog and cannot bear to see it mistreated. It isn't some dumb kiddie picture. It's about deep emotions, and represents the real world with all of its terrors and responsibilities.

The kid's name is Marty (Blake Heron). One day the dog follows him home. The dog has a welt over its eye, and we know how it got it; the opening scene shows a hunter named Judd (Scott Wilson) banging it with a gun butt. The dog is afraid of Judd and loves Marty, who names it Shiloh.

Marty's parents are a mailman named Ray (Michael Moriarty) and his wife, Louise (Ann Dowd), who would like to get a job as a manicurist because the family needs the money. They live in a rural area near a general story run by Mrs. Wallace (Bonnie Bartlett), whose husband, Doc (Rod Steiger), can patch up people or animals.

Marty's dad explains to him that the dog is Judd's property and they must return it, which they do, only to hear Judd promise that if the dog runs away again he'll beat it to within an inch of its life. The dog runs away again and comes to Marty, who hides it in a shed on the property. Then Shiloh is injured in a dogfight, and Marty can no longer keep the secret. His father is angry with him for concealing the dog, and for lying to him. Marty feels he had to lie to save Shiloh's life. He begs his mother to intervene: "Dad will never change his mind, and you'll never stand up to him," he says bitterly. His mother will not keep secrets from her husband and supports him, even though her heart breaks for her son. And the father is standing on principle.

So now you see this is real stuff, and not some nonsense about a brave dog fording creeks and rescuing families. It's real about Judd, too, who laughs when he hears the dog is named Shiloh: "I don't name my dogs. When I want them, I whistle. When I don't want them, I give them a kick." But Judd himself has been treated the same way. When Marty tells him, "A dog is like a kid. If you don't treat it right, it will run away," Judd says he cannot remember a time in his childhood when his back wasn't covered with welts—but he didn't run away.

What is remarkable about the film (which is written and directed by Dale Rosenbloom and based on a Newbery Award–winning novel by Phyllis Reynolds Naylor) is that it deals with real moral issues: with property, responsibility, and honesty, and with whether there is a higher good that justifies breaking ordinary rules. To the kid, saving a dog's life is more important than respecting a man's property. Maybe it is to his father, too, but when you are an adult you think twice about letting your son take a man's hunting dog away from him.

By the time the story has been resolved, we have seen a family deal with all the stages of an ethical crisis. And we have seen a boy start to become a man by going over to Judd's and offering to work to earn the money to buy the dog. Marty tells Judd, "All I had was your word. Ain't that worth something to you?" In saying that, he shows he has learned something about what his father was trying to teach him about his own word.

A lesser movie would be about whether the boy gets the dog. *Shiloh* is about whether the boy deserves the dog, can take responsibility for figuring out what's right, and can discover an honest way to get what he wants. This would be an ideal movie for parents and children to see together and talk about afterward. *Shiloh,* like all great family films, deals with real issues in real ways.

I remember, by the way, the day we got rid of that wall-to-wall carpeting. Hardwood floors were back in style.

Shiloh 2: Shiloh Season ★ ★ ★

PG, 96 m., 1999

Michael Moriarty (Ray Preston), Scott Wilson (Judd Travers), Zachary Browne (Marty Preston), Rod Steiger (Doc Wallace), Ann Dowd (Louise Preston), Bonnie Bartlett (Mrs. Wallace), Rachel David (Becky), Joe Pichler (David Howard), Marissa Leigh (Samantha). Directed by Sandy Tung and produced by Dale Rosenbloom and Carl Borack. Screenplay by Rosenbloom, based on novels by Phyllis Reynolds Naylor.

Shiloh 2: Shiloh Season recycles the same characters and, in a way, the same problems as the wonderful original film, but carries the message a little further. The first film was about a boy who is adopted by a dog, loves it, and wants to protect it from its cruel owner—even if that means lying to his parents. This sequel is about how people get to be cruel in the first place, and what you might be able to do to help them.

What's unique about both films, which are based on novels by Phyllis Reynolds Naylor, is that they're about hard ethical issues that kids can identify with. A boy's dog inspires fierce love and protectiveness, and if he thinks adults (even his parents) might be a threat to the dog, he will instinctively do what he can to protect it. Even lie.

Who is to say he is wrong? Yes, "lying" is wrong—but what if it's the only weapon at your disposal to protect a dog that depends on you? I don't think I'd be pleased if a son of mine betrayed his dog. On the other hand, I don't think I'd let him know that. I'd let him find out in other ways. Sometimes parents and children have to enact these passion plays to learn lessons that are deeper than words.

Shiloh 2 takes place once again in an isolated rural area populated only by the Prestons, their alcoholic neighbor Judd Travers, and the friendly folks at the general store. At one point it occurred to me that the lives of the entire Preston family—father, mother, son, daughters, and dog—were completely dominated by Travers, who is their only visitor and the subject of most of their conversations. But there's a kind of purity to the way the story narrows down to the key players.

Marty Preston (Zachary Browne), now on the edge of adolescence, has been able to buy the dog Shiloh from Travers (Scott Wilson). That pleases his dad and mom (Michael Moriarty and Ann Dowd), and also watchful old Doc Wallace (Rod Steiger), who runs the store with his wife and their granddaughter, who is about Marty's age. But now Travers is drinking heavily, hunting out of season, and trespassing on Preston land. And someone is picking on him—scratching his car, knocking over his mailbox, freeing his remaining dogs.

Who is it? There's a line of dialogue that gives us a good idea, but Travers thinks it's Marty. This leads to several charged confrontations between the hunter and Marty's dad (played by Moriarty with solemn authority). Then there are a couple of emergencies—one serious, one a false alarm—and Shiloh plays a role both times.

Scott Wilson once again brings a humanity to the tricky role of Judd Travers, who is a pathetic being. Yes, he kicks dogs. But he was kicked himself as a child, and is a lonely man, living in poverty. (He claims to support himself by hunting, but his only success during this movie comes when he sits on his front porch and picks off one squirrel.) Doc Wallace knows something about the Travers family, and what he tells Marty leads to the ending, in which a life is redeemed—maybe. (I liked the frankness with which Marty prays, after Travers is injured, that the man get better, "but maybe don't let his legs get good enough to go hunting.")

Families do not often attend "family movies" in theaters, unless they're Disney cartoons or TV spin-offs, but the original *Shiloh* was such a success on video that it justified a sequel. Both films demand to be discussed afterward by parents and their children. Neither is about the kind of dumb, empty-headed stuff that passes for children's entertainment. Kids are not stupid, and they wonder about issues like this. They may also suspect, as the movie observes, that "you have to be taught to be kind."

Sick: The Life & Death of Bob Flanagan, Supermasochist ★ ★ ★ ½

NO MPAA RATING, 90 m., 1997

A documentary directed and produced by Kirby Dick. Featuring Bob Flanagan and Sheree Rose.

A few months before he died, Bob Flanagan and Sheree Rose had an argument. She was angry with him for refusing to submit to her sexual discipline. He was angry because she couldn't see that he was dying—drowning in the fluids of cystic fibrosis—and could hardly breathe.

This bare outline makes Rose seem like a monster, but the reality was much, much more complicated. Years earlier, in 1982, Flanagan had signed a contract giving Rose "total control over my mind and body." They had a sadomasochistic relationship lasting fifteen years. At the end she was not being cruel, so much as expressing her fear of losing him. It sounds cruel because she speaks in the terms they used to express their love.

Sick: The Life & Death of Bob Flanagan, Supermasochist is one of the most agonizing films I have ever seen. It tells the story of a man who was born with cystic fibrosis, a disease that fills the lungs with thick, sticky mucus, so that breathing is hard and painful, and an early death is the prognosis. He was in pain all of his life, and in a gesture of defiance he fought the pain with more pain. With Sheree Rose as his partner, he became a performance artist, using his own body as a canvas for museum shows, gallery exhibits, lectures, and performances. He was the literal embodiment of the joke about the man who liked to hit himself with a hammer because it felt so good when he stopped.

Flanagan's masochism began early in life. He recalls forcing himself to sleep under an open window in the winter, and torturing himself by hanging suspended from his bedroom ceiling or the bathroom door ("My parents could never figure out why all the doors were off the jambs"). By the time he made it formal with Sheree Rose, he had already been a masochist for years. "Where was I?" his mother asks herself. "Did we only give him love when he was in pain? I don't know. He was in pain so much of the time."

How do you develop a taste for sticking nails into yourself? His parents recall that as a small child he had pus drained from his lungs by needles; since he felt better afterward, perhaps he identified the pain with relief. Later it became a sort of defiant gesture. His father says: "He's saying to God—'I'll show you!'" In Sheree Rose he found a woman who was a true dominatrix, not just a kinky actress with bizarre costumes. He also found a life partner, and the closeness of their relationship seems frightening at times; they seemed to live inside each other's minds.

What makes *Sick* bearable is the saving grace of humor. Apart from the pain he was born with and the pain he heaped on top of it, Bob Flanagan was a wry, witty, funny man who saw the irony of his own situation. We see video footage of his lectures, his songs, his poems. He takes one of those plastic "Visible Man" dolls they use in science class, and modifies it to illustrate his own special case. As he jokes, kids himself, and makes puns about pain, we are aware of the plastic tubes leading into his nose: oxygen from a canister he carries everywhere.

We are a little surprised to discover that from 1973 to 1995 he was a counselor at a summer camp for kids with CF, and around the campfire we hear him singing his version of a Dylan song, "Forever Lung." He was "scheduled" to die as a child, but lived until forty-two (two of his sisters died of the disease). He was a role model for CF survivors. We meet a seventeen-year-old Toronto girl named Sara who has cystic fibrosis and tells the Make-a-Wish Foundation her wish is to meet Bob Flanagan. She does. How does she deal with his sex life? "Bondage. I can relate to that. Being able to control *some*thing."

Flanagan and Rose collaborated on this film with the documentarian Kirby Dick. It is a last testament. He was very sick when the filming began, and he died in January 1996, almost literally on camera. We see and hear him gasping for his last breaths. If that seems heartless, reflect on his (unrealized) plans for a final artwork: "I want a wealthy collector to finance an installation in which a video camera will be placed in the coffin with my body, connected to a screen on the wall, and whenever he wants to, the patron can see how I'm coming along."

There are scenes in *Sick* that forced me to look away. I could not watch as Flanagan pierced his penis with a nail. But the scenes I did watch were, if anything, more painful. At the end, as Bob fights for breath and Sheree weeps and cares for him, what we are seeing is a couple that had something, however bizarre, that gave them the roles they preferred, and mutual reassurance. Now death is taking it all away.

After his death, Sheree Rose holds a large canister filled with the contents of Bob's lungs, removed at the time of the autopsy. There are pints of liquid there, manufactured by his disease in its determination to kill him. No one can say that Bob Flanagan, after his fashion and in his own way, did not fight back.

The Siege ★ ★ ½

R, 110 m., 1998

Denzel Washington (Anthony Hubbard), Annette Bening (Elise/Sharon), Bruce Willis (General Devereaux), Tony Shalhoub (Frank Haddad), Sami Bouajila (Samir Nazhde), Ahmed Ben Larby (Sheik Ahmed Bin Talal), Mosley Mohamed (Muezzin), Liana Pai (Tina Osu). Directed by Edward Zwick and produced by Lynda Obst and Zwick. Screenplay by Lawrence Wright, Menno Meyjes, and Zwick.

"What if they were black people? What if they were Italian?" These words are spoken by an unseen character in *The Siege*, but they get at the heart of the film, which is about a roundup of Arab Americans after terrorist bombs strike New York City. Okay, what if they *were* black or Italian? What if the movie was a fantasy about the army running rampant over the civil liberties of American Irish, Poles, Koreans? Wouldn't that be the same thing as rounding up the Arab Americans?

Not really, because the same feelings are not at stake. Of all our ethnic groups, only Arabs come from nations that are currently in a state of indefinitely suspended war with the United States. The vast majority of Arab-Americans are patriotic citizens who are happy to plunge into the melting pot with the rest of us (a point the movie does make), but a minority have been much in the news, especially after the World Trade Center bombing.

Many Americans do not draw those distinctions, and could not check off on a list those Arab countries we consider hostile, neutral, or friendly. There is a tendency to lump together "towelheads" (a term used in the movie). Arab-Americans feel vulnerable right now to the kinds of things that happen in this movie, and that's why it's not the same thing as targeting other ethnic groups. (By way of illustration, it is unlikely, even unimaginable, after recent history, that a fantasy like *The Siege* would be made about the internment of Japanese- or Jewish-Americans.)

Oh, the movie tries to temper its material. "They love this country as much as we do," one American says in the film, unaware of the irony in the "they" and "we." The hero, an African-American played by Denzel Washington, has an Arab-American partner (Tony Shalhoub) who is angered when his own son is mistreated. The heroine, a U.S. spy played by Annette Bening, grew up in Lebanon and has an Arab-American lover (although it's a little more complicated than that). But the bottom line is that Arab terrorists blow up New York buses, a packed Broadway theater, and FBI headquarters.

Martial law is declared, the army moves in, and Arabs are detained without any rights. There's cat-and-mouse stuff involving the tracking of Arab bad guys, the usual computer and satellite gimmicks, and suspenseful standoffs and shoot-outs. The dramatic outdoor mob, action, and army scenes are well handled by director Ed Zwick.

I'm not arguing that *The Siege* is a deliberately offensive movie. It's not that brainy. In its clumsy way it throws in comments now and then to show it knows the difference between Arab terrorists and American citizens. But the prejudicial attitudes embodied in the film are insidious, like the anti-Semitism that infected fiction and journalism in the 1930s—not just in Germany, but in Britain and America.

Watching the film, I felt uneasy. Events like those in the film are familiar. The World Trade Center was blown up in real life, not in a thriller. We've recently fired missiles at suspected terrorist centers. *The Siege* opens with actual footage of President Clinton commenting on television about those missiles, and the film implies that he is the president during the events in the story. Given how vulnerable our cities are to terrorism, and how vulnerable Arab-Americans are to defamation, was this movie really necessary?

The movie awkwardly tries to switch villains in the third act, adding an Orwellian twist. Its final thrust is against a military mindset that runs rampant over civil liberties. The FBI and its allies have a face-off with an American general (Bruce Willis) who becomes military commander of New York under martial law and has disdain for the Constitution. Denzel Washington has a good speech where he observes that the enemy doesn't have to destroy our liberties if we do it for ourselves.

By the end of the movie the filmmakers can truthfully say they tried to balance out the villains. But most audiences won't give it that much thought. They'll leave the theater thinking of Arabs (who are handled as an undifferentiated group), not of dangers to the Constitution—which can be dismissed as the fevers of one man (Willis), who is handled like a traditional megalomaniac. ("This is the land of opportunity," he tells Arab-Americans. "The opportunity to turn yourself in.")

Most people will not be watching a political movie, but a popcorn movie. They may even be a little restless during the speechmaking toward the end. They'll be comfortable with the Arab villains because that's what they've been taught on the news. True, at the present moment most of America's enemies in the world are Arab. But at one time or another, this country has been at war with the home nations of most of the major ethnic groups in America. And it was "we" who were at war—all of us. Japanese-Americans who fought in American uniform in World War II will not have to have the buried message of *The Siege* explained to them. ☞

Simon Birch ★★★

PG, 110 m., 1998

Ian Michael Smith (Simon Birch), Joseph Mazzello (Joe Wenteworth), Ashley Judd (Rebecca Wenteworth), Oliver Platt (Ben Goodrich), David Strathairn (Reverend Russell), Dana Ivey (Grandmother Wenteworth), Beatrice Winde (Hildie Grove), Jan Hooks (Miss Leavey), Jim Carrey (Adult Joe). Directed by Mark Steven Johnson and produced by Laurence Mark and Roger Birnbaum. Screenplay by Johnson.

Simon Birch is an unabashedly sentimental tearjerker. Either you stand back and resist it, or you plunge in. There was something about its innocence and spunk that got to me, and I caved in. A lot of that had to do with how likable some of the characters are. We go to the movies for a lot of reasons, and one of them is to seek good company.

The movie takes place in 1964, in a New Hampshire town that obviously had Grandma Moses as its city planner. It's about a friendship between two boys, one a gawky preadolescent named Joe, the other a dwarf named Simon who believes God has chosen him for a mission in life. The opening narration reveals that two of the characters will die during the course of the movie; that softens the shock when they do, and lets the entire movie play as bittersweet nostalgia. It's all framed in a flashback, as an adult Joe (Jim Carrey) revisits the scenes of his childhood.

Joe is your average kid. Simon Birch is not. Played by Ian Michael Smith with remarkable cockiness, he's the smartest person in Sunday school and possibly in town. He is very short and very cute, and very wise about the fact of his dwarfism. When Joe tells him a local girl finds him cute, he sniffs, "She means cute like a baby turtle is cute. Girls don't kiss baby turtles." How do you know? asks Joe. "I just know. If you were me you'd know too."

Joe and Simon are drawn together because they're both misfits. Joe (Joseph Mazzello) is a boy without a father; his mother, Rebecca (Ashley Judd), steadfastly refuses to name names. "I don't understand why she doesn't just tell you," Simon says. "You're already a bastard; might as well be an enlightened one." Rebecca is a sunny, loving mother whose one lapse has, if anything, improved her character.

The other key characters could all be from Norman Rockwell paintings. They include Simon's loutish parents, who don't like him; Rev. Russell (David Strathairn), the local minister; Grandma Wenteworth (Dana Ivey), Rebecca's mother; Miss Leavey (Jan Hooks), the Sunday school teacher who endures Simon's theological insights; and Ben (Oliver Platt), a man Rebecca meets on the train and brings home for supper. (The last time Rebecca met someone on the Boston & Maine, her mother recalls, she came home pregnant.)

Simon and Joe occupy a world of their own, swimming and boating and slipping invisibly around town. Simon's dwarfism doesn't prevent him from going everywhere and doing everything, and even taking his turn at bat in a Little League game; when he finally does get a hit, there are tragic consequences. Simon uses his size as a license to say exactly what he thinks on all occasions, loudly and clearly, as when Rev. Russell is asking God's help for a fund-raiser and Simon stands up on his pew to announce: "I doubt if God is interested in our church activities. If God has made the bake sale a priority, we're all in a lot of trouble."

All of this is a scene-raiser for the melodramatic climax, in which it appears that God has perhaps indeed made Simon a priority. There are people who will find Simon's big scene contrived and cornball but, as I said, it all depends on the state of mind you assign to the picture. I've been seeing a lot of silent films lately, in which incredibly melodramatic developments are a way of life: What matters is not that they're unlikely or sentimental, but that the movie presents them with sincerity, and finds the right tone.

The movie's a directorial debut for Mark Steven Johnson, author of the *Grumpy Old Men* movies. He seems to know his way around small towns and broad emotions. His story was "suggested" by the novel *A Prayer for Owen*

Meany, by John Irving, unread by me, although no doubt much more complex and ambiguous; Johnson goes for a purity of tone that children may identify with as much as adults.

Many of the scenes depend on the screen presence of Ian Michael Smith, making his movie debut with a refreshing brashness. Working with the more experienced Joseph Mazzello *(Radio Flyer, Jurassic Park),* he projects the confidence of a very bright small boy who has been the center of attention for a long time, and has learned to deal with it. By surrounding the boys with very nice people (the Ashley Judd and Oliver Platt characters) and not so nice people (the minister, the teacher), Johnson creates a film so direct and engaging that cynicism wilts in its sunny spirit.

A Simple Plan ★ ★ ★ ★

R, 123 m., 1998

Bill Paxton (Hank Mitchell), Billy Bob Thornton (Jacob Mitchell), Bridget Fonda (Sarah Mitchell), Brent Briscoe (Lou), Gary Cole (Baxter), Becky Ann Baker (Nancy), Chelcie Ross (Carl), Jack Walsh (Mr. Pederson). Directed by Sam Raimi and produced by James Jacks and Adam Schroeder. Screenplay by Scott B. Smith, based on his novel.

"You work for the American Dream—you don't steal it." So says a Minnesota family man early in *A Simple Plan,* but he is only repeating an untested theory. Confronted with the actual presence of $4 million in cash, he finds his values bending, and eventually he's trapped in a horror story of greed, guilt, and murder.

The materials of Sam Raimi's *A Simple Plan* are not unfamiliar, but rarely is a film this skillful at drawing us, step by step, into the consequences of criminal action. The central character is Hank Mitchell (Bill Paxton), who in a narration at the beginning gives us his father's formula for happiness: "A wife he loves. A decent job. Friends and neighbors that like and respect him."

His older brother, Jacob (Billy Bob Thornton), trapped in a lifetime of dim loneliness, would like to go out with a girl who really likes him, and someday farm the place they grew up on. Jacob's best friend, Lou (Brent Briscoe), basically wants to get by, get drunk, and hang out. Hank's pregnant wife, Sarah (Bridget Fonda), would like enough money so she could plan the week's dinners without checking the coupons in the grocery ads.

All of these dreams seem within reach when the three men stumble across an airplane that has crashed in a nature preserve. On board they find the body of the pilot, and a cache of $4 million in bills. "You want to keep it?" Hank asks incredulously. The others do. Soon he does too. It should be a simple plan to hide the money, wait until spring, and divide it among themselves. It's probably drug money anyway, they tell themselves. Who will know? Who can complain?

Hank is the smartest of the three, a college graduate. Jacob, bucktoothed and nearsighted, has never been very bright. Lou is a loose cannon. Can Hank keep them all under control? Some of the film's most harrowing moments show Hank watching in agonized frustration as the others make big, dumb blunders. Right after they find the money, for example, a law officer happens by, and what does Jacob do but blurt out to Hank: "Did you tell him about the plane? It sure sounded like a plane."

At home, Hank's wife, Sarah, at first agrees it would be wrong to keep the money, but she turns that moral judgment around in a snap, and is soon making smart suggestions: "You have to return some of the money, so it looks like no one has been there." All three men begin to dream of what they could do with the money. Then circumstances inspire one impulsive, reckless act after another—acts I will not reveal, because the strength of this film is in the way it leads its characters into doing things they could never have contemplated.

A Simple Plan is one of the year's best films for a lot of reasons, including its ability to involve the audience almost breathlessly in a story of mounting tragedy. Like the reprehensible *Very Bad Things,* it is about friends stumbling into crime and then stumbling into bigger crimes in an attempt to conceal their guilt. One difference between the two films is that *A Simple Plan* faces its moral implications instead of mocking them. We are not allowed to stand outside the story and feel superior to it; we are drawn along, step by step, as the characters make compromises that lead to unimaginable consequences.

The performances can only be described as flawless: I could not see a single error of tone or feeling. Paxton, Thornton, Fonda, and Briscoe don't reach, don't strain and don't signal. They simply embody their characters in performances based on a clear emotional logic that carries us along from the beginning to the end. Like Richard Brooks's *In Cold Blood* (1968), this is a film about ordinary people capable of monstrous deeds.

Thornton and Fonda have big scenes that, in other hands, might have led to grandstanding. They perform them so directly and simply that we are moved almost to tears—we identify with their feelings even while shuddering at their deeds.

Thornton's character, Jacob, has never been very bright, and has watched as Hank went to college and achieved what passes for success. At a crucial moment, when his brotherhood is appealed to, he looks at his friend Lou and his brother Hank and says, "We don't have one thing in common, me and him, except maybe our last name." He has another heartbreaking scene as they talk about women. Hank remembers the name of a girl Jacob dated years ago in high school. Jacob reveals that the girl's friends bet her $100 she wouldn't go steady with him for a month. As for Fonda, her best moment is a speech about facing a lifetime of struggling to make ends meet.

The characters are rich, full, and plausible. Raimi's direction and the screenplay by Scott Smith are meticulous in forming and building the characters, and placing them within a film that also functions as a thriller. There is the danger that the theft will be discovered. The deepening hole of crime they dig for themselves. Suspense over the source of the money. Mystery over the true identity of some characters. And two confrontations in the woods—one suspenseful, one heartbreaking.

All of this is seen against a backdrop of Minnesota in the winter (Raimi's friends the Coen brothers, who made *Fargo*, gave advice about shooting and lighting in the snow). The blanket of snow muffles voices, gives a soft edge to things, underlines the way the characters are isolated indoors, each in their own warm refuge. Outdoors, in the woods, foxes kill chickens and men kill each other. Angry black birds scramble to eat dead bodies. "Those things are always waiting for something to die so they can eat it," Jacob says. "What a weird job."

A Simple Wish ★ ½

PG, 95 m., 1997

Martin Short (Murray), Kathleen Turner (Claudia), Mara Wilson (Anabel), Robert Pastorelli (Oliver), Amanda Plummer (Boots), Francis Capra (Charlie), Ruby Dee (Hortense), Teri Garr (Rena). Directed by Michael Ritchie and produced by Sid, Bill, and Jon Sheinberg. Screenplay by Jeff Rothberg.

A Simple Wish has assembled all the trinkets and effects necessary for its story, without bothering to tell one. Here are the ingredients for a funny family movie about an incompetent fairy godperson (Martin Short), but there's nothing much to really care about, and characters go off on their own without it much mattering.

The movie stars Short as a trainee male godmother named Murray. We see him apparently flunking his godmother's exam in the funny opening credits, but evidently he passed it, because when a little girl needs a godmother, there he is. The girl's name is Anabel (Mara Wilson), and she's the eight-year-old daughter of a Central Park carriage driver (Robert Pastorelli) who dreams of being cast for the lead in the new Broadway musical *A Tale of Two Cities*.

Can Murray help him? Will he be able to edge out the less talented but more famous front-runner for the job? Not necessarily. Short, who comes across in some scenes amazingly like Pee-wee Herman, is a willing but incompetent godmother who lands them in Nebraska and is indirectly responsible for Mara's dad being turned into a bronze statue in Central Park.

Meanwhile, at cross-purposes to this plot, there's another story involving an evil former godmother named Claudia (Kathleen Turner) and her devoted sidekick Boots (Amanda Plummer), who looks like a regular in a punk bar. ("One night, in a weak moment," Claudia sighs to her, "I chose to tolerate your companionship.") Their objective is to steal lots of wands at the annual gathering of the fairy godmother's association, and in general take over the show. They see Murray as a gnat in the way of their plan.

The movie has been produced by three members of a famed showbiz family (Sid, Bill, and Jon Sheinberg), and the screenplay might be tilted a little too much in the direction of their interests. Most smaller children are not very familiar with Broadway musicals, auditions, sniffy producers, and egotistical stars, and while of course you can learn about such things and still enjoy a movie, *A Simple Wish* is sometimes a little too inside in its theatrical references.

Most of the children in the audience, alas, will never have seen a Broadway musical (given the quality of many of them, maybe I don't need that "alas"). When the movie's *Tale of Two Cities* goes for laughs with a big scene delivered from the guillotine, will kids know it's funny? Maybe the movie should have taken inspiration from the musical of *The Elephant Man* staged in the underrated comedy *The Tall Guy.*

Kathleen Turner can be very quirky, and Amanda Plummer is an eccentric original, but do they really have a purpose in this movie? When special effects are used to shatter Turner's mirror image into a thousand jagged pieces, the effect is sensational—but it would mean more if she and Plummer had been more carefully involved in the plot. Many of their scenes together read like a stand-alone double act.

Now. Will kids like it? I doubt it. When family audiences avoid inspired films like *The Secret Garden, The Little Princess,* and *Shiloh,* why would they choose a pallid exercise like this? One of the great fictions is that America has a large audience hungering for family films, which Hollywood won't supply. The truth is that Hollywood wants to make family films more than families want to see them. I imagine most of the kids in the target audience for *A Simple Wish* will see *Men in Black* instead.

Simply Irresistible ★ ★ ★

PG-13, 95 m., 1999

Sarah Michelle Gellar (Amanda Shelton), Sean Patrick Flanery (Tom Bartlett), Betty Buckley (Stella), Patricia Clarkson (Lois McNally), Dylan Baker (Jonathan Bendel), Christopher Durang (Gene O'Reilly), Larry Gilliard Jr. (Nolan Traynor). Directed by Mark Tarlov and produced by John Fiedler, Jon Amiel, and Joe Caracciolo Jr. Screenplay by Judith Roberts.

Simply Irresistible begins with one of the more unlikely Meet Cutes in movie history: Sarah Michelle Gellar chases a runaway crab up the trouser leg of the man she is destined to love. She owns one of those restaurants where all the customers know each other, like in a sitcom. I was settling down for a slow ride when somehow the movie caught hold and turned into an enchanting romantic comedy about people who float to the ceiling when they kiss. It's *Like Water for Chocolate* meets *Everyone Says I Love You.*

Gellar plays Amanda Shelton, whose restaurant in New York's SoHo is failing fast. No wonder. She's not such a good cook. Then one day a mysterious stranger appears in her vicinity and brings a magical crab. Yes, a magical crab. And the beady-eyed little crustacean sets itself up in her kitchen and somehow casts a spell. She becomes a great cook. An inspired cook. A cook so good that when the guy with the trousers tastes one of her desserts, he falls in love. "We kissed in a vanilla cloud," he tells his secretary. "This fog—it was warm, and it was wet, and it was like you could see what we were feeling."

The movie is as light as a soufflé, as fleeting as a breath of pumpkin pie on the wind from a widow's window. It is about almost nothing at all, except for a love story, the joy of eating, and a final sequence in a room that looks blessed by Astaire and Rogers.

Sarah Michelle Gellar is the star of TV's *Buffy the Vampire Slayer* and was in the original *I Know What You Did Last Summer,* where she was slashed by the Groton's Fisherman lookalike—a wise career move, freeing her from the sequel so she could make this movie. She plays Amanda Shelton perfectly straight, as a woman who is depressed by how she used to be a bad cook and now she is a great one. (I am reminded of the story about Lawrence Olivier, who moaned after a great performance as Othello, "Yes, but I don't know how I did it!")

Her new love is Sean Patrick Flanery, as Tom Bartlett, the manager of a new gourmet restaurant in the Henri Bendel store. (The second-string romance is between the grandson of Henri Bendel and Tom's secretary. They kiss after eating one of Amanda's eclairs.) Gellar is lovable, but this isn't a movie where the ground shakes, maybe because most of the love scenes take place while the couples are in midair. Nor are there any sex scenes per se. It's all soft, gauzy romance—a Valentine in which the *idea* of great love is disembodied from the old rumpy-pumpy.

When Tom recruits Amanda to cook for the premiere of his new restaurant, the movie generates a scene of simple, pure delight. It's a tough crowd (food critics, sniffy socialites), but after the appetizer, they're weeping with joy. After the entrée, transfixed in ecstatic meditation. Then dessert is served. If there is a heaven, this is its menu.

Simply Irresistible is old-fashioned and obvious, yes, like a featherweight comedy from the 1950s. But that's the charm. I love movies that cut loose from the moorings of the possible, and dance among their fancies. When Woody Allen waltzed with Goldie Hawn on the banks of the Seine and she floated in the air and just stayed up there, my heart danced too. And the closing scenes of *Simply Irresistible* are like that. It's not a great movie. But it's a charmer.

Six Days, Seven Nights ★ ★ ½

PG-13, 101 m., 1998

Harrison Ford (Quinn Harris), Anne Heche (Robin Monroe), David Schwimmer (Frank Martin), Jacqueline Obradors (Angelica), Temuera Morrison (Jager), Allison Janney (Marjorie), Douglas Westoh (Phillippe), Cliff Curtis (Kip). Directed by Ivan Reitman and produced by Reitman, Wallis Nicita, and Roger Birnbaum. Screenplay by Michael Browning.

Whenever pirates turn up in a romance set more recently than 1843, you figure the filmmakers ran out of ideas. *Six Days, Seven Nights* illustrates that principle. It's the kind of movie that provides diversion for the idle channel-surfer but isn't worth a trip to the theater. A lot of it seems cobbled together out of spare parts.

Harrison Ford and Anne Heche costar in an Opposites Attract formula that strands them on a South Pacific island. He once owned his own business, but simplified his life by moving to paradise as a charter pilot. She's a high-powered New York magazine editor (the third this month; Tina Brown should collect royalties). Heche and her would-be fiancé (David Schwimmer) arrive on the tropical isle, he proposes marriage, she accepts—and then hires Ford to fly her over to Tahiti for an emergency photo shoot.

When their plane crash-lands on an uninhabited island in a thunderstorm, Ford and Heche are thrown together in a fight for survival. (I would like to know what Ford's thoughts were in the scene where he dresses up in palm fronds to hunt birds). Back on the resort island, Schwimmer and Ford's friendly masseuse, an island seductress played by Jacqueline Obradors, mourn their missing lovers and seek consolation, or something, in each other's arms.

The screenplay by Michael Browning has little interest in the characters—certainly not enough to provide them with a movie's worth of conversation. It's devised along standard formula lines, and so desperate for a crisis that pirates conveniently materialize on two occasions simply to give the movie something to be about. If you want to see a movie that knows what to do with a man, a woman, and an island, see John Huston's *Heaven Knows, Mr. Allison,* in which Robert Mitchum and Deborah Kerr create atmosphere where Ford and Heche create only weather.

Not that they aren't pleasant enough to watch. Ford has a nice early drunk scene where he avoids the usual clichés and gives us a man who gets thoughtful and analytical in a sloshed sort of way. Heche is plucky and has unforced charm, and does a great job of looking searchingly into Ford's eyes while he talks to her. Meanwhile, Schwimmer and Obradors provide counterpoint, mirroring in low comedy what the stars are doing at a more elevated level.

Harrison Ford has an easy appeal in movies like this, and never pushes too hard. Anne Heche plays a nice duet with him. But their adventures on the island are like the greatest hits from other movies *(Butch Cassidy, Flight of the Phoenix),* and when they have a couple of well-written dialogue scenes toward the end, you wonder why two intelligent people like these need pirates in their movie.

The Sixth Man ★ ½

PG-13, 105 m., 1997

Marlon Wayans (Kenny Tyler), Kadeem Hardison (Antoine Tyler), David Paymer (Coach Pederson), Michael Michele (R. C. St. John), Kevin Dunn (Mikulski), Gary Jones (Gertz), Lorenzo Orr (Malik Major), Vladimir Cuk (Zigi Hrbacek). Directed by Randall Miller and produced by David Hoberman. Screenplay by Christopher Reed and Cynthia Carle.

The Sixth Man is another paint-by-the-numbers sports movie, this one about a college basketball team that makes it to the NCAA finals with the help of the ghost of one of its dead stars. Let's not talk about how predictable it is. Let's talk about how dumb it is.

The film starts with the childhood hoop dreams of a couple of brothers, Antoine and Kenny, who are coached by their father and hope to be stars one day. The father dies before he can see them realize their dream: They're both starters for the University of Washington Huskies. Antoine (Kadeem Hardison) is the dominant brother, the playmaker who gets the ball for the crucial last-minute shots. Kenny (Marlon Wayans) is a gifted player, but in his brother's shadow.

Then tragedy strikes. Antoine dunks the ball, falls to the court, and dies of heart failure on the way to the hospital. Kenny is crushed, and the Huskies embark on a losing streak until, one day at practice, Kenny throws the ball into the air and it never comes back down again.

Antoine, of course, has returned, this time as a ghost that only Kenny can see. And eventually Antoine returns to the court as an invisible sixth man on the Huskies team. He deflects the ball, tips in close shots, gives a boost to the Huskies, and trips up their opponents, and soon the team is in the NCAA playoffs.

Presumably *The Sixth Man* is intended to appeal to basketball fans. Is there a basketball fan alive who could fall for this premise? I'm not talking about the ghost—that's easy to believe. I'm talking about the details of the game.

I was out at the United Center last week for a big overtime contest between the Bulls and the SuperSonics. Along with thousands of other fans, I was an instant expert, my eyes riveted on every play. If the ball had suddenly changed course in midair, do you think we would have noticed? What if a ball dropped all the way through the basket and then popped back up again? What if a player was able to hang in midair twice as long as Michael Jordan?

My guess is that any one of those moments would have inspired a frenzy of instant replay analysis, and all three of them together would have induced apoplexy in announcer Johnny (Red) Kerr. But in *The Sixth Man*, audiences and commentators don't seem to realize that the laws of physics and gravity are being violated on behalf of the Huskies. Finally a woman sportswriter (Michael Michele) for the student paper uses the stop-action button on her VCR to replay a game, and notices that Kenny never even touched a ball before it went in.

I don't want to belabor technicalities here. I know the movie's premise is that nobody notices that the ghost is affecting the game. Because nobody notices, that frees the movie to proceed with its lethargic formula, right to the bitter end. (Will the team decide it has to win on its own? Will the ghost and his brother have to accept the fact of death? Will the Huskies be way behind at halftime of the big game? Will they win? Will the Sun rise tomorrow?)

You can't even begin to enjoy this game unless you put your intelligence on hold, or unless you're a little kid. A real, real, little, little kid. Why do Hollywood filmmakers hobble themselves in this way? Why be content with repeating ancient and boring formulas when a little thought could have produced an interesting movie? What if Kenny and Antoine had worked out a strategy to *secretly* affect the outcome of the game? What if they were aware that obvious tactics would be spotted? What if Kenny didn't tell his teammates about the ghost? What if Antoine, for sheer love of the game, took the other side once in a while?

The possibilities are endless. Movies like *The Sixth Man* are an example of Level One thinking, in which the filmmakers get the easy, obvious idea and are content with it. Good movies are made by taking the next step. Twisting the premise. Using lateral thinking. I imagine a lot of studio executives are sports fans. Would any of them be *personally* entertained by this movie? If this answer is "no"—

and it has to be—then they shouldn't expect us to be, either.

Slam ★ ★ ½

R, 100 m., 1998

Saul Williams (Raymond Joshua), Sonja Sohn (Lauren Bell), Bonz Malone (Hopha), Beau Sia (Jimmy Huang), Marion Barry (Judge). Directed by Marc Levin and produced by Levin, Richard Stratton, and Henri Kessler. Screenplay by Levin, Stratton, and Sonja Sohn.

Slam is a fable disguised as a slice of life, and cobbled together out of too many pieces that don't fit smoothly together. It's moving, but not as effective as it could have been. Inspired in part by the documentary *SlamNation,* it's the story of Ray, a Washington, D.C., prisoner whose life is transformed by poetry. And it also provides a glimpse of the world of competitive poetry slams, although Ray's story and the slam material don't seem to occupy the same level of intensity. Some scenes play like drama, others feel like they were grabbed documentary-style.

The movie stars Saul Williams, an effective actor, as Raymond Joshua, a young black man who is stopped by police who find four ounces of marijuana. He's innocent, he says, but he's advised by his public defender to cop a plea. That way he could get two to three years instead of up to ten. We can see he's stuck on the conveyor belt to prison, and a stern judge (played by former Washington mayor Marion Barry) gives him a weary lecture.

In prison, Ray's life is changed when he starts writing poetry and recites it one day in the prison yard, where the other inmates are (somewhat unconvincingly) transfixed. He attends a prison writing class, where Lauren, the teacher (Sonja Sohn), announces it's her last day: "They've cut this program." She is impressed by his writing and encourages him, and after he gets back on the street he finds her again, and enters her world of poetry slams. At one of them, she introduces him from the stage, and his poem is well received.

It's at about this point that the film loses its focus. Ray's arrest, conviction, and imprisonment were all filmed with realism. But the romance with Lauren seems out of another movie, and the scenes at poetry slams are awkwardly integrated: Either they weren't staged for this film, or the assistant director didn't have his extras under control.

Sometimes it works when characters are plugged into real events, but not this time. And having heard truly emotional, heartbreaking performances from slammers, I was underwhelmed by some of the material in this movie (the audiences, notoriously hard to please, are of course pushovers here).

The movie was made for about $1 million, but its shortcomings aren't because of the budget; they're because the director, Marc Levin, didn't decide clearly what level of reality to go for and stick to it. Better, maybe, to make a drama all the way through, and not unwind the tension with the semidoc poetry readings.

That approach would also have kept the focus on the relationship between Ray and Lauren, who are both well acted, and who are in an interesting dilemma: She's had hard times in her own past life, and while she wants to help an ex-con, she doesn't want to link her unfolding future to his problems. That Ray is a gifted poet doesn't make him an ideal mate.

There are issues lurking just out of sight here, but well known in the black community, about the shortage of eligible males and the reluctance of professional women to date beneath their economic level, but the movie doesn't really engage them. Lauren has some speeches that hint at what she's thinking, but then the movie dances away as if everything was simply a matter of the heart. We sense that Ray and Lauren are shaped more by the thousands of other relationship movies than by the specifics of their characters and their world. We sense their dialogue falling into the he-and-she patterns of screenplay formula—into the familiar rhythm in which attraction is followed by retreat and then by reluctant return and final acceptance.

To give the movie its due, there is an open ending, which is probably the right one; nothing is settled in Ray's life, and the movie doesn't try to squeeze a solution into 100 minutes. There is a lot of good material here, but unshaped and not sufficiently grappled with.

SlamNation ★★★

NO MPAA RATING, 91 m., 1998

A documentary directed and produced by Paul Devlin. Featuring Saul Williams, Jessica Care Moore, Beau Sia, Marc Smith, Mums the Schemer, Patricia Smith, Taylor Mali, and Daniel Ferri.

Poetry slams are a muscular verbal sport founded some twelve years ago in Chicago when a construction worker named Marc Smith got the idea of having poets read before a saloon audience. Their performances are graded from 1 to 10, like Olympic divers. The Green Mill, a tavern near Broadway and Lawrence in Uptown, is the birthplace of the slams, standing in relation to the sport roughly as Shakespeare's Globe does to drama.

Paul Devlin's *SlamNation* is a documentary about the 1996 National Poetry Slam, held in Portland, Oregon, with twenty-seven teams in the competition. The rules are simple: Four members to a team, every member must be a writer as well as a performer, no music, no props, no animal acts. There is a penalty for any poem that goes longer than three minutes. The judges are chosen from the audience. The performers are mostly dressed as if they're about to fix a leak in the basement.

Slams are nothing if not democratic. They are the only sport I'm aware of where the teams from Berwyn and San Francisco compete on the same field. (In 1996, Berwyn actually placed in the final four, led by its star, a slammer named Daniel Ferri, whose poem fiercely defends his baldness.) The documentary follows the New York team that eventually won the trophy (bronzed boxing gloves on a stack of books), and fielded four first-timers, including Saul Williams, who also stars in the fiction film *Slam.*

In evaluating the poetic content of the slams, one is tempted to take easy shots (poetry slams are to poetry as military music is to music?). Most of the material exists halfway between rap and Vachel Lindsay. Slams are essentially performance art, not literary art, and there is a shot of a New York book editor, sighing at his stack of slam manuscripts and observing that sometimes the poems don't translate well to the printed page.

Maybe that's because *SlamNation,* covering three semifinal rounds and the finals, inevitably focuses on the competition rather than the work.

I have had one personal experience of slam-style poetry, and it was unforgettable. In April 1998, at the annual meeting of the American Society of Newspaper Editors in Washington, D.C., the luncheon speaker was Secretary of State Madeleine Albright, who rattled off her speech as quickly as she could and hurried from the dais. Then the society's chairman called on a young woman to "give us one of your poems."

This was Patricia Smith, a friend of mine from her Chicago days, then a columnist for the *Boston Globe.* She performed a poem about a visit to a grade school class at which she asked, "How many of you know some dead people?" Almost every hand went up, she said, because all of these inner-city children knew dead people—many of them dead from drugs and gunshots. At the end a little girl thanked her for saying it was all right to know dead people. The girl was speaking of her own murdered mother.

This summary fails to capture the impact of Smith's poem, which surprised me to tears. I looked around the room and thought I had rarely seen so few words have such a strong impact.

Pat Smith, of course, was soon to get publicity of a different sort, when her paper accepted her resignation after she confirmed that some details of her columns had been made up. Making things up is not what a journalist is supposed to do, but it is what a poet is supposed to do. Seeing Smith again in *SlamNation,* as a member of the Boston team, I was reminded of the power of her words. She can see life and touch readers as few writers can. That is her vocation. Fiction and poetry exist to reach a different kind of truth. Maybe she had no business dealing with facts in the first place.

As for the other performers, I am prepared to believe that in context, uncut, seen as they should be, some of them have the same power. Others are basically soapbox orators with a new forum. In the cheerful anarchy of poetry slams, there is room for many styles. As a slammer named Jack McCarthy from Boston says: "You have to write one poem that everyone agrees is a poem. That qualifies you for your poetic license. After that, if you say it's a poem, it's a poem."

Slappy and the Stinkers ★ ★

PG, 78 m., 1998

B. D. Wong (Morgan Brinway), Bronson Pinchot (Roy), Jennifer Coolidge (Harriet), Joseph Ashton (Sonny), Gary LeRoi Gray (Domino), Carl Michael Lindner (Witz), Scarlett Pomers (Lucy), Travis Tedford (Loaf), Sam McMurray (Boccoli). Directed by Barnet Kellman and produced by Sid, Bill, and Jon Sheinberg. Screenplay by Bob Wolterstorff and Mike Scott.

The opening moments of *Slappy and the Stinkers* filled me with shreds of hope: Was it possible that this movie, about five kids who kidnap a sea lion, would not be without wit? The story opens in music class, where the teacher (B. D. Wong) slogs through Gilbert and Sullivan while the kids in the chorus giggle at lines like "my bosom swells with pride."

A nice touch. And I liked the way the kids waved their hands desperately for permission to go to the washroom. That rang a bell. And the irritation of the teacher ("My big number is coming up!"). But the movie is not, alas, interested in continuing such social observation. It's really a retread of the *Little Rascals* or *Our Gang* comedies, in which lovable scamps—freckled, towheaded, and gap-toothed—get up to mischief.

The setup: The stinkers, so named because they're always in trouble, are poor kids on scholarship at a posh private academy. Everything they touch turns to trouble. In a long and spectacularly unfunny opening sequence, they attach a leaf blower to a hang glider and the headmaster's desk chair in an attempt to "go where no kid has ever gone before." The contraption of course goes exactly where the screenplay requires it to go for a long time after we have lost interest in whether it goes anywhere.

Then the kids sneak away for a visit to the aquarium. There they get involved with Slappy, a sea lion who passes a lot of gas and provides the kids with an excuse to say "fart," which, I recall from my own grade school days, is a word kids adore so much they are rarely happier than when saying it. The kids, who have seen *Free Willy*, decide Slappy should be stolen from the aquarium and returned to the sea, although they have some second thoughts: "There's Willy!" they say, seeing a familiar whale tail on the horizon. "Hey, don't killer whales eat sea lions?"

The spectacle of Willy making a meal of Slappy right in front of the horrified kids will have to wait, unfortunately, for the Leslie Nielsen version of this picture. The best horror *Slappy and the Stinkers* can come up with is an evil sea lion–napper named Boccoli (Sam McMurray), who dreams of Slappy starring in a circus act. Boccoli (who with just a little more trouble could have been called Broccoli) is an unshaven chain-smoker with a broken-down van, and a lot of stuff falls on him, and he falls on a lot of stuff. His function is to take a lickin' and keep on kidnappin'.

We actually see a snippet of the sea lion's circus act, in which Slappy jumps through a ring of fire. If you can visualize a sea lion, you might ask yourself, how easy would it be for one to jump through such a ring? The same thought occurred to me, and I studied the stunt closely. My best guess is that what we are actually witnessing is an arrangement between a catapult and a large black Hefty garbage bag.

Along with hilarities involving a cattle prod, and scenes in which it appears that Slappy has learned to understand, if not to speak, English, there are a lot of sight gags in the film involving the teacher getting slushy drinks in his face, and the kids getting peanut butter and jelly sandwiches on theirs, and many close-ups of the little tykes shrieking and trying manfully to get their tongues around the big words in the dialogue.

Yeah, but will kids like it? I dunno. I never much liked the *Our Gang* and *Little Rascals* movies. The kids seemed too doggone cute. The Bad News Bears were a lot more fun, but, mister, I've seen *The Bad News Bears,* and these ain't them.

SLC Punk! ★ ★ ★

R, 97 m., 1999

Matthew Lillard (Stevo), Michael Goorjian (Bob), Annabeth Gish (Trish), Jennifer Lien (Sandy), Christopher McDonald (Father), Devon Sawa (Sean), Jason Segel (Mike), Summer Phoenix (Brandy). Directed by James Merendino and produced by Sam Maydew and Peter Ward. Screenplay by Merendino.

When people adopt a fearful and aggressive personal style, we forget that somewhere inside, hidden by the punk look, the haircuts, the body piercing, the chains, the tattoos, or the gang regalia, is a person who basically just wants to be loved and understood. Telling the world to go to hell is often the response of people who believe the world has told them to go to hell.

James Merendino's *SLC Punk!* knows that, and the essential sweetness of its hero is what makes the movie more than just an attempt to shock. It's a memory of Salt Lake City in 1985, the high Reagan era, when Stevo and Heroin Bob are, as far as they know, the only two punks in town. They embrace the anarchism embodied in Sex Pistols songs (and there is a hilarious stoned explanation of chaos theory), but the depth of their rebellion can be gauged by the fact that Heroin Bob (Michael Goorjian) has never taken heroin, and has an irrational fear of needles.

Stevo (Matthew Lillard) narrates the film, which is a nostalgic tour of his world, done in much the same tone as Ray Liotta's voice-overs in Scorsese's *GoodFellas.* He explains, he theorizes, he addresses the camera directly, he identifies the various characters and cliques. His approach is anthropological. The Stevo character simultaneously stands inside and outside his world; he keeps an ironic angle on his rebellion, but can't see himself living the life of his father, a former "activist," who now explains, "I didn't sell out. I bought in."

Stevo is stuck in a limbo of parties, music, hanging out, long discussions, recreational mind-altering, and uncertainty. His dad wants him to go to Harvard ("If you want to rebel there, you can do it"). Stevo wants to go to the University of Utah, "and get a 4.0 in Damage." He stays in Salt Lake City and there's a flashback to explain how he got to his current punk state: We see a young Stevo in the basement, playing with Dungeons & Dragons figures, and the future Heroin Bob comes in with a tape, tells him D&D sucks, "listen to this," and leads him out of dweebdom.

Stevo's college career passes, more or less, in the movie's fractured memory style, and Bob's girlfriend Trish (Annabeth Gish) introduces him to Brandy (Summer Phoenix), who asks him, "Wouldn't it be more rebellious if you didn't spend so much time buying blue hair dye and going out to get punky clothes?" There are also details about Stevo's home life (his parents have divorced, his dad having traded in the old wife on a new Porsche), and about the improvisational style of days spent seeing what turns up next.

The film could have taken a lot of cheap shots at the Mormon culture of Salt Lake City, but most of its local details are more in the way of reporting than of satire. Stevo laments, for example, the problems involved in such a basic act as buying a six-pack of beer in a state where only low-alcohol 3.2 beer is sold, and the clerks in the state-owned liquor stores are all cops and phone in tips if you even look like you're thinking of doing anything illegal. There is also a debate with customers in a convenience store about the "curse on the land" and the imminent arrival of Satan. Here we witness something I have long suspected, that the exaggerated fascination with Satan in some religious quarters is the flip side of the heavy metal/Goth/satanic thing. Whether you worship Satan or oppose him, he stars in your fantasies.

Matthew Lillard is an actor easy to dislike, and no wonder, since he often plays supercilious twits. Here his performance dominates the film, and he does a subtle, tricky job of being both an obnoxious punk and a kid in search of his direction in life. He's very good.

In this season of blaming everything on the movies, a film like *SLC Punk!* will no doubt inspire knee-jerk moralists to deplore its depiction of an anarcho-punk lifestyle. But remember: A movie isn't about what it's about, but about how it's about it. What *SLC Punk!* is *really* about is Stevo's ironic distance on his lifestyle—about the way he lives it and analyzes it at the same time. The message isn't "live this way," but "look at the way you live." There's a little something there for all of us.

Sliding Doors ★ ★

PG-13, 105 m., 1998

Gwyneth Paltrow (Helen), John Hannah (James), John Lynch (Gerry), Jeanne Tripplehorn (Lydia), Zara Turner (Anna), Douglas McFerran (Russell), Paul Brightwell (Clive), Nina Young (Claudia). Directed by Peter Howitt and produced by Sydney Pollack, Philippa Braithwaite, and William Horberg. Screenplay by Howitt.

Sliding Doors uses parallel time lines to explore the different paths that a woman's life might take after she does, and doesn't, find her lover in bed with another woman. I submit that there is a simple test to determine whether this plot can work: Is either time line interesting in itself? If not, then no amount of shifting back and forth between them can help. And I fear they are not.

The movie stars Gwyneth Paltrow as Helen, a London publicity executive who is fired for no good reason, and stalks out of her office in midmorning to take the underground train back home. In one scenario, she catches the train. In the other, she misses it because she's delayed, and the doors slide shut in her face. To save confusion, we will call these Scenarios A and B.

In A, Helen arrives home unexpectedly and finds her lover, Gerry (John Lynch), in the sack with his mistress, Lydia (Jeanne Tripplehorn). She confronts them, walks out, goes to a bar to get drunk, and runs into James (John Hannah). James recognizes her, because earlier he chatted her up on the train. Over the course of the next few days, Helen A is comforted by her best friend, gets her long hair cut and dyed blond, and begins to fall in love with James.

In Scenario B, Helen misses the train, and by the time she arrives home Lydia is already off the scene. But she begins to suspect things when she realizes two brandy glasses were on the dresser. Eventually Helen B finds out about Lydia, who is the kind of woman who gets a sadistic satisfaction out of popping up unexpectedly and threatening to blow Gerry's cover.

The film cuts backs and forth between A and B. It is clear that Gerry is a creep, Lydia is a Fatal Attraction, and James is a thoroughly nice bloke, although of course the requirements of Screenwriting 101 force the movie into a manufactured crisis in which it appears that James may have been lying to Helen A. There's even one of those scenes that madden me, in which James goes to Helen A's best friend's house, is informed of the misunderstanding, could say two or three words to clear it all up—but doesn't, because he is a puppet of the plot.

Gwyneth Paltrow is engaging as the two Helens, and I have no complaints about her performance. Pity about the screenplay. It requires her to appear to be unobservant, gullible, and absentminded as the faithless Gerry hems and haws through absurdly contrived emergencies. The worst moment comes when he opens the kitchen blinds and Lydia is standing right outside them, staring at him, and he slams them shut and tries to pretend nothing happened. What we have here is a particularly annoying movie gimmick in which the other person (Lydia, in this case) knows exactly when and where to position herself to create the shock effect. We aren't allowed to wonder how many hours, or days, she was posted outside, maybe in the rain, waiting for him to open the blinds.

I am grateful that the movie provides Helen A and Helen B with different haircuts, which helps tell the story lines apart (a bandage is used in the early scenes). But as we switched relentlessly back and forth between A and B, I found that I wasn't looking forward to either story. True, James is played by Hannah with warmth and charm, but to what effect? Is he interesting as a person? Does he, or anyone in the film, have much to say that's not at the service of the plot? I would have preferred Hypothetical Scenario C, in which Gwyneth Paltrow meets neither James nor Gerry, and stars in a smarter movie.

Slums of Beverly Hills ★ ★ ★

R, 91 m., 1998

Natasha Lyonne (Vivian), Alan Arkin (Murray), Marisa Tomei (Rita), Kevin Corrigan (Eliot), Eli Marienthal (Rickey), David Krumholtz (Ben), Jessica Walter (Doris), Carl Reiner(Mickey), Rita Moreno (Belle). Directed by Tamara Jenkins and produced by Michael Nozik and Stan Wlodkowski. Screenplay by Jenkins.

Slums of Beverly Hills was born to inspire a sitcom, and probably a pretty good one too. It's about a poor Jewish family that moves by night from one sleazy apartment to another, jumping the rent but always staying within Beverly Hills to take advantage of the educational system. Every move brings them into range of a fresh supply of wacky supporting characters.

The story's told through the eyes of Vivian (Natasha Lyonne), who will be a freshman in the fall, and is alarmed that her breasts have, in the words of her father, "sprouted overnight." Also sprouting is her sexual curiosity, which is enthusiastically encouraged by Eliot (Kevin Corrigan), the kid who lives across the hall of the latest pastel flea trap they've moved into. "I dropped out of school because I wanted to join the workforce," he tells her. "Doing what?" "Selling pot."

Dad is Murray Abramovitz, a sixty-five-year-old car salesman played by Alan Arkin as a man who seems to believe that if he had to have kids when he was fifty, he deserves everything he got. There are two boys in the family: Vivian's older brother Ben (David Krumholtz) and younger brother Rickey (Eli Marienthal), and they're all accustomed to being awakened at three in the morning and told to pack their stuff because the rent is due and, besides, Murray has found a "much nicer place that doesn't rob you blind."

Vivian thinks she hates her breasts. Her dad is always shouting at her to wear a bra, and the movie's best single shot is possibly the expression on her face when, under his orders, she puts on a bra under a skimpy halter top, creating a result more kinky than modest. "You've been blessed," the saleslady at the bra counter tells her. "Breasts are wonderful. You'll see."

She doesn't. But then life changes radically for the Abramovitzes when Rita (Marisa Tomei), the troubled daughter of Murray's rich brother, comes to stay with them. She's just gone over the wall of a rehab center, she's pregnant, and she enlists Vivian to help her deal with the rat who got her pregnant—an actor who does "Man of La Mancha" as a one-man show.

You can see the sitcom possibilities. The film, written and directed by Tamara Jenkins, is pitched pretty firmly at that level of ambition: broadly drawn characters, quick one-liners, squabbling family members, lots of sex. Yet it also has a certain sweetness, a good-hearted feeling for this family, which stays together and plugs away.

Alan Arkin is the key to the good feelings. He is a poor provider but a good father, who may skip out on the rent and be a lousy car salesman, but insists that his kids do their homework. One senses that his kids will grow up to be all right. Then there's his rich brother Mickey (Carl Reiner), who starts paying the rent in return for Murray taking his troublesome daughter off his hands. Mickey makes lots of money but has no class, and there's a painful scene in an airport restaurant where he blurts out crass insults, and Murray—who has been taking his handouts all his life—decides he's had enough.

Natasha Lyonne has the film's most important role, and is the key to the comedy. She does a good job of looking incredulous, and there's a lot in her life to be incredulous about. She also has a nice pragmatic approach to sexuality, as in a scene where she consults a plastic surgeon about on-the-spot breast reduction.

There are a couple of scenes that simply don't work, and the worst involves some tentative fooling around between Murray and Rita. I didn't believe it, I didn't like the way it played, and I think it should have been cut from the movie. It spoils the tone and introduces material that has no place in a story like this. The movie also grinds to a halt when Murray calls a black waiter "Jackson." Not funny, and not likely. But basically I enjoyed *Slums of Beverly Hills*—for the wisecracking, for the family squabbles, for the notion of squatters who stake a claim in a Beverly Hills where money, after all, is not the only currency.

Small Soldiers ★ ★ ½

PG-13, 110 m., 1998

David Cross (Irwin Wayfair), Jay Mohr (Larry Benson), Alexandra Wilson (Ms. Kegel), Denis Leary (Gil Mars), Gregory Smith (Alan Abernathy), Gregory Itzin (Mr. Florens), Dick Miller (Joe), Kirsten Dunst (Christy Fimple). Directed by Joe Dante and produced by Michael Finnell and Colin Wilson. Screenplay by Gavin Scott, Adam Rifkin, Ted Elliott, and Terry Rossio.

Small Soldiers is a family picture on the outside, and a mean, violent action picture on the inside. Since most of the violence happens to toys, I guess we're supposed to give it a pass, but I dunno: The toys are presented as individuals who can think for themselves, and there are believable heroes and villains among them. For smaller children, this could be a terrifying experience.

It's rated PG-13, but if the characters were human the movie would be a hard "R," just for the scene where characters get run over and chewed up by a lawn mower. I was a little amazed, indeed, by the whole concluding sequence, in which fireballs are lobbed, toy helicopters attack, and there's a struggle high in the air between killer toys and the movie's young hero, who are trying to electrocute each other. This is not a sequence a lot of gradeschoolers are ready for.

The movie's premise is intriguing. A toy company is purchased by a defense manufacturer, and the tough-skinned new owner (Denis Leary) orders his people to make "toys that actually do what they do in the commercials." Toys with batteries that don't run down, and minds of their own. His designers take him at his word and develop lines of toys using the company's X-1000 computer chip, which is also the brains of smart bombs and other military technology.

When these toys get into the marketplace, it's war. The toy characters are divided into two camps, the peaceful and zany Gorgonites and the professional killers of the Commando Elite. The problem is with the commandos, who are humorless martinets that strut through the movie looking like mercenaries and making threats like pro wrestlers. They are truly evil, and they throw off the movie's moral balance.

A lot of the other stuff in the movie is funny and entertaining, and, to be fair, all of the special effects are top drawer, seamlessly combining live action, models, and animation. (Industrial Light and Magic supplied some of them, and the figures were designed by Stan Winston.)

The Gorgonites are led by a pensive, thoughtful Yoda-figure named Archer (voice of Frank Langella). They include little guys who kind of grow on you, including Ocula, who is basically an eyeball with three limbs. The Commando Elite have names like Chip Hazard and Butch Meathook. One of the inside jokes is that many of their voices were supplied by veterans of the *Dirty Dozen,* while the Gorgonites are voiced by actors from *This Is Spinal Tap.*

The movie's human hero is Alan (Gregory Smith), a kid who inadvertently sets off the toy wars. His new girlfriend is Christy (Kirsten Dunst), who gets a shock when she sees Barbie-type dolls being fitted with X-1000 chips so that they can join the battle too. Among the adults are Alan's parents, who are taken out of action after the commandos use a mousetrap as a catapult to drop sleeping pills into their drinks.

Part of the inspiration for *Small Soldiers* may have come from *Toy Story,* where toy soldiers were among the characters. But too much of it may have come from Sid, the human kid in that movie who lived next door, and entertained himself by taking his toys apart and reassembling them in grotesque ways. In *Small Soldiers,* toys have unspeakable things happen to them, and many of them end up looking like horror props. Chip Hazard meets an especially gruesome end.

What bothered me most about *Small Soldiers* is that it didn't tell me where to stand—what attitude to adopt. In movies for adults, I like that quality. But here is a movie being sold to kids, with a lot of toy tie-ins and ads on the children's TV channels. Below a certain age, they like to know what they can count on. When Barbie clones are being sliced and diced by a lawn mower, are they going to understand the satirical purpose?

Roy Rogers's death earlier this year reminded me of how gentle and innocent his movies were. Sure, we called them "shoot-'em-ups," but Roy spent more time singing than shooting. Kids didn't leave the theater in a state of shock. Now they go to a kiddie movie, and there are scenes where toy characters are disemboweled and vivisected, and body parts crawl around in the street, separated from each other. Then there are other scenes that are perfectly innocent. We get two movies for the price of one. The nice movie would have been enough.

Smilla's Sense of Snow ★ ★ ★

R, 120 m., 1997

Julia Ormond (Smilla), Gabriel Byrne (The Mechanic), Richard Harris (Tork), Vanessa Redgrave (Elsa Lubing), Robert Loggia (Moritz Jasperson), Jim Broadbent (Lagermann), Peter Capaldi (Birgo Lander), Emma Croft (Benja). Directed by Bille August and produced by Bernd Eichinger and Martin Moszkowicz. Screenplay by Ann Biderman, based on the novel by Peter Hoeg.

Here is a movie so absorbing, so atmospheric, so suspenseful, and so dumb that it proves my point: The subject matter doesn't matter in a movie nearly as much as mood, tone, and style. *Smilla's Sense of Snow* is a superbly made film with one of the goofiest plots in many moons. Nothing in the final thirty minutes can possibly be taken seriously, and yet the movie works. Even the ending works, sort of, because the film has built up so much momentum.

Smilla stars Julia Ormond, who often plays sensuous women but here plays a cold and distant one, born in Greenland and now living in Copenhagen, where she keeps her distance and seems to be nursing an obscure wound or anger. Smilla's confidant is the little boy named Isaiah who lives in the building. He is an Inuit, a native Greenlander, and Smilla is half Inuit, and sometimes tells him stories based on the lore of their people.

One day she returns to her apartment building to find the boy's body crumpled on the ground. The official verdict is that he fell off the roof, but she has been to the roof and seen his footprints in a straight line running right over the edge. What was he running from? What frightened him so?

Smilla makes it her business to answer this question. The movie, which has so far been a character study, now becomes a crime procedural. She questions a helpful man at the coroner's, who notes mysteries about the autopsy. She discovers that the boy's father died in a mining accident, and learns from a retired mining company secretary (Vanessa Redgrave) of a secret company archive. She breaks into the archive by night and finds information about the accident and how it might be linked to events from 30 and 130 years ago.

She's aided in some of these investigations by her neighbor in the building, a man named The Mechanic (Gabriel Byrne). They are even drawn toward one another, although his motives are murky. What does it mean that she sees him at dinner with the head of the mining company (Richard Harris)? Less or more than it seems?

I cannot describe the impact of these scenes because they are so visceral. Ormond embodies Smilla—her iciness, her determination, her anger. She creates an interesting character, which is one of the hardest things to do in a movie: a character who intrigues us to such a degree that when she is doing nothing, we're reading motives into her inaction. Ormond has a beautiful face, less full here than in *Sabrina*, and the fact that she will not "let" it be beautiful—that she separates from the world around her with an almost painful defensiveness—makes her, paradoxically, more attractive. Byrne, who specializes in men that women love but shouldn't, plays a hesitant but smooth operator.

And then we arrive at the film's final passages. Smilla smuggles herself on board a ship to Greenland, and in one sequence hides inside a dumbwaiter with skills she must have learned from a Nancy Drew mystery. In Greenland . . . well, I wouldn't dream of telling you what's under the ice. But I sat in stunned amazement. I know *Smilla's Sense of Snow* is based on a best-selling novel by Peter Hoeg, and I assume all of this plot stuff must come from the book. But how absurd it all is. In the early 1960s, when American-International was cranking out a science-fiction thriller every other week, a plot like this would have been worthy of something like *Prehistoric Radioactive Worms from Outer Space.*

Never mind. The ending simply doesn't matter. The movie presents it, but isn't implicated in it. The movie is off somewhere else. *Smilla* was directed by Bille August, whose credits include *Pelle the Conqueror* (1988), and the strengths in both films are in the relationships between young children and adults who are moved by them. *Smilla* also works as a character study: We are intrigued by Smilla, by her quietness, by her strength. In a better world with more curiosity, we could have had this movie without any of the Greenland scenes. It could have been about Smilla and her neighbors. In our world movies need a plot, I guess, and so this one has one. Ignore it. It's irrelevant to the movie's power.

Smoke Signals ★ ★ ★

PG-13, 89 m., 1998

Adam Beach (Victor Joseph), Evan Adams (Thomas Builds-the-Fire), Irene Bedard (Suzy Song), Gary Farmer (Arnold Joseph), Tantoo Cardinal (Arlene Joseph), Cody Lightning (Young Victor), Simon Baker (Young Thomas). Directed by Chris Eyre and produced by Scott Rosenfelt and Larry Estes. Screenplay by Sherman Alexie, based on his book *The Lone Ranger and Tonto Fistfight in Heaven.*

"It's a good day to be indigenous!" the reservation radio DJ tells his American Indian listeners as *Smoke Signals* opens. We cut to the station's traffic reporter, who scrutinizes an intersection that rarely seems to be used. "A big truck just went by," he announces. Later in the film, we will hear several choruses of a song about John Wayne's false teeth.

Smoke Signals comes billed as the first feature written, directed, coproduced, and acted by American Indians. It hardly seems necessary to even announce that: The film is so relaxed about its characters, so much at home in their world, that we sense it's an inside job. Most films about Native Americans have had points to make and scores to settle, like all those earnest 1950s white films about blacks. Blaxploitation broke the ice and liberated unrehearsed black voices, and now here are two young Indians who speak freshly, humorously, and for themselves.

The film opens in Idaho on a significant day: the Fourth of July, 1976. It's significant not only for America but for the infant Thomas Builds-the-Fire, who is saved by being thrown from an upper window when his house burns down at 3 A.M. He was caught in the arms of Arnold Joseph (Gary Farmer), a neighbor with a drinking problem, who is eventually kicked out by his wife (Tantoo Cardinal) and goes to live in Phoenix. He leaves behind his son Victor Joseph (Adam Beach).

And then, twenty years later, word comes that Arnold has died. Victor has a deep resentment against his father, but thinks he should go to Phoenix and pick up his ashes. He has no money for the journey, but Thomas Builds-the-Fire (Evan Adams) does—and offers to buy the bus tickets if Victor will take him along on the trip. That would be a big concession for Victor, who is tall and silent and has never much liked the skinny, talkative Thomas. But he has no choice. And as the movie settles into the rhythms of a road picture, the two characters talk, and the dialogue becomes the heart of the movie.

Smoke Signals was written by Sherman Alexie, based on his book *The Lone Ranger and Tonto Fistfight in Heaven.* He has a good ear for speech, and he allows his characters to refer to the real world, to TV and pop culture and the movies (the reserved Victor, impatient with Thomas's chatter, accuses him of having learned most of what he knows about Indians by watching *Dances With Wolves,* and advises him to spend more time "looking stoic").

There are references to General Custer and the U.S. Cavalry, to John Wayne and to U.S. policies toward Indians over the years, but *Smoke Signals* is free of the oppressive weight of victim culture; these characters don't live in the past and define themselves by the crimes committed against their people. They are the next generation; I'd assign them to Generation X if that didn't limit them too much.

If they are the future, Arnold, the Gary Farmer character, is the past. Victor nurses a resentment against him, but Thomas is understandably more open-minded, since the man did, after all, save his life. There are a few flashbacks to help explain the older man, and although they're brief, they're strong and well done: We see that Arnold is more complicated than his son imagines, and able to inspire the respect of the woman he was living with in Phoenix (Irene Bedard).

Smoke Signals is, in a way, a continuation of a 1989 movie named *Powwow Highway,* which starred this same Gary Farmer as a huge, gentle, insightful man, and A Martinez as more "modern." It, too, was a road movie, and it lived through its conversations. To see the two movies side-by-side is to observe how Native Americans, like all Americans, are not exempt from the melting pot—for better and worse.

The director, Chris Eyre, takes advantage of the road movie genre, which requires only a goal and then permits great freedom in the events along the way. The two men will eventually obtain the ashes, we expect, and also some wisdom. Meanwhile, we can watch them discover one another: the taciturn, inward man who was abused as a child, and the orphan who, it's true, seems to have gotten his worldview at secondhand through the media.

There's a particular satisfaction in listening to people talk about what they know well and care about. The subject isn't as important as the feeling. Listen to them discuss the ins and outs of an Indian specialty known as "fry bread," and you will sense what they know about the world.

Snake Eyes ★

R, 99 m., 1998

Nicolas Cage (Rick Santoro), Gary Sinise (Kevin Dunne), Carla Gugino (Julia Costello), John Heard (Gilbert Powell), Stan Shaw (Lincoln Tyler), Kevin Dunn (Lou Logan), Michael Rispoli (Jimmy George), David Anthony Higgins (Ned Campbell). Directed and produced by Brian De Palma. Screenplay by David Koepp.

If Brian De Palma were as good at rewriting as he is at visual style, *Snake Eyes* might have been a heck of a movie. He isn't, and it isn't. It's the worst kind of bad film: The kind that gets you all worked up and then lets you down, instead of just being lousy from the first shot.

Now about that first shot. It's wonderful. It's a Steadicam take that runs on and on, seemingly forever. Nicolas Cage is on-screen for almost every second of it, as a corrupt Atlantic City cop who scuttles backstage and ringside at a heavyweight championship. He shakes down a creep, he places a bet, he has a chitchat with his old friend who is in charge of security, he talks on the phone with his wife and kid, he shmoozes with a sexy blonde who sits down next to him, and he's sitting right in front of the secretary of defense when the man is assassinated.

I'd have to look at the film very carefully to be sure how long this uninterrupted single shot is; it's possible that De Palma has hidden a couple of cuts in the middle of swish pans. No matter; he steals the crown here from the famous long takes by Scorsese in *GoodFellas* and Anderson in *Boogie Nights*, and it's virtuoso work, as the camera follows Cage up and down stairs and he never quits talking. Cage is wonderful, all the extras and supporting actors hit their marks right on time, the camerawork (by Stephen H. Burum) is perfectly coordinated, the energy level is high, there's great excitement, and I'm scribbling "terrific opening!" in my notes.

Alas, slowly at first and then with stunning rapidity, the movie falls apart. It has the elements for a good thriller, and De Palma still has some surprises up his sleeve, but it's a downhill slog.

The other key characters are played by Gary Sinise, as a navy officer who has taken over command of the security at the prizefight; Carla Gugino, as a woman with secret information she wants to deliver to the secretary of defense; and Stan Shaw as the defending champion.

A small cast, in a story using a structure De Palma has had fun with in the past, in films like *Blow Out* (1981). He shows an action and then repeats it from various points of view, adding information until a jigsaw of information falls into place. Occasionally we'll see a moment that doesn't seem to fit and then it will be explained later, and eventually the outlines of a conspiracy become clear.

There are nice ideas here, as when the Gugino character loses her glasses and has to flee from the bad guys without being able to see anything other than a blur. And moments when De Palma brutally rips up everything we thought we knew, and makes us start all over again. But there are also moments of dreadful implausibility. How likely is it, for example, inside a coliseum crawling with law enforcement, where thousands of fans have been forcibly detained, that no one would notice the heavyweight champ beating up a cop?

De Palma supplies one more fine shot, looking straight down through the ceilings of a series of hotel rooms until he finds the one he's looking for. But he's not on guard against lame dialogue, and at one point the desperate Gugino, looking for a place to hide and trying to convince a guy to take her upstairs to his room, actually says, "If you don't . . . I'll bet . . . somebody else will!"

Then comes an ending so improbable it seems to have been fashioned as a film school exercise: Find the Mistakes in This Scene. I can't describe it in detail without giving away too much of the plot, but imagine a grand climax in which a hurricane strikes Atlantic City and all of the key players find themselves standing outdoors in the middle of it, on live TV.

David Koepp, the writer, has been associated with some successful movies *(The Paper, Jurassic Park,* De Palma's *Carlito's Way,* and *Mission: Impossible).* What happened while he was writing this one? I would genuinely be curious to know how a professional screenwriter and an important director could both agree that *Snake Eyes* has a last act they're willing to sign their names to.

A Soldier's Daughter Never Cries

★★★½

R, 124 m., 1998

Kris Kristofferson (Bill Willis), Barbara Hershey (Marcella Willis), Leelee Sobieski (Channe Willis), Jane Birkin (Mrs. Fortescue), Dominique Blanc (Candida), Jesse Bradford (Billy Willis), Virginie Ledoyen (Billy's Mother), Anthony Roth Costanzo (Francis Fortescue). Directed by James Ivory and produced by Ismail Merchant. Screenplay by Ivory and Ruth Prawer Jhabvala, based on a novel by Kaylie Jones.

You can sense the love of a daughter for her parents in every frame of *A Soldier's Daughter Never Cries.* It's brought into the foreground in only a couple of scenes, but it courses beneath the whole film, an underground river of gratitude for parents who were difficult and flawed, but prepared their kids for almost anything.

The movie is told through the eyes of Channe, a young girl whose father is a famous American novelist. In the 1960s, the family lives in Paris on the Ile St. Louis in the Seine. Bill Willis (Kris Kristofferson) and his wife, Marcella (Barbara Hershey), move in expatriate circles ("We're Euro-trash"), and the kids go to a school where the students come from wildly different backgrounds. At home, Dad writes, but doesn't tyrannize the family with the importance of his work, which he treats as a job ("Typing is the one thing I learned in high school of any use to me"). There is a younger brother, Billy, who was adopted under quasi-legal circumstances, and a nanny, Candida, who turns down a marriage proposal to stay with the family.

All of this is somewhat inspired, I gather, by fact. The movie is based on an autobiographical novel by Kaylie Jones, whose father, James Jones, was the author of *From Here to Eternity, The Thin Red Line,* and *Whistle.* Many of the parallels are obvious: Jones lived in Paris, drank a lot, and had heart problems. Other embellishments are no doubt fiction, but what cannot be concealed is that Kaylie was sometimes almost stunned by the way both parents treated her with respect as an individual, instead of patronizing her as a child.

The overarching plot line is simple: The children become teenagers, the father's health causes concerns, the family eventually decides to move back home to North Carolina. The film's appeal is in the details. It re-creates a childhood of wonderfully strange friends, eccentric visitors, a Paris which was more home for the children than for the parents, and a homecoming which was fraught for them all. The Willises are like a family sailing in a small boat from one comfortable but uncertain port after another.

The movie was directed by James Ivory and produced by Ismail Merchant, from a screenplay by their longtime collaborator, the novelist Ruth Prawer Jhabvala. She also knows about living in other people's countries, and indeed many of Ivory's films have been about expatriates and exiles (most recently another American in France, in *Jefferson in Paris*). There is a delight in the way they introduce new characters and weave them into the family's bohemian existence. This is one of their best films.

Channe and young Billy are played as teenagers by Leelee Sobieski and Jesse Bradford. We learn some of the circumstances of Billy's adoption, and there is a journal, kept by his mother at the age of fifteen, which he eventually has to decide whether to read or not. He has some anger and resentment, which his parents deal with tactfully; apart from anything else, the film is useful in the way it deals with the challenge of adoption.

Channe, at school, becomes close friends

with the irrepressible Francis Fortescue (Anthony Roth Costanzo), who is the kind of one-off original the movie makes us grateful for. He is flamboyant and uninhibited, an opera fan whose clear, high voice has not yet broken, and who exuberantly serenades the night with his favorite arias. We suspect that perhaps he might grow up to discover he is gay, but the friendship takes place at a time when such possibilities are not yet relevant, and Channe and Francis become soul mates, enjoying the kind of art-besotted existence Channe's parents no doubt sought for themselves in Paris.

The film opens with a portrait of the Willises on the Paris cocktail party circuit, but North Carolina is a different story, with a big frame house and all the moods and customs of home. The kids hate it. They're called "frogs" at school. Channe responds by starting to drink and becoming promiscuous, and Billy vegetates in front of the TV set. Two of the best scenes involve a talk between father and daughter about girls who are too loose, and another, after Channe and a classmate really do fall in love, where Bill asks them if they're having sex. When he gets his answer, he suggests, sincerely, that they use the girl's bedroom: "They're gonna do it anyway; let them do it right."

A Soldier's Daughter Never Cries is not a textbook for every family. It is a story about this one. If a parent is remembered by his children only for what he did, then he spent too much time at work. What is better is to be valued for who you really were. If the parallels between this story and the growing up of Kaylie Jones are true ones, then James Jones was not just a good writer but a good man. ☞

Sonatine ★ ★ ★ ½

R, 89 m., 1998

Beat Kitano (Murakama), Tetsu Watanabe (Uechi), Aya Kikumai (Miyuki), Masanobu Katsumura (Ryoji), Susumu Terashima (Ken), Ren Ohsugi (Katagiri), Tonbo Zushi (Kitajima), Kenichi Yajima (Takahashi). Directed by Takeshi Kitano and produced by Masayuki Mori, Hisao Nabeshima, and Takeo Yoshida. Screenplay by Kitano.

"Maybe you're too rich for this business," a friend tells Murakama, the stone-faced gangster hero of *Sonatine.* Murakama, who rarely says anything, has let it slip that he is tired. Very tired. When he is not actually engaged in the business of being a yakuza, he simply stops moving at all and sits, staring into space, sometimes with a cigarette, sometimes not.

He is tired of living, but not scared of dying, because death, he explains, would at least put an end to his fear of death, which is making his life not worth living. When he explains this perfectly logical reasoning, you look to see if he is smiling, but he isn't. He has it all worked out.

Sonatine is the latest film to be released in this country by Takeshi Kitano, who wrote, directed, and edited it—and stars in it under his acting name, Beat Kitano. It arrives here only a month after *Fireworks,* his 1997 Venice Film Festival winner, but was made in 1993, the fourth of his seven films. He is the biggest star in Japan right now, and as a filmmaker one of the most intriguing.

This film is even better than *Fireworks.* It shows how violent gangster movies need not be filled with stupid dialogue, nonstop action, and gratuitous gore. *Sonatine* is pure, minimal, and clean in its lines; I was reminded of Jean-Pierre Melville's *Le Samourai* (1967), another film about a professional killer who is all but paralyzed by existential dread.

Neither movie depends on extended action scenes because neither hero finds them fun. There is the sense in a lot of American action movies that Bruce Willis or Arnold Schwarzenegger enjoy the action in the way, say, that they might enjoy a football game. Murakama and the French samurai (Alain Delon) do jobs—jobs they have lost the heart for, jobs that have extinguished in them the enjoyment of life.

As the film opens, Murakama and his crew are being assigned by a yakuza overlord to travel to Okinawa as soldiers on loan to an ally who is facing gang warfare. They sense that something is phony about the assignment. "The last time you sent us out," Murakama tells his boss, "I lost three men. I didn't enjoy that." Murakama is correct in his suspicions: The district he controls has become so lucrative that the boss wants to move in and take over.

These yakuza live by a code so deep it even

regulates their fury. Murakama administers a brutal beating to the boss's lieutenant, but they remain on speaking terms. Later, one yakuza stabs another in the stomach. Yet they sit side by side on a bus in Okinawa. "Ice cream?" says the guy who had the knife. "You stabbed me in the belly and it still hurts," the other replies, and we are not quite sure if he is rejecting the ice cream out of anger, or because he doesn't think it will stay down.

In Takeshi's universe, violence is as transient as a lightning bolt. It happens and is over. It means nothing. We sense that in a scene where three men play "paper, rock, scissors" to see who will get to point a pistol at his head and pull the trigger to see if there is a round in the chamber. We see it again in a chilling sequence where a gambler, who didn't want to pay protection, is dunked into the sea; Murakama gets into a conversation and almost forgets to notice how long the guy has been under. And we see it in the climactic battle scene, which is played entirely as flashes of lights against the windows of an apartment: Who else would have the wit, or the sadness, to leave the carnage offscreen?

Kitano was in a motorcycle accident a few years ago that paralyzed half his face. This film was made before the accident, but there's little difference between the way he appears here and in *Fireworks.* If ever there was an actor who could dispense with facial expression, he's the one.

The less he gives, the less he reveals, the less he says and does, the more his presence grows, until he becomes the cold, dangerous center of the story. And in his willingness to let characters languish in real time, to do nothing in between the moments of action, he forces us to look into their eyes and try to figure them out. Films that explain nothing often make everything clear. Films that explain everything often have nothing to explain.

Soul Food ★ ★ ★ ½

R, 115 m., 1997

Vanessa L. Williams (Teri), Vivica A. Fox (Maxine), Nia Long (Bird), Irma P. Hall (Big Mama), Michael Beach (Miles), Mekhi Phifer (Lem), Brandon Hammond (Ahmad), Jeffrey D. Sams (Kenny), Gina Ravera (Faith), Carl Wright (Reverend Williams), Mel Jackson (Simuel), John M. Watson Sr. (Uncle Pete). Directed by George Tillman Jr. and produced by Tracey E. Edmonds and Robert Teitel. Screenplay by Tillman Jr.

Soul Food tells the story of a big African-American family from Chicago with warm-hearted good cheer; in the way it cuts between stories of romance and trouble, it's like *Waiting to Exhale,* but more down-to-earth and believable—and funnier. It knows about how black families stay in constant communication down three or four generations and out to third cousins—how when a matriarch like the movie's Big Mama (Irma P. Hall) hosts a holiday dinner, there are going to be a lot of people in the house, and a lot of stories to catch up with.

The story is told through the eyes of Big Mama's grandson, Ahmad (Brandon Hammond), who introduces us to the key players, especially his mother and her two sisters. His mom and dad are Maxine (Vivica A. Fox) and Kenny (Jeffrey D. Sams). The oldest sister is Teri (Vanessa L. Williams), a successful attorney married to Miles (Michael Beach), who is also an attorney but wants to leave the law and follow his first love, music. The youngest sister, Bird (Nia Long, from *love jones*), has just married Lem (Mekhi Phifer) and opened a beauty shop with a loan from Teri.

Ahmad is young but observant, and starting with his clues we learn that Teri and Miles's marriage has lost its spark—Teri is a workaholic who's not interested in her husband's music. Bird and Lem are struggling, not least because of the shadowy presence of her former boyfriend (Mel Jackson). The whole family is apprehensive about the arrival back in town of Faith (Gina Ravera), who is thought to have been a stripper in California, and is well remembered for several loans she still hasn't paid back.

Oh, and the family extends further: It's a tribute to the script and direction by George Tillman Jr. that he makes them memorable, including the Reverend (Carl Wright) who is a faithful anchor at Big Mama's Sunday dinners, and the mysterious Uncle Pete (John M. Watson Sr.) who hasn't left his room in years. All of these people and more—including neighbors, church friends, and sometimes even the homeless—turn up at Big Mama's on Sundays for her famous soul food feasts, at which long-simmering family issues sometimes come to the boil before Big Mama puts the lid on.

"Big Mama" is not a nickname but an honorary title in a lot of African-American families, indicating a woman who has lived long, worked hard, and acted as an inspiration for many generations. That certainly describes my own mother-in-law, Mrs. Johnnie Mae Hammel, the first Big Mama I met, and it also describes the unforgettable character played by Irma P. Hall in this movie. She has an uncanny gift for seeing right to the heart of her family's strengths and weaknesses, and dishing out firm advice, spiritual sometimes and practical always.

That's until she has a stroke and is hospitalized in a coma. In one of the movie's key scenes, young Ahmad goes to visit her, and in a low-key, unemphasized way, seems to communicate telepathically. (He agrees with her about plans for the garden, even though she, of course, cannot speak.) Later, in the film's closing sequence, it is Ahmad who understands Big Mama's desires for the family and brings them about through some sneaky planning of his own.

The heart of the movie involves the three sisters, their stories and their marriages. The work of all the actors in these sequences—those playing the three couples, plus the two troublesome outsiders—is a reminder of how rich the African-American acting community has grown in recent years, with the renaissance in black-themed films. Williams does an observant job of playing Teri, the most successful woman in her family—ambitious, competitive, tired of picking up bills. She's happy to loan money to Bird (Long), but has a lifelong competition with Maxine (Fox) because she senses a happiness and marital security she'll never know.

Drama comes when Bird's ex-boyfriend pretends to help Lem get a job—and uses the opening to humiliate him. There's more trouble when Faith, the ex-stripper, needs a piano player and finds Teri's husband, Miles, available. It's unfortunate, in a way, that some of these developments lead to sexual situations that make this wonderful family film unsuitable for younger viewers.

Watching *Soul Food,* I reflected that in many ways it depicts a world that white audiences will find unfamiliar. Oh, Big Mama's family shares the same kinds of values, problems, worries, successes, and failures as whites. But movies and TV often focus only on a narrow wedge of black America, showing pimps and junkies, outlaw teenagers and con men, but ignoring the vast and substantial African-American middle and working classes. George Tillman says *Soul Food* is based in part on his own family, and I believe him, because he seems to know the characters so well; by the film's end, so do we.

Sour Grapes no stars

R, 92 m., 1998

Steven Weber (Evan), Craig Bierko (Richie), Jennifer Leigh Warren (Millie), Karen Sillas (Joan), Jack Burns (Eulogist), Viola Harris (Selma), Scott Erik (Teenage Richie), Michael Resnick (Teenage Evan). Directed by Larry David and produced by Laurie Lennard. Screenplay by David.

Sour Grapes is a comedy about things that aren't funny. It reminded me of *Crash,* an erotic thriller about things no one finds erotic. The big difference is that David Cronenberg, who made *Crash,* knew that people were not turned on by auto accidents. Larry David, who wrote and directed *Sour Grapes,* apparently thinks people are amused by cancer, accidental castration, racial stereotypes, and bitter family feuds.

Oh, I have no doubt that all of those subjects could be incorporated into a great comedy. It's all in the style and the timing. *Sour Grapes* is tone-deaf comedy; the material, the dialogue, the delivery, and even the sound track are labored and leaden. How to account for the fact that Larry David is one of the creators of *Seinfeld*? Maybe he works well with others.

I can't easily remember a film I've enjoyed less. *North,* a comedy I hated, was at least able to inflame me with dislike. *Sour Grapes* is a movie that deserves its title: It's puckered, deflated, and vinegary. It's a dead zone.

The story. Two cousins (Steven Weber and Craig Bierko) go to Atlantic City. One is a designer who wins a slot jackpot of more than $436,000. He was playing with quarters given him by the other guy. The other cousin, a surgeon, not unreasonably thinks he should get some of the winnings. If not half, then maybe a third. The winner offers him 3 percent.

This sets off several scenes of debate about what would be right or wrong in such a situation. Even a limo driver, hearing the winner's story, throws him out of the car: "You were playing with his money!" The losing doctor nevertheless gives his cousin a blue warm-up suit for his birthday, only to discover that the louse has given the suit away to an African-American street person.

So far all we have is a comic premise that doesn't deliver laughs. Now the movie heads for cringe-inducing material. We learn about the winner's ability to perform oral sex while alone. He's alone a lot because his wife is mad at him, but that's an opening for stereotyped Jewish mother scenes. The feud heats up until the enraged doctor lies to the winner: "You have terminal cancer. It's time to set your house in order." Ho, ho.

The winner wants to spare his mother the misery of watching her son die. So he gives her house key to the black bum in the warm-up suit and tells him to make himself at home. His plan: His mother will be scared to death by the sight of the black home invader. After she screams, we see the bum running down the street in Steppin' Fetchit style. Was there no one to hint to David that this was gratuitous and offensive?

Further material involves the surgeon getting so upset in the operating room that he reverses an X-ray film and removes the wrong testicle from a TV star—who then, of course, has to be told that they still had to go ahead and remove the remaining testicle. The star develops a castrato voice. Ho, ho.

This material is impossible to begin with. What makes it worse is the lack of lightness from the performers, who slog glumly through their dialogue as if they know what an aromatic turkey they're stuck in. Scene after scene clangs dead to the floor, starting with the funeral service that opens the film. The more I think of it, the more *Sour Grapes* really does resemble *Crash* (except that *Crash* was not a bad film). Both movies are like watching automobile accidents. Only one intended to be.

South Park: Bigger, Longer and Uncut ★ ★ ½

R, 80 m., 1999

An animated film with the voices of Trey Parker, Matthew Stone, Isaac Hayes, George Clooney, Minnie Driver, Mike Judge, and Eric Idle. Directed by Trey Parker and produced by Parker and Matt Stone. Screenplay by Parker, Stone, and Pam Brady.

The national debate about violence and obscenity in the movies has arrived in South Park. The "little redneck mountain town," where adult cynicism is found in the mouths of babes, is the setting for vicious social satire in *South Park: Bigger, Longer and Uncut.* The most slashing political commentary of the year is not in the new film by Oliver Stone, David Lynch, or John Sayles, but in an animated musical comedy about obscenity. Wait until you see the bedroom scenes between Satan and Saddam Hussein.

Waves of four-letter words roll out over the audience, which laughs with incredulity: People can't believe what they're hearing. The film has an R rating instead of NC-17 only because it's a cartoon, I suspect; even so, the MPAA has a lot of splaining to do. Not since Andrew Dice Clay passed into obscurity have sentences been constructed so completely out of the unspeakable.

I laughed. I did not always feel proud of myself while I was laughing, however. The movie is like a depraved extension of *Kids Say the Darnedest Things,* in which little children repeat what they've heard, and we cringe because we know what the words really mean. No target is too low, no attitude too mean or hurtful, no image too unthinkable. After making *South Park: Bigger, Longer and Uncut,* its creators, Trey Parker and Matt Stone, had better move on. They've taken *South Park* as far as it can go, and beyond.

If you've never seen the original Comedy Central TV show and somehow find yourself in the theater, you'll be jolted by the distance between the images and the content. The animation is deliberately crude, like elements cut out of construction paper. Characters are made of simple arrangements of basic geometrical shapes and solid colors. When they talk, their lips don't move; their entire heads tilt open in synch with the words. The effect is of sophisticated children slamming stuff around on the project table in first grade.

The story: A new R-rated movie has come to town, starring the Canadian stars Terrence and Phillip. It's titled *Asses of Fire.* (That's the mildest vulgarity in the movie, and the most extreme I can print in the paper.) The South Park kids bribe a homeless man to be their "adult guardian," attend the movie, drink in its nonstop, wall-to-wall language, and startle their class at school with streams of four-letter words.

One of their moms, deeply offended, founds the Mothers Against Canada (its acronym no doubt targeted at the cosmetics company). The neighbor to the north is blamed for all of the ills in U.S. society, Terrence and Phillip are arrested and condemned to death, and in retaliation the Canadian Air Force bombs the home of the Baldwin brothers in Hollywood. War is declared, leading to scenes your eyes will register but your mind will not believe, such as a USO show involving Winona Ryder doing unspeakable things with Ping-Pong balls.

The other plot strand begins after little Kenny is killed. (This is not a spoiler; little Kenny is killed in each and every episode of the TV series, always with the line, "Oh, my God! They've killed Kenny!") He goes to hell (we see Hitler and George Burns drifting past) and finds that Saddam Hussein, recently deceased, is having an affair with Satan. Saddam wants sex, Satan wants a meaningful relationship, and they inspire a book titled *Saddam Is from Mars, Satan Is from Venus.*

Key plot point: The deaths of Terrence and Phillip would be the seventh biblical sign of the apocalypse, triggering Armageddon. It's up to the South Park kids to save the world. All of this unfolds against an unending stream of satirical abuse, ethnic stereotyping, sexual vulgarity, and pointed political commentary that alternates common sense with the truly and hurtfully offensive.

I laughed, as I have reported. Sometimes the laughter was liberating, as good laughter can be, and sometimes it was simply disbelieving: How could they get away with this? This is a season when the movies are hurtling themselves over the precipice of good taste. Every week brings its new surprises. I watch as Austin Powers drinks coffee that contains excrement, and two weeks later I go to *American Pie* and watch a character drink beer that contains the most famous bodily fluid from *There's Something About Mary.* In *Big Daddy,* I see an adult role model instruct a five-year-old on how to trip in-line skaters, urinate in public, and spill the french fries of complete strangers in McDonald's.

Now this—a cartoon, but it goes far beyond anything in any of those live-action movies. All it lacks is a point to its message. What is it saying? That movies have gone too far, or that protests against movies have gone too far? It is a sign of our times that I cannot tell. Perhaps it's simply anarchistic, and feels that if it throws enough shocking material at the wall, some of it will stick. A lot of the movie offended me. Some of it amazed me. It is too long and runs out of steam, but it serves as a signpost for our troubled times. Just for the information it contains about the way we live now, maybe thoughtful and concerned people should see it. After all, everyone else will.

Note: Reading this again, I think it's more of a three-star review. The movie is unsettling, but that's a good thing; my doubts are a tribute to it.

The Spanish Prisoner ★ ★ ★ ½

PG, 112 m., 1998

Campbell Scott (Joe Ross), Rebecca Pidgeon (Susan Ricci), Steve Martin (Jimmy Dell), Ben Gazzara (Klein), Ricky Jay (George Lang), Felicity Huffman (McCune), Richard L. Freidman (Businessman). Directed by David Mamet and produced by Jean Doumanian. Screenplay by Mamet.

There are really only two screenwriters working at the moment whose words you can recognize as soon as you hear them: Quentin Tarantino and David Mamet. All of the others, however clever, deal in the ordinary rhythms of daily speech.

Tarantino we recognize because of the way his dialogue, like Mark Twain's, unfurls down the corridors of long inventive progressions, collecting proper names and trademarks along the way, to arrive at preposterous generalizations—delivered flatly, as if they were the simple truth.

Mamet is even easier to recognize. His characters often speak as if they're wary of the world, afraid of being misquoted, reluctant to say what's on their minds: As a protective shield, they fall into precise legalisms, invoking old sayings as if they're magic charms. Often they punctuate their dialogue with four-letter words, but in *The Spanish Prisoner* there is not a single obscenity, and we picture Mamet with a proud grin on his face, collecting his very first PG rating.

The movie does not take place in Spain and has no prisoners. The title refers to a classic con game. Mamet, whose favorite game is poker, loves films where the characters negotiate a thicket of lies. *The Spanish Prisoner* resembles Hitchcock in the way that everything takes place in full view, on sunny beaches and in brightly lighted rooms, with attractive people smilingly pulling the rug out from under the hero and revealing the abyss.

The hero is Joe Ross (Campbell Scott), who has invented a process that will make money for his company—so much money that when he writes the figure on a blackboard, we don't even see it, only the shining eyes of executives looking at it. ("The Process," he says. Pause. "And, by means of the Process, to control the world market." The missing words are replaced by greed.)

He works for Mr. Klein (Ben Gazzara), who has convened a meeting in the Caribbean to discuss the Process. Also on hand is George, a company lawyer played by Ricky Jay—a professional magician and expert in charlatans, who is Mamet's friend and collaborator. And there is Susan (Rebecca Pidgeon, Mamet's wife), whose heart is all aflutter for Joe Ross, and who is very smart and likes to prove it by saying smart things that end on a triumphant note, as if she expects a gold star on her report card. ("I'm a problem solver, and I have a heart of gold.")

To the Caribbean island comes a man named Jimmy Dell (Steve Martin), who may or may not have arrived by seaplane. We see how Mamet creates uncertainty: Joe thinks the man arrived by seaplane, but Susan thinks he didn't and provides photographic proof (which, as far as we can see, proves nothing), and in the end it doesn't matter if he arrives by seaplane or not; the whole episode is used simply to introduce the idea that Jimmy Dell may not be what he seems.

He seems to be a rich, friendly New Yorker, who is trying to conceal an affair with a partner's wife. He says he has a sister in New York, and gives Joe a book to deliver to her ("Might I ask you a service?"). Joe has thus accepted a wrapped package from a stranger, which he plans to take on board a plane; you see how our minds start working, spotting conspiracies everywhere. But at this point the plot summary must end, before the surprises begin. I can only say that anything as valuable as the Process would be a target for industrial espionage, and that when enough millions of dollars are involved, few people are above temptation.

The Spanish Prisoner is delightful in the way a great card manipulator is delightful. It rolls its sleeves to above its elbows to show it has no hidden cards, and then produces them out of thin air. It has the buried structure of a card manipulator's spiel, in which a "story" is told about the cards, and they are given personalities and motives, even though they are only cards. Our attention is misdirected—we are human and invest our interest in the human motives attributed to the cards, and forget to watch closely to see where they are going and how they are being handled. Same thing with the characters in *The Spanish Prisoner.* They are all given motives—romance, greed, pride, friendship, curiosity—and all of these motives are inventions and misdirections; the magician cuts the deck, and the joker wins.

There is, I think, a hole in the end of the story big enough to drive a ferry boat through, but then again there's another way of looking at the whole thing that would account for that, if the con were exactly the reverse of what we're left believing. Not that it matters. The end of a magic trick is never the most interesting part; the setup is more fun, because we can test ourselves against the magician, who will certainly fool us. We like to be fooled. It's like being tickled. We say, "Stop! Stop!" and don't mean it.

Spawn ★★★½

PG-13, 93 m., 1997

Michael Jai White (Al Simmons), John Leguizamo (Clown), Martin Sheen (Jason Wynn), Theresa Randle (Wanda), Nicol Williamson (Cogliostro), D. B. Sweeney (Terry Fitzgerald). Directed by Mark Dippe and produced by Clint Goldman. Screenplay by Alan McElroy, based on the comic books by Todd McFarlane.

Spawn is best seen as an experimental art film. It walks and talks like a big-budget horror film, heavy on special effects and pitched at the teenage audience, and maybe that's how it will be received. But it's more impressive if you ignore the genre and just look at what's on the screen. What we have here are creators in several different areas doing their best to push the envelope. The subject is simply an excuse for their art—just as it always is with serious artists.

Still, we can begin with the story. A man named Al Simmons (Michael Jai White) is happily married and at peace with himself, when he's recruited on a mission to destroy a biological warfare factory in North Korea. The mission is a setup. He is horribly burned and disfigured, and made captive of the forces of darkness. They offer him a deal: Lead the army of evil and he can see his wife again. He loves her, and he agrees.

That's what comic book writers call the "origination story," and *Spawn,* of course, is based on a famous series of comic books by Todd McFarlane, who made "Spiderman" the top-selling comic in history before jumping ship at Marvel to start his own company. After the setup, five years pass before the evil ones make good on their promise. Simmons by now is Spawn, seen either grotesquely scarred, or in an elaborate costume. He goes to his old home, sees his wife (Theresa Randle), now happily remarried, and is mistaken as a homeless man by everyone except his faithful little dog Spaz.

Most of the movie involves Spawn's efforts to break loose from his bargain with the devil, whose representative is Clown, a fat, wisecracking midget played with brilliant comic timing by John Leguizamo (who has little but his timing left to recognize after the special effects and makeup people have finished disguising him). Other key characters include Martin Sheen as Jason Wynn, a diabolical government agent who hopes to control the earth with biological blackmail, and Nicol Williamson as Cogliostro, Clown's enemy and a counterforce for good. Spawn has agreed to lead Armageddon for the powers of hell, but now finds himself trapped between good and evil.

And so on. I am sure there will be some who get involved at the plot level, but in comic books, and movies spawned by comic books, few things are ever really settled forever; the ending has to be left open for a sequel, and of course whole story lines can be negated (as happened at Marvel recently) just by explaining that impostors were at work. What matters is style, tone, and creative energy.

Spawn is the work of some of the most inventive artists now working in the area of digital effects. Its first-time director, Mark Dippe, worked on the dinosaurs of *Jurassic Park* and the shape-shifting villain of *Terminator 2.* The visual-effects coordinator is Steve "Spaz" Williams, once a resident genius at Industrial Light and Magic. They've gathered an expert creative team, and what they put on the screen are vivid, bizarre, intense images—including visions of hell that are worthy of Hieronymus Bosch.

Spawn himself is an extraordinary superhero, with smoking green eyeballs and two looks—scarred skin, or a uniform that makes Batman look underdressed. Clown is a shapeshifter who can impersonate almost anyone else in the movie; Leguizamo's features are buried in fat makeup and then transplanted by animation onto a grotesque clown's body. There is a dragonlike thing, the beast of hell, that is all tooth, eyeball, and disgusting, coiling tongue (an "overgrown gekko," it's called). And there are vast vistas of the expanse of hell, with countless souls writhing on clouds of flame, tortured by the very anonymity of their suffering.

Against this, and preventing the film from being even better, is a pretty sappy plot. Yes, I said that the subject is just an excuse for the art, but audiences don't always see it that way, and some are likely to complain that *Spawn* is basically just shallow setups for virtuoso special-effects sequences. And so it is. Michael

Jai White (who once played Mike Tyson on TV) makes a powerful Spawn with a presence both menacing and touching, and Clown is an inspired villain with one wicked one-liner after another ("You're Jimmy Stewart—and I'm Clarence"). But the Sheen and Williamson characters exist primarily just to nudge the plot along, and Theresa Randle's wife is underwritten; we want more about her feelings.

So the way to view the movie, I think, is to consider the story as the frame—necessary, but upstaged by what it contains, which in this case is some of the most impressive effects I've seen. The disciplines blend into one another: animation, makeup, costuming, process shots, morphing. They create a place and a look as specific as the places evoked in such films as *Metropolis* and *Blade Runner.* As a visual experience, *Spawn* is unforgettable.

Speed 2: Cruise Control ★ ★ ★

PG-13, 125 m., 1997

Sandra Bullock (Annie), Jason Patric (Alex), Willem Dafoe (Geiger), Temuera Morrison (Juliano), Brian McCardie (Merced), Christine Firkins (Drew), Michael G. Hagerty (Harvey), Colleen Camp (Debbie). Directed by Jan De Bont and produced by De Bont, Steve Perry, and Michael Peyser. Screenplay by Randall McCormick and Jeff Nathanson, based on a story by De Bont and McCormick.

I love the summertime. I love strolling down Michigan Avenue on a balmy June evening, past the tourists and the shoppers and the lovers and the people dawdling on their way home from work, and I love going into a theater for a sneak preview of a summer movie and buying popcorn and settling back in my seat and enjoying a movie containing:

—A chainsaw.

—An explosive device with a red digital readout that nobody will ever be able to see (this one is concealed inside a fake golf club).

—A villain who travels with jars of leeches to suck the copper poisoning from his blood.

—A sweet girl and her lover on a Caribbean cruise. He just happens to be a member of an LAPD SWAT team.

—The other passengers on the cruise, who just happen to include members of a diamond dealer's association, who have filled the ship's vault with treasure.

—The villain's plot to hijack and destroy the ship, steal the diamonds, and get revenge on the computer company whose "electromagnetic fields gave me copper poisoning," after which he was fired and cast aside.

All of these pleasures, and more, are in *Speed 2: Cruise Control,* which is a sequel to *Speed* in name only—since even the basic premise is different. In the first movie, if the bus stopped, everyone would get killed. In this one, if the ocean liner doesn't stop, everyone will get killed. It's a small twist, I grant you, but a decisive one.

The movie stars Sandra Bullock, from *Speed,* and Jason Patric as her boyfriend. (The dialogue explains that she split up with the Keanu Reeves character from the earlier film for a lot of reasons, one of them possibly being that he did not want to appear in the sequel.) They go on a cruise and are unlucky enough to pick the boat targeted for revenge by a villain named Geiger (Willem DaFoe), whose laptop computers can take over the ship's own systems and control them.

Bullock plays the same fetching character she played the first time: warm, likable, stuttering a little, calm under pressure. Unfortunately, considering that she was crucial to the success of *Speed,* the screenplay gives her a secondary role and hands most of the best scenes to Patric, who handles them like a traditional action hero. At one point he puts on scuba gear and dangles inches from the giant spinning props of the ocean liner, and at another point he shoots a seaplane with a speargun and reels himself in. These stunts make the original *Speed* look plausible.

The ship itself is, of course, supplied with a cross-section of typical passengers, who in addition to the diamond dealers include a fat-acceptance group and a deaf girl who gets trapped in an elevator and can't hear the abandon-ship alarm. The captain is thrown overboard early in the film, after Geiger explains his grievance. (Seems like a waste, somehow, to go to the trouble of lodging your complaint with someone you immediately kill.) Then it's up to the hero and his girlfriend to save the day.

I will leave you in suspense as to whether

they succeed. I will observe, however, that it's not every day (unless you live in New Orleans) that you get to see a ship crashing into a pier. The special-effects sequences in the movie are first-rate, especially that one. I know some of the houses on shore were models and that all kinds of fancy techniques were used, but the progress of the ship, as it crushes piers and condos, restaurants and trucks and cars, looks surprisingly real. And I was grateful to Jan De Bont, director of this film and the first one, for not overlooking such touches as The Dog Who Survives.

I chortled a few times. The first was at the digital readout. Why do mad bombers always go to the trouble of supplying them? There's not much room inside the head of a golf club (even a wood), so why waste space on a digital readout? I also chortled a few moments later, when the villain pulled out a piece of equipment labeled FIBER OPTIC CONVERTER in letters so large they could be read across the room. Doesn't mean much, but it sure looks good. And I will long treasure a moment when a computer asks Geiger, "Time to initiate?" and he types in, "Now."

Is the movie fun? Yes. Especially fun when the desperate Bullock breaks into a ship's supply cabinet and finds a chainsaw, which I imagine all ships carry. And when pleasure boaters somehow fail to see a full-sized runaway ocean liner until it is three feet from them. Movies like this embrace goofiness with an almost sensual pleasure. And so, on a warm summer evening, do I.

Sphere ★ ½

PG-13, 120 m., 1998

Dustin Hoffman (Dr. Norman Goodman), Sharon Stone (Beth Halperin), Samuel L. Jackson (Harry Adams), Peter Coyote (Barnes), Liev Schreiber (Ted Fielding), Queen Latifah (Fletcher). Directed by Barry Levinson and produced by Levinson, Michael Crichton, and Andrew Wald. Screenplay by Stephen Hauser and Paul Attanasio, based on the novel by Crichton.

Michael Crichton is the science-fiction author people read if they think they're too good for "regular" science fiction. Too bad. What they get in *Sphere*, now filmed by Barry Levinson, is a watered-down version of the sci-fi classic *Solaris*, by Stanislaw Lem, which was made into an immeasurably better film by Andrei Tarkovsky.

The underlying idea is the same: Humans come into contact with an extraterrestrial presence that allows their minds to make their thoughts seem real. The earlier novel and film challenged our ideas about human consciousness. *Sphere* functions more like a whodunit in which the plot's hot potato is tossed from character to character.

As the movie opens, an expert team is brought to the middle of the Pacific, where an amazing thing has been found on the ocean floor: a giant spacecraft, apparently buried for nearly 300 years, that still emits a distant hum—suggesting it is intact and may harbor life. The members of the team: a psychologist (Dustin Hoffman), a mathematician (Samuel L. Jackson), a biochemist (Sharon Stone), and an astrophysicist (Liev Schreiber). In command of a navy "habitat" on the ocean floor next to the ship is Peter Coyote. The habitat's small crew includes radio operator Queen Latifah, from *Set It Off*, who is on hand to illustrate Hollywood's immutable law that the first character to die is always the African-American.

The descent to the ocean floor, accompanied by much talk about depressurization, will be a disappointment to anyone who remembers the suspense in similar scenes in James Cameron's *Abyss*. And the introduction of the spacecraft is also a disappointment: Instead of the awe-inspiring first glimpses we remember from *Close Encounters* or even *Independence Day*, it's a throwaway. No wonder. The ocean-floor special effects are less than sensational, and the exteriors of the descent craft and the spacecraft are all too obviously models.

No matter, if the story holds our attention. At first it does. As long as we're in suspense, we're involved, because we anticipate great things. But *Sphere* is one of those movies where the end titles should be Peggy Lee singing "Is That All There Is?" The more the plot reveals, the more we realize how little there is to reveal, until finally the movie disintegrates into flaccid scenes where the surviving characters sit around talking about their puzzlements.

I have been careful to protect most of the film's secrets. I can be excused, I suppose, for revealing that what they find inside the spacecraft is, yes, a sphere. Where does this sphere come from? Who or what made it? How does it function? I am content to let it remain a mystery, so long as it entertains me, but after a promising start (it generates a *2001*-style hurtle through space and time), it just sits there, glowing and glowering, while the humans deal with the dangers of undersea life.

Hoffman, Jackson, Stone: These are good actors. How good is illustrated by how much they do with the flat, unyielding material. The last twenty minutes of the film are a slog through circular explanations and speculations that would have capsized lesser actors. They give it a good try, with dialogue that sounds either like characters analyzing the situation, or actors trying to figure out the plot.

Sphere feels rushed. The screenplay uses lots of talk to conceal the fact that the story has never been grappled with. The effects and the sets are pitched at the level of made-for-TV. The only excellence is in the acting, and even then the screenplay puts the characters through so many U-turns that dramatic momentum is impossible.

There are ideas sloshing around somewhere in the rising waters aboard the undersea habitat. The best one is an old science-fiction standby: Are humans mature enough to handle the secrets of the universe? Or are we but an infant species, whose fears and phobias prevent us from embracing the big picture? The last scenes are supposed to be a solemn confrontation of these questions, but they're punctuated by a special effects shot so puny and underwhelming that the spell is broken. That's all, folks. Put your hands together for Miss Peggy Lee.

Spice World ½★

PG, 93 m., 1998

Spice Girls (Themselves), Richard E. Grant (Clifford, the Manager), Claire Rushbrook (Deborah, the Assistant), Alan Cumming (Piers Cutherton-Smyth), Roger Moore (The Chief), George Wendt (Martin Barnfield), Meat Loaf (Dennis), Naoko Mori (Nicola). Cameos: Stephen Fry, Bob Hoskins, Elvis Costello, the Dream Boys, Bob Geldof, Elton John, Jonathan Ross. Directed by Bob Spiers and produced by Uri Fruchtmann and Barnaby Thompson. Screenplay by Kim Fuller.

The Spice Girls are easier to tell apart than the Mutant Ninja Turtles, but that is small consolation: What can you say about five women whose principal distinguishing characteristic is that they have different names?

They occupy *Spice World* as if they were watching it: They're so detached they can't even successfully lip-synch their own songs. During a rehearsal scene, their director tells them, with such truth that we may be hearing a secret message from the screenwriter, "That was absolutely perfect—without being actually any good."

Spice World is obviously intended as a ripoff of *A Hard Day's Night* (1964), which gave the Beatles to the movies. They should have ripped off more—everything they could get their hands on. The movie is a day in the life of a musical group that has become an overnight success, and we see them rehearse, perform, hang out together, and deal with such desperately contrived supporting characters as a trash newspaper editor, a paparazzo, and a manipulative manager.

All of these elements are inspired in one way or another by *A Hard Day's Night.* The huge difference, of course, is that the Beatles were talented—while, let's face it, the Spice Girls could be duplicated by any five women under the age of thirty standing in line at Dunkin' Donuts.

The Beatles film played off the personalities of the Beatles. The Spice Girls have no personalities; their bodies are carriers for inane chatter. The Beatles film had such great music that every song in it is beloved all over the world. The Spice Girls' music is so bad that even *Spice World* avoids using any more of it than absolutely necessary.

The film's linking device is a big double-decker bus, painted like a Union Jack, which ferries the Girls past London landmarks (so many landmarks I suspect the filmmakers were desperately trying to stretch the running time). This bus is of ordinary size on the outside but three times too wide on the inside; it is fitted with all the conveniences of Spice Girlhood, except, apparently, toilet facilities, leading to the unusual sight of the Girls jumping off for a quick pee in the woods. (They do everything together.)

So lacking in human characteristics are the Girls that when the screenplay falls back on the last resort of the bankrupt filmmaking imagination—a live childbirth scene—they have to import one of their friends to have the baby. She at least had the wit to get pregnant, something beyond the Girls since it would involve a relationship, and thus an attention span. Words fail me as I try to describe my thoughts at the prospect of the five Spice Girls shouting "push!"

Sprung ★ ½

R, 105 m., 1997

Tisha Campbell (Brandy), Rusty Cundieff (Montel), Paula Jai Parker (Adina), Joe Torry (Clyde), John Witherspoon (Detective), Jennifer Lee (Veronica), Clarence Williams III (Grand Daddy), Loretta Jean (Bride's Mother). Directed by Rusty Cundieff and produced by Darin Scott. Screenplay by Cundieff and Scott.

Sometimes it takes one movie to show you how good another movie was. *Sprung* provides that service for *Booty Call.* Both movies are sexcoms about two black couples. Both are cheerfully vulgar. Both have lots of sex and slapstick. *Booty Call* works. *Sprung,* despite containing a sweet relationship, doesn't.

The film begins with a manhunting woman named Adina (Paula Jai Parker) who convinces her somewhat shy friend Brandy (Tisha Campbell), a law clerk, to go partying. At a party, Adina exhibits her laserlike ability to calculate a man's worth by running an inventory on what he's wearing, while mental cash registers ring. She's fooled, though, by Clyde (Joe Torry), manager of a fast-food store, who flashes the keyring of a borrowed Porsche and "drops" a phony bank receipt.

When Adina and Clyde pair off, that leaves Brandy with Clyde's friend Montel (Rusty Cundieff, the film's director and cowriter). Cut to Clyde's apartment where, in the movie's worst miscalculation, he and Adina make love in a disturbingly animalistic scene that runs on and on and on to the world's loudest simultaneous orgasm—surpassing any possible comic purpose and simply becoming porno without the close-ups.

That scene throws the whole opening of the movie out of whack: In tone, effect, and length it breaks the rhythm and disturbs the tone, and it's a long time before we realize it had nothing to do with the rest of the plot. The other couple, Montel and Brandy, fall in love, and they're charming with one another—it would be a nice story if it weren't always being interrupted. But that happens regularly; Adina and Clyde plot to trick their friends to break up. Why? Because otherwise the couples will always be double-dating, and Adina and Clyde will have to spend too much time together.

Don't worry if you don't follow this. It has no connection to human life, and exists only in the terms of screenplay clichés. All that redeems it is the characters of Montel and Brandy; we care about them even though the movie does little to help us. There are well-written scenes in which Brandy, who's studying to be a lawyer, has to get over her snobbery and realize that Montel may indeed have a future in fast food.

Unfortunately, the good vibes in the movie are undermined by the dialogue, which makes a running gag out of the ability to put together long, ugly sentences full of insulting epithets; "pimp" and "buckwheat" are two I can print here. Why are there so many racial insults in black-oriented movies; isn't it time to declare a moratorium on insulting language?

Thinking back over the film, I can see how it might have been better. The plot might have worked if the characters had been allowed to emerge as halfway convincing people. Instead, there's a hyper quality to *Sprung,* as if Cundieff was concerned that a moment's pause or silence would sink the picture. It's amusing when he uses special effects (stars spin around Clyde's head, and Adina's inventory scene has cute visuals). But desperation created the sequence where Clyde plots to get Montel drunk and seduced by an old flame; Brandy's heart is broken when she overhears what she thinks are the sounds of love.

There is a nice extended sequence when Brandy and Montel first meet for lunch in the park. They like each other, they eat an obligatory hot dog, they talk and walk, and then, that evening, they happen upon a ballroom dancing party of middle-aged African-Americans, and spin onto the dance floor. Afterward they walk in the moonlight—and the next morning they're *still* in the park! It's like getting *Before Sunrise* as a bonus in the middle of a different movie.

Star Kid ★ ★ ★

PG, 101 m., 1998

Joseph Mazzello (Spencer Griffith), Joey Simmrin (Turbo Bruntley), Alex Daniels (Cyborsuit), Arthur Burghardt (Cyborsuit Voice), Brian Simpson (Broodwarrior), Richard Gilliland (Roland [Dad]), Corinne Bohrer (Janet Holloway), Ashlee Levitch (Stacey [Sister]), Lauren Eckstrom (Michelle). Directed by Manny Coto and produced by Jennie Lew Tugend. Screenplay by Coto.

How would you like to climb inside a glistening metallic superhero suit and be partners with the intelligent cyborg that controls it? If you were a shy twelve-year-old boy, picked on by bullies and your brat of a sister, you'd love it. *Star Kid* develops that fantasy in a lively action movie that young boys may especially enjoy—if their innocence hasn't already been hammered down by too much R-rated violence.

The movie stars Joseph Mazzello *(Jurassic Park, The River Wild)* as Spencer, a bright student whose imagination is centered on the adventures of a comic book hero named Midnight Warrior. He's got a hopeless crush on a girl at school named Michelle (Lauren Eckstrom), who also likes Midnight Warrior, and who would probably be his friend if he weren't paralyzed by shyness every time he tries to talk to her. At home, he has a preoccupied dad (Richard Gilliland) and a mean older sister (Ashlee Levitch) who gets resentful when she's required to baby-sit "the little scab juice."

One night everything changes for Spencer, when he sees a rocket land in a nearby junkyard. He scampers inside and finds the ship, still steaming, as it opens up to reveal a tall, glistening robotic cyborg inside. This creature, who looks like a detailed version of the visitor in *The Day the Earth Stood Still,* is inhabited by an intelligence that is quickly able to communicate with Spencer, inviting him to step inside and occupy his body.

We've already learned the back story. The creature was built by a race named the Trelkans, who look like Yoda with eczema, and are engaged in a struggle with the evil Broodwarriors. Spencer, once inside the suit, communicates face to face with a holographic image representing the cyborg's intelligence, and before long he's calling him Cy.

The movie's appeal is obvious: Inside the suit, Spencer becomes unbelievably strong and can do all kinds of neat stuff, like give the school bullies their comeuppance, impress Michelle, and let his sister see he's not a little scab juice anymore. There are comic scenes as Spencer awkwardly learns to control the suit, and then a climax when a Broodwarrior arrives on Earth for a final showdown.

Spencer is essentially living inside a comic book. A lot of action comics originate from the same premise—an ordinary guy like Clark Kent or Peter Parker is transformed into a paragon of strength and power. Adolescent readers like that; it suits their fantasies. *Star Kid,* written and directed by Manny Coto, has a sweet heart and a lot of sly wit, and the symbiosis between boy and cyborg is handled cleverly. For kids of a certain age, it pushes the right buttons.

Star Maps ★ ★

R, 95 m., 1997

Douglas Spain (Carlos), Efrain Figueroa (Pepe), Kandeyce Jorden (Jennifer), Martha Velez (Teresa), Lysa Flores (Maria), Annette Murphy (Letti), Robin Thomas (Martin), Vincent Chandler (Juancito). Directed by Miguel Arteta and produced by Matthew Greenfield. Screenplay by Arteta, based on a story by Arteta and Greenfield.

Sometimes while channel-surfing I'll linger with envy on the Spanish-language stations, where the dramas always seem steamier and more dramatic. I wish I spoke the language. I have the feeling I wouldn't be as bored. Characters make emotional declarations, bosoms heave, eyes flash, hair is tossed, faces are slapped, and there's lots of weeping, especially during emotional partings.

Star Maps is a movie that exists in the same emotional range, but it's in English, which is not necessarily an advantage, since you can almost always imagine better dialogue than the actors come up with in soft-core melodrama. The movie tells the story of a malevolent father named Pepe (Efrain Figueroa) who controls a string of young men on Hollywood street corners, who pretend to be selling maps to the stars' homes, but are actually male prostitutes.

As the film opens, Pepe's son Carlos (Douglas Spain), who dreams of being an actor, has returned from Mexico, where he was in amateur productions. He hopes his father's "connections" in showbiz will help him get his career started. His father immediately puts him out on the street as a hustler. It's a family tradition: Pepe's own father did the same to him.

Meanwhile, at home, life is chaotic. Pepe's wife, Teresa (Martha Velez), spends most of her time in bed, allegedly dying of cancer. Sometimes she has hallucinations in which she smiles and jokes with Cantinflas, the famous comedian. It was Teresa who sent young Carlos to her family in Mexico to get him away from the evil Pepe, and now that Carlos is back, Teresa has retreated into madness. Her daughter Maria (Lysa Flores), who has somehow escaped the family curse, warns Carlos that their father will destroy him. Meanwhile, another brother spends most of his time on the couch, eating. Occasionally he rouses himself to put on an S&M superhero costume and enact private fantasies.

Carlos doesn't much mind being a hustler, since for him it is good practice for the acting profession. But one day his luck changes when he meets Jennifer (Kandeyce Jorden), a TV star who is, she says, "looking for a nice little Mexican boy." The sex is good, and she decides she wants him around all the time, so she demands that he be written into her show. ("You're a Mexican stud. I'm helpless and white.") Jennifer's husband, who produces the show, is not pleased by this development.

Meanwhile, one of the better subplots involves the relationship between Pepe and Letti (Annette Murphy), his mistress, whom he also has working as a hooker. Letti, for some reason, trusts this monster, who exists on the fringes of Hollywood respectability, finding clients through bartenders (and promising clients "a guide to show you the more intimate parts of Hollywood"). Pepe is thrown out of a bar where he gets a lot of business after he beats up Letti, and that causes changes in the family's fortunes.

And there's more. Much more. *Star Maps* reads like a collision involving three or four scripts in different stages of development. It's a comedy, especially as Jennifer's writers try to rewrite a script to make use of Carlos. It's a tragedy, because Pepe is unspeakably evil and brutal. It's magic realism, as the mother chats with Cantinflas. And there are times when I think it's trying for parody, as when the sister, Maria, brings home the nice pharmacist who likes her, and Pepe puts on a horror show around the dinner table. (The pharmacist says, "Sir! This is no way to treat your daughter!" The father says, "I think she is probably a virgin. It's gonna cost you $50.")

Star Maps is not, to be sure, boring. But it is wildly unfocused. Is it about family abuse, prostitution, show business, dreams of fame, or what? It was written and directed by Miguel Arteta, who shows great energy and a dramatic drive, and with a more considered screenplay might have made a better movie. Walking out of the theater, I found myself wondering how this film is going to affect the lives of the people who really do sell maps to the stars' homes.

Starship Troopers ★ ★

R, 129 m., 1997

Casper Van Dien (Johnny Rico), Dina Meyer (Dizzy Flores), Denise Richards (Carmen Ibanez), Michael Ironside (Jean Rasczak), Jake Busey (Ace Levy), Neil Patrick Harris (Carl Jenkins), Clancy Brown (Sergeant Zim), Seth Gilliam (Sugar Watkins), Patrick Muldoon (Zander Barcalow). Directed by Paul Verhoeven and produced by Jon Davison and Alan Marshall. Screenplay by Ed Neumeier, based on the novel by Robert A. Heinlein.

Starship Troopers is the most violent kiddie movie ever made. I call it a kiddie movie not to be insulting, but to be accurate: Its action, characters, and values are pitched at eleven-year-old science-fiction fans. That makes it true to its source. It's based on a novel for juveniles by Robert A. Heinlein. I read it to the point of memorization when I was in grade school. I have improved since then, but the story has not.

The premise: Early in the next millennium, mankind is engaged in a war for survival with the Bugs, a vicious race of giant insects that colonize the galaxy by hurling their spores into space. If you seek their monument, do not look around you: Bugs have no buildings, no technology, no clothes, nothing but the ability to attack, fight, kill, and propagate. They exist not as an alien civilization but as pop-up enemies in a space war.

Human society recruits starship troopers to fight the Bugs. Their method is to machine-gun them to death. This does not work very well. Three or four troopers will fire thousands of rounds into a Bug, which like the Energizer Bunny just keeps on comin'. Grenades work better, but I guess the troopers haven't twigged to that. You'd think a human race capable of interstellar travel might have developed an effective insecticide, but no.

It doesn't really matter, since the Bugs aren't important except as props for the interminable action scenes, and as an enemy to justify the film's quasi-fascist militarism. Heinlein was, of course, a right-wing saber-rattler, but a charming and intelligent one who wrote some of the best science fiction ever. *Starship Troopers* proposes a society in which citizenship is earned through military service, and values are learned on the battlefield.

Heinlein intended his story for young boys, but wrote it more or less seriously. The one redeeming merit for director Paul Verhoeven's film is that by remaining faithful to Heinlein's material and period, it adds an element of sly satire. This is like the squarest but most technically advanced sci-fi movie of the 1950s, a film in which the sets and costumes look like a cross between Buck Rogers and the Archie comic books, and the characters look like they stepped out of Pepsodent ads.

The film's narration is handled by a futuristic version of the TV news crossed with the Web. After every breathless story, the cursor blinks while we're asked, "Want to know more?" Yes, I did. I was particularly intrigued by the way the Bugs had evolved organic launching pods that could spit their spores into space, and could also fire big globs of unidentified fiery matter at attacking spaceships. Since they have no technology, these abilities must have evolved along Darwinian lines; to say they severely test the theory of evolution is putting it mildly.

On the human side, we follow the adventures of a group of high school friends from Buenos Aires. Johnny (Casper Van Dien) has a crush on Carmen (Denise Richards), but she likes the way Zander (Patrick Muldoon) looks in uniform. When she signs up to become a starship trooper, so does Johnny. They go through basic training led by an officer of the take-no-prisoners school (Michael Ironside), and then they're sent to fight the Bugs. Until late in the movie, when things really get grim, Carmen wears a big, wide, bright smile in every single scene, as if posing for the cover of the novel. (Indeed, the whole look of the production design seems inspired by covers of the pulp space opera mags like *Amazing, Imagination,* and *Thrilling Wonder Stories.*)

The action sequences are heavily laden with special effects, but curiously joyless. We get the idea right away: Bugs will jump up, troopers will fire countless rounds at them, the Bugs will impale troopers with their spiny giant legs, and finally dissolve in a spray of goo. Later there are refinements, like fire-breathing beetles, flying insects, and giant Bugs that erupt from the earth. All very elaborate, but the Bugs are not *interesting* in the way, say, that the villains in the *Alien* pictures were. Even their planets are boring; Bugs live on ugly rock worlds with no other living species, raising the question of what they eat.

Discussing the science of *Starship Troopers* is beside the point. Paul Verhoeven is facing in the other direction. He wants to depict the world of the future as it might have been visualized in the mind of a kid reading Heinlein in 1956. He faithfully represents Heinlein's militarism, his Big Brother state, and a value system in which the highest good is to kill a friend before the Bugs can eat him. The underlying ideas are the most interesting aspect of the film.

What's lacking is exhilaration and sheer entertainment. Unlike the *Star Wars* movies, which embraced a joyous vision and great comic invention, *Starship Troopers* doesn't resonate. It's one-dimensional. We smile at the satirical asides, but where's the warmth of human nature? The spark of genius or rebellion? If *Star Wars* is humanist, *Starship Troopers* is totalitarian.

Watching a film that largely consists of interchangeable characters firing machine guns at computer-generated Bugs, I was reminded of the experience of my friend McHugh. After obtaining his degree from Indiana University, he spent the summer in the employ of Acme Bug Control in Bloomington, Indiana. One hot summer day, while he was spraying insecticide under a home, a trap door opened above his head and a housewife offered him a glass of lemonade. He crawled up, filthy and sweaty, and as he drank the lemonade, the woman told her son, "Now Jimmy—you study your books or you'll end up just like him!" I wanted to tell the troopers the same thing.

Star Trek: Insurrection ★ ★

PG, 103 m., 1998

Patrick Stewart (Picard), Jonathan Frakes (Riker), Brent Spiner (Data), LeVar Burton (LaForge), Michael Dorn (Worf), Gates McFadden (Crusher), Marina Sirtis (Troi), F. Murray Abraham (Ru'afo), Donna Murphy (Anij), Anthony Zerbe (Admiral Dougherty). Directed by Jonathan Frakes and produced by Rick Berman. Screenplay by Berman and Michael Piller.

A funny thing happened to me on the way to writing this review of *Star Trek: Insurrection.* I discovered that several of the key filmmakers disagree with the film's plot premise. Maybe that's why this ninth *Star Trek* saga seems inert and unconvincing.

Here's the premise: In a region of space known as the Briar Patch, an idyllic planet is home to a race known as the Ba'ku. They are members of a placid agricultural commune, tilling the neat rows of their fields, and then returning to a city whose neo-Greco-Roman architecture looks uncannily like the shopping mall at Caesars Palace. The Ba'ku are a blissful people, and no wonder: They have the secret of immortality. The "metaphasic radiation" generated by the planet's rings acts like a fountain of youth on their planet.

The planet and the Ba'ku are currently the subject of a cultural survey team, which looks down on them from something like a stadium press box, but remains invisible. Then Data (Brent Spinner), the android, goes berserk and makes hostages of the survey team. The *Enterprise* speeds to the scene, so that Captain Picard (Patrick Stewart) can deal with the crisis. The plot thickens when it is revealed that the Son'a race, which is also part of the Federation, was once allied with the Ba'ku. But the Son'a chose a different path and are now dying out—most visibly in the scrofulous countenance of their leader, Ru'afo (F. Murray Abraham).

The Son'a want the Ba'ku kidnapped and forcibly ejected from their planet. There are, after all, only 600 of them. Why should their little nature preserve be more important than the health and longevity of the Son'a and billions of other Federation citizens? Picard counters with the Federation's Prime Directive, which instructs that the natural development of any civilization must not be interfered with.

The plot of *Star Trek: Insurrection* deals with the conflict between the desperate Son'a and the blissful Ba'ku, and is further complicated when Picard falls in love with the beautiful Ba'ku woman Anij (Donna Murphy). "You explore the universe," she tells him, "but have you ever explored a single moment in time?" (Picard is so lovestruck he forgets that his answer would be, "Yes!") Further complications result when the metaphasic radiation leaks into the *Enterprise* and inspires Riker (Jonathan Frakes) and Troi (Marina Sirtis) to start acting like horny teenagers.

As the best minds in the Federation wrestled with the ethical questions involved, I was also asking questions. Such as, aren't the Ba'ku basically just living in a gated community? Since this Eden-like planet has only 600 inhabitants, why couldn't others use the planet as a spa, circling inside those metaphasic rings and bathing in the radiation, which is probably faster acting in space than down on the surface? After all, we're not talking *magic* here, are we?

Above these practical questions looms a larger philosophical one. Wouldn't it be *right* to sacrifice the lifestyles of 600 Ba'ku in order to save billions? "I think maybe I would," said Jonathan Frakes when I asked him that question after the movie's press screening. Frakes plays Riker and directed the film. "You've got to be flexible," said Stewart, who plays Picard. "If it had been left in the hands of Picard, some solution could have been found." "Absolutely!" said Spiner, who plays Data. "I think I raised that question more than once." "I had to be very narrow-minded to serve the character," confessed Murphy, who plays Anij.

I agree. Our own civilization routinely kills legions of people in wars large and small, for reasons of ideology, territory, religion, or geography. Would we contemplate removing 600 people from their native environment in order to grant immortality to everyone alive? In a flash. It would be difficult, indeed, to fashion a philosophical objection to such a move, which would result in the greatest good for the greatest number of people. But what about the rights of the Ba'ku? Hey, shouldn't they *volunteer* to help us all out? Especially since they need not die themselves?

The plot of *Star Trek: Insurrection* grinds through the usual conversations and crises, as the evil Ru'afo and his men carry forward their insidious plans, and Picard discovers that the Federation itself may be willing to play fast and loose with the Prime Directive. That's not exactly new; in the previous eight movies, there have in fact been many shots fired in anger at members of races who perhaps should have been left alone to "develop naturally"—presumably even if such development involves aggression and hostility. The overriding principle, let's face it, has been the Federation's own survival and best interests. So why not allow the Son'a the same ethnocentric behavior?

The movie is a work of fantasy, and these questions are not important unless they influence the film's entertainment value. Unfortunately, they do. There is a certain lackluster feeling to the way the key characters debate the issues, and perhaps that reflects the suspicion of the filmmakers that they have hitched their wagon to the wrong cause. The movie is shorter than the usual *Star Trek* saga, at 103 minutes, as if the central issue could not bear scrutiny at the usual length. Think how much more interesting it would have been if the Ba'ku had joined an interracial experiment to share immortality. What would happen if everyone in the Federation could live forever? Think how many more sequels there'd be.

Star Wars Episode I: The Phantom Menace ★ ★ ★ ½

PG, 133 m., 1999

Liam Neeson (Qui-Gon Jinn), Ewan McGregor (Obi-Wan Kenobi), Natalie Portman (Queen Amidala), Jake Lloyd (Anakin Skywalker), Pernilla August (Shmi Skywalker), Frank Oz (Yoda), Ian McDiarmid (Senator Palpatine), Oliver Ford Davies (Sio Bibble), Hugh Quarshie (Captain Panaka), Ahmed Best (Jar Jar Binks), Samuel L. Jackson (Mace Windu), Ray Park (Darth Maul), Peter Serafinowicz (Voice of Darth Maul), Ralph Brown (Ric Olie), Terence Stamp (Chancellor Valorum). Directed by George Lucas and produced by Rick McCallum. Screenplay by Lucas.

If it were the first *Star Wars* movie, *The Phantom Menace* would be hailed as a visionary breakthrough. But this is the fourth movie in the famous series, and we think we know the territory; many of the early reviews have been blasé, paying lip service to the visuals and wondering why the characters aren't better developed. How quickly do we grow accustomed to wonders. I am reminded of the Asimov story *Nightfall*, about the planet where the stars were visible only once in a thousand years. So awesome was the sight that it drove men mad. We who can see the stars every night glance up casually at the cosmos and then quickly down again, searching for a Dairy Queen.

Star Wars Episode I: The Phantom Menace, to cite its full title, is an astonishing achievement in imaginative filmmaking. If some of the characters are less than compelling, perhaps that's inevitable: This is the first story in the chronology, and has to set up characters who (we already know) will become more interesting with the passage of time. Here we first see Obi-Wan Kenobi, Anakin Skywalker, Yoda, and prototypes of R2D2 and C3PO. Anakin is only a fresh-faced kid in Episode I; in IV, V, and VI he has become Darth Vader.

At the risk of offending devotees of the Force, I will say that the stories in the *Star Wars* movies have always been space operas, and that the importance of the movies comes from their energy, their sense of fun, their colorful inventions, and their state-of-the-art special effects. I do not attend expecting to gain insights into human behavior. Unlike many movies, these are made to be looked at more than listened to, and George Lucas and his collaborators have filled *Phantom Menace* with wonderful visuals.

There are new places here—new *kinds* of places. Consider the underwater cities, floating in their transparent membranes. The Senate chamber, a vast sphere with senators arrayed along the inside walls and speakers floating on pods in the center. And other places: The cityscape with the waterfall that has a dizzying descent through space. And other cities—one city Venetian, with canals, another looking like a hothouse version of imperial Rome, and a third that seems to have grown out of desert sands.

Set against awesome backdrops, the characters in *Phantom Menace* inhabit a plot that is little more complex than the stories I grew up on in science-fiction magazines. The whole series sometimes feels like a cover from *Thrilling Wonder Stories* come to life. The dialogue is pretty flat and straightforward, although seasoned with a little quasi-classical formality, as if the characters had read but not retained *Julius Caesar.* I wish the *Star Wars* characters spoke with more elegance and wit (as Gore Vidal's Greeks and Romans do), but dialogue isn't the point anyway: These movies are about new things to look at.

The plot details (embargoes, blockades) tend to diminish the size of the movie's universe, anyway—to shrink it to the scale of a nineteenth-century trade dispute. The stars themselves are little more than pinpoints on a black curtain, and *Star Wars* has not drawn inspiration from the color photographs being captured by the Hubble telescope. The series is essentially human mythology, set in space but not occupying it. If Kubrick gave us man humbled by the universe, Lucas gives us the universe domesticated by man. His aliens are really just humans in odd skins. Consider Jar Jar Binks, a fully realized, computer-animated alien character whose physical movements seem based on afterthoughts. And Jabba the Hutt (who presides over the Pod race) has always seemed positively Dickensian to me.

Yet within the rules he has established, Lucas tells a good story. The key development in *Phantom* is the first meeting between the Jedi knight Qui-Gon Jinn (Liam Neeson) and the young boy Anakin Skywalker (Jake Lloyd)—who is, the Jedi immediately senses, fated for great things. Qui-Gon meets Anakin in a store where he's seeking replacement parts for his crippled ship. He soon finds himself backing the young slave in a high-speed Pod race—betting his ship itself against the cost of the replacement parts. The race is one of the film's high points, as the entrants rush between high cliff walls in a refinement of a similar race through metal canyons on a spaceship in *Star Wars.*

Why is Qui-Gon so confident that Anakin can win? Because he senses an unusual concentration of the Force—and perhaps because, like John the Baptist, he instinctively recognizes the one whose way he is destined to prepare. The film's shakiness on the psychological level is evident, however, in the scene where young Anakin is told he must leave his mother (Pernilla August) and follow this tall Jedi stranger. Their mutual resignation to the parting seems awfully restrained. I expected a tearful scene of parting between mother and child, but the best we get is when Anakin asks if his mother can come along, and she replies, "Son, my place is here." As a slave?

The discovery and testing of Anakin supplies the film's most important action, but in a sense all the action is equally important, because it provides platforms for special-effects sequences. Sometimes our common sense undermines a sequence (as Jar Jar's people and the good guys fight a 'droid army, it becomes obvious that the 'droids are such bad fighters they should be returned for a refund). But mostly I was happy to drink in the sights on the screen, in the same spirit that I might enjoy *Metropolis, Forbidden Planet, 2001, Dark City,* or *The Matrix.* The difference is that Lucas's visuals are more fanciful and the energy level of his film more cheerful; he doesn't share the prevailing view that the future is a dark and lonely place.

What he does have, in abundance, is exhilaration. There is a sense of discovery in scene after scene of *Phantom Menace*, as he tries out new effects and ideas, and seamlessly integrates real characters and digital ones, real landscapes and imaginary places. We are standing at the threshold of a new age of epic cinema, I think, in which digital techniques mean that budgets will no longer limit the scope of scenes; filmmakers will be able to show us just about anything they can conceive of.

As surely as Anakin Skywalker points the way into the future of *Star Wars*, so does *The Phantom Menace* raise the curtain on this new freedom for filmmakers. And it's a lot of fun. The film has correctly been given the PG rating; it's suitable for younger viewers, and doesn't depend on violence for its effects. As for the bad rap about the characters—hey, I've seen space operas that put their emphasis on human personalities and relationships. They're called *Star Trek* movies. Give me membranous underwater cities and vast, hollow senatorial spheres any day. ☞

Star Wars (Special Edition) ★ ★ ★ ★

PG, 125 m., 1977 (rereleased 1997)

Mark Hamill (Luke Skywalker), Harrison Ford (Han Solo), Carrie Fisher (Princess Leia), Peter Cushing (Grand Moff Tarkin), Alec Guinness (Ben (Obi-Wan) Kenobi), James Earl Jones (Vader's voice), Anthony Daniels (C3PO). Directed by George Lucas and produced by Gary Kurtz. Screenplay by Lucas.

To see *Star Wars* again after twenty years is to revisit a place in the mind. George Lucas's space epic has colonized our imaginations, and it is hard to stand back and see it simply as a motion picture because it has so completely become part of our memories. It's as goofy as a children's tale, as shallow as an old Saturday afternoon serial, as corny as Kansas in August—and a masterpiece. Those who analyze its philosophy do so, I imagine, with a smile in their minds. May the Force be with them.

Like *Birth of a Nation* and *Citizen Kane, Star Wars* was a technical watershed that influenced many of the movies that came after. These films have little in common, except for the way they came along at a crucial moment in cinema history, when new methods were ripe for synthesis. *Birth of a Nation* brought together the developing language of shots and editing. *Citizen Kane* married special effects, advanced sound, a new photographic style, and a freedom from linear storytelling. *Star Wars* combined a new generation of special effects with the high-energy action picture; it linked space opera and soap opera, fairy tales and legend, and packaged them as a wild visual ride.

Star Wars effectively brought to an end the golden era of early-1970s personal filmmaking and focused the industry on big-budget special-effects blockbusters, blasting off a trend we are still living through. But you can't blame it for what it did; you can only observe how well it did it. In one way or another all the big studios have been trying to make another *Star Wars* ever since (pictures like *Raiders of the Lost Ark, Jurassic Park*, and *Independence Day* are its heirs). It located Hollywood's center of gravity at the intellectual and emotional level of a bright teenager.

It's possible, however, that as we grow older we retain within the tastes of our earlier selves. How else to explain how much fun *Star Wars* is, even for those who think they don't care for science fiction? It's a good-hearted film in every single frame, and shining through is the gift of a man who knew how to link state-of-the-art technology with a deceptively simple, really very powerful, story. It was not by accident that George Lucas worked with Joseph Campbell, an expert on the world's basic myths, in fashioning a screenplay that owes much to man's oldest stories.

By now the ritual of classic film revival is well established: An older classic is brought out from the studio vaults, restored frame by frame, rereleased in the best theaters, and then relaunched on home video. With this "special edition" of the *Star Wars* trilogy (which includes new versions of *Return of the Jedi* and *The Empire Strikes Back*), Lucas has gone one step beyond. His special effects were so advanced in 1977 that they spun off an industry, including his own Industrial Light & Magic Co., the computer wizards who do many of today's best special effects.

Now Lucas has put IL&M to work touching

up the effects, including some that his limited 1977 budget left him unsatisfied with. Most of the changes are subtle; you'd need a side-by-side comparison to see that a new shot is a little better. There's about five minutes of new material, including a meeting between Han Solo and Jabba the Hut that was shot for the first version but not used. (We learn that Jabba is not immobile, but sloshes along in a kind of spongy undulation.) There's also an improved look to the city of Mos Eisley ("a wretched hive of scum and villainy," says Obi-Wan Kenobi). And the climactic battle scene against the Death Star has been rehabbed.

The improvements are well done, but they point up how well the effects were done to begin with: If the changes are not obvious, that's because *Star Wars* got the look of the film so right in the first place. The obvious comparison is with Kubrick's *2001: A Space Odyssey,* made ten years earlier, in 1967, which also holds up perfectly well today. (One difference is that Kubrick went for realism, trying to imagine how his future world would really look, while Lucas cheerfully plundered the past; Han Solo's Millennium Falcon has a gun turret with a hand-operated weapon that would be at home on a World War II bomber, but too slow to hit anything at space velocities.)

Two Lucas inspirations start the story with a tease: He sets the action not in the future but "long ago," and jumps into the middle of it with "Chapter 4: A New Hope." These seemingly innocent touches are actually rather powerful; they give the saga the aura of an ancient tale, and an ongoing one.

As if those two shocks were not enough for the movie's first moments, as the camera tilts up, a vast spaceship appears from the top of the screen and moves overhead, an effect reinforced by the surround sound. It is such a dramatic opening that it's no wonder Lucas paid a fine and resigned from the Directors' Guild rather than obey its demand that he begin with conventional opening credits.

The film has simple, well-defined characters, beginning with the robots R2D2 (childlike, easily hurt) and C3PO (fastidious, a little effete). The evil Empire has all but triumphed in the galaxy, but rebel forces are preparing an assault on the Death Star. Princess Leia (pert, sassy Carrie Fisher) has information pinpointing the star's vulnerable point, and feeds it into R2D2's computer; when her ship is captured, the robots escape from the Death Star and find themselves on Luke Skywalker's planet, where soon Luke (Mark Hammil as an idealistic youngster) meets the wise, old, mysterious Ben Kenobi (Alec Guinness) and they hire the freelance space jockey Han Solo (Harrison Ford, already laconic) to carry them to Leia's rescue.

The story is advanced with spectacularly effective art design, set decoration, and effects. Although the scene in the intergalactic bar is famous for its menagerie of alien drunks, there is another scene, when the two robots are thrown into a hold with other used droids, which equally fills the screen with fascinating throwaway details. And a scene in the Death Star's garbage bin (inhabited by a snake with a head curiously shaped like E.T.'s) is also well done.

Many of the planetscapes are startlingly beautiful, and owe something to Chesley Bonestell's imaginary drawings of other worlds. The final assault on the Death Star, when the fighter rockets speed between parallel walls, is a nod in the direction of *2001,* with its light trip into another dimension: Kubrick showed, and Lucas learned, how to make the audience feel it is hurtling headlong through space.

Lucas fills his screen with loving touches. There are little alien rats hopping around the desert, and a chess game played with living creatures. Luke's weather-worn "Speeder" vehicle, which hovers over the sand, reminds me uncannily of a 1965 Mustang. And consider the details creating the presence, look, and sound of Darth Vader, whose fanged face mask, black cape, and hollow breathing are the setting for James Earl Jones's cold voice of doom.

Seeing the film the first time, I was swept away, and have remained swept ever since. Seeing this restored version, I tried to be more objective, and noted that the gun battles on board the spaceships go on a bit too long; it is remarkable that the Empire marksmen never hit anyone important; and the fighter raid on the enemy ship now plays like the computer games it predicted. I wonder, too, if Lucas could have come up with a more challenging philosophy behind the Force. As Kenobi explains it, it's basically just going with the flow.

What if Lucas had pushed a little further to include elements of nonviolence or ideas about intergalactic conservation? (It's a great waste of resources to blow up star systems.)

The films that will live forever are the simplest-seeming ones. They have profound depths, but their surfaces are as clear to an audience as a beloved old story. The way I know this is because the stories that seem immortal—the Odyssey, the Tale of Genji, Don Quixote, David Copperfield, Huckleberry Finn—are all the same: a brave but flawed hero, a quest, colorful people and places, sidekicks, the discovery of life's underlying truths. If I were asked to say with certainty which movies will still be widely known a century or two from now, I would list *2001*, and *The Wizard of Oz*, and Keaton and Chaplin, and Astaire and Rogers, and probably *Casablanca* . . . and *Star Wars*, for sure.

Steam: The Turkish Bath ★ ★

NO MPAA RATING, 96 m., 1999

Alessandro Gassman (Francesco), Francesca d'Aloja (Marta), Halil Ergun (Osman), Serif Sezer (Perran), Mehmet Gunsur (Mehmet), Basak Koklukaya (Fusun), Alberto Molinari (Paolo), Carlo Cecchi (Oscar), Zozo Toledo (Zozo). Directed by Ferzan Ozpetek and produced by Paolo Buzzi and Ozan Ergun. Screenplay by Stefano Tummolini and Ozpetek.

One of the peculiarities of *Steam: The Turkish Bath* is that it's about the sexual passions of two actors who don't seem very passionate. As the movie opens, they're married. Both are tall, thin, dark, solemn, and secretive. He seems like a well-meaning wimp. She seems like the kind of woman who would close her eyes during sex and fantasize about tomorrow's entries in her Day Timer.

The film opens in Rome, where their marriage seems shaky. They find fault with each other, but in vague terms that don't give us useful insights. Then the man, named Francesco (Alessandro Gassman), flies to Istanbul, where he has been left some property by an aunt.

The building turns out to be a Turkish bath, closed but still fondly remembered in the neighborhood. Francesco makes friends with the family of Osman, the man who used to manage the bath. Osman lives next door with his wife, comely daughter and comelier son. In his home Francesco finds a warmth and cheer that was missing from his sterile existence in Rome, and soon he's languishing in the arms of the son, named Mehmet (Mehmet Gunsur). He extends his stay and begins to renovate the Turkish bath, planning to reopen it.

No one suspects a thing—not even Osman (Halil Ergun), who in the nature of things must have learned a little something about what can go on in the steam. The film is reserved about sex and shy about nudity, employing its greatest passion for travelogue scenes of Istanbul, a city of great beauty and character.

Then Marta (Francesca d'Aloja), Francesco's wife, arrives suddenly from Rome. The story tensions explode at a family dinner, although not quite in the way we expect (what Marta blurts out didn't surprise me, but I was amazed that this cool and well-mannered woman would make such an ugly scene). After moments of truth and revelation, there is a surprise ending that I found particularly unsatisfying.

Afterward, I found myself asking what exactly the point of the movie was. It is not a sex film; it's almost prudish in the reserve of its sex scenes. If it's a coming-out film, so what? Francesco's homosexuality is not a surprise to the audience or even, really, to his wife. If it is about how a man escapes from the fast lane in Rome and discovers the feeling of community in Istanbul—well, good for him.

Perhaps I would have cared more if the leads had been warmer, but both Gassman (son of Vittorio Gassman) and d'Aloja come across as cool and reserved. The Turks are much more fun: Gunsur, as the lover, is friendly and boyish, and Ergun, as the former custodian, is a cheerful man. Serif Sezer, as Ergun's wife and Gunsur's mother, is one of those beauties of a certain age who has lips that make you forget everything else except what it would be like to nibble them.

Stepmom ★ ★

PG-13, 124 m., 1998

Julia Roberts (Isabel Kelly), Susan Sarandon (Jackie Harrison), Ed Harris (Luke Harrison), Jena Malone (Anna Harrison), Liam Aiken

(Ben Harrison), Lynn Whitfield (Dr. Sweikert), Darrell Larson (Duncan Samuels), Mary Louise Wilson (School Counselor). Directed by Chris Columbus and produced by Wendy Finerman, Mark Radcliffe, Michael Barnathan, and Columbus. Screenplay by Gigi Levangie, Jessie Nelson, Steven Rogers, Karen Leigh Hopkins, and Ron Bass.

Sometimes all you have to do is look at the casting and you can guess where a movie will take you. If a movie named *Stepmom* costars Susan Sarandon and Julia Roberts, you know it's a tearjerker. (With Jennifer Jason Leigh and Neve Campbell, you know it's drenched in sex; with Jamie Lee Curtis and Drew Barrymore, in blood.) The current iconography of Sarandon and Roberts falls somewhere between feminist heroism and sainthood; if Roberts is the stepmom, you know she's not going to have fangs and talons.

Still, the art of a movie like this is to conceal the obvious. When the levers and the pulleys of the plot are concealed by good writing and acting, we get great entertainments like *Terms of Endearment.* When they're fairly well masked, we get sincere films like *One True Thing.* When every prop and device is displayed in the lobby on our way into the theater, we get Chris Columbus's *Stepmom.*

The movie begins one year after a fashion photographer named Isabel (Julia Roberts) has started dating a businessman named Luke (Ed Harris). She thinks it's time she can be trusted to take care of his two kids for the weekend. He has his doubts, maybe because she's "not used to kids," maybe because he still sees his ex-wife, Jackie (Susan Sarandon), as the perfect mother. It's a question of trust. Jackie doesn't trust Isabel (or like her). Luke likes her but is unsure. The kids have been tutored by their mother to resent this new woman in their dad's life.

The children are Anna (Jena Malone) and Ben (Liam Aiken). She's just starting to date. He's in the lower grades, and afraid of losing his mommy because of this new woman ("Mommy, if you want me to hate her, I will"). Isabel really loves Luke and would like to love the kids, if they would let her. But every time she's late with a school pickup, Jackie turns up like an avenging angel with sarcastic criticisms. One day Isabel takes the children to Central Park, where she's doing a photo shoot, and Ben wanders away. By the time he's found safely, Jackie is issuing ultimatums: "That woman is to have nothing else to do with my children."

That's act one. Act two, of course, is the gradual weakening of the emotional walls, as Isabel earns the trust of the children and Jackie learns to let go. (Spoiler warning.) The upbeat TV ads don't contain a hint of this, but, yes, just like Debra Winger in *Terms of Endearment* and Meryl Streep in *One True Thing,* the Sarandon character doesn't have long to live. When she gets bad news from her doctor, she realizes that Isabel will inevitably one day be taking care of her kids, and that she'd better ease the transition. Act three is the Kleenex stuff, including separate farewells between the mother and each child.

The problem with the movie is the way it jumps up and down on first, second, and third before sliding into home. The movie hasn't been written so much as constructed by its five screenwriters, and although Gigi Levangie and Ron Bass, credited first and last, no doubt elevated the sophistication of the dialogue, these are people whose lives are gripped in the mighty vise of plotting. The skill of the actors, who invest their characters with small touches of humanity, is useful in distracting us from the emotional manipulations, but it's like they're brightening separate rooms of a haunted house.

The movie is really about the Sarandon character. Harris is absent for much of the second half, until he turns up for a family photo. Sarandon can create characters of astonishing conviction (Sister Helen Prejean in *Dead Man Walking*). Here she has to be unreasonable for half the movie and courageous for the rest; there's not a rest period where she just gets to be this woman. Every scene has a purpose; we're reminded of the value of those brief pillow scenes in which directors like Ozu take a beat and let us see their characters simply being.

To be sure, *Stepmom* has a certain tact. It wants us to cry, but it doesn't hold a gun on us, like *Patch Adams,* and enforce its emotions with sentimental terrorism. Roberts and Sarandon are immensely likable people, and Harris here seems caring and reasonable in a thankless role. We would have enjoyed spending time with them, if they'd been able to pull themselves away from the plot. ☞

Still Crazy ★ ★ ★

R, 96 m., 1999

Stephen Rea (Tony), Billy Connolly (Hughie), Jimmy Nail (Les), Timothy Spall (Beano), Bill Nighy (Ray), Juliet Aubrey (Karen), Helene Bergstrom (Astrid), Bruce Robinson (Brian). Directed by Brian Gibson and produced by Amanda Marmot. Screenplay by Dick Clement and Ian La Frenais.

Still Crazy is a kinder, gentler version of *This Is Spinal Tap,* telling the story of a 1970s rock band that tries for a reunion twenty years after its last disastrous concert. Two decades have not been kind to the surviving members of Strange Fruit: One is a roofing contractor, one lives in a trailer in his mother's garden and hides from the tax man, one services condom machines in Ibiza, and even the one who held onto his money hasn't held onto enough of it. Two other members are dead.

None of the survivors remember the old days with much affection. There was jealousy, anger, and betrayal among band members, and the drugs and lifestyle didn't help. "God got tired of all that seventies excess," one observes. "That's why he invented the Sex Pistols." The band members have drifted out of touch, and like it that way.

But one day the keyboard man, Tony (Stephen Rea), is recognized in a restaurant by the son of the man who produced the disastrous 1977 concert at which Strange Fruit disintegrated. He suggests a reunion. Tony, who services the condom machines, still believes a little in the dream of rock 'n' roll (he wears Jimmy Hendrix's tooth around his neck). Besides, he needs the money, so he tracks down Karen (Juliet Aubrey), who was the group's secretary and gofer.

Together they go looking for the others, and find them: Ray Simms (Bill Nighy) is a cadaverous poseur living in a Victorian mansion with his bossy Swedish wife (Helena Bergstrom). He keeps his gold records in the crypt. Les Wickes (Jimmy Nail) is a roofer, tracked down by Tony on top of a church. Beano Baggot (Timothy Spall) works in a nursery, lives in a trailer, and fears a jail term from the tax authorities. Hughie (Billy Connolly) is the lead roadie. Brian (Bruce Robinson), the lead guitarist, disappeared long ago and is thought by everyone to be dead.

Not so reluctantly, the Fruit agree to do a "test tour" of Holland as a preliminary to a big seventies revival concert. They need the money. But they are all much decayed since their glory days, and only by not shaving and letting their hair grow rank are they able to conceal how bad they look—by looking worse.

Ray is a particularly dodgy case. Nagged by his wife, who micromanages every moment of his life, he's a recovering addict who is terrified of a fatal lapse back into drugs or booze. He stutters a little, makes profound statements that nobody else can quite understand, and cannot cope with the challenges of an ordinary day. His speech at a wedding reminds me of Rowan Atkinson's inept Mr. Bean.

The filmmakers must have personal experience with neurotic rock stars past their sell-by dates. The director, Brian Gibson, made the Tina Turner biopic *What's Love Got to Do With It,* and the writers are Dick Clement and Ian La Frenais, who wrote *The Commitments,* about an Irish group that would have been a garage band if they'd had a garage. They succeed in making Strange Fruit look and sound like a real band (the music was written and performed by various veterans of Foreigner, Spandau Ballet, Squeeze, and ELO), and there is an authenticity to the backstage desperation, as old wounds are reopened.

There are times when the film edges close to *Spinal Tap* territory, as when young fans are quick to boo the aging and uncertain group. In a way, the spirit of *Spinal Tap* hovers over the entire film, since its deadly aim has forever marked middle-aged rockers as targets of satire. But *Still Crazy* pays attention to the personalities of its heroes, and finds enough humor in reality, as when Ray slams his fiftieth birthday cake against the wall.

Some of the faces, especially Rea and Spall, are familiar from other recent British movies. But it's Bill Nighy who makes the most memorable impression. He conveys fear so well, especially that central kind of fear that forms when you can no longer trust yourself to do the right thing. There is a scene where he unwisely ventured onto some ice that cracks, and the way he handles it is unexpected, and right.

There aren't a lot of plot surprises in *Still Crazy* (the biggest surprise is telegraphed early on), and the ending is more or less as expected—indeed, as decreed by the comeback genre. But the characters are sharply defined and well written, and we come to like them. Twenty years ago they may have seemed like unapproachable rock gods, but now we see them as touching and vulnerable: Once they could do something fairly well, and now they have arrived at the stage in life where they can do it better—if they can do it at all.

The Substance of Fire ★ ★ ★

R, 102 m., 1997

Ron Rifkin (Isaac Geldhart), Timothy Hutton (Martin Geldhart), Tony Goldwyn (Aaron Geldhart), Sarah Jessica Parker (Sarah Geldhart), Eric Bogosian (Gene Byck), Lee Grant (Cora Cahn), Ronny Graham (Louis Foukold). Directed by Daniel Sullivan and produced by Jon Robin Baitz, Randy Finch, and Ron Kastner. Screenplay by Baitz.

The Substance of Fire, like *Shine*, involves a father who is descending into madness. In both films, the process is a result of the psychic wounding done by the Holocaust. And in both films we are not quite sure how we are expected to deal with the illness, which results in cruelty to the next generation. It would be simpler without the madness: A man is damaged by the Holocaust and visits his pain on his children. That is possible to understand. But insanity brings with it a certain license: Does it matter, after a point, what a mad person does? Can we blame them?

The fact that we ask such questions makes both movies more interesting. The Holocaust is often used in fiction as pure evil, to which our moral response is immediate and direct. In these films it is more complicated. The father in *The Substance of Fire* is Isaac Geldhart (Ron Rifkin), who as a child saw the Nazis burn books. Now he heads one of New York's most respected publishing houses and wants to publish a four-volume study of Nazi medical atrocities. This would seem destined to be a scholarly or academic work, but Isaac wants to print it like an art book and sell it for hundreds of dollars. He rejects an entire printing—at $200 per set wholesale—because the paper is not good enough.

What's going on here? Why must the book be so beautiful and expensive when its contents are as well contained in a paperback? Where is the market? Will the book appeal to those sometimes slightly ambivalent collectors of Nazi memorabilia? Isaac apparently wants the set to be handsome as a tribute to the aging scholar who spent his life writing it. He saw the Nazis burn books; now he will publish an elegant book about the Nazis. There is symbolism here, but hard to sort out.

Like Lear, Isaac has three children and is of an age to divide his kingdom among them. His oldest son, Aaron (Tony Goldwyn), who is gay, works with him in the publishing house. His other son, Martin (Timothy Hutton), teaches landscape architecture at Vassar. His daughter, Sarah (Sarah Jessica Parker), is an actress on a children's TV series ("I sing songs about trichinosis").

"Everybody in town knows your company is on the rocks," an agent (Eric Bogosian) tells Aaron. There's talk of a merger with Japanese interests, but they find the Nazi book "too morbid" and shy away from Isaac's developing mania. Aaron hopes to make some money by publishing a steamy novel by his lover. The father calls it "meretricious crap—a trashy novel by a sicko hipster. I wanted my time back after I read it." Isaac is probably right. But a business cannot be run as a charity.

The children, who all own stock in the company, meet with their father, and the meeting degenerates into a tirade against them. He fires his son. His daughter sides with her brother. The family is in disarray. At the same time it's clear that Isaac is losing his sanity. In the early scenes he's a literate, tart-tongued iconoclast. In the last scenes, like Lear, he ranges across the blasted heath of his office, denouncing his children and clinging to his fool—or, in this case, his faithful secretary. Soon he is holding imaginary conversations with his wife and offering to buy a man's shoes off his feet.

A line has been crossed, and we as viewers have to decide when it was crossed and how that affects our feelings. Was Isaac ever wholly sane? Was the four-volume edition ever a good idea? Certainly we like the old man (Ronny Graham) who wrote it. Does the Holocaust stop being a relevant factor in Isaac's life after he loses his mind—or is it, as the cause of the madness, more relevant than ever? What about Aaron's homosexuality? Does his father reject the lover's book as a way of rejecting his son's sexuality?

The Substance of Fire was written by Jon Robin Baitz, based on his stage play, which according to some reports was not as ambiguous. The film, directed by Daniel Sullivan, is brave, I think, to offer us a complicated scenario without an easy moral compass. *Shine,* by contrast, is much simpler: The young pianist's father lost his family in the Holocaust, is terrified of losing a family again, and thus becomes insanely possessive of his son. The son, torn between ambition and guilt, goes mad. Cut and dried. In *The Substance of Fire,* more complex issues lurk in the corners of the material.

It would be useful to know, for example, whether the four-volume work about medical atrocities contains any information likely to be of scientific benefit. Will it save lives? Or does it simply record sadistic experiments and their results? If so, what is the purpose of publishing it and reading it? Everything depends on context and tone; *Schindler's List* and *Ilsa, She-Wolf of the SS* both contain concentration camp commandants.

Leaving this movie, we want answers, and there aren't any (apart from an answer of sorts in a silly epilogue that plays like it was tacked on in a sentimental fit). Because the film is well written and acted, it holds our interest. Because its ideas remain murky, it frustrates our expectations. It's not a satisfying film, but that doesn't make it a bad one.

subUrbia ★★★½

R, 118 m., 1997

Jayce Bartok (Pony), Giovanni Ribisi (Jeff), Nicky Katt (Tim), Steve Zahn (Buff), Ajay Naidu (Nazeer), Samia Shoaib (Pakeesa), Amie Carey (Sooze), Dina Spybey (Bee-Bee), Parker Posey (Erica). Directed by Richard Linklater and produced by Anne Walker-McBay. Screenplay by Eric Bogosian, based on his play.

"Don't tell us about private property—this is America!" So says one of the slackers who hang out endlessly at the minimart of a strip mall in "subUrbia." He's shouting at the owners of a store, a Pakistani couple who feel, reasonably, that the constant presence of a half-dozen beer-swilling teenagers is not good for business. What the Pakistani store owner sees (and tells one of them in a devastating speech) is that the lives of these young people are on hold. They have no plans and few skills, and resentment is a poison in their souls.

subUrbia has been directed by Richard Linklater, whose movie *Slackers* gave a name to part of a generation, and whose *Dazed and Confused* caught much of its tone. Now, working from a screenplay by Eric Bogosian, he takes the despair of *Waiting for Godot* and tops it: His heroes aren't waiting as a mission, but as a lifestyle.

The movie is dark, intense, and disturbing. It takes place during a long night when the slackers in the parking lot are awaiting the appearance of a friend of theirs who has made it. His name is Pony (Jayce Bartok), and the last time they saw him he was the geek who was singing folk songs at the senior prom. Now, suddenly, amazingly, he is a rock star. He has promised to drop by and see them after his concert.

Among the slackers leaning against the brick wall, the dominant figure is Jeff (Giovanni Ribisi). He is darkly handsome, sardonic, intelligent, and utterly clueless. The depth of his alienation is established the first time we see him: He lives in a pup tent in his parents' garage, and communicates with his friends by cell phone.

He has been dating Sooze (Amie Carey), but that's about to end because she plans to move to New York and attend an art school. The fact that she has plans is a rebuke, in a way. In one of the movie's best scenes, she does a performance piece by the cold light of a bakery window, attacking testosterone as the enemy of civilization (her hit list ranges from Pope John Paul II to Howard Stern).

Their friends in the lot include Tim (Nicky Katt), an air force dropout who is hard at work perfecting his alcoholism; Sooze's best pal Bee-Bee (Dana Spybey), who is out of rehab but very shaky; and Buff (Steve Zahn), who cherishes his reputation as a nut who will do anything for attention. As they wait for Pony to arrive, they shift restlessly against the wall, perch on an iron bar, and sometimes fight new engagements in their running battle with the Pakistanis (Ajay Naidu and Samia Shoaib), who in this movie represent traditional American values.

Their conversation, originally written by Bogosian for a stage play, is talky, but I like that. It doesn't seem too theatrical to me, because these characters have absolutely nothing else to do except talk, and this barren corner of a suburban wasteland is literally their stage: They make their entrances and exits with a certain dramatic flair, as if reality stops when they are not here to watch it. Their suburb is perfectly named: Burnfield.

Pony eventually arrives, accompanied by his publicist (Parker Posey). They size up the situation but go with it; Pony tries to be nice, and the publicist tries to get lucky. One of Bogosian's inspirations is to avoid the predictable line in which Pony is a jerk or a big shot. He seems like a decent enough guy, unimpressed with his success, who only wants to hang out with the old gang. His chances of fitting in are destroyed immediately, of course, by his stretch limo, which underlines the fact that he's made it (however improbably) and they have not. Jeff's inferiority complex is painful in its twists and evasions, and it is revealing to watch him while Pony sighs about the thankless life of a rock star: "It's just airport, hotel, show, airport, hotel, show . . . you still living at your mom's house?"

This is the fourth Linklater film I've seen (he also made the smart, romantic *Before Sunrise*). All of them take place within a twenty-four-hour period, and involve characters who are between engagements. There is, I believe, a seductive quality to idleness. To be without ambition or plans is to rebuke those who have them: It is a refusal to enlist in the rat race, and there may even be a sad courage in it. But what Linklater sees is that it is so damned boring. Life without goals reduces itself to waiting. What it finally comes down to is airport, hotel, show—but without the airport, the hotel, or the show.

Summer of Sam ★ ★ ★ ½

R, 136 m., 1999

John Leguizamo (Vinny), Adrien Brody (Ritchie), Mira Sorvino (Dionna), Jennifer Esposito (Ruby), Michael Rispoli (Joey T), Saverio Guerra (Woodstock), Brian Tarantino (Bobby Del Fiore), Al Palagonia (Anthony), Ben Gazzara (Luigi), Bebe Neuwirth (Gloria). Directed by Spike Lee and produced by Lee and Jon Kilik. Screenplay by Lee, Victor Colicchio, and Michael Imperioli.

Spike Lee's *Summer of Sam* is his first film with no major African-American characters, but it has a theme familiar to blacks and other minorities: scapegoating. In the summer of 1977, when New York City is gripped by paranoid fear of the serial killer who called himself the Son of Sam, the residents of an Italian-American neighborhood in the Bronx are looking for a suspect. Anyone who stands out from the crowd is a candidate.

Lee's best films thrum with a wound-up energy, and *Summer of Sam* vibrates with fear, guilt, and lust. It's not about the killer, but about his victims—not those he murdered, but those whose overheated imaginations bloomed into a lynch mob mentality. There is a sequence near the end of the film that shows a side of human nature as ugly as it is familiar: the fever to find someone to blame, and the need to blame someone who is different.

We see the Son of Sam from time to time in the film, often as a shadowy presence, but his appearances are more like punctuation than drama. The story centers on several characters in a tightly knit neighborhood—one of those neighborhoods so insular that everyone suspects the killer may be someone they know. That's not because they think a killer must live among them, but because it's hard to imagine anyone living anywhere else.

The key characters are two couples. Vinny (John Leguizamo) is a hairdresser with a roving eye, married none too faithfully to Dionna (Mira Sorvino), who is a waitress in her father's restaurant. Ritchie (Adrien Brody) is a local kid who has mysteriously developed a punk haircut and a British accent. He dates the sexy Ruby (Jennifer Esposito), but leads a double life as a dancer in a gay club. The movie doesn't involve them in plot mechanics so much as follow them for human atmosphere; we get to know them and their friends and neighbors, and then watch them change as the pall of murder settles over the city.

Lee is a city kid himself, from Brooklyn, and makes the city's background noise into a sort of parallel sound track. There's the voice of Phil Rizzuto doing play-by-play as Reggie Jackson slams the Yankees into the World Series. The hit songs of the summer, disco and otherwise. The almost sexual quality of gossip; people are turned on by spreading rumors, and feed off each other's excitement. The tone is set by the opening shot of columnist Jimmy Breslin, introducing the film. It was to Breslin that the killer wrote the first of his famous notes to the papers, identifying himself as the monster, and saying he would kill again.

The *Summer of Sam* screenplay, written by Lee with Victor Colicchio and Michael Imperioli, isn't the inside, autobiographical job of a Scorsese film, but more of an analytical outsider's view. We learn things. There is a certain conviction in a scene where the police turn to a local Mafia boss (Ben Gazzara) for help from his troops in finding the killer; he has power in the neighborhood, this is known to everyone, and the cops put it to pragmatic use.

We watch Vinny, the Leguizamo character, as he cheats on his wife, notably with Gloria (Bebe Neuwirth), the sexpot at the beauty salon where he works. We watch as he stumbles on two of Sam's victims and returns home, chastened, believing God spared him, and vowing to start treating his wife better. In this neighborhood, it's personal; if you have a near brush with Sam, it's a sign. And Lee shows us Dionna wearing a blond wig on a date with her husband, because the killer seems to single out brunettes. She does it for safety's sake, but there's a sexual undercurrent: Wearing the wig and risking the wrath of Sam is kind of a turn-on.

The summer of 1977 was at the height of the so-called sexual revolution; Plato's Retreat was famous and AIDS unheard-of, and both of the principal couples are caught up in the fever. Vinny and Dionna experiment at a sex club, and Ritchie gets involved in gay porno films. In a confused way he believes his career as a sex worker is connected to his (mostly imaginary) career as a punk rock star. For him, all forms of show business feel more or less the same.

In the neighborhood, people hang around talking, speculating, killing time, often where the street dead-ends into the water. One of the regulars has a theory that Son of Sam is in fact Reggie Jackson (the killer uses a .44 handgun; Jackson's number is 44). The local priest is also a suspect; after all, he lives alone and can come and go as he wants. And then, slowly, frighteningly, attention becomes focused on Ritchie, the neighborhood kid who has chosen to flaunt his weird lifestyle.

Lee has a wealth of material here, and the film tumbles through it with exuberance. He likes the energy, the street-level culture, the music, the way that when conversation fails, sex can take over the burden of entertainment. And there is a deeper theme, too: the theme of how scapegoats are chosen. What's interesting is not that misfits are singled out as suspects; it's that the ringleaders require validation for their suspicions. At the end of the film, everyone's looking for Vinny. They need him to agree with their choice of victim—to validate their fever. It's as if they know they're wrong, but if Vinny says they're right, then they can't be blamed.

Summer of Sam is like a companion piece to Lee's *Do the Right Thing* (1989). In a different neighborhood, in a different summer, the same process takes place: The neighborhood feels threatened and needs to project its fear on an outsider. It is often lamented that in modern city neighborhoods, people don't get to know their neighbors. That may be a blessing in disguise.

Sunday ★ ★ ★

NO MPAA RATING, 93 m., 1997

David Suchet (Matthew/Oliver), Lisa Harrow (Madeleine Vesey), Jared Harris (Ray), Larry Pine (Ben Vesey), Joe Grifasi (Scotti Elster), Arnold Barkus (Andy). Directed by Jonathan Nossiter and produced by Nossiter, Alix Madigan, and Jed Alpert. Screenplay by James Lasdun and Nossiter.

Sunday opens like a documentary, watching the residents of a halfway house get up for the day, shave, dress, pour coffee, and continue what seem to be eternal arguments about what is or isn't "community property." Then it cuts outside, to the wintry gray streets of Queens, and what appears to be a large green plant walking down the street. The plant is in the arms of a woman who spots a man, walks up to him, and calls him Matthew Delacorta. He is, she says, the famous movie director, whom she met in London.

He is not. He is Oliver (David Suchet), a middle-aged man who lives in the shelter, where he is generally disliked, and spends his days wandering the streets. But he is so astonished to be addressed in this way that he goes along with the misunderstanding, pretending to be the director. The woman's name is Madeleine (Lisa Harrow), and she is a British actress, once a member of the Royal Shakespeare Company, but now reduced, she confesses, to playing "mutant zombies."

They talk. Their talk will occupy most of the movie—the best parts, certainly—as they sit in a diner, drink wine at her nearby home, and eventually have sex. But *Sunday* is not a romance, and they are not flirting but crying for help, for companionship, for another voice against the loneliness.

Sunday won the screenwriting award at the 1997 Sundance Festival (it also won the Grand Jury Prize), and its writing, by James Lasdun and the director, Jonathan Nossiter, is its best quality. It is about two people who were once good at what they did, who were "downsized" in one way or another, and who now feel stranded and worthless. "When they ask what do you do," he says, "they mean, who are you?" He eventually tells her who he was once, and what he is now.

She had a crisis in her career—a loss of voice, or perhaps a loss of the will to speak on stage—and notes that her agent mostly sends her horror roles: "I guess I'm too old to play a human being." Oliver could, in a way, make the same statement.

The movie plays a subtle game with the information they share with each other. "Tell me one of your stories," she says, over a glass of wine, and he tells her the literal story of this day in his life, which we have already glimpsed as it began in the shelter. It is the truth. Does she accept it as the truth, or continue to deceive herself that he is Matthew Delacorta?

We have to decide as the movie continues; some moments we would answer one way, some moments another. It's intriguing, how they play games with their dialogue; at times it's like a conversation with an artificial intelligence program, especially when the "director" uses her questions to inspire his answers—not so much confirming that he's Delacorta as letting her assert it.

One of the things the movie accepts without apology or question is the substantial flesh of these two middle-aged people. Suchet (who plays Hercule Poirot on television) has a potbelly, and Harrow (unforgettable in Gillian Armstrong's *The Last Days of Chez Nous*) has a tummy, smaller but definite. In one scene she lies on a bed, frankly revealing herself to his gaze, looking like a model for a Francis Bacon portrait—but Madeleine isn't ugly, as Bacon's subjects were made to seem; she is lovely, and more at home in her body than in her life.

The film takes this strong, simple material and surrounds it with a little too much artiness. There are cutaway shots to the dismal streets, shots of a fellow resident of the shelter singing for coins in the subway, and flashbacks to Oliver's daily routine. When Madeleine's husband and adopted daughter return home, there are hints that all is not right in their house—hints that add an unnecessary subtext.

But the heart of the film is strong. It is about two people who would rather build and share a fantasy together than do whatever else would have occupied them on this empty Sunday. "The hardest thing is having nothing to do," Oliver says about unemployment. "Every day is Sunday."

The Sweet Hereafter ★ ★ ★ ★

R, 110 m., 1997

Ian Holm (Mitchell Stephens), Sarah Polley (Nicole Burnell), Bruce Greenwood (Billy Ansell), Tom McCamus (Sam Burnell), Gabrielle Rose (Dolores Driscoll), Arsinee Khanjian (Wanda Otto), Alberta Watson (Risa Walker), Maury Chaykin (Wendell Walker). Directed by Atom Egoyan and produced by Egoyan and

Camelia Frieberg. Screenplay by Egoyan, based on the novel by Russell Banks.

A cold, dark hillside looms above the Bide-a-Wile Motel, pressing down on it, crushing out the life with the gray weight of winter. It is one of the strongest images in Atom Egoyan's *The Sweet Hereafter*, which takes place in a small Canadian town, locked in by snow and buried in grief after fourteen children are killed in a school bus accident.

To this town comes a quiet man, a lawyer who wants to represent the residents in a class-action suit. Mitchell Stephens (Ian Holm) lacks the energy to be an ambulance chaser; he is only going through the motions of his occupation. In a way he's lost a child, too; the first time we see him, he's on the phone with his drug-addicted daughter. "I don't know who I'm talking to right now," he tells her.

There will be no victory at the end, we sense. This is not one of those Grisham films in which the lawyers battle injustice and the creaky system somehow works. The parents who have lost their children can never get them back; the school bus driver must live forever with what happened; lawsuits will open old wounds and betray old secrets. If the lawyer wins he gets to keep a third of the settlement; one look in his eyes reveals how little he thinks about money.

Egoyan's film, based on the novel by Russell Banks, is not about the tragedy of dying but about the grief of surviving. In the film the Browning poem about the Pied Piper is read, and we remember that the saddest figure in that poem was the lame boy who could not join the others in following the Piper. In *The Sweet Hereafter*, an important character is a teenage girl who loses the use of her legs in the accident; she survives but seems unwilling to accept the life still left for her.

Egoyan is a director whose films coil through time and double back to take a second look at the lives of their characters. It is typical of his approach that *The Sweet Hereafter* neither begins nor ends with the bus falling through the ice of a frozen lake, and is not really about how the accident happened, or who was to blame. The accident is like the snow clouds, always there, cutting off the characters from the sun, a vast fact nobody can change.

The lawyer makes his rounds, calling on parents. Egoyan draws them vividly with brief, cutting scenes. The motel owners, Wendell and Risa Walker (Maury Chaykin and Alberta Watson), fill him in on the other parents (Wendell has nothing good to say about anyone). Sam and Mary Burnell (Tom McCamus and Brooke Johnson) are the parents of Nicole, the budding young C&W singer who is now in a wheelchair. Wanda and Hartley Otto (Arsinee Khanjian and Earl Pastko) lost their son, an adopted Indian boy. Billy Ansell (Bruce Greenwood) was following the bus in his pickup, and waved to his children just before it swerved from the road. He wants nothing to do with the lawsuit, and is bitter about those who do. He is having an affair with Risa, the motel owner's wife.

This story. It is not about lawyers or the law, not about small-town insularity, not about revenge (although that motivates an unexpected turning point). It is more about the living dead: About people carrying on their lives after hope and meaning have gone. The film is so sad, so tender toward its characters. The lawyer, an outsider who might at first seem like the source of more trouble, comes across more like a witness, who regards the stricken parents and sees his own approaching loss of a daughter in their eyes.

Ian Holm's performance here is bottomless with its subtlety; he proceeds doggedly through the town, following the routine of his profession as if this is his penance. And there is a later scene, set on an airplane, where he finds himself seated next to his daughter's childhood friend, and remembers, in a heartbreaking monologue, a time in childhood when his daughter almost died of a spider bite. Is it good or bad that she survived, in order now to die of drugs?

Egoyan sees the town so vividly. A hearing is held in the village hall, where folding tables and chairs wait for potluck dinners and bingo nights. A foosball table is in a corner. In another corner, Nicole, in her wheelchair, describes the accident. She lies. It is too simple to say she lies as a form of getting even, because we wonder—if she were not in a wheelchair, would she feel the same way? Does she feel abused, or scorned?

"You'd make a great poker player, kid," the lawyer tells her.

This is one of the best films of 1997, an unflinching lament for the human condition. Yes, it is told out of sequence, but not as a gimmick: In a way, Egoyan has constructed this film in the simplest possible way. It isn't about the beginning and end of the plot, but about the beginning and end of the emotions. In his first scene, the lawyer tells his daughter he doesn't know who he's talking to. In one of his closing scenes, he remembers a time when he did know her. But what did it get him?

Swept From the Sea ★★

PG-13, 114 m., 1998

Rachel Weisz (Amy Foster), Vincent Perez (Yanko), Ian McKellen (Dr. James Kennedy), Kathy Bates (Miss Swaffer), Joss Ackland (Mr. Swaffer), Tony Haygarth (Mr. Smith), Fiona Victory (Mrs. Smith), Tom Bell (Isaac Foster). Directed by Beeban Kidron and produced by Polly Tapson, Charles Steel, and Kidron. Screenplay by Tim Willocks.

Swept From the Sea is a plodding retelling of *Amy Foster*, not one of Joseph Conrad's best short stories. It follows the original more or less faithfully, except for the addition of a subtle element of homosexuality—which, if it had been less subtle, might have made the movie more intriguing.

The story involves a doomed love affair between a simple country girl and a Russian peasant who is swept onto the Cornish shore in 1888, after his emigrant ship sinks on its way to America. The peasant, whose hair, beard, and rags make him look like a wild man, speaks no English. He is feared by the locals—except for Amy Foster (Rachel Weisz), a local girl born in scandal and working for the Swaffers, a farm family. Amy is thought to be retarded, but it is more complicated than that; she was a student at the parish school for years, we learn, without making the slightest effort to read and write. Then she read and wrote for a month, to prove a point, and then stopped again.

Amy and the castaway, whose name is Yanko (Vincent Perez), fall in love, court, are married, and have a child. These events are closely monitored by James Kennedy (Ian McKellen), the local doctor, who shares the general feeling that Yanko is simpleminded until the Russian whips him at chess. With quiet hints and lingering looks, the film makes it clear that the doctor becomes attracted to the well-built Yanko, and resentful of Amy Foster for possessing his time and love.

Conrad's original story was narrated by Dr. Kennedy, who is not shy in describing Yanko's physical beauty, so the filmmakers are not unjustified in making his feelings more overt. Conrad has Kennedy speaking to the author of the tale, so that we got a narration within a narration. In the film, the doctor tells it instead to the bedridden Miss Swaffer, creating an unnecessary question: Why does he need to tell her things she already knows at firsthand? Better to simply eliminate the narrator and the flashbacks, and just tell the story from beginning to end.

The director is Beeban Kidron, whose films *(Antonia & Jane, To Wong Foo, Thanks for Everything, Julie Newman)* have been miles away from this sort of overwrought historical melodrama. She enters into the spirit of the enterprise with one of the most remarkable opening shots I have seen, as the camera sweeps over miles of ocean before rising to the top of a cliff and to the lonely figures of a mother and a child. There are also effective storm scenes, and the landscape is evoked as Conrad described it, as low and flat, a depressing setting for a population devoted enthusiastically to the hatred of outsiders.

This drabness is relieved by Amy's secret grotto, where she keeps treasures given to her by the ocean, and where she takes Yanko, also a gift of the sea; when they make love in the grotto's waters, however, I couldn't help wondering about the source of the shimmering underwater illumination.

I suppose the film can be excused for casting the slender and beautiful Rachel Weisz as Amy, described by Conrad as squat and dull-faced. The story is about two outsiders who find one another, and the movie remains faithful to that idea while adding another outsider, the doctor, who is never quite said to be homosexual but goes out of his way to be as near to Yanko as he can, as often as possible, and whose dislike of Amy extends to rudeness. At the end of the film, after the doctor has told Miss Swaffer (Kathy Bates) all that he knows about the histories of the two unfortunate people, she asks, "Did your own love blind you to hers?"

Kidron and her screenwriter, Tim Willocks, are not reaching in making Kennedy homosexual (certain lines in the story point in that direction). But why make his sexuality so understated many viewers will miss it? For fear of offending an audience that has turned up for a conventional period romance?

McKellen plays the character subtly and with restraint, even deliberate repression; there is the possibility the doctor has not acknowledged his sexuality and is responding only to unexamined feelings. But at the end, when the sad story has played out, there is a moment in which Dr. Kennedy lashes out, and the moment would play better and provide more of a dramatic shock if the movie had been clearer about the nature of the feelings he is expressing. As it is, *Swept From the Sea* is a disappointment, a film in which good and evil dutifully go through their paces, while the character who could have added complexity and intrigue remains, unfortunately, unrealized

The Swindle ★ ★ ★

NO MPAA RATING, 105 m., 1999

Isabelle Huppert (Betty), Michel Serrault (Victor), Francois Cluzet (Maurice), Jean-Francois Balmer (Monsieur K), Jackie Berroyer (Chatillon), Jean Benguigui (Guadeloupe Gangster), Mony Dalmes (Signora Trotti). Directed by Claude Chabrol and produced by Marin Karmitz. Screenplay by Chabrol.

While their comrades in the French New Wave are either dead (Truffaut, Malle) or work rarely (Godard, Resnais, Rivette), Claude Chabrol and Eric Rohmer soldier on, prolific and creative. Other directors give difficult birth to each new project, but they've created worlds that easily produce new stories—Rohmer the world of minutely observed romance, Chabrol the world of crime and depravity.

The Swindle is Chabrol's fiftieth film, made with the practiced ease of a master. It's typical of his droll confidence that a man sprawls asleep in a chair during a key scene involving death threats and the breaking of fingers—and typical of Chabrol's restraint that he never cuts to the sleeping man for a quick laugh, but only subtly reveals him on the edges of the screen.

The movie stars Isabelle Huppert and Michel Serrault as Betty and Victor (if those are indeed their real names). She's fortyish, he's seventyish, they're con artists, and it's impossible to say what their personal relationship is: Friends? Lovers? Relatives? Even a hint at the end is left ambiguous. (It's a tribute to the actors, and to Chabrol, that in any given scene they could convincingly have any one of those three relationships.)

The movie starts with a warm-up con game. Betty poses as an available woman in a casino, and reels in a wealthy hardware dealer. She spikes his drink, he passes out in his room, and she and Victor relieve him of some, but not all, of his money—so that when he comes to, he won't remember his wagers well enough to be sure he was robbed.

That caper establishes the working partnership. Then the film ventures into a more complicated con—so complicated we're never quite sure if Betty and Victor are even conning one another. Betty has latched onto a financial courier for a crime syndicate, and has her eyes on the millions of Swiss francs in his locked briefcase. "Swissss! Swissss!" Victor hisses cheerfully, relishing the superiority of Swiss to French francs.

The courier, Maurice (Francois Cluzet), is a polished man about Betty's age, and there's the hint of a romance between them. Or is that only in Victor's jealous eyes? Or is he really jealous? And is Betty planning to steal the money from Maurice and Victor? Or only from Maurice? Or is Victor planning to steal it from Betty? And what about the powerful criminals who consider the money, after all, to be their property?

The plot unfolds as an understated comedy. Serrault, who has made more than 150 films, seems to twinkle as he schemes. Huppert is, of course, famous for her impassivity (see her in *The School of Flesh*), but here she adds a kind of crazy flair, suddenly exaggerating a word or a gesture, as if amusing herself while going through the steps of a confidence charade. The movie adds sneaky little running jokes, like the way Serrault is forever being mistaken for an employee of whatever establishment he's in.

Or the way a meal is lovingly ordered (there's great food in almost all of Chabrol's films).

Chabrol has always been an admirer of Hitchcock, and here he displays a Hitchcockian touch from time to time, almost deliberately. Consider the scene where the three principals observe a dance performance at a winter resort: Betty says she is too warm and leaves, followed first by one man and then the other; as they walk down the aisle all eyes are upon them. It's a reminder of how Hitchcock liked to put characters at a public event where escape meant breaking the rules.

By the end of the film we may still be murky about just what Betty and Victor were planning, and about their true relationship. That's part of the fun. Magicians don't reveal their secrets lightly ("The trick is told when the trick is sold"), and neither do con men. The con man this time, of course, is Chabrol, who has conned us into enjoying the entire film without giving away his own secrets.

Switchback ★★

R, 121 m., 1997

Danny Glover (Bob Goodall), Dennis Quaid (Frank LaCrosse), Jared Leto (Lane Dixon), R. Lee Ermey (Sheriff Buck Olmstead), William Fichtner (Chief Jack McGinnis), Ted Levine (Deputy Nate Booker). Directed by Jeb Stuart and produced by Gale Anne Hurd. Screenplay by Stuart.

Switchback is not a good movie, but it does an admirable job of distracting us from how bad it is. If they'd thrown out the two leading characters and started all over with the locations, the lore, and the supporting actors, they might have had something here. Time and again the movie fascinates us with digressions, only to jerk back to the helpless main story line.

There are two threads to the action. One involves a long car journey through the West by Bob, a former railroad worker (Danny Glover), and Lane (Jared Leto), a hitchhiker with a secret in his past. The other involves Sheriff Buck Olmstead (R. Lee Ermey) of Amarillo, Texas, and Frank LaCrosse, an FBI agent (Dennis Quaid), who has just turned up in town.

The agent is on the trail of a serial killer. They've been involved in a cat-and-mouse game for months or years, but now the rules have changed: The killer has kidnapped the agent's young son, and so the bureau has pulled the agent off the case, because it would be a conflict of interest. Would it ever.

The rules of movies like this require that the serial killer must be one of the characters onscreen. We easily narrow the suspects to the railway worker or the hitchhiker—unless the FBI agent is an impostor, which is also a possibility. Clues are scattered prodigiously. The killer knows how to sever arteries with a scalpel. So does the hitchhiker, Lane, a former medical student. The killer is maybe driving a Cadillac lined with centerfold pinups. So is Bob. And what about Frank, the FBI man: How can he be so sure that the violent hostage-taker just arrested in Amarillo, who was driving another car linked to the serial killer, isn't the right man?

All of this is plot stuff, and unreels as plot stuff does. None of it is very interesting, especially since we know too soon who the serial killer is, and he's not very convincing. Yes, there's suspense about whether he'll kill again. But let's put it this way: After two of the possibilities save each other's lives, we doubt they'll go on to kill each other in the next act.

What I liked about the movie had nothing to do with any of the above. I found Dennis Quaid's FBI agent a monotonous bore (he plays the role with a flat monotone that sounds affected). I found Danny Glover's character too chatty and genial. I was, however, persuaded by Lane, the Jared Leto character, who can't be blamed for a strange movie coincidence: A guy in a bar collapses on the floor and Lane cries, "I'm a doctor!" and proceeds to use a knife, a soda siphon, and a plastic bottle to perform the exact same weird emergency surgery performed by David Duchovny in *Playing God.* I guess it was the luck of the draw which movie came out first.

But the real center of the movie is occupied, not by the nominal leads Glover and Quaid, but by Ermey as the Amarillo sheriff, who is in the middle of a tough reelection campaign. Ermey is the former Marine drill instructor who was hired by Stanley Kubrick as a technical adviser on *Full Metal Jacket,* and then given the role he was advising on. He plays a fully drawn, colorful, convincing character, whose dialogue rings with an authenticity the others lack. He steals every scene and what is left of the movie; he's so tough and authentic he can get away with dry understatements like, "You can see this whole experience has just devastated me."

I also liked the use of winter locations in Texas, New Mexico, and Utah. And the railroad lore involving getting trains through snowbound mountain passes. I liked the culture of the truck stops and the railroad bunkhouses, and the old rail workers warming their hands over stoves in cabooses. I liked the faces of the bit players—guys in bars and locomotives. And I liked the way a climactic scene was played out on a train (the film's writer-director, Jeb Stuart, cowrote *The Fugitive,* which also made good use of a train and the cold light of winter locations).

If we lived in a more venturesome and curious world, *Switchback* would have been about a sheriff fighting for reelection in Amarillo, and about some rail workers trying to get a train through a blizzard. No serial killers, no obsessed FBI agents, maybe just enough of a crime for the sheriff and his opponent (the slimy local police chief) to fight over. What we have here is a potentially good movie swamped by the weight of Hollywood formulas it is forced to carry.

Footnotes: I was amused to see Stuart recycling the always reliable "It's Only a Cat!" gimmick in an early scene. And the convention that whenever a stranger walks into a Western saloon, all the regulars immediately beat him senseless. Late in the film, when a character falls backward from a train, he shouts "Yee-ha!" and both the shot and the shout are homage to Kubrick's Dr. Strangelove.

T

Tango ★ ★ ★ ½

PG-13, 112 m., 1999

Miguel Angel Sola (Mario Suarez), Cecilia Narova (Laura Fuentes), Mia Maestro (Elena Flores), Juan Carlos Copes (Carlos Nebbia), Julio Bocca (Himself), Juan Luis Galiardo (Angelo Larroca). Directed by Carlos Saura and produced by Luis A. Scalella, Carlos Mentasti, and Juan Carlos Codazzi. Screenplay by Saura.

The tango is based on suspicion, sex, and insincerity. It is not a dance for virgins. It is for the wounded and the wary. The opening shots of Carlos Saura's *Tango,* after a slow pan across Buenos Aires, are of a man who has given his life to the dance, and has a bad leg and a walking stick as his reward. This is the weary, graceful Mario (Miguel Angel Sola), who is preparing a new show based on the tango.

At the same time, perhaps Mario also represents Carlos Saura. The movie, one of 1999's Oscar nominees, has many layers: It is a film about the making of a film, and also a film about the making of a stage production. We are never quite sure what is intended as real and what is part of the stage production. That's especially true of some of the dance visuals, which use mirrors, special effects, trick lighting, and silhouettes so that we can't tell if we're looking at the real dancers or their reflections. A special set was constructed to shoot the film in this way, and the photography, by the great three-time Oscar winner Vittorio Storaro, is like a celebration of his gift.

If the film is visually beautiful, it is also ravishing as a musical—which is really what it is, with its passionate music and angry dance sequences. It is said the musical is dead, but it lives here, and Saura of course has made several films where music is crucial to the weave of the story; his credits include *Blood Wedding, Carmen,* and *Flamenco.*

Early in the film, Mario visits a club run by the sinister Angelo Larroca (Juan Luis Galiardo), who asks him a favor: an audition for his girlfriend, Elena (Mia Maestro). Mario can hardly refuse, because Angelo owns 50 percent of the show. Mario watches Elena dance, and realizes she is very good. He begins to fall in love with her, which is dangerous; when he makes a guarded proposal at dinner, she says, "Come off it—you know who I'm living with!"

Yes, he does. So does his estranged wife, Laura (Cecilia Narova), who warns him off the girl. But Mario and Elena draw closer, until finally they are sleeping with each other even though Angelo has threatened to punish cheating with death. What adds an additional element to their romance is Mario's essential sadness; he is like a man who has given up hope of being happy, and at one point he calls himself "A solitary animal—one of those old lions who roam the African savanna."

Of course, there is always the question of how much of this story is real, and how much of it is actually the story of the stage production. Saura allows us to see his cameras at times, suggesting that what we see is being filmed—for this film? Back and forth flow the lines of possibility and reality.

There are several dance sequences of special power. One is an almost vicious duet between Elena and Laura. Another uses dancers as soldiers, and suggests the time in Argentina's history when many people disappeared forever. That time is also evoked by images of startling simplicity: Torture, for example, is suggested by light on a single chair. And there is also a sequence, showing mostly just feet and legs, that suggests the arrival of immigrants to Argentina. You see in *Tango* that there are still things to be discovered about how dancing can be shown on the screen.

Recently, for one reason or another, I've seen a lot of tango. A stage performance in Paris, for example, and the 1997 British movie *The Tango Lesson.* Apart from the larger dimensions of the dance, there is the bottom line of technical skill. The legs of the dancers move so swiftly and so close to one another that only long practice and perfect timing prevents falls—even injuries. With the tango you never get the feeling the dancers have just met. They have a long history together, and not necessarily a happy one; they dance as a challenge, a boast, a taunt, a sexual put-down. It is the one dance where the woman gives as good as she gets, and the sexes are equal.

The romantic stories in *Tango* reflect that

kind of dynamic. Mario and his estranged wife talk the way tango dancers dance. The early stages of Mario's seduction of Elena are like an emotional duel. The role of Angelo, the tough guy, is like a stage tango performance when a stranger arrives and tries to take command. It isn't real. It is real. It's all rehearsed, but they really mean it. It's only a show, but it reflects what's going on in the dancers' lives. It's only a dance. Yes, but life is only a dance.

The Tango Lesson ★ ★ ★ ½

PG, 101 m., 1997

Sally Potter (Sally), Pablo Veron (Pablo), Carlos Copello (Carlos), Olga Besio (Olga), Carolina Iotti (Pablo's Partner), Gustavo Naveira (Gustavo). Directed by Sally Potter and produced by Christopher Sheppard. Screenplay by Potter.

The Tango Lesson is a fictional film in which almost everything and everybody seems to be, in some sense, real. It's about a British film director named Sally, who is played by the British film director Sally Potter. She meets a great tango dancer named Pablo, who is played by the great tango dancer Pablo Veron. She says that if he gives her tango lessons, she will put him in a movie. She has put him in this movie. She is pretty damn fine at dancing the tango; she must have had some lessons somewhere.

For her pains in telling this story, Miss Potter has been slapped down by several critics. How dare she, a middle-aged woman, star herself in a love story where she falls in love with a tango dancer—and, even worse, is good enough to dance as his partner? This is "blatant narcissism" (Britain's *Empire* magazine), and "an act of wild hubris" *(The New York Times)*. "Talk about self-indulgence!" says a critic on the Internet.

Political correctness is not my favorite pose, and so I will not go into detail about the countless movies in which middle-aged (and, indeed, elderly) men seduce twenty-two-year-old models and jump out of airplanes while throwing bombs. I will note, however, that Sally Potter really does dance the tango herself in this film; it's not a stunt woman or special effects, and my theory is, if you've got it, flaunt it.

She also does other things very well. One of them is to delicately examine the tension between a man and a woman who are not really sexually destined for one another, but go through a mad moment of thinking they are—simply because they have idealized one another. If power is the ultimate aphrodisiac, then what could be sexier than the power you yourself have granted to another person by mentally supplying them with those qualities you find most dazzling? Sally and Pablo have "no chemistry," I read, and are "passionless." These are words that could only have been written by critics whose own ideas of passion are limited to the narrow range of testosterone emissions seen in most movies. The typical movie love story is about characters so young that proximity triggers tumescence. *The Tango Lesson* is not intended as a story about romantic passion achieved, but about passion sighted in the near distance, considered, flirted with, and regretfully declined. "We should set some limits," Sally tells Pablo after he stands her up on New Year's Eve. "It's better to sublimate our relationship in our work." Those are words you will not hear for many years between Tom and Nicole, Matt and Minnie, Will and Jada, or Johnny and Kate.

Potter is best known in North America for *Orlando*, her 1993 film starring Tilda Swinton as a character who lives four centuries, half as a man, half as a woman. Now here is another film about a character who dares to reinvent herself—whose future is not defined by her past. As the film opens, Sally is working on an artsy movie named *Rage*, which involves beautiful models and a legless fashion designer who pursues them in a wheelchair, shooting at them. Not surprisingly, the work is not going well; the opening shot of *Tango Lesson* suggestively shows Sally wiping her worktable clean.

She goes to Paris, wanders into a theater, sees Pablo dancing, and is entranced—more, I think, by the intricate sexiness of the dance than by the man himself. (The tango strikes me as aggressive foreplay performed with legs instead of genitals.) She visits Pablo, suggests that she might put him in a movie in return for dance lessons, and begins to study the tango.

The scenes are broken down into "lessons." Some of them are about dance, and others are about life. We visit Argentina, London, Paris again. Sally gets good. They perform together, but there is tension: As a director, she is accustomed to leading. As a male dancer, so is he. "You should do nothing!" he tells her. "When you dance—just follow! Otherwise you destroy my freedom to move."

There is an interesting underlying question here: All good artists are the undisputed rulers of their art. Novelists or painters are godlike tyrants who create every molecule of their work out of their own beings. Can two artists therefore collaborate, or must one always be the brush and the other the canvas? When a man and a woman dance the tango, is the man the artist and his partner's response the work he is creating? "I did everything he did," Ginger Rogers once said about Fred Astaire. "And I did it backwards, and in high heels."

The Tango Lesson considers but does not answer these questions. It contains truly virtuoso dance sequences, photographed in black and white by Robby Muller (who must agree with Astaire's fierce belief that color only distracts from dance on the screen). The duel between Potter and Veron is all the more fascinating because it is about the wisdom of passion, rather than the temptation. The score, partly composed by Potter, is so seductive that for the first time in years I walked out of the screening and down the street and bought the sound track.

Most dances are for people who are falling in love. The tango is a dance for those who have survived it, and are still a little angry about having their hearts so mishandled. *The Tango Lesson* is a movie for people who understand that difference.

Tarzan ★★★★

G, 88 m., 1999

With the voices of: Brian Blessed (Clayton), Glenn Close (Kala), Minnie Driver (Jane), Tony Goldwyn (Tarzan), Nigel Hawthorne (Professor Porter), Lance Henriksen (Kerchak), Wayne Knight (Tantor), Alex D. Linz (Young Tarzan), Rosie O'Donnell (Terk). Directed by Kevin Lima and Chris Buck and produced by Bonnie Arnold. Screenplay by Tab Murphy, Bob Tzudiker, and Noni White, based on the story "Tarzan of the Apes" by Edgar Rice Burroughs.

Something deep within the Tarzan myth speaks to us, and Disney's new animated *Tarzan* captures it. Maybe it's the notion that we can all inhabit this planet together, man and beast, and get along. The surface of the movie is adventure, comedy, and movement—there are sequences here as exciting as the ballroom scene in *Beauty and the Beast*—but underneath is something of substance. The most durable movie character in history emerges this time as a man who asks the question, "Why are you threatened by anyone different than you?"

This is not the confident Tarzan of so many Edgar Rice Burroughs novels and Johnny Weissmuller movies, discovering cities of gold. It is a Tarzan who knows from the day he compares his hand with the hand of Kala, the ape who has adopted him, that he is different. A Tarzan who is still different even after he meets other humans—because his experience is not the same. The movie doesn't insist on this thread of meaning, but it gives the movie weight. Like all the best Disney animated films, this one is about something other than cute characters and cheerful songs. It speaks even to the youngest members of the audience, who, like Tarzan, must have days when they feel surrounded by tall, rumbling, autocratic bipeds.

The movie is also a lot of fun. It has scenes that move through space with a freedom undreamed of in older animated films, and unreachable by any live-action process. Disney uses a process called Deep Canvas, a computer-assisted animation tool that handles the details during swoops through three dimensions. There's a sequence where Tarzan helps Jane escape from a band of monkeys, and as they hurtle through the treetops and loop-the-loop on byways of vines, it's like a roller-coaster ride.

The origin of Tarzan is one of the great masterstrokes of twentieth-century fiction. Burroughs, who never visited Africa, imagined it in much the same way that a child might, peering into a picture book of gorillas and elephants. The opening sequence of *Tarzan* encapsulates the story of how the young British baby and his parents were shipwrecked on the coast of Africa, built a treehouse, and lived in it. In the film, the infant is discovered by the curious gorilla Kala, after Sabor the leopard has killed his parents (offscreen, mercifully, although of course almost all Disney movies are about orphans in one way or another). She names the baby Tarzan, and brings it home to the family, where her mate, Kerchak, growls, "He can stay—but that doesn't make him my son!"

The look of the African forest is one of the great beauties of the film. There is such a depth to some scenes, and a feeling of great space in shots like the one where a waterfall tumbles off a mountain wall, while tiny birds make their way through the sky. Against this primeval wilderness, the Disney animators strike a sort of compromise with the laws of the jungle. Some animals (the leopard, for example) are true to their natures and are predators. Others, like the humanoid apes, are sentimentalized; Kala, voiced by Glenn Close, sounds like a suburban mom, and Terk, the wacky sidekick, sounds like—well, Rosie O'Donnell.

The leader of the pack, Kerchak (Lance Henrikson), is rumbling and distant, but there's an elephant who talks like a twelve-stepper ("I've had it with you and your emotional constipation"). Oddly, the animals have normal English dialogue when they are heard by one another, but are reduced to soft gutturals in the presence of outside humans. (Tarzan, who has been chatting with Kala for years, is reduced to talking in little coos after Jane turns up, and we are denied what would no doubt have been an invaluable scene in which Kala tells him the facts of life.)

Jane is voiced by Minnie Driver, as a peppy British girl with lots of moxie. She's come with her father, the walrus-faced Professor Porter (Nigel Hawthorne), to study the gorillas; their guide is Clayton (Brian Blessed), with the graying sideburns of Stewart Granger and the sneers of a Victorian villain. The human plot, as you can guess, includes Clayton's nefarious plans for the gorillas and Tarzan's defense of them. The more interesting plot involves the tug-of-war after Tarzan and Jane fall in love ("I'm in a tree with a man who talks with gorillas!"). Will he return to London with her, or will she stay in the jungle? Burroughs had one answer; Disney has another.

There are, of course, no Africans in this movie. (The opening song promises us a paradise unspoiled by man.) This may be just as well. The Tarzan myth doesn't take place in Africa so much as in a kind of archetypal wilderness occupied only by its own characters. Burroughs used some Africans in his books, but that was after Tarzan got involved in politics (fighting the Germans in South West Africa, for example). At the stage of the story where this film is set, the presence of any additional characters would be disastrous, because they would bring in the real world, and this story has to close out reality to work at all. (*The Lion King,* of course, didn't even have room for Tarzan.)

Tarzan, like *The Hunchback of Notre Dame,* represents another attempt by Disney to push the envelope of animation. Taking a page from the Japanese, where animation is an accepted art form for serious films, *Tarzan* isn't a kiddie cartoon but a movie that works on one level for children (who will like the "Trashin' the Camp" production number), and another for adults (who may stir at scenes like the one where the gorillas reveal themselves to their visitors). The Disney animators also borrow a technique that has been useful to the Japanese, of exaggerating the size of eyes and mouths to make emotions clearer.

I saw *Tarzan* once, and went to see it again. This kind of bright, colorful, hyperkinetic animation is a visual exhilaration. Animation cuts loose from what we can actually see, and shows us what we might ideally see. Like *Mulan* and *A Bug's Life,* this is a film where grown-ups do not need to be accompanied by a non-adult guardian. ☞

The Taste of Cherry ★

NO MPAA RATING, 95 m., 1998

Homayon Ershadi (Mr. Badii), Abdolrahman Bagheri (Taxidermist), Afshin Khorshid Bakhtiari (Soldier), Safar Ali Moradi (Soldier), Mir Hossein Noori (Seminarian). Directed and produced by Abbas Kiarostami. Screenplay by Kiarostami.

There was great drama at Cannes in 1997 when the Iranian director Abbas Kiarostami was allowed, at the last moment, to leave his country and attend the festival premiere of his new film, *The Taste of Cherry.* He received a standing ovation as he entered the theater, and another at the end of his film (although this time mixed with boos), and the jury eventually made the film cowinner of the Palme d'Or.

Back at the Hotel Splendid, standing in the lobby, I found myself in lively disagreement with two critics I respect, Jonathan Rosenbaum of the *Chicago Reader* and Dave Kehr of the *New York Daily News.* Both believed they had seen a masterpiece. I thought I had seen an emperor without any clothes.

A case can be made for the movie, but it would involve transforming the experience of viewing the film (which is excruciatingly boring) into something more interesting, a fable about life and death. Just as a bad novel can be made into a good movie, so can a boring movie be made into a fascinating movie review.

The story: A man in a Range Rover drives through the wastelands outside Tehran, crisscrossing a barren industrial landscape of construction sites and shantytowns, populated by young men looking for work. The driver picks up a young serviceman, asking him, at length, if he's looking for a job: "If you've got money problems, I can help." Is this a homosexual pickup? Kiarostami deliberately allows us to draw that inference for a time, before gradually revealing the true nature of the job.

The man, Mr. Badii (Homayon Ershadi), wants to commit suicide. He has dug a hole in the ground. He plans to climb into it and take pills. He wants to pay the other man to come around at 6 A.M. and call down to him. "If I answer, pull me out. If I don't, throw in twenty shovels of earth to bury me."

The serviceman runs away. Badii resumes his employment quest, first asking a seminarian, who turns him down because suicide is forbidden by the Koran, and then an elderly taxidermist. The older man agrees because he needs money to help his son, but argues against suicide. He makes a speech on Mother Earth and her provisions, and asks Badii, "Can you do without the taste of cherries?"

That, essentially, is the story (I will not reveal if Badii gets his wish). Kiarostami tells it in a monotone. Conversations are very long, elusive, and enigmatic. Intentions are misunderstood. The car is seen driving for long periods in the wasteland, or parked overlooking desolation, while Badii smokes a cigarette. Any two characters are rarely seen in the same shot, reportedly because Kiarostami shot the movie himself, first sitting in the driver's seat, then in the passenger's seat.

Defenders of the film, and there are many, speak of Kiarostami's willingness to accept silence, passivity, a slow pace, deliberation, inactivity. Viewers who have short attention spans will grow restless, we learn, but if we allow ourselves to accept Kiarostami's time sense, if we open ourselves to the existential dilemma of the main character, then we will sense the film's greatness.

But will we? I have abundant patience with long, slow films, if they engage me. I fondly recall *Taiga,* the eight-hour documentary about the yurt-dwelling nomads of Outer Mongolia. I understand intellectually what Kiarostami is doing. I am not impatiently asking for action or incident. What I do feel, however, is that Kiarostami's style here is an affectation; the subject matter does not make it necessary, and is not benefited by it.

If we're to feel sympathy for Badii, wouldn't it help to know more about him? To know, in fact, *anything at all* about him? What purpose does it serve to suggest at first he may be a homosexual? (Not what purpose for the audience—what purpose for Badii himself? Surely he must be aware his intentions are being misinterpreted.) And why must we see Kiarostami's camera crew—a tiresome distancing strategy to remind us we are seeing a movie? If there is one thing *The Taste of Cherry* does not lack, it is such a reminder: The film is such a lifeless drone that we experience it *only* as a movie.

Yes, there is a humanistic feeling underlying the action. Yes, an Iranian director making a film on the forbidden subject of suicide must have courage. Yes, we applaud the stirrings of artistic independence in the strict Islamic republic. But is *The Taste of Cherry* a worthwhile viewing experience? I say it is not.

Tea with Mussolini ★ ★ ½

PG, 117 m., 1999

Cher (Elsa), Judi Dench (Arabella), Joan Plowright (Mary), Maggie Smith (Lady Hester), Lily Tomlin (Georgie), Baird Wallace (Luca), Charlie Lucas (Luca [child]), Massimo Ghini (Paolo). Directed by Franco Zeffirelli and produced by Riccardo Tozzi, Giovannella

Zannoni, and Clive Parsons. Screenplay by John Mortimer and Zeffirelli, based on Zeffirelli's autobiography.

How accurate *Tea with Mussolini* is I cannot say, but it is based on the autobiography of the film director Franco Zeffirelli, who directed it, so we can be sure it is true to what he remembers, or wants to remember. The film tells of a boy named Luca, born out of wedlock to a clothing manufacturer in Florence. His mother is dead, his father's wife visits him at school to hiss that he is a bastard, and his best friend is an old expatriate Brit named Mary (Joan Plowright), who has been hired to turn him into a perfect English gentleman.

As the film opens in the early 1930s, we are told, the Italians and the British have a mutual love affair. We see it reflected in the daily lives of a gaggle of eccentric British ladies of more than a certain age, who gather in Doney's Tea Rooms and the galleries of the Uffizi to gossip—about each other, mostly. After Luca's father orders Mary to return him to the orphanage, she finds she cares for him too much, and takes him instead to live with her at the Pensione Shelley. And thus young Luca is plunged into the intrigues and artistic passions of the "Scorpioni," which is the nickname for the ladies with their stinging wit.

These ladies are played by a cast as eclectic as it is engaging. The grand dame of the Scorpioni is Lady Hester (Maggie Smith), the widow of the former British ambassador. The artistic soul of the group is Arabella (Judi Dench), who informs young Luca, "I have warmed both hands before the fires of Michelangelo and Botticelli." The most visible eccentric, in a congregation of flamboyance, is Georgie (Lily Tomlin), an archaeologist who works among the ruins in pants and overalls that match her cheerfully lesbian inclinations. Mary seems almost average in this company, a sweet lady who supports herself by typing florid Italian into sensible English.

And then there is Elsa Morganthal (Cher), an outlandish American who swoops in and out of Florence like a summer squall. She's an art collector, whose purchases are financed by a rich and absent husband (who is "too cheap to slip a poor girl a little Picasso"). Resembling Peggy Guggenheim, who made her headquarters in Venice, Elsa is loud, flamboyant, and unwise enough to fall in love with her chauffeur, a cad with patent-leather hair who sells fake art to her, steals her money, and when the time comes, betrays her to the fascists.

The character of Luca is a little overwhelmed by all of these outsize personalities, and indeed the movie might actually have been better without him. Yes, Luca is supposed to be Zeffirelli, and the director is telling his own story—but he seems to inhabit it mostly as an observer. The two actors engaged to play Luca aren't given much to say, and although as a young man Luca joins the Resistance, that activity consists mostly of lurking behind trees and appearing when he is required by the plot. Zeffirelli may look out through Luca's eyes, but not into a mirror.

The ladies supply quite enough entertainment all on their own. Lady Hester charges off to Rome for tea with Mussolini, who assures her that she and her British friends have nothing to worry about, and then poses for photos that will be useful propaganda (ambassador's wife has tea with dictator, finds him a nice chap). Soon, however, the brownshirts are breaking the windows of the tearoom, and the ladies are put under custody and shipped off to a beautiful mountaintop village.

The movie is heavier with events than with plot. Things are always happening, but it's hard to see the connections, and the material involving Elsa's love affair, Lady Hester's draft-dodging male relative, and Arabella's dog all coexists uneasily. (The draft dodger hides from the fascists by dressing in drag, only to finally snap, run into the street, cry out "I'm a man!" strip off his dress, and join the Resistance.) Elsa, the Cher character, meanwhile ignores the dangers for a Jew in Italy, and makes unwise statements such as, "Musso? I think his butt's too big to push around the dance floor."

I enjoyed the movie in a certain way, as a kind of sub–Merchant-Ivory combination of eccentric ladies and enchanting scenery. I liked the performances of the women (including Cher; people keep forgetting what a good actress she can be). I wanted to see more of Tomlin's bracingly frank archaeologist (why do movie lesbians have to recite so much dialogue that keys off their sexuality?). But the movie seemed the stuff of anecdote, not drama, and as the alleged protagonist, Luca/Franco is too young much of the time to play more than a bystander's role. Zeffirelli, of course, grew up to direct better movies *(Romeo and Juliet,* the Burton-Taylor *Taming of the Shrew,* the Mel Gibson *Hamlet)* and opera, and to speak flawless English.

Telling Lies in America ★★★

PG-13, 101 m., 1997

Kevin Bacon (Billy Magic), Brad Renfro (Karchy Jonas), Maximilian Schell (Mr. Jonas), Calista Flockhart (Diney), Paul Dooley (Father Norton). Directed by Guy Ferland and produced by Ben Myron and Fran Kuzui. Screenplay by Joe Eszterhas.

Cleveland, 1960. "I haven't been Billy Magic since Fort Worth," says the lanky, chain-smoking disc jockey. He has the grin of a man who is getting away with something. He is. *Telling Lies in America,* based on the memories of America's top-paid screenwriter, Joe Eszterhas, is about the kid who helps Billy get away with it, and does a lot of growing up in the process. He gets a break and loses his innocence at the same time.

Karchy Jonas (Brad Renfro) is a student at a Catholic high school attended mostly by rich kids, who call him "white trash." His father (Maximilian Schell) is a Hungarian immigrant, who was a professor in the old country but is a janitor in this one. Karchy works for an egg dealer in the local produce market, and has a crush on a girl who tells him she'll date him, but only if he's picked for Billy Magic's "High School Hall of Fame."

Hall of famers are supposed to be nominated by their classmates, but Karchy forges the signatures, sends them in, and wins. What he doesn't know is that Billy Magic is *looking* for a cheater. "You lie good, kid," Billy tells him, but even after he gives Karchy $100 a week, the kid won't admit he was lying. That's good. It's the time of the payola scandals, and Billy needs an underage bag man who can't be forced to testify.

Eszterhas, who has made a fortune with screenplays like *Basic Instinct* and *Showgirls,* has had this story in the works for fifteen years. Himself a Hungarian immigrant who came to Cleveland as a child, he remembers what success looked like from the outside. To Karchy, Billy Magic is a star. And the kid soon centers his life on the radio station, letting his grades slip because high school is no longer where he expects to find his future.

Kevin Bacon's work as the disc jockey is one of his best performances. He never pushes it too far: His style is laid-back cool rather than frantic. His lazy announcer's drawl suggests a cynicism developed during a career on too many stations under too many names. When the kid tells him he's got it made, Billy explains about his ex-wives, his child support payments, and the fact that his red Cadillac convertible is leased. He's one jump ahead of his next market.

Brad Renfro is assured and involving as Karchy. Amazingly, he's playing over his age; Renfro (so good as the young boy in *The Client* in 1994) was fourteen or fifteen when he played this seventeen-year-old; it is a nuanced performance, showing a character who has been so wounded by life (his mother is dead, his father embittered) that, yes, he'll lie to get what he wants. And in an unexpected twist at the end of the film, lying pays off. (At one point, he advises the girl to read *Huckleberry Finn*—a nod to his previous role, as Huck in *Huck and Jim.*)

The movie's weak point is Karchy's father, as played by Schell. Mr. Jonas is a weary assortment of clichés about immigrant dads; he always wears his hat in the house, has stringy hair, and needs a shave. We are told this man was a professor and famous doctor in Hungary. It is more likely that he would dress according to Old World standards, however old his clothes. He wouldn't seem so self-demeaning and clueless, forever moping around at home waiting for his son to walk in. A smarter character would have led to a better relationship.

But that's a small point. I liked this movie a lot—not just for Bacon and Renfro, but also for the work of the wonderfully named Calista Flockhart, as the girl who dates Karchy even after he unwisely tries to give her Spanish fly. What I'll remember best about the film is Billy Magic, who does what he does, knows what he knows, and is intimately familiar with the underside of fame.

Temptress Moon ★★

R, 115 m., 1997

Leslie Cheung (Zhongliang), Gong Li (Pang Ruyi), Kevin Lin (Pang Duanwu), He Saifei (Yu Xiuyi [Zhongliang's Sister]), Zhang Shi (Li Niangjiu), Lin Lianqun (Pang An), Ge Xiangting (Elder Qi), Zhou Yemang (Zhengda). Directed by Chen Kaige and produced by Tong Cunlin and Hsu Feng. Screenplay by Shu Kei, based on the story by Kaige and Wang Anyi.

Chen Kaige's *Temptress Moon* opens like one of those nineteenth-century novels with a cast of characters on the first page. In a helpful sequence added by Miramax, the film's U.S. distributor, we are introduced to the three central characters, first as children, then as adults, with their names printed on the screen under their faces. There is also a prologue, which scrolls up the screen as it is read aloud.

This is not window dressing. *Temptress Moon* is a hard movie to follow—so hard, that at some point you may be tempted to abandon the effort and simply enjoy the elegant visuals by the Australian cinematographer Christopher Doyle, who mirrors the labyrinthine story with his treatment of city streets and shadowed corridors, all circling back upon themselves.

Like almost all modern Chinese films, this one is ravishing to look at, but it is impossible to care deeply about, because Kaige's characters, once we have them straight, are not sympathetic or even very interesting. I found myself more absorbed in the backgrounds and contexts of the action—in the ceremony, for example, by which a family aide informs its members of a change of leadership.

The story centers on Zhongliang (Leslie Cheung), who as a boy was raised on the decadent country estate of the Pang family, where his playmate was Ruyi (Gong Li). Now follow this closely. In 1911, the family is headed by Old Master Pang. His son, Zhengda (Zhou Yemang), is married to Xiuyi (He Saifei), who is Zhongliang's sister—which is why Zhongliang is invited there in the first place. (Ruyi is Zhengda's sister.) Zhongliang's duties include preparing the opium pipes for the Pangs, father and son, and for his own sister. There is a murky flashback later in the film indicating that Zhengda forced Zhongliang to kiss Xiuyi—and there are shadowy implications of additional incest.

Whatever. Time passes. Zhongliang flees, eventually finding work in Shanghai as a gigolo who kisses women while stealing their pearls. Old Master Pang dies. Young Master Pang (Zhengda) becomes a witless basket case through opium addiction, and so Zhengda's sister, Ruyi, is made the acting head of the family. Knowing that Ruyi and Zhongliang were playmates as children, Zhongliang's criminal boss orders him back to the Pang estate, where the scenario is that he will use his skills as a gigolo to seduce Ruyi and gain control of the family's assets.

Ruyi is envisioned as a sort of caretaker until a suitable male heir can be groomed, but she seizes firm control immediately, and orders her late father's concubines out of the house (everyone is scandalized; surely they deserve a serene retirement?). But Ruyi is also addicted to opium, and the entire family seems bemused by its fumes.

Why do I feel like I'm sitting in an opera house, trying to absorb the convoluted synopsis before the curtain goes up? Somehow it seems as if Kaige could have covered the essential elements of his story with fewer characters, especially since the flashbacks mean that the key characters are played both by children and adults, further complicating things.

Bewildered, I turned to the Web to see what Asian critics of the film had written, and was relieved to find I was not alone: "This dazed and confused viewer found it hard to make out what the story was about" (S. Young, Singapore). "He has to be ambiguous and obscure. The man has a thing or two to say. You bet. But he (doesn't) say it straight. He has to say something by not saying it, say something that has something else inside it, or say one thing and mean another" (Long Tin, Hong Kong).

The film is, in any event, beautiful to behold—as is Gong Li, although by making her an opium addict Kaige requires her to be unfocused and addled, and that undercuts the intelligence that is key to her beauty.

The film and its director ran into difficulties with the Chinese government, as did Kaige's *Farewell My Concubine* (1993), which also starred

Gong Li and Leslie Chueng. The earlier film depicted homosexuality and suicide, which were frowned upon. I am not sure why *Temptress Moon* got into trouble. It presumably wouldn't concern the current regime that the 1920s are portrayed as a period of decadent capitalist excess, but I suspect there is a level of allegory in the story that eludes me. The film opens with the abdication of the old emperor in 1911; could we move the entire action forward to the death of Mao and decode the symbolism? You tell me.

10 Things I Hate About You ★ ★ ½

PG-13, 94 m., 1999

Heath Ledger (Patrick Verona), Julia Stiles (Katarina Stratford), Joseph Gordon-Levitt (Cameron James), Larisa Oleynik (Bianca Stratford), David Krumholtz (Michael Eckman), Larry Miller (Mr. Stratford), Andrew Keegan (Joey Donner), Susan May Pratt (Mandella), Gabrielle Union (Chastity), Allison Janney (Counselor), Daryl "Chill" Mitchell (English Teacher). Directed by Gil Junger and produced by Andrew Lazar. Screenplay by Karen McCullah Lutz and Kirsten Smith.

I'm trying to remember the last movie I saw that didn't end with a high school prom. *Ravenous,* maybe. Even the *next* film I've seen, *Never Been Kissed,* ends with a prom. The high school romance genre has become so popular that it's running out of new ideas, and has taken to recycling classic literature.

My colleague James Berardinelli made a list recently: *Clueless* was based on *Emma, She's All That* was inspired by *Pygmalion,* and *Cruel Intentions* was recycled from *Les Liaisons Dangereuses* (prompting Stanley Kauffmann to observe that it was better back in the days when high school students were allowed to take over the city government for a day, instead of remaking French novels). To this list we might also add the update of *Great Expectations,* Cinderella's true story in *Ever After,* and *William Shakespeare's Romeo and Juliet,* which was anything but. There's even *Rage: Carrie 2*—a retread of *Carrie,* a work that ranks in my opinion right up there with the best of Austen, Shaw, and Shakespeare.

10 Things I Hate About You is inspired, in a sortuva kinduva way, by Shakespeare's *The Taming of the Shrew,* in the same sense that *Starship Troopers* was inspired by *Titus Andronicus.* It doesn't remake Shakespeare so much as evoke him as a talisman by setting its story at Padua High School, naming its characters Stratford and Verona, making one of the heroines a shrew, etc. There is even a scene where the shrew is assigned to rewrite a Shakespeare sonnet.

And yet . . . gee, the movie is charming, even despite its exhausted wheeze of an ancient recycled plot idea (boy takes bribe to ask girl to prom, then discovers that he really likes her—but then she finds out about the bribe and hates him). I haven't seen that idea in almost two months, since *She's All That* (boy makes bet he can turn plain wallflower into prom queen and does, but falls in love with her, after which she discovers, etc., etc.).

The story this time involves two Seattle sisters. Bianca Stratford (Larisa Oleynik) is popular and wears a lot of red dresses. Her shrewish older sister Katarina (Julia Stiles) is unpopular, never dates, and is the class brain. (When the English teacher asks his class for reactions to a Hemingway novel, she snaps, "Hemingway was an alcoholic who hung around Picasso hoping to nail his leftovers.")

Two guys want to take Bianca to the prom. One is shy and likable. The other is a blowhard. But Bianca's father (Larry Miller) has forbidden her to date until her older sister Katarina starts going out. So a plot is hatched to convince Patrick (Heath Ledger), the school outlaw, to ask her to the prom. He takes a $300 bribe, but then realizes that Kat is actually quite lovely, etc., and really falls in love with her, after which, etc.

I think we simply have to dump the entire plot and appreciate the performances and some of the jolliest scenes. I liked, to begin with, the spirit of the high school teachers. Allison Janney is the sex-mad counselor, and Daryl "Chill" Mitchell is the English teacher who performs Shakespeare's sonnets as if they were rap lyrics. (I've got news for you: They work pretty well as rap, and I expect the album any day.)

I also liked the sweet, tentative feeling between Ledger and Stiles. He has a scene that brings the whole movie to an enjoyable halt. Trying to win her heart, he waits until she's on the athletic field, and then sings "I Love You Baby" over the P.A. system, having bribed the marching band to accompany him. Those scenes are worth the price of admission—almost. But then other scenes are a drag.

All teenage movies have at least one boring and endless party scene, in which everyone is wildly dressed, drunk, and relentlessly colorful (in *Never Been Kissed*, some of the kids come as the Village People). These scenes inevitably involve (a) a fight, (b) barfing, and (c) a tearful romantic breakup In Front of Everybody. That scene was tedious, and so was a scene where the would-be lovers throw paint balloons at each other. I know there has to be a scene of carefree, colorful frolic, but as I watched them rubbing paint in each other's hair I began to yearn for that old standby, the obligatory Tilt-a-Whirl ride.

I liked the movie's spirit, and the actors, and some of the scenes. The music, much of it by a band named Letters to Cleo, is subtle and inventive while still cheerful. The movie almost but not quite achieves liftoff against the gravitational pull of the tired story formula. Sometimes it's a mistake to have acting this charming; the characters become so engaging and spontaneous we notice how they're trapped in the plot. ☞

Tetsuo II: Body Hammer ★ ★ ★

NO MPAA RATING, 83 m., 1997

Tomoroh Taguchi (Tomoo Taniguchi), Nobu Kanaoka (Kana), Shinya Tsukamoto (Guy), Sujin Kim (Taniguchi's Father). Directed by Shinya Tsukamoto and produced by Fuminori Shishido, Fumio Kurokawa, Nobuo Takeushi, and Hiromi Aihara. Screenplay by Tsukamoto.

When Shinya Tsukamoto was growing up in Tokyo, there were still green and open spaces in the city—but now he sees it transformed into a towering, compacted mass of steel and concrete. This is not altogether a bad thing, he believes; both visions of the city attract him. But the inhabitants of the new Tokyo need to adapt in order to survive—have to become steel and concrete themselves—and that is what happens in the gruesomely fascinating images of *Tetsuo II: Body Hammer.*

The movie has many points in common with the original *Tetsuo* (1989), a black-and-white cult classic that became a fetish for some fans. The second film is not a sequel so much as another run at the same material, this time with more money, better special effects, and color (although the palate is mostly limited to dark grays and blues). Tsukamoto has an image in his mind of a human terrifyingly morphed into a machine and a weapon, and he creates nightmarish visions from this idea with only the most casual attention to plot.

The story involves a salaryman named Taniguchi (Tomoroh Taguchi), sort of a Clark Kent wearing horn-rimmed glasses and a neatly pressed shirt, whose child is kidnapped by skinhead cyborgs. Pursuing them, he mysteriously undergoes an experience in which his flesh mates with steel, and his body undergoes a transformation into a fearsome creature that looks like a dirty concrete block with arms and guns extruding from it, and exhaust pipes for ribs.

Tetsuo II doesn't rise (or stoop) to the level of conventional action or suspense; it's a design concept, a director's attempt to take some of the ideas in *Blade Runner* and some of the Schwarzenegger films and the Japanese animated films like *Akira* and extend them into grotesquerie. Japanese art has since the earliest times been fascinated by the possibilities in shape-changing, in creatures who take first one form and then another. Here we have the changes forced upon the ordinary hero by the very terms of his environment: Tokyo has reached some sort of critical mass in which flesh and steel combine, just as atomic reactions are created in the center of the Sun.

The movie's look is grim and grungy—heavy metal punk cyber-surrealism with undertones of S&M. Dialogue is scattered here and there, mostly in the form of cries, threats, and imprecations, but the bulk of the film consists of horrific confrontations between Taniguchi and his persecutors (led by Tsukamoto himself). There is an odd flashback, late in the film, that provides some sort of psychological underpinning for the events, but it's superfluous: Tsukamoto is painting a canvas, not a narrative, here—the vision is as complex, detailed, and obsessive as a painting by Bosch.

I assume that some of the shots are animation, or involve animation, but I can't be sure. Much of the action takes place at night, or in shadow, or in rain, and a typical shot will show a cyborg mutant monster lumbering piteously toward us, helpless to do anything except kill and maim. The film plays like an extended heavy-metal music video, and the sound track, insidious and hypnotic, is part of the effect.

Does *Tetsuo II: Body Hammer* succeed? Those who see it are not likely to forget it, and its images will linger as a warning of postapocalyptic urban critical mass. We already act for several hours every day like the extensions of our automobiles, telephones, computers, and television sets, so I suppose it is only a matter of time until we also take architecture and weaponry on board, and join Tsukamoto's future. It looks more like fate than destiny, but you can't have everything.

That Old Feeling ★

PG-13, 105 m., 1997

Bette Midler (Lilly), Dennis Farina (Dan), Paula Marshall (Molly), Gail O'Grady (Rowena), David Rasche (Alan), Jamie Denton (Keith), Danny Nucci (Joey). Directed by Carl Reiner and produced by Leslie Dixon and Bonnie Bruckheimer. Screenplay by Dixon.

Remember those little Scotty dogs kids used to play with? They were glued to magnets. If you pointed them one way, they jumped toward each other, and if you pointed them the opposite way, they jumped apart. Carl Reiner's *That Old Feeling* is an entire movie based on the dance of the Scotty dogs, and the characters in it act as mechanically as if they had big magnets strapped to their thighs.

The premise: A senator's son (Jamie Denton) gets engaged to the daughter (Paula Marshall) of a movie star and a journalist. He wants a big wedding. Her parents have been divorced for fifteen years and both have remarried. He insists on inviting everyone. She warns against it: "My parents hate each other with a nuclear capacity."

She is right. In no time at all her parents (Bette Midler and Dennis Farina) are insulting each other on the dance floor ("I could have had the entire rock 'n' roll hall of fame!" Bette shouts. "I turned down a Beatle for you."). This is, of course, painful to their current spouses: Farina's wife (Gail O'Grady) and Midler's husband (David Rasche). But not nearly as disturbing as when the fighting couple suddenly fall into each other's arms.

Okay. So now we have Farina and Midler fighting and loving and fighting and loving. The wheezy screenplay by Leslie Dixon now works out the other combinations with almost mathematical precision. First it must be established that the young groom is a prig. Then the plot must contrive to lock the bride into a hotel room with a paparazzo (Danny Nucci) who has been following her movie-star mother. Then Farina's wife must get drunk with the groom, with predictable consequences.

And so on. There is not a moment that is believable, but of course the movie is not intended as realism. It is intended as comedy. So consider this "funny" scene: Marshall and Nucci, locked in the hotel room, try to attract attention by dropping fruit from a balcony. Cops see them, but nod indulgently and walk on. Jeez. So the two continue to drop fruit, finally dropping a whole lot of fruit. End of scene, with a whole lot of fruit on the sidewalk. At least when David Letterman was dropping watermelons off of buildings he showed them hitting the sidewalk in slow motion.

What's in slow motion here is the progress of the plot. Every development is exhausting because we have arrived at it long, long before the characters. There are only two saving graces. One is that Bette Midler sings "Somewhere Along the Way" to Farina in a piano bar, very nicely. The other is that David Rasche has some funny dialogue. He is a self-help counselor with smarmy little slogans at his command: "It is important to dialogue and to language each other," he says, and he recommends "emotional valet parking" and says to Farina's wife: "Is any part of your body original? You are so at odds with your shadow self."

I liked his dialogue because it was smart and satirical. I liked the two young actors—Denton and Marshall—because they were fresh and appealing. Hell, I liked Farina and Midler too. I liked everyone: O'Grady, Nucci . . . make a list. They all seemed way too nice to have done anything to deserve this screenplay.

The Theory of Flight ★ ★ ½

R, 100 m., 1999

Helena Bonham Carter (Jane), Kenneth Branagh (Richard), Gemma Jones (Anne), Holly Aird (Julie). Directed by Peter Greengrass and produced by Ruth Caleb, Anant Singh, Helena Spring, and David Thompson. Screenplay by Richard Hawkins.

Godard said that the best way to criticize a movie is to make another movie. That has already been done in the case of *The Theory of Flight*, a British film about a young woman in a wheelchair who desperately desires to have sex. The movie that eclipses this one is *Dance Me to My Song*, an Australian film that played in 1998 at the Cannes Film Festival and silenced the audience with its stark courage. (It still lacks American distribution.)

The Theory of Flight stars Helena Bonham Carter as Jane, the young woman in the chair, who suffers from ALS and uses a voice synthesizer to help her communicate. It is a good performance—but just that, a performance. What is astonishing about *Dance Me to My Song* is that it was written by a young woman named Heather Rose, who has cerebral palsy, lives in a chair, communicates with a machine—and actually plays Julia, the heroine of her movie.

To compare Jane and Julia is not fair, since neither film could have known about the other and both are good-hearted. But I will do it anyway. Jane, the Bonham-Carter character, has had bad luck with her helpers, until she draws the quirky Richard (Kenneth Branagh), an artist who has been assigned to her after being sentenced to community service for having caused a lot of trouble when he jumped off a building with homemade wings.

Compare that idealized situation with the plight of Julia, in the Australian movie. Her disease is so advanced she can barely move, and she has been assigned a series of empty-headed and cruel companions who steal her money and let her lie in her own messes while they chatter on the phone.

Jane wants sex, and informs Richard by playing a little speech that she has programmed into her synthesizer. "Help me lose my virginity," she says. "I know realistically I'll never get the whole deal. But that doesn't mean I shouldn't get as much as I can."

For Julia it is not that easy (not that it is easy for Jane). She is a virtual captive of her apartment, has no way to meet other people, and in an astonishing sequence takes things into her own hands. Using her battery-powered chair, she escapes from her house and onto the sidewalk, where she accosts a young man and begins, in her own way, to seduce him. Consider that Heather Rose plays all of these scenes herself, without doubles, and is cruelly handicapped in speech and movement, and you will begin to guess how powerful it all becomes.

Both young women are frank in their speech. They like four-letter words, which growl out of their synthesizers like Stephen Hawking on a bad day. Both of their targets are at first disbelieving, then reluctant. And so on. Enough of the plots.

Recently I have been getting a lot of flak from readers who object to my review of *Patch Adams*, the Robin Williams film. How can I dislike this film, they ask, when its message is so heartwarming? The movie argues that doctors must care more for their patients, they inform me, and that laughter is the best medicine. Some of the letters are from people whose loved ones are critically ill, and have either endured impersonal medical treatment, or benefited from doctors and nurses who do care.

I agree with these correspondents that laughter is the best medicine. I agree that the personal touch is invaluable in the healing professions. But they have confused the message with the movie. Who could disagree with the sentiments in *Patch Adams*? And what do they have to do with the film's shameless and manipulative cynicism? I write back: "Remember, it's not what the movie is about—it's *how* it's about it!"

I wish I could rent a theater and show these good people a double feature of *The Theory of Flight* and *Dance Me to My Song*. Here are two movies that are essentially about the same thing. The British film uses big stars and cutes everything up (much of the plot involves whether Branagh can build a flying machine, and whether he and the young woman can overcome their personal versions of fear of flying). The Australian film is an act of the will by a cerebral palsy sufferer whose own achievement is even greater than her heroine's. (As anyone in Hollywood can tell you, it is a lot easier to get someone to sleep with you than to get a screenplay produced.)

The Theory of Flight is actually fairly enjoyable. At least it doesn't drown its message in syrup and cornball sentiment like *Patch Adams.* It has a lot of refreshing humor. But then, when you see the real thing, when you see *Dance Me to My Song,* you're struck by the difference. Two movies. Same story. Same objective. Similar characters. Similar situation. One is an entertainment. The other is a thunderbolt.

There's Something About Mary ★ ★ ★

R, 119 m., 1998

Ben Stiller (Ted), Cameron Diaz (Mary), Matt Dillon (Healy), Chris Elliott (Dom), W. Earl Brown (Warren), Lee Evans (Tucker), Lin Shaye (Magda), Jeffrey Tambor (Sully). Directed by Peter Farrelly and Bobby Farrelly and produced by Bradley Thomas, Charles Wessler, Frank Beddor, Michael Steinberg, and Mark S. Fischer. Screenplay by Ed Decter, John J. Strauss, and the Farrellys.

What a blessed relief is laughter. It flies in the face of manners, values, political correctness, and decorum. It exposes us for what we are, the only animal with a sense of humor. *There's Something About Mary* is an unalloyed exercise in bad taste, and contains five or six explosively funny sequences. Okay, five explosive, one moderate.

I love it when a movie takes control, sweeps away my doubts and objections, and compels me to laugh. I'm having a physical reaction, not an intellectual one. There's such freedom in laughing so loudly. I feel cleansed.

There's Something About Mary is the latest work by Peter and Bobby Farrelly, brothers whose earlier credits include *Dumb and Dumber* and *Kingpin.* Good taste is not their strong suit. *Dumb and Dumber* included a scene where a blind boy realizes his parakeet's head is held on with Scotch tape. *Kingpin* includes a scene where a bowler's artificial hand gets stuck in the ball and rolls down the alley, flop-flop-flop.

Now here is a movie about a woman who is beautiful, sunny, good, and pure, and inspires a remarkable array of creeps to fall into love with her. There's . . . just something about her. Mary is played by Cameron Diaz as a high school knockout who amazes the geeky Ted (Ben Stiller) by asking him to the prom even though he has pounds of braces on his teeth. ("I have a thing about braces," she muses, long after.)

Ted turns up proudly for the date, only to set off the first of the movie's uproariously funny sequences when he asks to use the toilet and then somehow catches in his zipper that part of the male anatomy one least wants to think about in connection with zippers. ("Is it the frank or the beans?" asks Mary's solicitous stepfather.)

In a lesser film, that would be that: The directors would expect us to laugh at his misfortune and the plot would roll on. Not the Farrelly brothers. When they get something going, they keep on building, daring themselves to top each outrage. I won't reveal how the scene develops, apart from noting the perfect timing involved with the unexpected close-up.

Thirteen years pass. Ted is still in love with Mary. He hires a sleazy investigator named Healy (Matt Dillon) to track her down. Healy, wearing one of those mustaches that shout "Distrust me!" finds her in Miami, discovers she is an unbelievable babe who is still single, and decides to grab her for himself. He tells Ted she weighs 250 pounds, has four children by three fathers, and has just shipped out for Japan as a mail-order bride.

Healy's trick is to eavesdrop on Mary's conversations, so he'll know just what she wants to hear. Among the things most important to her is her retarded brother Warren (W. Earl Brown), who doesn't like to have his ears touched. Healy poses as the person of her dreams (an architect with a condo in Nepal, who loves to work with retarded people), but he raises the suspicions of another of her suitors, Tucker (Lee Evans), who is an architect who uses crutches. Maybe.

Further plot description would be pointless. The plot exists, like all screwball plots, simply to steer us from one gag to the next. In the TV ads you may already have seen the moment when the dog of Mary's deeply tanned neighbor needs to have its heart restarted.

That's because the dog has been tranquilized. There is also a scene where the dog is on speed, and his human target does things with walls and furniture not seen since Donald O'Connor's "Make 'em Laugh" sequence in *Singin' in the Rain.*

Then there are the peculiar and intimate preparations Ted goes through in anticipation of his first date with Mary. I have paused here at the keyboard for many minutes, trying to decide how to describe them (a) in a family newspaper, and (b) without spoiling the fun. I cannot. I will simply observe in admiration that after the scene explodes in disbelieving, prolonged laughter, the Farrellys find a way to blindside us with a completely unanticipated consequence that sets us off all over again.

Among the other characters in the movie are Chris Elliott, as Dom, a friend of Ted's, who has a nervous eczema condition ("Do you know what it feels like to have a whitehead on your eyeball?"), and Magda (Lin Shaye), the neighbor whose tan makes her look like she's been put through the same process that produces Slim Jims. Magda is funny in a bizarre, over-the-top way, but Dom is more creepy than funny, or is it just that we're afraid we'll catch his skin rash?

Stanley Kauffmann, the great film critic of the *New Republic,* was on Charlie Rose's show the other night, sharing the discoveries of forty years as a film critic. What he has noticed over the years, he said, is that we are getting more good dramatic films than in the old days—but fewer good entertainments. It is easier to excel at drama than at comedy. I have no idea if Kauffmann will like *There's Something About Mary,* but his point applies for me: After months and months of comedies that did not make me laugh, here at last is one that did. ☞

The Thief ★★★

R, 97 m., 1998

Vladimir Mashkov (Tolyan), Ekatarina Rednikova (Katia), Misha Philipchuk (Sanya). Directed by Pavel Chukhrai and produced by Igor Tolstunov. Screenplay by Chukhrai.

It is clear fairly early in *The Thief* that the title character represents Stalin, and it's one of the strengths of the film that the symbolism never gets in the way of a convincing, heartbreaking story. The movie, one of the 1998 Oscar nominees for Best Foreign Film, never pushes too hard to make its point, but what's clear in every frame is the sense of hopelessness and betrayal in the years after World War II.

The movie is told through the eyes of Sanya, who is born on the roadside to a homeless mother in 1946, the first year of the Cold War. He is six when he and his mother are approached on a train by a man named Tolyan, who is dressed as an army officer and may once have been one—or perhaps not. Nothing about him is trustworthy, a lesson the mother and boy learn through many hard lessons.

"Uncle" Tolyan is a charming, mustachioed man, tall and robust in a land where many citizens seem weak, ill, and hungry. It takes money to be healthy, and Tolyan is a thief—not only of money and possessions, but also of hearts. The mother, Katia (Ekatarina Rednikova), falls for him almost on sight, but of course her situation is desperate and there are sound Darwinian reasons for choosing a healthy, strong mate when you are unable to provide for yourself and your child. He looks like shelter from the poverty and hopelessness of 1952.

For the boy (Misha Philipchuk), it is a little more complicated. He often has visions of his real father, who died before he was born but speaks to him and promises to return soon. Yet all little boys are impressed by soldiers, and when Tolyan (Vladimir Mashkov) asks Sanya to look after his revolver, the boy's eyes grow as wide as saucers. Soon the three are living together as a family, and the boy enters into an uneasy mixture of fear, respect, and love for the man.

Tolyan, it is true, is a charmer. He is popular in the series of boardinghouses where they take a room, or part of a flat, and meals are often communal affairs fueled by vodka. He likes to propose toasts to Stalin, and encourage the others to get drunk, and then steal into their apartments. It is not unknown for the mother and boy to get urgent messages to meet him, immediately, at the train station, and they live a nomadic existence. The army uniform and Tolyan's ability to bluff are protections against identity checks and police questions. So are his "wife" and "son."

The movie proceeds in two fronts. We gradually learn more about the real nature of Tolyan and his criminal activities, and at the same time the relationships among the three people deepen and grow more complicated. Sanya in particular is conflicted. He indulges the fantasy that his real father will return. He resents Tolyan for being a fake, a thief, and a philanderer. And yet he admires him, too, and feels both shame and pride when the man uses him to squeeze through a small window and open a flat to be burgled.

Behind, beneath, around everything is the everyday reality of life in Stalin's Russia. The most touching sequence in the movie shows a transfer of prisoners from a district prison to transport that will take them to Siberia. Their friends and relatives wait in the snow for a glimpse of them. The prisoners are released from jail and sent running down a gauntlet of men and dogs, as their loved ones shout out desperate messages.

Did ordinary Russians think of Stalin the way Sanya thinks of Tolyan? As a big, bluff provider who would protect them—as a liar and a thief, but not without charm? That is the implication lurking in every frame of *The Thief*, but the movie works because it doesn't insist on the parallels. And the final sequence, of disillusionment and betrayal, is the saddest, because in it Tolyan is finally reduced to telling the truth.

The Thin Red Line ★ ★ ★

R, 170 m., 1999

Sean Penn (First Sergeant Welsh), Adrien Brody (Corporal Fife), Nick Nolte (Lieutenant Colonel Tall), Jim Caviezel (Private Witt), John Cusack (Captain Gaff), George Clooney (Captain Bosche), Ben Chaplin (Private Bell), Woody Harrelson (Sergeant Keck), Elias Koteas (Captain Staros), John Travolta (Brigadier General Quintard). Directed by Terrence Malick and produced by Robert Michael Geisler, John Roberdeau, and Grant Hill. Screenplay by Malick, based on the novel by James Jones.

The actors in *The Thin Red Line* are making one movie, and the director is making another. This leads to an almost hallucinatory sense of displacement, as the actors struggle for realism, and the movie's point of view hovers above them like a high school kid all filled with big questions. My guess is that any veteran of the actual battle of Guadalcanal would describe this movie with an eight-letter word much beloved in the army.

The movie's schizophrenia keeps it from greatness (this film has no firm idea of what it is about), but doesn't make it bad. It is, in fact, sort of fascinating: a film in the act of becoming, a field trial, an experiment in which a dreamy poet meditates on stark reality. It's like horror seen through the detachment of drugs or dementia. The sound track allows us to hear the thoughts of the characters, but there is no conviction that these characters would have these thoughts. They all seem to be musing in the same voice, the voice of a man who is older, more educated, more poetic and less worldly than any of these characters seem likely to be. The voice of the director.

Terrence Malick is the director of two of the best films I have ever seen, *Badlands* (1973) and *Days of Heaven* (1978). *The Thin Red Line* feels like an extension of the second film, in which a narrator muses on the underlying tragedy that is sometimes shown on the screen, sometimes implied. Both films are founded on a transcendental sense that all natural things share their underlying reality in the mind of God. The film opens with a question: "Why does nature contend with itself?" It shows a crocodile, a killing machine. Later, as men prove more deadly than crocodiles, it shows a bird, its wing shattered by gunfire, pulling itself along the ground. In a way the film is not about war at all, but simply about the way in which all living beings are founded on the necessity of killing one another (and eating one another, either literally or figuratively).

The film opens with an idyll on a Pacific island. Two soldiers have gone AWOL and live blissfully with tribal people who exist in a prelapsarian state, eating the fruit that falls from the trees and the fish that leap from the seas, and smiling contentedly at the bounty of Eden. This is, the movie implies, a society that reflects man's best nature. But reality interrupts when the two soldiers are captured and returned to their army company for the assault on a crucial hill on Guadalcanal.

During the battle scenes, there will be flashbacks to the island idyll—and other flashbacks as a solider remembers his love for his wife. Against these simple pleasures is stacked the ideology of war, as expressed by a colonel (Nick Nolte) who read Homer at West Point ("in Greek") and is intoxicated to be in battle at last after having studied it so long. The plot of the second act of the film involves the taking of a well-defended hill, and the colonel prefers that it be attacked in a frontal assault; a captain (Elias Koteas) resists this plan as suicidal, and is right from a strategic point of view but wrong when viewed through the colonel's blood lust: "You are not gonna take your men around in the jungle to avoid a goddamn fight."

The soldiers are not well developed as individual characters. Covered in grime and blood, they look much alike, and we strain to hear their names, barked out mostly in one syllable (Welsh, Fife, Tall, Witt, Gaff, Bosche, Bell, Keck, Staros). Sometimes during an action we are not sure who we are watching, and have to piece it together afterward. I am sure battle is like that, but I'm not sure that was Malick's point: I think he was just not much interested in the destinies and personalities of individual characters.

It was not this way in the novel by James Jones, which inspired the screenplay. Jones drew his characters sharply, and indicated the ways in which each acted according to his ability and personality; his novel could have been filmed by Spielberg in the style of *Saving Private Ryan*. Malick's movie sees it more as a crapshoot. For defying his superior officers, the captain is offered first a court-martial, later a Silver Star, and then a Purple Heart. It is all the same. He is also transferred stateside by the colonel, and instead of insisting on staying with his men, he confesses he is rather happy to be going. This is not a movie of conventional war clichés.

The battle scenes themselves are masterful in creating a sense of the geography of a particular hill, the way it is defended by Japanese bunkers, the ways in which the American soldiers attempt to take it. The camera crouches low in the grass, and as Malick focuses on locusts or blades of grass, we are reminded that a battle like this must have taken place with the soldiers' eyes inches from the ground. The Japanese throughout are totally depersonalized (in one crucial scene, their language is not even translated with subtitles); they aren't seen as enemies, so much as necessary antagonists—an expression of nature's compulsion to "contend with itself." (One wonders what murky philosophical voice-over questions were floating above the Japanese soldiers in *The Thin Red Line*. Were they also dreaming about nature, immortality, humanity, and death?)

Actors like Sean Penn, John Cusack, Jim Caviezel, and Ben Chaplin find the perfect tone for scenes of a few seconds or a minute, and then are dropped before a rhythm can be established. We get the sense that we are rejoining characters in the middle of interrupted actions. Koteas and Nolte come the closest to creating rounded performances, and Woody Harrelson has a good death scene; actors like John Travolta and George Clooney are on screen so briefly they don't have time to seem like anything other than guest stars.

The central intelligence in the film doesn't belong to any of the characters, or even to their voice-over philosophies. It belongs to Malick, whose ideas about war are heartfelt but not profound; the questions he asks are inescapable, but one wonders if soldiers in combat ever ask them (one guesses they ask themselves what they should do next, and how in the hell they can keep themselves from being shot). It's as if the film, long in preproduction, drifted away from the Jones novel (which was based on Jones's personal combat experience) and into a meditation not so much on war, as on film. Aren't most of the voice-over observations really not about war, but about war films? About their materials and rationales, about why one would make them, and what one would hope to say?

Any film that can inspire thoughts like these is worth seeing. But the audience has to finish the work: Malick isn't sure where he's going or what he's saying. That may be a good thing. If a question has no answer, it is not useful to be supplied with one. Still, one leaves the theater bemused by what seems to be a universal law: While most war films are "antiwar," they are always antiwar from the point of view of the winning side. They say, "War is hell, and we won." Shouldn't antiwar films be told from the point of view of the losers? War was hell, and they lost. ☞

This Is My Father ★ ★ ★
R, 120 m., 1999

Aidan Quinn (Kieran O'Day), Moya Farrelly (Fiona Flynn), James Caan (Kieran Johnson), Gina Moxley (Mary Flynn), Colm Meaney (Seamus), Moira Deady (Mrs. Kearney), Stephen Rea (Father Quinn), John Cusack (Eddie Sharp, the Pilot), Brendan Gleeson (Officer Jim). Directed by Paul Quinn and produced by Nicolas Clermont and Philip King.

On my first trip to Ireland, in 1967, I was taken to a party after the pubs closed. There were bottles of whiskey and Guinness stout, someone had a concertina, and there was a singsong. In the bedroom, a couple was making out. Eventually they emerged to join the party, and I noticed that, to my young eyes, they were "old"—in their forties.

On the way home, I asked my friend McHugh about that, and he explained that they had been engaged for fifteen years, that they were putting off marriage until the man made more money, and until "family matters" got sorted out. Necking at parties was undoubtedly the extent of their sex lives, since intercourse before marriage was a mortal sin. I said I thought it was sad that two middle-aged people, who had loved each other since they were young, had put their lives on hold. "Welcome to Ireland," he said.

It is not like that anymore in Ireland, where some of the old customs have died with startling speed. But that is the Ireland remembered in *This Is My Father*, a film about lives ruled by guilt, fear, prejudice, and dour family pride. For every cheerful Irish comedy about free spirits with quick wits, there is a story like this one, about characters sitting in dark rooms, ruminating on old grudges and fresh resentments, and using the rules of the church, when convenient, as justification for their own spites and dreads.

The movie is said to be based on a true family story and has been made by Chicago's Quinn brothers. Aidan Quinn stars as an orphaned tenant farmer who falls in love with the daughter of the woman who owns the land he works. Paul Quinn directs. Declan Quinn, the cinematographer, is known for such work as *Leaving Las Vegas*. It is so much a family project that there is even a role for a friend, John Cusack, who drops in out of the sky in a small plane, lands on the beach, and figures in a scene as charming as it is irrelevant.

The heart of the story involves Kieran O'Day (Aidan Quinn) and Fiona Flynn (Moya Farrelly), who fall passionately in love in 1939. He is an orphan, being raised by a tenant couple named the Maneys (Donal Donnelly and Maria McDermottroe) on land owned by Fiona's mother, Mary (Gina Moxley). The mother has fierce pride, not improved by a drinking problem, and looks down on her neighbors. Of course she opposes a liaison between her daughter and a tenant.

This story is told in flashback. In the present day, we meet a sad, tired high school teacher (James Caan) whose mother is dying and whose life is going nowhere. He determines to go back to Ireland and search for his roots. In the village where his mother came from, he finds an old gypsy woman (Moira Deady) who remembers with perfect clarity everything that happened in 1939, and triggers the flashbacks. The modern story is almost not essential (we forget Caan in the midst of the flashback), but it does trigger a happy ending in which much is explained.

The key element in the romance between Kieran and Fiona, and the one that reminded me of my first visit to Ireland, is the way their sex lives are ruled by others, whose own real motives are masked under the cover of church law. Mrs. Flynn is spiteful, mean, and bitter, or she would find a way for her daughter to be happy. Kieran's love is all the more poignant because he sincerely believes himself to be an occasion of sin for Fiona, and castigates himself for endangering her immortal soul.

Fiona's mother pays lip service to the church, but her real motives are fueled by class prejudice and social climbing, and there is a cruel moment when she accuses Kieran of molesting her daughter. She also threatens the Maneys, who have raised him, with the loss of their land and livelihood. One scene which rings true to life is the way the village policemen, negotiating a tricky path between the laws of this world and the next, give Kieran broad hints about their plans for eventually arresting him—should he still be in the vicinity, of course. Sensibly, he is not, but the cost of his freedom is his happiness, and that price is underlined by a message which the Caan character discovers, and delivers several decades too late.

I believe *This Is My Father* is indeed based on true family stories (or legends, which are the same thing), because it insists on details that are more important to the narrator than to the listener. The entire construction of the Caan character, for example, is explained no doubt by a relative's visit back to the old country. The story might have been simpler, sadder, and sweeter if it had taken place entirely in 1939—but like all stories, it belongs to the teller, not the subject.

A Thousand Acres ★★

R, 104 m., 1997

Michelle Pfeiffer (Rose Cook Lewis), Jessica Lange (Ginny Cook Smith), Jason Robards (Larry Cook), Jennifer Jason Leigh (Caroline Cook), Colin Firth (Jess Clark), Keith Carradine (Ty Smith), Kevin Anderson (Peter Lewis), Pat Hingle (Harold Clarke). Directed by Jocelyn Moorhouse and produced by Marc Abraham, Lynn Arost, Steve Golin, Kate Guinzburg, and Sigurjon Sighvatsson. Screenplay by Laura Jones, based on the novel by Jane Smiley.

A Thousand Acres is an ungainly, undigested assembly of "women's issues," milling about within a half-baked retread of *King Lear*. The film is so unfocused that at the end of its very long 104 minutes, I was unable to say who I was supposed to like and who I was supposed to hate—although I could name several characters for whom I had no feelings at all.

The movie is set on the 1,000-acre Cook farm in Iowa, where the weathered and wise old patriarch, Larry (Jason Robards), is the most powerful farmer for miles around. Then he announces he has decided to retire and to divide his farm into three parts, giving shares to each of his daughters.

That's fine with Rose (Michelle Pfeiffer) and Ginny (Jessica Lange), who are married farm women—but Larry's youngest and most favored daughter, Caroline (Jennifer Jason Leigh), a lawyer, questions the wisdom of the plan. Larry instantly disowns her and later slams a door in her face, and as the other two daughters and their husbands begin running the farm, we figure it's only a matter of time until old Larry is out there in a raging storm, cursing the heavens.

We are correct, but *A Thousand Acres* wants only to borrow plot elements of *King Lear*, not to face up to its essentials. We are denied even the old man's heartbreaking deathbed scene—that goes to one of the daughters after her second bout with breast cancer. The movie repeats the currently fashionable pattern in which men are bad and fathers are the most evil of all; there is not a single positive male character in the movie, unless you count the preacher who says grace before the church supper.

The husbands of the two older daughters, indeed, are written so thinly that when one of them (Kevin Anderson) kills himself, we're not sure why (until it's belatedly explained) and don't much care, and when the other (Keith Carradine) goes off to Texas to work on a hog farm, his wife scarcely seems to notice he's gone. Along the way, in a development so badly handled it seems to belong in another movie, Caroline gets married in Des Moines and lets her sisters find out about it only through a wedding announcement in the local weekly; as nearly as I can recall, we never meet her husband, nor is he ever referred to again.

All white male patriarchs must be guilty of something in modern women's fiction, preferably the sexual abuse of their children, and I was not surprised to find out that Larry visited the bedrooms of Rose and Ginny. Rose describes the visits in lurid detail, but Ginny cannot remember, although they took place as late as her sixteenth year; her memory lapse, I think, serves to prolong the breathless scenes of description. ("Daddy might be a drinker and a rager," Ginny says, "but he goes to church!") The youngest daughter was apparently not molested, maybe because (in the movie's laborious Lear parallels) she was the most favored.

Among the other subjects dutifully ticked off are a husband's rejection of his wife after she has a mastectomy; a woman who has five miscarriages because no one told her the local drinking water was poisoned with pesticides; the alcoholism of the father and one of the husbands; the inadequate sexual performance of both husbands; the betrayal of Rose and Ginny by a handsome neighbor man (Colin Firth), who is such a cad he sleeps with both of them but tells only one about the other; and a man who buys a tractor that is three times bigger than he needs—a clear case of phallic compensation. Toward the end we get the tragedy of Alzheimer's, the heartlessness of banks, the problem of unnecessary lawsuits, and the obligatory "giant agricultural conglomerate."

All of these subjects are valid and promising and could be well-handled in a better movie. In *A Thousand Acres*, alas, they seem like items on a checklist. The movie is so distracted by both the issues and the Lear parallels that the characters bolt from one knee-jerk situation to the next.

Then there is the problem of where to place our sympathy. In *King Lear*, of course, we love Lear and his daughter Cordelia, and hate the two older sisters and their husbands. In *A Thousand Acres*, it cannot be permitted for a man to be loved or a woman to be hated, and so we have the curious spectacle of the two older sisters being portrayed as somehow favorably unfavorable, while the youngest, by eventually siding with her father, becomes a study in tortured plotting: She is good because she's a woman, suspect because she's a lawyer, bad because she sues the others, forgiven because her father evolves from monstrous to merely pathetic. Many of the closing scenes are set in a courtroom, providing the curious experience of a movie legal case in which the audience neither understands the issues nor cares which side wins.

The movie is narrated by Ginny, the Lange character, apparently in an effort to impose a point of view where none exists. But why Ginny? Is she better than the others? At the end of the film she intones in a solemn voice-over: "I've often thought that the death of a parent is the one misfortune for which there is no compensation." Say what? She doesn't remember her mother and is more than reconciled to the death of a father who (thanks to recovered memory) she now knows molested her. What compensation could she hope for, short of stealing him from his deathbed to hang him on a gallows?

A Thousand Acres is so misconceived it should almost be seen just to appreciate the winding road it travels through sexual politics. Many of the individual scenes are well acted (Michelle Pfeiffer and Jessica Lange are luminous in their three most important scenes together). But the film substitutes prejudices for ideas, formula feminism for character studies, and a signposted plot for a well-told story. The screenplay is based on a novel by Jane Smiley, unread by me, which won the Pulitzer Prize—which means that either the novel or the prize has been done a great injustice.

Three Lives and Only One Death

★★★

NO MPAA RATING, 123 m., 1997

Marcello Mastroianni (Mateo, Georges, Butler, Luc), Anna Galiena (Tania), Marisa Paredes (Maria), Melvil Poupaud (Martin), Chiara Mastroianni (Cecile), Arielle Dombasle (Helene), Feodor Atkine (Andre), Jacques Pieller (Tania's Husband), Jean-Yves Gautier (Mario), Pierre Bellemare (Radio Narrator), Lou Castel (Bum). Directed by Raul Ruiz and produced by Paulo Branco. Screenplay by Ruiz and Pascal Bonitzer.

I never tire of quoting Godard, who said the way to criticize a movie is to make another movie. For those left unsatisfied by David Lynch's *Lost Highway*, I offer Raul Ruiz's *Three Lives and Only One Death*. The fact that they both opened in Chicago on the same day was one of those serendipitous events that, according to Ruiz, happens all the time.

Three Lives stars Marcello Mastroianni in one of the last and most enchanting of his screen appearances. As if aware that time was running out, he plays four roles—or so we think, although by the end we learn there was perhaps only one. In a series of stories that first seem separate and then seem entwined, Mastroianni plays a man who shifts roles, costumes, and identities as readily as a street performer, moving effortlessly through his many lives.

In *Lost Highway*, one character disappears halfway through the film and another appears. How this happens and whether the characters are related (or perhaps are even the same person) I leave for you to discover—not because I hesitate to reveal the plot, but because I do not understand it. *Three Lives and Only One Death* is more complicated, but also more understandable; its complications are not added out of whimsy or the desire to frustrate, but as part of Ruiz's delightful storytelling game.

The first part of the film could be a story by Kafka; a man named Andre (Feodor Atkine) wakes up feeling out of sorts, says good-bye to his wife and daughter, and wanders out in search of cigarettes. He meets an engaging stranger (Mastroianni) who buttonholes him, plies him with champagne, and even pays him 1,000 francs an hour just to listen to his story.

And what a story. "I lived in your apartment twenty years ago," Mastroianni tells the man. "But," the man says, "my wife was living there then, with her first husband. . . ." Exactly. Mastroianni was the first husband. And now he wants to take up where he left off, back before . . . before . . . well, it's hard to explain precisely what happened, but it involves another apartment he moved into, one with strangely shifting walls and ceilings, which was inhabited by tiny fairies living in speeded-up time. When Andre doesn't seem eager to trade his own apartment for this magic place, he ends up with a hammer embedded in his head. Although this is not immediately fatal, it certainly indicates which way the wind is blowing.

The second story involves a man (Mastroianni again) who lectures at the Sorbonne. One day on his way to class he pauses, thinks, and abandons his teaching career to become a beggar. He is assaulted and then befriended by a prostitute, although it turns out she is not who, or what, she appears to be, either. (I like the moment when the professor's demanding mother spies on him through binoculars and discovers he makes more as a beggar than as a professor.)

In the third story, a young couple (played by Melvil Poupaud and Chiara Mastroianni, who is Mastroianni's daughter by Catherine Deneuve) receive a mysterious offer to occupy a luxurious chateau, where they are waited on by a butler (Mastroianni). And then there is a concluding segment in which a wealthy industrialist (Mastroianni) has invented a fictitious family, only to discover that its members are coming to visit him. It is here that the film reveals its overall plan: Perhaps Mastroianni has been playing only one man all of this time. Perhaps all of the roles were performances. Perhaps, I say. You tell me.

The movie has been compared to films by Luis Buñuel, the Spanish surrealist who loved to tell matter-of-fact stories about ordinary people who tried to behave in an everyday way while finding themselves in extraordinary circumstances. There is a bit of Buñuel here, and a little of *Groundhog Day,* too: Mastroianni's characters are never anything but sweet, calm, and reasonable as they negotiate life's bizarre twists. The movie works in two ways. Each of the "stories" has its own interior logic and charm. And then the overall picture, as it gradually develops, adds level upon mysterious level.

Ruiz seems to be an altogether more mature and complete filmmaker than the Lynch of *Lost Highway.* He is not simply toying with paradoxes and mysteries, but arranging them lovingly into a wicked pattern. Both directors are playing games, but Ruiz knows the rules. Comparing the two films, I am struck by the way both involve sexuality and violence, but in Ruiz such elements grow naturally out of the characters' lives, while in Lynch there is a rush toward lurid melodrama: pounding *noir* music, ominous rumbles, screams, distorted close-ups, fires, stabbings, shootings, rapes, sexual humiliation, all burying the characters beneath a flood of exhibitionism. Ruiz has more confidence in his story—and, it must be said, in his technique.

Three Seasons ★ ★ ★

PG-13, 113 m., 1999

Don Duong (Hai [Cyclo Driver]), Nguyen Ngoc Hiep (Kien An), Tran Manh Cuong (Teacher Dao), Harvey Keitel (James Hager), Zoe Bui (Lan), Nguyen Huu Duoc (Woody [Peddler]), Minh Ngoc (Truck Driver), Hoang Phat Trieu (Huy). Directed by Tony Bui and produced by Jason Kliot, Joana Vicente, and Tony Bui. Screenplay by Tony Bui, based on a story by Tony Bui and Timothy Linh Bui.

We require Asia to be ancient, traditional, and mysterious. It fills a need. We don't want to know that Hong Kong is a trade capital and Japan is an economic giant. We're looking for Shangri-La, for the sentimental fantasies of generations of Western writers who fell for the romantic idea of the East—and centuries of Eastern writers who did too.

Three Seasons, filmed in Ho Chi Minh City by Tony Bui, a twenty-six-year-old American born in Vietnam, allows us to enjoy fantasies which, in America, would be politically incorrect. Like the best-selling *Memoirs of a Geisha*, it romanticizes prostitution, makes poverty picturesque, transforms hardship into fable. We do not approve of small boys working as street peddlers, of young women organized to sell flowers for a cult, of hookers servicing rich businessmen and snubbing their own people. But because *Three Seasons* is so languorously beautiful, because it has the sentiment of a Chaplin film, because exotic customs and settings are so seductive, we change the rules. What is wrong in Chicago becomes colorful, even enchanting, in the former Saigon.

I say all this as a disclaimer, because I'm certainly not above the pleasures of a film like *Three Seasons*. Taken as reporting, it shows deplorable conditions. Taken as a fable, it's enchanting. Art often offers us such bargains; it is better to attend *La Bohème* than to freeze in a garret. No wonder *Three Seasons* won everything in sight at Sundance: Grand Jury Prize, Audience Award, and Best Cinematography.

The movie takes place in a modern Vietnam that, at first, looks like the past. Beautiful young women in tiny flat-bottomed boats paddle in shallow waters among flower pads. As they pick white lotus blossoms, they sing. The scene is overshadowed by a dark temple that looks abandoned. "It is the Teacher's house," one of the new girls is told. "He has not left it for years. None of us have ever seen him."

The newcomer, named Kien An (Nguyen Ngoc Hiep), is trucked with the others into the city to sell their flowers. We meet some of the others who live there. Woody (Nguyen Huu Duoc) is a boy of nine or ten who sells gum and cigarettes from a box that hangs from a strap around his neck. Hai (Don Duong) drives a cyclo (a bicycle rickshaw) and hangs out with his buddies near the luxury hotels, where the towels must be perfumed because "everyone we drive from there has a fresh smell." Lan (Zoe Bui) is a prostitute who works the big hotels; she runs from a shop, leaps into Hai's cyclo, and asks him to step on it.

Then there's James Hager (Harvey Keitel), the mysterious American who has spent weeks sitting in an aluminum chair on a sidewalk, smoking and staring into space. His story is more modern. He left a daughter behind in Vietnam, and has come back to find her, and "maybe make some kind of peace with this place." (Keitel is the film's executive producer, once again lending his presence to a director's first film; no actor has put himself more on the line in support of young filmmakers.)

The interlocking stories of these characters remind us not only of Chaplinesque sentimentality, but also of the poor street people of Italian neorealist films like *Bicycle Thief* and *Shoeshine*, and of the languorous beauty of recent Asian films like *The Scent of Green Papaya* and *Raise the Red Lantern*. Lisa Rinzler's cinematography makes the city and surrounding countryside look poor but breathtakingly beautiful, and even sad shots, like the little peddler standing in the rain, have a kind of poetic grace.

Of the stories, the one I responded to most deeply involved the hooker and the cyclo driver, who loves and respects her. One day she says her dream is to spend the whole night in an air-conditioned room. He asks her price ($50), wins that much in a race for cyclo drivers, and treats her to her dream. She is grateful, but resists his further advances: She somehow feels she is not entitled to ordinary human emotion.

There are touching, somewhat contrived, revelations involving the unseen Teacher, whose teaching seems far in the past. The song of the new young girl reminds him of the songs of the floating market in his childhood, "the only time I was pure and whole." And she discovers his secrets. The outcome of the story involving the American G.I. is less effective, because we've seen such material before.

Three Seasons is extravagantly beautiful, especially in scenes where artifice is permitted, as when an unlikely shower of spring blossoms floats down from the sky. It's a remarkably ambitious work by the twenty-six-year-old Bui, who financed it on a shoestring but makes it look expensive. It arrives billed as the first

American fiction film shot entirely in postwar Vietnam; although Bui acknowledges his script had to win government approval, he was allowed to portray prostitution and poverty—perhaps because the city is seen not in a documentary way, but through the lens of fable. The result may not reflect the Vietnam of reality, but it's as close to life as most romantic melodramas, which is probably the point. And it's a lot more interesting.

'Til There Was You ★ ½

PG-13, 114 m., 1997

Jeanne Tripplehorn (Gwen), Dylan McDermott (Nick), Sarah Jessica Parker (Francesca), Jennifer Aniston (Debbie), Craig Bierko (Jon), Nina Foch (Sophia Monroe), Alice Drummond (Harriet), Christine Ebersole (Beebee). Directed by Scott Winant and produced by Penney Finkelman Cox, Tom Rosenberg, and Alan Poul. Screenplay by Winnie Holzman.

Here is the most tiresome and affected movie in many a moon, a 114-minute demonstration of the Idiot Plot, in which everything could be solved with a few well-chosen words that are never spoken. The underlying story is a simple one: A man and a woman who are obviously intended for each other are kept apart for an entire movie, only to meet at the end. We're supposed to be pleased when they get together, I guess, although the movie ends with such unseemly haste that we never get to experience them as a couple.

'Til There Was You, directed by Scott Winant with a screenplay by Winnie Holzman, plays like half-digested remnants of a dozen fictional meals. We have flashbacks to the love stories of parents, college love affairs, shocking revelations about sexuality and parentage, a maladjusted former sitcom star, an architect who is a "perfectionist with low self-esteem," a ghostwriter who falls in love with a colorful old apartment building, not one but two colorful old ladies who stick to their guns, a restaurant that's an architectural nightmare, zoning hearings, bad poetry, endlessly falling rose petals, chain-smoking, gays in the closet, traffic accidents, and at the end of it all we have the frustration of knowing that 114 minutes of our lives have been wasted, never to be returned.

Oh, and we have disastrous casting decisions. I find it helpful, as a general rule, to be able to tell the characters in a movie apart. Several of the characters in this film (a gay college professor, an architect, and another guy) look so much alike I was forever getting them confused. They were all sort of would-be Pierce Brosnan clones. Since the plot depends on coincidental meetings (and close misses) involving people who should know each other but don't, and people who do know each other but shouldn't, the look alikes grow even more confusing. The casting director no doubt thought that since several of the leads have appeared on TV sitcoms, the audience would recognize them and not be distracted by superficial physical similarities. Sorry.

The plot: A former sitcom star (Sarah Jessica Parker) owns a wonderful old apartment complex that has been earmarked for replacement by a condo. She begins to date the architect (Dylan McDermott) who will design the condo. His hero is an old lady architect (Nina Foch) who is apparently the Frank Lloyd Wright of her generation. She designed the colorful old apartment complex, but he doesn't know that. (How likely is it that an architect would be unfamiliar with one of his famous mentor's key buildings in the city where he lives? Not very.)

Meanwhile, a ghostwriter (Jeanne Tripplehorn) is hired by the sitcom star to write her autobiography. The ghostwriter and the architect met when they were children at summer camp. They are destined to meet again, but keep missing each other by inches or minutes. Some of their near misses take place in a restaurant the architect designed.

This restaurant, of frightening ugliness, seems designed to keep personal injury lawyers in work. When Tripplehorn enters it for the first time, she can't get the door open. Then it flies open and she staggers across the entire room and bangs into something. Later, she beans herself on a low-flying sculpture, trips over a waiter, catches her heel in the floor, falls over a chair, etc. Did she train for a Three Stooges movie?

All of the movie's heartfelt scenes are tangential. They involve major characters talking to minor ones instead of to each other. There is the heartfelt talk between the architect and his mentor. The heartfelt talk between the ghostwriter and a dotty old lady (Gwen Verdon) who lives in the colorful old building (which the writer staggered into after a coincidental car crash). There is the heartfelt talk between the writer and her old father, who tells her the childhood legends the movie began with were all fiction. There is the heartfelt love scene between the writer and her college professor, who is later revealed to be gay, and then disappears from the movie just when we thought the story would be about him.

Many details are just plain wrong. Since the Tripplehorn character is a literature student, we expect her to be a fairly sophisticated writer. Yet when we hear one of her poems read (after it accidentally sticks to the bottom of an architectural model thrown out of a window—but never mind), it turns out to be written in rhyming couplets of the sort found beneath the needlework column in women's craft magazines. All of the characters smoke unpleasantly and want to stop, and one of the movie's near misses, where they almost meet, is an "N.A." meeting, which is described as "Nicotine Anonymous." Warning: Before dropping "N.A." into your conversation, be aware that most people think it stands for something else.

And what about those rose petals? Or lilac petals, or whatever they are? The courtyard of the colorful old building, we can clearly see, has no foliage above it. Yet petals drift down in endless profusion for days and weeks during every scene—so many, I sat through the end credits in the futile hope there would be mention of the Petal Dropper.

All comes together at the end. Landmarks are saved, hearts are mended, long-deferred love is realized, coincidences are explained, the past is healed, the future is assured, the movie is over. I liked the last part the best.

Titanic ★ ★ ★ ★

PG-13, 194 m., 1997

Leonardo DiCaprio (Jack Dawson), Kate Winslet (Rose DeWitt Bukater), Billy Zane (Cal Hockley), Kathy Bates (Molly Brown), Bill Paxton (Brock Lovett), Gloria Stuart (Rose Calvert), Frances Fisher (Ruth DeWitt Bukater), Bernard Hill (Captain E. J. Smith), David Warner (Spicer Lovejoy), Victor Garber (Thomas Andrews), Jonathan Hyde (Bruce Ismay). Directed by James Cameron and produced by Cameron and Jon Landau. Screenplay by Cameron.

Like a great iron Sphinx on the ocean floor, the *Titanic* faces still toward the West, interrupted forever on its only voyage. We see it in the opening shots of *Titanic*, encrusted with the silt of eighty-five years; a remote-controlled TV camera snakes its way inside, down corridors and through doorways, showing us staterooms built for millionaires and inherited by crustaceans.

These shots strike precisely the right note; the ship calls from its grave for its story to be told, and if the story is made of showbiz and hype, smoke and mirrors—well, so was the *Titanic*. She was "the largest moving object created by man," a character boasts. There is a shot of her, early in the film, sweeping majestically beneath the camera from bow to stern, nearly 900 feet long and "unsinkable," it was claimed, until an iceberg made an irrefutable reply.

James Cameron's 194-minute, $200 million film of the tragic voyage is in the tradition of the great Hollywood epics. It is flawlessly crafted, intelligently constructed, strongly acted, and spellbinding. If its story stays well within the traditional formulas for such pictures, well, you don't choose the most expensive film ever made as your opportunity to reinvent the wheel.

We know before the movie begins that certain things must happen. We must see the *Titanic* sail and sink, and be convinced we are looking at a real ship. There must be a human story—probably a romance—involving a few of the passengers. There must be vignettes involving some of the rest, and a subplot involving the arrogance and pride of the ship's builders—and perhaps also their courage and dignity. And there must be a reenactment of the ship's terrible death throes; it took two and a half hours to sink, so that everyone aboard had time to know what was happening, and to consider his actions.

All of those elements are present in Cameron's *Titanic*, weighted and balanced like ballast, so that the film always seems in proportion. The ship was made out of models (large and small), visual effects, and computer animation. You know intellectually that you're not looking at a real ocean liner—but the illusion is convincing and seamless. The special effects don't call inappropriate attention to themselves, but get the job done.

The human story involves an eighteen-year-old woman named Rose DeWitt Bukater (Kate Winslet) who is sailing to what she sees as her own personal doom: She has been forced by her penniless mother to become engaged to marry a rich, supercilious snob named Cal Hockley (Billy Zane), and so bitterly does she hate this prospect that she tries to kill herself by jumping from the ship. She is saved by Jack Dawson (Leonardo DiCaprio), a brash kid from steerage class, and of course they will fall in love during the brief time left to them.

The screenplay tells their story in a way that unobtrusively shows off the ship. Jack is invited to join Rose's party at dinner in the first-class dining room, and later, fleeing from Cal's manservant, Lovejoy (David Warner), they find themselves first in the awesome engine room, with pistons as tall as churches, and then at a rousing Irish dance in the crowded steerage. (At one point Rose gives Lovejoy the finger; did young ladies do that in 1912?) Their exploration is intercut with scenes from the command deck, where the captain (Bernard Hill) consults with Andrews (Victor Garber), the ship's designer, and Ismay (Jonathan Hyde), the White Star Line's managing director.

Ismay wants the ship to break the transatlantic speed record. He is warned that icebergs may have floated into the hazardous northern crossing, but is scornful of danger. The *Titanic* can easily break the speed record, but is too massive to turn quickly at high speed; there is an agonizing sequence that almost seems to play in slow motion, as the ship strains and shudders to turn away from an iceberg in its path, and fails.

We understand exactly what is happening at that moment because of an ingenious story technique by Cameron, who frames and explains the entire voyage in a modern story. The opening shots of the real *Titanic*, we are told, are obtained during an expedition led by Brock Lovett (Bill Paxton), a documentary filmmaker. He seeks precious jewels but finds a nude drawing of a young girl. In England, an ancient woman sees the drawing on TV and recognizes herself. This is Rose (Gloria Stuart), still alive at 101. She visits Paxton and shares her memories ("I can still smell the fresh paint"). And he shows her scenes from his documentary, including a computer simulation of the *Titanic*'s last hours—which doubles as a briefing for the audience. By the time the ship sinks, we already know what is happening and why, and the story can focus on the characters while we effortlessly follow the stages of the *Titanic*'s sinking.

Movies like this are not merely difficult to make at all, but almost impossible to make well. The technical difficulties are so daunting that it's a wonder when the filmmakers are also able to bring the drama and history into proportion. I found myself convinced by both the story and the saga. The setup of the love story is fairly routine, but the payoff—how everyone behaves as the ship is sinking—is wonderfully written, as passengers are forced to make impossible choices. Even the villain, played by Zane, reveals a human element at a crucial moment (despite everything, damn it all, he does love the girl).

The image from the *Titanic* that has haunted me, ever since I first read the story of the great ship, involves the moments right after it sank. The night sea was quiet enough so that cries for help carried easily across the water to the lifeboats, which drew prudently away. Still dressed up in the latest fashions, hundreds froze and drowned. What an extraordinary position to find yourself in after spending all that money for a ticket on an unsinkable ship. ☞

Tomorrow Never Dies ★ ★ ★

PG-13, 120 m., 1997

Pierce Brosnan (James Bond), Jonathan Pryce (Elliot Carver), Michelle Yeoh (Wai Lin), Teri Hatcher (Paris Carver), Goetz Otto (Stamper), Judi Dench (M), Desmond Llewelyn (Q), Samantha Bond (Miss Moneypenny). Directed by Roger Spottiswoode and produced by Barbara Broccoli and Michael G. Wilson. Screenplay by Bruce Feirstein.

James Bond has battled evil commies and megalomaniac madmen; perhaps it was only a matter of time until he faced off against a media baron—the only sort of figure in today's world that actually does seek global domination. His enemy in *Tomorrow Never Dies* wants to start a war in order to create headlines for the launch of his latest news channel. Just imagine what Rupert Murdoch and Ted Turner would like to do to each other and imagine either one of them doing it to the Chinese, and you'll get the idea.

Bond, played confidently and with a minimum of fuss by Pierce Brosnan, stumbles into the middle of the plot, masterminded by Elliot Carver (Jonathan Pryce), who owns newspapers, TV stations, and a gigantic Stealth warship that's invisible to radar. Carver's plan is ingenious: He'll use his satellites to draw a British warship off course, sink it with the Stealth ship, steal its nuclear warheads, and fire one at China, which will think it is under attack from the West. The only flaw in this plan, as far as I can see, is the likely nuclear destruction of most of Carver's biggest markets.

Bond films traditionally open with an elaborate scene built of stunts and special effects, and *Tomorrow Never Dies* doesn't break with custom: We see British military officials monitoring a "Terrorist Arms Bazaar on the Russian Border" (which border? who cares?). A hothead British general gives an order that leads to the likely detonation of nuclear weapons. Then Bond appears, steals the plane containing the warheads, uses its missiles to destroy all of his enemies, and takes off in it before . . .

But I dare not reveal too much. The plot has a lot of fun with the Carver character, played by Pryce in a platinum crew cut. He likes to write headlines and design front pages in advance of big news events, and then make them happen, although more than once he's premature in reporting the death of Bond. His wife, Paris (Teri Hatcher), happens to be a former lover of 007, and M (Judi Dench), head of the British secret service, makes a few tart suggestions about how Bond might make use of the connection.

The other Bond woman this time is a departure from many of 007's former teammates. She's Wai Lin, an agent for the "Chinese External Security Force," and she's played by Michelle Yeoh as a karate expert with formidable fighting and intelligence skills. Yeoh, of course, is a star in her own right, having toplined many Asian martial arts movies, and her presence in the movie is so effective that she'd be a natural to add to the other regulars, like M, Q, and Miss Moneypenny.

In its thirty-fifth year, the long-running Bond series has settled into a dependable formula, based on gimmicks, high-tech toys, chases, elaborate stunts, and the battle to foil the madman's evil schemes. The toys this time are a couple of BMW products: a motorcycle, used during an incredible chase scene over rooftops, and a car, which is remote-controlled by a handheld device with a touch pad. In one ingenious chase scene, Bond crouches in the backseat of the car while guiding it with the remote control.

All Bond movies include at least one Fruit Cart Scene, in which market stalls are overturned in a chase, and this one sets some kind of a record by having the carts destroyed by the blades of a helicopter that's chasing Bond and Wai Lin. There is also the obligatory Talking Killer Scene, in which the madman explains his plans when he should simply be killing Bond as quickly as possible ("Caesar had his legions, Napoleon had his armies, and I have my divisions—TV, newspapers . . .").

Is Pierce Brosnan better or worse as Bond than Connery, Lazenby, Moore, and Dalton? This is one of those questions (like why doesn't tomorrow ever die?) that can be debated but never answered. Basically, you have Connery, and then you have all of the rest. I enjoyed Brosnan in the role, although I noticed fewer Bondian moments this time in which the trademarks of the series are relished.

Yes, we have the usual double entendres and product placements (I find product placement distracting in most movies, but sort of anticipate them as part of the Bond formula). There's a high gloss and some nice payoffs, but not quite as much humor as usual; Bond seems to be straying from his tongue-in-cheek origins into the realm of conventional technothrillers.

Still, *Tomorrow Never Dies* gets the job done, sometimes excitingly, often with style. The villain, slightly more contemporary and plausible than usual, brings some subtler-than-usual satire into the film, and I liked the chemistry between Bond and Wai Lin (all the more convincing because the plot doesn't force it). The look of the film is authoritative; the scenes involving warships and airplanes seem sleek and plausible. There's gorgeous photography as a junk sails in a sea filled with peaks, and astonishing action choreography in the rooftop motorcycle chase. On the basis of this installment, the longest-running movie series seems fit for the twenty-first century.

Touch ★★½

R, 97 m., 1997

Christopher Walken (Bill Hill), Skeet Ulrich (Juvenal), Gina Gershon (Debra Lusanne), Bridget Fonda (Lynn Faulkner), Janeane Garofalo (Kathy Worthington), Lolita Davidovich (Antoinette Baker), LL Cool J (LL Cool J). Directed by Paul Schrader and produced by Lila Cazes and Fida Attieh. Screenplay by Schrader, based on the novel by Elmore Leonard.

There is a moment in Paul Schrader's *Touch* when all of the conflicting forces of this strange film seem to come together at once. It involves a young man named Juvenal, a former Franciscan who is able to heal people by touching them. On his body he bears the five stigmata—the marks of the wounds of Christ. He has met a woman named Lynn, who cares for him, and she is trying to bring order to his solitary existence by doing some laundry. "Do you think it's all right?" she asks him. "Stigmata blood going through the wash?"

Here we have a moment which probably reads as if it were intended to be funny or satirical. Probably it was written that way by Elmore Leonard, whose most bizarre novel inspired the screenplay. But it plays as if Lynn is asking the question in all seriousness. There's no attempt by the actress Bridget Fonda to punch up the moment, and it almost slips by without registering. A few people in the audience snickered uncomfortably, and fell silent: We are more comfortable with postcard angels than with saints who bleed like Christ.

The plot of *Touch* sounds like a comedy. But the experience of seeing the film is subduing; the movie plays in a muted key. Actors like Tom Arnold, who approach their characters more broadly, sound like they're talking too loudly in church. The dominant note is set by Skeet Ulrich, as Juvenal: He's sweet, soft-spoken, not sure what it all means. Schrader has said his movie has "a whole cast of ironic characters, with an existential character in the center." If the viewer doesn't figure this out, some scenes play very oddly.

As the movie opens, Juvenal finds himself comforting a blind woman (Conchata Ferrell) who has been beaten. He touches her, and she can see. This miracle excites a man named Bill Hill (Christopher Walken), who had a thriving evangelism business in the south, but moved it to Los Angeles, went broke, and was reduced to selling recreational vehicles. He thinks maybe Juvenal could put him back in business, but can't find out his last name because Juvenal is in a rehab center, and A.A. rules require anonymity. Bill recruits Lynn (Fonda) to pose as an alcoholic and infiltrate the center. (They're old friends; she was a baton twirler at his services.)

Juvenal sees through Lynn instantly. He touches her breast and says, "You were gonna tell me you have a lump here—maybe a tumor—and if it was malignant, would I help you?" That is what she was going to do. She falls under his spell. Also drifting through this milieu is a militant Catholic conservative (Tom Arnold) who heads a group called "Outrage!" which demonstrates in favor of the discarded Latin rite.

Elmore Leonard, whose novels have fueled such films as *Get Shorty* and *52 Pickup,* has never written a story with more possibilities and hazards. I'm not sure why Schrader was drawn to it. There may be a connection with his own background. Raised in a strict religion, he didn't see his first movie until he was seventeen. His writing credits include *Taxi Driver* and *Raging Bull,* but two of his directing credits might provide clues: *Mishima* is about a Japanese novelist who commits suicide as a statement of his medieval ideals, and *Hard Core* is about a fundamentalist father who seeks his daughter among the porn and drug users of San Francisco.

Schrader is serious about religion. He may no longer be a formal believer, but the lessons are in his blood, and in *Touch* I believe he was drawn to the serious implications of the story, not the comic possibilities. It is not in him to generate jokes with the stigmata. He correctly sees Walken and Arnold as figures of fun: Anyone who uses religion as an avenue to publicity and self-aggrandizement is missing the point, and that is always funny. But Juvenal does bleed from the wounds of Christ, and so must be approached in another way.

The story is cluttered by two unnecessary filler characters: Gina Gershon plays a TV talk show host, and Janeane Garofolo plays a newspaper reporter. They get involved with the Walken and Arnold stories and stumble into the possibility that Juvenal may be for real. But their subplots, using standard media-bashing techniques, don't pay off. Much more interesting (in a fascinating pure dialogue scene) is Lolita Davidovich as Antoinette, a stripper who figures in a brilliantly written barroom conversation about religion. It basically asks: What do you do when your religion calls your bluff and turns out to be real, and you can't get away with safe middle-class piety any more, but are called to behave like those fanatics in the Lives of the Saints?

Touch is not successful in any way I can easily describe. Its effect is like that of a ghost at a banquet. Comic actors deliver one-liners, and the screenplay serves up the usual easy shots against phony evangelists, and then this tender, sweet, confused young man wanders in and doesn't know what to make of his frightening power.

How should a reviewer rate a film like this? I am not "recommending" the picture because I don't think it delivers what any reasonable filmgoer is likely to expect from it. Unreasonable filmgoers are another matter. You know who you are.

Traveller ★ ★ ★

R, 100 m., 1997

Bill Paxton (Bokky), Mark Wahlberg (Pat), Julianna Margulies (Jean), James Gammon (Double D), Luke Askew (Boss Jack), Nikki Deloach (Kate), Danielle Wiener (Shane), Michael Shaner (Lip), Vincent Chase (Bimbo). Directed by Jack Green and produced by Bill Paxton, Brian Swardstrom, Mickey Liddell, and David Blocker. Screenplay by Jim McGlynn.

One of the pleasures of *Traveller* is trying to figure out how the scams work. Some of them are easy, like the con where they take worthless crankcase oil and sell it to homeowners as driveway sealant or to farmers as roofing tar. But the last one—a final scam involving two teams of con men dealing in counterfeit money—is so twisted that only later, after the movie, do you understand it.

Travellers are con men of Irish descent who belong to a tightly knit clan based in the American South and travel the highways looking for easy marks. As the film opens, a young man named Pat (Mark Wahlberg), whose father married outside the clan, has returned with his body for burial. His father was banished, but Pat wants back in. The head of the clan, Boss Jack (Luke Askew), won't have anything to do with him, but a traveller named Bokky (Bill Paxton) takes him under his arm, and they set out together for a life of crime.

If that's all there was to it, *Traveller* would be a standard road picture with a twist. There's more to it. Bokky and Pat pull a complicated scam on a bartender named Jean (Julianna Margulies), and then Bokky regrets it—she's a nice woman—and violates all of his own principles by returning her money. He likes her, and it's headed in the direction of love.

Meanwhile, the two men pick up a fellow traveller (James Gammon). They cooperate on some scams and like to exclaim, "This is the life!" while sitting in a cheap motel room drinking beer (there doesn't seem to be a lot of money in travelling). When Jean needs money for an operation for her daughter, Bokky winds up the incredibly complicated scam involving two kinds of money: real counterfeit money and phony counterfeit money. His intended mark is a bald fat man named Bimbo, played by Vincent Chase with a silky, insinuating quality; like Sydney Greenstreet, Chase is able to suggest he knows all about the sin and has no interest in salvation.

Chase in a way is the most interesting character in the movie. Paxton has an everyman quality that makes it possible to overlook his skill, but here he finds the right way to be true to his criminal career while still scamming: His heart is in the right place, even if his hand is in your pocket. As producer, he supervised the sound track, which has a lot of country swing. And Julianna Margulies, from *ER*, is able to make her bartender tired and hard-pressed, yet filled with promise for the future.

The movie is the directorial debut of Jack Green, the Oscar-winning cinematographer of many Clint Eastwood films (and of *Twister*, where he worked with Paxton). The screenplay by Jim McGlynn, which plays a little like something Eastwood might have made, is subtle and observant; there aren't big plot points but lots of little ones, and the plot allows us the delight of figuring out the scams. Too bad the ending is a surprisingly violent confrontation; that seems to be obligatory these days. The movie should have ended as it began, slyly.

Trekkies ★ ★ ★

PG, 86 m., 1999

A documentary directed by Roger Nygard and produced by Keith Border. Narrated by Denise Crosby and featuring LeVar Burton, Frank D'Amico, John de Lancie, James Doohan, Michael Dorn, Jonathan Frakes, DeForest Kelly, Walter Koenig, Kate Mulgrew, Anne Murphy, Nichelle Nichols, Leonard Nimoy, William Shatner, Brent Spiner, and George Takei.

When Barbara Adams of Little Rock, Arkansas, was called to serve as a Whitewater juror, she arrived dressed appropriately, in her opinion. She was in a lieutenant commander's uniform as commanding officer of the USS *Artemis*, the Little Rock unit of the Federation Alliance. In other words, she was a *Star Trek* fan.

When the judge demurred at her costume and she made national news, she refused to back down: "If the president himself were on trial," she said, "I would still wear the uniform. I am an officer in the Federation universe twenty-four hours a day." Plus, she was setting a good example: "I don't want my officers to ever be ashamed to wear their uniforms."

As Adams is making these statements in *Trekkies*, a new documentary, I was looking closely for any sign of a smile. She was dead serious. *Star Trek* is her life. Old soldiers get their dress uniforms out of mothballs to prove the point that "formal wear" can mean either a tuxedo or a military uniform. And Lieutenant Commander Adams honors her uniform in the same spirit.

Not everyone in *Trekkies* is as serious about the long-running series of TV programs and movies. But most of them are as obsessed. Consider Denis Bourguinon, a dentist in Orlando whose Star Base Dental is an office completely designed around a *Star Trek* motif. Even his aides and hygienists are in uniform. One says she held out for a year before putting on the outfit. What convinced her? "He told me I had to."

Then there is the Canadian man who has designed a motorized life-support chair like one seen in the series, and drives around town in it, only his head visible above what looks like a steam cabinet. Or the father-and-son team whose pickup looks like a lunar lander and might someday be able to "shoot a 1,000-foot beam." And consider the *Star Trek* auction where someone bid $40 for a half-filled water glass used by a cast member with a virus. The lucky bidder drank the rest of the water so he could have the virus too.

I've been vaguely aware of the further shores of *Star Trek* fandom through my mail and contact with audiences at screenings. And I've sensed a certain tone of awe about it in the voices of many cast members I've interviewed, from Leonard Nimoy and William Shatner on down, or up. It's not so much a hobby, more a way of life. "Somewhere in the world," Denise (Tasha Yar) Crosby, the film's narrator, informs us, "there is a *Star Trek* event every weekend." We meet Richard Arnold, a *Star Trek* consultant, who has visited 360 of them.

Trekkies and Trekkers evolved out of the older and broader-based science-fiction fandom, which began with mimeographed magazines in the 1940s and went on to sponsor gigantic WorldCons and influence the tone and jargon of the Web (many Web pages are mutated fanzines). Fandom began the tradition of dressing in the costumes of science-fiction characters, and *Star Trek* fandom is intensely involved in that side of things—to such a degree that the dentist and his wife cheerfully hint that many different species play roles in their fantasy lives.

To some degree, dressing up and role-playing in a *Star Trek* context may be a cover for cross-dressing impulses in general. To a much larger degree, it is probably just good fun. I was going to say "good, clean fun," but was reminded of an attractive black woman in the movie who, as Mistress Janeway, pens popular S&M fantasies with a *Star Trek* theme, in which aliens do things to one another that humans can hardly hope to appreciate.

Sinclair Lewis, who I believe invented the term "boosterism," would appreciate a uniquely American strain in Trekdom, which feels compelled, like so many popular movements, to cloak its fun in do-gooderism. Trekkies talk at length about how the world would be a saner and more peaceful place if the *Star Trek* philosophy ruled our lives. No doubt it would be a lot more entertaining, too, especially during root canals.

Trial and Error ★ ★ ★

PG-13, 106 m., 1997

Michael Richards (Richard Rietti), Jeff Daniels (Charles Tuttle), Alexandra Wentworth (Tiffany), Rip Torn (Benny Gibbs), Charlize Theron (Billie), Jessica Steen (Elizabeth Gardner), Austin Pendleton (Judge Graff). Directed by Jonathan Lynn and produced by Gary Ross and Lynn. Screenplay by Sara Bernstein and Gregory Bernstein.

There is a moment in *Trial and Error* when a woman in love finds out her man is engaged to another woman, and she handles it by telling him she understands. "Look," she says, "it's not a federal case." Then she walks outside his room and starts to cry. What I liked about that scene—especially in a comedy—is that it looked for the truth and not just for the easy sitcom laugh.

In a lazier or more routine movie, the woman—a waitress in a Nevada backwater town—would have exploded, or thrown things, or insulted the guy's fiancée, or done anything other than to react the way a real person might really react. That's why so many comedies aren't funny: They don't go for the humor of truth, but for the kind of machine-made insult comedy that sitcoms extrude by the yard.

Trial and Error has some very funny scenes in it—funny because they reflect the natures of the characters. (It has some other scenes that aren't so funny, when characters trip over things and knock things over and we doubt any human being would be so clumsy.) By the end of the film, we actually care what happens to the people in the film, and in a modern comedy, that's rare.

The movie is the starring debut of Michael Richards, a *Seinfeld* regular, who plays a so-so actor named Richard Rietti. He's planning to be the best man at the wedding of his friend Charles Tuttle (Jeff Daniels), a lawyer. Tuttle is engaged to marry the daughter of his boss at the law firm. He's dispatched to Nevada to defend the boss's distant relative, Benny Gibbs (Rip Torn), who is a con man and has been for fifty years. His latest stunt: selling "genuine copper engravings of the Great Emancipator" for $17.99 through the mail, and sending his victims a penny.

Richard sneaks ahead to the small town to throw a surprise bachelor party for Tuttle. Tuttle gets so drunk he can't appear in court the next day. Rietti pretends to be the lawyer, and when a continuance plea is rejected, he ends up facing a desperate choice: continue the masquerade and defend the client, or be arrested for impersonating a lawyer. The two friends work out a makeshift arrangement involving flash cards, horn toots, and other signals by which Tuttle tries, and fails, to control the phony lawyer.

A promising premise. And the director, Jonathan Lynn, has already proven he knows how to handle comedies about fish out of water in the courts of a small town: He made *My Cousin Vinny* five years ago. That was the film that won an Oscar for Marisa Tomei, and again this time he has a key role for a newcomer: Charlize Theron plays Billie, the waitress at the local hotel, who falls in love with Tuttle.

Rip Torn, all guilt and phony wounded dignity, makes the con man into a defendant who obviously should go to jail. Austin Pendleton has a lot of fun playing the judge, a man who finds the case increasingly incredible and hilarious. Jessica Steen has the key but thankless role of playing the prosecuting attorney, but the screenplay saves her from a one-note role by giving her priceless scenes where she cross-examines two of the defense witnesses: One is a "psychiatric expert" who is glib but seems to be about eighteen, and the other, the keystone of Rietti's Twinkie defense, is a "nutritional expert" who explains that the only difference between sugar and cocaine is a few molecules here and there.

The movie reminded me a little of some of Billy Wilder's work in the way he took the characters seriously, or at least as seriously as the material allowed, and got a lot of the laughs by playing scenes straight.

Jeff Daniels is invaluable in films like this (as he was in *Dumb and Dumber*) because he doesn't overplay or sound like he's going for a laugh. And Michael Richards makes the wise decision to play the courtroom scenes not as a buffoon, but as an intelligent guy who's seen too many courtroom movies.

I liked the love affair between the Daniels and Theron characters. I liked the way they seemed comfortable with one another, and the way she projected both love and sympathy. And in a crucial scene, where her eyes are filled with love and forgiveness, and she runs in slow motion across the street toward him, I liked the little touch that she looked both ways first. You'd be surprised how many movie heroines would run across the street without looking in a scene like that. Surprising more of them aren't traffic victims.

Trippin' ★★½

R, 92 m., 1999

Deon Richmond (Gregory Reed), Donald Adeosun Faison (June), Maia Campbell (Cinny Hawkins), Guy Torry (Fish), Aloma Wright (Louis Reed), Harold Sylvester (Willie Reed), Cleavon McClendon (Jamal), Bill Henderson (Gramps), Michael Warren (Shapik). Directed by David Hubbard (as David Raynr) and produced by Marc Abraham and Caitlin Scanlon. Screenplay by Gary Hardwick.

To judge by a lot of the movies I've been seeing, the most pressing issue of our time (indeed, the *only* issue in most movies about teenagers) is who to take to the senior prom. Faithful readers will know that this question has been raised in at least six movies already this year, and I'm not even counting the one about who Carrie II will kill at the prom.

Trippin' transports this issue to the African-American community, in a high-spirited comedy about a likable senior named Gregory Reed (Deon Richmond), who puts off everything until the last possible moment. When he approaches his parents with a request for "funds to finance my senior prom activities," they laugh at him: He hasn't even sent in his college applications yet, his dad points out. First things first.

Gregory's problem is that he lives in a world of daydreams. The movie opens with one—an island fantasy, shot in the style of a music video, with Gregory basking in the admiration of a brace of Hawaiian Tropics girls. A friend of his, who wears leg braces, inspires a daydream in which he becomes the Terminator crossed with RoboCop. And a visit to an army recruiting office triggers a fantasy in which Gregory receives the Medal of Honor—plus, the president tells him, "unreleased CDs from Tupac and Notorious B.I.G."

Gregory has fallen in love with Cinny Hawkins (the beautiful Maia Campbell), and would like to ask her to the prom—but lacks the funds and the courage. His friends advise him to impress her with his bright future, so he lies and says he's been given a full scholarship to UCLA. There's a sweet scene where they wander through a dock area, dreaming of the voyages they could take—on the sea and in life.

There seems to be, alas, a requirement that almost every movie about black teenagers include drugs somewhere in the plot. *Trippin'* supplies a no-good drug dealer who at one point has Gregory's friend hanging upside down from a crane, and the scenes involving this villain don't really seem necessary. I guess the crime stuff is there to provide the plot with prefab suspense, but it might have been more fun to develop Cinny's character more fully, since there's a lot more to her than simply beauty.

Trippin' does have some amiable scenes involving Gregory's family, including his strict dad (Harold Sylvester), his sympathetic mother (Aloma Wright), and Gramps (Bill Henderson), who has no truck with attempts to improve his nutrition, and bangs on the table while demanding pork sausage. And there's a no-nonsense teacher (Michael Warren) who tries to jolt Gregory out of his mind-trips and into some kind of organized approach to the rest of his life.

The movie is sweet, but predictable, and we get about three more daydreams than we really require. Deon Richmond and Maia Campbell both possess radiant smiles, which is important in a movie where a character's appearance supplies at least half of the character development. Whether Richmond and Campbell will someday be getting the kind of roles that go to Denzel Washington and Halle Berry is impossible to predict, but on the basis of their work here, it's not implausible.

Did I like the movie? Not enough to recommend it, except to someone who really wants to see another senior prom cliffhanger. Still, there are so many grim and gritty urban violence movies that it's good to see nice African-American kids in a comedy, even if it's so lacking in imagination that it finds it necessary to hang them upside down.

Troublesome Creek: A Midwestern ★★★

NO MPAA RATING, 88 m., 1997

A documentary directed and produced by Jeanne Jordan and Steven Ascher. Screenplay by Jordan and Ascher. Featuring Russel and Mary Jane Jordan and their family.

There were 6 million family farms in 1960, but there are only 2 million now. That is a fact. Mary Jane Jordan saw her beloved Ethan Allen dining room table sold at auction for only $105. That is an experience. The gift of every good reporter is to turn the facts into experiences, so that we can understand what they mean and how they feel. *Troublesome Creek: A Midwestern* sees the disappearance of the family farm through the eyes of one Iowa family, the Jordans, who have been farming the same land since 1867.

The movie is narrated by their daughter Jeanne and filmed by her husband, Steven Ascher. They codirected it during a series of several trips back to the farm from their home in Cambridge, Massachusetts. They present the story of her parents, Russ and Mary Jane Jordan, not as a tragedy but as a response to very hard times.

The Jordan place is what we all think of as a farm: It could be a movie set. There's a big clapboard house, lots of well-tended outbuildings, silos, hogs, cows, and rich flat fields. Russ worries about the livestock and crops, and Mary Jane worries about the bills; we often see her on the telephone, talking to her contact at the bank about another short-term loan. The Jordans are both about seventy. She was state 4-H president in high school. He once placed second in an Abe Lincoln look-alike contest.

They have a son, Jim, who is farming rented land nearby. "What many people fail to realize," Jeanne explains on the sound track, "is that sons have to move off the farm where they were born and work a rented farm until their father retires or dies and they can inherit the family place." Jim is the obvious heir since the other Jordan children have moved into town; there isn't a living for a big family from this land.

As the film begins, the Jordans face a crisis. Farm prices have fallen and they've gotten $70,000 in debt to the bank, in addition to their annual $150,000 loan. The local bank has been absorbed into a megabank named Norwest, which has a tower in Des Moines from which tidy young men telephone with news of "risk ratios." It is unlikely the Jordans can get more credit.

We see flashbacks to better days and photographs of all the Jordans who have worked this land, including the great-great-grandfather who came out to Iowa from Ohio after the Civil War. During a visit home, Jeanne and her husband join her parents in visiting the farm where she was raised—the rented farm her father worked while waiting for *his* father to retire. "When I was a child I didn't even know we rented this farm," she says. "I thought of it as home." The clothesline trees are still in the yard and a closet door still shows signs of an unwise orange paint job, but the farm is abandoned. "I wouldn't think a place could go down this bad in fifteen years," says Russ.

He looks a little like Gary Cooper. Mary Jane could pose for Bisquick commercials. They like to watch Westerns on TV, and their daughter casts their story as a "Midwestern," a last stand by heroic figures against the onslaught of the bankers.

Then more bad news arrives; the farm Jim rents is being sold. He owns equipment, but has no place to use it. Russ devises a plan. He and his wife will sell everything—their livestock, farm machinery, house, possessions, everything—to pay off the bank debt and keep the land. They'll move to town (they know a little house that's walking distance from Van's

Chat and Chew) and Jim will work the land with his machinery.

The film follows the preparations for the big auction sale with details that will be familiar to many who have never been on a farm. Mary Jane cannot bring herself to part with certain items—a plant stand, her collections of saucers and spoons—but she believes fondly that her treasured Ethan Allen dining room set, protected from scratches all these years with pads, will get a good price. I remember my mother speculating about the untold fortune she was convinced her Hummel figurines would bring.

The table goes for almost nothing. Mary Jane bites her lip in disbelief. But the plan keeps the wolf from the door for the time being, and Jim takes up the struggle of all the Jordans before him.

The underlying lesson is clear: Our state and federal farm policies do not really allow for family farms anymore. Corporations and conglomerates now farm the land, with men paid by the day or the week. Big banks don't much care. Small banks are sold to big banks. When Russ calls up Des Moines to tell the bankers he can pay off the loan, he says they're happy to hear the good news. "Daddy, that's just guilt!" his daughter tells him. "You don't have to make it so easy for them!"

In Gary Sinise's *Miles From Home* (1988), Richard Gere and Kevin Anderson starred as two brothers unable to make a go of their family's Iowa farm, which had been visited by Khrushchev as the "farm of the year" in 1959. Filled with drama and action, it was a pretty good film. Now here is the everyday face of the same story. Should we make it easier for family farms? Yes. Why? Because they represent something we think America stands for. Strange how for all the talk of individualism and resourcefulness from politicians, our country drifts every year closer to a totalitarianism of the corporation.

True Crime ★ ★ ★

R, 127 m., 1999

Clint Eastwood (Steve Everett), Isaiah Washington (Frank Beachum), Denis Leary (Bob Findley), Lisa Gay Hamilton (Frank's Wife), James Woods (Alan Mann), Diane Venora (Barbara). Directed by Clint Eastwood and produced by Eastwood, Richard D. Zanuck, and Lili Fini Zanuck. Screenplay by Larry Gross, Paul Brickman, and Stephen Schiff, based on the novel by Andrew Klavan.

Clint Eastwood's *True Crime* follows the rhythm of a newspaperman's day. For those who cover breaking news, many days are about the same. When they begin, time seems to stretch out generously toward the deadline. There's leisure for coffee and phone calls, jokes and arguments. Then a blip appears on the radar screen: an assignment. Seemingly a simple assignment. Then the assignment reveals itself as more complicated. The reporter makes some calls.

If there's anything to the story at all, a moment arrives when it becomes, to the reporter, the most important story in the world. His mind shapes the form it should take. He badgers sources for the missing pieces. The deadline approaches, his attention focuses, the finish line is the only thing visible, and then facts, story, deadline, and satisfaction come all at the same time. A deadline reporter's day, in other words, is a lot like sex.

Eastwood uses this rhythm to make *True Crime* into a wickedly effective thriller. He plays Steve Everett, a reporter for the *Oakland Tribune.* Steve used to work out east, but got fired for "screwing the owner's underage daughter." The movie's Web page says he worked for the *New York Times,* but this detail has been dropped from the movie, no doubt when the information about the owner's daughter was added. Now he's having an affair with the wife of Findlay, his city editor (Denis Leary).

Everett's personal life is a mess. His wife, Barbara (Diane Venora), knew he cheated when she married him, but thought it was only with her. Now they have a young daughter, but Everett seems too busy to be a good dad (there's a scene where he pushes her stroller through the zoo at a dead run). Everett's also a little shaky; he was a drunk until two months ago, when he graduated to recovering alcoholic.

He's assigned to write a routine story about the last hours of a man on death row: Frank Beachum (Isaiah Washington), convicted of the shooting death of a pregnant clerk in a convenience store. Both the city editor and the editor-in-chief (James Woods) know Everett is a hotshot with a habit of turning routine stories into federal cases, and they warn him against trying to save Beachum at the eleventh hour. But it's in Everett's blood to sniff out the story behind the story. He becomes convinced the wrong man is going to be executed. "When my nose tells me something stinks—I gotta have faith in it," he tells Beachum.

This is Eastwood's twenty-first film as a director, and experience has given him patience. He knows that even in a deadline story like this, not all scenes have to have the same breakneck pace. He doesn't direct like a child of MTV, for whom every moment has to vibrate to the same beat. Eastwood knows about story arc, and as a jazz fan he also knows about improvising a little before returning to the main theme.

True Crime has a nice rhythm to it, intercutting the character's problems at home, his interviews with the prisoner, his lunch with a witness, his unsettling encounter with the grandmother of another witness. And then, as the midnight hour of execution draws closer, Eastwood tightens the noose of inexorably mounting tension. There are scenes involving an obnoxious prison chaplain, and a basically gentle warden, and the mechanical details of execution. Cuts to the governor who can stay the execution. Tests of the telephone hot lines. Battles with his editors. Last-minute revelations. Like a good pitcher, he gives the movie a nice slow curve, and a fast break.

Many recent thrillers are so concerned with technology that the human characters are almost in the way. We get gun battles and car chases that we don't care about, because we don't know the people firing the guns or driving the cars. I liked the way Eastwood and his writers (Larry Gross, Paul Brickman, and Stephen Schiff) lovingly added the small details. For example, the relationships that both the reporter and the condemned man have with their daughters. And a problem when the prisoner's little girl can't find the right color crayon for her drawing of green pastures.

In England twenty-five years ago, traditional beer was being pushed off the market by a pasteurized product that had been pumped full of carbonation (in other words, by American beer). A man named Richard Boston started the Real Beer Campaign. Maybe it's time for a movement in favor of real movies. Movies with tempo and character details and style, instead of actionfests with Attention Deficit Disorder. Clint Eastwood could be honorary chairman.

The Truman Show ★ ★ ★ ★

PG, 104 m., 1998

Jim Carrey (Truman Burbank), Laura Linney (Meryl), Noah Emmerich (Marlon), Natascha McElhone (Lauren/Sylvia), Holland Taylor (Mother), Ed Harris (Christof), Brian Delate (Kirk), Paul Giamatti (Simeon). Directed by Peter Weir and produced by Scott Rudin, Andrew Niccol, Edward S. Feldman, and Adam Schroeder. Screenplay by Niccol.

The Truman Show is founded on an enormous secret, which all of the studio's advertising has been determined to reveal. I didn't know the secret when I saw the film, and was able to enjoy the little doubts and wonderings that the filmmakers so carefully planted. If by some good chance you do not know the secret, read no further.

Those fortunate audience members (I trust they have all left the room?) will be able to appreciate the meticulous way director Peter Weir and writer Andrew Niccol have constructed a jigsaw plot around their central character, who doesn't suspect that he's living his entire life on live television. Yes, he lives in an improbably ideal world, but I fell for that: I assumed the movie was taking a sitcom view of life, in which neighbors greet each other over white picket fences, and Ozzie and Harriet are real people.

Actually, it's Seaside, a planned community on the Gulf Coast near Panama City. Called Seahaven in the movie, it looks like a nice place to live. Certainly Truman Burbank (Jim Carrey) doesn't know anything else. You accept the world you're given, the filmmakers suggest; more thoughtful viewers will get the buried message, which is that we accept almost everything in our lives without examining it very closely. When was the last time you reflected on how really odd a tree looks?

Truman works as a sales executive at an insurance company, is happily married to Meryl

(Laura Linney), and doesn't find it suspicious that she describes household products in the language of TV commercials. He is happy, in a way, but an uneasiness gnaws away at him. Something is missing, and he thinks perhaps he might find it in Fiji, where Lauren (Natascha McElhone), the only woman he really loved, has allegedly moved with her family.

Why did she leave so quickly? Perhaps because she was not a safe bet for Truman's world: The actress who played her (named Sylvia) developed real feeling and pity for Truman, and felt he should know the truth about his existence. Meryl, on the other hand, is a reliable pro (which raises the question, unanswered, of their sex life).

Truman's world is controlled by a TV producer named Christof (Ed Harris), whose control room is high in the artificial dome that provides the sky and horizon of Seahaven. He discusses his programming on talk shows, and dismisses the protests of those (including Sylvia) who believe Truman is the victim of a cruel deception. Meanwhile, the whole world watches Truman's every move, and some viewers even leave the TV on all night as he sleeps.

The trajectory of the screenplay is more or less inevitable: Truman must gradually realize the truth of his environment and try to escape from it. It's clever the way he's kept on his island by implanted traumas about travel and water. As the story unfolds, however, we're not simply expected to follow it; we're invited to think about the implications. About a world in which modern communications make celebrity possible, and inhuman.

Until fairly recently, the only way you could become really famous was to be royalty, or a writer, actor, preacher, or politician—and even then, most people had knowledge of you only through words or printed pictures. Television, with its insatiable hunger for material, has made celebrities into "content," devouring their lives and secrets. If you think *The Truman Show* is an exaggeration, reflect that Princess Diana lived under similar conditions from the day she became engaged to Charles.

Carrey is a surprisingly good choice to play Truman. We catch glimpses of his manic comic persona, just to make us comfortable with his presence in the character, but this is a well-planned performance; Carrey is on the right note as a guy raised to be liked and likable, who decides his life requires more risk and hardship. Like the angels in *City of Angels,* he'd like to take his chances.

Ed Harris finds the right notes as Christof, the TV Svengali. He uses the technospeak by which we distance ourselves from the real meanings of our words. (If TV producers ever spoke frankly about what they were really doing, they'd come across like Bulworth.) For Harris, the demands of the show take precedence over any other values, and if you think that's an exaggeration, tell it to the TV news people who broadcast that Los Angeles suicide.

I enjoyed *The Truman Show* on its levels of comedy and drama; I *liked* Truman in the same way I liked Forrest Gump—because he was a good man, honest and easy to sympathize with. But the underlying ideas made the movie more than just an entertainment. Like *Gattaca,* the previous film written by Niccol, it brings into focus the new values that technology is forcing on humanity. Because we can engineer genetics, because we can telecast real lives—of course we must, right? But are these good things to do? The irony is, the people who will finally answer that question will be the very ones produced by the process. ☞

Turbulence ★

R, 100 m., 1997

Ray Liotta (Ryan Weaver), Lauren Holly (Teri Halloran), Brendan Gleeson (Stubbs), Hector Elizondo (Detective Aldo Hines), Catherine Hicks (Maggie), Rachel Ticotin (Rachel Taper), Ben Cross (Captain Sam Bowen). Directed by Robert Butler and produced by Martin Ransohoff and David Valdes. Screenplay by Jonathan Brett.

Turbulence thrashes about like a formula action picture that has stepped on a live wire: It's dead, but doesn't stop moving. It looks like it cost a lot of money, but none of that money went into quality. It's schlock, hurled at the screen in expensive gobs.

The plot involves an endangered 747 flight from New York to Los Angeles. It's Christmas Eve, and there are only about a dozen passengers on board, including two prisoners and their federal marshals (anyone who has flown around Christmastime knows how empty the planes always are). One prisoner gets a gun and shoots some of the marshals, after which the other prisoner—the really dangerous one—gets a gun and kills the rest, including both pilots and one flight attendant. He locks the remaining hostages in the "crew quarters," where they are forgotten for most of the picture.

This prisoner is Ryan Weaver (Ray Liotta), a.k.a. the Lonely Hearts Killer. He claims the evidence against him was faked by an L.A. cop (Hector Elizondo). In a performance that seems like an anthology of possible acting choices, Liotta goes from charmer to intelligent negotiator to berserk slasher to demented madman. My favorite moment is when he's covered with blood, the plane is buckling through a Level 6 storm, bodies are littered everywhere, and he's singing "Buffalo Gals, Won't You Come Out Tonight?"

This is one of those movies where you keep asking questions. Questions like, how much money does an airline lose by flying a 747 from New York to L.A. with a dozen passengers on board? Like, do passengers board 747s from the rear door? Like, can a 747 fly upside down? Like, have you ever seen Christmas decorations inside an airplane (lights and wreaths and bows and mistletoe)? Like, why don't the oxygen masks drop down automatically when the cabin depressurizes—and why do they drop down later, during a fire? Like, do storms reach as high as the cruising altitude of a transcontinental flight?

The big conflict involves the Lonely Hearts Killer and two flight attendants. One of them (Catherine Hicks) is strangled fairly early. The other (Lauren Holly) wages a heroic fight after both pilots are killed. It's up to her to fend off the madman and somehow land the big plane. Holly's performance is the key to the movie, and it's not very good: She screams a lot and keeps shouting "Ooohhh!" but doesn't generate much charisma, and frankly I wish the killer had strangled her and left the more likable Hicks to land the plane.

The 747 spends much time weathering a big storm ("It's a Level 6!" "Is that on a scale of 1 to 10?" "No! It's on a scale of 1 to 6!"). The storm causes all of the lights inside the plane to flash on and off, including the Christmas lights. That lends to extended sequences in which the attendant and the madman crawl around the aisles in darkness illuminated by lightning bolts—and then there's the big moment when the plane flies upside down and they get to crawl on the ceiling.

On the ground, events are monitored in the Los Angeles control tower. The pilot of another 747 (Ben Cross) talks the brave attendant through the landing procedure, while a stern FBI agent argues that the plane should be shot down by the Air Force before it crashes in an inhabited area. Eventually he orders a fighter plane to fire—although by then the plane is already over Los Angeles and looks as if it would crash more or less into Disneyland.

There are more questions. Like, if a 747 sheers off the roof of a high-rise restaurant, wouldn't that cause it to crash? Like, if a 747 plows through an outdoor billboard, wouldn't that cause it to crash? Like, if it sweeps all the cars off the roof of a parking garage, wouldn't that cause it to crash? Like, if it gets a truck caught in its landing gear, what would happen then? ("It's a Ford!" a sharp-eyed observer says, in a line that—for once—I don't think represents product placement.)

Oh, yes, there are many moments I will long remember from *Turbulence.* But one stands out. After Lauren Holly outsmarts and outfights the berserk killer and pilots the plane through a Level 6 storm, the FBI guy still doubts she can land it. "She's only a stewardess," he says. To which the female air traffic controller standing next to him snaps, "She's a—flight attendant!"

20 Dates ½★

R, 88 m., 1999

Myles Berkowitz (Himself), Richard Arlook (His Agent), Tia Carrere (Herself), Elisabeth Wagner (Elisabeth), Robert McKee (Himself). Directed by Myles Berkowitz and produced by Elie Samaha, Jason Villard, and Mark McGarry. Screenplay by Berkowitz.

20 Dates tells the story of Myles Berkowitz, a man who wants to make a film and to fall in love. These areas are his "two greatest failures, professional and personal," so he decides to make a film about going out on twenty dates. By the end of the film he has won the love of the lovely Elisabeth—maybe—but his professional life is obviously still a failure.

The film has the obnoxious tone of a boring home movie narrated by a guy shouting in your ear. We learn how he gets a $60,000 investment from a man named Elie Samaha and uses it to hire a cameraman and a soundman to follow him around on his dates. Elie is never seen on film, but is taped with an (allegedly) hidden recorder while he threatens Berkowitz, complains about the quality of the footage, and insists on sex, stars—and a scene with Tia Carrere.

Elie has a point. Even though $60,000 is a low budget, you can't exactly see the money up there on the screen. I've seen features shot for half as much that were more impressive. What's worse is that Berkowitz loses our trust early in the film and never regains it. I don't know how much of this film is real, if any of it is. Some scenes are admittedly staged, and others feel that way.

Even though Berkowitz presumably displays himself in his best light, I couldn't find a moment when he said anything of charm or interest to one of his dates. He's surprised when one woman is offended to learn she's being photographed with a hidden camera, and when another one delivers an (unseen) hand wound that requires twenty stitches. The movie's best dialogue is: "I could have sworn that Karen and I had fallen in love. And now, it's never to be, because I couldn't ever get close to her—at least not closer than ninety feet, which was specified in the restraining order."

One of his dates, Stephanie, is a Hollywood wardrobe mistress. He asks her for free costumes for his movie (if it's a documentary, why does it need costumes?). She leaves for the rest room, "and I never saw her again." Distraught, he consults Robert McKee, a writing teacher, and McKee gives him theories about screen romance, which are irrelevant, of course, to an allegedly true-life documentary.

And what about Elie? He sounds unpleasant, vulgar, and tasteless (although no more so than many Hollywood producers). But why are we shown the outside of the county jail during his last conversation? Is he inside? What for? He promises to supply Tia Carrere, who indeed turns up in the film, describing Elie as a "very good friend." She may want to change her number.

There's a 1996 film available on video named *Me and My Matchmaker*, by Mark Wexler, about a filmmaker who consults a matchmaker and goes on dates, which he films himself. It is incomparably more entertaining, funny, professional, absorbing, honest, revealing, surprising, and convincing than *20 Dates*. It works wonderfully to demonstrate just how incompetent and annoying *20 Dates* really is. ☞

The 24-Hour Woman ★ ★ ★

R, 95 m., 1999

Rosie Perez (Grace Santos), Marianne Jean-Baptiste (Madeline Labelle), Patti LuPone (Joan Marshall), Karen Duffy (Margo Lynn), Diego Serrano (Eddie Diaz), Wendell Pierce (Roy Labelle), Melissa Leo (Dr. Suzanne Pincus). Directed by Nancy Savoca and produced by Richard Guay, Larry Meistrich, and Peter Newman. Screenplay by Savoca and Guay.

The look in Grace's eyes is hard to describe as she watches her daughter, Daisy, take her first steps, and no wonder: She's seeing it on video. She missed her daughter's first birthday and the first steps because she was arrested trying to jump over a subway turnstile with a birthday present. And she yelled at the cop because she was so frustrated after a crazy day at work and then the struggle to find the toy, one of those overnight sensations that inspires buying panics at Toys-R-Us.

Grace, played at top speed by Rosie Perez, is a TV producer just finishing her first year as a working mom. She's at the end of her rope. First came the surprise news that she was pregnant. Then her husband, the host of the show, announced her pregnancy on TV. Then the executive producer (Patti LuPone) found out she's expected to deliver in November: "During sweeps!" Then the show made her pregnancy a ratings-winner on cable, and it got picked up by a network. Meanwhile Grace has been running herself ragged, trying to keep up.

Her mom smiles at Grace's faith that she can be a mother and hold a full-time job: "I remember when you were born. I was gonna write my novel while you slept." But Grace tries to juggle both lives, although hiring a nanny is an alarming experience: "So far all we've met are Nazi nurses and emotionally disturbed women with no skills." To balance her experience, there's the case of her new assistant, Madeline (Marianne Jean-Baptiste), who is returning to the workforce after taking time out for a family, and whose husband (Wendell Pierce) is playing househusband, not without grumbles.

The 24-Hour Woman is a message picture wrapped inside a screwball comedy, with a touch of satire aimed at TV talk shows. It doesn't all work, but it happens so fast we don't get stuck in the awkward parts. Rosie Perez's Grace is the engine that pulls the story with so much energy she seems to vibrate. Some will see her character as exaggerated. Not me. She's half-Brooklynite and half–TV producer, and from what I've seen of both species, hyperactivity is built in.

The only person on the show more driven than Grace is the Patti LuPone character, who has true tunnel vision and cares only about ratings and programming gimmicks (one of her segment titles: "Romancing the Stone: How to Kick-Start Your Man's Love Machine"). The message of the movie is that new mothers who want to work are pretty much on their own. They get more lip service than real help from their husbands, and fellow females at work are running too hard to pause for sisterhood. "Take your baby and go home," Joan shouts at her at one point. "I got a show to do here."

The movie's not an idealized *Ms.* magazine vision of a working mom breast-feeding between conference calls. Its message is more Darwinian: Motherhood releases powerful drives in a woman, which are good for her children but bad for her career. No matter how hard Grace tries, she can't get rid of the guilt when she's not with her baby. And the other people in her life, who do not share these mother's instincts, simply do not care as much, or at all.

The movie was directed and cowritten by Nancy Savoca, who in three earlier films also considered social institutions through a woman's eyes. Her *True Love* (1989) was about a bride who suddenly understood that she was being sacrificed on the altar of her family's expectations. Her *Dogfight* (1991) was about a woman who discovers she has been asked out on a date as part of a contest—four guys on their way to Vietnam are trying to see who can pick up the homeliest girl. And *Household Saints* (1993) was about a grandmother who was a devout Catholic, a mother and a husband who had drifted into secular ways, and a granddaughter who literally wanted to be a saint. Behavior that would have seemed admirable to the grandmother seemed like insanity to the mother.

Now comes *The 24-Hour Woman,* which one imagines contains some of Savoca's own experiences. Her casting of Rosie Perez is a good one, because Perez is the most grounded of actors; you can't find the slightest hint of theory or conceit in her performances, which seem founded on total identification with the character. She isn't a "working woman" or a "Puerto Rican yuppie" but simply Grace Santos, with her marriage, her kid, and her job. She doesn't have time for abstractions. This isn't the kind of movie that would make a working woman think twice about having a child. It would make her think twice about having a job. And if that's reactionary, then tough luck: What's a mom going to do when little Lily starts crying and only one person can comfort her?

TwentyFourSeven ★ ★

R, 96 m., 1998

Bob Hoskins (Alan Darcy), Frank Harper (Ronnie Marsh), Pamela Cundell (Auntie Iris), Danny Nussbaum (Tim), James Hooton (Knighty), Darren O. Campbell (Daz), Justin Brady (Gadget), Jimmy Hynd (Meggy). Directed by Shane Meadows and produced by Imogen West. Screenplay by Meadows and Paul Fraser.

I've never been able to understand why boxing is so often recommended as a worthwhile pastime for idle lads in depressed areas. As a possible avenue to future employment, it ranks well below the chances of making it in the NBA, and has the added inconvenience that you get hit all the time. There is, in fact, almost no legitimate job that depends on boxing skills, unless it be nightclub bouncing.

And yet there's a whole body of films about earnest reformers who look around the neighborhood, see young men who are unemployed and aimless, and decide that what they need is a boxing club. Just this year we've had Jim Sheridan's *The Boxer,* with Daniel Day-Lewis as an ex-IRA man who starts a club in Belfast, and now Shane Meadows's *TwentyFourSeven,* with Bob Hoskins starting a club in the British Midlands.

Although both seem to feel that practicing the manly art will help their members develop self-confidence and personal goals, I'm more persuaded by the theory that if they spend all day beating up each other they'll be too tired in the evening to beat up civilians. Another motive, in *The Boxer,* is to run the club along nonsectarian lines, so that Catholics and Protestants can pound each other without regard for sect or creed.

TwentyFourSeven takes place in a desolate postindustrial wasteland in England, where the unemployed are warehoused in government housing and spend their days watching the telly, visiting the pub, and weighing the possibilities of petty crime. Their idea of amusement is to spit in a friend's chips when he isn't looking.

Into this bleak prospect comes Bob Hoskins, a former local lad who remembers when there was a boxing club and times were better. He determines to start the club again, and recruits the local louts, including one who's better off than the others because his dad is a gangster. The gangster is happy to see his son's days fruitfully occupied and helps underwrite the club, although in an excess of zeal (or bad timing) he manages to knock Hoskins unconscious against his car, and then complains about the blood on his paint job.

Hoskins, as he often does, brings a sweetness and conviction to his character. He conducts an inarticulate romantic campaign aimed at a local shop girl who is not interested, and in one of the film's best scenes he takes an aged aunt dancing. There's a certain humor in the boxing sequences (the first match turns into a brawl), and a good feeling for local color. But the personal tragedy of the Hoskins character evolves unconvincingly from the story of the boxing club, and I was left with the curious impression that the director would have rather made a documentary and not told a story at all.

Twice Upon a Yesterday ★ ½

R, 92 m., 1999

Lena Headey (Sylvia Weld), Douglas Henshall (Victor Bukowski), Penelope Cruz (Louise), Gustavo Salmeron (Rafael), Mark Strong (Dave Summers), Eusebio Lazaro (Don Miguel), Charlotte Coleman (Alison Hayes), Elizabeth McGovern (Diane). Directed by Maria Ripoll and produced by Juan Gordon. Screenplay by Rafa Russo.

Twice Upon a Yesterday has the kind of title that promises you'll hate the movie, and in this case the movie doesn't disappoint. It's a tedious contrivance about a messy drunk who is given a second chance in life, only to discover that life has a grudge against him both times. The story gives us a London actor named Victor (Douglas Henshall), who breaks up with his girlfriend, Sylvia (Lena Headey), telling her he loves someone else. Then his new love wears thin and he discovers he loves Sylvia after all—too late, because she's moved on with her life.

Enter a fairy godmother–type figure, a barmaid played by Elizabeth McGovern, who steers him toward a couple of trash collectors who are meant to remind us of Don Quixote and Sancho Panza. They show him, in a trash bin, all of the parts of his life he has thrown away, and give him another chance—reeling the thread of time backward so that he can retrieve his fatal mistake with Sylvia.

But hold on a second. Movies like this are always blinded by their concern for the hero and *his* all-important second chance. What about Sylvia? Breaking up with Victor was the best thing that's ever happened to her, we feel—after having spent more time with him than we really want to, even if it is his movie. When he says, "I don't know where I am in time," how can we be sure he's confused by the plot machinations and not merely sloshed?

Victor is a bore who's smashed most of the time, and if the great wheels of the universe revolve to give him a second chance, is there no hope for the Sylvias? Are women simply a plot convenience for the hero? I ask even though the film was directed by a woman, Maria Ripoll. She should have known better.

Movies come in cycles, governed by some occult law of synchronicity, and recently there have been several movies about alternatives in time, with the characters trying first one and then another set of decisions. Divergent time lines figured in *Groundhog Day*, with Bill Murray living the same day until he got it right. Gwyneth Paltrow, in *Sliding Doors*, was snared in alternate time lines, romance, and adultery. The new German film *Run Lola Run* plays the same twenty minutes three different ways. And now here's poor Victor, stumbling into the past to try to repair the wreckage of his life.

Much depends, in these films, on whether we care for the hero. If we like him, we wish him well. Victor is not likable. There is, however, a character we like quite a lot: Louise (Penelope Cruz), who mysteriously replaces McGovern as the barmaid, and whom Victor falls in love with. I must not reveal too much about the plot—including exactly when, and why, this romance takes place—but trust me, if we wanted Victor to find happiness, it would be a lot easier to forgive him for finding it again and again.

Twilight ★ ★

R, 104 m., 1998

Paul Newman (Harry Ross), Susan Sarandon (Catherine Ames), Gene Hackman (Jack Ames), Stockard Channing (Verna), Reese Witherspoon (Mel Ames), Giancarlo Esposito (Reuben), James Garner (Raymond Hope), Liev Schreiber (Jeff Willis), Margo Martindale (Gloria Lamar), John Spencer (Captain Phil Egan), M. Emmet Walsh (Lester Ivar). Directed by Robert Benton and produced by Arlene Donovan and Scott Rudin. Screenplay by Benton and Richard Russo.

Before a concert, the orchestra members warm up by playing snatches of difficult passages from familiar scores. *Twilight* is a movie that feels like that: The filmmakers, seasoned professionals, perform familiar scenes from the world of *film noir*. They do riffs, they noodle a little, they provide snatches from famous arias. But the curtain never goes up.

The reason to see the film is to observe how relaxed and serene Paul Newman is before the camera. How, at seventy-two, he has absorbed everything he needs to know about how to be a movie actor, so that at every moment he is at home in his skin and the skin of his character. It's sad to see all that assurance used in the service of a plot so worn and mechanical. Marcello Mastroianni, who in his humor, ease, and sex appeal resembled Newman, chose more challenging projects at a similar stage in his life.

The other veterans in the cast are Gene Hackman, Susan Sarandon, and James Garner. They know as much about acting as Newman does, although the film gives them fewer opportunities to display it. Garner, indeed, is the man to call if you need an actor who can slip beneath even Newman's level of comfortability. But the movie's story is too obvious in its message, and too absurd in its plotting.

The message: The characters are nearing the end of the line. They know the moves but are losing the daylight. "Your prostate started acting up yet?" Garner asks Newman. After Newman's character is shot in the groin, the rumor goes around that he's no longer a candidate for the full monty. What kind of a private eye doesn't have any privates? For all of the characters, this is the last hurrah, and that's especially true for Hackman's, who is dying of cancer.

The plot: Harry, the Newman character, is described as "cop, private investigator, drunk, husband, father." He has failed at all of those roles, and now, sober, broke, single, and retired, he lives on the estate of Jack and Catherine Ames (Hackman and Sarandon), movie stars who are old friends. One day Jack gives him a package to deliver. At the address he's sent to, he discovers Lester, a dying man (M. Emmet Walsh) whom someone has already shot. When he goes to the man's apartment, he finds newspaper clippings from twenty years ago, about the death of Catherine Ames's first husband.

Were Catherine or Jack involved in the murder? Who was paying for the investigation? Harry wants to know. His trail leads him to Raymond Hope (Garner), a guy he knew on the force, who has made a lot of money as a studio security chief, and lives very well. It also leads to Catherine's bedroom. He's had a crush on her for years, but no sooner is there a romantic breakthrough than the intercom rings: Jack is having an attack.

Jack discovers Catherine's infidelity through

the kind of clue (she's wearing Harry's polo shirt) that seems left over from much older films. Harry knows Catherine was at the apartment where Lester died, because he smelled her perfume there. These are clues at the Perry Mason level, but the complete explanation, when it comes, doesn't depend on them. It's lowered into the film from the sky.

The screenplay, by director Robert Benton and his cowriter, Richard Russo, is bits and pieces. The movie appeals because we like the actors, not because we care about their characters. They're like living beings caught in a clockwork mechanism. Also caught are several characters who hang around the periphery without enough to do: Stockard Channing as a cop Harry's fooled around with in the past, and Giancarlo Esposito as a limo driver who turns up out of nowhere and becomes an inexplicable sidekick. Reese Witherspoon plays the sexpot Ames daughter.

Newman's previous film, *Nobody's Fool,* was also written and directed by Benton, based on a novel by Russo. It gave Newman one of his great roles, as an aging failure, still able to dream, hope, and repair the wreckage of a life. Here we have essentially the same character description, including the same roguish, unflagging sexuality, but the payoff isn't a rich human portrait, it's a contrived manipulation of arbitrary devices from old crime stories. Who cares?

Twin Town ★★

NO MPAA RATING, 99 m., 1997

Llyr Evans (Julian), Rhys Ifans (Jeremy), William Thomas (Bryn Cartwright), Dorien Thomas (Greyo), Dougray Scott (Terry), Biddug Williams (Mrs. Mort), Ronnie Williams (Mr. Mort), Huw Ceredig (Fatty), Rachel Scorgie (Adie). Directed by Kevin Allen and produced by Peter McAleese. Screenplay by Allen and Paul Durden.

When Bill Clinton warned the fashion industry about heroin chic, perhaps he could have steered it toward films like *Twin Town* from Wales or *Trainspotting* from Scotland—two films in which drugs play a role and chic definitely does not.

Twin Town is a grotty examination of sordid lives, a reminder that many colorful characters are colorful only from a distance. The movie takes place in Swansea, Wales, a town that the Welsh poet Dylan Thomas once referred to as "the graveyard of ambition"—and he was a local boy, mind you. I have friends who live there, and who assure me that most of the creeps in the film live on the other side of town. I hope for their sake they are right.

The story involves two families who work up an extremely unpleasant disagreement after the father of one clan falls off a ladder while working on a roof. Fatty (Huw Ceredig) is injured, and his twin grandsons see that as a golden opportunity for an out-of-court settlement. The roof belongs to Bryn Cartwright (William Thomas), a contractor, property developer, and occasional cocaine dealer, who takes great pride in the greens of the local football club, which he controls along with most of the rest of the town. Cartwright won't pay, and that leads to an undeclared war in which pet dogs are beheaded and house trailers are set on fire.

The twins are Julian (Llyr Evans) and Jeremy (Rhys Ifans). They're actually not twins, only brothers, but everyone calls them twins (and they are played by brothers, despite the difference in the spellings of their names). How to describe them? If you saw them coming, you'd lock up your daughters, your sheep, and perhaps even your turtles. Swansea is not the graveyard of their ambition, only because they never had any.

They live in a trailer on the outskirts of town, where the arts are manifested only in nail-painting. The Cartwrights live in a nicer house, where Bryn plays with model trains. The mothers in both families are dim-witted, and the children have not turned out well.

The plot veers uneasily between comedy and pathos, with episodes of gore. There are beatings, a murder, lots of drugs, two crooked and dim-witted cops, the savage destruction of a soccer field, a particularly unpleasant hanging method, and also, lest we forget, karaoke sessions, a massage parlor, and a peculiarly poetic ending involving a local choir (one can just glimpse, at times, what must be the very pleasant other side of town).

I was not sure where the movie wanted to go and what it wanted to do; this despite the fact that it goes many places and does too much. Somewhere buried within it is a sweeter, more lighthearted story about its feckless lads, and then the hard-edged *Trainspotting* angle seems to have been added. But while *Trainspotting* had a clear vision and found a way to move confidently between comedy and the appalling, *Twin Town* is less surefooted.

The movie's executive producers are Danny Boyle and Andrew McDonald, who were the director and producer of *Trainspotting.* Its director, Kevin Allen, is the brother of Keith Allen, an actor in *Trainspotting.* The connection is obvious: This film wants to do for (or to) Wales what the other did for Scotland. Some audiences will have trouble with the accents, but I find that in films like this (and Gary Oldman's much superior *Nil by Mouth*) it isn't the words but the music, and you can nearly always sense pretty easily what is being said. *Twin Town* makes things easier by using variations of the same four-letter word as roughly a sixth of its dialogue.

Two Girls and a Guy ★ ★ ★

R, 92 m., 1998

Robert Downey Jr. (Blake), Natasha Gregson Wagner (Lou), Heather Graham (Carla). Directed by James Toback and produced by Edward R. Pressman and Chris Hanley. Screenplay by Toback.

Sometimes the story behind a movie can bring an angle to what's on the screen. Consider *Two Girls and a Guy,* written and directed by James Toback, and starring Robert Downey Jr. The story involves a two-timing actor who returns to his Manhattan apartment to be confronted by both of his girlfriends, who've just found out about each other.

Here's the background:

—Toback and Downey worked together before, in *The Pick-Up Artist* (1987), where Downey played a compulsive womanizer who bounded through the streets of New York, fast-talking pretty girls. He was a cad and a liar, but likable; Pauline Kael wrote that "Downey, whose soul is floppy-eared, gives the movie a fairy-tale sunniness."

—James Toback himself is, or was, a notorious pickup artist. How notorious? The late *Spy* magazine once printed a double fold-out chart of his activity during just one month. With the names of his female targets running down the left-hand side of the page, the magazine used a grid to chronicle his various approaches, and how many of his favorite pickup lines ("I work closely with Warren Beatty") he used on each woman.

—When Downey was shown on television, being led to jail in handcuffs on drug charges, Toback was watching, and says he sat down immediately to write a screenplay for his old friend. "When I saw him in that orange jail jumpsuit, I knew he was ready to play this role," Toback told me at the 1997 Toronto Film Festival. Of course, perhaps Toback (whose screenplays include *The Gambler* and *Bugsy*) was also ready to write it; the film is confessional and contrite.

—*Two Girls and a Guy* was written in four days and filmed in just eleven, mostly inside a single apartment in SoHo. Not long after, Downey went back to court and eventually to jail, only to be released this month.

Downey is not floppy-eared or sunny in the new film, but he is resilient and unbowed. Confronted with both of his girlfriends (Heather Graham and Natasha Gregson Wagner), he talks and thinks quickly, saying he meant it when he told them both he had "never experienced real love" before.

"He decided consciously to start with both of us at the same time!" Lou (Wagner) says. And as they work it out, it appears he did meet them at about the same time. He saw each girl three nights of the week, excusing himself on the other nights because of the illness of his mother, whom neither one ever met.

The two women meet on his doorstep, break into his apartment, and are hiding there when he returns from a trip and leaves phone messages for them both. When he sees them, he's at a loss for words, but soon they come tumbling out; Toback in person is a torrential talker, and here Downey is as persuasive as a snake oil salesman and Wagner (Natalie Wood's daughter) fires out high-energy dialogue like Robin Williams.

What can be said, really? He's a cheating, lying SOB, and both women find even more colorful terms to describe him, both as a person and in terms of his various parts. The movie is essentially a filmed stage play, one of those idea-plays like Shaw liked to write, in which men and women ponder their differences and complexities. Is it true that men are polygamous by nature? It's much more complex than that, the movie suggests, especially after Lou suggests that her interest in Blake might expand to include Carla (Graham).

Downey, whatever his problems, is a fine actor, smart and in command of his presence, and he's persuasive here as he defends himself: "I'm an actor. And actors lie." There is a show-stopping scene when he looks at himself in a mirror and warns himself to get his act together. There are some notes in the movie that I could have done without, including an offstage gunshot and a tearjerker ending. But I enjoyed the ebb and flow of their time together.

What shows Toback has learned something since his days as a *Spy* cover boy is that the movie doesn't pretend any of these three people is *really* in love. They're playing at being in love, but essentially all three are soloists, looking out for themselves, and the women can sustain outrage only so long before they begin to seek additional amusements and possibilities. As for the man, well, he always told them his favorite song was "You Don't Know Me."

200 Cigarettes ½★

R, 97 m., 1999

Ben Affleck (Bartender), Casey Affleck (Tom), Janeane Garofalo (Ellie), Courtney Love (Lucy), Gaby Hoffmann (Stephie), Kate Hudson (Cindy), Martha Plimpton (Monica), Paul Rudd (Kevin), Guillermo Diaz (Dave), Brian McCardie (Eric), Christina Ricci (Val), Jay Mohr (Jack), Angela Featherstone (Caitlyn). Directed by Risa Bramon Garcia and produced by Betsy Beers, David Gale, and Van Toffler. Screenplay by Shana Larsen.

All those cigarettes, and nobody knows how to smoke. Everybody in *200 Cigarettes* smokes nearly all the time, but none of them show any style or flair with their cigarettes. And the cinematographer doesn't know how to light smoke so it looks great.

He should have studied *Out of the Past* (1947), the greatest cigarette-smoking movie of all time. The trick, as demonstrated by Jacques Tourneur and his cameraman, Nicholas Musuraca, is to throw a lot of light into the empty space where the characters are going to exhale. When they do, they produce great white clouds of smoke, which express their moods, their personalities, and their energy levels. There were guns in *Out of the Past*, but the real hostility came when Robert Mitchum and Kirk Douglas smoked at each other.

The cast of *200 Cigarettes* reads like a roll call of hot talent. They're the kinds of young stars who are on lots of magazine covers and have Web pages devoted to them, and so they know they will live forever and are immune to the diseases of smoking. I wish them well. But if they must smoke in the movies, can't they at least be great smokers, like my mother was? When she was smoking you always knew exactly how she felt because of the way she used her cigarette and her hands and the smoke itself as a prop to help her express herself. She should have been good; she learned from Bette Davis movies.

The stars of *200 Cigarettes*, on the other hand, belong to the suck-and-blow school of smokeology. They inhale, not too deeply, and exhale, not too convincingly, and they squint in their close-ups while smoke curls up from below the screen. Their smoke emerges as small, pale, noxious gray clouds. When Robert Mitchum exhaled at a guy, the guy ducked out of the way.

I suppose there will be someone who counts the cigarettes in *200 Cigarettes* to see if there are actually 200. That will at least be something to do during the movie, which is a lame and labored conceit about an assortment of would-be colorful characters on their way to a New Year's Eve party in 1981. Onto the pyre of this dreadful film are thrown the talents of such as Ben Affleck, Casey Affleck, Janeane Garofalo, Courtney Love, Gaby Hoffmann, Kate Hudson, Martha Plimpton, Paul Rudd, Guillermo Diaz, Brian McCardie, Jay Mohr, Christina Ricci, Angela Featherstone, and others equally unlucky.

Ricci and Love have the kinds of self-contained personalities that hew out living space for their characters no matter where they find themselves, but the others are pretty much lost. The witless screenplay provides its characters with aimless dialogue and meaningless confrontations, and they are dressed not like people who might have been alive in 1981, but like people going to a costume party where 1981 is the theme. (There is not a single reason, by the way, why the plot requires the film to be set in 1981 or any other year.)

Seeing a film like this helps you to realize that actors are empty vessels waiting to be filled with characters and dialogue. As people, they are no doubt much smarter and funnier than the cretins in this film. I am reminded of Gene Siskel's bottom-line test for a film: "Is this movie more entertaining than a documentary of the same people having lunch?" Here they are contained by small ideas and arch dialogue, and lack the juice of life. Maybe another 200 cigarettes would have helped; coughing would be better than some of this dialogue.

U

Ulee's Gold ★ ★ ★ ½

R, 115 m., 1997

Peter Fonda (Ulee Jackson), Patricia Richardson (Connie Hope), Jessica Biel (Casey Jackson), J. Kenneth Campbell (Bill Floyd), Christine Dunford (Helen Jackson), Steven Flynn (Eddie Flowers), Dewey Weber (Ferris Dooley), Tom Wood (Jimmy Jackson). Directed by Victor Nunez and produced by Nunez, Sam Gowan, and Peter Saraf. Screenplay by Nunez.

Peter Fonda was never an action hero in the first place. Tall, introverted, and sensitive, he was best cast in his breakthrough role as Captain America, a hippie motorcyclist on an odyssey in *Easy Rider* (1968). His films since are an undistinguished collection of action and exploitation pictures; the rare good film like *The Hired Hand* (1971) looks lonely in such company. Now, at fifty-seven, he has found the role of a lifetime—perhaps the role that points the way to a reborn career.

In *Ulee's Gold,* he plays Ulysses Jackson, a beekeeper in the Florida panhandle who has a lot on his mind. He was the only survivor of his Vietnam unit. His wife died six years ago. His son is in prison on a robbery charge, and he is raising his two granddaughters as best he can. He is a very lonely man, but he loves his work: "The bees and I have an understanding."

He hasn't spoken to his son, Jimmy (Tom Wood), in two years when one day a call comes. He goes to visit the boy in prison. The son asks for help: His wife, Helen (Christine Dunford), has turned up in bad shape, and is staying with Eddie and Ferris, the two guys Jimmy pulled the robbery with. Jimmy wants Ulee to get Helen and take care of her.

"She can just stay gone," Ulee says.

"She's sick, Dad," says Jimmy.

So Ulee drives his pickup truck down to where Ferris and Eddie (Dewey Weber and Steven Flynn) are holed up in a flophouse with Helen, who is strung out on drugs and madness. And he hauls Helen home, although not before the two men tell him they believe Jimmy hid $100,000 from the robbery, and they want it back—or they will come after the grandchildren.

A woman named Connie (Patricia Richardson, from *Home Improvement*) lives across the street from Ulee. She's a nurse, divorced twice, no children. The granddaughters like her, and when they see the shape their mother is in, they drag her across the street to help. Helen needs a lot of help: sedatives, restraints, the whole detox process. Ulee tries to thank her. "It's what I do," she says.

The elements are in place here for a fairly standard story in which Ferris and Eddie come looking for the money, and Ulee must defend his family, while falling in love, of course, with Connie—while the girls bond once again with their mother. But to look at events in that way would miss the whole purpose of *Ulee's Gold,* which is not about who prevails, but about what Ulee learns about himself.

The movie was written, directed, and edited by Victor Nunez, who sets all of his films in Florida and goes from strength to strength. His films include *Gal Young 'Un* (1979), about a backwoods widow's run-in with a con man; *A Flash of Green* (1984), with Ed Harris as a newspaper reporter, in one of his finest roles; and then, after too long a wait, the wonderful *Ruby in Paradise* (1993), with its luminous performance by Ashley Judd.

Nunez has a gift for finding the essence, the soul, of his actors; that's why Harris and Judd were so good, and why Peter Fonda here reveals a depth of talent we did not suspect. Nunez is attentive to the quiet in Fonda's nature, to the deeply buried anger, and to the intelligence. There is a situation late in this film that involves a gun, and the Fonda character handles it like a chessmaster, figuring out what the real threat is and how his opponents will react. Raised on routine movies, we figure Ulee will grab for the gun. Ulee is smarter and deeper than that.

The scenes between Fonda and Richardson are charged with quiet tension. Obviously she likes him. He tells her he is no longer good at—well, getting along with people. She understands. What happens between them happens slowly and tactfully. And Nunez is just as careful in the way he introduces Ulee's profession. We learn something about bees in this movie, and a lot about beekeepers, but *Ulee's*

Gold is not a documentary; all of the information is put to the use of the story, especially in a scene where one of the granddaughters uses bees in a parable she tells her mother. Basically, it comes down to: You take care of them, and they'll take care of you.

Ulysses' Gaze ★

NO MPAA RATING, 180 m., 1997

Harvey Keitel ("A"), Erland Josephson (Film Library Curator), Maia Morgenstern ("Ulysses' Wives"), Thanassis Vengos (Taxi Driver), Yorgos Michalakopoulos (Journalist Friend), Dora Volanaki (Old Woman). Directed by Theo Angelopoulos and produced by Eric Heumann. Screenplay by Angelopoulos, Tonino Guerra, and Petros Markaris.

Because it is a noble epic set amid the ruins of the Russian empire and the genocide of what was Yugoslavia, there is a temptation to give *Ulysses' Gaze* the benefit of the doubt: to praise it for its vision, its daring, its courage, its great length. But I would not be able to look you in the eye if you then went to see it, because how could I deny that it is a numbing bore?

A director must be very sure of his greatness to inflict an experience like this on the audience, and Theo Angelopoulos was so sure that when he won only the Special Jury Prize at the 1995 Cannes Film Festival, he made his displeasure obvious on the stage. He thought he should have won the Palme d'Or, which went instead to *Underground,* by Emir Kusturica, which was also three hours long and also set in the wreckage of Yugoslavia, but had at least the virtue of not being almost unendurable.

Ulysses' Gaze stars Harvey Keitel as a Greek movie director named "A," who returns to his roots thirty-five years after leaving for America. He seeks, he says, some rare old film footage: the first film ever shot in the Balkans. His odyssey (for so we must describe any journey in a movie with "Ulysses" in the title) takes him by taxi from Greece to the Albanian border, and then by boat to the cities of Skopje, Bucharest, and Sarajevo. ("Is this Sarajevo?" he asks at one point. If you have to ask, you're in the wrong place.) Along the way there are flashbacks to 1945 and 1946 when, as a friend in Belgrade tells him, "We fell asleep in one world and were rudely awakened in another."

You might be tempted to wonder why old film footage would be so important to "A" that he would risk his life traveling unprotected through a war zone to find it. Since Angelopoulos in fact directed this movie about such a man, and filmed it in the very same war zones, he would probably not be the man to ask.

The initial "A" undoubtedly stands for Angelopoulos, but why he chose Harvey Keitel to portray him is a mystery. Keitel is a great spontaneous actor, able to think on his feet and move around quickly in dialect, but here he acts as if someone has injected him with crazy glue. He's slow, measured, portentous, tedious, and his dialogue sounds like readings from an editorial translated imperfectly through several languages.

There are several women in the movie (the credits call them "Ulysses' Wives"), and they find themselves powerfully attracted to "A," a mystery only partly explained by the fact that they are all played by the same actress, Maia Morgenstern. They see him, he sees them, and soon the two of them are looking greatly pained. I was reminded of Armando Bo's anguished 1960s Argentinian soft-core sex films, which starred his wife, Isabel Sarli, whose agony was terrible to behold and could only be slaked in the arms of a man. "A" and the women make love in this movie as if trying to apply unguent inside each other's clothes.

There are some remarkable images. They are spaced throughout the film at roughly twenty-minute intervals. One shows a thin line of police separating demonstrators with torches, and other people with umbrellas. When the torchbearers press forward, the umbrellas undulate backward, in a scene reminiscent of the umbrella scene in Hitchcock's *Foreign Correspondent.* Similar crowds with umbrellas stand in squares, and in fields, and along the banks of rivers. One wonders if the umbrellas are important to the shots, or if the extras demanded them.

Another big image involves a huge statue of Lenin, which has been disassembled and placed aboard a barge. (For shipment . . . where? Where is there a demand for used Lenin statues these days?) The vast stone head looks forward, and Lenin's giant finger points the way, as "A" travels on the same barge. The image is so powerful that even its banality cannot diminish it.

The closing passages of the film have an immediacy; they're set in the middle of a war zone, and characters important to "A" are endangered. But one can easily think of much better films also shot under wartime conditions, particularly *Circle of Deceit,* shot by Volker Schlondorff during the fighting in Beirut, or Milcho Manchevski's *Before the Rain,* shot near the fighting in Yugoslavia.

What's left after *Ulysses' Gaze* is the impression of a film made by a director so convinced of the gravity and importance of his theme that he wants to weed out any moviegoers seeking interest, grace, humor, or involvement. One cannot easily imagine anyone else speaking up at a dinner table where he presides.

It is an old fact about the cinema—known perhaps even to those pioneers who made the ancient footage "A" is seeking—that a film does not exist unless there is an audience between the projector and the screen. A director, having chosen to work in a mass medium, has a certain duty to that audience. I do not ask that he make it laugh or cry, or even that he entertain it, but he must at least not insult its goodwill by giving it so little to repay its patience. What arrogance and self-importance this film reveals.

Unhook the Stars ★ ★ ★

R, 105 m., 1997

Gena Rowlands (Mildred), Marisa Tomei (Monica), Gérard Depardieu (Big Tommy), Jake Lloyd (J.J.), Moira Kelly (Ann Mary Margaret), David Sherrill (Ethan), David Thompson (Frankie), Bridgett Wilson (Jeannie). Directed by Nick Cassavetes and produced by Rene Cleitman. Screenplay by Cassavetes and Helen Caldwell.

If Gena Rowlands were getting a makeover on one of the chat shows, they'd tell her to cut her hair to a sensible length and stop trying to look like a 1950s sex bomb, but what her look tells you is that you get the whole package: She's bringing along the past, the glamour, and all those blowzy, confused, desperate women she played for her husband, the late John Cassavetes. You want my theory about the hairstyle? John liked it that way.

In *Unhook the Stars,* the directorial debut of their son, Nick Cassavetes, Rowlands plays a calmer version of the high-energy, neurotic heroines of *Opening Night, Love Streams, Minnie and Moskowitz, A Woman Under the Influence,* and all those other Cassavetes dramas in which the characters drank and smoked and tried to settle—right now!—things that could never be settled at all. In the current movie, she's a widow named Mildred, comfortably well-off, living in a house that's too big for her now that her husband has died. Her son is prospering in San Francisco, and her daughter has angrily moved out.

One day there's a knock on the door, and she opens it to find a neighbor she doesn't know, Monica (Marisa Tomei), with her small son J.J. (Jake Lloyd) in tow. Monica is obviously at the end of her rope, and we know why: Her husband, who likes to slap her around, has made life impossible, and she needs emergency baby-sitting, right now.

That's the setup for a film of gentleness and low-key romance. Mildred finds herself caring for a small child once again, and volunteers to do it on a daily basis. There's a hint of the old Cassavetes compulsiveness in a scene where she settles the kid down with the encyclopedia and begins to read, starting with "a, for a capella." Soon she and J.J. are best friends, and Mildred is tactfully trying to bring some order into Monica's life.

Monica is played by Tomei as the kind of borderline manic that the senior Cassavetes filled his films with. Nick sees her with more dimensions. Yes, she has a problem with anger. Yes, she drinks too much. Yes, she dates men as if they're a quick fix. ("This guy I'm going out with," she giggles to Mildred, "I don't even like him. Good thing I'm drinking.") But she is also a loving mom who is determined to raise her son as best she can, and who deals with an abusive spouse in a direct and decisive way.

Meanwhile, other issues are churning in Mildred's life. Her daughter (Moira Kelly), sullen and angry, has moved out to live with her boyfriend, in a relationship that clearly will not survive. Her son (David Sherrill) invites her out to San Francisco for a tour of his luxury townhouse, which includes a "mother-in-law apartment" just for her. But is she ready to sell her rambling house and move in with him?

And then there is the most unexpected development of all. Monica takes her to a bar one night, and she is picked up—yes, at her age!—by a French-Canadian truck driver (Gérard Depardieu) who seems to have fallen in love with her. They go on a date, he delivers her back home in his giant rig, and there is a kissing scene that only these two accomplished actors could have made work quite the way it does.

Unhook the Stars doesn't create a lot of contrived plot problems and then resolve them with dramatic developments. Each element of the screenplay (written by Nick Cassavetes and Helen Caldwell) is taken only as far as it will willingly go. Monica's husband doesn't go berserk, Mildred's daughter is rebellious but not insane, the truck driver is tactful in declaring his love, and even the inevitable separation between Mildred and J.J. is handled as the next step, rather than the last straw. The outcome is nicely open-ended, instead of insisting that Mildred do something concrete to provide a happy ending.

Unhook the Stars feels as if it may have been written for Rowlands, but who better to write for? What's interesting is how developed all of the characters are; Tomei doesn't have a supporting role but sort of a parallel one, and young Jake Lloyd is blunt and direct as J.J., zeroing in as children do on the subject at hand. Like his father, Nick Cassavetes has made a movie about a slice of life. But it is about manageable, not unmanageable, life. It has an underlying contentment.

Unmade Beds ★ ★ ½

NO MPAA RATING, 93 m., 1998

Brenda Monte (Brenda), Michael De Stefano (Michael), Aimee Copp (Aimee), Mikey Russo (Mikey). Directed by Nicholas Barker and produced by Steve Wax. Screenplay by Barker.

Brenda, sexy Italian, buxom, blond, 40s, seeks man to give her money and go away.

Michael, 40, 5-4, graying temples, seeks marriage, fears that "if I die a bachelor, all I will leave behind me is stuff."

Aimee, 28, 225 pounds, blond, wants husband, children; has job, health benefits.

Mikey, 50ish, screenwriter, doesn't date mutts: "I remember making love to three gorgeous women in 24 hours in 1974. One of those women would still be with me today if I was a faithful kind of a guy."

Those are the four protagonists in Nicholas Barker's *Unmade Beds,* a film that walks and talks like a documentary but is, I am assured, entirely scripted. Barker found his subjects by answering 400 personal ads in New York, and screening the advertisers until he had found four who projected humor, personality, and bleak desperation.

Early in the film he shows an Edward Hopper painting of empty urban windows, and the scenes of his film are separated by telephoto shots of New York apartment windows, some empty, others filled by people living their lives or simply looking out at the street below.

One of them is Brenda Monte, a tough-talking woman who has often been told she has a great body, "but now they add those three little words, 'for your age.'" Her problem: "My income is $2,000 a month. My expenses are $3,000." All she is to her teenage daughter "is a cash machine and a taxi." What she wants from a man is money.

Mikey Russo, the "screenwriter," has never sold a screenplay. His apartment, filled with erotic art, says one thing to women: They're there for sex. The medicine cabinet is stocked with all their needs, even toothbrushes. "I'm not cheap. They get Oral-Bs." We sense he doesn't have many visitors. He has himself paged to get out of buying dinner.

Aimee Copp has a nice smile and a warm laugh, but is overweight and desperate for a man. Her aunt recently called her and said she had checked with the whole family ("and I'm sure she did") and the family would be "okay" if she decided to have a child out of wedlock. In other words, they've given up any hope she will ever get married.

Michael De Stefano stands 5-4 and is sensitive about his height. He tells dates they can meet in a public place, and if they can't stand the sight of him, they can just walk away. He keeps talking about how everyone, even his parents, suspects he is gay.

All of these people use their real names in the movie. Whether we are seeing their real lives is a good question. This is not *cinema verité;* some scenes took ten takes. "The movie contains a lot of truth," Barker told a Toronto festival audience, "but precious little reality." A couple of the characters "tell major lies."

You know it's scripted anyway, because of two stylistic giveaways: The characters never stumble over words, and the camera continues unbroken dialogue passages while cutting from one angle to another. But, hey, Robert Flaherty scripted *Nanook of the North.* There's more than one path to truth.

The movie has moments that seem absolutely authentic, as when Aimee tells her friend she has always had a weight problem and will always have a weight problem, and she needs a man who is comfortable with that. There are other moments that feel scripted, as when Brenda says she shoplifts dog food because "they're God's creatures—I shouldn't have to pay for it."

Then again, maybe Brenda would say that. She's disarmingly direct, and the movie's best scene occurs when she conducts a guided critical tour of her body, dispassionately pointing out the parts that are holding up and the places that are starting to sag. I am not sure if I believe she really gets married to an immigrant for cash, but I believe every word of her description of her bridal trousseau, including the price she actually paid for her $400 dress.

At the end of the film, I concluded that Brenda will be okay, and the other three characters are single because getting married is the only thing that interests them. That can scare away a first date. It's a bad sign when a girl tells you she has her own health plan, and a guy points out the fresh toothbrushes. You don't sense a lot of confidence there. We never meet the immigrant Brenda goes to marry, but I'll bet there'd be a movie in *his* story.

Urban Legend ★★

R, 98 m., 1998

Alicia Witt (Natalie), Jared Leto (Paul), Rebecca Gayheart (Brenda), Robert Englund (Professor Wexler), Natasha Gregson Wagner (Michelle), Michael Rosenbaum (Parker), Loretta Devine (Reese), Joshua Jackson (Damon), Tara Reid (Sasha), John Neville (Dean Adams). Directed by Jamie Blanks and produced by Neal H. Moritz, Gina Matthews, and Michael McDonnell. Screenplay by Silvio Horta.

I really wish I knew more about music. There must be a name for the kind of loud, sudden chord that slasher movies depend on. You know the effect. The foreground is filled with the heroine, carefully framed so that we can see nothing behind her. She turns around, there's a shock cut to a big close-up of another face, and on the sound track we get the "thwaaaaank!" of the chord. Then we realize—hey, it's only Natalie! Or Brenda! Or Michelle!

"Sorry—didn't mean to scare you," Natalie/Brenda/Michelle says, while the heroine grins foolishly and both parties laugh with relief. I've got a tip for Natalie/Brenda/Michelle. When the campus is in the grip of a mad slasher, the dead outnumber the living in the dorms, and security guards start sliding through pools of blood—it is seriously uncool to sneak up silently behind someone and grab them by the shoulder. If they're packing, you're dead meat.

Urban Legend makes heavy use of what we may as well name the Creep Chord. It's the movie's punctuation mark. There's a moment of relief, and then the buildup, and then "thwaaaank!" Just to keep things interesting, about every third time it's not Natalie/Brenda, etc., but a slasher with an ax.

The slasher prowls the campus wearing one of those L. L. Bean subzero Arctic parkas where the fur lining on the hood sticks out so far that you can't see the face inside. If I were dean of students, I'd ban all forms of head covering for the duration of the emergency. Of course, the dean of students may *be* the killer; this movie doesn't waste a single character—every single person in it is possibly the slasher.

Still, you have to wonder why a person in a conspicuous parka isn't noticed creeping around the campus and even into a heated swimming pool area (sorry—that one's a false alarm; the person in the parka is an innocent who just happens to like to wear a subzero parka in hot and humid environments). I am reminded of *I Know What You Did Last Summer* (1997), in which the slasher dressed at all times in a slicker and a rubber rain hat, like the Groton's Fisherman, and yet was never noticed in a coastal resort town in summer when it was not raining.

Urban Legend is in the *Scream* tradition, which means that its characters are allowed to be aware of the traditions of their genre. In this case, the killings are deliberately planned to reenact famous urban legends. I will only reveal the opening example, in which a woman grows frightened when the alarming goon who runs the gas pumps tries to lure her inside the station. She beans him, breaks a window, and escapes back to her car—too late for him to warn her there's an ax murderer hiding in the backseat.

My favorite urban legend, the phantom Doberman, is overlooked by the movie, but it hits a lot of the other bases, including the babysitter who traces a threatening call and discovers it's coming from . . . upstairs. These kinds of movies used to star the dregs of the B-movie stables but the casts look a lot better these days; up-and-coming stars are assembled, and knocked off one by one. The real killer is the one person you would never, ever, not in a million years, even remotely suspect, unless your I.Q. is above 60.

The film is competently made, and the attractive cast emotes and screams energetically, and does a good job of unwisely grabbing each other by the shoulders. The gore is within reasonable bounds, as slasher movies go; oddly enough, today's truly violent movies are the comedies. The stars include Alicia Witt, Jared Leto, Natasha Gregson Wagner, Rebecca Gayheart, and Robert (Freddy Krueger) Englund, who is to slasher movies as the Quaker is to oatmeal.

Urban Legend is not art. But for its teenage audience, it serves the same purpose, which is to speed the meeting of like minds. Everybody knows how it works. The guy puts his arm casually around his date's shoulders. Natalie/Brenda/Michelle goes poking around in the abandoned campus building where the massacre took place years ago. The Creep Chord blasts out of the Dolby speakers, everyone jumps, and if in the confusion his hand slips south, well, who says cable will ever replace the theatrical experience?

U.S. Marshals ★ ★ ½

PG-13, 123 m., 1998

Tommy Lee Jones (Marshal Sam Gerard), Wesley Snipes (Sheridan), Robert Downey Jr. (John Royce), Joe Pantoliano (Deputy Marshal Cosmo Renfro), Kate Nelligan (U.S. Marshal Walsh), Irene Jacob (Marie), Daniel Roebuck (Biggs), Tom Wood (Newman). Directed by Stuart Baird and produced by Arnold Kopelson and Anne Kopelson. Screenplay by John Pogue, based on characters created by Roy Huggins.

I didn't expect *U.S. Marshals* to be the equal of *The Fugitive*, and it isn't. But I hoped it would approach the taut tension of the 1993 film, and it doesn't. It has extra scenes, needless characters, an aimless plot, and a solution that the hero seems to keep learning and then forgetting.

The hero is U.S. Deputy Marshal Sam Gerard, played by Tommy Lee Jones in a reprise of his costarring role in *The Fugitive*. The fact that they made this quasi-sequel without its original star (Harrison Ford) is a tribute to the strength of Jones's presence in the earlier film, where he had more dialogue than the lead. Jones made a big impression there, and won an Oscar. Here he hits the same marks with the same razor-edged delivery; everything's right about his performance except that it's in a rambling movie.

Take the opening sequence, where Jones disguises himself as a fast-food chicken to supervise a stakeout of a wanted man. There's a break-in, a fight, some violence, an arrest, TV interviews, a jailing, a tavern scene to celebrate, a reprimand by his superior (Kate Nelligan)—and all for what? So that the guy they caught can be put on a plane to a Missouri prison, and Sam Gerard can be put on the same flight—but not to guard the guy. No, Sam is flying on to Washington. The guy they caught and fought with is utterly unnecessary for the rest of the movie.

But also on that plane to Missouri is another character, played by Wesley Snipes. When we first see him he's a Chicago tow-truck driver. Another driver causes a crash, he's hospitalized, his prints are checked, and he's arrested and charged with the murders of two agents in New York. He protests that it's a case of mistaken identity. Is it?

Never mind that for a moment. Stop to consider. All you need for the movie to get rolling, is to establish the Snipes character and get him on that plane with Marshal Gerard. The marshal doesn't need a lot of establishing because (1) we know him from the earlier movie, and (2) Tommy Lee Jones can establish himself with three lines of dialogue, as he did in the first film.

By lingering over the chicken-suit raid, the movie has wasted time. More time is wasted by supplying a girlfriend for Snipes, played by Irene Jacob. This character is utterly superfluous. Example: She turns up at a cemetery in the middle of a shoot-out, flees with Snipes, can't make it over a wall, and is left behind. (That wall . . . hmmm. How can Snipes leap high enough to get atop the wall, but Jacob can't even jump high enough to reach his outstretched hand lowered to her?)

The movie gets rolling at around the twenty-five-minute mark, with a spectacular plane crash, reminding us of the train crash in *The Fugitive.* One prisoner escapes: Snipes. The marshal coordinates a manhunt that looks like it costs millions (helicopters, roadblocks for a twenty-mile radius, teams combing the woods, etc.). "We got a fugitive," he barks, in a line supplied as a convenience for the producers of the TV spots.

The State Department gets involved, revealing that Snipes is a bigger fish than anybody thought. And the marshal is supplied with a shadow: an agent named Royce (Robert Downey Jr.), who will follow him everywhere. They spar. "You sure you wanna get cute with me?" the marshal asks him. And, "I love that nickel-plated sissy pistol." Royce falls under the Law of Economy of Characters: A seemingly unnecessary sidekick will inevitably turn out to be—but you know how it goes.

The movie settles into a chase structure, with set pieces: a confrontation in a swamp, a cat-and-mouse game in a cemetery, and a chase through an old folks' home. It's there that the Snipes character commits the Fallacy of the Climbing Fugitive (fleeing man climbs stairs, tower, scaffold, etc., even though he can't possibly escape at the top unless he can fly). There is, however, a reason for him to climb—a spectacular escape that would have made Batman proud.

There is an explanation for all of this. We know or guess its outlines early in the film. The marshal figures it out, too ("This is a 'ruthless assassin' who keeps going out of his way to let people live"). He even discovers videotape evidence revealing the real story. And yet, in the cemetery, even when the evil Chinese agent tries to kill the fugitive, the marshal and his men still chase Snipes. It's like Gerard keeps absentmindedly overlooking what he's learned earlier in the film.

The result is unconvincing and disorganized. Yes, there are some spectacular stunts and slick special-effects sequences. Yes, Jones is right on the money, and Snipes makes a sympathetic fugitive. But it's the story that has to pull this train, and its derailment is about as definitive as the train crash in the earlier film.

U-Turn ★ ½

R, 125 m., 1997

Sean Penn (Bobby Cooper), Billy Bob Thornton (Darrell), Powers Boothe (Sheriff), Jennifer Lopez (Grace McKenna), Nick Nolte (Jake McKenna), Julie Hagerty (Flo), Joaquin Phoenix (Toby N. Tucker), Jon Voight (Blind Man), Claire Danes (Jenny), Laurie Metcalf (Bus Clerk), Liv Tyler (Girl in Bus Station). Directed by Oliver Stone and produced by Dan Halsted and Clayton Townsend. Screenplay by John Ridley.

Only Oliver Stone knows what he was trying to accomplish by making *U-Turn,* and it is a secret he doesn't share with the audience. This is a repetitive, pointless exercise in genre film-making—the kind of movie where you distract yourself by making a list of the sources. Much of the story comes from *Red Rock West,* John Dahl's 1994 film about a man and a wife who both try to convince a drifter to kill the other. And the images and milieu are out of Russ Meyer country; his *Cherry, Harry and Raquel* and *SuperVixens* contain the same red-neck sheriffs, the same lustful wives, the same isolated shacks and ignorant mechanics and car culture. *U-Turn* and *Cherry* both end, indeed, with a debt to *Duel in the Sun.*

I imagine Stone made this movie as sort of a lark, after the exhausting but remarkable accomplishments of *Nixon, Natural Born Killers, Heaven and Earth,* and *JFK.* Well, he deserves a break—but this one? Stone is a gifted filmmaker not afraid to take chances, to express ideas in his films and make political statements. Here he's on holiday.

Watching *U-Turn,* I was reminded of a concert pianist playing "Chopsticks": It is done well, but one is disappointed to find it done at all.

The film stars Sean Penn, in a convincing performance all the more admirable for being pointless. He plays Bobby, a man who has had bad luck up the road (his bandaged hand is missing two fingers) and will have a lot more bad luck in the desert town of Superior, Arizona. He wheels into town in his beloved Mustang convertible, which needs a new radiator hose, and encounters the loathsome Darrell (Billy Bob Thornton), a garage mechanic he will eventually be inspired to call an "ignorant inbred turtleneck hick."

While Darrell works on the car, Bobby walks into town. Superior is one of those backwater hells much beloved in the movies, where everyone is malevolent, oversexed, narrow-eyed, and hateful. There are never any industries in these towns (except for garages, saloons, and law enforcement) because everyone is too preoccupied by sex, lying, scheming, embezzling, and hiring strangers to kill each other.

Bobby quickly finds a sultry young woman named Grace (Jennifer Lopez) and is invited home to help her install her drapes and whatever else comes to mind. Soon her enraged husband, Jake (Nick Nolte), comes charging in, red-eyed and bewhiskered, to threaten Bobby with his life, but after the obligatory fight they meet down the road and Jake asks Bobby to kill his wife. Soon Grace will want Bobby to kill her husband (the *Red Rock West* bit), and the film leads to one of those situations where Bobby's life depends on which one he believes.

Superior, Arizona, is the original town without pity. During the course of his brief stay there, Bobby will be kicked in the ribs several dozen times, almost be bitten by a tarantula, shot at, and have his car all but destroyed—and that's all before the final scenes with the vultures circling overhead. Bobby comes across almost like a character in a computer game; you wipe him out, he falls down, stars spin around his head, and then he jumps up again, ready for action.

The film is well made on the level of craft; of course it is, with this strong cast, and Stone directing, and Robert Richardson as cinematographer. But it goes around and around until, like a merry-go-round rider, we figure out that the view is always changing but it's never going to be new. There comes a sinking feeling, half an hour into the film, when we realize the characters are not driven by their personalities and needs but by the plot. At that point they become puppets, not people. That's the last thing we'd expect in a film by Oliver Stone.

V

The Van ★★★

R, 100 m., 1997

Colm Meaney (Larry), Donal O'Kelly (Bimbo), Brendan O'Carroll (Weslie), Ger Ryan (Maggie), Ruaidhri Conroy (Kevin). Directed by Stephen Frears and produced by Lynda Myles. Screenplay by Roddy Doyle, based on his novel.

In three novels made into three movies, Roddy Doyle has brought to life the comic, poignant, resourceful people of a fictitious North Dublin suburb he calls Barrytown. They live so close together they're almost in each other's pockets, and are chronically short of cash (although there is somehow always money for drink). And they weather life's crises with imagination and resiliency.

The Van is the third of the trilogy, the story of two good buddies whose friendship is almost wrecked by their decision to go into business with an ancient and filthy fast-food truck they find rotting in someone's backyard. It has no engine and is caked with grease ("It's like the inside of a leper"), but as "Bimbo's Burgers," it embodies all their hopes.

The friends are Larry (Colm Meaney) and Bimbo (Donal O'Kelly). Meaney has been in all three of the Doyle films; he was the exasperated father of the pregnant teenager in *The Snapper* (1993) and the father of the young band leader in *The Commitments* (1991), and is underused as the mad-dog DEA agent in *Con Air.* He's a large man with a face that exudes goodwill in spite of everything—and the characters he plays usually have a lot of everything to be in spite of. As the film opens, he's locked in unemployment and consoling Bimbo over a pint of Guinness after Bimbo has been fired at the bakery.

One of the quiet gifts of all the Doyle films (the first directed by Alan Parker, the next two by Stephen Frears) is the richness of Dublin life you can spot in the margins. Consider Larry's home life. He presides uneasily over a household consisting of a daughter with a baby but no husband, and a son with a sharp tongue ("Who paid for that dinner in front of you, son?" "The state."). But there is an underlying happiness in the film, added to by his much-loved wife, Maggie (Ger Ryan), who is taking night school literature classes. The perfect note is struck by a subtle decorating touch: the framed portrait of John Wayne on the kitchen wall. (When the van is finally cleaned up and ready to be moved, it's to the call of "Take 'em to Missouri, men! Yee-haw!") Another touch: the kitchen "swear jar," where a contribution frequently has to be made because of the words that are the cornerstones of Larry's vocabulary.

The movie's action takes place during the summer of 1990, fondly remembered in Dublin because the Irish soccer team made it to the semifinals of the World Cup, defeating England and Romania along the way. Larry and Bimbo and all of their friends gather to watch the matches in pubs, cheering passionately and with utter conviction ("I love Ireland, Maggie!" a beery Larry cries, kissing his wife).

Their venture into business is inspired after they leave a pub after one match and the usual fast-food van, owned by Vietnamese, is gone. (The explanation is matter-of-fact: "They've got to be gone by dark or they'll get bricked by the kids.") Larry and Bimbo figure to clean up after the cup matches and down at the beach. And so they do, for a while, despite several problems (a breaded and deep-fried diaper is served to one customer in place of cod, and when another is ten pence short of the price for a burger, Larry takes a ten-pence bite out of it and hands it to the man).

The movie builds its comic scenes by close observation. Consider, for example, the Christmas dinner sequence, which combines Guinness with "Frosty the Snowman" and a mute, disapproving mother-in-law, and involves the theft of a candy bar from a child's Christmas basket. Or the scene where the two friends combine golfing and baby-sitting, taking along a snapper (baby) in its rainproof little stroller. Characters on the edges contribute to the overall atmosphere, especially Brendan O'Carroll as Weslie, a little man in a long plaid coat who always seems to know where he can get you a better price.

When I saw *The Van* for the first time at the Cannes Film Festival in 1996, I felt it was the least of the three films, and I still do, but it was trimmed of about five minutes of footage after Cannes and, seeing it again a year later, I found it quicker and more alive. It is also the most thoughtful, in a way, and the ending has a poignancy and an unresolved quality that is just right: These disorganized lives would not fit into a neat ending.

Varsity Blues ★ ★

R, 100 m., 1999

James Van Der Beek (Mox), Jon Voight (Coach Kilmer), Paul Walker (Lance Harbor), Ron Lester (Billy Bob), Scott Caan (Tweeder), Richard Lineback (Joe Harbor), Tiffany C. Love (Collette Harbor), Amy Smart (Julie Harbor). Directed by Brian Robbins and produced by Tova Laiter, Mike Tollin, and Robbins. Screenplay by W. Peter Iliff.

Varsity Blues is not your average sports movie. It brings an outsider viewpoint to the material, which involves a Texas high school quarterback who would rather win an academic scholarship than play football. The character, named Mox and played by James Van Der Beek of TV's *Dawson's Creek*, is a good kid—so good that at one point he asks himself why he's always being so good—and although the movie contains *Animal House*–style gross-outs, it doesn't applaud them.

The central struggle is between Mox and Coach Kilmer (Jon Voight, in another of a group of striking recent performances). Kilmer is a close-cropped martinet who addresses pep rallies with a vaguely Hitlerian salute, and has won two state titles and twenty-two district championships in thirty years. Now he wants the twenty-third, at any cost.

The movie takes place in a west Texas town not unlike the setting of *The Last Picture Show*, although the kids get away with even more these days. (When one steals a squad car and drives around town with his buddies and their girlfriends, all naked, that merely inspires some "boys will be boys" talk at the local diner.) Some plot elements are hard to believe (could a high school teacher get away with stripping at a nearby topless club?), but others, including the way players are injected with painkillers before a big game, feel truthful.

The movie was directed by Brian Robbins, who made the high-spirited *Good Burger* (1997), and here again we see the impulses of a satirist winking from behind the constraints of a genre. I enjoyed, for example, the subplot involving Mox's kid brother, the religion-obsessed Kyle, who makes his first entrance with a crucifix strapped to his back and by the end of the film has founded a cult with his playmates. Maybe his spirituality is inherited; their father asks Mox, "Did you pray for more playing time?"

The arc of the movie involves one football season, during which Coach Kilmer will or will not win his twenty-third title. Of course it ends with a Big Game and a Big Play, with seconds on the clock, but this is a movie that doesn't buy into all the tenets of our national sports religion; the subtext is that winning *isn't* everything.

One of Mox's friends is the enormous Billy Bob (Ron Lester), whose breakfast consists of pancakes chased down with syrup swigged straight from the bottle. Without revealing what happens to him, I will express my gratitude to Robbins and his writer, W. Peter Iliff, for not marching lockstep down the well-traveled road of inevitable developments. I also enjoyed the relationship between Mox and Lance (Paul Walker), the starting quarterback; instead of making Lance into the obligatory jerk, the movie pays more attention. To the standard role of the town sexpot, Tiffany C. Love brings a certain poignancy; she always goes for the starting quarterback, but she's not a slut so much as a realist.

All of this sounds as if *Varsity Blues* is a good movie, and parts of it are, but the parts never quite come together. Scenes work, but they don't pile up and build momentum. Van Der Beek is convincing and likable, Voight's performance has a kind of doomed grandeur, and the characters are seen with quirky humor. (When Billy Bob gets knocked cold during a game, for example, and the trainer asks him how many fingers he's holding up, Mox explains, "With Billy Bob, you gotta go true or false. Billy Bob, is he holding up fingers? Yes or no?") The movie doesn't quite get over the top, but you sense that Brian Robbins has the right instincts, and is ready to break loose for a touchdown.

Velvet Goldmine ★★

R, 127 m., 1998

Ewan McGregor (Curt Wild), Jonathan Rhys-Meyers (Brian Slade), Toni Collette (Mandy Slade), Christian Bale (Arthur Stuart), Eddie Izzard (Jerry Divine), Emily Woof (Shannon), Michael Feast (Cecil), Janet McTeer (Female Narrator). Directed by Todd Haynes and produced by Christine Vachon. Screenplay by James Lyons and Haynes.

Velvet Goldmine is a movie made up of beginnings, endings, and fresh starts. There isn't enough in between. It wants to be a movie in search of a truth, but it's more like a movie in search of itself. Not everyone who leaves the theater will be able to pass a quiz on exactly what happens.

Set in the 1970s, it's the story of the life, death, and resurrection of a glam-rock idol named Brian Slade, played by Jonathan Rhys-Meyers and probably inspired by David Bowie. After headlining a brief but dazzling era of glitter rock, he fakes his own death onstage. When the hoax is revealed, his cocaine use increases, his sales plummet, and he disappears from view. A decade later, in the fraught year of 1984, a journalist named Arthur Stuart (Christian Bale) is assigned to find out what really happened to Brian Slade.

Do we care? Not much. Slade is not made into a convincing character in *Velvet Goldmine,* although his stage appearances are entertaining enough. But a better reason for our disinterest is that the film bogs down in the apparatus of the search for Slade. Clumsily borrowing moments from *Citizen Kane,* it has its journalist interview Slade's ex-wife and business associates, and there is even a sequence of shots specifically mirroring *Kane*'s first interview with the mogul's former wife Susan.

Citizen Kane may have been voted the greatest of all American films (which it is), but how many people watching *Velvet Goldmine* will appreciate a scene where a former Slade partner is seen in a wheelchair, just like Joseph Cotten? Many of them will still be puzzling out the opening of the film, which begins in Dublin with the birth of Oscar Wilde, who says at an early age, "I want to be a pop idol."

I guess this prologue is intended to establish a link between Wilde and the Bowie generation of cross-dressing performance artists who teased audiences with their apparent bisexuality. Brian Slade, in the movie, is married to an American catwoman named Mandy (Toni Collette), but has an affair with a rising rock star named Curt Wild (Ewan McGregor), who looks like Kurt Cobain, is heedless like Oscar Wilde, and is so original onstage that he upstages Slade, who complains, "I just wish it had been me. I wish I'd thought of it." (His wife, as wise as all the wives of brilliant men, tells him, "You will.")

The film evokes snatches of the 1970s rock scene (and another of its opening moments evokes early shots from the Beatles' *A Hard Day's Night*). But it doesn't settle for long enough on any one approach to become very interesting. It's not a career film, or a rags-to-riches film, or an exposé, or an attack, or a dirge, or a musical, but a little of all of those, chopped up and run through a confusing assortment of flashbacks and memories.

The lesson seems to be that Brian Slade was an ambitious, semitalented poseur who cheated his audience once too often, and then fooled them again in a way only the movie and its inquiring reporter fully understand. In the wreckage of his first incarnation are left his wife, lovers, managers, and fans. It is a little disconcerting that the last twenty minutes, if not more, consist of a series of scenes that all feel as if they could be the last scene in the movie: *Velvet Goldmine* keeps promising to quit, but doesn't make good.

David Bowie (if Slade is indeed meant to be Bowie) deserves better than this. He was more talented and smarter than Slade, reinvented himself in full view, and in the long run can only be said to have triumphed (if being married to Iman, pioneering a multimedia art project, and being the richest of all non-Beatle British rock stars is a triumph, and I submit that it is). Bowie is also more interesting than his fictional alter ego in *Velvet Goldmine,* and if glam rock was not great music at least it inaugurated the era of concerts as theatrical spectacles, and inspired its audiences to dress in something other than the hippie uniform.

Todd Haynes, the director and writer, is an American whose first two films (*Poison* and

Safe) were tightly focused, spare, and bleak. *Safe* starred Julianne Moore as a woman allergic to very nearly everything—or was she only allergic to herself? These films were perceptive character studies. In *Velvet Goldmine,* there is the sense that the film's arms were spread too wide, gathered in all of the possible approaches to the material, and couldn't decide on just one.

Very Bad Things ★

R, 101 m., 1998

Christian Slater (Robert Boyd), Cameron Diaz (Laura Garrety), Daniel Stern (Adam Berkow), Jeanne Tripplehorn (Lois Berkow), Jon Favreau (Kyle Fisher), Jeremy Piven (Michael Berkow), Leland Orser (Charles Moore), Carla Scott (Tina), Russell B. McKenzie (Security Guard), Joey Zimmerman (Adam Berkow Jr.), Tyler Malinger (Timmy Berkow). Directed by Peter Berg and produced by Michael Schiffer, Diane Nabatoff, and Cindy Cowan. Screenplay by Berg.

Peter Berg's *Very Bad Things* isn't a bad movie, just a reprehensible one. It presents as comedy things that are not amusing. If you think this movie is funny, that tells me things about you that I don't want to know.

What bothers me most, after two viewings, is its confidence that an audience would be entertained by its sad, sick vision, tainted by racism. If this material had been presented straight, as a drama, the movie would have felt more honest and might have been more successful. Its cynicism is the most unattractive thing about it—the assumption that an audience has no moral limits, and will laugh at cruelty simply to feel hip. I know moral detachment is a key strategy of the ironic pose, but there is a point, once reached, which provides a test of your underlying values.

The film involves five friends who go on a bachelor party to Las Vegas. Kyle Fisher (Jon Favreau) is on the eve of marriage to the wedding-obsessed Laura (Cameron Diaz). His pals include a realty agent named Robert Boyd (Christian Slater), the antagonistic Berkow brothers Adam (Daniel Stern) and Michael (Jeremy Piven), and a mechanic named Charles (Leland Orser), who doesn't talk much.

In Vegas, there's a montage showing them gambling, tossing back shots, and snorting cocaine. A stripper named Tina (Carla Scott) arrives, does lap dances, and is steered into the bathroom by Michael. He lurches drunkenly about the room with her until her head is accidentally impaled on a coat hook. She's dead. (When I saw the film at the Toronto festival, the audience laughed at a shot showing her feet hanging above the floor. Why?)

Some of the men want to dial 911, but Robert takes charge. How will it look that a hooker has turned up dead in their suite? "Take away the horror of the situation. Take away the tragedy of her death. Take away all the moral and ethical considerations you've had drummed into you since childhood, and what are you left with? A 105-pound problem."

His solution? Cut her up and bury her in the desert. He browbeats the others into agreement, but then a black security guard enters with a complaint about noise. The guard (Russell B. McKenzie) sees the dead body, and Robert stabs him with a corkscrew. Now there are two bodies to dispose of, and the guys stride through a hardware store like the Reservoir Dogs.

The movie makes it a point that some of the guys are Jewish, and uses that to get laughs as they bury the bodies. Jewish law, one argues, requires that the body parts be kept together—so they should dig up the dismembered pieces and sort them out. "She's Asian," says another. "Do they have Jews in Asia?" The answer is yes, although surely such a theory would apply to anyone. They start rearranging: "We'll start with black. Then we'll go to Asian."

My thoughts here are complex. The movie is not blatantly racist, and yet a note of some kind is being played when white men kill an Asian and a black. Why then make it a point that some of them are Jewish? What is the purpose, exactly? Please don't tell me it's humor. I'm not asking for political correctness; I'm simply observing the way the movie tries to show how hip it is by rubbing our noses in race.

The events described take about thirty minutes. There is not a single funny thing that happens once the men get to Vegas (Diaz has some funny early stuff about the wedding). Nor is the aftermath funny, as the men freak out with guilt and fear. Robert makes threats to hold them in line, but more deaths follow, and the last act of the film spins out a grisly, unfunny, screwball plot. By the time of the wedding, when potentially comic material crawls back in over the dead bodies, it's way too late to laugh; the movie's tone is too mean-spirited and sour.

Very Bad Things isn't bad on the technical and acting level, and Slater makes a convincing engine to drive the evil. Peter Berg shows that he can direct a good movie, even if he hasn't. If he'd dumped the irony and looked this material straight in the eye, it might have been a better experience. His screenplay has effective lines, as when Robert coldly reasons, "What we have here was not a good thing, but it was, under the circumstances, the smart play." Or when he uses self-help platitudes to rationalize murder ("Given the fact that we are alive and they are not, we chose life over death").

But the film wants it both ways. At a Jewish funeral, the sad song of the cantor is subtly mocked by upbeat jazz segueing into the next scene. Mourners fall onto the coffin in a scene that is embarrassing, not funny. When a widow (Jeanne Tripplehorn) struggles with Robert, she bites his groin, and as he fights back we hear female ululations on the sound track. What's that about? I won't even get into the bonus material about her handicapped child and three-legged dog.

Very Bad Things filled me with dismay. The material doesn't match the genre; it's an attempt to exploit black humor without the control of tone necessary to pull it off. I left the theater feeling sad and angry. On the movie's Website, you can download a stripper. I'm surprised you can't kill her. ☞

Virus ★

R, 96 m., 1999

Jamie Lee Curtis (Kit Foster), William Baldwin (Steve Baker), Donald Sutherland (Captain Everton), Joanna Pacula (Nadia), Marshall Bell (J. W. Woods Jr.), Julio Oscar Mechoso (Squeaky), Sherman Augustus (Richie), Cliff Curtis (Hiko). Directed by John Bruno and produced by Gale Anne Hurd. Written by Chuck Pfarrer and Dennis Feldman, based on the Dark Horse Comic Book Series *Virus* by Chuck Pfarrer.

Ever notice how movies come in twos? It's as if the same idea descends upon several Hollywood producers at once, perhaps because someone who hates movies is sticking pins in his dolls. *Virus* is more or less the same movie as *Deep Rising*, which opened a year earlier. Both begin with small boats in the Pacific. Both boats come upon giant floating ships that are seemingly deserted. Both giant ships are inhabited by a vicious monster. Both movies send the heroes racing around the ship trying to destroy the monster. Both movies also have lots of knee-deep water, fierce storms, Spielbergian visible flashlight beams cutting through the gloom, and red digital readouts.

Deep Rising was one of the worst movies of 1998. *Virus* is easily worse. It didn't help that the print I saw was so underlit that often I could see hardly anything on the screen. Was that because the movie was filmed that way, or because the projector bulb was dimmed to extend its life span? I don't know and in a way I don't care, because to see this movie more clearly would not be to like it better.

Virus opens with berserk tugboat captain Donald Sutherland and his crew towing a barge through a typhoon. The barge is sinking and the crew, led by Jamie Lee Curtis and William Baldwin, want to cut it loose. But the barge represents the skipper's net worth, and he'd rather go to the bottom with it. This sequence is necessary to set up the skipper's avarice.

In the eye of the storm, the tug comes upon a drifting Russian satellite communications ship. In the movie's opening credits, we have already seen what happened to the ship: A drifting space cloud enveloped the *Mir* space station and sent a bolt of energy down to the ship's satellite dish, and apparently the energy included a virus that takes over the onboard computers and represents a vast, if never clearly defined, threat to life on Earth.

Sutherland wants to claim the ship for salvage. The crew board it and soon are fighting the virus. "The ship's steering itself!" one character cries. The chilling answer: "Ships don't steer themselves." Uh, oh. The methods of the virus are strange. It creates robots, and uses them to grab crew members and turn them into strange creatures that are half-man, half–Radio Shack. It's up to Curtis, Baldwin, and their crewmates to outsmart the virus, which seems none too bright and spends most of its time clomping around and issuing threatening statements with a basso profundo voice synthesizer.

The movie's special effects are not exactly slick, and the creature itself is a distinct letdown. It looks like a very tall humanoid figure hammered together out of crushed auto parts, with several headlights for its eyes. It crunches through steel bulkheads and crushes all barriers to its progress, but is this an efficient way for a virus to behave? It could be cruising the Internet instead of doing a Robocop number.

The last half-hour of the movie is almost unseeable. In dark dimness, various human and other figures race around in a lot of water and flashlight beams, and there is much screaming. Occasionally an eye, a limb, or a bloody face emerges from the gloom. Many instructions are shouted. If you can explain to me the exact function of that rocket tube that turns up at the end, I will be sincerely grateful. If you can explain how anyone could survive that function, I will be amazed. The last shot is an homage to *The African Queen,* a movie I earnestly recommend instead of this one.

Volcano ★ ½

PG-13, 104 m., 1997

Tommy Lee Jones (Mike Roark), Anne Heche (Dr. Amy Barnes), Don Cheadle (Emmitt Reese), John Corbett (Norman Caldwell), Keith David (Lieutenant Fox), Gaby Hoffman (Kelly Roark), Jacqueline Kim (Dr. Jaye Calder), John Carroll Lynch (Stan Olber), Michael Rispoli (Gator). Directed by Mick Jackson and produced by Andrew Davis and Neal H. Moritz. Screenplay by Jerome Armstrong and Billy Ray.

I expected to see a mountainous volcano in *Volcano,* towering high over Los Angeles. But the movie takes place at ground level; it's about how lava boils out of the La Brea Tar Pits, threatens a stretch of Wilshire Boulevard, and then takes a shortcut through the city sewer system. The ads say, "The Coast Is Toast," but maybe they should say, "The Volcano Is Drano."

This is a surprisingly cheesy disaster epic. It's said that *Volcano* cost a lot more than *Dante's Peak,* a competing volcano movie, but it doesn't look it. *Dante's Peak* had better special effects, a more entertaining story, and a real mountain. *Volcano* is an absolutely standard, assembly-line undertaking; no wonder one of the extras is reading a paperback titled *Screenwriting Made Easy.*

The movie stars Tommy Lee Jones, professional as always even in this flimsy story, as the chief of the city's Office of Emergency Management. He races through the obligatory opening scenes of all disaster movies (everyday life, ominous warnings, alarm sounded by hero scientist, warnings poo-pooed by official muckety-mucks, etc.). Soon manhole covers are being blown sky-high, subway trains are being engulfed by fireballs, and "lava bombs" are flying through the air and setting miniature sets on fire.

Jones is at ground zero when the La Brea Tar Pits erupt and lava flows down the street, melting fire trucks. Like all disaster movie heroes, he's supplied with five obligatory companions:

1. His daughter (Gaby Hoffmann), who comes along for the ride, gets trapped by a lava flow, is rescued, is taken to a hospital, and has to be rescued from the path of a falling skyscraper that her dad has blown up to redirect the lava flow.

2. The blond female scientist (Anne Heche), who warns that the first eruption is not the last, predicts where the lava will flow next, and at a crucial point explains to Jones that it will flow downhill, not uphill. He tells her at a critical moment: "Find my daughter!" She should have replied, "Hey, I'm the one who told you what the lava was going to do! Find her yourself! I'm needed here."

3. The African-American sidekick (Don Cheadle), whose function is to stand in the middle of the Office of Emergency Management and shout at Jones through a telephone. I don't know what he *did* at the office, but nobody else did anything either. One wall was covered by a giant screen showing hysterical anchors on the local TV news. Rows of grim technicians faced this wall, seated at computer terminals that showed the very same TV news broadcast. (All of the anchors are so thrilled to be covering a big story that they can scarcely conceal the elation in their voices.)

4. The Asian-American female doctor (Jacqueline Kim), who arrives at the scene, gives first aid to firemen and hero's daughter, and organizes the evacuation of Cedars-Sinai Hospital as the lava flows toward it. (She doubles as the wife of the man who builds the high-rise tower that Jones blows up.)

5. The dog. In a tiny subplot, we see a dog barking at the lava coming in the front door, and then grabbing his doggy bone and escaping out the back. When that happened, not a single dog in the audience had dry eyes.

Tommy Lee Jones is a fine actor, and he does what he can. Striding into the OEM control center, he walks briskly up to a hapless technician and taps on his computer keyboard, barking: "See that, that, and that? Now watch this!" He sounds like he means business, but do you suppose someone was actually paid for writing that line?

Various subplots are rushed on and off screen at blinding speed. At one point a troublesome black man is handcuffed by police, who later release him as the lava flow approaches. He's free to go, but lingers and says, "You block this street, you save the neighborhood—right?" The cops nod. Then he pitches in and helps them lift a giant concrete barrier. The scene is over in a second, but think how insulting it is: It doesn't take a rocket scientist to figure out they're trying to save the neighborhood, so the dialogue is for our benefit, implying that the black dude cares merely for "the neighborhood," and volunteers only when his myopic concerns have been addressed.

The lava keeps flowing for much of the movie, never looking convincing. I loved it when the firemen aimed their hoses way offscreen into the middle of the lava flow, instead of maybe aiming them at the leading edge of the lava—which they couldn't do, because the lava was a visual effect, and not really there.

I also chortled at the way the scientist warns that the first eruption "is not the last," and yet after the second eruption (when it is time for the movie to end), the sun comes out, everyone smiles, and she offers Jones and his daughter a lift home. Hey, what about the possibility of a third eruption? What about that story she told about the Mexican farmer who found a mountain in his cornfield?

The movie has one perfect line: "This city is finally paying for its arrogance!" Yes, and *Volcano* is part of the price.

W

Waco: The Rules of Engagement ★ ★ ★ ½

NO MPAA RATING, 135 m., 1997

A documentary directed by William Gazecki and produced by Gazecki and Michael McNulty.

Like many news-drenched Americans, I paid only casual attention to the standoff at Waco between the Branch Davidians and two agencies of the federal government. I came away with the vague impression that the "cult," as it was always styled, was a group of gun-toting crackpots, that they killed several U.S. agents, refused to negotiate, and finally shot themselves and burned down their "compound" after the feds tried to end the siege peacefully with tear gas.

Watching William Gazecki's remarkable documentary *Waco: The Rules of Engagement,* I am more inclined to use the words "religion" than "cult," and "church center" than "compound." Yes, the Branch Davidians had some strange beliefs, but no weirder than those held by many other religions. And it is pretty clear, on the basis of this film, that the original raid was staged as a publicity stunt, and the final raid was a government riot—a tragedy caused by uniformed boys with toys.

Of course, I am aware that *Waco* argues its point of view, and that there is, no doubt, another case to be made. What is remarkable, watching the film, is to realize that the federal case has not been made. Evidence has been "lost," files and reports have "disappeared," tapes have been returned blank, participants have not testified, and the "crime scene," as a Texas Ranger indignantly testifies, was not preserved for investigation, but razed to the ground by the FBI—presumably to destroy evidence.

The film is persuasive because:

1. It presents testimony from both sides, and shies away from cheap shots. We feel we are seeing a fair attempt to deal with the facts.

2. Those who attack the government are not simply lawyers for the Branch Davidians or muckraking authors (although they are represented) but also solid middle-American types like the county sheriff, the district Texas Rangers, the FBI photographer on the scene, and the man who developed and patented some of the equipment used by the FBI itself to film devastating footage that appears to show its agents firing into the buildings—even though the FBI insists it did not fire a single shot.

3. The eyes of the witnesses. We all have built-in truth detectors, and although it is certainly possible for us to be deceived, there is a human instinct that is hard to fool. Those who argue against the government in this film seem to be telling the truth, and their eyes seem to reflect inner visions of what they believe happened, or saw happen. Most of the government defenders, including an FBI spokesman and Attorney General Janet Reno, seem to be following rehearsed scripts and repeating cant phrases. Reno comes across particularly badly: Either she was misled by the FBI and her aides, or she was completely out of touch with what was happening.

If the film is to be believed, the Branch Davidians were a harmless if controversial group of religious zealots, their beliefs stretching back many decades, who were singled out for attention by the Bureau of Alcohol, Tobacco and Firearms for offenses, real or contrived, involving the possession of firearms—which is far from illegal in Texas. The ATF hoped by raiding the group to repair its tarnished image. And when four of its agents, and several Davidians, were killed in a misguided raid, they played cover-up and turned the case over to the FBI, which mishandled it even more spectacularly.

What is clear, no matter which side you believe, is that during the final deadly FBI raid on the buildings, a toxic and flammable gas was pumped into the compound even though women and children were inside. "Tear gas" sounds innocent, but this type of gas could undergo a chemical transition into cyanide, and there is a pitiful shot of an eight-year-old child's body bent double, backward, by the muscular contractions caused by cyanide.

What comes through strongly is the sense that the attackers were "boys with toys." The film says many of the troops were thrilled to get their hands on real tanks. Some of the law-enforcement types were itching to "stop standing around." One SWAT team member boasts he is "honed to kill." Nancy Sinatra's "These Boots Are Made for Walking" was blasted over loudspeakers to deprive those inside of sleep (the memory of that harebrained operation must still fill the agents with shame).

When the time came, on April 19, 1993, the agents were apparently ready to rock and roll. Heat-sensitive film taken by the FBI and interpreted by experts seems to show FBI agents firing into the compound, firing on an escape route after the fires were started, and deliberately operating on the side of the compound hidden from the view of the press. No evidence is presented that those inside started fires or shot themselves. Although many dead Davidians were indeed found with gunshot wounds, all of the bullets and other evidence have been impounded by the FBI.

Whatever happened at Waco, these facts remain: It is not against the law to hold irregular religious beliefs. It is not illegal to hold and trade firearms. It is legal to defend your own home against armed assault, if that assault is illegal. It is impossible to see this film without reflecting that the federal government, from the top on down, treated the Branch Davidians as if those rights did not apply.

Wag the Dog ★★★★

R, 97 m., 1998

Dustin Hoffman (Stanley Motss), Robert De Niro (Conrad Brean), Anne Heche (Winifred Ames), Woody Harrelson (Sergeant William Schumann), Denis Leary (Fad King), Willie Nelson (Johnny Green), Andrea Martin (Liz Butsky), Kirsten Dunst (Tacy Lime). Directed by Barry Levinson and produced by Jane Rosenthal, Robert De Niro, and Levinson. Screenplay by David Mamet and Hilary Henkin, based on the book *American Hero* by Larry Beinhart.

So, why *did* we invade Grenada? A terrorist bomb killed all those Marines in Beirut, the White House was taking flak, and suddenly our Marines were landing on a Caribbean island few people had heard of, everybody was tying yellow ribbons 'round old oak trees, and Clint Eastwood was making the movie. The Grenadan invasion, I have read, produced more decorations than combatants. By the time it was over, the Reagan presidency had proven the republic could still flex its muscle—we could take out a Caribbean Marxist regime at will, Cuba notwithstanding.

Barry Levinson's *Wag the Dog* cites Grenada as an example of how easy it is to whip up patriotic frenzy, and how dubious the motives can sometimes be. The movie is a satire that contains just enough realistic ballast to be teasingly plausible; like *Dr. Strangelove*, it makes you laugh, and then it makes you wonder. Just today, I read a Strangelovian story in the paper revealing that some of Russia's nuclear missiles, still aimed at the United States, have gone unattended because their guards were denied their bonus rations of four pounds of sausage a month. It is getting harder and harder for satire to stay ahead of reality.

In the movie, a U.S. president is accused of luring an underage "Firefly Girl" into an anteroom of the Oval Office, and there presenting her with opportunities no Firefly Girl should anticipate from her commander in chief. A presidential election is weeks away, the opposition candidate starts using "Thank Heaven for Little Girls" in his TV ads, and White House aide Winifred Ames (Anne Heche) leads a spin doctor named Conrad Brean (Robert De Niro) into bunkers far beneath the White House for an emergency session.

Brean, a Mr. Fixit who has masterminded a lot of shady scenarios, has a motto: "To change the story, change the lead." To distract the press from the Firefly Girl scandal, he advises extending a presidential trip to Asia, while issuing official denials that the new B-3 bomber is being activated ahead of schedule. "But there *is* no B-3 bomber," he's told. "Perfect! Deny it even exists!"

Meanwhile, he cooks up a phony international crisis with Albania. Why Albania? Nobody is sure where it is, nobody cares, and you can't get any news out of it. Nobody can even think of any Albanians except—maybe the Belushi brothers? To produce the graphic look and feel of the war, Brean flies to Hollywood and enlists the services of a producer named Stanley Motss (Dustin Hoffman), who is hard to convince at first. He wants proof that Brean has a direct line to the White House. He gets it.

As they watch a live briefing by a presidential spokesman, Brean dictates into a cell phone and the spokesman repeats, word for word, what he hears on his earpiece. (I was reminded of the line in *Broadcast News:* "Goes in here, comes out there.")

Motss assembles the pieces for a media blitz. As spokesmen warn of Albanian terrorists skulking south from Canada with "suitcase bombs," Motss supervises the design of a logo for use on the news channels, hires Willie Nelson to write the song that will become the conflict's "spontaneous" anthem, and fakes news footage of a hapless Albanian girl (Kirsten Dunst) fleeing from rapists with her kitten. (Dunst is an American actress, and the kitten, before it is created with special effects, is a bag of Tostitos.)

But what about a martyr? Motss cooks up "good old Shoe," Sergeant William Schumann (Woody Harrelson), who is allegedly rescued from the hands of the Albanians to be flown back for a hero's welcome. Shoe inspires a shtick, too: Kids start lobbing their old gym shoes over power lines, and throwing them onto the court during basketball games, as a spontaneous display of patriotism.

It's creepy how this material is absurd and convincing at the same time. Levinson, working from a smart, talky script by David Mamet and Hilary Henkin, based on the book *American Hero* by Larry Beinhart, deconstructs the media blitz that invariably accompanies any modern international crisis. Even when a conflict is real and necessary (the Gulf War, for example), the packaging of it is invariably shallow and unquestioning; like sportswriters, war correspondents abandon any pretense of objectivity and detachment, and cheerfully root for our side.

For Hoffman, this is the best performance in some time, inspired, it is said, by producer Robert Evans. (In power and influence, however, Motss seems more like Ray Stark.) Like a lot of Hollywood power brokers, Hoffman's Motss combines intelligence with insecurity and insincerity, and frets because he won't get "credit" for his secret manipulations. De Niro's Brean, on the other hand, is a creature born to live in shadow, and De Niro plays him with the poker-faced plausibility of real spin doctors, who tell lies as a professional specialty. Their conversations are crafted by Mamet as a verbal ballet between two men who love the jargon of their crafts.

"Why does a dog wag its tail?" Brean asks at one point. "Because the dog is smarter than the tail. If the tail was smarter, it would wag the dog." In the Breanian universe, the tail is smarter, and we, dear readers, are invited to be the dogs.

Waiting for Guffman ★ ★ ★

R, 84 m., 1997

Christopher Guest (Corky St. Clair), Eugene Levy (Dr. Allan Pearl), Fred Willard (Ron Albertson), Catherine O'Hara (Sheila Albertson), Parker Posey (Libby Mae Brown), Matt Keeslar (Johnny Savage), Lewis Arquette (Clifford Wooley), Bob Balaban (Lloyd Miller). Directed by Christopher Guest and produced by Karen Murphy. Screenplay by Guest and Eugene Levy.

Blaine, Missouri, was founded, we are told, 150 years ago by settlers who were trekking to the West Coast and stopped when their leader "smelled the salt air." Its place in history has been assured by two events: a wooden stool made in Blaine, presented to President William McKinley, led to the city becoming "stool capital of America." And in 1946, a flying saucer landed nearby. Within its radius it was "always sixty-seven degrees with a 40 percent chance of rain." Local residents were invited aboard for a potluck supper, and one of them still has no feeling in his buttocks.

Obviously such events cry out for dramatic treatment, and for its 150th anniversary Blaine obtains the services of Corky St. Clair (Christopher Guest), a "relocated" Broadway director who will stage an amateur theatrical pageant. Corky's credits include *Backdraft,* a musical based on the film about firemen. He allegedly has a wife named Bonnie, who has never been seen, although he buys all of her clothing and knows a great deal about depilatories.

Such is the setup for *Waiting for Guffman,* directed and cowritten by Guest, who was also the cowriter for *This Is Spinal Tap,* the very funny 1981 mock-documentary about a failing rock group. *Guffman* is not as insistently funny, perhaps because it has a sneaking fondness for its characters (*Spinal Tap* ridiculed its heroes with a true zeal). In a sequence that, I gather, was improvised by the actors themselves, a group of locals audition for Corky and the local music teacher (Bob Balaban), and we see Parker Posey's extremely literal interpretation of "Teacher's Pet."

Others in the audition include the local travel agents (Fred Willard and Catherine O'Hara), who have never been out of town but have travelers' imaginations and perform "Midnight at the Oasis." They consider themselves "the Lunts of Blaine."

The movie doesn't bludgeon us with gags. It proceeds with a certain comic relentlessness from setup to payoff, and its deliberation is part of the fun (as when it takes its time explaining the exact nature of the travel agent's plastic surgery). Some of the better laughs are deadpan, as when the travel agent and his wife take the local dentist (Eugene Levy) and his wife to dinner at a Chinese restaurant. It has a neon sign two stories high that announces CHOP SUEY; the travel agent asks, "How did you find this place?"

Much of the fun comes from the songs composed for the pageant (music and lyrics by Guest, Harry Shearer, and Michael McKean). They have the sound and the brio of 1940s musicals, and the literal-mindedness of people determined to shoehorn cosmic significance into a perspective. Tension is generated when it becomes known that a man named Guffman, a famous New York producer's agent, will attend opening night with the thought that "Red, White . . . and Blaine" might travel well to Broadway.

The comic tone of *Waiting for Guffman* has grown out of Second City (where most of the actors once worked) and the classic SCTV television show. Attention is paid not simply to funny characters and punch lines, but to small nudges at human nature. Consider, for example, Bob Balaban in an understated role as the long-suffering local teacher who knows how outrageous Corky St. Clair is, but never quite acts on his knowledge. Or listen to small touches as when the descendant of Blaine's original settlers sighs, "I know how the Kennedys must feel." Some of the laughs are so subtle you almost miss them, as when Corky warns the dentist that his horn-rimmed glasses would be out of place in a scene set in 1846—but neglects to remember his own earring.

If you see the film, don't leave before the closing credits, which include several "movie collectibles" that provide maybe the loudest laughs in the movie.

Waking Ned Devine ★ ★ ★

PG, 91 m., 1998

Ian Bannen (Jackie O'Shea), David Kelly (Michael O'Sullivan), Fionnula Flanagan (Annie O'Shea), Susan Lynch (Maggie), James Nesbitt (Pig Finn), Maura O'Malley (Mrs. Kennedy), Robert Hickey (Maurice), Brendan F. Dempsey (Jim Kelly), Dermot Kerrigan (Father Patrick), Eileen Dromey (Lizzy Quinn). Directed by Kirk Jones and produced by Glynis Murray and Richard Holmes. Screenplay by Jones.

Waking Ned Devine opens with the news that someone in the Irish hamlet of Tullymore (population fifty-three—uh, fifty-two) has won the National Lottery. Who could it be? The locals, who have lived in each other's pockets for years, snoop and gossip and seize upon the slightest deviation from habit as proof that someone expects a windfall. But there are no leads, and finally in desperation a chicken supper is held, at which the winner will perhaps be revealed. No luck. But one person doesn't attend the dinner: Ned Devine.

Jackie O'Shea (Ian Bannen) and Michael O'Sullivan (David Kelly) hasten to Ned's cottage to find him seated in front of the television set, clutching the winning ticket—and dead. The winnings, they are astounded to learn, are not several hundred thousand pounds, as they had assumed, but nearly 7 million pounds. A fortune! Alas, since Ned Devine is dead, the money will be recycled back into the kitty for next week's drawing.

Right? Not on your life. Jackie and Michael hatch a plan to fool the visiting official from Dublin, who after all has never laid eyes on Ned in his life (few have, outside of Tullymore). Michael will impersonate Ned. The whole town will of course have to be in on the scheme, and so Jackie and Michael draw up an agreement in which their friends and neighbors will join in the deception and share in the prize.

That's the premise of another one of those delightful village comedies that seem to spin out of the British isles at least annually. *Waking Ned Devine* can take its place with *Local Hero, The Snapper, The Full Monty, The Englishman Who Went Up a Hill and Came Down a Mountain, Brassed Off, Circle of Friends, Eat the Peach,* and many others. Why don't we have more small-town comedies like this from America? Why are small towns in the United Kingdom and Ireland seen as conspiracies of friends, while American small towns are so often depicted as filled with liars or wackos?

One of the joys of *Waking Ned Devine* is in the richness of the local eccentric population. There is, for example, the mean-spirited Lizzy Quinn (Eileen Dromey), who tools around on her battery-powered chair, scowling and spreading ill will. Contrast her with the hard-working Pig Finn (James Nesbitt), a handsome young pig farmer who loves Maggie (Susan Lynch). She loves him too, but not the way he smells. Either the pigs go or she does. And there is the substitute village priest (Dermot Kerrigan), filling in during the regular's vacation, who has solemn talks about theology with bright young Maurice (Robert Hickey), who says of a life devoted to the Lord: "I don't think I could work for someone I never met."

The treasure of the local population is Michael O'Sullivan, who is played by David Kelly in what can only be described as a performance arriving at the ultimate reaches of geezerdom. Kelly, with his twinkling eyes and turkey neck, is engaging, conspiratorial, and delighted by all things not too wicked. Stealing 6.8 million pounds from the lottery is, of course, not too wicked. Like Nigel Hawthorne in *The Madness of King George* or Simon Callow in *Four Weddings and a Funeral,* Kelly is one of those seasoned and expert actors who is well known in the United Kingdom (he was a character on *Fawlty Towers*), but will be a delightful discovery for North American audiences. There is a scene where he must get back to Ned Devine's cottage at breakneck speed to beat out the Lotto official from Dublin (Brendan F. Dempsey). Why he must dash down back lanes on a motorcycle while completely naked I will leave to you to discover; the sight inspires uproarious laughter.

That's one of the movie's big laughs. Another involves a telephone booth. Most of the time we're smiling more than laughing; we recognize the human nature involved in *Waking Ned Devine,* and we like the way Kirk Jones, the writer and director, throws up obstacles just to have fun leaping over them. One reason we like village comedies from Ireland and the United Kingdom is of course that they're funny. Another is to meet the characters and the actors, and enjoy the pleasure of their company. I have a feeling that an evening spent with David Kelly would be a merry one.

A Walk on the Moon ★ ★

R, 106 m., 1999

Diane Lane (Pearl Kantrowitz), Viggo Mortensen (Walker Jerome), Liev Schreiber (Marty Kantrowitz), Anna Paquin (Alison Kantrowitz), Tovah Feldshuh (Lilian Kantrowitz), Bobby Boriello (Daniel Kantrowitz). Directed by Tony Goldwyn and produced by Dustin Hoffman, Goldwyn, Jay Cohen, Neil Koenigsberg, Lee Gottsegen, and Murray Schisgal. Screenplay by Pamela Gray.

"Sometimes I just wish I was a whole other person," says Pearl Kantrowitz, who is the subject, if not precisely the heroine, of *A Walk on the Moon.* It is the summer of 1969, and Pearl and her husband, Marty, have taken a bungalow in a Catskills resort. Pearl spends the week with their teenage daughter, their younger son, and her mother-in-law. Marty drives up from the city on the weekends.

The summer of 1969 is, of course, the summer of Woodstock, which is being held nearby. And Pearl (Diane Lane), who was married at a very early age to the only man she ever slept with, feels trapped in the stodgy domesticity of the resort—where wives and families are aired while the man labors in town. She doesn't know it, but she's ripe for the Blouse Man (Viggo Mortensen).

The Blouse Man drives a truck from resort to resort. It opens out into a retail store, offering marked-down prices on blouses and accessories. Funny, but he doesn't look like a Blouse Man: With his long hair and chiseled features, he looks more like a cross between a hippie and the hero on the cover of a paperback romance. He senses quickly that Pearl is shopping for more than blouses, and offers her a free tie-dyed T-shirt and his phone number. The T-shirt is crucial, symbolizing a time when women of Pearl's age were in the throes of the Sexual Revolution. Soon Pearl is using the phone number. "I wonder," she asks the Blouse Man, "if you had plans for watching the moon walk?"

A Walk on the Moon is one small step for the Blouse Man, a giant leap for Pearl Kantrowitz. In the arms of the Blouse Man, she experiences sexual passion and a taste of freedom, and soon they're skinny-dipping just like the hippies at Woodstock. The festival indeed exudes a siren call, and Pearl, like a teenage girl slipping out of the house for a concert, finally sneaks off to attend it with the Blouse Man. Marty (Liev Schreiber), meanwhile, is stuck in the Woodstock traffic jam. And their daughter, Alison (Anna Paquin), who has gotten her period and her first boyfriend more or less simultaneously, is at Woodstock, too—where she sees her mother.

The movie is a memory of a time and place now largely gone (these days Pearl and Marty would be more likely to take the family to Disney World or Hawaii). It evokes the heady feelings of 1969, when rock was mistaken for revolution. To be near Woodstock and in heat with a long-haired god, but not be able to go there, is a Dantean punishment. But the movie also has thoughts about the nature of freedom and responsibility. "Do you think you're the only one whose dreams didn't come true?" asks Marty, whose early marriage meant he became a TV repairman instead of a college graduate.

Watching the gathering clouds over the marriage, Pearl's mother-in-law, Lilian (Tovah Feldshuh), sees all and understands much. If Pearl is not an entirely sympathetic character, Lilian Kantrowitz is a saint. She calls her son to warn him of trouble, she watches silently as Pearl defiantly leaves the house, and perhaps she understands Pearl's fear of being trapped in a life lived as an accessory to a man.

So the underlying strength of the story is there. Unfortunately, the casting and some of the romantic scenes sabotage it. Liev Schreiber is a good actor and I have admired him in many movies, but put him beside Viggo Mortensen and the Blouse Man wins; you can hardly blame Pearl for surrendering. (I am reminded of a TV news interview about that movie where Demi Moore was offered $1 million to sleep with Robert Redford. "Would you sleep with Robert Redford for a million dollars?" a woman in a mall was asked. She replied: "I'd sleep with him for 50 cents.")

The movie's problem is that it loads the casting in a way that tilts the movie in the direction of a Harlequin romance. Mortensen looks like one of those long-haired, bare-chested, muscular buccaneers on the covers of the paperbacks; all he needs is a Gothic tower behind him, with one light in a window. The movie exhibits almost unseemly haste in speeding Pearl and the Blouse Man toward love-making, and then lingers over their sex scenes as if they were an end in themselves, and not a transgression in a larger story. As Pearl and the Blouse Man cavort naked under a waterfall, the movie forgets its ethical questions and becomes soft-core lust.

Then, alas, there is the reckoning. We know sooner or later there will be anger and recrimination, self-revelation and confession, acceptance and resolve, wasp attacks and rescues. We've enjoyed those sex scenes, and now, like Pearl, we have to pay. Somewhere in the midst of the dramaturgy is a fine performance by Anna Paquin (from *The Piano*) as a teenage girl struggling with new ideas and raging hormones. Everytime I saw her character on screen, I thought: There's the real story.

Warriors of Virtue ★★

PG, 103 m., 1997

Angus Macfadyen (Komodo), Mario Yedidia (Ryan), Marley Shelton (Elysia), Chao-Li Chi (Master Chung), Dennis Dun (Chef Ming), Michael John Anderson (Mudlap), Jack Tate (Yun), Doug Jones (Yee), Don W. Lewis (Lai), J. Todd Adams (Chi), Adrienne Corcoran (Tsun). Directed by Ronny Yu and produced by Dennis Law, Ronald Law, Christopher Law, Jeremy Law, and Patricia Ruben. Screenplay by Michael Vickerman and Hugh Kelley.

I have always been amazed by the recuperative powers of young heroes who are snatched away from home and family and sent to struggle in distant fantasy worlds. Consider young

Ryan (Mario Yedidia), the hero of *Warriors of Virtue.* One moment he's balancing above a drainage whirlpool on a bet from a bully on the football team, and the next he's on the planet Tao, helping a race of kangaroo warriors fight the evil Komodo for control of the Lifespring.

Does he weep? Does he worry about his parents? Is he homesick? Not for a moment. He's a comic book fan who intuits, I guess, that he's been magically transported into a fantasy adventure, and soon he is getting briefed by the beautiful Princess Elysia (Marley Shelton) and wise old Master Chung (Chao-Li Chi) about the desperate state of affairs on Tao, where all but one Lifespring have been exhausted, and the vile Komodo (Angus Macfadyen) wants it for himself.

The key to this dilemma lies with Ryan, who in real life has a friend named Ming who is a virtuoso chef in a Chinese restaurant (he can land a ladle full of fried rice on a platter at ten paces). Ming is wise in the Zen master tradition, and shows Ryan an empty cocoon: As a child he released a beautiful moth from it, only to see the moth die because "I interrupted its journey" and it "needed its struggle." Likewise, Ryan must continue his journey. If he feels inadequate as the water boy on the football team, then he must prove himself. Ming gives him an old book that may contain the answers.

Warriors of Virtue is ambitious in its production, if not especially original. Its set design is by Eugenio Zanetti, who won an Oscar for "Restoration," and he does a good job of creating a forest planet with towering trees and an Everglades-like landscape that looks not unlike Yoda's setting in *The Empire Strikes Back.* The *Star Wars* movies are evoked in more than the setting; when Ryan opens the old book Ming gave him, he finds its pages blank, and on the sound track we hear, "The answer lies within you, Ryan"—which sounds uncannily Force-like.

On the planet of Tao, he finds Elysia and Master Chung (a Mr. Miyagi clone) helped by a group of five creatures who look like kangaroos but behave like a cross between Power Rangers and Ninja Turtles. The kangaroos represent the elemental forces of fire, metal, wood, water, and earth (the movie informs us these forces are more powerful than "guns, lasers . . . morphing"). As the evil Komodo schemes to drop the Roo Warriors through a trapdoor into death by spinning blades, only Ryan can save the day—if he can wrest the book from the scheming little person Mudlap (Michael John Anderson).

And so on. The movie looks better than it plays, and gets rather tiresome, especially since there is a limit to a Roo personality, Ryan is resolutely one-dimensional, and Angus Macfadyen (who played Robert the Bruce in *Braveheart*) makes Komodo into a villain who goes through the motions of evil but doesn't seem to have his heart in it.

At one point, Komodo wearily intones, "The center cannot hold; things fall apart." It's a slight misquotation from W. B. Yeats's poem "The Second Coming," but one is surprised to hear it at all, since everything said on the planet Tao presumably comes from within Ryan's mind, and he shows no signs of having read any book—except, of course, for Chef Ming's. The Yeats poem continues, "Mere anarchy is loosed upon the world." Call me a dreamer, but that sounds like an even more promising story idea than *Warriors of Virtue.*

Washington Square ★ ★ ★

PG, 115 m., 1997

Jennifer Jason Leigh (Catherine Sloper), Albert Finney (Dr. Austin Sloper), Maggie Smith (Aunt Lavinia), Ben Chaplin (Morris Townsend), Judith Ivey (Mrs. Almond). Directed by Agnieszka Holland and produced by Roger Birnbaum and Julie Bergman Sender. Screenplay by Carol Doyle, based on the novel by Henry James.

So often in Henry James it comes down to the same contest: On the one side, the yearnings of the heart, and on the other side, money. Usually it is old family money and the old family that controls it, sometimes hoping to restrict the freedom of a character *(The Ambassadors),* sometimes hoping to grant it *(Portrait of a Lady).* In James's short novel *Washington Square,* a rich doctor cannot believe anyone would value what he considers his plain and graceless daughter, and so assumes that the man she loves is after her money. That he may be right is, for her, no consolation.

Agnieszka Holland's new movie *Washington Square* makes of this situation a sad story about a young woman named Catherine (Jennifer Jason Leigh), who spends much of her life seeking the love of two men who do not deserve it. Her father, the wealthy Dr. Austin Sloper (Albert Finney), resents her because his wife died in giving birth to her. Her suitor, Morris Townsend (Ben Chaplin), likes her well enough if she comes with her father's money, but not so well otherwise. Her challenge is to find some measure of self-respect in a life where everyone seems to value her because of someone else's accomplishments.

Her father is an orotund monster who demands, and even receives, the love and obedience of his daughter. He sees her as a loyal helpmate, waiting with tea when he returns from work, content to spend the rest of her days as her father's meek little companion. Her lover is poor, must marry money or make it, and knows which course he prefers, although he is handsome and agreeable enough to feel his "attributes" are the equal of her own.

And the girl? "I've never thought of her as delightful and charming," the doctor says on one occasion, astonished that anyone else should. He is capable of astonishing cruelty, as when he tells her, "How obscene that your mother should give her life so that you can inhabit space on this earth." She is so intimidated that when asked, as a little girl, to give a recital for her father's friends, she can do no more than pee on the floor.

There are, however, weapons in her arsenal. She is not as plain as her father thinks, nor as lacking in spirit. And she has an ally in her father's sister, Aunt Lavinia (Maggie Smith), who is thrilled by romantic intrigue and does everything she can to further the courtship—if only because it provides her entertainment by allowing her to sneak off as a secret emissary.

The movie is set in the years before the Civil War in a newly prosperous section of Manhattan, where Dr. Sloper, as James tells us in his book, "was what you might call a scholarly doctor, and yet there was nothing abstract in his remedies—he always ordered you to take something." Sloper earns a good income, but came into his fortune by marrying a rich woman, and so is uniquely prepared to judge the motives of young Mr. Townsend.

For Catherine, Townsend's attention is liberating, offering a way out of her father's house. Still, she agrees to a year's European journey with her father, during which she is to reconsider her position. At the very summit of the Alps (how did they get there, dressed as they are?), her father asks, "Should you like to be left in such a place as this to starve?" He warns that Townsend will someday abandon her in just such a place, literally or figuratively. She cannot believe this, and we are not sure. Townsend is no worse, probably, than most of the young men produced by his materialistic society. The problem is, he is not nearly as good as Catherine thinks.

Jennifer Jason Leigh often plays women of brassy boldness *(Last Exit to Brooklyn, Kansas City,* and Dorothy Parker in *Mrs. Parker and the Vicious Circle).* What is remarkable is how she can also play a recessive character like Catherine so that every assertion seems like an act of courage. Her Catherine is based on quiet determination: She can either collapse or grow.

Holland is a director interested in the secrets behind family walls, as in her wonderful *The Secret Garden.* Here she takes a story that, in a modern rewrite, would be about child abuse, and she makes it into the story of how the doctor's fortune seems to shrink even as it grows—until it loses all its power to destroy Catherine's life. Henry James saw more humor in the story than Holland does (although Aunt Lavinia remains comic), but what they both understand is that in a family like this, everything depends on the money—unless nothing does.

The Waterboy ★

PG-13, 86 m., 1998

Adam Sandler (Bobby Boucher), Kathy Bates (Mama Boucher), Henry Winkler (Coach Klein), Fairuza Balk (Vicki Vallencourt), Jerry Reed (Red Beaulieu), Larry Gilliard Jr. (Derek Wallace), Blake Clark (Farmer Fran), Peter Dante (Gee Grenouille). Directed by Frank Coraci and produced by Robert Simonds and

Jack Giarraputo. Screenplay by Tim Herlihy and Adam Sandler.

I believe in giving every movie the benefit of the doubt. I walked into *The Waterboy,* sat down, took a sip of my delicious medium roast coffee, and felt at peace with the world. How nice it would be, I thought, to give Adam Sandler a good review for a change. Good will and caffeine suffused my being, and as the lights went down I all but beamed at the screen.

Then Adam Sandler spoke and all was lost. His character's voice is made of a lisp, a whine, a nasal grating, and an accent that nobody in Louisiana actually has, although the movies pretend that they do. His character is a thirty-one-year-old man who, soon after the film opens, is fired as the waterboy of a championship football team. Then he talks himself into a job with a team of losers, led by the insecure Coach Klein (Henry Winkler).

Bobby Boucher, the waterboy, is one of those people who is so insufferable, in a passive-aggressive way, that you have to believe they know what they're doing. No one could be that annoying by accident. I am occasionally buttonholed by such specimens. They stand too close, they talk too loudly, they are not looking at me but at an invisible TelePrompTer somewhere over my shoulder. If I were a man of action, I would head-butt them and take my chances with the courts.

The Waterboy tries to force this character into the ancient movie mold of the misunderstood simple little guy with a heart of gold. By the end of the movie we are supposed to like him, I think, especially as the whole school turns up in a candlelight vigil outside the hospital where he waits at the bedside of his (not) dying mother. There is only one way I can see myself liking this character. That would be if *The Waterboy,* like *That Obscure Object of Desire* and *Lost Highway,* had two different actors play the same character, so that by the end Bobby Boucher was being portrayed by Tom Hanks.

Kathy Bates has the best scenes in the movie, as Bobby's mother, a possessive and manipulative creature who has kept her son tied to her apron strings in their bayou cabin, which looks like it was furnished by the same artist who draws "How Many Mistakes Can You Find in This Picture?" Mama Boucher and Bobby share space with large animals and junk-shop treasures, and she serves giant swamp snakes, coiled in a tasty brew of herbs and spices. Bates makes her character work as a comic creation, and knows the line between parody and wretched excess.

Henry Winkler is luckless as Coach Klein, because he is given little to do other than be a creature of the plot. And the plot is that exhausted wheeze of a sports-movie formula, in which the hero is scorned by everyone until he comes off the bench, shows remarkable talent, and (a) wins or (b) loses the big game. (I do not want to reveal the ending, so you will have to guess for yourself which it is. If you voted for (b), you are reading the wrong movie critic.)

Do I have something visceral against Adam Sandler? I hope not. I try to keep an open mind and approach every movie with high hopes. It would give me enormous satisfaction (and relief) to like him in a movie. But I suggest he is making a tactical error when he creates a character whose manner and voice have the effect of fingernails on a blackboard, and then expects us to hang in there for a whole movie. ☞

The Wedding Singer ★

PG-13, 96 m., 1998

Adam Sandler (Robbie), Drew Barrymore (Julia), Christine Taylor (Holly), Allen Covert (Sammy), Matthew Glave (Glenn), Ellen Albertini Dow (Rosie), Angela Featherstone (Linda), Alexis Arquette (George). Directed by Frank Coraci and produced by Robert Simonds and Jack Giarraputo. Screenplay by Tim Herlihy.

The Wedding Singer tells the story of, yes, a wedding singer from New Jersey, who is cloyingly sweet at some times and a cruel monster at others. The filmmakers are obviously unaware of his split personality; the screenplay reads like a collaboration between Jekyll and Hyde. Did anybody, at any stage, give the story the slightest thought?

The plot is so familiar the end credits should have issued a blanket thank-you to a century of Hollywood love-coms. Through a torturous series of contrived misunderstandings, the boy and girl avoid happiness for most of the movie, although not as successfully as we do. It's your basic off-the-shelf formula in which two people fall in love, but are kept apart because (a) they're engaged to creeps; (b) they say the wrong things at the wrong times; and (c) they get bad information. It's exhausting, seeing the characters work so hard at avoiding the obvious.

Of course, there's the obligatory scene where the good girl goes to the good boy's house to say she loves him, but the bad girl answers the door and lies to her. I spent the weekend looking at old Astaire and Rogers movies, which basically had the same plot: She thinks he's a married man, and almost gets married to the slimy bandleader before he finally figures everything out and declares his love at the eleventh hour.

The big differences between Astaire and Rogers in *Swing Time* and Adam Sandler and Drew Barrymore in *The Wedding Singer* is that (1) in 1936 they were more sophisticated than we are now, and *knew* the plot was inane, and had fun with that fact, and (2) they could dance. One of the sad by-products of the dumbing-down of America is that we're now forced to witness the goofy plots of the 1930s played sincerely, as if they were really deep.

Sandler is the wedding singer. He's engaged to a slut who stands him up at the altar because, sob, "the man I fell in love with six years ago was a rock singer who licked the microphone like David Lee Roth—and now you're only a . . . a . . . wedding singer!" Barrymore, meanwhile, is engaged to a macho monster who brags about how he's cheating on her. Sandler and Barrymore meet because she's a waitress at the weddings where he sings. We know immediately they are meant for each other. Why do we know this? Because we are conscious and sentient. It takes them a lot longer.

The basic miscalculation in Adam Sandler's career plan is to ever play the lead. He is not a lead. He is the best friend, or the creep, or the loser boyfriend. He doesn't have the voice to play a lead: Even at his most sincere, he sounds like he's doing stand-up—like he's mocking a character in a movie he saw last night. Barrymore, on the other hand, has the stuff to play a lead (I commend you once again to the underrated *Mad Love*). But what is she doing in this one—in a plot her grandfather would have found old-fashioned? At least when she gets a good line (she tries out the married name "Mrs. Julia Gulia") she knows how to handle it.

The best laughs in the film come right at the top, in an unbilled cameo by the invaluable Steve Buscemi, as a drunken best man who makes a shambles of a wedding toast. He has the timing, the presence, and the intelligence to go right to the edge. Sandler, on the other hand, always keeps something in reserve—his talent. It's like he's afraid of committing; he holds back so he can use the "only kidding" defense.

I could bore you with more plot details. About why he thinks she's happy and she thinks he's happy and they're both wrong and she flies to Vegas to marry the stinker, and he . . . but why bother? And why even mention that the movie is set in the mid-1980s and makes a lot of mid-1980s references that are supposed to be funny but sound exactly like lame dialogue? And what about the curious cameos by faded stars and inexplicably cast character actors? And why do they write the role of a Boy George clone for Alexis Arquette and then do nothing with the character except let him hang there on screen? And why does the tourist section of the plane have fewer seats than first class? And, and, and . . .

Welcome to Sarajevo ★ ★

R, 102 m., 1998

Stephen Dillane (Henderson), Woody Harrelson (Flynn), Marisa Tomei (Nina), Emira Nusevic (Emira), Kerry Fox (Jane Carson), Goran Visnjic (Risto), James Nesbitt (Gregg), Emily Lloyd (Annie McGee). Directed by Michael Winterbottom and produced by Graham Broadbent and Damian Jones. Screenplay by Frank Cottrell Boyce, based on the book *Natasha's Story* by Michael Nicholson.

My confidence in *Welcome to Sarajevo* was undermined by the film's uncertain air of improvisation. Like Haskell Wexler's *Medium Cool*, which plunged into the midst of the riots at the 1968 Democratic Convention in Chicago, it combines fact and fiction, real and fake news footage, and actors side-by-side with local people. Wexler pulled it off. Michael Winterbottom, who made this film about a 1992 Sarajevo where the smoke seems to be still rising from the latest shellings, doesn't quite.

The movie centers itself on a group of journalists who take harrowing risks to cover a war that their editors and viewers back home aren't very interested in. Stephen Dillane plays Henderson, a British reporter who finds his latest big story has been pushed off the front page by the divorce of the Duchess of York. And Woody Harrelson plays Flynn, a high-profile news star on American TV, who walks into the range of sniper fire to aid a wounded altar boy—after first making sure, of course, that the cameras are rolling. His reasoning: "Well you know, oddly enough, back home no one has ever heard of Sarajevo and everyone has heard of me."

The story of Henderson forms the core of the movie. He's in anguish over the fates of children who are war victims, and narrates footage of a big UN plane taking off: "Children are dying in the most dangerous corner of the most dangerous city on earth—but this plane is flying out of here empty." He eventually takes things into his own hands, smuggling a young girl orphan out of Sarajevo by quasi-legal means, so that he and his wife can adopt her. This story thread is based on fact—British TV reporter Michael Nicholson and his wife adopted an orphan, and he wrote a book about it.

One can imagine a strong film about that part of the story. One can also imagine a film about war correspondents under fire and frustrated by an indifferent world. The problem is that Winterbottom has imagined both stories and several others, and tells them in a style designed to feel as if reality has been caught on the fly. What it more often feels like, alas, is the venerable Second City formula for improvisation—"Something wonderful right away!"—and too often we sense that the actors are drifting and the story is at sea.

That's especially true of the Woody Harrelson scenes. He's an interesting, intense actor, and a good choice for a character living recklessly under fire. But too often I got the feeling that Winterbottom, having imported American stars (Marisa Tomei is also in the cast), tried to plug them into spur-of-the-moment, spontaneous situations that didn't fit with the rest of the film. There's the feeling that the central characters don't really know each other as well as they should. The film arrives in fragments, without a sense of destination.

Films like this, of course, lament for the children—for helpless orphans and altar boys gunned down by partisan and sectarian snipers. But the snipers were altar boys only a few years ago, and altar boys grow up to become snipers. The film decries "violence" but doesn't name names: Much of the evil that has descended on this part of the world is caused by tribalism and religious fanaticism (when one group kills another in the name of their God, that is fanaticism).

So often there is a style of reporting events like the Bosnian tragedy in which words like "partisans" are used instead of "religious fanatics," because although a man might kill others for worshiping the wrong god, of course we must not offend his religion. *Welcome to Sarajevo* tiptoes around that awkwardness with easy pieties, in which an orphan is spared, a man is a hero, cynicism masks bravery—and the underlying issues are not addressed. A better and braver film about this part of the world is Milcho Manchevsky's *Before the Rain* (1995), which shows clearly how the circle of killing goes around and around, fueled by the mindless passion that my God, my language, my ancestors, give me the right to kill you.

Western ★★

NO MPAA RATING, 121 m., 1999

Sergi Lopez (Paco), Sacha Bourdo (Nino), Elisabeth Vitali (Marinette), Marie Matheron (Nathalie), Basile Sieouka (Baptiste), Jean-Louis Dupont (Policeman), Olivier Herveet (Hospital Doctor). Directed by Manuel Poirier and produced by Maurice Bernart. Screenplay by Poirier and Jean Francois Goyet.

Western is a road movie about a friendship between two men and their search for the love of the right woman. The roads they travel are in western France, in the district of Brittany, which looks rough and dour but, on the evidence of this film, has the kindest and most accommodating women in the world.

The Meet Cute between the men occurs when Paco (Sergi Lopez), a shoe salesman from Spain, gives a lift to Nino (Sacha Bourdo), a Russian who lived in Italy before moving to France. Nino tricks Paco and steals his car, and when the stranded Paco sees him on the street the next day, he chases him and beats him so badly Nino lands in the hospital. Paco visits him there, says he is sorry to have hit him so hard, and the men become friends. Since Paco has lost his job along with his car, they hit the road.

Road movies are the oldest genre known to man, and the most flexible, since anything can happen on the road and there's always a fresh supply of characters. Paco, who has always been a ladies' man, in fact has already found a woman: Marinette (Elisabeth Vitali), who befriended him after his car was stolen and even let him sleep overnight on her sofa bed. Soon they've kissed and think they may be in love, but Marinette wants a thirty-day cooling-off period, so the two men hitch around Brittany, depending on the kindness of strangers.

If Paco has always had luck with women, Nino has had none. He's a short, unprepossessing man with a defeatist attitude, and one day Paco stands next to him at the roadside, points to a nearby village, and says, "I'm sure that in that town, there has to be a woman for you." "Really?" "Yes, there is a minimum of one woman in every town in France for you."

This belief leads them to conduct a phony door-to-door survey as a ruse for finding the right woman for Nino, and along the way they make a new friend, Baptiste (Basile Sieouka), an African from Senegal in a wheelchair. He teaches them the "bonjour" game, in which they get points every time a stranger returns their greeting. "Go back where you came from!" one man snarls at Baptiste, who laughs uproariously; all three of these men are strangers in a foreign land.

The emotional center of the story comes when Paco meets a woman named Nathalie (Marie Matheron), who invites them home for dinner, likes the way Nino cooks chicken, and unexpectedly goes for Nino rather than Paco. This woman's lifestyle seems unlikely (she is a male daydream of an earth mother), but she provides the excuse for the film's ending—which is intended as joyous, but seemed too pat and complacent to me.

Western, directed and cowritten by Manuel Poirier, won the Grand Jury Prize, or second place, in 1997 at Cannes; that's the same prize *Life Is Beautiful* won in 1998. Set in France, it absorbed a certain offhand flair. The same material, filmed in America, might seem thin and contrived; the adventures are arbitrary, the cuteness of the men grows wearing, and when Nino has an accident with a chainsaw, we can see contrivance shading off into desperation.

The movie is slow-going. Paco and Nino are the kinds of open-faced proletarian heroes found more often in fables than in life. Their luck as homeless men in finding a ready supply of trusting and hospitable women is uncanny, even unbelievable. The movie insists on their charm, instead of letting us find it for ourselves. And although the leading actresses are sunny and vital, they are fantasy women, not real ones (who would be smarter and warier).

One of the women in the film collects children fathered by an assortment of men who capture her fancy and then drift away, apparently with her blessings. The movie smiles on this practice, instead of wondering how she found so many men so indifferent to their own children. By the end of the film she has given birth to her own orphanage, and could hire the family out as a package to the casting director for *Oliver Twist.* The jury at Cannes loved this, but I squirmed, and speculated that the subtitles and the European cachet gives the film immunity. In English, with American actors, this story would be unbearable.

What Dreams May Come ★ ★ ★ ½

PG-13, 113 m., 1998

Robin Williams (Chris Nielsen), Cuba Gooding Jr. (Albert), Annabella Sciorra (Annie Nielsen), Max Von Sydow (The Tracker), Rosalind Chow (Leona), Jessica Brooks Grant (Marie Nielsen), Josh Paddock (Ian Nielsen). Directed by Vincent Ward and produced by Stephen Simon and Barnet Bain. Screenplay by Ron Bass, based on the novel by Richard Matheson.

Vincent Ward's *What Dreams May Come* is so breathtaking, so beautiful, so bold in its imagination, that it's a surprise at the end to find it doesn't finally deliver. It takes us to the emotional brink, but it doesn't push us over. It ends on a curiously unconvincing note—a conventional resolution in a movie that for most of its length has been daring and visionary.

So, yes, I have my disappointments with it. But I would not want them to discourage you from seeing it, because this is a film that even in its imperfect form shows how movies can imagine the unknown, can lead our imaginations into wonderful places. And it contains heartbreakingly effective performances by Robin Williams and Annabella Sciorra. The movie is so good it shows us how it could have been better: It seems headed for a great leap, we can sense it coming, and then it settles. If Hollywood is determined to shortchange us with an obligatory happy ending, then it shouldn't torment us with a movie that deserves better.

I hesitate to reveal too many secrets, but the film's setup was so thoroughly publicized that you probably already know certain key facts. Save the review until later if you don't.

The facts you know from the ads and the trailers are that Chris and Annie (Williams and Sciorra) have a Meet Cute when their boats collide on a Swiss lake. They marry. They have two children. They are happy. Then both of the children are killed in an accident. Annie has a breakdown, Chris nurses her through, art works as therapy, they are somehow patching their lives back together—and then Chris is killed.

The film follows him into the next world, and creates it with visuals that seem borrowed from his own memories and imagination. In one sequence that is among the most visually exciting I have ever seen, he occupies a landscape that is a painting, and as he plucks a flower it turns to oil paint in his hand. Other parts of this world seem cheerfully assembled from the storage rooms of images we keep in our minds: Renaissance art, the pre-Raphaelites, greeting cards, angel kitsch (cherubs float past on plump clouds). Later, when Chris ventures into hell, the images are darker and more fearsome—Bosch crossed with Dali.

There is a guide in the next world named Albert (Cuba Gooding Jr.). Is he all that he seems? Now we have ventured beyond the information in the ads, and I will be more circumspect. The story, inspired by a novel by Richard Matheson, is founded on the assumption that heaven exists in a state of flux, that its inhabitants assume identities that please themselves, or us; that having been bound within one identity during life, we are set free. Heaven, in one sense, means becoming who you want to be.

And hell? "Hell is for those who don't know they're dead," says Albert. Or they know they're dead but don't know what the deal is. Or they won't go along with the deal. Many of those in hell are guilty of the greatest sin against God, which is despair: They believe they are beyond hope.

After the death of her children and husband, Annie has despaired and killed herself and gone to hell. Chris wants to find her: "I'm her soul mate." Albert says that's not possible: "Nothing will make her recognize you." But he acts as a guide and Chris ventures into hell, which, like heaven, has been realized with a visual intensity and originality that is astonishing. In this film the road to hell is paved, not with good intentions, but with the faces of the damned, bitter and complaining (the face and voice of Chris's father are played by the German director Werner Herzog).

What happens then, what happens throughout the film, is like nothing you have seen before. Vincent Ward is a New Zealand director whose works have not always reached a large audience, but have always dared for big ideas and bold visuals to express them. He made *The Navigator* (1988), about medieval Englishmen who tunnel to escape the plague—and emerge in the present. And then, in 1993, the great *Map of the Human Heart,* about the odyssey of an Eskimo boy from Alaska in the 1930s to London in the war, and from a great love affair to high adventure.

What Dreams May Come ends, like *The Navigator,* with the characters seeking their destiny in a cathedral—but this one, like many of the film's images, is like none you have seen before. It is upside down, the great vaulted ceilings providing a floor and a landscape. Since I have mentioned Herzog, I had might as well quote his belief that our century is "starving for great images." This film provides them, and also provides quiet moments of winsome human nature, as when a character played by

Rosalind Chow explains why she appears to be an Asian flight attendant, and when another, played by Max Von Sydow, explains the rules of the game as he understands them.

Robin Williams somehow has a quality that makes him seem at home in imaginary universes. Remember him in *Popeye, The Adventures of Baron Munchausen, Toys, Jumanji,* and in his animated incarnation in *Aladdin.* There is a muscular reality about him, despite his mercurial wit, that anchors him and makes the fantastic images around him seem almost plausible. He is good, too, at emotion: He brings us along with him. In Annabella Sciorra he has a costar whose own character is deeply unhappy and yet touching; her sin of despair was committed, we believe, because she loved so much and was so happy she cannot exist in the absence of those feelings.

And yet, as I've suggested, the movie somehow gathers all these threads and its triumphant art direction and special effects, and then doesn't get across the finish line with them. I walked out of the theater sensing that I should have felt more, that an opportunity had been lost. *What Dreams May Come* takes us too far and risks too much to turn conventional at the end. It could have been better. It could perhaps have been the best film of the year. Whatever its shortcomings, it is a film to treasure. ☞

Whatever ★ ★ ★

R, 112 m., 1998

Liza Weil (Anna Stockard), Chad Morgan (Brenda Talbot), Frederic Forrest (Chaminski), Kathryn Rossetter (Carol Stockard), Marc Riffon (Martin), Dan Montano (Zak), John G. Connolly (Woods), Gary Wolf (Eddie). Directed by Susan Skoog and produced by Ellin Baumel, Michelle Yahn, Kevin Segalla, and Skoog. Screenplay by Skoog.

Whatever is a movie that knows how a lot of kids survive the teenage years through sheer blind luck. Others die or have their lives destroyed because their luck is bad. Most people, I imagine, keep teenage secrets that still make them cringe years later—memories of stupid chances they shouldn't have taken, and relief that they weren't caught.

Anna, the heroine of *Whatever,* is not a bad girl but she is an unhappy one, and she drifts into danger without even giving it much thought. Isn't it amazing how everything a girl has been taught all her life sometimes means nothing in the face of temptation by a boy who is reckless and stupid, but seems to offer freedom?

It's the early 1980s. Anna (Liza Weil) attends high school in New Jersey. Her best friend, Brenda (Chad Morgan), values herself so lightly that she has sex with guys just to get her hands on their jugs of wine. Anna is taking art classes and hopes to be accepted by Cooper Union, a good school in Manhattan. Her teacher (Frederic Forrest), an aging hippie in a time warp, urges her to do her thing. Anna lives with her mother (Kathryn Rossetter) and unpleasant younger brother; they often prepare their own meals while their mother is out on dates with a married man she hopes will pay their bills.

Anna is smart, but not a good student. She's not into booze and sex the way her friend Brenda is, but she figures, without giving it much thought, that these are areas where she might as well do some experimenting. She has a crush on a kid named Martin (Marc Riffon), who has been out of town but now returns from his self-styled wanderings with lessons about "the passion of one's existence." A lot of the time Anna spends doing nothing while listening to bad music.

The movie unfolds episodically. Brenda suggests cutting school and taking a trip to New York. Anna visits Cooper Union but doesn't really connect. They pick up a couple of twenty-five-year-olds in a bar. They pretend to be older than they are. Something embarrassing happens that will turn into a funny story many years from now, when the confusion and pain have been outgrown.

Back in New Jersey, there are a couple of guys hanging around who have already done time in a reformatory, and are low-level would-be drug dealers who suggest a trip to Florida. Brenda wants to go. Anna agrees passively. This trip could produce the turning point in her life; it could result in trouble that would last for years. The way it turns out, and the subtle way those scenes are written and acted, give us a glimpse inside the character of one of the guys—who has probably already taken the wrong turn himself, but still has his feelings.

The movie was written and directed by Susan Skoog, who accepts a difficult challenge by making Anna neither a rebel nor an endangered good girl, but simply an average person whose potential, if any, is still wrapped up inside adolescent confusion and resentment. She's at a stage. She doesn't express herself very well and often clams up, and the counselor at high school is exasperated because she seems to be drifting into trouble without much meaning to. She gets into trouble for smoking in the school restroom, and we sense she doesn't even care if she smokes or not—she just thinks she ought to.

Movies like this depend on observation. Yes, there's some plot, especially when Brenda seizes an occasion to strike back at the stepfather who has abused her. But it's significant that Brenda takes action, not Anna—who usually has no particular action in mind. She's along for the ride. Doesn't care how, doesn't know where. The suspense involves whether she'll avoid trouble long enough to grow out of the stage where she allows herself to drift into it. Seeing a movie like this could do a lot of kids some good. Parents, I suspect, would find it terrifying.

When the Cat's Away ★ ★ ★

R, 95 m., 1997

Garance Clavel (Chloe), Zinedine Soualem (Jamel), Renee Le Calm (Madame Renee), Olivier Py (Michel), Arapimou (Gris-Gris), Romain Duris (Drummer). Directed by Cedric Klapisch and produced by Aissa Djabri, Farid Lahouassa, and Manuel Munz. Screenplay by Klapisch.

Here is a movie about a young woman named Chloe, who has no luck with men, considers herself desperately lonely, and then finds out what loneliness is when she loses her cat. She's a little mouse, and *When the Cat's Away* tells the story of how she plays. But it is all so much more tricky than that.

The French love to make these pictures that are about attitude and personal style. The one thing you know is that the movie is not going to be about the cat's loss, or the cat's return, or even the cat's life or death.

In an American movie the heroine would think the cat's fate was terribly important, and so would the filmmakers. But Cedric Klapisch, who wrote and directed *When the Cat's Away,* realizes that the movie is really about a woman who has nothing better to do than obsess about her cat.

Chloe (Garance Clavel) lives in a district of Paris that was until recently rather shabby and neglected, which meant that people could count on spending their lives there without being annoyed. When she decides to go on vacation, she needs someone to look after the cat (named Gris-Gris), and the waiter in the local café suggests Madame Renee (Renee Le Calm), an elderly cat woman who lives in an apartment nearby.

Chloe parks Gris-Gris with Madame Renee, goes on vacation (the director compresses the entire holiday into one postcard shot), and returns to find Madame Renee in distress because the cat has run away. Chloe now sets about finding the cat, aided by Madame Renee's network of cat ladies, and by a simpleminded fellow named Jamel (Zinedine Soualem), who helpfully risks his life on rooftops, usually in search of the wrong cat.

The disappearance of Gris-Gris compounds Chloe's isolation. "Why am I all alone?" she asks her gay roommate, who is lonely himself. "Guys scare you," he says. "That's why you have a roommate who's gay." She goes awkwardly into a bar, but doesn't know any of the right pickup behavior, and ends up being accused in the toilet of trying to steal another woman's boyfriend. Not that Chloe's love life is quite that adventuresome; in one scene, the guy seems to hurry through the mechanics of sex because he's eager to make a phone call.

All of this takes place in a kind of casual, offhand way: Chloe exudes the sense of living in her city, of being rooted in the neighborhood, of being not a character in a movie but someone you might see or hear about. And many of the other characters really do live in the district, and are playing themselves—particularly Madame Renee, a short, frizzy-haired, strongly opinionated little woman who is so uninhibited and convincing you'd never guess she's a real cat lady, playing herself.

The movie reminds us of what it must have been like to live in cities before air conditioning sealed the windows and television ended leisurely conversations on the front steps. Now we live in containers, like cargo on a ship. In Chloe's Paris, people have a good sense of who lives next door and upstairs, and when she finally meets the neighborhood rock 'n' roll musician, she and everyone else have been listening to his drums for weeks. Of course, this is changing; the district is being gentrified, and familiar old merchants are being replaced by high-priced shops.

The movie is made in the tradition of Eric Rohmer, who is the master of this sort of film. In his many movies, most recently *Rendezvous in Paris,* he follows people into the casual moments of their lives, and allows them coincidences and mistakes. Klapisch does the same thing. *When the Cat's Away* is like a very subtle, curious, edgy documentary in which we get interested in Chloe because she has lost her cat, and by the end almost have to be reminded that the cat is missing.

When We Were Kings ★ ★ ★

PG, 85 m., 1997

A documentary film directed by Leon Gast and produced by David Sonenberg, Gast, and Taylor Hackford. Featuring Muhammad Ali, George Foreman, James Brown, B. B. King, Don King, Spike Lee, Norman Mailer, Miriam Makeba, George Plimpton, and Mobutu Sese Seko.

The heavyweight title fight between Muhammad Ali and George Foreman in Zaire on October 30, 1974—the "Rumble in the Jungle"—is enshrined as one of the great sports events of the century. It was also a cultural and political happening. Into the capital of Kinshasa flew planeloads of performers for an "African Woodstock," TV crews, Howard Cosell at the head of an international contingent of sports journalists, celebrity fight groupies like Norman Mailer and George Plimpton, and, of course, the two principals: Ali, then still controversial because of his decision to be a conscientious objector, and Foreman, now huggable and lovable in TV commercials but then seen as fearsome and forbidding.

"I'm young, I'm handsome, I'm fast, I'm strong, and I can't be beat," Ali told the press. They didn't believe him. Foreman had destroyed Joe Frazier, who had defeated Ali. Foreman was younger, bigger, and stronger, with a punch so powerful, Norman Mailer recalled, "that after he was finished with a heavy punching bag it had a depression pounded into it." Ali was thirty-two and thought to be over the hill. The odds were seven-to-one against him.

The Zaire they arrived in was a country much in need of foreign currency and image refurbishment. Under the leadership of Mobutu Sese Seko ("the archetype of a closet sadist," said Mailer), the former Belgian Congo had became a paranoid police state; the new stadium built to showcase the fight was rumored to hold 1,000 political prisoners in cells in its catacombs.

Don King, then at the dawn of his career as a fight promoter, had sold Mobutu on the fight and raised $5 million for each fighter. The "African Woodstock," featuring such stars as B. B. King, James Brown, and Miriam Makeba, was supposed to pay for part of that. For Ali, the fight in Africa was payback time for the hammering he'd taken in the American press for his refusal to fight in Vietnam. For Foreman, it was more complicated. So great was the pro-Ali frenzy, Foreman observed, that when he got off the plane the crowds were surprised to find that he was also a black man. "Why do they hate me so much?" he wondered.

Leon Gast's *When We Were Kings* is like a time capsule; the original footage has waited all these years to be assembled into a film, because of legal and financial difficulties. It is a new documentary of a past event, recapturing the electricity generated by Muhammad Ali in his prime. Spike Lee, who with Mailer and Plimpton provides modern commentary on the 1974 footage, says young people today do not know how famous and important Ali was. He is right. "When I fly on an airplane," Ali once told me, "I look out of the window and I think, I am the only person that *everyone* down there knows about." It is not bragging if you are only telling the truth.

The original film apparently started as a concert documentary. Then the fight was delayed because of a cut to Foreman's eye. The concert went ahead as scheduled, and then the fighters, their entourages, and the press settled down to wait for the main event. No one really thought Ali had a chance—perhaps not even Ali, who seems reflective and withdrawn in a few private moments, although in public he predicted victory.

How could he have a chance, really? Hadn't the U.S. government taken away his prime years as a fighter after he refused to fight in Vietnam? ("I ain't got no quarrel with the Viet Cong," he explained.) Wasn't Foreman bigger, faster, stronger, younger? History records Ali's famous strategy, the "Rope-a Dope Defense," in which he simply outwaited Foreman, absorbing incalculable punishment until, in the eighth round, Foreman was exhausted and Ali exploded with a series of rights to the head, finishing him.

Was this, however, really a strategy at all? The film gives the impression that Ali got nowhere in the first round and adopted the "Rope-a-Dope" almost by default. Perhaps he knew, or hoped, that he was in better condition than Foreman and could outlast him if he simply stayed on his feet. It is certain that hardly anyone in Zaire that night, not even his steadfast supporter Cosell, thought Ali could win; the upset became an enduring part of his myth.

When We Were Kings captures Ali's public persona and private resolve. As heavyweight champion during the Vietnam War, he could easily have arrived at an accommodation with the military, touring bases in lieu of combat duty. Although he was called a coward and a draft dodger, surely it took more courage to follow the path he chose. And yet it is remarkable how ebullient, how joyful he remained even after the price he paid; how he is willing to be a clown and a poet as well as a fighter and an activist.

Seeing the film today inspires poignant feelings; we contrast young Ali with the ailing and aging legend, and reflect that this fight must have contributed to the damage that slowed him down. It is also fascinating to contrast the young Foreman with today's much-loved figure; he, too, has grown and mellowed. When the movie was made all of those developments were still ahead; there is a palpable tension, as the two men step into the ring, that is not lessened because we know the outcome.

The Whole Wide World ★ ★ ★

PG, 105 m., 1997

Vincent D'Onofrio (Robert E. Howard), Renee Zellweger (Novalyne Price), Ann Wedgeworth (Mrs. Howard), Benjamin Mouton (Clyde Smith), Chris Shearer (Truett). Directed by Dan Ireland and produced by Carl-Jan Colpaert, Kevin Reidy, Ireland, and Vincent D'Onofrio. Screenplay by Michael Scott Myers, based on the memoir "One Who Walked Alone" by Novalyne Price Ellis.

The pulp magazines that flourished from the 1920s through the 1950s were one of the great trashy entertainment media of our century. I got in at the end of the period, as the big-format classic pulps like *Thrilling Wonder Stories* were being pushed aside by television and replaced on the newsstands by more respectable digest-sized mags like *Analog, Galaxy,* and *F&SF.* But I haunted used bookstores and brought home old pulps in cardboard boxes strapped to the back of my bike, and late into the night I'd read their breathless stories and feel faint stirrings of unfamiliar emotions as I examined their covers, on which desperate women in big titanium brassieres squirmed in the tentacles of bug-eyed monsters.

The great pulps came in four flavors: science fiction, Westerns, romance, and crime. Of these, the brand-new genre was SF, baptized by Hugo Gernsback in his pioneering magazine *Amazing Stories.* The skilled pulp writers could move from one genre to another, sometimes using pseudonyms because they had more than one story in an issue. The crime mags gave birth to *film noir* and the great writers like Hammett, Chandler, and their heirs. They also gave rise to the image of the writer as romantic loner, slaving at his typewriter in a rented room, a cigarette in his mouth and a bottle on the floor, working for peanuts.

Robert E. Howard bought that image lock, stock, and truncheon. He was by his own admission "the greatest pulp writer in the whole wide world," a mainstay of the famous fantasy/horror magazine named *Weird Tales.* The best of his creations was Conan the Barbarian, who had a rebirth in the 1970s in two Schwarzenegger movies and in some fifty Conan paperbacks written under license by modern-day hacks. By then Howard was long dead.

The Whole Wide World is based on a 1988 memoir of Howard, written by a woman named Novalyne Price Ellis, who was a retired Louisiana schoolteacher when the Conan boom came along. Disturbed by portraits of Howard as some kind of loony loner, she wrote the book to recall her own romance with Howard more than fifty years earlier. Her memories have served him well, even though he was probably loony and a loner given to statements like "the road I walk, I walk alone," which are not designed to inspire confidence in the bosom of a potential fiancée.

Howard is played in the film by Vincent D'Onofrio as a tall, broad, open-faced Texas boy who likes to wear white shirts and suspenders. Novalyne is Renee Zellweger, who was magical as Tom Cruise's romantic partner in *Jerry Maguire* and is charming here, too, as a small-town schoolteacher who dreams of being a writer and talks her date into taking her to meet his friend Bob Howard, who really was one.

Bob and Novalyne like each other immediately, but Bob comes with a great deal of emotional baggage. He lives at home with an almost invisible father and an ailing mother he dotes upon. In another sense he lives in his head and in his stories; Novalyne hears him at his typewriter, pounding the keys while shouting out his prose at the same time: "When women felt those tree-trunk arms around their waists, they melted like butter!"

The two young people have a sweet, innocent courtship, with much talk but little sex; Howard appreciates her as an audience but does not quite seem to see her as a woman until, realizing they have no future, she starts dating a more conventional young man in town. Then he is betrayed, not because she left him, but because she abandoned their vision—a vision that had him promising her he could deliver the best sunsets in Texas right on order, as if he were God. Somehow in his film Ireland implies the tenderness that an old woman might still feel for the boy she once loved; there is an echo here somewhere of Joyce's short story "The Dead."

Howard's inner emotional life is obviously in turmoil. "Robert is real close to his mother," the family doctor observes, and Bob changes her soiled linen, combs her hair, and coos to her in between banging out bloodcurdling adventures on his typewriter. Novalyne sees him striding down the street trying out new dialogue, and Ireland uses subtle devices on the sound track to suggest that Howard's fantasy world was as real to him as any other.

Howard was not a great writer, but he was a great storyteller, like Edgar Rice Burroughs, Doc Smith, and the other masters of pulp. For a teenage boy his stories were so enthralling that I can only pity today's kids who have to make do with tamer fiction. His books indeed still sell, maybe because readers can sense the utter conviction behind the muscular prose. The pulps "don't pay much," he tells Novalyne, "a half-cent a word, mostly—so I stretch my yarns." It was the kind of writer's bravado he loved, to discuss his work in mercenary terms. He knew, and she guessed, he stretched them because he didn't want to leave them. He was afraid to.

Why Do Fools Fall in Love ★★

R, 115 m., 1998

Halle Berry (Zola Taylor), Larenz Tate (Frankie Lymon), Vivica A. Fox (Elizabeth Waters), Lela Rochon (Emira Eagle), Paul Mazursky (Morris Levy). Directed by Gregory Nava and produced by Paul Hall and Stephen Nemeth. Written by Tina Andrews. Screenplay by Andrews.

Frankie Lymon was thirteen when he had his big hit record and twenty-five when he died. The record fell like a gift from the sky, hit the top of the charts, and can still be heard on the golden oldies stations. The rest of his life played like the flip side. *Why Do Fools Fall in Love* tells the story of how he married three women (at least according to them), got into trouble with drugs and the army, and self-destructed prematurely, leaving his ex-wives and/or widows squabbling in court over the estate.

There are several angles this material might have been approached from, and the director tries several without hitting on one that works. By the end of the film we're not even left with anyone to root for; we realize with a little astonishment, waiting for the court verdict, that we don't care who wins.

The movie is not really about Frankie Lymon (Larenz Tate), who remains an enigma. Nor does it have many insights into the three claimants to his estate: Zola Taylor (Halle Berry), a singer with the Platters, who was his first girl and his second wife; Elizabeth Waters (Vivica A. Fox), a shoplifter who loved him so much she became a hooker to pay for his drug rehab; and Emira Eagle (Lela Rochon), a church-going waitress who was there when he needed her after he was drafted into the army and sent to Georgia for training.

What made Frankie run? The movie clearly doesn't know. It sets the story against a convincing backdrop of the 1950s rock 'n' roll industry, provides some high-energy musical sequences, and finds moments of drama as Frankie is beaten by drug money collectors, steals a mink stole from one woman to give to another, and threatens to throw dogs out the window—all while somehow remaining a lovable madcap. Well, most of the time.

The usual generic conventions seem missing. There is no real sense of loss in Frankie's death, since his early promise, if genuine, was so quickly dissipated. There is no sense that he betrayed the three women: He loved them all, after his fashion, and was so needy he simply reached out to the closest one. An awkward courtroom scene at the end belatedly tries to pin some of the blame on a record producer (Paul Mazursky), who stole cowriting credit and perhaps a lot of Frankie's profits, but the producer, if guilty, was still not responsible for most of the events in the movie. Frankie was. His song should have been, "When I'm Not With the One I Love, I Love the One I'm With."

The movie's director is Gregory Nava, whose artistry in films like *El Norte, My Family,* and *Selena* seems missing this time: His films usually proceed from passion and commitment, and here the inspiration seems to be missing. It's as if someone read about Lymon's three wives in court and decided it would be a great story without ever deciding what the story was.

The four principal actors all provide the spectacle of talent without purpose: They do what they can with their characters and their scenes, but the screenplay doesn't provide them with an arc or a purpose. When their characters reappear, we haven't been waiting for them. When they're offscreen, we don't miss them. That's true even of Frankie, who is missing a fair amount of the time.

What approach might have worked? Hard to say. Maybe the whole thing should have been seen exclusively through Frankie's eyes, as a kid who has his fifteen minutes of fame at an early age and then dines out for the rest of his life on other people's memories. That would have meant jettisoning the whole court case and its flashbacks, but the court stuff doesn't work anyway. Maybe straight chronology would have been a better idea, allowing Frankie to be the focus, and allowing us to follow his moves more clearly from one woman to the next and back again. As it stands, *Why Do Fools Fall in Love* never convinces us its story is worth telling, and never finds a way to tell it, even if it is.

Wide Awake ★ ★

PG, 90 m., 1998

Joseph Cross (Joshua Beal), Timothy Reifsnyder (Dave O'Hara), Dana Delany (Mrs. Beal), Denis Leary (Mr. Beal), Robert Loggia (Grandpa Beal), Rosie O'Donnell (Sister Terry), Julia Stiles (Neena Beal). Directed by M. Night Shyamalan and produced by Cary Woods and Cathy Konrad. Screenplay by Shyamalan.

In an opening scene of *Wide Awake,* the fifth-grade kids in a Catholic school have a spirited discussion about whether the unbaptized can get into heaven. This rang a bell. Morning religion class in my grade school was much the same; the nuns tried to teach us principles, and we were always getting sidetracked on technicalities.

When *Wide Awake* observes moments like these in the classroom, it's an entertaining film. I liked, for example, Rosie O'Donnell's performance as Sister Terry, a Philadelphia Phillies fan, and was reminded of my own teacher, Sister Marie Donald, who was also our basketball coach. A film accurately remembering Catholic school in the pre–Vatican II era could be a charmer.

But the movie has higher and, I'm afraid, more contrived goals. Its hero is young Joshua (Joseph Cross), who has been depressed ever since his beloved grandfather (Robert Loggia) died of bone marrow cancer. He mopes about his granddad's room, he doesn't want to get up for school, he is the despair of his parents (Dana Delany and Denis Leary) and annoys his sister (Julia Stiles). Finally he announces to his best friend, Dave (Timothy Reifsnyder), that he's going on a mission to find out if his grandfather is okay.

Joshua's mission, which occupies much of the movie, involves his demand for a sign from heaven. Along the way, he also sneaks into a girls' school to cross-examine a cardinal and holds a photo of the pope hostage in the rain. Does he get his sign? The movie is rated PG, a tip-off that it does not end with Joshua taking a tough position in favor of existential nothingness. (It is clever how the movie hides the "sign" in plain view all along.)

I wonder who the movie was made for. Smaller kids, I'm afraid, will find it both slow and depressing, especially the parts about why God allows bad things to happen. The health problems of Dave, the best friend, may also come as an unsettling shock. Older kids, on the other hand, are likely to find it too cute, and adults are better advised to see the French film *Ponette*, a more intelligent treatment of a child asking hard questions about heaven.

The film does have some pleasures, however. One of them is Rosie O'Donnell's performance. Although I can relate to her cheerful energy on television, I've not been a fan of her work in movies—especially not in *Exit to Eden* (1994), where she played a dominatrix as if her whip didn't fit.

In *Wide Awake*, however, she finds a role that she seems comfortable in and creates a character I would have liked to see more of. Becoming a nun is sometimes seen as a renunciation of independence and freedom, but for some women it is liberating—a role they feel relaxed in, allowing them to express themselves. Movies give us priests and nuns who are tortured and neurotic, but O'Donnell's Sister Terry seems happy and fulfilled; her role suits her personality.

As for the rest of the movie: Well, Joseph Cross is an effective and convincing little performer, but I always felt I was looking at a movie, not the actions of a real little boy. At the end of his film, when he reads his essay to his class, I asked myself if fifth-graders really thought and wrote like that. No, I decided, they don't. But screenwriters do.

The Wife ★ ★ ★

R, 101 m., 1997

Julie Hagerty (Rita), Tom Noonan (Jack), Wallace Shawn (Cosmo), Karen Young (Arlie). Directed by Tom Noonan and produced by Scott Macaulay and Robin O'Hara. Screenplay by Noonan.

Jack's eyes dart around the table like a cat waiting to pounce. He looks at his wife and their guests, shields his own thoughts, and occasionally drops another word into the conversation just to see what effect it will have. He is as frightening as a madman with a knife—curious about whether he can goad the others to an explosion, a damaging revelation, or self-destruction.

Jack (Tom Noonan) is supposed to be a therapist. Well, so is his wife, Rita (Julie Hagerty). They practice those brands of therapies you learn out of best-sellers on the counter near the scented candles and the angel bookmarks. Jack's secret is that he gets off on manipulation and control. He has manipulated Rita into becoming his cotherapist, although we suspect she doesn't much believe in herself or their practice. She has ludes and booze stashed around the house like magic talismans. They talk in gentle tones to one another, as if recovering from much damage in the past.

Their house is a comfortable cabin in the country, near a frozen lake that Jack sometimes visits, even late at night in the winter, carrying a torch. This is the kind of house where every decorating touch seems planned for its secret effect; the dining room table has a four-sided triangular lamp in its center—a low lamp, so that everyone at dinner is lit from beneath, as in a horror movie. When the lamp is turned brighter, it hums.

As the movie opens, indeed, dinner guests have arrived. Cosmo (Wallace Shawn), one of their clients, has brought his wife, Arlie (Karen Young), to meet his therapists. He has a hidden motive: He wants them to see that he's telling the truth when he says how hostile and crazy she is. Arlie is a onetime topless dancer who is still proud of her body; we dread, correctly, that at some point in the evening she will display her still-marketable assets. (Ever notice how the more a woman wants to show you her breasts, the less you want to see them?)

Rita is unhappy about the unexpected company, but then she's unhappy about everything. Jack is delighted, and insists on an impromptu dinner party. The conversation races through the conventional niceties at a breakneck speed, as Jack steers it into verbal games of truth and pain. And watch his eyes, as he feasts on the unhappiness he inspires. Arlie does her topless act, and Cosmo at one point does a dance that looks for all the world like an animated version of a Thurber drawing.

The Wife can be compared to *Who's Afraid of Virginia Woolf?* in the sense that it consists of two couples, much booze, and a long evening. There is a key difference. Here, only one character is the gamemaster and the other three are his victims. It makes for a whole new set of possible moves.

Tom Noonan is an actor and writer whose name you may not recognize, although his face and body might ring a bell. He's tall, balding, and born to play Death in *The Seventh Seal.* This is his second film based on probing conversational fun and games. His *What Happened Was . . .*, in 1993, was about a blind date between two people so desperate that eventually each can hardly bear to look upon the other. Here he ups the stakes.

One could say this is a filmed version of a stage play, and so it is (the stage version was named *Wifey*). But I think this material benefits from being filmed. It craves the close-ups. Four people on a stage would be too far away. We need to be trapped in the eerie light of that dinner table, or the flickering torch, or the candles, or the headlights; all of the illumination in this film seems like a last stand against all-encroaching darkness.

Wild America ★ ★

PG, 107 m., 1997

Jonathan Taylor Thomas (Marshall Stouffer), Devon Sawa (Mark Stouffer), Scott Bairstow (Marty Stouffer), Frances Fisher (Agnes Stouffer), Jamey Sheridan (Marty Stouffer Sr.). Directed by William Dear and produced by James G. Robinson, Irby Smith, and Mark Stouffer. Screenplay by David Michael Wieger.

A lot of movies begin with the information that they're based on true stories. *Wild America* ends with that information—wisely, since it would be impossible to watch the movie without hooting and hollering if you had the slightest suspicion you were supposed to believe the stuff on the screen.

The film tells the story of the three irrepressible Stouffer brothers—Marshall, Mark, and Marty—who dream of growing up to make movies about wild animals. In the late 1960s, when the two older boys are teenagers and the youngest is maybe eleven or twelve, they buy a used 16mm camera and talk their parents into letting them make a wildlife photo odyssey from their southern home to the mountains of the West. They have only a few weeks, because it's August and they have to be back for school in the fall. We follow them through a series of adventures that I, for one, (a) doubt ever happened, (b) doubt could happen in a two- or three-week period, and (c) doubt could happen without one, two, or perhaps all three young Stouffers ending up like their namesakes, as reheatable entrées.

First stop, Alligator Hell, an alligator preserve where the boys rent a boat and head into the swamp at night with flashlights. Needless to say, they find alligators. They also find themselves overboard—splashing in the water as the giant beasts attack them and flashlight beams reflect off rows of wicked alligator teeth. They all escape alive. Whew!

After a brief respite with some skinny-dipping British girls (who do not endanger the PG rating), the boys head out West, where a subtitle informs us they have arrived at the "High Country." Why do we need to be told it's the High Country? Because there's snow on the ground. Of course, there is snow on mountain peaks even in August, but my rudimentary knowledge of wild animals leads me to believe that hibernating bears and snakes, etc., head for warmer climes farther down on the slopes. A bear that is still hibernating in August is dead, or agoraphobic.

Not in this movie. The boys are searching for the Cave of the Sleeping Bears. Most bears hibernate alone, but this legendary cave is sort of like a dorm. From a mysterious woman with a scarred face, who lives in a cabin, they get secret information, and soon they have found the very cave itself. Film footage of this could make their fortune.

Alas, the mouth of the cave is guarded by dangerous snakes. Thinking fast, the boys throw snow into the cave to cool the snakes and neutralize them. Now hold on a second. Wouldn't the temperature inside a cave be the same as outside? If there's snow on the ground, wouldn't the cold-blooded snakes be asleep, unless they built campfires for themselves?

Not in this movie. The lads venture into the cave, which, sure 'nuf, is filled with sleeping bears (who do not know that farther down the mountain it's summertime and the livin' is easy). They make a lot of noise and shine their flashlights around and wake the bears, which rumble and roar alarmingly and loom over the lads until (I am not making this up) the lads lull them back to sleep by singing that popular bear lullaby, "Mountain Dew."

More adventures ensue. Back home, the youngest boy goes on a solo flight in his dad's restored antique aircraft, while Dad (in the hospital after a truck accident) looks on with horror and pride. It's a stunt to demonstrate to strict old Dad, in the words of a son, that "I doubt this family is gonna stay together unless you let every one of us be who he needs to be."

It seemed to me that Dad was less a curmudgeon than a sensible father. There is a difference between letting a teenage boy realize his dream, and letting him wake sleeping bears and rassle with gators. (I won't even mention the moose attack, or the adventure on the air force bombing range.)

The film ends with the Stouffers showing their film footage to a crowd in the local gymnasium, and a few years later, on "Aug. 6, 1977," their first nature film premiered on NBC-TV, "narrated by Robert Redford." All of the boys have since gone on to careers as photographers and naturalists, for which I applaud them, while wondering how much of *Wild America* can be true. I imagine the animal hijinks in the film will be entertaining for younger viewers, as true-life adventures often are. But—caution, kids! Do not experiment with throwing snow at deadly snakes. And if you find yourself in the Cave of the Sleeping Bears, go out the same way you came in, as quietly as you possibly can.

Wilde ★ ★ ★ ½

R, 116 m., 1998

Stephen Fry (Oscar Wilde), Jude Law (Lord Alfred Douglas), Vanessa Redgrave (Lady Speranza Wilde), Jennifer Ehle (Constance Wilde), Gemma Jones (Lady Queensberry), Judy Parfitt (Lady Mount-Temple), Michael Sheen (Robert Ross), Zoe Wanamaker (Ada Leverson), Tom Wilkinson (Marquis of Queensberry). Directed by Brian Gilbert and produced by Marc Samuelson and Peter Samuelson. Screenplay by Julian Mitchell, based on the book *Oscar Wilde* by Richard Ellmann.

"Wickedness," Oscar Wilde said, "is a myth invented by good people to account for the curious attractiveness of others." Wilde himself was considered in some quarters the most wicked man of his time, in others the most attractive—a gifted artist who was a martyr to convention.

At the very peak of his fame, after his play *The Importance of Being Earnest* opened to wild success in 1895, Wilde was convicted of "gross indecency," and spent his few remaining years in prison or decline. A century later his reputation, personal and professional, could not stand higher, and this new biopic joins two new stage productions in celebrating his rise, fall, and immortality. If he were alive today he would no doubt describe his homosexuality as a good career move.

Wilde's personal tragedy would be of little lasting interest were it not for the enduring popularity of his work, and the sensational nature of his fall. There were no doubt as many homosexuals in Wilde's day as there are now, but most of them either repressed their feelings or kept them secret. Homosexual behavior was, after all, against the law. It was Wilde's misfortune to fall in love with a reckless and vain young man who hated his pigheaded father, and wanted to use Wilde's fame as a taunt.

Worse luck that the father was the marquess of Queensbury, a famous figure in boxing and horse racing. Still worse luck that when the marquess left an insulting message at Wilde's club, Wilde unwisely sued him. And dashedly bad luck that the marquis's attorneys were able to produce in court "rent boys" from a male brothel, who testified that the marquis was correct in describing Wilde as a sodomite.

Consider that a century later gay men are being knighted, and you see what bad timing it was to be born in 1854. In another sense, Wilde's genius required a backdrop of Victorian stuffiness. Many of the people in his audiences understood what he was writing between the lines, but accepted it as funny and daring—as long as it stayed between the lines. ("Earnest," for example, was in Wilde's time a synonym for "gay.") Wilde was famous for his quips and one-liners, which survive because they almost always contain a center of truth. With immense self-enjoyment, he punctured hypocrisy ("I never take any notice of what common people say, and I never interfere with what charming people do").

Brian Gilbert's *Wilde*, with a screenplay by Julian Mitchell, based on Richard Ellmann's famous biography, has the good fortune to star Stephen Fry, a British author, actor, and comedian who looks a lot like Wilde and has many of the same attributes: He is very tall, he is somewhat plump, he is gay, he is funny, he makes his conversation into an art. That he is also a fine actor is important, because the film requires him to show many conflicting aspects of Wilde's life: How he loved his wife and children, how his homosexuality was oriented not so much toward the physical as toward the idealistic, how he was so successful for so long in charming everyone in his life that he actually believed he could charm an English courtroom out of a sentence for sodomy.

Wilde was the dandy as superstar; in the years before mass media, he wrote best-sellers and long-running plays, and went on enormously popular lecture tours (the film opens with him down in a silver mine in Nevada, reading poetry to the miners and beaming upon their muscular torsos). He invented the type exploited by the later Elvis Presley: the peacock in full plumage, kidding himself.

Born in Dublin, he came out of Ireland more or less expecting to behave as a heterosexual, and was sincere in his marriage to Constance (Jennifer Ehle). He loved his children, and the movie uses one of his children's stories as a counterpoint. But when a young Canadian houseguest named Robbie (Michael Sheen) boldly approached him in the parlor late one night, Wilde responded. He might have settled into an existence of discreet bisexuality had it not been for his meeting, some years later, the beautiful young Lord Alfred Douglas (Jude Law), known as "Bosie"—who was, if Wilde had only realized it, more interested in his fame than his body.

Bosie liked to flirt and flaunt. There is a scene in a restaurant where the two men smoke, smile, and hold hands, while all of London seems to look on. Bosie did that to shock. Wilde did it because he was a genuinely sweet man who believed in expressing his feelings, and was naive about how much leeway he'd be given because of his fame. Bosie's physical interest in Wilde soon waned, and he took the playwright to a famous male brothel, which Wilde seems to have seen as an opportunity to expose handsome working-class lads to the possibilities of higher culture.

It is so sad how ripe Wilde was for destruction. We can see the beginning of the end in an extraordinary scene in a restaurant, where Wilde calmly charms the tough, angry marquess of Queensbury (Tom Wilkinson). The marquess is happy to exchange tips about fly-fishing, but warns Wilde to stay away from his son (ironic, since Wilde was the seduced, not the seducer). Soon it all comes down to a humiliating courtroom scene, despite the desperate advice of loyal Robbie to stay far away from the law. Those who know of Wilde at thirdhand may be under the impression that the marquess hauled him into court; actually, it was Wilde who sued the marquess for slander.

Stephen Fry brings a depth and gentleness to the role that says what can be said about Oscar Wilde: That he was a funny and gifted idealist in a society that valued hypocrisy above honesty. Because he could make people laugh, he thought they always would. Bosie lived on for years, boring generations of undergraduates with his fatuous egotism. He grew gross and ugly. Wilde once said that he could forgive a man for what he was, but not for what he became.

Wild Man Blues ★ ★ ★

PG, 104 m., 1998

A documentary film directed by Barbara Kopple and produced by Jean Doumanian. With Woody Allen, Soon-Yi Previn, Letty Aronson, Eddy Davis, and others.

Early in *Wild Man Blues,* as they arrive in Europe, a subtitle identifies one of the women with Woody Allen as "Letty Aronson, Woody Allen's sister," and the other simply as "Soon-Yi Previn." One can only speculate how long a subtitle it would have taken to explain *her* presence. "Theoretically, this should be fun for us," Allen observes at the start of a tour with his New Orleans jazz band. Theoretically, it should, but the greatest pleasure for Woody seems to be having his worst fears confirmed. An omelet in Spain seems "vulcanized." A gondola ride in Venice leads to seasickness. An audience in Rome is "anesthetized, like a jury." In Milan he worries that the hotel might bread their laundry.

Wild Man Blues, Barbara Kopple's documentary about the tour, could be retitled *The Innocents Abroad*—although Woody, sixtyish, not Soon-Yi, twenty-fiveish, is the innocent. What was I expecting from this scrutiny of Allen on tour with the adopted daughter of his former companion Mia Farrow? Perhaps something slightly scandalous—the aging rake flaunting his Asian girlfriend in continental hot spots. But it's not like that at all.

Woody and Soon-Yi, who was soon to become his wife, seem to have a stable and workable relationship, in which Allen plays his usual role as the dubious neurotic, and Miss Previn is calm and authoritative—a combination of wife, mother, and manager. She seems to be good for him. Whether he is good for her, of course, has been a matter of controversy, but this film supports what Allen said when their affair was first revealed: "The heart has its reasons."

Soon-Yi seems more like the adult in the partnership. At one point, she advises him to be more animated when he appears on stage with his band. "I'm not gonna bob my head or tap my feet," he says. "They want to see you bob a little," she says, and he gets defensive: "I'm appropriately animated for a human being in the context in which I appear." But at the next concert, he bobs a little.

Little romantic passion is revealed on-screen, perhaps because of mutual reticence. At one point, checking into another of the vast hotel suites they occupy, Woody looks around hopefully for a real king-size bed, instead of two twin beds pushed up against each other. No luck. He frets that he could fall into the crack between the two beds and get stuck. Here is an example of their morning conversation: She: "The shower was excellent, wasn't it?" He: "Yes, great pressure."

The ostensible purpose of the documentary is to showcase Allen's seven-piece band and its music. But the audiences come to see Woody more than to listen to the music, and so do we. The music is entertaining, and the crowds like it (except for the stone-faced concertgoers in Rome, who look like they paid for their benefit tickets by donating blood). Eddy Davis, the banjo player and musical director, remembers that he first met Allen at Mister Kelly's in Chicago in the 1960s, and even then "he was a serious clarinetist."

Apparently terrified that he might say something funny and betray his serious calling as a musician, Allen introduces the numbers with the gravity of a heart surgeon announcing his next incision. Forced to attend a series of receptions before or after the concerts, he deals graciously with some fans, impatiently with others. When an official in black tie announces, "I present to you my wife," Allen nods and says, "This is the notorious Soon-Yi Previn."

Kopple made the Oscar-winning documentaries *Harlan County, USA* and *American Dream,* both about labor disputes. She might seem an unlikely choice for this material, but no doubt her track record gained Allen's trust. To his credit he hasn't exercised veto power over the results (if he had, he probably would have removed his observation that as a child Soon-Yi "was eating out of garbage pails").

In a closing sequence, Woody and Soon-Yi visit the director's elderly parents in New York. His father, examining various trophies presented to Woody on tour, seems more interested in the quality of the engraving than in the honors. His mother admits she would have preferred "a nice Jewish girl" to Soon-Yi, and wonders if her son might not, after all, have been more successful as a pharmacist.

Woody seems at times to be inviting his parents' comments with leading questions, and the reunion has been interpreted by some as illustrating his "Jewish self-hate," but that's a charge sometimes misused to punish anything other than perfect piety and filial regard. So Woody didn't like Hebrew school? I was bored during Catechism. A lot of Protestant kids would rather play baseball than go to Sunday school. That's not self-hate; it's human nature.

Wild Things ★ ★ ★

R, 113 m., 1998

Kevin Bacon (Ray Duquette), Matt Dillon (Sam Lombardo), Neve Campbell (Suzie Toller), Theresa Russell (Sandra Van Ryan), Denise Richards (Kelly Van Ryan), Daphne Rubin-Vega (Gloria Perez), Robert Wagner (Tom Baxter), Bill Murray (Ken Bowden), Carrie Snodgress (Ruby). Directed by John McNaughton and produced by Rodney Liber and Steven A. Jones. Screenplay by Stephen Peters.

Wild Things is lurid trash, with a plot so twisted they're still explaining it during the closing titles. It's like a three-way collision between a soft-core sex film, a soap opera, and a B-grade *noir.* I liked it. This being the latest example of Florida *noir* (hot on the high heels of *Palmetto*), it has a little of everything, including ominous shots of alligators looking like they know more than they're telling.

The movie solidifies Neve Campbell's position as the queen of slick exploitation, gives Matt Dillon and Kevin Bacon lots of chances to squint ominously, and has a sex scene with Denise Richards (of *Starship Troopers*) that is either gratuitous or indispensable, depending on your point of view. Plus it has Bill Murray as a storefront lawyer who delivers twenty minutes of hilarity, which at the time is the last thing we're expecting.

Movies like this either entertain or offend audiences; there's no neutral ground. Either you're a connoisseur of melodramatic comic vulgarity, or you're not. You know who you are. I don't want to get any postcards telling me this movie is in bad taste. I'm warning you: It *is* in bad taste. Bad taste elevated to the level of demented sleaze.

The plot: Matt Dillon plays Lombardo, a high school teacher who was "educator of the year" and has an engraved crystal goblet to prove it. As the movie opens, he writes SEX CRIMES on the board at a school assembly, and introduces speakers on the subject, including police officers Duquette (Bacon) and Perez (Daphne Rubin-Vega). In the back of the room, a student named Suzie (Neve Campbell) stalks out, suggesting which part of her anatomy one of the speakers can kiss. I wasn't sure if she was referring to Bacon or Dillon, but this is the kind of plot where it works either way.

Then we meet Kelly Van Ryan (Denise Richards), the richest kid in the upscale Florida enclave of Blue Bay. She's got the hots for Mr. Lombardo. She follows him home, asks for rides, washes his Jeep, and turns up in his living room so thoroughly wetted-down she reminds us of the classic Hollywood line about Esther Williams: "Dry, she ain't much. Wet, she's a star!" Later, we see her leaving the teacher's humble bungalow, looking mad.

Why is she mad? I will tread carefully; a publicist was stationed at the door of the screening, handing out letters begging the press not to give away the ending. The problem is, the ending of this film begins at the forty-five-minute mark and is so complicated, I doubt if it *can* be given away. What sets up everything, in any event, is Kelly's testimony that she was raped by Mr. Lombardo—and the surprise testimony of Suzie that she was too.

Suzie lives in a trashy trailer out behind an alligator farm run by Carrie Snodgress. But Kelly lives on the right side of town, in manorial splendor, with her bikini-wearing, martini-drinking mom (Theresa Russell), who has had an affair with Lombardo. Hearing her daughter has been raped by him, Mom is enraged, and snarls, "That SOB must be insane to think he can do this to me!" That's the kind of dialogue that elevates ordinary trash into the kind that glows in the dark. Here's another line, after a murder: "My mother would kill me if she knew I took the Rover!"

Bill Murray lands in the middle of this pie like a plum from heaven. Wearing a neck brace as part of an insurance scam, Murray runs his shabby storefront law office like a big downtown spread; when he asks his secretary to "show Mr. Duquette his way out," all she needs to do is look up and say, "Good-bye," since the door is in arm's reach of everything else in the office.

Without giving away the ending, that's about all I can tell you. See the movie and you'll understand how very much I must leave unsaid. The director is John McNaughton, whose work includes two inspired films, *Henry: Portrait of a Serial Killer* and *Normal Life.* He likes to show audiences how wrong their expectations are by upsetting them. That worked in *Henry* as grim tragedy, and it works here as satire.

Don't leave when the end titles start to roll. Credit cookies (those little bonus scenes they stick in between Key Grip and Location Catering) are usually used for outtakes showing Matthau and Lemmon blowing their lines, or Jackie Chan breaking his legs. In *Wild Things,* McNaughton does something new: flashbacks, showing us stuff that was offscreen the first time around. The movie is still explaining itself as the curtains close, and then the audience explains it some more on its way out of the theater.

Wild Wild West ★

PG-13, 107 m., 1999

Will Smith (James T. West), Kevin Kline (Artemus Gordon), Kenneth Branagh (Dr. Arliss Loveless), Salma Hayek (Rita Escobar), Ted Levine (McGrath), Frederique Van Der Wal (Amazonia), Musetta Vander (Munitia), Sofia Eng (Miss Lippenreider), M. Emmet Walsh (Coleman). Directed by Barry Sonnenfeld and produced by Sonnenfeld and Jon Peters. Screenplay by S. S. Wilson, Brent Maddock, Jeffrey Price, and Peter S. Seaman, based on a story by Jim Thomas and John Thomas.

Wild Wild West is a comedy dead zone. You stare in disbelief as scenes flop and die. The movie is all concept and no content; the elaborate special effects are like watching money burn on the screen. You know something has gone wrong when a story is about two heroes in the Old West, and the last shot is of a mechanical spider riding off into the sunset.

Will Smith and Kevin Kline costar, as special federal agents who are assigned by President U. S. Grant to investigate the disappearance of lots of top scientists. They stumble over a plot to assassinate Grant by a megalomaniac who wants to give half the country back to Britain and Spain, and keep the rest in the hands of the villain. Salma Hayek teams up with them, as a woman who says her father was one of the kidnapped geniuses. The bad guy (Kenneth Branagh) is a mad inventor who makes giant steam-powered iron tarantulas and spiders, which are not very practical in Monument Valley, but who cares?

Certainly not anyone in the movie. Smith and Kline have so little chemistry they seem to be acting in front of rear-projections of each other. They go through the motions, but there's no eye contact. Imagine Bill Clinton and Kenneth Starr as partners in a celebrity golf tournament.

The Kline character is said to be a master of disguise, and first appears in drag as a dance hall girl, wearing a false plastic bosom so persuasive that when a siren turns up later in the movie, her décolletage looks unconvincing by comparison. That doesn't stop Smith from giving her cleavage a few jolly thumps, and then telling a white lynch mob he was simply following the example of his African ancestors, who communicated by pounding on drums—and bosoms, I guess. (In a movie where almost nothing is funny, the race references are painfully lame.)

One of the running gags is about how the Kline character can invent almost anything, right on the spot. He rigs a rail car so that it can shoot people into the air, have them fall through openings that appear in the roof, and land in a chair. The rig works in opposition to the first law of motion, but never mind: In a movie where anything can happen, does it matter that anything does?

Kenneth Branagh's character has no body from the waist down, but operates from a clever wheelchair and, later, with mechanical legs. He has weird facial hair and lots of bizarre plans, and an evil general on his payroll has a weird miniature ear trumpet permanently screwed into the side of his face. His gigantic artificial war machines look like they were recycled from *Star Wars,* right down to their command cockpits.

There are moments when all artifice fails and you realize you are regarding desperate actors, trapped on the screen, fully aware they've been left hanging out to dry. Consider an early scene where Will Smith and a sexy girl are embracing in a water tank when the evil General McGrath rides into town. Smith is made to look at McGrath out of a knothole, while continuing to make automatic midair smooching movements with his lips—as if he doesn't realize he's not still kissing the woman. Uh, huh.

Wild Wild West is so bad it violates not one but two rules from *Ebert's Bigger Little Movie Glossary.* By casting M. Emmet Walsh as the train engineer, it invalidates the Stanton-Walsh Rule, which states that no movie starring Harry Dean Stanton or M. Emmet Walsh can be altogether bad. And by featuring Kevin Kline without facial hair, it violates the Kevin Kline Mustache Principle, which observes that Kline wears a mustache in comedies but is clean-shaven in serious roles. Of course, Kline can always appeal on the grounds that although he is clean-shaven in his principal role here, he sports facial hair in three other roles he plays in the movie—or perhaps he could use the defense that *Wild Wild West* is not a comedy.

William Shakespeare's A Midsummer Night's Dream ★ ★ ★

PG-13, 115 m., 1999

Kevin Kline (Nick Bottom), Michelle Pfeiffer (Titania), Rupert Everett (Oberon), Stanley Tucci (Puck [Robin]), Calista Flockhart (Helena), Anna Friel (Hermia), Christian Bale (Demetrius), Dominic West (Lysander), David Strathairn (Theseus), Sophie Marceau (Hippolyta). Directed by Michael Hoffman and produced by Leslie Urdang and Hoffman. Screenplay by Hoffman, based on the play by William Shakespeare.

"Reason and love keep little company together nowadays."

So says Bottom in Shakespeare's *A Midsummer Night's Dream,* and he could be describing the play he occupies. It is an enchanted folly, suggesting that romance is a matter of chance, since love is blind; at the right moment we are likely to fall in love with the first person our eyes light upon. Much of the play's fun comes during a long night in the forest, where a mischief-maker anoints the eyes of sleeping lovers with magic potions that cause them to adore the first person they see upon awakening.

This causes all sorts of confusions, not least when Titania, the Fairy Queen herself, falls in love with a weaver who has grown donkey's ears. The weaver is Bottom (Kevin Kline), and he and the mischievous Puck (Stanley Tucci) are the most important characters in the play, although it also involves dukes, kings, queens, and high-born lovers. Bottom has a good heart and bumbles through, and Puck (also called Robin Goodfellow) spreads misunderstanding wherever he goes. The young lovers are pawns in a magic show: When they can't see the one they love, they love the one they see.

Michael Hoffman's new film of *William Shakespeare's A Midsummer Night's Dream* (who else's?) is updated to the nineteenth century, set in Italy, and furnished with bicycles and operatic interludes. But it is founded on Shakespeare's language and is faithful, by and large, to the original play. Harold Bloom complains in his wise best-seller *Shakespeare: The Invention of the Human* that the play's romantic capers have been twisted by modern adaptations into "the notion that sexual violence and bestiality are at the center of this humane and wise drama." He might approve of this version, which is gentle and lighthearted, and portrays Bottom not as a lustful animal but as a nice enough fellow who has had the misfortune to wake up with donkey's ears—"amiably innocent, and not very bawdy," as Bloom describes him.

Kevin Kline is, of course, the embodiment of amiability, as he bashfully parries the passionate advances of Titania (Michelle Pfeiffer). Her eyes have been anointed with magical ointment at the behest of her husband, Oberon, (Rupert Everett), who hopes to steal away the young boy they both dote on. When she opens them to regard Bottom, she is besotted with love and inspired to some of Shakespeare's most lyrical poetry:

> I'll give thee fairies to attend on thee;
> And they shall fetch thee jewels from
> the deep,

And sing, while thou on pressed flowers
dost sleep.

Meanwhile, more magical potions, distributed carelessly by Puck, have hopelessly confused the relationships among four young people who were introduced at the beginning of the play. They are Helena (Calista Flockhart), Hermia (Anna Friel), Demetrius (Christian Bale), and Lysander (Dominic West). Now follow this closely. Hermia has been promised by her father to Demetrius, but she loves Lysander. Demetrius was Helena's lover, but now claims to prefers Hermia. Hermia is offered three cruel choices by the duke, Theseus (David Strathairn): marry according to her father's wishes, go into a convent, or die. Desperate, she flees to a nearby wood with Lysander, her true love. Helena, who loves Demetrius, tips him off to follow them; maybe if he sees his intended in the arms of another man, he will return to Helena's arms.

The wood grows crowded. Also turning up at the same moonlit rendezvous are Bottom and his friends, workmen from the village who plan to rehearse a play to be performed at the wedding of Theseus and *his* intended, Queen Hippolyta (Sophie Marceau). And flickering about the glen are Oberon, Titania, Puck, and assorted fairies. Only the most determined typecasting helps us tell them apart: As many times as I've been through this play in one form or another, I can't always distinguish the four young lovers, who seem interchangeable. They function mostly to be meddled with by Puck's potions.

Hoffman, whose wonderful *Restoration* recreated a time of fire and plague, here conducts with a playful touch. There are small gems of stagecraft for all of the actors, including Snout, the village tinker, who plays a wall in the performance for the duke, and makes a circle with his thumb and finger to represent a chink in it. It's wonderful to behold Pfeiffer's infatuation with the donkey-eared Bottom, whom she winds in her arms as "doth the woodbine the sweet honeysuckle gently twist"; her love is so real, we almost believe it. Kline's Bottom tactfully humors her mad infatuation, good-natured and accepting. And Tucci's Puck suggests sometimes that he has a darker side, but is not so much malicious as incompetent.

Midsummer Night's Dream is another entry in Shakespeare's recent renaissance on film. After *Much Ado About Nothing,* Ian McKellen's *Richard III,* Al Pacino's documentary *Looking for Richard,* Laurence Fishburne as *Othello,* Branagh's *Hamlet,* Helena Bonham Carter in *Twelfth Night,* Baz Luhrmann's modern street version of *Romeo and Juliet,* the Lear-inspired *A Thousand Acres,* the remake of *Taming of the Shrew* as *10 Things I Hate About You,* and the bard's celebration in *Shakespeare in Love,* we can look ahead to the forthcoming *Hamlet* with Ethan Hawke, Branagh's *Love's Labour's Lost,* Mekhi Phifer as Othello in the modern urban drama *O,* and Anthony Hopkins in *Titus,* based on the rarely staged Titus Andronicus ("All Rome's a wilderness of tigers").

Why is Shakespeare so popular with filmmakers when he contains so few car chases and explosions? Because he is the measuring stick by which actors and directors test themselves. His insights into human nature are so true that he has, as Bloom argues in his book, actually created our modern idea of the human personality. Before Hamlet asked, "To be, or not to be?" dramatic characters just were. Ever since, they have known and questioned themselves. Even in a comedy like *Midsummer,* there are quick flashes of brilliance that help us see ourselves. "What fools these mortals be," indeed.

Wing Commander ★

PG-13, 100 m., 1999

Freddie Prinze Jr. (Blair), Saffron Burrows (Deveraux), Matthew Lillard (Maniac), Tcheky Karyo (Paladin), Jurgen Prochnow (Gerald), David Suchet (Sansky), Ginny Holder (Rosie Forbes), David Warner (Tolwyn). Directed by Chris Roberts and produced by Todd Moyer. Screenplay by Roberts.

Jurgen Prochnow, who played the submarine captain in *Das Boot,* is one of the stars of *Wing Commander,* and no wonder: This is a sub movie exported to deep space, complete with the obligatory warning about the onboard oxygen running low. "Torpedoes incoming!" a watch officer shouts. "Brace yourself!" It's 500 years in the future. If the weapons developed by the race of evil Kilrathi only inspire you to "brace yourself," we might reasonably ask what the Kilrathi have been doing with their time.

Other marine notes: "Hard to port!" is a command at one point. Reasonable at sea, but in space, where a ship is not sailing on a horizontal surface, not so useful. "Quiet! There's a destroyer!" someone shouts, and then everyone on board holds their breath, as there are subtle sonar "pings" on the sound track, and we hear the rumble of a giant vessel overhead. Or underhead. Wherever. "In space," as *Alien* reminded us, "no one can hear you scream." There is an excellent reason for that: Vacuums do not conduct sound waves, not even those caused by giant destroyers.

Such logic is, of course, irrelevant to *Wing Commander,* a movie based on a video game and looking like one a lot of the time, as dashing pilots fly around blowing up enemy targets. Our side kills about a zillion Kilrathi for every one of our guys that buys it, but when heroes die, of course, they die in the order laid down by ancient movie clichés. The moment I saw that one of the pilots was an attractive black woman (Ginny Holder), I knew she'd go down, or up, in flames.

The plot involves war between the humans and the Kilrathi, who have refused all offers of peace and wish only to be targets in the crosshairs of video computer screens. Indeed, according to a Web page, they hope to "destroy the universe," which seems self-defeating. The Kilrathi are ugly turtleoid creatures with goatees, who talk like voice synthesizers cranked way down, heavy on the bass.

Against them stand the noble earthlings, although the film's hero, Blair (Freddie Prinze Jr.) is suspect in some circles because he is a half-breed. Yes, his mother was a Pilgrim. Who were the Pilgrims? Humans who were the original space voyagers and developed a gene useful for instinctively navigating in "space-time itself." (Just about all navigation is done in space-time itself, but never mind.) Pilgrims went too far and dared too much, so timid later men resented them—but if you need someone to skip across a Gravity Hole, a Pilgrim is your man.

There are actors on board capable of splendid performances. The commander of the fleet is played by David Warner, who brings utter believability to, alas, banal dialogue. Two of the other officers, played by Tcheky Karyo and Prochnow, are also fine; I'd like to see them in a real navy movie. Prinze shows again an easy grace and instant likability. Matthew Lillard, as a hotshot pilot named Maniac, gets into a daredevil competition with the Holder character, and I enjoyed their energy. And the perfectly named Saffron Burrows has a pleasing presence as the head of the pilot squadron, although having recently seen her in a real movie (Mike Figgis's *The Loss of Sexual Innocence,* at Sundance), I assume she took this role to pay the utility bills.

These actors, alas, are at the service of a submoronic script and special effects that look like a video game writ large. *Wing Commander* arrived at the end of a week that began with the death of the creator of *2001: A Space Odyssey.* Close the pod bay door, Hal. And turn off the lights.

The Wings of the Dove ★ ★ ★ ½

R, 103 m., 1997

Helena Bonham Carter (Kate Croy), Linus Roache (Merton Densher), Alison Elliott (Millie Theale), Charlotte Rampling (Aunt Maude), Elizabeth McGovern (Susan), Michael Gambon (Kate's Father), Alex Jennings (Lord Mark). Directed by Iain Softley and produced by Stephen Evans and David Parfitt. Screenplay by Hossein Amini, based on the novel by Henry James.

What happens in Henry James takes place deep within stories where, on the surface, the characters go languidly about their lives of privilege. They subscribe to a code of what is done and what is not done. They know exactly what it means to be a gentleman or a lady; those titles are like decorations, to be worn invisibly at social occasions. And then in the privacy of their souls, some of James's characters darkly contemplate getting their way no matter what.

The Wings of the Dove is the cold-blooded story of two British lovers who plot to deprive a rich American girl ("the richest orphan in the world") of her heart and her inheritance. What makes it complicated—what makes it James—is that the two lovers really do like the rich girl, and she really does like them, and everyone eventually knows more or less precisely what is being done. The buried message is that when it comes to money, sex, love, and death, most people are prepared to go a great deal further than they would admit. There is, if you know how to look for it, incredible emotional violence in the work of Henry James.

This new film of his famous novel makes two significant changes. It moves the action up slightly, from 1902 to 1910. And it makes the British woman a little more sympathetic than she was in the original. The second change flows from the first. James's story, which he began writing in 1894, embedded the characters in the world of Victorian propriety. By 1910, the actions they contemplate, while still improper, were not unthinkable; modern relativism was creeping in. Kate Croy, whose desire fuels the story, was more selfish and evil in the James version; the film softens her into someone whose actions can almost be defended as pragmatism.

Kate, played with flashing eyes and bold imagination by Helena Bonham Carter, is a poor girl with a tenuous foothold in society. Her father is a penniless drunkard. Her mother is dead. She is taken in by her wealthy Aunt Maude (Charlotte Rampling), who wants to marry her off to the best advantage—perhaps to Lord Mark (Alex Jennings). But Kate loves Merton Densher (Linus Roache), an ill-paid journalist who cheerfully admits he doesn't believe the things he writes. Maude forbids the marriage, and even threatens to cut off the weekly shillings she pays Kate's father.

What is Kate prepared to do? Characters talk a great deal in Henry James, but are sometimes maddeningly obscure about what they mean (does any other novelist use the word "intercourse" more frequently, while not meaning by that word or any other what we immediately think of?). They talk much less in this film, where facial expressions imply the feelings that are talked around in the novel. My guess is that Kate might have eventually married the odious Lord Mark, while continuing quietly to see Merton Densher.

But that is not necessary. At a dinner party, she meets Millie Theale (Alison Elliott), the rich young American, and discovers that Millie has an unnamed disease, possesses hardly a protector in the world except for her traveling companion (Elizabeth McGovern), and intends to see Europe and die. One of the things Millie wants to experience in Europe is romance; she doesn't say so, but she is looking for a man, and when she sees Merton, she asks Kate about him.

"He's a friend of the family," Kate replies—a lie of omission, because Kate and Merton are secretly engaged. Kate's plan is clear. She will accompany Millie to Venice. Merton will join them there. Millie will fall in love with Merton, marry him, die, and leave him her fortune. Merton will then have the money he needs to marry Kate. This scheme unfolds only gradually in the James novel, emerging from behind leisurely screens of dialogue and implication. It is more clear in the film, especially in a dark, atmospheric scene where Kate and Merton walk down deserted Venetian passages. She tells him she is returning to London, and outlines what she expects him to do. Then, to seal the bargain, they have sex for the first time. (They do it standing up against the old stones of Venice; one imagines the ghost of James turning aside with a shudder.)

Iain Softley's film, written by Hossein Amini, emphasizes Kate's desperation and downplays her cold calculation. It softens the villainy of Merton by making it clear how desperately Millie does want to be involved in a romance with him; is he simply granting her dying wish? There is another fugitive strand of affection in the film that I did not sense in the book: Millie and Kate genuinely like one another, and it's almost as if they strike an unexpressed bargain, in which Kate lets Millie have the use of Merton—lets her find what she came to Europe for. The money is crucial, of course, but too vulgar to be discussed.

In its stark outlines, this plot would be at home on a daytime talk show ("Sold her lover to a dying rich girl"). But the film sets it at a time when standards were higher, when society had clear expectations of moral behavior. The reason we're so fascinated by the adaptations of James, Austen, Forster, and the others is that their characters think marriage, fidelity, chastity, and honesty are important. In modern movies many characters have no values at all.

In *The Wings of the Dove* there is a fascination in the way smart people try to figure each other out. The film is acted with great tenderness. If the three central characters had been more forthright, more hedonistic, we wouldn't care nearly as much. But all three have a certain tact, a certain sympathy for the needs of the others. At the end, when Millie knows the score, she can at least be grateful that she got to play the game.

The Winslow Boy ★ ★ ★ ½

G, 110 m., 1999

Nigel Hawthorne (Arthur Winslow), Jeremy Northam (Sir Robert Morton), Rebecca Pidgeon (Catherine Winslow), Gemma Jones (Grace Winslow), Guy Edwards (Ronnie Winslow), Matthew Pidgeon (Dickie Winslow), Colin Stinton (Desmond Curry), Aden Gillett (John Watherstone). Directed by David Mamet and produced by Sarah Green. Screenplay by Mamet, based on the play by Terence Rattigan.

The Winslow Boy, based on a play set in 1912, is said to be a strange choice for David Mamet, whose work usually involves lowlifes and con men, gamblers and thieves. Not really. This film, like many of his stories, is about whether an offscreen crime really took place. And it employs his knack for using the crime as a surface distraction while his real subject takes form at a buried level. *The Winslow Boy* seems to be about a young boy accused of theft. It is actually about a father prepared to ruin his family to prove that the boy's word (and by extension his own word) can be trusted. And about a woman who conducts two courtships in plain view while a third, the real one, takes place entirely between the lines.

The movie is based on a 1940s play by Terence Rattigan, inspired by a true story. It involves the Winslow family of South Kensington, London—the father a retired bank official, wife pleased with their life, adult daughter a suffragette, older son at Oxford, younger son a cadet at the Royal Naval Academy. One day the young cadet, named Ronnie, is found standing terrified in the garden. He has been expelled from school for stealing a five-shilling postal order.

In a scene that establishes the moral foundation for the entire story, his father, Arthur, calls him into the study after dinner and demands the truth, adding, "A lie between us cannot be hidden." Did he steal the money? "No, father, I didn't." The father is played by Nigel Hawthorne *(The Madness of King George),* who is stern, firm, and on the brink of old age. He believes his son and calls in the family solicitor to mount a defense. Soon one of the most famous attorneys in London has been hired: Sir Robert Morton (Jeremy Northam), who led the defense of Oscar Wilde. The father devotes his family's large but finite resources to the expensive legal battle, which eventually leads to the older son being brought home from Oxford, servants being dismissed, and possessions being sold. Arthur's wife, Grace (Gemma Jones), protests that justice is not worth the price being paid, but Arthur persists in his unwavering obsession.

The court case inspires newspaper headlines, popular songs, public demonstrations, and debates in Parliament. It proceeds on the surface level of the film. Underneath, hidden in a murk of emotional contradictions, is the buried life of the suffragette daughter, Catherine (Rebecca Pidgeon). She is engaged to the respectable, bloodless John Watherstone (Aden Gillett). She has known for years that Desmond, the family solicitor (Colin Stinton), is in love with her. As the case gains notoriety, John's ardor cools: He fears the name Winslow is becoming a laughingstock. And as John fades, Desmond's hopes grow. But the only interesting tension between Catherine and a man involves her disapproval of the great Sir Robert Morton, who rejects her feelings about women's equality and indeed disagrees with more or less every idea she possesses.

It is an interesting law of romance that a truly strong woman will choose a strong man who disagrees with her over a weak one who goes along. Strength demands intelligence, intelligence demands stimulation, and weakness is boring. It is better to find a partner you can contend with for a lifetime than one who accommodates you because he doesn't really care. That is the psychological principle on which Mamet's hidden story is founded, and it all leads up to the famous closing line of Rattigan's play, "How little you know about men." A line innocuous in itself, but electrifying in context.

In a lesser film, we would be required to get involved in the defense of young Ronnie Winslow, and there would be a big courtroom scene and artificial suspense and an obligatory payoff. Mamet doesn't make films on automatic pilot, and Rattigan's play is not about who is right, but about how important it is to be right. There is a wonderful audacity in the way that the outcome of the case happens offscreen and is announced in an indirect manner. The real drama isn't about poor little Ronnie, but about the passions he has unleashed in his household—between his parents, and between his sister and her suitors, declared and undeclared.

A story like this, when done badly, is about plot. When done well, it is about character. All of the characters are well-bred, and brought up in a time when reticence was valued above all. Today's audiences have been raised in a climate of emotional promiscuity; confession and self-humiliation are leaking from the daytime talk shows into our personal styles. But there's no fun and no class in simply blurting out everything one feels. Mamet's characters are interesting precisely because of the reserve and detachment they bring to passion. Sixty seconds of wondering if someone is about to kiss you is more entertaining than sixty minutes of kissing. By understanding that, Mamet is able to deliver a G-rated film that is largely about adult sexuality.

That brings us to the key performances by Jeremy Northam and Rebecca Pidgeon, as Sir Robert and the suffragette. Pidgeon's performance has been criticized in some circles (no doubt the fact that she is Mrs. Mamet was a warning flag). She is said to be too reticent, too mannered, too cold. Those adjectives describe her performance, but miss the point. What her critics seem to desire is a willingness to roll over and play friendly puppy to Sir Robert. But Pidgeon's character, Catherine, is not a people-pleaser; she is scarcely interested in knowing you unless you are clever enough to clear the hurdle of her defenses. Her public personality is a performance game, and Sir Robert knows it—because his is too. That's why their conversations are so erotic. Spill the beans, and the conversation is history. Speak in code, with wit and challenge, and the process of decryption is like foreplay.

The Winter Guest ★ ★ ½

R, 110 m., 1998

Phyllida Law (Elspeth), Emma Thompson (Frances), Gary Hollywood (Alex), Arlene Cockburn (Nita), Sheila Reid (Lily), Sandra Voe (Chloe), Douglas Murphy (Sam), Sean Biggerstaff (Tom). Directed by Alan Rickman and produced by Ken Lipper, Edward R. Pressman, and Steve Clark-Hall. Screenplay by Sharman Macdonald.

Winter in Scotland is as muted as a wake. So far north the sun is slow to rise and early to set, and a day can be blindingly bright or always seem like twilight. *The Winter Guest* follows four sets of characters through a day in a Scots village, and its purpose is not to draw a lesson or tell a story, but to evoke a mood. To see this film is like spending a day in a village near St Andrews, and with a shock I realized I had once lingered for an afternoon in this village, or one much like it—in August, when the days were long and the trees were green.

Everything is different in winter. The people disappear inside and count on one another. The film opens with a well-coifed woman in her sixties, in a long fur coat, making her way across a field in bitter cold. This is Elspeth (Phyllida Law), and she is on her way to the house of her daughter Frances (Emma Thompson). She fears losing her. Frances's husband has died, and she has retreated into an angry silence beyond mourning. Perhaps she will leave Scotland and move to Australia with her teenage son, Alex (Gary Hollywood).

Alex has an admirer. Her name is Nita (Arlene Cockburn), and she has a crush on him. Early on the day of the film she ambushes him with a snowball, and at first they scuffle but then they begin to talk, and by the end of the day they will be boyfriend and girlfriend, with all the uncertainty that that means at their age.

There are two boys walking by the frozen sea. It is a school day, but they have stayed away, and no one will look for them here. They are Sam (Douglas Murphy) and Tom (Sean Biggerstaff), and the emptiness of the town and the quiet of the weekday has made them a little more serious than they planned; they look about twelve or thirteen, and tentatively talk about more serious things than they would have six months ago.

Two old ladies wait for a bus. They are Lily (Sheila Reid) and Chloe (Sandra Voe), and they are connoisseurs of funerals. Like the girl in *Huckleberry Finn* who loved to mourn, they find something cheerful about the rituals of death. They scour the death notices and compare notes on funerals past; they are old enough and ordinary enough that no one ever questions them when they attend a funeral; they look like the relatives you are sure you have forgotten.

The Winter Guest, based on a play by Sharman Macdonald, follows these four couples and listens to them. There isn't a lot of interaction between them, although Alex does bring Nita home, and she does talk with Frances. Since there is no plot engine to drag them all to the same station, we're forced to decide why they find themselves in this film, and what connection they have. Is the Winter Guest death? Do these couples represent four stages of life? Childhood, courtship, parenthood, and old age?

The central strands involve Elspeth and Frances. Phyllida Law and Emma Thompson are mother and daughter in real life, and in the film they have the familiarity of a lifelong couple. They know each other's speech rhythms. They look alike. When Frances closes herself off and refuses to talk, the worry lines between Elspeth's eyes seem real—the stress of a mother who loves a daughter and cannot reach her. Frances at one point buries her ears in the bathwater to block out words she doesn't want to hear, but it's hard to ignore someone if you're also concerned about them—and Frances is worried that Elspeth is growing older and soon will not be able to take care of herself.

The other three couples have defined roles. They are sure who they are, and more or less clear on how they should be acting on this winter day. But Elspeth and Frances are unsprung. The death of Frances's husband has changed everything, redefined it, ended a stage of life. There is so much pain that talking about it is unbearable, and so the mother and daughter talk around it.

The Winter Guest is the directing debut of Alan Rickman, an actor who makes intelligent British films *(Truly, Madly, Deeply; Sense and Sensibility)* and makes big money as a villain in American films *(Die Hard)*. He has great command here of look and tone, and I felt I knew what it would be like to wander the streets of that village in Scotland. But the film left me feeling strangely hollow. Perhaps it was meant to. At the end there is an emptiness, like stepping into air, or like a play interrupted after the first act.

Without Limits ★ ★ ★

PG-13, 118 m., 1998

Billy Crudup (Steve Prefontaine), Donald Sutherland (Bill Bowerman), Monica Potter (Mary Marckx), Jeremy Sisto (Frank Shorter), Billy Burke (Kenny Moore), Matthew Lillard (Roscoe Devine), Dean Norris (Bill Dellinger), Gabe Olds (Don Kardong). Directed by Robert Towne and produced by Tom Cruise and Paula Wagner. Screenplay by Towne and Kenny Moore.

Without Limits is the second recent film about Steve Prefontaine, the legendary American runner who brought his sport into the headlines and helped topple the creaky amateur athletic establishment. Like *Prefontaine* (1997), it focuses on the star's abrasive personality and his refusal to pace himself; the only way he wanted to win was by "flat-out leading all the way." By the time he died in a road accident, he held most of the American distance records, and one of them still stands.

Why two movies about Steve Prefontaine? Because two directors wanted to make them, and neither one backed down. *Prefontaine* was by Steve James *(Hoop Dreams)*, starred Jared Leto, and had former marine drill sergeant R. Lee Ermey as the legendary Oregon coach Bill Bowerman. *Without Limits* is by Robert Towne (screenwriter of *Chinatown*, writer-director of *Personal Best*), stars Billy Crudup, and has Donald Sutherland playing Bowerman.

The earlier film focuses more on Prefontaine's stubborn battle with the AAU and other amateur bodies that essentially dictated the terms under which Americans could run. It makes it clear that a late invitational meet in Oregon with Finnish athletes was held as a deliberate challenge to the amateur establishment. Towne's film is less quirky, more a conventional sports movie, but it benefits by giving more attention to the relationship between Pre and Bowerman.

And Sutherland's performance is the film's treasure. Watching the way he gently tries to direct his headstrong young star, we are seeing a version of Phil Jackson's zen and the art of coaching. "What do you think a track coach *does,* Pre?" he asks at one point, since Pre seems to think the coach's primary function is to frustrate him. Sutherland brings a deep patience to Bowerman, who understands that running is a matter of endurance and strategy as well as heart: "Men of Oregon, I invite you to become students of your events." Pre thinks heart is enough, and explains his success simply: "I can endure more pain than anyone you've ever met."

The film follows Pre from his early sports failures (he was no good at football) and into running, where he quickly drew attention. The earlier film points out that his legs were short for a runner, and of unequal length; this one sees him more as naturally gifted, but heedless with his talent. We follow his progress from record to record, and from girlfriend to girlfriend (Mary Marckx, played by Monica Potter, is the true love, but he shuts her out of his life for obscure reasons). Everything leads up to the 1972 Munich Olympics, marred by the terrorist attack on Israeli athletes.

But the point of the story is contained in the epilogue. Pre returns to Oregon as an amateur who is expected to work at menial jobs (he becomes a bartender) and live at the poverty line (he gets a mobile home) while training for the next Olympics. Other countries support their athletes, and Pre leads a campaign to reform America's rules. He makes no attempts to win friends, and in *Prefontaine* he tells a press conference: "To hell with love of country; I'm looking out for me."

Without Limits is less interested in the politics and the crusade, and sees Pre more in personal, psychological terms. I prefer the earlier approach, which contains more information about why Pre is important even today. Robert Towne's affecting *Personal Best* (1982) told the story of a talented woman runner in terms of both her sport and her romantic involvement with another woman athlete; Prefontaine is more interesting as a public figure than a private one.

Woo ★ ½

R, 80 m., 1998

Jada Pinkett Smith (Woo), Tommy Davidson (Tim), Duane Martin (Frankie), Michael Ralph (Romaine), Darrel M. Heath (Hop), Dave Chappelle (Lenny), Paula Jai Parker (Claudette), LL Cool J (Darryl). Directed by Daisy V. S. Mayer and produced by Beth Hubbard and Michael Hubbard. Screenplay by David C. Johnson.

Woo is about a collision between black lifestyles when a sexpot looking for "someone impulsive and exciting" ends up with a middle-class professional, and puts him through a severe psychosexual test-drive. When the smoke clears, she's revealed as not quite as streetwise as she pretends, and he turns out to have a few personality secrets concealed behind that white collar. Along the way, the movie touches on subjects usually sidestepped in African-American films, including the discomfort of black professionals around "country" behavior.

Jada Pinkett Smith stars as Woo, a girl who likes to party and is looking for a man. Her transvestite psychic friend predicts that a dynamic Virgo is in her future, but she doubts it. That night, she drops in on her cousin Claudette (Paula Jai Parker) and her boyfriend, Lenny (Dave Chappelle), but they want to be alone together, so Lenny talks his friend Tim (Tommy Davidson of *In Living Color*) into taking her out. Tim is a law clerk, studying for the bar; Woo suspects a bore, but agrees to the date when she finds out he's a Virgo.

That's the setup for a movie constructed so loosely that I had the feeling some of the characters were introduced after we'd already met them. The film is a series of episodes in which Woo and Tim demonstrate to each other's satisfaction (and certainly to ours) that they have no business being out on a date with one another—although, of course, after they survive assorted bizarre adventures a certain camaraderie grows up between them. As hostages of each other, they develop reciprocal Stockholm syndrome.

The running joke is that Tim doesn't know much about women or, for that matter, black culture. Fixed up on the blind date with Woo, he goes across the hall to get tips from his neighbor Darryl (LL Cool J), who supplies him with a kit containing various stimulants and preventives, and a cassette of absolutely guaranteed romantic music ("by the time you get to side B, you should be naked").

Woo is not in the mood to be wooed, however, and the evening breaks down into episodes like the one in an Italian restaurant, where polite Tim doesn't get very far with the waiter, but Woo (who turns out to speak Italian) does. Then she sees an old friend through the window, and their reunion essentially demolishes the restaurant.

Movies like this don't really establish their characters and draw much of the humor out of their personalities; they go for quick payoffs, easy slapstick and in-jokes based on insults and code words. It's harmless and sometimes entertaining, but compared to Tommy Davidson's previous film, *Booty Call* (1997), or for that matter Jada Pinkett Smith's work in *Set It Off* and *The Nutty Professor,* it's lightweight and disposable.

The X Files: Fight the Future ★ ★ ★

PG-13, 122 m., 1998

David Duchovny (Agent Fox Mulder), Gillian Anderson (Agent Dana Scully), Martin Landau (Kurtzweil), Armin Mueller-Stahl (Strughold), Blythe Danner (Cassidy), Mitch Pileggi (Director Skinner), William B. David (Cigarette-Smoking Man), John Neville (Well-Manicured Man). Directed by Rob Bowman and produced by Chris Carter and Daniel Sackheim. Screenplay by Carter.

As pure movie, *The X Files* more or less works. As a story, it needs a sequel, a prequel, and Cliffs Notes. I'm not sure even the filmmakers can explain exactly what happens in the movie and why. It doesn't make much difference if you've seen every episode of the TV series or none: The film is essentially self-contained, and that includes its enigmas. X-philes will probably be as puzzled at the end as an infrequent viewer like myself.

Puzzled, but not dissatisfied. Like *Mission: Impossible,* this is a movie that depends on surface, on mystery, on atmosphere, on vague hints and murky warnings. Since the underlying plot is completely goofy, it's probably just as well that it's not spelled out. If it were, this would play more like a seminar on the works of Whitley Strieber. Instead, producer-writer Chris Carter, who conceived the TV series, reassembles his basic elements in a glossy extravaganza that ends, apparently, with humankind facing precisely the same danger it did at the beginning.

The story involves, of course, Mulder and Scully, who call each other "Mulder!" and "Scully!" so often they must be paid by the word. FBI agents Fox Mulder (David Duchovny) and Dana Scully (Gillian Anderson) have been investigating a cover-up of aliens among us. Yanked off their X-files and assigned to an antiterrorism unit, they get involved in the explosion of a Dallas high-rise.

The alien conspiracy theorist Kurtzweil (Martin Landau) tells Mulder some of the bombing victims were already dead, and the blast was a plot to account for their bodies. (There is a shot of the ruined building, its front blasted away, that evokes disturbing memories of the Oklahoma City tragedy; that shot could have been removed from the film with absolutely no loss.)

We already know something about the dead bodies. The film opens in "North Texas, 35,000 B.C." (a long time before it was north Texas), with prehistoric men encountering violent, creepy, leaky beings in a cave. In "Present Day: North Texas," a kid falls into the same cave, and sluglike beings slither into his nose and eye sockets. What are these?

"The original inhabitant of this planet," we eventually learn, and a mighty patient inhabitant, too, if it had to wait for us to evolve. The alien creatures are a "virus," and yet they also seem to have bodily form, unless they inhabit hijacked bodies, which they can indeed do, although that begs the question of what they were to begin with, who built the large object we see in the final scenes, etc.

It's tricky work, not giving away the plot of a movie you don't understand. The story is less concerned with the aliens than with the cover-up, and there are several scenes (maybe one too many) of agents Scully and Mulder being grilled by an FBI panel about their misdeeds. I can't fault the FBI here. If I were investigating unreliable field agents and they told me they spent the weekend in Antarctica, I'd want to know what they were smoking.

Speaking of smoking, the Cigarette-Smoking Man (known on the Web as the Cancer Man) is in the movie, of course. Has there ever been a more thankless role? William B. David, who plays him, has to inhale, exhale, or light up every time we see him. The Well-Manicured Man (John Neville) has more to do, as does Director Skinner (Mitch Pileggi), but the best supporting performance is by Landau, as a desperate man who lurks in the back booths of shady bars, passing info to the X-agents.

What does he know? What's being covered up? Why are all the powerful men having the secret meeting in London? If you watch the show you will guess it has something to do with covering up the Aliens Among Us. What are they doing here? What are their hopes and plans? There's dialogue in which we get the answers to these questions, I guess, but they didn't fit together for me. And when the large unnamed object appears at the end, I wanted to know where it came from, where it was going, what it was leaving behind, and why. I also wanted a better look at it (the special effects are too cloudy).

There is little real drama, as such, in *The X Files.* Mulder and Scully are in love with one another, but sublimate all their feelings into their work. Do they kiss? Would I tell you? Do their lips meet? Is that one question, or two? They spend much of their time gaining unchallenged entry into vast installations that should be better guarded. One of these installations involves corn and bees. Why? We are told, but I didn't believe it. Nor do I understand why humans cooperate with the aliens; what sort of Faustian bargain has been struck?

Much has been made of the fact that *The X Files* is not so much a film based on a TV series as a continuation of that series in film form. The movie feeds out of last season and into the next one. No final answers are therefore provided about anything; it's as if, at the end of *Casablanca,* the airplane circled around and landed again. But I liked the way the movie looked, and the unforced urgency of Mulder and Scully, and the way the plot was told through verbal puzzles and visual revelations, rather than through boring action scenes. And it was a relief to discover that the guys in the black helicopters are just as clueless as the rest of us. ☞

Y

Year of the Horse ★

R, 108 m., 1997

Featuring Neil Young, Billy Talbot, Poncho Sampedro, Ralph Molina. Directed by Jim Jarmusch and produced by L. A. Johnson.

Year of the Horse plays like *This Is Spinal Tap* made from antimatter. Both films are about aging rockers, but *Year of the Horse* removes the humor and energy, portraying Neil Young and Crazy Horse as the survivors of a death march. There are times, indeed, when Young, his hair plastered flat against his face with sweat, his eyes haunted beneath a glowering brow, looks like a candidate for a mad slasher role.

The film, directed by Jim Jarmusch, follows a 1996 concert tour and intercuts footage from 1986 and 1976 tours. It's all shot in muddy earth tones, on grainy Super 8 film, Hi Fi 8 video, and 16 mm. If you seek the origin of the grunge look, seek no further: Young, in his floppy plaid shirts and baggy shorts, looks like a shipwrecked lumberjack. His fellow band members, Billy Talbot, Poncho Sampedro, and Ralph Molina, exude vibes that would strike terror into the heart of an unarmed convenience store clerk.

This is not a fly-on-the-wall documentary. Jarmusch's interviews take place in a laundry room where the band members and Young's father sit on straight chairs and meditate on the band's long and lonely road. Young muses on "the trail of destruction I've left behind me," and there is solemn mention of departed band members ("Neil once said they were dropping like flies").

These séances are intercut with concert footage, during which the band typically sings the lyrics through once and then gets mired in endless loops of instrumental repetition that seem positioned somewhere between mantras and autism. The music is shapeless, graceless, and built from rhythm, not melody; it is amusing, given the undisciplined sound, to eavesdrop later as they argue in a van about whether they all were following the same arrangement.

The older footage is not illuminating. One high point, from a visit to Glasgow in 1976, is a meal in a restaurant that is interrupted when the fabric flowers in the centerpiece catch fire. The band members try smothering the flames with napkins and extinguishing them with orange juice, and eventually they join the woman who owns the place in sadly eyeing the ashes.

Later in the film, Jarmusch himself appears on camera, reading to Young from the Old Testament, a book the musician seems unfamiliar with. Jarmusch reads the parts where an angry God tells his people how he will punish them, and Young looks like God's tribulations are nothing he hasn't been through more than once.

If there is a theme to the band's musings, it is astonishment that they have been playing together for so long. They play with other groups, but when they come together, they say, there is a fusion. With touching self-effacement, Young tells Jarmusch, "The band is called 'Neil Young and Crazy Horse,' but I know it's really 'Crazy Horse.' My new jacket says 'Crazy Horse.' The others say 'Neil Young and Crazy Horse,' but mine just says 'Crazy Horse.'" Yes, but wouldn't the point come across a little better if theirs just said "Crazy Horse" too?

Your Friends and Neighbors ★ ★ ★

R, 99 m., 1998

Jason Patric (Cary), Nastassja Kinski (Cheri), Ben Stiller (Jerry), Catherine Keener (Terri), Aaron Eckhart (Barry), Amy Brenneman (Mary). Directed by Neil LaBute and produced by Steve Golin and Jason Patric. Screenplay by LaBute.

Neil LaBute's *Your Friends and Neighbors* is a film about monstrous selfishness—about people whose minds are focused exclusively on their own needs. They use the language of sharing and caring when it suits them, but only to their own ends. Here is the most revealing exchange in the film:

"Are you, like, a good person?"

"Hey! I'm eating lunch!"

The movie looks at sexual behavior with a sharp, unforgiving cynicism. And yet it's not really about sex. It's about power, about enforcing your will on another, about having what you want when you want it. Sex is only the medium of exchange. LaBute is merciless. His previous film, *In the Company of Men,* was about two men who play a cruel trick on a woman. In this film, the trick is played on all the characters by the society that raised and surrounded them. They've been emotionally shortchanged and will never hear a lot of the notes on the human piano.

LaBute's *Your Friends and Neighbors* is to *In the Company of Men* as Tarantino's *Pulp Fiction* was to *Reservoir Dogs.* In both cases, the second film reveals the full scope of the talent, and the director, given greater resources, paints what he earlier sketched. In LaBute's world, the characters are deeply wounded and resentful, they are locked onto their own egos, they are like infants for which everything is either "me!" or "mine!" Sometimes this can be very funny—for the audience, not for them.

Of course they have fashionable exteriors. They live in good "spaces," they have good jobs, they eat in trendy restaurants, and are well-dressed. They look good. They know that. And yet there is some kind of a wall closing them off from one another. Early in the film, the character played by Aaron Eckhart frankly confesses that he is his own favorite sexual partner. A character played by Catherine Keener can't stand it when her husband (Ben Stiller) talks during sex, and later, after sex with Nastassja Kinski, when she's asked, "What did you like the best?" she replies, "I liked the silence best."

Ben Stiller and Keener are a couple; Eckhart and Amy Brenneman are a couple. In addition to Kinski, who works as an artist's assistant, there is another single character played by Jason Patric. During the course of the movie these people will cheat on and with one another in various ways.

A plot summary, describing who does what and with whom, would be pointless. The underlying truth is that no one cares for or about anybody else very much, and all of the fooling around is just an exercise in selfishness. The other day I spent a long time looking at the penguins in the Shedd Aquarium. Every once in a while two of them would square off into a squawking fit over which rock they were entitled to stand on. Big deal. Meanwhile, they're helpless captives inside a system that has cut them off from their full natures, and they don't even know it. Same thing in this movie.

LaBute, who writes and directs, is an intriguing new talent. His emphasis is on writing: As a director, he is functional, straightforward, and uncluttered. As a writer, he composes dialogue that can be funny, heartless, and satirical all at once. He doesn't insist on the funny moments, because they might distort the tone, but they're fine, as when the Keener character tells Kinski she's a writer—"if you read the sides of a tampon box." She writes ad copy, in other words. Later, in a store, Kinski reads the sides of a tampon box and asks, "Did you write this?" It's like she's picking up an author's latest volume in a bookstore, although in this case the medium is carefully chosen.

The Jason Patric character, too, makes his living off the physical expression of sex: He's possibly a gynecologist (that's hinted, but left vague). The Aaron Eckhart character, who pleasures himself as no other person can, is cheating on his wife with . . . himself, and likes the look of his lover. The Brenneman character is enraged to be treated like an object by her new lover, but of course is treated like one by Eckhart, her husband. And treats him like one. Only the Kinski character seems adrift, as if she wants to be nice and is a little puzzled that Keener can't seem to receive on that frequency.

LaBute deliberately isolates these characters from identification with any particular city, so we can't categorize them and distance ourselves with an easy statement like, "Look at how they behave in Los Angeles." They live in a generic, affluent America. There are no exteriors in the movie. The interiors are modern homes, restaurants, exercise clubs, offices, bedrooms, bookstores. These people are not someone else. In the immortal words of Pogo, "We has met the enemy, and it is us."

This is a movie with the impact of the original stage production of Albee's *Who's Afraid of Virginia Woolf.* It has a similar form, but is more cruel and unforgiving than *Carnal Knowledge.* Mamet has written some stuff like this. It contains hardly any nudity and no physical violence, but the MPAA at first slapped it with an NC-17 rating, perhaps in an oblique tribute to its power (on appeal, it got an R). It's the kind of date movie that makes you want to go home alone.

You've Got Mail ★ ★ ★

PG, 116 m., 1998

Tom Hanks (Joe Fox), Meg Ryan (Kathleen Kelly), Parker Posey (Patricia Eden), Jean Stapleton (Birdie), Steve Zahn (George Pappas), David Chappelle (Kevin Scanlon), Greg Kinnear (Frank Navasky). Directed by Nora Ephron and produced by Lauren Shuler Donner and Nora Ephron. Screenplay by Nora Ephron and Delia Ephron.

The appeal of *You've Got Mail* is as old as love and as new as the Web. It stars Tom Hanks and Meg Ryan as immensely lovable people whose purpose it is to display their lovability for two hours, while we desperately yearn for them to solve their problems, fall into one another's arms, and get down to the old rumpy-pumpy.

They meet in a chat room on AOL, and soon they're revealing deep secrets (but no personal facts) in daily and even hourly e-mail sessions. The movie's call to arms is the inane chirp of the maddening "You've Got Mail!" voice (which prompts me to growl, "Yes, and I'm gonna stick it up your modem!"). But the e-mail is really just the MacGuffin—the device necessary to keep two people who fall in love on-line from finding out that they already know and hate each other in real life.

The plot surrounds Hanks and Ryan not only with e-mail lore, but with the Yuppie Urban Lifestyle. It's the kind of movie where the characters walk into Starbucks and we never for a moment think "product placement!" because, frankly, we can't imagine them anywhere else. Where the generations are so confused by modern mating appetites that Joe Fox (the Hanks character) can walk into a bookstore with two young children and introduce them as his brother and his aunt ("Matt is my father's son, and Annabel is my grandfather's daughter").

Kathleen, the Meg Ryan character, runs the children's bookshop she inherited from her mother. She and her loyal staff read all the books, know all the customers, and provide full service and love. Joe Fox is the third generation to run a chain of gigantic book megastores. When the new Fox Books opens around the corner from Kathleen's shop, it's only a matter of time until the little store is forced out of business. Kathleen turns for advice and solace to her anonymous on-line friend—who is, of course, Joe.

And yet this is not *quite* an Idiot Plot, so called because a word from either party would instantly end the confusion. It maintains the confusion only up to a point, and then does an interesting thing: allows Joe to find out Kathleen's real identity while still keeping her quite reasonably in the dark. And, oh, the poignant irony, as Joe has to stand there and be insulted by the woman he loves. "You're nothing but a suit!" she says. "That's my cue," he says. "Good night." And as he nobly conceals his pain, we are solaced only by the knowledge that sooner or later the scales will fall from her eyes.

The movie was directed by Nora Ephron, who first paired Hanks and Ryan in *Sleepless in Seattle* (1993) and has made an emotional, if not a literal, sequel. That earlier film was partly inspired by *An Affair to Remember*, and this one is inspired by *The Shop Around the Corner*, but both are really inspired by the appeal of Ryan and Hanks, who have more winning smiles than most people have expressions.

Ephron and her cowriter, her sister Delia, have surrounded the characters with cultural references that we can congratulate ourselves on recognizing: Not only Jane Austen, but the love affair carried on by correspondence between George Bernard Shaw and Mrs. Patrick Campbell. Not only *The Godfather* (which "contains the answers to all of life's questions") but Anthony Powell and Generalissimo Franco. (It is one of the movie's quietly hilarious conceits that the little store's elderly bookkeeper, played by Jean Stapleton, was in love years ago with a man who couldn't marry her "because he had to run Spain.")

The plot I shall not describe, because it consists of nothing but itself, so any description would make it redundant. What you have are two people the audience desires to see together, and a lot of devices to keep them apart. There is the added complication that both Hanks and Ryan begin the movie with other partners (Parker Posey and Greg Kinnear—respectively, of course). The partners get dumped without much fuss, and then we're left with these two lonely single people, who have neat jobs but no one to rub toes with, and who are trapped by fate in a situation where he is destroying her dream, and she is turning to him (without knowing it is him) for consolation. Perfect.

The movie is sophisticated enough not to make the megastore into the villain. Say what you will, those giant stores are fun to spend time in, and there is a scene where Kathleen ventures anonymously into Joe's big store for the first time and looks around, at the magazine racks and the café and all the books—and then there's the heartbreaking moment when she overhears a question in the children's section, and she knows the answer but of course the clerk doesn't, and so she supplies the answer, but it makes her cry, and Joe overhears everything. Whoa. ☞

Z

Zero Effect ★ ★ ★ ½

R, 115 m., 1998

Bill Pullman (Daryl Zero), Ben Stiller (Steve Arlo), Ryan O'Neal (Gregory Stark), Kim Dickens (Gloria Sullivan), Angela Featherstone (Jess), Hugh Ross (Bill), Sara Devincentis (Daisy), Matt O'Toole (Kragen Vincent). Directed by Jake Kasdan and produced by Lisa Henson, Janet Yang, and Kasdan. Screenplay by Kasdan.

Zero Effect opens with the key character offscreen. His name is Daryl Zero, he's the best private detective in the world, and he's a recluse who prefers to be represented in public by a hireling. Sounds like the setup for a comedy, but this is one of those movies that creeps up on you, insidiously gathering power. By the end, I was surprised how much I was involved.

The hireling, named Steve Arlo, is played by Ben Stiller as a dry, detached functionary. He represents Zero at a meeting with a millionaire named Stark (Ryan O'Neal), who wants to find some lost keys—one of them to a safe-deposit box. Stark is being blackmailed by someone who may have access to the secret of dark deeds in the past.

Arlo enjoys spinning amazing tales about Zero. He's the kind of guy who feels personally enhanced by his boss's qualities. "He has a deeply nuanced understanding of human nature," Arlo says of Zero, but when we see Zero he looks more like a case for treatment. He lives behind a steel door with six locks on it. He eats little except for tuna fish from a can. And he likes to bounce on the bed while singing very bad folk songs of his own composition.

Yet this man is indeed an investigative genius, and soon he's meeting a young woman named Gloria (Kim Dickens) and using his sense of smell to tell her she's a paramedic. Zero is strangely split: He's hopelessly incompetent in his personal life, but when he goes into P.I. mode he's cool, competent, suave, and self-confident. Using Arlo as his assistant, he begins to unravel a murder that took place more than two decades ago, and leads to a trail of hidden identities.

To describe the details of the case would be wrong. They lead to surprises and reversals that are among the movie's pleasures (the last scenes force us to rearrange almost everything we thought we knew about the plot). The movie was written and directed by Jake Kasdan, son of the writer-director Lawrence Kasdan, and it's an exercise in devious construction—like one of those Ross Macdonald novels in which the sins of the fathers are visited upon the children.

If the plot is ingenious, it's the personal stuff that makes the movie increasingly delightful. Daryl Zero is baffled and challenged by Gloria, who is one of the few people he's ever met whose mind he can't more or less read. She fools him. She's shielded. She intuitively understands him the way he understands other people. When he claims to be in town at an accountant's convention, she finds a way to check that: She asks him to do her income tax.

Midway through the movie, I was being nudged by echoes of another story, and then I realized that *Zero Effect* was probably inspired by the relationship between Sherlock Holmes and the faithful Watson—Holmes, who could sit in his study and use pure deduction to solve a crime. When Zero describes his methods, he sounds Holmesian: "Objectivity . . . and observation. The two obs."

If Zero is like Holmes, Gloria is certainly like Irene Adler, from *A Scandal in Bohemia.* She was the one woman for Holmes, the one who got under his skin and into his mind. And as Gloria begins to have that effect on Zero, a softening and humanizing takes place: He becomes less weird, less insistent on his peculiar rituals, more like a guy.

Zero Effect begins, as I said, like a comedy—one not a million miles away from the kind of private-eye parody David Spade or Mike Myers might make. The Bill Pullman character, the first time we see him, seems like a goofy, off-the-shelf weirdo. But Pullman, from *While You Were Sleeping* and *Independence Day,* can drop the facade and let you see the complications inside. He also costarred in *Sleepless in Seattle,* and it's uncanny, by the end of *Zero Effect,* how much this private-eye caper has started to touch some of the same notes. ☞

The Best Films of 1998

1. *Dark City*

The best film of 1998 was also one of the more obscure. It opened without a compelling campaign and was yanked before it could find an audience. Now, on video, it's beginning to build a reputation that may eventually link it with *Blade Runner*, another slow starter that gained cult status.

The movie is set in a *noir* city run by the Strangers, aliens who use it as a laboratory to study humans. They erase human memories every midnight and shape-shift the city into new configurations for fresh experiments. The hero (Rufus Sewell) is aided by a mysterious doctor (Kiefer Sutherland) to break loose from the mind-wiping, and remembers vaguely an earlier life that may have involved a beautiful young woman (Jennifer Connelly). Meanwhile, a police inspector (William Hurt) tries to make sense of a crime. The closing shots reveal the true nature of all that has gone before.

I responded so strongly to the film because it was intelligent, intriguing, darkly atmospheric, and most of all because it was visually breathtaking. Werner Herzog tells us we need new images or we will die. Alex Proyas's *Dark City* was visionary in the tradition of *Metropolis, The Cabinet of Dr. Caligari, 2001,* and *Blade Runner.* It was a daring act of the imagination. So strongly did I feel about it that for the first time I agreed to do a commentary sound track for the DVD video, where you can hear me talking for two hours about the film's mysteries and beauties. (I don't get royalties.) Like *Babe: Pig in the City, Pleasantville, The Truman Show,* and *What Dreams May Come, Dark City* started from scratch to reimagine a world.

2. *Pleasantville*

Gary Ross's film pointed the way to the new freedom that computer-generated images have given filmmakers. He imagined two modern-day young people who are magically transported back in time to the insides of a black-and-white 1950s sitcom. Nothing ever changes in the sitcom world, but they bring the seeds of the future, and soon color is blooming in the black-and-white society.

One of the pleasures of the film was figuring out what triggered the color shifts. (It was not simply sex, but insight or change.) Another was to enjoy the wit with which paradoxes were handled in a world closed to space and time. (In geography class, students learned that when you got to the end of Main Street, it just started all over again.)

The film stirred debate. Some argued that the stable and predictable 1950s were preferable to the social upheaval in which we now reside. Others said the 1950s were, in fact, more revolutionary than today—that reverse time travel could do us some good. Still others said the 1950s were great if you didn't happen to be female or nonwhite. Whatever you said, the movie got you talking. Not many great entertainments also inspire social introspection.

3. *Saving Private Ryan*

Steven Spielberg's epic was one of the most involving war movies ever made. Using enormous resources of men and technique, he recreated the landing at Omaha Beach with such power and immediacy that movie battle scenes would never seem quite the same again. His film's opening act is one of the great sustained acts of filmmaking.

Then the film fell into more conventional but still thought-provoking channels, as an officer (Tom Hanks) and his men are assigned to venture into dangerous territory to find a private whose brothers have been killed in combat. Saving him is thought to be useful propaganda—but the war looks different at ground level than from the Pentagon.

Saving Private Ryan was a powerful experience. Spielberg knows how to make audiences weep better than any director since Chaplin in *City Lights.* But weeping is an immediate response, and this film also embodies ideas. After the immediate experience begins to fade, the implications remain, and grow.

4. *A Simple Plan*

Three men in a wintertime forest preserve find a crashed plane that has $4 million on board. They figure it's probably drug money, that no one will come forward to claim it, and that it might be a simple matter for them to keep the money themselves. Almost immediately this decision involves them in a crime, and their values, held for a lifetime but never really tested, begin to disintegrate.

Sam Raimi's film runs sure and deep. It has an uncanny sense of time and place, and it never rushes as it follows its characters from one fateful decision to the next. Strong, Oscar-worthy performances by Bill Paxton as the college graduate, Billy Bob Thornton as his unlucky brother, Brent Briscoe as the third man, and Bridget Fonda as Paxton's wife, who gives what seems at the time like practical advice.

5. *Happiness*

Todd Solondz's painful and funny film showed desperate people reaching out from the loneliness they were drowning in. Some were obviously pathetic, in apartment buildings that are warehouses of strangers. Others, like a Little League dad who was a psychiatrist, seemed more normal, but was trapped in a role far removed from the depraved center of his libido.

Solondz made it difficult for audiences to take a stand on these people: Tragedy kept shifting into farce or satire, and then back again. When the film premiered at Cannes, some wondered if it would ever find an audience. It did surprisingly well at the box office, perhaps because audiences realized that Solondz wasn't simply manipulating situations for shock value, but was rotating them like specimens under a microscope, to see how they looked from various angles.

6. *Elizabeth*

The story was intriguing, but the visuals multiplied its depth and fascination. Cate Blanchett starred as Elizabeth I, her life in danger as she takes the throne as a young and untested ruler, and then grows in office into perhaps the greatest of British monarchs. Around her, advisers steer her away from (or toward) trouble; kings want her hand for political reasons, but her first true love is a disappointment, and eventually she "becomes" a virgin.

Shekhar Kapur, an Indian director, used the palette of his subcontinent to portray Elizabeth, her court, and her architecture in the colors and texture of medieval India. The film is largely set in vast, echoing halls, their pillars reaching up into the shadows. He is attentive to the rustle of dresses and the clank of armor, and gives us a barge on the Thames like a houseboat on a lake in Kashmir. Action is glimpsed through iron filigree screens, dresses are rich with embroidery, hairstyles are ornately elaborate, and yet there is the feeling that just out of sight of these riches are the rats in the kitchen and the slop pots in the halls.

7. *Babe: Pig in the City*

Set aside for the moment the question of whether this film is "too dark" for children (set aside too the fact that many children see slasher and horror movies on video). Consider this *Babe* sequel as a film for adults. It is an unending parade of wonderments and visual delights, linked to a story that is Dickensian in its richness of character and the boldness of its villains.

Babe, the clever pig, is marooned in the city with Mrs. Hoggett, and finds refuge in a boardinghouse that is friendly to animals. There he meets an astonishing array of new friends (some dubious), and gets involved in startling adventures. Yes, some were bothered by the plight of the bull terrier who almost drowned—but isn't it interesting that the dog's dilemma upset more folks than the loss of a billion lives in *Armageddon*? Maybe it actually touched people. Maybe they cared. The movie's visual imagination and art direction were astonishing.

8. *Shakespeare in Love*

A rowdy, irreverent movie with as many different tones as a Shakespeare play: high and low comedy, coincidences, masquerades, jokes about itself, topical references, exits and entrances with screwball timing. It begins as a backstage comedy, filled with lore about the Elizabethan stage and its ambitious young scribbler, Shakespeare (Joseph Fiennes), and then widens into a love story as young Will falls in love with the beautiful Viola (Gwyneth Paltrow) whose rich father is buying her a nobleman with title attached.

Much gender confusion as Paltrow plays a woman auditioning to play a man, and later plays a man playing a woman. Meanwhile, Shakespeare struggles to write *Romeo and Ethel, the Pirate's Daughter,* before his love for Viola shows him the way to *Romeo and Juliet.* Would you be surprised to find that Viola and Shakespeare eventually find themselves acting in one of the great love scenes?

9. *Life Is Beautiful*

The film falls more or less into two halves. In the first, Roberto Benigni plays a man whose entire personality is dominated by his clown's perspective. In Mussolini's prewar Fascist Italy, he uses humor to handle every situation. Then war clouds descend, and the clown and his family are placed in concentration camps, where the hero desperately uses humor to make it all seem like a game to his young son.

The first half is important, because unless we fully understand that comedy is the *only* weapon in the hero's arsenal, we might be offended by the second half. As it is, we are deeply moved. Benigni and his wife, Nicoletta Braschi, play the married couple; he wrote and directed a film of delicacy and power—and humor.

10. *Primary Colors*

I composed this list soon after President Clinton had been impeached by the House of Representatives. A year earlier, *Wag the Dog* was tenth on my list. In recent months "wag the dog" has become the first fictional phrase to enter the political language since "Catch-22," and indeed the events of the surreal weekend of impeachment and bombing seemed eerily foreshadowed.

With *Primary Colors,* Mike Nichols made a film based on the traits and faults that seem to have led Clinton to the present moment. It was based on a best-selling novel written by an insider, who used gossip and speculation to study the president's weaknesses, his strengths, his charms—and how he seemed for a long time to be unsinkable. The film was a box-office disappointment, maybe because audiences were satiated by the subject. But John Travolta's performance as the president was a subtle and substantial achievement, and Emma Thompson provided insights into how the president's wife reacted and coped. Nothing that has happened since this film was released has caused me to question its instincts.

Special Jury Prize

At Cannes and other festivals, a "jury prize" is offered as a sort of equal first to films that deserve a place beside the winners. In recent years I've declared a five-way tie for eleventh place. Here are the jury prizes this year, alphabetically:

—*Character.* Mike van Diem's Dutch film won the Oscar last March as Best Foreign Film, and deserved to. It tells the story of a cold and stony bailiff and his lifelong hatred for a son born out of wedlock. Is he as evil as he seems? Not quite. But nearly.

—*High Art.* Lisa Cholodenko's film stars Ally Sheedy, in an impressive return to acting, as a burnt-out photographer who lives in virtual seclusion with her lover, an actress who once worked for Fassbinder but now lives for cocaine. When a young magazine editor (Radha Mitchell) discovers their ménage in the apartment upstairs, the photographer is tempted to resume her life.

—*Men With Guns.* John Sayles is one of the most admirable and ambitious of American independent directors, and in this film he sets his story in an unnamed Central American country where, to the peasants, it doesn't much matter whether the men with guns are government forces or rebels—since neither side has any respect for those who live on the land.

—π. Such an odd, challenging, quirky film! Directed by Darren Aronofsky, it stars Sean Gullette as a reclusive genius who seeks the answer to the deepest puzzle in mathematics, while Wall Streeters, orthodox Jews, and cabalists grow obsessed with his secrets. Visually and in its narrative, a film that feels like it is inside genius—or madness.

—*The Truman Show.* Jim Carrey stars in Peter Weir's Orwellian comedy about a man who doesn't realize his entire life has been lived on TV. Inside a vast world constructed just for him, Truman doesn't know his every moment fascinates a worldwide audience.

The Chuck Jones Award

Named for the genius behind Bugs Bunny, Daffy Duck, Wile E. Coyote, and the Road Runner, this special prize is shared this year by five animated films that dramatized the ways in which feature-length cartoons are breaking away from the "children and family" category and growing up into full-bodied entertainments. The winners, alphabetically:

—*Antz* enters into a microscopic world—an ant colony beneath Central Park—and makes it into a world so vast and threatening that comparisons with *Star Wars* are not unjustified. Woody Allen voiced the hero, who explains, it's not easy when you're the middle child in a family of 5 million.

—*A Bug's Life,* similar in theme but original in look and treatment; ants fight off domination by cruel grasshoppers, as the heroic Flik (Dave Foley) devises ingenious last-minute stratagems.

—*Kiki's Delivery Service,* by the Japanese animation genius Hayao Miyazaki, tells the story of a young witch in training, who goes to a new city, gets a job, and saves her friend from a dirigible crash. Miyazaki's *My Neighbor Totoro* has found big audiences, and now *Kiki* is also a video best-seller.

—*Mulan* was Disney's story about a young Chinese girl who disguised herself as a boy in order to take her father's place in the war against the Huns. Once again, a larger theme and freer artwork continued the liberation of animation from older formulas.

—*The Prince of Egypt* was Dreamworks' year-end retelling of the story of Moses, with visuals inspired by De Mille's *The Ten Commandments* and a story that made free with the facts (were Moses and Ramses really sibling rivals?). Visually splendid, using the freedom of animation to get a true epic feel.

Top Ten Sleepers

Some films seem to open and close in a parallel universe to the world of full-page ads and TV interviews. Here are ten films, bold and creative, you might not even have heard of.

—*Affliction,* Paul Schrader's film with Nick Nolte as the battered adult son of the overbearing James Coburn; based on a novel by Russell *(The Sweet Hereafter)* Banks.

—*Clockwatchers,* by Jill Sprecher, starring Toni Collette, Parker Posey, and Lisa Kudrow in the story of desperate office temps in a hostile corporate environment.

—*Deja Vu,* by Henry Jaglom, a no-holds-barred romance about fate, synchronicity, coincidence, and love that literally spans the generations.

—*Insomnia,* by Erik Skjoldbjaerg of Norway, stars Stellan Skarsgard in the best police procedural of the year, about a cop who commits a crime in the course of an investigation, and finds that his partner, without knowing it, is looking for him.

—*Little Dieter Needs to Fly,* by Werner Herzog, is a documentary about the amazing experiences of Dieter Dengler, a German who enlisted in the U.S. Navy, was shot down over Laos, and survived untold hardships, which are re-created by Dengler and Herzog in an unexpected way.

—*Love Is the Devil,* by John Maybury, stars Derek Jacobi as the great but scruffy British painter Francis Bacon, who creates masterworks and hangs out in a dank drinking club with bohemian drunks and just plain drunks. The movie brilliantly sidesteps its inability to show Bacon's paintings by filming its visuals in the style of his work.

—*Nil by Mouth,* written and directed by Gary Oldman, is based on his life and his father, an alcoholic who presided over a family of great disorder and emotional chaos.

—*A Soldier's Daughter Never Cries,* by James Ivory, is inspired by a happier childhood memory, a novel by Kaylie Jones, daughter of James Jones *(The Thin Red Line),* about growing up in Paris as the child of unconventional but loving parents (Kris Kristofferson and Barbara Hershey).

—*Your Friends and Neighbors,* by Neil LaBute, listens and watches as self-centered, success-driven moderns obsessively monitor their own happiness while occupying vacuums that make the results meaningless.

—*Zero Effect,* by Jake Kasdan, stars Ben Stiller as the hireling to brilliant detective

Daryl Zero (Bill Pullman), a modern Sherlock Holmes who lurks in his chambers—until he meets a woman as smart as he is.

Top Ten Runners-Up

Beloved, with Oprah Winfrey as Toni Morrison's heroine, a haunted former slave visited by the ghost of her daughter; *Drifting Clouds,* by Finland's Aki Kaurismaeki, a dour and winsome comedy about downsizing in Helsinki; *Hilary and Jackie,* the story of cellist Jacqueline du Pre and her sister and rival; *Living Out Loud,* an offbeat comedy about loneliness, with Holly Hunter, Danny DeVito, and Queen Latifah; and *Love and Death on Long Island,* with John Hurt as a British writer infatuated by an American teen idol (this film and performance are more interesting than the somewhat similar *Gods and Monsters*).

Also, *Out of Sight,* based on the Elmore Leonard tale, dazzlingly directed by Steven Soderbergh with George Clooney and Jennifer Lopez; David Mamet's *The Spanish Prisoner,* with Campbell Scott and Steve Martin in a labyrinthine con game; the uproariously funny *There's Something About Mary;* Terrence Malick's strong, poetic *The Thin Red Line;* and Vincent Ward's *What Dreams May Come,* with its startling visualizations of heaven and hell.

Drew Barrymore

Toronto, November 1998—It's like, you know, I'm talking with Drew Barrymore and she is like so drowning me in words, and I'm like so getting it, and I'm thinking like, here is a girl who is like still only twenty-three years old and has been in like thirty movies and already grown *beyond* the problems that most people her age still soooo don't know how to handle.

I've always liked her work. I'm like such a defender of movies that opened and closed in a minute, like *Gun Crazy* and *Mad Love* and even *Poison Ivy,* and it's like she has a throne forever in the movie hall of fame for playing the little girl in *E.T.,* but her career is still mostly ahead of her.

And I'm sitting here at the keyboard thinking this story is going to have like such long paragraphs because a paragraph can't end until you get to the period, and Drew Barrymore's speech is punctuated only with commas, semicolons, and the words "like" and "and." Being in the room with her is like inhaling a shot in one of those oxygen bars.

This is at the Toronto Film Festival last September. I've just seen her in *Home Fries,* a quirky comedy. She plays a pregnant fast food worker who falls in love with the stepson of the louse who got her pregnant, after the stepson (Luke Wilson) and his no-good brother (Jake Busey) have scared the guy to death on instructions from their creepy mother (Catherine O'Hara). It's the kind of movie where Barrymore has dialogue like, "You can't be the father and the brother at the same time. That's the kind of thing that messes kids up."

Last summer, she also starred in *Ever After,* an enchanting retelling of the Cinderella story, where we discover all the things the Brothers Grimm left out. It's an elegant period romance and Barrymore glows in it: You see the star quality that made her grandfather, the troubled, legendary John Barrymore, into one of the great actors of the century.

And she's not the weirdo for a change. Even in *Home Fries,* with its twisting plot and dark humor, she's kind of the sane center, the character who looks at events with a level eye and can tell the fools from the villains.

"This girl Sally is just so sweet and unassuming and going through life but not blindly," Barrymore said, "but at the same time, rather than focusing on everything, she likes watching moths on the wall. Like that to her is a beautiful moment."

Which is a sample of the rush of her prose. She continues: "I love that. I love that so much, especially in this crazy, tumultuous world where we get so wrapped up in things, that she can sit there and have that kind of Zen appreciation."

It's a change of pace from some of your seductresses and killers.

"All that matters to me is that physically, emotionally, spiritually, mentally, verbally, you know, accents, dialogue, wardrobe, you know, personalities, backstories, cultures, everything, I want to be different in every movie. And if, you know, you play a couple of characters that have a similar genre, can you depict that they do have differences, no matter what? All that matters to me is that I get to be every different type of person: bad, good, indifferent. Maybe my choices at times have seemed odd, but I read these scripts and knew I had to be these people.

"For a while, you know, when I was like sixteen to twenty, I like . . . I had like this total wild streak in me and yet I wasn't wild at all but I loved playing these wild characters. I just . . . you know, it's cathartic and you do become these people and it was really fun for me. I love movies more than anything."

I wanted to get to the stuff about the total wild streak, but not yet. I asked her what she loved most about the movies.

"Ummm. Life. What feels right to you. What kind of message you wanna put out there. It's all in what you respond to. I loved *Used Cars,* but I also loved Cocteau's *Beauty and the Beast.* You can't watch those in the same mood."

You liked Cocteau's *Beauty and the Beast*?

(Not the Disney version, but the famous and eerie fable directed by the French poet and filmmaker in 1946.)

"My favorite."

That's where Spike Lee got that shot.

"Which one?"

You know the shots he uses where the people glide down the sidewalk without walking?

"Exactly, yes. And Cocteau's *Orpheus.* I mean, when he falls back on that bed and it looks like he's falling into water or when he sits in that car—it's just a shot of a man in a car but the poetry that's spoken through the radio, it's so incredibly beautiful that you get lost in the words. I mean, when he walks down that corridor and the human arms are coming out of the walls holding the candles . . . oh my God!"

You seem to be more into movies than a lot of movie actors. With a lot of people in the business, all that matters is how big the box office was on Friday night.

She nodded. "I try to remember, as an actor and now as a producer, that the gross isn't that important. A lot of my favorite films, the films that make a big difference in my life—the ones I go to, you know, medicinally—that I need in my life and revisit all the time, I have no idea what the numbers were."

But some movies are successful with everyone. I remember the night Spielberg's *E.T.* had its world premiere at Cannes, and the audience stood and cheered and cheered. Were you there that night?

"Yes I was."

Like in the front row of the balcony? With Spielberg?

"Yes, yes."

I've never seen such a response from an audience.

"He made a film for everyone. There are those few films that reach the masses. Which is so cool when you tap into that."

You mentioned you're a producer now.

"My next film. It's called *Never Been Kissed,* and you'll love it—well, at least you'll love that it's like set at the *Chicago Sun-Times.* My character is one of the head copy editors at the *Sun-Times* and her dream is to be a reporter but she has no social skills whatsoever and none of the mechanisms that I think a reporter really needs to be a good one. She's the antithesis of that, and she gets an opportunity, because she's the youngest one there, to go back into high school and find out what kids are like today."

She goes back to high school undercover?

"And poses as a student. And what you find out is why she's so lacking in people skills and why she's so smart at such a young age; she had the worst high school experience, like, known to man. Like, just the epitome of how rough and raw and terrifying those years can be and she just relives the whole thing. But she's like, no, this time I can go back. I'm sophisticated; I can do it this time. But no, not at all. She goes back and they hate her again; they just hate her. They're like kids who want nothing to do with her; she cannot like get in there to save her life, and it's like, how do you love yourself with what God gave you? How do you find the beauty within yourself for who you are? It's about the underdog inside of all of us, and I love that because it doesn't skip over the awkwardness. As such a dork I love it. I got to have more fun in this movie—I got to go for it."

Who's in it with you?

"Molly Shannon, who, omigod, she's so good and so real."

As a high school student?

"No, she works at the *Sun-Times* with me. She's Anita from classifieds and we're best friends, and John C. Reilly, who is just so amazing, is the editor. And then the owner of the paper, this man who just sort of like haphazardly sends people on these assignments, is Garry Marshall, and then David Arquette plays my brother."

I was noticing that the line of her profile is so much like John Barrymore's. With all this talk about loving movies, I said, you probably love all your grandfather's films.

"Oh, incredibly so. He's the one I feel closest to. I mean, I love the rest of my family so much, and yet he's the one that I know I'm directly plugged into. He's my moon so I see him every night. And when I see films like *A Bill of Divorcement,* it kills me. I can't think straight for like a week when I watch him holding Katharine Hepburn and crying because he's lacked a life with this daughter of his. And then when I watch him in *Twentieth Century,* what I love so much is the range. He was an amazing comedian but he was also incredibly dramatic. He was real but he was magical; he could do everything. I see him doing things that remind me of me or my father."

When she was a teenager, Drew made the supermarket papers every week with rumors of drinking and drugs. Now it's clear she's passed through that stage. I nudged the topic into the conversation.

"I've had the pleasure of experiencing the ups and downs," she said. "I have a deep appreciation for what I get to do, because I did have it taken away from me for a while due to certain circumstances. And it's like, you can become really freaked out from something like that but instead it made me realize how lucky I am to be here. And now maybe because of all the hard work I've done, maybe that's why it's coming to me now, so easily. I wanna jump through the fiery hoops and singe my hairs off my body doing it, you know."

If everything had gone smoothly for you, you'd probably be insufferable, I said.

"I'd be just a bore."

You'd think that everything was blessed.

"I like it when life makes you work for things and gives you trials and tribulations that you have to overcome. Although it was harsh going through it in public, because then people do think you have a problem—when you're just experimenting like every other kid, you know."

But you're under a magnifying glass.

"The only thing that was hard at the time was when people didn't trust me for work. Because I never messed up at work and when they said I did, that was so painful for me. But you take negatives and turn them into your strengths, so everything that's happened has happened for not only a reason but a great reason."

We had to stop talking. We both had movies to see. I asked her if I could take her picture.

"Take the profile," she grinned. "The famous profile."

I took the profile.

Michael Caine

Toronto, September 1998—Michael Caine likes to talk. Some actors hide in the mountains, or huddle in private clubs with their friends. Caine opens restaurants. Then he sits in a table near the door—not counting the customers, just pleased to see them.

"It's just sort of a hobby, you know," he said.

But if you had no movie career at all, you'd still be successful because of your restaurants. Am I right?

"Yeah, yeah. But it's a hobby and it stays a hobby. I don't spend a lot of time working at it. My partners do all the work. I do it for my own amusement really. Wherever I live, if there isn't a restaurant I want to go to of a certain type, then I open it. That's all. For selfish reasons."

I remember in Budapest, this was in 1981, Caine jotting down the address of Langan's Brasserie in London and telling me to try it the next time I was in town. And walking into Langan's and seeing him at a table near the front, savoring a cigar. He is well-fixed. When he makes a movie, it is because he has a reason to make it. No more *Jaws 4* for him.

"I opened Langan's because London didn't have a brasserie like La Coupole in Paris. It's just a hobby. What I've been doing is, I went away, it must have been about five or seven years ago, and took a year off to write my autobiography. I took another year off because I didn't write it the first year. Then I took another year off. Then I started looking at scripts to do my sort of mini-comeback. But I couldn't find anything. I got scripts where I told them, 'Not only will I not do this, but my professional advice is, you shouldn't make the film.'"

In 1993, Caine filmed *On Deadly Ground,* with Steven Seagal as a hero fighting against Caine's evil, polluting, ecologically unsound oil tycoon. Then came the years off, which would have been better timed if they had started just one picture sooner. Then in 1997, Caine reappeared in Bob Rafelson's *Blood and Wine,* with one of his best performances ever, as a dying British burglar. He deserved an Oscar nomination, and for that matter his costar Jack Nicholson did work in the movie that was miles better than the performance he won an Oscar for in *As Good As It Gets.*

Now comes *Little Voice,* with Caine as Ray Say, a failing British club promoter who dreams of turning his career around after discovering, in a small northern town, a reclusive young woman (Jane Horrocks) who does not talk much, but can sing exactly, yes, *exactly,* like Marilyn Monroe, Shirley Bassey, Billie Holiday, Judy Garland, and other pop idols.

Ray Say is Caine's kind of character, an easy-living chum with a well-hidden mean streak, who allows himself to be taken home by needy widows. One such escort, played by Brenda Blethyn, is Little Voice's mother. She brings Ray into the parlor, pours a drink and suggests, "Let's roll about." After she puts "It's Not Unusual" on the turntable, a voice from upstairs counters with "That's Entertainment," and Ray knows he has discovered a new star.

The movie was a big hit in September at the Toronto Film Festival. That's where we were talking, in a café at the Four Seasons. Caine had been doing interviews all morning, and looked as if he rather enjoyed it; like a politician, he does not resent the attention of the press.

"The screening last night seemed to get a good reception," he said. "Or do they cheer at everything? Do they usually stand on their hands?"

Well, they're Canadians, you know. Sometimes they just file out.

"Well, we didn't get that. We got a standing ovation for about two minutes. I'd never seen the picture and I thought it was magical. A lot of this stuff was new to me. Like Ewan McGregor's performance. I wasn't there when they filmed those scenes. It's a very sensitive, small, intimate performance. I loved it. I was very impressed with everybody in it, from Brenda right through to Jim Broadbent."

McGregor plays the telephone lineman who is in love with Jane Horrocks. Because she rarely leaves her room, he courts her from the cherry-picker on his telephone truck. Jim Broadbent, the substantial star of many British and Irish comedies, plays Mr. Boo, owner of a local club where Ray Say tries to get Little Voice a booking.

"One of the interviewers," Caine said, "asked me, 'Do you see the film as a homosexual metaphor?' I said, 'Homosexual metaphor?' I'm thinking to myself, I don't think I played Ray Say very gay. Do you? It turns out he was talking about the girl. She had a domineering mother, and she was in the closet, and she came out, and she was Marlene Dietrich. I was stunned by that. I kept answering his questions by rote. I was still thinking about it."

I think of it more as a showbiz metaphor, I said. The plain little wallflower starts to sing and a star is born, that sort of thing.

"Yeah. Jane Horrocks went off and recorded all of those songs. And at a press conference a lot of people said it must have been expensive getting the rights for her to mime to all those people. She does it so well they don't realize that it's not them; it's her. That's really her singing."

It really is. But she sounds so uncannily like the singers she's imitating that it was wise for the movie to announce, in the first end credit, that Horrocks did her own singing.

"When you see how tiny she is, you wonder where the voice comes from," Caine said. "She sounds like a belter—like Garland and Bassey."

The Ray Say character is on his last legs when Little Voice enters his life. He's down to managing an elderly knife-thrower who hurls blades at his wife to the strains of "Rawhide."

"Especially if you were British," Caine said, "you would know that, since he's a Londoner, going farther north means he's not only dying from a business point of view—he's dying geographically. The normal Cinderella story is the boy who was born in the north and makes it to London. This guy's gonna wind up in Scotland, which for an Englishman is . . ."

Words failed him. "But I loved the character. I've always loved reprehensible people because they're so much more interesting to play on screen. And now as I've been getting to my age, I get the better things to do. You're not just the guy who gets the girl, loses the girl, and gets the girl. You're the villain, you're the father, you're the . . ."

Dying British crook in *Blood and Wine*, I interrupted. One of your best performances.

"It just didn't work, did it?" said Caine.

Blood and Wine must have broken Bob Rafelson's heart, because that's as good a picture as he's made, I said, of the director who also made *Five Easy Pieces*.

"I thought it was a wonderful movie," Caine said. "I asked someone what they thought was wrong with it. He said, 'No one to root for.' Everybody was an (bleep), he said. Next, I'm playing Doctor Large in John Irving's *The Cider House Rules*. He's an abortionist who runs an orphanage."

Who's directing it?

"Lasse Hallstrom. I find it difficult to say his name without saying 'Lassie.' Lasse Hallstrom.

I've never met him, but on the phone he sounds just like a Swede."

He ordered a pot of tea and leaned back with his arm resting on the table.

"If I make a bad film, it's a mistake now. In my early days, I didn't know what a good film or a bad film was, and I was trying to make some money. As it happens I was lucky. I made some good films. The good films are almost as accidental as the bad films. But now I knew *Little Voice* wasn't a bad film. I know *The Cider House Rules* is not a bad film. I'm at a stage now where if someone would say, here's $2 million to make *Jaws 5*, well, I did it before. But I wouldn't do it again."

He made the fourth *Jaws* movie, *Jaws: The Revenge*. He was filming it in the Bahamas and couldn't go to Hollywood for the Academy Awards in 1986, the year he won an Oscar for *Hannah and Her Sisters*. Not the sort of film one would choose to pass up the Oscars for.

Did you know there's a continuity error in that *Jaws* picture? I asked.

"I've never seen it," Caine said thoughtfully.

You know the scene where your pontoon plane lands on the water and the shark eats it?

"Yeah."

And everybody's standing around on the yacht in tears because you've gone down with the shark?

"And I come up the other side."

You climb on board.

"Yeah.

With a dry shirt.

He laughed gleefully. "It was a dry shirt, yeah. What happened was, we stood there for so long waiting for the camera to turn over, and it was so hot the shirt dried out in the sun."

Jane Horrocks was in the restaurant and came over to our table to chat for a moment. When she left I mentioned to Caine that she was a lot smaller than I had imagined, after seeing her in *Little Voice, Life Is Sweet*, and *Absolutely Fabulous*. You never know how tall people really are, I said, because the movies can make them look the same size.

"I did a picture with Elizabeth Taylor," he said, "and she stood on a box for the whole movie to be level with me, and for three years everybody thought I was five-feet-six because everybody knew how short Elizabeth was."

Alan Ladd spent his whole career on a box.

"That was my shortest audition. He was doing *The Red Berry* in England about paratroopers and they said, 'Next,' and it was my turn. I opened the door and walked in and the guy looked up and he went, 'Next!' And I hadn't said anything. 'Next!' he repeats.

"I said, 'Can't I audition or do something?'"

"'No,' he said, 'look at your left.' There was a mark on the doorway. Anyone who was over the mark was out. It was my shortest audition. You had to be shorter than Alan Ladd."

They say that on *Boy on a Dolphin*, the director wanted a shot where Ladd and Sophia Loren were walking and talking, and they dug a trench for her. She had to walk in the trench.

"No wonder the guy was a drunk. I mean, the humiliation of all that. He was about four-feet-eleven or something. But Veronica Lake must have been small because they always used her."

He wasn't four-feet-eleven, I said. Was he?

"About that. He was tiny, but he had big heels on. You wonder how a guy like that becomes a star, you know, because he wasn't a stage actor with a great reputation."

You gotta think like an optimist, I said. Look at Danny DeVito.

"Did you hear about the pessimist who came to visit America?" Caine asked. "He complains about the shop signs. They all say, 'Yes, we're open!' And he says they should say, 'No, we're open!'"

Tom Cruise

Los Angeles, July 1999—Tom Cruise had just flown in from Australia, and he was tired and sad. Sad because he was talking about the new Stanley Kubrick movie, and Stanley wasn't there to pitch in.

"I haven't really talked about the movie, you know," he said. "The pressure of going through this without Stanley being there also. Stanley, who was gonna do everything, you know, suddenly . . ."

Dying, last March, just four days after a completed version of *Eyes Wide Shut* was screened for Cruise and his wife, Nicole Kidman, who were the costars, and for Robert Daly and Terry Semel, the top executives at Warner Bros.

"Nic had laryngitis from her play," Cruise said, remembering his feelings after seeing the first cut of the movie they'd spent three years on. "She couldn't talk, so she was writing notes to me as I was talking to Stanley over the phone from New York. We were so excited and proud. Then I had to fly off to Australia. I was meeting with John Woo, and we had a month of pre-production on the new movie. Nic was gonna follow with the kids. I got in on Saturday. Stanley and I were supposed to talk on Sunday. He'd call me in the middle of the night. 'You're asleep?' 'No, Stanley, what's up?' Instead I got a call from Leon (Vitale), who worked with him for many years and said, 'Tom, Stanley Kubrick has passed away.'"

Cruise paused and toyed with a glass of mineral water. We were talking on Sunday, the day after the Los Angeles preview screening of *Eyes Wide Shut.*

"Well, he had made thirteen perfect visions, Stanley Kubrick, and I'm just proud to have been part of it."

Like all of Kubrick's films, *Eyes Wide Shut* was made in strict secrecy. Rumors flew about the picture: It was about Cruise and Kidman as two sex therapists. It was hard-core porn. It was . . .

"Stanley would just say, let them keep talking," Cruise smiled. "Now it's such a relief to actually be able to discuss the picture. It's also—it's strange. It has a bittersweetness. At night, you hear Stanley's voice."

The film has sex as its subject matter, along with trust, fidelity, and jealousy. But the Cruise character never has sex with anyone during the movie, and that sets up the movie's final line of dialogue, a punch line that will gain a certain immortality.

He plays a rich Manhattan doctor. He and Kidman have one child. She tells him a story one night about how she was so filled with lust for a strange man that she would have left everything—husband, home, child—just to have sex with that man. The story fills him with anger and jealousy, and he sets out on a dangerous odyssey through the sexual underworld, which leads to a masked orgy in a country estate. A wealthy friend of his seems to be involved, and there is the possibility that dread secrets lurk just beneath the surface.

It's all based on a book, *Traumnovelle,* by Arthur Schnitzler—a book Kubrick didn't want them to read. The book was a starting point, not a destination. Kubrick worked obsessively on every scene, rehearsing, rewriting, involving Cruise, Kidman, and the other actors in discussions about motives. I got the sense that the movie evolved from the collaboration; one reason for the secrecy might have been that Kubrick himself didn't know for sure what the movie was finally going to be about.

"Stanley had worked on this and thought about it for about twenty-eight years," Cruise said. "The apartment in the movie was the New York apartment he and his wife, Christianne, lived in. He re-created it. The furniture in the house was furniture from their own home. Of course, the paintings were Christianne's paintings. It was as personal a story as he's ever done. When he first wanted to do it, it was after *Lolita* (1962), and Christianne told me she said, 'Don't . . . oh, please don't . . . not now. We're so young. Let's not go through this right now.'

"They were young in their marriage, and so he put it off and put it off. He was working on "A.I." (a planned film involving artificial intelligence) and was waiting for the technology to get to where he needed it. So he put that on hold, and it was just the perfect time to do this project."

Sometimes, Cruise said, it was just the three of them in a room. Kubrick would send the crew away. There was no deadline. They had all the time in the world.

"The crew wasn't ever there when we were rehearsing. We'd rehearse and he'd rewrite and he'd say, 'Well, what would you guys do here?' or 'What happened here?' And without talking about what the scene was *about,* you know, we'd discuss details of behavior or dialogue. 'What makes sense?' he would say. And finally, 'Okay, well, that makes sense.' We'd rehearse and he'd rewrite and it got to the point that it was in your bones. Just in your bones."

What was your feeling, I asked, about that article in the *New Yorker* by Frederic Raphael, the coauthor of the screenplay? It was an article that painted a harsh portrait of Kubrick as a self-hating megalomaniac.

Cruise made a face. "He wouldn't have written it if Stanley had been alive. Opportunistic. Self-serving. Inaccurate. I don't know that man at all and I've never met him. It's been interesting seeing how people have behaved afterward."

This was Cruise's first newspaper interview about the movie, although he had talked a few weeks earlier to a team from *Time* magazine. As he spoke, it was like listening to him relive his thoughts. They didn't come out in neat sound bites, like the typical movie star interview where everything has been said a dozen times before. Cruise has obviously been through a deep creative experience, and was only now surfacing and looking at it more objectively.

"I'm glad Nic and I didn't make this movie in the first or second year of our marriage," he mused. "The stuff we were talking about, confronting together with Stanley, was volatile and intense. The characters are very much at odds. When you're talking about jealousy or raw emotions that bring men to their knees at times, it can be crippling."

Everyone who has worked with Kubrick returns with stories of perfectionism, of the same shot being taken dozens of times, of days spent on a single scene.

"But it was funny," Cruise said, "how he was truly optimistic about the schedule. I'd show up on the set and we'd find ourselves singing a song, goofing around, and we'd rehearse the scene, and he'd ask, 'What are we gonna shoot the rest of the week?' And I'd say, 'Oh, Stanley, please don't say that!' Because at the end of the week, we'd still be working on that same scene, and he would laugh at himself."

The small crews meant less pressure, Cruise said.

"Stanley bought time when he made a movie. He was not at the mercy of a studio. I'm used to working. I'll work fifteen hours a day and I'll work very hard to try to make something work. But if he felt that I was tired or the scene wasn't working, he never panicked. He knew he had the time. No matter what, he could always go back and take time to fix it. He never locked himself in."

Despite all the rumors about the film, I said, your character never has sex with anyone. It's not a movie about sex but about what sex represents.

"Sex itself wasn't what interested Stanley. The movie's about many things, but especially the dynamic of a relationship that's affected by the raw emotions of obsession and jealousy. About how one little event in your life can take you off into such debilitating emotions."

When your character goes to the address where the orgy is being held . . .

"I think he was driven by his emotions," Cruise said. "He didn't want to go back home. He was absolutely driven by what his wife said to him. He was heading right for Dante's Inferno. He's consumed by the image of his wife he has created in his mind."

We see that fantasy image in monochrome, as he imagines his wife making love to the stranger she described. Then, at the orgy, surrounded by masked and hooded figures and nude women, he sees pure lust unbridled by morals, conduct—even personalities.

It was that scene that created the movie's problems with the MPAA Classification and Rating Administration, which gave the film an R rating only after certain images at the orgy were masked by digitally created figures who are superimposed between the viewer and some of the action.

"Stanley was concerned through editing," Cruise said, "that certain shots would get an NC-17. Stanley committed to an R rating."

But it's an adult movie.

"Listen, at sixteen, I would have been interested in seeing what Stanley Kubrick had to say; I think I was seven years old when my father took me to *2001*. He felt that he wanted an R for the movie. He committed to an R for the picture and he felt that the changes would affect the form but not the content."

The Cruise character glides from one room of the chateau to another, in long, unbroken, elaborate shots. To cut out the offending images would destroy the exquisite rhythm. Therefore, blotting them out with digital additions was the only alternative.

When both versions of the famous sixty-five-second scene were shown at the preview, I said, a lot of people didn't like the strategy.

"Well, it's a shame if people feel that. But it doesn't change the content of the movie. Not a frame is touched on this, except just in form. I think when audiences see the movie, that won't be an issue for them."

Well, it might be, since for Kubrick, form and content and style are all so closely linked. Isn't it a shame, I said, that America is the only country with no workable adult category, so that everything has to be cut and squeezed and compromised to get the R rating?

"With the NC-17—there are papers that won't run NC-17 ads, television stations that won't have NC-17 promos . . ."

But wouldn't a Kubrick picture with Tom Cruise be just the opportunity to overturn all that?

"You're preaching to the converted here. But Stanley made the decision, you know. He wanted this and there's nothing I could have done."

Did he say he would add digital figures in the forefront?

"Yes, that's what he was exploring when he was in the editing process and what he discussed. He didn't want to cut into the shots, but he felt that if he took the digital effects and just covered, you know . . . because he wanted to deliver an R rating."

But when he was shooting it, obviously he thought it *was* an R rating, because otherwise he would have had real people standing there instead of adding digital figures later.

Cruise sighed. "There aren't any real rules with the MPAA, you know. There aren't any rules like, 'Look, you can say three swear words or sixteen swear words, but you can't have fornication in various positions, blah, blah, blah.' He worked very hard on that sequence. What's really even more important in this scene is the people in the masks watching. His composition is stunning."

I agreed, and said something about how there'd someday be a director's cut on video.

"But this *is* Stanley's cut," Cruise said. "I would not have supported anything that Stanley hadn't approved or didn't want. There's absolutely no way that would have happened. I mean, before he died, we went through a lot of details about how the movie was going to be released, how he wanted things handled, where he wanted the print developed. All of these issues. Stanley did everything. Only Stanley."

Also see my interview with Terry Semel.

Catherine Deneuve

Cannes, France, May 1999—"You personally are responsible for the redesign of the steps to the Palais des Festivals," I reminded Catherine Deneuve, the legendary beauty.

She laughed ruefully.

"Yes, but I wish I hadn't been responsible. Because there was a sort of panic that night, I remember it so well. . . ."

It was the opening night of the new Palais at the Cannes Film Festival, circa 1981: The vast new hall for the showing of films, with two great theaters and countless little ones, and terraces clinging to the walls. In the upper reaches, the art of cinema was celebrated. In the halls far below street level, movies were sold by the pound.

"Like a cross between a parking garage and a machine-gun emplacement," said Billy "Silver Dollar" Baxter, who served as sidewalk superintendent during construction. "The Death Star," Red Reed said, when he first regarded the finished building. Within minutes of its completion, vines were being planted everywhere, watered by the tears and prayers of the architects.

And then came the great opening night of the new Palais, which replaced a more humble building at the other end of the Croisette. The older building had featured, more by accident than design, a grand staircase up which paraded the stars of the evening's projections, pausing on the red carpet for the paparazzi and the adoring fans.

The new Palais took the idea of that staircase and magnified it into something Mussolini might have ordered over the telephone. The red carpet began at the curb where the limousines disgorged the stars. It proceeded for twenty yards to a staging area flanked by bleachers for the paparazzi. The stars paused, turned, and chatted gaily—trying not to block one another's shots, as the flashbulbs exploded like firecrackers.

Then the carpet ascended perhaps fifteen stairs, where there was another landing, this one covered by a canopy of television lights. Here the stars paused for the television networks of the world, while breathless fashion commentators did a play-by-play on who had gowned Miss Deneuve, Miss Moreau, and Miss Adjani, and who had armored Miss Madonna.

Then another twenty steps, and then a vast landing where Gilles Jacob, director of the festival, greeted his friends and waved them inside.

Meanwhile, flanking both sides of the carpet, all the way up the stairs, officers of the French National Police Honor Guard stood at attention in their formal uniforms, framing the entrance. There are three levels of cops at Cannes: (1) honor guardsmen, with white gloves, plumes, swords, helmets, striped pants, and shiny shoes; (2) uniformed police, ready to hurl back strikers, gate-crashers, and demonstrators; and (3) troops in riot gear and gas masks, standing by in buses behind the Palais, in case the film is *really* bad.

On that great night when the new Palais was inaugurated, a human traffic jam developed. Stars from below continued to ascend, but stars above did not disappear inside, and soon the women in their gowns and high heels were teetering precariously.

"I remember so well," said Deneuve. There could have been a sort of domino effect, the first arrivals falling back and carrying everyone on down before them, tiara over teakettle, into a glamorous heap at the bottom.

Deneuve, who feared for her safety, was not diplomatic at the press conference the next day. She announced that she would never again ascend that staircase until it had been redesigned.

"But the steps were too short and too high!" she said here the other day, remembering. So they rebuilt the stairs, making them lower and more gradual—a pleasure to ascend, everyone agrees.

Miss Deneuve was in the Hotel Martinez, where she was granting interviews about the two Cannes entries she stars in this year: *Pola X*, based on Herman Melville's novel *Pierre*, in which she plays a mother with a too healthy, or is it unhealthy, affection for her son; and *Le Temps Rétrouvé*, an adaptation of the classic by Marcel Proust, the novelist whose game plan was to spend a third of his life experiencing, and then two-thirds remembering what he had experienced, while enclosing himself in a cork-lined bedroom to shut out additional experiences, lest he fall behind.

"You've gone to the Oscars," I said. "You've seen how brutal it all is. The stars are crushed together into a tiny area, and shouted at and herded like cattle down a red carpet so narrow that four friends cannot fit while arm-in-arm."

"I have been there only once," Deneuve said. That was in 1992, when she was nominated for Best Actress for *Indochine*. "I did not realize it would be that close, that small."

"Here at Cannes," I said, "you ascend, you pause, you turn, the photographers shoot you, the TV cameras photograph your gown, you ascend, you stop again, you are visible to the throngs of fans surging against the police barricades, you are high enough that they can see you bathed in the golden lights."

"Yes," said Deneuve, "tonight we will arrive, fifteen of us in the cast, and pause for the photographs."

Fifteen! I thought. To assemble a cast of fifteen in the Academy Awards entrance area, they'd have to pose piggyback.

"But now the academy is building a new theater in Los Angeles," I said. "It is obvious to me that you should serve as the consultant on the design of the entrance area. You could explain to them how important it is to move gracefully, uncrowded, unhurried."

"Yes, you're right," Deneuve said. "After the experience I've had, I could be of some help."

"After all," I said, "the women spend all day making themselves look beautiful."

"All day?!?" said Deneuve. "They've been working all *day?* They've been working for months! I've heard that in America they even have . . . beauty consultants!"

"Yes," I said gallantly, "but we have need of them—while for you, Miss Deneuve, all a beauty consultant could possibly tell you would be, whatever it is you're doing, keep right on doing it."

"But the crowding at the Oscars! That's, don't you think, very American?" asked Deneuve. "To spend so much time to make things perfect, and then treat it all like a sport, you know. All of that sophistication and at the end, it's just a big fight."

"Yes," I said. "They wear designer gowns and are pushed down the carpet like football fans. And instead of an elegant, elevated area where they can pause and turn and smile, and be televised wearing their fabulous gowns, what do they do? They climb up three steps to Army Archerd's dais, so he can ask the audience to predict the winners on an Applause-O-Meter."

"My, my, my," Catherine Deneuve said. "Yes, I will be so pleased to give them any benefit of my experiences."

She took a thoughtful sip of her Evian.

"My, my."

Mel Gibson

Chicago, February 1999—Thirteen things I learned while talking with Mel Gibson:

1. When he prepared to play Porter, the antihero of his film *Payback*, he thought of a fence-

post with splinters: no problem, unless you rub him the wrong way.

2. "Although Porter is morally reprehensible, he fulfills all of the classic elements of the mythic hero. He does all of those beats, except he's anti: He does them in a bad way."

3. The movie was shot in Chicago, but not so you'd notice. "Maybe if you're a native you'll recognize the street signs, but you don't see skyscrapers, and it's more like a generic, older, urban gritty city."

4. The look of the film is dark, with blue-greens and a lot of shadows: "We wanted it down and dirty. I mean even the film process. If it looked too bright, they would actually do something to bring it down a little bit. The bleach bypass process, it's called. The colors are muted and the contrasts are more contrasty. In our dreams, we thought of shooting in 16mm black and white, and blowing it up to 35 so it was really grainy, and then we'd actually put scratches on the negative. But that's just not such a good idea—especially for the overseas market."

5. He is not known for his wardrobe. "My whole approach to wardrobe is, throw it in a suitcase and make sure they don't press it, for Pete's sake, so I can try to display some rumpled charm. Actually, I'm just a pig. I've got coffee stains on my pants. I think they're coffee stains, anyway."

6. "I'm as vain as the next guy. I have a facade on right now. But you can't see it, because it's reality-based."

7. He has six children and his wife is expecting their seventh. "I'd be lost without this woman. She does everything for me. But I like to get involved with the bonding and the changing of diapers. I figure if I change theirs today, they'll change mine in twenty or thirty years."

8. He's been hearing rumors that he'll make another *Mad Max* movie, "but Kevin Costner already made all those movies, didn't he? Jeez, what a bitchy thing to say!"

9. His Australian accent in the original *Mad Max* was dubbed by producers afraid that American audiences wouldn't understand him. "I got dubbed by some Utah cowboy. I saw a reel of it and it sounds like a gladiator movie: 'Romans—run!'"

10. He likes making action pictures: "Film is built for kinetic movement and crash and burn. It's a great tool for spectacles. But if it's not rooted to something a little higher, you're just kicking your butt around the corner. You can only take so much of that. You have to have some sort of foundation to explode from."

11. The movie's payoff is a double cross involving a telephone, and "I cooked that up after it was already shot. The movie didn't have a conclusion. It's the producer's job to work on that stuff and get it to happen. I was the producer. We reshot some stuff for two weeks. Bang!"

12. The film's original director, Brian Helgeland, didn't approve of the changes: "There was all this weird stuff going around about how Brian was fired from the picture, but that's not so. He opted not to do the reshoots. He was busy, and he felt he was compromising his artistic integrity to change a frame. And you have to respect him for sticking by his guns. But, hey, I have no problem with artistic integrity. I'll just walk right around it. I have people to answer to. Studios who give you all that money to work with."

13. In the movie, he comes closer than anyone since James Bond to losing that part of the anatomy that the action hero most requires: "And then it's, good-bye, low angle."

Tom Hanks

Chicago, July 1998—Tom Hanks has been described as a Hollywood everyman, an actor who elevates the ordinary to an art form. Maybe that's why Steven Spielberg chose him for the lead in *Saving Private Ryan.* The movie's message is that World War II was not won by gung ho, over-the-top heroes, but by brave, frightened civilians who somehow got the job done.

The first time we see Hanks clearly for very long, he's on Omaha Beach, trying to exercise leadership in a chaotic situation, with the dead and dying piled all around him. Throughout the film, we never feel we're watching a movie hero; his Captain Miller was once a civilian, is now in command, and is trying desperately to do the best he can.

"The reality is that only 10 percent of the guys who went ashore on D-day were combat veterans," Hanks was telling me during a Chicago visit last week. "Miller is one of them, because he'd already seen some hideous action in Italy, so he is a terrified man because he is an experienced man. He has no naïveté that says it's going to be easy.

"Larger-than-life characters make up about 0.01 percent of the world's population. By and large, it was all elbows and asses on that beach, guys scared to death. Maybe if you're really good you're able to operate on pure instinct as opposed to pure panic. We won the war because of ordinary guys who did the right thing at the right time."

The landing in France, which occupies the first thirty minutes of the film, was a bloodbath. But that's not the way it was portrayed to the folks back home. The film's story line is about a sentimental gesture: an attempt, in the face of carnage everywhere, to spare a private named Ryan because three of his brothers had already died. The top brass think that will look good in the papers and help civilian morale. But it makes no sense to Captain Miller and his men, who have to risk their lives in a public relations gesture.

When they find Ryan, I said, and decide to stay with him and help defend the bridge, they're bringing meaning to a situation which up until then has been absurd.

"Yes," Hanks said. "And you might wonder why they make that decision. We always had this problem with the story: Why do they stay? There are two lines of dialogue that made everything work, as far as I was concerned. One is said by Private Ryan: 'These are the only brothers I have left.' The other is said by my character: 'Things have taken a turn for the surreal here.' All rules are off and nothing makes sense anymore and this is the last thing we should be doing but yet we're going to do it."

When Spielberg sent his cast through a week of basic training, only Hanks knew what they were in store for.

"I had worked with (marine drill sergeant) Dale Dye in *Forrest Gump;* he trained me for the Vietnam sequences. I went in knowing that it would be a full-blown experience and Dye was not gonna compromise for a moment. The other guys, I think, were anticipating camping in the woods and maybe learning a couple of things and sitting around the campfire.

"By the time the third day came around, it was cold and miserable and people began to get sick and they just didn't understand how getting yelled at by this gray-haired guy was gonna make them better actors. But in the course of this meeting we had, I said, 'Look, this is our rehearsal. Never again on this movie will we have it all to ourselves; we've got our characters, we've got the equipment, we've got stuff to learn, and it's not about dialogue. It's about our own individual motivations and monologues.'

"And Dale Dye said, 'You guys aren't just actors putting on some uniform and running around on the beach saying, "pow, pow, I got you." You're embodying the lives and uniforms of men who did something for real and you're not going to do them dishonor.' He said this while we're all standing in the freezing rain, and there was no arguing with that."

Perhaps as a result, the ensemble acting in *Saving Private Ryan* is seamless and convincing, and the actors project a weariness and an underlying despair: It is good to know you're doing the right thing, but no comfort to know you'll quite possibly get killed.

One of the film's technical advisers was Stephen Ambrose, whose books about the landings in France paint a different picture than the glory in the old Hollywood movies. What made Ambrose mad, Hanks said, is the notion that soldiers "never knew what hit them." There was nothing about suffering terrible wounds and waiting in the mud, wet and cold for hours with your blood draining out.

"I've never even seen movies where guys threw up on the landing craft," he said. "In Ambrose's books you learn these guys were ankle deep in seawater and vomit. They'd been out there for four hours in flat-bottomed landing craft in heavy seas. And they were told that Omaha Beach would be a lunar wasteland by the time they got there. The B-17 bombers were going to pulverize the defensive position so badly that the physical landmarks weren't even gonna be there. But in reality the B-17s dropped their bombs deep inside France and might have killed some cows and that's about it. So everything went wrong from the very first moment.

"The first day of shooting the D-day sequences, I was in the back of the landing craft and that ramp went down and I saw the first 1-2-3-4 rows of guys just getting blown to bits. In my head, of course, I knew it was special effects, but I still wasn't prepared for how tactile it was. The air literally went pink and the noise was deafening and there's bits and pieces of stuff falling all on top of you and it was horrifying."

Maybe the first third of the movie is what makes the final third so compelling. Knowing what they'd been through, knowing what they were surely going to go through again, Captain Miller and his men don't choose the easy way out. Their war had gone too far to justify, any longer, a public relations gesture.

Werner Herzog

Telluride, Colo., September 1998—There is no such thing as a casual conversation with Werner Herzog. When I run into him at a film festival, my heart quickens because I know I am going to be told amazing things, all delivered with the intense air that we are sharing occult knowledge.

Here he is sitting in front of me at the Telluride Film Festival next to André Gregory of *My Dinner with André.* If André had dinner with Werner, it would last a week.

Herzog's latest film, *Little Dieter Needs to Fly,* is going into release around the country. It is the story of a German who joined the U.S. Air Force, was shot down in Vietnam, and underwent jungle experiences so harrowing that at one point he essentially invited a snake to devour him, and the snake declined.

Herzog himself always looks as if he has just trekked out of the rain forest, and often has. "You look thin," I told him.

"I returned a week ago from Peru," the German director said, nodding. "I lost twenty pounds. I hacked my way through the jungle. I am making a film about a doomed aircraft flight that I was almost a passenger on. It was the day before Christmas. I paid $20 to the clerk as a bribe. She promised me I had a seat. But this airline, almost all of their planes were grounded, and in the rush I did not get my seat after all.

"The plane went down in the jungle. After a week, the search was called off. After eleven and a half days, a young girl crawled out of the jungle. She was the only survivor. I took her back to the site of the crash, which was very hard to find. At the same time, I revisited the locations of my movies *Aguirre: The Wrath of God* and *Fitzcarraldo*—where I pulled the steamship through the jungle."

He shrugged. "All overgrown now. No sign that anyone was ever there."

Both of those films starred Klaus Kinski, he of the fearsome countenance, who fought bitterly with Herzog. There is a story that Herzog pulled a gun on Kinski and ordered him to work or be killed. There is also the story (documented in Les Blank's documentary *Burden of Dreams*) that Herzog refused to use models and special effects. He insisted on building a real steamship and really pulling it through the real jungle with real ropes and winches, and when the German engineers predicted that the ropes would snap and whip around and cut everyone in two, Herzog simply sent the engineers home.

"A native Indian offered to kill Kinski for me," Herzog told me, as we still stood in the aisle at Telluride. "Which I had to decline, because I needed him."

A few years ago at Telluride, Herzog showed me tapes of two recent documentaries he had made, one about the Jesuses of Russia—men who dress as Jesus and walk the streets—and another about villagers who believe that if they crawl out onto a lake when the ice is still thin enough, they can see the angels who live in the city under the water.

They were both astonishing documentaries. The Jesuses reminded me of the story in Salman Rushdie's novel *The Moor's Last Sigh* about the Lenins of Russia—actors who dressed as Lenin and recited his memorized speeches so peasants could get the message in the age before television. The difference between the Lenins and the Jesuses is that the Lenins presumably existed, but the Jesuses were made up. Herzog's "documentary" was fiction.

Herzog moves freely through the spheres of fact, fiction, legend, myth, and invention. He is the first to tell you that not every detail of *Little Dieter Needs to Fly* is ice-cold documentary fact. Yes, that is really Dieter on the screen, and yes, he was really shot down in Vietnam and underwent horrifying experiences. But his image of Death as a jellyfish? "I found it for him," Herzog says.

He is willing to push beyond documentary fact, he says, in his quest for underlying truth.

"The weakness of *cinema verité* documentaries is that they can never go any deeper. They can only reach the surface of what constitutes truth in cinema. Deeper truth can only be found in poetry, because then you start to fabricate. The world is simply there. It is what men find in it and bring to it that is truth. I am in search of the fathomless."

Was he really scheduled to be a passenger on that doomed flight? I believe him.

Neil LaBute

Chicago, August 1998—Neil LaBute's new film doesn't take place in Los Angeles or New York or . . . anywhere in particular. There is not a single outdoor establishing shot anywhere in it. "Yeah," says LaBute. "There's no shot of the apartment building we're about to go into, in case you've forgotten what it looks like." The movie is entirely filmed in interiors: homes, restaurants, clubs, a grocery store.

And the characters don't have names. Or at least they never refer to each other by name. "That's true to life," LaBute says. "When you're talking to someone, you don't use their name. We've been talking for an hour and I have never used your name and you have never used mine."

We are having the kind of conversation you might find in a film like LaBute's *Your Friends and Neighbors.* Or in his first film, *In the Company of Men,* which I thought was one of the best films of 1997. We are seated in a hotel café . . . somewhere . . . hunched together over the table, speaking urgently, rapidly.

A little earlier, I'd been talking with Jason Patric, one of the stars of the film, who also co-produced it. He observed that the film contains no insert shots. Those are the extreme close-ups of details like hands or spoons or eyes. By not pulling back and not pushing in, LaBute creates a dispassionate, analytical visual style: He is regarding these characters from a certain distance. He wants us to think about what they say and how they behave, and what their values are.

"If you set the movie in Los Angeles," Patric told me, "audiences would say, 'Yeah, look at the way they live in L.A.' Or put it in New York: 'Wow, those New Yorkers.'"

Instead, these are people who live in settings, not a city. Settings for themselves. Their living rooms. Their clubs. Their beds. The movie is about six characters played by Amy Brenneman, Aaron Eckhart, Catherine Keener, Nastassja Kinski, Jason Patric, and Ben Stiller, who sleep with each other in various combinations but are basically sleeping with themselves. "Nobody satisfies me like I do," one of the characters says early in the film.

LaBute observes: "There's a little mantra throughout the film, of people saying 'Is it me?' It's often used, but never for introspection. When you have a character like Aaron's who's still saying, 'Is it me?' at the end, when he's lying alone in bed, you realize there are people who will just absolutely look anywhere but at themselves to find the cause of the problem."

The movie almost studiously avoids telling us exactly what any of these people do for a living—except for Kinski, who is an "artist's assistant," a job description that inspires some quiet irony. (Jason Patric's character has been called a gynecologist in some reviews, but LaBute says that's just speculation.) The characters don't really seem to care about their work, except to the degree that it gives them money, status, and toys. They're like kids waiting for the school bell so their hedonistic pleasures can begin. They're the kind of people one imagines, no doubt unfairly, that cigar magazines are published for.

"They're into control of their lives," LaBute said. "The masters and mistresses of their universes. Jason's character, who seems like a selfish monster, is simply saying, 'This is my life. That's a fact. People get in the way. I'm sorry, but I have to right that wrong.'"

Among the people who get in their ways are their sex partners, and one of the movie's dialogue masterstrokes is when the Catherine Keener character, after possibly her first experience of lesbianism, is asked, "What did you like the best?" and replies, "I liked the silence best." She hates it when her lovers insist on talking during sex. She's not interested in what they're thinking. She wants them to shut up and take care of business.

LaBute is one of the most distinctive, hard-edged, challenging new directors to emerge in the decade. He is not a showman or a flashy stylist (although his films are built on a deep understanding of style), but a moralist, a critic, a director obsessed with the way we live now. He sees a sort of Post-Everything Period, in which the characters spin down into material comforts and moneymaking concerns, have no curiosity about culture or society, and devote themselves with the single-mindedness of medieval monks to the contemplation of consumer goods. Among the things they consume are each other.

LaBute is a substantial, bearded man in his thirties who made his first film, *In the Company of Men,* in Fort Wayne, Indiana, while teaching at local colleges. He'd already written both that script and *Your Friends and Neighbors,* but decided to start with the smaller film and its three major characters, "to avoid that equation where people look at your film and say what a shame it was you didn't have this or that. You look at that film, and it has everything it needs."

The first film was financed in bits and pieces, including $10,000 in traffic accident settlements that were invested by a couple of his friends. The new film, more expensive and with bigger names, is recognizably from the same director, who listens to how people talk with the same sort of ironic attention as David Mamet. His people are cold, but not monsters: "This is just a couple of weeks. They can change."

Because his films are often described as merciless and uncompromising, he makes a point of saying *Your Friends and Neighbors* is also, in a way, a comedy.

"We didn't work to offend the audience. You make a movie for people to see. But to provoke them, to engage them in some way—that's the best thing I think you can do. The worst criticism in the world doesn't come from a movie critic. It's an audience member who uses you as two hours of air-conditioning because you fit the time slot before the pool opens. And then never tells another person about what you've done. That is the most damning thing, that your sphere of influence lasts only until they get to their car door."

Audiences don't treat LaBute films that way. Of course, some of his characters might.

Spike Lee

Cannes, France, May 1999—David Berkowitz, the Son of Sam killer, sits repentant in his cell and says he wishes that Spike Lee would just let him alone. He does not approve of Lee's new film, *Summer of Sam.* Berkowitz, who has not seen the film, no doubt assumes it is about him and his crimes. He may be surprised to discover he is a supporting character with just a couple of walk-ons, and a brief dialogue scene in which a dog does most of the talking.

The emphasis in *Summer of Sam* is on "summer" as much as on "Sam." It's set in the summer of 1977, when Spike Lee was a sophomore who came home to Brooklyn from Morehouse College in Atlanta. It was the summer of a heat wave, the summer the Yankees led the league and won the Series, and the summer Spike Lee decided he wanted to be a movie director.

"I was twenty," Lee told me. "I couldn't find any work, I'd gotten a Super 8 camera as a gift for Christmas, I picked up the camera, and I went out to shoot."

It was also the summer when the city was paralyzed by fear. A serial killer, at first called "the .44-caliber killer," was murdering couples on lovers' lanes, and sending notes to newspaper columnist Jimmy Breslin and others, detailing his plans and promising more deaths. Whole neighborhoods shut down after dark. Discos closed early, or didn't open.

"It was mayhem, chaos," Lee remembered. "No going to bars at night. People were terrified. And the *Post* and the *Daily News* had the big headlines. Double-digit circulation gains. It was a feeding frenzy. New York City had never had a serial killer before."

Lee's film takes place in an Italian-American neighborhood in the Bronx, and is about how the citywide paranoia affected a small group of friends and neighbors. John Leguizamo and Mira Sorvino star as a troubled young married couple, and Adrien Brody plays a neighborhood kid who suddenly develops a British accent and a punk look. There are many other characters, including a Mafia boss (Ben Gazzara) who gets an appeal from the police: Maybe his troops can find the killer. The film is introduced by the real Jimmy Breslin ("There are 8 million stories in the Naked City," he intones, as if he'd been waiting a long time for the chance to say those words in a movie). And soon the .44-caliber killer has a new name, "Son of Sam," which is how he signs his letters to Breslin and the newspapers.

Summer of Sam is not a police procedural. It is not about the search for the killer. It is not about his crimes but about their effect. Its real subject is scapegoating—how the neighborhood is affected by the notion that it may be harboring a killer, and how everyone who acts even slightly out of the ordinary becomes a suspect.

From his jail cell, Berkowitz runs a home page (www.inetworld.net/hutrcc/david.htm)

that celebrates his status as a born-again Christian. He says he knows "without any doubt" that Jesus has forgiven him. "I am so sad about this," he says of Lee's movie, "and I know many old wounds will be opened. For those who have lost a loved one, they will have to relive the violent death of their family member over and over as the years go by."

He may be relieved to know that the real climax of the film is not the story of his capture, but the story of a witch-hunt that springs into being at about the same time. The movie *Summer of Sam* most resembles not a crime docudrama, but Lee's own *Do the Right Thing.* Both films are about a tightly knit neighborhood where tempers fray as the heat rises, and any differences (ethnic, racial, sexual, economic, or lifestyle) are magnified.

Lee and I had lunch at Cannes a few days after his movie played there in the Directors' Fortnight. He is a Cannes regular; the 1986 screening there of *She's Gotta Have It* launched his career, and the premiere of *Do the Right Thing* in 1989 remains the most electrifying memory I have from the festival. His films have all been primarily about African-American characters, until this one, which has only a few smaller roles for blacks.

At first, he said, he was planning only to produce it. The actor Michael Imperioli came to him with a script cowritten by Victor Colicchio and based on memories of that summer. Lee said he would read it. "I loved the script," he said. "We sent it out, but nobody bit. This was during postproduction on *He Got Game* (1998), and the other project I was working on was not coming along so fast; I needed a film for the summer and so I took another look at this script, which was then called *Anarchy in NYC,* and I decided to do it."

The result was the most exciting film I saw at Cannes this year, a fast-moving collage that shows an easy knowledge of New York neighborhood life, where the big city is made up of neighborhoods that sometimes feel too small. So focused on their own neighborhood are the characters, indeed, that they assume any citywide story is really about them. If Son of Sam is found, they seem to feel, he will be found living on their block.

The press feeds their conviction. The Son of Sam killings created a new news genre. These days, when a high-profile crime occurs, it immediately gets a name ("Tragedy in the Rockies"), and the news channels give it a logo and a theme song. In 1977, news outlets covered crime, but they didn't turn it into "nonstop continuing coverage." The daily headlines about Son of Sam changed that.

"Before Son of Sam," Lee said, "no one had ever used the term 'serial killer' before. At least he named himself 'Son of Sam.' The media only came up with .44-caliber killer. Then he wrote his letter to Breslin, and said he got instructions from a dog, and all."

That summer, Lee recalled, he backed into filmmaking. "My counselor at Morehouse told me I had to choose a major, so I chose mass communications. I was lucky that I found something I was passionate about. Very lucky. Because up to that point, I had no idea what I was gonna do. That summer of '77 was pivotal because I was a young man in the world just trying to find my place; discovering who I was and asking, what am I gonna do? I remember the baseball season, I remember the songs, and I remember the way the whole city was fixated on the killings."

There were reports, I said, that *Summer of Sam* ran into problems with the MPAA ratings board. That cuts were necessary to avoid an NC-17 rating.

"Yeah. There's a scene with John and Mira where originally you see his butt move, but now we have an optical way to slow-dissolve, so you don't."

They don't like the rhythmic movements?

"They count 'em. And there are a couple of shots in Plato's Retreat (a notorious sex club of the 1970s) that we had to take out too. But they said nothing about the violence in the film. Just the sexual content."

This is a movie, I said, where people are blasted away...

"Those scenes never came up. If they'd asked me, I would have preferred to make a couple of changes in the violence rather than the sexual content."

David Berkowitz would probably agree.

George Lucas

New York, May 1999—The day may never come when kids can make *Star Wars* movies in their bedrooms, but next year they'll have the equipment to do it with. The new Sony Playstation II, which is set for release in 2000, will allow its owners to create and play games in real time. The computers that made *Star Wars Episode I: The Phantom Menace* were not that fast. They cost a lot of money. The PSII will retail at around $200.

George Lucas is shaking his head at these factoids. We are sitting in a New York hotel talking about the hidden side of the *Star Wars* saga—its technology. No live-action films have ever used more animation, more muppetry, and more computer-generated images than the *Star Wars* series, and there is scarcely a shot in *Phantom Menace* that doesn't involve at least one element that wasn't visible to the actors while they were on the set. Lucas estimates, indeed, that 95 percent of the shots use digital effects, and that's apart from other kinds of special-effects trickery.

All of this costs money, but the price is coming down. I remember a day in 1990 when I visited Lucas at his Skywalker Ranch and he explained that he'd put the *Star Wars* saga on hold until computers got fast enough and cheap enough to allow him to create any image he could dream up. Now that day is not only here for Lucas, but is approaching at warp speed for ordinary computer owners.

"It's coming in leaps and bounds," Lucas told me. "You know something funny? I have a computer game company, and we have a relationship with Sony, and we're desperately trying to get our hands on the Playstation II so we can start developing games for it. But you can't bring it into the country because it's classified as a supercomputer!"

He shook his head in delight. This was on the day after *Phantom Menace* had screened in New York, and we'd started out to talk about it, but the conversation veered into technology, and he started talking faster and faster.

"I just finished this movie which is kinda state-of-the-art, you know. Nobody's been able to do some of these things. We've created full 3-D digital characters and 3-D environments that are photo-realistic, and we were sitting there being extremely proud of ourselves—boy, we're way ahead of everybody.

"And then they put this toy on the desk that is more powerful than anything we're using. It can re-create what we're doing in the movie. I mean, it's like we struggled for four years to get there and a year from now, it's gonna be available to everybody. It's not quite the same quality as what we're putting on film, but it's high enough quality for TV. It's astounding."

Whenever I talk with Lucas, we get off on tangents like this. I think it's because technology is where his imagination is really centered. Yes, he cares deeply about the *Star Wars* universe, and yes, he can talk at length about the Midichlorins, submicroscopic beings who live within our cells. But when the history of twentieth-century cinema is written, Lucas will be singled out as an inventor and innovator. Most directors see technology as the way to get their stories told. Lucas, I suspect, sees stories as a way to drive breakthroughs in technology.

It has indeed been sixteen years since the previous *Star Wars* movie, *Return of the Jedi*, but that wasn't downtime. Lucas was busier than ever, with the wizards at his Industrial Light and Magic Co. leading the charge in special effects (the dinosaurs in *Jurassic Park* were by Lucas as well as Spielberg).

Now comes the dawn of unimaginable computing speed, cheap. Five million instructions a second? In a toy?

"The thing about the Playstation II," George Lucas was saying, "is that it works in real time. We didn't make *Phantom Menace* in real time. Some of the shots in the film took forty-eight hours to render. We had huge, giant computers cranking every minute of the day. Here they're doing it in real time as you sit there."

Help me to understand something, I said. How can they put that much computing in a $200 toy?

"I was just as blown away as you were. I looked at it and thought, this is going way too fast. I can't keep up. It's mind-boggling. What they've accomplished is just beyond comprehension, if you know anything about computers."

Somewhere, I said, there will be kids inspired by you, who can create their own fantasies on these machines.

"One thing about *Star Wars* that I'm really proud of is that it expands the imagination. That's why I like the *Star Wars* toys. The best part of playing with toys is lying on the rug and moving your little critters around while you're telling a little story to yourself: 'This guy is gonna go and get that guy . . .' and, you know. I think that's a very healthy thing for children, to be able to create their own little worlds, to have their imaginations sparked by something like *Star Wars,* and then be able to re-create that, and play with it, and make new stories.

"Well, that kind of play has progressed, and now it exists on the Internet. There are Websites that do nothing but create little *Star Wars.* They make little films and some of them are very sophisticated. They're using bits and pieces from movies, and cutting them up, and adding stuff; they're making trailers, they're making short films and they're using digital betacams, and then they're broadcasting them on Websites with names like *Star Wars* Fans Movie Festival.

"It's just a matter of time before these little movies start getting longer, and they stop being based on copyrighted property, and they start creating their own characters and broadcasting those. They're just using home digital cameras and Macintoshes with PhotoShop, and they're creating effects and things that aren't quite at the level where we're doing them—but they're close enough to where you say, gee, this is interesting.

"It's happening at light speed. And now you've got these games where they'll be able to create that same kind of thing in real time. The amazing thing about the Playstation is, you can just walk down the hall and say, 'Let's turn left,' and you go left. And it's in the same resolution as the Pixar film called *Jerry's Game,* which won the Academy Award. The characters aren't super photo-realistic, but they're way beyond anything you'll see in a video game today.

"That's a Web phenomenon. That whole thing was created by the Web and it's broadcast on the Web. It's not really a *Star Wars* event. The *Star Wars* thing was sort of the catalyst, but we're gonna live in a very, very different world ten years from now."

Lucas chuckled. "It's a little scary," he said, "but a lot of fun."

And where do you go next? I asked. You have more than $200 to spend on your next machines. People keep talking about how one day we'll just feed all of Marilyn Monroe's performances into a computer, and out will come a new Monroe performance, just as convincing as anything she ever did in her lifetime. You create a convincing character in *Phantom Menace* with the alien Jar Jar Binks, who is completely computer-generated, interacts three-dimensionally with humans in every one of his scenes, and has a captivating personality.

"People say, 'Oh, you're gonna replace actors, and it's all gonna be digital,'" Lucas said. "But in the end, you know, Ahmed Best was the actor who played the part of Jar Jar Binks. He was on the set, he played the scenes with the actors, and then we based the computer images on his performance. I saw him on the stage in *Stomp* and hired him because of his way of body movement.

"In the auditions I auditioned body movement because I wasn't sure whether I was gonna use the voice or not. But just like it happened with Tony Daniels in the first film (the actor who did the voice for the robot C3PO), once an actor gets into that part they kinda become the character. So you have an actor like Ahmed who's there performing on the set with everybody else. And then, with a digital character, you have to bring in a second actor who has the same skills as the first one. Only *this* actor has other skills, too—because he's an animator. Animators are actors too. They have to understand how to move faces, and how to get expressions and how to create a motion.

"So you end up actually having to hire two actors to create one character. And it's twice as hard to build a digital character as it is to just hire an actor and have him say the lines on the set. An alien is one thing, but I think it'll be a long, long time before anybody's digitally creating human actors."

He grinned. "One day they may have Jack Nicholson–type computers, but in our lifetimes, human actors are safe."

Bill Paxton

Los Angeles, December 1998—Bill Paxton has an Oscar contender and a giant gorilla movie coming out within a couple of weeks of each other, and that's the story of his career. He makes little movies *(One False Move, Boxing Helena, Indian Summer)* and big ones *(True Lies, Apollo 13, Twister).* In the big ones he is a stalwart leading man—like his hero, the fellow Texan Ben Johnson, whose every word sounded like the simple truth. In the little ones, he plays regular guys who get twisted into strange traps of crime and guilt.

Paxton has received the reviews of his career for *A Simple Plan*. He stars with Billy Bob Thornton in the story of three Minnesota hunters who discover $4 million in a crashed airplane and think they can get away with keeping it. Both Paxton and Thornton are likely Oscar nominees, and the picture is as good as any this year.

On Christmas Day, another Paxton movie opens: *Mighty Joe Young*, a remake of the 1949 classic about a giant gorilla that is taken from its African home and soon terrifies Hollywood. In this one, Paxton falls in love with Charlize Theron, who has known Mighty Joe since their childhood together.

Mighty Joe Young has spectacular special effects: The gorilla scales the facade of Graumann's Chinese Theater and later rescues an imperiled child from atop a Ferris wheel.

A Simple Plan is direct, unadorned drama, as the unlikely conspirators (also including Brent Briscoe as the third hunter and Bridget Fonda as Paxton's wife) find their lives destroyed by greed and paranoia.

Paxton's acting approach is similar in both pictures, if you make allowances for the different tones. He plays scenes straight and . . . reasonably, I guess you could say. No reaching for effects. In that, he resembles Ben Johnson (1918–1996), who starred in the original *Mighty Joe Young* and a lot of Westerns and won an Oscar for *The Last Picture Show* in 1971.

"Growing up in Texas and Oklahoma, Ben Johnson was more famous than John Wayne to some of us," Paxton said. "I knew him. I worked with him on a low-budget film years ago, and we'd sit around at night while waiting for a shot. We'd chew cloves and he'd tell me all these great stories about the films he'd worked on, including *Mighty Joe Young*—which really put him on the map, a little like me and *Twister*. They didn't need to get Humphrey Bogart and Lauren Bacall for the picture because they were gonna sell it on the effects, but it got him on the board and he ended up getting to do movies like *Last Picture Show*. It was so bizarre to be asked to play the Ben Johnson role in *Mighty Joe Young*."

When Mighty Joe climbs the Chinese theater, the poster out front is for another Ben Johnson classic, *Wagonmaster*. "I told Ron Underwood, the director, there had to be a Ben Johnson tribute in there somewhere."

The story behind *A Simple Plan* is a longer one.

"My father sent me the book when it was in hardback. He said, 'You'll love it. It's got a lot of hair on it. You were born to play this part.' I said, 'Dad, I'll never get to do this.' And for five years there was a whole list of actors and directors who kinda marched through it. Billy Bob and I were set to do these roles in 1997 and then it fell apart. That was the cruelest twist for an actor, to get a part you dreamed you'd get and then they decide to scrap the whole thing."

John Boorman *(Deliverance, The General)* was originally set to direct, but wasn't available when the pieces fell into place. The final choice seemed an unlikely one: Sam Raimi, known for his horror work, such as the *Evil Dead* films. But Raimi's work on the film shows flawless control of mood and tone as the characters work themselves into a tragic hole.

For Paxton, *A Simple Plan* was an intensely personal movie: "Every day you're taking a final exam as an actor. You had to be so naked in this role. But I had a good relationship with Billy Bob from *One False Move*, where we worked together. And the relationship that we were able to put into this movie is so personal to both of us. I have an older brother, Bob, who's not unlike Billy's character. We were always really close. I've had a life where things have worked out for me beyond my wildest dreams, and my brother's had just the opposite.

"Billy Bob's a very impromptu actor. He'll kinda look at a scene and then he'll put it in his own words. There's a scene where I'm just tryin' to kinda calm him down and he says, 'Do you feel evil? I do. I feel evil.' And I start massaging his shoulders. I remembered that when my dad would put us to sleep at night, he'd say, 'Everything relaxes . . . your head relaxes . . . your neck relaxes . . .' That's where we got that."

The two movies are opening so close together because *Mighty Joe Young* was moved back from its original summer opening, he said. "They still had a lot of special-effects work to do. Same story as *Titanic*. But this is more of a Christmas picture anyway, because it has a lot of charity and a lot of heart to it. And I think they were a little worried about getting backed up against *Godzilla*.

"This is a different kind of gorilla. Joe is a noble beast; he's kind of our ancestor. He comes into the world like an innocent; he's brought here and exploited, and finally he's fighting for his life. And as for the effects: In some of the other creature features you'll see the legs moving or you'll see a head turn, but in our movie you see a fully articulated animal, from head to toe, running across open fields and such."

It's true. The camera is free to circle Joe even while he's moving; the gorilla isn't locked into an area of the screen as in many special effects. Then again, in *A Simple Plan,* there aren't any special effects.

Paxton seems at home both ways. He may not have to wait as long as Ben Johnson for his Oscar.

Rosie Perez

Park City, Utah, February 1999—What's it like to premiere your new film in the mountains of Utah? "I hate the altitude thing," Rosie Perez says. "Ooohhh, it's so bad. I couldn't do anything. I just had to lay down. My gums hurt. My teeth hurt. My jaws. It's funny. My knees locked in. When we finally got to the condo, they hadn't plowed yet. It's like right up to like my thigh. We were cracking up, but I like the cold weather better than the hot weather."

You do? I asked.

"I really, really do. I hate goin' on vacation like in the Caribbean and Puerto Rico."

Really?

"Really. Really. I might die and go to Alaska."

And we're off and rolling. You don't have a conversation with Rosie Perez. You try to keep up with her stream of consciousness, as she races from comedy to passion. Sometimes in the middle of lifeless movies, I ask myself, how would this movie be different if Rosie Perez were in it? The answer is: I wouldn't be bored.

Perez was at the Sundance Film Festival for the premiere of *The 24-Hour Woman,* her new movie about a TV producer named Grace who gets pregnant and tries to juggle motherhood with a high-powered professional life. The movie is by Nancy Savoca *(Dogfight, Household Saints),* who is half Italian and half Argentine, and originally wrote the role for an Italian-American.

"I got a call," Perez said. We were sitting at a place called the Grubsteak, in one of those booths hewn out of a mighty log. "My manager says Nancy Savoca wants to talk to me. I'm sayin', wow, she was on my wish list and I love her films and then my manager says, 'Before you get too excited, she's offering you the role of the receptionist, and it's kinda small but it's a very good part.' I read the script and I was blown away, but not by the receptionist. I wanted to play Grace.

"When I got the script, Grace was an Italian-American woman. I told Nancy, 'I'm gonna pass on your offer for the receptionist. I want the lead. It spoke to my soul. And it has comedy, it has drama, it's complex, it's a well-rounded character.' I felt as if she's rushing to end the lunch so I really thought like I blew it. But a few weeks later she calls and says, 'When I originally wrote the movie it was for a Latin-American, but the people who were tryin' to get me financing for the film said I'd have a better chance gettin' it financed if I made it something else.' Really? And she goes, 'Yeah, so maybe it was meant that we met.' And I said, 'You mean you're not gonna change anything?' She says, 'No. Instead of your parents speaking Italian, they'll speak Spanish.' I said, 'Oh my God, I can't believe it.'"

So it was a go. But just then, Perez said, her agent called with a big-money offer on a high-profile picture. She asked Savoca if *The 24-Hour Woman* could be pushed back a little. "'How dare you?' says Savoca. 'You tell me you have passion for the script and now you're gonna tell me—why? Are they offering you more money?' I felt really quiet. She says, 'Listen, if you wanna take it, tell me now so I can move on.' I say, 'I'll tell you in the morning.' I tell my fiancé, 'I'm goin' to bed! I'm turning into everything I say I'm not!' And he says, 'What's your heart telling you to do?' And I go, 'But we can use the money.' He's like an independent filmmaker too."

Somewhere in here Perez had ordered a shrimp and cilantro thing wrapped in a tortilla, and was splashing hot sauce on it.

"The next day Nancy calls me, and says, 'Listen! As passionate as you were of me, I am with you now. You could do this other film and get paid and have a good financial year. But no one's gonna remember your fifteen or twenty minutes on film and you're just gonna be the girl in the film and it's all gonna be about the men. Because I know the film that you're talkin' about.' And she did too. She goes on, 'People are gonna remember *The 24-Hour Woman.*'

"So I hang up, and my fiancé says, 'What'd she say?' And I go, 'I hate her! I hate her! I hate her!' He goes, 'You hate her 'cause she's a lot like you.' I go, 'No, no! She's not!' He goes, 'You two are just alike and that's why you're gonna bump heads.' And I went, ahhhhh! And that next night I couldn't sleep all night and I called her and I said let's do it."

Whew. There's as much suspense and drama when Rosie Perez decides to take a role as when most actresses play one. Her fiancé, by the way, is named Seth Rosenfeld; I couldn't sneak that into the previous two paragraphs because Rosie was talking too fast. Anyway, they made the movie, which is not about a superwoman but about an all-too-human woman who has a little girl named Daisy and tries to produce a morning talk show at the same time. It's not easy.

"Some people ask what the movie is trying to say," Perez said. "I go, there *is* no definitive answer. She's not gonna tell you how to do it and she's not gonna male-bash and she's not gonna say you can have it all. What she's saying is—look, this is the real deal. We all gotta figure it out for ourselves. And it's difficult, and success is relative and you gotta figure out what it means to you. Grace always thought her career was everything. But she starts to say, okay, maybe what I wanted isn't really what I wanted, and I'm scared. But she doesn't wanna tell anybody that because she's supposed to be the consummate professional. She's one of these showbiz women where she's supposed to be one of the boys. Only she isn't."

There is a moment in the movie when things are going badly at work and Grace's husband is more focused on his own acting career than on their so-called shared duties, and Daisy is crying all night, and Grace says she's beginning to understand child abuse.

"Yeah," said Perez. "She's beginning to understand when women like throw their kids out the window. Of course she would never do it. But she's at the end of her rope. And some of the financial backers were debating that. They were like, 'Is that gonna be a little harsh for the audience?' And Nancy goes, 'I'm stickin' to it. That's how you feel. That's really how you feel. The question is, are you gonna act upon it?' Of course not. But you can have those feelings, you know."

I first noticed Rosie Perez in Spike Lee's *Do the Right Thing*, where she played Lee's girlfriend. It was a good role, but not a showcase. That came with *White Men Can't Jump*, where she played Woody Harrelson's girlfriend and proved herself one of the few actresses capable of shouting him to a standstill.

Once again, the role wasn't written for a New Yorker of Puerto Rican ancestry. Once again, Rosie walked in and grabbed it.

"There was nothing to say his girlfriend *couldn't* be Puerto Rican. I went into the audition and I delivered the lines and Ron Shelton, the director, told me, 'Say that line again?' And the line went, 'You got hustled.' And he says, 'You say that like you understand that point of view. Like you've been there.' And he goes, 'Most of the girls that auditioned—they would either cry or get emotional or laugh. Like the line was beyond their comprehension. You said it like—yeah, he got hustled.'"

It's part of the Perez legend that she started as a dancer on the TV show *In Living Color*. The legend is wrong. She was the choreographer and segment producer: "They asked me if I wanted to be a Flygirl and I said, no! No, I don't wanna worry about being skinny and fitting into those outfits and having my hair done every day and the makeup and no, I said, I really wanna choreograph. It's really more of who I am."

After the Spike Lee film and *White Guys*, she got an Oscar nomination for her work in *Fearless* (1993) as a woman who survives a plane crash and consoles a fellow survivor, Jeff Bridges. And she had a career high in Alex Rockwell's *Somebody to Love* (1994), which became a hit on video after the U.S. distribution got caught in a financial dispute. In that one, she was a taxi dancer with a crush on a broken-down former TV star played by Harvey Keitel.

"It broke my heart when people couldn't see *Somebody to Love*," she said. "Absolutely broke it. You gotta go out there and sell your picture. I'm at the distributor's office every day on *The 24-Hour Woman*, driving them crazy: We need more promotion, we need more this, we need more that. I asked for 5,000 fliers of the movie poster. They go, 'What for?' I say, 'I have friends and we're gonna make sure everybody sees it.' They say I don't have to do that. I say yes, I do; I've learned the hard way how this system works.

"So I'm passing out fliers and someone comes up to me and goes, 'Don't you have no shame?' I go, no, this is my art; this is what I live for. This is nothin'. Van Gogh cut off his ear for his art. I'm not tryin' to cut off my ear. I'm not humiliating myself. I believe in my work and I want people to see it, period, and I would do anything without losing my integrity and this is not part of losin' my integrity."

Just the opposite, if anything.

Gary Ross

Chicago, October 1998—The cliché is: In the 1950s in America, we were all a little like Ozzie and Harriet. In the decadent 1990s, we're descending into Armageddon. Gary Ross's film *Pleasantville* argues the opposite: In the 1950s we were leading blinkered lives, but it's been steady progress ever since, into today's society where change is seen as an opportunity, not a threat.

"It's an anticynical movie," Ross was telling me. "It strips you of some armor."

The movie, which is one of this year's top Oscar contenders, opens in the present, with a teenage brother and sister fighting over the channel-changer. Folksy old Don Knotts comes along and offers them a unit with more "oomph," and—zap!—they've been magically transported into one of those 1950s sitcoms where father knows best. But the kids bring along the seeds of change, and before long people and paintings and flowers are turning from black and white into full color, as they realize their inner potential.

Magical transformations are at the heart of all of Gary Ross's films. As a writer, he wrote *Big,* in which Tom Hanks played a kid who found himself inside the body of an adult, and *Dave,* in which Kevin Kline played a man who looked like the president, was recruited to work as his double—and then eerily found himself mistaken for the real thing.

Now comes Ross's first film as a director, one of those movies that starts out like a predictable comedy and then gets deeper and better until by the end we're kind of astonished by how far we've been taken. It's a comic social fable like *Forrest Gump,* where the message develops sneakily from the material. It's the best kind of commentary, subversive in a palatable way, like Orwell's *Animal Farm.*

"Yeah, it's intentionally kind of Orwellian," Ross said. "It starts out as a little parable and then it starts undercutting things."

We were having tea one afternoon during the Chicago Film Festival, where the movie played on its way to its current engagements around the country. Ross is one of these guys you picture in a home workshop, building everything himself, and he was proud of the special effects that allowed *Pleasantville* to create that world of black and white being gradually assaulted by color. In many frames, one character will be color, the world will be black and white—and that isn't as easy to do as it might seem.

"This is more digital than any movie ever made," he said, "and it was all done right in my office. Home grown. We bought and rented equipment and hired the right people. Which just shows how special effects have been . . . democratized."

Yeah. Because they used to cost millions and be done by geniuses in white lab coats, and Ross was claiming he had 1,700 special-effects shots in the movie (as compared to 500 in *Titanic*) and it cost only about 10 percent of his budget.

"Basically I'm shooting in color and then I'm desaturating the environment around the color to create black and white. But we had to make it look like real black and white. If you just desaturate color film it looks terrible. It looks flat. So we electronically amp up the contrast, so you get the richer blacks and whiter whites—so it pops. You have to hard-light the sections of the frame that are black and white so it looks like an old black-and-white movie while we soft-light the parts of the frame that are color, you know."

Well, not exactly. But I get the drift, and I like his enthusiasm as he describes how he created the film's unique look. "I mean, these people in color are becoming more real, not less, right? So if we just used the old colorization method of shooting in black and white and applying color on top of it, that would look pasty and phony."

Pleasantville combines color and black and white so effectively, indeed, that the effects stop being effects and become the world of the film. And we begin to figure out the principle by which some people turn into color and others remain black and white. It's not just a sexual awakening, although that accounts for the transformation of the 1950s sitcom housewife played by Joan Allen. It can also be artistic inspiration (as with the soda jerk who wants to be a painter, played by Jeff Daniels), or it can be sudden insights, or new knowledge pumped in from outside.

The underlying message is that in the 1950s things seemed hunky-dory because everyone conspired to agree that they were. But then comes a moment when there's a little Dave Brubeck on the sound track, and things start to loosen up, and the future starts to invent itself. "Social oppression is just an extension of things we're afraid of in ourselves," Ross said. "It goes deeper, in some ways, than any of the isms—sexism, racism, fascism. We project our own fear or self-loathing on other people. In a conflict-free environment everyone is your neighbor and everyone can smile. It's when your fears become tested, when you're faced with change, that society opens up."

Joan Allen and William H. Macy, the Chicago-trained actors chosen to play the complacent 1950s married couple, find themselves at the cutting edge of change in the movie. She embraces it, he fears it. Ross liked working with them.

"She's the most self-effacing actor I've ever met," he said. "She's shy. I've never met a shy actor before. She's able to go to this place where she's demure, and then she breaks loose. There's no limitation on what she can do. She looks so right cooking in pearls. What would your husband think if you didn't cook in pearls? And then Bill has that patriarchal thing going in; that square jaw kind of voice, and then he's a great actor beneath it."

There may be academy nominations for them, and the film. When I observed that *Pleasantville* was opening during the autumn, which is always said to be Oscar season, Ross smiled, sipped his tea, and said, "I can't say it's an accident."

Eduardo Sanchez and Dan Myrick

Chicago, July 1999—Eduardo Sanchez is working as a bartender and Dan Myrick is driving a blueprint truck and they're out of film school in Florida and going nowhere fast, and Ed says: "We've got that woods movie. We gotta do that woods movie." Nothing else was happening for them. Ed made a movie named *Gabriel's Dream* in 1991. "It was a financial and emotional nightmare," he says. Unfortunately, that described his experience, not the plot. Nothing else had panned out. "But every time Dan and I would pitch the woods movie, people would be like, intrigued."

And so they made the woods movie. For the cost of a new car.

"A normal new car," Ed says.

"Not a Maserati," says Dan.

"The average new car," Ed says. "What's the average fairly good new car cost now?"

Twenty grand? I ask.

"Ballpark," Ed says.

They get two cameras. One is a 16mm with synch sound. The other is an RCA Hi8 camcorder.

"Just a consumer-grade $500 camera," Ed says.

"From Circuit City," Dan says. "We bought two and returned one of them."

"That cut our budget in half," says Ed.

This was their plan. They would make a fake documentary about three young filmmakers walking into the Black Hills Forest of Maryland in search of the legendary Blair Witch. The entire movie would consist of footage allegedly shot by the three characters. The movie would open with the information that all three disappeared in the woods, but "a year later, their footage was found."

The result is *The Blair Witch Project*, which is both (a) footage that looks like it was shot by three people wandering around in the woods with two cheap cameras, and (b) the hottest independent film of the year, a surprise hit at Sundance and Cannes, and a hit with preview audiences because, yes, it is convincing and scary.

If *Blair Witch* looks like it was really shot by the three people in the movie, that's because it really was.

"The actors were actually the camera operators," Dan told me at the Cannes Film Festival.

"And we shot it all in real time," Ed said. We were sitting in the gardens of the Grand Hotel, a long way from bartending and blueprint trucks.

How did you find the actors? I asked.

"We auditioned for over a year," Dan said.

"We found Mike Williams, Joshua Leonard, and Heather Donahue, and we told them the film was gonna be in an entirely improvised environment. Gregg Hale, our producer, helped set up the logistics of the system. We set them loose in the woods with a Global Positioning System (an inexpensive portable computing device that uses a satellite signal to pinpoint a position on a map). We had our own GPS handset. That enabled us to rendezvous with the actors in the woods without having to interact with them, so they could remain in character."

They made up the movie as they went along?

"We told Heather: 'This is your house; this is your room. Ad-lib an intro to the documentary you are making.' And from then on everything was real time."

"When they arrived at a restaurant," Ed said, "we had actors planted in the restaurant, but they didn't know who was an actor and who wasn't. We just had them interview whoever they wanted to, asking the locals what they'd heard about the Blair Witch. Some of the people they chose were our actors."

You had the luxury of being able to burn hours and hours of film, I said, because it was costing you nothing.

"Once they were in the woods," Dan said, "every two or three hours or so, we'd give them directing notes. Each of them got their own notes and they couldn't show them to each other."

"We had a base camp," Ed said, "and we could get in radio contact with them. We shadowed them as they went through the woods and then we reviewed the tapes at each checkpoint. They'd find a cache with script notes and fresh batteries, and leave their footage. And then they would go back to their tent and get back into character again and just be lost; be out there . . ."

He grinned. "And then, at night, they go to sleep and at three in the morning they start hearing weird noises and they wake up . . ."

"It's us, running around the tent," Dan said. "They react to that and then we sneak away and in the morning they find the little rock piles, the arrangements of twigs, the omens."

"They had no idea what was coming," said Ed. "Their prime directive was to shoot everything, to roll film on everything that's weird or whatever."

The actors had no idea how long they would be wandering around in the woods, the directors said. Sometimes only one of them was provided with information about a scene, and the others just reacted. Other times, only two had directions. Sometimes they were really lost.

"We had a pretty detailed outline," Ed said, "but a lot of the moments in the film, there was no way we could have scripted them."

The real name of the forest area they used was Seneca Creek State Park. Walkie-talkies were used for Mayday situations; the code word was "bulldozer" if someone broke an ankle or fell in a well.

In making a fake documentary, they said, they paid a lot of attention to details. Many fake docs are all too obviously faked, and experienced viewers can spot the fakery, particularly when the camera always seems to be in the right place at the right time; in real life, cameramen can't always anticipate the next development.

"The whole goal was to avoid convenient cutaways," Ed said. "There's no pre-shot of them walking through the woods. Sometimes events happen and the camera is in the wrong place. Things happen offscreen."

"Like the scene where there's a noise outside the tent," Dan said. "When the camera comes on, the scene has already started. They would have been asleep when the noise first occurred."

They said they liked pseudodocumentaries like the Big Foot movie, and the *In Search of* . . . programs with Leonard Nimoy.

"We went back and kinda reexamined all those documentaries and they still creeped us out, even as adults," Dan said. "Then we started talking about the theory that the edits in those films killed the realism—killed the horror. When they cut a certain way, you know it's fiction. We came up with the idea of making a film that feels completely real."

"Where the camera's not conveniently in the right place," Ed said. "In the fake films, you'll see a guy anticipating something before it happens. You used to be able to fool people that way, but today, with all the cop shows showing real footage of arrests, and with everyone owning a camcorder, people are more sophisticated."

For the same reason, the film never says definitely whether there's a witch or not. The ending, frightening as it is, is ambiguous. As I was walking out of the Sundance screening at midnight, people assured me it was a "real" documentary. When I disagreed, they said they'd "heard" it was, or remembered reading in a paper about the disappearance of the three documentarians. Thus do urban legends bloom; everybody knows a "friend" who is the source of the story.

"The explanation could be supernatural," Dan said. "Things are just inexplicable enough to leave that open to interpretation. But we don't just show you or tell you. That would be a disappointment. I think people's own conception of the bogeyman is much scarier than anything we could have shown on the screen."

"Yeah," said Ed. "This is a monster that still lives in your brain as you leave the theater."

John Sayles

Cannes, France, June 1999—John Sayles has two movies in release these days, but he takes a credit on only one of them. *Limbo* is his Cannes premiere. It's a story set in Alaska that starts as a romance and ends as a cliff-hanger. And the other movie, which you may also have heard of, is *The Mummy.*

Sayles makes no bones about it: He supports his filmmaking by working as a script doctor, one of the busiest in Hollywood. "I work fast," he told a panel of would-be filmmakers here at Cannes. And he gets paid well. Then he takes those paychecks and finances his own kinds of movies, working entirely outside the studio system. When he's finished with a film, he offers it as a package for distribution. That gives him more independence than all but a handful of the most powerful directors.

John Sayles, tall and lean with craggy, leading-man looks, is the patron saint of American independent filmmaking. He and his wife and producing partner, Maggie Renzi, have collaborated on good and great films of surprising variety, from *Lone Star* in Texas to *Matewan* in West Virginia, *The Secret of Roan Inish* in Ireland to *City of Hope* in New Jersey, *Passion Fish* in Louisiana to *Men with Guns* in South America.

Starting with such early titles as *Return of the Secaucus Seven, Brother From Another Planet, Lianna,* and *Baby, It's You,* Sayles and Renzi have hacked their own path through the underbrush of American filmmaking, demonstrating that it is possible to make your own films in your own way, year after year, successfully. All you need is money.

That's where *The Mummy* comes in. Yes, Sayles was one of the script doctors on it. He didn't bring it up; I did. He's discreet about his house calls. At the Cannes panel, for example, one of his fellow panelists was Ron Howard. Sayles did some work on Howard's *Apollo 13* screenplay, but neither one mentioned it—not because they wanted to hide it, but because it wasn't relevant. Almost every Hollywood movie goes through rewrites, and top writers like Sayles, Elaine May, and Robert Towne have big paydays for their moonlighting. It's the rare script that gets filmed more or less exactly as it was written—except, of course, Sayles's screenplays for his own movies.

Script-doctoring can produce funny stories. The doctors are often called in by insecure executives who know little about the business except how to protect their jobs. Sayles's rewrite on *The Mummy* was several years ago, when director Joe Dante was attached to the project. ("George Romero was on it twice, fifteen years apart," Sayles mused.) Dante told the studio he wanted to set the movie in Los Angeles instead of Egypt. "I don't know why you wanna make it a contemporary movie," a Universal exec fretted. "Why don't you make it a period movie, like the original?"

Sayles snorted gleefully. "Joe had to point out to this guy that the original movie wasn't a period piece *set* in 1932. It was actually *filmed* in 1932—so it *was* contemporary."

Sayles's titles as a script doctor are like a universe lurking beneath his own films. He's worked on *The Howling, Battle Beyond the Stars, Sword of the Ninja, The Quick and the Dead, Mimic,* and countless others. All for money, but all with love: He's not a snob, and likes action movies even though he doesn't make them himself.

Or if he does, they're films like *Limbo,* in which the action, even including some killing, isn't the point of the film but serves as a way to land the characters in unanticipated situations. The film takes place in Juneau, Alaska, a place so isolated that every road out of town ends in the wilderness. Here he gives us characters who are inhabiting their own kinds of limbo: A cannery worker (David Strathairn) who is ending a marriage and trying to forget the two lives lost on his fishing boat; and a lounge singer (Mary Elizabeth Mastrantonio) ending a relationship and more or less at the end of the road for club acts. She has a daughter (Vanessa Martinez) who's fed up with her mother's poor choice in men, but it looks for a time as if this story will involve a happy relationship.

But then things happen. It would be unfair to the movie to discuss the twists in detail. The plot takes a U-turn, and what looked like a love story turns into a wilderness experience. And then into something else.

"The only movie I can think of that resembles it in form was *Something Wild* by Jonathan Demme," Sayles told me one afternoon at lunch, the day of the movie's Cannes screening. "There you start out and it's a screwball comedy, it could be Ryan O'Neal and Barbra Streisand—and all of a sudden, you're in this thriller."

The three main characters end up in a situation, he said, "that's like a chess game. Every move you make limits the number of possible moves remaining for you."

What the movie does is confront the characters with the danger of humans and the implacable indifference of the wilderness. "It's a ten-minute walk from the center of Juneau to where you can be attacked by a bear or fall into a glacier," Sayles said. "Or you go up kayaking with your friends," said Maggie Renzi, "and you tip over and you'll be dead in that water in minutes."

"In Juneau," Sayles said, "you can see the tower of the radio station while you're dying. You don't have to go that far. One of the things *Limbo* is about is how we romanticize nature. We're nostalgic for nature, until we get put into a position where (we're) not prepared and (we've) gotta survive. It's not a picture postcard. It (nature) doesn't care whether you make it or not. Very few people really want to go down the river without the people who are going to make them lunch."

The film's ending, which can only be described as unexpected from every possible point of view, struck me as perfect. Some audience members at Cannes booed it, but then at Cannes they'll boo the typefaces on the title cards. Sayles has arrived at the only possible ending that doesn't cheat or manipulate—that reflects the reality of the situation the characters are in.

Sayles and Renzi are like the godparents of the Sundance Generation. They've been making indee films so long it's in their nature; their films aren't a journey to Hollywood studio paychecks, but a destination. When it comes to making films on your own, by yourself, with financing found anywhere, they took the baton from John Cassavetes and passed it on to the Sundancers.

And yet Sayles's films aren't exercises in style, like so many Sundance titles. They aren't about thirty-somethings smoking cigarettes and sitting in diners and dabbling in crime and talking in epigrams. They're about something, about relationships, society, politics.

"Our frame of reference is entirely different," Renzi said, "because we started doing this twenty years ago. We're not naturally grouped together with the young people who are making movies like *Go*."

Or all the other Tarantino-influenced films, I said. *Go* was pretty good, but as a film it's unthinkable without the example of *Pulp Fiction*. Tarantino has left us such an endless legacy.

"We have a name for *Pulp Fiction*," Renzi said, smiling. "We call it *The Spawning*. Because it spawned so many rip-offs. I wish there'd be more spawnings of movies about a place, about a community, about a culture, about a political movement, about an idea. I hear all these people saying, 'Oh, I love John Sayles.' I think well, if you love him so much, why don't you try imitating him a little bit, and see what happens?"

Terry Semel

Los Angeles, July 1999—In two days Terry Semel would announce his resignation as chairman of Warner Bros. But that was still his secret when we had a long talk about the MPAA rating system and the studio's decision to censor Stanley Kubrick's *Eyes Wide Shut*.

As all the world now knows, digital cutouts were superimposed on parts of an orgy scene in Kubrick's final film to qualify it for an R rating. The decision, allegedly approved by Kubrick himself, has generated protests from moviegoers outraged that they cannot see the master's final film in its unaltered version.

The film was premiered in its original version at Warner's Burbank screening room on July 10. Then Jan Harlan, Kubrick's associate, introduced a rough demonstration of the digital masking, which superimposes figures in front of parts of the image.

The studio certainly deserves credit for its frankness in showing both versions; dozens of films are silently edited every year to get the R rating. Great directors like Kubrick are not spared. Among films the MPAA demanded changes in are Martin Scorsese's *Casino*, Spike Lee's *Summer of Sam*, and Oliver Stone's *Natural Born Killers*.

Even though the studio was frank in showing both versions of the now-famous sixty-five-second scene, it lacked the will to bite the bullet and release Kubrick's preferred cut in an NC-17 or "unrated" version.

That's what I wanted to talk with Semel about on July 13. Two days later, he and longtime colleague Robert Daly resigned as the top executives at Warner Bros., after a long partnership that had kept the studio atop Hollywood for years. Perhaps the idealism behind my questions seemed naive to Semel; if we can believe a report by Neal Travis in the *New York Post*, Semel and Daly resigned because big Warner stockholder Ted Turner hated the movie.

The well-connected columnist wrote on July 16: "My sources say that when Turner finally got to view the late Stanley Kubrick's last film . . . he exploded. I'm told he 'couldn't believe' that Daly and Semel would give Kubrick final and absolute control of the movie, right down to the marketing strategy. One source claims that Ted . . . demanded of Daly and Semel that they have it drastically recut and shortened, arguing that since Kubrick was dead, all former agreements were canceled. They refused to go along with him—and now they are out."

If Travis is right, Semel and Daly deserve credit for preserving the film in its almost original form, instead of editing it under the instructions from Atlanta. Turner, who admits he sees only two or three movies a year, has shaky taste or judgment when it comes to serious movies. He led the charge to colorize many black-and-white classics, including *Casablanca*, and discontinued that vandalism only when the marketplace rejected his wares.

When I talked with Semel, I wanted to discuss the ratings system in general. It was clear that Kubrick's complete vision would have to await the "director's cut" on video, but I wanted to know why Warner didn't simply grit its teeth and release *Eyes Wide Shut* with the NC-17. Certainly a Kubrick film with Cruise and Kidman would only have benefited from the resulting controversy.

"NC-17 is not our business," Semel said flatly. "We're not in the NC-17 business. When one looks at *Eyes Wide Shut* perhaps there was not a huge difference between what would be an R, what would be an NC-17. But NC-17 is a whole industry. It includes triple-X-rated porno films. So to us, that's just not a business that we're in. Never have been."

This bald statement by the head of a studio stands as a final refutation to years of Jack Valenti's bullroar about how the NC-17 was any kind of an improvement on the X rating it replaced. When the rating system was established in the late 1960s, X was a rating that meant, simply, "adults only." Major studios made and released X movies. Then hard-core porn embraced the X and made it unsavory. It became difficult to advertise X-rated movies, and some theaters had leases forbidding them to book them.

I suggested years ago that an A rating be inserted between the R and the X to provide a workable, usable adult category. X would remain to denote hard-core; A would allow adult movies of redeeming artistic or social merit to escape the curse of the X. I debated Valenti on TV and in print, but he held firm, eventually renaming X (which the MPAA never copyrighted!) to NC-17 (which was copyrighted). Now there was a category for these difficult pictures, he said.

But there was not, because NC-17 to this day is confused with X. Note that even Semel, who is well informed, made the mistake of confusing NC-17 with self-rated "triple-X" porno pictures.

Why should America, which dominates the global movie business, have no practical, workable, usable adults-only category? Why must *every* major studio movie be made available to those under seventeen (with the obligatory "adult guardian," blah, blah)? Why is it *necessary* for this movie to be available to people under seventeen?

"I don't suggest that it is. I think that's why it's rated R. It isn't really being made available for people under seventeen unless their parents approve."

But we know that millions of underage kids sneak into R-rated movies every year, I said.

"Now that's a different issue. That's unfair. You're gonna ask, how well is it enforced? But it would be the same if no one was enforcing NC-17 or R or PG-13."

Well, perhaps a category that clearly said "adults only" would draw a line in the sand, unlike the R rating, which is winked at. Perhaps the industry doesn't *want* a category that requires them to turn away customers with dollars in their hands.

"Well, I don't see anything wrong with an NC-17 film," Semel said, "but I also think we should have the right to decide what business we want to be in."

That's the whole problem, I said. I don't want you to be in the porno business. But NC-17 *means* porno to everyone. That's why there needs to be a nonpornographic adult rating. Kids under seventeen always have the right to see a movie with their parents at home on video—but adults are being denied the right to see Stanley Kubrick's original cut.

"I think we've already been around that. This is a decision Stanley made, and his decision was to have an R rating in America, and to qualify his film for the broadest adult audiences in each of the major countries. The R rating does signify that you can bring your child if you choose to. NC-17 says under no circumstances can you bring a child."

Apparently, I said, the Hollywood studios believe that there should not be any movie that people under seventeen can't see—because they will not make an NC-17 movie.

"Well, subject to the parents. When my children want to go to the theater, we talk about what they want to see and my wife or I make that decision."

I agree it's great for kids and great for parents, I said. It's not great for adults who want to see a director's preferred cut.

"Okay, help me for second," Semel said. "What you're saying is a movie like *Natural Born Killers* or *Eyes Wide Shut*, which might not have qualified for R, would have qualified for something beyond R but not quite an NC-17, which has a connotation of X."

Yes. Both Canada and England have such an intermediate category before you get to pornography.

"I think you're right. So there'd be a category that would say it's more than an R..."

But still within the pale. It would give the studios a choice. I understand you when you say you're not in the business of making NC-17. When the X rating was first promulgated it was a respectable rating and studios made X-rated films, like *Midnight Cowboy*. You don't have that freedom now.

"I don't disagree," Semel said. "Of course, as things stand now, with NC-17, your possibilities for advertising the film diminish enormously. I don't think there's a network in our country that would play a TV spot for either an X or an NC-17 film."

Valenti assured me, I remembered, when they changed from X to NC-17 that would quiet those objections. It didn't work out that way.

"Even if you have an R-rated film today," Semel said, "you often find you can't advertise it until 9 P.M. or later. There are some R-rated films that they will permit, but many they won't. If you have something past an R-rated film, you have a hard time advertising it at all."

That's why you need that A category between the R and NC-17!

"Assuming the networks would see that as acceptable."

If it were broached as a positive thing, as an example of greater responsibility...

"I think they look at it differently," Semel said. "We're looking at the artistic values of what we're trying to create. They're saying if your movie can qualify for an R, they'll run the advertising."

I wonder if, even as we spoke, Semel was thinking about his conversations with philistines like Turner, whose reaction to a film he apparently lacks the emotional capacity to understand is simply to cut it. Whose regard for the artistic integrity of Stanley Kubrick is zero (as opposed to Semel, who probably gets an A-minus).

"We're getting caught coming and going," Semel sighed. "A long time ago I talked with Stanley, and he said, 'I really would like everyone to at least see the difference between the two versions.' And I said, 'Stanley, it's never been done before; it's gonna create some anger, some jealousy, and some hate.' But Stanley wanted the press to see both versions so they would be able to see the difference."

About that, I have thought long and hard. When it came to controlling the public presentation of his films, Kubrick was a chessmaster, foreseeing every move. Is it possible that Kubrick knew he'd have to insert digital figures to block out certain material—but that he also knew that if both versions were shown to critics, they would (correctly) see the "Austin Powers version" as a travesty? Was this whole controversy foreseen by Kubrick? Is he smiling now?

"I don't think there's gonna be any perfect system," Semel sighed again. "Here's the primary question: If we created another adult category, would that be acceptable to advertise on TV? Or would it fall into the same dilemma as everything else past the R?"

Well, that's the question, all right. On the answer hinges the right of adult Americans to see a movie as its director made it.

Ian Michael Smith

Chicago, September 1998—When Ian Michael Smith got his first chance to try out for a movie, his parents said "no way." And so did he.

"Our hospital got a fax from this movie called *The Mighty,* saying everyone shorter than a certain height could test for this role," he was explaining to me. "But dwarfs have been portrayed badly and really kinda mistreated by the entertainment industry, so we turned them down. But then my parents read the book, and it was a great book. So I tried out, but I didn't get the part."

That was for a movie based on the best-selling children's novel *Freak the Mighty,* which stars Kieran Culkin, brother of Macaulay, in what is no longer a role for a dwarf.

"But then the casting director called back," Ian said. "It was the same casting director for both movies. They said they'd shown the producers my tape and they liked it: 'You wanna try out for another movie?' Which was surprising, because earlier I had thought it was cool but it would never happen again."

You had no plans to become an actor?

"No. And now I'm in the movie biz."

And he's on a coast-to-coast press tour for *Simon Birch,* an uncommonly affecting new movie in which Ian Michael Smith plays the title character, who is eleven years old, weighs about thirty-five pounds, stands a few inches over three feet, and believes he must have been selected by God for some special task.

Smith's family comes from Chicago's western suburbs, where his dad, Steve, is a management consultant, and his mother, Gayle, is a former high school band director. When Ian was three, he stopped growing and was diagnosed with Morquio's syndrome, which will limit his height but allows him a normal life span—and more-than-normal interests, judging from his press kit bio, which says he's into every possible after-school activity.

"The press kit is the cut-down version," Ian said. "I've had to cut stuff down a lot because one year I had no free time at all outside of all the activities."

What did you leave out?

"Oh, Cub Scouts and stuff like that."

In the movie, Ian plays Simon, a dwarf whose best friend, Joe (Joseph Mazzello), is also a misfit in their little New Hampshire town. Joe's mother (Ashley Judd) refuses to tell anyone who his father is; Simon not unreasonably observes: "I don't understand why she doesn't just tell you. You're already a bastard; you might as well be an enlightened one."

Simon talks like that, and so does Ian, who is startlingly bright and composed for his age, and articulate on the subject of dwarfism. When I tell him that, he explains: "People with dwarfism as a rule find out everything about it. If you haven't heard of, like, everything about your kind of dwarfism you probably don't even know you have dwarfism."

During the Chicago stop on the movie's press tour, Ian and his parents and young Joseph Mazzello and his mother camped out at the Four Seasons, and I talked to them all at once. He was being followed around, Ian said, by a TV crew doing a story on a day in his life.

"Like on Oprah's show once they followed a grown-up dwarf around in everyday life. And everyone in the dwarf community said that was great for dwarfism; it kinda made dwarfism known."

What do people misunderstand about dwarfism?

"They don't know we can lead normal lives. It used to be if you were a dwarf you couldn't get work anywhere but in the entertainment biz. So we're trying to show that we can work elsewhere and stay away from showbiz a bit. Like right now we can go into business anywhere, but it used to be that people would say, 'If I hired you, my boss would fire me.' But not anymore."

I asked Joe Mazzello what he found out from Ian about dwarfism.

"Well, Ian basically told me all there is that I needed to know. I wanted to be his friend and I didn't really like talking about that kind of stuff because I just wanted to kinda put that aside and just be normal friends."

Since Mazzello has been in a lot of high-profile films like *Jurassic Park,* I asked Ian if he'd seen him before—if he was a movie buff.

"No, not really. Actually before this I'd never heard of Joe."

Joe, who was sitting next to him, grinned.

"You hadn't heard of Jim Carrey either," he said. Carrey plays Mazzello's character as a grown-up.

"Yes, I had," Ian said.

"Ian had to ask the director, Mark Steven Johnson, who Carrey was. Ask Mark, he'll tell ya."

"Yes, I had heard of Carrey," Ian repeated calmly.

"Jim Carrey was cast in the middle of the movie," Joe said, "and Mark came up to me and told me about it and I was all excited. Then he went to Ian and said, 'Ian, Jim Carrey's gonna be in this movie!' Ian goes, 'Who?' He didn't know who he was."

"That's a lie!" Ian said, bouncing up. "That is a lie. A complete lie." He and Mazzello seemed to be doing this as a routine.

"Everyone on this movie knows it's the truth," Joe said.

"I'd heard of him because I read the book *Ace Ventura,*" Ian said.

Hello? I said. You found out about Jim Carrey by *reading the book?*

Ian said he was more of a reader than a moviegoer: "The only movies I know anything about are *Star Wars.*"

You strike me as having a director's personality, I said.

"I do?"

You wouldn't have any difficulty ordering people around.

"I don't think so either, in that regard," he said.

How is this going to change your life? I asked. Are you looking for other roles?

"No, I'm not really looking for anything right now. But I'm definitely gonna keep being in plays and stuff."

Do you have a different career path in mind?

"Yeah. I've wanted to be a lawyer since second grade. We had a mock trial over a book called *Superfudge,* about whose fault it was that a toddler falls off a jungle gym and loses his two front teeth. I was one of the lawyers and I won."

Have you always been the smartest kid in class?

"Yeah, I guess," Ian said thoughtfully, "I've been the one who reads the most. But not the smartest-in-math guy, though. There's a guy—he eats math, he drinks math, he sleeps math."

"There's a kid in my school like that," Joe said. "He was on like the math team and he like always won first place in national."

"Continental Math League," Ian said.

"I don't know; I wasn't a part of it," Joe said.

"I'm guessing it's Continental Math League," Ian said firmly.

So you're on track to be a lawyer? I asked.

"Yeah."

What kind of law?

"I have no idea. Maybe movie law."

Now that's really swimming with the sharks, I said.

"Sounds like it," said Ian, brightening at the prospect.

Todd Solondz

Toronto, October 1998—It is a disturbing movie. People don't know how to think about it. They laugh, and then they squirm. Afterward, they get into heated discussions, some calling it trash, others insisting it's a masterpiece. *Happiness* is like a challenge hurled at audiences who think movies should come with built-in viewing instructions—with cues to the appropriate response.

The movie is the standard-bearer of the New Geek Cinema—the movement by many young filmmakers to combine outrageous behavior with self-aware irony. The parents of the New Geeks are David Lynch and Quentin Tarantino; the many grandparents include Ed Wood and Russ Meyer. The tradition includes that night in Paris in the 1920s when Salvador Dali and Luis Buñuel showed their shocking *Un Chien Andalou,* and Buñuel loaded his pockets with rocks to throw if the audience attacked him.

What is curious about *Happiness* is that, in addition to everything else, the film is . . . touching. Its characters include a pedophile, an obscene phone caller, and a woman who cuts up her doorman and keeps him in plastic bags in the freezer ("Everyone uses Baggies. That's why we can relate to this crime"). We hear the phone calls, but the worst transgressions remain offscreen; the movie doesn't sensationalize the behavior of its characters, but regards the forlorn and desolate lives that produce it. Yet it is not an entirely serious or sincere film; moments of metaphysical insight will be followed by shots that could be found in *There's Something About Mary.*

The movie takes place in suburban New Jersey, where three sisters occupy a spectrum: One is a contented homemaker, one is a depressed loser, and one is, or thinks she is, a successful poet. The homemaker's husband is a psychiatrist and a pedophile. The poet's neighbor is a miserable loner who makes dirty phone calls. Across the hall from them lives a chirpy fat girl who has the parts in her freezer. The mother of the sisters depends on Valium; their father wants a divorce. Other characters enter briefly, offering happiness that they do not provide.

Telling their stories, director Todd Solondz moves from ridicule to compassion and back again. This kind of unsettling, off-balance filmmaking is a high-wire act. Directors risk spectacular falls. Imagine this metaphor: Solondz is up on the wire, working without a net. He leaves the safety of his perch. He skips rope, and we laugh. He almost falls, and we gasp. He produces a knife and amputates a thumb. We scream and look away as the blood drips to the sawdust below. He reveals it was only an illusion. We are relieved. Now he falls for real, and catches himself on the wire, which really does sever his thumb. We recoil, but by now we are also analyzing our own reactions to this spectacle. He climbs back up on the wire. His act does not end when he reaches the other side. It ends with him still balanced in the center of the wire, which trembles. It is a long way down.

"It's a tricky movie," Solondz was telling me. We were talking after the recent Toronto Film Festival screening of the film, which had already won the Critics' Prize at Cannes and played at Telluride. He looked, well, like a nerd. It may almost be calculated. Would anybody wear glasses like that by accident?

"The thing that seems to unsettle people is that there are characters whose behavior may be abhorrent, repellent, repugnant. And yet we can't dismiss these characters. They can't be reduced to the pedophile, the obscene phone caller, the lady who dismembers her what-have-you. They have hearts and minds and lives that are bleeding. I care and, in a certain sense, I am asking the audience to care, for people who might be the last people in the world we want to care for."

"In a certain sense." That's what's trickiest about *Happiness.* In a certain sense he wants us to care, and in another sense, or maybe it's the same sense, he wants us to laugh. After his fat neighbor confesses to having killed the doorman by twisting his neck (after he had raped her), the phone caller replies, "We all have our plusses and minuses." They are sitting in an all-night diner, where she then orders dessert.

Do we laugh or do we cry? "If I laugh at any mortal thing," wrote Byron, "'tis that I may not weep." We want to laugh at the phone caller, and we do, a couple of times. But as he crosses off names in his phone book, we sense his despair. He is a damaged person, who tells his psychiatrist he is "boring, boring, boring"—and is. Conversation with a woman strikes him dumb. His nose seems permanently blocked; he breathes through his mouth, giving himself an expression of perpetual puzzlement. If we sympathize with him, it is not because we approve of his phone calls. It is that we see that he must make them; they may be all that keeps him from suicide. (Of course then Solondz gives another twist to the screw by having him call a woman who wants him to keep talking—calling his bluff.)

"People have asked me, 'Ugh! Why did you make a film about these people? They're so unlikable.' Well, I like them. I happen to care deeply for these characters. The way these people respond to the film says more about them than about me as a filmmaker. They say my characters are so ugly. It never struck me that way. I don't see them as ugly. They are all suffering."

What are they looking for? What would make them happy? To be loved. Early in the film, a rejected suitor grabs back the ashtray he has just given his former girlfriend and snarls, "This is for the girl who loves me for who I am."

"To my mind, there are two kinds of happiness," Solondz told me. "What interests me about the title is not the ironic aspect, but what's not ironic. On the one hand, there is the happiness of buying a car or having sex. It's a superficial happiness. On the other hand, there's a kind of transience and contentment. It relates more to compassion or tolerance. The second kind is more elusive. You can't put a name to it. The distinction between these two kinds of happiness is lost on these characters."

They seek happiness, though, in ways that are antisocial at the best and immoral and criminal at worst.

"The film is not about pedophilia or about obscene phone calls or anything like that," Solondz said. "These are devices that get to the larger themes of alienation, isolation, and the struggle to connect. It's not even about sex. We live in a country where alienation is more acutely felt than anywhere else in the world. We lack a sense of family, of a community that shapes one's identity. My sister lives in Boston, my brother lives in L.A., my parents lived in Arizona, and yet we're from a 'close family,' and there's no irony intended."

As *Happiness* went around the festival circuit, it was joined by other examples of the New Geek Cinema like *Thursday* and *Very Bad Things.* (I mean the term as descriptive, not negative; some Geek films are good and others are appalling.) At the same time, the top box-office hit in America was the New Geek film *There's Something About Mary,* which had audiences roaring with laughter at scenes that once would have gotten exhibitors arrested.

"I was at Telluride," Solondz said, "and there was a moderator who said, 'In ten years they'll remember 1998 as the year of *Happiness, Something About Mary,* and Monica Lewinsky's dress.' I couldn't have anticipated the Lewinsky scandal, and yet it seems inevitable, given the way our culture has been heading, that this sort of thing would happen. It's not even a conscious effort on my part to be in tune. There's nothing in my movie taboowise that you won't see on a TV talk show any day of the week. It's all out there.

"There's a difference, though. On TV it tends to be discussed in a dual way. On the one hand there's a righteous moralism—people saying 'rape is bad' as if there were an argument. And then the other side is 'look at this horrible, horrible crime,' as they move in for the close-up. At the extreme close-up there comes a titillating sort of entertainment. There's a kind of freak show aspect: the moralistic and exploitative attitudes at the same time."

Yes. Like in the original carnival geek shows, where a drunk would bite the head off a live chicken, while the guy with the microphone lectured the audience about wet brain and the dangers of alcoholism. The difference in a film like *Happiness* is that you never see the chicken and you never get the lecture. You see the geeks and have to infer their sadness and imagine their sins. The most frightening thing about the movie is that it may not be showing sideshow attractions, but people who walk among us. "The mass of men," said Thoreau, "lead lives of quiet desperation."

Steven Spielberg

Chicago, July 1998—It is an interesting moral equation, Steven Spielberg was saying. When three brothers in the same family are all killed during World War II, the army chief of staff promises their mother that the fourth brother will be brought home alive. Then he orders an eight-man squad to go out and get him. The men must penetrate terrain still being violently contested by the Nazis.

"So what you're doing," Spielberg said, "is sending eight people out, all of whom have parents, to rescue one boy and send him back to his mom when any or all of these kids, along the mission route, could be killed. That was the central tug that made me want to tell the story."

Simple, ironic math. But *Saving Private Ryan* raises it to another order. If the movie had been made in 1944, he agreed, the film would have ended with Private Ryan being found, and saved, and brought back for a reunion with his mother. Spielberg's film doesn't make it that simple.

"There was a sentiment that Hollywood put out there in the 1940s," he said, "when they cooperated with Roosevelt to make movies extolling the virtues and nobility of the war. They would never have allowed the story to be told this way. They weren't willing, in those days, to show America the dark side of the face of war."

So is Spielberg's revisionist story an antiwar film? Not at all. It accepts the necessity of the war, and its heroes reject the easy symbolism of saving Private Ryan and confront what they are really there for, which is to kill enemy soldiers and win the war and try not to get killed themselves.

Is this you, I asked Spielberg, remembering the war movies you saw as a kid, and wanting to make one that was less upbeat, that wasn't locked into a formula?

"This is me being fifty-one years old and my dad being eighty-one, and he fought in Burma," he said. "And my wanting to acquit his war with honor, as opposed to just using his war as the backdrop for a big action-adventure picture."

The story really begins when the squad, led by Tom Hanks, finds Private Ryan (Matt Damon). At that point, they all—the searchers, the private, and the men he's fighting with—have to decide what to do next. Ryan and his group are defending an important bridge. If he stays, he's making a simple statement: The war is worth fighting, and it's worth dying for.

Saving Private Ryan is a film that means a lot to Spielberg, who brought along his star, Tom Hanks, on a visit to Chicago to talk about it. When the historians look back over his career, they'll find, I suspect, that his films fall into two categories: the great popular entertainments that he seems to make with natural ease, and the more difficult, tricky films that he slips in between them. *Saving Private Ryan* goes on the list with titles like *Schindler's List, The Color Purple,* and *Empire of the Sun.* The dinosaurs of *Jurassic Park* occupy other spheres of his talent.

He is the most successful filmmaker of his generation, and perhaps of any generation. No one has made movies seen by more people, and yet at his best Spielberg is more than just popular; he has the spark of the artist. In *Saving Private Ryan,* he takes genre material and rotates it until it reveals its truthful, difficult side. Beneath the action and the wartime dialogue is an unblinking acceptance of the nature of war.

Part of that rotation turns away from traditional action heroes and toward the kinds of soldiers who actually did fight the war: not John Wayne, but English teachers from Pennsylvania and Iowa farm boys. In casting Tom Hanks as his lead, Spielberg smiled: "I was trying very hard to imagine what actor would not immediately want to use his teeth to pull out a pin from a hand grenade. And Tom Hanks just sprang to mind."

Matt Damon, who plays Private Ryan, is a star after *Good Will Hunting* and other titles, but when Spielberg cast him, he'd only seen him in *Courage Under Fire.*

"Robin Williams introduced us. I thought he had a great American 'everyboy' look, and he was also a fine actor. Who knew he was gonna go off and become a movie star overnight and win the Academy Award for Screenplay? And not be the anonymous actor I had in mind? But he looked the part. You know, the people in World War II actually looked different than people look today. A lot of the people I cast in this picture, I was looking at their faces, to match the faces I saw on the newsreels."

How do we look different now?

"We look more innocent. In those days, all the boys looked like men. Today boys seventeen or eighteen years old look like children, but back then, the sixteen-, seventeen-, eighteen-year-old face actually looked sometimes like a twenty-nine- to thirty-five-year-old face. If you look at all those guys coming down the gangplanks in the documentary footage, they all look much older than they actually were."

The movie stars back then, too, I said. Robert Mitchum never looked young. He always looked forty, until he started looking sixty. Is there something in our society that created that difference in perception?

Spielberg grinned. "Bottled water! I don't know what it is. I think in the 1940s we looked a lot more like our ancestors who came over on ships to settle here from other countries. Today, the one country that still has faces from the 1940s are the Australians. Australian boys look as grown up as the boys looked fifty years ago."

It's true that his cast, for the most part, looks weathered and beaten. Only the timid young translator, who speaks German and French but has never fired at anyone, looks like a kid. And what happens inside him by the end of the movie is one of the story's most unblinking messages.

Looking at the film, you can see how physically and mentally demanding it must have been, especially in the combat scenes as waves of landing craft hit the beaches and many soldiers are massacred by Nazi machine guns before they even get their feet wet. The haggard exhaustion on the faces of the actors in some shots cannot simply be acting.

"It was a mentally demoralizing experience for us," Spielberg said, "because we shot in continuity, from beginning to end. We were all reliving the story together. The last film I shot in continuity was *E.T.* I did that to help the kids understand where they were coming from and where they were going in the story. So literally yesterday was a page ago and tomorrow would be a page later.

"I did that again in this picture, but I didn't realize how devastating that was going to be for the whole cast to actually start off with Omaha Beach and survive that as a film team, and then move into the hedgerows, move into the next town, as we all began to get whittled down by the storytelling."

You held a boot camp for these guys. Did you go through it yourself?

"No. One of the gratuities about being a director is that you can volunteer yourself out of difficult details. I didn't do the boot camp, but they had to. A regular soldier does four months of boot camp and these guys did six days. But I wanted to put them through boot camp not just to familiarize them with how to hold a weapon and how to clean and fire it—but because I wanted them to respect what it was like to be a soldier."

We sense that reality in the extraordinary opening sequence, as landing craft arrive at Normandy to find the Nazi resistance much fiercer than predicted. Those who got ashore walked over dead bodies. Most of them had never been in combat before. One has his arm blown off and stoops over to pick it up, as if he'll need it later. It was a bewildering, terrifying hell. Usually war pictures break down into individual acts of action or heroism. Here we see waves of helpless soldiers mowed down. In the landing crafts, before they arrive at the beach, we see them vomiting and shaking and praying: not the vision Hollywood offered in the 1940s.

"You see it the way it was," Spielberg said. "It's easy to point out a couple of shots that are obviously very graphic, but it's the accumulation of the sequence on Omaha Beach that's supposed to help the audience understand the physical experience of combat. I didn't want to do something I've done with many of my other movies—allowing the audience to be spectators. Here I wanted to bring the audience onto the stage with me and demand them to be participants with those kids who had never seen combat before in real life, and get to the top of Omaha Beach together."

As we approach the end of the century, I said, I've been thinking that it's the first century that has been recorded on film, in fact and fiction. And a film like this deals with the key event of the century.

"I think it is the key—the turning point of the entire century. It was as simple as this: The century either was going to produce the baby boomers or it was not going to produce the baby boomers. World War II allowed my generation to exist."

World War II made our future possible.

"The baby boomers owe a big debt of gratitude to the parents and grandparents—who we haven't given enough credit to anyway—for giving us another generation."

That's me too.

"That's you too. And me."

Julia Sweeney

Chicago, February 1999—When she found out her brother Mike had cancer, Julia Sweeney dealt with that fact in different ways. One was to have her brother move into her house so she could care for him. Another was to talk about it every Sunday night in a comedy club.

"It was a little tiny club," she said. "Fifty seats. Dark and intimate. It was more like calling a girlfriend and just ranting—getting everything off my chest. Or like a therapy session."

Sometimes she talked about the sad and scary times, but more often she talked about the human comedy. Her parents moved in, too, and so after finally getting her first house of her very own, she felt as if she'd moved back home. Even a lot of the furniture was the same.

"I remember one Sunday I did a whole thing about my mother and elevators, and how she drives me crazy in the way she pushes buttons. When you're with somebody that many hours, just the way they get on elevators drives you crazy. It made it less upsetting at the time because I could see how to make it into a funny story. I've always been able to tell funny stories about my life, but I never thought that was part of my talent or my art, until I did this."

This is *God Said, "Ha!"*—an eighty-nine-minute film in which Sweeney, who is best known for her work on *Saturday Night Live*, stands alone on a stage and talks about a year in her life when cancer visited her family, and is very funny about it. Cancer is not a laughing matter. But people who have cancer, and those who love them, can be. What did the man say in the poem? We laugh, that we may not weep.

If laughter is the best medicine, then certainly Sweeney's kind of laughter, based on sympathy and understanding, is the best kind—not the silly red noses in *Patch Adams*, but humor generated by a woman who sees the absurdity of malignant little cells that go off on their own and start causing trouble. Why, she wonders at one point, does cancer only strike the parts we need? "Why can't there be cancer of the fat?"

When she first started talking about her family and her worries, Sweeney said, she wondered if people would be in tune. "It was like I'd been on Mars and was telling people about this experience that no one could relate to. Then I found out that everyone could relate to it. *Everyone.* But at first, with my background in comedy, I didn't find the right note. A friend took me out to breakfast and said, 'You need to let the sad come in. You're afraid to not have people laughing while you're onstage.' And I thought, yeah, that's right—because it's not like I trained as an actor, really. I was an accountant and did sketch comedy. So I started cutting jokes and adding to my descriptions of people. It was funny and sad and poignant, and it just got so much richer."

The movie makes lovable comic characters of her parents, who moved down from Washington and into the house with Julia and Mike; finding the bedrooms occupied, Julia moved to a little cottage in the backyard, which she called her office, and sometimes, looking through the window at her parents in the big house, she had to remind herself it was *her* house. One time she and her boyfriend, Carl, were in the house alone and took advantage of the empty bedroom, only to realize her parents had come home and then, tactfully, left: "I started getting warning calls from them announcing, 'We're in San Diego, and we're leaving now, and we should be home in about forty-five minutes.'"

Mike's cancer was not the only bad luck the family had that year, although the other developments should be revealed only during the course of the film; *God Said, "Ha!"* is a process of discovery.

"When I started doing it onstage," she remembered, "nobody knew anything about what was going to happen. They just knew it was a one-woman comedy about a woman whose parents move in and drive her nuts. We didn't want to push that cancer thing because we thought we wouldn't get anyone to come to the theater. But it's okay to know that my brother gets cancer because in the first two minutes you find out about it; it's not like a big plot point is revealed later. It's the setup. This is what happened and he moved in and here we go."

I've seen the film three times, at the Floating Film Festival, the Toronto Film Festival (where we did this interview), and recently at a Chicago screening. I felt each time as if I were actually seeing Mike and Julia's parents and the house with its inherited furniture that was trucked down from Spokane. Sometimes mental images are more vivid than actual ones.

"People asked, why don't we put a picture of your real family at the end, or a picture of the house? But I thought, no. People create their own. They make Mike in their head and they make my mom the way they see her. I listen to a lot of radio drama and a lot of books on tape, and I love imagining it."

Sweeney says she learned a lot of things from *God Said, "Ha!"* and one of them was that she was a writer. The monologue and the movie are not just stand-up bits, but a rounded dramatic experience with pacing and subtle development. Earlier, she'd had to get used to the idea that she was a comic actor, a profession she sort of backed into.

"Sometimes when I hear about people coming out of the closet, that's how I felt about being an actress. I felt like I was really an accountant. I made $10,000 during the year I did freelance accounting. I did all the accounting on *Rainman* for United Artists. My cohorts in accounting were all buying houses and stuff, and I was trying to figure out how to pay rent. I knew inside that I was a performer, but I was too embarrassed to tell anyone because it was socially unacceptable.

"It was like a religious experience in a way, because I had to get to the point where I didn't care what people thought. And I might try for years and not succeed. And it was another three years before I got on *Saturday Night Live*, so it was a struggle there for a while."

On *SNL*, her best-known character was the androgynous person known as "Pat." She made a movie as Pat after leaving the show, wrote some other screenplays, and then Mike moved in. After that year and the material it produced, she did more screenplays, appeared on *George and Leo*, a short-lived sitcom with Judd Hirsch and Bob Newhart, and is working on a movie about a Catholic girls' school that goes co-ed. And she has her house to herself again.

Did your parents see the show? I asked, wondering how they reacted to her comic version of them.

She smiled. "At the time I started working on this stuff, I didn't think of my parents ever seeing it. Then I thought, I'll just take it to San Francisco and see how it goes. And it got these really nice reviews, and unbeknownst to me, my parents have friends in San Francisco, and they heard all about it, so they flew to San Francisco . . ."

And walked into the theater?

"No, I met 'em at the airport. At least I knew they were coming."

How would it have been if you looked out from the stage and saw them in the audience one night?

"I would have had a heart attack. So I tried to protect myself and the audience, because I thought I can't give that audience a bad performance just because my parents are in the audience. So I took them out and said, 'Now look, I'm gonna mimic you for comedic benefit, you know, and it's not gonna be easy for you to take. . . .' I worked myself up into this lather about how I was an artist and a writer and how I couldn't be encumbered by worrying about if somebody's feelings are gonna get hurt.

"I had my script and I thought, I'll read them all the parts that are most offensive and they can just have their reaction right now so I don't have to worry onstage. And I got a quarter of the way through and my mom said, 'Oh, stop! You know, we can handle a lot.' And then she just changed the subject and it was really neat. Like they really didn't care. I think they could see it was loving. They just wanted me to do well."

And she did. One gets the feeling, seeing the film, that the parts that are true are very true, and the other parts are even truer.

John Travolta

Los Angeles, January 1999—I was thinking back to a day at the 1994 Cannes Film Festival when I had lunch with John Travolta after the screening of *Pulp Fiction*. It was clear that the movie represented the rebirth of his career, and he wryly observed that, after all, his career seemed to consist of one comeback after another.

First came TV's *Welcome Back, Kotter, Saturday Night Fever*, and *Grease* in the late 1970s and *Urban Cowboy* in 1980. Then it was nine years before his next big hit, *Look Who's Talking*, in 1989. And another five years (including two dismal *Look Who's Talking* sequels) before *Pulp Fiction* renewed a career that has rarely stepped wrong since; his hits have included the Hollywood crime comedy *Get Shorty* (1995), the John Woo action extravaganza *Broken Arrow* (1996), and the new-age *Phenomenon* (1997), in which a mysterious development multiplies a simple man's intelligence.

Now comes an ambitious, straight dramatic role, ranking with the underrated *Blow Out* (1981) and *Primary Colors*. In *A Civil Action*, he plays a personal injury lawyer who unwisely gets emotionally involved in representing the parents of twelve children who possibly died of leukemia after drinking polluted water.

This is not your usual Hollywood lawyer, with the big courtroom scene in the last reel. The movie, written and directed by Steven Zaillian *(Searching for Bobby Fischer)*, is based on the best-selling book by Jonathan Harr, winner of the National Book Award for nonfiction. It is about law in the real world: not about truth and justice, but about strategy, reality, and how firms can go broke by taking the wrong case.

For Travolta, it's a good role and a wise career move, taking him into the realm of straight drama. One can imagine Al Pacino, Dustin Hoffman, Brad Pitt, or Nick Nolte playing the character. Travolta was ready for it.

"My commitment is so much deeper than

when I was a kid," he said. "In those days I was happy that I had a film career, but I needed to sow my oats. At this point I feel more dedicated to acting, and my choice and judgment have improved. I'm lucky to get the first shot at a script like this, and this time I'm smart enough to say yes, where years ago I used to say no."

He's a pleasant, soft-spoken guy. He likes to be liked. Zaillian uses that quality in *A Civil Action,* where Travolta plays a lawyer who wants to think of himself as hard-boiled. The lawyer takes on only cases he thinks he can win; his firm eats the costs, hoping for a big share of the settlement. When Travolta's character gets personally involved, the movie gets fascinating: Instead of treating that as a plus, it shows how emotion can actually work against the client's best interests. The lawyer points out the mistakes that others make by caring too much. Then he makes the same mistakes himself.

"It was interesting, in the first half of the movie, to turn off all my sensitivities and instincts to be empathetic and sympathetic," Travolta said. "We've all met cold, distant, arrogant people. But to try to portray one is really a great challenge. That was different for me."

In one scene early in the movie, Travolta's character even has a little speech about how much various categories of deaths are "worth" in a personal injury suit. He sounds like a financial analyst.

"He's the most complex character I've ever played," Travolta said. "That's because he doesn't always know which way he's going. His firm is going broke, that's for sure. Is he working from ego, professionalism, or what?"

His opponent in the film, played by Robert Duvall in a performance of masterful small touches, is a technician who lurks behind a facade of folksy eccentricity. One of the intriguing things about the Duvall character is that he is almost always right about the case, the law, the strategy, and the outcome.

"He knows I'm not as wise as he is," Travolta said. "I'll still make the mistakes even if he tells me about them. But he gives me warning points and ultimately that $20 scene is the big pivotal moment for both of us. It's my favorite scene in the movie."

That's the scene where Duvall puts a $20 bill on the bench between them, in a courtroom corridor, and asks Travolta to add six zeros to it, and settle out of court for that sum. Duvall believes he'll win, but it's worth $20 million to cover his bet.

"From his perspective, it's that simple," Travolta said.

So he should take the money? *A Civil Action* isn't about solving immediate problems. It's about what happens when emotions grow so deep they swamp a rational legal strategy.

A Civil Action came after another fine performance by Travolta in *Primary Colors,* where he played a presidential candidate not a million miles apart from Bill Clinton. The movie made my best ten list for its insights into the political drama that has been playing out all year, but did only moderately well at the box office.

"It was a success but not a megasuccess," Travolta said. "I think that political films have a sort of ceiling in how many people they will appeal to. It's like Westerns have a certain market. Because the timing was so acute (the movie was released during the early Lewinsky furor), people thought it might be a superhit, but actually it did exactly what I expected it to do."

Turning back to *A Civil Action,* Travolta said he'd only recently finished the voice-over narration for the film.

"When I went to say, 'If you had to do it all over again, would you do it?'—well, how Zaillian structured that question just moved me so."

I know what he means. Most films don't leave room for such doubts. At the end of *A Civil Action,* you're left with a guy who has all the right feelings and instincts, and maybe needed some of the wrong ones.

Oprah Winfrey

Chicago, October 1998—After she finished reading Toni Morrison's novel *Beloved,* Oprah Winfrey said, "I called Toni and said to her, 'You know, I loved this book—but do people tell you they have to keep going over it?' And she said, 'That, my dear, is called reading.'"

When Winfrey decided she wanted to produce the movie *Beloved* and play the lead, a former slave named Sethe, there was concern that audiences would be distracted because Sethe was the famous Oprah Winfrey. "When everyone was saying to me, how are you gonna be able to lose yourself in this role?" Winfrey said, "I was thinking, 'That, my dear, is called acting.'"

Watching the film, one is of course aware that Oprah Winfrey (and Danny Glover, Thandie Newton, and other actors) are on the screen. But there's no glitch, because the performances and story have been so strongly joined by director Jonathan Demme that the actors simply melt into it.

"The studio did a test screening in San Francisco," Winfrey told me, "and in the audience comments nobody referred to me—which they saw as a positive. I guess people lost the Oprah factor immediately."

We were sitting in her office at Harpo Studios on Chicago's near west side, an office more like a sitting room with overstuffed sofas, understated art, and lots of flowers. She'd just finished taping two shows back-to-back, and plopped down in front of a big mug of designer coffee. I have been talking with Oprah in one way or another ever since I was once on her talk show in Baltimore, and one thing stays the same: her conversational style, confiding, informal, but direct. You sense right away why people open up to her on television and relate to her show. She's playing straight.

The day we talked, she had just turned down what would have certainly been the highest-rated show in her history, an interview with Monica Lewinsky. "I do not pay for interviews," she said simply. "My producers were like, 'How can you say no? It's the biggest interview of the year.' I said, 'Watch me say no.'"

I tried to picture the Lewinsky interview, if Oprah had gone through with it, knowing Lewinsky would then own the tape. I couldn't. I don't think Winfrey could have finished the show. Her whole persona is about controlling her own destiny—owning herself. No wonder she was powerfully attracted by *Beloved,* which is about a woman who tastes twenty-eight days of what freedom feels like, and is willing to kill her daughter rather than see her taken back into slavery.

For years it seemed, however, that the Pulitzer Prize–winning novel might not ever be filmed. Certainly Toni Morrison had no burning desire to see it on the screen. Winfrey was a voracious reader for years before she started Oprah's Book Club and became the most influential reader in America. Reading *Beloved,* she remembers, she was touched by the slave experience more deeply than ever before. And she embarked on a ten-year process, through many screenplay drafts and several setbacks, to get the movie made.

The book and movie are both told in a series of interlocking flashbacks that piece together the anguished memories of Sethe, a woman who kills her daughter rather than see her be returned to the slave-owning plantation she had escaped. As the film opens, it is 1873 and the freed Sethe is living with another daughter, Denver (Kimberly Elise), in a frame house on the outskirts of Cincinnati. They are joined by Paul D. (Danny Glover), a man she knew from the plantation. Her house is haunted by a poltergeist, and soon the ghost arrives in physical form: Beloved (Thandie Newton), a thin, spectral presence who walks and speaks oddly, as indeed she should, because she is a two-year-old inhabiting an adult body.

"It is important to understand why a woman would be so driven by the slave experience that she could kill her own children," Winfrey told me. We were looking through a book of photographs and diary entries she made during the filming.

"Toni spoke to me of 'that iron-willed, arrogant Sethe.' And I had trouble with the term 'arrogant.' And Toni said, 'When I tell you she's arrogant, believe it. She's arrogant.' Arrogant, in her unwavering confidence, without one moment of doubt that the decision that she made to take the life of her children was the right decision."

Winfrey said the novel was inspired by the true story of a slave named Margaret Garner. "And the real Margaret Garner not only killed one child, and attempted to kill all of them, but then was taken back for stealing property, was sold downriver to New Orleans, and jumped overboard again with another child. That child drowned and she was pulled back out of the water and sent south. And in the true story, she wasn't even tried for murder. She was tried for stealing property, because they weren't considered human.

"She just was so defiant and iron-willed that she would not be taken, under any circumstances. And what I came to understand is, that's what happens when you've known freedom. It's the fact that she experienced twenty-eight days of freedom that drove her to that. Had she not had the twenty-eight days she might have gone back. She might very well have made another choice.

"In the process of making this movie, I went there. I went there. I said to Toni that I knew the stories but I never felt the stories. I got for the first time what every slave knows—that the beatings, the mistreatment by Master, going to the fields, working hard—that doesn't in any way come close to the spiritual and emotional explanation of what slavery is. It's the loss of self, the loss of your own humanity. It's not being able to have a will to choose."

In the film, there is a speech where Sethe talks of her twenty-eight days of freedom. It was one of the hardest scenes in the movie for Winfrey, she said.

"I did four takes and I couldn't get through it. I was hysterical. The hardest line for me was when she says, 'Look like when I got here I love my children more because as long as I knew we were in Kentucky they really weren't mine to love.'

"I had read the book, but in acting the scene I was going to the knowing place. What does that mean? It means that every time a slave woman or man went to the fields they came back home knowing that their children might not be there. If Master decides he wants to sell 'em, they're gone. They're not yours; they don't belong to you.

"And another hard, hard line of dialogue to get through was what she said about freedom: 'Wake up in the mornin' and decide for myself what to do with the day.' That line was life-transforming for me. It was the purest definition of freedom. But to say that line was hard, hard, hard. Until I was in the moment with Danny, I never thought that it would be that hard. Finally Jonathan Demme said to me, 'We're gonna turn the camera around on Danny and let you come back and try again tomorrow.' I felt like a failure. I'm blowing it. But I really needed to come back because I was so emotional about it. I had lost touch with Sethe. Because she just tells it; she just tells it. She's not all in it; she just tells it."

Demme was helpful at other moments, Winfrey said, when her own emotions about the material threatened to overwhelm how Sethe would feel about it. After all, Sethe has lived this life. She's come to terms with it.

There is a scene, for example, where the unseen ghost hurls Sethe's dog against the wall. Winfrey says she first played it in a very emotional way, rushing over to the injured dog. "Then Jonathan had a conversation with me. He said, 'I don't know how you're feeling about the dog hitting the wall, but I don't think she's gonna be surprised to see it. Do you?' And I realized she wouldn't be. And he goes on, 'Because she's been in that house living with this ghost and the ghost has done all kinds of unspeakable things. So I don't think she's gonna be shocked at all. I think she's gonna be resigned and sad that baby ghost just won't leave this house alone.'"

Winfrey got up and brought over two framed documents she had in her office. They were the bills from slave auctions held more than 150 years ago. There were first names in a column down the left-hand side, and then neatly written prices: $400, $275 . . .

On the set of *Beloved,* she said, she used these documents to help her prepare for the day.

"I had these in my trailer. Before some scenes, I would light candles and say their names. These are ledgers from plantations. I would say their names and their ages and their prices, and this one where they are listed along with the cows and how many plows and how many mules. I would try to call them in. Call them in with a sense of reverence, because I always thought that this was bigger than my own little self.

"The first meeting that I had with Jonathan Demme," she said, "he was concerned about how I was going to lose the Oprah persona, was going to play the character. And I said I didn't know if it could be acted as much as channeled. I felt like I had to open up and receive, as opposed to trying to go in and find."

I've read, I said, that when you wander in the woods of your farm in Indiana you sometimes feel that there are slave spirits close to you.

"I do," she said, "but I'm reluctant to go too far with that because once you start talking about spirits, that's kinda open to, you know, weird interpretations. I haven't seen a spirit but I certainly have felt the presence of them in doing this film. Many, many, many times over."

And you also went through this actual experience where they re-created the slave experience, they blindfolded you, and put you through some of the same ordeals?

"Yes, in Maryland I went through all that.

That's where I really touched the dark space. I originally wanted to do the exercises just as a matter of physicality. Like okay, what's it like to be barefoot in the woods and in the hot sun? I was gonna try to experience a part of the Underground Railroad for a couple of days. Sitting under a tree during that experience, though, I touched the dark, hollow, death-without-salvation place. 'Oh, that's what it is,' I thought. That's what it is."

Alfre Woodard

Toronto, September 1998—It started like this. We were talking about her film, *Down in the Delta,* where Alfre Woodard plays a hard-drinking woman from the Chicago projects who gets a fresh start on her uncle's farm in the Mississippi Delta. It is a good film, strong and touching, the directorial debut of the writer Maya Angeḷou. I said to Woodard, "You've never really made yourself available for exploitation films, have you?"

"How do you mean, made myself available?"

You haven't been in them.

"Okay."

Have you? I'm trying to think...

"No!"

And that started us on an extraordinary conversation about the position of a gifted black actress in America today. But before we get to it, pause for a moment to consider her career.

Alfre Woodard has had more success than most young women who start out hoping for employment as an actor. She's starred in twenty-eight films and a lot of stage and TV work—everything from the Arena Stage in Washington to the New York Shakespeare Festival. Her first big movie role was for Robert Altman, as the hotel manager in *Health* (1979). She was nominated for an Oscar in 1984, for *Cross Creek.* She's played Winnie Mandela opposite Danny Glover, and a Bob Cratchit-y secretary opposite Bill Murray's Scrooge, and the seamstress who designs Holly Hunter's winning costume for the *Miss Firecracker* contest, and the title role of Isiah Thomas's mother in *A Mother's Courage: The Mary Thomas Story.* As a social worker, she advised Farrah Fawcett to take it easy in *Extremities.* As a veteran's counselor, she supported John Ritter as a Vietnam vet affected by Agent Orange in *Unnatural Causes.* As a straight-talking nurse, she challenged Mary McDonnell's paralyzed soap actress in *Passion Fish.* As the judge in *Primal Fear,* she presided over a key scene with Richard Gere as the lawyer for an accused murderer of an archbishop.

Now, in *Down in the Delta,* she gives one of her very best performances as a self-destructive Chicago woman named Loretta, with two children, one gifted, one autistic. She lives with her mother (Mary Alice) in a high-rise project and spends her days watching TV, hanging out, and drinking. Her life is going nowhere. Her mother lays down the law: Either she moves back to the family farm in Mississippi, or she gets kicked out.

She moves. On the Delta, her Uncle Earl (Al Freeman Jr.) helps her get her feet back on the ground. It's an uncommonly affecting family drama, also starring Esther Rolle as Earl's wife, Annie, who has Alzheimer's. And there are convincing performances by Kulani Hassen as the autistic daughter and Mpho Koaho as a bright son who hangs out on Rush Street, making money photographing tourists.

So, as I was saying, she hasn't made any exploitation films and she hasn't played stereotyped gangsters' girlfriends. In a time of limited choices for African-American actresses, she has not made a single choice simply to get the work.

"I would love to be a gangster's girlfriend," she tells me. "But I want *Bonnie and Clyde.*"

This was last September at the Toronto Film Festival, where we had a long talk the day after *Down in the Delta* first screened.

"I want my characters to be as complex as human beings can be. But they're not complex as written in most pictures with predominantly black casts, so I can't be in them. I'd like a legitimate story about a real person who does rob banks. In that one, I'd love to be the bad girl. But in some stereotyped role about who they think black people are and how they think we talk and what they think our values are..."

You could hear the quiet unhappiness in her voice.

"I've heard for twenty-five years now that 'we have to tell our stories.' But the stories they give the money to are the stories that say: Look! We're black! They're not seeing human beings. I'm interested in stories about people that you might actually know. But nobody wants to bankroll it unless you explain the whole time that you're black. Or talk about how the white man is at the middle of everything. You know what? You don't talk about the fact that you're black every day."

I think back over her roles and I see, yes, they have that in common: They are about individual people. None of them require the word "black" in front of the job description in order to explain the role.

"Real black people are hardly ever represented in American cinema and television," she said. "Nobody knows who we are, because it's been popular to keep us exotic. People think they're very liberal and hip, making movies about street types. But black people have never known many of the kinds of edgy black characters that are in the movies. Once you admit that a person is a human being, that their story is universal and you can identify with them, then they can't just be put in the 'black' category. Gangsters, all those wacky blacks that populate the black films—that's why they're supported by Hollywood. It's so that you can think, 'I'm not like that.' And whenever that hair stands up on your arm when a black guy walks too close and you didn't see him coming—that's where it comes from.

"You know what it is? It's technologically advanced Jim Crow. It's like the days when you kept people separate and you had children running away from black people because they were taught to be afraid. Once people know each other they know it's not true. But the movies are teaching the world that black Americans are all hip-hop and drugs and crime and dangerous.

"I can't tell you what it's like, as a person who is traveling, and I'm on the Riviera, I'm standing in Siberia, anywhere, and have a person turn to me and say some little catchy B.S. jive they've heard from a movie. The only thing they know about me, as a person in my skin, is that they might be able to get some drugs from me, they might be able to screw me, they might be able to get me to help them steal something. They learned it at the movies. It is just amazing to me that black people are not angrier than they are."

She made a face. "So yes, I'd rather see pictures about people doing whatever they're doing, and I'm moved, and I'm reminded of myself."

That's the test of a role for you?

"It's just that, as an actor, I can't be in something I don't believe. I just don't have those kinda balls. So the only thing I can do is be honest. I don't mind going to *see* a piece of fluffy, wacky junk, because I want to see the people who are in it. But do it myself? To be on that set working fourteen, fifteen, sixteen hours a day, saying that stuff—I couldn't do it. Not even so much from a moral point of view but because it would bore me. I'd be acting like I needed to be somewhere else."

She paused, picked up a coffee cup, put it down again.

"I'll tell you something else. Maybe if I was beautiful in that way that white people and African-American people crave for African-American women to look, maybe I'd be offered more of that. Then I'd have to decide, Oohhh, am I gonna show my butt?"

Don't you think you're beautiful?

"In the way that Americans, white *and* black Americans, think black women are beautiful? No. It's like, frankly, I don't get asked to do sexy scenes because I am not considered beautiful by American standards. I'd like to believe that I would still make the same choices but—see, that's the thing. People think I'm such a righteous black woman because they've seen me doing that on film, and they haven't seen me shaking my tits on film. They think I'm earnest and 'strong' in that stereotypical way that people use 'strong' when they talk about women. All I can think of when they say 'strong woman' is somebody who can lift things. It deprives the person of their humanity and their complexity.

"So I'm strong. But I was never offered the things that Meryl and Sigourney, Michelle and all my contemporaries are offered. Because they're being offered roles as human beings in complex situations—life situations. The things I'm being offered are like O.P.P. or the Mary Thomas story. Now, of course, I'm gonna choose Mary Thomas. But then people start to think that I am only that. I could live and die and people would still have no idea who I am, but for however long my name lasts, that's what I'll be reported as. Strong, righteous black woman.

"We don't know who the hell people really were. You take Harriet Tubman. I'm trying to get a picture made about her. What do you think when you hear her name? The way they always portray her, she's got on her little bonnet, she's got her little Bible. She *walked* all over the country, and the first thing she bought when she got to freedom was a gun, and she used it. That is not how she is presented to us."

Loretta, your character in *Down in the Delta,* seems very human, very natural, not righteous . . .

"I was attracted to Loretta. I knew I could do her. It was actually her disorganized, failing self, at the beginning of the story, that I was attracted to—more than her success at the end. That person at the end is easy to like, but I'm interested in the person at the beginning who can't get it together.

"What word would you call her, at the beginning of the film? She's not successful at being a sturdy human being. She's somebody that's drunk and loud or angry, always wrong and fighting. I'm attracted to people like that, as long as they're still attractive as human beings. I'm drawn, because I see fire there. I'd rather hang out and have a cup of tea while she had a glass of whiskey, just to hear what she had to say, because I know there'd be currents around her.

"We want to say she's a terrible person. But there have always been people like her in my life. You didn't support them in hurting themselves, but you also didn't toss them away. People like Loretta have lives and friends like me. And they have families, and people who care about them."

I like that scene, I said, where she's in the crack house but she won't take the strong stuff because that could be the beginning of the end. She has that much self-respect and survival instinct. She's thinking, I'm getting drunk every day, but I have enough sense to realize that I don't need any more problems than I have right now.

"Yeah. I've found a way to manage. I'm not trying to kill myself. There's a blues song: 'I ain't drunk, I'm just drinking.' I did a lot of thinking about Loretta. I decided she dropped out of high school as a sophomore. The school system let her glide through. She's never been able to get a good job because she can't read. There's that scene when she applies at the supermarket.

"She's in an urban environment, Chicago, where you can fall through the cracks. If she had been down in the Delta with her family, she would have had people who own land, people who are watching your back for you. When people live close to the land, there is a place for you. If you can't read or add, there's something for you to do. There's nothing for you to do in cities, especially in blighted environments, where it gets multigenerational so fast. All the roots are on top. There's nobody older than anybody else.

"It's her family that saves her. In any family there will be teachers, there will be inspired holy people, there will be crooks. It is the foundation that allows a person to become who they would like to become. So she actually gets to have a shot. If you put a plant in the right soil, food, water, and sunlight, it may not grow into the most fabulous orchid you ever saw. But it will do what an orchid does."

High School Killers

I am asked by CNN and CBS if violent movies might have helped create the climate that led to the tragic high school shooting incident in Littleton, Colorado. My feeling is that CNN and MSNBC may be more to blame. The saturation coverage of these incidents writes a scenario for disturbed young people: Hey, that could be me they're talking about!

Movies are the scapegoat whenever something bad happens. As a society, we find it difficult to accept tragedy. It must have a cause. There must be a way we can fix it. When young men walk into a school and open fire, it must be because of movies they saw, or music they listened to, or satanic cults, or drugs.

It is assumed that there are lots of movies about kids shooting up high schools. There are not. The most dramatic one, Lindsay Anderson's *If* . . . , came out in 1968 and is remembered only by movie critics. Most high school movies are about who is going to the senior prom. Those that show troubled kids *(The Basketball Diaries)* depict them as losers no one would want to copy. These movies are morality lessons. There are also countless slasher movies (the *Scream* series, etc.), but they don't glorify the killing and are in a long tradition of pop horror.

Yet my phone rings when another tragedy occurs, and I am asked if the movies are to blame. They need lots of sound bites, because there isn't enough footage to fill up the airtime unless the stark facts are stretched out by speculation about the "cause" and "climate." And, of course, there are the endless profiles of the shooters, illustrated with yearbook photos.

Watching this coverage on every channel, am I watching the seeds for the next tragedy? No troubled kid wants to be like the troubled kid in some movie that makes the kid look like a deluded, drug-crazed loser. But you can be sure he's watching the coverage of the latest shooting. On TV he sees photos of the suspects. He hears them talked about for hours. He sees interviews with their friends, neighbors, teachers, employers, coworkers, clergymen, coaches, and the last kids to talk to them before the rampage. They get a neat name ("The Trench Coat Mafia") and the news programs devise graphic logos to identify the "continuing coverage."

What does the disturbed viewer of such coverage conclude? Here is the way to become famous, to get everyone talking about you, and to go out in a blaze of glory.

The last two times a tragedy like the Littleton shooting occurred, my newspaper did not put the story on the front page. The *Sun-Times* argued (correctly, I believe) that such coverage does more harm than good. On the day after Littleton, when every other paper headlined the tragedy, the *Sun-Times* headlined atrocities in Kosovo—which is, in the balance, the more important story. The Littleton killings were covered inside the paper. Such a story is sad and sensational, but its outlines are familiar, and all of the expert analysis could be boiled down to: "Yes, sick people do evil things."

God forbid, there may be more tragedies like the one in Littleton. If there are, the same news formulas will be hauled out again, and new logos designed, and experts will wonder if the movies made them do it. If the shooters survive the next time, it might be useful to quiz them about how carefully they followed the news coverage of the Littleton incident. I'll predict they didn't miss a minute of it.

Eyes Wide Shut Sparks Rating System Controversy

Los Angeles, July 1999—Sixty-five seconds of Stanley Kubrick's final film, *Eyes Wide Shut,* will be digitally masked so that the film can qualify for an R rating. Saturday night on its Burbank lot, Warner Bros. screened both Kubrick's original version and a rough draft of a studio-censored sequence. It wasn't a pretty sight.

In the film, a doctor played by Tom Cruise gate-crashes a costumed sex orgy in a mansion outside New York. Wearing a mask like the other participants, he is led by a nude woman through rooms where various sex acts are taking place before small groups of onlookers.

In the Kubrick version, the sex acts, mostly seen at a distance of several feet, are clear but not detailed (no genitalia are visible). In the R-rated version, additional digitized characters have been placed between the participants and the camera. Instead of seeing two orgy participants full length, for example, we see their heads and feet, with the back of a cloaked figure blotting out everything in between.

The two versions were introduced by Jan Harlan, Kubrick's executive producer, who said the digital changes had been approved by Kubrick, while agreeing that both he and the late director would have preferred the original version.

The reaction of the invited audience of critics and film people ranged from silence to outrage. My own feeling was that the altered version is a travesty. (I called it "the Austin Powers version," in honor of the famous sequence where teapots and cushions block the view of Austin's private parts.) It results from the failure of the MPAA's rating system to provide a viable adult rating, and the unwillingness of the studio to bite the bullet and release the film that Kubrick gave them.

Loud objections were voiced by several Canadian critics, because the American R-rated version will be released all over North America, even though Canada has a workable adult rating that would have accommodated Kubrick's cut.

The movie as a whole is a strong and important work, a worthy final chapter to a great director's career. It stars Cruise and his wife, Nicole Kidman, as a Manhattan married couple whose argument over imagined infidelity leads to a long night during which the wandering Cruise encounters a prostitute, witnesses assorted sexual situations, and eventually ends up at the secret orgy. In form if not style or content, it resembles Martin Scorsese's *After Hours* (1985), in which a character wanders for a night through the sexual underworld.

The movie is an adult film in every atom of its being. Kubrick, Cruise, Kidman, and the other participants intended it that way. In its original version, as the producer Harlan readily stated on Saturday night, it would have qualified for the NC-17 rating ("no one under 17 admitted"). But the NC-17 rating is so rarely applied that it exists in limbo. Besmirched by associations with hard-core pornography, it is a kiss of death because many theaters will not show NC-17 films, and some newspapers and broadcast outlets will not accept advertising for it.

If only Warner Bros. had taken the occasion of this final Kubrick film to confront the system! A Tom Cruise film directed by Stanley Kubrick, with reams of advance publicity, could have been successfully released rated NC-17, or even "unrated, for adults only." But the studio's contract with Kubrick required an R-rated film.

The studio cites the contract in its defense, but of course, it is a contract with itself and can be waived. The only pragmatic reason for desiring an R rating is to maximize profits by making it available in more theaters and to younger filmgoers.

"When he shot that scene, Stanley was absolutely convinced it was R-rated," Harlan said. "In postproduction, it became clear that it was not. Working with the MPAA, we devised the idea of using digital figures in the foreground to qualify for an R rating." He implied that this was done with Kubrick's knowledge before the director's death in March, although final postproduction on the digital changes is still under way, and only a rough approximation was shown on Saturday night.

The result is likely to please no one. The "Austin Powers version" will distract attention from Kubrick's work as a whole, because audiences will be trying to spot the digital effects just at the moment when, in Kubrick's original cut, a sense of erotic dread is building. It will produce an R-rated film which is not, in fact, appropriate for most viewers under 17—with or without adult guardians. It will have the result of making the film more, not less, accessible to younger audiences, while denying adult audiences the power of Kubrick's original vision.

As a result of what it learned at Saturday night's screening, Warner Bros. should do the right thing and release Kubrick's original cut—either as NC-17 or as "unrated." At the very least, it should make that version available on separate screens for adults-only audiences in major American markets and throughout Canada.

Babe in the Woods

The most enchanting film of the year is going down in flames. *Babe: Pig in the City,* which will make a surprising number of "best 10" lists, has been crushed by *A Bug's Life* and by wrong-headed publicity. It's outta here.

The destiny of *Pig2* can't be explained by saying audiences didn't like it, because audiences didn't see it. Critics generally loved it. People tell me it's the best film they've seen in a long time. The "failure" of *Pig2* lies with its marketing, and with the way people gather and store information.

—Marketing: Because it had a tie-in with a fast-food chain, Universal was unwilling to change *Babe's* opening date, which was November 25, the day before Thanksgiving—despite clear omens that the date was suicide for the pig. Why? Because Disney's *A Bug's Life* was opening on the same day. You simply don't open any children's film against a new animated feature from Disney. (Another omen: *Rugrats* was making millions from young Nickelodeon fans.)

—Information Storage: People are busy and don't make a study of new movies. They can process perhaps one or two facts about most films. The scientist Richard Dawkins has named these little infonuggets "memes." They're like genes, except they hop from mind to mind instead of from generation to generation.

By mid-November, those who cared at all had stored two memes about *Babe: Pig in the City:* (1) It was over budget and late. (2) The studio was concerned that it was "too dark." After the movie opened, they could add a third factoid: It was a flop.

Do you want to see a movie that is a flop, too dark for kids, and was late and over budget? Of course not, because all your information is negative.

What if I were to say that the film was late because the director was working to make the special effects better? That the budget is all up there on the screen, since there were no big star salaries? That the subject matter is "dark" only in the same way that *Bambi* and *Dumbo* are dark? That because the film is intelligent and creative enough to delight adults, it may indeed be too challenging for younger children, but that for kids eight and up, it may become one of their favorite films?

Okay, I'm telling you all that. Movie critics across the land have said much the same things. This is probably the year's second-best reviewed film, after *Saving Private Ryan.* But we movie critics labor under the handicap of having seen the film—unlike the scribes on the financial pages and the cable news pundits, who pass on the box-office "buzz."

Why is it bigger news that *Pig2* flopped than that *Pig2* is a great movie? Because the head of Universal got fired after the pig's flop—by corporate bosses who thereby brilliantly made absolutely sure that the headlines about *Pig2* in its first week would be negative.

In this swamp of bad news, all I can do is wave for attention, and repeat: *Babe: Pig in the City* is a magical, original, daring, wonderful movie, one of the year's best. Take my word for it. I've actually seen it.

Beloved and Happy Endings

The film *Beloved,* which cost $75 million and has grossed only about $22 million, proves that mainstream audiences will not support a serious film on black themes.

Or so the movie industry pundits conclude. There is much head-shaking over the film's failure at the box office. The successful African-American TV producer Deborah Pratt *(The Net)* told me this week that in the current climate it is almost impossible to get an ambitious black-themed movie financed at a major studio.

I believe her. But I don't believe *Beloved* failed because mainstream audiences rejected a serious black film. I believe audiences, black and white, rejected a depressing film they did not understand.

Imagine if *Schindler's List* had been about a Holocaust survivor who killed her infant daughter to spare her from the gas chambers. That the daughter's adult ghost returned years later in the flesh. And that the story was told in complex flashbacks, so that some viewers never did understand that the dead child and the adult visitor were the same person. That film would have fared no better with audiences than *Beloved.*

I admired *Beloved.* It is a good, powerful movie. But I've spoken with many people who were confused and depressed by it. "Who are these kinds of movies supposed to appeal to anyway?" wrote *Sun-Times* columnist Mary A. Mitchell. "*Beloved* gives us nothing to celebrate and everything to mourn."

The lesson is one Hollywood has known for decades: Mass audiences want happy endings.

It was the genius of Steven Spielberg to enter the horror of the Holocaust and emerge from it with a story that contained heroism, triumph, and not one but two happy endings. TV's *Roots* celebrated endurance and found triumph at the end of its story.

I am at the Hawaii Film Festival, where the other night we saw a Chinese film that ended with a double suicide. I had an hour between movies, and darted into a nearby Korean noodle shop. Other moviegoers had the same idea, and because the café was so small we were all soon talking about the film.

"I hated it," one jolly Chinese-American woman told me. Her three friends nodded in agreement. "Not once have I seen a Chinese film that was happy. I know they have a lot of troubles over there—but sometimes they must have a good day!"

The other customers laughed in agreement. And I thought: Ordinary people buy tickets in order to have more entertaining things happen to them in the theater than might happen outside.

That describes several recent nonexploitation black-oriented films that have returned impressive profits. Consider *Soul Food, love jones, Waiting to Exhale, The Bodyguard, Amistad,* and *Once Upon a Time When We Were Colored.* How many people know that the top-grossing American independent film of 1997 was Kasi Lemmons's *Eve's Bayou,* a serious film without a single white character? It outgrossed all those indie films about young white guys on the make, sitting around in diners and smoking cigars. Maya Angelou's *Down in the Delta,* starring Alfre Woodard, was an audience favorite at the Toronto Film Festival and is likely to do well.

Hollywood executives survive by trying to do exactly what worked for someone else. Therefore, if *Beloved* has failed, black films are out. They don't blame the film, but the genre. I have no doubt that eventually there will be a film about slavery that will "cross over" and make enormous profits at the box office. And I can promise you this: It will have a happy ending.

Home Movies with Hef

Los Angeles—There are three official movie nights at the Playboy Mansion. Friday nights are for classic films, Sundays for new releases, and Wednesday night for films chosen by popular demand. "You ought to drop in on Friday," Hugh Hefner's daughter, Christie, told me. "Hef does the notes himself."

The mansion stands in Holmby Hills, west of Beverly Hills, but it could be in the English countryside, with its neo-Gothic battlements and the fountain splashing in its forecourt. I brought along Russ Meyer, the celebrated filmmaker, who had photographed half of the first dozen Playboy Playmates.

We entered the entrance hall, which looked uncannily like a set for an elegant horror film. Straight ahead, overlooking the lawn, was a bar where I ordered a Diet Pepsi, official drink of the mansion, and said hello to some of Hef's regular moviegoers. Ray Anthony, the orchestra leader, was there, and Robert Blake, the actor.

Hef materialized, wearing his customary pajamas and smoking jacket. A glass of iced Pepsi was pressed into his hand without comment.

"What Oscar parties are you going to?" he asked.

"My wife and I will go to the Miramax party," I said. "That's always a lot of fun. And we're invited to the *Vanity Fair* party . . ."

"So was I," Hef said gloomily, "but I can't go."

"Why not?"

"They're so strict with their invitations. You're only allowed one guest."

"So?"

"I'm dating twins."

Russ Meyer's face brightened. "You, sir, are a great inspiration," he said.

"They're going to be late to the movie," Hef said. "One is at the hairdresser's. When one dates twenty-two-year-olds, one pays the price."

"Twins?" I said.

"Mandy and Sandy. Delightful girlfriends. Luckily they get along well with Candy, who I was dating when I met them."

"So you might have three dates on Oscar night?"

"It was suggested that I walk in with one twin, leave her inside, and then walk in with the other one," Hef said. "But how many girls can you walk in with?"

A gong sounded. "Time to eat," Hef said briskly. Movie Night followed a tight schedule. The group, perhaps eighteen or twenty, drifted into the dining room, where a chef sliced prime rib onto our plates. Hef sat at the head of a long oval table. The seats on either side of him were reserved for Mandy and Sandy, but since they were missing, Russ and I were invited to sit there.

"I was here for the grand opening of the mansion," I told Hef, remembering peacocks on the lawns and Playmates splashing in the grotto. "I wrote that you were the Gatsby of your time."

Hef nodded thoughtfully. It occurred to me that considering Gatsby's difficulties, this was not as high a compliment as I had intended.

"Since I started to date again," Hef said, "after the divorce, we've been swamped by the press. Bill Zehme wrote a piece in *Esquire.* That started everything. Then we got the *New York Times,* the *London Telegraph,* the *Los Angeles Times, Time* magazine . . ."

"I read that Hollywood's young turks are hanging out here now," I said.

"Leonardo DiCaprio was here the other night," Hef said.

I sensed, however, that Friday Night at the Movies was taken too seriously to permit the mansion to be overrun by cover-kids from *Entertainment Weekly.* The guests were members of Hef's inner circle—heavy-duty film buffs, for whom these nights were in the nature of a devotion.

I quoted something Gore Vidal had written: That as he looked back over his life, he realized that he had enjoyed nothing—not art, not sex—more than going to the movies. Hef looked as if he could think of a modified version of that sentiment. "Okay, movie time!" he said, getting up. We filed into the Great Hall, where sofas were lined up facing a big screen. Two full-sized 35mm projectors stood at the back of the room.

Hef waited, just slightly impatiently, until everyone was seated, and then held up a hand for silence. He produced a yellow legal pad and introduced the movie. "Hef does his own research every Friday afternoon," Chuck McCann, the actor, whispered to me.

Tonight's feature was *Treasure Island*—the 1934 MGM version with Jackie Cooper and Wallace Beery. They had not gotten along well on the set, Hef told us. His remarks dealt with the four earlier silent versions of the story and the 1950 Robert Newton version, but he left out the 1972 version with Orson Welles as Long John Silver, perhaps as an act of mercy.

Meyer and I sat right behind Hefner. During the movie young women materialized in the dark and slipped in next to Hef. Mandy? Sandy? He gave them a smooch of welcome, and then returned his attention to the adventures of Long John Silver.

After the movie, Hef repaired to his private quarters. "Look at this," Chuck McCann said. He led me into a passage between the walls where we found a full-sized pipe organ. "It's concealed behind a screen in the Great Hall," he said. "Sometimes we show silent films with live music. *The Phantom of the Opera* was sensational."

Hef reappeared in a black suit and open-necked white shirt. We were introduced to Mandy and Sandy, who were wearing matching outfits with bare midriffs. They were on their way to a party. McCann, Meyer, and I lingered, talking about the greatness of old movies.

Looking for the bathroom at the end of the evening, I wandered into the kitchen. It was enormous, with spotless stainless steel everywhere. On a shiny counter, two plates were laid out, wrapped in Saran Wrap. One held half a grapefruit, the other slices of tomato. Hef's bedtime snack, I guessed. Living well is its own reward.

On Oscar night, after the ceremony, I co-hosted a TV program that included live reports from the various parties around town. There were six monitors facing me, and on one of them, just before midnight, I saw Hugh Hefner arriving at a party with Mandy, Sandy, and six other dates. Must not have been *Vanity Fair*'s.

Honoring Elia Kazan

The questions about Elia Kazan's honorary Oscar have no simple answers. When the eighty-nine-year-old director of *On the Waterfront, A Streetcar Named Desire,* and *East of Eden* accepts his Lifetime Achievement Award from the motion picture academy on March 20, there will probably be as many boos as cheers. I will be doing neither: just watching silently.

There is no question that Kazan deserves the award for his work in film and the theater. More than any other single person, he presided over the modernization of American film acting. From the dawn of cinema until the late 1940s, actors' styles ranged from the melodramatic to the mannered to the realistic and relaxed—and then came Kazan with actors like Marlon Brandon, Eva Marie Saint, and James Dean, to change everything, even our ideas of what was realistic.

The Method, the new style was called, and it took shape at the Actors Studio, which Kazan cofounded. It advised actors to reach within themselves for emotional touchstones to apply to the characters they were playing. It could also became a fearless exercise in self-revelation, and when Brando appeared in *Streetcar* and *Waterfront,* there was the feeling he was baring his soul to the camera. Great stars of earlier years would have been too protective of their images to put themselves on display like that.

Those key films changed American movie acting for good. Kazan, however, did something else to assure his immortality. At the time of the congressional witch-hunts, when the House Un-American Activities Committee made unconstitutional probes into the political beliefs of citizens, Kazan named names. In 1952, he told HUAC of colleagues who were allegedly Communist Party members. He did it, he says, for two reasons: because he didn't want to lose his ability to work, and because he thought communism represented a genuine threat to democracy.

He did, ironically, lose the ability to work in some ways: He knew, he said, he'd never get the right to direct another play by Arthur Miller, whose *Death of a Salesman* he brought to Broadway. And, of course, his testimony helped others to lose *their* freedom to work. But he was right about communism. It has become clear over the years that Soviet communism was not what it claimed—that when all the dead are added up, Stalin's toll of innocent victims was comparable to Hitler's.

The problem with Kazan's testimony is that the evil of communism and the danger of subversion were not really the point. The purpose of the "un-American" hearings was to smear—to enforce guilt by association, to use congressional power to destroy careers in a way that would not have been proper in a courtroom.

Kazan was being asked to supply the names of people who, in most cases, had not belonged to the party for years—who were communists when that was perfectly legal, and indeed when America and Russia were allies. The witch-hunts were show trials, just like those under Stalin. They assumed that the end justified the means (the same rationale used by the Ken Starr circus). They used the threat of contempt of Congress to coerce American citizens into answering questions that no citizen should be asked by such a forum. They created a hysteria that was a greater threat to our freedoms than the feeble American Communist Party ever represented.

So Kazan cooperated with an illegal and immoral investigation. That is the point. To name names was to give legitimacy to unconstitutional demagoguery. Even the staunchest anti-communist could, and should, have refused to answer such questions. Now, nearing the end of his life, Kazan is being honored for his work. It is work worthy of honor. It is right to give him the Oscar—and right, perhaps, not to applaud, but simply to observe.

Phantom Menace Offers Exhilarating Visual Spectacle

There's a certain disconnect between George Lucas and the most fervent *Star Wars* fans. Lucas is at heart a techie, who finds less fascination in the story of *Star Wars* than in the making of it. He'd rather talk about digital animation than about Anakin Skywalker. The fans, on the other hand, approach the *Star Wars* saga as a secular religion: *Star Wars Episode I: The Phantom Menace* is important to them not because 95 percent of the shots contain digital effects, but because it reveals the origins of the boy who will grow up to be Darth Vader.

As early reactions to the movie appear, they seem to split along the same fault line. Those who are fascinated by technique find it an exhilarating visual experience, proving that what Lucas can conceive, computers can achieve. Those obsessed by the story find it more prologue than payoff, a setup for the next two films that contains lots of action but not enough heart.

My own position is in the first camp. With all the will in the world, I cannot bring myself to care seriously about the Trade Federation, the relationship of Anakin and Luke Skywalker, or the microscopic beings that reside inside our cells and are intimately attuned to the Force. What I do care about are great visuals. I have always felt an immediate connection to astonishing sights on the screen, from *Metropolis* to

2001 to the *Star Wars* saga to *Dark City* and, yes, *Babe: Pig in the City.* Watching *The Phantom Menace,* I was filled with wonderment at such sights as a city in the clouds, a Senate chamber inside a vast sphere, an underwater city of floating globes, a double-jointed alien named Jar-Jar, and a triumphant victory march into a vast imperial setting.

Those sights existed first inside the imagination of George Lucas, and next inside the memory chips of computers. Talking to the human actors who coexisted with the digital effects in the film, I found they were as astonished as I was at the settings they found themselves in. "We shot one scene in a parking lot," the actress Natalie Portman told me. "We were in costumes standing in front of a big blue screen. Now we're in this city in the sky, with big waterfalls and towers and spaceships. . . ."

Why are great, imaginative visuals important? Because they stir our dreams. Two weeks ago I was in Minneapolis for a tribute to Werner Herzog, the great German director whose own visuals include a man afloat on a raft in the Amazon with gibbering monkeys. Herzog believes that as a civilization we cannot live without being nourished by new images; that movies are being deadened by the boring routine of scenes showing car chases, gunfire, and people on telephones.

Not everyone responding to the first screening of *The Phantom Menace* would agree with his notion. Those attending advance showings of the movie were sworn to secrecy, yet reviews and reactions to the movie appeared ten minutes after the first screening was over. One writer found that he was distracted by the thought that Jar-Jar, the alien who is one of the key characters in *Menace,* was computer-generated: The alien was, he said, not much more convincing than Jessica Rabbit.

That's not how I felt. I was intrigued by Jar-Jar's oddness, as I was by such earlier *Star Wars* inhabitants as Yoda, Jabba the Hut, Chewbacca, or the regulars in the bar on the planet Tatooine. Too many science-fiction movies give us aliens who look like humans with funny heads. When Spielberg gave us spindly child-creatures in *Close Encounters,* I found that fascinating. And when Lucas gives us Jar-Jar, with his eyes perched on stalks growing atop his kangaroo/rabbit/donkey head, with his weirdly backward speech, with his body language that seems generated by second thoughts, I am delighted. If it takes animation to make a creature like that—well, I'm glad they can do it.

One of the hazards faced by *The Phantom Menace* is that the way has been so thoroughly prepared for it by the first three *Star Wars* movies and the genre they inspired. I remember seeing the original *Star Wars* in 1977 and being stirred by the immensity of the vast spaceship appearing from behind the top of the screen and rumbling forward to reveal its unimaginable size. Now that method of introducing a ship has become a standard procedure. First devised by Kubrick in *2001,* perfected by Lucas, it has been used in *Alien, Starship Troopers, Wing Commander,* and most of the *Star Trek* movies.

The fresh delight we felt when we first saw C3PO and R2D2 is likewise not the same as seeing their earlier incarnations in *Phantom Menace.* The pod-race in *Menace* is to some degree inspired by the scenes in *Star Wars* where rocket fighters zoomed down the tall outer canyons of the enemy command vessel. Those sights can never be new for us again; we've internalized the *Star Wars* universe, and even its creator can only return to it.

What Lucas can and does do is create new kinds of places. His planetary cities in *Phantom Menace* seem inspired by ancient Greece and Rome, by the architectural forms of the Renaissance, and by the cityscapes designed by Luytens for nineteenth-century British imperial capitals like New Delhi. They aren't constructed of sets and matte drawings, so there's no feeling that they end just a foot outside the frame. Instead, benefiting from computer-generated imagery, they stretch as far as the eye can see, and the camera can pan freely across them; one cityscape in particular looks like a fantasy conceived by Sir John Soane, the British architect who drew watercolors in which all of his buildings, real and imagined, jostled each other in a vast landscape.

What I missed in *The Phantom Menace,* and what I hope Lucas is able to supply in the next two films, is more imagination applied to the look of outer space itself, and more original planets. Many of his planetscapes are, once again, frankly based on (and shot in) the forests and deserts of Earth. Some alien planets must look very odd and contain forms of vegetation that look nothing like trees and plants and grasses. Perhaps he could seek inspiration in the life-forms that cluster around heat vents on the ocean floor, where life exists without light.

As for the look of space, in *Phantom Menace* it is still limited to twinkling pinpricks of light on a dark background, and then huge planetary hemispheres. The photographs taken by the Hubble telescope show a much more colorful cosmos of colliding stars, pinwheel galaxies, vast clouds of interstellar gases, and terrifying events on the thresholds of black holes.

In *Star Wars* this vision of space hardly exists, and the stories entail commutes between worlds where the issues involve such earthbound notions as trade agreements, boycotts, embargoes, lines of royal succession, and secrets of parentage. What if a truly alien threat appeared? Some permutation of chaos theory that threatens the universe with destruction? A close call with a black hole? A kind of life-form that plays with the minds of its visitors (this idea has been explored by a lot of science fiction)? Meanwhile, electron microscopes are revealing the world of the unimaginably small. I hope the next *Star Wars* movies journey inside the heart of the atom, to where the microscopic soul mates of the Force live, and show us something of their existence.

Now that Lucas can show literally anything—now that digital magic has supplied a canvas for his imagination—perhaps it's time to widen the scope of the *Star Wars* saga beyond its space-opera parameters. The limitation of a lot of science fiction is self-imposed. The genre allows the consideration of literally anything we can imagine, and yet most science fiction, especially in the movies, involves human social structures seen against a cosmic backdrop. As the poet e. e. cummings once wrote, "Listen: there's a hell of a good universe next door; let's go."

Outrage in Toronto

Toronto, September 1998—It is unhip to admit to being offended by anything in the new movies, and indeed it's pretty hard to offend me, but a film named *Thursday* crossed the line this week at the Toronto Film Festival. Watching it, I felt outrage. I saw a movie so reprehensible I couldn't rationalize it using the standard critical language about style, genre, or irony. The people associated with it should be ashamed of themselves.

The film is the first work by Skip Woods, a young Texan whose style owes a great deal to Quentin Tarantino, and whose experience of the world seems based on the violent films he recycles and tries to surpass. There is a "plot," but essentially the film is a series of geek-show sequences in which characters are tortured, raped, murdered, and dismembered in between passages of sexist and racist language.

Here is a head count: innocent East Asian female grocery clerk, shot in cold blood after argument over coffee. Black cop, shot dead. Black Rastafarian heroin dealer plans to kill hero, but is overcome, bound with duct tape ("You guys always call it 'duck tape'"), and hung upside down in a garage.

Dominatrix in red leather minidress enters, tapes hero to chair, rapes him. Her head is blown off in midclimax by another visitor, who wants drugs and money, and retapes hero to chair, preparing to slice him with power saw. Hero will not bleed to death because visitor has brought along propane torch to cauterize wounds ("I once cut on a girl for sixteen hours before she died").

Hero frees self, knocks chain saw man unconscious, hangs him in garage. Cop arrives, is in on the deal, offers to fix everything if money is handed over. Is shown people hanging upside down in garage, shoots them without asking who they are, leaves. In the middle of this carnage, the dominatrix narrates a flashback about dope-smoking black smack dealers who are gunned down by hero and friend, after which black girl enters room and is killed. (A later flashback doubles back to explain that the girl was eight months pregnant.) The dialogue is heavy with the n-word and its usual satellites. The n-word is no longer neutralized by being used primarily by blacks, but is used by whites among themselves.

I don't object to these events in the abstract (any subject matter can be appropriate for a film), but to their tone. The film expects audiences to process the sad images through filters of irony—it trusts they'll evade a moral response by using a shield of laughter.

The tortured and peculiar festival program notes for *Thursday*, written by Noah Cowan, who introduced the film, speak of "a streak of 'white rage'—not racist reaction, but the desperation of those (largely white) newly enriched Americans to preserve their economic place at any cost—and a rigid ethical structure that would please any Talmudic scholar."

I will save the scholars to analyze Cowan's comments themselves. But after seeing *Thursday*, I wonder: What are these characters raging about or against? No one's done anything to them. They're the murderers and torturers. Their "economic place" has been attained by selling drugs and stealing. And we will need to call that scholar back in to explain why it is not racist (in this film, and *Very Bad Things*, which Cowan also mentions) to blow away virtually every black, Asian, or Indian character without, for the most part, establishing them as anything more than nonwhite targets.

In the question-and-answer session after the screening, the Toronto audience, apparently unshockable, opened by reverently asking Woods the usual boilerplate questions, such as, "Did the actors do a lot of improvisation in the movie?" A woman said, "I've seen women raped in a lot of movies, but I can't recall seeing a man before." Applause, as if the cinematic rape scorecard had been evened. "I think that scene was easier for Paulina than for Tom," Woods said. Laughter.

I should have kept my mouth shut. The proper forum for a critic is in a review. But the Q&A session came to a close without a single question that seemed aware of the moral issues raised by the film.

I heard myself asking Woods: "Do you have any insights about black people that have not been borrowed from drug movies?"

"I don't think I understand the question," he said.

"How simple can I make it?" I asked, and rephrased it. His answer touched briefly on the fact that "everybody knows" Rastafarians control a lot of the heroin trade ("Well, not all Rastafarians," he amended), and then he went on to explain that, anyway, the black drug dealers were only seen in a flashback narrated by the woman, and we have no way of knowing if her story was true or not. With a hairsplitting evasion like that, Woods is squirming free. The fact, of course, is that images on a screen have reality whether or not they are "true."

"Hey, it's your movie," an audience member shouted encouragingly to Woods. But no, it isn't. Once the director releases a film, it is the audience's movie, to embrace, reject, and think about as it chooses.

My revulsion wasn't just about the portrayal of blacks. It was about the cheapness with which all human life was portrayed—and about the movie's confidence that an audience in the age of irony would find it uncool to be offended. There was a passage of dialogue midway in this film that was so vile and cruel, I found my temples pounding. Will someone boo or hiss, I wondered? Then came a cheap, throwaway laugh line, and the audience gratefully laughed: See, it was all a joke.

One audience member said the movie "blew me away" like Quentin Tarantino's *Reservoir Dogs* (a much better film). Quentin Tarantino is a great director and *Pulp Fiction* was the best film of its year, but he has set loose the junior carrion hounds of Hollywood. They don't understand that it's not what a movie is about, but how it's about it. Tarantino, a master of tone and style, makes movies with an attitude toward risky subject matter; he understands, shapes, and redeems it. These New Geeks make movies that simply exploit it: They make depravity into a stand-up routine.

Godard said the way to criticize a movie is to make another movie. I am grateful to Skip Woods for one thing. All week I have been grappling with my thoughts about Todd Solondz's *Happiness*, the most controversial film at Toronto and Telluride (and Cannes) this year. *Thursday* snapped *Happiness* into perspective for me, helping me to see that Solondz is a genuine artist, that he earns his right to his subject matter by the skill with which he frames it and the thoughtfulness that underlies it.

On the way out of the theater, a woman informed me that I was "a real a——" for speaking out. For her to sit approvingly through *Thursday* and then find my statement offensive provides, I think, a scary measure of her values. Outside in the night air, other audience members caught up with me on the sidewalk and said they agreed with me. They'd been thinking some of the same things, they said. But they hadn't wanted to offend anyone.

Notes on the New Geek Cinema

Toronto, September 1998—Toronto was an edgy festival for people like myself who are convinced that anything can theoretically be a legitimate subject for a film. Movies about the Holocaust, child abuse, rape, and reckless murder have had audiences cringing and critics embroiled in nose-to-nose debates in the lobbies. The director John Waters has coined a term for them: Feel-Bad Comedies. So have I: The New Geek Cinema.

There are those who think some subjects should be forbidden. My belief is: If a film is going to consider areas that are dangerous or fraught with emotion, then it has to convince the audience it has the right. It can do that seriously, or with humor, or with intelligence or satire—but it has to earn its way. It can't just dine out on controversy.

My thoughts on the most extreme example of this new genre, *Thursday,* are in the previous essay. Here are notes on other films that are opening soon:

—*Happiness,* by Todd Solondz, is the most controversial film of the year. It is about the messy and sordid private lives of several lonely people, who seek happiness in ways they would not want you to know about. In the most talked-about scene, a father who is a pedophile (he has assaulted a friend of his young son) engages in a serious and honest discussion with his son, in which he fully answers every question about what he has done, and why.

—*Very Bad Things,* by Peter Berg, is about five friends who go to Vegas on a bachelor party. They get high on booze and coke, and one of their number, while assaulting a call girl in the bathroom, violently throws her against a wall. A metal clothes hook penetrates her brain. When a security guard comes to investigate, he's stabbed to death with a corkscrew. The men decide to cover up the deaths and bury the bodies in the desert. There is an arguably unnecessary conversation identifying some of the killers as Jews; the victims are an Asian and a black.

—*Apt Pupil,* by Bryan Singer *(The Usual Suspects),* is about a high school kid (Brad Renfro) who realizes an old man (Ian McKellen) is in fact a Nazi death camp murderer. Threatening blackmail, he forces the old man to tell him "what it was like." During the course of the film, the old man, who harbors great rages, attempts to throw a neighbor's cat into a lighted gas oven (he may succeed; the film's shifty editing seems to have it both ways). There is no indication that the boy is horrified by the man's Nazi past; he is more like a fascinated voyeur.

I should add that *Very Bad Things* is intended as a comedy. *Apt Pupil,* based on a Stephen King novella, plays as a horror film. *Happiness* cannot easily be categorized, but I think it stands above the other films, not with them. (Two other new films that are superficially similar, *Clay Pigeons* and *Home Fries,* are more traditional character-driven comedy thrillers that contain a lot of gore but stay within generally acceptable boundaries.)

All of these films owe something to John Carpenter's *Halloween* (1978), an enormous success that suggested a way into Hollywood for unknown young directors. If you don't have major stars and you don't have a big budget, then the genre itself can be your selling point. Horror films, like sex films, do not depend on marquee names. The content itself is the star.

Horror as a genre has been expanded, in some of these films, by a mean streak of cruelty, masked as irony. Once horror films sympathized with victims who were being threatened. Then they started using point-of-view shots to identify with the slashers, instead of the victims. In recent years there are two more refinements: (1) a single victim is not enough, and most of the movies string together snuff scenes like an all-hit radio format; and (2) there is a fascination with bizarre kinds of pain and torture not seen since the Marquis de Sade on a good day.

Combine these ingredients with the two most easily assimilated trademarks of Quentin Tarantino (colorfully arcane and vulgar dialogue, and labyrinthine plotting) and you have the elements that the New Geeks are exultantly recycling.

What some of these directors do not seem to realize is that *films are really about something.* They are not just exercises in style. Not all racism, women-hating, and monstrous torture can be cloaked in the forgiving veil of irony. The New Geeks see the surfaces of Tarantino, and do not begin to guess the depths.

Having been through *Pulp Fiction* twice on a shot-by-shot basis over a period of days with audiences at the Universities of Colorado and Virginia, I can tell you that his film contains three crucial elements many of the others lack: three-dimensional characters, comedy that undercuts violence instead of feeding on it, and a quality of redemption.

The characters in *Pulp Fiction* and the gentler *Jackie Brown* are people with heft and depth, who get involved in violence for reasons that are made clear. The characters in *Thursday* and *Very Bad Things* are not people at all, but carriers for behavior.

Say what you will about the violence in *Pulp Fiction,* the characters are mostly horrified by it, and the humor is in their reactions (as in the overdose sequence). In many of the geek films, the intermediate level has been eliminated, and the violence *itself* is supposed to be funny.

In the New Geek Cinema, victory is the only redemption. At the end of these films, the living are the winners, and dead are the losers, and victory consists of getting away with everything. Period.

Of the films I've mentioned here, the one that best understands what it is doing and incorporates a moral vision is Todd Solondz's *Happiness.* It has probably been attacked more than the others, but it's the one that faces up to the consequences of its content and has a genuine sympathy for most of its characters. The others, to one degree or another, raise disturbing questions. *Thursday* crosses the line, and a person of healthy sensibility should, I believe, be appalled by it.

As these films fan out into theaters, it will be interesting to see how they are received. My guess is that the most extreme films will do the best, and the more challenging ones, like Happiness, may have a harder time of it. People can absorb a great deal of cruelty and inhumanity as long as they're not required to think about it or make any moral judgments. As the twentieth century has proven.

Celebrating the Master of Cinema

August 13, 1999—Nineteen years after his death, he remains as famous as any director in movie history—even Steven Spielberg. Other directors have had their films remade, but only Alfred Hitchcock made one so monumental that another director, a good one, actually tried to duplicate it, shot by shot. Gus Van Sant's *Psycho* (1998) was a bad idea, but it's the thought that counts.

Hitchcock, who was born a century ago today, remains not only the Master of Suspense but a grandmaster of the cinema, whose films are so distinctive that anyone familiar with his work can spot one after just a few shots.

Hitchcock was content, with very few exceptions, to make films about crime and guilt. There are no philosophical statements in his work, except ironic ones. Nothing is ever taken quite seriously. He used big stars, flamboyant locations, audacious camera strategies. By making a cameo appearance near the beginning of almost all of his films, he became personally famous at a time when most people never ever thought about a film's director. When most serious directors scorned television, he became even more famous with a weekly half hour program, *Alfred Hitchcock Presents.* How well-known did he become? Using only a few curved lines, he was able to draw a caricature of himself that is instantly recognizable.

This case history would seem to add up to a man who was famous in his time but is now perhaps half-scorned, half-forgotten, past his sell-by date (the evolution of Cecil B. deMille's reputation comes to mind). But Hitchcock's stature is as great as it ever was. Witness the controversy over the recent poll by *Sight and Sound,* the British film magazine, which asked directors to vote on Hitchcock's ten best films. There was outrage when the list did not include *Rebecca, Strangers on a Train,* and *Rear Window.* And for that matter, where were *Suspicion* and *Spellbound*? (The top ten: *Psycho, Vertigo, Notorious, The Birds, North by Northwest, Shadow of a Doubt, Foreign Correspondent, Frenzy, The Lady Vanishes,* and *Marnie.*) Name another director who could make *Strangers on a Train* and not have it ranked as one of his best ten films.

Hitchcock's favorite plot is often summarized as: the Innocent Person Wrongly Accused. From Cary Grant in *North by Northwest* to Ingrid Bergman in *Notorious,* his characters were often blameless but seemed guilty from a certain point of view. In explaining this obsession, Hitchcock never tired of telling the story of how, when he was a young boy who had misbehaved, his father sent him down to a London police station with a note asking the desk sergeant to lock him up to teach him a lesson. Years later, Hitchcock said that on his tombstone he wanted these words: *You see what can happen to you if you are not a good boy.*

Born in London, Hitchcock broke into silent films as a gofer, artist, and writer. The first of his own films, *The Pleasure Garden* was shot in Germany at the height of Expressionism, and throughout his career, he liked strange camera angles, dramatic shadows, weird juxtapositions, unexpected visual revelations. His first big hits were *The Man Who Knew Too Much* (1934) and *The 39 Steps* (1935), and after the huge success of *The Lady Vanishes* (1938), he was soon summoned to Hollywood by producer David O. Selznick. Their 1940 production of *Rebecca* won the Oscar as best picture; ironically, it was a macabre romance and did not have the kind of suspense for which Hitchcock was most famous.

The great stars dropped everything to work for Hitchcock. James Stewart and Cary Grant made four films with him. Ingrid Bergman, Joseph Cotten, Joan Fontaine, Henry Fonda, Joel McCrea, Grace Kelly, Kim Novak, and Paul Newman appeared in his pictures. He liked to use a big star, he said, "because you can leave out the first reel, which establishes the character; the audience already knows him." He liked cool blonds (Novak, Kelly, Eva Marie Saint, Tippi Hedren, Janet Leigh) and took delight in disheveling them. His male leads didn't play rugged but vulnerable, and it took courage for Stewart to display the weaknesses of the wheelchair-bound hero in *Rear Window* and the erotically obsessed man in *Vertigo.*

Fascinated by the technical side of the movies, Hitchcock worked meticulously on his scripts, hiring artists to draw storyboards of every shot; he claimed when the screenplay was finished, it was all downhill. He set himself technical challenges. *Lifeboat* (1944) took place entirely within a small boat, and *Rope* (1948) was knotted together out of unbroken ten-minute takes, so it looked like the whole movie was made in one shot. *Rear Window* (1954) gave Stewart a pair of binoculars and, in a virtuoso sequence, had him piece together a possible murder out of clues glimpsed through windows. In *Psycho* (1960), Hitchcock played with audience expectations by focusing entirely on a big star (Leigh) before killing her off a third of the way through the movie.

Psycho has been called the most influential of his films, ushering in the current period of screen violence. His best film was *Vertigo* (1958); it contains a scene where Novak emerges from a ghostly green mist while Stewart watches her. In his face is exaltation: He has re-created the image of the lost woman he is obsessed with. In her face is pain: She is not only the image of that woman, but in fact *was* that woman, a fact she cannot reveal—because, having cruelly deceived him, she loves him.

The moral and psychological ambiguities of that scene are so complex that you can only cringe, or shiver, or pity them both.

In Memoriam

Lord Grade

Lord Lew Grade, a titan of the British entertainment industry, died in London, Sunday, December 13, 1998, at the age of ninety-one. For many years he was a colorful fixture at the Cannes Film Festival, where after the box-office failure of his film Raise the Titanic! *he held a press conference to announce, "It would have been less costly to lower the ocean." This is a memory from the early 1980s, when Lord Grade's path crossed that of Billy (Silver Dollar) Baxter, another Cannes legend, famed for calling all waiters "Irving." It is reprinted from my book* Two Weeks in the Midday Sun *(Andrews McMeel Publishing, 1987).—Roger Ebert*

I still do not fully understand how Billy Baxter convinced Lord Lew Grade, then the millionaire boss of England's largest film conglomerate, to take Billy and a group of his friends on the inaugural cruise of his lordship's brand-new yacht. But there are a lot of things I do not understand about Silver Dollar Baxter, one of them being how a character from out of the pages of Damon Runyan could survive and even flourish in these pale days of ordinary people.

Silver Dollar Baxter got his nickname because for many years he arrived at Cannes with 2,000 American silver dollars, which he bestowed as tips. "You think this is something?" he once explained. "You shoulda seen what I paid in air freight to get them over here. I gotta send them in advance, because you try to get through customs with 2,000 silver dollars, you're gonna be explaining things for hours. My banker handles it."

"Do you call your banker Irving?"

"Yeah. Irving Trust."

Baxter's silver dollars are still held as lucky charms in the pockets of many of the waiters in Cannes, who have waited in vain in recent years for his return. At the Majestic, he brought excitement to the room.

Even during the darkest days of the twenty-five-cent franc, when a round of drinks at the Majestic could easily run $100, Billy grabbed the checks. So great was his generosity that certain other customers began to take his hospitality for granted and would sign his room number to their bar bills. To stop such fraud, Billy appeared at the 1982 festival with a small rubber stamp, which reproduced his signature and added underneath, "None genuine without this mark."

Billy's genius was to boldly cut through bureaucracy with his own loud personality. In 1980, he pulled off his single greatest stunt by issuing his own credentials to the festival. This was in connection with a Cannes television special that he had convinced Lord Grade to underwrite.

"These guys over here are all hung up on anything that looks official," he said. "They issue you a permit to take a crap. But half of the guards can't read, and besides, they don't got the time, because there's always a riot going on."

Taking advantage of this situation, Billy had a New York job shop print up dozens of official-looking credentials for the "World International Television Network" ("I shoulda added 'Global,'" he moaned). He attached the photographs of his friends to the cards, had the cards laminated and strung them on a chain so they could hang them around their necks. Only guards with sharp eyes might be expected to read the personal details on the cards and learn that each and every one of Billy's friends was exactly the same height, weight, and age, and had the same hair and eye color. Billy signed all of the credentials himself. "What this document certifies," he chortled, "is that it is worn by the bearer." I still have mine. It got me into screenings where the guards were waving away people with genuine tickets.

Billy had a genius for sweeping up people who had no idea who he was and introducing them to other people he wanted to meet. "Sir Lord!" he boomed one night to Lord Grade, "meet Miss Boop-a-Doop-a-Dee from Venezuela." Instead of remembering names, he often simply improvised them, along with identities, credits, and national origin. "She directed the winning film in last year's festival. That's why she gets to come to the bar in her underwear."

Miss Boop-a-Doop-a-Dee was, in fact, Edy Williams, the starlet who has become famous for traveling all the way to Cannes every year to take off her clothes while standing in the public fountains. Lord Grade looked prepared to believe that she was a director from Venezuela. Indeed, he looked prepared to believe almost anything about her. The only thing the seventy-five-year-old lord couldn't believe was that he had walked into the Majestic bar.

"Irving!" Baxter shouted, beginning his unvarying litany. "Brang 'em on! Johnny Walker! Red Label! Generous portion! Clean glass! Pas de soda! Pas de ice! And clean up this shit!"—his arm indicating a glass table piled high with Xeroxes of Edy's latest press clippings. Baxter settled down next to Grade, accepted the offer of one of the lord's foot-long cigars, rubber-stamped the bill, and fell into deep conversation.

Whatever Baxter said to Lord Grade that night was sufficient, apparently, for the lord to agree that Baxter and his friends were the natural choices as guests for the inaugural cruise of his yacht, scheduled in two days.

I went along on that cruise, and the memory of it is still a wonderment to me. Spare me the stories of the great con men of the past; I ate Lord Grade's fresh strawberries and listened to his stories because Silver Dollar Baxter had worked his magic.

The morning after whispering in his lordship's ear and rubber-stamping his bar bill, Billy settled down in the Majestic bar to compose a personal note to the lord. "Dear Lord Lew," he wrote, "Here is a list of the people you should invite to your yacht on Sunday. All good people. Signed, B.B." He licked the flap of the envelope and sealed it.

"Signed with the sign of the Double B," he said. "My personal voucher that his lordship is gonna enjoy their acquaintanceship."

The next morning, Billy was pacing nervously up and down in front of the Majestic, scanning the boulevard for signs of Grade's rented limousines.

"Rex Reed originally said he doesn't know if he could make it," Baxter said. "He says he's gotta interview Monica Vitti, for chrissakes. I told him he can interview her any year but this is his lordship's inaugural cruise."

"Do you mean the yacht hasn't sailed before?"

"Naw. It's twenty years old—back when they made real yachts. I mean, Lord Lew bought it yesterday, so he hasn't seen it yet. We're all gonna be walking up and down the harbor, looking for the right boat, so anyway, it's nine o'clock this morning and my phone rings, and it's Sexy Rexy wanting to know when we sail. Here come the limos now."

We all piled in—the usual crew of film critics like Kathleen Carroll, Rex Reed, Andrew Sarris, Molly Haskell, Alexander Walker, and Richard and Mary Corliss, all ready for our audience with the man who had made *Voyage of the Damned, Jesus of Nazareth,* and *Love and Bullets.* It was possible that not a single one of us had ever admired any film Grade had produced.

We drove down the Croisette and twenty miles along the coast, past the Hotel du Cap d'Antibes, and toward the yacht harbor at Antibes. Billy provided a running commentary: "In terms of the status order, first you got the guys in town in rooms costing merely $250 a day. Then you got the guys out here, who are so big they don't even go into town. To come all the way to the Cannes Film Festival and never even set foot in Cannes—that's class. Then what you get, up at the top of the heap, is guys like Lord Lew, who buy a yacht for a few million and anchor it offshore, but close enough in so the big shots at the Hotel Cap can see it and eat their hearts out. You get any bigger than that, you're Niarchos, you float in with your private navy. Look at that!" He pointed to an elegant villa at the edge of the sea. "That used to be Jack Warner's house. Now they're having picnics on his private beach. He'd kill 'em!"

The limos pulled up to the harbor, and there was Grade, pacing nervously by his gangplank. He was wearing gray flannel trousers, a blue blazer, and a Panama hat. In his hand was one of the $25 cigars he fancies from the vaults of Davidoff's on Jermyn Street.

"I was growing nervous," Grade said. "I thought perhaps you hadn't been able to find the yacht."

"You kidding?" Baxter asked. "A yacht this size, you could fire off a machine gun."

Baxter led his parade of film critics aboard,

and held an inspection of the ship's crew, which was standing at attention. "Any of you guys named Irving?" he asked. He passed out free flight bags that said "American Express Travel Service" on them.

For an hour or two, we wandered the yacht while it sailed near the shore from Antibes to Cannes. Grade spoke of his latest project to Richard Corliss: "*The Muppet Movie.* I have the biggest stars. Charles Bronson and Miss Piggy." Then it was time for luncheon. A table in the shade was spread with linen and covered with cold smoked salmon, rare roast beef, iced lobster tail, caviar, salade mesclun, and fresh strawberry tarts. Far away across the blue waters of the Cote d'Azur, the hapless tenants of the Hotel du Cap shaded their eyes on the verandas of their thousand-dollar rooms and squinted enviously at Lord Lew, rocking at anchor.

"I have been thinking," Grade told us, "of writing my autobiography. My life has been filled with coincidences. When I began in London, for example, I had an office across from the Palladium. Now I own the Palladium."

"What an amazing coincidence," Rex Reed said.

"I began as a dancer," Grade said. "I did a double act with my brother, Lord Delfont. I was a natural at the Charleston, but the others I had to finesse. It was called 'eccentric dancing.' Like this." He stood up, clasped his hands above his head, and bumped to an imaginary rhythm.

"We played Paris, Germany . . . we were always broke. Those were the days. I remember I was in love with twins. Two lovely girls. Dancers. I couldn't make up my mind between them." He sighed at lost opportunities.

Luncheon drew to a leisurely close, punctuated by tarts. I dozed off in the midday sun, and was awakened by a quickening tempo in Lord Grade's voice.

"Television—television!" he was saying. "What an impact. With one successful program, we reach ten times as many people as with a hit movie. My most successful television program was, of course, *Jesus of Nazareth,* directed for me by Franco Zeffirelli. Do you know that a survey was taken of 6,525 people. Forty percent of them said they had learned the most about Jesus from my program. Twenty-one percent named the Bible. Thirty percent named the church."

"Let's see," Rex Reed said. "That still leaves 9 percent undecided."

Lord Grade sighted sternly down his cigar at Reed.

"The survey," he said, "was taken before the reruns."

Stanley Kubrick

Stanley Kubrick, one of the greatest of film directors, and perhaps the most independent and self-contained, is dead at seventy. The creator of *2001: A Space Odyssey* died early Sunday morning, March 7, 1999, at his country home north of London.

Even in a century when film directors fashioned images as strong-willed visionaries, Kubrick stood out from the crowd. He became legendary for his total independence, his disdain for studio interference, and his indifference to publicity and "image." He made great films entirely outside conventional commercial formulas.

At the time of his death he had just completed *Eyes Wide Shut,* an erotic thriller starring Tom Cruise and Nicole Kidman, who devoted more than a year of their careers to his exacting demands. Kubrick had been working on it for a long time, brushing off Warner Bros.' hopes that it could be released last year.

But "he had finished it," his friend Joe Hyams told me. "A print was shown on Thursday night in New York to just four people—Tom, Nicole, and (studio executives) Terry Semel and Bob Daley. They loved it."

Kubrick's death "was a bolt from the blue," said Hyams, an executive vice president at the studio. "He had been working every day, those eighteen-hour days. He was such a perfectionist." Pending a coroner's report, Hyams said, it was assumed that the cause of death was a heart attack while the director slept.

In recent decades Kubrick's contract with Warner Bros. specified simply that he would make a film of his own choice, at a cost to be determined, and the studio would release it exactly as he supplied it to them. Even at a time when powerful directors have the right of "final cut," this arrangement was extraordinary; at Warner's, only Kubrick and Clint Eastwood enjoyed it. "Whatever those guys want, they get," Hyams said.

Kubrick was rarely photographed and had

not given an interview in years. He did most of his business dealings by phone. His estate in the English countryside included editing and sound facilities, and he was famous for creating his own locations instead of traveling to them; his Vietnam movie *Full Metal Jacket* was shot entirely in England, and of course so was *2001*, which took place in space.

Some have called *2001* the greatest film of the century. Certainly it was the most inimitable—an epic with little dialogue for much of its length, special effects that have not been surpassed for their grandeur, an enigmatic ending that is still argued about, and human characters so wooden they were upstaged by a talking computer. When orbiting American astronauts were asked what the view was like, they replied, "Like in *2001*."

Kubrick worked slowly in recent years, marching to the sound of his own drum. His prestige was so great that he could command the services of top stars like Cruise and Jack Nicholson, who put other projects on hold to accommodate Kubrick's lengthy shooting schedules and demands for many takes of every shot.

Matthew Modine, who starred in Kubrick's *Full Metal Jacket*, told me that after he questioned the director's high number of takes, "He told me that on *The Shining* Jack Nicholson would arrive on the set sort of knowing his lines. After six takes he would know them. After twenty takes he would know what they meant. After fifty takes he would start to play around with them in interesting ways. And after one hundred takes, he began to really feel them."

"He was the ultimate perfectionist," recalled the director Gregory Nava, who consulted with Kubrick on the Spanish-language version of *Eyes Wide Shut*. "He would call a dozen times a day. No detail was too small."

Indeed, Kubrick was said to have his own computer database of the theaters where his movies were shown, and it was not unheard-of for the phone in a projection booth to ring if Kubrick heard reports that his work was being shown out of focus or at the wrong brightness.

"I screamed for months and months," Shelley Duvall once told me about her work in Kubrick's *The Shining*. "I thought I'd lose my mind. He wanted to get it just right. There was a scene where the camera preceded (actor) Roberts Blossom in a long tracking shot around three legs of a hotel corridor, and he did it maybe ninety times—because he wanted the crosshairs in the viewfinder to be exactly on the actor's forehead at every moment."

Born in the Bronx in 1928, Kubrick was a fast starter; he got his first job, as a staff photographer for *Look* magazine, when he was only seventeen, and had made two short documentaries by the age of twenty-two. Kubrick's desire for control may have had its beginnings then: Glossy magazine photographers in those days were free-ranging buccaneers who called their own shots, and Kubrick brought the same approach to his first two features, which he financed himself: *Fear and Desire* (1953), which he later suppressed, and *Killer's Kiss* (1955).

Kiss has its admirers, but with his next two films Kubrick emerged as a distinctive talent. *The Killing* (1956) starred Sterling Hayden in the story of a racetrack robbery, and *Paths of Glory* (1957) starred Kirk Douglas in what is considered one of the greatest of antiwar films. Three years later, Douglas insisted on Kubrick as director of the epic *Spartacus* (1960), which Kubrick later said he disliked, although it has many defenders.

Kubrick moved to England in 1961, partly to isolate himself from Hollywood interference, and in 1962 made *Lolita*, with James Mason, Shelley Winters, Peter Sellers, and Sue Lyon as the "nymphet" of the title. Many believed the Vladimir Nabokov novel could not be filmed; Kubrick made the heroine fifteen instead of twelve, and had a critical and popular success.

But it was with *Dr. Strangelove* (1963) that he had his greatest early hit. Starring Sellers again, in three roles, and Hayden as "General Jack D. Ripper," the film treated nuclear war as fodder for a black comedy. It still seems fresh and new today.

The film's success allowed Kubrick to write his own ticket for the rest of his career, and in 1968 he produced his masterpiece, *2001: A Space Odyssey*, which is on most lists of the ten greatest films. Its success was all the more extraordinary because it was plotless—a frankly experimental film that traced man's evolution from the first tool-using apes to the ultimate tool—a spaceship to escape our birth planet.

Kubrick's *A Clockwork Orange* (1971) starred Malcolm McDowell as a violent lout in a fearsome world of the near future; its prophetic vision was so disturbing that the movie is banned in Britain to this day. *Barry Lyndon* (1975), a period piece based on a Thackeray novel and starring Ryan O'Neal, was one of his less successful films. Then came Nicholson in the horror film *The Shining* (1980), based on a Stephen King novel and including the star's trademark line, "Heeeere's Johnny!"

Full Metal Jacket (1987) began with marine basic training (he hired a real drill instructor, R. Lee Ermey, to play himself) and continued with combat footage set in Vietnam. And then there was a long hiatus as the director worked on various projects that never went before the cameras. One, titled *A.I.*, was about artificial intelligence, and would have returned to the world of HAL 9000, the computer in *2001*.

Now there is one more title: *Eyes Wide Shut.* Filmed in complete secrecy, it is said to be unusually explicit in its sex scenes. Before Thursday's screenings, Warner's executives had seen no footage except for a two-minute trailer that was so bold, I was told, that one exec said, "I don't know whether to be angry or relieved that Stanley left off the studio logo."

At a time when major movies can cost $50,000 to $100,000 a day to shoot, Kubrick's shooting schedules of many months were possible because he knew exactly what he wanted, and used the smallest possible crews.

"He doesn't believe in waste," Modine told me. "On *Full Metal Jacket,* sometimes he had only six people. One day he had a set lit, and he told the electrician, 'Okay, this set is lit and it's not going to change, so I don't need you here anymore.' So he sent the guy over to work on the wiring on his house."

Akira Kurosawa

Akira Kurosawa, one of the greatest of all film directors, died September 6, 1998, in Tokyo. He was eighty-eight. His later years were spent in near-blindness, and yet he continued to work, sketching scenes with the paper only inches from his eyes, and his final film was made only five years ago.

Of the postwar giants who redefined the art of the cinema, what other director, save perhaps Sweden's Ingmar Bergman, could claim so many masterpieces? The titles are like a roll call of greatness: *Stray Dog, Rashomon, Ikiru, The Seven Samurai, Throne of Blood, The Hidden Fortress, The Idiot, Yojimbo, High and Low, Red Beard, Dersu Uzala, Kagemusha, Ran,* and many more.

He combined two qualities not always found together in filmmakers: He was a visual stylist and a thoughtful humanist. His films had a daring, exhilarating visual freedom, and a heart of deep human understanding. He often made movies about heroes, but their challenge was not simply to win; it was to make the right ethical choice.

His films fall into three overlapping categories. There were the samurai dramas, steeped in Japanese history, like *The Seven Samurai* (remade by Hollywood as *The Magnificent Seven*) and *The Hidden Fortress* (which inspired the characters R2D2 and C3PO in *Star Wars*). There were the literary adaptations, from sources like Shakespeare and Dostoyevsky but also from American crime writers. And there were the contemporary stories, about ordinary people faced with ethical dilemmas.

Few Japanese directors would have thought to adapt one of Ed McBain's crime stories, for example, but Kurosawa, reading *King's Ransom,* found the materials for one of his most challenging films, *High and Low* (1962). A wealthy man is told his son has been kidnapped. He must sell everything to raise the ransom. Then it's discovered that the kidnapper mistakenly kidnapped the son of the millionaire's chauffeur instead. Is this boy worth the same ransom? As the eyes of the millionaire and the workingman meet in a shot of stunning power, Kurosawa confronts the question of whether all lives are equal.

The same question was approached in another way in *Kagemusha* (1980), about a thief who looks exactly like a warlord who has just died. To keep the death a secret, the lord's men install the double in his position. To have the power, the position, the costumes, and the riches of a lord, but not to be the lord, is the dilemma of the "shadow warrior."

And consider the beloved *Ikiru* (1952), in which an old man works at a meaningless job as head of a city bureau. Told he will die, he passes through suicidal depression and drunken escape before finally determining to accomplish one final thing, a children's playground, to give his life meaning.

What does a man's life mean? Kurosawa

himself faced that question in the 1970s, when, after the commercial failure of *Red Beard* (1965) and *Dodes-ka-den* (1970), he was unable to find financing for new films. He attempted suicide. Then, in 1975, Russian funds were found for his only non-Japanese film, *Dersu Uzala,* about a friendship between a famous explorer and a simple guide. It won the Oscar for Best Foreign Film (his second, after *Rashomon*), and yet still he could not find funds to work in Japan, where he was considered too old and noncommercial. Finally in 1980, with backing from American directors who admired him, he made *Kagemusha,* and in 1985 he made *Ran,* his adaptation of *King Lear,* which won a special award at Cannes.

Those two late epics are among the most ravishing visual achievements in the history of the cinema. Individual shots—troops pouring down a flight of steps like water finding its level, or a horse dying on a battlefield, or the fading old king surrounded by the bright flags of his court—summarize the whole tone and feeling of the stories.

Throughout his career Kurosawa was criticized in Japan as "too Western." The criticism came because he often used Western stories and music, and also, said the critic Donald Richie, because his films were the statements of an individual and did not remain within the genres beloved in a conformist society. His samurai films portrayed individuals faced with choices rather than loyal functionaries.

Kurosawa was born in 1910, and his taste was shaped when he studied Western art in school. He emerged as a director in the postwar years, at first with routine work approved by the American occupation authorities, and then, starting with *Stray Dog* (1949) and *Rashomon* (1950), entirely on his own. He was known for his long associations with the actors Toshiro Mifune *(Rashomon, Seven Samurai, Throne of Blood, Yojimbo,* and *Red Beard),* and Takashi Shimura, who gained immortality as the bureaucrat in *Ikiru.*

Kurosawa's late films were the meditations of an old man at peace with himself. There was *Akira Kurosawa's Dreams* (1990), a series of eight short stories suggested by his fantasies, and *Rhapsody in August* (1991), an attempt to deal with the bomb; he created a Japanese-American character (Richard Gere) to embody Kurosawa's belief that the war took place between governments, not people.

His last film was *Madayayo* (1993). It has never been distributed in America, but was shown here once, in March 1998 at Facets Cinematheque in Chicago. It tells of a beloved old professor whose students gather once a year for his birthday. He drinks a ritual glass of beer at the parties and then shouts out, "Not yet!"—because he is not yet dead.

"Take myself, subtract movies, and the remainder is zero," Kurosawa once said. And in an interview in 1993, after *Madayayo,* he said: "I hope that all the people who have seen this picture will leave the theater feeling refreshed, with broad smiles on their faces." That could be his epitaph.

Roy Rogers

I can't remember the name of a single Roy Rogers movie. That's because I saw some of them before I was able to read, and all of them before I started paying attention to titles. They weren't movies. They were that part of life that was known as the Saturday matinee.

This was at the Princess Theater on Main Street in Urbana, Illinois. It cost nine cents to get in. For your money you got two features, five color cartoons (they were always called "color" cartoons), a newsreel, coming attractions, a chapter of a serial, and the ads for the Urbana Pure Milk Co. and the Busey Bank. Four hours later you were disgorged into the daylight again.

One of the movies was always a Western. It usually starred Roy Rogers, Gene Autry, Hopalong Cassidy, Rex Allen, or those two lesser heroes whose tastes seem ever more peculiar with the passing of the years, Lash LaRue and Whip Wilson.

"Hoppy" went through a period of enormous popularity, but year in and year out, Roy Rogers was the top choice, because he was King of the Cowboys. We knew all about him: how his palomino was named Trigger, his wife was named Dale Evans, and his dog was named Bullet (that was their relative order of importance).

Dale Evans was, by default, the Queen of the Cowgirls, and in my mind she ranked beside the Queen of England, who was the only other queen I had heard of—except, of course, for Mary, Queen of the May.

Roy Rogers always looked vaguely Asian to me. Something about his eyes: They were wise and serene, and they looked merry when he smiled. He had an open, happy face, and he never seemed to get as alarmed as Gene Autry, or as angry as Hoppy. Life was good for him. He sang a song, he palled around with Dale, he was friends with Gabby Hayes and the Sons of the Pioneers, and bad guys seemed relieved to surrender to him. Maybe they hoped he'd sing to them in jail.

The plots of those Saturday afternoon Westerns were utterly inconsequential, because we spent half of every movie fighting with each other and running back and forth to the rest room. We hated kisses, but Roy never kissed girls—just Trigger. We cheered when Roy's posses chased bad guys across the range. When we got outside, we made guns of our hands by pointing our fingers straight ahead and our thumbs straight up, and going "Pow! pow!" And when we ran, we slapped our thighs with our open palms, and that was supposed to symbolize riding a horse. I guess we were Roy, and our blue jeans were Trigger.

Roy Rogers lived on and on. His wife wrote best-sellers. His name was on a chain of restaurants. Sometimes you'd see him on television. When Trigger died, he had the horse stuffed, and I heard a story, possibly apocryphal, that he said, "When I die, I want to be stuffed and put right up there on Trigger." And Dale said, "Now, Roy, don't you go gettin' any ideas about me!"

I suppose in the next few days they'll show some old Roy Rogers movies on TV. If you watch one, notice how gentle it is, and how innocent. How little violence there is. How the action can come to a halt for a song around the old campfire: "Happy trails to you . . ."

Gene Siskel

For the first five years that we knew one another, Gene Siskel and I hardly spoke. Then it seemed like we never stopped. We began as film critics for the two morning papers in Chicago, both still in our twenties and eager to establish ourselves—preferably at the other's expense. When we were asked to work together on a TV show, we both said we'd rather do it with someone else. Anyone else.

At first the relationship on TV was edgy and uncomfortable. Our newspaper rivalry was always in the air between us. Gene liked to tell about the time he was taking a nap under a conference table at the television station, overheard a telephone conversation I was having with an editor, and scooped me on the story. I got scooped more than once; it really hurt in 1997 when he sat down to talk about the movies with Bill Clinton.

He considered himself a reporter as well as a critic, and he was one of the best I ever knew. It was typical of Gene that when he got interested in the Chicago Bulls, it wasn't just as a fan, but as an expert; he knew as much about the Bulls as most of the sportswriters who covered them. It was consistent with his reporter's orientation that some of his favorite films were documentaries, like *Hoop Dreams.*

After his surgery in May 1998, his first public appearance was at a Bulls game. It was important to him that he be there. And it was typical of Gene's determination that he returned to the job as soon as he could. Two weeks after his surgery, he was watching movies on tape in his hospital room and phoning in his reviews to *Siskel & Ebert.* Soon he was back in the show's balcony, and in print at the *Tribune* and *TV Guide,* and on the air at CBS.

Someone else might have taken a leave of absence then and there, but Gene worked as long as he could. Being a film critic was important to him. He liked to refer to his job as "the national dream beat," and say that in reviewing movies he was covering what people hoped for, dreamed about, and feared.

Because the movies could do such a powerful job of reaching into the minds and emotions of audiences, he took it personally when they disappointed him—when they were lazy and stupid. He told me about a proud moment as a father: He asked one of his daughters how she'd liked a movie, and she told him that, well, she didn't. "Some kids think they're supposed to be polite and just say they liked a film," he said, "but I've always told my children it's important to make up your own mind."

He was ferociously honest in his opinions. He didn't care about seeming fashionable. When he picked *Babe: Pig in the City* as the best movie of 1998, some people thought it was a strange choice. I didn't. The movie was on my top ten list, too, and I knew why Gene admired it: It was original, it was trying to do something new, it had been overlooked in the flood of more mainstream products, and it had something worthwhile to say. It stood for what he stood for.

When Gene saw a movie he really admired, he almost glowed. Toward the end of the screening of *Fargo,* he walked over to me in the dark and whispered, "This is why I go to the movies." When he saw a movie he hated, he liked to suggest that filmmakers ask themselves this question: "Is my film more interesting than a documentary of the same actors having lunch together?"

Gene kept private about the state of his health in the months after his surgery. I understood why. He wanted to protect his family from the attention that might result. He wanted the focus to remain on his film criticism, and although it was obvious sometimes that he walked slowly and was in pain, I never once heard him complain. He carried on with a bravery it is hard to imagine.

We did the TV show together for twenty-four years. It was a strange format: Two ordinary-looking guys from Chicago, sitting in a balcony talking about the movies. One question we were asked, again and again, was: "Do you really hate each other?" There were days at the beginning of our relationship when the honest answer sometimes was "yes." It was unnatural for two men to be rivals six days of the week and sit down together on the seventh. But over the years respect grew between us, and it deepened into friendship and love.

Telluride Film Festival

Telluride, Colorado—Most film festivals trumpet their offerings, bragging about their premieres and stars. The Telluride Film Festival treats its films like a poker player treats his hole cards. One imagines Bill Pence and Tom Luddy, the cofounders, looking at the programs from Montreal, Toronto, and Venice, and sneaking another peek at their hands.

Telluride never announces its schedule in advance. You have to fly to Denver, take a commuter flight to Montrose, and then drive ninety minutes into the Rocky Mountains, all on spec. When you get there, they tell you what they're showing. Usually it's something amazing.

It was at Telluride that I first saw *Sling Blade, Roger & Me, My Dinner with André, My Left Foot, The Crying Game, Au Revoir les Enfants, Reservoir Dogs,* and *Henry: Portrait of a Serial Killer.* But apart from the premieres, the festival devotes at least half of its screenings to tributes, revivals, discoveries, and silent films with live accompaniment. I know people who hardly even go to the new films at Telluride, figuring they can catch up with them later.

A few hints of the twenty-fifth anniversary program have leaked out, however. This year, one of the three winners of the Telluride Medal will be the actress Meryl Streep, whose autumn release *Dancing at Lughnasa* will be premiered there. I know this because I've been asked to do the Q&A with her onstage. The reedited *original* version of Orson Welles's *Touch of Evil,* which was canceled at Cannes because of the protests of Welles's daughter Beatrice, will be screened at Telluride. I know that because Jonathan Rosenbaum of the *Chicago Reader* was one of the expert consultants on the project.

King Vidor's silent classic *The Crowd* (1925) will be the silent film; I know that because *Variety* said so in its advance story, which also announced that this year's guest programmer will be the director Peter Bogdanovich. And I've heard that Stanley Kauffmann, the legendary film critic of *The New Republic,* will be there on the occasion of his fortieth anniversary with the magazine.

I can also predict that the great German director Werner Herzog will be in attendance, because he almost always is. When Pence and producer Tom Luddy cofounded the festival a quarter-century ago, Herzog was one of their first supporters, and in those early days, before screenings took every moment of the day and night, he ran an annual softball game.

In the early years Telluride was a tiny festival, with less than 1,000 people attending; now it has expanded into a small festival, with some 3,500 people expected. The crowds have outgrown the tiny Sheridan Opera House, the Nugget theater, the Community Center, the Mason's Hall, and Elks Park; now a new portable cinema is erected in the high school gym every year, complete with Dolby sound. But the town and the crowds are still small enough that you can count on running into almost everybody you know, and especially at the combination Labor Day picnic and panel discussion.

Of the festivals I attend, Cannes is the most important, Toronto is the most useful, and Telluride is the most fun. That's partly because of the spectacular setting in the mountains, partly because it's small, and mostly because Pence and Luddy program with such imagination. They've shown films that weren't supposed to exist and honored filmmakers who weren't thought to still be alive. Once they pulled off a double play, showing the long-lost *Napoleon* (1927) to its ninety-one-year-old director, Abel Gance. Screenings like that are worth driving up a mountain for.

Telluride Celebrates Twenty-five Years with Retrospectives

September 3, 1998—For its twenty-fifth anniversary celebration, which more or less coincides with the first century of film, the Telluride Film Festival is plunging gleefully into the past. Although there's the usual selection of premieres, at least half of the screenings this year are retrospectives: a look at 1928, the last great year of silent film; personal selections from the festival's guest programmers over the years; and a salute to black and white.

The festival was to get rolling with a tribute to Meryl Streep and the premiere of John Boorman's new film *The General*, which won him the Best Director Award at Cannes. Also premiering Thursday: *I'm Losing You*, by Bruce Wagner, about the way they live now in Hollywood; Rolf de Heer's *Dance Me to My Song*, a film starring cerebral palsy patient Heather Rose in what is said to be a wrenching performance; and Todd Solondz's *Happiness*, one of the most controversial offerings at Cannes, about a group of depressed, solitary losers and their sometimes perverse searches for what they would define as happiness.

Streep's tribute comes a day before the premiere of her new film, *Dancing at Lughnasa*, based on Brian Friel's play about an Irish family in the 1930s. Pat O'Connor *(Circle of Friends)* directs. Streep has two much-heralded releases this fall, *Lughnasa* and *One True Thing*, about women who cope with bad times in radically different ways: one with almost biblical strength, the other through becoming a Martha Stewart clone. Either could win her an Oscar nomination.

The other tributes this year are to the great cinematographer Vittorio Storaro *(Apocalypse Now, The Last Emperor)* and Susumu Hani, the seventy-year-old Japanese director. The Telluride Silver Medallion will be presented to Stanley Kauffmann, observing his fortieth year at *The New Republic*.

This year's Telluride lineup is heavily influenced by nostalgia for the twenty-four remarkable festivals that went before. Former guest programmers have been asked to pick one film they'd like to see revived; the only requirement was that it be in black and white. Their choices range widely: Performance artist Laurie Anderson picks *Dial H-I-S-T-O-R-Y*, which combines Don DiLillo's prose with footage of skyjackings; experimental filmmaker Stan Brakhage (who will be honored with a documentary about his work) chooses Charles Laughton's surreal classic *The Night of the Hunter;* festival cofounder James Card chooses Ingmar Bergman's *Smiles of a Summer Night;* John Boorman, whose *The General* is about a man who bucks the IRA, chooses another film on the same theme, John Ford's *The Informer.*

This year's guest programmer, director Peter Bogdanovich, will show his 1971 documentary *Directed by John Ford*, lead a tribute to Ford's work, and also introduce a newly re-edited version of Orson Welles's *Touch of Evil*, which reflects the director's original ideas before the studio re-cut it.

Telluride usually programs something you are simply never going to be able to see anywhere else, and this year that would be the program hosted by filmmaker Murray Lerner about the ups and downs of 3-D films. The principles behind 3-D were known even before the movies began; the Steriopticon was a device that allowed viewers to peer at photos that seemed to be in 3-D. There have been booms in 3-D movies over the years, mostly notably in the early 1950s and 1970s, but mostly it's been bust—the viewers ultimately find it a nuisance. Now the new IMAX 3-D process, startlingly good, may resurrect the technique again.

It's rare to see silent films in 35mm, and this year's festival offers some masterpieces: not only the tribute to great films of 1928, the last year before sound *(The Crowd, The Wedding March, The Last Command)*, but also a restored version of Sergei Eisenstein's 1924 debut film *Strike*, with a live accompaniment by the Alloy Orchestra, annual Telluride visitors who achieve an amazing bandwidth of music and sound effects. Not to be outdone, the nine-piece Octour de France Orchestra is here to accompany a screening of the 1928 film *The Man Who Laughs*, which put Universal on the map.

As you wander from theater to theater, from the quaint Sheridan Opera House to the state-of-the-art Max to the Quonset hut Community Center, you're reminded of what riches the movies have to offer. So many new films are just clones of recent successes. Telluride finds such treasures. You sit in the dark and look at a silent classic while three guys up front go berserk in the midst of a forest of sound equipment, and you feel a tingle of joy.

One cloud looms on the horizon. Several, actually. The hurricane lashing Mexico is expected to send weather up this way, and the laid-back announcers on the local community radio station are warning of "significant" rainfall. Well, we didn't come here to enjoy the great outdoors.

Work Reflects Meryl Streep's Gift for Characterization

September 4, 1998—If there's one thing she can't stand, Meryl Streep said, it's the sensation that another actor is watching her act while they do a scene together. That sense of scrutiny stands outside the scene and makes it difficult for her to work. She wonders if it isn't one of the reasons *The French Lieutenant's Woman* didn't succeed for her: "It didn't get my rocks off," she said, smiling charmingly during an onstage conversation at the twenty-fifth Telluride Film Festival. "I don't know any other way to say it."

Streep was here as the first of this year's winners of the Telluride Medallion, and after an hour-long look at full-length scenes from many of her films, she took to the stage for a refreshingly informal discussion of her work.

Looking at the scenes was a reminder of what an astonishing gallery of women she has played over the years: the woman waiting for her soldier lover in *The Deer Hunter*, the brainy ex-wife in *Manhattan*, the concentration camp survivor in *Sophie's Choice*, the nuclear plant worker in *Silkwood*, the Danish author in *Out of Africa*, the Skid Row survivor in *Ironweed*, the Australian woman accused of murdering her baby in *A Cry in the Dark*, the drug-addicted actress in *Postcards from the Edge*, the Italian-born Iowa housewife in *The Bridges of Madison County*.

Those were the clips that were shown. An equally interesting program could show her political worker in *The Seduction of Joe Tynan*, the divorced mother in *Kramer vs. Kramer*, the resistance fighter in *Plenty*, and so on. What is impressive, seeing the scenes one after another, is that although she is of course a master of characters and accents, she is above all gifted at getting inside their skins, so that each character is fresh and new.

Asked about that gift, she said she had always been interested in the specific differences between people, and that she and her good pal Tracey Ullman love to explore the quirks of accents and behavior together. "I like to be a conduit," she said.

There's a moment in *The Deer Hunter* when she holds up a sweater she's knitted and finds it much too large for Robert De Niro, and then, before taking it away, allows her fingers to tap lightly across his chest. "Well, because he was so beautiful!" she said, to laughter, and then said little gestures come and go in various takes, and it's up to the director to find what he likes.

In the clip from *The French Lieutenant's Woman*, she said, she felt she could see Jeremy Irons looking at her performance—but then the issue was complicated because, in a way, he was supposed to be: The film cut back and forth between the Victorian story and the relationship between Streep and Irons as the modern actors playing the nineteenth-century characters.

"It never really worked for me one way or the other," she mused. Were you thinking that even when you made the film? she was asked. "Lord, no! I was thinking, it's time for me to breast-feed. Only years and years later do these thoughts come to me."

The biggest laugh of the evening came when critic Stanley Kauffmann stood up to ask a question and she asked him one instead: "When you were teaching at Yale Drama School and I was put on probation—how did you vote? For or against?" Kauffmann said he was a part-timer without a vote, and was allowed to ask his question, which was about the way he thought she put an Italian peasant woman's walk into the character in *The Bridges of Madison County*.

Streep's new film *Dancing at Lughnasa*, about an Irish family in the 1930s, will premiere here, and she has another important autumn film, *One True Thing*, about a perfect housewife married to an imperfect English teacher, that opens soon. The one thing that influences her choices, she mused, was her family: "I have three daughters. I wouldn't want to make a film I didn't want them to see."

The Telluride festival continues through Labor Day weekend with premieres and revivals, and remains the only festival that film industry pros attend for fun. So far I've counted a dozen important directors here who do *not* have new films to promote or deals to sign, and are simply here to see the movies. Fancy that.

Central Station Is Early Favorite at Telluride

September 6, 1998—At every Telluride Film Festival, there's always the film that everyone loves, and the film that everybody stammers about because they can't put their feelings into words.

At the halfway point in this year's festival, the audiences love *Central Station*, the story of a friendship between an old lady and a homeless young boy in Brazil. And the film they can't get a handle on is *Happiness*, which is about characters so pathetic and perverse you watch them with a kind of horror.

There are a lot of other good films here, too—the best selection in several years, although the revivals and retrospectives are so good that it's a shame, really, to take up time with the new films at all. They'll open eventually in theaters. But I will never, ever again in my life be able to have an experience like the one I had last night, watching a restored print of the 1928 silent film *The Man Who Laughs*, accompanied by a twelve-piece orchestra from France.

Silent films are everywhere at Telluride this year, led by guest director Peter Bogdanovich's morning screenings of classics from 1928, "the greatest year in the history of the movies." That was also the last year before the talkies took over; "just when we had it right, it ended," Chaplin mourned. In one day here I began at 9:30 A.M. with a screening of King Vidor's *The Crowd*, and ended late that night with *The Man Who Laughs*, starring Conrad Veidt in Victor Hugo's melodrama about a child whose face is permanently carved into a smile to make him a sideshow attraction. As an adult, he falls in love with a blind girl, and then discovers that his real father was the duke of . . . but the plot grows complex. The film has the kind of heedless joy that happens when every other shot is a plunge into excess.

The festival's popular favorite, *Central Station*, by Walter Salles, stars the great Brazilian actress Fernanda Montenegro, as a former schoolteacher who ekes out a living by writing letters for illiterates in the Rio train station. Against her will she becomes the protector of a young boy (Vinicius de Oliveira) after his mother is struck and killed by a bus. They are adversaries at first, and then grow closer as they set out on a perilous journey across the vast nation, looking for the boy's father. The film has the simplicity and power of titles like *Bicycle Thief* and *Pixote*, and is being positioned by Sony Classics for Best Picture and Actress Oscar nominations.

Happiness, on the other hand, is not exactly an audience favorite. But that doesn't mean it's not a remarkable film—the new work by Todd Solondz, whose *Welcome to the Dollhouse* was about an unpopular junior high school girl who fought back against life. *Happiness* assembles a gallery of desperately lonely and unhappy inverts, including a man who makes obscene phone calls and another who molests the young friend of his son. "The funniest film ever to explore sexual obsession," the program notes say. Not everyone was laughing, and some were squirming. It's amusing to ask people if they "liked" it and hear them wonder how that word applies to this difficult but brilliant film. *Happiness* won the Critic's Prize at Cannes this year but was dropped like a hot potato by its original distributor. It will cause a lot of discussion when it opens.

Another much-discussed film, but this one with a happy ending, is Rolf de Heer's *Dance Me to My Song*, an extraordinary Australian work that was written by Heather Rose, who also stars in it—even though she has cerebral palsy and communicates through a computer and a speaking machine. As the film opens, she's at the mercy of a stupid and cruel "caregiver" who neglects and insults her. Using her motorized wheelchair and her lively intelligence, she tries to figure a way out of her dilemma. In the opening shot, the heroine seems hopeless and alien. By the end, we identify more with her than with the normals in the story.

Audiences are also applauding *The General*, by England's John Boorman, which stars Brendan Gleeson in a powerful performance as an Irish master criminal who makes the mistake of crossing the IRA. Boorman won Best Director at Cannes for the film, which shows how crime has a life of its own and seeks to exist in the cracks of society—even in Ireland, where the cracks are already pretty well filled.

There are lots of other films to write about from Telluride, where by the light of the full moon, festivalgoers walk home at midnight in the crisp mountain air, still talking about what they've seen.

Restored Welles Classic Is Screened at Telluride

September 7, 1998—"This is the world premiere of a movie made in 1958," Peter Bogdanovich said in introducing the first public screening of Orson Welles's restored *Touch of Evil*. And in a sense he was right. Welles's *noir* tragicomedy was reedited by Universal Pictures after he finished it; the studio even shot extra scenes and slapped them in before shipping the movie out as the bottom half of a double bill.

"When I saw the film in 1958, I thought it was . . . a little lacking," confessed Janet Leigh, one of the stars, who was here for the unveiling of the restored version. "Tonight I could see what we had all worked for."

Welles, whose *Citizen Kane* (1941) was recently voted the greatest American film, never worked in Hollywood again after *Touch of Evil* opened to disappointing business and reviews. After seeing Universal's version of his film, he fired off a fifty-eight-page memo detailing the changes he wanted made, but the memo was ignored.

"In 1967," director Bogdanovich recalled, "I was working on a book about Welles, and Charlton Heston walked into my office with a copy of the memo." Bogdanovich intended to include the memo in the book, but it didn't reach print until *Chicago Reader* critic Jonathan Rosenbaum, a Welles expert, published it in *Film Quarterly*.

For producer Rick Schmidlin and Oscar-winning editor Walter Murch, the memo was a guide for their painstaking restoration of the film Welles intended. As nearly as possible, they carried out every one of his instructions, and in the version that played here it was easier to follow the plot, which seemed muddled in the earlier version.

The movie takes place in a sleazy Mexican-American border town, where the corrupt local sheriff (Welles) tries to frame a Mexican official (Heston) on a drug and murder charge. The cast is incredibly rich. Janet Leigh plays Heston's new wife, Marlene Dietrich is the local madam, Dennis Weaver is the loony night man at the hotel, and there's even a cameo for Zsa Zsa Gabor. The movie is going out into national release this month.

"My husband asked me why in the world I was coming up here for this screening," Leigh told me after the event. "I said that this was something we had started forty years ago, and it was time to finish it. They cheated Orson. And they cheated us. This is vindication."

* * *

The most enchanting of the films I've seen here this year is *Autumn Tale*, by Eric Rohmer, the French director who has great warmth and curiosity and watches patiently as people work out their romantic destinies. He is one of my favorite directors anyway, but this time he has surpassed himself, with the story of a forty-fiveish woman (Beatrice Romandi) who runs a vineyard and despairs of ever finding a man—until her friend takes out a personal ad and arranges for her to meet a likely candidate.

That's about all there is to the story, which surrounds the would-be couple with friends, children, and rivals. But it is told so lovingly, with such humor and good cheer, that the audience actually applauded once at nothing more than a smile.

* * *

Bruce Wagner is a novelist who takes Hollywood lifestyles for his subjects, and now in his first film he has made a hard-edged, involving, very intelligent examination of Hollywood's extended families—extended through divorce, remarriage, affairs, and even the quasi-familial relationships with agents and business partners.

I'm Losing You stars Frank Langella, in a subtle and strong performance as a TV producer and star who learns he has perhaps a year to live. He keeps his death sentence a secret at first from his son (Andrew McCarthy) and adopted daughter (Rosanna Arquette), and meanwhile their lives spin around other secrets, such as the true story of Arquette's birth parents. The movie is hip and knowing about the mating and business customs of show business, and touching in the way it shows its characters as humans, not just as caricatures.

* * *

Need a documentary be the literal truth in every shot? Not according to the great documentarian Robert Flaherty, who in films like *Nanook of the North* directed his real characters in scripts he felt would best reveal their lives and customs. An absorbing new documentary named *Endurance* uses the same approach to re-create the life of Haile Gebrselassie, the Ethiopian

Olympic champion who has been called the best distance runner in the world.

He was born one of eight children in a one-room hut in the countryside, and ran miles each day to school. The film casts young men to play him at various times in his life, and Gebrselassie himself is seen relatively rarely—except in footage where he sets a new 10,000-meter record. The movie gives us insights into his background that would have been impossible, I imagine, using any other approach.

Telluride Festival Celebrates Human Films

September 8, 1998—In the blazing noon sun of Labor Day, on a panel discussion in Elks Park, the veteran critic Stanley Kauffmann put his finger on the kinds of films that the Telluride Film Festival does *not* exist to support: movies made of special effects and technology.

"Ingmar Bergman always says that the greatest subject of the movies is the human face," Kauffmann said. "In recent years we've seen a growth in films that are not about faces and stories, but about technology. This trend started with Stanley Kubrick, with *2001*, and it's accelerating. It is now possible to make an entire movie with machines, without really involving human stories at all."

Sitting next to him on the panel, I thought how true that was, and meditated on some of the recent films I'd seen, like *Armageddon*, which were really about nothing—or nothing except for mindless spectacle manufactured by special effects. That movie starred Bruce Willis, but for all the humanity embodied in the role, it could have starred Robby the Robot.

Such thoughts come to one at Telluride, which is like an annual recess where the film world can play and dream before the bell rings and everybody goes back inside to start counting the grosses.

Other true words were spoken by San Francisco critic B. Ruby Rich, who regretted the great emphasis on "production values," when the most interesting films are often those heavy on characters and ideas but light on budgets. For many years, she said, independent films were penalized because they just didn't look expensive enough; only now that Sundance is seen as a supermarket for hot young directors are the indie (and women's and black and gay) films getting a more "professional" gloss.

On another panel discussion, about the Hollywood golden age that began with *Bonnie and Clyde* in 1967 and ended with *One Flew Over the Cuckoo's Nest* in 1975, several directors who flourished in those days recalled a time when a script could get filmed without countless memos and input from "executives" whose job is to sniff out originality and squish it.

"I remember discussing making *Point Blank* with Lee Marvin," John Boorman remembered. "We met in a London hotel. We both hated the script. He said he would do the film on one condition, and threw the script out the window. He committed on a conversation. That can't happen anymore."

Directors were in charge at that time, Boorman said. Today, the power resides first with the studios, then with stars, then with producers and agents, and only then with directors.

The result is assembly-line filmmaking, endless recycling of predictable formulas. Executives who are not creative protect their jobs by remaking last week's hits. Commenting on a series of clips from golden-age classics like *Five Easy Pieces*, director Michael Ritchie said: "None of those films had a happy ending. Today, you know the happy ending, engineered by the studio, is going to be there."

Even rarer is the ambiguous ending. The last film I saw at Telluride this year was the observant, thoughtful, funny, sad *My Son the Fanatic*, by Udayan Prasad, about a British cab driver from Pakistan. In Manchester, he drives the night shift, growing friendly with a hooker and then recommending her to a heartless visiting businessman. At home, his marriage is sterile, but there is cause for cheer: His son is engaged to the daughter of the police chief inspector. Then the son breaks off the match ("I don't want to bring up my children in this country") and joins a fundamentalist Islamic group.

The driver (Om Puri), values his friendship with the hooker (Rachel Griffiths), even though he is alarmed when it turns physical. "Am I to spend all the rest of my days sitting behind the wheel, without the touch of a human hand?" he asks, justifying himself to a friend who immigrated from Pakistan when he did. This new relationship challenges his morals, but his son's group "imposes mad values," he thinks, and at the end of an eventful film he pours himself a drink, and thinks, and thinks. That is an effective ending for the film, but you can bet in Hollywood it would have been assigned a happy one.

The romance in *My Son the Fanatic* is not the kind of simpleminded lunacy that passes for adult relationships in most modern movies. Neither is the romance in Eric Rohmer's *Autumn Tale*, a glowing film. For now let's set aside the details of the film and look at how Rohmer works. His plot (a woman's best friend places a personal ad for her and secretly arranges for her to meet a likely candidate for marriage) could be the stuff of soap opera, sitcom, or paperback romance. But not the way Rohmer approaches it.

A director who is still inventive and curious at seventy-eight, he has two valuable qualities: patience and attention. He allows us to meet the characters. To hear them talking, to see them living. They explain themselves. They discuss their lives. He's in no hurry to get to the payoff (and indeed the film has no love scene). He involves us in the lives of these people, and in what Bergman means by their faces. We grow to know them and care for them.

The challenge for the actors (especially Marie Riviere, as the widow) is enormous. The camera is not interested in their "acting" so much as in their essence, and as Rohmer attentively regards these people, we find ourselves in synch with their breathing and their inner natures. It's scary, almost, the way the movie cuts free of conventional pacing and allows us into the characters' real time.

The film was introduced by its producer, the director Barbet Schroeder, who said Rohmer has his ideas long in advance of filming, but doesn't write a word of the script until he has spent weeks talking with the actors, "so that they will never have to say anything they wouldn't really say."

Schroeder told a story about one of Rohmer's earlier films, *Claire's Knee* (1971). "There is a scene in that movie where they pick a rose," he said. "Rohmer knew where the scene would be shot, and there he planted that rose, one year earlier, so that it would bloom just on time."

Sometimes at Telluride it feels as if we are all planting roses, before we return to the land of the artificial flowers.

Toronto Film Festival

Toronto, Canada—The program for the Toronto Film Festival falls with the thud of the Yellow Pages. This year more than 300 films from fifty-three countries will be shown at the largest and most important film festival in North America and, as usual, the crowds will be lining up for everything—literally everything. If your movie can't fill a theater at this festival, you might as well cut it up and use it to floss with.

Toronto's reach is wide. It embraces the two nightly Galas, which are often much-hyped premieres of major fall openings. It includes Special Presentations, which are to Galas as the Un Certain Regard category is to the official competition at Cannes. It includes, this year, special seasons of new films from Africa (sixteen titles) and Japan (nineteen). Then there are eighty-four other foreign films in the Contemporary World Cinema section.

And nine new documentaries. And thirty films in the Discovery section—mostly new directors. And seven classic revivals, including films by Losey, Korda, Powell, Welles, Buñuel, and Satyajit Ray. And fourteen titles in the category called simply The Masters, and devoted to new work by such great directors as Eric Rohmer, Shohei Imamura, Arturo Ripstein, John Boorman, Carlos Saura, and the Taviani brothers. And sixty-three new Canadian films. And a movie every night in the Midnight Madness series—titles that either are, will be, or should be cult movies. And on and on. Did I forget to mention the career retrospective for Darezhan Omirbaev from Kazakhstan?

Toronto is one of the few "destination" festivals—an event attended by people from out of town. Such prestigious festivals as New York and Chicago are essentially hometown events, but movie lovers, both civilians and professionals, fly to Toronto from all over; in that respect, it's like Cannes, Berlin, Sundance, and Telluride. The newspapers assign platoons of reporters and critics to cover it (no star, however obscure, can munch a bran muffin unpublicized), and the big studios use the festival's two weekends to premiere the fall product they have the highest hopes for.

Among the high-profile premieres this year are *Antz*, the DreamWorks animated film; James Ivory's *A Soldier's Daughter Never Cries*, with Kris Kristofferson playing a character inspired by novelist James Jones; *Dancing at Lughnasa*, starring Meryl Streep in the film of Brian Friel's celebrated play; John Waters's *Pecker*, with Edward Furlong as a fast-food worker whose photos are embraced by the New York art world; Helena Bonham Carter and Kenneth Branagh in *The Theory of Flight*, about a work-release prisoner assigned to a woman with Lou Gehrig's disease; Ben Stiller as a drug-addicted TV writer in *Permanent Midnight;* Christina Ricci in *Desert Blue*, about slim prospects for a teenager in a town of eighty-nine people; *The Imposters*, the new film by Stanley *(Big Night)* Tucci, starring Tucci and Oliver Platt as stowaways on a cruise ship; *Rushmore*, with Jason Schwartzmann as a prep schooler who is a lousy student but hyperactive in campus activities; Cameron Diaz in *Very Bad Things*, about a bachelor party that ends in murder; Cate Blanchett as *Elizabeth*, the story of England's sixteenth-century monarch; and *The Judas Kiss*, with FBI agent Emma Thompson on the trail of the kidnapper of a computer genius.

Some of the best-received films at earlier festivals will get their North American launches at Toronto, including *Life Is Beautiful*, Roberto Begnini's Cannes winner about an Italian clown who fights the Nazis with laughter; Eric Rohmer's heartwarming love story *Autumn Tale*, which charmed audiences at Telluride; Ken Loach's *My Name Is Joe*, with Cannes Best Actor winner Peter Mullen as a recovering alcoholic facing tough times; Theo Angelopoulos's *Eternity and a Day*, this year's Cannes winner; *The General*, which won John Boorman the Best Director prize at Cannes; and the Cannes and Telluride favorite *Claire Dolan*, by Lodge Kerrigan, starring Emily Watson *(Breaking the Waves)* as a prostitute who thinks she can detach from her work.

Film fans in Toronto plan their vacations around the festival. I've sat next to people who were seeing their fifth film of the day. The press corps is so large that six theaters are used for the press screenings. The festival venues are strung out along the axis of the Toronto subway system, so it's easy to travel between theaters, and fans plan their schedules with military precision.

When the Toronto festival started, its official name was "The Festival of Festivals." The name was changed at just about the time when the title became accurate. Since Cannes is basically a trade fair, Toronto is the world's top festival for—well, for moviegoers.

Gross-Out Comedy Reaches New Low in *Very Bad Things*

September 14, 1998—One week after the gross-out comedy *There's Something About Mary* reached No. 1 at the box office, here's Cameron Diaz back again in an even grosser movie—one that makes *Mary* look positively tasteful by comparison.

Very Bad Things, which had its world premiere at the Toronto Film Festival, tests the limits of what a general audience picture can contain. Although my review will wait until the movie opens, word will be quickly spreading from a capacity crowd that was urged by writer-director Peter Berg to shout at the screen: "Hit it back! It can take it!"

Diaz has a supporting role as a twenty-seven-year-old who is focusing obsessively on her upcoming marriage. Most of the movie involves a Las Vegas bachelor party and its aftermath, as her fiancé, Jon Favreau, is joined by buddies Christian Slater, Jeremy Piven, Daniel Stern, and Leland Orser in a wild booze-and-drugs orgy that ends with them burying bodies in the desert. And that's only the start of the very bad things.

It's not the story that's startling, really, but the gruesome, violent tone. The events in *Very Bad Things* could occur in lots of different kinds of movies, but Berg seems intent not only on pushing the envelope but slashing and burning it.

The question occurs: Is Hollywood going to get involved in a race to outgross itself? There were those who were offended by *There's Something About Mary*, but at heart it was a romantic screwball comedy, and it got away with murder because it was really, truly funny. A movie doesn't climb to the top of the box-office charts in its eighth week unless the word of mouth is extraordinary: Moviegoers are obviously telling their friends about it, and taking them to see it at theaters that shake with laughter.

If laughter can redeem borderline subject matter, one wonders how much laughter it will take to redeem *Very Bad Things*, which involves mayhem so gruesome it upstages the previous recordholder, *Shallow Grave*, especially in the vivisection and burial department. There are racial themes sure to make audiences uncomfortable (two of the victims are black and Asian; several of the heroes talk much of their Jewishness). And although the later stages of the movie relax into somewhat more conventional slapstick, the Vegas scenes seem inspired by gore and slasher movies more than by comedy.

Will this mixture work at the box office? I heard a lot of laughter and some applause at the Toronto premiere. But, less obviously, to be sure, I sensed that many audience members were watching in thoughtful silence.

* * *

What a contrast was *After Life*, the new film by Japan's Hirokazu Kore-Eda, whose *Maborosi* was one of the best films of 1997. The new film has a premise that sounds simplistic, but the film reaches surprising emotional insights.

It's about a way station between this world and the next, where the newly deceased are asked to choose one memory that they wish to preserve. The memory is then reenacted and filmed by the way station staff, and after viewing it, the visitors move on to the next level of the afterlife, with only that one memory left to them.

What will the newcomers choose? What will it mean? How will their choices affect the staff members? The movie takes its seemingly sentimental premise and uses it to examine how memory works selectively to interpret our loves to ourselves.

* * *

"I expect the total transformation of their lives the moment they get on the bus," declares a Manhattan tour bus guide named Timothy (Speed) Levitch, in a weirdly infectious new documentary by Bennett Miller named *The Cruise*. Levitch clears about $200 a week improvising into the microphone as he conducts tours, or "cruises," informing and amazing his Gray Line passengers with such information as, "You are five blocks from where Dorothy Parker died of alcoholism and despair."

Levitch is a cast-iron original, with his adenoidal voice, blinding sports coats, unruly mane of curly hair, and flat-footed gait. He seems utterly confident about who he is and what he does, but an oddness creeps in, and we suspect there's more to the story. He seems to be projecting his entire psyche onto the city and the tour.

Here he is on architecture: "I identify with the anger and inferiority that some of the smaller buildings feel." Louis Sullivan's terra-cotta Manhattan skyscraper is, he feels, orgasmic, and he describes its sex life in detail. Of the Brooklyn Bridge, he says, "Eleven people have jumped off this bridge and survived. One of my cruising dreams would be to get those people together on a cruise."

He became a tour guide, he explains "to meet and seduce women." That's why he rebels at the requirement that he wear the Gray Line's official uniform, a red shirt: "You are not ever gonna get lucky in a red shirt."

Pot Pie Is Comfort Food Tradition for Friends of Christy

September 14, 1998—Every year at the Toronto Film Festival we gather, the friends of George Christy, to have lunch in the Four Seasons Hotel. This is a tradition going back so far that no one except George remembers how it started, or what it represents. Christy, who writes the "Good Life" column for the *Hollywood Reporter*, invites some seventy of the chosen to a private dining room, where we eat chicken pot pie and gossip among ourselves.

The pot pie is a story in itself. One year George served pot pie, and Garth Drabinsky, then the chief honcho of Cineplex Odeon, pronounced it excellent. The following year, chicken pot pie was served again in his honor. And the year after that. We have had pot pie now for five or six years running.

George stands up every year and makes a toast thanking the chefs of the Four Seasons for working so closely with him in planning the menu, and we all think, "chicken pot pie again."

This year, there were phone calls for a week beforehand among the friends of George, who are all aware that Drabinsky is involved in a nasty legal battle with Mike Ovitz and others who have taken over Livent, the company Drabinsky founded to stage vast spectacles such as *Ragtime* in rehabbed palaces such as Chicago's old Oriental, now under reconstruction.

Would Drabinsky still be invited? Would chicken pot pie still be served? Yes, and yes. As it happens I was seated only one person away from Drabinsky, and I observed we had him to thank for the chicken pot pie.

"It is very good pot pie," he observed. "One of the best I have tasted."

"I got a lot of peas this year," I said. "Last year I got only one pea."

"George no doubt spoke to the chefs."

I looked around the room, seeing Rosanna Arquette and Helena Bonham Carter, Mekhi Phifer, and John Waters with his little pencil mustache, good Donald Sutherland and Cameron Diaz with her merry smile, Edward Furlong and former Canadian prime minister Brian Mulroney, director Norman Jewison and his wife, Dixie, and all of the other friends of George, all blissfully eating their pot pie.

Naomi Campbell, who is filming in Toronto, popped into the room for a second, and George took her from table to table.

"The last time I saw you," I said, "Harvey Weinstein was bidding $50,000 for your navel ring."

This was at a charity auction at Cannes. Campbell, who was the auctioneer, informed Weinstein that her navel ring was not up for auction. "Sixty thousand," he reasoned.

"He paid the money but he never got the ring," she said. "It was all for charity."

"I'll bet he didn't really want the ring," I said, as an unsettling image flashed into my mind of the bear-like Miramax chief with a pierced navel.

Soon George Christy returned to our table. The genius of George and his column is that he knows everyone in show business and likes, and is liked by, a high percentage of them. His column runs stories about parties and premieres, benefits and soirees, festivals and fundraisers, all illustrated with dozens of tiny photos of the rich and famous, sometimes shown in conversation with the poor and famous. It is a column nobody in the biz ever misses, especially if they want to see how they would look on a postage stamp.

"Did you notice that I had the chicken pot pie again this year?" George asked Garth.

Garth looked down at his little porcelain pot, which was entirely empty, he having used a soup spoon to scoop out the last morsels of pot pie. Perhaps he reflected that the printed menu advertised

Chicken Pot Pie George Christy
In honor of Garth Drabinsky

"Yes, I did," he said, manfully suppressing no doubt an urge to add, "Everyone at this luncheon has been talking to me about nothing but pot pie, pot pie, pot pie."

Well, if you are chatting with a man who is involved in a big and messy public dispute and you have a subject like pot pie at hand, my advice is, stick to the pot pie. If I should meet President Clinton in the next few days, for example, pot pie will be at the tip of my tongue.

Someone asked Drabinsky about the Lewinsky scandal.

"Well, after what I've been though, I have a great deal of sympathy for him," Drabinsky said. "This is costing me a year of my life. More than a million dollars in legal fees. And what did I do? I'm fifty years old. Where do I go from here?"

"You'll bounce right back and still be doing marvelous things when you're seventy-five," a friend reassured him.

Yes, he no doubt thought, and if I do, I'll still be eating this pot pie.

Riker's *City* Is Film to Treasure

September 15, 1998—Sometimes in the middle of the hustle and hype you find a little film that exists simply because it needs to. Here at the Toronto Film Festival the hotel lobbies are jammed with celebs wearing the T-shirts and baseball caps of each other's movies. There is nothing to advertise *The City*, not even a free lead pencil with the title printed on it, but here is a movie to treasure.

It tells four stories about recent illegal immigrants to New York City. They come from Mexico and farther south in Latin America, and they carry the hopes of their families at home that they will send back money from the promised land. It doesn't work that way.

Although the TV news and music videos

have drilled us to think of Latin Americans in terms of flash and style, music, and sometimes drugs, the characters in this movie come from an entirely different world. They are hardworking people, men mostly, who come from a world where they were respected. After all, anyone who goes to the trouble of becoming an illegal immigrant is, by definition, one of the most confident and ambitious citizens in his home community. The losers would be afraid to try.

New York, we see, offers little. Men line the streets hoping to be hired as day laborers, and the cops threaten to sweep them away—for the crime of wanting to work. They're paid fifteen cents apiece to scrape and hammer the mortar off of old bricks. In another story, a woman gets a job in a garment sweatshop, where piecework workers are hired and fired on whim. A man lives in his car and supports himself with a portable Punch and Judy show; he wants to enroll his daughter in school, which is their legal right, but because he has no permanent address no school will have her. And in a more hopeful story, a young man meets a woman and they fall in love—but the city defeats them after all.

The City (La Ciudad) was written and directed by David Riker, who comes out of the New York University Film School; fellow graduates such as Spike Lee and Martin Scorsese have also been interested in the streets. It was photographed by Harlan Bosmajian, whose black-and-white work is realistic and poetic. One is reminded of *Bicycle Thief.*

* * *

It is a rare autumn that does not bring at least one movie about British royalty. All nations have two histories—their own and England's. The prize entry this fall is obviously *Elizabeth,* which premiered here this week and immediately inspired Oscar talk for Cate Blanchett's performance as Elizabeth I, the Virgin Queen.

We see her first as a tall, regal young girl with flowing red hair, who laughs and plays and is dangerously naive about the intrigues at court. Her half-sister Mary, a Catholic, is advised to have Elizabeth, a Protestant, put to death. But Mary dallies and dies, and Elizabeth ascends to a throne that controls no treasury, no army, and a pitiful navy. The French conspire with her rival Mary of Guise in Scotland to overthrow her, but she grows in office and eventually gives her name to the greatest age in British history.

Blanchett deserves the praise she is getting, and her costars include Geoffrey Rush and Richard Attenborough. But the appeal of the movie is as much in its look and feel as in its performances. Director Shekhar Kapur *(Bandit Queen)* and cinematographer Remi Adefarasin remind us that the Elizabethan age was a time of gloomy, damp dwellings and earthy simplicity, where shadows and distances could conceal conspiracies. Rarely has a time and place added so much to a royal story.

* * *

The loudest buzz at Toronto, as it was at Telluride and last May at Cannes, is all about *Happiness,* the film by Todd Solondz that cannot be discussed without the word "controversial" somewhere in the same sentence. I've written about it before, and will indeed have an audience with Solondz himself. I have no idea how the film, which is about people whose dysfunctions range from the depraved to the criminal to the merely pathetic, will be received by audiences. But festivalgoers are intrigued, because they don't know what to make of it; it fits no known category.

* * *

It's not a film festival unless you see movies by accident. I went to what I thought was a screening for *Clay Pigeons,* with Vince Vaughn and Janeane Garafolo in a rough Montana story, and when the lights went down I found myself watching *Fire Eater,* from Finland, about children left behind by a mother who leaves with the Nazis. And yesterday I walked out of a movie with a painfully shrill sound track and was talked into the theater next door by a persuasive publicist who was sure I should see *Fated Vocations,* perhaps the least commercial title of the year, about a troupe of Vietnamese singers. I admired both films, although I am not sure they will be opening soon in a theater near you.

Toronto Festival Is Movie Marathon

September 16, 1998—We are a little past the halfway point of the twenty-third Toronto Film Festival, and my colleagues are looking more hollow-eyed and gaunt than usual. It is a strange occupation, going to three or four movies a day, and critics begin to resemble fishlike creatures from unlit caverns. This year is worse than usual because the facilities are better.

Millions have been spent to enlarge the Varsity theaters, where most of the press screenings are held, and where before there were two screens there are now, I dunno, nine or ten. Because there are more screenings, critics feel guilty if they don't attend more movies; they scurry from one room to another, surfing on the buzz.

This ordeal is made merry by the sight of at least two or three critics falling flat on their faces at every screening. That's because the theaters feature "stadium seating," which means that every row is a little higher than the one in front of it. That would be splendid except that the steps in the aisles do not match the levels of the seat rows.

"Excuse me," a latecomer will politely whisper, "but is that seat taken?" "No," comes the whispered response, followed by sudden cries of alarm as the latecomer pitches forward into the laps of three or four patrons, and popcorn flies everywhere. Leaving after the movie, they trip over the step and fall into the aisle.

I am reminded of the inaugural year of the new Palais des Festivals at Cannes, where the grand exterior staircase was built at too steep a pitch, and in the crush of paparazzi it appeared that a domino effect might send the cream of the French cinema rolling and tumbling to the bottom, with Gérard Depardieu landing atop Catherine Deneuve and squishing untold beauty out of the world. Cannes rebuilt the staircase, and the Varsity theaters may have to fine-tune those stairs.

* * *

Despite these occupational hazards, I have been having a good time because the films are fine and there are more than 300 of them. Some of them will open in the next week or two and will get their reviews then. Others deserve special attention.

One is *God Said, "Ha!"* This is a performance film by Julia Sweeney, formerly of *Saturday Night Live* (you may remember her character, the omnigendered Pat). The film is simply Sweeney onstage in front of an audience, talking about a year in her life during which her brother developed a virulent form of cancer, and other bad things happened, too—although I will leave the film with its surprises.

The film is not a dirge of bad news but a brave and funny reshaping of the material. Just as she had finally broken free of her large Irish-American family from Seattle and bought her own little house in Los Angeles, her brother fell ill—and brother, father, and mother all moved in with her, along with a lot of heirloom furniture, which was so familiar that it created the eerie hallucination that *she* had moved back in with *them.*

Like all good performance films, *God Said, "Ha!"* plays not like a monologue but like a radio drama. Sitting here now, I can picture the little home and the midnight trip to the hospital as if I'd seen them in a movie. The film works as comedy, and yet its feelings are real; I imagine it would be a healing experience for any family dealing with cancer.

* * *

Down in the Delta is the first film directed by poet Maya Angelou, and it's not so much a story as a fable of memory and recovery. It stars Alfre Woodard as a woman who lives in the Chicago projects with her mother (Mary Alice), her son, and her brain-damaged daughter. The Woodard character is unemployed and unemployable (no math skills), and spends her days drinking and smoking weed. Her mother sees that she's headed for worse, and sends her and her children south for the summer, to her only brother (Al Freeman Jr.), who lives on the family homestead in the Mississippi Delta with his wife, who has Alzheimer's.

The story centers around a family heirloom, a silver candelabra, that at first seems like an obvious story gimmick, and then takes on deeper meanings, until finally it represents the very history of this family. Al Freeman, so wonderful in *Once Upon a Time When We Were Colored,* has some of the same strengths here, as a man who sees well, feels deeply, and chooses his moments. And Woodard's performance moves quietly from the despair of the opening scenes to the hope of the closing ones. At a festival where gimmicks, cynicism, and the flavor of the month are routinely overpraised, here is a film of real worth that might make a difference for some of its viewers.

* * *

It has become a tradition for Toronto moviegoers to take a week's vacation and book themselves into nonstop movies from dawn until midnight. At a Vietnamese musical, I sat next to Barbara Strange, who plans to see forty-five movies, takes no breaks for meals, and exists, she said, "on bottled water, dried apricots, and mixed nuts." At another I met John MacInnis, a market researcher, who will see thirty-five movies this year: "For the first week after the festival, they all blur into one long movie. Then slowly the high points emerge from the fog."

A Soldier's Daughter Is a Hit at Toronto Fest

September 17, 1998—I can't identify with a lot of the families I see in movies. They aren't like my family and I doubt if they're like anyone's. The family in *A Soldier's Daughter Never Cries* isn't like anyone else's family, either, but I never doubted for a moment that it existed. The movie could be advertised with a line like, "Apart from the fact that my dad was an alcoholic novelist and we were raised in the expatriate colony in Paris in the 1960s, I had a typical American childhood."

The movie, which is one of the hits of the twenty-third Toronto Film Festival, is based on an autobiographical novel by Kaylie Jones, the daughter of the novelist James Jones *(From Here to Eternity, The Thin Red Line)*. In the 1960s, her parents lived in Paris in a spacious apartment on the Ile St. Louis, which is between the two banks of the Seine, and their lives were likewise split between Left and Right Bank values.

The movie stars Kris Kristofferson as the novelist (called Bill Willis), Barbara Hershey as his sexpot but sensible wife, LeeLee Sobieski as the daughter, Samuel Gruen as an adopted son, and Anthony Roth Costanzo as an extraordinarily original character—the heroine's young schoolmate who is crazy about the opera.

I will be reviewing the film next week, so further details can wait. What I want to say now is that the film is so particular in the way it evokes the inner life of this family; how it is not afraid to be oddball or perplexing in the way it shows a bohemian couple trying to be good parents. How it incorporates all of the traumas and anxieties of a novelist's life into the family fabric, without making the movie all about the writer. *A Soldier's Daughter* was directed by James Ivory, and is one of his very best works. It is kind of exciting to watch a film that assumes you are intelligent enough to care about the family without a series of easily grasped plot points.

* * *

I missed the tribute to the great cinematographer Vittorio Storaro *(Last Tango in Paris, Apocalypse Now)* at Telluride, because I didn't think I'd ever get another chance to see the silent classic *The Man Who Laughs* with a twelve-piece French orchestra. That was the right decision, I think, but now that I've caught up with the latest film Storaro has photographed, I'm reminded once again what a master he is.

Carlos Saura's *Tango* is set in Argentina and is about the tango and a director who is making a tango film, and that's about all of the plot I want to divulge right now. You can assume that the dancing and the music are splendid.

Storaro's contribution is to make the visuals reflect the complexity of the dance form. The tango involves "one body with four legs," and often the dancers' legs move at dizzying speed between and around each other's, so that a viewer is not always quite sure where the balance of gravity lies, and who is leading, and what is rehearsed and what is inspiration.

Storaro's shots do the same thing. He uses reflections, and tricks with mirrors, and back-projection screens, and pullbacks that reveal shots are not what they seem. Meanwhile, the screenplay itself is also allowing the characters to flick back and forth between levels of reality as their bodies do in the tango. In another kind of movie, one might be annoyed by Storaro's trickery, but the tango is a dance that combines passion with detachment, wildness with rigidity, and so does Storaro's camera here.

* * *

As I write there are lots more movies to see, but a few titles seem to be emerging as audience favorites: Roberto Benigni's *Life Is Beautiful*, about a comedian who uses humor to shield his son from the Holocaust; John Boorman's *The General*, with its absorbing performance by Brendan Gleeson as a Dublin criminal; Todd Solondz's *Happiness*, easily the most controversial film of the festival; Eric Rohmer's gentle, seductive story of middle-aged love, *Autumn Tale; Elizabeth*, the lush royal biography starring Cate Blanchett in a showcase role; *Central Station*, about the old woman and the orphan boy in Rio; *Rushmore*, about the worst student in a prep school, who is also the smartest student; *After Life*, by Japan's Hirokazu Kore-Eda, about a way station between earth and heaven; and *The Mighty*, based on the children's classic about a partnership between a big, slow boy and a small, fast one. There are more than 300 films, and I haven't seen most of them, so that's a sample, not a complete list.

Hope Survives Amidst the Mayhem at Toronto Festival

September 21, 1998—Reeling after a week of too many films built on too much mindless brutality, I found *Little Voice* and *Mixing Nia* like soothing reassurances that there were still filmmakers with heart and humor. The general view at this year's Toronto Film Festival is that a lot of ambitious new flickers are engaged in a game of one-upmanship in violence, and may have out-stripped even the audience appetite for mayhem.

Certainly the heroine of *Mixing Nia* is a refreshing change from some of the twisted nut cases in many other films. She has ideas, a personality, values, and other qualities unknown to the New Geek Cinema.

Played by Karyn Parsons (of *Fresh Prince of Bel Air*), she's the daughter of a white father and a black mother who works in an ad agency until she refuses to work on an account pitching cheap beer to young blacks. She thinks maybe she'll write a novel. But that goes badly, and meanwhile her romantic life involves shaky relationships with two men: the teacher of her African-American writing workshop (Isaiah Washington) and her former partner at the ad agency (Eric Thal).

The debut movie was written and directed by Alison Swan, an NYU film school graduate from Bermuda, and she's too smart to present easy answers. Instead, as racial and ideological questions spill over into everyday decisions, she depends on Nia's common sense to muddle through.

Parsons is right for the title role because she keeps the material in perspective with a saving sense of humor; she has good timing in small, subtle double takes as she reacts to what people think she wants to hear. Swan said in the Q&A afterward that she wanted to let all the characters have their say, and they have it, although Nia doesn't get many answers that way. The movie's buried insight, I think, is that valid human relationships begin with feeling and honesty, not abstractions.

* * *

Little Voice is one of the great audience favorites of the last days of the twenty-third Toronto festival. It stars Michael Caine, Brenda Blethyn, and Jane Horrocks in a delightful British comedy, in which Caine is a desperate showbiz promoter and Horrocks is a goofy girl who never leaves her room and hardly ever speaks—but can do uncanny imitations of the records she listens to incessantly, by Marilyn Monroe, Billie Holiday, Shirley Bassey, and Judy Garland.

The first credit at the end of the film informs us that Horrocks (the star of *Absolutely Fabulous* on TV) did all of her own singing, which is amazing; since she's so good the audience assumes she's miming.

* * *

Antz, the big new DreamWorks animated comedy, was featured at the closing night gala. It uses clever animation to create ants with some of the facial features of the stars who voice them, including Woody Allen, Sharon Stone, Sylvester Stallone, and Christopher Walken. Allen's dialogue, as a worker ant who becomes a revolutionary, is very funny. "It's tough to feel loved," he says, "when you're the middle child in a family of 5 million."

* * *

This year's festival solidified Toronto's position as a festival second only to Cannes. Its timing helps; September is the launch month for the festival-type films of the autumn. The only cloud on the horizon: rumors that Cannes may switch to September. Oddly enough, Toronto is now so big and well established that Cannes may be the first to blink.

Films of Wide Variety Are Honored at Toronto

September 21, 1998—The public and the critics were far apart in choosing their favorites at this year's Toronto Film Festival—selecting titles that could almost be viewed as opposites.

Life Is Beautiful, the gentle, powerful tragicomedy by Italy's Roberto Benigni, won the Air Canada People's Choice Award, which is determined by a weighted ballot of moviegoers on their way out of the screenings. Benigni stars as a clown who uses humor, his only weapon, to try to save his son from death in a concentration camp. His wife, Nicolette Braschi, costars as the clown's wife and the boy's mother.

Happiness, the much-discussed portrait of loneliness, perversion, and desperation by Todd Solondz, won the Metro Media Award, voted on by some 740 members of the international press corps that covered the festival. The film follows a loosely related group of characters who desperately try to maintain acceptable facades while pursuing private depravities.

In a way, the Toronto awards repeated recent history. At Cannes in May, *Life Is Beautiful* won the Jury Prize, and *Happiness* won the Critics' Prize.

The separate Rothman's World International Critics Award, decided by a jury of members of the International Film Critics' Association (FIRPRESCI), was shared by *West Beirut*, by Ziad Doueiri of Lebanon and France, and *Praise*, by John Curran of Australia. The first film follows two Muslim friends who are students in a Catholic school in Beirut in the first days of the civil war in Lebanon. The second is about an unlikely love affair between two loners in a down-and-out hotel.

The $15,000 CityTV award for best first Canadian feature film went to Don McKellar's *Last Night*, in which Earth has but a few more hours before destruction, and a group of characters decide in intensely personal ways how to spend them.

The $25,000 award for best Canadian film cosponsored by CityTV and the city of Toronto, went to Robert Lepage for *No*, which follows a troupe from Montreal to the 1970 Osaka world's fair and subtly contrasts the Japanese No drama with the Quebec separatist cry of "No!"

Runners-up for the People's Choice Award were Kirk Jones's *Waking Ned Devine*, an Irish comedy, and Walter Salles's *Central Station*, about an odyssey in Brazil as an old woman helps a young orphan find his father.

An estimated 250,000 moviegoers attended this year's Toronto festival, which has become North America's most important, and draws tourists from all over the world. When it was founded twenty-three years ago, the New York and Chicago festivals were the major autumn showcases for the same kinds of films, but the Toronto and Ontario governments provided financial support that allowed Toronto to develop into a major source of prestige and tourism dollars, eclipsing both of the American cities.

Sundance Film Festival

Park City, Utah—The future of the American film industry holds its annual convention at the Sundance Film Festival. For the next ten days, new independent films and documentaries will unspool all over town, in every possible performance space: Wherever two or three people gather together, they're probably looking at a movie.

The opening night film is *Cookie's Fortune*, directed by Robert Altman, an independent filmmaker in every atom of his being, and at seventy-two a hero for the younger filmmakers gathering here. The movie stars Glenn Close as a fierce southern dame whose unruly family (mother Pat Neal, sister Julianne Moore, daughter Liv Tyler) severely tests her patience.

The Altman film is high profile, and other movies during the festival also feature big names, but the soul of Sundance is in the low-budget first features that have survived a rigorous selection process. In past years the festival has made such discoveries as Steven Soderbergh *(sex, lies and videotape)*, Quentin Tarantino *(Reservoir Dogs)*, Edward Burns *(Brothers McMullen)*, Neil LaBute *(In the Company of Men)*, and Terry Zwigoff *(Crumb)*.

In its early days the Sundance festival, then known as the USA Film Festival, was essentially an attempt by Park City Realtors to call attention to the town; as a juror in an early year, I was taken on a tour of condos. But in 1981, Robert Redford founded the Sundance Institute at his resort above Provo, as a workshop for aspiring writers and directors. And a few years later he took over direction of the struggling festival, renaming it. Even then, Sundance was partially an excuse for Hollywood agents to write off their ski holidays—until Soderbergh's *sex, lies and videotape* was premiered here, went on to win the Palme d'Or at Cannes, and transformed Sundance into a marketplace for hopeful filmmakers and those who would feed off them.

Park City is not the most festival-friendly

city on earth, and every year visitors return with horror stories of sold-out screenings, shaky projection, and towed cars (the city hires freelancers who collect a bounty for every vehicle they impound). Some screening rooms are improvised out of motel meeting rooms, with folding chairs on risers and a 16mm projector right in the middle of the crowd, but the situation was much improved last year with the opening of the new Eccles Theater, a spacious state-of-the-art venue.

Other films are shown in the local library, in the antique Egyptian theater on Main Street, in a shopping mall duplex, and in rooms carved out of convention meeting spaces. In the way the festival employs every possible theater space, Sundance resembles Telluride, with two differences: Everything is not within walking distance, and there is usually a lot of snow on the ground.

It is impossible, of course, to predict what wonderful discoveries will emerge from this year's event. By definition, they remain to be discovered. Having examined the program, I know I am looking forward to seeing Steven Maler's *The Autumn Heart*, with Tyne Daly and Ally Sheedy as a reconciling mother and daughter; Frank Whaley's *Joe the King*, with Noah Fleiss and Ethan Hawke, about an alcoholic's son; Toni Kalem's *A Slipping-Down Life*, with Lili Taylor starring in an adaptation of an Anne Tyler novel about a rock fan; Guy Ritchie's *Lock, Stock and Two Smoking Barrels*, already a hit in the United Kingdom; Errol Morris's *Mr. Death*, about a Holocaust denier; Christopher Menaul's *The Passion of Ayn Rand*, with Helen Mirren in the title role; and *American Pimp*, a documentary by the Hughes brothers *(Menace II Society)*.

There's also a special section this year devoted to the emerging Native American cinema; the usual cross section of foreign films, documentaries, and shorts; a tribute to the independently spirited Laura Dern; and a fifteenth-anniversary revival of Gregory Nava's *El Norte*, the first of the Sundance Institute projects to reach the screen.

And then, of course, there's the competing Slamdance festival, a piggyback event of films rejected by Sundance for one reason or another. This year, Slamdance is also sponsoring workshops, including one by John Chua titled *How to Make a Film With No Money and Sell It to a TV Network*. Now that's the spirit.

The Business of Movies Is Center Stage at Sundance Fest

January 25, 1999—At most film festivals, 90 percent of the audience members are civilians and 10 percent are employed in the industry. At Sundance, the ratio is reversed. Screenings here consist of pitches, bids, deal-making, business card exchanging, and schmoozing, interrupted by movies.

"I wanted to recapture the feelings I had here a few years ago," producer Gale Anne Hurd was telling me before the screening of a movie named *Valerie Flake*. "I was remembering what it was like in 1992, when we were here with *The Waterdance*. Before everything got so crazy. I even flew here coach class, just to get in the spirit."

Producers like Hurd do not usually fly coach class. She's a heavy hitter whose credits include *Aliens* and both *Terminator* films. But she has also produced films like *The Waterdance*, a Sundance hit about a man's painful adjustment to an accident that leaves him paralyzed. Everybody understands that while *Terminator 2* was born to be a box-office champion, Sundance films need tender, loving care.

That's why Rosie Perez is here, plugging her new movie, *The 24-Hour Woman*. She plays a TV producer who has her first child, and tries to juggle the demands of her job and motherhood. The movie was written and directed by Nancy Savoca *(Dogfight, Household Saints)*, who doesn't follow the easy formulas of Hollywood packages but shows how very complicated it is to fight with your boss, your husband, and your heart, all at the same time.

"I've been doing everything I can think of to help this picture," Perez told me at lunch. "I asked the producers to print up 5,000 flyers to be handed out. They wanted to know, like, why? I said because we gotta get the word out there, because the days of platforming are long gone and a picture has to open strong to have a chance."

She used friends to pass out the flyers in New York, where the movie opens in two weeks, and passed out a lot of them herself. "I had my heart broken by a movie called *Somebody to Love* (1994), which was my first starring role and my best work, and the producer got in some kind of a fight, and although it made a lot of money in Europe, it hardly even opened here. Went right to video. You have to fight for your work."

At Sundance, they're fighting. More than 800 features were screened before the final selection was made, but just making the cut here isn't enough: You have to generate buzz. You have to be sure people see your movie and not the other six movies playing at the same time.

There is a movie here named *Chillicothe*, and I don't know anything about it, but I do know that three different people have pitched it to me, and one invited me to the *Chillicothe* party and another gave me a *Chillicothe* baseball cap. The way postcards, flyers, screening schedules, posters, and gimmicks are spread around town, Park City feels like a high school on the day before the election for prom queen.

The festival opened with the premiere of Robert Altman's new film *Cookie's Fortune*, which was very warmly received; it's a comedy set in Holly Springs, Mississippi, where everyone seems to know everything about everyone else. That makes it complicated when it appears to some people that a murder has been committed. Glenn Close and Charles Dutton costar as the daughter of a local matriarch and her best friend.

"Festivals are important," Altman told the audience, "because new stories have to be told and new directors have to be found, and they need a showcase." He recalled that his own early career got a boost when his *M*A*S*H* (1970) was a hit at Cannes ("a festival that used to be pretty good and is still okay," he said, with a grin to Sundance sponsor Robert Redford).

Walk five minutes down the street here, and you see a movie star—maybe six. I was leaving the press office when I ran into Val Kilmer, who was with Frank Whaley, an actor whose first directing effort, *Joe the King*, premiered here. Kilmer was wearing full snow regalia—ski sweater, down vest, muffler. Whaley, who often plays neurotic busybodies, was dressed as for another planet, in a black turtleneck and a black leather jacket. His movie stars Noah Fleiss in a remarkable performance as a young teenager from a troubled home who is in the early stages of a life of crime; Kilmer is his alcoholic father.

The day ended with *Valerie Flake*, which made an obvious impression on its audience. It stars Susan Traylor as a woman whose husband is dead, and who is dealing with it through anger, hostility, and isolation—even years later. The character is smart and articulate, and has a deliberately cruel style that cuts through all the ordinary rituals of grief. Traylor embodies the role, and in her ferocity might have reminded Gale Anne Hurd of the way Eric Stoltz, as the hero of *The Waterdance*, lashed out against his paralysis. It's the kind of movie where people walk out saying, "I don't know who they think will come to see this, but I'm glad I did."

No Shortage of Dreams at Sundance Film Festival

January 25, 1999—You have to go to something like Robert Redford's annual "filmmakers' brunch" to sense the level of ambition, hope, and need at the Sundance Film Festival.

You understand that the festival is a showcase (some say a trade fair) for independent filmmakers. You know that a lot of them are here with their first or second movies and a game plan to make a sale, find distribution, win awards, and generate buzz.

You know that when you meet the filmmakers one at a time. But when there are a couple of hundred in the same room, the sheer level of psychic desire is almost overwhelming.

Redford holds his annual brunch more than an hour's drive from Park City, at his Sundance Institute, up in a canyon above Provo. This is where his Sundance Institute holds workshops for aspiring directors, writers, and actors every summer. A lot of those summer sessions have borne fruit over the years; sitting at a table right in front of the podium during Redford's greeting speech was Gregory Nava, whose *El Norte* (1983) was the first of the Sundance projects to be released.

There are people here who hope the institute's good fortune will rub off on them. Here is Princess Peter-Raboff, from Fairbanks, Alaska, a Native American screenwriter who polished her *Silent Raven* at the institute last summer: "It was an unbelievable opportunity to work with professionals and learn more about the craft. Redford really makes a difference to filmmakers like me."

In another corner, Noah Stern and Michael

Kastenbaum are passing around invitations to the screening of *The Invisibles*, which Stern directed and Kastenbaum produced. Stern I've met before: He was the film critic at the *Daily Illini* at the University of Illinois. He's made more than a dozen films, average cost $6,000. The new one, shot on location in Paris, cost around $9,000, he says: "You have no idea how little money a film can be made for."

After the brunch is officially over, it looks like everyone in the room wants to have a word with Redford. He doesn't hurry away, but remains, patiently listening to stories, hopes, plans, and pitches. Watching it all is Gary Farmer, the towering Native American actor from Toronto, who is here with a documentary: "It's about corn. Corn is an incredibly interesting subject when you approach it in terms of my people's tradition."

Not far away is Michael Epstein, "born in Rogers Park, Chicago, now living in Brooklyn," who is here with his documentary *Hitchcock, Selznick and the End of Hollywood.* "There's a brand-new print of *Notorious*," he reports. "It's beautiful."

Next I run into Toni Kalem, an actress you may remember from *Private Benjamin*, where she played the toughest private in the army. "I bought the rights to Anne Tyler's novel *A Slipping-Down Life* years ago," she says. "At first I wanted to star in it. Then I wanted to direct it." It stars Lili Taylor as a woman with no aims in life (she works in costume as a rabbit) until she becomes obsessed by a local rock star (Guy Pearce, in sideburns and lanky hair, looking utterly unlike his clean-cut cop in *L.A. Confidential*).

And here's Cauleen Smith, from L.A. via the Bay Area, with her first feature, *Drylongso.* "That's an old African-American slang word for ordinary or everyday people," she tells me. "My movie is about a young black woman who photographs black men because she thinks they're an endangered species. Then one day she meets a woman who started presenting herself as a man, at first to hide from her boyfriend, then because she found it allowed her to move around the city more freely." This is a first film too.

So many dreams in this room. So much hope. If I had been doing this story a few years ago, I might have written: "And here was Quentin Tarantino, a former video store clerk, who talked Harvey Keitel into appearing in his first film. It's called *Reservoir Dogs*, and it's great, he assures me."

They're all great, if you listen to the filmmakers. Sometimes they're right.

Persistence Is Key for Fledgling Director

January 25, 1999—So this kid accosts me while I'm standing in the lobby before the Robert Altman film. "You gotta see my film," he says, pulling a videocassette from the depths of his goose-down parka.

"I just can't," I say. "Believe me. People try to give me tapes six times a day. I'm here to see the movies, and I don't have a VCR, and there's no room in my luggage, and besides, I can't review a movie that isn't going to open anywhere."

"But this is a great film," the kid says.

"I hope it is," I say, "and when it opens in a theater, I hope I agree with you."

"But it's only twenty minutes long! So how long would it take for you to see it?"

"Twenty minutes," I say, after a quick mental calculation. "But like I said . . ."

"Yeah, yeah," he says.

"So now you probably think I'm a seven-letter word."

"No," he says, "but someday I'll be a great director, and I will remind you of this moment."

"Good luck," I say. "No, really."

At that point the story should end. If it did, it would be like a dozen other conversations I've had here at Sundance, where my employer is not paying my expenses so I can sit in my room watching home videos by kids who are gonna be great someday. But this story doesn't end there.

Saturday afternoon I'm standing in the coffee shop of the Yarrow Inn, a motel where press screenings are held. There is a large-screen TV behind me. It's tuned to ESPN. I'm talking to the three stars of a movie named *The Outfitters.* They're all sitting in front of the fireplace: Paul Le Mat *(American Graffiti, Melvin and Howard)*, Danny Nucci *(The Rock)*, and Sarah Lassez.

A voice in my ear says: "All you have to do is turn around. My movie is on the TV set."

It's the kid. The giant-screen TV is no longer

tuned to ESPN. Now we are looking at *Bobby Loves Mangos*, and it says "A Film by Stuart Acher."

"What'd you do? Bribe the manager?" I ask.

"Kind of," he says.

"But I have to go to a press screening in ten minutes," I say.

"I'll have them hold it for you," he assures me. "I work here."

"Hold it?" I say. "They're not gonna keep three dozen people waiting so that . . ."

"Don't miss the opening scene," he says.

It takes a certain unrelenting determination to pitch your project at Sundance. Ordinary social inhibitions do not apply.

I sit down next to Danny Nucci. We look at the screen. A school principal arrives at work. His secretary gives him a package. He goes into his office. It is a videocassette made by one of his students named Bobby. Bobby is currently about eight years old, but on the tape he looks about forty. It is a tape from the future. Bobby wants to warn the principal about a school bus accident that is going to happen the next Friday. Fifty students will be killed. Bobby will survive only because he eats mangos, which he's allergic to, and so he's kept home from school.

"This looks like a professional film," I say quietly to Nucci.

"Look at the editing," Nucci says. "He knows where to put his camera, how to move around, when to go in for a close-up."

The story continues. "This is really good," I whisper to Nucci. Le Mat looks over and nods. I look around. There is now a crowd of maybe fifteen people watching the TV. They're absorbed in the story. It's a fascinating premise, and it develops like *Twilight Zone* meets *Groundhog Day.*

Finally I have to rush to the press screening. I tell Acher he is obviously a director of professional caliber. I'm almost late for the screening. They're not holding it for me.

Afterward, I come out into the hallway, and there's Acher again. He wants to know if I want to see the rest of the film. I would, I say, but right now I have to go to another screening.

I get some facts. He's twenty-two years old, the film was his thesis project at Boston University, "and two companies are interested." (At Sundance, the phrase "two companies are interested" is automatically attached to every unsold project.)

I walk into the lobby of the Yarrow and run into David Eick, a senior vice president of the USA Network. He's here looking for stuff. I tell him about the kid and his film. Eick is intrigued. We go back into the coffee shop. The kid talks the manager into putting the film back on the TV again. As I leave, Eick is watching it, with Acher right next to him.

Will Eick buy it as a short? Will he offer Acher a deal to develop it as a made-for-TV feature? Will Miramax hear about it and start a bidding war? Will Stuart Acher become a great director? There are a million stories at the festival, and this is one of them.

Buzz Is in the Air at Sundance

January 26, 1999—Of course I've seen all the wrong films so far at the Sundance Film Festival, according to the helpful touts who whisper in my ear before every screening. It is always this way. You think you're seeing wonderful films, and everybody assures you that you've missed the masterpieces and are hopelessly out of the buzz loop.

If I am to believe what I hear, the biggest bidding war this year is over *Happy, Texas*, a movie about two escaped convicts posing as a gay theatrical couple, who are hired to direct the annual Little Miss Fresh-Squeezed Beauty Pageant. William H. Macy plays the secretive local sheriff.

The audience favorite is said to be *Three Seasons*, the first American feature to be shot in Vietnam since the war, interweaving four stories of transition. It has received two standing ovations, unheard-of at Sundance. And the underground buzz is about *The Blair Witch Project*, a weird experimental horror film, which had only a couple of small screenings, although fest director Geoff Gilmore tells me he's slotting it in for another showing. I'll report on all three films later in the festival.

Meanwhile, I am left with the films I have actually seen, many of them very good. I have been telling the touts about them, so they can share the anguish of having missed the best films. Actual reviews will await their openings. Here are notes:

Ravenous, by the British director Antonia

Bird *(Mad Love)*, is a very dark Western about an isolated army cavalry unit in the wintertime California mountains, and how cannibalism is introduced into their circle by a vampirish outcast. This is one of the creepiest and most unusual horror films in many a moon, starring Guy Pearce, Jeffrey Jones, Jeremy Davies, and Robert Carlyle as the stranger with odd tastes.

Mr. Death is the latest documentary by Errol Morris *(Fast, Cheap and Out of Control)*. He finds odd subjects, and Fred A. Leuchter Jr. is one of the oddest: an engineer who specializes in designing updated and "humane" electric chairs, gas chambers, and lethal injection machines. His business is booming until he takes a commission from Holocaust deniers to study the gas chambers at Auschwitz. He claims they wouldn't have worked; experts attack his methods, and his death business falls off.

The Loss of Sexual Innocence is one of the most daring and innovative films in the festival, by Mike Figgis *(Leaving Las Vegas)*. It has the kind of freedom of form seen in works by Kieslowski and Tarkovsky, as it examines the way sex, guilt, and knowledge interact in several lives; the background story is an interracial version of *Paradise Lost*. Julian Sands and Saffron Burrows star.

Lock, Stock and Two Smoking Barrels is already a hit in the United Kingdom; it's a twisted crime comedy about villains and double crosses, told in a style halfway between *film noir* and MTV. Sting stars in a cast of hot young Brits and Scots.

Valerie Flake stars Susan Traylor in one of the year's most uncompromising performances, as a woman whose bitter and aggressive style conceals deep wounds. She meets a very nice guy (Jay Underwood), patient and understanding, and his niceness seems to make her suffer even more. Bleak, darkly comic, wholly original.

A Slipping-Down Life stars Lili Taylor, a heroine at Sundance, as a small-town woman whose life is pointless, she feels, until she grows obsessed with a local rock singer (Guy Pearce, again) and carves his name in her forehead. Oddly enough, this leads not to a movie about stalking, but to a romance: The singer falls in love with her, although their relationship is far from simple.

Home Page is a haunting documentary set at the time when the Web was shifting from individual anarchists to corporate megasites. It centers on Justin Hall, bright, articulate, and with a peculiar hairstyle, as his Web page makes him an early Web superstar, and then follows him on an odyssey to San Francisco, where he intersects with the Web empires of *Wired* magazine and Internet pioneer Howard Rheingold. Justin and others talk of their on-line friendships (their lives seem primarily devoted to producing fodder for their Web pages); the movie wonders how fulfilling their virtual relationships really are.

Guinevere is a comic and touching love story about a twenty-year-old (Sarah Polley) who meets a much older wedding photographer (Stephen Rea) and falls for his bohemian lifestyle and his encouragement; she has low self-esteem, and he helps her to flower. But is this because he has a big heart, or because it's a good way to score with chicks?

Sundance featured two tributes this year. Laura Dern, whose acting has distinguished such independent films as *Smooth Talk, Wild at Heart, Rambling Rose*, and *Citizen Ruth*, was honored at the Piper-Heidsieck Tribute to Independent Vision. Isabella Rossellini was the emcee, Peter Bogdanovich discussed her work in *Mask*, and I joined her for an onstage Q&A. The night before, Gregory Nava and Anna Thomas, director and producer of *El Norte*, were honored by a fifteenth-anniversary screening of their epic classic, which was the first of the Sundance Institute summer workshop screenplays to make it to the screen.

Six more films tomorrow. Gotta get some sleep. The buzz goes on.

Teenage Boys Are Focus of Big-Studio Attention

January 26, 1999—Teenage boys.

Those two words have become a mantra at this year's Sundance Film Festival. They're buzzwords reflecting the gloom among those who love independent films. They explain why, even in the midst of one of the healthiest Sundance festivals, there are those who worry about the future of films that try to be different.

"Teenage boys" is shorthand for the following thought process:

1. Hollywood studios are mesmerized by the desire to win the weekend box-office race. Every newspaper and TV show in the land faithfully repeats the weekend scorecard, anointing one film the "winner" and clucking over the poor performances of others.

2. Therefore, studios want to make films that "open strong." Movies where the crowds are lined up for the first show on Friday.

3. Most people have real lives, and cannot drop everything at a moment's notice to rush out to the first Friday screening.

4. Teenage boys can, and do. And they like loud, noisy movies with a lot of action and violence, and some, but not too much, sex. Their favorite genres are horror, science fiction, and teenage gross-out comedies. Certain big-name stars can turn them out almost automatically; the A-list currently includes Jim Carrey, Adam Sandler, and the young stars of the *I Know What You Did Last Summer*–style teenage slasher films.

5. Therefore . . . but you can fill in the rest yourself.

The studios are looking for immediate returns. Older audiences take longer to make up their minds about a movie. They read the reviews, they talk to their friends, they make plans, they go in a week or two. That's too slow for the impatient Hollywood bookers. Movies used to be allowed to "find an audience." They grew through word of mouth, over weeks and months. No longer. Now they have to perform immediately, or die.

This is, of course, gloomy news for independent films and those who make and love them. The phrase "independent film" is hard to define, and no longer means nonstudio pictures. What it does mean is nonmainstream, nonformula pictures. Movies that are different from one another. Movies that try for something new, and challenge you. Just the kind of movies teenage boys hate. (Of course, many teenage boys are informed and astute about the movies, but we're talking hard box-office cash here.)

Because independent films tend to be better than Teenage Boy Movies, they get a lot of attention at awards time. Two years ago the Oscars were dominated by indie entries. This year, the leading contenders include *Shakespeare in Love*, *A Simple Plan*, *Elizabeth*, *Life Is Beautiful*, and *Pleasantville*. Because you read a lot about those titles, you get the impression that indie films are doing okay. Not so.

I've been hearing for months from people complaining that none (repeat, none) of those titles are playing in their towns. Although big cities are good enough for such films, the Hollywood-based block bookers peer into their computers and decide that smaller cities (and smaller states) are too backward, I guess. Anyone who lives in a small town is consigned by the booking wizards to horror, explosions, and blockbusters. Complaints to the local theater manager are useless. His responsibility is to preside over a refreshment-counter operation; he has nothing to say about the movies he shows.

Items of evidence:

—At a screening here, I ran into Jake Eberts, a man with an almost perfect last name. He's one of the best-known independent producers, with credits like *Driving Miss Daisy*, *Dances With Wolves*, and *A River Runs Through It*, the acclaimed Robert Redford film about the connections between trout fishing and life.

"When we finished *River Runs Through It* in 1992," he told me, "we could hardly find a distributor for it. All the studios thought it was a hard sell. Columbia finally took it, and of course we had a big success. But today, if I were going out with that film, I don't think I could sell it. It would go straight to video."

Trout fishing? Lessons about life? Not for teenage boys.

—At another screening, I ran into Gary Meyer, an executive with the new Sundance theater chain.

"Amazing news," he said. "After seventeen years in limbo, the rights to the Beatles' *Yellow Submarine* have finally been cleared. And it's been restored with a remastered digital sound track!"

"Fabulous," I said. *Yellow Submarine* was a 1968 animated film starring the Beatles in a Peter Max–inspired pop art fantasy, as they save the people of Pepperland from the Blue Meanies. It has ten Beatles songs, including "All You Need Is Love," "When I'm 64," "Nowhere Man," "Eleanor Rigby," and a version of "Lucy in the Sky with Diamonds" that Pauline Kael said "is a stunning use of stylized human figures, an apotheosis of Rogers and Astaire."

You have not seen this on TV, and it is not

available on video because of legal problems over the rights. Now it would be perfect for a big-screen theatrical release, right? Wrong.

"Frank Mancuso at MGM loves it, but his people want to take it straight to video," Meyer told me. "They say there's no theatrical market for the film. They say audiences don't care about the Beatles."

For "audiences," read "teenage boys." Beatles? Animation? "When I'm 64"? Not for teenage boys. (Even so, the execs are astonishingly wrongheaded; my guess is that *Yellow Submarine* in theaters would be a major source of found money for MGM, which could use some.)

—On Monday night, actress Laura Dern was honored at the Piper-Heidsieck Tribute to Independent Vision. Her entire career is a list of important independent films, including *Smooth Talk*, *Mask*, *Blue Velvet*, *Wild at Heart*, *Rambling Rose*, and *Citizen Ruth*.

I joined her onstage for a Q&A session, and we looked at clips from her career, including one from *The Baby Dance*, which played on cable TV last year. She plays a young woman who agrees to bear a baby for an affluent older couple.

"TV offers a home for films like this," she said. "There's more freedom for difficult stories. I remember in 1980 seeing Robert Redford's *Ordinary People* (which won Oscars for Picture, Supporting Actor, and Redford's direction). A film about a family and its problems and how it gets through them. Today, that film would be made for cable TV. It wouldn't be considered for theatrical release."

A family? Problems? Emotional confrontations? Lack of communication? Not for teenage boys.

Right now there is no more gripping movie playing in America than Sam Raimi's *A Simple Plan*. If and when it gets some Oscar nominations, maybe for Best Picture and Billy Bob Thornton's acting, it may be distributed half as widely as *Patch Adams*. It did "go wide" on January 22—but not so wide that people aren't still asking me why it's not in their town.

For those who love inventive and daring films, there are three glimmers of hope on the horizon.

—Build theaters dedicated to independent, foreign, and documentary films. Redford's Sundance theaters and the Landmark Corp. have both announced multiplexes for the Chicago market and other big cities; small towns have to wait.

—Cable TV. A movie plays on TV, and reaches a larger audience than it ever could in theaters. Three channels are dedicated to indie films: Bravo, the Independent Film Channel, and Sundance. Of course, many local cable systems don't carry them. That's why I got a satellite dish. Made-for-TV movies are produced by such as HBO, Showtime, TNT, and USA. Some of them are very good.

—Digital filmmaking. A few years ago, video was scorned by filmmakers, who insisted on celluloid. Now its quality has improved so much that a theatrical-quality film can be shot inexpensively on video. Yesterday I saw a documentary named *Home Page*, about people who live their lives through their Web pages. Director Doug Block said he shot it with a Super-8 camera. Looked fine to me. If video cinematography can allow filmmakers to cut production costs in half or more, it will be easier for them to make their films.

There is one other solution, suggested sardonically during a conversation I was having in a restaurant about the Teenage Boy Problem. We must have been talking loudly enough to be overheard. A woman at the next table smiled and said, "Better schools, that's the answer. We have to start turning out smarter teenage boys."

Death and Denial

January 29, 1999—One of the most talked-about films at this year's Sundance Film Festival focuses on a man named Fred A. Leuchter, Jr., whose unusual business (designing electric chairs and other lethal devices) brings him into contact with those who deny the Holocaust really happened. A meek and extremely literal man, he agrees to conduct an "investigation" of the death chambers at Auschwitz, and concludes that no deadly gas was employed there. His finding flies in the face of overwhelming evidence that some 500,000 victims were asphixiated there.

The documentary, *Mr. Death: The Rise and Fall of Fred A. Leuchter Jr.*, is by Errol Morris, America's most intriguing and sometimes perplexing documentarian. It is not about whether gas was used at Auschwitz (although it concludes that Leuchter is mistaken), but about the kind of personality that can flourish in the presence of evil. Leuchter fits the mold of a Holocaust denier, but in fact his denial goes even deeper than that, goes right down to bedrock: In his plodding and ingratiating way, he denies common sense.

There is always the danger, in films about dangerous subjects, that the film will have an unintended effect. Truffaut wondered if there could be such a thing as an antiwar film, since film by its very nature argues in favor of its protagonists; war is bad, but still we cheer for our side. A long article about *Mr. Death* in a recent *New Yorker*, by Mark Singer, muses on the relationship between Morris and Leuchter, and wonders whether the film will create sympathy in some viewers for the self-styled death engineer.

Here at Sundance, I've talked with people who fear *Mr. Death* may give pleasure to those who deny the Holocaust. Certainly the *Leuchter Report* is a prized document of the loony fringe, and has been widely distributed for a decade. My response has been: Since the film does not agree with Leuchter, indeed portrays him as a limited man of great self-delusion, Errol Morris cannot be held responsible for conclusions arrived at by viewers who may be eager to interpret it according to their own prejudices. No film is safe from fools.

In Morris's film, which he says is still not in its final form, we see amateur movies of Leuchter's trip to Auschwitz—where he chipped away at walls and ceilings and brought his samples back to America to be analyzed. They produced so little residue of cyanide that he concluded the "alleged gas chamber" could not have been used for that purpose. He also argues from the physical remains at Auschwitz that the chambers would have leaked, killing guards and other prisoners. There are no airtight gaskets, he says, or ventilation outlets.

The film rebuts Leuchter's conclusions. The hired chemist who analyzed the samples was never told where they came from or what they were, and says on camera that he pulverized them before his analysis; since cyanide by its nature would penetrate bricks only to the depth of one-tenth of a human hair, he says, by crushing the chips to powder before testing them, he had diluted the sample and "the results were meaningless." It is also true that the site had been exposed to decades of decay, weather, and vandalism (many of its bricks ended up cannibalized for nearby home construction), so that Leuchter could have no accurate idea of what the chambers looked like during the war.

Still, Leuchter himself is a deeply ambiguous figure, as the subjects of Morris's documentaries always are. I remember the operators of pet cemeteries in *Gates of Heaven* (sincere or ridiculous?) and the subjects of *Fast, Cheap and Out of Control*, who have devoted their lives to training nature to do what it is not in nature's nature to do. The topiary gardener, spending decades clipping shrubs to look like animals, has a single-mindedness that reminds me of Leuchter; they live with tunnel vision.

Mr. Death begins with a portrait of Leuchter as a death consultant, explaining why some electric chairs "cook the meat too much," and why he'd like to design a "lethal injection machine" like a dental chair, so the condemned could die in comfort. (He's enthusiastic about the possibilities for letting them watch TV or listen to music while fading away.) The contrast between his "humane" methods and the stark fact of execution is so bizarre that Morris just lets his camera sit there and regard him.

When Leuchter is hired in 1988 by the anti-Semite Ernst Zundel, author of *Did Six Million Really Die?* there is some question about whether he fully understands the implications of his work. Indeed, as he clambers about Auschwitz chipping at walls, he looks like a parody of a scientist; his study is so limited he is like the blind man examining an elephant. (Zundel commissioned the report as part of his defense after being charged in Canada with distributing hate literature.)

The film refutes Leuchter, but does it create sympathy for him? Yes, of course it does. Here is a man who lost his wife and his business because he conducted a sincere (if misguided and wrongheaded) study. State prison officials stopped hiring him after he was identified as a friend of neo-Nazis.

My feeling is that those who watch movies bear a responsibility for using their intelligence. Only the stupid or the willfully misguided could get the wrong message from *Mr. Death;* attentive viewers will see it as a document illustrating Hannah Arendt's concept of the "banality of evil"—a modern case study of a man with blinders on, obsessed with his own limited definition of his duty, oblivious to the big picture or any moral implications.

Among documentaries about the Holocaust, this one is invaluable, because instead of simply repeating familiar facts, it demonstrates the very process of self-deception that made the Holocaust possible. Fred Leuchter would agree that the Holocaust had at least one victim—himself. And in his ruefulness we hear echoes of war criminals, complaining they were "only doing their jobs."

As this unremarkable middle-aged man talks about designing better electrocutions, hangings, and poisonings while respecting "the dignity of the condemned man," we hear the same kind of technology in a moral void that designed the mechanics of the Holocaust. Humans are capable of building mental firewalls between their evildoing and their ordinary lives. Perhaps we even see a connection between the Holocaust and capital punishment—between any presumptions that the state is innocent when it takes lives.

Three Seasons Wins Grand Slam at Sundance

February 1, 1999—A first-generation Vietnamese-American has scored the first grand slam in the history of the Sundance Film Festival feature competition, by winning both the Grand Jury Prize and the Audience Award.

Tony Bui, born in Vietnam, raised in California, won for *Three Seasons*, a poetic interweaving of three stories in modern-day Vietnam. Harvey Keitel has the only American role, as an ex-marine searching for his daughter. Other stories involve a rickshaw driver who loves a prostitute, and the world of child street vendors. The first American fiction film to be shot in Vietnam, it also won for Best Cinematography.

In the documentary category, the Grand Jury Prize went to *American Movie*, the story of the making of a basement-budget horror film in Wisconsin. Filmmakers Chris Smith and Sarah Price followed dedicated would-be director Mark Borchardt, of Menominee Falls, as he hustled friends, his parents, and an uncle (who had some money in the bank) to make the straight-to-video *Coven* (which the ever-optimistic Borchardt reported has sold seventy copies—"fifty here at Sundance").

The Audience Award for Best Documentary, voted on by filmgoers, went to *Genghis Blues*, by Evanston, Illinois, filmmakers Roko and Adrian Belic. The film begins with a bet years ago by physicist Richard Feynman: Can you find Tuva on the map? By a strange process, that leads to blind blues singer Paul Pena learning the obscure Tuvan technique of throat-singing, which can produce four notes at once.

The Filmmakers Trophies are voted by directors at the festival. This year the feature winner was *Tumbleweeds*, by Gavin O'Connor, starring Janet McTeer as a feisty southern woman. For documentaries, the winner was *Sing Faster: The Stagehands' Ring Cycle*, by Jon Else, a comic look at the backstage world of San Francisco opera as seen by the stagehands.

It was a year for revisiting Vietnam. The directing award for docs went to Barbara Sonneborn, for *Regret to Inform.* She lost a husband in Vietnam and went back looking for closure; in a deeply affecting movie, she talks to widows from both sides of the war. In the feature category, the best director was Eric Mendelsohn, for *Judy Berlin*, about a discouraged young man's reunion with an old classmate whose dreams are still ahead.

The Freedom of Expression Award, sponsored by Playboy, went to *The Black Press: Soldiers Without Swords* by Stanley Nelson. It's the story of a century of newspapers serving African-Americans. The Waldo Salt Screenwriting Award went to Audrey Wells, whose *Guinevere* starred Sarah Polley as a young girl who falls in love with an older photographer (Stephen Rea).

Special Jury Prizes went to Steve Zahn for his performance in *Happy, Texas*, as an escaped convict who impersonates a gay pageant director, and to Scott King's *Treasure Island.* In the documentary category, the Special Jury winner was *On the Ropes*, by Nanette Burstein and Brett Morgen, who followed three boxers from a New York gym and found a heartbreaking story in one of them, a mother of two with a chance at the Golden Gloves belt.

The Jury Prize for Latin American Cinema went to *Santitos*, by Alejandro Springall of Mexico. The World Cinema Award was shared by *Run Lola Run* by Tom Tykwer of Germany, and *Train of Life* by Radu Milhaileanu of France.

For documentary cinematography, Emiko Omori won for *Rabbit in the Moon* (she also shot parts of *Regret to Inform*). For a dramatic film, Lisa Rinzler's camera work continued the victorious night for *Three Seasons*.

Victory at Sundance often means significant box-office results and even Academy Awards. The top financial winner this year was *Happy, Texas*, picked up by Miramax for a reported $2.5 million—plus an unprecedented guarantee (for indie films) of a share of the grosses. Another film that seems destined for wide audiences is *The Blair Witch Project*, picked up by Artisan, which truly frightened even the blasé Sundance audience with its premise: Three filmmakers go into the forest in search of a legendary witch, and only their film is found two years later.

Buzz Abounds at Sundance

February 1, 1999—How long has it been since I saw a film that was really scary, instead of just going through the motions of scary? Most horror films are merely exercises in ritualized surprise, but a low-budget film named *The Blair Witch Project* shook up Sundance audiences with its gathering sense of menace.

The film, directed by Eduardo Sanchez and Daniel Myrick, begins with a stark announcement: A few years ago, three filmmakers walked into the hills of Maryland in search of a legendary local witch. "Two years later, their tapes were found." The film consists entirely of video and 16mm film allegedly shot by the filmmakers, as a walk in the woods turns into a terrifying nightmare.

Walking out of the screening, I was with a group of people who actually thought it was a documentary. I told them it was fiction that cleverly used the techniques of fact. "Those performers weren't actors," one said. "They were too real." In the Salt Lake City airport, I ran into Michael Williams, who plays one of the three. "Yeah," he said, "after every screening, people were surprised to see me alive."

Blair Witch won no awards at Sundance, but was one of the most buzzed-about films. Some of the others:

—*Three Seasons*, which became the first feature to win both the Grand Jury Prize and the Audience Award, is the first U.S. film shot in Vietnam. Tony Bui, born there, raised here, combines realism with romance and sadness in his interlocking stories about an ex-marine (Harvey Keitel) searching for his daughter, a rickshaw driver who falls for a hooker, and some kids who live in the streets. It received standing ovations from Sundance audiences.

—Chris Smith's *American Movie*, which won the Grand Jury prize for documentary, is a harrowing and hilarious documentary about a would-be filmmaker from Menominee Falls, Wisconsin, and his heroic effort to film a horror film named *Coven*.

Mark Borchardt, tall, gangly, and bearded, is the hopeful producer, director, and star, and enlists his buddies and family in the effort. An elderly uncle is persuaded to invest his savings, convinced it will all come to nothing. Local actors are recruited; one firmly corrects Mark's mispronunciation of "coven," and another allows his head to be pounded into a cabinet that does not break easily.

—Of all the films I saw at Sundance, the best was *The War Zone*. It's the first directing job by actor Tim Roth, whose roles range from *Reservoir Dogs* and *Pulp Fiction* to *Rob Roy*. In its story, tone, pacing, images, performances, and effect, it is as well made as the work of a seasoned professional; Roth takes a story filled with hazards and tells it triumphantly.

His film takes place in a wintry season in Devon, within a family that seems close and happy, and is not. It is slowly, painfully, subtly revealed that the father is raping his teenage daughter. This becomes known to the younger son, and how he deals with that information provides the film's central story. The father's behavior shows how humans are capable of building mental firewalls between evildoing and their ordinary lives.

—*On the Ropes*, a doc that won a Special Jury prize, tells the story of three boxers based in a gym in Bedford-Stuyvesant. One of them, a mother of two named Tyrene, grabs our hearts. She lives in a house with a crackhead uncle, but raises her children to achieve straight A's in school, and seems poised for a Golden Glove belt after knocking out the current female champion.

Then crack is found in her house, and she is charged with possession and dealing—wrongly, we feel. The judicial system fails her; an incompetent attorney and an uncaring judge figure in a courtroom scene that makes you want to shout at the screen. Now she's in prison, but filmmakers Nanette Burstein and Brett Morgen say she may be paroled in September. She's still in training.

—*Happy, Texas* was the big money winner, purchased by Miramax for $2.5 million and a piece of the profits. It's a weirdly original comedy about two convicts (Jeremy Northam and Steve Zahn) who are mistaken for a gay couple hired to produce the local Little Miss Fresh-Squeezed Beauty Pageant. The sheriff of Happy (William H. Macy) makes discoveries about his own sexuality, while local teacher Illeana Douglas falls in what she thinks is futile love.

—Barbara Sonneborn's husband was killed in Vietnam as a young man; she visits that land in *Regret to Inform* to try to come to grips what happened three decades ago. She talks with other war widows—American and Vietnamese—in a film that approaches the war from a different viewpoint than all the other Vietnam films. There is great sadness in the memories of the women, including one who seriously considered hammering her husband's hand while he slept, to keep him out of uniform. She didn't, and he's dead.

—*A Walk on the Moon* stars Diane Lane as a Jewish mother in the world of upstate New York summer resorts in the late 1960s. The women and children spend the week, the husbands drive up on weekends. She finds herself attracted to the "blouse man" (Viggo Mortensen), whose retail truck makes regular calls. And there is the siren lure of the nearby Woodstock festival, reminding her that all of her options were put on hold when she married.

—There are those who think the Japanese director Hirokasu Kore-Eda is at the top of the new generation of directors. His first film, *Maborosi* (1997), was a masterpiece, and he is back with *After Life*, the story of a heavenly way station where the newly dead are asked to make a film of just one memory from their entire lifetimes. It opens in the spring.

—*La Ciudad (The City)*, by David Riker, tells related stories of illegal immigrants from Central and South America, trying to make lives in New York. Everyone agrees it is a wonderful film; no one seems to know if it would be "commercial." One of the sad underlying themes at Sundance this year was a general lack of confidence in the national movie audience, which is thought to attend only empty-headed entertainments; distributors are afraid to sink money into films they really love.

—*Go*, the second film by Doug Liman *(Swingers)*, is yet another post-Tarantino pastiche of lowlifes whose stories occupy parallel time tracks. But it's a superior example of the form, as grocery clerks, drug dealers, cops, and actors in trouble get enmeshed in interlocking violence and intrigue. It doesn't make the mistake of the superficially similar *Very Bad Things*, which went so far with its bad things that the humor could never recover.

—*Sugar Town* is Los Angeles, in the comedy by Allison Anders and Kurt Voss about the music business. Once-hot rockers, studio musicians, and actors wheel and deal, love and hate, and date, in a series of sometimes delightful comic vignettes. Rosanna Arquette, Ally Sheedy, and Michael des Barres are among the stars, in a movie where the dialogue is as inside as this week's *Variety*.

The Kid Makes Contact!

February 2, 1999—The kid made a deal!

Well, maybe. Faithful readers will recall the persistent Stuart Acher, a twenty-two-year-old Boston film school graduate who accosted me on the opening night of the Sundance Film Festival with a video, which he freed from the depths of his goose-down vest and pressed upon me with the assurance that he would soon be a great director.

I told him I was not at Sundance to view videos by directors of the future, however great. But a few days later, in the coffee shop of the Yarrow Inn, a voice in my ear advised: "All you have to do is turn around. My movie is on the TV set."

So it was. Acher had persuaded the manager to switch off ESPN and fill the sixty-inch screen with Acher's tape, named *Bobby Loves Mangos.* I watched it. What else could I do? I liked it. Maybe he'll make a successful pitch, I mused, and history will be made. After all, even Scorsese was once a kid trying to get his scripts read.

Four days passed. I was back in the Yarrow

for a screening. Here came the kid, dialing down the volume on his headset.

"I made a contact!" he says.

"Someone's producing your film?" I ask.

"Not exactly," he says. "But I showed it to a Universal executive, and he says if I come to L.A., he'll introduce me to people. He thinks it could be developed into a viable project!"

"How did he happen to see the video?" I ask.

"I overheard him on his way into a press screening and found out who he was," Acher said. "Then, when I saw him in the coffee shop, I threw the video back into the TV and showed him a printout of your article."

His quarry was Ted Perkins, director of international distribution for Universal. I contacted Perkins, who informed me he did indeed believe Acher "could develop a viable feature concept if he broadened the scope of the drama and upped the stakes."

He has already made some suggestions along those lines, Perkins said, adding: "I promised that if he ever comes to L.A., I will recommend him to every agent and manager I know. No doubt his career will take off from there. I hope he gives me a first-look on the resulting films!"

The Sundance festival is crawling with kids who have a video in their parka and a script in their jeans. They're all trying to get someone to pay attention. It takes a certain relentless determination.

Perkins added: "Stuart represents the quintessence of what makes the indie sector tick—a drive by creative young people to get noticed, get produced, get taken seriously at all costs. This whole business is built on perseverance. Stuart's got it in spades. His shoestring-budget film is both a revelation and a warning to Hollywood: Creativity doesn't particularly need to cost a lot of money."

Will Acher make a deal? Will he make the movie? Wait, there's more.

"Wanna see another great short?" he asked me.

"You have another one?"

"No, but my friend Kirsten Holly Smith does." He produced a blonde from behind a billboard that said, "TURN OFF CELL PHONES BEFORE SCREENINGS."

"Hi," Kirsten said. "I star in this movie. It's called *Isle of Lesbos*, and it's a musical."

"You directed it yourself?"

"No, it was directed by Jeff B. Harmon. He's, like, Bozo's son?"

"She's gonna be a great actress someday," Acher assures me.

"When you get your deal at Universal, will you cast her in *Bobby Loves Mangos*?" I ask.

"We'll cross that bridge when we come to it."

See Answer Man entry on page 841.

Cannes Film Festival

Cannes, France—One year I arrived in Cannes a little early, two days before the festival was scheduled to begin, and watched the waiters on the famous terrace of the Carlton Hotel as they loaded the good furniture into trucks and unloaded the weather-beaten rattan that I had come to know and love.

The expensive chairs are for rich tourists during the months when Cannes is the jewel of the Riviera. The rattan is for the ten days when hordes of maddened paparazzi are likely to leap onto chairs to get a better angle for their shots of the French starlet Lolo Ferrari, whose breasts are much larger than necessary.

Cannes goes crazy during these days in May; it is not merely the center of the movie world, but also of the publicity world. National TV networks park their trailer trucks out behind the Palais des Festivals, pointing their big satellite dishes at the sky to beam back breathless reports to Madrid, London, Tokyo, Rome, and Frankfurt. Limousines disgorge stars, who walk slowly up the red carpet of the outside staircase, and turn to display the latest fashions from the Paris design houses. And the biggest star of all may be Harvey Weinstein, head honcho of Miramax films, because he has the biggest checkbook for buying the kinds of films they show at Cannes.

They will not be showing *Star Wars: The Phantom Menace* or *Eyes Wide Shut* this year, although in the past they've unveiled such blockbusters as *E.T.*, and they do have this summer's third most talked-about film, *The*

Blair Witch Project. And they will be showing the new films of Takeshi Kitano, the hottest director in Japan right now, and Canada's Atom Egoyan, and Spain's Pedro Almodovar, and Mexico's Arturo Ripstein, and Britain's Peter Greenaway. They were going to show the new film by China's Chen Kaige, until he withdrew it, although it may be back in the lineup by the festival's end (the Chinese have been sensitive over the years to slights, real and otherwise, although they will not hold the bombing of their Belgrade embassy against the French).

Cannes has a tradition of discovering new American directors every year, and although this year's discoveries are, of course, still undiscovered, the 1999 selection includes an honor roll of leading U.S. independents. In competition are new films by Tim Robbins *(The Cradle Will Rock)*, Jim Jarmusch *(Ghost Dog: The Way of the Samurai)*, John Sayles *(Limbo)*, and David Lynch *(The Straight Story)*.

There will be special screenings out of competition for Kevin Smith, whose *Dogma* has already stirred controversy for its religious views, Jon Amiel *(Entrapment)*, and Steven Soderbergh *(The Limey)*. Ron Howard will see if his *EDtv* stirs up more excitement in Europe than it did in America. And Spike Lee will be playing in a sidebar event with *Summer of Sam*, about the serial killer "Son of Sam." The film has been dogged by rumors of a possible NC-17 rating; it will be one of the hottest films of the festival.

Some films cause shoving matches at the turnstiles, and they're usually the ones that have to do with movies. One of this year's most eagerly awaited films is *My Best Fiend* (yes, fiend, not friend), a film about the legendary and creepy German actor Klaus Kinski by his friend and enemy Werner Herzog, who shipped him into the heart of the Amazon for *Aguirre, the Wrath of God* and *Fitzcarraldo*, and made him into a vampire wraith in *Nosferatu*. Perhaps this film will settle for once and all whether Herzog and Kinski actually plotted to murder each other during those steamy jungle ordeals.

Some films at Cannes are shown in the best venues in the world, the vast auditoriums inside the Palais; the theater Lumiere, named for the French inventor of the cinema, has the largest screen I have ever seen, and is packed from the daily 8:30 A.M. press screening until the black-tie premieres late at night. Other films unspool all over town. The Director's Fortnight is in a cavernous bunker beneath the Noga Hilton hotel, and you can see filmgoers trudging back and forth along the Boulevard Croisette, which follows the beach for a mile or so between the two venues.

Then there is the sidebar selection called Un Certain Regard, for films by directors that the festival has, yes, a certain regard for. One of them is David Mamet, whose *The Winslow Boy* will play. And there is the Critics' Week, which is much too picky to have anything to do with the official festival, and this year sniffed that it could find no American films worthy of screening.

The Marketplace, home to some 5,000 buyers and sellers of more commercial films, holds screenings in the local theaters along the crowded shopping street of the rue d'Antibes. Hotel suites are filled with VCR machines, playing films that can't afford to rent theater space. And down in the basement of the Palais, there is a man who will sell you videotapes by the pound.

The head of the jury this year is the Canadian director David Cronenberg, whose *eXistenZ* and the Cannes entry *Crash* confused the movie ratings boards by presenting activities that looked like sex, but involved unfamiliar orifices (in *eXistenZ*, the characters have "bioports" opening into their spines). The best-known of his jurors are actors Holly Hunter and Jeff Goldblum, filmmaker George Miller *(Babe, Pig in the City)* and French director Andre Techine *(My Favorite Season, Thieves)*.

An estimated 50,000 people will attend the festival in one capacity or another. That includes pickpockets, hookers, and the sidewalk salesmen of fake Gucci bags—who all hold their annual conventions here. "It's a funny thing," a veteran critic once said. "Every year, I can't wait to get here. And I can't wait to leave."

Hollywood Blockbusters Absent at Cannes

May 13, 1999—If Gilles Jacob, the overlord of the Cannes Film Festival, had gotten his way, the Palais des Festivals would have been trembling with the THX sound track of *The Phantom Menace.* Jacob likes to open his festival with a blockbuster, just to remind everyone what a movie is before they disappear into intense screenings of tortured adaptations of obscure novels by Herman Melville.

But George Lucas and 20th Century-Fox didn't grant Jacob his wish, preferring to hold the press premiere of the new *Star Wars* picture at a popcorn palace in Manhattan. I attended that screening last Friday, at a location so secret that the press had to be bused to an "undisclosed location," where we were greeted by the cameras of the TV gossip shows, which had somehow discovered it.

The picture and sound were indeed splendid at the screening (Lucas's producer, Rick McCallum, assured me "only 1 percent of the theaters in America meet our technical standards"). But it wasn't as overwhelming as it would have been at Cannes, in a vast, 3,500-seat house with the largest screen I have ever seen and the best sound. Perhaps *Phantom Menace* would have been greeted more warmly here, where visual style is highly valued, than in New York, where many critics found the new movie lacking in its "human relationships."

Call me a hopeless innocent, but I don't go to a *Star Wars* movie to see human relationships, not even when they involve aliens and androids. I go to see amazing sights, real big and loud, one after another.

Denied *Phantom Menace*, and also denied the premiere of Stanley Kubrick's *Eyes Wide Shut*, which he would have liked to show, Jacob opened his festival here Wednesday greeted by headlines like "H'WOOD ABSENT IN FORCE" *(Hollywood Reporter)* and "U.S. GO HOME!" *(Le Film Francais)*. But there is no absence of Americans at the fifty-second festival, only of high-profile Hollywood megafilms.

"America is fast vanishing from Cannes," wrote the industry-centered *Reporter*. Yet this year's festival is like a roll call of the biggest names in independent North American filmmaking. Can a festival be said to lack Americans when it premieres new films by Spike Lee, John Sayles, David Lynch, Jim Jarmusch, Kevin Smith, Steven Soderbergh, and Tim Robbins? Not to mention Canada's Atom Egoyan? What's interesting is that most of those directors were first put on the map at Cannes, where their early films were successful. (It was here that I first saw *Do the Right Thing, Brother from Another Planet, Wild at Heart, Down by Law, sex, lies, and videotape*, and *Bob Roberts*.)

If *Phantom Menace* had opened the festival, I would, of course, have gone to see it again. But it did not, and so it was off to La Pizza, down by the old yacht harbor, instead. Experience has taught me that after flying all night from America and arriving in a state of severe time dislocation, there is nothing like a comfortable seat at an evening screening for a deep sleep.

The opening night film I would have slumbered through was *The Barber of Siberia*, by the Russian Nikita Milhalkov. It is a nineteenth-century story about a beautiful young American woman (Julia Ormond) who poses as the daughter of the inventor of a gigantic machine to shave down the forests of Siberia; her assignment is to seduce the bureaucrat who could approve this project. How good was it? I spent the morning running into colleagues who found many different and colorful ways of telling me it was unbelievably bad.

My own festival kickoff was the press screening of *Pola X*, by Leos Carax, a French adaptation of Melville's *Pierre*, a nineteenth-century story about a young man's idyllic relationship with his mother and his happy plans for marriage, all destroyed by the appearance of a strange, dark woman who claims to be his father's secret daughter.

Strange, isn't it, how what seems gloriously melodramatic in a nineteenth-century story has a way of becoming absurd in a modern context? Pierre, played by Gérard Depardieu's son Guillaume, spends his days chatting with his seductive and often nude mother (Catherine Deneuve) and racing on his motorcycle to the bed of his fiancée before encountering his dark and wounded sister and running off to Paris with her, where they find quarters in an abandoned factory that is being used for recording sessions by an orchestra whose members pound fifty-five-gallon drums while chickens run between their legs. Young Depardieu's performance features the gradual destruction of his body in a series of beatings, woundings, and motorcycle accidents (the family pastime). He begins as a golden-haired Adonis and ends by lurching about Paris like the hunchback of Notre Dame. *Pola X* exists outside the categories of good and bad; it is a magnificent folly.

Cannes is preceded every year by an international television convention in April, during which many visitors invariably find themselves robbed, kidnapped, raped, or pickpocketed.

The opening day's trade papers at this festival are always filled with horror stories from the earlier one, alarming arriving Americans with the same apprehension that Europeans feel when they rent a car at Miami airport. The new twist this year involves pirates on motorbikes who waylay luxury cars on the road to Cap d'Antibes. My theory is that anyone in a luxury car who can't run a motorbike off the road is just asking for trouble.

Bimbos and Convergence

May 14, 1999—Bimbos and convergence. Those are the two topics that come to mind for your Cannes correspondent. I will see nine movies this weekend and hope to have some good ones to write about in my next dispatch. But . . . convergence! I have been talking about nothing else.

First the bimbos, however, because all Cannes reports must include some mention of starlets on the beach, etc., if only to reassure my editors, who are concerned that I will ruin my eyesight peering at tortured adaptations of obscure novels by Herman Melville, as covered in my last report.

Ever since Robert Mitchum was embraced by a topless starlet in 1949 and put Cannes on the map, young women have flocked to the Riviera during the festival to frolic in the surf and be photographed. The theory is that this will make them famous.

I cannot remember the name right now of any starlet who actually became famous in that way, but they must get a rush—a "frisson," as the French put it—simply by walking out to the end of the Carlton pier, dropping their bathrobe, and being surrounded by several dozen baying paparazzi, who knee and elbow one another in their eagerness to record on film the sight of a well-filled bikini, since such a sight has not been previously seen by anyone on earth more than several thousand times.

Do the starlets think their likenesses are whisked by wirephoto around the world? I have never seen a single cheesecake shot from Cannes on the AP wire. I predict my editors will not be able to find a single example to run with this story. (I also predict they will, however, spare no effort in their search.) My own feeling is that the paparazzi take the bikini photos because they are expected to; it is their way of upholding the honor of their profession. They make their livings by selling photographs of Harvey Weinstein signing checks.

Yet bimbo eruptions are expected again this year. I learn by the trade papers that Hugh Hefner is expected to arrive with a bevy of Playmates, including no doubt Mandy and Sandy, the twins he is dating. Mike Myers, whose new Austin Powers movie will open in June, will be here with the Fembots. I am not sure what they are, but I predict the emphasis will be on "fem" and not on "bots." And every year a man named Ron Rice turns up with the Hawaiian Tropic girls. Their purpose is to publicize Hawaiian Tropic. I am not sure if that is a condom or a fruit punch, but you see I did remember the brand name.

Convergence! I was at a cocktail party last night thrown by the Bravo Channel and Independent Film Channel for the operators of important American cable systems. I go to a dinner like this every year. Last year, faithful readers will recall, the French movie star Gérard Depardieu attended the dinner, and thrust his tongue down the throats of several startled cable tycoons' wives (and/or cable tycoonesses). "Did he kiss you?" I asked a woman who was recalling her experience. "If you can call it a kiss," she said, "when he bends over you so far that your hair is sweeping the floor."

Depardieu had just finished filming a miniseries for Bravo/IFC, which he was theoretically going to promote by his appearance, although his remarks were all about a new project which he hoped the cable moguls would also finance. The next day, he turned over his motorcycle and severely rearranged several bones. (This year's festival opened with *Pola X*, which stars Depardieu's son Guillaume, in a film where he had a motorcycle accident—as did Catherine Deneuve, playing his mother. It is the family pastime.)

Anyway, that was last year, when the focus was still on stars and movies—all the traditional stuff. This year, I found myself talking to a woman who is working on the merger between MediaOne and AT&T. And to a man who wants to combine cable with pay-for-view and put it all on the Web. And a woman who told me that realtors are being asked by clients if new houses have fiber-optic Web access.

I even saw an old friend, Milos Stehlik,

founder of Facets Multimedia in Chicago. The first time I met Milos, he was showing Werner Herzog films on a 16mm projector in a deconsecrated church (patrons were advised to bring their own pillows as the pews were hardwood). Now Milos, too, is being "converged." Since Facets is the largest single source of specialist, foreign, art, and silent video in the world, he is being courted by the Bravo/IFC people as a consultant and collaborator on their new Foreign Film Channel.

Convergence! What does it mean? It means that the telephone, television, and the Internet will all come into your home in the same way, from the same provider, and be used more or less interchangeably. You will make phone calls, watch TV, buy or rent videos, send e-mail, play video games, manage your portfolio, and buy at retail, all with the same integrated technology, which will appear on a computer monitor, an HDTV set, a wall-size screen, or on the insides of your eyeballs.

"Imagine this," said an enthusiastic MediaOne executive, after saying no to three trays of canapés. "Imagine it is the last year of the nineteenth century, and you are being offered the opportunity to combine the gas company, the water company, the electric company, the telephone company, and the post office—all into one emerging utility!"

"There would be money to be made?" I guessed.

"How about instead of a $35 phone bill today, we could bill the same consumer $150 a month for phone, cable, Internet, pay-for-view, everything?"

"Sign me up!"

She sighed. "The problem is that the entire nation needs to be wired with fiber-optic cable," she said. "AT&T has spent $2 billion a year for the last three years, and that's a drop in the bucket. Nobody can find enough trained workers to install the cable. Providers are cannibalizing each other's employees. It's all front-end investment. The payoff will be unbelievable, but it's down the road."

"Meanwhile," I said, "Web delivery of video still means a picture the size of a postage stamp, that refreshes every ten seconds and spends the rest of the time telling me it is 'buffering.'"

"It's coming," she said, in a tone nicely balanced between intractability and glee. "It's all coming."

Walking back to my hotel, I passed the old harbor, where yachts have rocked at anchor since time immemorial. My mind was filled with a vision for the future. Of a time when one could walk into any room of the house and flick on a remote control device, no doubt surgically embedded in a fingernail, and summon up wall-sized 3-D Internet images of Mandy, Candy, and the Fembots. And hear them. Or perhaps it would be enough to see them.

Crashing with Jerry

May 17, 1999—Readers of Chicago gossip columns have long been familiar with the name of Jerry Berliant, shadow to the stars. I was first introduced to him by late Cubs announcer Jack Brickhouse, at the fifteenth anniversary of Disney World. "He's the world's greatest gate-crasher," Brickhouse told me, while Berliant carefully pretended not to hear. "You'll be seeing a lot of him."

I have. I've seen Berliant at the Oscars and the Emmys, at television conventions and the Kentucky Derby, and as he stood beaming behind political candidates during their acceptance and/or concession speeches. Yesterday I was making an espresso stop in the bar of the Majestic Hotel, and he materialized, brimming with news.

"Yeah, Tom Rosenberg is here, from Lakeshore Entertainment," he was saying. "Hefner's been on his yacht all morning. Did you see Faye Dunaway? She's here for *Bonnie and Clyde.* Yeah, I've had a good year. I was in Palm Springs during their film festival. Yeah, they do a good job with it. And the Hamptons, they have a nice little festival. I was up there. Yeah, I like the Riviera. I was in San Tropez the other day. Nice, Monte Carlo . . . after Cannes I'm going to drive up through Switzerland and down through Italy. See some friends. Yeah."

Gossip columnists with enormous overhead don't collect half the intelligence that Berliant gathers, I reflected, and yet he seems to exist on air. This is a festival where seasoned journalists despair of getting into screenings and parties. Where muscular gorillas in monkey suits bar your entry to every door. Where directors have been refused entry to their own screenings. The

American Pavilion is fenced off inside a high-security compound in this year of Kosovo, with passes checked at the gate, and yet when I stopped off later for a quick sandwich, there was Berliant, working the room.

Last night my wife, Chaz, and I joined the South African producer Anant Singh and his wife, Vanashree, for dinner. Afterward, we took taxis to the Hotel du Cap d'Antibes for a quick drink. This is a hotel where the rooms start at $2,000 a night and payment is required in cash—no plastic. Where Miramax's Harvey Weinstein gave orders last year that the Bellini cocktails were on him, and got a bar tab for $14,000. The papers have been filled with reports of millionaires being robbed, kidnapped, insulted, etc., on their way to and from the hotel. When we arrived at the gate a uniformed guard with a checklist demanded our names and admitted us only because we were meeting Monsieur Singh, a guest.

We walked into the lobby bar. "Nice to see you," said Jerry Berliant. "Yeah, Sean Connery's still down at the restaurant."

Miramax's Weinstein Minces No Words

May 17, 1999—Harvey. Only one name is necessary. At the Cannes Film Festival, Harvey Weinstein of Miramax is the most important person because he is the most powerful holder of the keys to the American market for specialized films. It isn't simply that he guided Italy's *Life Is Beautiful* to three Oscars and a $55 million payday in the U.S. market—but that he masterminded the campaign to get it into last year's Cannes festival in the first place, overcoming the doubts of festival honcho Gilles Jacob.

The outspoken Weinstein is not shy about describing his role in such scenarios. Here at Cannes on a rainy Monday morning, I was asked to do a Q&A session with him, sponsored by the *Hollywood Reporter* at the American Pavilion. He spoke so bluntly that he began to keep a running count of whom he was offending.

Among his targets:

—American TV networks, which have *never*, he said, shown a French or Italian film in prime time—not even one dubbed into English.

—U.S. senators who attack violence in films but vote against gun registration and control legislation.

—20th Century-Fox president Bill Mechanic, who criticized Miramax's spending on the Oscar campaign for *Shakespeare in Love*, but "wasn't heard from last year, when they spent ten times as much on the campaign for *Titanic*."

—Cannes boss Gilles Jacob, who didn't want to admit *Life Is Beautiful* into last year's official competition until Weinstein screened it for Jewish leaders and key French film people, convincing Jacob that the comedy did not make inappropriate use of the Holocaust. It won the Cannes Jury Prize before going on to conquer world markets.

Weinstein made headlines earlier this year when he told *Le Monde* that Europeans should continue their quota system for limiting the number of American films shown on their TV networks. "Why not?" he asked—when U.S. networks have a "secret boycott" of French and Italian films. He's hopeful, he said, that *Life Is Beautiful* will get a network slot "when they hear how well we've dubbed it." Subtitles, of course, are completely out of the question for the networks.

"But the network executives must have already seen the film," I said, "and they must assume you'll dub it well. Hasn't at least one network programmer already approached you about first rights to the film?"

"Not one."

Weinstein defended his company's aggressive campaigns to win Oscars (he has collected thirty), saying, "I don't think we should be criticized for supporting our films."

He entered a guilty plea, however, on charges that the company buys more films than it can release. At this year's Independent Spirit Awards, Miramax got an honorary Shelf Award for having the most acquisitions still on the shelf. "It's true," he said. "I'll see a film I like, and sometimes find out nobody is trying to buy it, and I'll buy it, and then sometimes our hopes or plans don't work out."

This year, he said, Miramax plans to acquire only "about two" outside films, down from ten last year. He confirmed reports that the deal for one of those titles, the Sundance hit *Happy,*

Texas, included a promise to release it by October. (His scaled-down acquisition plans didn't keep him from being mobbed after the session by hopeful filmmakers who pressed cassettes, scripts, and pitches into his hands.)

Weinstein's top priority at this year's festival, he said, is a successful launch for *Dogma*, the controversial Kevin Smith film that has been criticized for possibly being offensive to Catholics.

"People who have seen it say it gave them a real spiritual experience," Weinstein said. "That's not what it's about, but still . . ."

Is it true that Disney, Miramax's parent company, objected to the film?

"Not any more," he said, "because I bought it. I'm releasing it personally. Disney isn't involved."

As for a possible link between violent films and high school shooting tragedies, Weinstein said many attacks on films were by the same people who oppose gun legislation. He wondered if extensive TV news coverage of teenage shooters might not be inspiring copycats.

"A few years ago," he said, "major league baseball had an epidemic of players mobbed by fans, of strippers running onto the field, and so on. Baseball simply agreed not to televise such incidents, and now they've dropped off by 95 percent—because you can no longer see yourself on TV." He suggested that newspapers and TV not use the names and photographs of teenage shooters, "so other kids won't get the idea they can get famous that way."

As for today's film content, he simply sighed, naming three unsuccessful recent Miramax releases that were made for family audiences. (One was made "for my mother, Miriam, who counted 156 f-words in a movie and asked me why I was always talking about my commitment to great writing.") The titles were *Wide Awake*, *The Mighty*, and Maya Angelou's *Down in the Delta*, and all three were box-office disappointments. "Even at the Magic Johnson cinemas, where people were thanking us for releasing Maya's film, *Patch Adams* was doing all the business," he said.

The Cannes festival wanted to show *The Phantom Menace* on its opening night, but was turned down by filmmaker George Lucas and 20th Century-Fox. I asked Weinstein what he would have done in the same situation.

"I think the festival needs to find a better relationship with the Hollywood studios," he said. "Not on a one-film basis, but continuing."

The relationship is bad right now?

"It could be improved," he said, in an uncharacteristic attack of diplomacy.

Cannes Is Abuzz Over *Blair Witch Project*

May 19, 1999—Here, in a nutshell, is the dream of every young movie director in America:

1. Obtain $800 digital camcorder at Circuit City.
2. Shoot feature film on $20,000 budget.
3. Save on cost of cinematography by training actors to operate cameras themselves.
4. Enter film at Sundance, where it generates biggest buzz. Festival forced to schedule extra screenings to accommodate demand.
5. Weigh many distribution offers, accept best one.
6. Fly to Cannes, where film is invited to Directors' Fortnight.
7. Sit on terrace overlooking gardens of Grand Hotel, giving interviews about your vision, release strategy, next project, and so on.

Eduardo Sanchez and Daniel Myrick are, as they say, living that dream. They wrote and directed *The Blair Witch Project*, a horror film. It is already the third most-buzzed-about film of the summer, after *The Phantom Menace* and *Eyes Wide Shut*.

I saw the movie last January. It is not easily forgotten. It begins with the announcement that three young documentary filmmakers ventured into the woods in search of a legendary witch. "Two years later," we are told, "their footage was found."

The movie consists entirely of what purports to be the actual footage of the doomed documentary. Sanchez and Myrick obtained a Hi-8 camcorder and a lightweight 16mm film camera, gave them to three actors, and sent them off into the woods. Literally.

Until I talked with them here, I didn't realize how cleverly the film's footage was devised. I imagined a traditional shoot, in which the crew followed the actors through the woods, clicking off shots from the script.

Not at all. "We tried to stage the experience so they were having it while they were shooting it," Sanchez told me. "For example, we showed our actress a house and told her this was where she lived, this was her room, blah-blah. We told her to be ready to leave home at a given time. On schedule, the other two actors arrived. They all started filming everything. They went to a restaurant for breakfast. Some of the customers and waitresses were planted by us, but they didn't know which ones. Then we told the actress to make some notes for her little speech explaining the mission to these two guys she had recruited as her crew."

We see all of that happening, as it's shown spliced together from handheld footage from the two cameras. Then the three documentary makers venture off into the woods.

"We followed them at a distance," Myrick said. "We gave them GPS devices so they could find their locations. At certain times they were supposed to find checkpoints, with fresh batteries for the cameras, and instructions on what to do next. And they were just supposed to film everything."

One night after they pitch their tent and go to sleep, they're awakened at 3 A.M. by strange noises. The cameras click on in the darkness, and then flashlights illuminate their frightened faces.

"The noise was us," Sanchez and Myrick told me. "We were rustling around in the leaves outside the tent."

Because every single shot in the movie is obtained from unrehearsed *cinema verité* cameras, it has such a convincing documentary look that some audiences think the film has to be for real.

"In most horror films," Myrick said, "you know it's not real because the camera knows where to look before the scary thing happens. In this film, the camera is always a little late, swinging around to catch something that has already started happening."

What were their influences? "Classic horror that really scares you, like *The Exorcist*," said Sanchez. "And movies where they go looking for something legendary, like *In Search of Big Foot*," said Myrick. "You know, Big Foot probably does exist."

* * *

The legendary German director Werner Herzog arrived here with a real documentary scarcely less scary than *Blair Witch*. Titled *My Best Fiend*, it's the story of his relationship with the late actor Klaus Kinski, whose towering rages held crews and directors in a reign of terror—except for Herzog.

The title—"fiend," not "friend"—is a pun on their love-hate relationship. Herzog became convinced as a boy that it was his destiny to direct Kinski in a film. Kinski actually lived under the same roof with Herzog, his mother, and his four siblings for several months, on one occasion locking himself into the bathroom for two days and reducing every single porcelain fixture "to grains the size of sand."

Kinski starred for Herzog in *Aguirre, the Wrath of God*, *Fitzcarraldo*, *Nosferatu*, *Woyzeck*, and *Cobra Verde* (in which he ran wild inside a mob of hundreds of naked, spear-wielding warrior Amazons). When the actor threatened to walk off one of Herzog's difficult locations in the Peruvian rain forest, the director told him: "I have eight bullets in this gun. If you leave, by the time you reach that river bend, you will have seven bullets in your head, and the eighth one is for me."

Ha! says Kinski in his autobiography—it is a lie, because he had the gun, not Herzog. Ha! says Herzog in his film. Kinski knew his autobiography would not sell unless he said shocking things, so Herzog helped him use the dictionary to look up vile words he could use in describing the director.

So much did the Indians of the Amazon hate Kinski, Herzog says, that one day they approached him with an offer to kill the actor. "I needed Kinski for a few more shots, so I turned them down," Herzog says. "I have always regretted that I lost that opportunity." Is he kidding? Sure.

* * *

For years, every Cannes official screening has opened with an elegant logo showing a staircase climbing up out of the sea and reaching to the stars. This year, alas, the classic simplicity has been replaced by a hideous new design, in which a multifaceted zirconium tree ornament zigzags up a staircase while shedding digital debris. If it works, don't fix it.

Austin Powers, Shut Up!

May 21, 1999—The original *Austin Powers* received good reviews when it was released in 1997. But now its ingrate writer and star, Mike Myers, has launched a campaign to drive all the major movie critics at this year's Cannes Film Festival stark raving mad.

A gigantic advertising kiosk for the forthcoming *Austin Powers: The Spy Who Shagged Me* has been erected directly beneath the windows of the Splendid Hotel, where the critics for *Time*, *Newsweek*, *Entertainment Weekly*, and the *Los Angeles Times* have their rooms, along with your faithful correspondent. The kiosk is equipped with powerful loudspeakers that repeat ad slogans, music, and sample dialogue from the movie over and over and over and over and over again, from late afternoon until late at night. There is also a sound effect that may be, well—shagging.

Readers will recall that two years ago Planet Hollywood moved into premises on the ground level of the Splendid, and kept journalists awake with high-decibel personal appearances by Bruce Willis, who usually dropped by about 1 A.M. After the hotel protested, the Planet dialed down its act. This year, ironically, the only place in the neighborhood where you can't hear the *Austin Powers* audio attack is . . . inside Planet Hollywood.

New York of the '70s Captured in *Summer of Sam*

May 23, 1999—Spike Lee's *Summer of Sam* has the right title. It isn't a film about David Berkowitz, the serial killer who named himself Son of Sam—but about the summer of 1977, when his bloody string of murders coincided with a heat wave, a Yankees World Series victory, and skirmishes in the ongoing American cultural war.

Lee's film, which premiered here in the Directors' Fortnight, is the most exciting I've seen at Cannes so far this year. It comes billed as his first film not about an African-American subject, but it might better be described as his first with no major black characters—because the subject is scapegoating, something black Americans know a lot about.

As Son of Sam's body count grows and the city is paralyzed, a group of young Bronx men begin to look for suspects to fit the killer's profile—and center on such misfits as a cab driver (works nights), a priest (drinks, has strange ideas), a homosexual, and a kid from the neighborhood who has adopted a punk lifestyle and wears his hair in weird spikes. Just as a long, hot summer day brought underlying prejudice to a boil in Lee's masterpiece *Do the Right Thing*, so does Sam-inspired paranoia generate violence during *Summer of Sam*.

The movie is electric, driven, feverish. Lee includes perhaps a dozen major characters. His leads, played by John Leguizamo and Mira Sorvino, are Vinny and Dionne, a guilt-ridden, sexually insecure hairdresser and his wife, a waitress so worried about their marriage that she even asks one of his former girlfriends what turns him on. Their social life centers on discos, until Bronx nightlife shuts down under the Sam-inspired curfew of fear.

Other characters: a gangster (Ben Gazzara) asked by the cops to use his people to find the killer. The punk, who affects a British accent and switches in mid-movie from spiked hair to a yellow Mohawk. Cops. A man with a barking dog. Sexually adventurous wives. TV reporters. Vinny's friends. And columnist Jimmy Breslin and slugger Reggie Jackson, who in their own ways reflected the texture of the city that summer.

Lee shows an instinctive grasp for the rhythms of New York neighborhood life: the crowded booths in pizza restaurants. Bars, clubs, living rooms. Hanging out where the street ends and the river begins. Going to Times Square looking for action. Drugs. A sound track from the hits of that summer. The cars. The shock when an old, established Italian-Catholic neighborhood is challenged by sexual and women's lib, gays, punks, hippies—as they said in the 1970s, the whole enchilada.

* * *

What goes around, comes around, they said during the summer of Sam. I was at Cannes for the premieres of films by Francis Coppola *(Apocalypse Now)* and John Huston *(Under the Volcano)*. Now I am here for the premieres of films by their daughters, Sofia Coppola *(The Virgin Suicides)* and Anjelica Huston *(Agnes Browne)*.

The Coppola film tells the story of a suburban Lisbon family: science teacher dad and housewife mom (James Woods and Kathleen Turner) and their five beautiful blond daughters (Kirsten Dunst is the most beautiful), all of whom commit suicide in the same tragic year. The Huston film is about an Irish woman (played by Huston) who runs her own market stall. Her husband dies, she buries him, she continues to raise her brood, and she cements her bond with her best friend, another woman who works in the market. A man comes along—a nice man—and she has to decide if she wants to go through the whole man thing again.

The Virgin Suicides, with its sense of puzzlement and mystery about deaths that cannot be explained, reminded me of a quite different film, *Picnic at Hanging Rock*, which was also about an inexplicable disappearance. *Suicides* received strongly favorable reviews, and is said to be a favorite for the Camera d'Or Award, given to the best first film.

Agnes Browne is another of the new wave of Irish films in which particular characters are seen so closely that you want to laugh and cry at the same time. It might seem a reach for Huston to direct and star in a film about an Irish working woman, but recall that she was born and raised in Ireland (where her father, to be sure, lived in his own castle). Her Agnes is convincing, involving, and (this is important) very thoughtful but not too bright.

* * *

Still more going around and coming around: Eighteen years ago I saw *Chariots of Fire* here at Cannes. It was booed by the French and dismissed by the British, but America took it to heart and it won an Oscar as the year's best picture. It was produced by David Puttnam and directed by Hugh Hudson, and I remember having dinner with them after the premiere, at an unusually quiet party that seemed to have little to celebrate; the consensus was that the film hadn't impressed the audience.

Tonight I went to another premiere of a film produced by Puttnam and directed by Hudson. It was *My Life So Far*, the story of the first ten years of a boy raised as part of a large and eccentric family on a great estate in Scotland. Father (Colin Firth) is "an inventor and a genius" who bets his fortune on sphagnum moss. Mother (Mary Elizabeth Mastrantonio) has an uncle (Malcolm McDowell), a millionaire who returns from France with a bride half his age (Irene Jacob). All is narrated through the eyes of young Frazier, wonderfully played by Robbie Norman, who studies books from his grandfather's library and stuns a dinner party with his reasoning about how his mother and aunt might go into prostitution.

David Puttnam is now Lord Puttnam. His film played at the Miramax charity premiere for AMFAR, Elizabeth Taylor's AIDS charity. Guests proceeded afterward to Moulin du Mougins, in the hills above Cannes, for dinner and an auction so successful it has raised $10 million in seven years (including Harvey Weinstein's $50,000 bid for Naomi Campbell's navel ring).

"This is my last film and my last Cannes," Puttnam said somewhat winsomely, introducing the evening. What does that mean? I asked him. "I'm in the House of Lords now, and helping to direct the government's education policy," he said. "I thought perhaps I could handle two careers, but it can't be done. So there you have it."

At one point Puttnam was actually brought to America and given the reins of a major studio, Columbia Pictures. But his tastes were said to be too venturesome and not mass-market enough. He mused about his Hollywood adventure: "I was too English, too middle-class, and too nice." The evening was cochaired by Miramax mogul Harvey Weinstein, who cheerfully acknowledged he was none of the three.

Kevin Smith's *Dogma* Screened at Cannes

May 24, 1999—Kevin Smith's *Dogma* had its first public screening here, and the world did not end. Not even in the film. The apocalyptic comedy, which has stirred charges of blasphemy in some Catholic circles, played at midnight Friday in the Cannes film festival, after press screenings earlier in the day. There was much laughter and no visible outrage.

Yet the film is being handled gingerly by Harvey and Bob Weinstein, the brothers who produced it for Miramax, a Disney subsidiary, and then purchased it from Disney for $12 million to spare the parent company controversy. There was a prescreening party Friday night for Smith and his cast members (Ben Affleck, Linda Fiorentino, Salma Hayek, Alan Rickman, Jason Mewes) at the Majestic Hotel's beach restaurant, but the invitations were carefully worded, "Bob and Harvey Weinstein invite you . . .". There was no mention of Miramax.

Versions of the screenplay have been circulating on the Web for months, and opponents of *Dogma* have taken exception to a lot of the dialogue and situations. For example, Fiorentino, who works as a counselor in an abortion clinic, is presented as a distant descendant of Jesus. George Carlin plays a cardinal who heads a "Catholicism WOW!" campaign that replaces the crucified Christ with a "Buddy Jesus" who winks and gives the thumbs-up sign. And Affleck and Matt Damon play exiled angels who hope to sneak back into heaven through a loophole, after Carlin declares a plenary indulgence for anyone who walks through the doors of his New Jersey church.

Phrases like "plenary indulgence" are understood by Catholics but not many others, and indeed *Dogma*, whatever its status as blasphemy, is more drenched in Catholic concepts, terminology, and teachings than any other film I've ever seen. Non-Catholics should be issued a catechism at the theater door.

Like Kevin Smith, I went to Catholic schools for eight years, and the dialogue in the movie was like a homecoming for me. Setting aside the liberal use of the f-word, which functions like punctuation in modern movie dialogue, *Dogma* plays like those long theoretical conversations we used to have about technicalities of Catholic law ("Sister, what if you miss making your Easter duty, but then you cross the International Date Line . . ."). Smith's dialogue is funny and smart, getting laughs with concepts and paradoxes that would be beyond the reach of many filmmakers.

What the film does do, for better or worse, is to assume that all Catholic teachings are literally true.

"Maybe it's not the Catholic Church that should be upset, but every other religion," Smith was musing early Saturday morning, as we drank coffee beside the still-deserted pool of the Majestic Hotel. "Other religions should be like—Hey, dude, wait a second! The world is going to end because of *Catholic dogma?* What about Judaism, Buddhism, the Methodists?"

In the film, the fallen angels take out victims with machine guns. Christ is temporarily out of action after getting trapped between the spiritual and temporal state because he's mugged in human form after returning to Earth to play Skee-Ball. And at the end, God appears. Well, not literally God (who is such an overwhelming sight that if you looked at her you would explode), but God in human form, appearing on the church steps and bringing reconciliation to the world (while resisting what must have been a great temptation to sing "What If God Was One of Us?").

The film does indeed end on a note of redemption—something I know all too well, because after I was caught sneaking out before the end, I was required to go back and see the ending by Father Harvey.

Here's what happened. The press screening began late, at 11:15 A.M. I was scheduled to interview Spike Lee at 1 P.M. At 1:10 P.M., when the film had not yet ended, I slipped out of the theater because I didn't want to keep Spike waiting. Weinstein saw me and dispatched his minions to request that I look at the last reel, "because you have to see the redemption." I dutifully reported back to the theater early Saturday for the last ten minutes, before going to talk to Kevin Smith.

This kind of hands-on attention to detail reveals how concerned Weinstein is that the film be seen as a whole, and not as a collection of possibly blasphemous sound bites. My own suspicion is that *Dogma* will play funnier and be more entertaining for Catholics than for any other group. Stand back to get the big picture, and the movie isn't blasphemous so much as devout by an extremely indirect route.

"This whole thing is a hearsay controversy," said Smith, who attends church every Sunday, and whose wife, Jennifer, is expecting their first child. "Maybe people saw earlier drafts on the Web. My stuff often reads more harsh than the way it plays out. My sister read my screenplay for *Chasing Amy* and chewed me a new rear end; she said it was vulgar and misogynist. When she saw the movie, she asked me what I cut out. 'Nothing,' I said. 'It's all in the delivery.' Stuff comes across a lot different on the screen when it's coming out of a well-honed actor's mouth."

A lot of that dialogue involves impassioned (sometimes violent) arguments about Church teachings. In an age of secular films, where the world of religion is completely absent, *Dogma*'s characters hurl theological fine points at one another in impassioned tirades. I was reminded of how George Bernard Shaw's characters debated weighty issues in the midst of melodrama and comedy.

"I almost feel like it's a recruiting film," Smith

said. "It's pro-faith. I want to grab the people attacking the film and tell them, 'Hey, dude, I'm doing your job while you sit here and politicize. I don't hear you out there tub-thumping for Christ.' And I don't remember reading anything in the Bible where Christ was like, 'Go out amongst men, and make sure they don't say anything bad about me.'"

Cannes Award Ceremony Filled with Surprises

May 24, 1999—By the time I walked into my hotel after the Cannes Film Festival award ceremony on Sunday night, the verdict was already in. "Scandale!" cried the desk clerks in unison, summarizing the television coverage. Cannes was reeling after a list of winners so unexpected and generally unpopular that the TV commentators were rolling their eyes. The instant verdict was that jury president David Cronenberg, the unorthodox Canadian, had led his jury into the hinterlands of cinema and camped there.

Only one of the alleged favorites won anything. That was Pedro Almodovar, the Spanish director of *All About My Mother*, whose prize as Best Director drew a standing ovation from the glittering audience in the Palais des Festivals—partly because they approved, but mostly, it was clear, to send a message that at last the jury had produced an acceptable winner. As the applause escalated into a demonstration, Cronenberg leaned over for a rueful word with his fellow juror actor Jeff Goldblum.

The Palme d'Or, or first prize, went to *Rosetta*, a French-Belgian film by brothers Luc and Jean-Pierre Dardenne, starring Emille Dequenne as a teenage outsider. She won as Best Actress, to the astonishment of many who noted that the popular Spanish actress Marisa Paredes, who starred in both the Almodovar film and *No One Writes to the General*, by Mexico's Arturo Ripstein, was in the audience. (Likely winners are unofficially advised by the festival to attend the ceremony.)

The Grand Jury Prize, or second place, which last year went to the wildly popular *Life Is Beautiful*, by Roberto Benigni, went this year to the gray, glacial, and raw *L'Humanite*, by Bruno Dumont. It was a police procedural about a dour cop who investigates a brutal child murder while enduring a life of utter depression. I admired it for the defiant courage of its alienation and despair—but was in a minority, judging by the votes of panels of critics in each of the eight daily festival newspapers.

Although the jury theoretically gives only one award to a film, *L'Humanite* won two more. Best Actor went to its star, Emmanuel Schotte, who onstage behaved exactly like his character, regarding the audience as if they were bugs and he a microscope. Severine Caneele, his costar, shared the Best Actress award with *Rosetta*'s Dequenne. She was the first Cannes winner in memory who was missing a front tooth.

The Jury Prize, or third place, went to *The Letter*, by Manoel de Oliveira of Portugal. It starred Chiarra Mastroianni, daughter of Catherine Deneuve and Marcello Mastroianni, as a young woman on the rebound from a bad love affair, who marries an older doctor who has admired her since she was a teenager. Although I saw most of the entries, I did not see *The Letter;* colleagues argued over whether it was the second or third worst film in the festival.

At ninety-one, de Oliveira is the oldest active director in the world today. That inspired a joke by the veteran French actor Michel Piccoli, who stood up to announce the winner of the Camera d'Or, for best first film, and said de Oliveira had won it. Ho, ho. Actually, the Camera d'Or went to *Marana Simhasabab*, by Morali Nair of India.

Piccoli's was not the least successful speech of the evening. The Palme d'Or was introduced by the French actress Sophie Marceau (James Bond's next girlfriend), who looked windswept, began with "What a day!" and rambled aimlessly about how "there are more important things than movies—sick children, for example," until the audience booed and whistled, and the mistress of ceremonies, the poised English actress Kristen Scott Thomas, firmly interrupted her and asked Cronenberg for the name of the winner.

Other prizes went to *Molach*, a Russian-German film about Hitler, for Best Screenplay, and to *The Emperor and the Assassin*, by China's Chen Kaige, for Best Set Design.

There's no quota system at Cannes, but festival boss Gilles Jacob is said to encourage the jury to distribute its awards so that major film-producing nations are not snubbed. It did not escape notice that Cronenberg's jury had no award for his fellow Canadian Atom Egoyan, and also shut out every American in the competition, a roll call of independent legends: Tim Robbins, Jim Jarmusch, David Lynch, and John Sayles.

At the end of the day, the only English-language film that won anything was *The Blair Witch Project*, the low-budget horror film, which won the Prix de la Jeunesse, or youth prize, voted on by a jury of seven critics between the ages of eighteen and twenty-five. Quite possibly Gilles Jacob was wondering if he should have asked the kids to take a look at the official competition while they were at it.

Boos Abound for Jury's Selections at Cannes

May 25, 1999—The survivors of the fifty-second Cannes Film Festival met at the Nice airport like applicants for an emergency airlift. The carnage of the awards ceremony was still fresh in our minds. A jury led by the Canadian director David Cronenberg had produced a list of awards so peculiar that it is safe to say no one understood it except Cronenberg—and perhaps some, but not all, of his jury members. "Perverse," *Variety* called the verdict.

"What I heard," said Todd McCarthy, *Variety*'s well-connected chief film critic, "is that Cronenberg was a firm leader who imposed his views on the rest of the jury. He kept saying, 'Small films! Small films!' Some even said he browbeat them. This was Cronenberg's handpicked jury, and the winners very much reflected his choices."

True, the jury included two actors (Holly Hunter and Jeff Goldblum) who had worked for Cronenberg, and others who perhaps shared his tastes. Every jury reflects the tastes of its president, a fact acknowledged a few years ago by one disgruntled loser who thought he got the wrong award, and made a speech in which he gave "no thanks to the midget" (jury president Roman Polanski).

But usually the awards reflect the tastes of at least some well-informed members of the audience. Not this year. At the awards ceremony, the audience reaction moved from incredulity to boos and outrage, and finally provoked an outright demonstration. When the single popular choice was announced (Spain's Pedro Almodovar for Best Director), the audience gave him a standing ovation, one that was too loud and too long to be simply for Almodovar, especially since many of the audience members pivoted to look directed at Cronenberg and his jurors, who were making "What? Me worry?" faces.

Cronenberg's jury gave the coveted Palme d'Or to *Rosetta*, a small Belgian film, unseen by me, about a disturbed young girl whose mother is an alcoholic. She lives in a trailer and moves from job to job, fighting to avoid her mother's fate. It may be a fine film (Ken Turan of the *Los Angeles Times* called it "heartbreaking and uplifting"). But few even saw it because it was slotted last, on Saturday afternoon—a time traditionally earmarked by festival boss Gilles Jacob for a film he thinks has no chance of winning, since the jury has already formed its shortlist.

The film also won a Best Actress award for its star, Emilie Dequenne, whose tearful acceptance speech was interrupted by boos and jeers—probably not so much against her as against the jury, which by then was in the doghouse.

That made two awards for *Rosetta*. After the Polanski jury gave *Barton Fink* three awards in 1991, Jacob decreed that in the future no single film could take home more than two prizes, but Cronenberg ignored him, and gave no less than three awards to Bruno Dumont's *L'Humanite*, an unremittingly grim French-Belgian police melodrama described by *Variety* as "the slowest murder investigation ever filmed" and by Turan as "completely insane . . . had most viewers tearing at their hair . . . personal cinema reduced to the level of absurdity."

L'Humanite won the Special Jury Prize and awards for both of its actors. (Since that meant the Best Actress award was shared, maybe *L'Humanite* technically won only 2.5 awards.) When *L'Humanite*'s Jury Prize was announced, McCarthy said, the audience "hooted so vehemently at Dumont when he ascended the stage that the director basically turned away from the audience and directly thanked the jury for 'understanding.'"

The glamorous closing night audience in the Palais des Festivals was underwhelmed by the awards for the costars of *L'Humanite*, Emmanuel Schotte, who played the policeman, and Severine Caneele, who plays his neighbor and figures in three sex scenes in which the final score is Animalistic Jiggling 3, Eroticism 0. Ceneele's prize must have come as a surprise; if she'd had an inkling she might win, she might have gone to the dentist and had her missing incisor replaced. The jury itself seemed a little nonplussed when Schotte accepted his award, since he behaved onstage exactly as he does in the film: dim, slow-speaking, gape-mouthed, expressionless. Was it even a performance?

It is possible to create a justification for *L'Humanite* (perhaps the Popeye Defense—"It am what it am"). I certainly admired it more than Turan did. It unfolded with a sort of unremitting, grim horror that kept the audience in their seats, if unwillingly. It is also possible to understand why the Jury Prize, or third place, went to *The Letter*, by Manoel de Oliveira of Portugal. He is ninety-one years old and a vigorous legend. The fact that he did *not* get a standing ovation perhaps reflects the audience's general disgust—that, and the fact that everyone I spoke to hated the film. The panels of international critics assembled by each of the eight dailies at Cannes graded *The Letter* pretty near the bottom of the field.

In the unique construction of the Cannes awards, there is a mistress of ceremonies. This year it was the unflappable, French-speaking British actress Kristen Scott Thomas. She stands behind a podium on the left. The jury files on and sits in two rows on the right. As the emcee announces each category, a star comes onstage—not to present the award, but to introduce the category with some scripted boilerplate about how important writers are, or actors, or cinematographers, or whatever. Then the emcee asks the jury president to read the winner, which he does.

This would seem to be a foolproof system, but it broke down when Sophie Marceau, the French actress, breezed onstage to introduce the Palme d'Or. You may remember her from the recent David Spade film *Lost and Found*, unless you understandably tried to forget him, her, and the film as quickly as possible. She is the next James Bond girl, and on the basis of her Cannes performance may be named Ditzy Galore.

Announcing airily that she had a speech but wasn't going to read it, she launched into a rambling discussion apparently on the topic of "what is film." Films are often "merde," she helpfully informed the audience. There are more important things, like sick children. Furthermore . . .

The audience was booing and whistling, and Kristen Scott Thomas interrupted her, asking Cronenberg somewhat prematurely for his selection, which he announced so quickly that the audience could conveniently just keep on booing. At the Nice airport, two of the actors who were backstage with Marceau chatted: "She seemed okay until she went on." "That must have been when the Ecstasy kicked in."

I do not for a moment pretend that my own taste encompasses the world of possible winners. It is quite possible for a film to win Cannes, be widely admired by people I respect, and still leave me cold. Last year's *Taste of the Cherry*, by Abbas Kiarostami, is an example. I remember standing in the lobby of the Hotel Splendid debating it with that excellent critic Dave Kehr, who admired it highly.

This year, again in the Splendid lobby, I said to Kehr, "You and I often have quite different favorites. I suppose you liked Cronenberg's winners?"

"Not exactly," he said.

Cronenberg's jury worked by commission and omission. It pointedly shut out every single English language film in competition, including work by Canada's Atom Egoyan, America's John Sayles, Tim Robbins, Jim Jarmusch, and David Lynch, and England's Michael Winterbottom and Peter Greenaway. The movie world is so dominated by English-language films that in the video store down from my hotel I was able to find exactly one DVD of a French film *(Ridicule)*. The world, "oui," but the jury, "non!"

What message was Cronenberg sending? We might start by looking at two of his own recent films, the Cannes winner *Crash* and this summer's *eXistenZ*. Both of them deal with forms of sexuality that are not erotic or even understandable to most people. The first is about fetishists who are turned on by car crashes, broken bones, wounds, etc. The second is about virtual reality at a time when computers jack directly into the spine through "bio-ports," and sex is in the imagination. I admired both films; neither film makes any particular effort to please a mass audience.

At Cannes, where every hotel drips with advertising billboards and the biggest event of the week was arguably Sean Connery's visit, perhaps Cronenberg was striking a blow not just for the small film, but for the film that insists on directorial style over audience expectations. Most moviegoers choose titles that will show them, they hope, exactly what they want to see. The willingess to accept a director's vision, even if it's not your own, is the sign of a moviegoer who has advanced from passive, childlike consumerism into a more advanced understanding of the cinema.

But of course not every difficult film is worth the time, many directors have visions interesting only to themselves, and some films are just plain bad. One can agree with Cronenberg's purpose and still question his judgment: Are these really the titles to make a stand with? Cannes audiences are not unsophisticated. Most of the critics at the festival have a certain standing, just to be able to get credentials. Coming from so many different nations and critical traditions, if they collectively dislike a film, can the jury be right and all of them wrong?

Ah well. It's the business of a jury to stir up controversy, and second-guessing is commonplace at Cannes. But when two French films win the top prizes and the mostly French audience boos and whistles and stomps its feet, you get the feeling that next year's jury will be presided over by someone more mainstream. Bruce Willis, maybe.

AFI's 50 Greatest Screen Legends

Why the AFI's List Is Nutty

June 15, 1999—A list that claims to name the fifty greatest movie stars will be released today by the American Film Institute in anticipation of its three-hour CBS special tonight, "AFI's 100 Years . . . 100 Stars."

Forgive me if I do not applaud. While I can understand the interest in the AFI's earlier list of the "100 Greatest American Films," however odd and skewed it might have been, I draw the line at a ranking of human beings.

Any organization that believes it can take a vote and decide if John Wayne should rank higher than Spencer Tracy has no understanding of movies, no understanding of acting, and no common sense. When I learned that Vegas oddsmakers offered even money on Katharine Hepburn's chances of placing first among the women, my skin crawled.

Actors can be good, even great. They can be mediocre, even bad. They can, I suppose, be ranked in a way—by a director preferring one to another, for example. But a movie star by definition is one of a kind. Stars pass beyond ordinary categories and create a new category of their own, containing one person. That is what makes them stars.

Should Katharine Hepburn rank "higher" than Bette Davis? Who's better—Jimmy Stewart or James Cagney? This is insanity.

How was this nutty enterprise conducted? The American Film Institute drew up a list of 500 potential "greatest stars," using whatever arcane and occult methods it has devised (I picture Shirley MacLaine down in the basement with a crystal ball, or Bruce Willis picking names from a bowl). These names were then mailed out to an arbitrary list of film actors and crafts workers, historians, critics, and other "cultural leaders," who were asked to select the twenty-five "greatest" males and females (no category for Lassie or Rin-Tin-Tin, although Miss Piggy will appear on the TV special). I received a ballot, which may still be buried on my desk somewhere unless I remembered to throw it out.

The 500 finalists were limited to those who debuted in or before 1950, or those who debuted later, but have died. The TV program title refers to "100 stars" because fifty living stars will appear on it to welcome the immortals into the Pantheon. (There may be some overlapping; Shirley Temple Black, who will host the special, is also nominated; would you guess that her chances of being selected are excellent?)

Lists of celebrities are, of course, a wonderful device for TV shows, newspaper stories, magazine articles, and whatnot. They provide a convenient method for cannibalizing the entertainment value of famous people without having to pay them, or do any reporting, research, or thinking. Their value, if any, depends on who draws them up. Certainly the AFI's list of 100 great films encouraged some people to rent them, and the institute claims that its No. 1 film, *Citizen Kane,* had its rentals increase by "more than 1,600 percent."

The primary purpose of the AFI lists is to raise money. The TV special is a revenue spinner, and then there are tie-ins with video stores, a special label sticker for video cassettes and discs, and various other promotions. The AFI does many worthy things, but this trivialization of our movie heritage is not one of them.

Because the lists are destined for commercial use, of course the finalists are skewed. The "great films" list included no documentaries or experimental films, for example, and few silent films. So inept were the voters that they succeeded in including no title by Buster Keaton, arguably the greatest actor-director in American films. Also no Garbo, no Astaire and Rogers—where did they find these voters?

Tonight we will see what actors they come up with. I confidently predict that silent stars will again be underrepresented; that while we will get a pious nod for Mary Pickford, Charlie Chaplin, Lillian Gish, and (perhaps) Keaton and Douglas Fairbanks Sr., there will be no room for Lon Chaney or Louise Brooks. Among sound stars, look for Bob Hope but not W. C. Fields, and draw your own conclusions. Will Robert Mitchum make it? If he doesn't, they should declare a mistrial.

There must be a better way for the AFI to raise money. If I were one of the stars picked to cohost tonight's special (the list includes Alec Baldwin, Mike Myers, Billy Bob Thornton, and Cher), I'd just mail in a check and spare myself the embarrassment.

AFI's Great Stars

June 16, 1999—Humphrey Bogart is just a little greater than Cary Grant, and they are both a little greater than James Stewart. Katharine Hepburn is a smidgen greater than Bette Davis, and Ingrid Bergman is not quite as great as Audrey Hepburn, but they are both greater than Greta Garbo.

So we learn from a list of the "50 greatest screen legends," announced by the American Film Institute on a three-hour CBS special that played Tuesday night. We also learn that degrees of greatness can be measured, and that stars who were one of a kind are now one of 25. Well, at least they didn't get left off the list altogether.

The AFI's list was obtained after a ballot of 500 finalists was mailed to several hundred film types, who were asked to vote on the greatest stars. No one seems to have questioned the nutty notion that such a ballot would be meaningful or useful.

The payoff for the AFI is rich: It gets the revenue from the TV special, plus a tie-in with Blockbuster, which will feature 100 classic titles in its stores. Fifty of the titles will be by the 50 "greatest stars" and the other 50 will be by each of the 50 star presenters on the special—which helps to explain their presence on the show.

The AFI will use the money in its campaign to preserve old films. This is a good cause. It does not, however, validate the notion that movie stars can be ranked from one to 25. Better, perhaps, to list them alphabetically—or raise the money another way. Movie memorabilia is pulling in big money. Maybe the AFI could hold an auction of celebrity artifacts.

Looking at the list, I see that some of my concerns in an earlier article were needless. Four stars whose films did not make the earlier AFI list of the "100 Greatest Films" have now at least ranked among the greatest stars: Buster Keaton, Greta Garbo, Fred Astaire (No. 5 among the men), and Ginger Rogers (No. 14 among the women—even though, as she pointed out, "everything he did, I did backwards, and wearing heels"). And Robert Mitchum squeaks in at 23, which is a great relief, since he embodies *film noir.*

By making a 1950 cutoff date (nominees' careers had to start before 1950, or they had to be dead), the AFI avoided the danger of an avalanche of Toms, Arnolds, Demis, and Julias crushing the old-timers. Only four of the men (Brando, Peck, Douglas, and Poitier) and five of the women (Katharine Hepburn, Taylor, Temple, Bacall, and Loren) are still alive. To the degree that the list encourages video rentals of some of their best films, it is of course a good thing, since some younger moviegoers believe movie history began with *Star Wars.*

Looking at the list, I am at a loss to play the role of learned commentator. What does it prove that Chaplin is 10th and Keaton 21st (except that voters were probably not familiar with the films of either)? That the two comedians are the only two silent stars among the men? (No Douglas Fairbanks Sr., no Lon Chaney, no Rudolph Valentino.) That two of the top five actresses spoke Swedish as their native language? I don't know. I truly don't.

But I do have an idea for a sequel: "50 More Great Screen Legends." Or the AFI could even list the "50 Greatest American Directors," although that wouldn't generate such great TV ratings. Do I sound disillusioned? Sorry, but to me the great stars are unique, individual, INCOMPARABLE, and shouldn't be ranked like Derby entries.

Here are the lucky winners:

1.	Humphrey Bogart	Katharine Hepburn
2.	Cary Grant	Bette Davis
3.	James Stewart	Audrey Hepburn
4.	Marlon Brando	Ingrid Bergman
5.	Fred Astaire	Greta Garbo
6.	Henry Fonda	Marilyn Monroe
7.	Clark Gable	Elizabeth Taylor
8.	James Cagney	Judy Garland
9.	Spencer Tracy	Marlene Dietrich
10.	Charlie Chaplin	Joan Crawford

11.	Gary Cooper	Barbara Stanwyck
12.	Gregory Peck	Claudette Colbert
13.	John Wayne	Grace Kelly
14.	Laurence Olivier	Ginger Rogers
15.	Gene Kelly	Mae West
16.	Orson Welles	Vivien Leigh
17.	Kirk Douglas	Lillian Gish
18.	James Dean	Shirley Temple
19.	Burt Lancaster	Rita Hayworth
20.	The Marx Brothers	Lauren Bacall
21.	Buster Keaton	Sophia Loren
22.	Sidney Poitier	Jean Harlow
23.	Robert Mitchum	Carole Lombard
24.	Edward G. Robinson	Mary Pickford
25.	William Holden	Ava Gardner

Questions for the Movie Answer Man

Academy Awards

Q. Why is it that the Academy only seems to remember movies that were released later in the year? I thought for sure that either Holly Hunter or Queen Latifah would have been nominated for *Living Out Loud* and both were overlooked. This has happened in prior years and I was curious as to why that consistently happens.

—Suzanne Rudolph, West Chester, Pennsylvania

A. I've written before about the Academy Attention Span problem: Movies released more than four months before year's end are penalized. But *Living Out Loud* came out in November, and so it doesn't fit that theory. Okay, here's another reason: It was not a big box-office hit. Although there are exceptions, the Oscar voters tend not to vote for movies that didn't make a lot of money. They don't like to embrace box-office mediocrity because they're afraid it may be catching. The Independent Spirit Awards, held in a big tent on the beach in Santa Monica on the day before the Oscars, has no such superstition, and indeed this year's awards are being hosted by Queen Latifah.

Accents

Q. I just read Ken Griggs's letter about foreign accents in movies in your Answer Man column. He should go see *Ever After*. The setting is France, the names are French, the characters are French, most of the actors are American, yet the characters speak British English. Go figure. I would argue that the actors should not have had any accents at all. Why do directors feel the need to stick in accents when they clearly do not belong? One of my pet peeves has always been movies that are set in another country, where all the characters are from that country, and would clearly be speaking to one another *in their own language*. Yet the movie always shows the characters speaking accented English. If we are to assume that we are being given a glimpse into the characters' world, but, for the sake of the English-speaking audience, everything is portrayed in English, *there should be no accent*. I mean, really, when two Russians speak to each other in Russian, do they think, "My god, what a thick accent I have!"

—JoAnne Vicente, Toronto, Ontario

A. Only if they're from Tashkent.

AFI Lists

Q. The strangest of many selections on the AFI's list of the Greatest 100 American Films is *The Third Man*, at number fifty-seven. Of course this movie would rank in the top ten of most cinema lover's lists (and could easily have taken the place of *The Graduate* at number seven). But why is it on a list of American films at all? This was a British film if ever there was one.

—Mark H. Cohen, Atlanta, Georgia

A. The director, Carol Reed, and the author, Graham Greene, were British. It was shot in Vienna. Two of the stars (Joseph Cotten and Orson Welles) were American, one was British (Trevor Howard), and one Italian (Alida Valli). The producer, David O. Selznick, was American. Certainly *The Third Man* is always claimed by the British cinema, and for that matter we might ask how, exactly, *Lawrence of Arabia* and *Bridge on the River Kwai*, both by the very British David Lean, are "American" films. (Apparently they qualify because of American studios' financing.)

In a larger sense, the entire AFI list has been a fiasco. Hardly anyone is happy with it. It has been attacked for its lack of African-American films, for its puny handful of films about women, and for overlooking most of the silent era (including Buster Keaton). True, it was never intended to be a politically correct "balanced" list—but as it stands, it could be called "The 100 Greatest Relatively Recent Popular Studio Films Mostly about White Males."

Many people have mentioned, as you do, *The Graduate* being too high at number seven (is there anyone, including its director, who thinks it is a greater film than *2001*, at number twenty-two, or *City Lights* at seventy-six?). Other films apparently got in on the basis of their past reputations. I recently screened *High Noon* (number thirty-three) as a candidate for my "Great Movies" series, and rejected it as, frankly, just not a very good film. I choose Howard Hawks's great *Red River* instead.

The bottom line: The AFI list is an arbitrary selection of 100 titles from an equally arbitrary selection of 400 tiles, chosen by an arbitrary group of voters, many of whom have bad taste and are uninformed about film history.

Q. I understand that the American Film Institute is doing a follow-up on its 100 Greatest Films list by holding a ballot for the 100 Greatest Actors. Who, in your opinion, is the greatest actor in film history?

—Casey Anderson, Schaumberg, Illinois

A. Only a barking idiot would attempt to answer such a question, so I beg to disqualify myself. It is important to understand that all such lists are a silly waste of time, since they prove nothing except that a given group of people voted on a list of names compiled by another group of people. (That also describes the Academy Awards, but at least on the Oscarcast we get to see the faces of the losers.) The AFI lists are not drummed up out of some serious regard for cinema history, but in order to raise funds for the institute through a TV special and tie-ins with video sales. They also inspire the waste of tons of newsprint and hours of broadcast time, as pundits boviate about the relative merits of Roy Rogers versus Gene Autry. Both of those names are actually on the AFI list of finalists, by the way, along with William Boyd. I was crushed to see Whip Wilson and Lash LaRue omitted. I was relieved, however, to find that the AFI finalists include Buster Keaton, whose works were completely ignored on the 100 Greatest Films list, even though he may have been the greatest actor/director of all time. My advice? Hand out trophies to Keaton, Robert Mitchum, Marilyn Monroe, and Lillian Gish, and call it a day.

Q. In your January 24 Answer Man column, you responded to the question, "Who is the greatest actor in film history?" with the statement, "Only a barking idiot would attempt to answer such a question." I was reading through your 1996 Video Companion, and when I got to *Last Tango in Paris* I was shocked to read the line, "[Marlon Brando] makes it absolutely clear why he is the best film actor of all time." I won't debate your assessment of Brando, but as for your contradiction—well, to quote Steve Buscemi in *Fargo*—"What gives, man?"

—Thad Jantzi, Vancouver, British Columbia

A. The answer is obvious. I am a barking idiot. In my defense: The question involved the balloting for a new AFI list of the Greatest Movie Actors. Such lists are meaningless. When I say Marlon Brando is the best, that is at least my opinion, for what it's worth. When hundreds of people are polled on a list of hundreds of names, it's statistically likely that the winning total won't be anywhere near a majority of the votes cast. Instead of calling the winner the best actor of all time, you could with equal accuracy boast that he got 7 percent of the votes.

Q. In regard to the Answer Man's comment about the pointlessness of "Best Lists" (such as the AFI's upcoming list of the "greatest actors and actresses"), here are the first two entries in *Entertainment Weekly*'s list of the "100 Greatest Television Moments."

#1—The Kennedy Assassination

#2—Mary Tyler Moore throwing her hat in the air

'Nuff said.

—David J. Bondelevitch, Studio City, California

A. "Best lists" share with phone-in telephone polls the admirable journalistic attributes that they can be made to resemble useful information, and can be illustrated with photographs of popular people.

Antz

Q. I just saw *Antz*, and was amazed at the way in which the animators were able to capture the particular nuances of body language and speaking patterns of the actors voicing the characters. What kind of software program did the people at DreamWorks use to capture this effect, and were the character designs created before or after the voices were cast?

—Zack Smith, Raleigh, North Carolina

A. Raman Hui, lead character designer on *Antz*, says: "From the very beginning we knew Woody Allen was going to do the voice of Z. With that in mind, we created a lot of designs that reflect different characteristics of Woody. Some earlier designs even looked like a caricature of Woody. We moved away from that because we wanted to create a new character named Z instead of having Woody Allen be Z. When the animators did the animation, they put a percentage of Woody's mannerisms into the acting (but not totally). Most of the other character designs were started before we knew their voices. When we knew for sure about the voices, we did some adjustment and expressions study to make sure the voices would work with the designs. We used PDI's proprietary facial animation software, developed by Dick Walsh and Beth Hofer."

Armageddon

Q. While I can't fault you for overlooking a minor detail in a film as ridiculous as *Armageddon*, the movie does answer your question about how the drillers were able to walk around normally despite the asteroid's puny gravity. It was because they had little booster packs on their backs to push them down, simulating gravity. However, every time one of our brave explorers bent over at the waist, those boosters *should* have sent them scooting backward across the asteroid's surface at nearly the same rate as a freefall on Earth. I'm betting that either (a) the writers failed physics miserably, or (b) they were betting that the bulk of the American populace failed physics miserably.

—Dominic Armato, Burbank, California

A. And when they were down in the holes they dug for the bombs, did they have to turn their boosters off in order to get up to the surface again?

Q. About those explosions in outer space in *Armageddon*—space is a vacuum, so of course you couldn't see explosions, and there wouldn't be fireballs, because—no oxygen! What gives?

—Gordon "Buzz" Hannan, Chicago, Illinois

A. Plus, in space, no one can hear you scream, unless you happen to be watching this movie.

Q. Please tell Gordon (Buzz) Hannan of Chicago, who said we should not be able to see explosions in outer space films like *Armageddon*, that what we see, including explosions, results from light (either direct or reflected) and this is unimpaired in a vacuum. If it was not, we could not see the Sun, Moon, stars, etc. He also said you couldn't see fireballs, because of the lack of oxygen. It is true explosions require oxygen to work, but rockets fire in outer space because their fuels include oxygen components; it is entirely feasible that explosives for use in space could do the same. You really should consult someone more knowledgeable before printing nonsense from homegrown "experts." I have never taken a course in physics, but science is not that hard.

—Thomas P. Breen Jr., McHenry, Illinois

A. I consulted Richard J. Gaylord, professor in the Department of Materials Science and Engineering at the University of Illinois at Urbana, who replies:

"Thomas Breen is half right (and therefore half wrong). Light does travel in a vacuum, so anything producing light would be visible through space. However, explosions do not require oxygen. Explosions are simply the result of a chemical reaction, so even if the material combusting does not contain oxygen, a fireball could result which would then be seen. There is no oxygen in the Sun and we can see it 'burning.' By the way, science can, in fact, be quite hard when you do it right."

Q. If you look carefully toward the end of *Armageddon*, it appears that the same piece of film was used twice. There is a scene in the master control room on Earth as the explosive charge detonates on the asteroid, showing a jubilant crowd scene. In the right foreground an air policeman holds his head with both hands in joy. A few more scenes pass, and it is announced that the asteroid has been destroyed; a reaction shot of the control room is shown and we see in the right foreground an air policeman holding his head with both hands, etc. I caught this repetition quite by accident. I have seen scenes repeated in films before, usually low-budget action films that flop the negative of a scene so the movement is reversed, but I have not noticed this practice in high-budget pictures. Have you noticed this practice—done to fill time or replace a scene that didn't work, I presume?

—Tom Butters, Indianapolis, Indiana

A. Very alert work! No, I haven't noticed the practice before. Oddly enough, in the screening I attended, most of the audience members were holding their heads in both hands, although not with joy.

Q. A recent Answer Man discussed films which use the same shot twice, often reversed left to right. When I watched *Anaconda* a while back, I was dumbfounded by a shot which was obviously run backward. In the shot, the main characters' boat travels across the screen while a waterfall flows upward. While this is not exactly the same thing as reversing a negative, it is definitely an interesting screwup.

— Zach Fine, University of Washington

A. Sometimes editors feel that the movement in a shot must go in one direction and not another, in order to fit into the flow of a sequence. They trust you will be looking at the foreground action, and not the waterfall. It's not that filmmakers aren't aware of sneaky moments like that—but that they believe they can direct your eyes away from them.

Q. Did you notice in *Armageddon* that during one of the first drilling scenes on the asteroid, there's grass underneath the actors' feet and underneath the drilling rig known as the "armadillo"? If I recall correctly, the temperature on the behemoth was reportedly minus 200 degrees or so, making it unsuitable for any type of greenery. Maybe Bruckheimer has discovered a new strain of sod.

—Chris McIlroy, Salt Lake City, Utah

A. This certainly adds credence to the theory that life arrived on Earth from outer space. Maybe golf did too.

Austin Powers: The Spy Who Shagged Me

Q. You made it clear that you didn't think *Austin Powers: The Spy Who Shagged Me* was very good, but I saw a commercial for the movie recently where they were rattling off positive quotes, and I was shocked to see that you were quoted as saying, "Big laughs!" I assume that you did say this, but it was clearly taken out of context. Don't you think that it is a little unethical?

—Chad M. Roberts, Seattle, Washington

A. A little, but I did say it, and so they're playing by the rules. And hey, *Austin Powers* does have some monster laughs. (Let's see how long that takes to get into print!)

Q. AAAaarrrrgghh! Roger Ebert COME BACK. Dr. Idiotevil clearly has a shill behind the reviewer's desk! How can you possibly justify giving such a favorable review to such a nasty little boy flick like *Austin Powers: The Spy Who Shagged Me*? Isn't anyone going to be responsible enough to question taste and good judgment in entertainment ever again? This movie is nauseating garbage that is not fit for children or other humans to see. Where are the responsible humans who footed the bill for this ode to the potty? Mike Myers, you should be ashamed of yourself.

—Linda Hart, San Mateo, California

A. Your response is based on my *negative* but somewhat affectionate 2.5-star review. If I'd given it 3 stars, we might have lost you. Little boy movies seem to be just what America wants right now; the movie set a three-day record of $54.7 million, and Mike Myers, to paraphrase Liberace, is laughing all the way to the potty.

Babe: Pig in the City

Q. I've been hearing that *Babe: Pig in the City* is too dark, and that darkness is a trend in kid's movies. This sentiment is being blamed for *Babe*'s less than stellar box-office performance. I saw *Babe* and thought that while it was more intense than most children's movies of late, it wasn't as intense as such classics as *Willy Wonka and the Chocolate Factory*, and that any darkness was justified by the unabashedly optimistic ending. In your opinion, are children's movies becoming too dark for younger viewers?

—Paul Bogosian, Watertown, Massachusetts

A. *Babe: Pig in the City*, one of the year's most magical films, has been the victim of two widely publicized factoids. One is that the film was hammered at the box office by *A Bug's Life* (true). The other is that it was "too dark for children." Not true. Troublesome for very young children, perhaps. But enchanting and original for anyone else. Dark themes are not new in children's films. Consider the deaths in *Bambi*, or Mrs. Jumbo's chaining in *Dumbo*. Reflect, too, that an alarming number of today's kids routinely see videos of R-rated slasher and horror movies. *Babe* is unlikely to cause many nightmares.

Q. I went to see *Babe: Pig in the City* and I loved it. It is a brilliant piece of work and a rare sequel that outdoes the original. I also found it to be the most ambitious family film I have ever seen. It will easily make my top ten. I was extremely saddened on how the film flopped badly at the box office. I cannot believe such garbage as *The Waterboy* and *Rugrats* is doing so well. Films like *Babe: Pig in the City* are the ones that inspire me to become a filmmaker. Why did it do so poorly at the box office?

—Michael Pereira, Toronto, Ontario

A. When it comes to family movies, you can't trounce the Mouse. Universal should never, ever, have opened on the same day as a Disney animated picture. Six weeks either way on the opening date, and the picture's history would have been dramatically different.

Q. I just saw the Golden Globe nominations, and *Babe: Pig in the City* is nowhere in there. Not for best script, not for best direction, not for nothing. I consider this a scandal. I'd like Congress to investigate.

—Don Hinkle, Green Village, New Jersey

A. Hey, *Dark City* isn't in there, either. It is important to understand (1) the Globe voters are mostly not film critics but celebrity and gossip writers; (2) the Globes exist as a pretext for a profitable TV show; (3) if the voters *were* film critics, they would just go and vote for films on the basis of quality, and hurt the TV ratings. Still, it must be said that on the whole this year's Globe nominations are not bad, for what they are. They're more judicious than in years past when the fix sometimes seemed to be in.

Q. In your review of *Babe: Pig in the City*, you said, "Mrs. Hoggett gets involved in a weird bungee-like session of chandelier-swinging." I thought the scene was funny because it seemed to be an homage to one of director George Miller's previous films, *Mad Max Beyond Thunderdome*, where Mel Gibson and others fought like that.

—Steve Aronson, Northbrook, Illinois

A. You have to be right.

Q. The financial failure of *Babe: Pig in the City* is, I fear, a major watershed in the history of movies. Seeing this film was at once an elating and depressing experience. An enchanting movie from start to finish, *Pig in the City* certainly *feels* like a blockbuster. All the jokes are great, and you can practically hear where the audience would explode with applause and laughter—except that there is nary an audience to be found. The lonely, cavernous theaters showing this movie (and not for much longer, to be sure) are a clear sign of our culture's collectively deprived imagination. Like *Willie Wonka and the Chocolate Factory*, *Pig in the City* is a children's art film in the best possible sense. Unlike some current hit "kids' films," it is good-hearted, noncynical, and glorious fun: It enriches the cinematic experience rather than cheapens it.

—Craig Simpson, Reynoldsburg, Ohio

A. Well of course I totally agree. But Universal Studios not only picked the wrong weekend to open (against Disney) but sealed the movie's fate by firing the studio head after it flopped—this assuring that the only headlines most people saw were about how the film was such a flop it got the guy fired. Maybe it will come into its own on video. Remember, *Willie Wonka*, now enshrined as a classic, did only so-so in theaters.

Beloved

Q. I read *Beloved* several years ago and think it is the greatest novel of the last half of this century. But for those who haven't read the book, the TV ads are going to result in a great shock when they see the movie. According to the ads, it is about a bunch of happy slaves dancing around in the woods. My God, I hope they haven't messed that story around. Those promos are an insult to Toni Morrison.

—Guenvuer Burnell, Kent, Ohio

A. No matter what a movie is about, it is the absolute policy of all Hollywood studios to produce TV ads that promise the audience a good time, every time. They haven't messed the story around.

Black and White

Q. Recently I've seen three films in black and white: *Pleasantville*, *π*, and *Celebrity*. *Pleasantville*'s black and white was essential to the plot. *π*'s black and white seemed to complement the stark world of Max Cohen and his obsessions; also, it was shot on a micro budget. I can't even start to wonder why Woody Allen's *Celebrity* was shot in b&w.

—John J. Fink, Pompton Lakes, New Jersey

A. Perhaps Allen shot *Celebrity* in b&w because it was a veiled homage to Fellini's *La Dolce Vita*, one of my own favorite b&w films. The fact is that color is the wrong choice for many films, and it's a shame that directors have the b&w option taken away from them because studios fear that would hurt the eventual TV sale. Their thinking is about thirty years out of date. When most TV sets were b&w, color was a novelty, and color programming got higher ratings. Now that everything is in color, b&w is the treat—and when I'm channel surfing, I pause on b&w channels out of curiosity. As a general rule, b&w programming is likely to be more entertaining than color, because it has to be—to get on the air.

Q. I've read with great interest your comments concerning the benefits of black-and-white films, and I couldn't agree more. In fact, I have actually taken several videos, turned the color off on my TV, and watched them! It's amazing how many poor or average movies are improved somehow by having them in black and white. It gives the film more depth, more surrealism—an almost *film noir* edge and mystery. This isn't to say that the latest Pauly Shore movie is improved, of course, but you know what I mean. What do you think of my practice?

—Bob Sassone, video columnist, *Boston Herald*

A. Although I am opposed to colorizing black-and-white movies, I must confess that I have occasionally decolorized color movies, and find that they frequently play better that way, especially if the color is either garish or faded. Recently I found that *The Barefoot Contessa* made the transition especially well.

The Blair Witch Project

Q. I recently read your review of the Coen brothers' *Fargo*. The opening sentence of the second paragraph reads "The film is 'based on a true story' that took place in Minnesota in 1987." It does say this at the beginning of the film, but I have read it was just a stunt by the Coen brothers to add a sense of authenticity to the movie. I think that's an ingenious technique. Do you know of any other films that have done something like this?

—Jonathan Coleman, New Orleans, Louisiana

A. *The Blair Witch Project*, the winner in the buzz sweepstakes at the just-concluded Sundance festival, claims to be made out of documentary footage shot by three filmmakers who disappeared while searching the woods for a legendary witch. On my way out of the theater, I talked to several people who were convinced the film was real.

Q. I'm confused and hope you might help me. A few months ago, I saw a digital film in Orlando entitled *The Last Broadcast*, the plot of which is nearly identical to *The Blair Witch Project*. With all the talk about *Blair Witch*, I haven't heard *The Last Broadcast* mentioned at all. What gives?

—Glenn Mobley, Orlando, Florida

A. *The Last Broadcast* is described as the story of an investigation of the Jersey Devil by two cable TV hosts and two fans, who go into the wild to film a documentary. One of them is eventually charged with murder. Without having seen it, I can't say how close it is to *Blair Witch,* but of course it's common for similar movies to be made simultaneously. By the time it was aired in March 1998, *Blair Witch* was already in the can. *Last Broadcast* got some good reviews, and may get a new lease on life if *Blair Witch* does as well as expected.

Q. Just saw *The Blair Witch Project.* Here's some food for thought. Mary Brown spoke of seeing a creature that was hairy like a man/beast and had a weird-looking face. She herself seemed to be a man dressed like a woman. She had a weird face, and we could not see if her body was hairy. She was referred to as "Crazy Mary." Could this be the witch? Mary knew about the documentary, saw their equipment, and could have followed them into the woods, using witchcraft to torment them.

—Vincent Santino, Phoenix, Arizona

A. Like *2001* and *Pulp Fiction, The Blair Witch Project* seems destined to inspire endless interpretations. My own best guess is that *something* was there in the woods (how else to explain the twigs and slime?) but that the movie ends without a solution.

A Bug's Life

Q. I've been watching for years how "blooper" reels went from the credit sequences of Burt Reynolds/Hal Needham films, to their current popularity at the end of major films and television shows. But the question I have is about the bloopers for *A Bug's Life:* How can a film planned and animated with care and complete control *have* a blooper reel? I mean, did they go to the expense of computer animating bloopers that took place when the character voices were being recorded? What's next? News bloopers? PBS bloopers?

—Jeff Young, Lake Elsinore, California

A. Yes, they went to the expense of deliberately making the bloopers, which were so popular with audiences that on December 18 *new* bloopers were added to the end of *A Bug's Life* in theaters. The video release of the film will include all of the different bloopers.

Burton's *Hamlet*

Q. I was surprised to hear that a print of Richard Burton's 1964 performance of *Hamlet* has been found. I understand it was shown in movie theaters for just two performances and then all prints were supposed to have been destroyed. A streaming video of the movie is being shown on the www.aentv.com Website. The picture is the size of a soda cracker of course, but the sound comes through tolerably well. They have the whole three and half hours. Do you know if there are plans to bring this out on DVD or perhaps even release it to theaters again?

—Bruce Worthen, Salt Lake City, Utah

A. Burton's famous stage performance, directed by John Gielgud, was filmed live over several nights, and shown on a roadshow basis in 1964. Then the prints were indeed to be destroyed. After the actor's death, his widow, Sally, found one print in his Switzerland home. It was restored by the British Film Institute and is now being sold on the Web, along with audio cassettes and CDs of the same performance. I saw the film in 1964, and the Web samples bring back the impact of that experience. What a wonderful voice Burton had!

A Civil Action

Q. How could *A Civil Action* use the names of Beatrice and W. R. Grace in the movie, and show W. R. Grace's trademarked name? I would assume if both companies had their preference they would not have their names mentioned at all.

—Joshua McFeeters, Madison, Wisconsin

A. I would assume the same. But what would an expert say? I'm writing this column on my laptop, en route to Chicago from the Sundance Film Festival, and who should be across the aisle, also returning from Sundance, but Burton Joseph, the famed Chicago first amendment attorney. He advises: "It isn't a violation of the law to identify individuals or companies involved in a public controversy. Wide latitude is given to depict even uncomplimentary events, and in order to bring a successful action for libel, the plaintiff would have to show that the producer knew that what he represented was untruthful, and depicted it anyway. Under the circumstances involved in *A Civil Action*, the producers could reasonably rely upon the publication in the book of the facts on the screen." (Mr. Joseph has kindly agreed to waive his usual fee, and will not bill you for this opinion.)

Closed Captions

Q. I watch many movies on my television with the closed captioning turned on, and have noticed that what the characters say is often different from what is displayed on the screen. Does the closed captioning text come straight from the shooting script? If so, this would imply that the actors are improvising and adding to many of their lines. Or is it that the cc text is simply a truncated version of the script?

—Ian Skinner, Victoria, British Columbia

A. I referred your question to Henry Kisor, book editor of the *Chicago Sun-Times*, whose memoir *What's That Pig Outdoors: A Memoir of Deafness* is a modern classic. He replies: "Closed captioning in the movies is an art of compromises. Often it is impossible for the person doing the captioning to present the script verbatim. The actors may be speaking too rapidly, or speaking almost on top of one another, crowded also by sound and visual effects. In order for the captions to remain on-screen long enough for the average viewer to register and understand, they often must be foreshortened. Words and sometimes phrases are left out or otherwise altered. True, in some cases subtleties of language are lost in the compromises that need to be made. Captioners do use scripts, but they also follow the actual filmed dialogue. If the actors improvise, the captioners present the improvisations."

Credits

Q. I've noticed that Barry Sonenfeld's opening credits all have the same, hand-drawn appearance. I know he used to be a cinematographer, and I don't know of his personal artistic credits beyond that, but the *Addams Family* movies, *Get Shorty* (I think), and *Men in Black* are all titled in the same hand. Does he do these credits himself, or did he just keep hiring the same titler over and again?

—Jeff Young, Lake Elsinore, California

A. A Columbia Tri-Star rep says Pablo Ferro did the credits on the two *Addams Family* movies and *Men in Black*. He did not do *Get Shorty*.

Dark City

Q. As a fellow film critic, I would like to ask a question regarding my choice (so far) as the best film of 1998. I saw *Dark City* back when it was first released, and the entire audience arose and gave the film a standing ovation. But it must have been a great group of people, because since then, all I've heard is negative comments, even from complete strangers who've seen my T-shirt (I bought it and love it). I would like to know how the films *2001: A Space Odyssey* and *Blade Runner* were received by the public. They are obviously among the best science-fiction films ever made; I've heard rumors that both were hated by the public. Is this true?

—Boyd Petrie, Salt Lake City, Utah

A. *Dark City* was also my choice as the best film of 1998. It's the kind of visionary science-fiction movie that requires a smart, attentive audience; it doesn't just pound the gape-jaws with special effects. At the University of Colorado at Boulder last April, I went through it a scene at a time with about 1,000 students over the course of a week, and the more closely we looked, the more it impressed us. *2001* and *Blade Runner* were also slow starters at the box office, but eventually achieved cult status.

Q. I note you picked *Dark City* as the best film of the year. I recently watched the film on DVD and, like every good DVD should, it contained some additional commentary tracks. Strange that one of these should be by a certain Roger Ebert. Does that make you on commission?

—Mark Weal, Southhampton, England

A. No, but it's a good question. I do not receive royalties from the disc's sales, and did not receive a payment for doing the commentary track. A fee was offered, which I suggested be used instead to press a laser disc so that I could do a shot-by-shot workshop on the film last April at the University of Colorado, in preparation for taping the commentary track. The track was a labor of love.

Dead Body in *The Wizard of Oz*

Q. I apologize for resurrecting The Question That Will Not Die less than twelve months after its last appearance in the Answer Man, but after an extended argument with a friend of mine I feel compelled to write. The QTWND involves the rumor that there is a dead body hanging in the background of a shot in *The Wizard of Oz*. You claimed this is an urban legend. Unfortunately my friend seems convinced of a mass studio cover-up conspiracy. Can you provide me with more ammunition?

—Dominic Armato, Burbank, California

A. Ask your friend what the odds are that a dead body could remain unnoticed, dangling from a tree, in full view of several hundred people, while a full-blown musical number is filmed around it on an MGM sound stage. If they wanted to cover up the death—wouldn't cutting down the body before filming the scene be the *first thing* they'd do? I quoted *Wizard* expert David J. Bondelevitch in an earlier AM column: "The man in the background is a sound man (a boom operator, to be precise). He was not electrocuted, he was simply stupid and got in the shot when he shouldn't have." Advise your friend to cut way back on his viewing of *The X Files* and drop out of those Internet discussions about Area 51.

Digital Films and Projection

Q. In one of your articles from Sundance, you mentioned digital documentaries. But what about digital features? Will these find any kind of distribution? What form of exhibition could they hope for? I am about to produce a digital feature myself, and at the very most I was hoping for it to be picked up by Film Threat Video or some other little video distribution chain, but what's the buzz? Is there any hope for a digital feature to be seen in theaters? Or to be picked up by a larger company?

—Jack Bennett, Blacksburg, Virginia

A. The technology now exists for prints of acceptable quality to be made with digital video cameras. Professional models can cost upward of $10,000, but a home model, priced between $800 and $2,000, is capable of shooting a theatrical movie. Video is not yet capable of recording dazzling images of the sort we associate with movies like *Lawrence of Arabia*, but it's fine for low-budget features. *The Blair Witch Project*, a Sundance entry with lots of buzz, was shot mostly on video, with some 16mm. Another entry, *The Invisibles*, cost only $9,000. One video expert told me, "This will be the last Sundance where a majority of the films were shot on film." This development could reduce the below-the-line cost of a feature from 30 to 90 percent, putting filmmaking at last within the means of ordinary people.

Q. George Lucas has announced he will be shooting and hopefully exhibiting Episode II of the *Star Wars* saga exclusively with digital technology. There will be no physical film stock, just memory bites in a computer. Will this look as clear and realistic as "old-fashioned" movies? Could shooting movies on actual film go the way of the Dodo?

—Matt Wilson, Los Angeles, California

A. Lucas has spent twenty years and millions of dollars pioneering new levels of digital technology, and what he has helped make possible in movie production is truly incredible. But digital *projection* is another matter altogether. Call it what you will, it's high-tech television. Bill Mechanic, head of 20th Century–Fox, told me he tried to talk Lucas out of showing *Phantom Menace* in four theaters using digital projection. No luck. Fans sampling the digital screenings will be closely quizzed on their impressions, and I will await that feedback with interest. Meanwhile, Lucas says he plans to make the next *Star Wars* film all digital—no film—from first shot to consumer.

That's kind of sad, because experts say the best digital projection is not yet a match for current film technology, and there is a new film system named MaxiVision, developed by

Dean Goodhill, that projects film at forty-eight frames per second—twice the current rate—and would produce astonishing results for Lucas. Digital projection systems have been estimated to cost $70,000 per theater. MaxiVision can be retrofitted to existing 35mm projectors for a fraction of the cost, and the projectors can show both twenty-four- and forty-eight-fps films. Steven Poster, vice president of the American Society of Cinematographers, tells me the MaxiVision picture is breathtakingly superior to current film projection, not to mention video.

Since some perceptual psychologists argue that film and video are perceived differently by the mind (film creates an alpha state, resembling reverie, while video produces a beta state, resembling hypnosis), digital video projection might in fact destroy the moviegoing experience as we know it. I hope Lucas doesn't lead the movie industry down the digital rabbit hole.

In June I was able to see MaxiVision demonstrated. I've also seen digital projection, as demonstrated at Cannes. MaxiVision is incomparably superior. We stand at a crossroads between a superior film picture, and an alarming switch to video. Digital video can be very good, but it is not film and never will be.

Q. I recently saw the "digital" projection of *Phantom Menace* (at the Burbank 14 theaters—the Texas Instruments version). While it's hard to gauge the full effects of a new technology on a film one has already seen, nonetheless I found the experience seriously lacking. To tell you the truth, I felt like I was watching a giant TV screen. My friend (who can't wait until DVD is the norm simply based on the fact that videotape loses its sharpness over time) loved it. Afterward, when I expressed my displeasure about the new format, he basically said I had been "brainwashed" into not liking it by your comments. Honestly though, I think I would have had the same reaction regardless of what you said. There's simply something "different" about film and this digital stuff.

—Jeff Taplin, United Talent, Los Angeles, California

A. I support DVD, films shot on digital, and digital special effects, but I believe that digital projection in theaters is, at this point, a case of the emperor not having any clothes. The digital demo I saw at Cannes was just simply not as good as film. But here is another opinion:

Q. I went to all three theaters playing *The Phantom Menace* with digital in L.A. this weekend and was unimpressed with the Hughes/JVC equipment (which was at two of the three screens), but stunned and amazed by the near perfection of the Texas Instruments projector. It was, amazingly enough, better than film. I know you hate to read that, but it was. Not that I have closed my mind to your preferred system. I really would love to know more about it and hopefully, end up seeing it.

—David Poland, TNT Rough Cut Website columnist, Los Angeles, California

A. I have not yet seen *Phantom Menace* in digital, and I want to. But what you saw is not quite the same as what millions of moviegoers would see, any more than the crystal-clear film screenings in Westwood are the same as those in cheapo theaters that turn down the wattage to extend the life of their projector bulbs. You saw a custom-built installation with squads of TI acolytes hovering in the booth. As yet no foolproof system for delivering a digital film to thousands of theaters exists, and one likely candidate—satellite—would involve compression and compromised picture quality. Digital projection is also likely to create nightmares for moviegoers, since few theaters will want to replace their underpaid projections with an expensive trained computer systems specialist. How would you like it if the movie went down as often as the computers at your bank? Meanwhile, the film-based MaxiVision48 is cheaper, uses existing film technology, and is more than twice as good as the best digital projection. The danger is that digital mania will seduce the movie industry into throwing out a century of experience in favor of a problematic system that is not even cheaper, once you factor in the $150,000 per-screen installation and the high costs of in-booth maintenance. That would be a tragedy.

Donnie Brasco

Q. I recently watched *Donnie Brasco* on TV. Can you tell me what Al Pacino was supposed to be doing at the end? He put some things in a drawer—left the drawer pulled out on purpose, put on glasses, and walked out the door. What are we supposed to think happened to him? Did I miss something?

—Mary Fran Purse, Northfield, Illinois

A. He knows he's going to his death, and is leaving those valued possessions for his wife to find, as kind of a message of love.

Drag Queens

Q. I just saw an advertisement for a film called *Billy's Hollywood Screen Kiss.* I do *not* have anything against homosexuals, but my question is this: Why do so many "gay movies" revolve around drag queen performances? Every "gay" movie has some sort of drag queen/disco sequence in it. It's as if the movies believe that if you're gay, you automatically find yourself drawn to divas à la Streisand. Just take a look at *Priscilla, To Wong Foo, The Birdcage, La Cage,* and *Love! Valour! Compassion!* Even *Philadelphia* threw in a drag party. Here's an idea: Make a "gay" movie where the sexuality is secondary to the characters' intellect, personality, and charm.

—Paul West, Seattle, Washington

A. I referred your question to San Francisco film critic B Ruby Rich, who coined the term "New Queer Cinema" and whose new book, *Chick Flicks: Theories and Memories of the Feminist Film Movement,* deals with gay topics, among others. She replied: "It is true that drag is the most popular representation of homosexuality in the movies. But that's a phenomenon not of the New Queer Cinema but rather of 'straight' Hollywood. It's the image that heterosexuals want to see: cute, campy, gay critters that are just so fun and not threatening at all. It's such a beloved stereotype that it even makes money at the box office, which is why it appears on screen over and over and over. The other new favorite is the gay best friend, such as Rupert Everett in *My Best Friend's Wedding.* Once upon a time, that was actually the most prevalent lesbian role, not that she was ever labeled as such—no, she was the 'spinster' best friend or sidekick to the star, wisecracking, not falling for the crap rolled out by the romantic narrative. Think of *Mildred Pierce*'s gal at the cash register. The independent films made by gay and lesbian filmmakers generally have had little use for drag."

Dut-da or Da-da?

Q. At the beginning of movies distributed by 20th Century–Fox, the Fox logo is accompanied by music. It goes:

Dut-da-da-daaa det-dit-det-det-dit-dit-det-dut-da-da-daaa

Only sometimes the fanfare finishes with:

Da-da-da-daaa da-da-da-daaaaa da-da-da —DAAAAAA (det-det-det-daaaa)

My question is, what is the difference between movies that get the full treatment and movies that don't get the big finish? This question has plagued me for years.

—Norman Taylor, Plano, Texas

A. A 20th Century–Fox spokesperson says: "The original music was written in 1934 by Alfred Newman for Daryl Zanuck's newly formed production company, 20th Century Pictures. This fanfare was carried over when the company became 20th Century Fox Corp. in 1935. In 1954, a longer version of the fanfare was developed with an additional seven seconds of music, for films that were in Cinemascope. This version was first used for *The Robe.* As years went on, either one or the other was used until 1994; since then all films begin with the longer version."

DVD

Q. MGM recently made an announcement that they will release the following DVDs in the pan-and-scan format only: *Kingpin, The Secret of NIHM, A Fish Called Wanda.* I was wondering if you agree (or disagree) that this is a step backward for DVD. Even though I do not like the P&S format, I do believe the consumer should have a choice and that all DVDs should include both formats. I do believe the exclusion of wide screen on these titles is just plain laziness on MGM's part.

—Jeff Lockhart, Vancouver, British Columbia

A. "Pan and scan," of course, means that a wide-screen format has its edges sliced off so that the amputated remainder will fill a standard TV screen. "Letterboxing" is the term for movies that use black bands at top and bottom so the viewer can see the entire picture as the director originally intended it. Anyone who loves the movies wants to see the original version, without all the distracting compromises that P&S requires. There are deluded or thoughtless viewers who complain that their whole TV screen isn't filled up. The beauty of the DVD process is that there is room on a disc for *both* letterbox *and* pan and scan. That means the format is ready for the new wide-screen digital TVs, and for the new generation of front projectors that can fill a wide screen. MGM's decision to deprive customers of the choice is small-minded and deceitful. It is always depressing to realize that there are people who make a living from the movies but have no respect or love for the medium.

Dying Is Easy, Comedy Is Hard

Q. In your piece about this year's Oscar nominations, you quote the "old actor's deathbed lament" that "dying is easy; comedy is hard." Which old actor was that?

—Charlie Smith, Chicago, Illinois

A. I wish I knew. Edmund Gwenn is credited with a very similar phrase in the book *Hollywood Anecdotes.* My editor at the *Sun-Times* insists it was Edmund Kean. I searched the Web using the exact wording of the phrase, and found it attributed to Kean. Also to Gwenn. Also to Nell Gwyn, Sir Donald Wolfit, Edwin Booth, and John Barrymore. *Bartlett's Familiar Quotations* steers clear and doesn't deal with it at all.

Editing Rhythm

Q. I might be exaggerating, but it seems that the average cut in many movies today is often a few seconds at most. It often feels as if I'm watching TV and someone else is flipping the channels. Woody Allen's *Manhattan Murder Mystery* is an excellent example of a movie with subtle, but long takes. I watch it on DVD frequently, and I've noticed that entire scenes are sometimes single cuts of upward of two to three minutes. However, the camera moves around so subtly it is easy not to notice. It's refreshing to realize that the actors are actually "acting." I think even I could be an actor if I only had to prepare for several seconds at a time.

—Daniel DeJarnatt, San Francisco, California

A. No doubt about it, movies have shorter average cuts these days. Part of the reason is the popularity of the new AVID editing systems, which make it so easy to cut quickly that it takes a good editor to find the right rhythm. Some directors believe that young viewers, weaned on MTV and commercials, have short attention spans. But I think shorter cuts require a *longer* attention span, because if they don't involve you along in the progress of a scene, you have to hold it in memory.

Q. I had the pleasure last night of watching *Big Night* on video. Your review mentions the unbroken closing shot of Secondo preparing the omelet. I thought this was one of the most brilliant scenes I have come across. We don't know what happens after the Big Night but we know that Secondo will continue to take care of things and that Primo accepts his younger brother's caregiving. I would appreciate hearing any more thoughts that you may have on the scene. It has really taken hold of me.

—Chris Wilkinson, Toronto, Ontario

A. Godard said that every edit is a lie. Cooking that omelet in a montage would have been a TV commercial. Cooking it in one unbroken shot was a performance. Even audience members not consciously aware that there were no edits would understand in a deeper way that Secondo loved to cook.

8 MM

Q. I'm puzzled by the seeming moral indifference to the subject matter of *8 MM.* The "snuff film" theme seems to have barely raised any eyebrows (yours included), in sharp contrast to the recent uproar surrounding *Lolita.* Why is the latter considered untouchable, while the former attracts an audience outwardly apathetic to its much darker subject?

—George Patrice, DeKalb, Illinois

A. The remade *Lolita* was indeed shown on cable TV to less furor than might have been anticipated. But the answer to your question hinges on this fundamental point: A film is not moral or immoral because of its subject matter, but because of how it *treats* its subject matter. I believe that *8 MM* dealt with its subject responsibly; I wrote, "It deals with the materials of violent exploitation films, but in a nonpornographic way; it would rather horrify than thrill." Also, of course, morality resides in the viewer, not the film, which is why censors believe it is correct for them to view dirty movies.

Enemy of the State

Q. Many moviegoers have noticed parallels between the Gene Hackman character in *Enemy of the State* and his classic character Harry Caul in Francis Coppola's *The Conversation* (1973). Here are some more. The clerk in the electronics store addresses Brill as "Harry." And the identity photo of Brill in the NSA's database is a shot of Gene Hackman from *The Conversation.*

—Bill Mullins, Huntsville, Alabama

A. Also, when Hackman takes Will Smith into his secret hideout, the setup, with electronic equipment locked behind steel mesh, is very similar to his rig in *The Conversation.*

Entrapment

Q. In *Entrapment,* a main part of the plot is that the two main characters will gain ten seconds off the clock by "stealing" a tenth of a second every minute for one hour. But wait—just add that up. Pull off your shoes if you have to. Okay now, do you see the problem? That adds up to *six* seconds! What rule of Movie Math am I overlooking?

—Dave Walsh, Bloomington, Illinois

A. You're forgetting that nobody in a movie theater is willing to pull off their shoes. Have you ever taken a good look at the floor?

Eyes Wide Shut

Q. I read in Mr. Showbiz: "Once again, Europeans prove more amenable to sex and nudity than their American counterparts. British cinemagoers will be treated to sixty-five more seconds of orgiastic sex in the explicit Tom Cruise–Nicole Kidman *Eyes Wide Shut* than will Stateside audiences. So much for Stanley Kubrick and so much for Tom Cruise's vow that the film wouldn't be cut." Your feelings?

—Paul Idol, Ft. Lee, New Jersey

A. The sixty-five seconds are still in the American version, but with digitally-produced figures standing in front of crucial parts of the screen to block the sight of sexual activity. Both Britain and Canada have workable categories for adult films. America is the only major moviegoing nation in which, for all practical purposes, no studio film can be adults-only. The NC-17 rating, like the X before it, has been surrendered to pornography. Obviously there should be an A rating between the R and the NC-17, to accommodate just such films as *Eyes Wide Shut.* Canadians meanwhile are in an uproar that they have to see the American version even through they have a category perfectly able to accept Kubrick's preferred cut. Cultural imperialism marches on.

Q. Thank you for speaking out about the travesty that Warner Brothers is perpetuating with *Eyes Wide Shut.* I originally read about the digitally altered sixty-five seconds in Richard Schickel's *Time* magazine article. This is truly a sad day for film enthusiasts. I believe that it is time for someone to step in and deal with the MPAA's perversion of their power. There seems to be no rhyme or reason to their decisions. For example, the original tag line of the *South Park* movie, "All Hell Breaks Loose," was rejected due to the use of the word "hell." The MPAA claims the rating system is only to inform potential viewers about objectionable subject matter, but it is farcical for them to act as if their rulings have no effect on a film's box-office potential, especially the stigmatized NC-17. I will still see *Eyes Wide Shut,* because I love Stanley Kubrick's work and consider him a true artist. That does not change the fact that I am extremely disappointed in Warner Brothers. Although they are in business to make money, it would be nice to see them strive to support those filmmakers who have an artistic vision, rather than solely support mind-numbing dreck such as *Wild, Wild West.*

—Jeremy Slate, Tallahassee, Florida

A. America sleeps better at night knowing that the offensive "All Hell Breaks Loose" was not part of the campaign for *South Park: Bigger, Longer, and Uncut,* a title the MPAA did not object to. The MPAA serves a useful purpose as a guide for parents. But as an unintended side effect, it prevents adults from seeing films as their directors intended them to be seen.

Still, it's not fair to single out Warner Brothers as a villain. True, the studio digitally altered the film; reportedly that was also Kubrick's desire, to get the R rating. But Warners deserves credit for showing both versions to critics at the Los Angeles premieres. Movies are silently cut all the time to qualify for the R rating; we learn about it only after the fact, when the video "director's cut" shows what was left out of the theatrical release. By screening *ESW* pre- and postdigital, the studio was at least able to demonstrate that digital masking was better than cuts which would have disrupted the flow of Kubrick's mesmerizing cinematography.

Q. My question concerns the backward speech read over the speakers in the initial (pre–rumpy pumpy) gathering at the masquerade ball in *Eyes Wide Shut.* It is obvious that something is being said backward, but I don't particularly want to bring recording equipment into the theater to find out what it is.

—Matt Thiesen, Maple Grove, Minnesota

A. The orgy master is saying, "Paul is dead." Just joking. Actually, I believe that's a foreign language and not backward speech at all. I'd appreciate hearing from anyone who argues otherwise.

Fake Documentaries

Q. What is your opinion on the "fake documentary" genre in film? I recently saw *Unmade Beds* by Nicholas Barker, and was more distracted than anything else by attempting to view what was "real" and what wasn't. What is the motivation behind such films? I truly enjoy documentaries, but can such a film be called a legitimate nonfiction piece?

—Ian Visser, Toronto, Ontario

A. As long as the director is not actually trying to fabricate falsehoods in order to mislead the audience, I have no problem with any stylistic approach. Even in "real" documentaries so much is controlled by selection and editing that they are inevitably the director's subjective take on the subject.

Family Movies

Q. The wire services recently carried a story reporting that a study has revealed that the average G-rated film had five times the gross profit and a 31 percent higher return on investment than the average R-rated film. What is your take on this? If G-rated films make more money, why don't we see more of them?

—Paul Chinn, Rochester, Minnesota

A. This survey from the conservative Dove Foundation recycles a statistical error that was discredited by *Variety* when Michael Medved publicized a similar claim several years ago. It is based on a simple but subtle flaw: A handful of films dominates a small category, and that leads to misleading results. Relatively few G-rated films are released in a year (most family films are PG or PG-13), and the category is dominated by the hugely profitable Disney animated cartoons, skewing the statistics. So okay, why don't studios make more animated features? They'd love to, and DreamWorks, Warner Bros., and Universal have all jumped into the genre, with titles like *Antz, Space Jam,* and *Prince of Egypt.* They've had success, but not the huge grosses that Disney enjoys. It's not that easy to make an animated megahit.

An article by Karl Zinsmeister in the magazine *American Enterprise,* commenting on this survey, says, "The dirty little secret of Hollywood is that lots of incredibly unprofitable amoral junk gets made solely because the story titillates some Brentwood producer." The *real* dirty little secret is that all movies are made with the hope of profit—and American families do not, in general, attend "family films." In recent years critics including myself have praised such titles as *The Secret Garden, The Little Princess, White Fang, Babe: Pig in the City, Shiloh, Alaska, My Neighbor Totoro, Children of Heaven, Star Kid, Madeline, The Mighty,* etc. Families have enthusiastically stayed away from these films.

Gattaca

Q. I recently rented *Gattaca*, and found that it suffers in one aspect that seems to plague almost every film where music is performed. The pianist with twelve fingers who is seen and heard performing is supposedly playing a piece that is only possible to play with twelve fingers. Hogwash!! Anyone who has taken rudimentary piano lessons would know that the piece is very easy to play, and by no means requires twelve fingers. Directors will put their actors through boot camp for war films, have them hang out with cops for police films, even have them go through simulated astronaut training, and yet they can't take a few minutes to show Jack Nicolson the approximate places to put his hands when playing the piano *(As Good as It Gets)*. I realize that several films have done an excellent job at making the actors look as though they're actually playing *(Shine, Brassed Off)*, and I realize that many people wouldn't even know the difference, but at the same time, I'm sure fewer people know what combat is like, or what it's like to be in outer space.

—Daniel Peitsch, Ann Arbor, Michigan

A. Yeah, and why don't they show those hotshot young "sex symbols" the proper way to make love?

The General

Q. John Boormann's *The General*, a black-and-white film when it played in theaters, has been released in *color* on VHS, not black and white! But the DVD has both versions.

—Paul West, Seattle, Washington

A. Quite true. The VHS version is in color, and is also panned-and-scanned. The DVD version has color on one side of the disc and b&w on the other, and both sides are letterboxed. My source at Sony says Boorman preferred the film in b&w, but shot it in "desaturated color" with an eye to the VHS and television markets. DVD users are assumed to prefer the real thing. My advice to VHS users: Turn down the color. This film's soul is black and white.

The General's Daughter

Q. In your review of *The General's Daughter* you mentioned that the seediness of the movie was hard to take. I want to give you my view, which is that this was an antirape film, and the violence, sexual seediness, and promiscuity was the whole point of the story. My husband had a similar view to yours; he didn't think it was "necessary" to show the rape—it could have been implied. He thought it was horrible to watch. But did anyone say Spielberg should have just "implied" the violence in *Saving Private Ryan*? NO! That's what made it a great antiwar film. I thought *The General's Daughter* was a powerful, beautifully-done film that really depicted the horror of rape, and what it does to the victim psychologically

—Judy Carr, Tucson, Arizona

A. *Saving Private Ryan* was, in my opinion, a prowar film, about a war that most people feel it was necessary for us to fight. Movies generally tend to argue in favor of what they show, no matter what they say about it. Of course *The General's Daughter* was against rape, but by lingering in the scenes in which the victim is staked to the ground, strangled, etc., it assured that those are the images that linger in the mind.

Happiness

Q. I have a theory about Todd Solondz's movie *Happiness*. I think Allen, the loner who makes obscene phone calls, and Billy, the son of the pederast, are intended to be the same person, seen at two different stages in life. Take a look at their similar physical characteristics, then factor in what Billy might grow up to become after living the childhood he is in. I thought of this when I saw the movie for a second time and noticed that Todd Solondz draws slight attention to both characters' glasses being removed before going to sleep. When I started to think about the other similarities, I was convinced.

—Josh Harris, Los Angeles, California

A. Todd Solondz replies: "Few people who wear glasses do not take them off before going to sleep. If there is such a connection to be made between Allen and Billy, it is unconscious and unintentional—though certainly not unmeaningful. At the end of the movie I do, in fact, feel particularly hopeful for the fates of these two characters: Both of them have known love."

Happy Endings

Q. I recently bought David Fincher's *The Game* on video and enjoyed it again immensely. But as the end credits rolled, I realized I was profoundly angered by the ending of the film. When Van Orton jumps off the edge of the building, Christine screams his name, we see visions of his father—and BANG! we go into the Hollywood Ending where everyone's happy again. Why must American studios believe that you cannot make a decent film without everyone smiling at the end? *The Game* would've been one of my favorite films of all time if Van Orton had died. Alas, I'm stuck with the ending that suspiciously feels like a quick rewrite. As if a test audience didn't like the original downbeat ending maybe? I'm referring to the "Gonna cheer some more sheep" line at the end. That sounds like it was written in a hurry. What is the deal with this type of thing?

—David Rayfield, Brisbane, Australia

A. Studio executives, who can conceive of only happy endings, are notorious for wording test questions so that test audiences can reply in only one way. "Did you want Van Orten to die?" is a question that gets a "no," while "did you like the ending of the film?" might get a yes. If *Casablanca* were remade, everybody would get on the plane.

He Got Game

Q. Unless a really good song comes out the rest of the year, my favorite from a film in 1998 is clearly Public Enemy's "He Got Game" from the Spike Lee film of the same name. The song has the great lyrics and sound of the best of PE songs, and it is truly inspired by the movie. But is it even eligible for Best Original Song? Though there are new lyrics and beats, the song heavily samples Buffalo Springfield's "For What it's Worth." If PE is disqualified for sampling, Aerosmith's "I Don't Wanna Miss a Thing" from the wretched *Armageddon* may be the favorite—another blatant example of a non-movie-inspired song (it sounds like it was written in the eighties for Bon Jovi). If it wins and "He Got Game" (as "original" and integral to its film as any song this year) loses, a hypocritical injustice will be done. Am I correct?

—Robert Sterling, Los Angeles, California

A. Spike Lee, whose opinion of the Academy is well known, tersely replies: "It has no chance of being nominated."

Isms

Q. I was reading your review of *There's Something About Mary* and was absolutely shocked to find that you are a bigot. Your statement that we are "the only animal with a sense of humor" is pure species-ism. Recent books on various ape societies make it quite clear that members of the ape species have a definite sense of humor. Moreover, just because other species may not show a human-like manifestation of a sense of humor does not mean they don't have one. They may in fact have a better sense of humor than humans. It seems to me possible, if not likely, that animals possess the full range of emotional responses that humans do but they just don't communicate it to us, maybe because they know that animal jokes are only funny to other animals.

—Prof. Richard J. Gaylord, University of Illinois, Urbana, Illinois

A. A guy goes into a bar with a duck under his arm. The bartender says, "Where'd you get the pig?" The duck says, "He's a human."

Q. I recently saw *John Carpenter's Vampires* and have to admit that I enjoyed it. However, I felt the film had a strong misogynist tone that made me a bit queasy. I refer to Daniel Baldwin's constant slapping around of Sheryl Lee's character. I'm not a die-hard feminist, but I was pretty offended.

—Lindsay Nelson, Austin, Texas

A. It all depends on how you look at it. He treated her very badly if she was a woman, but she got what she deserved if she was a vampire.

Laser Pointers

Q. Here on the coast the latest annoyance is even worse than people who talk during movies. At some films, teenagers have started using laser pens to throw little moving dots of light on the screen. They especially use them to highlight key areas during nude scenes. Theaters are throwing the offenders out or confiscating the pens. What do you think?

—Ronnie Barzell, Los Angeles, California

A. If this practice discourages attendance at the kinds of movies that attract such cretins, in the long run it could be good for the cinema and perhaps for Western Civilization.

Lethal Weapon 4

Q. Just saw *Lethal Weapon 4*, which I thought was sub-par except for that terrific car-trailer chase scene. What threw me most about the movie was that any sense of fair play has been pretty much abandoned by our heroes. Riggs fakes an injury to get out of a boxing match, and the cops grind an innocent perp's face into the pavement, and it's just the wacky hijinks of another day on the job for the LAPD. The scene that most unnerved me was the finale, in which Riggs and Murtaugh double up on Jet Li. I always thought the idea was that fistfights be resolved mano a mano. Wasn't that how you could spot the villain in old movies—he was the coward who wouldn't fight the hero alone? Didn't Mel Gibson wave off Danny Glover's help at the end of the first *Lethal Weapon*, when he's fighting with Gary Busey? What's happened since then? Have the rules changed?

—Tim Carvell, New York City, New York

A. Riggs and Murtaugh are obviously students of the Hong Kong cinema, and know that when you're up against Jet Li, if you want to live, you cheat.

Letterboxing

Q. Remember all the fuss a couple of years ago when *Pulp Fiction* was first released on video? Miramax had wisely chosen to produce the film in both "pan-and-scan" and wide-screen "letterbox" formats. It took some major arm twisting to get the video chain Blockbuster to offer both versions of the video to its customers. In the end, they did finally rent out one wide-screen copy per store of the film. Well, here we go again. Only this time the public was not so "lucky." When *Titanic* was released it was produced in both "letterbox" and "pan-and-scan" formats. However, none of the three Blockbusters in my city were renting any wide-screen versions. I can only assume that most if not all Blockbuster stores across the nation are also doing the same thing. Needless to say, this is a real shame. If ever a film deserved to be seen in its original aspect ratio it's *Titanic*. It is nice that the purchase price is low enough that one can order the letterbox version to buy, but it's a crime that the thousands of consumers who will rent this movie from the nation's largest video chain will have no choice but to settle for seeing the version that Blockbuster feels is most "marketable."

—Mark Bendiksen, College Station, Texas

A. Incredible, but true. Blockbuster is not making the uncut version available for rental. Stephanie Cota, public relations coordinator for Blockbuster, says so many of their customers prefer the cropped version that they have no plans to release a wide-screen version for rental. Wide screen is available for purchase but not for rental. That means that people renting at Blockbuster will not be able to see up to 40 percent of the original width of the image. Such slicing and dicing on the spectacular special effects of the final hour is sad to contemplate. Blockbuster has had a traditional unwillingness to acknowledge letterboxing, and, indeed, a top executive of the company once revealed to me that he had no idea what it was. Yet many consumers are increasingly insisting on letterboxing. This is a case where the ship has sailed, leaving Blockbuster in port.

Life Is Beautiful

Q. I recently saw Roberto Benigni's terrific *Life Is Beautiful*, and wonder about a possible oversight. What ever came of the last riddle Dr. Lessing presented to Guido at the dinner party—the one he thought represented a duck? I kept waiting for the answer and it never came.

—Matt Ramm, Birmingham, Alabama

A. A Miramax rep says, "The riddle is never explained in the film."

Q. Roberto Benigni—is he for real? I loved it when he climbed up on the backs of the seats after winning his Best Actor Award, but what if he had fallen off and broken a leg?

—Ronnie Barzell, Los Angeles, California

A. Then he would have hopped onstage with one leg instead of two. Or maybe walked on his hands. I am not sure, though, that you can lie down in the firmament and make-a love to everybody with-a your leg in a cast.

Q. Seems like the revisionism is already setting in over Roberto Benigni. He delighted everyone on Oscar night, but now Richard Roeper asks in the *Sun-Times*, "How can he toss around words like 'firmament' and 'tranquillity' and turn such clever phrases as 'oceans of generosity' if he has such a limited grasp of the language?" Roeper also suggests that Benigni's *Life Is Beautiful* isn't exactly original. He writes, "I kept thinking, *Jerry Lewis is a damn genius.* For it was Lewis who explored similar turf nearly thirty years ago in the most notorious unreleased film in history: *The Day the Clown Cried.* In 1972, Lewis directed himself in the role of Helmut Dork, an emaciated, seventy-seven-year-old clown at Aushwitz who entertained children with his wacky antics in an effort to keep them distracted from their ultimate fate." Your reaction?

—Charlie Smith, Chicago, Illinois

A. The Jerry Lewis film is not rumored to be a work of genius. As for its plot, it depends on how you look at it. "It is not a comedy," reports David Thomson in his *Biographical Dictionary of Film.* "It is about a circus clown employed by the Nazis to assist in the killing of children in concentration camps." Somehow that doesn't sound like the same approach. As for Benigni's "limited grasp of the language"—he speaks English imperfectly but with enthusiasm, deliberately cultivating a colorful vocabulary, and has appeared in English-language movies such as Jim Jarmusch's *Night on Earth* and *Down by Law*, and *Son of the Pink Panther.* His acceptance speeches could not have been so artful unless he knew exactly what he was doing; his word choices were part of the joke.

Little Voice

Q. My husband thinks he heard Jane Horrocks mimic Julie Andrews in *Little Voice.* I think it must have been someone else; Andrews is of the wrong era to join Shirley Bassey, Marilyn Monroe, Judy Garland, Marlene Dietrich, etc. Or maybe my husband and I are of the wrong era. Does someone have a list of all the "voices" that come from LV's throat?

—Amy Hoffman, Cambridge, Massachusetts

A. Jayna Pakman of Miramax says: "Marilyn Monroe, Gracie Fields, Shirley Bassey, Judy Garland (both as herself and as Dorothy in *Wizard of Oz*), Billie Holliday, Cilla Black, and Marlene Dietrich."

Locations

Q. Recently I rewatched *Starship Troopers* and noticed a location that struck me as familiar. The location was the long glass hall area used for the scene where the young stars get their new military assignments. This has to be the same hall area used in *Men in Black.* Could you please confirm my hunch, and also give some background behind this now famous locale?

—Charles N. Ogan, Naperville, Illinois

A. According to Columbia spokesman Jeff Marden, these were not the same locations.

Q. Have you noticed that all the kind, decent, down-to-earth movie characters now come from Wisconsin? Several examples come to mind immediately, and *The American President* and *Contact* went out of their way to establish their protagonists' stately origins. The cheese state has clearly replaced Minnesota as the screenwriter's favorite "normal" state (I wonder if *Fargo* had anything to do with it), and Pennsylvania is running a distant third. I think it has something to do with all three states combining farm life with access to a major city; the character can seem both salt-of-the-earth and worldly.

—Matt Chaput, Toronto, Ontario

A. And of course the hero of *Ed's Next Move* made a big deal of coming from Wisconsin. Also, the salt-of-the-earth filmmaker heroes of *American Movie*, this year's Sundance-winning documentary, are from Menominee Falls. Kind of makes you forget all about Ed Gein.

Q. Have you read E. Annie Proulx's book *The Shipping News*? I recently read that production of the movie based on the book has been delayed because of location issues. John Travolta, who hopes to star, wants to shoot in Maine (he has a home there). Director Fred Schepisi left the project because he wanted to shoot in Newfoundland. The book takes place in Newfoundland, and I haven't read a book in the past ten years in which the geographic location was so instrumental to the novel. Newfoundland is like a character in the book. I hate when stars do this! I'm not green enough to think every movie is filmed "on location." But this book deserves it! Am I a biased Newfoundlander? YES!

—Mike Spearns, St. John's, Newfoundland

A. I was in Minneapolis last weekend to do a Q&A session with the great German director Werner Herzog at the Walker Art Center, which showed his movies all month. Herzog believes in the "voodoo of location"—that locations seep into performances and photography and give a special texture to the film. That's why his *Aguirre, the Wrath of God* and *Fitzcarraldo* were shot hundreds of miles inside the South American rain forests, and why for *Nosferatu* he used some of the same locations employed in Murnau's silent classic. Newfoundland is not Maine. Maine is not Newfoundland. Some movies can be shot anywhere. Some cannot. Those that cannot usually turn out to be the best ones.

Logos

Q. Any significance to the twenty-two stars that surround the Paramount Pictures logo?

—John Kumiega, Lansing, Illinois

A. A Paramount rep says, "No, it's just our design."

Madeline

Q. Regarding *Madeline*, try reading the stories or check out the cartoon series. The girls are not visiting Paris, they live there! *They are French!!!* And they should speak with a French accent! From the clips, it sounds like these little girls are talking with an English accent. This is a basic and major error on the part of the producers—as bad as *Dr. Zhivago* in an Italian accent. That English (UK) accent keeps hitting us in the face like a dirty dish rag. Official protests should be coming from the French government over the international insult of this movie. At least the girls in the cartoon series speak English with a French accent. You probably also eat at Au Bon Pain for the French food. The only thing close to French on that menu is the croissants, which were not invented in France.

—Ken Griggs, Park Forest, Illinois

A. But the movie is AMERICAN!!! In French movies, the Americans speak in FRENCH!! Yet the U.S. government has not protested this international insult. Another thing close to French on that menu is the prices.

Q. In your review of *Madeline*, you said you hoped people would discover the books that Ludwig Bemelmans wrote for grown-ups, and that his writing should be "studied by anyone who wants to learn how to put a sentence together without any nails." Titles and recommendations, please?

—Charlie Smith, Chicago, Illinois

A. If you're a movie fan, a good place to start would be *Dirty Eddie*, his Hollywood novel. My own favorite is *Now I Lay Me Down to Sleep*. Basically, you can't go wrong. Bemelmans is a treasure without price, a master of prose style, piercing observation, and the human comedy. The Book of the Month Club brought out a matched set of five or six titles a couple of years ago, which you may be able to find.

Mafia! a.k.a. *Jane Austen*

Q. The new movie *Mafia!* was originally titled *Jane Austen's Mafia!*? I like the original title better. Perhaps distant family of Jane Austen's threatened to sue, or a Jane Austen society was up in arms about this, or maybe there was some sort of mass Jane Austen fan backlash. I'm very curious about the change.

—Jeff Braun, Seattle, Washington

A. Nope, no mass backlash from Jane Austin fans. Quite the contrary. According to the film's director, Jim Abrahams, the studio marketing team found that a majority of the target market did not know who Jane Austen was.

The Mask of Zorro

Q. I recently rented *The Mask of Zorro,* and was struck by the scene in which young Zorro hides in the confessional to escape Don Rafael's impending army detail. The beautiful Elena enters and begins confessing her sins to Zorro, whom she believes is the priest. She claims to be guilty of violating the fourth commandment, which Zorro mistakes as murder, but which Elena believes to be dishonoring her mother and father. I am quite certain that honoring one's mother and father is the fifth commandment. Was this a joke, or an unintentional slip?

—Daniel A. Silver, Boston, Massachusetts

A. In the Jewish and Catholic traditions, "Honor thy father and thy mother" is the fourth commandment, but in the Protestant tradition, it is the fifth. If Elena and Zorro are Catholics (a good bet since we find them in a confessional), Elena is right and Zorro is wrong, since "Thou shalt not kill" is the fifth commandment. If he is a Protestant, he is still wrong, since in that tradition the fourth commandment is "Keep holy the Sabbath" and the fifth is "Honor thy father and mother."

The Matrix

Q. Maybe one reason *The Matrix* seemed like rehashed material was that it is a pretty transparent biblical allegory. Computers enslave the humans as the Romans enslaved the Jews, and Neo (Reeves) is the prophesied Jesus while Cypher acted as Judas. The original VR simulation was a world without sin, but humankind was flawed, and the VR had to be changed to include suffering. Names like "Trinity" and "Apoc" are direct references. Reeves's ascent toward heaven in the final scene completes the biblical semiotics. The only places where the allegory was not straightforward were where the Hollywood Studio Plot™ had to step in.

—Josh Powers, San Mateo, California

A. Quite true. Neo is referred to as "the One," and "Neo" is an anagram for "One." Also, of course, "Agent Smith" is an anagram for "I'm the Angst," and "Morpheus" spells "Push Rome."

Q. I was wondering how they shot those rotating stills in *The Matrix.* An example would be the kung-fu training scene where Laurence Fishburne jumps up into the air and hangs there while the movie pans around him making it look like 3-D. I first saw this effect in a music video and have been intrigued ever since. I've also seen this same effect in one of the Gap commercials.

—Jose Francisco Roa, Manchester, New Hampshire

A. Such an effect can be done with Dayton Taylor's Virtual Camera technique, which the Answer Man has discussed before. (It's explained at www.virtualcamera.com/.) It can also be done with images manipulated by computer. Sometimes, they "fly" actors or their doubles with hidden wires and then manipulate those images.

Q. I saw *The Matrix.* Did'ja notice that all of the street coordinates in the cyber world ("Balbo," "Franklin," "Wabash," "Lake," etc.) are also streets in Chicago? It's a bummer to spend your whole life floating in a tank of orange viscous fluid—but at least it's comforting to know that someone remembered the directions to "Mr. Beef."

—James Stevens, Lisle, Illinois

A. The screening room where I saw the movie is near the corner of Wabash and Lake, and I expected Keanu Reeves to burst through the door. Stranger things have happened in there. The screening of the Spice Girls movie, for example.

Q. A recent Answer Man column noted how the street names in *The Matrix* were also streets in Chicago. There's obviously a bug in *The Matrix:* the Chicago street names are combined with the landmarks and company logos of Sydney, Australia. And for some strange reason, all the streets in this strange city are "one way," and it's difficult to see into the interiors of cars for all the reflections. Does this have anything to do with the fact that Australians drive on the other side of the road?

—Murray Chapman, Internet Movie Database

A. Inspired by your e-mail address, I went to www.imdb.com, the most invaluable single movie site on the web, and discovered that *The Matrix* locations were indeed in Sydney, Australia.

Memorabilia

Q. That auction price of $250,000 for the Cowardly Lion's costume—a record? What was the old record? Does it mean Planet Hollywood has millions of dollars of inventory hanging on its walls?

—Casey Anderson, Schaumberg, Illinois

A. The lion's costume broke a three-year-old record of $145,500, which was the winning bid for John Travolta's white disco suit from *Saturday Night Fever.* So says Gene Siskel, who owned the suit for many years after outbidding Jane Fonda at a charity auction. (He paid $2,000.) Only a few movies are so special that their props fetch prices in this range. Among them: *Gone With the Wind, Casablanca, Citizen Kane, The Wizard of Oz,* and the *Star Wars* series. The "eye" plate for Hal 9000, the computer in *2001: A Space Odyssey,* would probably earn in the same high range if it were ever auctioned.

Message in a Bottle

Q. I saw *Message in a Bottle* at a sneak preview the other night. How is it that the heroine's newspaper builds up this big story, sells thousands of papers with it, spends untold sums in research on it, and then as soon as the heroine says there's no story, her boss just walks away from it with a shrug?

—Steve Bailey, Jacksonville Beach, Florida

A. The paper is the *Chicago Tribune,* which may help answer your question. Right now I am looking forward to *Never Been Kissed,* the new Drew Barrymore movie, in which she plays a *Chicago Sun-Times* reporter who pretends to be a high school student. Hey, have you seen that TV show *Early Edition*? Its hero prevents problems by magically getting tomorrow's *Sun-Times* a day early. They considered using the *Tribune,* but found that tomorrow's *Tribune* was so much like today's *Sun-Times* that it just wasn't much help.

Missing Scenes

Q. I realize scenes used in promos are not always in the movie when you see it, but I was surprised that the massage scene wasn't in *Living Out Loud* when I went to see it here in San Antonio. I asked the theater manager why it wasn't there since they referred to it in what was obviously the following scene. He swears the movie arrived that way. Then *People* magazine referred to this hot new actor, Eddie Cibrian, who gives Holly Hunter a massage, and how much attention he got at the premiere. Is it usual for scenes to be removed after a show has premiered, or did San Antonio just get a botched copy?

—Hollis Osburn, San Antonio, Texas

A. A spokesman for New Line Cinema replies: "All prints of *Living Out Loud* were shipped by New Line Cinema with the scene in question. Any subsequent edits were not made with the authorization of the filmmakers or the studio." Perhaps an individual exhibitor found the scene offensive and removed it. Or maybe Eddie Cibrian has a fan in the projection booth who has added the scene to a private collection.

Movie Critics

Q. *All-Movie Guide* ran an ad looking for reviewers. Pay is $400 a week, and you must be able to review 50–100 films a week. Okay, say the average film is around two hours. You would have to watch movies twenty-eight hours a day, seven days a week, to watch 100 movies. When would you find time to write the reviews? Hey, there are only twenty-four hours in a day to begin with! Even if you only reviewed the minimum of fifty films, that's still fourteen hours a day seven days a week just watching the suckers. They seem to want people to make up the reviews without watching the movies.

—W. C. Martell, Studio City, California

A. Many of the vast compendiums of movie "reviews" are actually ripped off from other books, and compiled by freelancers who have not seen many of the movies they pass judgment on. The best of the freelancers, of course, steal from me.

Q. Have enjoyed your attacks over the years on the blurbmeisters who grind out favorable quotes for ads. But there was a quote in Friday's *Sun-Times* that was truly strange. It was for Clint Eastwood's *True Crime*, and it quoted Joanna Langfield of *The Movie Minute*, whatever that is, saying the movie was "A TRUE POTBOILER!" Hello?

—Emerson Thorne, Chicago, Illinois

A. The ad appeared around the country. *Webster's* defines *potboiler* as "a work of art or literature, often inferior, produced only to make money." Obviously at least one member of the Warner Bros. advertising department was not familiar with the meaning of the word. As for Joanna Langfield, either (a) she also does not know what it means, or (b) she has written her first negative review, and we should send her congratulatory telegrams.

Q. An oft-mentioned criticism of today's movie critics is that they are "too critical," that they've either been doing the job too long, or that they consider themselves such "film experts" that they judge a movie on "artistic" designs, rather then on the enjoyability. With your recent search for guest hosts on TV, this might be an interesting time to add someone not affiliated with the film industry. Someone who doesn't have a degree in film; someone who normally doesn't review movies; and someone who doesn't gain or lose from a film review. Basically, someone who sees these films through the relatively unjaded eyes of a "regular human being."

—Patrick M. Geahan, Midland, Michigan

A. I could not agree with you more. We need more critics like me, who has no film degree and can judge *Speed 2* on enjoyability! Your insight is so valuable I recommend you apply it to surgeons, dentists, lawyers, accountants, and airplane pilots. These professions are also overloaded with jaded people with degrees, who cannot see their specialties through the eyes of regular human beings. I have even heard alarming rumors of overcompetence in the Midland Fire Department.

Q. Given all the films you view professionally, my question for you is, do you have some technique of clearing your mind between films, much as a gourmet might clear his palate with sherbet between courses, or something like that, so you can have at least some degree of fresh experience?

—Timothy E. Klay, Louisville, Kentucky

A. I go downstairs and get a turkey on whole wheat with lettuce, onion, and mustard.

Q. So here I am in the dark watching *Nosferatu* and scribbling down notes about all sorts of new images and I realize that in a proper movie theater you scribble without seeing and hope that your pen strokes don't clobber other pen strokes that are already on the page. I assume that when you're reviewing movies you are also writing notes to yourself somehow. To voice them into a cassette recorder could be obnoxious to nearby viewers. Do you have a lighted paper pad of some sort? Or a pen that emits a small cone of light? What technology would you like to see developed for note-taking in the dark? Would you ever consider taking advantage of a TV screen you hold in your lap (a fourteen-inch backlit LCD of some kind) that you could use to draw directly onto the movie itself, circling things like the TV sportscasters do on *Monday Night Football*, with their light pens?

—Evan Reidell, Cambridge, Massachusetts

A. I use the Levenger Pocket Briefcase, a little leather gizmo with three-by-five card storage and a slot to hold the active card. There is enough light from the screen so I can see where not to write. Sometimes I cannot read my handwriting, of course. In the past I have tried a Palm Pilot with the special alphabet (too distracting while watching a movie) and a Newton (handwriting recognition excellent, but backlit screen a distraction to those around me). I find that three-by-five cards work best, and do not yearn for an electronic substitute. Professional film critics frown sternly on amateurs who turn up with illuminated pens and/or clipboards with built-in lights. They are annoying to those around you. The *Monday Night Football* thing would be useless while watching a movie, but if the pen strokes could be captured on a DVD and linked to an audio commentary, that would be a wonderful bell and/or whistle.

Movie Math

Q. I appreciate how you regularly inform your readers about how some sleazy theater owners run their projectors on "low" lamp intensity in order to save money. I have another annoyance. Many movie theaters, even in big cities, do not allow the entire movie credits to roll before they start: 1) closing the screen curtains, 2) turning up the lights, and 3) noisily bringing in the brooms and garbage bags to clean up. Some movie companies have caught onto this and have deliberately added a scene or two to the very end of the movie so that you *have* to sit through the credits.

—Bob Makarowski, New York City, New York

A. Credit cookies are an effective way to keep the audience seated, but only if the audience knows they're coming. Half the audience I joined for *Austin Powers: The Spy Who Shagged Me* was on its feet before the first cookie appeared. I agree with you that the credits and the end music are included in the admission price; demand a refund if you're shortchanged.

Q. This is in response to the person who felt shortchanged because movie employees would come in during the ending credits banging trash cans and brooms. You have to understand that most large theaters carry more than one major movie at a time. So, while *The Phantom Menace* is getting out in one theater, *Big Daddy* is getting out five minutes later in another. In order to clean all the theaters in time sometimes they have to clean while the credits are still rolling.

—Jacob Galvez, Phoenix, Arizona

A. Try this Movie Math: If they let the credits roll, the movies would still end at the same times, relative to one another. So early banging solves nothing.

MPAA Ratings System

Q. I was driving past our local cinemultiplex and noticed on the marquee, *Gone With the Wind* (G) beneath *Madeline* (PG). How can *GWTW* get a G rating when it contains scenes of war, mutilated soldiers, the famous "street of death," and the death of a child, while *Madeline* gets a PG? The reason quoted in your review of *Madeline* was that it got the PG for a single "damn." Certainly *GWTW* has the most famous "damn" in the history of cinema.

—David M. Arnold, Brookfield, Wisconsin

A. Joan Graves, cochair of the Motion Picture Code and Ratings Administration, says *Gone With the Wind* was originally rated in 1971. Once a film is rated it keeps that rating —unless, on a rerelease, the distributor chooses to resubmit it. For its current rerelease, *GWTW* was not resubmitted. *Madeline*, of course, was given a PG this year. Ms. Graves said that if *GWTW* were to be submitted today, it would probably not get a G rating.

Q. The TV advertisements for *Antz* include the line when "Z" says he doesn't want to drink from the "caboose" of another creature. Yet, when I saw the movie in a theater, the word "caboose" was replaced with the word "anus." Like so many other recent "family" movies, this one had to include an unnecessary gross-out joke. The word "caboose" is not only more "palatable," but I think it sounds funnier anyway. So which word was in the original script?

—Greg Anderson, Huntsville, Utah

A. The line occurs as ants are drinking nectar from the anuses of aphids, which ants do all the time. I first learned of this ant gourmet behavior in high school biology class, where Mr. Dimmick never once, as I recall, found it necessary to use the word "caboose." The word was switched in the TV ad because our society finds accurate scientific and medical terminology more offensive than hayseed euphemisms.

Q. Why is *Shakespeare in Love* rated R? Were the MPAA reviewers replaced for one day by NFL officials? There is nothing in *Shakespeare* that a teenager couldn't handle. In fact, that is the exact audience who should see this picture, as it provides a wonderful introduction to the Bard and situations that may have inspired his art.

—Douglas Trapasso, Boston, Massachusetts

A. They're bean-counters. *Shakespeare in Love* gets an R, and so does *8 MM*. *Shake-*

speare has a little mild nudity and some bawdiness. *8 MM* contains rough sex, sadistic violence, and representations of snuff films. Any category big enough to contain both of those titles is so commodious it's meaningless. We need an A rating, between the R and the NC-17, to distinguish films that are not hard-core porno but are nevertheless clearly for adults only. The MPAA won't take this obvious step because of pressure from exhibitors terrified of losing a few ticket sales.

Q. I read an article that says Spike Lee may return to the editing room to cut his latest opus down from NC-17 to R. Besides the box office, what factors into these decisions? Why would Lee ever want to tamper with his own vision? Why can't we simply accept NC-17 films? I think NC-17 should be applied much more often; it provides strong information about the content of the movie.

—Paul West, Seattle, Washington

A. Spike Lee is indeed faced with the possibility of an NC-17 for *Summer of Sam,* his much-awaited film about David Berkowitz, the serial killer known as Son of Sam. I understand he is reediting to avoid the rating. His distributor, Touchstone, like most major studios, doesn't like NC-17 because the rating makes it hard to advertise a picture or play it in some theaters. NC-17 was supposed to avoid the curse of X, but has simply replaced it. For years I have suggested an A rating *between* R and NC-17 (or X). A would simply denote "for adults only but not pornography." It would provide a service to moviegoers, it would give more freedom to filmgoers, and NC-17 would take the heat. It makes perfect sense. The MPAA opposes A, however, because it has panic attacks at the thought of any rating that would cause them to turn away paying customers. The result: Serious filmmakers like Lee pay the price, and we're the losers.

Q. I'm writing as a parent who is shocked and appalled at what has been done to a great story like *Doctor Dolittle.* Why would they make a movie for children with a rating like PG-13? Teenagers and adults wouldn't want to go to a movie like this, so why make it for them? I shudder to think how many children will end up at it just because their parents aren't paying attention to the ratings.

—Cindy Helgason, Des Moines, Iowa

A. The PG-13 reflects an emphasis on bodily functions, as when a pigeon poops on a villain, and Dolittle, as a little boy, takes the advice of his dog and sniffs the rear end of the school principal. Yes, the movie has some gross-out moments, but it's comparatively tame, and the overall tone is kind of sweet. I think the studio is aiming to attract teenagers and adults (Murphy is the box-office draw), and didn't intend to remake a G-rated children's film. All the same, I know many parents are concerned about the specific content of films, and I recommend Screen It! which is an *incredibly* detailed on-line guide to the content, tone, tenor, language, sexuality, violence, action, implications, and example-setting of current movies. It's on the Web at (www.screenit.com/index.html).

Q. I've been following your arguments for an A rating to be placed between the R and the NC-17. Another problem is theater owners who become a ratings board all on their own, effectively overruling the MPAA when they see fit. When I saw *The Wood,* the theater was packed with young teenagers. I guess that about 50 percent of the audience was between the ages of twelve and seventeen. Funny, considering the same theater would not allow those teenagers to purchase a ticket for *Eyes Wide Shut,* despite the fact that they are both rated R. So the theater decided that some R-rated films are worse than others.

— Jason Ihle, East Northport, New York

A. The problem is that the R category has been stretched to the bursting point because there is no other place for a movie to go. Some theater owners sensibly decide on their own which films are truly for older audiences, and which ones got the R only on technicalities. R is so bloated because NC-17 is identified with porn, and is not a practical, workable choice for a film in mass distribution. My point is that the A should *not* replace the NC-17, but come between the R and NC-17, creating a clear category for films that are intended for adults but do not cross the line into hard-core pornography. Jack Valenti and I had a spirited airing of our views in columns in *Variety* last week, and I was encouraged that Peter Bart, *Variety*'s editor, wrote an open letter to Valenti arguing that there was something to be said for the A rating.

Valenti keeps talking about the rights of parents and teenagers. The R category addresses those rights. Now it is time for adults to have the right to see movies as their directors prefer them to be seen.

Q. If I ever meet Jack Valenti, I want to tell him of my experience seeing *Eyes Wide Shut*. There were about 100 people in the theater, exactly one of whom looked under eighteen. That one was a boy of about ten who was there with a man of about forty, presumably his father. (I'll withhold my opinion of a father who would take his young son to *Eyes Wide Shut* when *Tarzan* was playing in the same multiplex.) The boy sat right in front of me, so I couldn't help but notice his restlessness. During the sex scenes he seemed embarrassed to be with his father; during the rest of the film he seemed bored. So if we had the A rating that you propose, 99 of the 100 people in the theater would have been able to see Kubrick's film the way it was intended (rather than the *Austin Powers* version) and the ten-year-old would have been sent to *Tarzan*. I know Mr. Valenti would object to this, but I'm not sure why.

—Michael David Smith, Urbana, Illinois

A. Could it be that Valenti and his bosses, the theater owners, oppose *any* category that would actually prevent them from selling tickets? Is this a question of artistic freedom, or retailing?

Mulan

Q. In your review of Disney's *Mulan* you wrote: "The story this time isn't a retread of a familiar children's classic, but original material." I thought you might be interested to know that *Mulan* is in fact based on an epic poem from ancient Chinese folklore. It is almost as well-known to the Chinese as *The Iliad* is to the Greeks. The full name of the protagonist is actually Kwa Mulan, "Kwa" being the family name. The male-female duality in Mulan's psyche and strength is echoed in her very name: "Kwa" means "flower" in Chinese, "Mu" means wood, and "Lan" means orchids. It's a pity that Disney altered an integral part of the original story, which is that Mulan was as proficient in the martial arts as she was in sewing and poetry. This is because she was an only child and her father had no sons to whom he could pass on his martial arts skills. I'm convinced *Mulan* might have been intended partially as an icebreaker for Disney's emerging markets in China. Regardless, I am glad that Disney borrowed from my favorite Chinese epic.

—Mina Chung, Beltsville, Maryland

A. What I should have said is that Disney didn't base the movie on a *Western* children's classic, as it often does. Since Disney is the dominant global source of children's entertainment, it's good to see it reaching out to other cultures for its source material.

Q. Your review of *Mulan* is predictably incomplete. "The message here is standard feminist empowerment," you say. No. The message here also is empowerment for transgendered persons such as myself. This is far from a standard message for any movie, much less for an animated film with a hopefully large children's audience. Society has put so many restrictions on transgendered people's chances to simply be themselves. But just as I didn't want to play sports as a boy but would rather play house or dolls, just as I found myself enjoying wearing the clothes of women, Mulan finds herself not wanting to follow the so-called rules of her assigned gender. The message from "Pinocchio" of "let your conscience be your guide" is the true message of *Mulan*. When they need to, even her fellow soldiers abandon convention and dress up like women (and seem a little freer and happier for it). It's a beautiful moral to the story, one that transgendered children especially need to hear so they don't go through years of self-hatred: It's okay to be one's self.

—Jennifer Wendy Michael Gilbert, also known as Dave, Chicago, Illinois

A. Sorry I had to edit your longer letter for space; I hope I got the essence. I am not convinced that Mulan does in fact believe she is a boy who has been mistakenly born inside a girl's body; I believe she is a girl who pretends to be a boy simply in order to take her father's place in the army. She is not, however, happy with the roles assigned to women in her society, which is why she flees the matchmaker and an arranged marriage. That's why I think the message is essentially feminist.

Cross-dressing and gender-based disguises are a central theme in Asian folklore. I believe they reflect a desire to escape from the limitations of one's own sex, rather than a desire to be of another sex. This trend continues to this day: In modern Tokyo, teenage girls go to a wildly popular stage show in which all of the "boys" are girls.

National Board of Review

Q. Now that *Gods and Monsters* has been given the award as Best Film of 1998 by the National Board of Review, the question arises—who are they? I pulled out a 1960 issue from my inherited postwar collection of their magazine, *Films in Review*, and found this statement on the back cover: "The National Board of Review is an independent, nonprofit organization of public-spirited citizens founded in 1909 to represent the interests of the motion picture public . . . , etc." I called New York information for their number; no listing. I take it that within the circle of film critics, this group is something of an enigma? Who appoints them?

—Tom Norris, Braintree, Massachusetts

A. I have never met anyone who has met a member of the National Board of Review. The director John Boormann recently told me that he attended one of their award banquets at the Tavern on the Green in Central Park, and met several other award winners. There was a celebrity host to hand out the prizes. "After I got back home," he mused, "I realized that I had not met a single person claiming to be a member of the National Board of Review."

Needles

Q. A lot of the time when an actor is shown being injected with drugs, the needle looks like something you would use on a horse. I doubt that the actors are actually injected with anything, yet the effect looks pretty real. Is this a special-effects needle or do they use a real one on the actor (or body double) with a harmless substance? A movie I just saw with Ewan MacGregor called *Nightwatch* showed an actress being injected in the neck with one of these and it made me wonder.

—Keith Silcox-Ingersoll, Ontario, Canada

A. One of the most memorable needle injections of recent years occurred in *Pulp Fiction*, when Uma Thurman was skewered with a needle straight through the breastbone and into the heart. So I turned to the coauthor of that screenplay, Roger Avary, for an answer.

He replies: "In reality, the needles that junkies and diabetics use are these tiny little things, not much longer than an inch. That, of course, won't do in most films. When I see a needle on screen, I want it to scare me. In my movie *Killing Zoe* I never actually showed a needle touching an arm, because what you imagine is far worse than what I could afford to do. But if I had wanted to, and had my actors felt game, we could have injected a little saline, or some vitamins, into their system. Stage needles (the ridiculous-looking ones out of *Dr. Phibes*) never look real. If most junkies had one of these monster-sized needles they'd shred up their arms because the process of shooting up is such a mess. In the case of the actress in *Nightwatch*, I tend to think that it was a fake syringe with a collapsible needle. I can't imagine many actors who'd allow you to jab a needle into the jugular. I guess the answer to your question is that in film, which is a medium of trickery, you use whatever trick will accomplish the effect you're looking for."

New Geek Cinema

Q. While I agree with your description of and complaints about what you term the "New Geek Cinema," I was wondering how you chose the word "geek." Traditionally, the word "geek" has been almost synonymous with "nerd," evoking an image of a scrawny social outcast with greasy hair and bad hygiene. Lately, the term has been coopted by techies who, pocket protectors or no, have succeeded in life by doing the same things that made them punching bags as kids. In its mildest form, "geek" now describes electronic gear-heads who speak mostly in model numbers ("I gotta couple 1200s and a 58 feeding my Rane; I can mix your 303 and 909 in with that"). What connotation of "geek" are you thinking of when you speak of these nouveau-Tarantino poseurs?

—Ed Horch, Bridgewater, New Jersey

A. The word "geek" has its origins in carnival sideshows, where it referred to the man who did disgusting things like biting the heads off of live chickens. Imagine him wearing a pocket protector, and you've got it.

October Sky

Q. In your review of *October Sky*, you mentioned that it was based on the book *Rocket Boys*, by Homer H. Hickam Jr. Here is an interesting footnote: Universal refused to go with the original movie title, which was also *Rocket Boys*. So the filmmakers were forced to come up with something else. Thus it became *October Sky*—which is an anagram of *Rocket Boys*!

—Mary Jo Kaplan, New York City, New York

A. How could anyone possibly think *October Sky* was a better title than *Rocket Boys*? The original title leaps off the page and vividly summarizes the movie's concept; *October Sky* sounds like the title of an album by Wyndham Hill. Here are some other new and improved titles: *A Span at River Vying, A Pale Heroes' Knives, I Fail But Use Life, The Ale Biz,* and *Dither the Lenin.*

One True Thing

Q. Did I miss something or was there a mirror image shot in *One True Thing*? In the scene where Rene Zellweger's character first overhears her mother talking with her father's friend it looked like a mirror image because all the lettering on the books were backward. And there's a later scene in the same room where everything is reversed. Why would they do that? Was it a heavy-handed way to symbolize a world in turmoil, or were the filmmakers sloppy?

—Mark Rennie, San Jose, California

A. Jessie Beaton, the producer of *One True Thing* says: "Yes, there was a mirror in the scene this reader talks about. It was not a mistake nor was it symbolic; it was just the way they composed the shot. Earlier in the movie, in a scene that was cut, there was a scene where Rene Zellweger enters her bedroom and you see the mirror."

The Opposite of Sex

Q. The funniest, best-written movie I've seen this year is *The Opposite of Sex*. When I watched it on video today, I was horrified to discover they'd taken out one of my favorite lines! In her narration, DeDee says that Matt almost got fired from his job at Kinko's. In the theater, the line finished, "and you know how hard it is to get fired from Kinko's. It's like the post office. You practically have to start shooting people." I rewound twice and checked my hearing, and the answer was clear: The last part of the line was taken out from the video release. This was a line they even used in the print advertisements, if I recall correctly. What happened?

—Tim Tori, Glendale, California

A. Don Roos, director of the film, explains: "Your reader is correct. It was a line used, unwisely, as it turns out, in the print advertising. Some lawyer from Kinko's was offended and protested to the studio, and we agreed to remove it from the video version (it would have been prohibitively expensive to remove it from the theatrical prints). I took so many swipes at so many institutions and people in this movie—there really isn't anybody left to offend—that I can't complain if one of those swipes failed to make it to video. And I need the people at Kinko's to like me because sometimes they throw in free brads."

Out of Sight

Q. I recently saw *Out of Sight* and noticed Michael Keaton's character seemed very similar in that movie to his character in *Jackie Brown*. So I looked back in the novel *Rum Punch* and saw that Keaton's character was also named Ray Nicolet, the part he is playing in *Out of Sight*. Is he playing the same character here?

—Steve Dermentzis, Scotia, New York

A. Yes. Both movies are based on novels by Elmore Leonard, who carried Nicolet over.

Pajamas

Q. Re your review of *Holy Man:* I am from India and there is no such thing as "Gandhi Pajamas" there. Is it an American term for the "Kurta Pyjama" (which is the Indian term for Murphy's attire)?

—Navneeth Rao, Minneapolis, Minnesota

A. No, it is my term for the Kurta Pyjama. Sorry.

The Parent Trap

Q. The new version of *The Parent Trap* repeats the gimmick of having one actress (Lindsay Lohan) playing twins. Which is less expensive, hiring actual twins, or using technology to duplicate one person?

—Willie Holmes, Chicago, Illinois

A. Regarding your first question: It would be cheaper to hire twins than to pay for the special-effects technology, and indeed the Olsen twins starred in *It Takes Two* (1995), which was, like *The Parent Trap*, about twins who play Cupid.

Q. At the end of Disney's remake of *The Parent Trap*, a closing credit dedicates the movie to "Hallie." I know that Hallie Meyers-Shyer, the daughter of producer/directors Charles Shyer and Nancy Meyers, was credited as one of the girls in the camp. Was this simply a tribute to the child or did something happen to her?

—Len Klatt, Los Angeles, California

A. Suzanne Farwell, Nancy Meyers's assistant, says: "So many movies feature boys as the hero that Nancy and Charles wanted to make a movie where the hero is a girl (or girls, in this case). Nancy says that *The Parent Trap* empowers girls who are the exact age of her daughter, Hallie. Nancy and Charles wanted Hallie to have this to look back on for the rest of her life, as a film that her parents made as a valentine to her. In 1987, Nancy and Charles dedicated their *Baby Boom* to their other daughter, Annie, who was seven-years old at the time."

Patch Adams

Q. *Patch Adams* was universally loathed by critics, but it is a huge box-office success. Conventional wisdom is that if a movie sucks, word of mouth will quickly diminish its box office. So, it seems safe to conclude that people actually like it. This brings up the age-old question: Do people generally have bad taste, in the eyes of critics? Do critics see so many movies that they are more aware of hackneyed formulas and overt manipulation? Are they watching a film differently?

—Mike Spearns, St. Johns, Newfoundland

A. Most of the critics, alert to formula screenplays and plot manipulation, said *Patch Adams* was a cynical exercise in audience manipulation. They're fighting each other in the race to name it the year's worst. Yet, many audience members loved it. I think this may involve different ways of looking at a movie. Buy it, and you like it. Allow yourself to observe the cheap tricks and shameless plot twists (i.e., the fate of the girlfriend), and you start to squirm. I suggest watching it several times, until the artifice and calculation become obvious. See how long it takes you to become really offended by the scene where the bald little chemotherapy patients are trotted into the hearing room with their red clown noses. If Patch were half the doctor he claims to be, he'd shout: "Good God! Those kids have suppressed immune systems! Get them out of here before they catch pneumonia and die!"

Payback

Q. I read in *Premiere* about the reediting of *Payback* by star and producer Mel Gibson, against director Brian Helgeland's will. Reportedly, Gibson made the changes because he felt he was not heroic enough and the ending was too ambiguous. I was surprised that Helgeland lost the battle with Gibson because he had won an Oscar for *L.A. Confidential* and his name (I thought) carried clout. As a film student, I have become wary of this issue, since I recall similar instances with *Hard Target, Waterworld,* and *American History X.* Is this a common practice, for studios to side with actors over directors?

—Nate Bundy, Antrim, New Hampshire

A. Helgeland defended his cut, and would not make changes. Gibson, as producer, felt the movie needed more punch at the end. The surprise involving the telephone (both the setup and the payoff) was added by Gibson. I personally liked it, although I would enjoy seeing Helgeland's cut. Regarding clout: Gibson also won an Oscar *(Braveheart)*, and his name carries more clout, in a town where clout is the name of the game.

The Phantom Menace

Q. Lucasfilm has been threatening to withhold further promotional materials for *Star Wars Episode I: The Phantom Menace* from theaters if the posters and preview trailers are not returned by January 14, 1999. Why must *all* the promotional materials be withheld from the public as collector's items?

—Jeff Young, Lake Elsinore, California

A. I consulted Andy Ihnatko, the Answer Man's *Star Wars* guru, who adds: "A pal of mine who's a theater manager confirms that the boys at Lucasfilm are being *very* tight with the stuff. They consider the posters and other materials property of Lucasfilm, and are demanding proof that they never leave the theater. If that gorgeous one-sheet should go "missing," the theater absolutely won't get a replacement, though no one believes that a stolen poster will cost them a booking. The trailer is a different matter. Managers are willing to play Chicken with the posters, but the consequences of not returning the trailer intact to Lucasfilm could not have been more menacing if they had been voiced by James Earl Jones himself, according to my pal."

Q. *Star Wars* is not in the future as you mistakenly believe!!! It is set in the past. Duh!!! Obviously you neglected to wear your glasses, and couldn't read the introduction to the story shown at the beginning of the movie.

—Julie E. Waltz, Livermore, California

A. I wrote that George Lucas "doesn't share the prevailing view that the future is a dark and lonely place." Should I have said "the past"? Many readers wrote with this contention, including Fenton House of Saskatoon, and Ian Gajadharsingh of Cincinnati, who points out the opening narration speaks of events "long, long ago." This belief that the *Star Wars* films are set in the past is common, but possibly mistaken. The stories are indeed set in the past of the film's internal history, but not necessarily in the past of the movie audience. Since we know that George Lucas originally conceived nine stories in the series (of which we have now seen episodes one, four, five, and six), the opening narrative "crawl" is obviously written from a time after the ninth episode has already taken place. Therefore, *Episode I: The Phantom Menace* takes place "long ago"—in the eyes of a narrator who is writing after the ninth episode is over. When that narrator lives relative to us is an excellent question.

Q. I ask you to think about one issue with *Phantom Menace*. Look at how George Lucas portrays women in this film. It's pretty backward. The main female character, the Queen, spends the entire film making cumbersome costume changes, even at true heights of danger. Is this a good model for women leaders today, let alone in the future? Her attendants have equally vapid things to do, like walk around with blank stares in orange bathrobes—no weapons allowed. Jabba the Hutt is once again surrounded by his harem of female stereotypes and two other female aliens (blue ones with head appendages) are seen giving a manicure to the kid's opponent in the chariot race. Great role models, eh? Later we briefly see two female fighter pilots, but they come out of nowhere and smack of tokenism. Further, until Lucas actually blows up a female fighter pilot in one of his films, we know he'll never view them as equals.

—Dave Monks, San Francisco, California

A. Wouldn't blowing up just one female fighter pilot smack of tokenism? Just to be on the safe side, I say blow up a manicurist too.

Q. In *Phantom Menace*, in the Imperial Senate scene, with all the floating podia, just after Queen Amidala gives her speech and calls for a new chancellor, I *swear* to you that one of the alien races cheering her on is none other than E.T. I wouldn't lie to you, man.

—Scot Murphy, Highland Park, Illinois

A. I also thought I caught a glimpse of E.T., but to be doubly sure, I consulted Andy Ihnatko, the Answer Man's ultimate authority for all things Starwarian. He replies: "Absolutely. Imagine that the screen image is cut into five equal vertical strips (12345). When the Senate starts chanting, "VOTE NOW! VOTE NOW! VOTE NOW!" lock your eyes around the center of Strip Four. There you'll find three ETs. Sharp-eyed viewers—or dedicated *SW* fans—will notice that practically every alien species ever shown in the four movies is present somewhere in that scene. Earlier in the scene (in Strip Two) you'll see a pair of Wookiees, for instance."

Q. Like some of the people who recently differed with you, I originally believed the *Star Wars* saga was set in the past ("A long time ago . . .). But now I'm certain it's set in the future, for one reason: Jar Jar Binks uses the phrase "Exsqueeze me?"—a phrase coined in 1992 by Mike Myers in *Wayne's World.* Watch for "I'm not worthy" when Jar Jar appears in Episode Two. Not!

—Ryan Hopak, Hollywood, California

A. Even more proof *Star Wars* is set in the future: Don't they use the word "hello"? It wasn't coined until the invention of the telephone.

Q. How do you feel about the attacks on *The Phantom Menace,* which insinuate that George Lucas is racist in his depiction of the alien characters, who are said to mimic ethnic stereotypes? I feel this notion is ridiculous.

—Tommy Sigmon, Chicago, Illinois

A. Any movie of blockbuster proportions lures part-time critics out of the woodwork, to practice their punditry where it is not always appropriate. *Phantom Menace* is a visually superb extravaganza aimed at about a twelve-year-old IQ. Jar Jar Binks is a goofy and likable alien with some amusing moves; the actor and dancer Ahmed Best brings offbeat originality to the body language. That's it. People who think the character is racist are barking up the wrong stereotype. I get so tired of the PC police.

Here's another insight, from reader Steven Bailey, of Jacksonville Beach, Florida: "I don't know why everyone's so down on Jar Jar; I found him pretty amusing myself. I thought the scene where Jar Jar dodges the blue globes was a direct homage to Buster Keaton's famous boulder-dodging scene in *Seven Chances,* and I thought it was just as funny. Nobody else in America has even mentioned this."

Q. Regarding the "pink zone" that the laser-sword fencers pass through in *Phantom Menace,* you quote George Lucas as saying, "That's one of those areas I'll probably fix in the Special Edition." What? Has Lucasfilm become the Microsoft of moviemaking—releasing an inadequately quality-controlled product, and planning to fix the bugs later? Lucas's explanation doesn't answer your reader's question: What *is* that pink zone? Yes, it's a set of forcefields designed to separate and delay the people running through it. But why would anyone build such a thing? Is Naboo some kind of puzzle-crazed society where the engineers drop huge, elaborate, clever, energy-wasting contraptions in the middle of utility catwalks, just for fun? I suspect that when the hard-core *Star Wars* fans analyze this film frame by frame, they'll look at the wall switch that Darth Maul hits to activate the pink zone, see a label written in the *Star Wars* alphabet, get out their secret *Star Wars* code books and decipher its real name: "Plot Device."

—Chris Rowland, Plainsboro, New Jersey

A. Reminds me that the pipes labeled GNDN in the *Star Trek* movies stand for "Goes Nowhere, Does Nothing." My guess is that the pink zone was a bright idea that didn't pay off, and Lucas is frank enough to admit it.

Pleasantville

Q. In *Pleasantville,* how would the folks know the names of the colors if their whole world was black and white? Or even what colors are?

—Guenvuer Burnell, Kent, Ohio

A. In one sense, this question inspires an easy answer ("Gee, they wouldn't!"). In another, it involves theories of color perception and visual cognition. Oliver Sacks, who has written about blind people who had their sight restored but found it difficult to interpret what they saw, would no doubt be fascinated by the case of a color-blind community suddenly confronted by colors. (Sacks's story of the restoration of sight inspired the movie

At First Sight, with Val Kilmer and Mira Sorvino.)

Q. I recently saw *Pleasantville* and enjoyed it. There was one perplexing element. Bud incites the mayor and through his provocation the man gains color. It is therefore assumed that anger is the cause of the mayor's coloration. However, when the noncolored people are destroying Mr. Johnson's malt shop and burning books, they are livid and yet unchanged. How could director Gary Ross overlook this loophole?

—Joanna Campbell, Woodinville, Washington

A. Gary Ross tells me: "The process by which b&w characters gain color is very random. That's kinda the point of the movie, that you can't tie the universe up in a bow. To me, people turn to color not out of passion, not out of feeling or depth of feeling, but when that thing that is missing is discovered and their potential becomes realized; the duality in their life is gone and they're whole."

Prince Known as Artist

Q. Earlier in the decade the musician Prince changed his name to an unpronounceable symbol. He has since been referred to as "the Artist formerly known as Prince." Since then, Spike Lee made his movie *Girl 6*. I picked up the box in the movie rental store the other night, and there it was: "Music by Prince." If the Artist wants his name to be an unpronounceable symbol, then why was "Prince" spelled out in readable English in the credits?

—Ricky Stilley, Carrollton, Georgia

A. A rep for Spike Lee says the songs featured in the movie *Girl 6*, were recorded while the Artist was still known as Prince.

Prizes

Q. What's with the ad campaign for *Beloved*? It refers to "Pulitzer Prize–winner Toni Morrison." PULITZER Prize? What about the NOBEL Prize? I think the Nobel is a little more prestigious! Does the studio's marketing department think the public can't identify the Nobel?

—David Martinez, San Jose, California

A. A rep for Touchstone Pictures argues that *Beloved* won the Pulitzer Prize, and the ad refers to the novel, not the author. Name recognition for the Nobel shot up dramatically, however, with this week's award to the discoverers of Viagra.

Projection and Theaters

Q. Last week I went to see the advance screening of π at Piper's Alley. The movie started twenty-five minutes late, and then it was projected with a grossly distorted aspect ratio. The film looked as if it was stretched out horizontally. It seems like every movie I see has some problems with the screening. The lights don't go off, the projector shakes, the movie starts out of focus, the focus goes out of whack when the reels change. The breaking of the projectionist's union is having a detrimental effect on the quality of the movie experience. I'm curious—how much money are the chains saving per screening? It can't be significant. A projectionist at a multiplex handles several screens simultaneously. We're entitled to a competent screening. I'm not a bleeding-heart liberal. I'm a selfish consumer looking out for Number One.

—Alex Strasheim, Chicago, Illinois

A. Yours is one of many complaints I have received recently about incompetent projection. A friend had problems in two attempts to see *Saving Private Ryan* at the same prominent North Side theater—the first time because the projection simply stopped, the second time because it began an hour late. At another theater recently, the entire corps of Chicago movie critics waited two hours for a movie to begin. My advice: Demand a refund not only for your ticket, but also for your refreshments.

Q. Last night my husband and I went to see *Gone With the Wind*. The film did not fill the entire theater screen. The shape of the projected image was like it was made for a square TV screen rather than the rectangular movie screen. When I asked the manager about it, she said that was the way they made films back in 1939. I say "Bull!" I think we got ripped off. What do you say?

—Ellen Bedrosian, Tenafly, New Jersey

A. The theater manager was absolutely correct. Prior to 1954, all movies were made in a ratio of 1 to 1.33, which means the picture was four feet wide for every three feet high. Then wide screen ratios were introduced, as Hollywood sought ways to compete with television. If *GWTW* had been altered to make it appear to be in wide screen, the picture would have lost as much as 25 percent of its height, leading to a Rhett Butler with no hair and a Scarlett O'Hara with no chin.

Q. Kudos to Warner Bros. for their restoration of *The Wizard of Oz*. I was particularly excited about WB's decision to release some prints in the new Technicolor process and the original 1 to 1.33 ratio. However, I noticed a disturbing problem at the Marcus Cinema in Addison. Although 85 percent of the screen was as bright and vibrant as I expected, it appeared dark around the bottom and right edges. I examined the projection window and noticed that duct tape was used to mask the screen image. What's up? I understand that modern projectors are probably not fitted for old aspect ratios, but why would the distributor agree to showing the film at this location if the only solution for the ratio problem was ragged duct tape?

—Joe Bosslet, Schaumburg, Illinois

A. Theater chains are cutting every corner they can in the projection booth. After the latest settlement with the projectionist's union, there are only about 100 projectionists still at work in this area. Many of them must single-handedly tend all the screens at a multiplex, and do not have time for special challenges like *Wizard*.

Q. In your recent review of *Virus*, you commented: "It didn't help that the print I saw was so underlit that often I could see hardly anything on the screen. Was that because the movie was filmed that way, or because the projector bulb was dimmed to extend its life span?"

A dirty secret is that movies are underlit in most theaters. Films are produced with the intent that they be projected at the brightness of sixteen foot-lamberts. Field research by Kodak found that they are often shown at eight to ten foot-lamberts, well under the SMPTE standard for brightness. To get theaters up to this and other standards, Kodak is introducing the Screencheck Experience program. The underlighting of screens may be acceptable for a few movies—lest you see the entirety of their badness—but in general it unnecessarily degrades the theater experience.

—Carl Donath, Rochester, New York

A. I've seen thousands of movies and I believe the Screencheck Experience program would only confirm that *Virus* was severely deprived of foot-lamberts when I saw it in a Chicago theater not a million miles from the Water Tower. Martin Scorsese, who travels with a light meter, once told me movies are projected at the correct brilliance in New York and Los Angeles, because that's where the filmmakers live, and they squawk. In a lot of other places, he said, the theaters turn down the juice to save on the replacement costs of expensive bulbs.

Q. I'm a freelancer assigned a story by *Newsweek*'s Japan edition about a movie theater in Lombard called Premium Cinema. It features comfortable leather seats, a nice restaurant, valet parking, a coat check, etc. Do you think such a concept will catch on? I was thinking perhaps people have complained to you about the rudeness of theatergoers.

—Don Babwin, Chicago, Illinois

A. I have not been to the theater and cannot testify from personal experience. Of course the concept is tempting, and I see no downside to it. It is optimistic, however, to assume that the audience in such a theater would not talk during the movie. My suspicion is that they would talk even more than the usual audience, especially if drinks are served.

Q. Re your Answer Man item on theaters that have dim images on the screen because they turn down the juice to extend the life of expensive bulbs: You quoted Martin Scorsese as saying movies are projected at the correct brilliance in New York and Los Angeles, "because that's where the filmmakers live, and they squawk." Based on my experiences here in LA, at least 50 percent of the theaters here show movies too dimly as well. Bulbs are expensive, several hundred dollars apiece. And they burn out pretty quickly; sometimes they get dim after a few months. Multiply that cost by an eighteen-plex and you'll see why they are usually dim.

—David Bondelevitch, Studio City, California

A. A scandal. Undercover reporters should be sent to theaters with light meters.

Q. I saw *The Thin Red Line* twice during its first run in theaters and loved it. Last night, I decided to see it again in a second-run theater. The theater temperature was cold enough to hang meat. The projection bulb seemed dim, and the theatrical aspect ratio (which is 2.35:1 for the film) was only 1.85:1. Shouldn't we be entitled to the same viewing experience regardless of the price?

—Daniel Smith, Athens, Alabama

A. This is a subject that gnaws at me. Martin Scorsese gave me the explanation several years ago: Theater chains all over the country turn down the wattage on their projectors in hopes of extending the life of their expensive bulbs. An expert from Eastman Kodak told the Answer Man a few months ago that some theaters dim the bulbs by one-third! And not just in second-run houses, but in first-run too. Moviegoers in some cities may never have seen a properly-lit image. The result: sad, dim, washed-out movies. This is stupid for two reasons: (1) discerning customers never return to such theaters, and (2) according to the veteran Chicago movie publicist and distributor John Iltis, *the practice does not extend the life of the bulbs!* As for showing movies in the correct ratio—screen ratio is a concept that has escaped many theaters.

Q. I'm writing to amplify the Answer Man's comments about turning down the wattage to extend the life of projector bulbs in movie theaters. I'm an electrical engineer. The answer is, yes, it *does* extend the life of projector bulbs when you dim them, but not by any significant amount. I did some hand-waving calculations based on a 3000W Xenon bulb from Sylvania, for which I happened to have a table of physical properties handy. If you were to run it at 2000W, you'd extend its life—by 2.3 percent! Wattage is a small factor among many others affecting the life of a bulb.

—Hank Graham, Seattle, Washington

A. Readers! Clip this item and mail it to any theater where you have been victimized by a picture that is suspiciously dim. If daytime skies are not bright in a movie, or if interiors seem too murky, you may be the target of a penny-pinching exhibitor. I'm not talking about dark movies—I'm talking about underlit screens. The Answer Man has quoted both director Martin Scorsese and scientists from Eastman Kodak as saying many theaters turn down the wattage to extend bulb life. The irony is that their only real achievement is to cheat their customers.

Psycho Remake

Q. Last week I was at Universal Studios and saw that construction had started on what looked to me like sets for the upcoming remake of *Psycho*. The tour guide didn't mention it, so after the tour I asked her to confirm my suspicion. After a bit of beating around the bush, she said that the construction was for *Psycho*, but that she wasn't supposed to say anything about it. Why do production companies sometimes try to hide what they are working on? I've run into similar situations at Universal before—notably the most recent Batman installment. During its filming a tour guide told me he had "no idea" what movie the street with all the fake ice and signs that read "Gotham City" had been prepared for.

—Dominick Cancilla, Santa Monica, California

A. In some cases, the productions have not yet been officially announced. In others, they're trying to confuse tourists with cameras, who might take shots of sets that the studio doesn't want to be publicly revealed. It would spoil the illusion, for example, to see an icy Batman street with palm trees in the background.

Q. Today, I read that a remake of Alfred Hitchcock's *Psycho* is shooting this summer with Gus Van Sant as the director and Anne

Heche taking the Janet Leigh role and Vince Vaughn the Tony Perkins role. My first reaction is—"why?" There are great novels and screenplays floating around that don't get made, and here comes yet another remake of a film that was plenty good the first time around. If a film was popular and successful, a remake automatically has things going against it from audiences who liked the first one. So, why?

—Vicki Halliday, New York City, New York

A. Even stranger, Van Sant is reportedly following Hitchcock's original script. Reports on the Web call it a "re-creation" instead of a remake. Dominick Cancilla of Santa Monica e-mails me: "If this is indeed the case, the film would, in essence, be more kabuki than cinema." My feeling is that the project is not only an affront to Hitchcock, but a waste of Van Sant's talent. The Answer Man's frequent correspondent David J. Bondelevitch, of Los Angeles, thinks perhaps Van Sant was attracted by "the intellectual experiment of testing whether Hitch's direction was so brilliant that it will transcend the casting." Ouch.

Q. Re Gus Van Sant's remake of Hitchcock's *Psycho:* Do you think Van Sant will go so far as to also re-create Hitchcock's original trailer (in which he showed the audience the sets and explained what went on in each set)?

—Ed Slota, Warwick, Rhode Island

A. That's one of the most famous previews in movie history, with the rotund Master of Suspense in his black suit leading a guided tour of the Bates home and motel. Assuming you think the remake is a good idea in the first place (I have grave doubts), then why not remake the trailer too? Of course, that would fly in the face of current studio wisdom, which says the coming attractions have to summarize and reveal the entire movie. On the other hand, in this case everybody knows the whole movie anyway.

Q. A friend of mine reports a rumor regarding the upcoming *Psycho* remake. She says all the talk about a shot-for-shot remake is just a smoke screen. What Gus Van Sant actually plans to do is copy only the first half of the movie, lure the audience into thinking they're getting a straight remake, and then go off in a completely different direction. I was dubious until she pointed out that's exactly what Hitchcock did with *Psycho,* where he suddenly kills off the main character. What do you think? Is there still hope?

—Eric Brochu, Regina, Saskatchewan

A. That would at least give the movie a reason for being. If I believed the rumor, I wouldn't print it and spoil the surprise. But I mentioned it to John Boorman, the British director whose film *The General* was playing at the Chicago Film Festival, and he said he'd actually met the actor who is playing the psychiatrist in the film: "And there is no reason to leave in the scene where the psychiatrist explains Norman Bates's problems unless you are faithfully remaking the entire film." True. Even Hitchcock's greatest admirers feel the film stops dead with the hilariously inappropriate "explanation."

Q. Why is everyone making a big deal about the new *Psycho* movie? I haven't heard anything bad about Chris Reeve's remake of *Rear Window.*

—Mark Sauer, St. Louis, Missouri

A. Frankly, that's not such a hot idea, either. Most movies can be remade (I am reminded of how *To the Shores of Tripoli* was remade as *Rip Goes to War,* with the John Payne role being played by a dog). But a few special movies are quite simply one of a kind, and to remake them is to court resentment and disaster.

Q. The great Sir Alfred Hitchcock was a busy worker right up until his death, and was working on a film when he died. From what I've heard, the screenplay and carefully-drawn storyboards were finished. My question is, why hasn't anyone opted to make *this* film? Wouldn't this have been a better idea for Gus Van Sant than a remake of Hitch's best-known work?

—Jeff VanDreason, Syracuse, New York

A. In 1977 and 1978, Hitchcock worked on a screenplay titled *The Short Night* with Ernest Lehman *(North by Northwest)* and David Freeman, but Hitch's biographer Donald Spoto says the script was never finished. If it had been, or if other finished scripts survive—yes, those would be more interesting projects than squirting juice into the Frankenstein's monster of the *Psycho* remake.

Q. I agree almost completely with your reviews of both *Psycho* films, but I must point out that the voice of the policeman in the remake was unaltered. That is James Remar's actual voice, and one of the few bits of casting that worked well, I thought.

—David J. Bondelevitch, Studio City, California

A. Remarkable. I wrote that Remar "has a speaking voice which, I think, has been electronically tweaked to make it deeper." It sounded eerie. Love to hear him sing "Asleep in the Deep."

The Red Violin

Q. I loved *The Red Violin*, but was left with one thing that bugged me. Isn't Morritz, the character played by Samuel L. Jackson, short a violin at the end? He replaced the real one with the copy that he had borrowed. What is he going to give that collector or museum back as a replacement?

—Marian Moore, Harvey, Louisiana

A. Beth English, publicity director for Lions Gate Films, replies, "Morritz is not short a violin at the end of the film. He replaced the real one with a copy that he had not borrowed, as you suggest in your question, but purchased from a private collector in London. This copy of a Bussotti violin was made at about the same time as the Red Violin."

Refreshments

Q. At what point exactly did the price for a *small* soda at the movies become more expensive than *three* forty ounces of beer? Heck, although a bottle of beer in a bar costs more or less the same as a soda at the movies, at least you get a buzz and look a lot cooler with a brewski in your hands instead of a plastic flexi-straw in your mouth.

—Chad Polenz, Schenectady, New York

A. It's a matter of simple economics. In the opening weeks of a movie's run, the studio grabs 70 percent of the ticket price, or more. Take out amusement taxes, and the theater isn't even breaking even on the ticket sale. Most of its profit comes from the refreshment stand. Look at it this way. If they didn't sell refreshments, a ticket might cost twice as much. At least this way you have the illusion that you're getting something for your extra money. People who buy a ticket but don't buy refreshments are essentially being subsidized by the rest of us.

Q. I'm writing about the Answer Man remark of yours regarding movie profits. You stated that we people who do not buy at the concession stands are being subsidized by others who do. 1) I'm allergic to chocolate. 2) I don't like the "liquid" that's put on popcorn. It's real butter or nothing for me. 3) If they raise the price because of me, so be it! I have a choice to buy or not. That's the American way, okay? I don't like snide remarks.

—Cara Williams, Blue Island, Illinois

A. So be it! I was simply pointing out that your local theater makes most of its money at the refreshment counter and sends most of the ticket price to the studios. If theaters didn't sell refreshments, an $8 ticket would cost about $12. It's the American Way.

Remakes

Q. Geez, is it true that Rhino Films is planning a remake of *Beyond the Valley of the Dolls*? How can such a film possibly be improved upon? Aside from remuneration, I'd assume you're not enthralled by the prospect?

—Kevin Driscoll, Scotts Valley, California

A. I've heard the same report. Rhino has not contacted Russ Meyer, who directed it, or the screenwriter (me). Some films can be remade and others cannot. Whatever you may think of it, *Beyond the Valley of the Dolls* is one of a kind. What makes it special is not just the story but the style, the period, the actors, the direction, the whole feel of the film.

Return to Paradise

In my review of the thriller *Return to Paradise*, I recklessly described the plot as "a variation of the Prisoner's Dilemma," which is a famous ethical and mathematical puzzle. I have before me letters from Kristy L. Towry of the University of Texas, Joshua Cherry of the University of Utah and others, informing me that it is not the Prisoner's Dilemma at all, but another logical puzzle altogether. Since they use mathematical formulae I cannot understand, I am sure they are correct.

I was trying to say that the plot avoids the clichés of most thrillers, and instead presents the characters with an exquisite moral challenge. In the movie, three friends vacation in Malaysia. Two return to America. The third is caught with all of their mutually-owned drugs, in a large enough quantity that he will get the death penalty unless his friends return and admit some of the ownership. If two friends return, they'll each have to serve three years. If one returns, he'll have to serve six years. If neither returns, their friend hangs.

In the movie, assuming that the death of the friend is undesirable, the best outcome for A, B, and C would be for A and B to serve three years, and C to live. The best strategy for A or B *individually* would be to stick the other guy with six years, serve no time, and C still lives. But the risk, of course, is that if both A and B use that strategy, C dies. Watching the movie, I was quietly amazed that the screenplay, by Bruce Robinson and Wesley Strick, was actually building suspense with ideas instead of explosions.

Roscoe's Chicken and Waffles

Q. In your review of *Rush Hour*, you mention that it has "even a reference to Roscoe's Chicken and Waffles, of *Jackie Brown* fame." This appears to presume Roscoe's is a fictional place invented in the *Jackie Brown* film. Let me assure you that Roscoe's is a *real place* in Los Angeles, with two locations I know of. I've enjoyed their hot fried chicken and waffles many times, in their improbably rough/refined place on Pico, filled with both street folk and stars, nearly all black, while even more improbable music (often Barbra Streisand or other mid-road white artists) argues with the whole scene. It's a treat.

—John Nagy, Los Angeles, California

A. I knew Roscoe's was a real place, but let's face it: More people heard of it in *Jackie Brown* than have visited it in life. I believe your recommendation, because, in the movie, a guy allows himself to be locked into a car trunk just because he's promised chicken and waffles as his reward.

Q. Re this Roscoe's Chicken and Waffles thing I keep seeing in your column, about how the restaurant was mentioned in both *Jackie Brown* and *Rush Hour*. The first movie to mention Roscoe's was a little 1988 comedy film called *Tape Heads*, starring John Cusack and Tim Robbins as two would-be music video producers. Their first job was doing a commercial for Roscoe's. Heavy, pounding 1980s rap music played while Roscoe sang into the camera about how he was "gonna give you the bird." The highlight was animated chicken legs and wings dancing with waffles.

—Roger B. Domian, Chicago, Illinois

A. Lee Benson of Brisbane, Australia, and Chris Martin of San Diego were among several other readers who also remembered the *Tape Heads* mention. Now the question becomes: Which came first, Quentin Tarantino's first viewing of *Tape Heads*, or his first visit to Roscoe's?

Rounders

Q. What did Matt Damon's character in *Rounders* determine about John Malkovich's character from his eating of the Oreos?

—Joseph Gonzales, Waco, Texas

A. Malkovich plays Teddy KGB, a Russian-American gangster and ace poker player who provides the ultimate test of the skill and nerve of Mike, the Matt Damon character. Teddy KGB likes to eat Oreos while he plays. Mike spots his "tell"—a poker term for an opponent's unconscious way of revealing whether he has the cards or is bluffing. The Oreos have been much discussed in the Internet discussion group rec.gambling.poker, where John Harkness of Toronto writes: "If he breaks it in front of his face, it means nothing. If he breaks it to the side of his head, as if listening to it, he's got the nuts."

Q. In *Rounders*, I found the final game confusing. What hand did Matt Damon's character have? I saw the hole cards, but the "common" cards were on the screen too briefly for me to register. When he announced his hand to "KGB," it didn't seem possible. For that matter, what hand did "KGB" have that would have kept him in that pot to the end?

—Steven Stine, Buffalo Grove, Illinois

A. I appealed again to poker expert John Harkness, who in another life is a Toronto film critic. He replies: "Damon flopped the nut straight—he had 8-9, the board came 6-7-10. (Of course, the play of the hand is foreshadowed in the tape of the World Series that Mike watches on video.) I assumed all along that KGB had a pair of tens in his hand. When I was watching the movie, I found myself thinking, 'Don't pair the board,' because I assumed that KGB was holding three tens and a pair on the board would give him the full house. Other arguments were for the A-10, that he had a pair of tens on the flop and caught his second pair with the A on the river and so moved all in, but I always put him on the three of a kind."

I heard from many poker players, by the way, who disagreed with the Harkness theory about Teddy KGB's Oreo cookie "tell" in the movie.

Q. Sorry to be contradictory, but John Harkness's answer regarding Teddy KGB's "tell" was wrong. KGB actually splits the Oreo in two natural halves, leaving a cream-filling side and a plain side. He breaks them the same way every time: next to his right ear. The "tell" is that he eats the cream-filling side first if he has the cards, the plain side first if he does not. It's an amazing moment in the film, unspoiled by voice-over narration; the careful observer knows what happens the second Damon's character does.

—Matt Bailey, Madison, Wisconsin

A. My "tell" is, if I dip the Oreo in milk, I am about to fold, since any delay would result in the soaked Oreo losing that residual crunch.

Q. There's a scene in the movie *Rounders* when Matt Damon watches a group of judges playing poker. There is one judge without a speaking role that looks to me like Guido Calabrisi, former dean of the Yale Law School, now an appellate judge. Am I right?

—Steve Shapiro, Wallingord, Connecticut

A. A Miramax spokesman says: "There are six players: Martin Landau as Abe Petrovsky, Richard Mawe as Professor Eisen, Michael Lombard as D. A. Shields, Tom Aldredge as Judge Marinacci, Beeson Carroll as Judge Kaplan, Matthew Yavne as Professor Greene.

Rush Hour

Q. I just saw *Rush Hour*, which I enjoyed. However, I noticed with dismay that it joined a trend of movies that think having a child curse is funny (I am thinking of *The Wedding Singer*, but I am sure there are more). Nothing is sacred in this day and age, but I can't buy this. Neither movie needed the extra lines by the children, and I don't think it does anything for kids to see this. Whats next? I shutter to think.

—Michael A. Taylor, Okinawa, Japan

A. This trend started with the famous line "penis breath" in Spielberg's *E.T.* Its spiritual godfather is Art Linkletter, whose "Kids Say the Darnedest Things" delighted in kids who knew not what they said. I think a lot depends on the context.

Saving Private Ryan

Q. I'm confused by crucial details of *Saving Private Ryan*, and it's driving me nuts. There are four key German soldiers throughout the film, and I'm not sure if they're all the same guy (warning—spoilers ahead!):

#1. The German prisoner blindfolded and released by Miller (Tom Hanks) at the bunker.

#2. The German who stabs Mellish (Adam Goldberg).

#3. The German who shoots Miller.

#4. The German executed by Upham (Jeremy Davies).

I think 1, 2, and 4 are the same guy, but is 3 also the same?

—Michael Whalen, Lewisville, Texas

A. I wasn't sure, either, and am grateful to Mary Jo Kaplan of the CompuServe ShowBiz Forum, who informs the Answer Man: "I called my contacts at DreamWorks publicity just now to see if we could get the bottom line about which German was which. This is what they told me (more spoilers ahead!):

1. The German who is released is referred to for convenience as "Steamboat Willie."

2. Steamboat Willie does *not* stab Mellish (Goldberg). That is a different German. I thought it was the same guy, but they flat out said, "No, it is not."

3. But Steamboat Willie *is* the German who shoots Miller (Tom Hanks).

4. And yes, Steamboat Willie *does* call out to Upham, "Upham!" before Upham shoots him.

Q. I recently saw *Saving Private Ryan.* I have one problem with the film. When some of the officers hit Omaha Beach, their rifles were in plastic bags. Plastic was not invented yet. How could Spielberg and his advisers make such a mistake?

—Nancy Geraci, Park Ridge, Illinois

A. Plastic had indeed been invented by then. Leo Hendrik Baekeland, a Belgian who moved to America, cooked up the first form of manufactured plastic in 1907. He called it Bakelite. Many soldiers in World War II, however, preferred another product to protect the barrels of their weapons: condoms.

Q. I heard that the violence in *Saving Private Ryan* is so extreme that it was threatened by the MPAA with the NC-17 rating. Is that true?

—Charlie Smith, Chicago, Illinois

A. I asked Steven Spielberg about that during his recent visit to Chicago, and he said: "I heard that story too. I even know its source: one of our trade publications in Los Angeles. It was a speculation on the part of the person who wrote the article. They never talked to anybody at the MPAA; they just speculated that, because my name was associated with it, the movie got an 'R' instead of an 'NC-17,' which is absolutely not true at all. The MPAA gave it a 'R' rating with no cuts. Often they will give you an 'R' rating and say, if you make these twenty cuts you can earn a 'PG-13.' And I assume they would give you an 'NC-17' and say with ten cuts that might get you to an 'R'—but they gave us an unqualified 'R' with very strong language. They did put a real strong rider next to the rating, but it was an 'R' rating from the beginning. As for myself, I'm saying strongly that no one fourteen or younger should see the film."

Set Pieces

Q. What does it mean when a scene in a movie is referred to as a "set piece"? Is it that the set itself is somehow involved in the scene, or that the set is just really huge and expensive?

—Chris McCaleb, Chicago, Illinois

A. Neither. A set piece is an assignment given to you by a teacher to demonstrate that you have mastered the fundamentals of your subject. When a movie scene is described as a set piece, that means the director has done it primarily to show how technically clever he is. *Armageddon,* for example, is a feature-length set piece.

Shakespeare in Love

Q. I enjoyed the heck out of *Shakespeare in Love,* but was distracted by one thing: Where oh where did Gwyneth Paltrow's hair go when she was rehearsing on stage for the part of Romeo? At night with William she has long, flowing blond hair, and in the day she has a short cut. I know the movie isn't supposed to be realistic, but this was going too far.

—Michael Whalen, Brooklyn, New York

A. Mark Schaeffer of the CompuServe Showbiz Forum replies: "It's all accounted for in the movie. After Viola auditions as 'Thomas Kent,' and flees the theater when Will asks her to remove her hat, she instructs her nurse to buy her 'a boy's wig.' Later, when John Webster exposes her charade by dropping a mouse down her collar, we see her accidentally knock the wig off her head, and her flowing blond hair falls beautifully down to her shoulders."

Q. The young kid (with the mice) in *Shakespeare in Love* gives his name at one point. Is he an actual historical character that I should know or is it an inside joke reference to someone in Hollywood?

—Mark Sachs, San Rafael, California

A. The mean little kid is John Webster, who was about sixteen years younger than Shakespeare. He grew up to write blood-soaked dramas such as *The Duchess of Malfi* and *The White Devil,* in which he wrote:

But keep the wolf far thence that's foe to men,
For with his nails he'll dig them up again.

Q. *Shakespeare in Love* is a wonderful film; thanks for recommending it. However, much of the film appears to have been inspired by *No Bed for Bacon*, written in 1940 by Caryl Brahms and S. J. Simon. Although there are major differences between the film and the book, the similarities in characters and story lines are too close and too many to be sheer coincidence. The story concerns Viola Compton, a lady at the court of Queen Elizabeth, who is having an affair with the Earl of Essex. She sees Shakespeare rehearsing one of his plays, and decides that she wants to be an actor. She disguises herself as a young man and is hired by Shakespeare. In the movie, the heroine is named Viola, she is having an affair with Lord Wessex, she disguises herself, etc. The first time Shakespeare appears in the movie, he is practicing his signature, spelling it many different ways. This is a running gag through the book. At the end of the book, Shakespeare, thinking of Viola, begins to write "Shall I compare thee to a summer's day . . ." Same in the movie. Even the joke about coming up with the right play title, *Romeo and Ethel*, seems to originate from the book, where Shakespeare struggles over *Love's Labour Won*!

—John and Rosalie Price, Palo Alto, California

A. Here's the response from Miramax, the film's distributor: "Neither of the two writers of *Shakespeare in Love*, Marc Norman and Tom Stoppard, have read the book, although Stoppard is familiar with it. The similarities are minor; the differences are major. Given that these are two fictional works set in the Elizabethan theater drawing on the same facts and events, historical characters, lore, and the work of the Bard himself, it shouldn't surprise anyone that they contain superficial similarities. For example, the different spellings of Shakespeare's signature is a historical in-joke that every English lit major would know. In *Shakespeare in Love*, the final spelling is 'Shagsbeard,' a play on Shakespeare's impotency problems.

"Similarly, characters such as Queen Elizabeth and Lord Essex, as well as Henslowe and Burbage, are all rooted in historical fact. As for Viola disguising herself as a young man, this too is based on the fact that in Elizabethan times, women were not allowed to act, thus the need for a disguise. The film's original heroine was called Belinda until just before shooting, when Viola was substituted in a nod to the film's *Twelfth Night* ending. Also, *Love's Labour's Won* is a different kind of Shakespearean in-joke than calling a play *Romeo and Ethel*. In *Shakespeare in Love*, the joke is that Shakespeare has come up with the wrong play title. In *No Bed for Bacon*, Shakespeare never has time to work on *Love's Labour's Won*, which is the real-life title of Shakespeare's famous lost play. Both jokes draw on knowledge of Shakespeare and his work but they are not related."

Q. What's your take on the controversy over this year's Oscar winner? Do you believe, as DreamWorks and some others have charged, that Miramax "bought" the Oscar by spending so much money on its campaign for *Shakespeare in Love*?

—Susan Lake, Urbana, Illinois

A. If Miramax bought the Oscar, then that means academy members can be bought—that they have no taste of their own, and are swayed by ads in the trade papers, free video cassettes, etc. I don't believe that. I believe that when voters regard the precious Academy ballot, they mark it for the movie they admired the most. They're not always right (I thought *Saving Private Ryan* was the better film). But they're sincere.

In the morning-after recriminations, it was even pointed out that *Ryan* bought more pages in the trade papers than *Shakespeare*. Ah, yes, said the other side, but Miramax bought lots of ads in the mainstream press and on TV. True, but then again, *Shakespeare in Love was* in a lot of theaters during that period. When *Ryan* opened, DreamWorks bought lots of mainstream ads.

The fact is that any movie opening late in the year has an enormous advantage over a movie that opened eight months earlier. Voters remember it better. Their admiration is fresh. The autumn is known as "Oscar Season" for a reason. Tom Hanks reminded me on Oscar night that *Forrest Gump* was a summer picture that won for Best Picture. Yes, and *Silence of the Lambs* was a February release. But the fact remains that most Oscars go to films released in the last three months of the year. If *Saving Private Ryan* had opened in December, I'm sure it would have won the big prize.

The Siege

Q. Thanks you for your criticism of *The Siege*. The movie is not about entertainment, but about denigrating the image of Arab Americans in particular and Muslims in general. This movie was made to create a psychological association between terrorism and Islam. I can see nothing in this film other than hatred. It serves no purpose other than creating a dark and ugly image for a beautiful religion. Being a Muslim, I found this movie offensive because of the correlation drawn between my religion and violence.

—Louay Hallak, Chicago, Illinois

A. Many of those who enjoyed the film would not have enjoyed seeing their own religions and ethnic groups treated in the same way.

A Soldier's Daughter Never Cries

Q. My husband and I just saw *A Soldier's Daughter Never Cries*. One scene seemed out of place. The principal comes into the classroom to ask Francis about his father and she appears to float into and out of the room. Did you notice this? Why would they choose to make only one scene surreal when the rest of the movie is just mildly unusual?

—Colleen Healy Ruff, Scottsdale, Arizona

A. This technique—placing a character on a moving platform to make them seem to glide instead of walking—has been used more than once by Spike Lee. The first time I saw it was in Jean Cocteau's *Beauty and the Beast* (1946). It is surreal, and I think that's the point: To heighten the importance of the scene.

Sound Tracks

Q. For years now I have noticed that many movie trailers use music from other movies instead of the music from the movie being advertised. *Jack Frost* and *Saving Private Ryan* both use the theme from *The American President* in the trailer. *Rookie of the Year* humorously used the theme from *The Natural* as a backdrop. To my mind this is false advertising. The themes from successful motion pictures, especially those with a positive emotional payoff, can subliminally influence a person's judgment in determining whether or not the movie is appealing. What is your opinion of this situation?

—Jay Todtman, Valley Stream, New York

A. Often the score for the new movie isn't yet available when they're cutting the trailers. In such a case, using older music for its associations is a standard practice. Unethical? Well, all trailer music is designed to inspire the desire to see the movie. But oddly enough, right after your communication came the following message from John Beal of Beverly Hills, who *does* compose original trailer music. He writes: "As you have pointed out to your readers, scores from previously released films are frequently used in trailers—often to attempt some sort of subliminal connection with another hit film. But many trailers have original scores actually composed for the marketing of the film. I am the leading composer of these original scores for the marketing campaigns for some truly wonderful (and not-so-wonderful) films, and have finally gotten around to releasing a double CD album of my scores for nearly seventy trailers over the past decade." Beal's web address is www.beal-net.com/john.

Q. I just watched (sort of, while painting the sunroom) *Jurassic Park: The Lost World* again, and was reminded of something that really amused my husband and me when we first saw the movie—the names of Roland and Van Owen. They are obviously a reference to the song "Roland the Headless Thompson Gunner" on the late 1970s Warren Zevon album featuring "Werewolves of London." Listen to the song. Do you know who got those names in there? Whose joke was that?

—Linda Reed-Warren, Champaign, Illinois

A. David Koepp, who wrote the screenplay for *The Lost World*, replies: "I'm so happy somebody picked up by Warren Zevon reference. 'Roland the Headless Thompson Gunner' is one of my favorite songs, and since Roland is a mercenary in the song, that seemed like a good name for the hunter-for-hire in our movie. While I was at it, I thought it would be fun to make the last name of his nemesis Van Owen, like in the song. It's okay to use my name as a source for this. I'm not afraid of anyone who has a room in their house called a sunroom."

Special Effects

Q. How is the effect of bullets hitting a windshield accomplished—especially when an actor is sitting behind the windshield being "hit" by the bullets?

—Keith Silcox-Ingersoll, Ontario, Canada

A. I asked Steven Poster, expert lensman and an editor of *American Cinematographer,* who replies: "When an actor gets shot through a windshield and the audience sees the bullet go through the glass, a small pellet is shot from a device called a Trunnon Gun mounted inside the car and shooting away from the actor (wouldn't want to make any mistakes). This device is remotely triggered simultaneously with a 'bullet hit' mounted on the actor. These bullet hits are small explosions mounted on a steel plate with plastic bags filled with movie blood and then taped to the actor under the clothes. If the entire windshield is to blow, a small explosive device is mounted on the glass out of camera range. When it is exploded the entire windshield cracks and crazes but doesn't fall out because of the safety glass. This is called a full breaker. Sometimes it is combined with a Trunnon gun to make it look like the bullet took out the entire window."

Speed 3—A Contest

Q. No interview with Sandra Bullock seems complete nowadays without her bringing up her disgust with herself for agreeing to star in *Speed 2.* It appears to be the pivotal moment of her professional career; she begs our forgiveness. You recently expressed irritation at Bullock's mea culpa tour for *Speed 2,* a movie that you gave three stars to, going against the critical consensus. Do you think she is truly contrite, or is she trying to curry favor with the critics to establish herself as a serious actress after the film's critical savaging?

—Lloyd A. White, Rockville, Maryland

A. The dissing of *Speed 2* has become a popular folk ritual, as if no worse movie has ever been made. Ms. Bullock has cravenly joined in. She would be performing more of a service if she warned us about *Forces of Nature.* Yes, I gave *Speed 2* three stars—and, yes, I was correct, if the movie is seen for what it is, a genre action picture. I am grateful to movies that show me what I haven't seen before, and *Speed 2* had a cruise ship plowing through a pier and right up the main street of a Caribbean village. I recently spent a week at the University of Colorado, where, in a small and futile gesture of support for the movie, I announced a contest for a short film to be named *Speed 3.* Contest rules: No longer than five minutes, and must involve something that cannot stop moving. Finalists will be shown next year at CU's Conference on World Affairs, and the winner gets a standing ovation, plus a copy of the DVD of *Speed 2,* autographed (by me, since I wouldn't think of causing any more pain to Ms. Bullock). Send entries to Prof. Russell Wiltse, Film Studies, Campus Box 316, Boulder, CO 80309-0316. Deadline is March 1, 2000. Do NOT contact me directly!

Spoilers

Q. The box of David Mamet's *The Spanish Prisoner* shows a photograph of Steve Martin pointing a gun at Campbell Scott on a boat. It goes without saying that this spoiler snapshot from the movie's penultimate scene reveals a number of key secrets. By contrast, *The Spanish Prisoner* trailer craftily displayed a pistol being pointed at somebody, but cut away before the identity of the gun-toter was revealed. The foolish video cover negates the effort put into creating a scintillating trailer. Who designs video box covers? Why are they so ignorant of the film's narrative?

—Andrew Nutting, Notre Dame, Indiana

A. The people who design many video boxes have only one mission, and that is to persuade browsers that a film contains sex or, preferably, violence. I'd guess that more than half the video boxes in the typical Blockbuster display guns, cleavage, or both. You are quite right that the *Spanish Prisoner* box gives away the crucial plot twist. Will you have another look at it and see if you can find a shot of Rebecca Pidgeon's chest?

Star Wars

Q. In preparation for the release of the new *Star Wars* movie, some friends and I were watching the new Special Edition of *Return of the Jedi* on video. At a point early in the film, a blinded Han Solo is hanging upside down from the side of one of Jabba the Hutt's skiffs. He is attempting to help Lando, whose leg has just been grabbed by the Sarlacc, by aiming a gun at the tentacle that was wrapped around his leg. The dialogue is as follows.

LANDO: "No, wait! I thought you were blind!"

HAN: "It's all right. I can see a lot better now."

This surprised me. It seemed as if Han Solo's line had been changed. I went back and checked an older version of the film, and indeed, the original Han Solo line was, "It's all right. Trust me." Why would George Lucas change a line in the film, which not only offered a chuckle, but seemed more like what the wisecracking character of Han Solo would have indeed said?

—John A. Adams, St. Paul, Minnesota

A. Karen Rose of Lucasfilm Ltd. says she did a lot of research before being able to supply this answer: "The sound mixes for all three films in the original *Star Wars* trilogy were produced before the days of fully automated digital mixing studios, and each film actually had several different sound mixes, depending on where and when you saw it. These mixes were almost like live performances in the subtle variation they sometimes produced between, for example, stereo and monaural versions of the movie sound track.

"*Star Wars* sound designer Ben Burtt recalls that the battle around the Sarlacc Pit was the most cut and recut sequences in all of *Return of the Jedi*. Several editors tried their hands at reworking this sequence as George Lucas worked to get a satisfactory result, and John Williams even went back and scored the sequence a second time. During filming, many lines of ad-lib dialogue were filmed in addition to the scripted lines, giving the editors many alternatives to choose from. The 'trust me' version of Han Solo's line ended up most widely distributed in video and laser disc, but as the last version of the sound mix was prepared, Lucas became concerned that Han's clearing vision was not satisfactorily explained in the course of the action, and so his final directorial choice was the "I can see a lot better" line. This was the line that went into the archived version of the sound mix, and it was this master that was followed for the remixing of the *Return of the Jedi* Special Edition."

Stepmom

Q. *Stepmom* has a line that made me cringe. When Ed Harris is telling Susan Sarandon that he's marrying Julia Roberts, the waiter comes over to the table and says to Harris, "Can I get anything for your wife?" Sarandon abruptly responds, "I am not his wife!" Now this was obviously done to get an audience reaction, and the writers must have thought they had a terrific tag line. But the fact is that it just doesn't work. I have been to many restaurants, and never, ever have I heard a waiter assume that the person you are with is your spouse. That's just plain dumb, and was created to get an "ooooohhhh" out of the audience. Well I say "booooo."

—Bradley Richman, New York City

A. Yeah, waiters learn to be canny about not making *any* assumptions about the relationships between customers ("another drink for your parole officer?").

Stuart Archer

Q. That kid you wrote about from Sundance—the one who got so many people to look at his short film, and then went to Hollywood in search of fortune. How did he make out?

—Charlie Smith, Chicago, Illinois

A. Stuart Acher tells me: "I signed with Larry Kennar at Writer's and Artists, and plan to move to L.A. Meanwhile, my agent (that has a nice ring to it) is setting up screenings of *Bobby Loves Mangos* at the various studios, for executives. The eventual plan is to go out with the feature of *Mangos* as a spec sometime next month."

Read my Sundance essay on Acher's success in persuading people to see his film.

Subliminal Images

Q. Have you ever read *Flicker* by Theodore Roszak? It is a work of fiction that tells a fascinating story of subliminal images that are incorporated in films to achieve an unconscious reaction. Roszak is a well-known social scientist (he coined the term "counterculture") and at the end of this book, claims that this is a "secret history of movies." Also, I have witnessed the use of subliminal imaging first-hand, in William Friedkin's *Cruising*. It is a scene halfway through the movie, where the killer stabs a man he has tied up in the back. By playing this frame by frame on my VCR, there is a two-second shot that is clearly pornographic in nature. When the movie is played normally, it cannot be seen. I have heard rumors that *The Exorcist* is drenched in such images as the "death mask" and that sounds of pigs being slaughtered are woven into the sound track. I have a sinking feeling that maybe it is not just Mr. Friedkin doing this in his films. I want to assure you I'm not a fanatic that thinks Satan speaks to us via Motley Crue records.

—John M. Harrison, Newark, Delaware

A. The use of single-frame or superimposed "subliminal" images and (subaural?) sounds is common throughout film history. *The Exorcist* does indeed contain single frames in which a Satanic head is superimposed on Linda Blair's face. There's that brief shot of Norman Bates's desiccated mother at the end of *Psycho*. The sound track of Scorsese's *Raging Bull* incorporates animal cries and bird shrieks into the noises of the prizefight crowds. The advent of freeze-frame features makes hidden shots easy to find—and has also, of course, turned up some naughty frames that Disney animators never thought anyone would see.

Synchronicity

Q. The cartoon animators at Termite Terrace always put some reference to something or other (politics, films, etc.) in their Merrie Melodies and/or Looney Tunes for yucks. One has always made me curious. Yosemite Sam is chasing Bugs, comes to a closed door that is locked, bangs, knocks, yells to be let in, and then calmly looks at the camera and says, "Notice I didn't say Richard." What was *that* in reference to?

—Frank Mendez, Dallas, Texas

A. I presented this seemingly unanswerable question to Leonard Maltin, an expert on animation and author of *Of Mice and Magic: A History of American Animated Cartoons*. He told me: "That was a topical reference to a popular song called 'Open the Door, Richard,' the lyrics of which consisted of a guy haranguing his friend to open his locked door and let him in. The scene occurs in *High Diving Hare*, I believe."

And now for an example of synchronicity almost too eerie to report. After typing the paragraph above, I was idly leafing through the new catalog for Separate Cinema, dealers in rare African-American movie posters (Box 114, Hyde Park, NY 12538), and my eye fell on a listing for the poster of *Open the Door, Richard!*—a 1946 comedy starring Richard "Dusty" Fletcher. The poster is yours for $25.

This gets stranger. After typing *both* of the above paragraphs, I went to a screening of the new movie version of *Lolita*, and heard, on its sound track, the song "Open the Door, Richard."

Q. I've noticed a trend the past couple of years that I can't figure out. It seems that two major studios will release films within weeks of each other that appear to be nearly identical in concept. Last year we had *Volcano* and *Dante's Peak*. This past summer it was *Deep Impact* and *Armageddon*. Now in the fall we have two animated insect films, *Antz* and *A Bug's Life*. What's going on here?

—Jack Hagerty, Livermore, California

A. Synchronicity is the generally accepted explanation. Ideas seem to be in the air, ripe for plucking by more than one studio. What's interesting is that when it becomes obvious that two similar projects are in the works, neither studio is inclined to blink, since that would concede they think the other studio can do a better job. It's not the story peg, anyway, that makes a movie good, but how it's handled.

Q. I've seen mention of the similarities between *Stag* and *Very Bad Things*, and between the two movies named *Jack Frost*, both about walking, talking snowmen. Here's another example of how they make two of everything. There is a 1996 direct-to-video movie named *Just Your Luck*, starring Virginia Madsen and Sean Patrick Flannery. The plot: A guy in a diner discovers he is holding a winning lottery ticket worth $6 million. He keels over dead from a heart attack. The rest of the people in the diner decide to cash the ticket and split up the money. Someone's been spending too much time in the video store, eh?

—Ed Slota, Warwick, Rhode Island

A. Maybe we should wake up Ned Devine and tell him about it.

Q. As you know, *Easy Rider* (1969) is famous for the lines, "We made it!" "We blew it!" Recently I was watching *Point Blank* (1967). Lee Marvin and his partner are robbing a pair of couriers at Alcatraz, and after the partner, whose name is Reese, shoots the two couriers, they have the following exchange:

Reese (elated): We made it!

Marvin (sadly): We blew it!

Point Blank came out two years prior to *Easy Rider*, and it would not surprise me if Peter Fonda and Dennis Hopper had seen and enjoyed it.

—Craig Simpson, Reynoldsburg, Ohio

A. Yes, but then again the dialogue itself is not of such stunning originality that anyone can claim it. Now if Lee Marvin and Dennis Hopper had both said, "Oh, what a rogue and peasant knave am I," we could really nail it.

Talking in the Movies

Q. I have become so strident on the topic of people who talk during movies that many of my closest friends refuse to go to a theater with me. I almost always end up rudely and profanely telling someone to shut the hell up. My most recent episode was at *Saving Private Ryan*, where a middle-aged woman behind me felt the need to point out several times during the invasion of Normandy that Tom Hanks was bleeding from the ears. I finally wheeled around and snarled, *"damnit, I want quiet back there!"* Silence fell. Some might suggest I ask politely, but I've discovered it doesn't really work. However, my more direct approach will almost certainly get me beaten up eventually. So how do we bring silence to the average movie theater? I've come up with an idea. Since your average multiplex has about 8 zillion screens, why don't they designate "talking" and "nontalking" theaters? Those who want to talk and crunch popcorn and screw around with laser pointers can gather with their brethren, and those of us who want to watch the movie we paid to see can watch in peace.

—W. Gamache, Calgary, Alberta

A. This is an excellent idea. You could be employed to toss a percussion bomb into the talking theaters from time to time.

Tall Actors

Q. My father, who is six-foot-four, insists that today's movies are populated by dwarves. The sight of Tom Cruise or Dustin Hoffman sets him into apoplexy. He says—I'm not exaggerating—that tall actors are discriminated against because of some sort of Hollywood conspiracy. I try to tell him that there are plenty of tall actors and that the proportion of tall, short, and average height is probably no different among movie stars than in the rest of the country. He tells me I'm not paying attention.

—Mike Holtzclaw, *Daily Press*, Newport News, Virginia

A. You are basically correct; actors come in many shapes and sizes. Close-ups are a great equalizing device (consider what an amazing impact Danny DeVito has in anything he does). Actresses who are taller than average (Sigourney Weaver, Saffron Burrows) sometimes have trouble getting cast opposite insecure stars, but it says something for Tom Cruise (who is not short but of average height) that he loves to work with his taller wife. Here's a theory to try out on your dad: Stars of both sexes tend to have larger heads, in relationship to body size, than the average person. That allows them to dominate in closer shots.

Tarzan

Q. I just saw *Tarzan* and loved the movie. My question is: Were my eyes deceiving me, or did Mrs. Potts and Chip from *The Little Mermaid* make cameo, albeit nonspeaking, appearances during the "Trashin' the Camp" scenes? Of course many teapots and teacups (with chips) look alike so it may be my mind creating a link that is simply not there.

—Jim Tsai, Philadelphia, Pennsylvania

A. Thomas Schumacher, president of Walt Disney Feature Animation and Theatrical Production, replies: "Yes indeed, good catch. That was in fact Mrs. Potts. Her cameo seemed a fitting tribute and you'll be comforted to know she is one of the few items not 'trashed' in that sequence."

Technical Terms

Q. In your review of *Urban Legends*, you mused: "There must be a name for the kind of loud, sudden chord that slasher movies depend on." I've been told by a composer that it's called a "sting."

—Chris Rowland, Plainsboro, New Jersey

A. Or a "stinger," according to other mail I've received. My other favorite movie composer jargon is "Mickey Mouse music," which refers to music that exactly mirrors the physical actions of characters on the screen

Q. There is an editing technique, used frequently in film and television, in which the audio track of the next scene is cut to before the visual scene is. Thus the viewer hears as much as a full line of dialogue from the following scene before the visual image is edited to actually show the speaker. This technique is very effective in conveying a feeling of linked, forward plot movement. My question is, what is this editing technique called? There must be a simple name to describe it, as opposed to the paragraph it took me to explain it.

—Daniel Welch, Wheaton, Illinois

A. I asked Thelma Schoonmaker, the gifted editor of such Martin Scorsese classics as *Raging Bull* and *GoodFellas*, for an answer. She replies: "The term your questioner is looking for is 'sound overlap' or 'sound prelap.' He is right that the device does convey a feeling of linked forward movement. It is also used sometimes when you are having difficulty with a transition and a sound overlap can trick the eye into accepting what might, otherwise, be an awkward cut."

10 Things I Hate About You

Q. I saw *10 Things I Hate About You* last night. In the movie, they need to find a student willing to date Kat (the "shrew") and one candidate says, "Maybe if we were the last two people alive and there were no sheep. Are there sheep?" I was intrigued by the fact that in the movie he says "sheep" but in the coming attractions previews he says "goats." This is obviously related to what can and can't be said in G-rated previews, but I fail to see how "goats" is less offensive than "sheep."

—Christian Morin, Vancouver, British Columbia

A. This is just the old bait and switch.

The End

Q. What happened to "The End"? Most movies now finish with a freeze/fadeout and the credits scroll. Bring back "The End"!

—Jim Coughlin, Oak Park, Illinois

A. I read your question and realized it had been years since I'd seen a new film that ended with "The End." I turned for an answer to Richard Neupert, professor of film studies at the University of Georgia and author of *The End: Narration and Closure in the Cinema*, who informs me: "My understanding is that unions and craft guilds got new concessions once the studio days ended, so that all creative personnel would get their names cited (partly because they were all "independent" now rather than studio employees), so by the mid-1960s it became routine to include all the names at the end of the movie. That does not of course mean that the words 'The End' were no longer needed, but partly because of more popular 'theme songs' that run over the credits, 'The End' may have seemed a bit inappropriate. By the early 1960s, the more modern art films made the sort of classical genre endings typical of *Casablanca* (camera and main characters separate, orchestral reprise, super of words 'The End') look old-fashioned. But the big dividing motive seems to have been the need to include all pertinent names, so now many films fade into the credit sequence. I agree that the sudden appearance of 'The End' is much more satisfying, and even a famous art film like *The 400 Blows* ended with the French 'Fin' over the final freeze frame."

Q. Re the Answer Man exchange about how the words "The End" have disappeared from the movies. Right off the bat, I can think of Ron Howard's recent movies *(The Paper, Apollo 13)* and Disney's animated *The Hunchback of Notre Dame*. Personally, I *prefer* the contemporary trend of ending on a freeze-frame or a fade-out. I'm a middle-school English teacher, and I have to work very hard to get my students over the bad habit of ending simple paragraphs with "The End." I tell them, "Know how I know that you've come to the end? Because *after* the end, you've written nothing else!" If moviegoers need "The End" to convince them that the movie's over, our country's literacy level is even worse than I've often feared.

—Steven Bailey, Jacksonville Beach, Florida

A. I've been part of audiences so noisy they needed "The Beginning."

Q. Re the Answer Man's discussion of the disappearance of the words "The End" at the end of modern movies: Audiences no longer require it. Once they've seen every scene that was in the trailer, they know that the movie's over.

—Tim Carvell, New York, New York

A. Either that, or they see Jackie Chan with his leg in a cast.

Q. Regarding the Answer Man's long-running discussion of the decline of the words "The End" at the ends of movies: My favorite was the use of "Fin" at the end of *A Fish Called Wanda*.

—Julia Moore, Akron, Ohio

A. Heh, heh. Dennis Thompson of West Palm Beach, Florida, points out that *Madeline* also ends with "Fin," which would make sense for a film set in France. He adds, "My daughter asked me what it meant and I said "the end," to which she replied, "We better go, then."

There's Something About Mary

Q. I saw a story about how the Farrelly brothers, directors of the surprise gross-out summer smash *There's Something About Mary*, are considering a "cleaned up" version that could get a PG or PG-13 rating. At first, I figured this was a suit-wearing executive's pinhead decision, but it turns out to be the Farrelly brothers themselves. Or so they claim. What's up with that and what do you think about it?

—Robert Sterling, Los Angeles, California

A. I suggest the new film be retitled *There's Not Much About Mary*. It is a spectacularly bad idea. The laughter in *Mary* is inspired specifically by how it gets away with so much. People laugh despite themselves—not believing what they see on the screen. Take out those moments, and what do you have left? A sweet little love story? I am reminded that the PG-13 version of *Saturday Night Fever* flopped dismally. Market surveys showed that everyone under seventeen who wanted to see the R-rated version already had. The Farrellys have already grossed $140 million with *Mary*, which is still doing big business. They should pocket their profits and move on.

Q. Near the end of *There's Something About Mary*, there's a scene in which Ted, the Ben Stiller character, touches the ear of Warren, the retarded brother—and, for the first time in the movie, Warren doesn't go berserk when his space is violated. When I saw this, my guess was that they would later show Brett Favre touching the ear and getting pummeled, making Mary realize that Ted was the guy for her. This didn't happen and I didn't think more about it until the credits, which include outtakes and silly stuff. Included is a scene where Favre touches Warren's ear and gets sacked. I wonder if the scene was shot for the picture, but later edited out.

—Alan Podmore, Canoga Park, California

A. Codirector Peter Farrelly says you're correct. The scene with Brett Favre getting sacked by Warren was filmed with the intention of using it. In the editing process they decided it made the living room sequence too long, and cut it. The Farrellys think the audience already "gets it" when Ted touches Warren's ear and gets away with it.

The Thin Red Line

Q. Settle a bet: What *is* "the thin red line?"

—Greg Nelson, Chicago, Illinois

A. Michael Mullen of the James Jones Literary Society tells me: "Jones himself answers this question with a couple of quotes that appear at the beginning of the book:

Then it's Tommy this, an' Tommy that,
An' Tommy, 'ow's your soul?
But it's "Thin red line of 'eroes,"
When the drums begin to roll—

—Kipling

And, "There is an old midwestern saying: 'There's only a thin red line between the sane and the mad.'"

The Thirteenth Floor

Q. I just saw *The Thirteenth Floor*, and I noticed in one of the scenes in the 1940s world, that there was a grand swimming pool. Wasn't this the same pool that was in *Cruel Intentions*? Both are Sony movies, and were probably produced at the same time. Since when have studios recycled sets? Did Reese Witherspoon and Craig Bierko bump into each other unexpectedly?

—Eric Knopp, San Francisco, California

A. A Sony Pictures rep says the pool of the Biltmore Hotel in downtown Los Angeles was used for both films.

Time Passing

Q. You say in your *Life Is Beautiful* review, that at a certain point "several years pass, offscreen." Please don't forget to tell us if that happens *on*-screen in another movie, so I can alert the family that I'll be taking a bit longer than usual at the cineplex.

—Zoltan Karpathy, Santiago, Chile

A. You bet. Uh, let's see. It happens onscreen in *Jack Frost.*

Titanic

Q. If I didn't know better, I'd say that *Titanic* has just sunk again. What was the most popular film on the planet a year ago now seems to have gone in the opposite direction, and *Titanic*-bashing is a fashionable sport. Witness its plunge in IMDB's rankings from the top 20 to nowhere on the top 250! Why? Is this a straightforward case of overexposure? Or has its popularity inspired many to attack it to prove their taste is superior to that of the masses?

—Murray Leeder, Calgary, Alberta

A. The intensity of your remembered enjoyment of a movie fades over a period of time, and you turn, not against the picture, but against the silent rebuke of your remembered enthusiasm. The rankings in the Internet Movie Database are an interesting curiosity, but not a scientific reflection of reality. *Titanic* is certain to remain a favorite film for many decades.

Q. As a fan of *Titanic*, I was dismayed to hear there are serious rumors flying around Hollywood about a sequel. The story will be that Jack really didn't die. He was rescued and spent three years in a coma. When he awakens he only remembers his tango with Rose in the car. Leo will be offered $30 million to star! Are these rumors true? I'm sure James Cameron wouldn't touch this, would he?

—Kari Pontinen, Minneapolis, Minnesota

A. This is an urban legend. No sequel is planned. It is true, of course, that when a movie becomes the top-grossing hit of all time, there is enormous pressure to generate a sequel. But although any silly plot device could easily resurrect Jack, the problem is that a *Titanic* sequel would have to involve more than Jack and Rose—it would also need a centerpiece at least as spectacular as the sinking of the ship. Jack and Rose could I suppose be reunited, marry, and book passage on the *Hindenberg*, but by then they would have aged out of the tango category and into the fox-trot.

Q. A friend of mine has told me they'll be releasing a longer version of *Titanic*, as if three-plus hours wasn't enough. When is this five-hour video supposed to be released?

—Mike Colfin, Queens Village, New York

A. Dorrit Ragosine of Paramount home video replies: "There has been much speculation regarding an extended version of *Titanic*, but a five-hour (or even a four-hour) expanded version would be literally impossible given the available materials. Although James Cameron is flattered that fans would want to view a longer picture, the film as theatrically released is the director's cut, and there are no plans to create or release a modified or extended version."

Titles

Q. I recently heard a rumor regarding *I Still Know What You Did Last Summer*. Originally it was to be titled *I Know What You Did Last Summer 2: Did You Think I Forgot?* Any truth?

—Jenn Clarke, Miami, Florida

A. According to the Internet Movie Database, these were the movie's working titles: *I Know What You Did Last Summer 2*, *I Know What You Did Last Summer . . . the Story Continues*, *I Know What You Did Last Summer: The Sequel*, *I Know What You Did Two Summers Ago*, and *I Still Know*.

Q. I am confused about the title to the film *I Still Know What You Did Last Summer*. Technically, shouldn't it be called *I Still Know What You Did The Summer Before Last*? After all, the hit-and-run incident happened not last summer, but the previous one before.

—Travis Eddings, Fayetteville, Arkansas

A. An excellent insight. And while we're at it, shouldn't *The Other Side of the Mountain, Part 2* have been titled *This Side of the Mountain*?

Q. The Answer Man tweaked the silly title *I Still Know What You Did Last Summer*. When it comes to stupid sequel names, personally I find it impossible to outdo *The Neverending Story II*.

—Michael Jennings, Sydney, Australia

A. I dunno. I was browsing in a video store just yesterday, and came across *Steven King's Sometimes They Come Back*, and its sequel, *Stephen King's Sometimes They Come Back . . . Again*.

Trailers

Q. What is with the growing trend for Hollywood to feature scenes from a movie in the trailer—then the scene never appears in the film? I understand that scenes are often cut from a film—but why make it a part of the trailer? For example: *The Devil's Own* had a huge love scene between Brad Pitt and Natascha McElhone in the trailer but not in the film. In the trailer for *200 Cigarettes*, Ben Affleck says, "By the way, I'm not gay. I get that a lot, and no, I am not gay." In *EDtv*, Woody Harrelson walks on his hands down the stairs and falls. Not in the film. This is irritating false advertising. I already don't like trailers to begin with, and this doesn't help.

—Jason Steele, Chicago, Illinois

A. Trailers are edited weeks or sometimes months before the movie has been finished, which is why they often use music from older movies, instead of from their own scores. They're shipped out and actually playing in theaters while editors and directors are still sweating over their final cut—where a scene, no matter how well it works in the trailer, has to work in the movie, or out it goes.

The Truman Show

Q. Re your Answer Man item about *The Truman Show* print that turned up in New York with French end credits. This is no big mystery. The answer is Quebec. All major films must be released up there in French as well as English. Reels occasionally do get switched, and I'll bet that somewhere along the line, either at the lab or during shipment, wires got crossed. It's rare, but not unprecedented; it happened to us last year, when half a dozen theaters in the L.A. area got prints of *Absolute Power* with a couple of reels in French.

—Mike Schlesinger, vice president, Sony Pictures Repertory

A. Hey, getting the wrong French dialogue happens all the time. When Groucho Marx was made a Chevalier of Arts and Letters at the Cannes Film Festival, he turned to the festival president and asked, "Voulez-vous couchez avec moi?"

20 Dates

Q. Re your review of the movie *20 Dates*, in which you reported on how producer Elie Samaha kept nudging the director to use the star Tia Carrere: Thought you might like to know that Elie Samaha and Tia Carrere are currently married (and, judging from the huge ring on her finger in the scene she appears in, were also probably married at the time of the film). Although I doubt that would heighten your enjoyment of the film, it does probably explain why Samaha was so insistent on putting her in the movie.

—Jeff Taplin, United Talent, Los Angeles, California

A. As you went on to point out, that means that the film's director, Myles Berkowitz, technically only went out on nineteen dates. But you know what? At least Tia Carrere has a dazzling smile, and when it appeared at the end of that dreadful film, it was like finding a diamond in a Cracker Jack box. Not that I have anything against Cracker Jacks.

Very Bad Things

Q. A friend of mine raised a very good point concerning *Very Bad Things.* Wouldn't the management at the Las Vegas hotel become suspicous that one of their security guards never returned after investigating a noise complaint? The room had to have been booked under Boyd's (or another character's) name. Wouldn't that have made them easy to track down? That portion of the film would have made more sense had only the prostitute been killed. But, I suppose the accidental death of a hooker just isn't "shocking" enough for whatever target audience this film was aimed for. Are we only supposed to start giving a damn after the murder of a hardworking family man? Does Hollywood truly believe we're that jaded?

—Carter Siddall, Toronto, Ontario

A. Apparently so.

Video Rental Standards

Q. While I was picking out a video last night, two guys came in with a case of beer each (no Canadian jokes please). They were looking through the Action section. For some reason, *Dead Man Walking* was filed under Action.

GUY1: What about this one?
GUY2: Nope. Saw it. There's nothing but acting in it.

—Mike Spearns, St. John's, Newfoundland

A. If you see Guy 2 again, tell him I thought his criticism was perceptive and accurate.

VirtualCamera

Q. There's a new visual effect I've seen on television, and I don't know how it's done. It's used in the Gap "Jump, Jive, an' Wail" commercial, the Matchbox 20 "Real World" video, and the ABC *Two of a Kind* sitcom intro. The effect: You see a fixed shot of a motion-filled scene (people jumping, horses running, cereal pouring); the action suddenly freezes, with people or objects suspended in midair, and the scene rotates as if the camera is dollying around it; the camera stops moving and motion resumes. In some cases, an unfrozen person continuously moves in the scene as if time has stopped around him or her. The effect is startlingly good in the Gap ad. I'm guessing that two cameras are used, one each in the initial and final angles, and 3-D computer modeling is used to create the intermediate angles.

—Chris Rowland, Plainsboro, New Jersey

A. You are looking at VirtualCamera, a patented process devised a few years ago by Dayton Taylor. I wrote about it a year ago in *Yahoo Internet Life* magazine. Here's how it works. Taylor places still cameras in a ring around his target event, and fires them all at once. Then he transfers the still images from each camera to motion picture film. When the film plays, our point of view circles the event, which is frozen in time. The technology to do this has been available since the invention of movies—but nobody ever thought of it, until Taylor did. He wrote me about the process soon after he first tested it, and I mentioned it to Steven Spielberg, who engaged in a correspondence with Taylor. Spielberg and I talked about what kind of a movie moment might be appropriate for VirtualCamera. Perhaps a great turning point, like the assassination of Lincoln or Gandhi, the death of Christ, or, obviously, anything new at The Gap. Taylor has an explanation and demo at www.virtualcamera.com/.

That led to some feedback:

In a recent column the Answer Man explained Dayton Taylor's VirtualCamera technique, which is used to freeze part of the action while the rest continues. I mentioned a conversation with Steven Spielberg about great moments in history or fiction for which the V.C. process would be the right stylistic choice. That inspired a lot of responses, and here are two of the most intriguing, plus a clarification:

Brian Jones, Atlanta, Georgia: Thank you for explaining the coolest effect lately, the VirtualCamera. I first saw it used in a Sting video and immediately found it striking. Here's a possibility: Alec Guinness falling onto the plunger in *Bridge Over the River Kwai.* Start with Guinness and the plunger in view; he's looking toward the camera, at the bridge, and says, "What have I done?" Then, when he starts falling, "virtual dolly" around until the bridge is in view so that as he hits the plunger, we release the freeze, and get to see the bridge blow up.

Mike Robertson, Austin, Texas: The VirtualCamera process seems to me the key to filming Nicholson Baker's novel, *The Fermata,* the story of a man who can stop time and yet move through the motionless world around him.

Charlie White, Milwaukee, Wisconsin: I, too, believed that Dayton Taylor was responsible for that effect in the Gap "Khakis Swing" spot until I was assigned by *Post* magazine to report on the spot. I was all ready to write a technical description about the VirtualCamera array technique that Taylor uses, when I found out that the spot wasn't done by him at all. It was directed by fashion photographer and music video director Matthew Ralston using two 35mm motion picture cameras and some fancy software running on SGI computers.

The Waterboy

Q. When a film such as *The Waterboy* grosses $39 million in its first weekend, how can you justify doing what you do? What's the point?

—R. Pockmire, Chicago, Illinois

A. If it had grossed $78 million, there would have been twice as much point. How many people have *you* heard nostalgically recalling what a terrific time they had at that movie? Compared, say, to *Forrest Gump*—another film about an intellectually-challenged overachiever?

Q. Why do you think you have had very similar reactions to the movies of Adam Sandler and Jim Carrey early movies? Are you not allowing for the possiblility that Sandler will grow on you as Carrey has? Though I do not think Sandler is as talented as Carrey, they both put out a great deal of effort, are both naturally comically talented, and both fulfill a need we have to laugh without thought, to simply cackle at the antics of someone who has the gift to make us forget for just a little while through the power of laughter. Only one star? Watch *The Waterboy* again, forget that his Cajun accent isn't right on target or that you may not like Sandler's character. Forget sappy endings that don't work. Just tell me that Sandler alone, with his energy, doesn't deserve at least another star and perhaps more of an open mind for future movies.

—Jason Peevy, Mobile, Alabama

A. I hope, I really do, that Adam Sandler grows on me, because I am going to be seeing his movies for a long, long time. Re your suggestion that I watch *The Waterboy* again while forgetting his accent, his character, and the movie's ending: That would do the trick if I could also forget the beginning and the middle.

Wet Streets

Q. Why, in scenes set on city streets, are the streets dry in daytime, but always wet at night?

—Doug Williams. Clearwater, Florida

A. Dry streets are boring to photograph at night. But cinematographers have discovered that if they hose them down, they show up much better and create interesting reflections. Thus, wet streets at night, even in desert towns.

What Dreams May Come

Q. It occurred to me while watching *What Dreams May Come* that this could have been a new silent film. The plot was simple enough to have been conveyed with a few cue cards. The dialogue was so clunky as to actually distract from the astonishing visuals ("Sometimes when you win, you lose."). You could use Elgar or Mahler perhaps for orchestration and you've got a better context to really appreciate Ward's artistry. I bet it would even increase the film's moral and dramatic impact. What do you think? Could the silent film ever come back?

—Nicole Cody, Memphis, Tennessee

A. I've been teaching a class on silent films this year and have been astounded all over again by the power of the medium. The use of music instead of dialogue makes it easier for the movie to absorb us in a reverie state. Audiences will accept a film with very little dialogue (or, in a case of action films like *Armageddon*, dialogue that need not all be comprehended). But they resist silent films. The only silent films of recent years were Mel Brooks's *Silent Movie* (1976) and Charles Lane's *Sidewalk Stories* (1989). However, revivals of silent films are booming around the country, and their video sales are strong.

Where to Sit?

Q. In your Answer Man book, you say that you like to sit twice as far back as the screen is wide. How do you determine the width of the screen, and then translate that into distance from the front? Do you estimate the width, or ask the management? And then, do you physically pace off the distance?

—Steve Hoffman, Seattle, Washington

A. I just do a simple triangulation, employing a pocket sextant.

Wish Fulfillment

Q. I had to bite my tongue from laughing when Sam Neill's character showed up near the end of *The Horse Whisperer*. I kept thinking he had fulfilled his dying plea from *The Hunt for Red October*. After being shot, Sam Neill's dying words in *Hunt* were (in a thick Russian accent): "I would like to have seen Montana."

—David J. Bondelevitch, Studio City, California

A. An autographed copy of *Roger Ebert's Video Companion* to you, and to the reader who sends the funniest similar example of a character's wish in one movie being fulfilled in another. Send to: Wish Fulfillment, Box 146829, Chicago, IL 60614.

That item inspired a flood of entries, and a later Answer Man column devoted to the best of them. Here are some examples:

* To begin with, doesn't *The Horse Whisperer* represent the *second* time that Sam Neill's character Captain Borodin from *The Hunt for Red October* fulfills his dying wish to see Montana? In *Jurassic Park*, Sam Neill's first scene as a paleontologist is identified as being near Snakewater, Montana. (Larry N. Christiansen, St. Paul, Minnesota; also spotted by Andrew Tice of Lebanon, Pennsylvania, and Connie L. Merchant of Rochester, New York)

* Halfway into *Forrest Gump*, a sneering Lt. Dan (Gary Sinese) tells Gump (Tom Hanks), "The day you become a shrimp boat captain, I will be your first mate. The day you become a shrimp boat captain is the day I become an astronaut!" Gary Sinese, of course, became an astronaut in his very next film, *Apollo 13*, also with Tom Hanks. (Craig Simpson, Reynoldsburg, Ohio; also spotted by Patrick Chizeck of Chicago, and Cal Bray Snowmass Village, Colorado)

* Reverse wish-fulfillment: In *Forrest Gump* that Gary Sinise, as Lt. Dan, mourns after his legs are cut off that he'll "never be an astronaut." This prediction is confirmed in *Apollo 13*, when it is not amputated legs, but suspicion that he was exposed to measles that keeps him earthbound. In both films, Tom Hanks listens to his disappointment. (Adam Remsen, Ames, Iowa)

* In *Demolition Man*, Sandra Bullock's character says to Sylvester Stallone's character, "while you were sleeping . . ." That just happens to be the title of her next film. (Cal Bray, Snowmass Village, Colorado)

* How about anti-wish-fulfillment? In *Bull Durham*, Kevin Costner, as Crash Davis, says, "I believe Lee Harvey Oswald acted alone." Later he played Kennedy conspiracy buff Jim Garrison in Oliver Stone's *JFK*." (Brian J. Carr, West Chester, Pennsylvania; also spotted

by Tom Cammaleri, Newbury Park, California, and Chuck Hopkins, Columbus, Ohio)

* Parker Posey's character in *Waiting for Guffman* dreams of moving to New York where she can have a lot of fun and meet guys. All you need to do is watch *Party Girl* to see that her wish did indeed come true. (Jeff Schmidt, Coon Rapids, Minnesota)

* Eddie Murphy's fabulously wealthy prince in *Coming to America* tosses a big wad of cash to two bums in the street. They are Ralph Bellamy and Don Ameche, whose Randolph and Mortimer Duke were ruined by Murphy and Dan Aykroyd in *Trading Places.* Bellamy looks wide-eyed at the money and exclaims, "Mortimer! We're back!" (Eric Berman, Indianapolis, Indiana)

* Here's a twist on wish-fulfillment in which an actor fulfills another actor's wishes in a film. In *Platoon,* Tom Berenger barks at Willem Dafoe, "Who do you think you are, Jesus Christ?" Dafoe should have replied, "No, but I'll be portraying him in my next film, *The Last Temptation of Christ.*" (Joe Collins, Chicago; also spotted by Chuck Hopkins, Columbus, Ohio)

* In Trey Parker's *Cannibal: The Musical,* a character named Cooge Noon, played by Dian Bachar, often talks and sing about his only wish in life, to lose his virginity. He never does, and he dies in the end. In Parker's comedy, *Orgazmo,* Bachar's character finally gets to see some action and gets his wish fulfilled. (Mike Babitsky, Old Bridge, New Jersey)

* In *How to Marry a Millionaire,* Lauren Bacall's character was trying to persuade the older millionaire that there are many older men who are still attractive and alluring. She compared him to the old guy who starred in *The African Queen*—her husband, Humphrey Bogart. (Jacqueline Iacullo, Chicago)

* In *Lethal Weapon,* Mel Gibson says, "I did (shoot) a guy in Laos from a thousand feet in a high wind. Maybe two or three guys in the world could have made that shot." No doubt he did it while he was in Laos in *Air America.* (Tom Cammaleri, Newbury Park, California)

* In *Star Trek: First Contact,* Captain Picard (Patrick Stewart) is intent on obtaining revenge on an enemy, the Borg. He gets maniacal about it, and a character named Lily stamps into his office and compares him to Captain Ahab chasing after Moby-Dick. Patrick Stewart went on to portray Captain Ahab in a recent cable movie version of *Moby-Dick.* (Marianne Stranich, Chicago)

* In *Batman Forever,* Jim Carrey as the Riddler says, in his final scene, "How could I forget?" in an eerie whisper. In *Liar, Liar,* Carrey says the same line in the same way when asked if he remembered his client's boyfriend. (Thomas Torrey, South Windsor, Connecticut)

* Daryl Hannah starred in a movie some time ago called *Summer Lovers.* In that movie there was one scene where she wished she was a mermaid. As you know, her wish was granted in her later movie *Splash.* (Carl Malmfeldt, San Ramon, California)

* Reverse wish-fulfillment: In Spike Lee's *Jungle Fever,* there is a scene in which actress Debi Mazar portrays a bigoted girlfriend of Annabella Sciorra and declares to her: "I'll never have a sexual relationship with a black man!" In *Malcolm X,* Mazar plays a character named Peg who does have sex with a black man. (Joseph Strickland, Chicago)

* In *GoodFellas,* Joe Pesci's character brutally kills Billy Batts, played by Frank Vincent. Mr. Vincent gets his own back, however, in *Casino,* in which he does away with Pesci with a shovel to the head! (Ian Waldron-Mantgani, Liverpool, England)

* In *Broadcast News,* a woman bored by Holly Hunter's conference speech yells at her to "Shut up!" She gets her wish—Miss Hunter refuses to talk in *The Piano.* (Ian Waldron-Mantgani, Liverpool, England)

* In *Pulp Fiction,* Peter Green as Zed says the line, "Feed it to the gimp." And in *The Usual Suspects,* Peter Green as Redfoot says that same exact line when asked what he should do about some drugs recovered. (Thomas Torrey, South Windsor, Connecticut)

* In *No Way Out,* Gene Hackman plays a high-ranking Washington official whose philandering ways lead him to accidentally murder his mistress. Close associates try to create a cover-up, unknowingly implicating the hero of the movie (Kevin Costner) as the

murderer. In the movie *Absolute Power,* Gene Hackman plays a high-ranking Washington official whose philandering ways lead to him accidentally murdering his mistress, and close associates try to create a cover-up, unknowingly implicating the hero of the movie (Clint Eastwood) as the murderer. *Absolute Power* is fun to watch if you pretend that the character that Gene Hackman plays is the same one from *No Way Out,* ten years later, and still murdering mistresses. (Chuck Hopkins, Columbus, Ohio)

And I'll add one of my own. In *Citizen Kane,* Orson Welles and Joseph Cotten were boyhood friends, "thrown out of all the best schools together," before Welles grows up and eventually goes on a collecting tour of Europe, leaving Cotten behind to work as a writer. In *The Third Man,* Welles is once again an old chum who has gone to Europe, but this time he sends for Cotten, a writer, asking him to join him.

The free book goes to Ian Waldron-Mantgani, who submitted the two most amusing entries.

The Wizard of Oz

Q. The Yellow Brick Road led to the Wizard. I always wondered where Dorothy would have ended up had she taken the Red Brick Road.

—Bradley Richman, New York City, New York

A. Alan Podmore of the CompuServe ShowBiz Forum has this theory: "The yellow brick road led to the Emerald City. Green is one color counterclockwise on the color wheel from yellow and purple is one color counterclockwise from red. So the red brick road must lead to the Purple (Grape?) City."

Woody Allen

Q. Any comments on Woody Allen's assertion that his film received a bad review because the writer didn't like him?

—Alan Podmore, Canoga Park, California

A. Allen told *Indie,* a film magazine, that Maureen Dowd of the *New York Times* attacked his film *Deconstructing Harry* because "she doesn't like me." Dowd described the movie as "a tiresome Manhattan whine about a weaselly, overcivilized, undermoralized, terminally psychoanalyzed terminator," adding that Allen's movies are "about nothing except his creepy obsessions." My comments: (1) Yes, I would agree she doesn't like him. (2) Allen has often described himself in more or less the same terms Dowd uses, so she's going to have to do better than that. (3) You'd be surprised how many good films are about their weaselly, overcivilized, undermoralized, terminally psychoanalyzed directors' creepy obsessions.

The X Files

Q. *The X Files* obviously took place in summer, as evidenced by the complaints about the heat in Dallas, the lack of overcoats in Washington, D.C., the corn crops, and the copious sweat in all locations. Therefore, the sun should not have been brightly shining in Antarctica. That continent should have been in the middle of its dark and stormy winter.

—Denise Leder, Las Vegas, Nevada

A. Either (a) you have spotted a technical error, or (b) Mulder and Scully only *thought* they were in Antarctica, and in fact were on an elaborate fake set constructed as part of the conspiracy. That would explain how they got from the United States to Antarctica so suspiciously quickly.

Q. In your review of *The X Files,* I'm glad you mentioned the shot evoking the Oklahoma City bombing. I enjoyed the movie, but like you, I wondered if some viewers might have old wounds reopened by that particular sight. Surely there must have been another way to evoke the shock. What are filmmakers thinking of when they do things like that?

—Steve Bailey, Jacksonville Beach, Florida

A. The shot, showing a building with its facade in shreds, deliberately echoes Oklahoma City. For the filmmakers, perhaps it represents the thin line between real and fictional conspiracies. I thought it was disturbing and unnecessary.

You've Got Mail

Q. I think I'm the only American to have been bored by *You've Got Mail.* I'd love to see a really good film about finding romance on-line (my wife and I met online about three years ago). I thought the whole "big corporation swallowing little bookseller" angle was dopey. Hey, it's a film about finding love on-line, so why doesn't Meg's character try to sell books on-line? That would have been a fun ending, and more relevant to the film's cyber-veneer: Meg keeps the bookstore and thrives, because she's getting customers from the entire planet, while Hanks's megastore only does so-so, because it's just getting people from the surrounding area.

—Ed Driscoll, San Jose, California

A. Yeah, and after she takes it public for $200 million, she buys out Hanks and fires him, only to discover this is the same guy she loves on-line. There wouldn't be a dry eye in the brokerage.

Zero Effect

Q. I recently listened to the alternate audio commentary track on the DVD version of *Zero Effect* and noticed that the film's director, Jake Kasdan, plays a word game throughout the film. Every so often he mentions a key word. Then, by the end of his commentary, the words reveal this sentence: "That spooky rumbling is a distant timpani." Is there any significance to why he chose this particular sentence?

—Rob Mathiowetz, Oshkosh, Wisconsin

A. Jake Kasdan replies: "Re the Case of the Timpani of Questionable Significance: For those unfamiliar with the whole 'commentary track' thing, the central idea is this—the director and/or other creative forces behind a film are locked in a small recording booth for duration of said film, as it rolls on video tape. An open microphone records their incoherent ramblings, anecdotes, and nervous jokes. No interviewer. No context. Just uninterrupted talk. The result is recorded onto an alternate digital track on the DVD, so viewers can press a button and hear a sports-broadcast-like color commentary as they watch the movie.

"As I sat at the studio, preparing to do this, the engineer and I started speculating about how many people, between that moment and the end of time, would ever actually listen to the whole thing. Thus, the Word Game of Dubious Conception. One word every ten or twenty minutes—and the aggregate sentence creates proof of having listened to the entire commentary track. I would, I thought, use this opportunity to launch a sort of club, the Secret Society of Zero People.

"The sad part of this story is that, in the course of the movie, I lost track of where I was going with the sentence, and recklessly dropped an article into a totally irresponsible spot, treating 'timpani' as a singular, when in fact the word is the plural of 'timpano.' So embarrassing. A few have come forward with the sentence and, needless to say, I love them. They've all been polite enough to avoid the subject of the syntax problem. As to the original question, 'Does the sentence have any significance?' The answer is—Yes."

Glossary Entries

Ebert's Bigger Little Movie Glossary, an expanded edition with twice as many entries as the original book, was published in May 1999. But the entries keep rolling in; the stock of movie clichés seems nowhere near exhausted. Here are the latest entries.

* * *

Catch-Up Movie. A film that frustrates the audience because the characters spend the bulk of the film slowly and laboriously learning information that the audience was given during the first ten minutes. See *In Dreams.*

—Stuart Cleland, Evanston, Illinois

Crazy Collage Syndrome. Psychotic stalkers sublimate their destructive impulses by creating a collage of newspaper clippings, candid photos, and charcoal sketches of their victims. This collage is glued to the wall of the stalker's one-room apartment, to be found by police officers bursting in just after the stalker has fled.

—Joe Zarrow, Herndon, Virginia

Dramatic Desk Sweep. In a fit of anger or frustration, main character dramatically sweeps everything off desk. We never see anyone replace items, but surface is in perfect order in later scenes. Only exception: If one item was a framed photo of a dead lover or family member, the glass will be cracked, giving photo deeper meaning.

—Kim Costello, Downers Grove, Illinois

Economy Class Crashes. No airplane that disappears out of sight over hills, treetops, or buildings ever lands safely; instead, a fireball explodes behind the foreground object.

—R. E.

Florence Nightingale Rule. Throughout movie history, no clean cloth has ever been the right size to be used as a bandage without first being torn in two.

—R. E.

Friendless Orphan Rule. No character who lacks parents may have friends or extended family. Holidays must be spent alone, preferably talking to a cat.

—Mary Riley, Chicago, Illinois

Inevitable Exit Line. Whenever a movie character says he is definitely, absolutely, irrevocably *not going*—the next shot shows him going.

—R. E.

It's Only the Drain Syndrome. Whenever there are offscreen noises of sexual activity, it is always revealed that they are caused by something else.

—R. E.

Less Action, More Talk. The difference between a romantic comedy and a sex comedy is that in the first the tension involves when they'll stop talking and make love, and in the second when they'll stop making love and start talking.

—R. E.

Mummy's Other Curse, The. Even though they have been sealed in airtight sarcophagi for millennia, all movie mummies are incredibly dusty.

—R. E.

Roll Over, Beethoven, etc., Obligatory Reveal. When one character is romantically obsessed with another and calls them at home in the middle of the night, and they answer the phone while propped up on one elbow, when they flop back down the shot will inevitably reveal they are not alone in bed.

—R. E.

Sliding Heroine Scale. When a hero and heroine "meet cute" in a fight scene, she always emerges victorious. Later the same hero she defeated will defeat a villain she is no match for. See *Robin Hood: Prince of Thieves, The Lion King.*

—Joseph Greenia, Chicago, Illinois

Smudge-Proof Screen Kiss. After a passionate kiss, the male star never has lipstick smudged around his lips, no matter how bright or glossy the lips of the female. Exception: If it is a nerdy teenager who has been kissed by a beautiful, older woman, he will always have lipstick smeared on his face. Also, his hair will be disheveled and his glasses askew.

—Kim Costello, Downers Grove, Illinois

Stay Put, Don't Do Anything Rule. When during an action movie an adult tells the smaller person to hide and not move and not do *anything*, the smaller person will invariably not stay there and will either get into trouble, or inadvertently save the day.

—David Taylor, Oak Park, Illinois

Ugly Dog Theory. In a comedy, whenever someone is being pummeled with insults, it's always the last and most seemingly innocent insult that evokes a heated response. Example: "You're ugly, your mother is ugly, your brother is ugly, and your dog is ugly!" Response: "You can't talk that way about my dog!"

—Scott Honea, Corsicana, Texas

Reviews Appearing in Previous Editions of the *Video Companion/Movie Yearbook*

A

Title	Edition
About Last Night . . . , 1986, R, ★★★★	1998
Above the Law, 1988, R, ★★★	1995
Above the Rim, 1994, R, ★★★	1995
Absence of Malice, 1981, PG, ★★★	1998
Absolute Power, 1997, R, ★★★½	1998
Accidental Tourist, The, 1988, PG, ★★★★	1998
Accompanist, The, 1994, PG, ★★★½	1998
Accused, The, 1988, R, ★★★	1998
Ace Ventura: Pet Detective, 1994, PG-13, ★	1998
Ace Ventura: When Nature Calls, 1995, PG-13, ★½	1998
Addams Family, The, 1991, PG-13, ★★	1997
Addams Family Values, 1993, PG-13, ★★★	1998
Addicted to Love, 1997, R, ★★	1998
Addiction, The, 1995, NR, ★★½	1997
Adjuster, The, 1992, R, ★★★	1998
Adventures of Baron Munchausen, The, 1989, PG, ★★★	1998
Adventures of Ford Fairlane, The, 1990, R, ★	1992
Adventures of Huck Finn, The, 1993, PG, ★★★	1998
Adventures of Priscilla, Queen of the Desert, The, 1994, R, ★★½	1998
After Hours, 1985, R, ★★★★	1998
After the Rehearsal, 1984, R, ★★★★	1998
Against All Odds, 1984, R, ★★★	1998
Age of Innocence, The, 1993, PG, ★★★★	1998
Agnes of God, 1985, PG-13, ★	1989
Airplane!, 1980, PG, ★★★	1998
Airport, 1970, G, ★★	1996
Airport 1975, 1974, PG, ★★½	1996
Aladdin, 1992, G, ★★★	1998
Alaska, 1996, PG, ★★★	1999
Alex in Wonderland, 1971, R, ★★★★	1998
Alice, 1990, PG-13, ★★★	1998
Alice Doesn't Live Here Anymore, 1974, PG, ★★★★	1998
Alien Nation, 1988, R, ★★	1994
Aliens, 1986, R, ★★★½	1998
Alien^3, 1992, R, ★½	1997
Alive, 1993, R, ★★½	1997
All Dogs Go to Heaven, 1989, G, ★★★	1998
Allegro Non Tropo, 1977, NR, ★★★½	1995
Alligator, 1980, R, ★	1990
All Night Long, 1981, R, ★★	1986
All of Me, 1984, PG, ★★★½	1998
. . . All the Marbles, 1981, R, ★★	1986
All the President's Men, 1976, PG, ★★★½	1998
All the Right Moves, 1983, R, ★★★	1998
All the Vermeers in New York, 1992, NR, ★★★	1998
Almost an Angel, 1990, PG, ★★½	1995
Altered States, 1980, R, ★★★½	1998
Always, 1989, PG, ★★	1997
Amadeus, 1984, PG, ★★★★	1998
Amarcord, 1974, R, ★★★★	1998
Amateur, 1995, R, ★★½	1996
American Buffalo, 1996, R, ★★½	1999
American Dream, 1992, NR, ★★★★	1998
American Flyers, 1985, PG-13, ★★½	1995
American Gigolo, 1980, R, ★★★½	1998
American Graffiti, 1973, PG, ★★★★	1998
American in Paris, An, 1952, G, ★★★½	1997
American Me, 1992, R, ★★★½	1998
American President, The, 1995, PG-13, ★★★★	1998
American Tail: Fievel Goes West, An, 1991, G, ★★½	1998
American Werewolf in London, An, 1981, R, ★★	1998
Amityville II: The Possession, 1982, R, ★★	1988
Amos & Andrew, 1993, PG-13, ★★½	1995
Anaconda, 1997, PG-13, ★★★½	1998
Angel at My Table, An, 1991, R, ★★★★	1998
Angel Heart, 1987, R, ★★★½	1998
Angelo My Love, 1983, R, ★★★½	1995
Angels and Insects, 1996, NR, ★★★½	1999
Angels in the Outfield, 1994, PG, ★★	1996
Angie, 1994, R, ★★½	1997
Angus, 1995, PG-13, ★★★	1998
Anne Frank Remembered, 1996, PG, ★★★½	1999
Annie, 1982, PG, ★★★	1998
Annie Hall, 1977, PG, ★★★½	1998
Another 48 HRS, 1990, R, ★★	1996
Another Woman, 1988, PG, ★★★★	1998

B

Betrayed, 1988, R, ★★ 1993
Betsy's Wedding, 1990, R, ★★ 1993
Beverly Hillbillies, The, 1993, PG, ½★ 1995
Beverly Hills Cop, 1984, R, ★★½ 1998
Beverly Hills Cop II, 1987, R, ★ 1995
Beyond Rangoon, 1995, R, ★★★ 1998
Beyond the Limit, 1983, R, ★★½ 1989
Beyond Therapy, 1987, R, ★ 1988
Beyond the Valley of the Dolls, 1970, NC-17, Stars N/A 1997
Big, 1988, PG, ★★★ 1998
Big Bang, The, 1990, R, ★★★ 1995
Big Brawl, The, 1980, R, ★½ 1986
Big Business, 1988, PG, ★★ 1993
Big Chill, The, 1983, R, ★★½ 1998
Big Easy, The, 1987, R, ★★★★ 1998
Big Foot, 1971, PG, ½★ 1990
Big Red One, The, 1980, PG, ★★★ 1996
Big Squeeze, The, 1996, R, ★ 1999
Big Town, The, 1987, R, ★★★½ 1998
Bill & Ted's Bogus Journey, 1991, PG-13, ★★★ 1998
Billy Bathgate, 1991, R, ★★ 1993
Billy Jack, 1971, PG, ★★½ 1993
Bird, 1988, R, ★★★½ 1998
Birdcage, The, 1995, R, ★★★ 1999
Bird on a Wire, 1990, PG-13, ★★½ 1993
Birdy, 1985, R, ★★★★ 1998
Bitter Moon, 1994, R, ★★★ 1998
Black Cauldron, The, 1985, PG, ★★★½ 1987
Black Marble, The, 1980, PG, ★★★½ 1998
Black Rain (Michael Douglas), 1989, R, ★★ 1993
Black Rain (Japan), 1990, NR, ★★★½ 1998
Black Robe, 1991, R, ★★½ 1994
Black Stallion, The, 1980, G, ★★★★ 1998
Black Stallion Returns, The, 1983, PG, ★★½ 1986
Black Widow, 1987, R, ★★½ 1991
Blade Runner, 1982, R, ★★★ 1998
Blade Runner: The Director's Cut, 1992, R, ★★★ 1997
Blame It on Rio, 1984, R, ★ 1987
Blaze, 1989, R, ★★★½ 1998
Blind Date, 1987, PG-13, ★★½ 1988
Blink, 1994, R, ★★★½ 1998
Bliss, 1997, R, ★★★½ 1998
Blood and Wine, 1997, R, ★★★½ 1998
Blood Simple, 1985, R, ★★★★ 1998
Blown Away, 1994, R, ★★ 1996
Blow Out, 1981, R, ★★★★ 1998
Blue, 1994, R, ★★★½ 1998
Blue Chips, 1994, PG-13, ★★★ 1998
Blue Collar, 1978, R, ★★★★ 1998
Blue Kite, The, 1994, NR, ★★★★ 1998
Blue Lagoon, The, 1980, R, ½★ 1991
Blues Brothers, The, 1980, R, ★★★ 1998
Blue Sky, 1994, PG-13, ★★★ 1998
Blue Steel, 1990, R, ★★★ 1998
Blue Velvet, 1986, R, ★ 1998
Blume in Love, 1973, R, ★★★★ 1998
Blush, 1996, NR, ★★½ 1999
Bob Roberts, 1992, R, ★★★ 1998
Bodies, Rest and Motion, 1993, R, ★★ 1994
Body Double, 1984, R, ★★★½ 1998
Bodyguard, The, 1992, R, ★★★ 1998
Body of Evidence, 1993, R, ½★ 1994
Body Snatchers, 1994, R, ★★★★ 1998
Bogus, 1996, PG, ★★★ 1999
Bolero, 1984, NR, ½★ 1993
Bonfire of the Vanities, The, 1990, R, ★★½ 1998
Boomerang, 1992, R, ★★★ 1998
Boost, The, 1988, R, ★★★½ 1998
Booty Call, 1997, R, ★★★ 1998
Bopha!, 1993, PG-13, ★★★½ 1998
Born on the Fourth of July, 1989, R, ★★★★ 1998
Born Yesterday, 1993, PG, ★ 1994
Bostonians, The, 1984, PG, ★★★ 1998
Bound, 1996, R, ★★★★ 1999
Bound by Honor, 1993, R, ★★ 1994
Bounty, The, 1984, PG, ★★★★ 1998
Boyfriends and Girlfriends, 1988, PG, ★★★ 1998
Boys, 1996, PG-13, ★★ 1999
Boys on the Side, 1995, R, ★★★½ 1998
Boy Who Could Fly, The, 1986, PG, ★★★ 1996
Boyz N the Hood, 1991, R, ★★★★ 1998
Brady Bunch Movie, The, 1995, PG-13, ★★ 1997
Brainscan, 1994, R, ★★ 1995
Brainstorm, 1983, PG, ★★ 1986
Bram Stoker's Dracula, 1992, R, ★★★ 1998
Brassed Off, 1997, R, ★★★ 1998
Braveheart, 1995, R, ★★★½ 1998
Brazil, 1985, R, ★★ 1998
Breakdown, 1997, R, ★★★ 1998
Breakfast Club, The, 1985, R, ★★★ 1998
Breaking Away, 1979, PG, ★★★★ 1998
Breaking In, 1989, R, ★★★ 1995

Breaking the Waves, 1996, R, ★★★★ 1999
Breakin' 2—Electric Boogaloo, 1984, PG, ★★★ 1995
Breathless, 1983, R, ★★½ 1989
Brewster's Millions, 1985, PG, ★ 1988
Bridges of Madison County, The, 1995, PG-13, ★★★½ 1998
Brief History of Time, A, 1992, NR, ★★½ 1994
Bright Angel, 1991, R, ★★★½ 1998
Bright Lights, Big City, 1988, R, ★★★½ 1998
Brighton Beach Memoirs, 1986, PG-13, ★★ 1989
Bring Me the Head of Alfredo Garcia, 1974, R, ★★★★ 1998
Broadcast News, 1987, R, ★★★★ 1998
Broadway Danny Rose, 1984, PG, ★★★½ 1998
Broken Arrow, 1996, R, ★★ 1999
Bronx Tale, A, 1993, R, ★★★★ 1998
Brother from Another Planet, The, 1984, PG, ★★★½ 1998
Brother's Keeper, 1993, NR, ★★★★ 1998
Brothers McMullen, The, 1995, R, ★★★ 1998
Brubaker, 1980, R, ★★½ 1991
Buddy Holly Story, The, 1978, PG, ★★★½ 1998
Bugsy, 1991, R, ★★★★ 1998
Bugsy Malone, 1976, G, ★★★½ 1998
Bull Durham, 1988, R, ★★★½ 1998
Bulletproof, 1996, R, ★★ 1999
Bulletproof Heart, 1995, R, ★★★ 1998
Bullets Over Broadway, 1994, R, ★★★½ 1998
'Burbs, The, 1989, PG, ★★ 1992
Burden of Dreams, 1982, NR, ★★★★ 1998
Burglar, 1987, R, ★ 1989
Buster, 1988, R, ★★★ 1998
Buster and Billie, 1974, R, ★★★ 1995
Butcher's Wife, The, 1991, PG-13, ★★½ 1997
Butley, 1974, NR, ★★★★ 1987
Butterfly Kiss, 1996, R, ★★ 1999
Bye Bye Brazil, 1979, NR, ★★★★ 1996
Bye Bye, Love, 1995, PG-13, ★★ 1996

C

Cabaret, 1972, PG, ★★★½ 1998
Cable Guy, The, 1996, PG-13, ★★ 1999
Cactus, 1987, NR, ★★★ 1998
Caddyshack, 1980, R, ★★½ 1998
Cadillac Man, 1990, R, ★★ 1994
California Split, 1974, R, ★★★★ 1998
Caligula, 1980, NR, no stars 1990
Camille Claudel, 1989, R, ★★★½ 1998
Candyman, 1992, R, ★★★ 1998
Candyman: Farewell to the Flesh, 1995, R, ★★ 1996
Cannery Row, 1982, PG, ★★½ 1987
Cannonball Run, The, 1981, PG, ½★ 1991
Cannonball Run II, 1984, PG, ½★ 1988
Cape Fear, 1991, R, ★★★ 1998
Carlito's Way, 1993, R, ★★★½ 1998
Carmen, 1984, PG, ★★★★ 1998
Carmen (dance), 1983, R, ★★★★ 1995
Carnival of Souls, 1962, NR, ★★★ 1997
Carrie, 1976, R, ★★★½ 1998
Carried Away, 1996, R, ★★★ 1999
Carrington, 1995, R, ★★★★ 1998
Car Wash, 1976, PG, ★★★½ 1995
Casablanca, 1942, NR, ★★★★ 1997
Casino, 1995, R, ★★★★ 1998
Casper, 1995, PG, ★★★ 1998
Casualties of War, 1989, R, ★★★ 1998
Cat People, 1982, R, ★★★½ 1998
Cat's Eye, 1985, PG-13, ★★★ 1986
Caught, 1996, R, ★★★ 1999
Caveman, 1981, PG, ★½ 1986
Celestial Clockwork, 1996, NR, ★★★ 1999
Celluloid Closet, The, 1995, NR, ★★★½ 1999
Celtic Pride, 1996, PG-13, ★★ 1999
Cement Garden, The, 1994, NR, ★★★ 1998
Cemetery Club, The, 1992, PG-13, ★★★ 1998
Chain Reaction, 1996, PG-13, ★★½ 1999
Chamber, The, 1996, R, ★★ 1999
Chances Are, 1989, PG, ★★★½ 1998
Chaplin, 1993, PG-13, ★★ 1994
Chapter Two, 1980, PG, ★★ 1992
Chariots of Fire, 1981, PG, ★★★★ 1998
Chase, The, 1994, PG-13, ★★½ 1995
Chasing Amy, 1997, R, ★★★½ 1998
Chattahoochee, 1990, R, ★★½ 1992
Child's Play, 1988, R, ★★★ 1998
China Moon, 1994, R, ★★★½ 1998
China Syndrome, The, 1979, PG, ★★★★ 1998
Chinatown, 1974, R, ★★★★ 1998
Chocolat, 1989, PG-13, ★★★★ 1998
Choose Me, 1984, R, ★★★½ 1998
Chorus Line, A, 1985, PG-13, ★★★½ 1998
Christiane F., 1981, R, ★★★½ 1998
Christine, 1983, R, ★★★ 1998
Christmas Story, A, 1983, PG, ★★★ 1998
Christopher Columbus: The Discovery, 1992, PG-13, ★ 1994

Chuck Berry Hail! Hail! Rock 'n' Roll, 1987, PG, ★★★★ 1998
Chungking Express, 1996, PG-13, ★★★ 1999
Cinderella, 1950, G, ★★★ 1997
Cinema Paradiso, 1989, NR, ★★★½ 1998
Circle of Friends, 1995, PG-13, ★★★½ 1998
Citizen Kane, 1941, NR, ★★★★ 1998
City Hall, 1996, R, ★★½ 1999
City Heat, 1984, PG, ½★ 1991
City of Hope, 1991, R, ★★★★ 1998
City of Joy, 1992, PG-13, ★★★ 1995
City of Lost Children, 1995, R, ★★★ 1998
City of Women, 1981, R, ★★½ 1991
City Slickers, 1991, PG-13, ★★★½ 1998
City Slickers II: The Legend of Curly's Gold, 1994, PG-13, ★★ 1995
Claire's Knee, 1971, PG, ★★★★ 1998
Clan of the Cave Bear, 1985, R, ★½ 1989
Clash of the Titans, 1981, PG, ★★★½ 1998
Class Action, 1991, R, ★★★ 1995
Class of 1984, The, 1982, R, ★★★½ 1995
Class of 1999, 1990, R, ★★ 1992
Clean and Sober, 1988, R, ★★★½ 1998
Clean, Shaven, 1995, NR, ★★★½ 1998
Clerks, 1994, R, ★★★ 1998
Client, The, 1994, PG-13, ★★½ 1998
Cliffhanger, 1993, R, ★★★ 1998
Clifford, 1994, PG, ½★ 1995
Clockers, 1995, R, ★★★½ 1998
Close Encounters of the Third Kind: The Special Edition, 1980, PG, ★★★★ 1998
Close to Eden, 1992, NR, ★★★ 1998
Clueless, 1995, PG-13, ★★★½ 1998
Coal Miner's Daughter, 1980, PG, ★★★ 1998
Cobb, 1994, R, ★★ 1996
Coca-Cola Kid, The, 1985, NR, ★★★ 1987
Cocktail, 1988, R, ★★ 1993
Cocoon, 1985, PG-13, ★★★ 1998
Cocoon: The Return, 1988, PG, ★★½ 1997
Code of Silence, 1985, R, ★★★½ 1998
Cold Comfort Farm, 1995, PG, ★★★ 1999
Cold Fever, 1996, NR, ★★★ 1999
Color of Money, The, 1986, R, ★★½ 1998
Color of Night, 1994, R, ★½ 1996
Color Purple, The, 1985, PG-13, ★★★★ 1998
Colors, 1988, R, ★★★ 1998
Coma, 1978, PG, ★★★ 1995
Come Back to the 5 & Dime, Jimmy Dean, Jimmy Dean, 1982, PG, ★★★ 1998
Come See the Paradise, 1991, R, ★★★ 1998
Comfort of Strangers, The, 1991, R, ★★½ 1994
Coming Home, 1978, R, ★★★★ 1998
Commitments, The, 1991, R, ★★★ 1998
Company of Wolves, The, 1985, R, ★★★ 1987
Competition, The, 1981, PG, ★★★ 1995
Compromising Positions, 1985, R, ★★ 1987
Con Air, 1997, R, ★★★ 1998
Conan the Barbarian, 1982, R, ★★★ 1998
Conan the Destroyer, 1984, PG, ★★★ 1998
Coneheads, 1993, PG, ★½ 1995
Congo, 1995, PG-13, ★★★ 1998
Contact, 1997, PG, ★★★½ 1998
Continental Divide, 1981, PG, ★★★ 1998
Conversation, The, 1974, PG, ★★★★ 1998
Cookie, 1989, R, ★★ 1992
Cook, the Thief, His Wife and Her Lover, The, 1990, NR, ★★★★ 1998
Cool Runnings, 1993, PG, ★★½ 1995
Cop, 1988, R, ★★★ 1998
Cop and a Half, 1993, PG, ★★★ 1995
Cops and Robbersons, 1994, PG, ★★ 1995
Copycat, 1995, R, ★★★½ 1998
Corrina, Corrina, 1994, PG, ★★½ 1997
Cotton Club, The, 1984, R, ★★★★ 1998
Country, 1984, PG, ★★★½ 1998
Country Life, 1995, PG-13, ★★★½ 1998
Coupe de Ville, 1990, PG-13, ★½ 1992
Cousins, 1989, PG-13, ★★★½ 1998
Cowboys, The, 1972, PG, ★★½ 1991
Craft, The, 1996, R, ★★ 1999
Crash, 1997, NC-17, ★★★½ 1998
Crazy People, 1990, R, ★★ 1992
Creator, 1985, R, ★★½ 1987
Creepshow, 1982, R, ★★★ 1995
Cries and Whispers, 1973, R, ★★★★ 1998
Crimes and Misdemeanors, 1989, PG-13, ★★★★ 1998
Crimes of Passion, 1984, R, ★½ 1994
Crimson Tide, 1995, R, ★★★½ 1998
Critters, 1986, PG-13, ★★★ 1998
Crocodile Dundee, 1986, PG-13, ★★ 1998
Cronos, 1994, NR, ★★★ 1998
Crooklyn, 1994, PG-13, ★★★½ 1998
Crossing Delancey, 1988, PG, ★★½ 1995
Crossing Guard, The, 1995, R, ★★½ 1997
Cross My Heart, 1987, R, ★★½ 1989
Crossover Dreams, 1985, PG-13, ★★★ 1995
Crossroads, 1985, R, ★★★½ 1998
Crow, The, 1994, R, ★★★½ 1998
Crucible, The, 1996, PG-13, ★★ 1999
Crumb, 1995, R, ★★★★ 1997
Crusoe, 1989, PG-13, ★★★½ 1995
Cry-Baby, 1990, PG-13, ★★★ 1998
Cry Freedom, 1987, PG, ★★½ 1997

Crying Game, The, 1992, R, ★★★★ 1998
Cry in the Dark, A, 1988, PG-13, ★★★ 1998
Curdled, 1996, R, ★★ 1999
Cure, The, 1995, PG-13, ★★½ 1996
Curly Sue, 1991, PG, ★★★ 1998
Curse of the Pink Panther, 1983, PG, ★½ 1986
Cutthroat Island, 1995, PG-13, ★★★ 1998
Cutting Edge, The, 1992, PG, ★★½ 1994
Cyborg, 1989, R, ★ 1992
Cyrano de Bergerac, 1990, PG, ★★★½ 1998

D

Dad, 1989, PG, ★★ 1993
Daddy Nostalgia, 1991, PG, ★★★½ 1998
Dadetown, 1996, NR, ★★ 1998
Damage, 1993, R, ★★★★ 1998
Dances With Wolves, 1990, PG-13, ★★★★ 1998
Dance With a Stranger, 1985, R, ★★★★ 1998
Dangerous Ground, 1997, R, ★★ 1998
Dangerous Liaisons, 1988, R, ★★★ 1998
Dangerous Minds, 1995, R, ★½ 1997
Daniel, 1983, R, ★★½ 1987
Dante's Peak, 1997, PG-13, ★★½ 1998
Dark Crystal, The, 1982, PG, ★★½ 1991
Dark Eyes, 1987, NR, ★★★½ 1998
Dark Half, The, 1993, R, ★★ 1994
Dark Obsession, 1991, NC-17, ★★★ 1998
D.A.R.Y.L., 1985, PG, ★★★ 1998
Date with an Angel, 1987, PG, ★ 1989
Daughters of the Dust, 1992, NR, ★★★ 1998
Dave, 1993, PG-13, ★★★½ 1998
Dawn of the Dead, 1979, R, ★★★★ 1998
Day After Trinity, The, 1980, NR, ★★★★ 1998
Day for Night, 1974, PG, ★★★★ 1998
Daylight, 1996, PG-13, ★★ 1999
Day of the Dead, 1985, R, ★½ 1992
Day of the Jackal, The, 1973, PG, ★★★★ 1998
Days of Heaven, 1978, PG, ★★★★ 1998
Days of Thunder, 1990, PG-13, ★★★ 1998
Dazed and Confused, 1993, R, ★★★ 1998
D.C. Cab, 1983, R, ★★ 1986
Dead, The, 1987, PG, ★★★ 1998
Dead Again, 1991, R, ★★★★ 1998
Dead Calm, 1989, R, ★★★ 1998
Dead Man Walking, 1995, R, ★★★★ 1999
Dead of Winter, 1987, PG-13, ★★½ 1993
Dead Poets Society, 1989, PG, ★★ 1998
Dead Pool, The, 1988, R, ★★★½ 1998
Dead Presidents, 1995, R, ★★½ 1998
Dead Ringers, 1988, R, ★★½ 1993
Dead Zone, The, 1983, R, ★★★½ 1998
Dear America: Letters Home from Vietnam, 1988, PG-13, ★★★★ 1998
Dear God, 1996, PG, ★ 1999
Death and the Maiden, 1995, R, ★★★ 1998
Death in Venice, 1971, PG, ★★½ 1994
Deathtrap, 1982, R, ★★★ 1998
Death Wish, 1974, R, ★★★ 1998
Death Wish II, 1982, R, no stars 1993
Death Wish 3, 1985, R, ★ 1993
Deceived, 1991, PG-13, ★★ 1993
Deep Cover, 1992, R, ★★★½ 1998
Deer Hunter, The, 1978, R, ★★★★ 1998
Defence of the Realm, 1987, PG, ★★★ 1998
Defending Your Life, 1991, PG, ★★★½ 1998
Delta Force, The, 1985, R, ★★★ 1998
Denise Calls Up, 1996, PG-13, ★★ 1999
Dennis the Menace, 1993, PG, ★★½ 1995
Desert Hearts, 1985, R, ★★½ 1988
Desperado, 1995, R, ★★ 1997
Desperate Hours, 1990, R, ★★ 1992
Desperately Seeking Susan, 1985, PG-13, ★★★ 1998
Devil in a Blue Dress, 1995, R, ★★★ 1998
Devil's Own, The, 1997, R, ★★½ 1998
Diabolique, 1955, NR, ★★★½ 1999
Diabolique, 1995, R, ★★ 1997
Diamonds Are Forever, 1971, PG, ★★★ 1998
Diary of a Mad Housewife, 1970, R, ★★★ 1996
Dice Rules, 1991, NC-17, no stars 1992
Dick Tracy, 1990, PG, ★★★★ 1998
Die Hard, 1988, R, ★★ 1998
Die Hard 2: Die Harder, 1990, R, ★★★½ 1998
Die Hard With a Vengeance, 1995, R, ★★★ 1998
Dim Sum, 1985, PG, ★★★ 1998
Diner, 1982, R, ★★★½ 1998
Dirty Dancing, 1987, PG-13, ★ 1995
Dirty Harry, 1971, R, ★★★ 1998
Dirty Rotten Scoundrels, 1988, PG, ★★★ 1998
Disclosure, 1994, R, ★★ 1996
Discreet Charm of the Bourgeoisie, The, 1972, PG, ★★★★ 1998
Distinguished Gentleman, The, 1992, R, ★★ 1994
Diva, 1981, R, ★★★★ 1998
Divine Madness, 1980, R, ★★★½ 1998
D.O.A., 1988, R, ★★★ 1998
Doc Hollywood, 1991, PG-13, ★★★ 1998
Doctor, The, 1991, PG-13, ★★★½ 1998
Doctor Zhivago, 1965, PG-13, ★★★ 1997

E

Explorers, 1985, PG, ★★ 1987
Exposed, 1983, R, ★★★½ 1998
Exterminator, The, 1980, R, no stars 1990
Extreme Prejudice, 1987, R, ★★★ 1998
Extremities, 1986, R, ★ 1989
Eye for an Eye, 1996, R, ★ 1999
Eye of the Needle, 1981, R, ★★★ 1998
Eyewitness, 1981, R, ★★★ 1998

F

Fabulous Baker Boys, The, 1989, R, ★★★½ 1998
Face/Off, 1997, R, ★★★ 1998
Fade to Black, 1980, R, ★★½ 1991
Faithful, 1996, R, ★★½ 1999
Falcon and the Snowman, The, 1985, R, ★★★★ 1998
Falling Down, 1993, R, ★★★ 1998
Falling from Grace, 1992, PG-13, ★★★★ 1998
Falling in Love, 1984, PG-13, ★★ 1987
Fame, 1980, R, ★★★½ 1998
Family Business, 1989, R, ★★★ 1998
Fanny and Alexander, 1983, R, ★★★★ 1998
Fantasia, 1940, G, ★★★★ 1997
Far and Away, 1992, PG-13, ★★ 1994
Farewell My Concubine, 1993, R, ★★★★ 1998
Farewell, My Lovely, 1975, R, ★★★★ 1998
Farewell to the King, 1989, PG, ★★★ 1998
Fargo, 1995, R, ★★★★ 1999
Farinelli, 1995, R, ★★ 1996
Far Off Place, A, 1993, PG, ★★ 1994
Faster Pussycat! Kill! Kill!, 1965, NR, ★★★ 1997
Fast Times at Ridgemont High, 1982, R, ★ 1994
Fatal Attraction, 1987, R, ★★½ 1998
Fatal Instinct, 1993, PG-13, ★½ 1995
Father of the Bride, 1991, PG, ★★★ 1998
Father of the Bride Part II, 1995, PG, ★★½ 1997
Fat Man and Little Boy, 1989, PG-13, ★½ 1992
Fearless, 1993, R, ★★★ 1998
Fear of a Black Hat, 1994, R, ★★★ 1998
Feeling Minnesota, 1996, PG-13, ★★★ 1999
Fellini's 8½, 1963, NR, ★★★★ 1997
Fellini's Roma, 1973, R, ★★★★ 1998
Female Perversions, 1997, R, ★★★½ 1998
Ferris Bueller's Day Off, 1986, PG-13, ★★★ 1998
Few Good Men, A, 1992, R, ★★½ 1997
Field, The, 1991, PG-13, ★ 1993
Field of Dreams, 1989, PG, ★★★★ 1998
Fiendish Plot of Dr. Fu Manchu, The, 1980, PG, ★ 1986
Fifth Element, The, PG-13, ★★★ 1998
52 Pick-Up, 1986, R, ★★★½ 1997
Final Analysis, 1992, R, ★★½ 1995
Final Conflict, The (Omen III), 1981, R, ★★ 1987
Final Countdown, The, 1980, PG, ★★ 1988
Firefox, 1982, PG, ★★★½ 1998
Fire in the Sky, 1993, PG-13, ★★½ 1994
Firestarter, 1984, R, ★★ 1987
Firm, The, 1993, R, ★★★ 1998
First Blood, 1982, R, ★★★ 1998
Firstborn, 1984, PG, ★★ 1987
First Deadly Sin, The, 1980, R, ★★★ 1986
First Knight, 1995, PG-13, ★★ 1997
First Wives Club, The, 1996, PG, ★★ 1999
Fish Called Wanda, A, 1988, R, ★★★★ 1998
Fisher King, The, 1991, R, ★★ 1994
Fitzcarraldo, 1982, PG, ★★★★ 1998
Five Easy Pieces, 1970, R, ★★★★ 1998
Five Heartbeats, The, 1991, R, ★★★ 1998
Flamingo Kid, The, 1984, PG-13, ★★★½ 1998
Flashback, 1990, R, ★★★ 1998
Flashdance, 1983, R, ★½ 1994
Flash Gordon, 1980, PG, ★★½ 1988
Flash of Green, A, 1985, NR, ★★★ 1987
Flatliners, 1990, R, ★★★ 1998
Fled, 1996, R, ★★ 1999
Flesh and Bone, 1993, R, ★★ 1995
Fletch, 1985, PG, ★★½ 1995
Fletch Lives, 1989, PG, ★½ 1995
Flintstones, The, 1994, PG, ★★½ 1997
Flipper, 1995, PG, ★★ 1999
Flirt, 1996, NR, ★★ 1999
Flirting, 1992, NR, ★★★★ 1998
Flower of My Secret, The, 1996, R, ★½ 1999
Fly Away Home, 1996, PG, ★★★½ 1999
Fog, The, 1980, R, ★★ 1988
Fool for Love, 1985, R, ★★★ 1998
Fools Rush In, 1997, PG-13, ★★★ 1998
Footloose, 1984, PG, ★½ 1995
Forever Young, 1992, PG, ★★½ 1994
Forget Paris, 1995, PG-13, ★★★½ 1998
For Keeps, 1988, PG-13, ★★★ 1998
For Love or Money, 1993, PG, ★★ 1995
Formula, The, 1980, R, ★★ 1987
For Queen and Country, 1989, R, ★★ 1992

Forrest Gump, 1994, PG-13, ★★★★ 1998
Fort Apache, The Bronx, 1981, R, ★★ 1987
For the Boys, 1991, R, ★★ 1993
48 HRS, 1982, R, ★★★½ 1998
For Your Eyes Only, 1981, PG, ★★ 1998
Four Friends, 1981, R, ★★★★ 1998
Four Rooms, 1995, R, ★★ 1998
1492: Conquest of Paradise, 1992, PG-13, ★★★ 1996
Fourth Protocol, The, 1987, R, ★★★½ 1998
Fourth War, The, 1990, R, ★★★ 1998
Four Weddings and a Funeral, 1994, R, ★★★½ 1998
Fox and the Hound, The, 1981, G, ★★★ 1998
Foxes, 1980, R, ★★★ 1998
Frances, 1983, R, ★★★½ 1998
Frankie and Johnny, 1991, R, ★★½ 1995
Frankie Starlight, 1995, R, ★★★½ 1998
Frantic, 1988, R, ★★★ 1998
Fraternity Vacation, 1985, R, ★ 1990
Freeway, 1997, R, ★★★½ 1998
Free Willy, 1993, PG, ★★★½ 1998
French Kiss, 1995, PG-13, ★★ 1997
French Lieutenant's Woman, The, 1981, R, ★★★½ 1998
Frenzy, 1972, R, ★★★★ 1998
Fresh, 1994, R, ★★★★ 1998
Freshman, The, 1990, PG, ★★★½ 1998
Friday the 13th, Part II, 1981, R, ½★ 1993
Fried Green Tomatoes, 1992, PG-13, ★★★ 1998
Friends of Eddie Coyle, The, 1973, R, ★★★★ 1998
Frighteners, The, 1996, R, ★ 1999
Fright Night, 1985, R, ★★★ 1996
Fringe Dwellers, The, 1987, PG-13, ★★★½ 1996
From Dusk Till Dawn, 1996, R, ★★★ 1999
From the Journals of Jean Seberg, 1996, NR, ★★★½ 1999
Frozen Assets, 1992, PG-13, no stars 1994
Fugitive, The, 1993, PG-13, ★★★★ 1998
Full Metal Jacket, 1987, R, ★★½ 1998
Full Moon on Blue Water, 1988, R, ★★ 1992
Funeral, The, 1996, R, ★★★ 1999
Funny Farm, 1988, PG, ★★★½ 1998
F/X, 1985, R, ★★★½ 1998
F/X 2: The Deadly Art of Illusion, 1991, PG-13, ★★ 1993

G

Gambler, The, 1974, R, ★★★★ 1998
Gandhi, 1982, PG, ★★★★ 1998
Garden of the Finzi-Continis, The, 1971, R, ★★★★ 1998
Gates of Heaven, 1978, NR, ★★★★ 1998
Gauntlet, The, 1977, R, ★★★ 1998
George of the Jungle, 1997, PG, ★★★ 1998
George Stevens: A Filmmaker's Journey, 1985, PG, ★★★½ 1996
Georgia, 1996, R, ★★★½ 1999
Germinal, 1994, R, ★★★ 1998
Geronimo: An American Legend, 1993, PG-13, ★★★½ 1998
Getaway, The, 1994, R, ★ 1995
Get on the Bus, 1996, R, ★★★★ 1999
Getting Away With Murder, 1995, R, ★★ 1999
Getting Even with Dad, 1994, PG, ★★ 1995
Getting It Right, 1989, R, ★★★★ 1998
Gettysburg, 1993, PG, ★★★ 1998
Ghost, 1990, PG-13, ★★½ 1998
Ghost and the Darkness, The, 1996, R, ½★ 1999
Ghostbusters, 1984, PG, ★★★½ 1998
Ghost in the Shell, 1995, NR, ★★★ 1999
Ghosts of Mississippi, 1996, PG-13, ★★½ 1999
Ghost Story, 1981, R, ★★★ 1989
Ginger and Fred, 1986, PG-13, ★★ 1987
Girl in a Swing, The, 1989, R, ★★½ 1994
Girl 6, 1995, R, ★★ 1999
Girls Town, 1996, R, ★★★ 1999
Give My Regards to Broad Street, 1984, PG, ★ 1986
Gladiator, 1992, R, ★★★ 1996
Glengarry Glen Ross, 1992, R, ★★★½ 1998
Gloria, 1980, PG, ★★★ 1998
Glory, 1989, R, ★★★½ 1998
Go-Between, The, 1971, PG, ★★★½ 1998
Godfather, The, 1972, R, ★★★★ 1998
Godfather, Part II, The, 1974, R, ★★★ 1998
Godfather, Part III, The, 1990, R, ★★★½ 1998
Gods Must Be Crazy, The, 1984, PG, ★★★ 1998
Gods Must Be Crazy II, The, 1990, PG, ★★★ 1998
Godspell, 1973, G, ★★★★ 1998
Godzilla 1985, 1985, PG, ★ 1988
Golden Child, The, 1986, PG-13, ★★★ 1998
Goldeneye, 1995, PG-13, ★★★ 1998
Gone With the Wind, 1939, NR, ★★★★ 1997
Goodbye Girl, The, 1977, PG, ★★★ 1998

Heidi Fleiss, Hollywood Madam, 1995, NR, ★★★★ 1999
Hellbound: Hellraiser II, 1988, R, ½★ 1990
Hell Night, 1981, R, ★ 1986
Henry and June, 1990, NC-17, ★★★ 1998
Henry V, 1989, NR, ★★★½ 1998
Henry: Portrait of a Serial Killer, 1986, NR, ★★★½ 1998
Her Alibi, 1989, PG, ½★ 1993
Hercules, 1997, G, ★★★½ 1998
Hero, 1992, PG-13, ★★ 1994
Hero and the Terror, 1987, R, ★★ 1991
Hidden, The, 1987, R, ★★★ 1996
Hidden Agenda, 1990, R, ★★★ 1998
Hidden Fortress, The, 1958, NR, ★★★★ 1997
Hideaway, 1995, R, ★★★ 1998
High Anxiety, 1978, PG, ★★½ 1995
Higher Learning, 1995, R, ★★★ 1998
High Hopes, 1989, NR, ★★★★ 1998
Highlander 2: The Quickening, 1991, R, ½★ 1993
High Road to China, 1983, PG, ★★ 1987
High School High, 1996, PG-13, ★½ 1999
High Season, 1988, R, ★★★ 1998
History of the World—Part I, 1981, R, ★★ 1995
Hitcher, The, 1985, R, no stars 1990
Hocus Pocus, 1993, PG, ★ 1995
Hoffa, 1992, R, ★★★½ 1998
Hollywood Shuffle, 1987, R, ★★★ 1998
Homage, 1996, R, ★★½ 1999
Home Alone, 1990, PG, ★★½ 1998
Home Alone 2: Lost in New York, 1992, PG, ★★ 1995
Home and the World, The, 1986, NR, ★★★ 1987
Home of Our Own, A, 1993, PG, ★★★ 1998
Home of the Brave, 1986, NR, ★★★½ 1998
Homeward Bound: The Incredible Journey, 1993, G, ★★★ 1998
Homeward Bound II: Lost in San Francisco, 1996, G, ★★ 1999
Homicide, 1991, R, ★★★★ 1998
Honey, I Blew Up the Kid, 1992, PG, ★½ 1994
Honey, I Shrunk the Kids, 1989, PG, ★★ 1995
Honeymoon in Vegas, 1992, PG-13, ★★★½ 1998
Honkytonk Man, 1982, PG, ★★★ 1998
Hook, 1991, PG, ★★ 1994
Hoop Dreams, 1994, PG-13, ★★★★ 1998
Hoosiers, 1987, PG, ★★★★ 1998
Hope and Glory, 1987, PG-13, ★★★ 1998
Horseman on the Roof, The, 1995, R, ★★★ 1999
Hotel Terminus, 1988, NR, ★★★ 1996
Hot Shots, Part Deux, 1993, PG-13, ★★★ 1998
Hot Spot, The, 1990, R, ★★★ 1996
House Arrest, 1996, PG, ★ 1999
Household Saints, 1993, R, ★★★★ 1998
Housekeeping, 1988, PG, ★★★★ 1998
House of Games, 1987, R, ★★★★ 1998
House of the Spirits, The, 1994, R, ★★ 1995
House on Carroll Street, The, 1988, PG, ★★★ 1998
House Party, 1990, R, ★★★ 1998
House Party 2, 1991, R, ★★ 1993
Housesitter, 1992, PG, ★★★ 1998
Howards End, 1992, PG, ★★★★ 1998
Howling, The, 1981, R, ★★ 1992
Howling II, 1986, R, ★ 1987
How to Make an American Quilt, 1995, PG-13, ★★ 1997
Hudsucker Proxy, The, 1994, PG, ★★ 1997
Hugh Hefner: Once Upon a Time, 1992, NR, ★★★ 1996
Hunchback of Notre Dame, The, 1995, G, ★★★★ 1999
Hunger, The, 1983, R, ★½ 1991
Hunt for Red October, The, 1990, PG, ★★★½ 1998
Husbands and Wives, 1992, R, ★★★½ 1998
Hype!, 1997, NR, ★★★ 1998

I

Iceman, 1984, PG, ★★★★ 1998
Idolmaker, The, 1980, PG, ★★★ 1998
If Looks Could Kill, 1991, PG-13, ★★★ 1995
If Lucy Fell, 1996, R, ★ 1999
I Like It Like That, 1994, R, ★★★ 1998
Il Ladro di Bambini, 1993, NR, ★★★★ 1998
I'll Do Anything, 1994, PG-13, ★★★ 1998
I Love You to Death, 1990, R, ★★★ 1998
I, Madman, 1989, R, ★★★ 1996
Imaginary Crimes, 1994, PG, ★★★½ 1998
Imagine: John Lennon, 1988, R, ★★★ 1997
Immediate Family, 1989, PG-13, ★★ 1992
Immortal Beloved, 1995, R, ★★★½ 1998
I'm Not Rappaport, 1997, PG-13, ★★½ 1998
Impromptu, 1991, PG-13, ★★½ 1994
Impulse, 1990, R, ★★★ 1998
In Country, 1989, R, ★★★ 1998
Incredible Shrinking Woman, The, 1981, PG, ★★½ 1991

Incredibly True Adventure of Two Girls in Love, The, 1995, R, ★★★ 1998
Indecent Proposal, 1993, R, ★★★ 1998
Independence Day, 1996, PG-13, ★★½ 1999
Indiana Jones and the Last Crusade, 1989, PG-13, ★★★½ 1998
Indiana Jones and the Temple of Doom, 1984, PG, ★★★★ 1998
Indian in the Cupboard, 1995, PG, ★★ 1997
Indian Runner, The, 1991, R, ★★★ 1996
Indian Summer, 1993, PG-13, ★★★ 1998
Indochine, 1993, PG-13, ★★½ 1994
I Never Promised You a Rose Garden, 1977, R, ★★★ 1996
I Never Sang for My Father, 1971, PG, ★★★★ 1998
Infinity, 1996, PG, ★★★ 1999
Infra-Man, 1976, PG, ★★½ 1996
Inkwell, The, 1994, R, ★★★ 1995
Inner Circle, The, 1992, PG-13, ★★★ 1996
Innerspace, 1987, PG, ★★★ 1996
Innocent, The, 1995, R, ★★★ 1998
Innocent Blood, 1992, R, ★★ 1994
Innocent Man, An, 1989, R, ★½ 1993
Insignificance, 1985, R, ★★★ 1996
Interiors, 1978, PG, ★★★★ 1998
Intersection, 1994, R, ★ 1995
Interview With the Vampire, 1994, R, ★★★ 1998
Intervista, 1993, NR, ★★½ 1995
In the Line of Fire, 1993, R, ★★★½ 1998
In the Mood, 1987, PG-13, ★★★ 1995
In the Mouth of Madness, 1995, R, ★★ 1996
In the Name of the Father, 1994, R, ★★★ 1998
Into the Night, 1985, R, ★ 1987
Into the West, 1993, PG, ★★★½ 1998
Invasion USA, 1985, R, ½★ 1987
Inventing the Abbotts, 1997, R, ★★ 1998
I.Q., 1994, PG, ★★★½ 1998
Ironweed, 1988, R, ★★★ 1998
Iron Will, 1994, PG, ★★ 1995
Irreconcilable Differences, 1984, PG, ★★★½ 1995
Ishtar, 1987, PG-13, ½★ 1994
I Shot Andy Warhol, 1995, NR, ★★★½ 1999
I Spit on Your Grave, 1980, R, no stars 1990
It Could Happen to You, 1994, PG, ★★★½ 1998
It's All True, 1993, G, ★★★ 1997
It's a Wonderful Life, 1946, NR, ★★★★ 1997
It's My Party, 1995, R, ★★★ 1999
It Takes Two, 1995, PG, ★★ 1997
I've Heard the Mermaids Singing, 1987, NR, ★★★½ 1998
I Wanna Hold Your Hand, 1978, PG, ★★½ 1994

J

Jack, 1996, PG-13, ★½ 1999
Jack and Sarah, 1996, R, ★★★ 1999
Jackie Chan's First Strike, 1997, PG-13, ★★★ 1998
Jacknife, 1989, R, ★★★ 1996
Jack's Back, 1988, R, ★★★ 1996
Jack the Bear, 1993, PG-13, ★★★ 1996
Jacob's Ladder, 1990, R, ★★★½ 1998
Jacquot, 1993, NR, ★★★½ 1996
Jade, 1995, R, ★★ 1997
Jagged Edge, 1985, R, ★★★½ 1998
James and the Giant Peach, 1995, PG, ★★★ 1999
Jamon Jamon, 1994, NR, ★★★½ 1998
Jane Eyre, 1995, PG, ★★★½ 1999
Jason's Lyric, 1994, R, ★★★ 1998
Jaws, 1975, PG, ★★★★ 1998
Jaws the Revenge, 1987, PG-13, no stars 1993
Jazz Singer, The, 1980, PG, ★ 1987
Jean de Florette, 1987, PG, ★★★½ 1998
Jefferson in Paris, 1995, PG-13, ★★ 1997
Jeremiah Johnson, 1972, PG, ★★★ 1998
Jerry Maguire, 1996, R, ★★★ 1999
Jesus of Montreal, 1990, R, ★★★½ 1998
Jewel of the Nile, The, 1985, PG, ★★★ 1998
JFK, 1991, R, ★★★★ 1998
Jimmy Hollywood, 1994, R, ★★½ 1997
Jingle All the Way, 1996, PG, ★★½ 1999
Joe Vs. the Volcano, 1990, PG, ★★★½ 1998
Johnny Dangerously, 1984, PG-13, ★★ 1993
Johnny Got His Gun, 1971, R, ★★★★ 1998
Johnny Handsome, 1989, R, ★★★½ 1998
Johnny Mnemonic, 1995, R, ★★ 1996
johns, 1997, R, ★★★ 1998
Jo Jo Dancer, Your Life Is Calling, 1986, R, ★★★ 1998
Josh and S.A.M., 1993, PG-13, ★★ 1995
Journey of August King, The, 1996, PG-13, ★½ 1999
Journey of Hope, 1990, NR, ★★½ 1995
Journey of Natty Gann, The, 1985, PG, ★★★ 1998
Joy Luck Club, The, 1993, R, ★★★★ 1998
Jude, 1996, R, ★★★ 1999
Judge Dredd, 1995, R, ★★ 1996
Ju Dou, 1991, NR, ★★★½ 1998

M

Madness of King George, The, 1995, NR, ★★★★ 1998
Major Payne, 1995, PG-13, ★★★ 1998
Making Love, 1982, R, ★★ 1988
Making Mr. Right, 1987, PG-13, ★★★½ 1998
Malcolm X, 1992, PG-13, ★★★★ 1998
Malice, 1993, R, ★★ 1995
Mambo Kings, The, 1992, R, ★★★½ 1998
Manchurian Candidate, The, 1962, PG-13, ★★★★ 1997
Manhattan, 1979, R, ★★★½ 1998
Manhattan Murder Mystery, 1993, PG, ★★★ 1998
Manhattan Project, The, 1986, PG-13, ★★★★ 1998
Man in the Moon, The, 1991, PG-13, ★★★★ 1998
Mannequin, 1987, PG, ½★ 1990
Manny and Lo, 1996, R, ★★★½ 1999
Man of Iron, 1980, NR, ★★★★ 1998
Manon of the Spring, 1987, PG, ★★★★ 1998
Man Who Loved Women, The, 1983, R, ★★ 1988
Man Who Would Be King, The, 1975, PG, ★★★★ 1998
Man Without a Face, The, 1993, PG-13, ★★★ 1998
Man With Two Brains, The, 1983, R, ★★ 1995
Map of the Human Heart, 1993, R, ★★★★ 1998
Margaret's Museum, 1997, R, ★★★½ 1998
Marie, 1985, PG-13, ★★★ 1987
Marriage of Maria Braun, The, 1979, R, ★★★★ 1998
Marrying Man, The, 1991, R, ★★★ 1995
Mars Attacks!, 1996, PG-13, ★★ 1999
Marvin's Room, 1997, PG-13, ★★★½ 1998
Mary Reilly, 1996, R, ★★★ 1998
Mary Shelley's Frankenstein, 1994, R, ★★½ 1997
M*A*S*H, 1970, R, ★★★★ 1998
Mask, 1985, PG-13, ★★★½ 1998
Mask, The, 1994, PG-13, ★★★ 1998
Masquerade, 1988, R, ★★★ 1998
Matilda, 1996, PG, ★★★ 1999
Matinee, 1993, PG, ★★★½ 1998
Maurice, 1987, R, ★★★ 1998
Maverick, 1994, PG, ★★★ 1998
Max Dugan Returns, 1983, PG, ★★½ 1986
Maxie, 1985, PG, 1/2★ 1987
Maybe . . . Maybe Not, 1996, R, ★★★ 1999
May Fools, 1990, R, ★★★ 1998
M. Butterfly, 1993, R, ★★½ 1995
McCabe and Mrs. Miller, 1971, R, ★★★★ 1998
Me and My Matchmaker, 1996, NR, ★★★ 1999
Mean Streets, 1974, R, ★★★★ 1998
Medicine Man, The, 1992, PG-13, ★½ 1994
Meeting Venus, 1991, PG-13, ★★★ 1995
Melvin and Howard, 1980, R, ★★★½ 1998
Memoirs of an Invisible Man, 1992, PG-13, ★★½ 1994
Memories of Me, 1988, PG-13, ★★★½ 1998
Memphis Belle, 1990, PG-13, ★★★ 1998
Menace II Society, 1993, R, ★★★★ 1998
Men Don't Leave, 1990, PG-13, ★★ 1991
Men in Black, 1997, PG-13, ★★★ 1998
Men of Respect, 1991, R, ★ 1992
Mephisto, 1981, NR, ★★★★ 1998
Mermaids, 1990, PG-13, ★★★ 1998
Merry Christmas, Mr. Lawrence, 1983, R, ★★½ 1991
Meteor Man, The, 1993, PG, ★★½ 1995
Metro, 1997, R, ★★★ 1998
Metropolis, 1926, NR, ★★★★ 1997
Metropolitan, 1990, PG-13, ★★★½ 1998
Miami Blues, 1990, R, ★★ 1993
Miami Rhapsody, 1995, PG-13, ★★★ 1998
Michael, 1996, PG, ★★★ 1999
Michael Collins, 1996, R, ★★★ 1999
Micki & Maude, 1984, PG-13, ★★★★ 1998
Microcosmos, 1997, G, ★★★★ 1998
Midnight Clear, A, 1992, R, ★★★ 1998
Midnight Cowboy, 1969, R, ★★★ 1997
Midnight Run, 1988, R, ★★★½ 1998
Midsummer Night's Sex Comedy, A, 1982, PG, ★★ 1997
Mighty Aphrodite, 1995, R, ★★★½ 1998
Mighty Ducks, The, 1992, PG, ★★ 1994
Mighty Morphin Power Rangers™: The Movie, 1995, PG, ½★ 1997
Mighty Quinn, The, 1989, R, ★★★★ 1998
Milagro Beanfield War, The, 1988, R, ★★½ 1993
Miles From Home, 1988, R, ★★★ 1998
Milk Money, 1994, PG-13, ★ 1996
Miller's Crossing, 1990, R, ★★★ 1998
Miracle Mile, 1989, R, ★★★ 1998
Miracle on 34th Street, 1994, PG, ★★★ 1998
Mirror Has Two Faces, The, 1996, PG-13, ★★★ 1999
Misery, 1990, R, ★★★ 1998
Mishima, 1985, R, ★★★★ 1998

Miss Firecracker, 1989, PG, ★★★½ 1998
Missing, 1982, R, ★★★ 1998
Mission, The, 1986, PG, ★★½ 1993
Mission Impossible, 1996, PG-13, ★★★ 1999
Mississippi Burning, 1988, R, ★★★★ 1998
Mississippi Masala, 1992, R, ★★★½ 1998
Mo' Better Blues, 1990, R, ★★★ 1998
Moderns, The, 1988, NR, ★★★ 1998
Mommie Dearest, 1981, PG, ★ 1998
Mona Lisa, 1986, R, ★★★★ 1998
Money Pit, The, 1986, PG-13, ★ 1991
Money Train, 1995, R, ★½ 1997
Monkey Trouble, 1994, PG, ★★★ 1998
Monsieur Hire, 1990, PG-13, ★★★★ 1998
Monsignor, 1982, R, ★ 1987
Month by the Lake, A, 1995, PG, ★★★½ 1998
Monty Python's Meaning of Life, 1983, R, ★★½ 1995
Moonlighting, 1982, PG, ★★★★ 1998
Moon Over Parador, 1988, PG-13, ★★ 1993
Moonstruck, 1987, PG, ★★★★ 1998
Morning After, The, 1986, R, ★★★ 1996
Mortal Thoughts, 1991, R, ★★★ 1998
Moscow on the Hudson, 1984, R, ★★★★ 1998
Mosquito Coast, The, 1986, PG, ★★ 1993
Motel Hell, 1980, R, ★★★ 1996
Mother, 1997, PG-13, ★★★½ 1998
Mother Night, 1996, R, ★★½ 1999
Mother's Day, 1980, R, no stars 1991
Mountains of the Moon, 1990, R, ★★★½ 1998
Mr. and Mrs. Bridge, 1991, PG-13, ★★★★ 1998
Mr. Baseball, 1992, PG-13, ★★★ 1998
Mr. Destiny, 1990, PG-13, ★★ 1992
Mr. Holland's Opus, 1996, PG, ★★★½ 1999
Mister Johnson, 1991, PG-13, ★★★ 1998
Mr. Jones, 1993, R, ★★★ 1998
Mr. Mom, 1983, PG, ★★ 1987
Mr. Saturday Night, 1992, R, ★★★ 1995
Mr. Wonderful, 1993, PG-13, ★½ 1995
Mrs. Doubtfire, 1993, PG-13, ★★½ 1998
Mrs. Parker and the Vicious Circle, 1994, R, ★★★½ 1998
Mrs. Winterbourne, 1996, PG-13, ★★½ 1999
Much Ado About Nothing, 1993, PG-13, ★★★ 1998
Mulholland Falls, 1996, R, ★★★½ 1999
Multiplicity, 1996, PG-13, ★★½ 1999
Muppet Christmas Carol, The, 1992, G, ★★★ 1998
Muppet Movie, The, 1979, G, ★★★½ 1998
Muppets Take Manhattan, The, 1984, G, ★★★ 1998
Muppet Treasure Island, 1996, G, ★★½ 1999
Murder at 1600, 1997, R, ★★½ 1998
Murder in the First, 1995, R, ★★ 1996
Murder on the Orient Express, 1974, PG, ★★★ 1998
Muriel's Wedding, 1995, R, ★★★½ 1998
Murphy's Romance, 1985, PG-13, ★★★ 1998
Music Box, 1990, PG-13, ★★ 1993
Music Lovers, The, 1971, R, ★★ 1993
Music of Chance, The, 1993, NR, ★★★ 1998
My Beautiful Laundrette, 1986, R, ★★★ 1998
My Best Friend's Wedding, 1997, PG-13, ★★★ 1998
My Bodyguard, 1980, PG, ★★★½ 1998
My Brilliant Career, 1980, NR, ★★★½ 1998
My Cousin Vinny, 1992, R, ★★½ 1998
My Dinner with André, 1981, NR, ★★★★ 1998
My Fair Lady, 1964, G, ★★★★ 1997
My Family, 1995, R, ★★★★ 1998
My Father's Glory, 1991, G, ★★★★ 1998
My Father the Hero, 1994, PG, ★★ 1995
My Favorite Season, 1995, NR, ★★★ 1999
My Favorite Year, 1982, PG, ★★★½ 1998
My Fellow Americans, 1996, PG-13, ★★½ 1999
My Girl, 1991, PG, ★★★½ 1998
My Girl 2, 1994, PG, ★★ 1995
My Heroes Have Always Been Cowboys, 1991, PG, ★★ 1992
My Left Foot, 1989, R, ★★★★ 1998
My Life, 1993, PG-13, ★★½ 1995
My Mother's Castle, 1991, PG, ★★★★ 1998
My Own Private Idaho, 1991, R, ★★★½ 1998
My Stepmother Is an Alien, 1988, PG-13, ★★ 1993
Mystery Science Theater 3000: The Movie, 1996, PG-13, ★★★ 1999
Mystery Train, 1990, R, ★★★½ 1998
Mystic Pizza, 1988, R, ★★★½ 1998
My Tutor, 1983, R, ★★★ 1986

N

Nadine, 1987, PG, ★★½ 1993
Naked, 1994, NR, ★★★★ 1998
Naked Gun, The, 1988, PG-13, ★★★½ 1998
Naked Gun 2½: The Smell of Fear, The, 1991, PG-13, ★★★ 1998
Naked Gun 33⅓: The Final Insult, 1994, PG-13, ★★★ 1998

O

Only When I Laugh, 1981, R, ★ 1987
Only You, 1994, PG, ★★★½ 1998
On the Edge, 1986, PG-13, ★★★½ 1989
On the Right Track, 1981, PG, ★★½ 1986
On the Road Again, 1980, PG, ★★★ 1998
Opening Night, 1978, PG-13, ★★★ 1998
Operation Condor, 1997, PG-13, ★★★ 1998
Ordinary People, 1980, R, ★★★★ 1998
Orlando, 1993, PG-13, ★★★½ 1998
Orphans, 1987, R, ★★½ 1993
Othello, 1952, NR, ★★★ 1997
Othello, 1995, R, ★★ 1998
Other People's Money, 1991, PG-13, ★★★½ 1998
Outbreak, 1995, R, ★★★½ 1998
Outlaw Josey Wales, The, 1976, PG, ★★★ 1998
Out of Africa, 1985, PG, ★★★★ 1998
Out of the Blue, 1982, R, ★★★½ 1998
Outrageous Fortune, 1987, R, ★★ 1993
Out to Sea, 1997, PG-13, ★★★ 1998
Overboard, 1987, PG, ★★★ 1995

P

Pacific Heights, 1990, R, ★★ 1993
Package, The, 1989, R, ★★★ 1998
Pale Rider, 1985, R, ★★★ 1998
Pallbearer, The, 1996, PG-13, ★★★ 1999
Palookaville, 1996, R, ★★★ 1999
Panther, 1995, R, ★★½ 1996
Paper, The, 1994, R, ★★★½ 1998
Paper Chase, The, 1973, PG, ★★★★ 1998
Paperhouse, 1989, PG-13, ★★★★ 1998
Paradise, 1991, PG-13, ★★ 1993
Paradise Road, 1997, R, ★★ 1998
Parenthood, 1989, PG-13, ★★★★ 1998
Parents, 1989, R, ★★ 1993
Paris Is Burning, 1991, NR, ★★★ 1996
Paris, Texas, 1984, R, ★★★★ 1998
Pascali's Island, 1988, PG-13, ★★★ 1998
Passage to India, A, 1984, PG, ★★★★ 1998
Passenger 57, 1992, R, ★★★ 1998
Passion Fish, 1993, R, ★★★★ 1998
Paternity, 1981, PG, ★★ 1986
Patriot Games, 1992, R, ★★½ 1995
Patton, 1970, PG, ★★★★ 1998
Patty Hearst, 1988, R, ★★★ 1998
PCU, 1994, PG-13, ★★ 1995
Peeping Tom, 1960, NR, ★★★½ 1997
Peggy Sue Got Married, 1986, PG-13, ★★★★ 1998
Pelican Brief, The, 1993, PG-13, ★★★ 1998
Pelle the Conqueror, 1988, NR, ★★★½ 1998
Pennies from Heaven, 1981, R, ★★ 1986
People vs. Larry Flynt, The, 1996, R, ★★★★ 1999
Perez Family, The, 1995, R, ★★★ 1998
Perfect, 1985, R, ★½ 1987
Perfect Candidate, A, 1996, NR, ★★★ 1999
Perfect World, A, 1993, PG-13, ★★★★ 1998
Performance, 1970, R, ★★½ 1993
Permanent Record, 1988, PG-13, ★★★★ 1998
Personal Best, 1982, R, ★★★★ 1998
Personal Services, 1987, R, ★★★½ 1998
Persuasion, 1995, PG, ★★★½ 1998
Peter's Friends, 1992, R, ★★★½ 1998
Phantom, The, 1996, PG, ★★★½ 1999
Phantom of Liberty, The, 1974, R, ★★★★ 1998
Phenomenon, 1996, PG, ★★★ 1999
Philadelphia, 1994, PG-13, ★★★½ 1998
Physical Evidence, 1989, R, ★★ 1992
Piano, The, 1993, R, ★★★★ 1998
Picnic, 1996, PG, ★★ 1999
Picnic at Hanging Rock, 1980, PG, ★★★½ 1998
Picture Bride, 1995, PG-13, ★★★ 1998
Pillow Book, The, 1997, NR, ★★★½ 1998
Pink Cadillac, 1989, PG-13, ★ 1992
Pink Flamingos, 1997, NC-17, no stars 1998
Pinocchio, 1940, G, ★★★★ 1997
Pirates of Penzance, 1983, G, ★★ 1986
Pixote, 1981, R, ★★★★ 1998
Places in the Heart, 1984, PG, ★★★ 1998
Planes, Trains and Automobiles, 1987, R, ★★★½ 1998
Platoon, 1986, R, ★★★★ 1998
Playboys, The, 1992, PG-13, ★★½ 1995
Player, The, 1992, R, ★★★★ 1998
Play It Again, Sam, 1972, PG, ★★★ 1998
Play Misty for Me, 1971, R, ★★★★ 1998
Plenty, 1985, R, ★★★½ 1998
Plot Against Harry, The, 1970, NR, ★★★½ 1998
Pocahontas, 1995, G, ★★★ 1998
Poetic Justice, 1993, R, ★★★ 1998
Point Break, 1991, R, ★★★½ 1998
Point of No Return, 1993, R, ★★★ 1998
Poison Ivy, 1992, R, ★★½ 1994
Police Academy, 1984, R, no stars 1994
Poltergeist, 1982, PG, ★★★ 1996
Pompatus of Love, The, 1996, NR, ★★ 1999
Ponette, 1997, NR, ★★★½ 1998

Q

R

Re-Animator, 1985, NR, ★★★ 1998
Red, 1994, R, ★★★★ 1998
Red Heat, 1988, R, ★★★ 1998
Red Rock West, 1994, R, ★★★½ 1998
Reds, 1981, PG, ★★★½ 1998
Red Sonja, 1985, PG-13, ★½ 1987
Ref, The, 1994, R, ★★★ 1998
Regarding Henry, 1991, PG-13, ★★ 1994
Relic, The, 1997, R, ★★★ 1998
Remains of the Day, 1993, PG, ★★★½ 1998
Renaissance Man, 1994, PG-13, ★½ 1995
Rendevous in Paris, 1996, NR, ★★★½ 1999
Repo Man, 1984, R, ★★★ 1998
Rescuers Down Under, The, 1990, G, ★★★ 1998
Reservoir Dogs, 1992, R, ★★½ 1998
Restoration, 1996, R, ★★★½ 1999
Return of the Jedi (Special Edition), 1997, PG, ★★★★ 1998
Return of the Living Dead, 1985, R, ★★★ 1987
Return of the Secaucus Seven, 1981, NR, ★★★ 1998
Return to Oz, 1985, PG, ★★ 1987
Revenge, 1990, R, ★★½ 1993
Revenge of the Nerds II, 1987, PG-13, ★½ 1990
Revenge of the Pink Panther, 1978, PG, ★★★ 1995
Reversal of Fortune, 1990, R, ★★★★ 1998
Rhapsody in August, 1992, PG, ★★★ 1998
Rhinestone, 1984, PG, ★ 1987
Rich and Famous, 1981, R, ★★½ 1987
Richard Pryor Here and Now, 1983, R, ★★★★ 1996
Richard Pryor Live on the Sunset Strip, 1982, R, ★★★★ 1996
Richard III, 1996, R, ★★★½ 1999
Richie Rich, 1994, PG, ★★★ 1998
Rich in Love, 1993, PG-13, ★★★ 1998
Rich Man's Wife, The, 1996, R, ★★½ 1999
Ridicule, 1996, R, ★★★½ 1999
Right Stuff, The, 1983, PG, ★★★★ 1998
Rising Sun, 1993, R, ★★ 1995
Risky Business, 1983, R, ★★★★ 1998
Rita, Sue and Bob Too, 1987, R, ★★★ 1996
River, The, 1985, PG-13, ★★ 1991
River Runs Through It, A, 1992, PG, ★★★½ 1998
River's Edge, 1987, R, ★★★½ 1998
River Wild, The, 1994, PG-13, ★★ 1997
Road House, 1989, R, ★★½ 1993
Road Warrior, The, 1982, R, ★★★½ 1998
Robin Hood: Prince of Thieves, 1991, PG-13, ★★ 1997
RoboCop, 1987, R, ★★★ 1998
RoboCop II, 1990, R, ★★ 1995
RoboCop 3, 1993, PG-13, ★½ 1995
Rob Roy, 1995, R, ★★★½ 1998
Rock, The, 1996, R, ★★★½ 1999
Rocketeer, The, 1991, PG-13, ★★★ 1998
Rocky, 1976, PG, ★★★★ 1998
Rocky II, 1979, PG, ★★★ 1998
Rocky IV, 1986, PG, ★★ 1993
Rocky V, 1990, PG-13, ★★ 1993
Rocky Horror Picture Show, The, 1975, R, ★★½ 1998
Roger & Me, 1989, R, ★★★★ 1998
Romancing the Stone, 1984, PG, ★★★ 1998
Romeo Is Bleeding, 1994, R, ★★ 1995
Romy and Michele's High School Reunion, 1997, R, ★★★ 1998
Rookie of the Year, 1993, PG, ★★★ 1996
Room with a View, A, 1985, PG-13, ★★★★ 1998
Rosalie Goes Shopping, 1990, PG, ★★★ 1998
Rose, The, 1979, R, ★★★ 1998
Rosewood, 1997, R, ★★★½ 1998
Rough Magic, 1997, PG-13, ★★ 1998
Roujin-Z, 1996, PG-13, ★★★ 1999
'Round Midnight, 1986, R, ★★★★ 1998
Roxanne, 1987, PG, ★★★½ 1998
Ruby, 1992, R, ★★ 1994
Ruby in Paradise, 1993, NR, ★★★★ 1998
Rudy, 1993, PG, ★★★½ 1998
Rudyard Kipling's The Jungle Book, 1994, PG, ★★★ 1998
Runaway Train, 1985, R, ★★★★ 1998
Running on Empty, 1988, PG-13, ★★★★ 1998
Running Scared, 1986, R, ★★★ 1995
Run of the Country, The, 1995, R, ★★½ 1997
Rush, 1992, R, ★★★ 1996
Russia House, The, 1990, R, ★★ 1995
Ruthless People, 1986, R, ★★★½ 1998

S

Sabrina, 1995, PG, ★★★½ 1998
Safe, 1995, NR, ★★★ 1998
Safe Passage, 1995, PG-13, ★★ 1996
Saint, The, 1997, PG-13, ★★ 1998
St. Elmo's Fire, 1985, R, ★½ 1987
Saint Jack, 1979, R, ★★★★ 1998
Saint of Fort Washington, The, 1994, R, ★★★ 1998

T

Title	Edition
Tequila Sunrise, 1988, R, ★★½	1994
Terminal Velocity, 1994, PG-13, ★★	1996
Terminator 2: Judgment Day, 1991, R, ★★★½	1998
Terms of Endearment, 1983, PG, ★★★★	1998
Terror Train, 1980, R, ★	1986
Tess, 1980, PG, ★★★★	1998
Testament, 1983, PG, ★★★★	1998
Tex, 1982, PG, ★★★★	1998
Texas Chainsaw Massacre, The, 1974, R, ★★	1995
Texasville, 1990, R, ★★★½	1998
That Obscure Object of Desire, 1977, R, ★★★★	1998
That Old Feeling, 1997, PG-13, ★	1998
That's Dancing!, 1985, PG, ★★★	1998
That's Entertainment!, 1974, G, ★★★★	1998
That's Entertainment! III, 1994, G, ★★★½	1998
That Thing You Do!, 1996, PG, ★★★	1999
That Was Then . . . This Is Now, 1985, R, ★★	1987
Thelma & Louise, 1991, R, ★★★½	1998
Thelonious Monk: Straight, No Chaser, 1989, PG-13, ★★★½	1998
Theremin: An Electronic Odyssey, 1995, NR, ★★★½	1998
Therese, 1987, NR, ★★★½	1996
They Call Me Bruce, 1983, PG, ★★	1986
They Shoot Horses, Don't They?, 1970, PG, ★★★★	1998
Thief, 1981, R, ★★★½	1996
Thieves Like Us, 1974, R, ★★★½	1998
Thin Blue Line, The, 1988, NR, ★★★½	1998
Thing, The, 1982, R, ★★½	1995
Things Change, 1988, PG, ★★★	1998
Things to Do in Denver When You're Dead, 1996, R, ★★½	1999
Thin Line Between Love and Hate, A, 1996, R, ★★½	1999
35 Up, 1992, NR, ★★★★	1998
36 Fillette, 1989, NR, ★★★½	1996
Thirty-two Short Films About Glenn Gould, 1994, NR, ★★★★	1998
This Boy's Life, 1993, R, ★★★½	1998
This Is Elvis, 1981, PG, ★★★½	1998
This Is My Life, 1992, PG-13, ★★★	1996
This Is Spinal Tap, 1984, R, ★★★★	1998
Three Men and a Baby, 1987, PG, ★★★	1998
Three Men and a Little Lady, 1990, PG, ★★	1994
Three Musketeers, The, 1993, PG, ★★	1995
3 Ninjas Kick Back, 1994, PG, ★★½	1995
Three of Hearts, 1993, R, ★★★	1996
Threesome, 1994, R, ★★★	1996
3 Women, 1977, PG, ★★★★	1998
Throw Momma from the Train, 1987, PG-13, ★★	1993
Thunderheart, 1992, R, ★★★½	1998
THX 1138, 1971, PG, ★★★	1998
Ticket to Heaven, 1981, R, ★★★½	1998
Tie Me Up! Tie Me Down!, 1990, NR, ★★	1993
Tiger's Tale, A, 1988, R, ★★	1989
Tightrope, 1984, R, ★★★½	1998
'Til There Was You, 1997, PG-13, ½★	1998
Tim Burton's Nightmare Before Christmas, 1993, PG, ★★★½	1998
Time Bandits, 1981, PG, ★★★	1998
Timecop, 1994, R, ★★	1997
Time of Destiny, A, 1988, PG-13, ★★★½	1998
Times of Harvey Milk, The, 1985, NR, ★★★½	1997
Tin Cup, 1996, R, ★★★	1999
Tin Drum, The, 1980, R, ★★	1988
Tin Men, 1987, R, ★★★	1998
To Be or Not To Be, 1983, R, ★★★	1998
To Die For, 1995, R, ★★★½	1998
To Gillian on Her 37th Birthday, 1996, PG-13, ★★	1999
Tokyo Story, 1953, G, ★★★★	1997
To Live, 1994, NR, ★★★½	1998
To Live and Die in L.A., 1985, R, ★★★★	1998
Tom and Viv, 1995, PG-13, ★★½	1996
Tommy, 1975, PG, ★★★	1998
Too Beautiful for You, 1990, R, ★★★½	1998
Tootsie, 1982, PG, ★★★★	1998
Topaz, 1970, PG, ★★★½	1998
Top Gun, 1986, PG, ★★½	1998
Top Secret!, 1984, R, ★★★½	1998
Torch Song Trilogy, 1988, R, ★★★½	1998
To Sleep With Anger, 1990, PG, ★★½	1993
Total Recall, 1990, R, ★★★½	1998
Toto le Heros, 1992, NR, ★★½	1994
Tough Enough, 1983, PG, ★★★	1986
Tough Guys Don't Dance, 1987, R, ★★½	1993
To Wong Foo, Thanks for Everything! Julie Newmar, 1995, PG-13, ★★½	1997
Toys, 1992, PG-13, ★★½	1994
Toy Story, 1995, G, ★★★½	1998
Track 29, 1988, R, ★★★	1996
Trading Places, 1983, R, ★★★½	1998
Trainspotting, 1996, R, ★★★	1998

Trees Lounge, 1996, R, ★★★½ 1999
Trespass, 1992, R, ★★½ 1994
Trial, The, 1994, NR, ★★½ 1996
Trial and Error, 1997, PG-13, ★★★ 1998
Tribute, 1981, PG, ★★★ 1996
Trip to Bountiful, The, 1985, PG, ★★★½ 1998
Tron, 1982, PG, ★★★★ 1998
Troop Beverly Hills, 1989, PG, ★★ 1994
Trouble in Mind, 1985, R, ★★★★ 1998
True Believer, 1989, R, ★★★ 1996
True Colors, 1991, R, ★★ 1994
True Confessions, 1981, R, ★★★ 1996
True Lies, 1994, R, ★★★ 1998
True Love, 1989, R, ★★★ 1996
True Romance, 1993, R, ★★★ 1998
True Stories, 1986, PG-13, ★★★½ 1998
Truly, Madly, Deeply, 1991, NR, ★★★ 1998
Trust, 1991, R, ★★ 1994
Truth About Cats and Dogs, The, 1996, PG-13, ★★★½ 1999
Truth or Dare, 1991, R, ★★★½ 1998
Tucker: The Man and His Dream, 1988, PG, ★★½ 1993
Tune in Tomorrow . . . , 1990, PG-13, ★★½ 1993
Turbulence, 1997, R, ★ 1998
Turk 182!, 1985, PG-13, ★ 1987
Turning Point, The, 1977, PG, ★★★½ 1998
Turtle Diary, 1985, PG-13, ★★★½ 1998
Twelfth Night, 1996, PG, ★★★½ 1999
12 Monkeys, 1996, R, ★★★ 1999
Twenty Bucks, 1994, R, ★★★ 1996
28 Up, 1985, NR, ★★★★ 1998
29th Street, 1991, R, ★★★ 1996
Twice in a Lifetime, 1985, R, ★★★½ 1998
Twilight Zone—the Movie, 1983, PG, ★★★½ 1998
Twins, 1988, PG, ★★★ 1998
Twin Town, 1997, NR, ★★ 1998
Twister, 1995, PG-13, ★★ 1999
Two Bits, 1996, PG-13, ★½ 1999
Two Deaths, 1996, R, ★ 1999
Two English Girls, 1972, R, ★★★★ 1998
Two Jakes, The, 1990, R, ★★★½ 1998
Two Much, 1996, PG-13, ★½ 1999
Two of a Kind, 1983, PG, ½★ 1986
2001: A Space Odyssey, 1968, G, ★★★★ 1997
2010, 1984, PG, ★★★ 1996

U

Uforia, 1985, PG, ★★★★ 1998
Ulee's Gold, 1997, R, ★★★½ 1998
Umbrellas of Cherbourg, The, 1996, NR, ★★★½ 1999
Unbearable Lightness of Being, The, 1988, R, ★★★★ 1998
Uncle Buck, 1989, PG, ★½ 1993
Un Coeur en Hiver, 1993, NR, ★★★½ 1998
Under Fire, 1983, R, ★★★½ 1998
Under Siege, 1992, R, ★★★ 1996
Under the Volcano, 1984, R, ★★★★ 1998
Unforgiven, 1992, R, ★★★★ 1998
Unhook the Stars, 1997, R, ★★★ 1998
Universal Soldier, 1992, R, ★★ 1994
Unlawful Entry, 1992, R, ★★★ 1996
Unmarried Woman, An, 1978, R, ★★★★ 1998
Unstrung Heroes, 1995, PG, ★★★½ 1998
Untamed Heart, 1993, PG-13, ★★★ 1996
Until September, 1984, R, ½★ 1987
Until the End of the World, 1992, R, ★★ 1994
Untouchables, The, 1987, R, ★★½ 1994
Unzipped, 1995, PG-13, ★★★ 1998
Up Close and Personal, 1996, PG-13, ★★★ 1999
Up the Creek, 1984, R, ★★★ 1989
Up the Sandbox, 1973, R, ★★★ 1996
Used Cars, 1980, R, ★★ 1994
Used People, 1992, PG-13, ★★ 1994
Usual Suspects, The, 1995, R, ★½ 1997

V

Vagabond, 1986, NR, ★★★★ 1998
Valley Girl, 1983, R, ★★★ 1998
Valmont, 1989, R, ★★★½ 1998
Vanishing, The, 1991, NR, ★★★½ 1998
Vanishing, The, 1993, R, ★ 1994
Vanya on 42nd Street, 1994, PG, ★★★½ 1998
Verdict, The, 1982, R, ★★★★ 1998
Very Brady Sequel, A, 1996, PG-13, ★★½ 1999
Vice Versa, 1988, PG, ★★★½ 1998
Victor/Victoria, 1982, R, ★★★ 1998
Videodrome, 1983, R, ★½ 1988
Vincent, 1989, NR, ★★★★ 1998
Vincent & Theo, 1990, PG-13, ★★★½ 1998
Violets Are Blue, 1986, PG-13, ★★★ 1987
Virtuosity, 1995, R, ★★★ 1998
Vision Quest, 1985, R, ★★★½ 1998
Visions of Eight, 1973, NR, ★★★ 1998
Visions of Light: The Art of Cinematography, 1993, NR, ★★★½ 1998
Visitors, The, 1996, R, ★★ 1999

Vixen, 1969, X, ★★★ 1996
Volcano, 1997, PG-13, ★½ 1998

W

Wages of Fear, The, 1953, NR, ★★★★ 1997
Waiting for Guffman, 1997, R, ★★★ 1998
Waiting to Exhale, 1995, R, ★★★ 1998
Walkabout, 1971, PG, ★★★★ 1998
Walk in the Clouds, A, 1995, PG-13, ★★★★ 1998
Wall Street, 1987, R, ★★★½ 1998
WarGames, 1983, PG, ★★★★ 1998
War of the Roses, The, 1989, R, ★★★ 1998
War Party, 1989, R, ★ 1991
War Room, The, 1994, NR, ★★★½ 1998
Watcher in the Woods, The, 1981, PG, ★★ 1986
Waterdance, The, 1992, R, ★★★½ 1998
Waterworld, 1995, PG-13, ★★½ 1997
Wayne's World, 1992, PG-13, ★★★ 1998
Wayne's World 2, 1993, PG-13, ★★★ 1998
Weavers: Wasn't That a Time!, The, 1982, PG, ★★★★ 1998
Wedding, A, 1978, PG, ★★★½ 1998
Wedding Banquet, The, 1993, NR, ★★★ 1998
Weeds, 1987, R, ★★★ 1996
Weekend at Bernie's, 1989, PG-13, ★ 1992
Week's Vacation, A, 1980, NR, ★★★½ 1998
Weird Science, 1985, PG-13, ★★★½ 1998
Welcome Home, 1989, R, ★★ 1992
Welcome Home, Roxy Carmichael, 1990, PG-13, ★★ 1993
We're No Angels, 1990, PG-13, ★★★ 1998
Wes Craven's New Nightmare, 1994, R, ★★★ 1998
Wetherby, 1985, R, ★★★★ 1998
We Think the World of You, 1989, PG, ★★★ 1996
Whales of August, The, 1987, NR, ★★★ 1998
What's Eating Gilbert Grape?, 1994, PG-13, ★★★★ 1998
What's Love Got to Do With It, 1993, R, ★★★½ 1998
When a Man Loves a Woman, 1994, R, ★★★★ 1998
When Harry Met Sally . . . , 1989, R, ★★★ 1998
When We Were Kings, 1997, PG, ★★★ 1998
Where Angels Fear to Tread, 1992, PG, ★★ 1994
Where the Boys Are, 1984, R, ½★ 1987
Where the Buffalo Roam, 1980, R, ★★ 1991
Where the Day Takes You, 1992, R, ★★★ 1996
Where the Green Ants Dream, 1985, NR, ★★★ 1988
Where the Heart Is, 1990, R, ★½ 1992
While You Were Sleeping, 1995, PG, ★★★ 1998
Whistle Blower, The, 1987, PG, ★★★½ 1998
White, 1994, R, ★★★½ 1998
White Fang, 1991, PG, ★★★ 1998
White Fang 2: Myth of the White Wolf, 1994, PG, ★★★ 1998
White Hunter, Black Heart, 1990, PG, ★★★ 1998
White Man's Burden, 1995, R, ★★ 1997
White Men Can't Jump, 1992, R, ★★★½ 1998
White Mischief, 1988, R, ★★★ 1998
White Nights, 1985, PG-13, ★★ 1988
White Palace, 1990, R, ★★★½ 1998
White Sands, 1992, R, ★★ 1994
White Squall, 1996, PG-13, ★★★ 1999
Who Framed Roger Rabbit, 1988, PG, ★★★★ 1998
Whole Wide World, The, 1997, PG, ★★★ 1998
Whore, 1991, NC-17, ★★★ 1996
Who's the Man, 1993, R, ★★★ 1998
Wide Sargasso Sea, 1993, NC-17, ★★★½ 1998
Widows' Peak, 1994, PG, ★★★½ 1998
Wife, The, 1997, R, ★★★ 1998
Wild America, 1997, PG, ★★ 1998
Wild at Heart, 1990, R, ★★½ 1997
Wild Bill, 1995, R, ★★ 1997
Wild Bunch, The, 1969, R, ★★★★ 1997
Wildcats, 1985, R, ★½ 1990
Wild Orchid, 1990, R, ★ 1994
Wild Orchid II: Two Shades of Blue, 1992, R, ★★ 1994
Wild Reeds, 1995, NR, ★★★ 1998
Wild West, 1993, NR, ★★ 1995
Willard, 1971, PG, ★★ 1991
William Shakespeare's Romeo & Juliet, 1996, PG-13, ★★ 1999
Willie and Phil, 1980, R, ★★★ 1996
Willie Wonka and the Chocolate Factory, 1971, G, ★★★★ 1998
Willow, 1988, PG, ★★½ 1994
Wind, 1992, PG-13, ★★★ 1998
Wings of Courage, 1996, G, ★★★ 1999
Wings of Desire, 1988, NR, ★★★★ 1998
Winter of Our Dreams, 1983, R, ★★★ 1998
Wired, 1989, R, ★½ 1993
Wise Guys, 1986, R, ★★★½ 1998

X, Y, Z

Note: The right hand column is the year in which the review last appeared in *Roger Ebert's Video Companion* or *Roger Ebert's Movie Yearbook.*

Index

C

D

E

F

H

I

L

M

O

P

Q

R

S

U

V

W

X

Y

Z